Student Companion

WITH PRACTICE AND PROBLEM SOLVING

TEACHER'S GUIDE

Boston, Massachusetts • Chandler, Arizona • Glenview, Illinois • Upper Saddle River, New Jersey

This work is protected by United States copyright laws and is provided *solely for the use of teachers and administrators* in teaching courses and assessing student learning in their classes and schools. Dissemination or sale of any part of this work (including on the World Wide Web) will destroy the integrity of the work and is *not* permitted.

Acknowledgements **Illustration:** Stephen Durke: 57, 258, 293; Jeff Grunwald represented by Wilkinson Studios, Inc.: 330, 346, 397, 404, 420; Phil Guzy: 473, 572; XNR Productions: 480 **Photo:** All photographs not listed are the property of Pearson Education; **Back Cover,** © Bon Appetit/Almay; **Page 30,** Pete Saloutos/zefa/Corbis; **226,** John Wells/Photo Researchers, Inc.; **319,** Eric Hood/iStockphoto; **488,** Ron Kimball/kimballstock; **496,** iStockphoto; Andy Crawford/Dorling Kindersley; **519,** M.C. Escher's "Symmetry E56" © 2009 The M.C. Escher Company-Holland. All rights reserved. www.mcescher.com; **579,** Matthias Tunger/Photonica/Getty Images; **589,** amana images inc./Alamy.

ISBN-13: 978-0-785-46937-7
ISBN-10: 0-785-46937-0
4 5 6 7 8 9 10 V042 13 12 11

Contents

Welcome to **Geometry!**

Your Prentice Hall Geometry program is designed to help you achieve mastery of Geometry topics. Your *Prentice Hall Geometry Student Companion* is written to support you as you study. Your Student Companion is designed to work with your Student Edition textbook and PowerGeometry.com by providing a place to practice the concepts, skills, and vocabulary you'll learn in each lesson.

Using the Geometry Student Companion

Your Student Companion provides daily support for each lesson by targeting the following areas:

- **Vocabulary** Building your math vocabulary is an important part of success this year. You'll use your Student Companion to learn and understand the vocabulary words you need for Geometry.
- **Got It?** You'll use your Student Companion to check your understanding of example problems from your Student Edition.
- **Lesson Check** You'll use your Student Companion to make sure you're ready to tackle your homework.
- **Practice and Problem Solving** You'll use your Student Companion to practice the skills you've learned in the lesson.

Together, these sections will help you prepare to master the topics covered in your Student Edition — and lead to a successful year in Geometry.

Using PowerGeometry.com

All your Student Companion pages are available for downloading and printing from PowerGeometry.com.

1-1 Nets and Drawings for Visualizing Geometry

Vocabulary

Review

Identify each figure as *two-dimensional* or *three-dimensional*.

1. 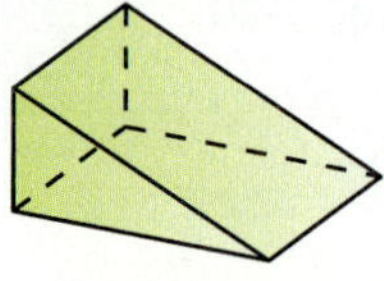

three-dimensional

2. 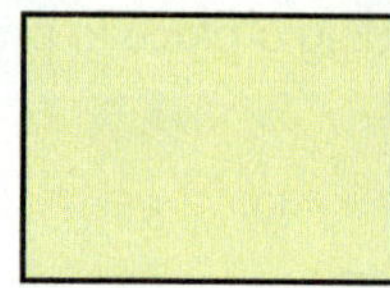

two-dimensional

3. 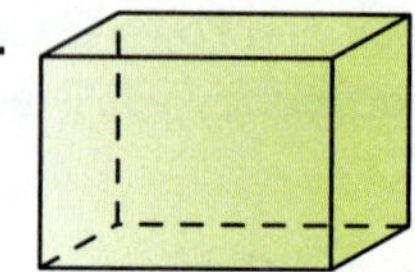

three-dimensional

Vocabulary Builder

polygon (noun) PAHL **ih gahn**

Definition A **polygon** is a two-dimensional figure with three or more sides, where each side meets exactly two other sides at their endpoints.

Main Idea: A **polygon** is a closed figure, so all sides meet. No sides cross each other.

Examples: Triangles, rectangles, pentagons, hexagons, and octagons are **polygons**.

Use Your Vocabulary

Underline the correct word(s) to complete each sentence.

4. A *polygon* is formed by two / three or more straight sides.
5. A circle is / is not a *polygon*.
6. A triangle / rectangle is a *polygon* with three sides.
7. The sides of a *polygon* are curved / straight.
8. Two / Three sides of *polygon* meet at the same point.

Cross out the figure(s) that are NOT *polygons*.

9. 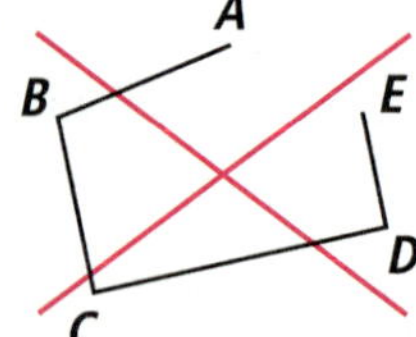

10. 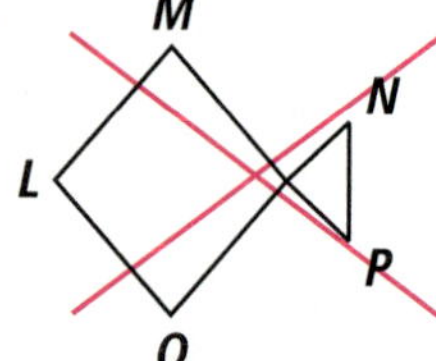

11. 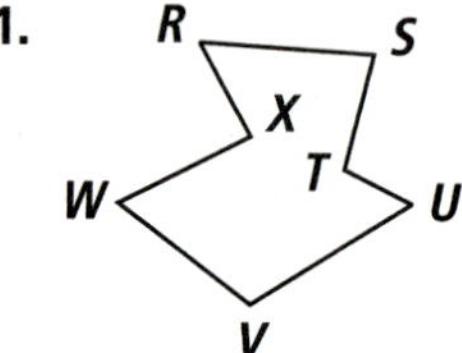

Underline the correct words to complete the sentence.

12. A *net* is a two-dimensional / three-dimensional diagram that you can fold to form a two-dimensional / three-dimensional figure.

13. Circle the *net* that you can NOT fold into a cube.

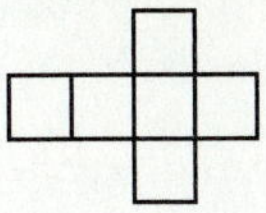

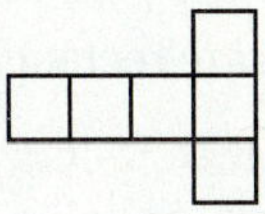

Use the net of a cube at the right for Exercises 14 and 15.

14. Suppose you fold the net into a cube. What color will be opposite each face?

red — orange

blue — yellow

green — purple

15. Suppose you fold the net into a cube. What color is missing from each view?

green

red

blue

Problem 1 Identifying a Solid From a Net

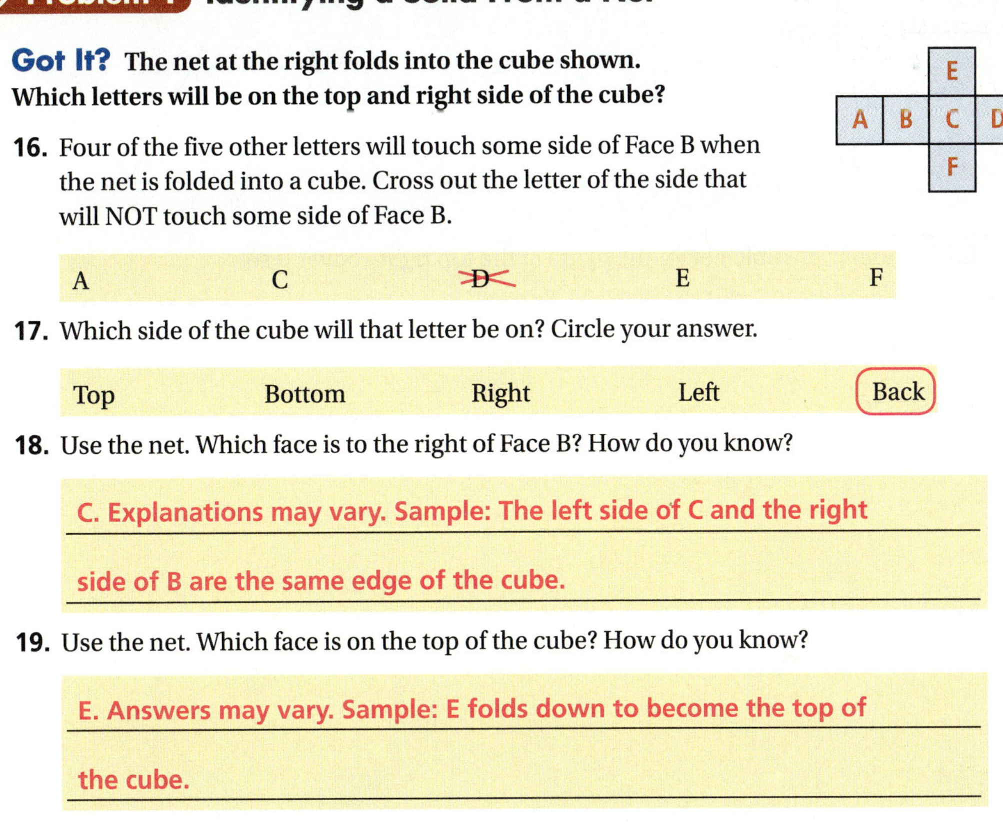

Got It? **The net at the right folds into the cube shown. Which letters will be on the top and right side of the cube?**

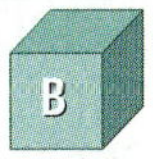

16. Four of the five other letters will touch some side of Face B when the net is folded into a cube. Cross out the letter of the side that will NOT touch some side of Face B.

A   C   ~~D~~   E   F

17. Which side of the cube will that letter be on? Circle your answer.

Top   Bottom   Right   Left   Back

18. Use the net. Which face is to the right of Face B? How do you know?

C. Explanations may vary. Sample: The left side of C and the right side of B are the same edge of the cube.

19. Use the net. Which face is on the top of the cube? How do you know?

E. Answers may vary. Sample: E folds down to become the top of the cube.

Problem 2 Drawing a Net From a Solid

Got It? **What is a net for the figure at the right? Label the net with its dimensions.**

Write T for *true* or F for *false*.

T **20.** Three of the faces are rectangles.

F **21.** Four of the faces are triangles.

T **22.** The figure has five faces in all.

23. Now write a description of the net.

Answers may vary. Sample: The net has three rectangles and two triangles that fold to form the figure above.

24. Circle the net that represents the figure above.

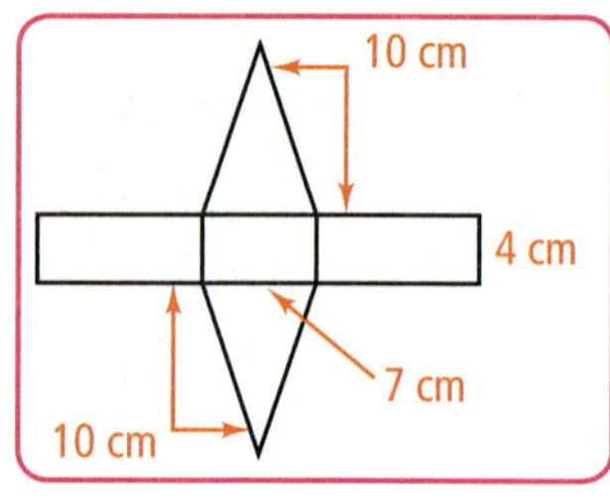

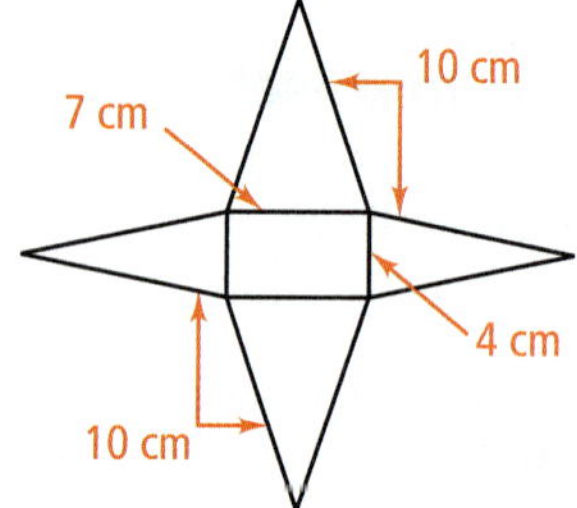

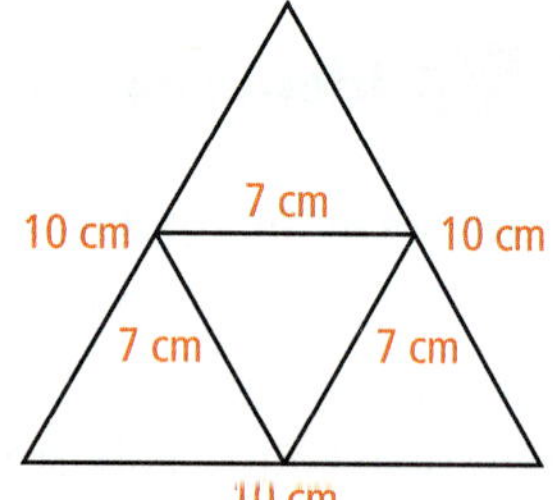

25. **Reasoning** Is there another possible net for the figure at the top right above? If so, draw it.

Problem 3 Isometric Drawing

Got It? What is an isometric drawing of this cube structure?

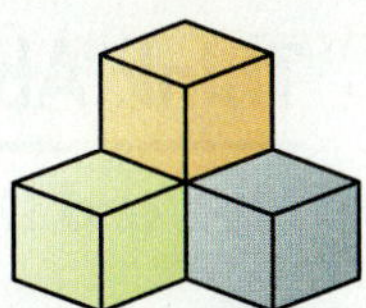

26. The cube structure has

24 edges that you can see and

16 vertices that you can see.

27. The isometric dot paper shows 2 vertices and 1 edge of the cube structure. Complete the isometric drawing.

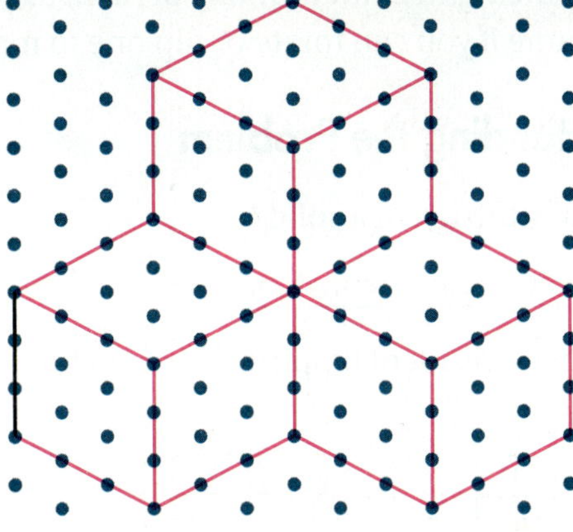

Lesson Check • Do you UNDERSTAND?

Vocabulary Tell whether each drawing is *isometric*, a *net*, or *neither*.

28. Does the drawing at the right show the surfaces of a three-dimensional figure as one folded-out flat surface?

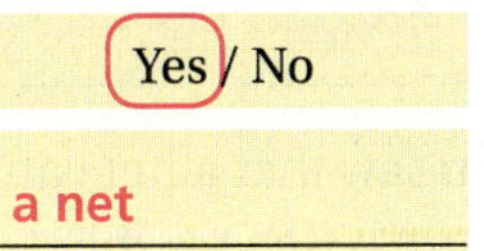

Yes / No

29. Is the drawing *isometric*, *a net*, or *neither*?

a net

30. Does the drawing at the right show the top, front, and sides of a three-dimensional figure using slanted lines to show depth?

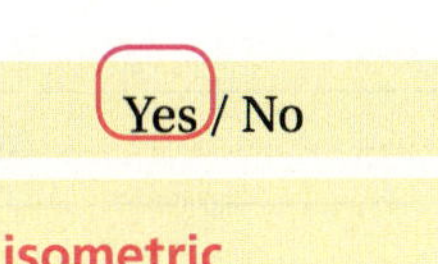

Yes / No

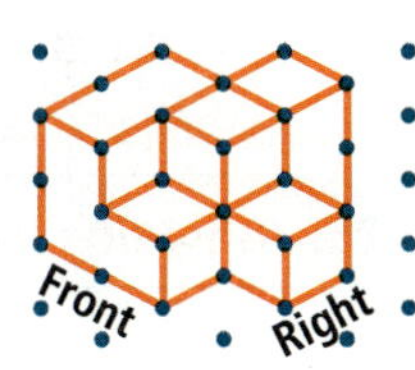

31. Is the drawing *isometric*, *a net*, or *neither*?

isometric

Math Success

Check off the vocabulary words that you understand.

☐ net ☐ isometric drawing ☐ orthographic drawing

Rate how well you can ***use nets, isometric drawings, and orthographic drawings.***

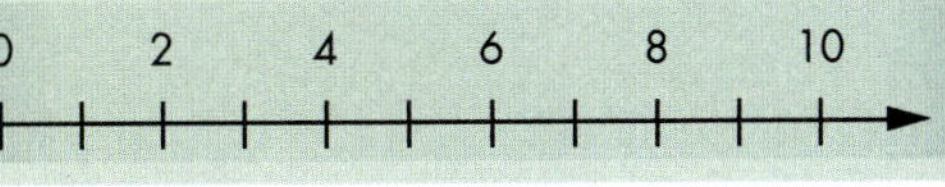

Name ______________________ Class ____________ Date ____________

1-1 Think About a Plan

Nets and Drawings for Visualizing Geometry

Multiple Representations There are eight different nets for the solid shown at the right. Draw as many of them as you can. (*Hint:* Two nets are the same if you can rotate or flip one to match the other.)

Understanding the Problem

1. What is the net of a solid?

   A net is a two-dimensional pattern that you can fold to form a three-dimensional figure.

2. What is a result of flipping the net below? Of rotating it? Answers may vary. Sample:

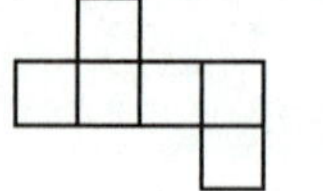

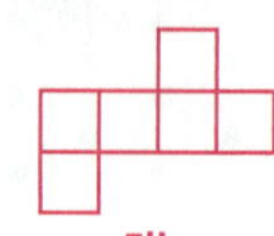

Flip

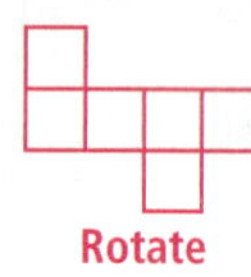

Rotate

Planning the Solution

3. Visualize unfolding the solid so that the base shares an edge with all four triangles. Then visualize unfolding the solid so that the base shares an edge with three triangles. Are the nets that result the same? Explain.

   The nets are different because you cannot superimpose them with a flip or a turn.

4. In Step 3, you saw that a net can have three or four triangles that share an edge with the square base. Are there other possibilities? If so, what are they? Are these the only possibilities?

   The base can share one, two, three, or four edges with the triangles. These are the only possibilities.

Finding the Answer

5. Are there other nets that have three or four triangles that share an edge with the square base? Explain.

   No; any other such net can be superimposed on one of the nets from Step 3 by a flip or a rotation.

6. There are four nets that have two triangles that share an edge with the base. For each of these, the triangles may either be on opposite or adjacent sides of the base. Draw each net.

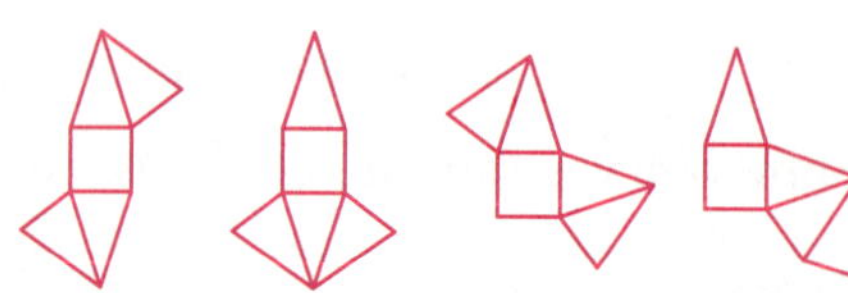

7. How many nets have only one triangle touching the base? Draw as many of them as you can. There are two such nets.

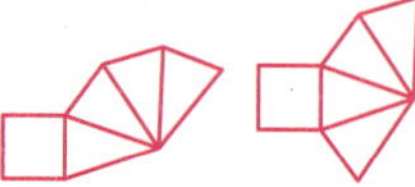

Name ______________________ Class ____________ Date ____________

1-1 Practice

Form K

Nets and Drawings for Visualizing Geometry

Match each three-dimensional figure with the sketch of its net.

1. 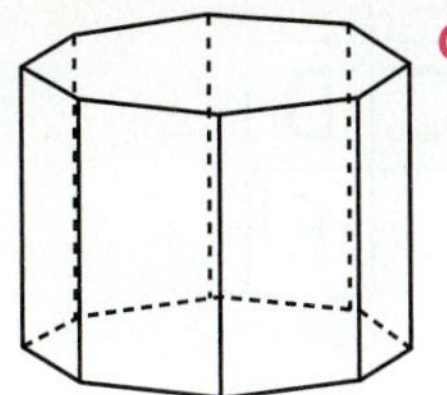 C

2. 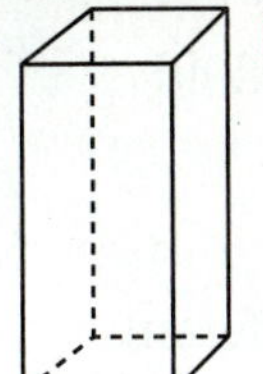 B

3. 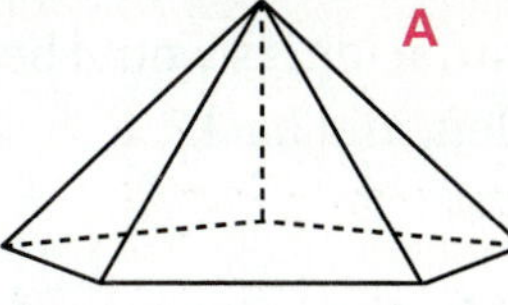 A

A. 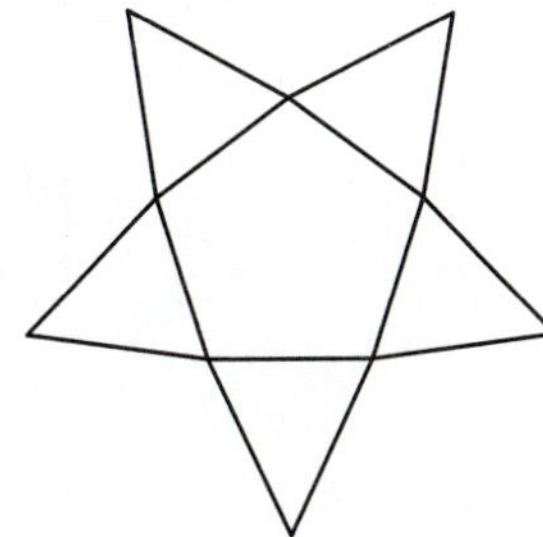

B. 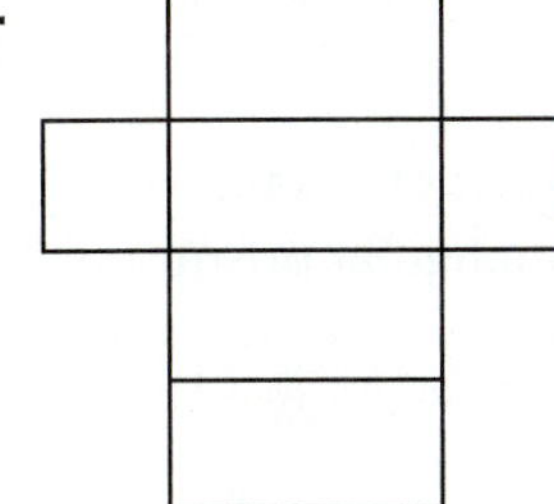

C. 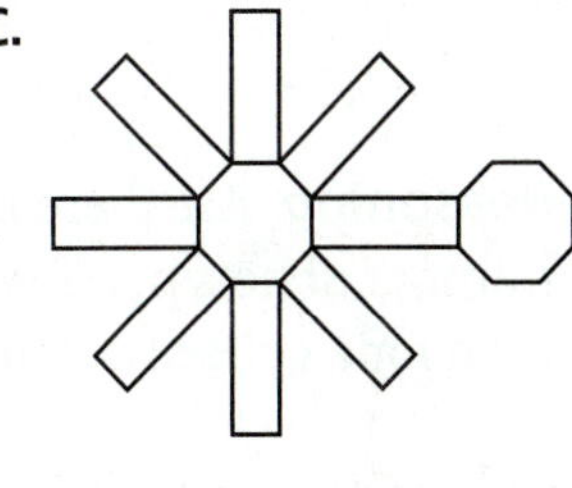

Draw a net for each figure. Label the net with its dimensions. To start, visualize opening the end flaps of the prism.

4. 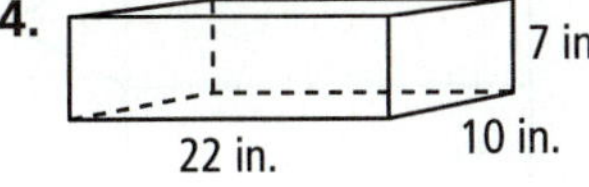

Answer net for 4:
7 in.
10 in.
7 in.
10 in.
22 in.

5. 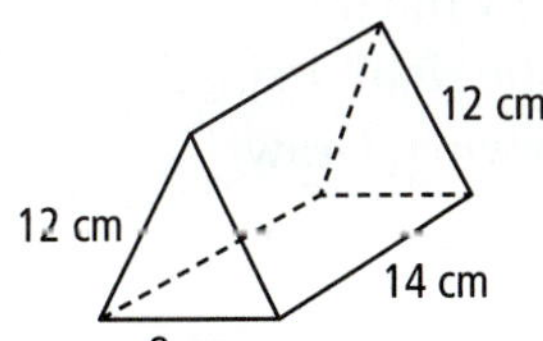

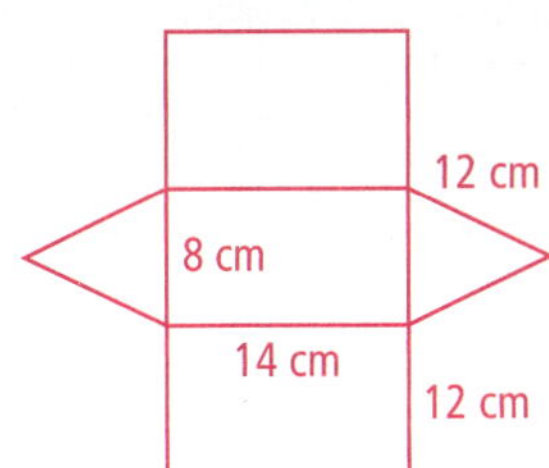

6. 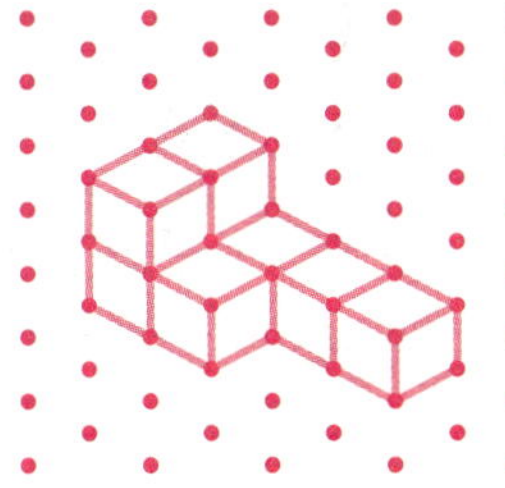

Make an isometric drawing of each cube structure on isometric dot paper. To start, draw the front edge.

6. 

7. 

7. 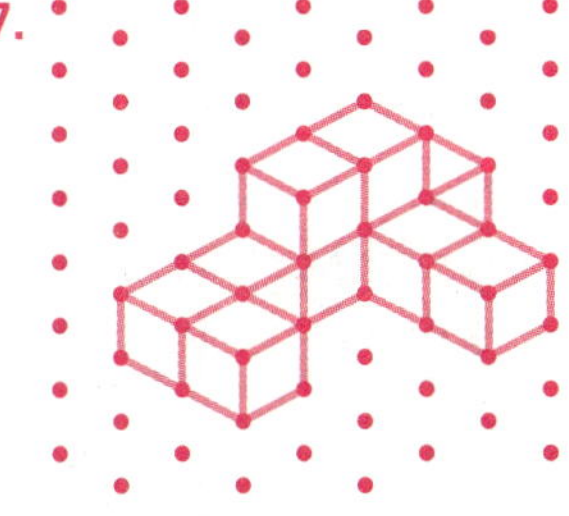

Name ______________________ Class ____________ Date ____________

1-1 Practice (continued)

Form K

Nets and Drawings for Visualizing Geometry

8. **Visualization** If the net shown at the right were folded so that side A is the front of the cube, what letters would be on the top, bottom, right, left, and back? **E; F; C; B; D**

9. **Multiple Representations** How many different nets can you make for a cube? Draw at least five nets. **Eleven; check students' work.**

10. **Reasoning** Are there more, fewer, or the same number of nets possible for a rectangular prism than for a cube? Explain. **Answers may vary. Sample: Same number; a cube is a rectangular prism, but more cube nets are identical.**

11. **Open-Ended** Make an isometric drawing of a structure you can build using six cubes. **Check students' work.**

12. **Error Analysis** A classmate drew the net of a triangular prism shown at the right. Explain the error in your classmate's drawing. Draw the net correctly. **The bases need to be on opposite sides of the net.**

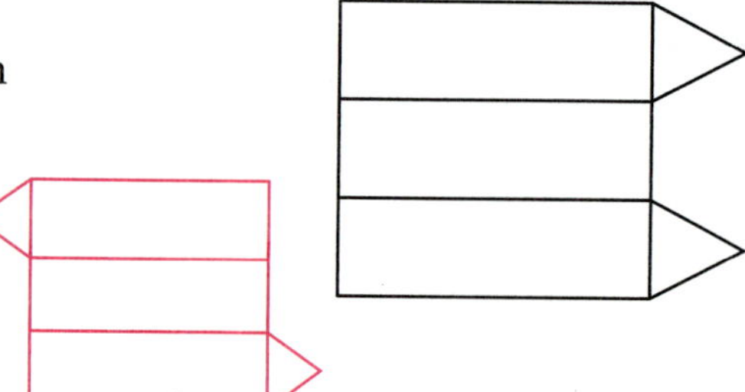

Match the package with its net.

13. 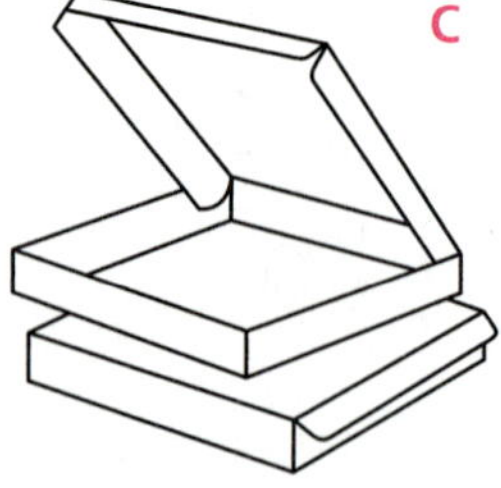 **C**

14.  **A**

15.  **B**

A. 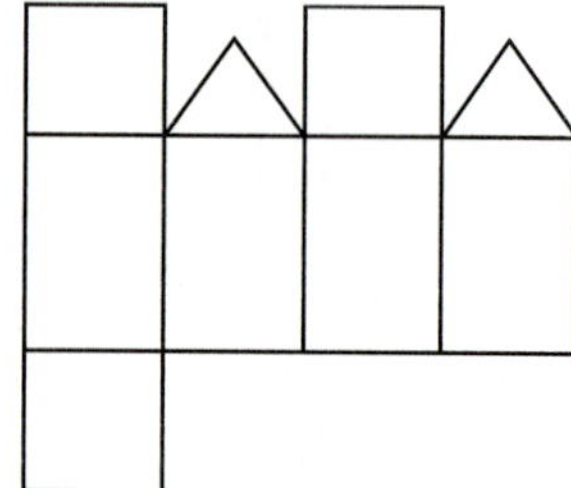

B. 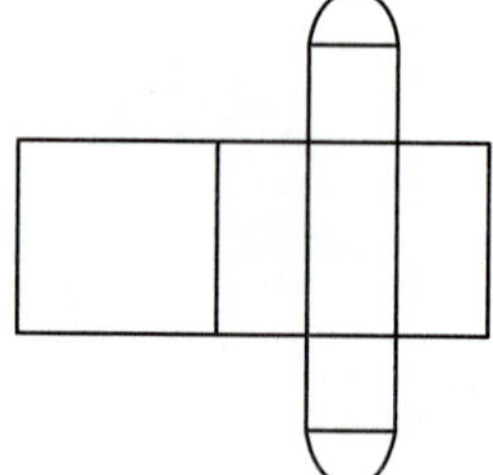

C. 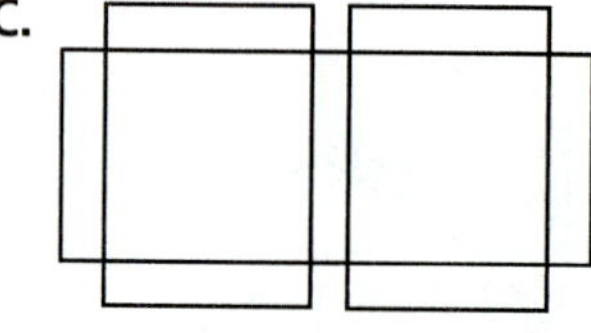

Name ______________________ Class ____________ Date ____________

1-1 Standardized Test Prep

Nets and Drawings for Visualizing Geometry

Multiple Choice

For Exercises 1–3, choose the correct letter.

1. Which three-dimensional figure matches the net shown at the right? A

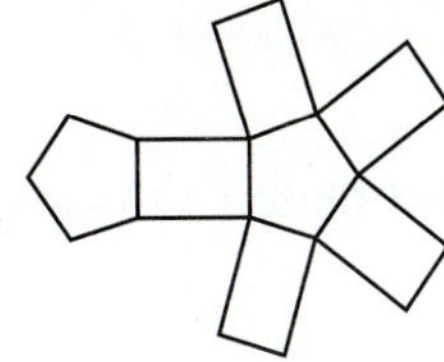

A 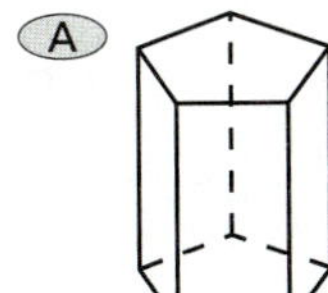
B 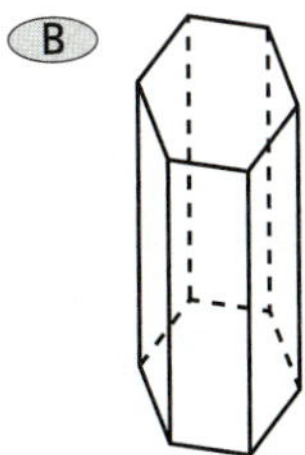
C 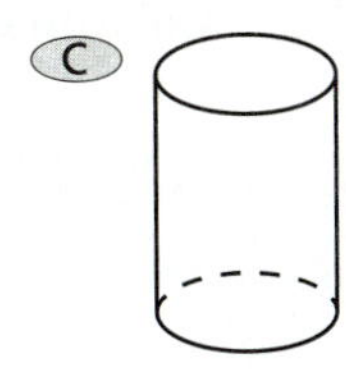
D 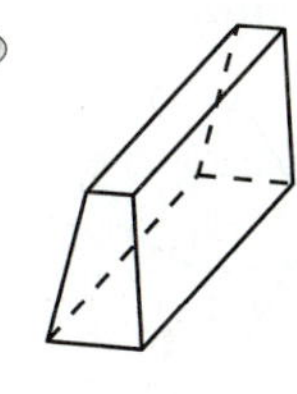

2. Which cube structure matches the isometric drawing shown at the right? I

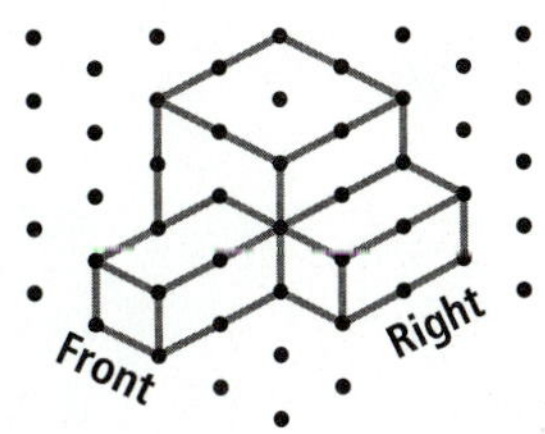

F 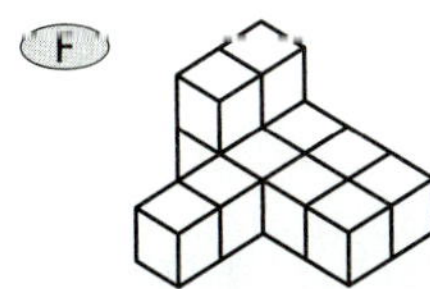
G 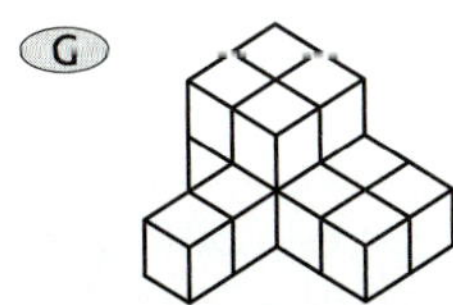
H 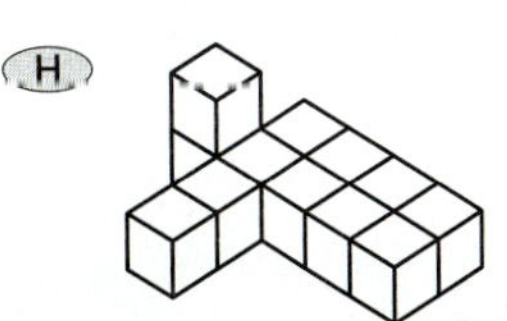
I 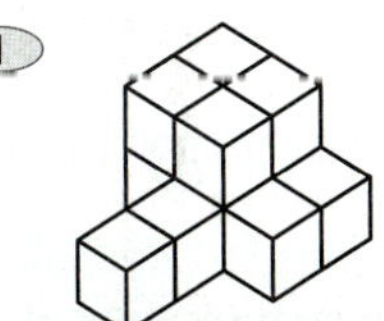

3. Which top view of an orthographic drawing matches the isometric drawing shown at the right? B

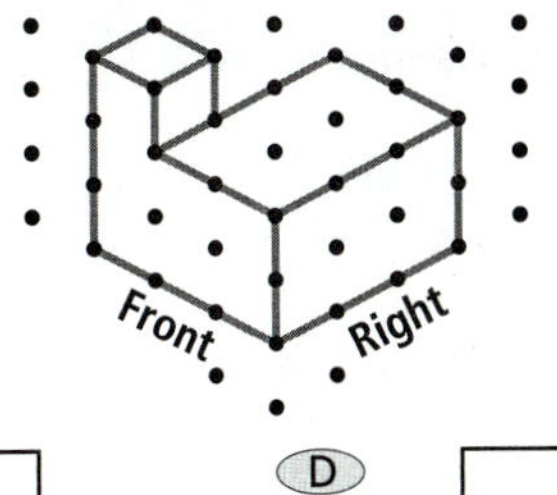

A 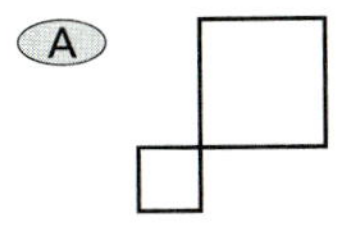
B 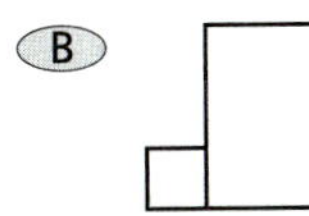
C 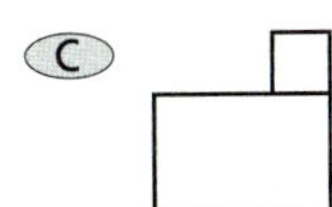
D 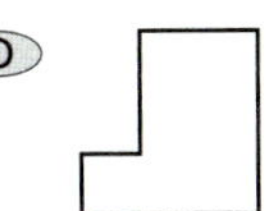

Short Response

4. You are building a small shed. You want to describe the area of the ground the shed will cover. Which type of drawing, isometric or orthographic, would best represent the area? Why? [2] orthographic; sample: It includes a bird's-eye or top-down view, which gives the building's footprint on the ground. [1] correct answer with incomplete explanation [0] incorrect answer with no explanation given

Points, Lines, and Planes

Vocabulary

Review

Draw a line from each *net* in Column A to the three-dimensional figure it represents in Column B.

Column A | **Column B**

1.

2.

3.

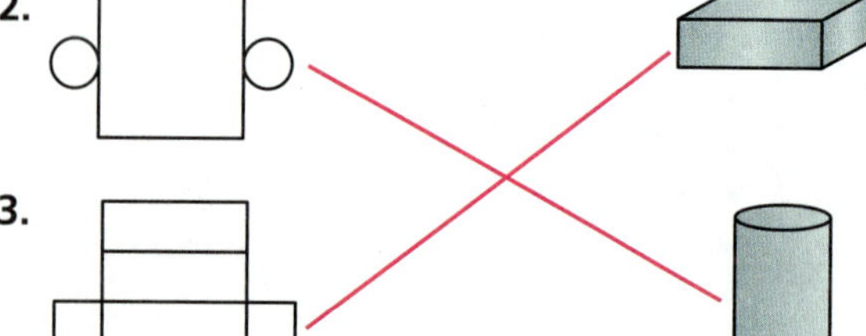

Vocabulary Builder

conjecture (noun, verb) **kun JEK chur**

Main Idea: A **conjecture** is a guess or a prediction.

Definition: A **conjecture** is a conclusion reached by using inductive reasoning.

Use Your Vocabulary

Write *noun* or *verb* to identify how the word *conjecture* is used in each sentence.

4. You make a *conjecture* that your volleyball team will win. noun

5. Assuming that your sister ate the last cookie is a *conjecture*. noun

6. You *conjecture* that your town will build a swimming pool. verb

Key Concept Undefined and Defined Terms

Write the correct word from the list on the right. Use each word only once.

	Undefined or Defined Term	Diagram	Name
7.	point	A •	A
8.	line	line ℓ through A and B	$\overleftrightarrow{AB}$
9.	plane	plane P with points A, B, C	P
10.	segment	A —— B	$\overline{AB}$
11.	ray	A —— B →	$\overrightarrow{AB}$
12.	opposite rays	← A C B →	$\overrightarrow{CA}$, $\overrightarrow{CB}$

line
opposite rays
plane
point
ray
segment

Draw a line from each item in Column A to its description in Column B.

Column A	Column B
13. plane HGE	intersection of $\overline{AB}$ and line z
14. $\overline{BF}$	plane AEH
15. plane DAE	line through points F and E
16. line y	intersection of planes ABF and CGF
17. point A	plane containing points E, F, and G

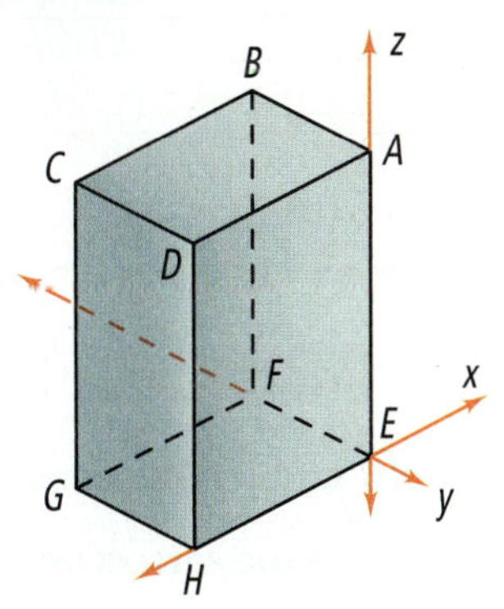

Points that lie on the same line are *collinear points*. Points and lines that lie in the same plane are *coplanar*. All the points of a line are coplanar.

Problem 1 Naming Points, Lines and Planes

Got It? What are two other ways to name $\overleftrightarrow{RS}$?

Underline the correct word or letter to complete each sentence.

18. $\overleftrightarrow{RS}$ is a line / segment.

19. The lowercase letter that represents $\overleftrightarrow{RS}$ is ℓ / m.

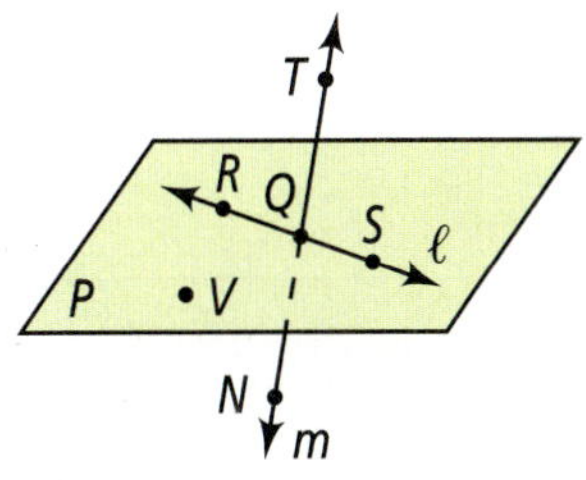

20. Circle the points that are on $\overleftrightarrow{RS}$.

N *P* *Q* *R* *S* *T* *V*

21. Cross out the lines that do NOT name $\overleftrightarrow{RS}$.

$\overleftrightarrow{NQ}$ $\overleftrightarrow{NT}$ $\overleftrightarrow{PV}$ $\overleftrightarrow{QR}$ $\overleftrightarrow{QS}$ $\overleftrightarrow{RQ}$ $\overleftrightarrow{SQ}$ $\overleftrightarrow{SR}$

Problem 2 Naming Segments and Rays

Got It? Reasoning $\overrightarrow{EF}$ and $\overrightarrow{FE}$ form a line. Are they opposite rays? Explain.

For Exercises 22–26, use the line below.

22. Draw and label points *E* and *F*. Then draw $\overrightarrow{EF}$ in one color and $\overrightarrow{FE}$ in another color.

23. Do $\overrightarrow{EF}$ and $\overrightarrow{FE}$ share an endpoint? Yes / No

24. Do $\overrightarrow{EF}$ and $\overrightarrow{FE}$ form a line? Yes / No

25. Are $\overrightarrow{EF}$ and $\overrightarrow{FE}$ opposite rays? Yes / No

26. Explain your answer to Exercise 25.

Answers may vary. Sample: The rays point in opposite directions but they do not share an endpoint so they are not opposite rays.

Lesson Check • Do you UNDERSTAND?

Are $\overrightarrow{AB}$ and $\overrightarrow{BA}$ the same ray? Explain.

Underline the correct symbol to complete each sentence.

27. The endpoint of $\overrightarrow{AB}$ is *A* / *B*.

28. The endpoint of $\overrightarrow{BA}$ is *A* / *B*.

29. Use the line. Draw and label points *A* and *B*. Then draw $\overrightarrow{AB}$ and $\overrightarrow{BA}$.

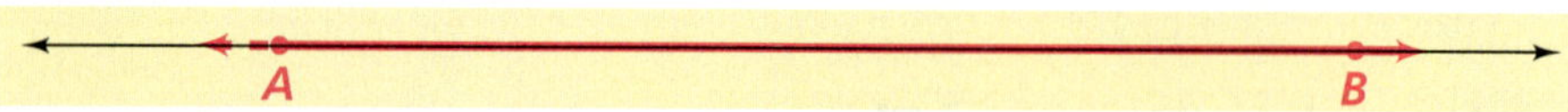

30. Are $\overrightarrow{AB}$ and $\overrightarrow{BA}$ the same ray? Explain.

No. Explanations may vary. Sample: They point in opposite directions and have different endpoints.

Points, Lines, and Planes

Vocabulary

Review

Use the diagram at the right. Complete each statement with the correct word from the list below.

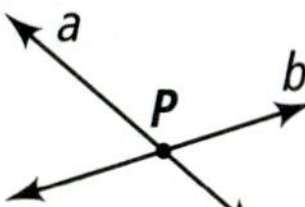

intersect intersecting intersection

1. Line *a* and line *b* _?_ at point *P*. intersect

2. The _?_ of lines *a* and *b* is point *P*. intersection

3. The diagram shows two _?_ lines. intersecting

Vocabulary Builder

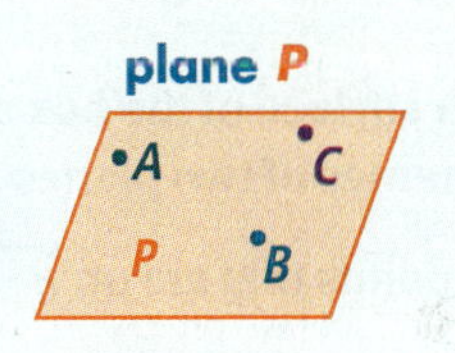

plane (noun) playn

Related Word: coplanar

Definition: A **plane** is represented by a flat surface that extends without end.

Word Origin: The word **plane** comes from the Latin *planos*, which means "flat."

Math Usage: A **plane** contains infinitely many points. You can name a **plane** by one capital letter or by at least three noncollinear points in the **plane**.

Use Your Vocabulary

Write T for *true* or F for *false*.

F 4. A *plane* has length, width, and height.

T 5. A *plane* extends without end.

T 6. All points in a line are *coplanar*.

F 7. All points in a *plane* are *collinear*.

take note

Postulates 1-1, 1-2, 1-3, and 1-4

8. Complete each postulate with *line, plane,* or *point.*

Postulate 1-1 Through any two points there is exactly one __?__. line

Postulate 1-2 If two distinct lines intersect, then they intersect in exactly one __?__. point

Postulate 1-3 If two distinct planes intersect, then they intersect in exactly one __?__. line

Postulate 1-4 Through any three noncollinear points there is exactly one __?__. plane

Write P if the statement describes a *postulate* or U if it describes an *undefined term.*

U **9.** A point indicates a location and has no size.

P **10.** Through any two points there is exactly one line.

P **11.** If two distinct planes intersect, then they intersect in exactly one line.

P **12.** If two distinct lines intersect, then they intersect in exactly one point.

Problem 3 Finding the Intersection of Two Planes

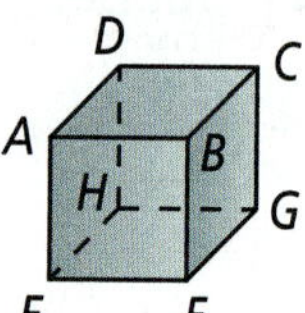

Got It? **Each surface of the box at the right represents part of a plane. What are the names of two planes that intersect in $\overleftrightarrow{BF}$?**

13. Circle the points that are on $\overleftrightarrow{BF}$ or in one of the two planes.

(A) (B) (C) *D* (E) (F) (G) *H*

14. Circle another name for plane *BFG*. Underline another name for plane *BFE*.

<u>*ABF*</u> *BCD* (*BCG*) *CDH* *FGH*

15. Now name two planes that intersect in $\overleftrightarrow{BF}$. Answers may vary. Accept any variation of

ABE, ABF, BFE, AFE, *BFC, BFG, CBG, and CFG.*

Use the diagram at the right for Exercises 16–19.

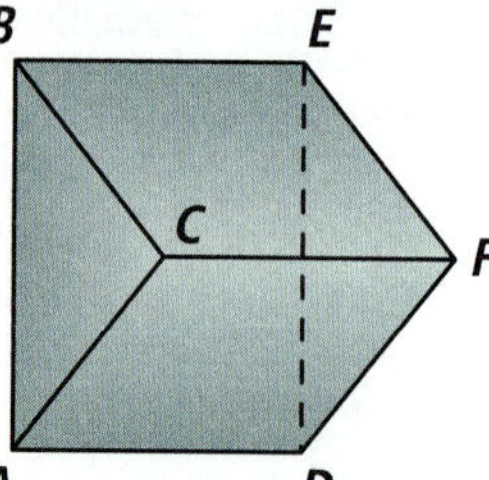

16. The intersection of plane *DFC* and plane *ACB* is $\overleftrightarrow{AC}$.

17. The intersection of plane *CBF* and plane *ACF* is $\overleftrightarrow{CF}$.

18. The intersection of plane *DFE* and plane *BEF* is $\overleftrightarrow{EF}$.

19. Name two planes that do NOT intersect. Answers may vary. Accept any version of the plane names.

plane *ABC* plane *DEF*

Problem 4 Using Postulate 1-4

Got It? **What plane contains points L, M, and N? Shade the plane.**

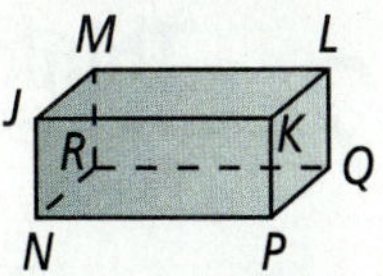

20. Use the figure below. Draw $\overline{LM}$, $\overline{LN}$, and $\overline{MN}$ as dashed segments. Then shade plane LMN.

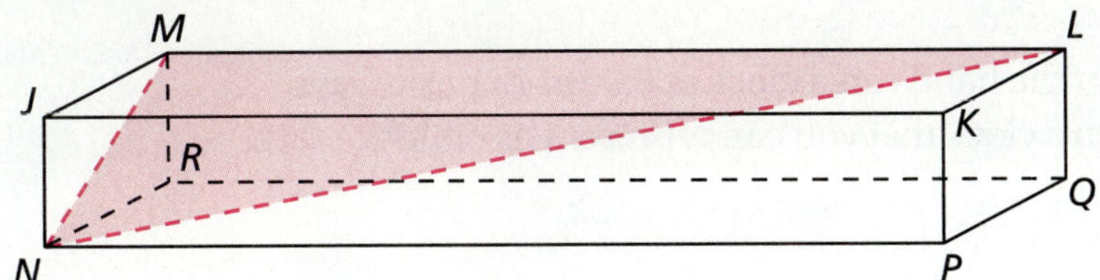

Underline the correct word to complete the sentence.

21. $\overline{LM}$, $\overline{LN}$, and $\overline{MN}$ form a triangle / rectangle .

22. Name the plane. Answers may vary. Accept any of

LMN, MNL, NLM, MLN, LNM, NML

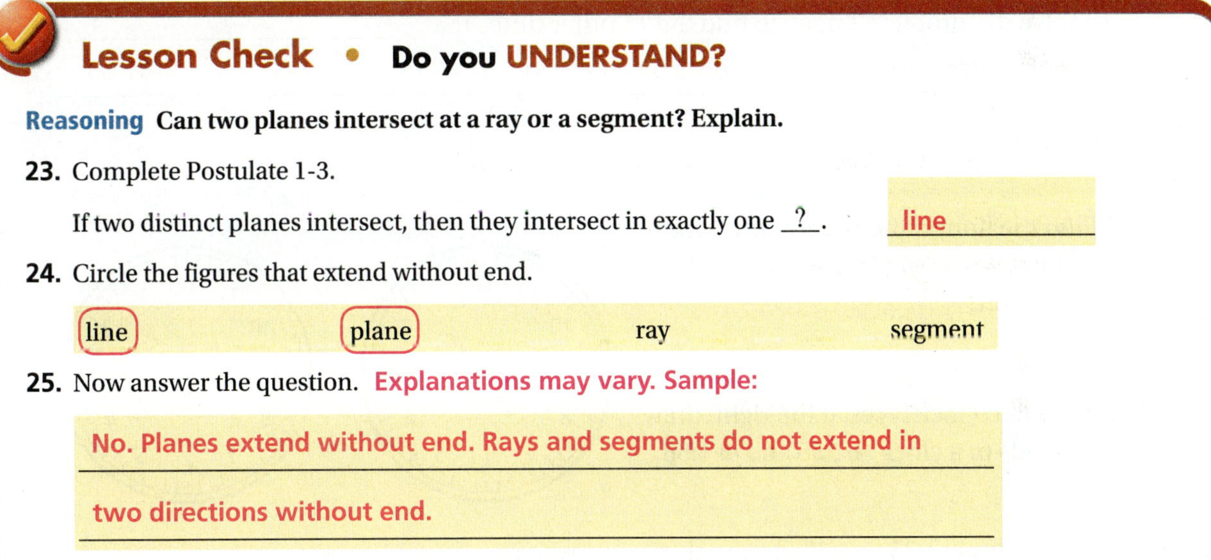

Lesson Check • Do you UNDERSTAND?

Reasoning **Can two planes intersect at a ray or a segment? Explain.**

23. Complete Postulate 1-3.

If two distinct planes intersect, then they intersect in exactly one __?__. line

24. Circle the figures that extend without end.

line plane ray segment

25. Now answer the question. Explanations may vary. Sample:

No. Planes extend without end. Rays and segments do not extend in two directions without end.

Math Success

Check off the vocabulary words that you understand.

☐ point ☐ line ☐ plane ☐ segment ☐ ray ☐ postulate ☐ axiom

Rate how well you ***understand points, lines, and planes.***

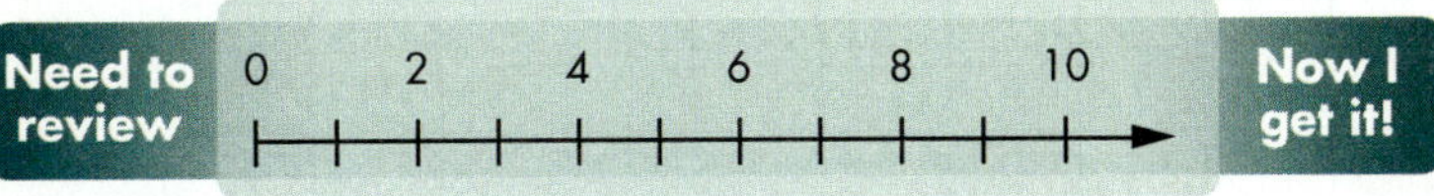

Name ______________________ Class ____________ Date ____________

1-2 Think About a Plan

Points, Lines, and Planes

Estimation You can represent the hands on a clock at 6:00 as opposite rays. Estimate the other 11 times on a clock that you can represent as opposite rays.

Know

1. Opposite rays are two rays that share the same endpoint and form a line.
2. The hands on the clock represent rays. At 6:00, these rays form opposite rays.

   This means they form a straight line.

Need

3. To solve the problem I need to find the 11 other times that the hands of a clock form a straight line.

Plan

4. When the hour hand is between 1 and 2 o'clock, what will the minute hand be between?

   somewhere between the 7 and 8

5. On the two clock faces at the right, draw the hands of a clock at 1:35 and at 1:38.

6. At which time, 1:35 or 1:38, do you think opposite rays form? Explain.

   Answers may vary. Sample: Opposite rays form at 1:38. Even though 1 and 7 are opposite each other on the clock face, the minute hand is not at 7 when the hour hand is at 1, so the hands are not opposite rays at 1:35.

7. Complete the table to show all of the times when the hands on a clock represent opposite rays. Answers may vary. Note that 6:00 is the only "exact" time. Reasonable estimates might be within 2 min of these times.

Hour	6	7	8	9	10	11	12	1	2	3	4
Time when opposite rays form	6:00	7:05	8:10	9:15	10:20	11:25	12:30	1:35	2:40	3:45	4:50

Name ______________________ Class ____________ Date ____________

1-2 Practice

Form K

Points, Lines, and Planes

Use the figure at the right for Exercises 1–4. Note that line *r* pierces the plane at *X*. It is not coplanar with *V*.

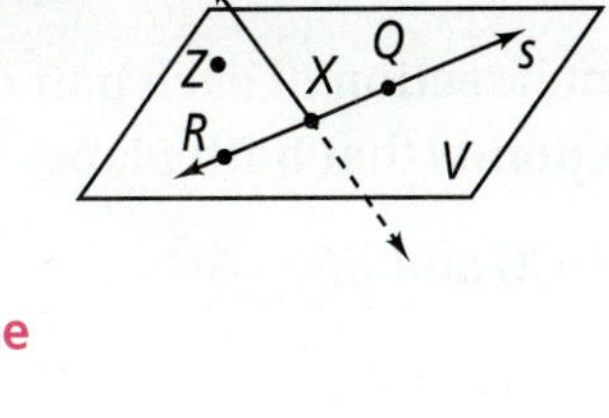

1. What are two other ways to name $\overleftrightarrow{QX}$?

   To start, remember you can name a line by any _?_ points on the line or by _?_ lowercase letter. two; one

   Two other ways to name $\overleftrightarrow{QX}$ are line _?_ and _?_.
   s; Answers may vary. Sample: $\overleftrightarrow{XQ}$

2. What are two other ways to name plane *V*?
   Answers may vary. Sample: *XQZ*; *RZQ*

3. Name three collinear points. *R*, *X*, and *Q*

4. Name four coplanar points. *Z*, *R*, *X*, and *Q*

Use the figure at the right for Exercises 5–7.

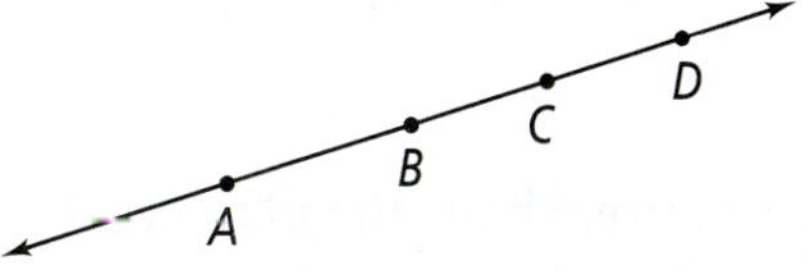

5. Name six segments in the figure. To start, remember a segment is part of a line that consists of _?_ endpoints. two

   Six segments are $\overline{AB}$, $\overline{BC}$, _?_, _?_, _?_, and _?_. $\overline{CD}$; $\overline{AC}$; $\overline{AD}$; $\overline{BD}$

6. Name the rays in the figure. Answers may vary. Samples: $\overrightarrow{AB}$ or $\overrightarrow{AC}$ or $\overrightarrow{AD}$; $\overrightarrow{BC}$ or $\overrightarrow{BD}$; $\overrightarrow{CD}$; $\overrightarrow{DC}$ or $\overrightarrow{DB}$ or $\overrightarrow{DA}$; $\overrightarrow{CB}$ or $\overrightarrow{CA}$; $\overrightarrow{BA}$

7. a. Name the pairs of opposite rays with endpoint *C*.
   Answers may vary. Samples: $\overrightarrow{CD}$ and $\overrightarrow{CA}$ or $\overrightarrow{CB}$

   b. Name another pair of opposite rays.
   Answers may vary. Samples: $\overrightarrow{BA}$ and $\overrightarrow{BD}$ or $\overrightarrow{BC}$

For Exercises 8–12, determine whether each statement is *always, sometimes,* or *never* true.

8. Plane *ABC* and plane *DEF* are the same plane. sometimes

9. $\overleftrightarrow{DE}$ and $\overleftrightarrow{DF}$ are the same line. sometimes

10. Plane *XYZ* does not contain point *Z*. never

11. All the points of a line are coplanar. always

12. Two rays that share an endpoint form a line. sometimes

Name ______________________ Class ____________ Date ____________

1-2 Practice (continued) Form K

Points, Lines, and Planes

Use the figure at the right for Exercises 13–21.

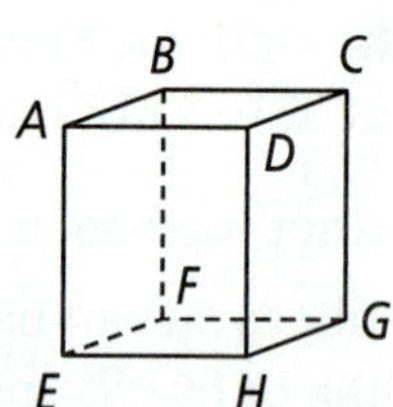

Name the intersection of each pair of planes. To start, identify the points that both planes contain.

13. planes *DCG* and *EFG* $\overleftrightarrow{GH}$

14. planes *EFG* and *ADH* $\overleftrightarrow{EH}$

15. planes *BCG* and *ABF* $\overleftrightarrow{BF}$

Name two planes that intersect in the given line. To start, identify the planes that contain the given line.

16. $\overleftrightarrow{CD}$ *ABC* and *DCG*

17. $\overleftrightarrow{DH}$ *DHG* and *DHE*

18. $\overleftrightarrow{EF}$ *EFG* and *EFB*

Copy the figure. Shade the plane that contains the given points.

19. *A, B, C*

20. *C, D, H*

21. *E, H, B*

19.

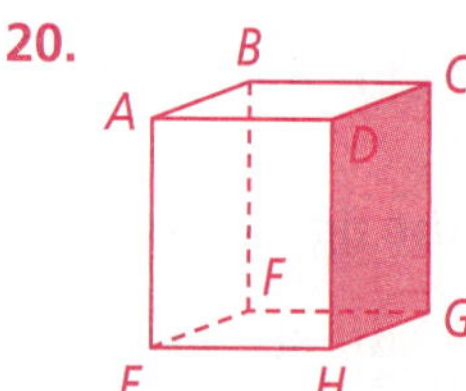

20.

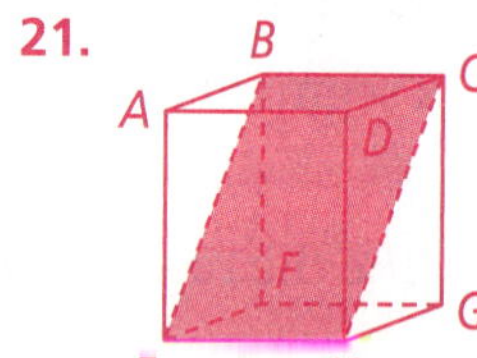

21.

Postulate 1-4 states that any three noncollinear points lie in one plane. Find the plane that contains the first three points listed. Then determine whether the fourth point is in that plane. Write *coplanar* or *noncoplanar* to describe the points.

22. *P, T, R, N* coplanar

23. *P, O, S, N* coplanar

24. *T, R, N, U* noncoplanar

25. *P, O, R, S* noncoplanar

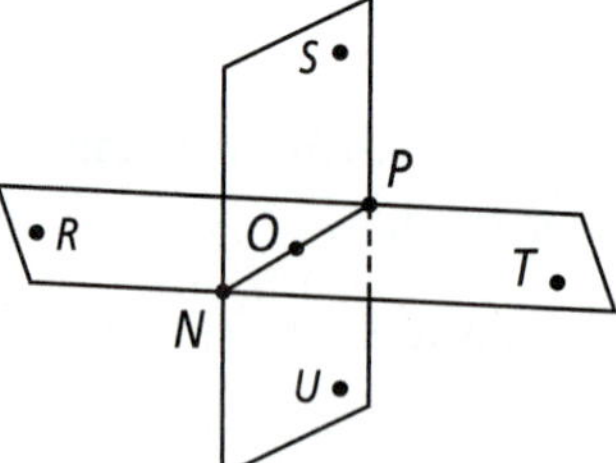

Use the diagram at the right. How many planes contain each line and point?

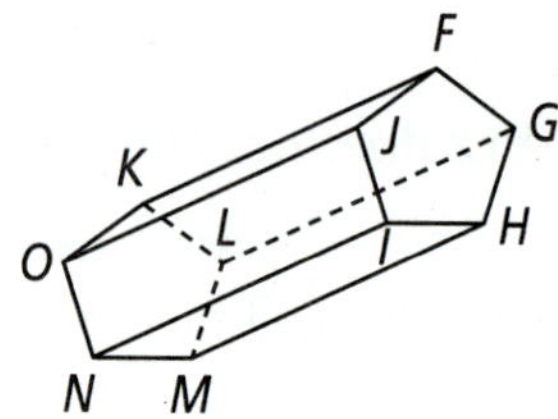

26. $\overleftrightarrow{KL}$ and *G* 1

27. $\overleftrightarrow{HM}$ and *F* 1

28. $\overleftrightarrow{JI}$ and *G* 1

29. $\overleftrightarrow{NM}$ and *M* infinitely many

Name ________________________ Class ____________ Date ____________

1-2 Standardized Test Prep

Points, Lines, and Planes

Multiple Choice

For Exercises 1–7, choose the correct letter.

1. Look at the figure at the right. Where do planes *ACE* and *BCD* intersect? B

A $\overleftrightarrow{AD}$ C $\overleftrightarrow{CB}$

B $\overleftrightarrow{CD}$ D $\overleftrightarrow{BF}$

2. Which of the following are opposite rays? I

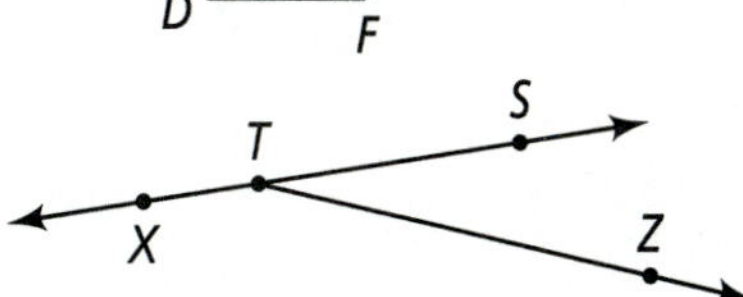

F $\overrightarrow{TS}$ and $\overrightarrow{XS}$ H $\overrightarrow{TS}$ and $\overrightarrow{TZ}$

G $\overrightarrow{TX}$ and $\overrightarrow{TZ}$ I $\overrightarrow{TS}$ and $\overrightarrow{TX}$

3. What is the smallest number of distinct points that can define a plane? B

A 2 B 3 C 4 D infinite

4. At how many points can two distinct lines intersect? F

F 1 G 2 H 3 I 4

5. In the figure at the right, which line is the same as $\overleftrightarrow{ED}$? B

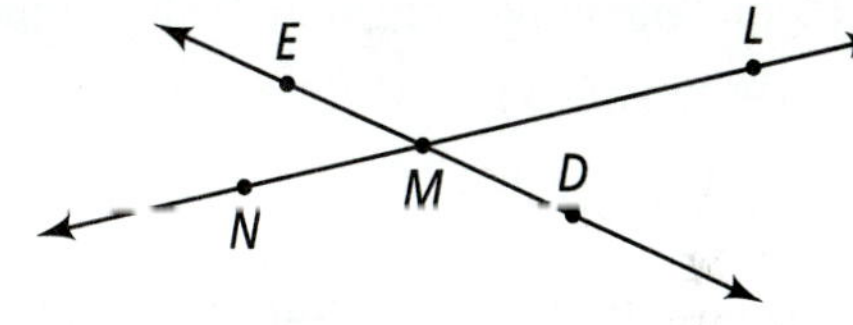

A $\overleftrightarrow{ML}$ C $\overleftrightarrow{NL}$

B $\overleftrightarrow{DM}$ D $\overleftrightarrow{MN}$

6. If two lines are coplanar, which of the following must be true? H

F The lines intersect.

G The lines never intersect.

H All points on the lines are coplanar.

I The lines share at least one point.

7. What is the intersection of two distinct, non-parallel planes? B

A a point B a line C a line segment D a ray

Short Response

8. Point *C* does not lie on $\overleftrightarrow{XY}$. Can point *C* lie in the same plane as $\overleftrightarrow{XY}$? Explain.

[2] Yes; *X*, *Y*, and *C* are noncollinear, and any three noncollinear points are coplanar.
[1] answer correct, but explanation missing, incomplete, or incorrect
[0] no explanation given

1-3 Measuring Segments

Vocabulary

Review

Draw an example of each. Answers may vary. Samples are shown.

1. *point*

• A

2. $\overleftrightarrow{AB}$

3. $\overrightarrow{DF}$

Vocabulary Builder

segment (noun) SEG **munt**

Definition: A **segment** is part of a line that consists of two endpoints and all points between them.

Main Idea: You name a **segment** by its endpoints.

segment *HJ*

H J

Use Your Vocabulary

Complete each sentence with *endpoint, endpoints, line,* or *points.*

4. A *ray* has one _?_. endpoint

5. A *line* contains infinitely many _?_. points

6. A *segment* has two _?_. endpoints

7. A *segment* is part of a _?_. line

Place a check ✓ if the phrase describes a *segment*. Place an ✗ if it does not.

 **8.** Earth's equator

✓ **9.** the right edge of a book's cover

 **10.** one side of a triangle

take note

Postulate 1-5 Ruler Postulate

Every point on a line can be paired with a real number, called the *coordinate* of the point.

Problem 1 Measuring Segment Lengths

Got It? Use the number line to find TV and SV.

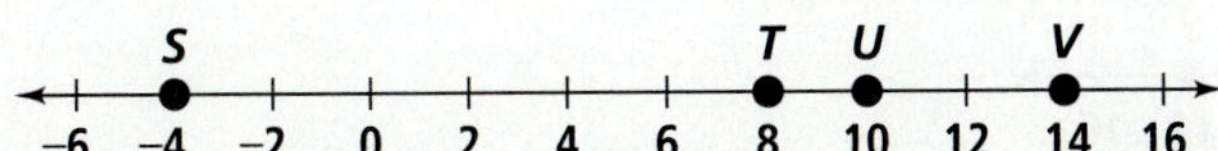

11. Find TV and SV. Write a justification for each statement.

$TV = \lvert 8 - 14 \rvert$	Definition of distance	$SV = \lvert -4 - 14 \rvert$
$TV = \lvert 6 \rvert$	Subtract.	$SV = \lvert -18 \rvert$
$TV = 6$	Find the absolute value.	$SV = 18$

take note — Postulate 1-6 Segment Addition Postulate

If three points A, B, and C are collinear and B is between A and C, then $AB + BC = AC$.

Given points A, B, and C are collinear and B is between A and C, complete each equation.

12. $AB = 5$ and $BC = 4$, so $AB + BC =$ 5 + 4 and $AC =$ 9.

13. $AC = 12$ and $BC = 7$, so $AC - BC =$ 12 − 7 and $AB =$ 5.

Problem 2 Using the Segment Addition Postulate

Got It? In the diagram, $JL = 120$. What are JK and KL?

14. Write a justification for each statement.

$JK + KL = JL$	Segment Addition Postulate
$(4x + 6) + (7x + 15) = 120$	Substitute.
$11x + 21 = 120$	Simplify.
$11x = 99$	Subtract 21 from each side.
$x = 9$	Divide each side by 11.

15. You know that $JK = 4x + 6$ and $KL = 7x + 15$. Use the value of x from Exercise 14 to to find JK and KL. Find JK and KL.

$4(9) + 6 = 36 + 6 = 42$ and $7(9) + 15 = 63 + 15 = 78$

16. $JK =$ 42 and $KL =$ 78.

Problem 3 Comparing Segment Lengths

Got It? Use the diagram below. Is $\overline{AB}$ congruent to $\overline{DE}$?

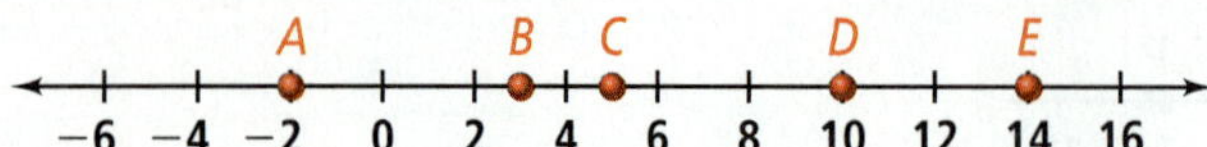

In Exercises 18 and 19, circle the expression that completes the equation.

17. $AB = ■$

$-2-2$	$\lvert -2-2 \rvert$	(circled) $\lvert -2-3 \rvert$	$\lvert -2-4 \rvert$

18. $DE = ■$

$3-14$	$10+14$	$\lvert 5-14 \rvert$	(circled) $\lvert 10-14 \rvert$

19. After simplifying, AB = 5 and DE = 4.

20. Is $\overline{AB}$ congruent to $\overline{DE}$? Explain. Explanations may vary. Sample:

No. Segments with different lengths are not congruent.

The *midpoint* of a segment is the point that divides the segment into two congruent segments.

Use the number line below for Exercises 21–24.

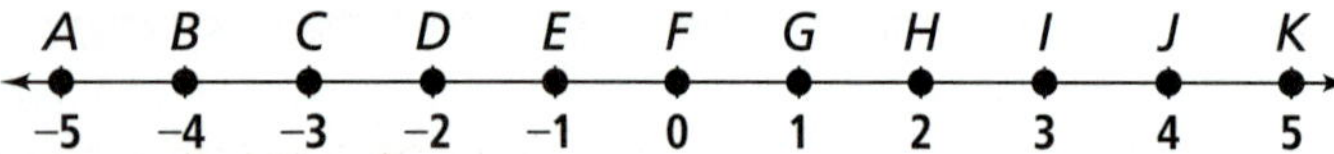

21. Point F is halfway between points B and J.

22. The midpoint of $\overline{AE}$ is point C.

23. Point H divides $\overline{EK}$ into two congruent segments.

24. Find the midpoint of each segment. Then write the coordinate of the midpoint.

	$\overline{AG}$	$\overline{DH}$	$\overline{AK}$
Midpoint	D	F	F
Coordinate	−2	0	0

25. Find the coordinate of the midpoint of each segment.

	segment with endpoints at −4 and 2	segment with endpoints at −2 and 4
Coordinate of midpoint	−1	1

26. Circle the expression that relates the coordinate of the midpoint to the coordinates of the endpoints, x_1 and x_2.

$x_1 + x_2$	(circled) $\frac{(x_1 + x_2)}{2}$	$\frac{(x_1 - x_2)}{2}$

Problem 4 Using the Midpoint

Got It? *U* is the midpoint of $\overline{TV}$. What are *TU*, *UV*, and *TV*?

8x + 11 12x − 1
T U V

28. Use the justifications to complete the steps.

Step 1 Find *x*.

$TU = UV$	Definition of midpoint
$8x + 11 = 12x - 1$	Substitute.
$8x + 11 + 1 = 12x - 1 + 1$	Add 1 to each side.
$12 = 4x$	Subtract 8*x* from each side.
$3 = x$	Divide each side by 4.

Step 2 Find *TU* and *UV*.

$TU = 8 \cdot 3 + 11 = 35$	Substitute 3 for *x*.
$UV = 12 \cdot 3 - 1 = 35$	Substitute.

Step 3 Find *TV*.

$TV = TU + UV$	Definition of midpoint
$= 35 + 35$	Substitute.
$= 70$	Simplify.

Lesson Check • Do you UNDERSTAND?

Vocabulary Name two segment bisectors of $\overline{PR}$.

ℓ
P Q R S T
2 3 4 5 6

Underline the correct word or symbol to complete each sentence.

29. A bisector / midpoint may be a point, line, ray, or segment.

30. The midpoint of $\overline{PR}$ is point *P* / *Q* / *R*.

31. Line ℓ passes through point *P* / *Q* / *R*.

32. Two bisectors of $\overline{PR}$ are Q and ℓ.

Math Success

Check off the vocabulary words that you understand.

☐ congruent segments ☐ coordinate ☐ midpoint ☐ segment bisector

Rate how well you can *find lengths of segments.*

Need to review 0 2 4 6 8 10 Now I get it!

Name ____________________ Class __________ Date __________

1-3 Think About a Plan

Measuring Segments

If $AD = 12$ and $AC = 4y - 36$, find the value of y. Then find AC and DC.

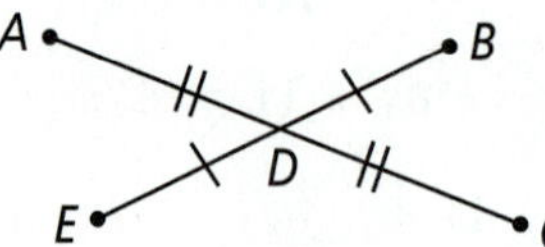

Understanding the Problem

1. What are the two congruence relationships that the diagram shows?
   $AD = DC$, $BD = DE$
2. What is the value of DC? 12
3. Write an equation that describes the relationship between AC, DC, and AD.
   $AC = AD + DC$

Planning the Solution

4. How can you use the equation in Exercise 3 above to find the value of y?
   Substitute the given values for AC and AD, and the value of DC, into the equation above.

Getting an Answer

5. Write an equation for y using the method described in Exercise 4 above.
   $4y - 36 = 12 + 12$ or $4y - 36 = 24$
6. Solve for y.
   $y = 15$
7. $AC = 4y - 36$. Substitute the value of y to find AC.
   24
8. Check your answer. Does it make the equation that you wrote in Step 5 true? yes

Name ______________________ Class ____________ Date ____________

1-3 Practice

Form K

Measuring Segments

Find the length of each segment. To start, find the coordinate of each endpoint.

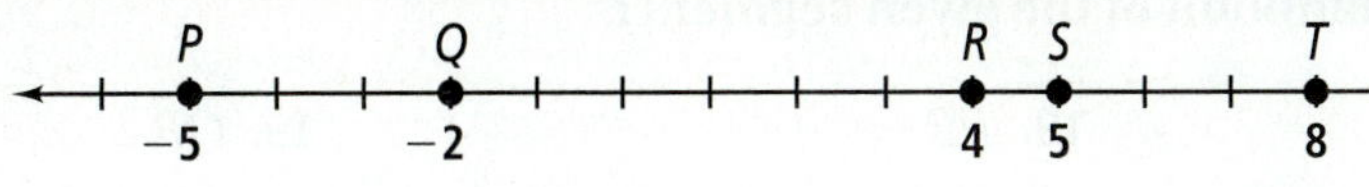

1. $\overline{PR}$ 9

2. $\overline{QT}$ 10

3. $\overline{QS}$ 7

Use the number line at the right for Exercises 4–6.

4. If $GH = 31$ and $HI = 11$, then $GI =$ 42.

5. If $GH = 45$ and $GI = 61$, then $HI =$ 16.

6. **Algebra** $GH = 7y + 3$, $HI = 3y - 5$, and $GI = 9y + 7$.
   a. What is the value of y? 9
   b. Find GH, HI, and GI. 66; 22; 88

Use the number line below for Exercises 7–9. Tell whether the segments are congruent. To start, use the definition of distance. Use the coordinates of the points to write an equation for each distance.

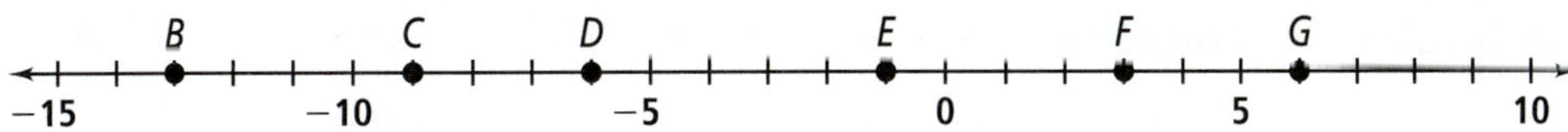

7. $\overline{CE}$ and $\overline{FD}$ no

8. $\overline{CD}$ and $\overline{FG}$ yes

9. $\overline{GE}$ and $\overline{BD}$ yes

For Exercises 10–12, use the figure below. Find the value of KL.

10. $KL = 3x + 2$ and $LM = 5x - 10$ 20

11. $KL = 8x - 5$ and $LM = 6x + 3$ 27

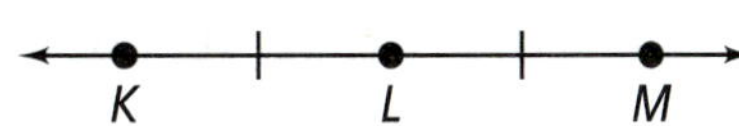

12. $KL = 4x + 7$ and $LM = 5x - 4$ 51

On a number line, the coordinates of D, E, F, G, and H are −9, −2, 0, 3, and 5, respectively. Find the lengths of the two segments. Then tell whether they are congruent.

13. $\overline{DG}$ and $\overline{DH}$ 12 and 14; no

14. $\overline{DE}$ and $\overline{EH}$ 7 and 7; yes

15. $\overline{EG}$ and $\overline{GH}$ 5 and 2; no

16. $\overline{EG}$ and $\overline{FH}$ 5 and 5; yes

Name ______________________ Class ____________ Date ____________

1-3 Practice (continued) — Form K

Measuring Segments

Suppose the coordinate of P is 2, $PQ = 8$, and $PR = 12$. What are the possible coordinates of the midpoint of the given segment?

17. $\overline{PQ}$
6 or −2

18. $\overline{PR}$
8 or −4

19. $\overline{QR}$
12, 4, 0 or −8

Visualization **Without using your ruler, sketch a segment with the given length. Use your ruler to see how well your sketch approximates the length provided.** Check students' work.

20. 5 cm

21. 8 in.

22. 8 cm

23. 12 cm

24. 85 mm

25. 5 in.

26. Suppose point J has a coordinate of −2 and $JK = 4$. What are the possible coordinates of point K? −6 and 2

27. Suppose point X has a coordinate of 5 and $XY = 10$. What are the possible coordinates of point Y? 15 or −5

Algebra **Use the diagram at the right for Exercises 28–32.**

N
Q
R
O
P

28. If $NO = 17$ and $NP = 5x - 6$, find the value of x. Then find NP and OP. 8, $NP = 34$, $OP = 17$

29. If $RO = 6 + x$ and $OQ = 2x + 1$, find the value of x. Then find RO, OQ, and RQ. 5; $RO = 11$, $OQ = 11$, and $RQ = 22$

30. If $NO = 3x + 4$ and $NP = 10x - 10$, find the value of x. Then find NO, NP, and OP. 4.5; $NO = 17.5$; $OP = 17.5$; $NP = 35$

31. If $RO = 5x$ and $RQ = 12x - 20$, find the value of x. Then find RO, OQ, and RQ. 10; $RO = 50$, $OQ = 50$, and $RQ = 100$

32. **Vocabulary** What term describes the relationship between $\overline{NP}$ and $\overline{RQ}$?
They are segment bisectors of each other because they divide each other in half.

33. **Reasoning** If $KL = 5$ and $KJ = 10$, is it possible that $LJ = 5$? Explain.
Yes; if L is between K and J, and L is on the segment $\overline{KJ}$, then $LJ = 5$.

Name ______________________ Class ____________ Date ____________

1-3 Standardized Test Prep

Measuring Segments

Gridded Response

Solve each exercise and enter your answer on the grid provided.

1. What is the length of $\overline{BD}$?

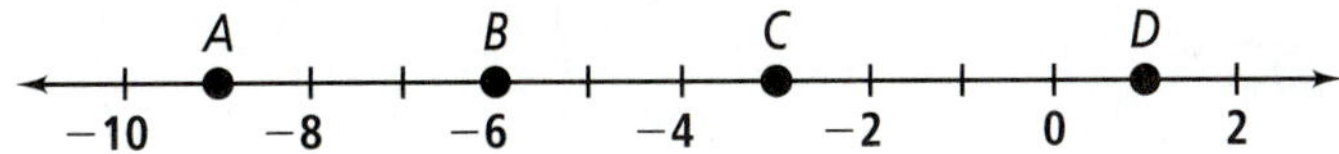

2. Points G, H, and I are collinear and H is between G and I. If $GH = 12$ and $GI = 23$, what is HI?

3. Look at the diagram below. If $XY = 7$ and $XZ = 30$, what is the value of t?

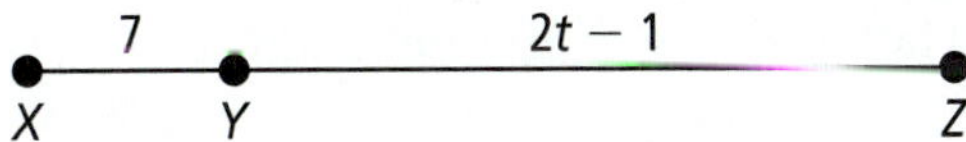

For Exercises 4 and 5, use the figure at the right.

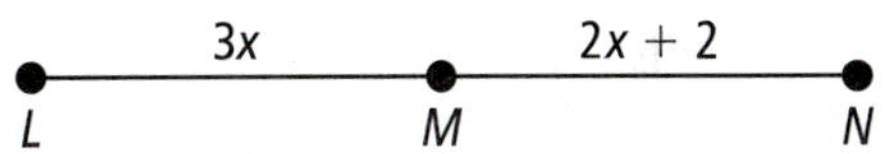

4. M is the midpoint of $\overline{LN}$. What is LM?

5. What is LN?

Answers

1. 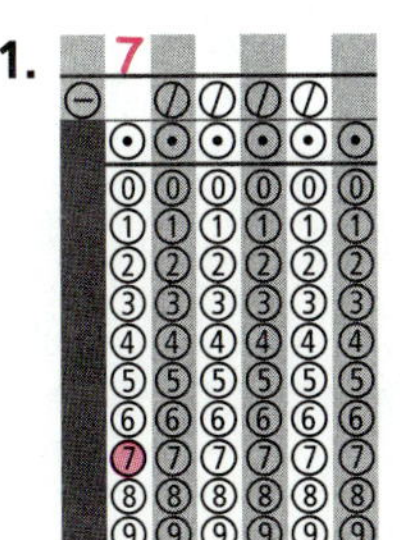

2. 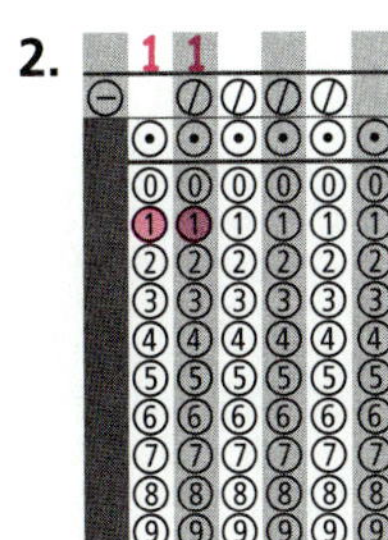

3. 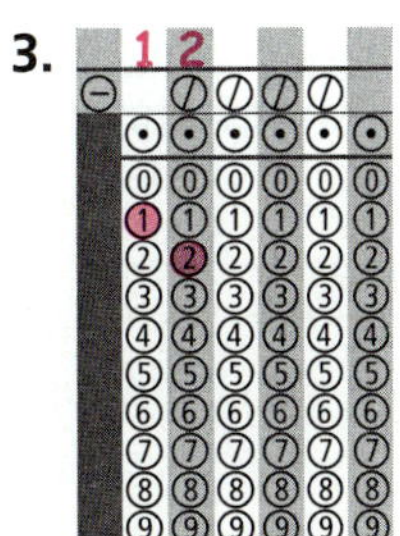

4. 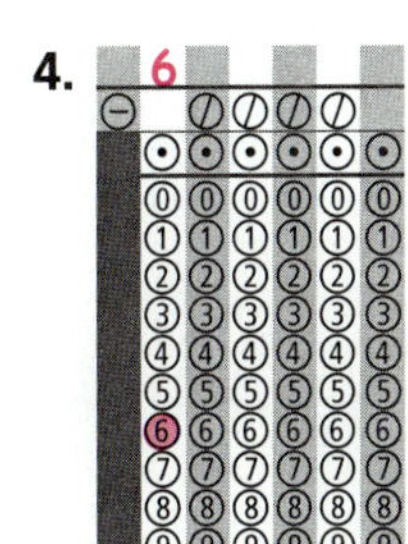

5. 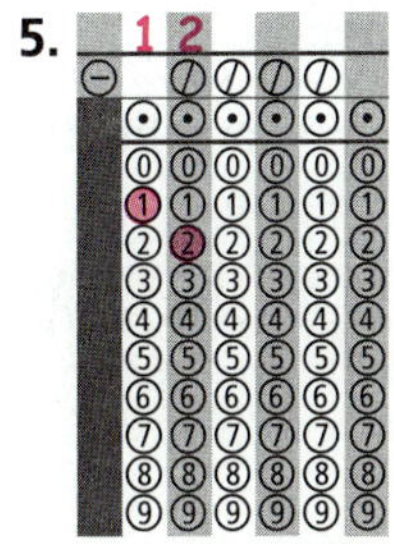

1-4 Measuring Angles

Vocabulary

Review

Write T for *true* or F for *false*.

F **1.** $\overrightarrow{AB}$ names a *ray* with endpoints *A* and *B*.

T **2.** You name a *ray* by its endpoint and another point on the *ray*.

Vocabulary Builder

angle (noun, verb) ANG **gul**

Other Word Forms: angular (adjective), angle (verb), angled (adjective)

Definition: An **angle** is formed by two rays with the same endpoint.

Use Your Vocabulary

Name the rays that form each *angle*.

3. 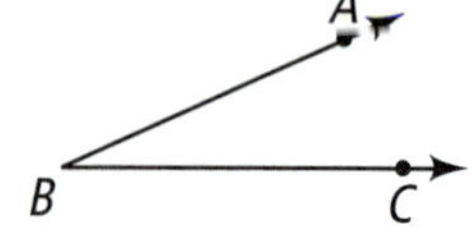

$\overrightarrow{BA}$ and $\overrightarrow{BC}$

4. 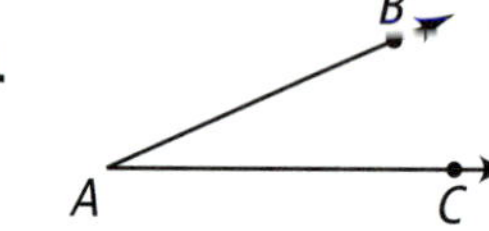

$\overrightarrow{AB}$ and $\overrightarrow{AC}$

take note Key Concept Angle

Definition	How to Name It	Diagram
An **angle** is formed by two rays with the same endpoint. The rays are the **sides** of the angle. The endpoint is the **vertex** of the angle.	You can name an angle by • its vertex • a point on each ray and the vertex • a number	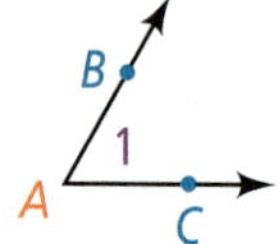

For Exercises 5–8, use the diagram in the Take Note on page 28. Name each part of the angle.

5. the *vertex*

A

6. two points that are NOT the vertex

B and C

7. the *sides*

$\overrightarrow{AB}$ and $\overrightarrow{AC}$

8. Name the angle three ways.

by its *vertex*

∠A

by a point on each side and the vertex

∠BAC

by a number

∠1

Problem 1 Naming Angles

Got It? What are two other names for ∠*KML*?

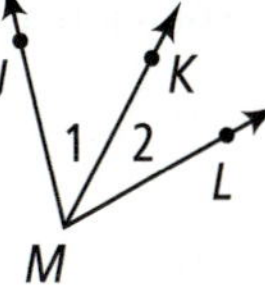

9. Cross out the ray that is NOT a ray of ∠*KML*.

$\overrightarrow{MK}$ ~~$\overrightarrow{MJ}$~~ $\overrightarrow{ML}$

10. Circle all the possible names of ∠*KML*.

∠1 (∠2) ∠*JKL* ∠*JMK* ∠*JML* ∠*KMJ* (∠*LMK*)

take note

Key Concept Types of Angles

11. Draw your own example of each type of angle. Angles may vary. Samples are given.

acute	right	obtuse	straight
$0 < x <$ 90	$x =$ 90	90 $< x <$ 180	$x =$ 180

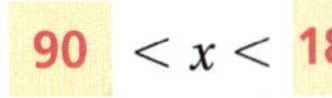
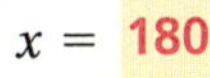
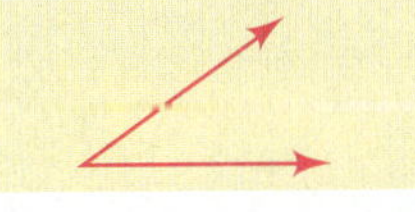
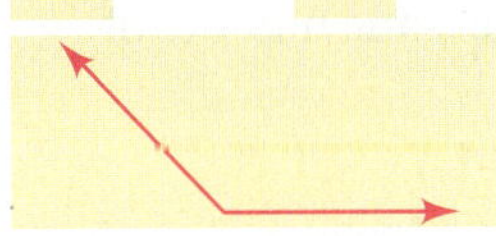

In the diagram, $m\angle ABC = 70$ and $m\angle BFE = 90$. Describe each angle as *acute, right, obtuse* or *straight.* Give an angle measure to support your description.

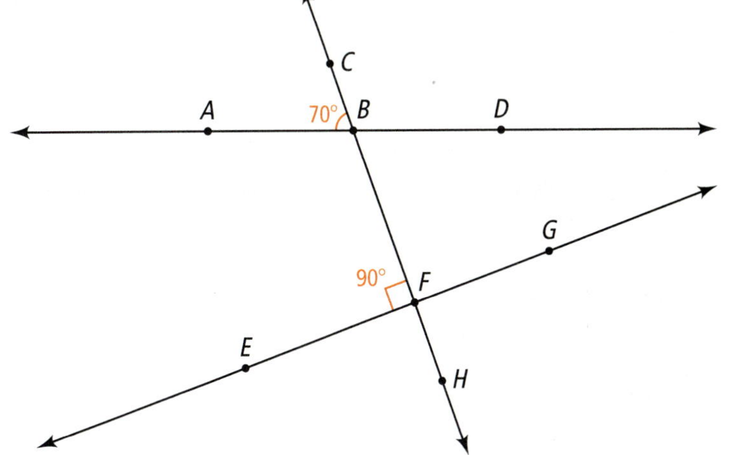

12. ∠*ABC*

acute; 70°

13. ∠*CBD*

obtuse; 110°

14. ∠*CFG*

right; 90°

15. ∠*CFH*

straight; 180°

Problem 2 Measuring and Classifying Angles

Got It? What are the measures of $\angle LKH$, $\angle HKN$, and $\angle MKH$ in the art below? Classify each angle as *acute, right, obtuse,* or *straight.*

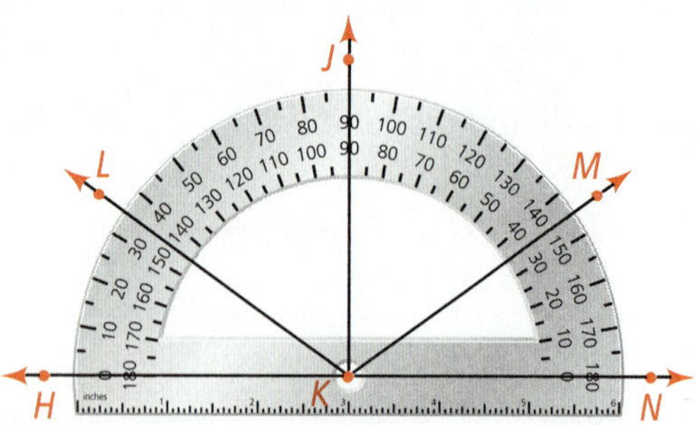

16. Write the measure of each angle. Then classify each angle.

$\angle LKH$	$\angle HKN$	$\angle MKH$
35°	180°	145°
acute	straight	obtuse

Problem 3 Using Congruent Angles

Got It? Use the photo at the right. If $m\angle ABC = 49$, what is $m\angle DEF$?

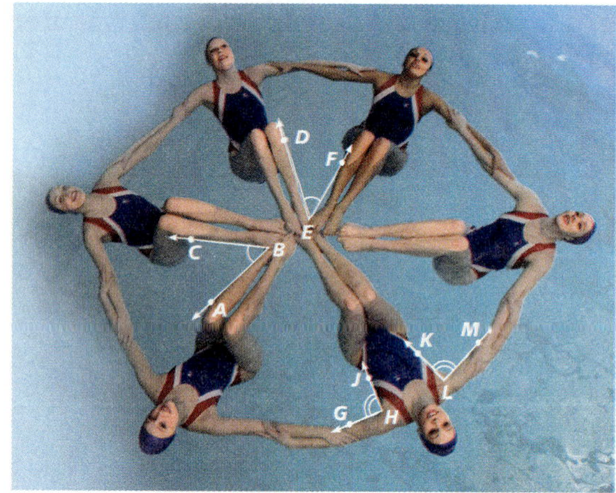

17. $\angle ABC$ has 1 angle mark(s).

18. The other angle with the same number of marks is $\angle$ DEF.

19. Underline the correct word to complete the sentence.

The measure of $\angle ABC$ and the measure of the angle in Exercise 18 are equal / unequal.

20. $m\angle DEF =$ 49

take note

Postulate 1-8 Angle Addition Postulate

If point B is in the interior of $\angle AOC$, then $m\angle AOB + m\angle BOC = m\angle AOC$.

21. Draw $\angle ABT$ with point L in the interior and $\angle ABL$ and $\angle LBT$.

Angles may vary. Sample:

A, L, B, T

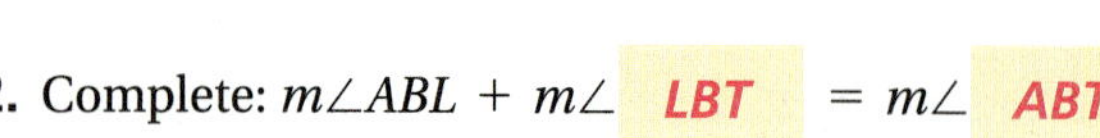

22. Complete: $m\angle ABL + m\angle$ LBT $= m\angle$ ABT

Problem 4 Using the Angle Addition Postulate

Got It? $\angle DEF$ is a straight angle. What are $m\angle DEC$ and $m\angle CEF$?

C
(11x − 12)°
(2x + 10)°
D E F

23. Write a justification for each statement.

Statement	Justification
$m\angle DEF = 180$	A straight angle measures 180°.
$m\angle DEC + m\angle CEF = 180$	Angle Addition Postulate
$(11x - 12) + (2x + 10) = 180$	Substitute.
$13x - 2 = 180$	Simplify.
$13x = 182$	Add 2 to each side.
$x = 14$	Divide each side by 13.

24. Use the value of x to find $m\angle DEC$ and $m\angle CEF$.

$m\angle DEC = 11x - 12 = 11(\ 14\ ) - 12 = 142$

$m\angle CEF = 2x + 10 = 2(14) + 10 = 28 + 10 = 38$

Lesson Check • Do you know How?

Algebra If $m\angle ABD = 85$, what is an expression to represent $m\angle ABC$?

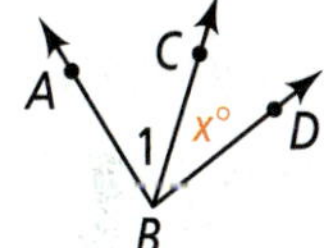

25. Use the justifications at the right to complete the statements below.

Statement	Justification
$m\angle ABC + m\angle CBD = m\angle ABD$	Angle Addition Postulate
$m\angle ABC + x = 85$	Substitute.
$m\angle ABC + x - x = 85 - x$	Subtract x from each side.
$m\angle ABC = 85 - x$	Simplify.

Math Success

Check off the vocabulary words that you understand.

☐ acute angle ☐ obtuse angle ☐ right angle ☐ straight angle

Rate how well you can *classify angles.*

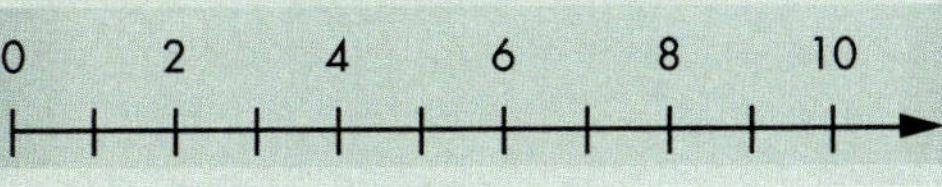

Name ______________________ Class ____________ Date ____________

1-4 Think About a Plan

Measuring Angles

Use the diagram at the right. Solve for *x*. Find the angle measures to check your work.

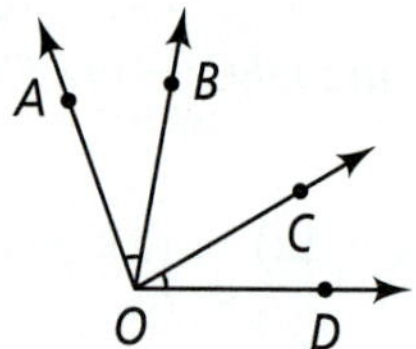

$m\angle AOB = 4x - 2$, $m\angle BOC = 5x + 10$, $m\angle COD = 2x + 14$

Understanding the Problem

1. The diagram shows that $\angle AOB$ and $\angle COD$ are congruent.

2. So, $m\angle AOB =$ $m\angle COD$.

Planning the Solution

3. How can you use the information in Step 2 to write an equation for *x*?

   Substitute the given values of $m\angle AOB$ and $m\angle COD$ into the equation in Exercise 2.

4. Write an equation for *x*.

   $4x - 2 = 2x + 14$

Getting an Answer

5. Solve for *x*. $x = 8$

6. Find the measures of the angles by substituting for *x*.

   $m\angle AOB =$ 30

   $m\angle BOC =$ 50

   $m\angle COD =$ 30

7. Measure the angles using a protractor to check your answers. Are they reasonable?

   yes

Name ______________________ Class ____________ Date ____________

1-4 Practice

Form K

Measuring Angles

Name each shaded angle in three different ways. To start, identify the rays that form each angle.

1.

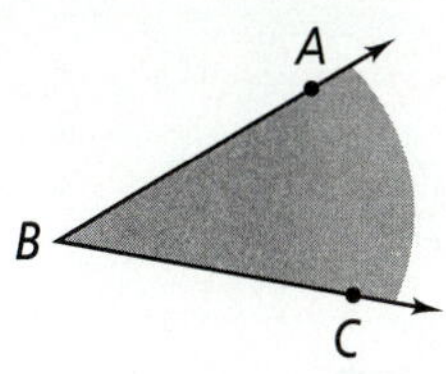

∠ABC, ∠CBA, ∠B

2.

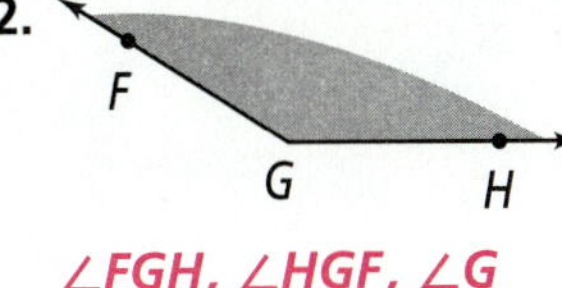

∠FGH, ∠HGF, ∠G

3.

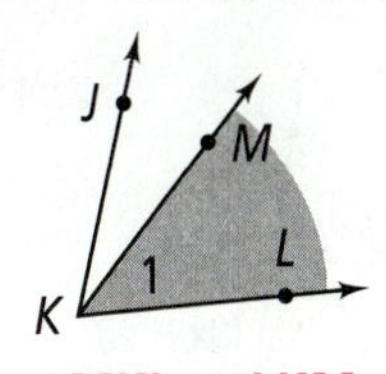

∠MKL, ∠LKM, ∠1

Use the diagram below. Find the measure of each angle. Then classify the angle as *acute, right, obtuse,* or *straight.*

4. ∠*AFB*

To start, identify ∠*AFB*. Then use the definition of the measure of an angle to find *m*∠*AFB*.

$m\angle AFB = |\boxed{180} - \boxed{130}| = \boxed{50}$

This angle is a(n) __?__ angle. acute

5. ∠*AFD* 140; obtuse

6. ∠*CFD* 65; acute

7. ∠*BFD* 90; right

8. ∠*AFE* 180; straight

9. ∠*BFE* 130; obtuse

10. ∠*AFC* 75; acute

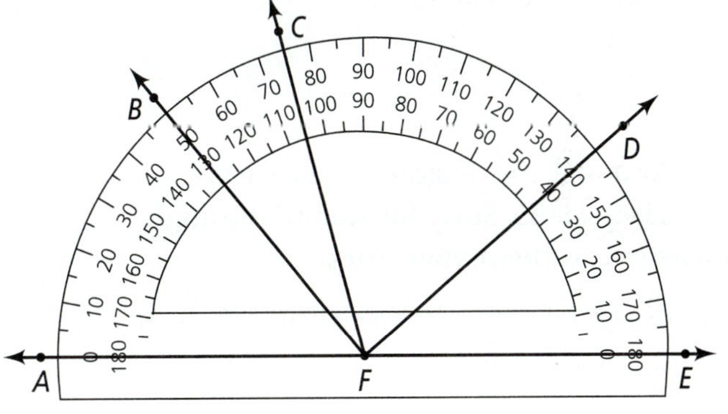

Use the diagram at the right. Complete each statement.

11. ∠*MIG* ≅ $\boxed{\angle JIH}$

12. ∠*PMJ* ≅ $\boxed{\angle GHQ}$

13. If *m*∠*KJL* = 30, then *m*∠$\boxed{MJI}$ = 30.

14. If *m*∠*LMP* = 100, then *m*∠*QHG* = $\boxed{100}$.

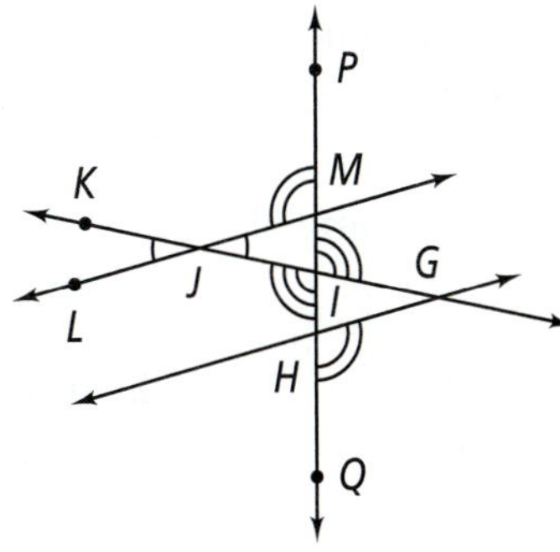

Name ______________________ Class ____________ Date ____________

1-4 Practice (continued) — Form K

Measuring Angles

15. If $m\angle FHI = 142$, what are $m\angle FHG$ and $m\angle GHI$?

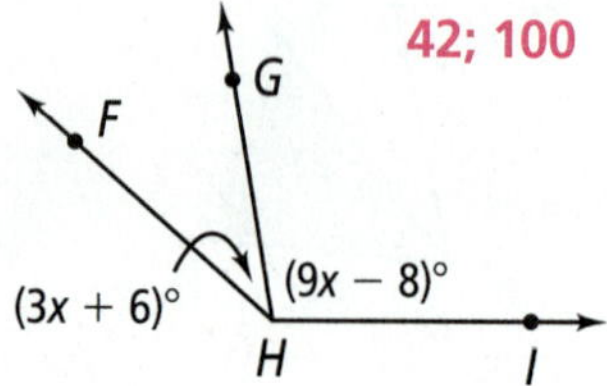

42; 100

16. $\angle JKL$ is a right angle. What are $m\angle JKM$ and $m\angle MKL$?

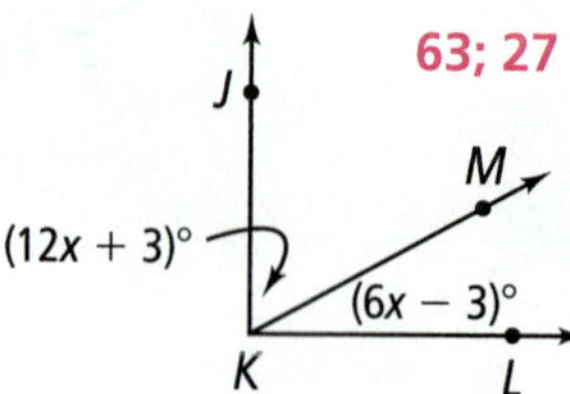

63; 27

Use a protractor. Measure and classify each angle.

17. 162; obtuse

18. 58; acute

19. 100; obtuse

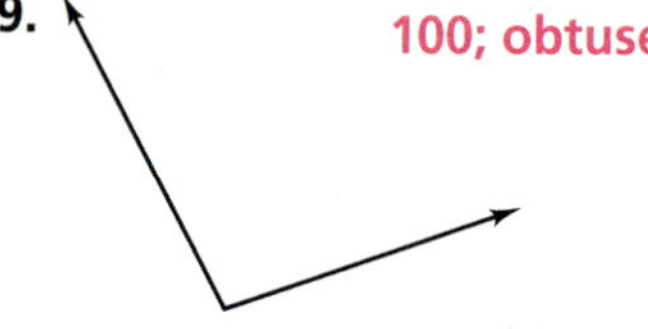

20. 90; right

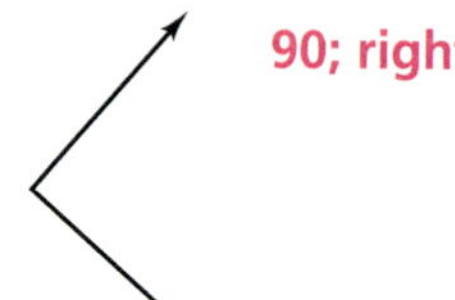

Algebra **Use the diagram at the right for Exercises 21–23. Solve for *x*. Find the angle measures to check your work.**

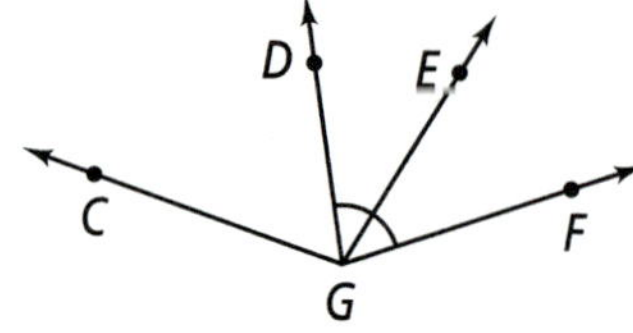

21. $m\angle CGD = 4x + 2$, $m\angle DGE = 3x - 5$, $m\angle EGF = 2x + 10$ 15; 62; 40; 40

22. $m\angle CGD = 2x - 2$, $m\angle EGF = 37$, $m\angle CGF = 7x + 2$ 14; 26; 37; 37; 100

23. If $m\angle DGF = 72$, what equation can you use to find $m\angle EGF$? $2x = 72$

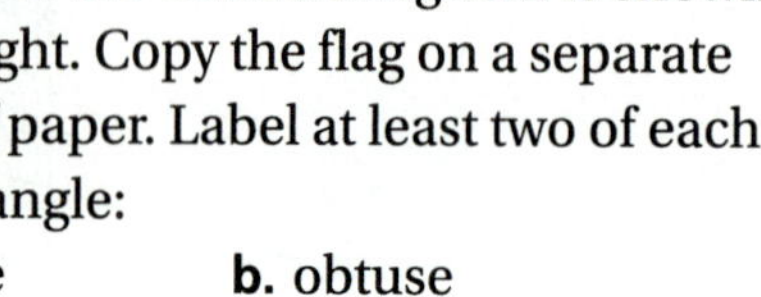

24. The flag of the United Kingdom is shown at the right. Copy the flag on a separate piece of paper. Label at least two of each type of angle:

a. acute **b.** obtuse

c. right **d.** straight Check students' work.

Name ______________________ Class ____________ Date ____________

1-4 Standardized Test Prep

Measuring Angles

Multiple Choice

For Exercises 1–5, choose the correct letter.

1. What is $m\angle BAC$? A

Ⓐ 25

Ⓑ 50

Ⓒ 130

Ⓓ 155

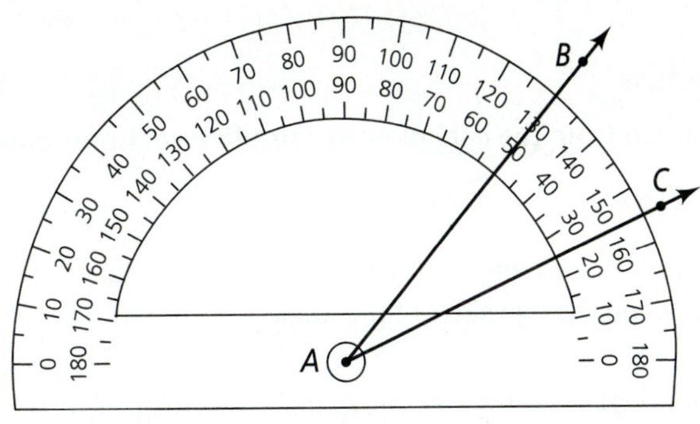

2. What is another name for $\angle 4$? H

Ⓕ $\angle VWS$ Ⓗ $\angle SVW$

Ⓖ $\angle SWV$ Ⓘ $\angle WVT$

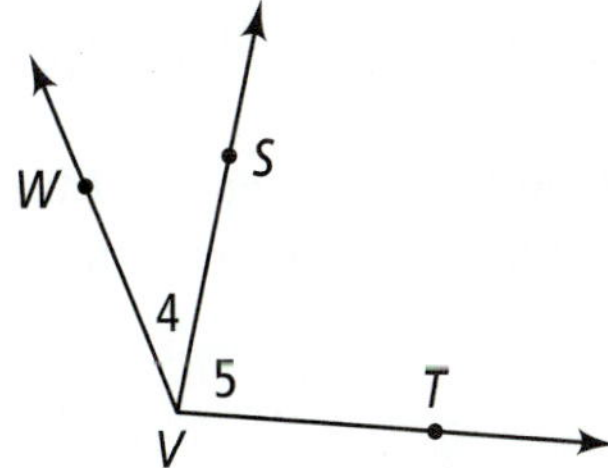

3. $m\angle KLM = 129$ and $m\angle MNO = 129$. What is true about these two angles? B

Ⓐ They are both acute angles. Ⓒ They are both right angles.

Ⓑ They are congruent. Ⓓ They are both straight angles.

4. $m\angle MRT = 133$. What is $m\angle MRN$? H

Ⓕ 24 Ⓗ 46

Ⓖ 48 Ⓘ 87

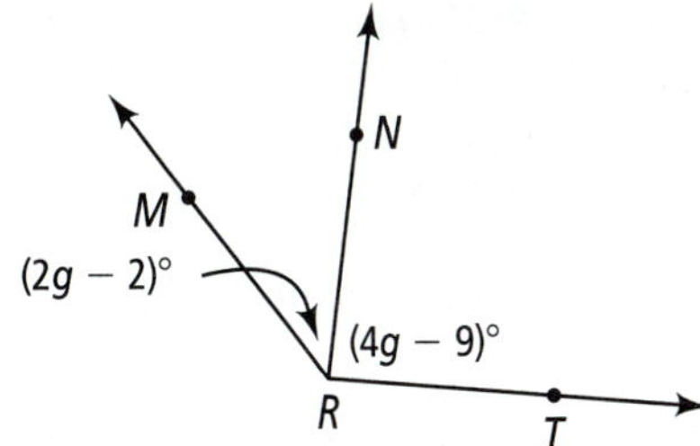

5. $\angle LJB$ and $\angle IJM$ are congruent. If the sum of the measures of the angles is 90, what type of angle are they? A

Ⓐ acute Ⓑ obtuse Ⓒ right Ⓓ straight

Short Response

6. $m\angle RNY + m\angle GNC = 128$ and $\angle RNY \cong \angle GNC$. What is true about these two angles? [2] They are both acute angles and they each measure 64. [1] only one of two characteristics listed [0] no characteristics listed

1-5 Exploring Angle Pairs

Vocabulary

Review

Use a word from the list below to complete each sentence. Use each word just once.

interior rays vertex

1. The _?_ of an *angle* is the region containing all of the points between the two sides of the angle. interior

2. When you use three points to name an *angle*, the _?_ must go in the middle. vertex

3. The sides of $\angle QRS$ are _?_ RS and RQ. rays

Use the figure below for Exercises 4–7. Identify each angle as *acute, right, obtuse,* or *straight.*

4. $\angle SRV$ obtuse

5. $\angle TRS$ acute

6. $\angle TRQ$ right

7. $\angle VRQ$ straight

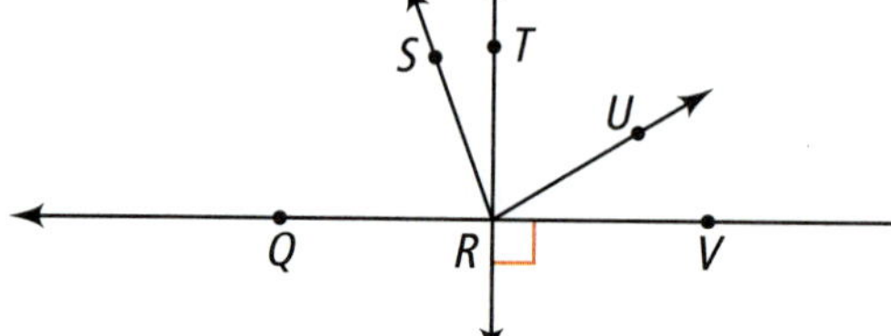

Vocabulary Builder

conclusion (noun) **kun KLOO zhun**

Other Word Forms: conclude (verb)

Definition: A **conclusion** is the end of an event or the last step in a reasoning process.

Use Your Vocabulary

Complete each sentence with *conclude* or *conclusion*.

8. If it rains, you can _?_ that soccer practice will be canceled. conclude

9. The last step of the proof is the _?_. conclusion

take note

Key Concept Types of Angle Pairs

Angle Pair	Definition
Adjacent angles	Two coplanar angles with a common side, a common vertex, and no common interior points
Vertical angles	Two angles whose sides are opposite rays
Complementary angles	Two angles whose measures have a sum of 90
Supplementary angles	Two angles whose measures have a sum of 180

Draw a line from each word in Column A to the angles it describes in Column B.

Column A	Column B
10. supplementary	∠1 and ∠2
11. adjacent	∠2 and ∠3
12. vertical	∠2 and ∠5
13. complementary	∠3 and ∠6

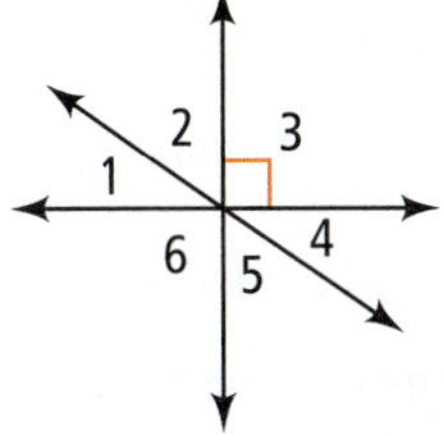

Problem 1 Identifying Angle Pairs

Got It? Use the diagram at the right. Are ∠*AFE* and ∠*CFD* vertical angles? Explain.

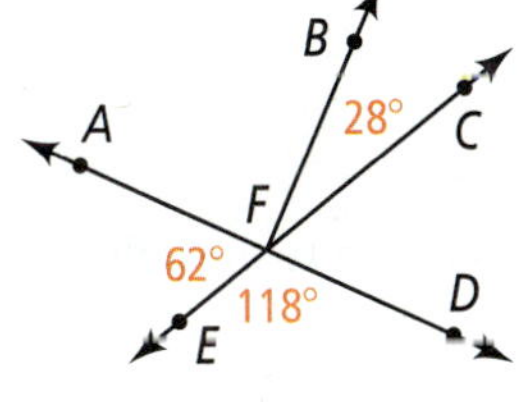

14. The rays of ∠*AFE* are $\overrightarrow{FE}$ and $\overrightarrow{FC}$ / $\overrightarrow{FA}$.

15. The rays of ∠*CFD* are $\overrightarrow{FC}$ and $\overrightarrow{FD}$ / $\overrightarrow{FA}$.

Complete each statement.

16. $\overrightarrow{FE}$ and $\overrightarrow{FC}$ are opposite rays.

17. $\overrightarrow{FA}$ and $\overrightarrow{FD}$ are opposite rays.

18. Are ∠*AFE* and ∠*CFD* vertical angles? Yes / No

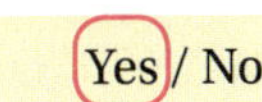

Problem 2 Making Conclusions From a Diagram

Got It? Can you conclude that $\overline{TW} \cong \overline{WV}$ from the diagram? Explain.

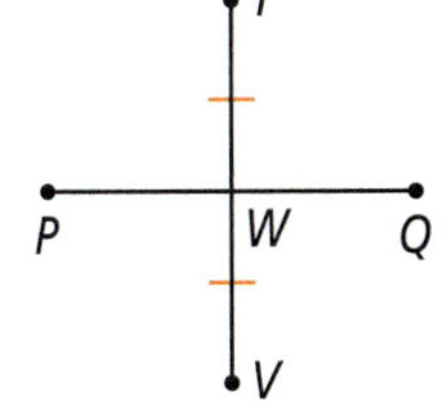

19. Circle the items marked as congruent in the diagram.

$\overline{PW}$ and $\overline{WQ}$ $\overline{TW}$ and $\overline{WV}$

∠*TWQ* and ∠*PWT* ∠*TWQ* and ∠*VWQ*

20. Can you conclude that $\overline{TW} \cong \overline{WV}$? Why or why not? Explanations may vary. Sample:

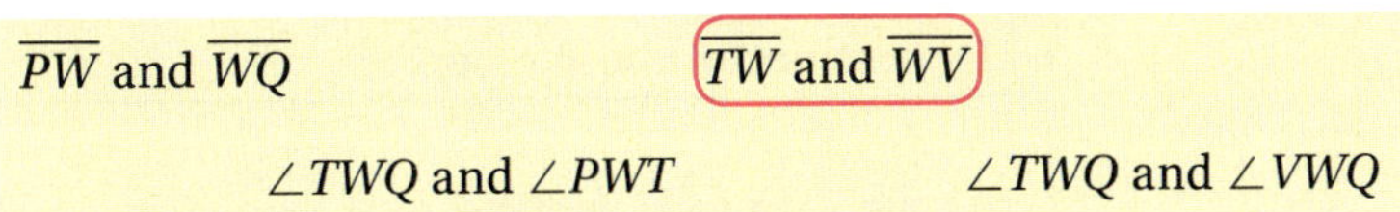

Yes. Congruence marks are on $\overline{TW}$ and $\overline{WV}$.

take note

Postulate 1-9 Linear Pair Postulate

If two angles form a linear pair, then they are supplementary.

21. If $\angle A$ and $\angle B$ form a linear pair, then $m\angle A + m\angle B =$ 180.

Problem 3 Finding Missing Angle Measures

Got It? $\angle ADB$ and $\angle BDC$ are a linear pair. $m\angle ADB = 3x + 14$, and $m\angle BDC = 5x - 2$. What are $m\angle ADB$ and $m\angle BDC$?

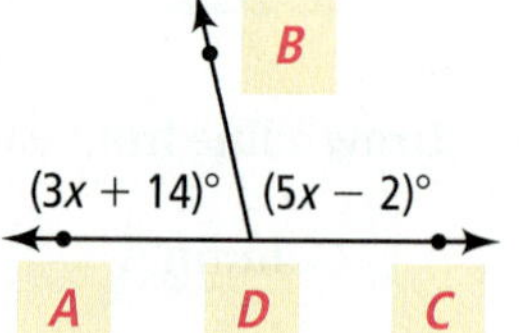

22. Complete the diagram of $\angle ADB$ and $\angle BDC$ by writing the letter name of each point.

23. Write *complementary, supplementary,* or *vertical* to complete the statement below.

$\angle ADB$ and $\angle BDC$ are _?_ angles. supplementary

24. Circle the equation you can solve to find the value of x.

$3x + 14 = 5x - 2$ $\quad$ $(3x + 14) + (5x - 2) = 90$ $\quad$ $(3x + 14) + (5x - 2) = 180$ (circled)

25. Use your answer to Exercise 24 to find the value of x.

$$m\angle ADB + m\angle BDC = 180$$
$$(3x + 14) + (5x - 2) = 180$$
$$8x + 12 = 180$$
$$8x = 168$$
$$x = 21$$

26. Substitute the value for x in each expression.

$m\angle ADB = 3x + 14$
$= 3 \cdot 21 + 14$
$= 63 + 14$
$= 77$

$m\angle BDC = 5x - 2$
$= 5 \cdot 21 - 2$
$= 105 - 2$
$= 103$

Problem 4 Using an Angle Bisector to Find Angle Measures

Got It? $\overrightarrow{KM}$ bisects $\angle JKL$. If $m\angle JKL = 72$, what is $m\angle JKM$?

27. Write a justification for each step.

$m\angle JKM = m\angle MKL$ — Definition of angle bisector

$m\angle JKM + m\angle MKL = m\angle JKL$ — Angle Addition Postulate

$2m\angle JKM = m\angle JKL$ — Substitute.

$m\angle JKM = \frac{1}{2}m\angle JKL$ — Divide each side by 2.

28. Complete.

$m\angle JKL =$ 72, so $m\angle JKM =$ 36.

29. Now complete the diagram below.

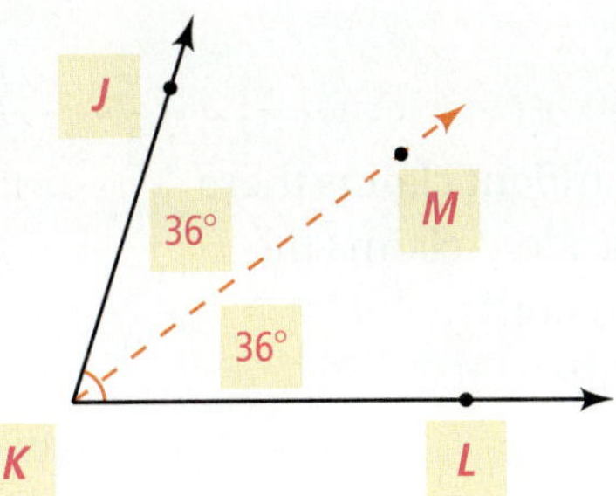

Lesson Check • Do you UNDERSTAND?

Error Analysis **Your friend calculated the value of *x* below. What is her error?**

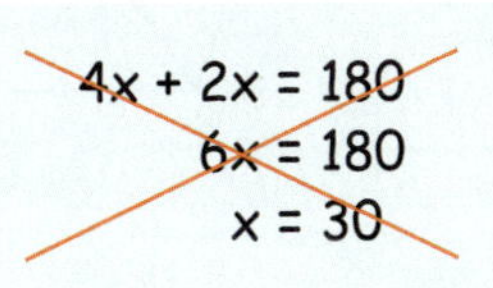

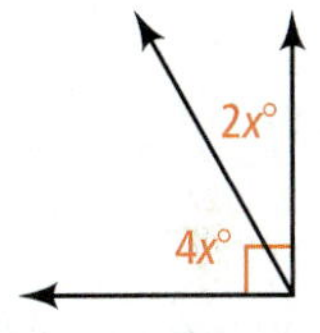

30. Circle the best description of the largest angle in the figure.

acute　　obtuse　　right　　straight

31. Complete: $4x + 2x =$ 90

32. What is your friend's error? Explain.

Answers may vary. Sample: She thought a right angle measures 180°, so she set the sum of the angle measures equal to 180.

Math Success

Check off the vocabulary words that you understand.

☐ angle　☐ complementary　☐ supplementary　☐ angle bisector　☐ vertical

Rate how well you can *find missing angle measures.*

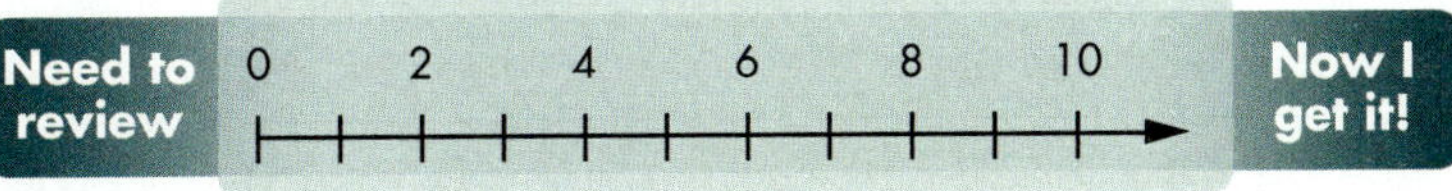

Name ______________________ Class __________ Date __________

1-5 Think About a Plan

Exploring Angle Pairs

Reasoning When $\overrightarrow{BX}$ bisects $\angle ABC$, $\angle ABX \cong \angle CBX$. One student claims there is always a related equation $m\angle ABX = \frac{1}{2}m\angle ABC$. Another student claims the related equation is $2m\angle ABX = m\angle ABC$. Who is correct? Explain.

Understanding the Problem

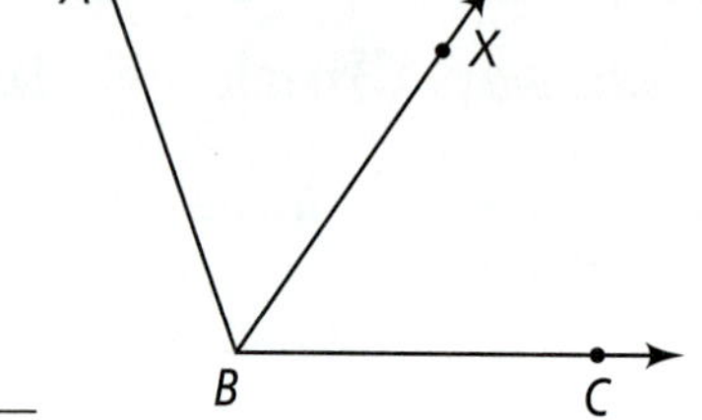

1. What does it mean for $\overrightarrow{BX}$ to bisect $\angle ABC$?

Answers may vary. Sample: $\overrightarrow{BX}$ cuts the angle in half.

2. How is $m\angle ABC$ related to $m\angle ABX$ and $m\angle CBX$?

Answers may vary. Sample: $m\angle ABC = m\angle ABX + m\angle CBX$

3. How are $m\angle ABX$ and $m\angle CBX$ related?

They are equal.

Planning the Solution

4. Based on your answers, write an equation relating $m\angle ABC$ and $m\angle ABX$.
Answers may vary. Sample: $2m\angle ABX = m\angle ABC$

5. Based on your answers, write an equation relating $m\angle ABC$ and $m\angle CBX$.
Answers may vary. Sample: $2m\angle CBX = m\angle ABC$

6. Based on your answers, write an equation relating $m\angle ABX$ and $m\angle CBX$.
Answers may vary. Sample: $m\angle ABX = m\angle CBX$

Getting an Answer

7. Do any of your equations match an equation given in the exercise?

yes

8. Can you show using algebra that one of your equations is equivalent to another equation in the exercise? Explain.

Yes; answers may vary. Sample: Divide both sides of the equation by 2 to get the equation $m\angle ABX = \frac{1}{2}m\angle ABC$.

9. Which student is correct? Explain.

Both students are correct. Answers may vary. Sample: The two equations are equivalent.

Name ______________________ Class ____________ Date ____________

1-5 Practice

Form K

Exploring Angle Pairs

Use the diagram at the right. Is each statement true? Explain.

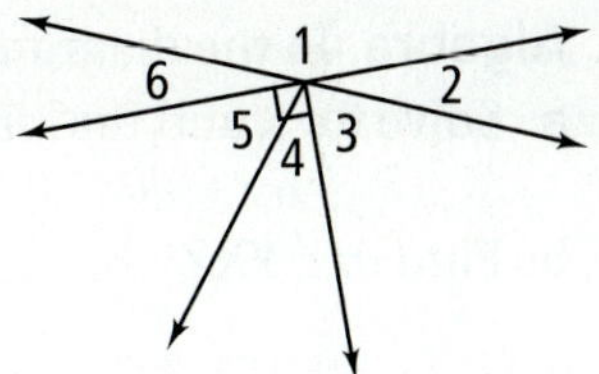

1. ∠5 and ∠4 are supplementary angles.
   No; they are complementary.

2. ∠6 and ∠5 are adjacent angles.
   Yes; they have a common side and vertex.

3. ∠1 and ∠2 are a linear pair.
   Yes; they are adjacent angles whose noncommon sides are opposite rays.

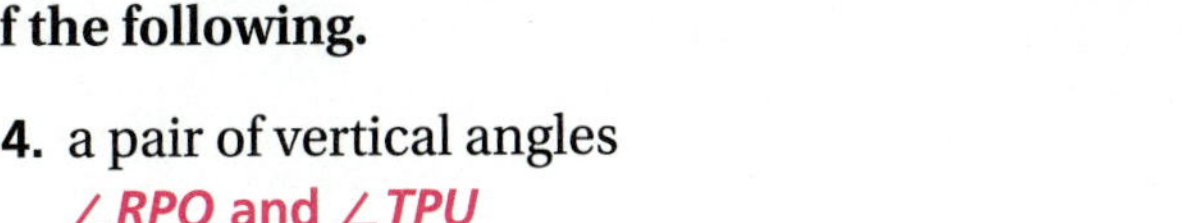

Name an angle or angles in the diagram described by each of the following.

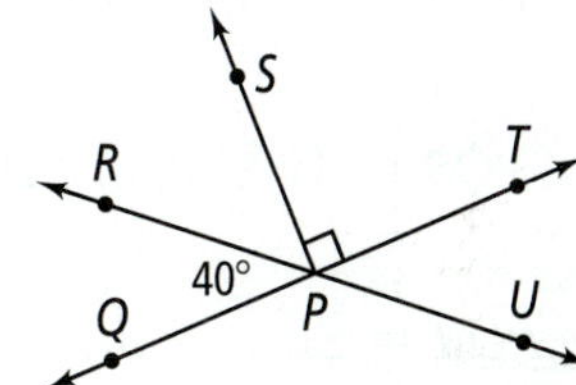

4. a pair of vertical angles
   ∠RPQ and ∠TPU

5. supplementary to ∠RPS ∠SPU

   To start, remember that supplementary angles are two angles whose measures have a sum of [180].

6. a pair of complementary angles ∠QPR and ∠RPS or ∠RPS and ∠UPT

   To start, remember that complementary angles are two angles whose measures have a sum of [90].

7. adjacent to ∠TPU ∠SPT, ∠RPT, ∠QPU, ∠RPU, and ∠QPT

For Exercises 8–11, can you make each conclusion from the information in the diagram? Explain.

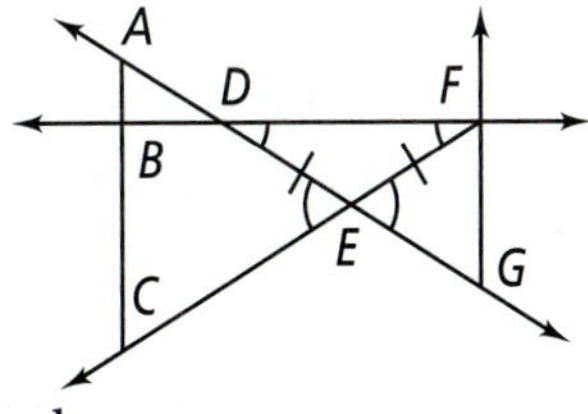

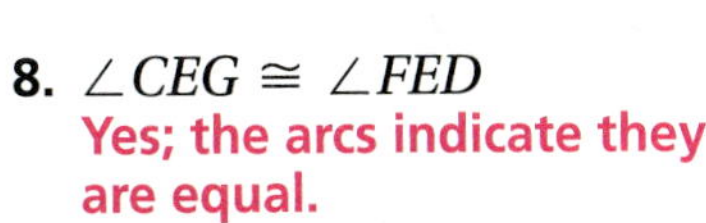

8. ∠CEG ≅ ∠FED
   Yes; the arcs indicate they are equal.

9. $\overline{DE} \cong \overline{EF}$
   Yes; they are marked as ≅.

10. ∠BCE ≅ ∠BAD
    no; not enough information

11. ∠ADB and ∠FDE are vertical angles.
    Yes; their sides are opposite rays.

Use the diagram at the right for Exercises 12 and 13.

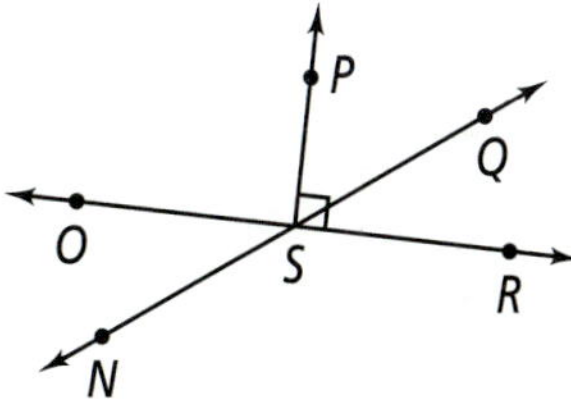

12. Name two pairs of angles that form a linear pair.
    Answers may vary. Sample: ∠NSO and ∠QSO; ∠NSP and ∠QSP; ∠OSP and ∠RSP; ∠OSQ and ∠RSQ

13. Name two pairs of angles that are complementary.
    ∠PSQ and ∠QSR, ∠PSQ and ∠NSO

Name _______________ Class _______________ Date _______________

1-5 Practice (continued) Form K

Exploring Angle Pairs

14. Algebra In the diagram, $\overrightarrow{XY}$ bisects $\angle WXZ$.

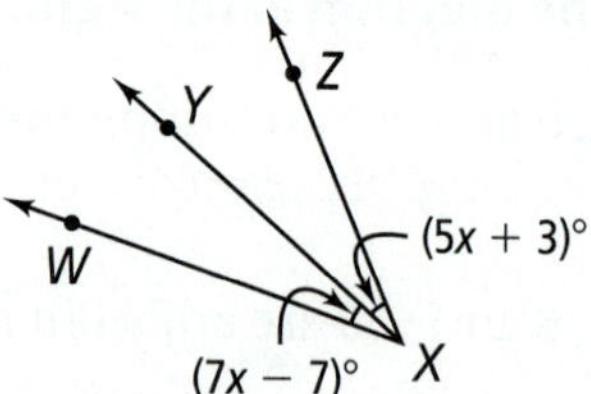

a. Solve for x and find $m\angle WXY$. 5; 28

b. Find $m\angle YXZ$. 28

c. Find $m\angle WXZ$. 56

Algebra $\overrightarrow{QR}$ **bisects** $\angle PQS$**. Solve for** x **and find** $m\angle PQS$**.**

15. $m\angle PQR = 3x, m\angle RQS = 4x - 9$ 9; 54

16. $m\angle PQS = 4x - 6, m\angle PQR = x + 11$ 14; 50

17. $m\angle PQR = 5x - 4, m\angle SQR = 3x + 10$ 7; 62

18. $m\angle PQR = 8x + 1, m\angle SQR = 6x + 7$ 3; 50

Algebra Find the measure of each angle in the angle pair described.

19. The measure of one angle is 5 times the measure of its complement. 75 and 15

20. The measure of an angle is 30 less than twice its supplement. 70 and 110

21. Draw a Diagram Make a diagram that matches the following description. Answers may vary. Sample:

- $\angle 1$ is adjacent to $\angle 2$.
- $\angle 2$ and $\angle 3$ are a linear pair.
- $\angle 2$ and $\angle 4$ are vertical angles.
- $\angle 4$ and $\angle 5$ are complementary.

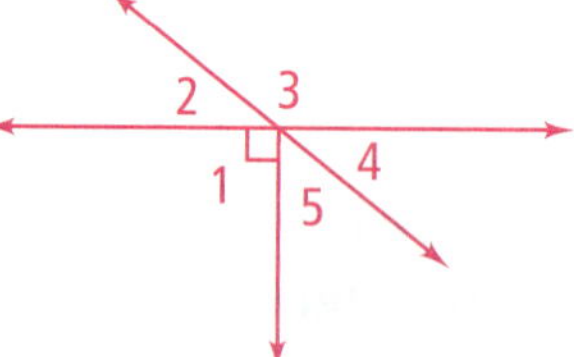

In the diagram at the right, $m\angle HKI = 48$**. Find each of the following.**

22. $m\angle HKJ$ 90

23. $m\angle IKJ$ 42

24. $m\angle FKG$ 42

25. $m\angle FKH$ 132

26. $m\angle FKJ$ 138

27. $m\angle GKI$ 138

Name ______________________ Class ____________ Date ____________

1-5 Standardized Test Prep

Exploring Angle Pairs

Multiple Choice

For Exercises 1–6, choose the correct letter.

1. $\angle CDE$ and $\angle FDE$ are supplementary, $m\angle CDE = 3x + 10$, and $m\angle FDE = 6x + 8$. What is $m\angle FDE$? D

   (A) 18 (B) 64 (C) 108 (D) 116

2. $\overrightarrow{SV}$ bisects $\angle RST$. If $m\angle RSV = 64$, what is $m\angle RST$? I

   (F) 32 (G) 64 (H) 116 (I) 128

Use the diagram at the right for Exercises 3 and 4.

3. Which of the following pairs are vertical angles? C

   (A) $\angle 1$ and $\angle 2$ (C) $\angle 2$ and $\angle 5$

   (B) $\angle 2$ and $\angle 3$ (D) $\angle 4$ and $\angle 5$

4. Which of the following pairs are supplementary? F

   (F) $\angle 1$ and $\angle 2$ (H) $\angle 2$ and $\angle 3$

   (G) $\angle 2$ and $\angle 5$ (I) $\angle 4$ and $\angle 5$

Use the diagram at the right for Exercises 5 and 6.

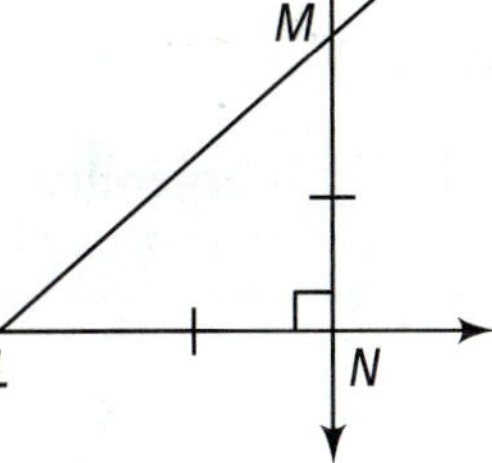

5. Which of the following conclusions can you make from the information in the diagram? B

   (A) $\angle MNL \cong \angle LMN$ (C) $\overline{LM} \cong \overline{MN}$

   (B) $m\angle MNL = 2m\angle LMN$ (D) $LM = 2MN$

6. Which of the following conclusions cannot be made from the information in the diagram? H

   (F) $\overline{MN} \cong \overline{LN}$ (H) $\angle NLM$ is supplementary to $\angle NML$.

   (G) $\angle NLM \cong \angle NML$ (I) $\angle NLM$ is complementary to $\angle NML$.

Short Response

7. $\angle ABC$ and $\angle DBE$ are vertical angles, $m\angle ABC = 3x + 20$, and $m\angle DBE = 4x - 10$. Write and solve an equation to find $m\angle ABC$ and $m\angle DBE$.

   [2] $3x + 20 = 4x - 10$; $m\angle ABC = m\angle DBE = 110$ [1] correct equation and wrong solution or correct answer with no equation [0] both equation and solution wrong

1-6 Basic Constructions

Vocabulary

Review

Draw a line from each word in Column A to its symbol or picture in Column B.

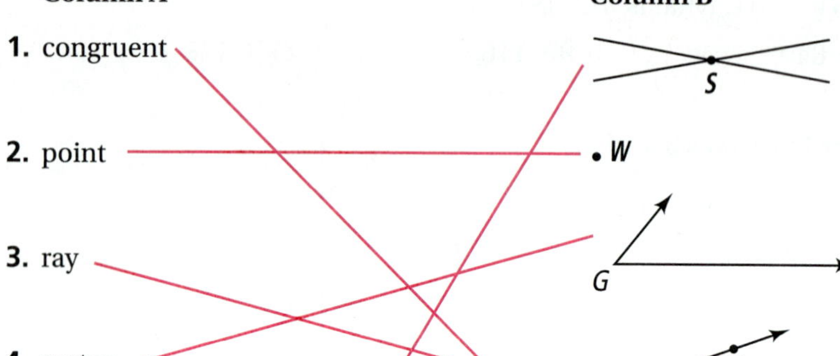

Vocabulary Builder

perpendicular (adjective) pur pun DIK yoo lur

Definition: **Perpendicular** means at right angles to a given line or plane.

Example: Each corner of this paper is formed by **perpendicular** edges of the page.

Non-Examples: Acute, obtuse, and straight angles do not have **perpendicular** rays.

Use Your Vocabulary

6. Circle the figure that shows *perpendicular* segments.

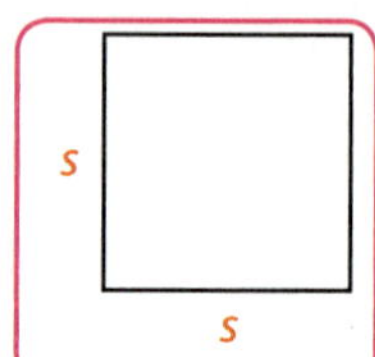

Problem 1 Constructing Congruent Segments

Got It? Use a straightedge to draw $\overline{XY}$. Then construct $\overline{RS}$ so that $RS = 2XY$.

7. A student did the construction at the right. Describe each step of the construction.

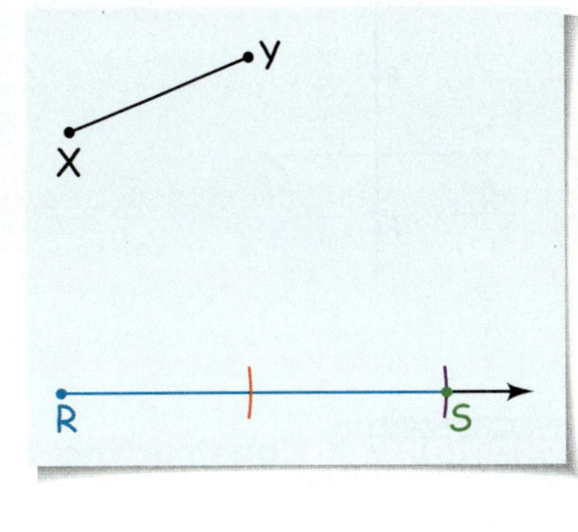

Step 1 Use a straightedge to draw $\overline{XY}$.

Step 2 Draw a ray with endpoint *R*.

Step 3 Draw an arc with compass point at *R* and opening *XY*.

Step 4 Draw another arc with the compass point at the intersection.

Step 5 Label the point of intersection *S*.

Problem 2 Constructing Congruent Angles

Got It? Construct $\angle F$ so that $m\angle F = 2m\angle B$ at the right.

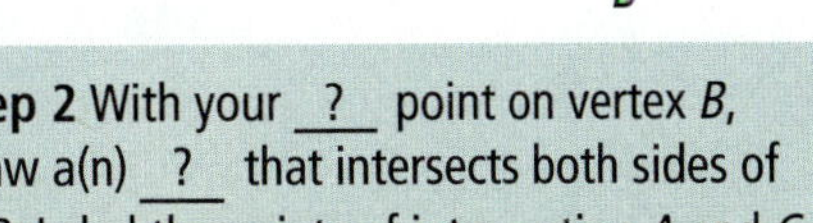

8. Use *arc* or *compass* to complete the sentence(s) in each step. In the large box, construct $\angle F$.

Step 1 Use a straightedge to construct a ray with endpoint *F*.

Step 2 With your _?_ point on vertex *B*, draw a(n) _?_ that intersects both sides of $\angle B$. Label the points of intersection *A* and *C*.

compass / arc

Step 3 Use the same compass setting. Put the _?_ point on point *F*. Draw a long _?_ and label its intersection with the ray as *S*.

compass / arc

Step 4 Open the _?_ to the length of $\overline{AC}$. With the compass point on point *S*, draw an _?_. Label where this arc intersects the other arc as point *T*.

compass / arc

Step 5 Use the same compass setting. Put the _?_ point on point *T*. Draw an _?_ and label its intersection with the first _?_ as point *R*.

compass / arc / arc

Step 6 Draw $\overrightarrow{FR}$.

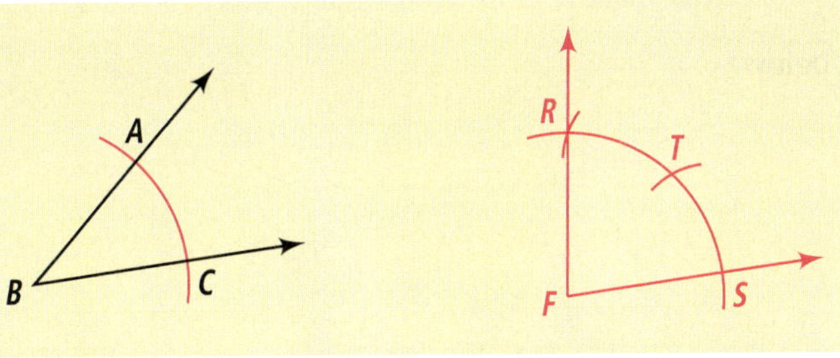

A *perpendicular bisector* of a segment is a line, segment, or ray that is perpendicular to the segment at its midpoint.

9. Circle the drawing that shows the perpendicular bisector of a segment.

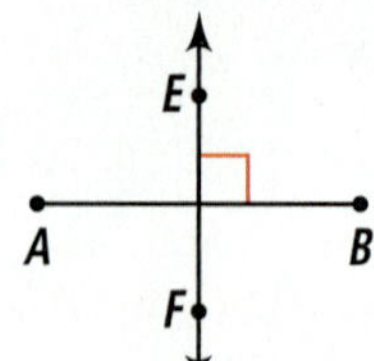

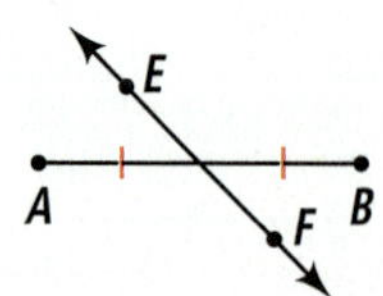

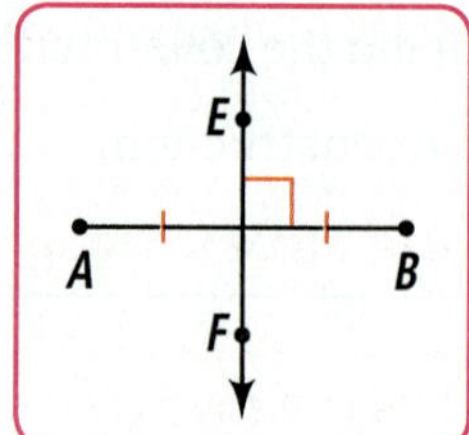

Problem 3 Constructing the Perpendicular Bisector

Got It? **Draw $\overline{ST}$. Construct its perpendicular bisector.**

10. **Error Analysis** A student's construction of the perpendicular bisector of $\overline{ST}$ is shown below. Describe the student's error.

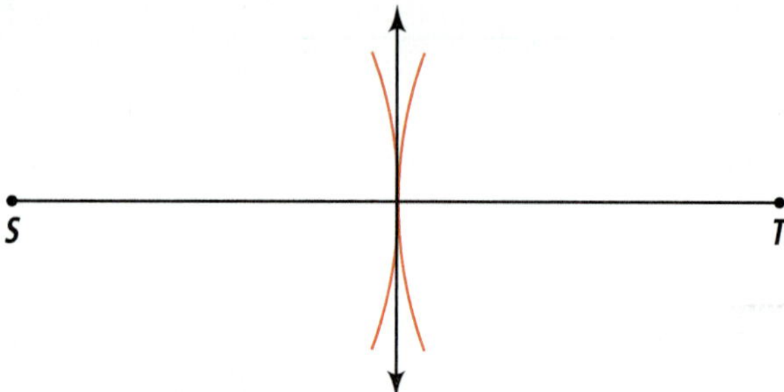

Answers may vary. Sample: The student did not make the opening of the arc drawn from points S and T greater than $\frac{1}{2}ST$.

11. Do the construction correctly in the box below.

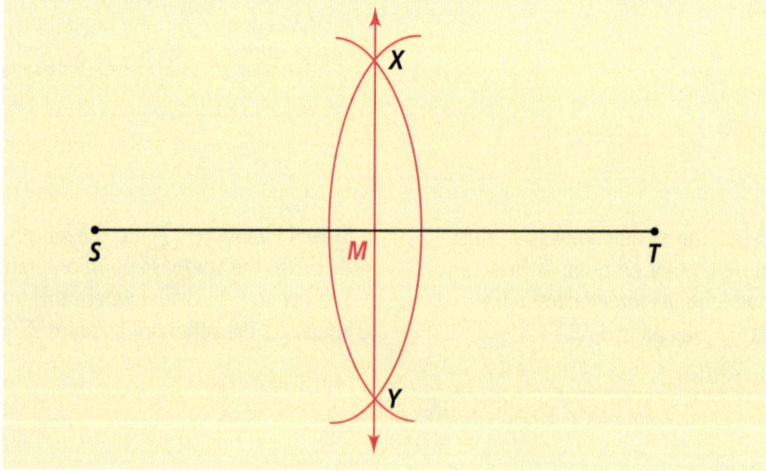

Problem 4 Constructing the Angle Bisector

Got It? Draw obtuse $\angle XYZ$. Then construct its bisector $\overrightarrow{YP}$.

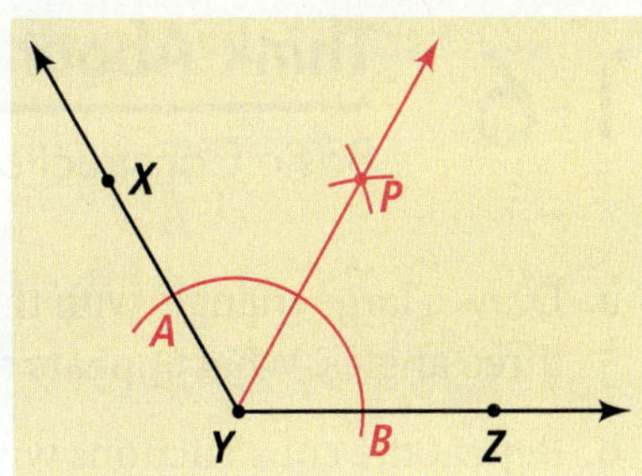

12. Obtuse $\angle XYZ$ is drawn in the box at the right. Complete the flowchart and do each step of the construction.

Step 1 Put the compass point on vertex Y. Draw an arc that intersects the sides of $\angle Y$. Label the points of intersection *A* and *B*.

↓

Step 2 Put the compass point on point *A* and draw an arc. With the same / a different compass setting, draw an arc using point *B*. Be sure the arcs intersect. Label the point where the two arcs intersect *P*.

↓

Step 3 Draw $\overrightarrow{YP}$.

Lesson Check • Do you UNDERSTAND?

Vocabulary What two tools do you use to make constructions?

Draw a line from each task in Column A to the tool used in Column B.

Column A	Column B
13. measure lines	compass
14. measure angles	protractor
15. construct arcs	ruler
16. construct lines	straightedge

Math Success

Check off the vocabulary words that you understand.

☐ straightedge ☐ compass ☐ construction ☐ perpendicular bisector

Rate how well you can *construct angles and bisectors.*

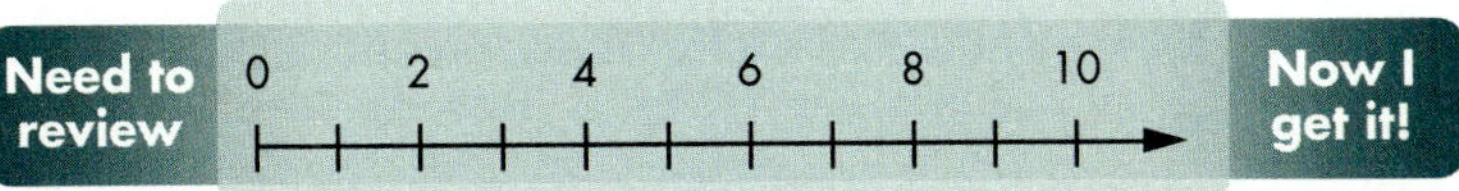

Name ______________________ Class __________ Date __________

1-6 Think About a Plan

Basic Constructions

a. Draw a large triangle with three acute angles. Construct the bisector of the three angles. What appears to be true about the three angle bisectors?

b. Repeat the constructions with a triangle that has one obtuse angle.

c. **Make a Conjecture** What appears to be true about the three angle bisectors of any triangle?

1. In this problem, you will draw three rays for each triangle. Each ray starts at a vertex and passes through the interior of the triangle.

a. What is the maximum number of points of intersection between the rays? 3

b. What is the minimum number? 1

2. On a separate piece of paper, draw $\triangle ABC$ such that all three angles are acute angles and the triangle takes up most of the paper.

Check students' drawings of an acute $\triangle ABC$.

3. In your own words, what are the steps for drawing the angle bisector of $\angle A$?

Answers may vary. Sample: Draw an arc centered at *A* that crosses its two rays at *X* and *Y*. Draw arcs with the same radius from *X* and *Y* that intersect at *Z*. Draw a ray from *A* through *Z*.

4. Draw the angle bisector of $\angle A$. Then draw the angle bisectors for $\angle B$ and $\angle C$.

Answers may vary. Check students' drawings of angle bisectors drawn at $\angle A$, $\angle B$, and $\angle C$.

5. On a separate piece of paper, draw $\triangle DEF$ such that one of the three angles is an obtuse angle and the triangle takes up most of the paper. Construct the angle bisectors for $\angle D$, $\angle E$, and $\angle F$.

Answers may vary. Check students' drawings of obtuse $\triangle DEF$ with angle bisectors at $\angle D$, $\angle E$, and $\angle F$.

6. How many points of intersection are there for the three angle bisectors of $\triangle ABC$? 1

7. How many points of intersection are there for the three angle bisectors of $\triangle DEF$? 1

8. Suppose a friend draws $\triangle DHI$. Without looking at the triangle, what do you think will be true of the three angle bisectors of its angles?

They will intersect at a single point.

Name ______________________ Class ____________ Date ____________

1-6 Practice

Form K

Basic Constructions

For Exercises 1–9, draw a diagram similar to the given one. Then do the construction. Check your work with a ruler or protractor.

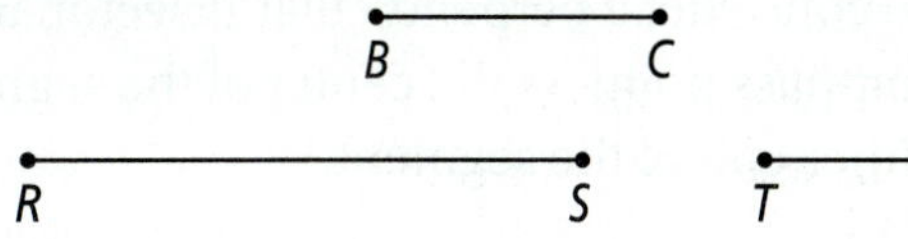

1. Construct $\overline{QR}$ congruent to $\overline{BC}$.

   To start, draw a ray with endpoint *Q*.

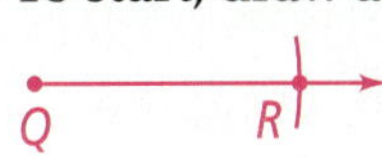

2. Construct $\overline{LM}$ so that $LM = 3BC$.

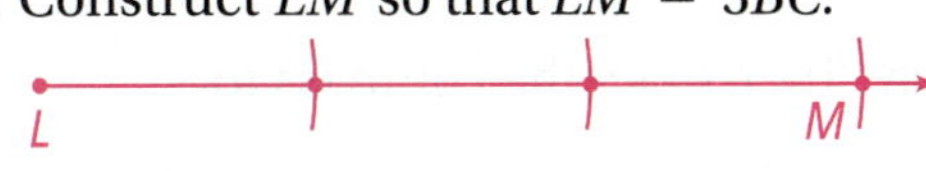

3. Construct $\overline{XY}$ so that $XY = RS + TU$.

   To start, construct a segment congruent to $\overline{RS}$.

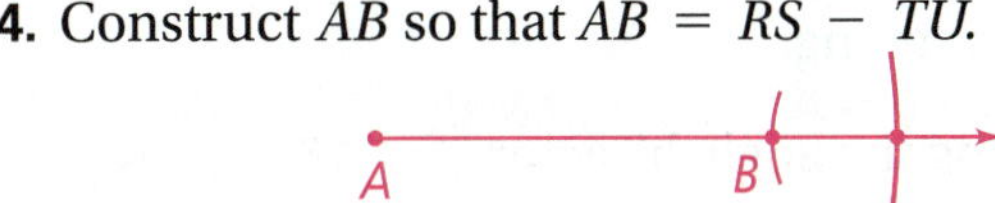

4. Construct $\overline{AB}$ so that $AB = RS - TU$.

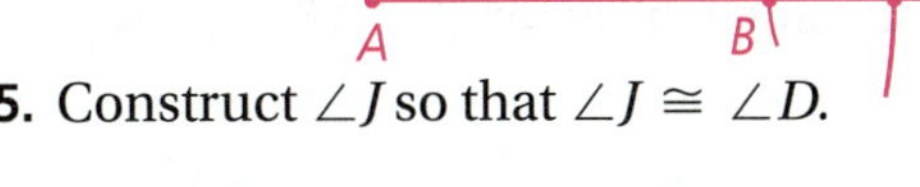

5. Construct $\angle J$ so that $\angle J \cong \angle D$.

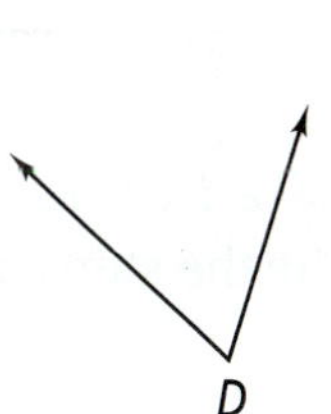

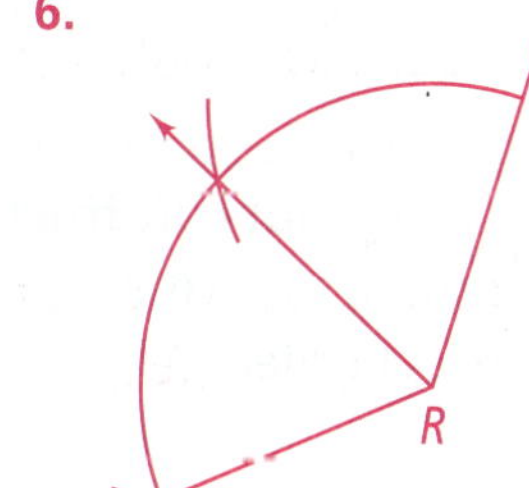

6. Construct $\angle R$ so that $m\angle R = 2m\angle D$.

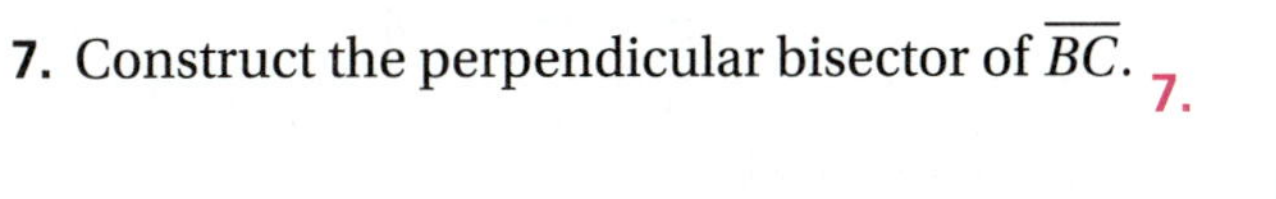

7. Construct the perpendicular bisector of $\overline{BC}$.

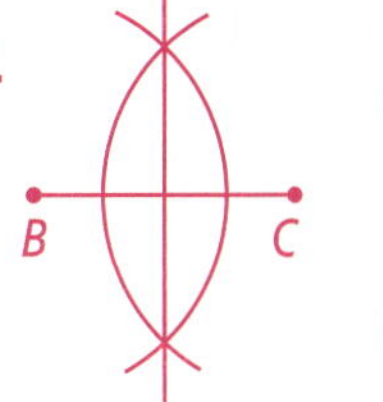

8. Construct the perpendicular bisector of $\overline{RS}$.

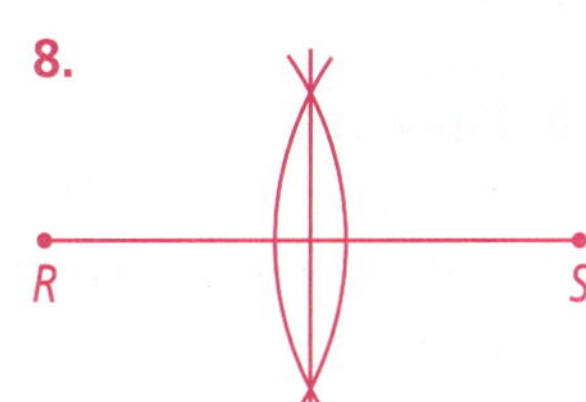

9. Draw acute $\angle FGH$. Then construct its bisector.

   To start, draw acute angle *FGH*.

   Answers may vary. Sample:

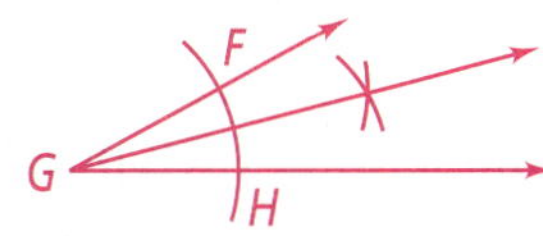

Sketch the figure described. Explain how to construct it. Then do the construction.

10. $\overrightarrow{OM}$ bisects obtuse angle $\angle NOP$.

    Answers may vary. Sample: Draw an obtuse angle. Put the compass on the vertex and draw an arc that intersects both sides of the angle. Put the compass on one of the points where the arc intersects the side and draw an arc. Do this on the other point, using the same compass setting. Draw a line through the intersection of the two arcs and the vertex.

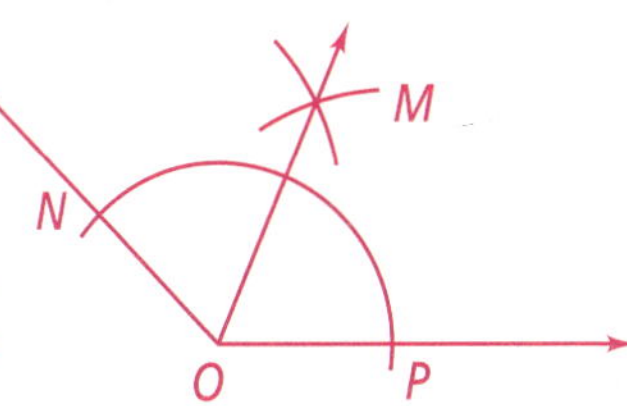

Name ______________________ Class ____________ Date ____________

1-6 Practice (continued)

Form K

Basic Constructions

Tell whether each statement is *true* or *false*. If false, rewrite the statement correctly.

11. To construct a perpendicular bisector, the first step is to place the compass point on the center of the segment. Then draw arcs on either end of the segment.
False; the first step is to put the compass point on both endpoints, and, using the same compass setting, draw arcs.

12. To construct a congruent segment, first draw a ray. Then open the compass to the length of the original segment.
true

13. To construct an angle bisector, first place your compass point on one side of the angle and draw an arc in the center of the angle. Then from a point on the other side, draw an arc using the same compass setting.
False; first place your compass point on the vertex and draw an arc that intersects both sides of the angle. Then from each point of intersection draw two intersecting arcs using the same compass setting.

14. The steps for constructing $\angle B \cong \angle E$ are listed below in the wrong order. Rewrite the steps in the correct order. **D, C, E, A, B**

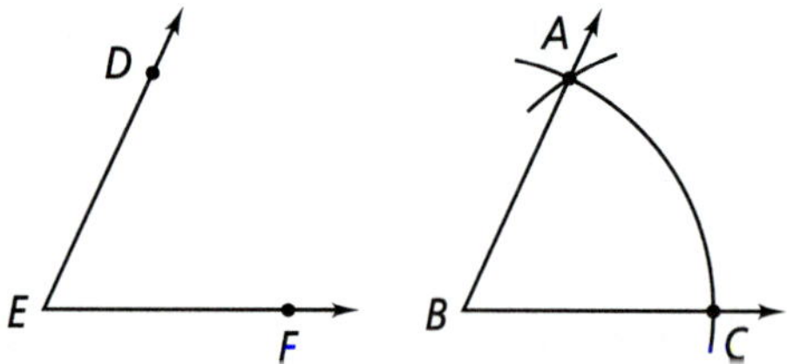

A. Open the compass to the length of *DF*. Using this setting, put the compass point on *C*. Draw an arc to locate point *A*.

B. Draw $\overline{BA}$.

C. Put the compass point on *E* and draw an arc that intersects the sides of $\angle E$. Label the points of intersection *D* and *F*.

15. Sample:

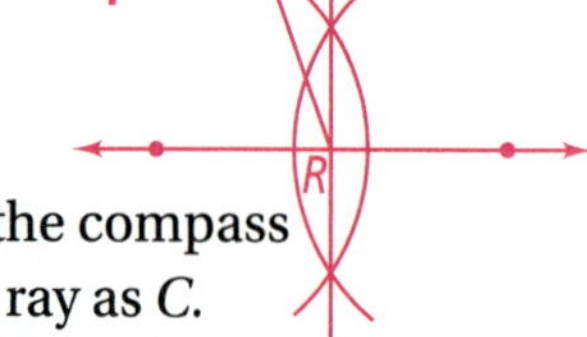

D. Draw a ray with endpoint *B*.

E. Keep the compass on the same setting. Then put the point of the compass on *B* and draw an arc. Label the point of intersection with the ray as *C*.

For Exercises 15 and 16, copy $\angle 1$ and $\angle 2$. Construct each angle described.

15. $\angle R$; $m\angle R = m\angle 1 + m\angle 2$

16. $\angle S$; $m\angle S = m\angle 2 - m\angle 1$

16. Sample:

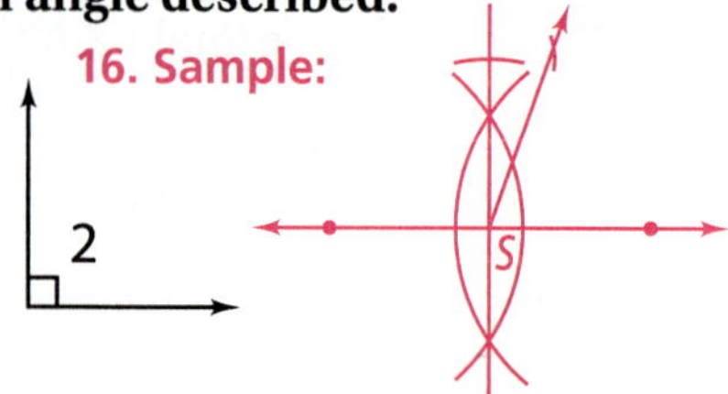

Name ______________________ Class ____________ Date ____________

1-6 Standardized Test Prep

Basic Constructions

Multiple Choice

For Exercises 1–4, choose the correct letter.

1. You are asked to construct a segment congruent to $\overline{AB}$. As a first step, you draw a ray. Which of the following, if true of the ray, would be most helpful? B

(A) The ray is drawn on the paper shorter than $\overline{AB}$.

(B) The ray is drawn on the paper longer than $\overline{AB}$.

(C) The ray is drawn parallel to $\overline{AB}$.

(D) The ray is drawn perpendicular to $\overline{AB}$.

2. Which of the following must be true about a perpendicular bisector and the segment it bisects? I

(F) The perpendicular bisector and the segment bisect each other.

(G) The angle of intersection depends on the length of the line segment.

(H) The perpendicular bisector intersects the segment at a 45° angle.

(I) The perpendicular bisector intersects the segment at a 90° angle.

3. Which of the following is true about the bisectors of a segment in a plane? C

(A) Every segment has exactly one bisector.

(B) Every segment has exactly two bisectors.

(C) Every segment has infinitely many bisectors.

(D) Every segment has infinitely many perpendicular bisectors.

4. Which of the following materials is not used when making basic constructions? F

(F) a ruler (G) a compass (H) a straightedge (I) a pencil

Extended Response

5. How do you construct a perpendicular bisector of $\overline{AB}$? Use three steps.

[4] 1) Put the compass point on *A*. Open the compass to wider than $\frac{1}{2}AB$. Then draw a long arc. 2) Put the compass point on *B*. Draw another long arc that intersects the first arc at two points. Label the points of intersection as *X* and *Y*. 3) Draw $\overline{XY}$. Label $\overline{XY}$ as the perpendicular bisector of $\overline{AB}$. [3] three steps but not all clear [2] two good steps and one wrong step [1] some steps shown [0] no steps shown

Midpoint and Distance in the Coordinate Plane

Vocabulary

Review

Use the figure at the right for Exercises 1–6. Write T for *true* or F for *false*.

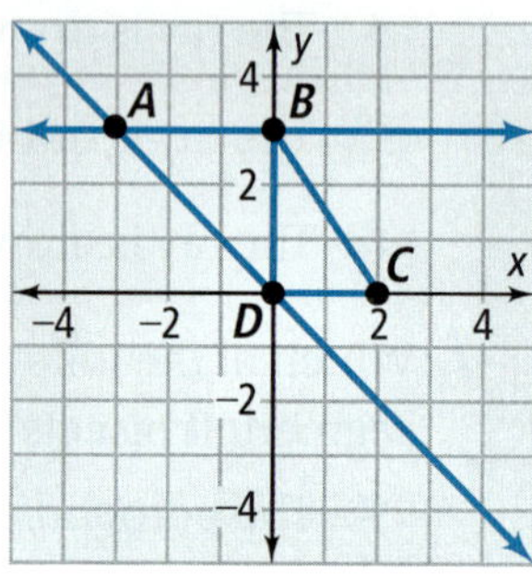

T **1.** A *segment* has two endpoints.

F **2.** A *segment* is named with two arrowheads.

T **3.** $\overline{AB}$ is a segment of $\overleftrightarrow{AB}$.

F **4.** The *segment* with endpoints B and C can only be named $\overline{BC}$.

T **5.** $\overline{BD}$ is on the y-axis.

F **6.** Two opposite rays form a *segment*.

Vocabulary Builder

midpoint (noun) MID poynt

Definition: A **midpoint** of a segment is a point that divides the segment into two congruent segments.

Use Your Vocabulary

Use the figure at the right for Exercises 7–9.

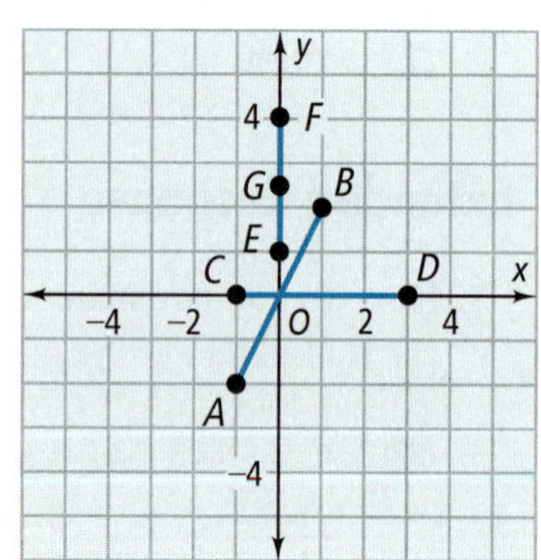

7. The *midpoint* of $\overline{EF}$ is $G($ 0 , 2.5 $)$.

8. The *midpoint* of $\overline{AB}$ is (0 , 0), or the origin.

9. The *midpoint* of $\overline{CD}$ is (1 , 0).

Key Concept Midpoint Formulas

take note

On a Number Line	In the Coordinate Plane
The coordinate of the midpoint M of $\overline{AB}$ with endpoints at a and b is $\frac{a+b}{2}$.	Given $A(x_1, y_1)$ and $B(x_2, y_2)$, the coordinates of the midpoint of $\overline{AB}$ are $M\left(\frac{x_1+x_2}{2}, \frac{y_1+y_2}{2}\right)$.

10. How do you know when to use each midpoint formula?

Use $\frac{a+b}{2}$ when you are finding a midpoint on a number line. Use $M\left(\frac{x_1+x_2}{2}, \frac{y_1+y_2}{2}\right)$ when you are finding a midpoint on a coordinate plane.

11. Complete the diagram below.

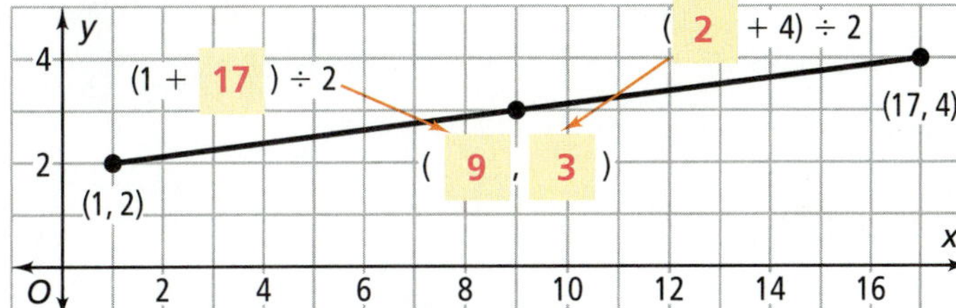

Problem 1 Finding the Midpoint

Got It? $\overline{JK}$ **has endpoints at −12 and 4 on a number line. What is the coordinate of its midpoint?**

12. Circle the formula you will use.

$\frac{a+b}{2}$ (circled) $\qquad \frac{a-b}{2} \qquad M\left(\frac{x_1+x_2}{2}, \frac{y_1+y_2}{2}\right) \qquad M\left(\frac{x_1-x_2}{2}, \frac{y_1-y_2}{2}\right)$

13. Find the coordinate of the midpoint.

$\frac{-12+4}{2} = \frac{-8}{2} = -4$

14. Label points J and K and their coordinates and graph the midpoint on the number line below.

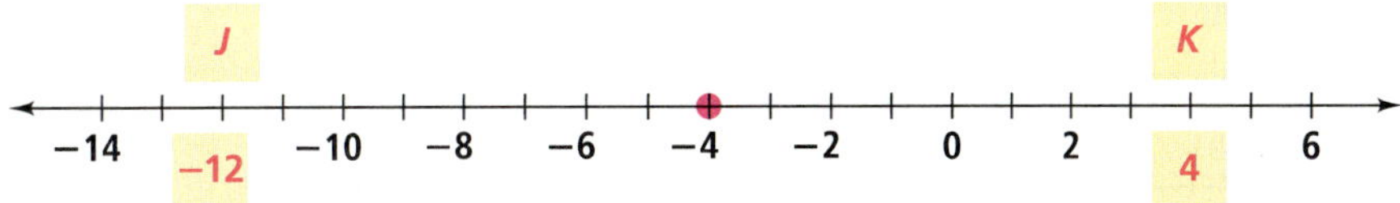

Problem 2 Finding an Endpoint

Got It? **The midpoint of $\overline{AB}$ has coordinates $(4, -9)$. Endpoint A has coordinates $(-3, -5)$. What are the coordinates of B?**

15. Circle the correct description of the coordinates of the given points.

ordered pairs real numbers

16. Complete the equations below.

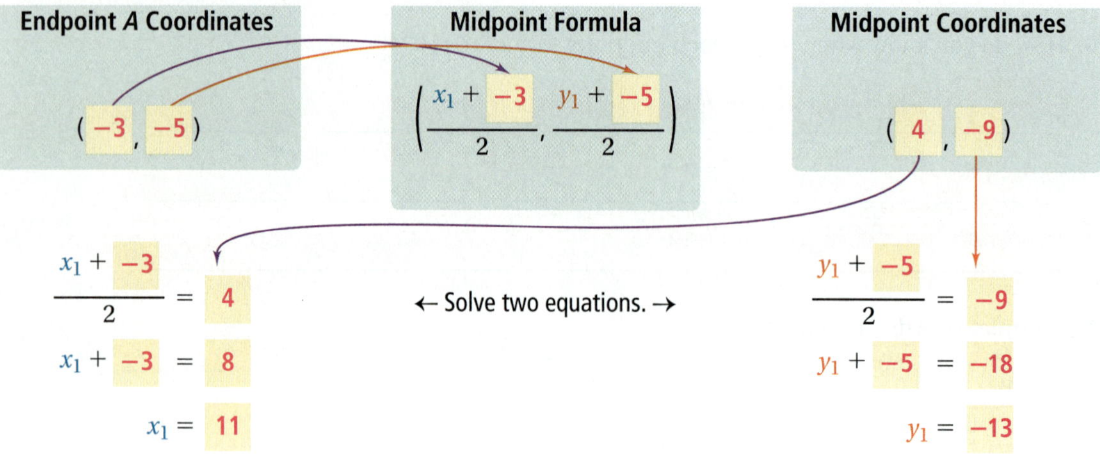

$\frac{x_1 + -3}{2} = 4$ ← Solve two equations. → $\frac{y_1 + -5}{2} = -9$

$x_1 + -3 = 8$ $y_1 + -5 = -18$

$x_1 = 11$ $y_1 = -13$

17. The coordinates of endpoint B are (11 , −13).

Lesson Check • Do you UNDERSTAND?

Error Analysis **$\overline{XY}$ has endpoints at -3 and 7. Shelby calculates the midpoint of $\overline{XY}$. What is her error?**

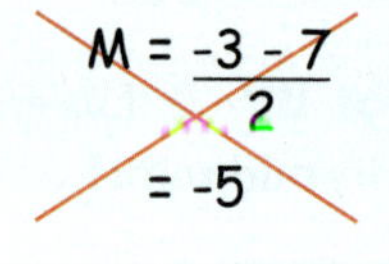

18. Circle the correct description of the coordinates of the given endpoints.

ordered pairs real numbers

19. Underline the correct word to complete the sentence.

The coordinate of the midpoint is the average / difference of the coordinates of the endpoints.

20. Draw $\overline{XY}$ on the number line below.

21. What is the error? Answers may vary. Sample:

She subtracted the coordinates of the endpoints to find the average.

She should have added the coordinates to find the average.

Midpoint and Distance in the Coordinate Plane

Vocabulary

Review

1. A right triangle contains one angle that measures 90.

Complete each statement with *hypotenuse* or *leg*.

2. The longest side of a *right triangle* is the _?_. hypotenuse

3. In a *right triangle,* each of the sides that form the right angle is a _?_. leg

4. Circle the *right triangle.*

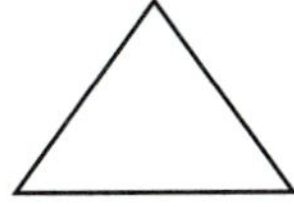
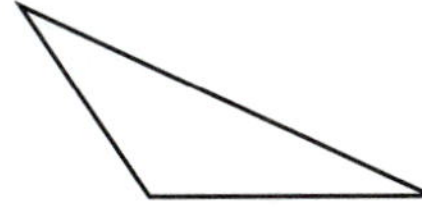
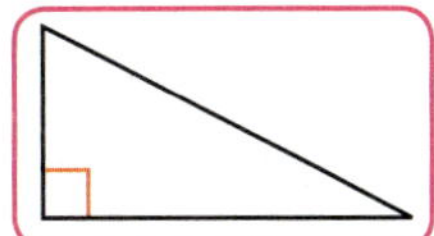

Vocabulary Builder

distance (noun, verb) DIS tuns

Related Word: distant (adjective)

Main Idea: **Distance** is a measurement of length. **Distance** is measured in units such as inches, feet, centimeters, and meters.

Definition: **Distance** is the amount of space between two objects, locations, points, lines, or figures.

Use Your Vocabulary

Determine whether the word *distance* is used as a *noun* or a *verb* in each sentence. Circle the correct choice.

5. Seven miles is a *distance* too great to walk in one hour. noun / verb

6. He tries to *distance* himself from other runners in the race. noun / verb

7. I see a mountain in the *distance.* noun / verb

take note

Key Concept The Distance Formula

The distance between two points $A(x_1, y_1)$ and $B(x_2, y_2)$ is $d = \sqrt{(x_2 - x_1)^2 + (y_2 - y_1)^2}$.

The Distance Formula is based on the Pythagorean Theorem.

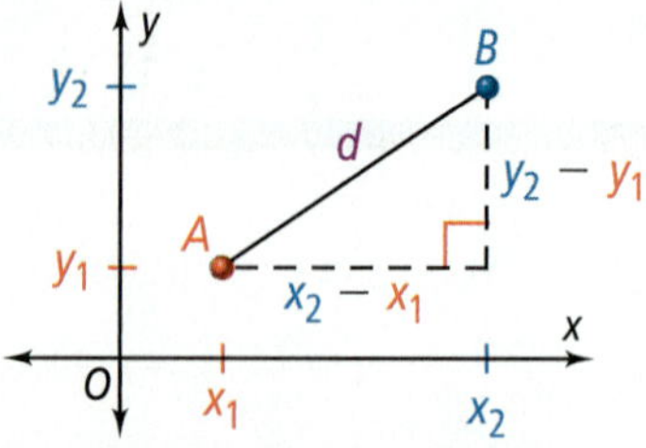

c
b
a
$a^2 + b^2 = c^2$

Use the diagrams above. Draw a line from each triangle side in Column A to the corresponding triangle side in Column B.

Column A	Column B
17. $y_2 - y_1$	a
18. $x_2 - x_1$	b
19. distance, d	c

Problem 3 Finding Distance

Got It? $\overline{SR}$ **has endpoints** $S(-2, 14)$ **and** $R(3, -1)$**. What is** SR **to the nearest tenth?**

20. Complete the diagram at the right.

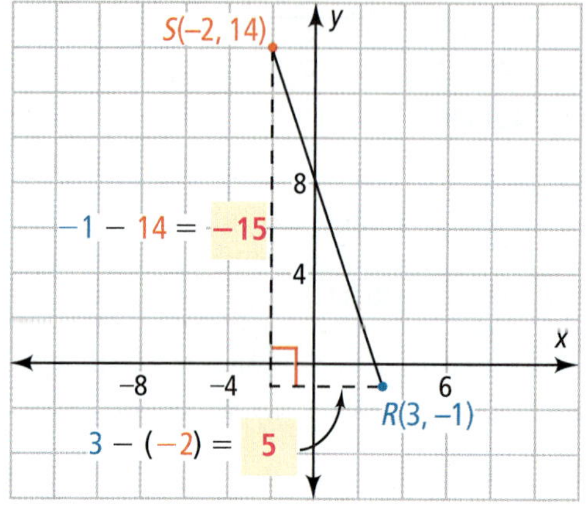

21. Let $S(-2, 14)$ be (x_1, y_1) and let $R(3, -1)$ be (x_2, y_2). Use the justifications and complete the steps below to find SR.

$d = \sqrt{(x_2 - x_1)^2 + (y_2 - y_1)^2}$	Use the Distance Formula.
$SR = \sqrt{(3 - (-2))^2 + (-1 - 14)^2}$	Substitute.
$= \sqrt{(5)^2 + (-15)^2}$	Subtract.
$= \sqrt{25 + 225}$	Simplify powers.
$= \sqrt{250}$	Add.
≈ 15.8	Use a calculator and round to the nearest tenth.

Problem 4 Finding Distance

Got It? On a zip-line course, you are harnessed to a cable that travels through the treetops. You start at Platform *A* and zip to each of the other platforms. How far do you travel from Platform *D* to Platform *E*? Each grid unit represents 5 m.

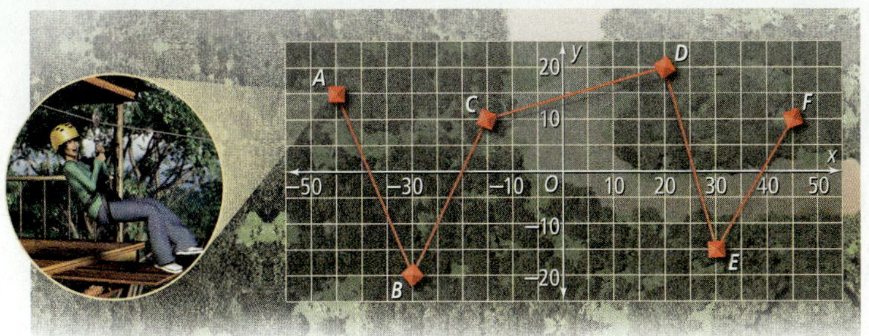

22. The equation is solved below. Write a justification for each step.

$$d = \sqrt{(x_2 - x_1)^2 + (y_2 - y_1)^2}$$ Use the Distance Formula.

$$DE = \sqrt{(30 - 20)^2 + (-15 - 20)^2}$$ Substitute.

$$= \sqrt{10^2 + (-35)^2} = \sqrt{100 + 1225} = \sqrt{1325}$$ Simplify.

23. To the nearest tenth, you travel about 36.4 m.

Lesson Check • Do you UNDERSTAND?

Reasoning **How does the Distance Formula ensure that the distance between two different points is positive?**

24. A radical symbol with no sign in front of it indicates a positive / negative square root.

25. Now answer the question. Answers may vary.

Sample: The radical in the Distance Formula represents a positive square root.

Math Success

Check off the vocabulary words that you understand.

☐ midpoint ☐ distance ☐ coordinate plane

Rate how well you can *use the Midpoint and Distance Formulas.*

Need to review 0 2 4 6 8 10 Now I get it!

Name ______________________ Class ____________ Date ____________

1-7 Think About a Plan

Midpoint and Distance in the Coordinate Plane

Do you use the Midpoint Formula or the Distance Formula to find the following?

a. Given points K and P, find the distance from K to the midpoint of $\overline{KP}$.

b. Given point K and the midpoint of $\overline{KP}$, find KP.

Understanding the Problem

1. What does the Midpoint Formula help you find?

a point

2. What does the Distance Formula help you find?

a distance

Planning the Solution

3. What does part (a) of the problem ask you to find?

a distance

4. What does part (b) of the problem ask you to find?

a distance

Getting the Answer

5. What formula would you use for part (a)?

the Distance Formula

6. What formula would you use for part (b)?

the Distance Formula

7. In Steps 5 and 6, how could you explain why you need to use one formula instead of the other?

Answers may vary. Sample: In neither part (a) nor in part (b) does the question ask for a point.

Name ______________________ Class ____________ Date ____________

1-7 Practice — Form K

Midpoint and Distance in the Coordinate Plane

Find the coordinate of the midpoint of the segment with the given endpoints.

1. 9 and 6 To start, write the Midpoint Formula. Let $a = 9$ and $b = 6$.

   The coordinate of the midpoint is $\frac{a+b}{2} = \frac{\boxed{9} + \boxed{6}}{2} = \boxed{7.5}$.

2. −2 and 7 2.5
3. −3 and −13 −8
4. −8 and 12 2

Find the coordinates of the midpoint of $\overline{LM}$.

5. $L(0, 0)$, $M(9, 3)$ Use the Midpoint Formula.

   x-coordinate of midpoint is $\frac{x_1 + x_2}{2} = \frac{\boxed{0} + \boxed{9}}{2} = \boxed{4.5}$

   y-coordinate of midpoint is $\frac{y_1 + y_2}{2} = \frac{\boxed{0} + \boxed{3}}{2} = \boxed{1.5}$

   The coordinates of the midpoint are $(\boxed{4.5}, \boxed{1.5})$.

6. $L(2, -1)$, $M(3, 6)$ (2.5, 2.5)
7. $L(-3, 14)$, $M(10, -4)$ (3.5, 5)
8. $L(-7, -4)$, $M(5, -10)$ (−1, −7)
9. $L(9\frac{1}{2}, -2\frac{1}{4})$, $M(-3\frac{3}{4}, 1\frac{1}{2})$ $(2\frac{7}{8}, -\frac{3}{8})$

The coordinates of point S are given. The midpoint of $\overline{RS}$ is (6, −10). Find the coordinates of point R.

10. $S(0, 8)$ (12, −28)
11. $S(9, -3)$ (3, −17)
12. $S(-2, -7)$ (14, −13)

For each graph, find the coordinates of the midpoint of $\overline{CD}$.

13. 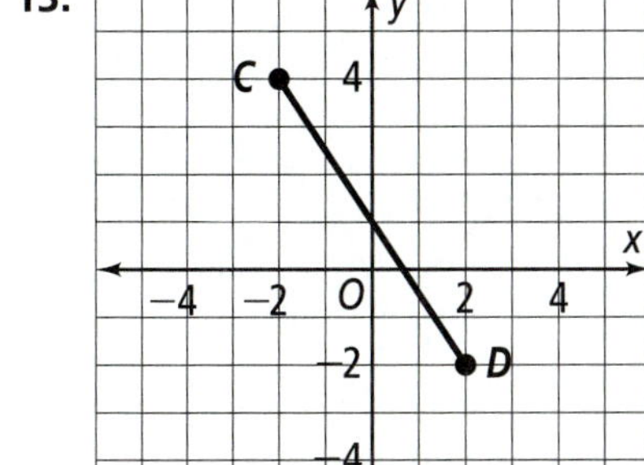

(0, 1)

14. 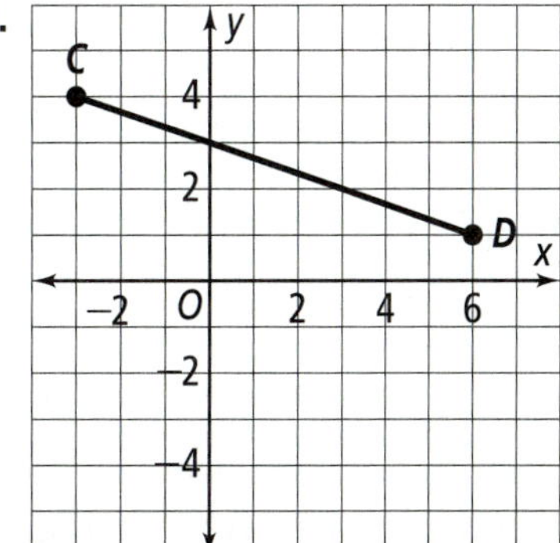

(1.5, 2.5)

Name ______________________ Class ____________ Date ____________

1-7 Practice (continued) — Form K

Midpoint and Distance in the Coordinate Plane

Find the distance between each pair of points. If necessary, round to the nearest tenth.

15. $K(0, 5)$, $L(7, 9)$ — Write the Distance Formula.

Substitute (0, 5) for (x_1, y_1) and (7, 9) for (x_2, y_2).

$$d = \sqrt{(x_2 - x_1)^2 + (y_2 - y_1)^2} = \sqrt{(7 - \boxed{0})^2 + (9 - \boxed{5})^2} = \boxed{8.1}$$

16. $C(-2, 6)$, $D(10, -8)$ 18.4

17. $W(-3, -5)$, $X(-9, 4)$ 10.8

18. $G(-12, -11)$, $H(5, -9)$ 17.1

19. $A(6, 2)$, $B(-3, -1)$ 9.5

For Exercises 20–24, use the map at the right. The units of the map are in miles. Find the distance between the cities to the nearest tenth.

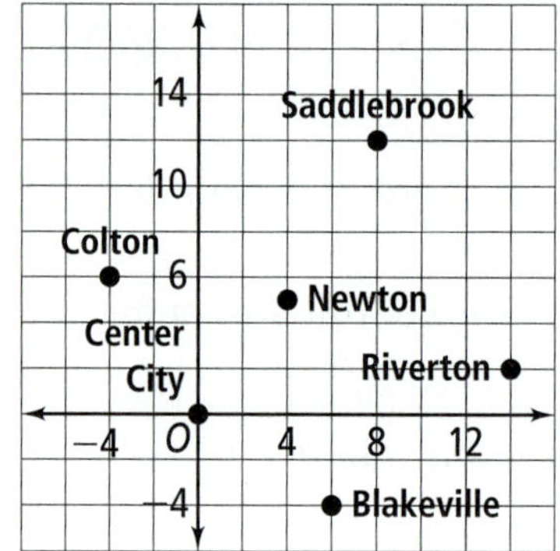

20. Colton and Riverton 18.4 mi

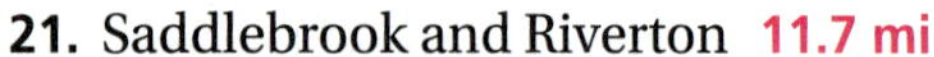

21. Saddlebrook and Riverton 11.7 mi

22. Saddlebrook and Colton 13.4 mi

23. Blakeville and Newton 9.2 mi

24. List the cities in order of greatest to least distance from Center City.
Saddlebrook, Riverton, Blakeville and Colton, Newton

The units of the trail map at the right are in kilometers. Suppose the trails are straight. Find the distance you would travel along each trail to the nearest tenth of a kilometer.

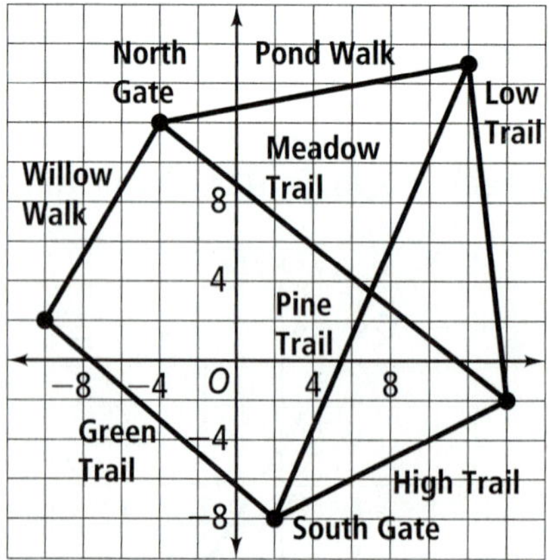

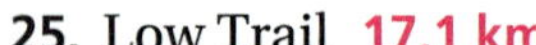

25. Low Trail 17.1 km

26. Willow Walk 11.7 km

27. Pond Walk 16.3 km

28. Meadow Trail 22.8 km

29. Starting at South Gate, you walk to North Gate on Green Trail and Willow Walk. How much farther would you have to walk if you took High Trail to Meadow Trail? 8.9 km

Name ______________________ Class ____________ Date ____________

1-7 Standardized Test Prep

Midpoint and Distance in the Coordinate Plane

Multiple Choice

For Exercises 1–7, choose the correct letter.

1. What is the other endpoint of the segment with midpoint −3 and endpoint −7? C

   (A) −11   (B) −5   (C) 1   (D) 4

2. The endpoints of $\overline{ST}$ are $S(2, -2)$ and $T(4, 2)$. What are the coordinates of the midpoint of $\overline{ST}$? F

   (F) (3, 0)   (G) (0, 3)   (H) (3, −2)   (I) (3, 2)

3. What is the distance between $A(-8, 4)$ and $B(4, -1)$? C

   (A) 7   (B) 10   (C) 13   (D) 17

4. The midpoint of $\overline{XZ}$ is Y. Which of the following is true? I

   (F) $XZ = XY$ (G) $XZ = \frac{1}{2}XY$ (H) $YZ = \frac{1}{2}XY$ (I) $YZ = \frac{1}{2}XZ$

Use the graph at the right for Exercises 5 and 6.

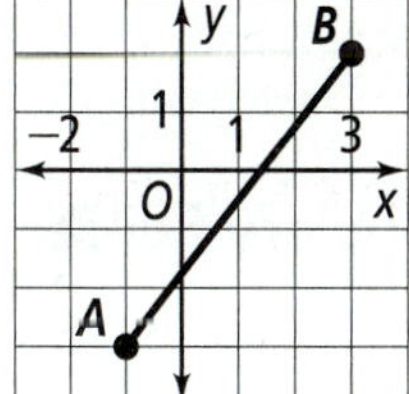

5. According to the graph, what is the midpoint of $\overline{AB}$? B

   (A) (1, 0)   (C) (1, 0.5)

   (B) (1, −0.5)   (D) (1.5, −0.5)

6. According to the graph, what is AB to the nearest tenth? I

   (F) 2.2   (G) 3   (H) 5   (I) 6.4

7. The midpoint of $\overline{CD}$ is $M(-3, -7)$. If the coordinates of C are $(-2, -10)$, what are the coordinates of D? A

   (A) (−4, −4)   (B) (−1, −13)   (C) (−2.5, −8.5)   (D) (−5, −17)

Short Response

8. The midpoint of $\overline{AB}$ is in Quadrant IV, and $\overline{AB}$ is parallel to the y-axis.

   a. What quadrant or quadrants cannot contain either point A or B? Explain.

   [2] II and III; the line segment is vertical and at the right of the origin, so it cannot be in Quadrant II or III.

   b. What else can you determine about points A and B?

   At least one point must be in Quadrant IV. [1] missing an answer or explanation [0] no correct answers or explanations

1-8 PART 1 Perimeter, Circumference, and Area

Vocabulary

Review

1. Cross out the shapes that are NOT *polygons*.

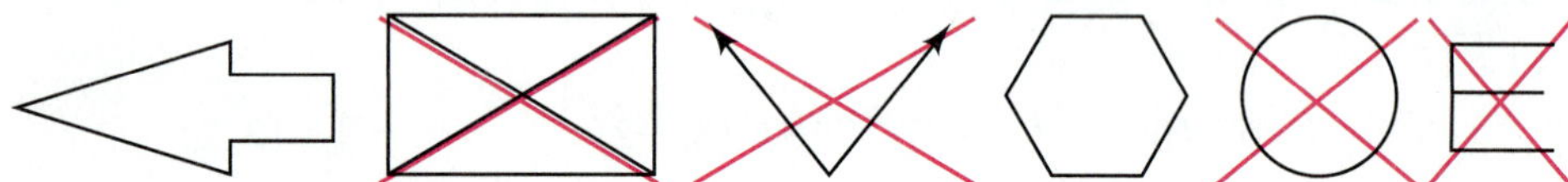

2. Write the name of each figure. Use each word once.

triangle square rectangle circle

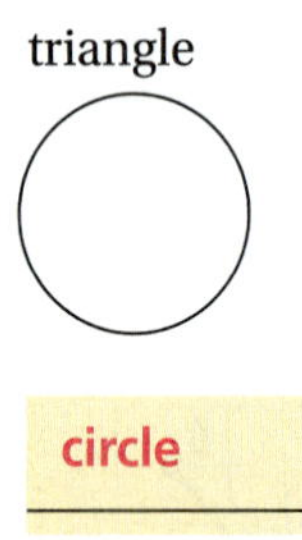

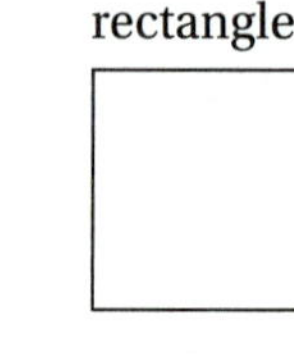
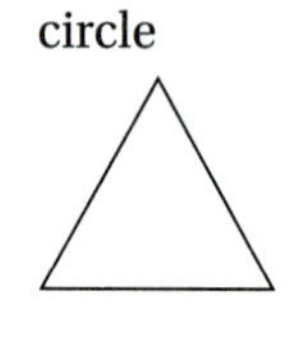

circle rectangle square triangle

Vocabulary Builder

perimeter (noun) puh RIM uh tur

Definition: The word **perimeter** comes from the Greek *peri-*, which means "around," and *metron*, which means "measure." **Perimeter** is the distance around a figure.

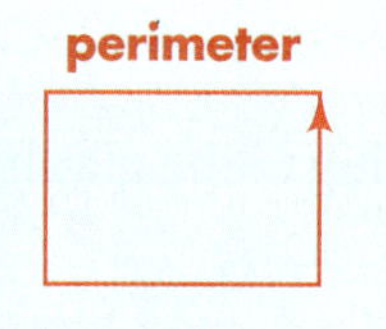

Math Usage: **Perimeter** is the sum of the lengths of the sides of a polygon or the length of a closed curve, such as a circle.

Use Your Vocabulary

Draw a line from each word in Column A to its definition in Column B.

Column A	Column B
3. circumference	distance around a polygon
4. *perimeter*	number of square units in a figure
5. area	distance around a circle

take note

Key Concept Perimeter and Circumference

6. Label the parts of each of the figures below.

Square

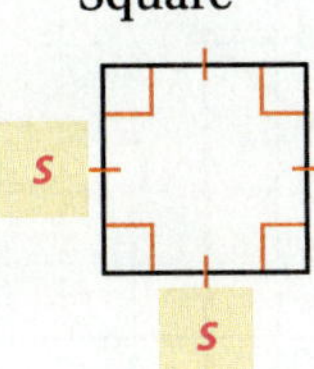

$P = 4s$

Triangle

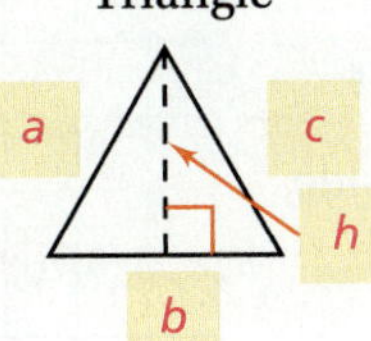

$P = a + b + c$

Rectangle

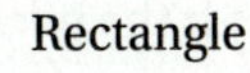
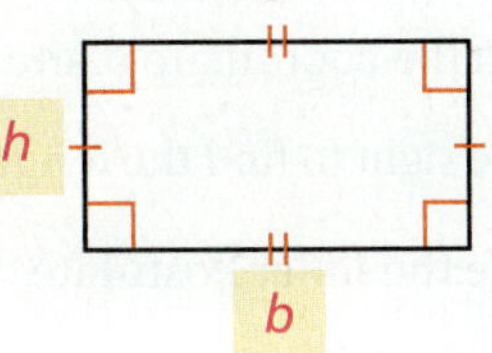

$P = 2b + 2h$

Circle

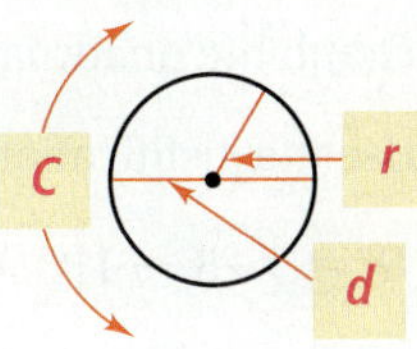

$C = \pi d$ or $C = 2\pi r$

Problem 1 Finding the Perimeter of a Rectangle

Got It? **You want to frame a picture that is 5 in. by 7 in. with a 1-in.-wide frame. What is the perimeter of the picture?**

7. The picture is 5 in. by 7 in.

8. Do you need to find the perimeter of the ouside frame? Yes / (No)

9. Circle the formula that gives the perimeter of the picture.

$P = 4s$ ($P = 2b + 2h$) $P = a + b + c$ $C = \pi d$

10. Solve using substitution.

$P = 2b + 2h$
$= 2(5) + 2(7)$
$= 10 + 14$
$= 24$

11. The perimeter of the picture is 24 in.

Problem 2 Finding Circumference

Got It? **What is the circumference of a circle with radius 24 m in terms of π?**

12. **Error Analysis** At the right is one student's solution. What error did the student make?

Answers may vary. Sample: The student used a diameter of 24 m instead of a radius of 24 m.

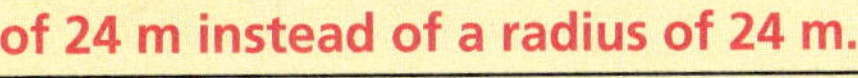

24 m
$c = \pi d$
$c = \pi(24)$
$c = 24\pi$

13. Find the correct circumference.

$C = 2\pi r$
$= 2\pi(24)$
$= 48\pi$

Problem 3 Finding Perimeter in the Coordinate Plane

Got It? **Graph quadrilateral *JKLM* with vertices $J(-3, -3)$, $K(1, -3)$, $L(1, 4)$, and $M(-3, 1)$. What is the perimeter of *JLKM*?**

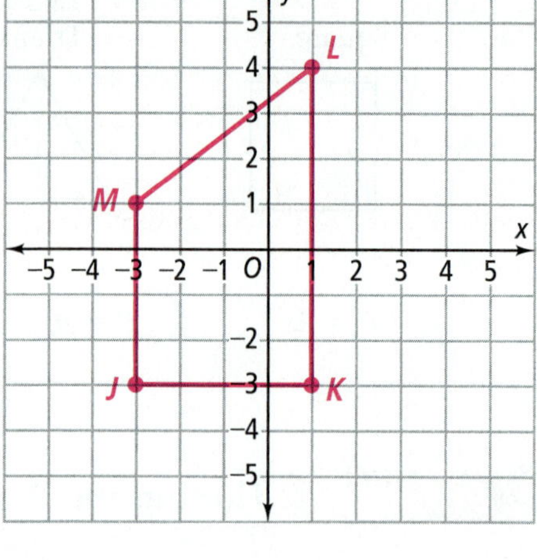

11. Graph the quadrilateral on the coordinate plane at the right.

12. Use the justifications at the right to find the length of each side.

$JK = |-3 - 1|$ Use the Ruler Postulate.

$= 4$ Simplify.

$KL = |4 - -3|$ Use the Ruler Postulate.

$= 7$ Simplify.

$JM = |-3 - 1|$ Use the Ruler Postulate.

$= 4$ Simplify.

$ML = \sqrt{(1 - (-3))^2 + (4 - 1)^2}$ Use the Distance Formula.

$= \sqrt{(4)^2 + 3^2}$ Simplify within the parentheses.

$= \sqrt{16 + 9}$ Simplify powers.

$= \sqrt{25}$ Add.

$= 5$ Take the square root.

13. Add the side lengths to find the perimeter.

$JK + KL + JM + ML = 4 + 7 + 4 + 5 = 20$

14. The perimeter of *JKLM* is 20 units.

Lesson Check • Do you UNDERSTAND?

What is the perimeter of a rectangle with base 3 in. and height 7 in.?

15. In the space below, draw a sketch of the rectangle. Label each side with its length.

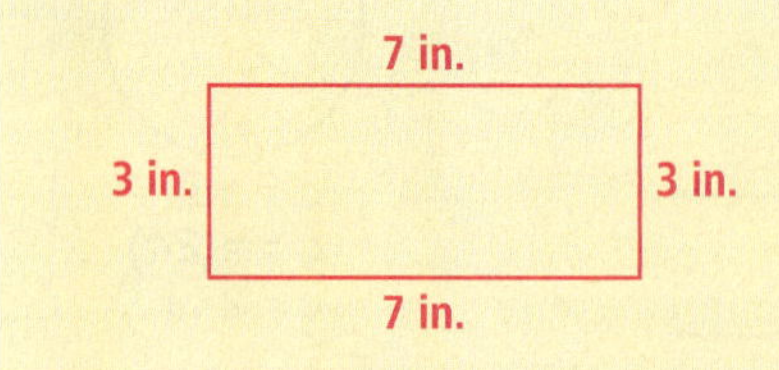

16. Circle the expression(s) that you could use to find the perimeter.

$3 + 7$ $2 \cdot 3 \cdot 7$

$2(3 + 7)$ (circled) $3 \cdot 7$

$3 + 7 + 3 + 7$ (circled)

17. The perimeter of the rectangle is 20 in.

Perimeter, Circumference, and Area

Vocabulary

Review

Write T for *true* or F for *false*.

T **1.** *Circumference* is the distance around a circle.

T **2.** The distance around a field is its *perimeter*.

F **3.** *Perimeter* is measured in square units.

4. Write *perimeter* or *circumference* to describe each measurement below.

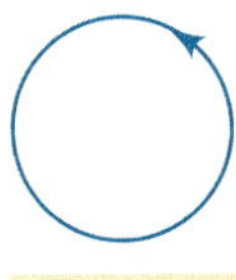

circumference

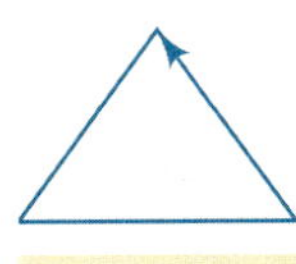

perimeter

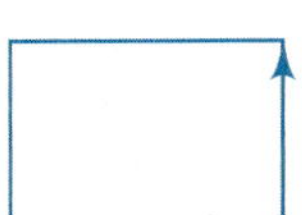

perimeter

Vocabulary Builder

consecutive (adjective) **kun SEK yoo tiv**

Related Word: sequence

Definition: **Consecutive** means following in order without interruption.

Example: The numbers 2, 4, 6, 8, . . . are **consecutive** even numbers.

Non-Example: The numbers 1, 3, 2, 5, 4, . . . are NOT **consecutive** numbers.

Use Your Vocabulary

Draw a line from each sequence of letters in Column A to the next *consecutive* letter in Column B.

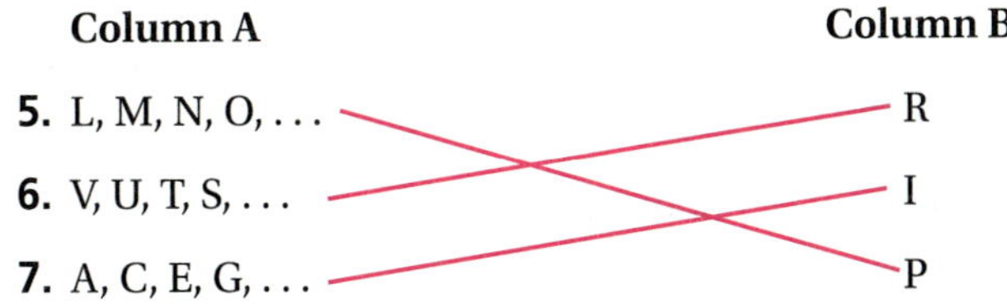

take note

Key Concept Area

Square	Triangle	Rectangle	Circle
$A = s^2$	$A = \frac{1}{2}bh$	$A = bh$	$A = \pi r^2$

8. Circle possible perimeter measurements. Underline possible area measurements.

81 ft^2 4π cm 29 mm 27 yd^2

Problem 4 Finding Area of a Rectangle

Got It? **You are designing a poster that will be 3 yd wide and 8 ft high. How much paper do you need to make the poster? Give your answer in square feet.**

Underline the correct word to complete each sentence.

9. Find the area / perimeter of the poster.

10. The number of yards is greater than / less than the equivalent number of feet.

11. You need your answer in square feet, so convert the width of the poster from yards to feet.

1 yd = 3 ft, so 3 yd = 3 · 3 = 9 ft

12. Find the amount of paper you need to make the poster.

$A = bh$
$= (9)(8)$
$= 72$

13. You need 72 square feet of paper.

Problem 5 Finding Area of a Circle

Got It? **The diameter of a circle is 14 ft. What is the area of the circle in terms of π?**

14. Label the diameter and radius of the circle at the right.

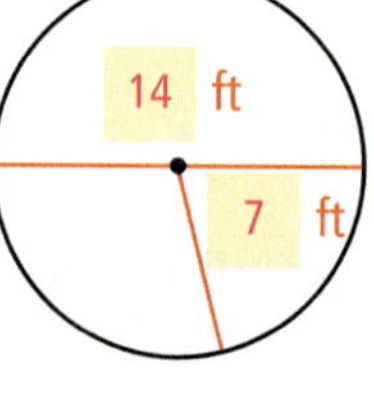

15. Use the formula $A = \pi r^2$ to find the area of the circle in terms of π.

$A = \pi r^2$
$= \pi(7)^2$
$= 49\pi$

16. The area of the circle is 49 π ft^2.

take note

Postulate 1-10 Area Addition Postulate

17. The area of a region is the sum / difference of the areas of its nonoverlapping parts.

Problem 6 Finding Area of an Irregular Shape

Got It? Reasoning **The figure below shows one way to separate the figure at the left. What is another way to separate the figure?**

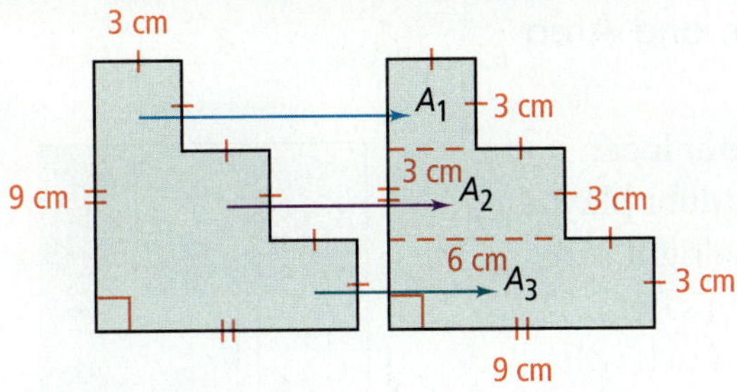

18. Draw segments to show two different ways to separate the figure. Separate the left-hand figure into three squares. Drawings will vary. Samples are given.

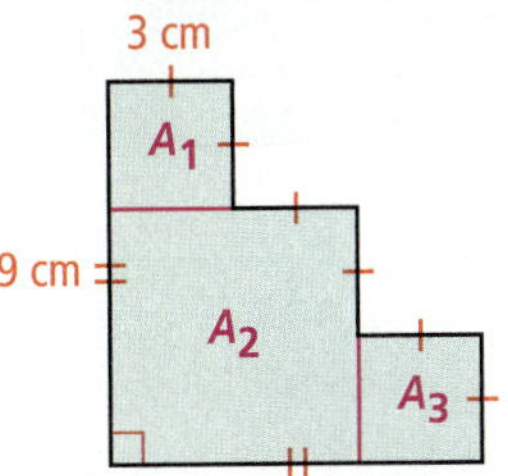

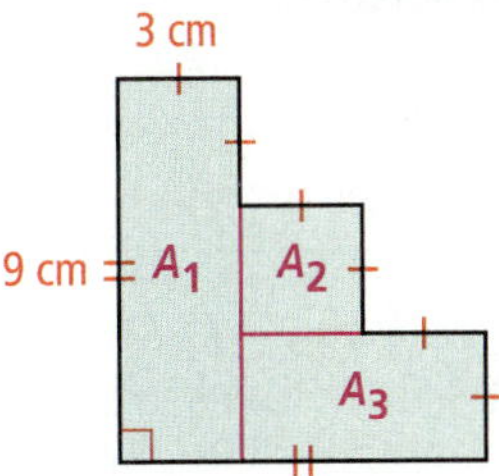

Lesson Check • Do you UNDERSTAND?

Writing **Describe a real-world situation in which you would need to find an area.**

19. Suppose you want to paint your room. Explain why you need to find an area.

Answers may vary. Sample: You need to find the area of the walls so you can buy enough paint.

Math Success

Check off the vocabulary words that you understand.

☐ perimeter ☐ area

Rate how well you can *find the area of irregular shapes.*

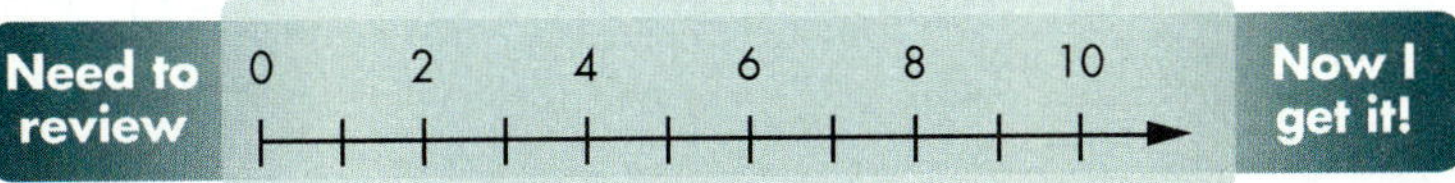

Name ______________________ Class ____________ Date ____________

1-8 Think About a Plan

Perimeter, Circumference, and Area

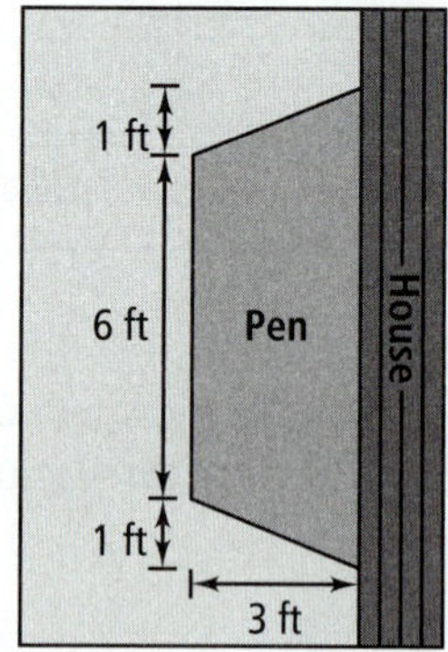

Pet Care You want to adopt a puppy from your local animal shelter. First, you plan to build an outdoor playpen along the side of your house, as shown on the right. You want to lay down special dog grass for the pen's floor. If dog grass costs \$1.70 per square foot, how much will you spend?

Understanding the Problem

1. What are you trying to find?

   What is the cost of the grass for the playpen?

Planning the Solution

2. What additional information do you need to know to answer the question?

   Answers may vary. Sample: the area of the playpen

3. How will you use that additional information to answer the question?

   Answers may vary. Sample: Multiply the area by \$1.70 to find the cost.

Getting the Answer

4. How can you find the area of the playpen?

   First break it down into triangles and a rectangle. Find the areas of these figures and then add the areas. Multiply the length by the width (6×3) for the rectangle and add the area of the two triangles on the sides ($2 \times \frac{1}{2} \times 1 \times 3$).

5. How do you find the total cost of the grass?

   Multiply the area by \$1.70.

6. What is the total cost of the grass? Show your work.

   Area $= 6 \times 3 + 2[\frac{1}{2}(1)(3)] = 21$ ft^2; cost $= 21 \times \$1.70 = \$35.70$

Name ______________________________ Class ____________ Date ____________

1-8 Practice

Form K

Perimeter, Circumference, and Area

Find the perimeter of each figure.

1. 14 in., 3 in.

Substitute 14 for b and 3 for h in the formula for perimeter of a rectangle.

$P = 2b + 2h = 2(\boxed{14}) + 2(\boxed{3}) = \boxed{34}$ in.

2. 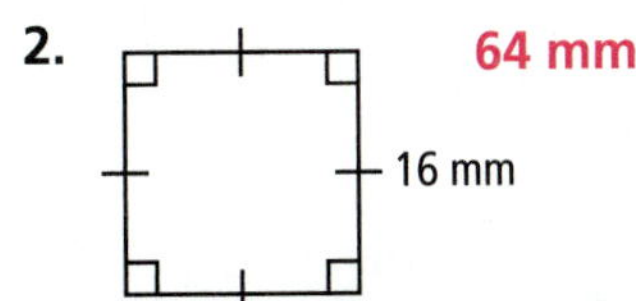

64 mm

3. 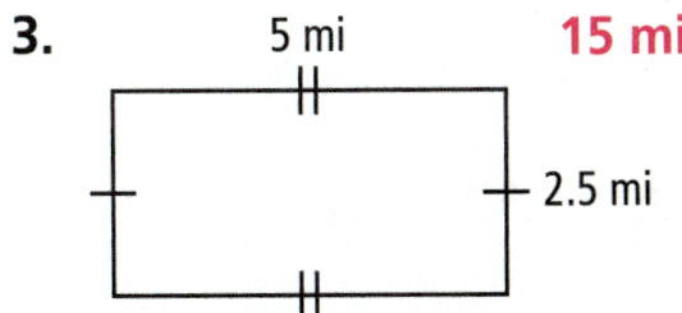

15 mi

4. Mrs. Henderson wants to put wallpaper border around her living room. The room is 18 ft by 22 ft. How many feet of border are needed? 80 ft

Find the circumference of circle G in terms of π.

5. 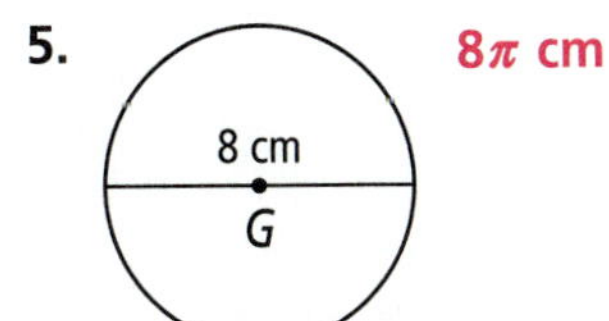

8π cm

6. 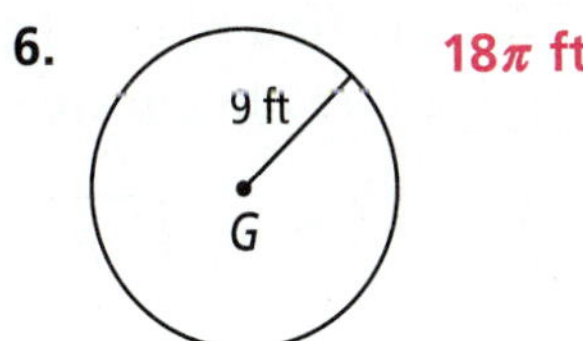

18π ft

7. 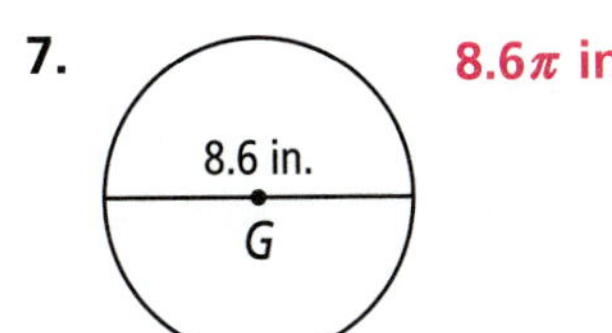

8.6π in.

8. 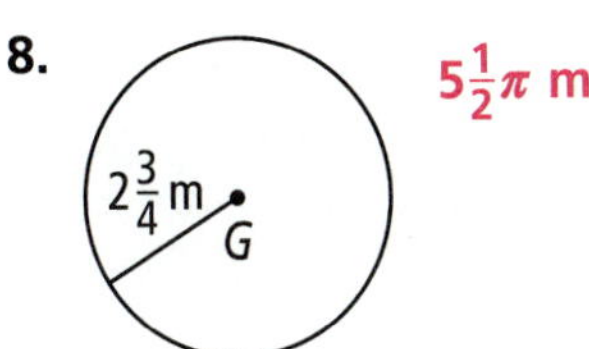

$5\frac{1}{2}\pi$ m

Coordinate Geometry **Graph each figure in the coordinate plane. Find each perimeter.**

9. $D(-3, 1)$, $E(-3, 3)$, $F(2, 3)$

Check students' graphs.

To start, graph the figure.

Find DE using the Distance Formula.

$D = \sqrt{(x_2 - x_1)^2 + (y_2 - y_1)^2} = \sqrt{(-3 - \boxed{-3})^2 + (3 - \boxed{1})^2} = \boxed{2}$

$P = DE + EF + FD = \boxed{2} + \boxed{5} + \boxed{5.4} = \boxed{12.4}$

10. $Q(-1, 0)$, $R(2, 3)$, $S(3, -3)$, $T(-1, 3)$ Check students' graphs; 17.1

Name ______________________ Class ____________ Date ____________

1-8 Practice (continued)

Form K

Perimeter, Circumference, and Area

Find the area of each rectangle with the given base and height.

11. 3 ft, 8 in.

To start, convert 3 ft to inches to make the units the same. Then substitute for b and h in the area formula.

$3 \text{ ft} \cdot \frac{12 \text{ in.}}{1 \text{ ft}} = \boxed{36} \text{ in.}$

$A = bh = \boxed{36} \cdot \boxed{8} = \boxed{288} \text{ in.}^2$

12. 28 in., 2 yd **2016 in.^{2}**

13. 8 ft 6 in., 2 ft **17 ft^2**

14. 64 mm, 20 cm **128 cm^2**

15. 3.2 m, 70 cm **2.24 m^2**

16. A restaurant owner wants to put a cement patio behind his restaurant so people can eat outside. The patio will be 16 ft wide and 25 yd long. What will the area of the patio be? **1200 ft^2**

Find the area of each circle in terms of π.

17.

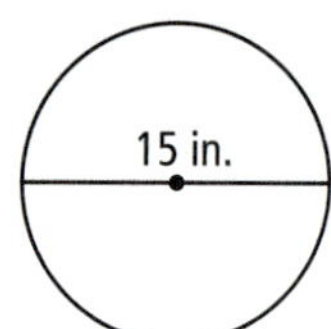

To start, find r from the given diameter. Then substitute r in the area formula for a circle.

$A = \pi r^2 = \pi \cdot \boxed{7.5}^2 = \boxed{56.25\pi \text{ in.}^2}$

18.

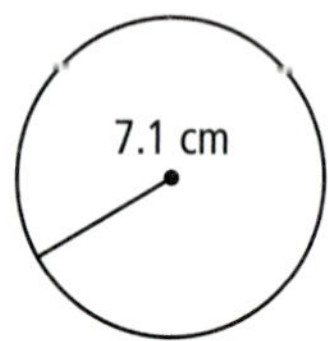

50.41π cm^2

19.

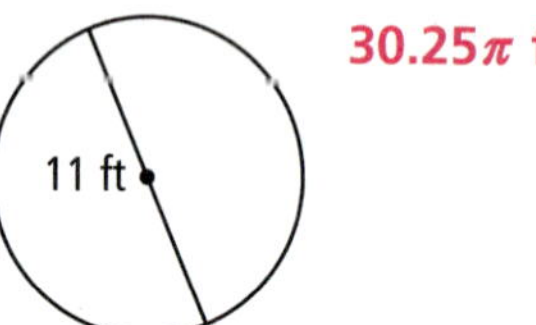

30.25π ft^2

Find the area of each circle using an approximation of π. If necessary, round to the nearest tenth.

20. $r = 9$ in. **254.3 in.^{2}**

21. $d = 13$ m **132.7 m^2**

22. $r = 5.8$ ft **105.6 ft^2**

Find the area of the shaded region. All angles are right angles.

23.

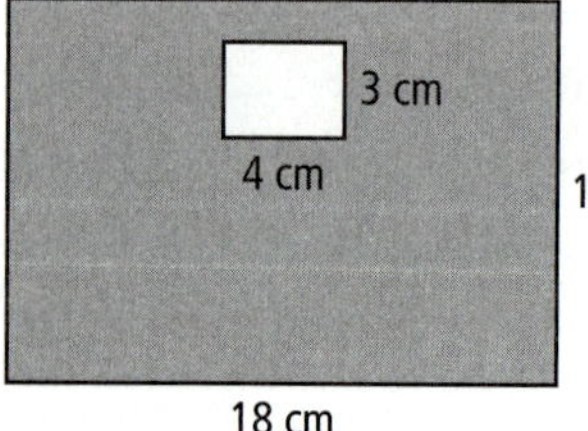

204 cm^2

24.

108 m^2

Name ______________________ Class ____________ Date ____________

1-8 Standardized Test Prep

Perimeter, Circumference, and Area

Multiple Choice

For Exercises 1–6, choose the correct letter.

1. A 12-ft-by-15-ft swimming pool has a 3-ft-wide no-slip surface around it. What is the outer perimeter of the no-slip surface? A

A 78 ft B 78 ft^2 C 198 ft D 198 ft^2

2. What is the circumference of the circle at the right in terms of π? I

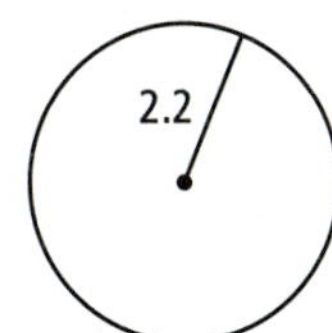

F 1.1π H 2.2π

G 1.21π I 4.4π

3. What is the perimeter of $\triangle PQR$ with vertices $P(-2, 9)$, $Q(7, -3)$, and $R(-2, -3)$ in the coordinate plane? D

A 21 units B 25 units C 34 units D 36 units

4. You are tiling a kitchen floor that is 10 ft wide by 4 yd long. How many square yards of tile do you need? F

F $13\frac{1}{3}$ yd^2 G $13\frac{1}{2}$ yd^2 H 20 yd^2 I 40 yd^2

5. The diameter of $\odot Z$ is 5 in. What is its area in terms of π? C

A 2.5π in.^{2} B 5π in.^{2} C 6.25π in.^{2} D 25π in.^{2}

6. All angles in the figure at the right are right angles. What is the area of the figure? I

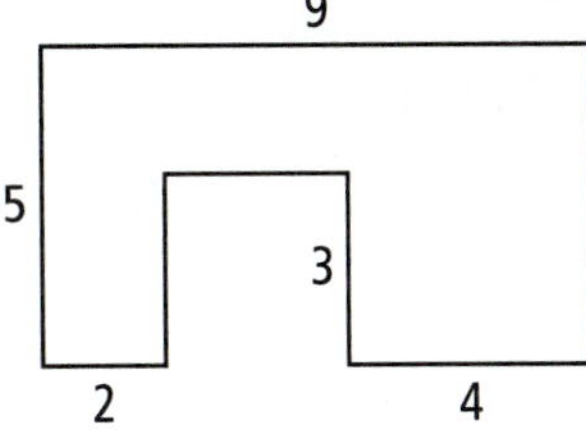

F 14 H 28

G 18 I 36

Short Response

7. a. If two squares have the same area, what do you know about the measures of their sides? Explain.

The area of a square is the measure of the length of the side squared. So, the measures of both squares' sides are the same.

b. If two rectangles have the same area, what do you know about the measures of their sides? Explain.

The area of a rectangle is the product of the measures of their sides. So, the product of the measures of both rectangles' sides is the same. [2] Both answers and explanations are correct. [1] missing answer or explanation [0] both answers incorrect or missing explanations

2-1 Patterns and Inductive Reasoning

Vocabulary

Review

Tell whether the statement is a *conjecture*. Explain your reasoning.

1. All apples are sweet.

   Yes. Answers may vary. Sample: It is an opinion.

2. The sun sets in the west.

   No. Answers may vary. Sample: It is a fact.

Vocabulary Builder

reason (noun, verb) REE zun

Related Words: reasonable (adjective), reasonably (adverb)

Definition: A **reason** is an explanation.

Main Idea: A logical argument uses **reasons** to arrive at a conclusion.

Use Your Vocabulary

3. Complete each statement with the appropriate form of the word *reason*.

NOUN	In a logical argument, you state each _?_.	reason
ADJECTIVE	The student did a _?_ job on the last math test.	reasonable
ADVERB	The workers cleaned up _?_ well after the party.	reasonably
VERB	To make a good decision, we _?_ together.	reason

Write R if the estimate is *reasonable* or U if it is *unreasonable*.

U 4. $32 + 11 + 6 \approx 60$

R 5. A 15% tip on \$36 is \$6.

Problem 1 Finding and Using a Pattern

Got It? **What are the next two terms in the sequence?**

45, 40, 35, 30, . . .

For Exercises 6–9, circle the correct answer.

6. Do the numbers increase or decrease?

7. Does the amount of change *vary* or remain *constant*?

8. Which operation helps you form the next term?

9. Which number helps you form the next term?

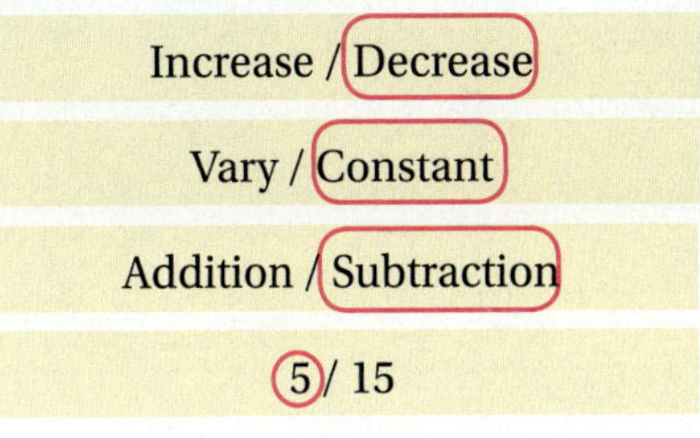

10. Now find the next two terms in the sequence.

25 20

Problem 2 Using Inductive Reasoning

Got It? **What conjecture can you make about the twenty-first term in R, W, B, R, W, B, ...?**

11. Complete the table.

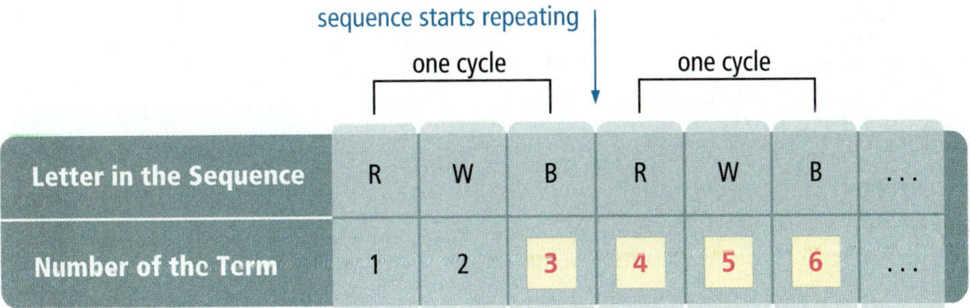

Letter in the Sequence	R	W	B	R	W	B	. . .
Number of the Term	1	2	3	4	5	6	. . .

12. There are 3 letters in the pattern before it starts repeating.

13. R is the 1st term, 4th term, 7th term, ...

W is the 2nd term, 5th term, 8th term, ...

B is the 3rd term, 6th term, 9th term, ...

Underline the correct words to complete the sentence.

14. The twenty-first term is

one more than a multiple of 3 / two more than a multiple of 3 / a multiple of 3.

15. Now make a conjecture.

The twenty-first term of the sequence is B.

Problem 3 Collecting Information to Make a Conjecture

Got It? What conjecture can you make about the sum of the first 30 odd numbers?

16. Complete the table.

Number of Terms	Sum
1	1 = 1 = 1 • 1
2	1 + 3 = 4 = 2 • 2
3	1 + 3 + 5 = 9 = 3 • 3
4	1 + 3 + 5 + 7 = 16 = 4 • 4
5	1 + 3 + 5 + 7 + 9 = 25 = 5 • 5
⋮	⋮

17. Now make a conjecture.

The sum of the first 30 odd numbers is 30 · 30, or 900.

Problem 4 Making a Prediction

Got It? What conjecture can you make about backpack sales in June?

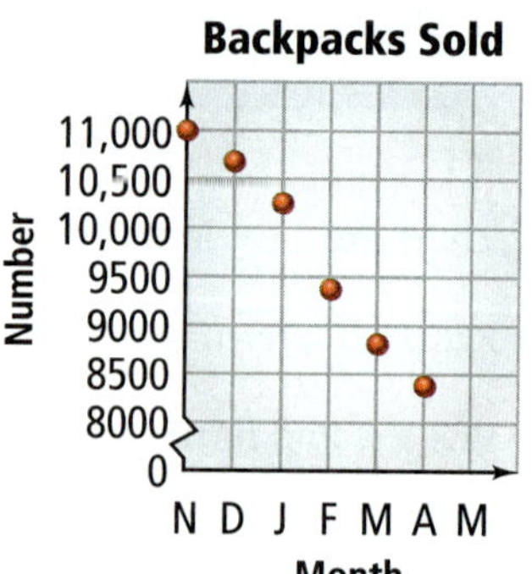

For Exercises 18–22, write T for *true* or F for *false*.

T **18.** The graph shows a pattern of points.

F **19.** Each month, the number of backpacks sold increases.

T **20.** The change in sales varies from month to month, so you need to estimate this change.

T **21.** If sales change by about 500 each month, you can subtract 500 from April's sales to estimate May's sales.

F **22.** If sales change by about 500 each month, you can add 500 to May's sales to estimate June's sales.

23. Now make a conjecture about backpack sales in June.

About 7500 backpacks will be sold in June.

Problem 5 Finding a Counterexample

Got It? **What is a counterexample for the conjecture?**

If a flower is red, it is a rose.

24. Circle the flowers below that are or can be red.

(rose) bluebell (carnation) (geranium) (tulip)

25. Is every flower you named a rose? Yes / (No)

26. Write a word to complete the counterexample. Answers may vary.

A __?__ is a red flower but it is not a rose.

Accept any of carnation, geranium, tulip.

Lesson Check • Do you UNDERSTAND?

Compare and Contrast **Clay thinks the next term in the sequence 2, 4, . . . is 6. Given the same pattern, Ott thinks the next term is 8, and Stacie thinks the next term is 7. What conjecture is each person making? Is there enough information to decide who is correct?**

Choose the letter that describes the rule for each sequence.

A Multiply by 2 **B** Add 2, add 3, add 4, ... **C** Add 2

C **27.** 2, 4, 6, 8, ...

A **28.** 2, 4, 8, 16, ...

B **29.** 2, 4, 7, 1, ...

C **30.** Clay's conjecture

A **31.** Ott's conjecture

B **32.** Stacie's conjecture

33. Circle the correct answer.

Are two numbers enough to show a pattern? Yes / (No)

Math Success

Check off the vocabulary words that you understand.

☐ inductive reasoning ☐ conjecture ☐ counterexample

Rate how well you can *use inductive reasoning.*

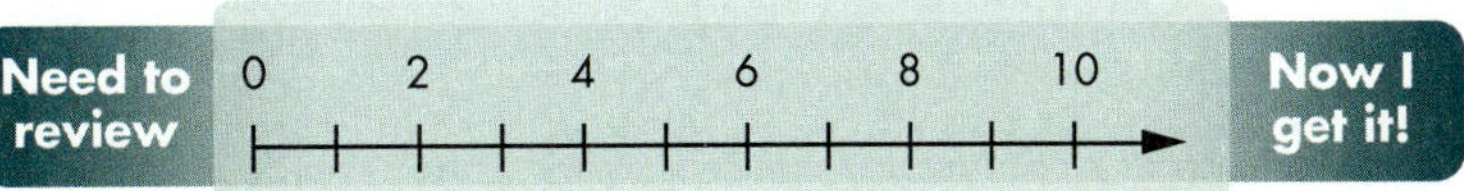

Name ______________________ Class ____________ Date ____________

2-1 Think About a Plan

Patterns and Inductive Reasoning

Bird Migration During bird migration, volunteers get up early on Bird Day to record the number of bird species they observe in their community during a 24-h period. Results are posted online to help scientists and students track the migration.

Bird Count

Year	Number of Species
2004	70
2005	83
2006	80
2007	85
2008	90

a. Make a graph of the data.

b. Use the graph and inductive reasoning to make a conjecture about the number of bird species the volunteers in this community will observe in 2015.

Understanding the Problem

1. What does the problem ask you to predict?

the number of bird species volunteers will observe on Bird Day in 2015

2. What approach to organizing the data is suggested in the problem?

The problem suggests using a graph of the data.

Planning the Solution

3. On your graph, what data should be represented by the horizontal axis?

years

4. On your graph, what data should be represented by the vertical axis?

number of bird species

5. Graph the data on the grid at the right. Don't forget to label the axes.
Check students' graphs. Sample shown at the right.

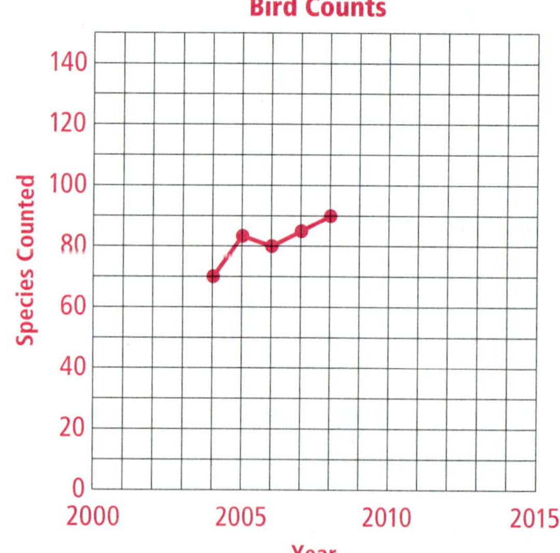

Getting an Answer

6. Look at the data points. Is there an upward or downward trend? What is the approximate increase or decrease in the number of bird species observed per year?

upward; increases by about 5 species per year

7. Based on the pattern in the graph of the data, how many bird species do you think will be observed in 2015? **about 125**

Name ______________________ Class ____________ Date ____________

2-1 Practice

Form K

Patterns and Inductive Reasoning

Find a pattern for each sequence. Use the pattern to show the next two terms.

1. 2, 3, 5, 7, 11, 13, . . . 17, 19

To start, look for a relationship between terms.

The terms are consecutive _?_ numbers. prime

2. $1, \frac{1}{4}, \frac{1}{16}, \frac{1}{64}, \ldots \frac{1}{256}, \frac{1}{1{,}024}$

Each term is one-quarter the value of the term preceding it.

3. III, V, VII, IX, . . . XI, XIII

Each term is a consecutive odd roman numeral.

4.

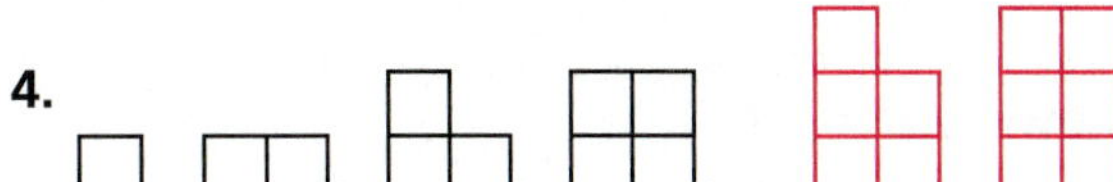

Successive terms alternate adding a box to the left column and then to the right column.

Use the sequence and inductive reasoning to make a conjecture.

5. What is the 12th figure in the sequence?

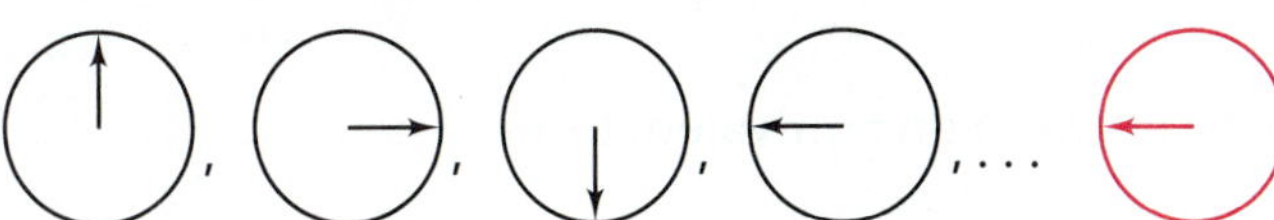

6. What are the coordinates of the point in the 8th figure in the sequence? (−2, −5)

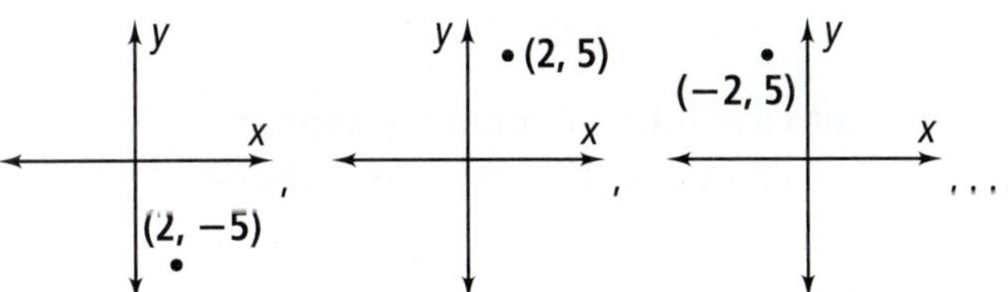

Make a conjecture for each scenario. Show your work.

7. the sum of the first 100 even numbers The sum is 10,100; the sum equals $n(n + 1)$, where n is the number of terms.

To start, find the first few terms of the sequence and look for a pattern.

$2 = 2 \qquad = 1 \times 2$

$2 + 4 = 6 \qquad = 2 \times \boxed{3}$

$2 + 4 + \boxed{6} = \boxed{12} \qquad = 3 \times \boxed{4}$

$2 + 4 + 6 + \boxed{8} = \boxed{20} \qquad = \boxed{4} \times \boxed{5}$

8. the product of an even and odd number

Even; the product of every even and odd number is an even number.

Name ______________________________ Class ____________ Date ____________

2-1 Practice (continued) — Form K

Patterns and Inductive Reasoning

Find one counterexample to show that each conjecture is false.

9. The product of two positive numbers is greater than either number. $0.5 \times 2 = 1$

To start, write a statement that describes a counterexample:

Find two positive numbers with a product less than __?__. one of the numbers

10. The difference of two integers is less than either integer. $5 - (-2) = 7$

11. Known: $AB = BC$

Conjecture: B is the midpoint of $\overline{AC}$. *B* is the vertex of isosceles $\triangle ABC$.

Find a pattern for each sequence. Use inductive reasoning to show the next two terms.

12. $\frac{2}{16}, \frac{2}{7}, \frac{1}{2}, \frac{4}{5}, \ldots$ $\frac{5}{4}, \frac{6}{3}$ or $1\frac{1}{4}, 2$

To start, look for a pattern by writing terms in an equivalent form.

$\frac{1}{\boxed{8}}, \frac{2}{7}, \frac{\boxed{3}}{6}, \frac{4}{5}, \ldots$

13. $-13, 8, -5, 3, -2, \ldots$ $1, -1$

14. A student dips a high-temperature wire into a solution containing sodium chloride (salt). He passes the wire through a flame and observes that doing so produces an orange-yellow flame. The student does this with additional salt solutions and finds that they all produce an orange-yellow flame. Make a conjecture based on his findings.
Salt solutions will produce an orange-yellow flame in a flame test.

15. 1, 3, 9, 27, 81, . . . 243, 729

16. 12, 0.5, 6, 3, 18, . . . 54, 972

Draw the next figure in each sequence.

17. 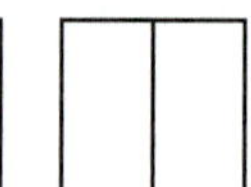 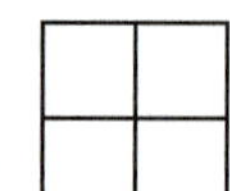 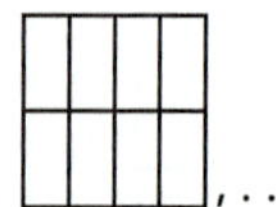 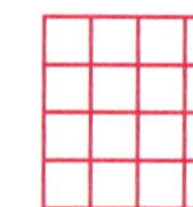, . . .

18. 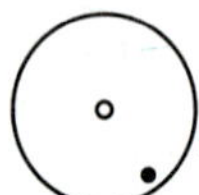 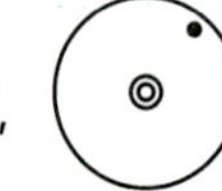 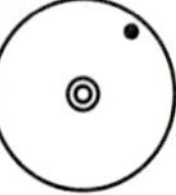 , . . . 

Name ______________________ Class ____________ Date ____________

2-1 Standardized Test Prep

Patterns and Inductive Reasoning

Gridded Response

Solve each exercise and enter your answer on the grid provided.

1. What is the next term of this sequence?

   1, 3, 5, 8, 11, 15, 19, 24, . . .

2. What is the next term of this sequence?

   $\frac{1}{2}, \frac{2}{6}, \frac{3}{18}, \frac{4}{54}, \ldots$

3. What is the next term of this sequence?

   −5, 5, −6, 6, −7, 7, −8, . . .

4. What is the missing term in this sequence?

   0.95, 0.85, 0.90, 0.80, __?__, 0.75, 0.80, . . .

5. Jim makes the following conjecture.

   Other than 1, there are no numbers less than 100 that are both perfect squares and perfect cubes.

   What is a counterexample that proves his conjecture false?

Answers

1. 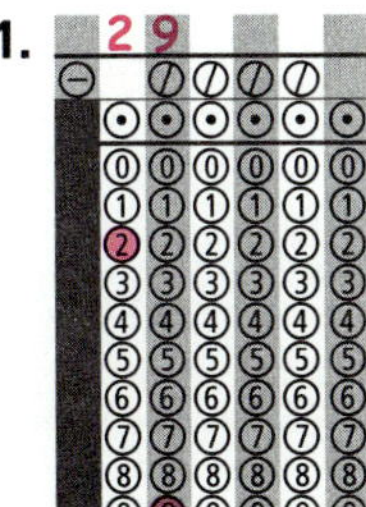

2. 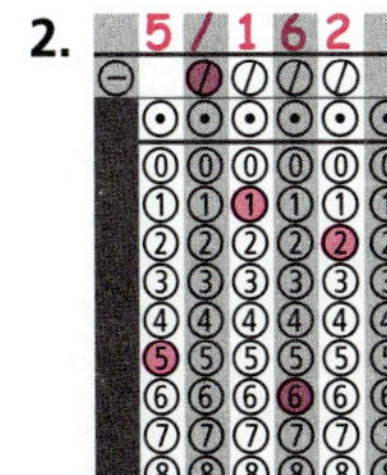

3. 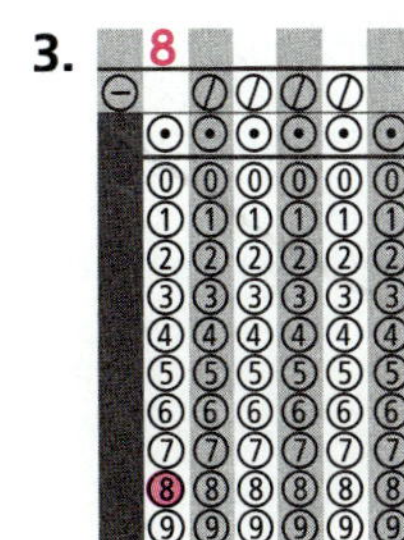

4. 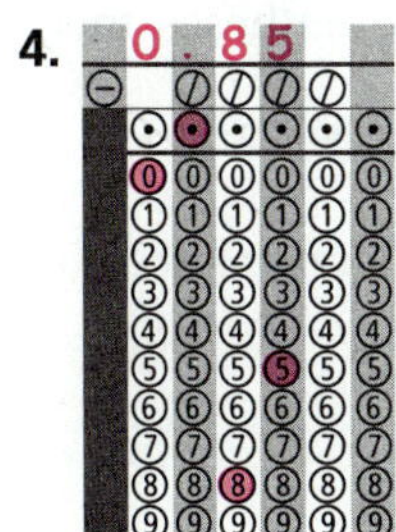

5. 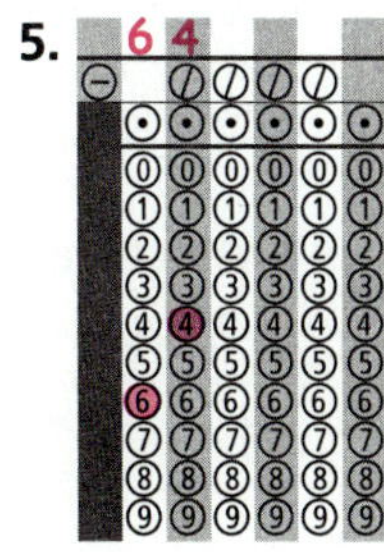

2-2 PART 1 Conditional Statements

Vocabulary

Review

Underline the *conclusion* of each statement.

1. If the weather is nice, we will go swimming.
2. If I exercise, then I will be strong.
3. If my friend works at her job this weekend, she won't go to the movies on Saturday.
4. If I ride my bike to softball practice, then I will get there on time.

Vocabulary Builder

conditional (noun) **kun DISH un ul**

Other Word Form: condition (noun)

Related Words: hypothesis, conclusion

Definition: A **conditional** is an *if-then* statement.

Example: The statement, "If two angles are vertical angles, then they are congruent," is a **conditional**.

Use Your Vocabulary

Place a ✓ in the box of the statement is a *conditional*. Place an ✗ in the box if it is not a *conditional*.

✓ **5.** If an angle measures 90, then it is a right angle.

✗ **6.** A pentagon is a polygon.

✓ **7.** If points lie on the same line, they are collinear.

✗ **8.** Work within parentheses, then multiply.

✓ **9.** If $x = 6$, then $x + 12 = 18$.

✗ **10.** A net is a two-dimensional diagram that you can fold to form a three-dimensional figure.

take note

Key Concept Conditional Statements

Definition	Symbols	Diagram
A **conditional** is an if-then statement.	$p \rightarrow q$	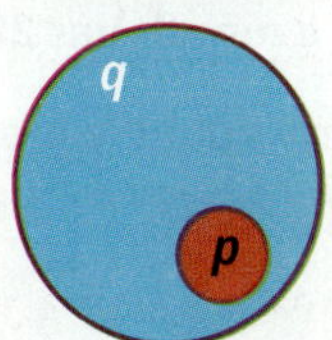
The **hypothesis** is the part p following *if*.	Read as "If p then q"	
The **conclusion** is the part q following *then*.	or "p implies q."	

11. If p = tears and q = sadness, what are two ways to read $p \rightarrow q$?

If tears, then sadness.

Tears imply sadness.

Problem 1 Identifying the Hypothesis and the Conclusion

Got It? **What are the hypothesis and the conclusion of the conditional?**

If an angle measures 130, then the angle is obtuse.

Complete each sentence with *if* or *then*.

12. The hypothesis is the part following _?_.

If

13. The conclusion is the part following _?_.

then

14. Circle the hypothesis. Underline the conclusion.

If (an angle measures 130), then <u>the angle is obtuse</u>.

Problem 2 Writing a Conditional

Got It? **How can you write "Dolphins are mammals" as a conditional?**

15. Circle the correct statement.

(All dolphins are mammals.) All mammals are dolphins.

Underline the correct words to complete each statement.

16. The set of <u>dolphins</u> / mammals is inside the set of dolphins / <u>mammals</u>.

17. The <u>smaller</u>/larger set is the hypothesis and the smaller / <u>larger</u> set is the conclusion.

18. Use your answers to Exercises 16 and 17 to write the conditional.

If _?_, then _?_.

If an animal is a dolphin,

then it is a mammal.

Problem 3 Finding the Truth Value of a Conditional

Got It? **Is the conditional *true* or *false*? If it is false, find a counterexample.**

If a month has 28 days, then it is February.

19. Cross out the month(s) that have at least 28 days.

~~January~~ ~~February~~ ~~March~~ ~~April~~ ~~May~~ ~~June~~

~~July~~ ~~August~~ ~~September~~ ~~October~~ ~~November~~ ~~December~~

20. Is the conditional *true* or *false*? Explain.

False. Explanations may vary. Sample: Every month has at least 28 days.

Lesson Check • Do you know HOW?

What are the hypothesis and the conclusion of the following statement? Write it as a conditional.

Residents of Key West live in Florida.

21. Label the Venn diagram with the words *Florida* and *Key West*.

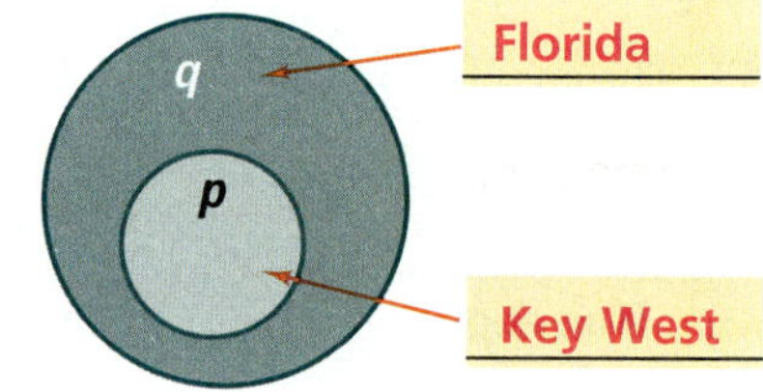

22. Circle the hypothesis. Underline the conclusion.

(are residents of Key West) <u>live in Florida</u>

23. Now write the conditional.

If people are residents of Key West,

then they live in Florida.

Lesson Check • Do you UNDERSTAND?

Error Analysis **Your classmate rewrote the statement "You jog every Sunday" as "If you jog, then it is Sunday." What is your classmate's error? Correct it.**

24. Circle the hypothesis and underline the conclusion of your classmate's conditional.

If (you jog), then <u>it is Sunday</u>.

25. Circle the counterexample for your classmate's conditional.

You don't jog, and it is not Sunday. (You also jog on Saturday.)

26. Write the conditional that best represents "You jog every Sunday."

If it is Sunday, then you jog.

2-2 PART 2 Conditional Statements

Vocabulary

Review

1. The conditional at the right is false. Complete the *counterexample* below.

   A whale lives in the ocean, but it is not a(n) fish.

If an animal lives in the ocean, then it is a fish.

Vocabulary Builder

converse (noun) KAHN vurs

Related Words: convert, conversion

Word Source: The prefix *con-*, which means "together," and *vertere*, which means "to turn," come from Latin. So, a **converse** involves changing the order of more than one thing.

Math Usage: The **converse** of a conditional exchanges the hypothesis and the conclusion.

Use Your Vocabulary

Finish writing the *converse* of each statement.

2. **Statement:** If I study, then I pass the Geometry test.

   Converse: If ?, then I study.

   I pass the Geometry test

3. **Statement:** If I am happy, then I laugh.

   Converse: If ?, then ?.

   I laugh | I am happy

4. **Statement:** If I have a summer job, then I can buy a new bicycle.

   Converse: ?.

   If I can buy a new bicycle, then I have a summer job.

take note

Key Concept Related Conditional Statements

Statement	How to Write It	Symbols	How to Read It
Conditional	Use the given hypothesis and conclusion.	$p \to q$	If p, then q.
Converse	Exchange the hypothesis and the conclusion.	$q \to p$	If q, then p.
Inverse	Negate both the hypothesis and the conclusion of the conditional.	$\sim p \to \sim q$	If not p, then not q.
Contrapositive	Negate both the hypothesis and the conclusion of the converse.	$\sim q \to \sim p$	If not q, then not p.

Use the statement below to write each conditional.

$\angle A$ measures 98, so $\angle A$ is obtuse.

5. **Conditional** If _?_, then _?_.

   If $\angle A$ measures 98, then $\angle A$ is obtuse.

6. **Converse** If _?_, then _?_.

   If $\angle A$ is obtuse, then $\angle A$ measures 98.

7. **Inverse** If *not* _?_, then *not* _?_.

   If $\angle A$ does not measure 98,

   then $\angle A$ is not obtuse.

8. **Contrapositive** If *not* _?_, then *not* _?_.

   If $\angle A$ is not obtuse,

   then $\angle A$ does not measure 98.

Problem 4 Writing and Finding Truth Values of Statements

Got It? **What are the converse, inverse, and contrapositive of the conditional statement below? What are the truth values of each? If a statement is false, give a counterexample.**

If a vegetable is a carrot, then it contains beta carotene.

Finish writing each statement.

9. **Converse:** If a vegetable contains beta carotene, then _?_. it is a carrot

10. **Inverse:** If a vegetable is not a carrot, then _?_. it does not contain beta carotene

11. **Contrapositive:** If a vegetable does not contain beta carotene, then _?_. it is not a carrot

12. Underline the correct word to complete each sentence.

The converse is true / <u>false</u>. The inverse is true / <u>false</u>. The contrapositive is <u>true</u> / false.

13. Give counterexamples for the statements that are false.

Answers may vary. Sample: A sweet potato is a counterexample for both the converse and the inverse.

Lesson Check • Do you UNDERSTAND?

Reasoning **Suppose a conditional statement and its converse are both true. What are the truth values of the contrapositive and inverse? How do you know?**

Write T for *true* or F for *false*.

T 14. A conditional and its contrapositive are equivalent statements.

T 15. The converse and inverse of a statement are equivalent statements.

F 16. Equivalent statements have different truth values.

T 17. When a conditional statement is true, the contrapositive is true.

F 18. When the converse of a statement true, the inverse is false.

19. What are the truth values of the contrapositive and inverse when a conditional statement and its converse are both true? How do you know? Explanations may vary. Sample:

Both are true. A conditional and its contrapositive are equivalent. The converse and inverse are equivalent. Equivalent statements have the same truth value.

Math Success

Check off the vocabulary words that you understand.

☐ conditional ☐ hypothesis ☐ conclusion

☐ converse ☐ inverse ☐ contrapositive

Rate how well you can *write conditional statements*.

Need to review 0 2 4 6 8 10 Now I get it!

Name ______________________ Class ____________ Date ____________

2-2 Think About a Plan

Conditional Statements

Error Analysis Natalie claims that a given conditional and its contrapositive are both true. Sean claims that the given conditional is true but its contrapositive is false. Who is correct and how do you know?

Understanding the Problem

1. What is the main point of disagreement between Natalie and Sean?

   Sample: Natalie thinks that a conditional and its contrapositive are both true. Sean thinks that only the conditional is true.

2. Do you think it is possible to write a conditional statement that is true, but has a false contrapositive? Explain.

   Sample: No; a conditional statement has the same truth value as its contrapositive.

3. How could you use examples of true and false conditionals to decide who is correct?

   Sample: You could write some conditional statements that you know are true and test whether the contrapositives are true. You could write some conditional statements that you know are false and test whether the contrapositives are false.

Planning the Solution

4. Use a table to test some conditional statements. Write several conditional statements and their contrapositives. Use the table to show their truth values. One example has been completed for you. Use additional paper if necessary. **Answers may vary. Sample:**

Conditional	True or false?	Contrapositive	True or false?
If a dog has spots, then the dog can fly.	false	If a dog cannot fly, then the dog does not have spots.	false
If a glass is half full, then the glass is half empty.	**true**	**If a glass is not half empty, then the glass is not half full.**	**true**

Getting an Answer

5. What does the pattern in your table tell you about whether Natalie or Sean is probably correct?

   Natalie is correct. If the original conditional is true, then its contrapositive must be true. Either both the conditional and contrapositive are true, or both are false.

Name ______________________ Class ____________ Date ____________

2-2 Practice

Form K

Conditional Statements

Identify the hypothesis and conclusion of each conditional.

1. If the shoe fits, then you can wear it.

   To start, identify the *if* and *then* portions of the statement.

   If the shoe fits, then you can wear it.

   Hypothesis (*p*): The shoe fits; Conclusion (*q*): You can wear it.

2. If you are a lawyer, then you passed the bar exam.

   Hypothesis (*p*): You are a lawyer; Conclusion (*q*): You passed the bar exam.

3. If it is a fish, then it lives in water.

   Hypothesis (*p*): It is a fish; Conclusion (*q*): It lives in water.

Write each sentence as a conditional.

4. Robert Oppenheimer spoke eight languages.

   To start, identify the *if* part of the statement and rewrite it as a hypothesis.

   If a person was Robert Oppenheimer, then he could speak eight languages.

5. Purple and yellow are complementary colors.

   If two colors are purple and yellow, then they are complementary.

6. A decibel is a measurement of the intensity of a sound.

   If it is measured in decibels, then it is the intensity of a sound.

Write a conditional statement that each Venn diagram illustrates.

7. 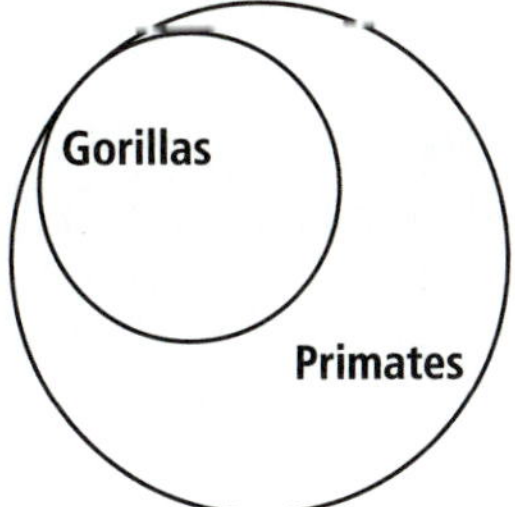

   If the animal is a gorilla, then it is a primate.

8. 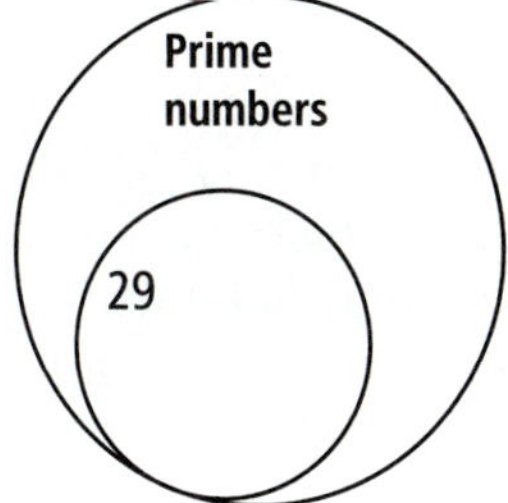

   If the number is 29, then it is a prime number.

Determine if the conditional is *true* or *false*. If it is false, find a counterexample.

9. If an animal has wings, then it is a bird. False; a bat has wings, but it is not a bird.

10. If it is after sunset, you can see the stars. False; you cannot see stars on a cloudy night.

Name ______________________ Class ____________ Date ____________

2-2 Practice (continued)

Form K

Conditional Statements

Write the converse, inverse, and contrapositive of the given conditional statement. Determine the truth value of all four statements. If a statement is false, give a counterexample.

11. Three points not on the same line are noncollinear. **True; Converse: If three points are noncollinear, then they are not on the same line; true. Inverse: If three points are on the same line, then they are collinear; true. Contrapositive: If three points are collinear, then they are on the same line; true.**

12. Obtuse angles have measures greater than 90. **True; Converse: If an ∠ has a measure greater than 90, then it is obtuse; true. Inverse: If an ∠ is not obtuse, then it does not have a measure greater than 90; true. Contrapositive: If an ∠ does not have a measure greater than 90, then it is not obtuse; true.**

13. If you do not live in Tampa, then you do not live in Florida. **False; You could live in Orlando. Converse: If you do not live in Florida, then you do not live in Tampa; true. Inverse: If you live in Tampa, then you live in Florida; true. Contrapositive: If you live in Florida, then you live in Tampa; false. You could live in Orlando.**

14. If n is an even number, then n is divisible by 2. **True; Converse: If n is divisible by 2, then n is an even number; true. Inverse: If n is not an even number, then n is not divisible by 2; true. Contrapositive: If n is not divisible by 2, then n is not an even number; true.**

Write the converse of each statement. If the converse is true, write *true.* If it is not true, provide a counterexample.

15. If it is snowing, then it is cloudy.
If it is cloudy, then it is snowing; false; it could be overcast without precipitation of any sort falling.

16. All rectangles are quadrilaterals.
If a figure is a quadrilateral, then it is a rectangle; false; a quadrilateral does not necessarily have 90° angles or parallel opposite sides.

17. All students like chocolate.
If a person likes chocolate, then he or she is a student; false; a chocolate lover could be a businessperson or a pre-school-aged child.

18. All right triangles have two or more congruent angles.
If a triangle has two or more congruent angles, then it is a right triangle; false; two equilateral triangles can be congruent, but neither is a right triangle.

Name ______________________ Class ____________ Date ____________

2-2 Standardized Test Prep

Conditional Statements

Multiple Choice

For Exercises 1–4, choose the correct letter.

1. What is the hypothesis of the given statement? A

If pigs had wings, you could fly.

(A) Pigs have wings.
(B) You can fly.
(C) Pigs do not have wings.
(D) You cannot fly.

2. Which statement is the converse of the given statement? H

If you make an insurance claim, then your rates will go up.

(F) If your insurance rates do not go up, then you have not made a claim.
(G) If you do not make an insurance claim, then your rates will not go up.
(H) If your insurance rates go up, then you have made an insurance claim.
(I) If you make an insurance claim, then your rates will not go up.

3. Which statement is the contrapositive of the given statement? A

If a person is a banjo player, then the person is a musician.

(A) If a person is not a musician, then the person is not a banjo player.
(B) If a person is not a banjo player, then the person is a musician.
(C) If a person is not a banjo player, then the person is not a musician.
(D) If a person is a musician, then the person is a banjo player.

4. How are the two statements given below related to each other? H

X: If you run for 10 minutes, then you will raise your heart rate.

Z: If you do not run for 10 minutes, then you will not raise your heart rate.

(F) *Z* is the contrapositive of *X*.
(G) *Z* is the converse of *X*.
(H) *Z* is the inverse of *X*.
(I) *Z* is the retrograde of *X*.

Short Response

5. What are the inverse and the contrapositive of the following conditional?

If a movie is a comedy, then it is funny.

[2] Inverse: If a movie is not a comedy, then it is not funny. Contrapositive: If a movie is not funny, then it is not a comedy. [1] Only one answer is written correctly. [0] Neither answer is written correctly.

2-3 Biconditionals and Definitions

Vocabulary

Review

Underline the *hypothesis* in each statement.

1. If it rains on Friday, I won't have to cut the grass on Saturday.
2. If I go to sleep early tonight, then I won't be late for school tomorrow.
3. A triangle is equilateral if it has three congruent sides.
4. I'll know how to write biconditionals if I can identify a hypothesis and a conclusion.

Vocabulary Builder

bi- (prefix) by

Definition: *bi-* is a prefix that means having two.

Examples: A *bicycle* has two wheels. Someone who is *bilingual* speaks two languages fluently.

Use Your Vocabulary

Draw a line from each word in Column A to its meaning in Column B.

Column A	Column B
5. biannually (adverb)	occurring every two hundred years
6. biathlon (noun)	a two-footed animal
7. bicentennial (adjective)	having two coasts
8. bicoastal (adjective)	supported by two parties
9. biped (noun)	occurring every two weeks
10. bipartisan (adjective)	occurring every two years
11. biplane (noun)	a plane with two sets of wings
12. biweekly (adjective)	a two-event athletic contest

Key Concept Biconditional Statements

A *biconditional* combines $p \rightarrow q$ and $q \rightarrow p$ as $p \leftrightarrow q$.

You read $p \leftrightarrow q$ as "p if and only if q."

13. Complete the biconditional.

A ray is an angle bisector __?__ it divides an angle into two congruent angles.

if and only if

Problem 1 Writing a Biconditional

Got It? What is the converse of the following true conditional? If the converse is also true, rewrite the statements as a biconditional.

If two angles have equal measure, then the angles are congruent.

14. Identify the hypothesis (p) and the conclusion (q).

p: two angles have equal measure

q: the angles are congruent

15. Circle the converse ($q \rightarrow p$) of the conditional.

If two angles do *not* have equal measure, then the angles are *not* congruent.	If two angles are congruent, then the angles have equal measure. (circled)	If two angles are *not* congruent, then the angles do *not* have equal measure.

16. Now write the statements as a biconditional ($p \leftrightarrow q$).

Two angles have equal measure if and only if the angles are congruent.

Problem 2 Identifying the Conditionals in a Biconditional

Got It? What are the two conditionals that form this biconditional?

Two numbers are reciprocals if and only if their product is 1.

17. Identify p and q.

p: two numbers are reciprocals

q: their product is 1

18. Write the conditional $p \rightarrow q$.

If two numbers are reciprocals,

then their product is 1.

19. Write the conditional $q \rightarrow p$.

If the product of two numbers is 1,

then they are reciprocals.

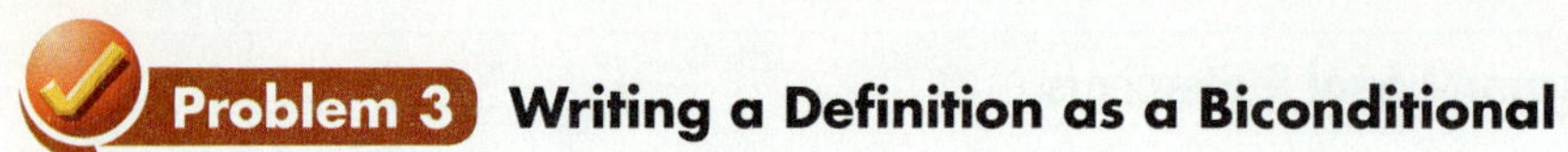

Problem 3 Writing a Definition as a Biconditional

Got It? **Is this definition of *straight angle* reversible? If yes, write it as a true biconditional.**

A straight angle is an angle that measures 180.

20. *Reversible* means you can reverse *p* and q in the conditional.

21. Write the conditional.

If an angle is a straight angle,

then it measures 180.

22. Write the converse.

If an angle measures 180,

then it is a straight angle.

23. Write the biconditional.

An angle is a straight angle,

if and only if it measures 180.

Problem 4 Identifying Good Definitions

Got It? **Is the following statement a good definition? Explain.**

A square is a figure with four right angles.

24. Write the *conditional.*

If a figure is a square, then it has four right angles.

25. Write the *converse.*

If a figure has four right angles, then it is a square.

26. Which statement is true, the *conditional*, the *converse*, or *both*?

the conditional

27. Is the definition of a square a good definition? Explain.

No. Explanations may vary. Sample: The converse of the conditional is not true.

Lesson Check • Do you UNDERSTAND?

Compare and Contrast **Which of the following statements is a better definition of a linear pair? Explain.**

A linear pair is a pair of supplementary angles.

A linear pair is a pair of adjacent angles with noncommon sides that are opposite rays.

Use the figures below for Exercises 28–31.

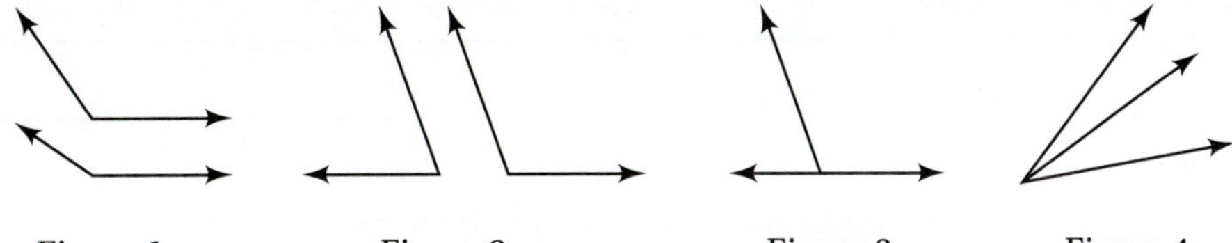

Figure 1 Figure 2 Figure 3 Figure 4

Underline the correct number or numbers to complete each sentence.

28. Figure(s) 1 / 2 / 3 / 4 show(s) linear pairs.

29. Figure(s) 1 / 2 / 3 / 4 show(s) supplementary angles.

30. Figure(s) 1 / 2 / 3 / 4 show(s) adjacent angles.

31. Figure(s) 1 / 2 / 3 / 4 show(s) adjacent angles whose noncommon sides are opposite rays.

32. Underline the correct word to complete the sentence.

Supplementary angles are always / sometimes / never linear pairs.

33. Write the better definition of a linear pair.

A linear pair is a pair of adjacent angles with noncommon sides that are opposite rays.

Math Success

Check off the vocabulary words that you understand.

☐ biconditional ☐ conditional ☐ hypothesis ☐ conclusion

Rate how well you can *use biconditionals*.

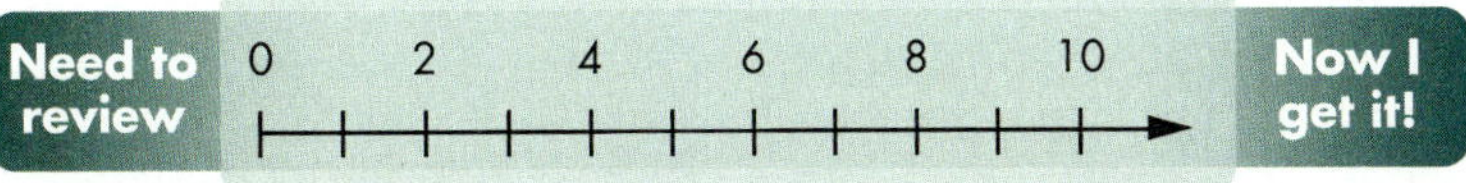

Name ____________________ Class ____________ Date ____________

2-3 Think About a Plan

Biconditionals and Definitions

Error Analysis Your friend defines a right angle as an angle that is greater than an acute angle. Use a biconditional to show that this is not a good definition.

1. What is your friend's statement?

   A right angle is an angle that is greater than an acute angle.

2. The exercise tells you to use a biconditional. What would be a good first step before you write a biconditional?

   Answers may vary. Sample: First write the definition as a conditional statement.

3. Rewrite your friend's statement as a biconditional.

   An angle is a right angle if and only if it is greater than an acute angle.

4. Now write the two conditionals that make up the biconditional. Fill in the blanks to complete the two conditional statements.

   a. If an angle is a(n) right angle, then the measure of the angle is greater than the measure of a(n) acute angle.

   b. If the measure of an angle is greater than the measure of a(n) acute angle, then the angle is a(n) right angle.

5. Look at the two conditionals. Are both conditionals true? Explain.

   The first of the two conditionals is true, but the second is not true. Obtuse angles also have measures that are greater than the measures of acute angles.

6. What would be the best way to explain that your friend's definition is not a good definition?

   The converse of the original definition is not true. Writing it as the two conditionals that make up a biconditional shows that it only works in one direction.

Name ______________________ Class ____________ Date ____________

2-3 Practice — Form K

Biconditionals and Definitions

Each conditional statement below is true. Write its converse. If the converse is also true, combine the statements as a biconditional.

1. If point B lies on $\overline{AC}$, then $AB + BC = AC$.

   To start, determine the hypothesis (p) and conclusion (q) of the statement.

   p: Point B lies on __?__. $\overline{AC}$ q: $AB + BC =$ __?__ AC

   If $AB + BC = AC$, then point B lies on $\overline{AC}$; true. Point B lies on $\overline{AC}$ if and only if $AB + BC = AC$.

2. If two lines intersect to form adjacent congruent angles, then the lines are perpendicular. If two lines are perpendicular, then they intersect to form adjacent congruent angles; true. Two lines are perpendicular if and only if they intersect to form adjacent congruent angles.

3. If two angles are right angles, then they are congruent.
   If two angles are congruent, then they are right angles; false.

4. If a point is on the perpendicular bisector of a segment, then it is equidistant from the endpoints of the segment. If a point is equidistant from the endpoints of a segment, then it is on the perpendicular bisector of the segment; true. A point is on the perpendicular bisector of a segment if and only if the point is equidistant from the endpoints of the segment.

Write the two statements that form each biconditional.

5. The product of two numbers is a perfect square if and only if the two numbers are identical. If the product of two numbers is a perfect square, then the two numbers are identical; If two numbers are identical, then the product of the numbers is a perfect square.

6. A number is a terminating decimal if and only if it contains a finite number of digits. If a number is a terminating decimal, then the number contains a finite number of digits; If a number contains a finite number of digits, then it is a terminating decimal.

7. A figure is three-dimensional if and only if it has length, width, and height.
   If a figure is three-dimensional, then the figure has length, width, and height.
   If a figure has length, width, and height, then it is three-dimensional.

Test each statement below to see if it is reversible. If so, write it as a true biconditional. If not, write *not reversible.*

8. A linear pair consists of two angles with measures that sum to 180.

   To start, rewrite the statement as an if-then conditional statement.

   If two angles __?__, then __?__.
   are a linear pair; the sum of their measures is 180;
   Two angles are a linear pair if and only if the sum of their measures is 180.

9. Two angles that are complements of the same angle are congruent. not reversible

Name ______________________ Class ____________ Date ____________

2-3 Practice (continued)

Form K

Biconditionals and Definitions

Is each statement below a good definition? If not, explain.

10. Linear pairs of angles are two adjacent angles that share one side, and the sides they do not share are opposite rays. **yes**

11. A leap year is a year that has 366 days because one day is added to the month of February. **yes**

12. A documentary movie does not have actors and does not have a script. **No; the definition is not reversible.**

13. A light duty truck is any motor vehicle that weighs less than 4500 lb and can carry a payload of up to 4000 lb. **yes**

14. A light bulb gives off light and is hot to the touch. **No; this definition excludes fluorescent light bulbs and does not mention electricity.**

15. Opposite rays are two rays that share the same endpoint. **No; opposite rays must form a line.**

Tell whether each conditional and its converse form a true biconditional.

16. Any fraction is in simplest form if the only common factor of the numerator and denominator is 1 or -1. **true**

17. For two integers a and b, the product ab is even if at least one of the integers, a or b, is even. **truc**

18. If a figure is a square, then it is a rectangle. **Not true; the converse is false: If a figure is a rectangle, then it is a square.**

19. If a triangle is equilateral, then its angles each measure 60. **true**

Write each statement as a biconditional.

20. If two angles are supplementary, the sum of their measures is 180 degrees. **Two angles are supplementary if and only if the sum of their measures is 180 degrees.**

21. In the equation $y = ax^2 + bx + c$, if a is positive, the parabola opens upward. **A parabola opens upward if and only if a is positive in the equation $y = ax^2 + bx + c$.**

Name ______________________ Class ____________ Date ____________

2-3 Standardized Test Prep

Biconditionals and Definitions

Multiple Choice

For Exercises 1–3, choose the correct letter.

1. Which statement is a good definition of a rectangle? C

   (A) A rectangle is a shape with four sides.

   (B) A rectangle is a shape with two pairs of parallel sides.

   (C) A rectangle is a quadrilateral with four congruent angles.

   (D) A rectangle is a parallelogram with four congruent sides.

2. Conditional: If a triangle is scalene, then the triangle has no congruent sides. F

   Which statement shows the conditional written as a true biconditional?

   (F) A triangle is scalene if and only if it has no congruent sides.

   (G) If a triangle has no congruent sides, then the triangle is scalene.

   (H) If a triangle has some congruent sides, then the triangle is not scalene.

   (I) A triangle is equilateral if and only if it is not scalene.

3. Biconditional: A triangle is equilateral if and only if the triangle has three congruent angles.

   Which choice shows the two conditionals that make up the biconditional? B

   (A) If a triangle has three sides, then it is equilateral. If the triangle is equilateral, then it has three sides.

   (B) If a triangle is equilateral, then it has three congruent angles. If a triangle has three congruent angles, then it is equilateral.

   (C) If a triangle is scalene, then the triangle is not equilateral. If a triangle is equilateral, then the triangle is not scalene.

   (D) An equilateral triangle has symmetry. If a triangle has symmetry, it is equilateral.

Short Response

4. Write this definition as a true biconditional two different ways.

   Definition: A rhombus is a parallelogram with four congruent sides.

   [2] A figure is a rhombus if and only if it is a parallelogram with four congruent sides. A parallelogram has four congruent sides if and only if it is a rhombus.
   [1] The student writes just one form of the biconditional correctly.
   [0] The student writes no correct forms of the biconditional.

2-4 Deductive Reasoning

Vocabulary

Review

Write the *converse* of each conditional.

1. If I am thirsty, then I drink water.

   If I drink water, then I am thirsty.

2. If the car outside is wet, then it rained.

   If it rained, then the car outside is wet.

Vocabulary Builder

deduce (verb) dee DOOS

Related Words: deductive (adjective), deduction (noun)

Definition: To **deduce** is to use known facts to reach a conclusion.

Main Idea: When you use general principles and facts to come to a conclusion, you **deduce** the conclusion.

Example: Your friend is wearing red today. He wears red only when there is a home game. You use these facts to **deduce** that there is a home game today.

Use Your Vocabulary

Complete each statement with a word from the list. Use each word only once.

deduce   deduction   deductive

3. You use _?_ reasoning to draw a conclusion based on facts. deductive

4. The conclusion of your reasoning is a _?_. deduction

5. The teacher will not _?_ that a dog ate your homework. deduce

Property Law of Detachment

Law	Symbols
If the hypothesis of a true conditional is true, then the conclusion is true.	If $p \to q$ is true and p is true, then q is true.

Problem 1 Using the Law of Detachment

Got It? **What can you conclude from the given information?**

If there is lightning, then it is not safe to be out in the open.
Marla sees lightning from the soccer field.

6. Underline the hypothesis of the conditional. Circle the conclusion.

If there is lightning, then it is not safe to be out in the open.

Underline the correct word or phrase to complete each sentence.

7. "Marla sees lightning from the soccer field" fits / does not fit the hypothesis.

8. It is safe / not safe to be on the soccer field.

Property Law of Syllogism

You can state a conclusion from two true conditional statements when the conclusion of one statement is the hypothesis of the other statement.

If $p \to q$ is true and $q \to r$ is true, then $p \to r$ is true.

Complete each conclusion.

9. If it is July, then you are on summer vacation.

If you are on summer vacation, then you work in a smoothie shop.

Conclusion: If it is July, then you work in a smoothie shop.

10. If a figure is a rhombus, then it has four sides.

If a figure has four sides, then it is a quadrilateral.

Conclusion: If a figure is a rhombus, then it is a quadrilateral.

Problem 2 Using the Law of Syllogism

Got It? **What can you conclude from the given information? What is your reasoning?**

If a whole number ends in 0, then it is divisible by 10.
If a whole number is divisible by 10, then it is divisible by 5.

11. Identify p, q, and r.

p: a whole number ends in 0

q: a whole number is divisible by 10

r: a whole number is divisible by 5

12. Decide whether each part of the given information is *true* or *false*. Write T for *true* or F for *false*.

T $p \to q$ T $q \to r$ T $p \to r$

13. Circle the part of the Law of Syllogism that you will write.

$p \to q$ $q \to r$ ($p \to r$)

14. Now write your conclusion.

If a whole number ends in 0, then it is divisible by 5.

Problem 3 Using the Laws of Syllogism and Detachment

Got It? **What can you conclude from the given information? What is your reasoning?**

If a river is more than 4000 mi long, then it is longer than the Amazon.
If a river is longer than the Amazon, then it is the longest river in the world.
The Nile is 4132 mi long.

15. Identify p, q, and r in the given information.

p: a river is more than 4000 mi long

q: a river is longer than the Amazon

r: a river is the longest river in the world

16. Use the Law of Syllogism to complete the conditional.

If a river is more than 4000 mi long.

then it is the longest river in the world.

17. Use the Law of Detachment and the conditional in Exercise 16 to write a conclusion.

The Nile is the longest river in the world.

Lesson Check • Do you know HOW?

If possible, make a conclusion from the given true statements. What reasoning did you use?

If a figure is a three-sided polygon, then it is a triangle.
Figure *ABC* is a three-sided polygon.

18. Identify p and q in the first statement.

p: a figure is a three-sided polygon

q: a figure is a triangle

19. Underline the correct words to complete each sentence.

The second statement matches the <u>hypothesis</u> / conclusion of the first statement.

I can use the Law of <u>Detachment</u> / Syllogism to state a conclusion.

20. Write your conclusion.

Figure *ABC* is a triangle.

Lesson Check • Do you UNDERSTAND?

Error Analysis **What is the error in the reasoning below?**

~~Birds that weigh more than 50 pounds cannot fly. A kiwi cannot fly. So, a kiwi weighs more than 50 pounds.~~

21. Write "Birds that weigh more than 50 pounds cannot fly" as a conditional.

If a bird weighs more than 50 pounds, then it cannot fly.

22. Write the hypothesis of the conditional in Exercise 21.

a bird weighs more than 50 pounds

Underline the correct word to complete each sentence.

23. "A kiwi cannot fly" matches the hypothesis / <u>conclusion</u> of the conditional.

24. The student incorrectly applied the Law of <u>Detachment</u> / Syllogism.

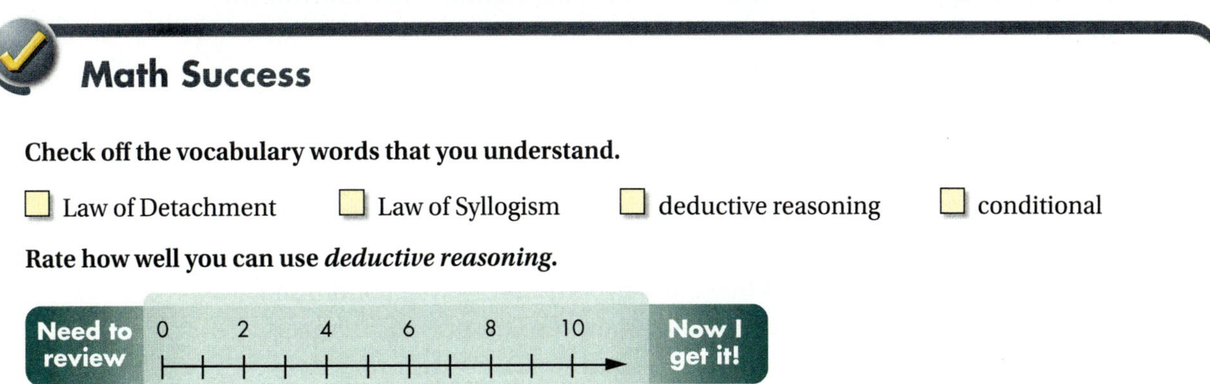

Math Success

Check off the vocabulary words that you understand.

- ☐ Law of Detachment
- ☐ Law of Syllogism
- ☐ deductive reasoning
- ☐ conditional

Rate how well you can use *deductive reasoning*.

Name ______________________ Class ____________ Date ____________

2-4 Think About a Plan

Deductive Reasoning

Writing Give an example of a rule used in your school that could be written as a conditional. Explain how the Law of Detachment is used in applying that rule.

Understanding the Problem

1. What is the problem asking you to do?

   Answers may vary. Sample: Write a school rule as a conditional. Then show how the rule is applied using the Law of Detachment.

Planning the Solution

2. List a school rule that could be written as a conditional.

   Example: Do not park your car in spaces marked "reserved" or your car will be towed.

   Sample: You will be given a 30-minute detention after getting three tardy slips.

Getting an Answer

3. Rewrite the school rule as a conditional.

   Example: If you park your car in a space marked "reserved," then your car will be towed.

   Sample: If you are tardy to class three times, then you will be given a 30-minute detention.

4. Identify the hypothesis and the conclusion of the conditional you wrote for the school rule.

   Example: Hypothesis: You park your car in a space marked "reserved."

   Conclusion: Your car will be towed.

   Sample: Hypothesis: You are tardy to class three times. Conclusion: You will be given a 30-minute detention.

5. The Law of Detachment states that if the hypothesis of a true conditional is true, then the conclusion is true. Explain how the Law of Detachment is used when applying your school rule.

   Sample: The conclusion of the rule is the consequence for breaking the rule. So, when the conditions of the hypothesis are met, then the consequence will result. So, when you get a third tardy slip, the consequence will be that you get a 30-minute detention.

Name _______________ Class _______________ Date _______________

2-4 Practice

Form K

Deductive Reasoning

If possible, use the Law of Detachment to make a conclusion. If it is not possible to make a conclusion, tell why.

1. If you pass a road test, you will get your driver's license.

   Tamara passed her road test. Tamara got her driver's license.

   To start, identify the hypothesis (p) of the first conditional.
   Then compare it to the second statement.

2. If an angle is a right angle, then it is not acute.

   $m\angle Q \neq 90$ No conclusion can be drawn because the second statement does not match the hypothesis of the given conditional.

3. If you swim 100 m in less than 90 s, you will be on the swim team.

   Jeremy swam 200 m in 190 s. No conclusion can be drawn because the second statement does not state how much time it took to swim 100 m.

4. If you arrive at the theater by 2:00 P.M., you can see the show.

   Julie arrived at the theater at 1:45 P.M. Julie can see the show.

5. If a triangle has one obtuse angle, then it is an obtuse triangle.

   $\triangle ABC$ has an acute angle. No conclusion can be drawn because the second statement does not match the hypothesis of the given conditional.

If possible, use the Law of Syllogism to make a conclusion. If it is not possible to make a conclusion, tell why.

6. If the sum of the digits in a number is 9, then the number is divisible by 9.

   If a number is divisible by 9, then it is divisible by 3.

   To start, identify the conclusion of the first statement.
   Then identify the hypothesis of the other statement and compare.
   If the sum of the digits in a number is 9, then the number is divisible by 3.

7. If an animal has hair, it is a mammal.

   If an animal gives birth to live young, it is a mammal.
   No conclusion can be drawn; the statements have the same conclusion.

8. If a language is Spanish, it is a Romance language.

   If a language is a Romance language, it has Latin roots.
   If a language is Spanish, then it has Latin roots.

9. If two angle measures sum to 180, then the angles are supplementary.

   If two angle measures sum to 90, then the angles are complementary.
   No conclusion can be drawn; neither conclusion matches the hypothesis of the other statement.

Name ______________________ Class ____________ Date ____________

2-4 Practice (continued) Form K

Deductive Reasoning

Use the Law of Detachment and the Law of Syllogism to make conclusions from the following statements. If it is not possible to make a conclusion, tell why.

10. If you live in Santa Monica, you live in California.
If you live in California, you live on the West Coast.
Cheryl lives in Santa Monica. **Cheryl lives on the West Coast.**

11. If you eat yogurt, you are eating food from the dairy group.
If you eat food from the dairy group, you are getting calcium.
Lenny does not eat yogurt. **No conclusion is possible about Lenny because he may or may not eat other foods from the dairy group.**

Write the first statement as a conditional. If possible, use the Law of Detachment to make a conclusion. If it is not possible to make a conclusion, tell why.

12. Citrus fruits grow in warm climates.
Oranges are citrus fruits.
If a fruit is a citrus fruit, then it grows in warm climates. Oranges grow in a warm climate.

13. All quadrilaterals are polygons.
ABCD is a quadrilateral.
If a figure is a quadrilateral, it is a polygon. *ABCD* is a polygon.

14. All Italians are Europeans.
Gia is European.
If you are Italian, you are European. No conclusion can be made because it is not stated that Gia is Italian.

15. Every child likes ice cream.
Karen likes ice cream.
If a person is a child, then she or he likes ice cream. No conclusion can be made because it is not stated that Karen is a child.

For Exercises 16–18, assume that the following statements are true.

A. If it is Tuesday, then Tom has art class.

B. If Julie has a soccer game, then it is Wednesday.

C. If it is a weekday, then Sarah has homework.

D. If it is not Saturday, then Manuel does not have tennis practice.

E. Julie has a soccer game.

Use only the information given above. For each statement, write *must be true, may be true,* or *is not true.* Explain your reasoning.

16. Sarah has homework. **Must be true. Julie has a soccer game, so today is Wednesday. Wednesday is a weekday, so Sarah has homework.**

17. Tom has art class. **May be true. Julie has a soccer game, so today is Wednesday. We know Tom has art on Tuesday, but he may also have art on Wednesday.**

18. Manuel has tennis practice. **Is not true. Julie has a soccer game, so today is Wednesday. Manuel only has tennis practice on Saturday.**

Name ______________________ Class ____________ Date ____________

2-4 Standardized Test Prep

Deductive Reasoning

Multiple Choice

For Exercises 1–3, choose the correct letter.

1. Which statement is a valid conclusion based on the argument? C

If a polygon is a regular pentagon, then the polygon has exactly five congruent angles.

The polygon is a regular pentagon.

A. Therefore, the polygon is a rectangle.

B. Therefore, the polygon is a regular quadrilateral.

C. Therefore, the polygon has exactly five congruent angles.

D. Therefore, the polygon has congruent sides.

2. Using the Law of Syllogism, which of the following completes the statement to form a valid conclusion? G

If it is snowing heavily, then school will be canceled.

If school is canceled, the big test will not be given today.

It is snowing heavily, therefore

F. look out for the snowplows while driving to school.

G. the big test will not be given today.

H. the roads will be hard to drive on.

I. you should call the school to see if school is canceled.

3. Using the Law of Detachment, which statement is a valid conclusion? B

If Jordin has a temperature of 100° or more, then Jordin should stay home from school.

Jordin has a temperature of 101°.

A. Jordin should see the school nurse.

B. Jordin should stay home from school.

C. Jordin should take his temperature again.

D. Jordin has a temperature of 100° or more.

Short Response

4. Use the Law of Syllogism to make a valid conclusion.

If a blub is screaming, then a frot is swimming.

If a frot is swimming, then a greep is flinging.

[2] The student writes the complete conclusion: If a blub is screaming, then a greep is flinging. [1] The student writes, "A greep is flinging." [0] The student writes no correct conclusions.

2-5 Reasoning in Algebra and Geometry

Vocabulary

Review

1. Circle each *equation*.

$2(a - 5)^2$ $3x + 2 = 4$ $5 + 3^4$ $9 < x - 2$

Write an *equation* to represent each problem.

2. Sara has five more than twice the number of apples that Gregg has. If Sara has 21 apples, how many apples does Gregg have?

Answers may vary but must be equivalent to $2x + 5 = 21$.

3. Your brother does one less than twice the number of chores that you do. If he does seven chores, how many chores do you do?

Answers may vary but must be equivalent to $2x - 1 = 7$.

Vocabulary Builder

justify (verb) JUS tuh fy

Related Words: justice (noun), justification (noun), justifiable (adjective), justly (adverb)

Definition: To **justify** a step in a solution means to provide a mathematical reason why the step is correct.

Main Idea: When you **justify** an action, you explain why it is reasonable.

Use Your Vocabulary

4. Draw a line from each equation in Column A to the property you would use to *justify* it in Column B.

Column A	Column B
$3 + 7 = 7 + 3$	Associative Property of Addition
$12(4) = 4(12)$	Associative Property of Multiplication
$2 \cdot (5 \cdot x) = (2 \cdot 5) \cdot x$	Commutative Property of Addition
$1 + (9 + 53) = (1 + 9) + 53$	Commutative Property of Multiplication

Key Concept Properties of Equality

5. Complete the graphic organizer.

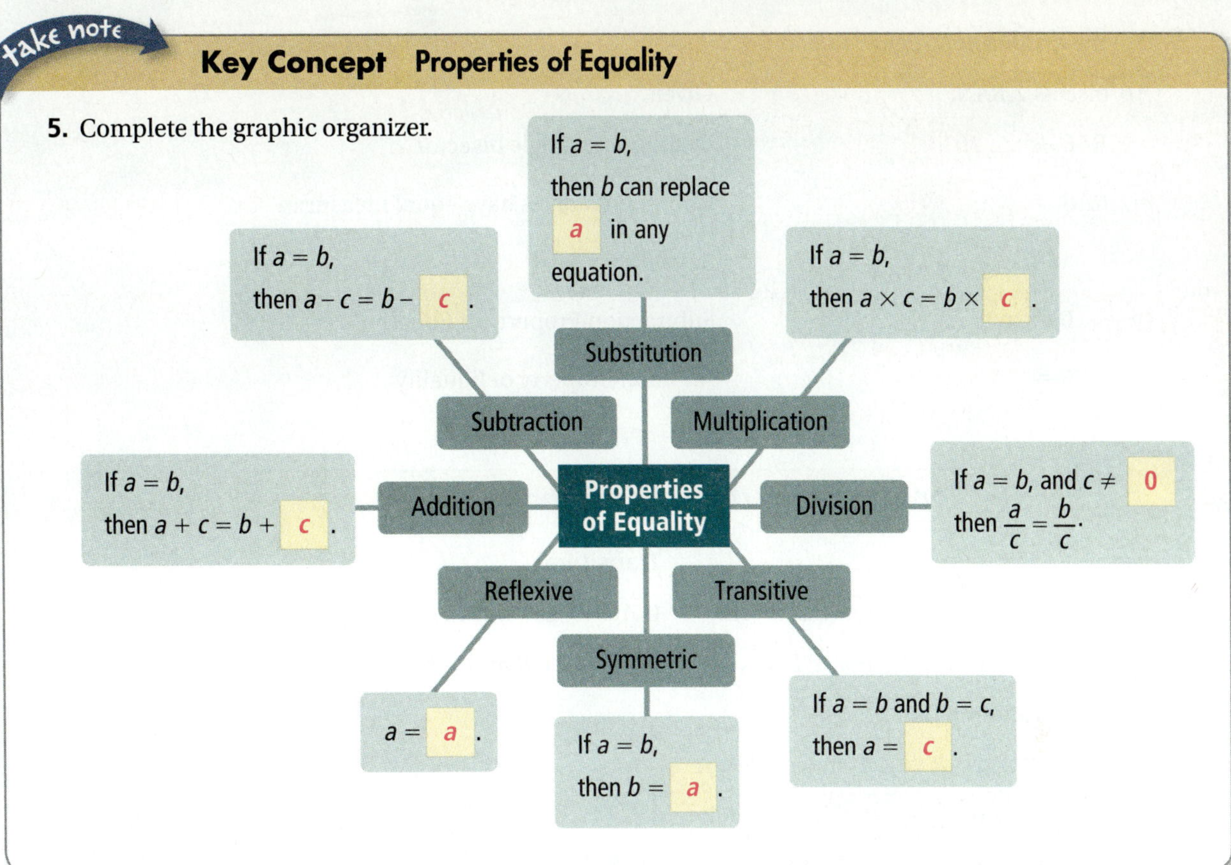

Key Concept The Distributive Property

Use multiplication to distribute a to each term of the sum or difference within the parentheses.

Sum

$a(b + c) = ab + ac$

Difference

$a(b - c) = ab - ac$

Use the Distributive Property to simplify each expression.

6. $5(24) = 5(20 + 4)$
$= 5(20) + 5(4)$
$= 100 + 20$
$= 120$

7. $17(3) = (20 - 3)(3)$
$= 20(3) - 3(3)$
$= 60 - 9$
$= 51$

Problem 1 Justifying Steps When Solving an Equation

Got It? What is the value of x? Justify each step.

Given: $\overrightarrow{AB}$ bisects $\angle RAN$.

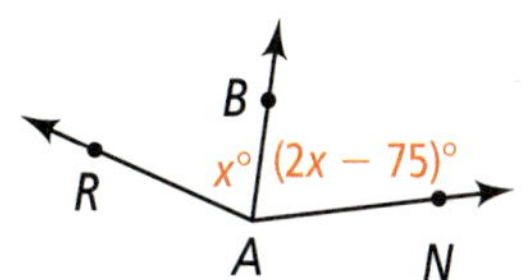

8. Circle the statement you can write from the given information.

$\angle RAB$ is obtuse. $\angle RAB \cong \angle NAB$ (circled) $\angle NAB \cong \angle RAN$

9. Use the justifications below to find the value of x.

$\overrightarrow{AB}$ bisects $\angle RAN$.	Given
$\angle RAB \cong \angle$ NAB	Definition of angle bisector
$m\angle RAB = m\angle$ NAB	Congruent angles have equal measures.
$x =$ $2x - 75$	Substitute.
$0 =$ $x - 75$	Subtraction Property of Equality
$75 =$ x	Addition Property of Equality

take note

Key Concept Properties of Congruence

Reflexive	Symmetric	Transitive
$\overline{AB} \cong \overline{AB}$	If $\overline{AB} \cong \overline{CD}$, then $\overline{CD} \cong \overline{AB}$.	If $\overline{AB} \cong \overline{CD}$ and $\overline{CD} \cong \overline{EF}$, then $\overline{AB} \cong \overline{EF}$.
$\angle A \cong \angle A$	If $\angle A \cong \angle B$, then $\angle B \cong \angle A$.	If $\angle A \cong \angle B$ and $\angle B \cong \angle C$, then $\angle A \cong \angle C$.

Complete each statement.

10. If $\angle P \cong \angle R$ and $\angle R \cong \angle A$, then $\angle P \cong \angle$ A.

11. If $\angle X \cong \angle N$ and $\angle$ N $\cong \angle Y$, then $\angle X \cong \angle Y$.

12. If $\angle L \cong \angle T$ and $\angle T \cong \angle$ Q, then $\angle L \cong \angle Q$.

Problem 3 Writing a Two-Column Proof

Got It? **Write a two-column proof.**

Given: $\overline{AB} \cong \overline{CD}$ **Prove:** $\overline{AC} \cong \overline{BD}$

13. The statements are given below. Write a reason for each statement.

Statements	Reasons
1) $\overline{AB} \cong \overline{CD}$	1) Given
2) $AB = CD$	2) Congruent segments have equal measure.
3) $BC = BC$	3) Reflexive Property of Equality
4) $AB + BC = BC + CD$	4) Addition Property of Equality
5) $AC = BD$	5) Segment Addition Postulate
6) $\overline{AC} \cong \overline{BD}$	6) Definition of congruence

Lesson Check • Do you UNDERSTAND?

Developing Proof **Fill in the reasons for this algebraic proof.**

Given: $5x + 1 = 21$

Prove: $x = 4$

Statements	Reasons
1) $5x + 1 = 21$	1) ?
2) $5x = 20$	2) ?
3) $x = 4$	3) ?

14. The first step in a proof is what you are given / to prove.

Underline the correct word(s) to complete each sentence. Then circle the property of equality that justifies the step.

15. First, the number 1 was added to / subtracted from each side of the equation.

Addition Property of Equality   Subtraction Property of Equality   Reflexive Property

16. Then, each side of the equation was multiplied / divided by 5.

Division Property of Equality   Multiplication Property of Equality   Transitive Property

17. Now write a reason for each step.

1) Given

2) Subtraction Property of Equality

3) Division Property of Equality

Math Success

Check off the vocabulary words that you understand.

☐ Reflexive Property   ☐ Symmetric Property   ☐ Transitive Property

☐ proof   ☐ two-column proof

Rate how well you can *use properties of equality and congruence in proofs.*

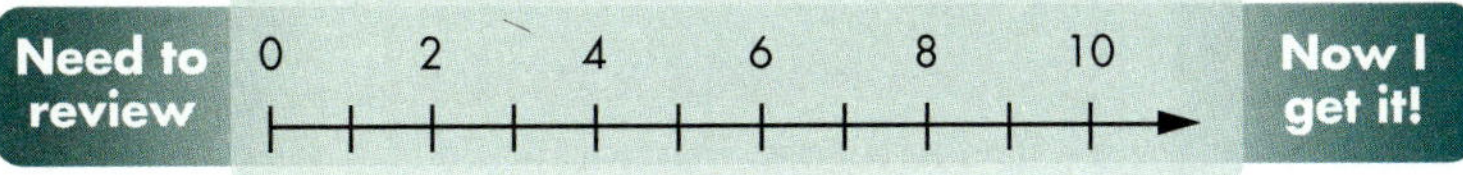

Name ______________________ Class ____________ Date ____________

2-5 Think About a Plan

Reasoning in Algebra and Geometry

Write a two-column proof.

Given: $KM = 35$

Prove: $KL = 15$

Know

1. What information are you given? Where does this information belong in the proof?

   $KM = 35$; It belongs in the first line with the reason "Given."

2. Use the figure. What information do you know from the figure?

   $KL = 2x - 5$; $LM = 2x$

Need

3. To solve the problem, what will you need to prove? Where does this statement belong in the proof?

   I need to prove that KL is equal to 15; The statement will be the last line in the proof.

Plan

4. You can determine information using the figure. Analyze the figure. What equation can you write?

   $KL + LM = KM$

5. How can you use the equation and the information you know to find the value of x?

   Substitute the values for KL, LM, and KM. Solve for x.

6. How can you use the value of x to show that $KL = 15$?

   Substitute the value of x into $2x - 5$, the value of KL.

7. Use the space below to write the proof.

Statements	Reasons
1) $KM = 35$	1) Given
2) $KL + LM = KM$	2) Segment Addition Postulate
3) $2x - 5 + 2x = 35$	3) Substitution Property
4) $4x - 5 = 35$	4) Combine like terms using the Associative and Distributive Properties
5) $4x = 40$	5) Addition Property of Equality
6) $x = 10$	6) Division Property of Equality
7) $KL = 2(10) - 5$	7) Substitution Property
8) $KL = 15$	8) Simplify.

Name ______________________ Class ____________ Date ____________

2-5 Practice — Form K

Reasoning in Algebra and Geometry

Algebra **Fill in the reason that justifies each step.**

1. $\frac{2}{3}x + 6 = 14$ Given

$3(\frac{2}{3}x + 6) = 42$ **a.** ? Mult. Prop. of =

$2x + 18 = 42$ **b.** ? Distr. Prop.

$2x = 24$ **c.** ? Subtr. Prop. of =

$x = 12$ **d.** ? Div. Prop. of =

2. $2(x - 12) = 40$ Given

$2x - 24 = 40$ **a.** ? Distr. Prop.

$2x = 64$ **b.** ? Add. Prop. of =

$x = 32$ **c.** ? Div. Prop. of =

3. 2x − 2 4(x + 1)

A C B

$AB = 50$ Given

$AC + CB = AB$ **a.** ? Segment Add. Post.

$2x - 2 + 4(x + 1) = 50$ **b.** ? Subst. Prop. of =

$2x - 2 + 4x + 4 = 50$ **c.** ? Distr. Prop. of =

$6x + 2 = 50$ **d.** ? Combine like terms

$6x = 48$ **e.** ? Subtr. Prop. of =

$x = 8$ **f.** ? Div. Prop. of =

Name the property of equality or congruence that justifies going from the first statement to the second statement.

4. $QR + LM = 20$

$QR = 20 - LM$

To start, determine which operation changes the first statement to the second statement.

Subtr. Prop. of =

5. $\overline{ST} \cong \overline{ST}$

$\overline{ST} \cong \overline{ST}$

Refl. Prop. of ≅

6. $3x = y$

$x = \frac{y}{3}$

Div. Prop. of =

7. $6x - 3$

$3(2x - 1)$

Distr. Prop.

Name ______________________ Class ____________ Date ____________

2-5 Practice (continued) — Form K

Reasoning in Algebra and Geometry

8. Developing Proof Fill in the missing statements or reasons for the following two-column proof.

Given: $\overrightarrow{AB}$ is the bisector of $\angle CAD$.

Prove: $x = 9$

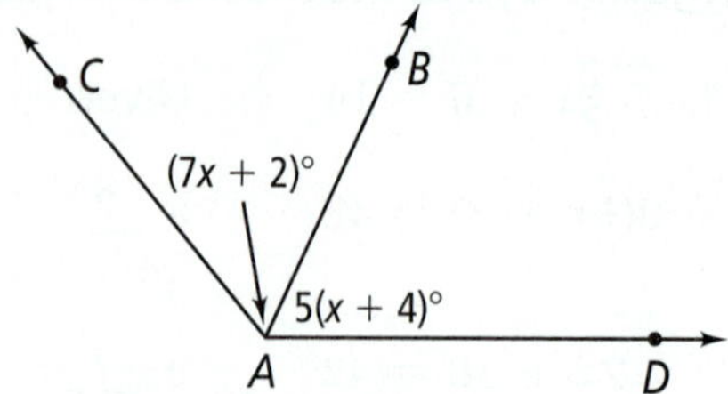

Statements	Reasons
1) $\overrightarrow{AB}$ is the bisector of $\angle CAD$.	1) Given
2) $\angle CAB \cong \angle BAD$	2) ? Def. of a bisector
3) $m\angle CAB \cong m\angle BAD$	3) $\cong$ angles have equal measures.
4) $7x + 2 = 5(x + 4)$	4) ? Subst. Prop. of =
5) $7x + 2 = 5x + 20$	5) ? Distr. Prop.
6) ? $2x = 18$	6) ? Subtr. Prop. of =
7) ? $x = 9$	7) ? Div. Prop. of =

Use the given property to complete each statement.

9. Addition Property of Equality

If $a = b$, then $a + 6 = b$? . $+ 6$

10. Symmetric Property of Congruence

If $\overline{LM} \cong \overline{GH}$, then $\overline{GH} \cong$? . $\overline{LM}$

11. Distributive Property

$10x - 5 = 5 \cdot ($? $)$ $2x - 1$

12. Multiplication Property of Equality

If $\frac{2}{5}x = 10$, then $2x =$? . 50

13. Substitution Property of Equality

If $JK = 20$ and $AB + JK = XY$, then ? $= XY$. $AB + 20$

14. Transitive Property of Congruence

If $\angle R \cong \angle Z$ and $\angle Z \cong \angle F$, then ? $\cong \angle F$. $\angle R$

Name ____________________ Class ____________ Date ____________

2-5 Standardized Test Prep

Reasoning in Algebra and Geometry

Multiple Choice

For Exercises 1–6, choose the correct letter.

1. According to the Transitive Property of Equality, if $TX = XY$, and $XY = YZ$, then $TX = \square$. C

   (A) TX (B) XY (C) YZ (D) TZ

2. What property is illustrated by the statement, if $KL = LM$, then $LM = KL$? G

   (F) Reflexive Property of Equality
   (G) Symmetric Property of Equality
   (H) Transitive Property of Equality
   (I) Division Property of Equality

Use the list of reasons below for Exercises 3–6. Choose the correct reason for each algebraic statement.

(A) Subtraction Property of Equality
(B) Combine like terms.
(C) Distributive Property
(D) Division Property of Equality

Statements	Reasons
$3(x + 2) + 1 = 8$	Given
$6x + 6 + 1 = 8$	3) ? C
$6x + 7 = 8$	4) ? B
$6x = 1$	5) ? A
$x = \frac{1}{6}$	6) ? D

Extended Response

7. Write a two-column proof.

   Given: A is the midpoint of $\overline{ZP}$.

   $XY = ZA$

   Prove: $XY = AP$

X Y

Z A P

[4] Statements	Reasons
1) A is the midpoint of ZP and $XY = ZA$.	1) Given
2) $ZA = AP$	2) Definition of midpoint
3) $XY = AP$	3) Transitive Property of Equality

[3] The student provides a thorough proof but a minimal number of statements, or fails to provide reasons or provides incomplete reasons; [2] The student provides a logical proof but fails to provide reasons or provides incomplete reasons; [1] The student provides a two-column proof format with the given included in the proof. [0] The student does not provide a proof that shows reasons.

2-6 Proving Angles Congruent

Vocabulary

Review

Complete each sentence with *proof* or *prove*.

1. Galileo wanted to _?_ that the planets revolve around the sun. prove

2. His observations and discoveries supported his theory but were not a _?_ of it. proof

Vocabulary Builder

theorem (noun) THEE uh rum

Definition: A **theorem** is a conjecture or statement that you prove true.

Main Idea: You use definitions, postulates, properties, and previously proven theorems to prove **theorems.**

Use Your Vocabulary

Write T for *true* or F for *false*.

F 3. A postulate is a *theorem*.

T 4. A *theorem* may contain definitions.

F 5. An axiom is a *theorem*.

Complete each statement with *lines, planes,* or *points.*

6. **Postulate 1-1** Through any two _?_ there is exactly one line. points

7. **Postulate 1-2** If two distinct _?_ intersect, then they intersect in exactly one point. lines

8. **Postulate 1-3** If two distinct _?_ intersect, then they intersect in exactly one line. planes

9. **Postulate 1-4** Through any three noncollinear _?_ there is exactly one plane. points

take note

Theorem 2-1 Vertical Angles Theorem

Vertical angles are congruent.

10. If $\angle A$ and $\angle B$ are vertical angles and $m\angle A = 15$, then $m\angle B =$ 15 .

Problem 1 Using the Vertical Angles Theorem

Got It? **What is the value of x?**

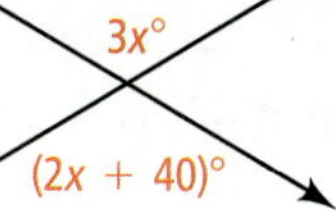

11. Circle the word that best describes the labeled angle pair in the diagram.

corresponding   perpendicular   (vertical)

12. Circle the word that best describes the relationship between the labeled angles in the diagram.

(congruent)   perpendicular   supplementary

13. Use the labels in the diagram to write an equation.

$3x =$ $2x + 40$

14. Now solve the equation.

$$3x = 2x + 40$$
$$3x - 2x = 2x - 2x + 40$$
$$x = 40$$

15. The value of x is 40 .

Problem 2 Proof Using the Vertical Angles Theorem

Got It? **Use the Vertical Angles Theorem to prove the following.**

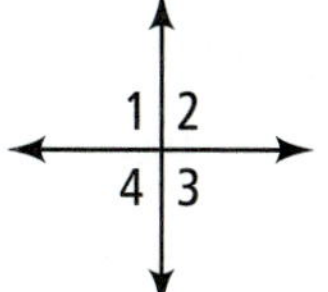

Given: $\angle 1 \cong \angle 2$

Prove: $\angle 1 \cong \angle 2 \cong \angle 3 \cong \angle 4$

16. Write a reason for each statement below.

Statements	Reasons
1) $\angle 1 \cong \angle 2$	1) Given
2) $\angle 1 \cong \angle 3$	2) Vertical angles are $\cong$.
3) $\angle 2 \cong \angle 4$	3) Vertical angles are $\cong$.
4) $\angle 1 \cong \angle 2 \cong \angle 3 \cong \angle 4$	4) Transitive Property of Congruence

take note

Theorem 2-2 Congruent Supplements Theorem

If two angles are supplements of the same angle (or of congruent angles), then the two angles are congruent.

If $\angle 1$ and $\angle 3$ are supplements and $\angle 2$ and $\angle 3$ are supplements, then $\angle 1 \cong \angle 2$.

17. Complete the diagram below to illustrate Theorem 2-2.

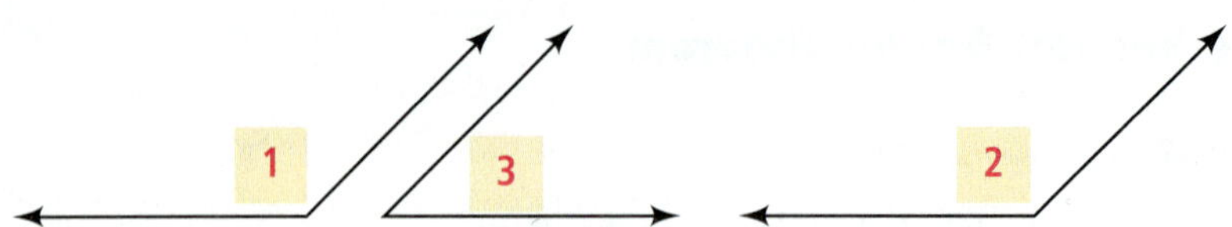

18. If $m\angle D = 135$ and $m\angle G = 45$ and $\angle F$ and $\angle G$ are supplements, then $m\angle F =$ 135 .

If $\angle A$ and $\angle B$ are supplements and $m\angle C = 85$ and $m\angle B = 95$, then $m\angle A =$ 85 .

Problem 3 Writing a Paragraph Proof

Got It? **Write a paragraph proof for the Vertical Angles Theorem.**

Given: $\angle 1$ and $\angle 3$ are vertical angles.

Prove: $\angle 1 \cong \angle 3$

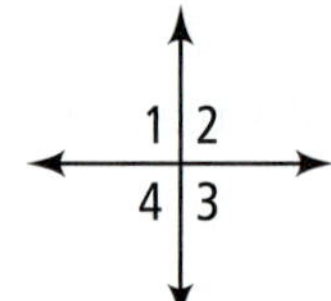

Circle the correct word to complete each sentence.

19. $\angle 1$ and $\angle 3$ are _?_ angles because it is given. — supplementary / vertical (circled: vertical)

20. $\angle 1$ and $\angle 2$ are _?_ angles because they form a linear pair. — supplementary / vertical (circled: supplementary)

21. $\angle 2$ and $\angle 3$ are _?_ angles because they form a linear pair. — supplementary / vertical (circled: supplementary)

22. $m\angle 1 + m\angle 2 = 180$ because the sum of the measures of _?_ angles is 180. — complementary / supplementary (circled: supplementary)

23. $m\angle 2 + m\angle 3 = 180$ because the sum of the measures of _?_ angles is 180. — complementary / supplementary (circled: supplementary)

24. By the _?_ Property of Equality, $m\angle 1 + m\angle 2 = m\angle 2 + m\angle 3$. — Reflexive / Transitive (circled: Transitive)

25. By the _?_ Property of Equality, $m\angle 1 = m\angle 3$. — Subtraction / Symmetric (circled: Subtraction)

26. Angles with the same _?_ are congruent, so $\angle 1 \cong \angle 3$. — properties / measure (circled: measure)

take note

Theorem 2-3 Congruent Complements Theorem

If two angles are complements of the same angle (or of congruent angles), then the two angles are congruent.

27. $\angle A$ is a supplement of a 165° angle. $\angle B$ is a complement of a 75° angle. Circle the relationship between $\angle A$ and $\angle B$.

complementary   congruent (circled)   supplementary

Theorems 2-4 and 2-5

Theorem 2-4 All right angles are congruent.

Theorem 2-5 If two angles are congruent and supplementary, then each is a right angle.

28. If $\angle R$ and $\angle S$ are right angles, then $\angle R$ $\cong$ $\angle S$.

29. If $\angle H \cong \angle J$ and $\angle H$ and $\angle J$ are supplements, then $m\angle H = m$ $\angle J$ $=$ 90.

Lesson Check • Do you know HOW?

What are the measures of ∠1, ∠2, and ∠3?

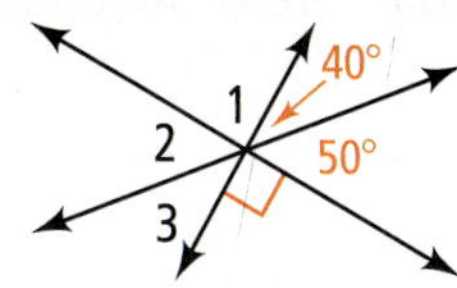

30. Cross out the theorem you CANNOT use to find an angle measure.

Congruent Complements Theorem ~~Congruent Supplements Theorem~~ Vertical Angles Theorem

31. $m\angle 1 =$ 90 **32.** $m\angle 2 =$ 50 **33.** $m\angle 3 =$ 40

Lesson Check • Do you UNDERSTAND?

Reasoning **If ∠A and ∠B are supplements, and ∠A and ∠C are supplements, what can you conclude about ∠B and ∠C? Explain.**

34. Since $\angle A$ and $\angle B$ are supplements, $m\angle A + m\angle B =$ 180.

35. Since $\angle A$ and $\angle C$ are supplements, $m\angle A + m\angle C =$ 180.

36. By the Transitive Property of Equality, $m\angle A$ $+ m\angle B =$ $m\angle A$ $+ m\angle C$.

37. By the Subtraction Property of Equality, $m\angle B =$ $m\angle C$, so $\angle B \cong$ $\angle C$.

Math Success

Check off the vocabulary words that you understand.

☐ theorem ☐ paragraph proof ☐ complementary ☐ supplementary ☐ right angle

Rate how well you can *write proofs.*

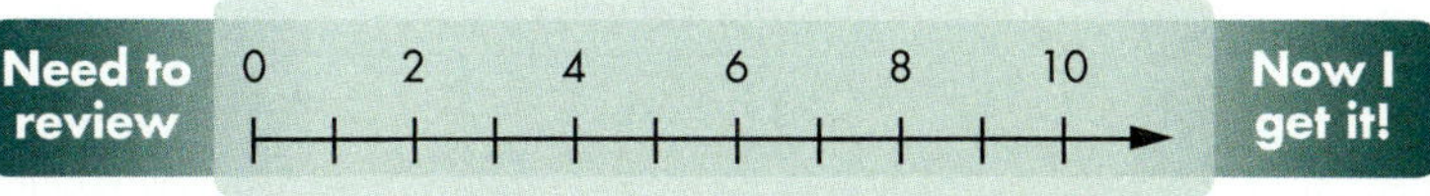

Name ______________________ Class ____________ Date ____________

2-6 Think About a Plan

Proving Angles Congruent

Reasoning Explain why this statement is true:
If $m\angle ABC + m\angle XYZ = 180$ and $\angle ABC \cong \angle XYZ$, then $\angle ABC$ and $\angle XYZ$ are right angles.

Understanding the Problem

1. The statement is a conditional. Break the conditional down into its parts. What is the hypothesis?
   $m\angle ABC + m\angle XYZ = 180$ and $\angle ABC \cong \angle XYZ$

2. What is the conclusion of the conditional?
   $\angle ABC$ and $\angle XYZ$ are right angles.

3. What makes an angle a right angle? It has a measure of 90.

4. What does the symbol $\cong$ mean about the angles? It means that they are congruent.

Planning the Solution

5. For the statement to be true, the sum of the measures of the two angles must equal 180 and the angles must have the same measure.

6. Write an equation to represent the hypothesis. Because $\angle ABC \cong \angle XYZ$, they have the same measure, so use the same variable m to represent the measure of each angle. $m + m = 180$

7. Simplify the equation. $2m = 180$

Getting an Answer

8. What is the value of m? 90

9. Does this value of m mean that $\angle ABC$ and $\angle XYZ$ are right angles?
   yes

10. How can you explain why the statement is true?
    Since both angles have the same measure, if you multiply that measure by 2, you get 180. The number 90 is the only number which when added to itself, equals 180. Since right angles have a measure of 90, then the statement must be true.

Name ______________________ Class __________ Date __________

2-6 Practice

Form K

Proving Angles Congruent

Find the value of each variable.

1. 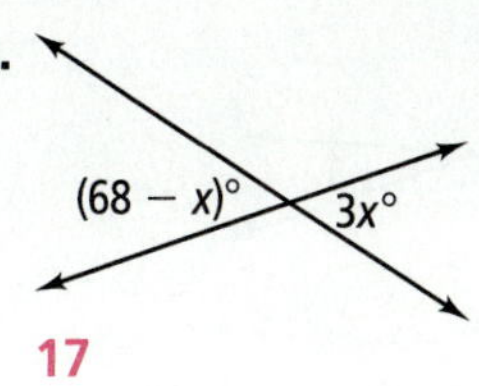

17

To start, identify the relationship between the marked angles in the diagram.

The marked angles are _?_. vertical angles

Then write an equation to express this relationship.

_?_ = _?_ $68 - x$; $3x$

2. 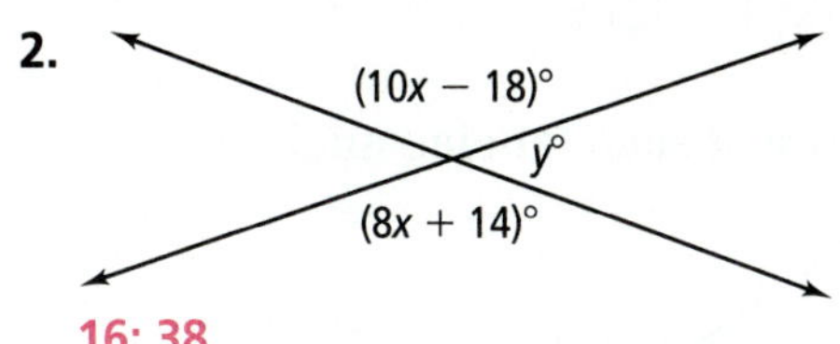

16; 38

3. 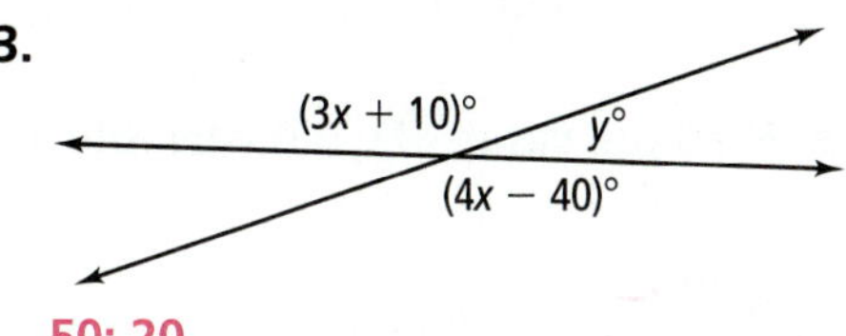

50; 20

Find the measures of the labeled angles in each exercise.

4. Exercise 1 51

5. Exercise 2 142; 38

6. Exercise 3 160; 20

Developing Proof **Complete the following proof by filling in the blanks.**

7. Given: $\angle 1 \cong \angle 2$

Prove: $\angle 3 \cong \angle 4$

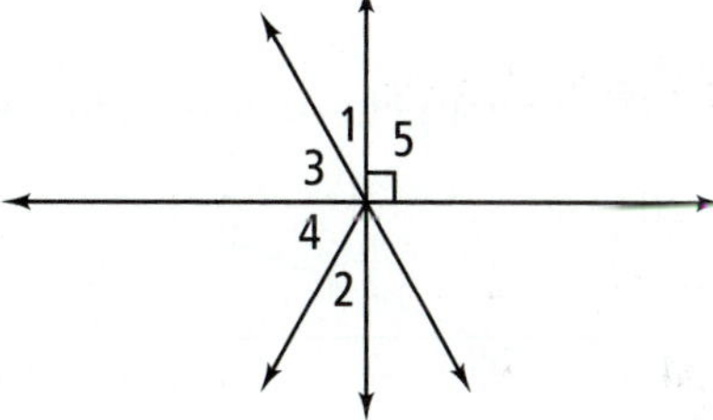

Statements	Reasons
1) $\angle 1 \cong \angle 2$	1) Given
2) $m\angle 1 + m\angle 3 + m\angle 5 = 180$	2) _?_ ∠ Add. Post.
3) $m\angle 1 + m\angle 3 + 90 = 180$	3) _?_ Subst. Prop. of =
4) $m\angle 1 + m\angle 3 = 90$	4) _?_ Subtr. Prop. of =
5) $m\angle 4 + m\angle 2 = m\angle 5$	5) _?_ Vert. ⦞ Thm.
6) $m\angle 4 + m\angle 2 = 90$	6) _?_ Subst. Prop. of =
7) $m\angle 4 + m\angle 1 = 90$	7) _?_ Subst. Prop. of =
8) $m\angle 4 = m\angle 3$	8) _?_ Congruent Complements Thm.

8. Reasoning $\angle A$ and $\angle B$ are adjacent complementary angles. $\angle C$ is supplementary to the angle formed by $\angle A$ and $\angle B$. What can you conclude about $\angle C$? Explain. It is a right angle; $m\angle A + m\angle B = 90$ and $m\angle A + m\angle B + m\angle C = 180$. By the Subtr. Prop. of =, $m\angle C = 90$.

Name ______________________ Class ____________ Date ____________

2-6 Practice (continued)

Form K

Proving Angles Congruent

9. Developing Proof Fill in the blanks to complete the paragraph proof below.

Given: $\angle 1 \cong \angle 4$

Prove: $\angle 2 \cong \angle 3$

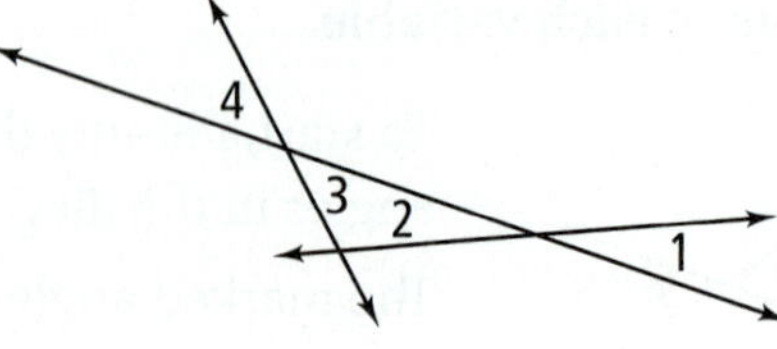

$\angle 1 \cong \angle 4$ because it is given. $\angle 1 \cong \angle 2$ by the __?__. $\angle 2 \cong \angle 4$ by the __?__. $\angle 3 \cong \angle 4$ by the __?__. It follows that __?__ $\cong$ __?__ by the __?__.

Vert. ∠s Thm.; Trans. Prop. of ≅; Vert. ∠s Thm.; ∠2; ∠3; Trans. Prop. of ≅

Algebra **Find the value of each variable and the measure of each labeled angle.**

10.

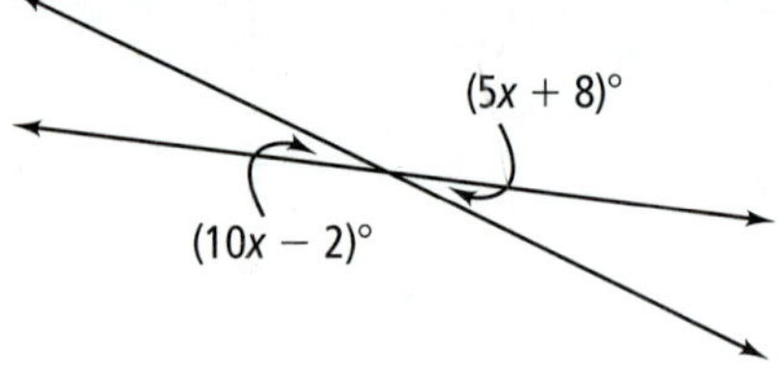

2; 18

11.

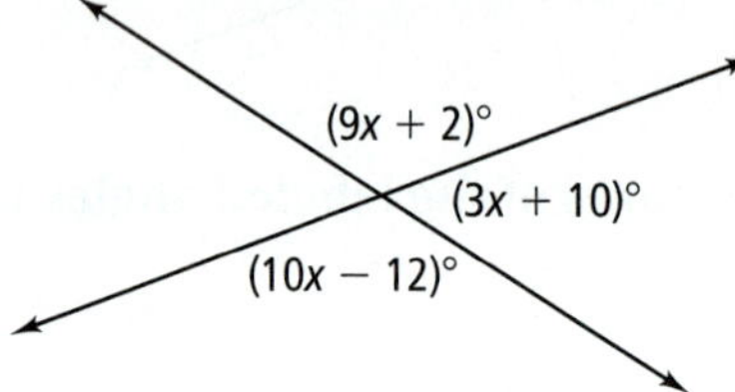

14; 128; 52

Name two pairs of congruent angles in each figure. Justify your answers.

12.

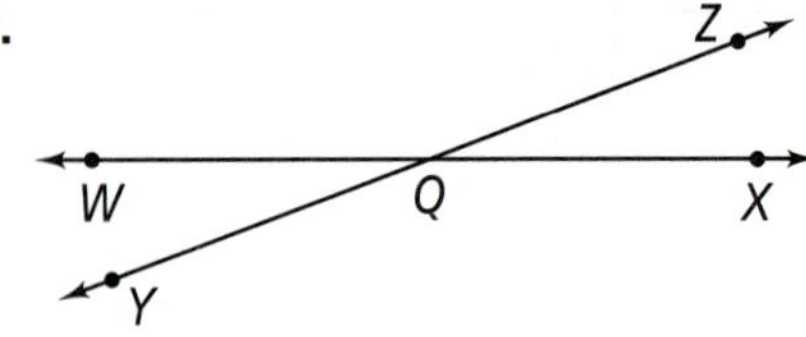

∠WQY ≅ ∠ZQX **and** ***∠WQZ ≅ ∠YQX*** **by Vert. ∠s Thm.**

13.

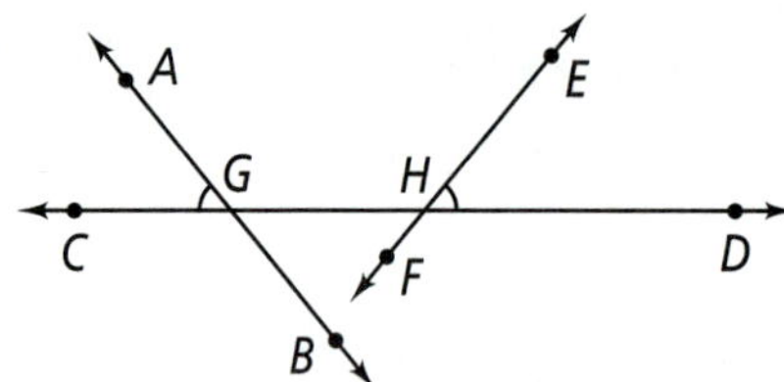

∠AGC ≅ ∠BGH ≅ ∠EHD ≅ ∠GHF **by Vert. ∠s Thm. and Trans. Prop. of ≅;** ***∠AGH ≅ ∠EHG ≅ ∠FHD ≅ ∠CGB*** **by Vert. ∠s Thm. and ≅ Supp. Thm.**

Algebra **Find the measure of each angle.**

14. $\angle A$ is three times as large as its complement, $\angle B$. **67.5; 22.5**

15. $\angle A$ is 21 less than twice as large as its supplement, $\angle B$. **113; 67**

16. $\angle A$ is congruent to its supplement, $\angle B$. **90; 90**

17. $\angle A$ is 18 more than five times its complement, $\angle B$. **78; 12**

Name ______________________ Class __________ Date __________

2-6 Standardized Test Prep

Proving Angles Congruent

Multiple Choice

For Exercises 1–5, choose the correct letter.

1. $\angle A$ and $\angle B$ are supplementary, and $\angle A$ and $\angle C$ are supplementary. Which conclusion is valid? D

   A $\angle B$ and $\angle C$ are supplementary.

   B $\angle B$ and $\angle C$ are complementary.

   C $\angle B$ and $\angle C$ are acute.

   D $\angle B$ and $\angle C$ are congruent.

2. The measure of $\angle B$ is one-half the measure of its complement. What is the measure of $\angle B$? F

   F 30 G 45 H 60 I 90

3. $\angle T$ and $\angle R$ are vertical angles. $m\angle T = 3x + 36$ and $m\angle R = 6x - 9$. What is the measure of $\angle T$? B

   A 15 B 81 C 87 D 99

Use the figure at the right for Exercises 4 and 5.

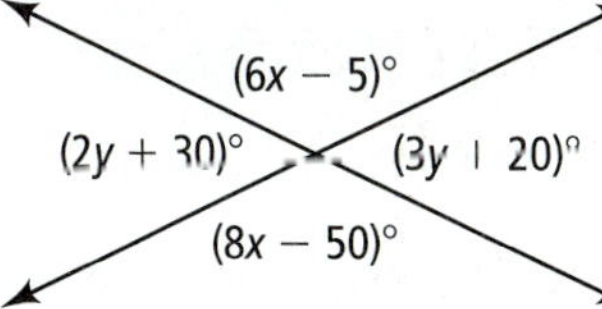

4. What is the value of x? G

   F 8.9 H 16.8

   G 22.5 I 27.5

5. What is the value of y? D

   A −10 C 2

   B −2 D 10

6. $\angle A$ and $\angle B$ are complementary angles. If $m\angle A = 5x - 2$, and $m\angle B = 3x + 4$, what is the value of x? H

   F 3 G 6 H 11 I 22.25

Short Response

7. In the figure at the right, if $m\angle 1 = 37$, and $\angle 1 \cong \angle 3$, what is $m\angle 4$? Explain.

   [2] 53; $m\angle 1 = m\angle 3$, and $m\angle 3 + m\angle 4 = 90$.
   So, $m\angle 4 = 90 - m\angle 3 = 90 - m\angle 1 = 90 - 37 = 53$.
   [1] missing answer or explanation [0] answer and explanation both missing

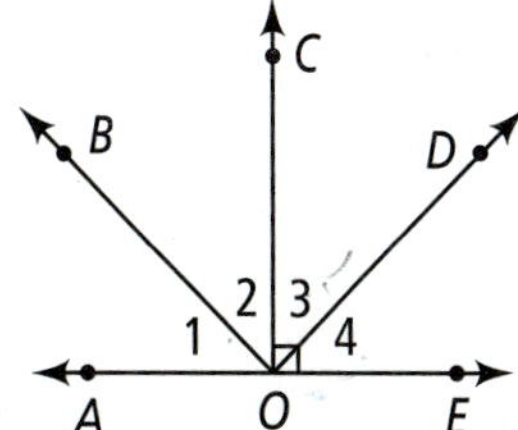

3-1 Lines and Angles

Vocabulary

Review

Write T for *true* or F for *false*.

T 1. You can name a *plane* by a capital letter, such as *A*.

F 2. A *plane* contains a finite number of lines.

T 3. Two points lying on the same *plane* are coplanar.

T 4. If two distinct *planes* intersect, then they intersect in exactly one line.

Vocabulary Builder

parallel (noun) PA **ruh lel**

Definition: *Parallel* lines lie in the same plane but never intersect, no matter how far they extend.

The symbol for **parallel** is ∥.

Use Your Vocabulary

5. Circle the segment(s) that are *parallel* to the *x*-axis.

$\overline{AB}$ (circled) $\overline{BC}$ $\overline{CD}$ (circled) $\overline{AD}$

6. Circle the segment(s) that are *parallel* to the *y*-axis.

$\overline{AB}$ $\overline{BC}$ (circled) $\overline{CD}$ $\overline{AD}$ (circled)

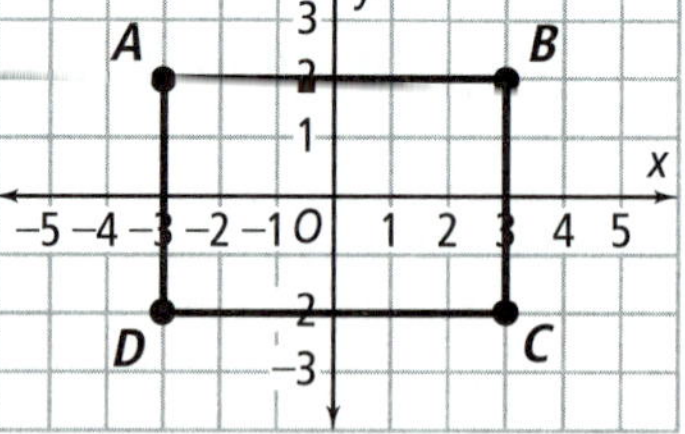

7. Circle the polygon(s) that have two pairs of *parallel* sides.

rectangle (circled) parallelogram (circled) square (circled) trapezoid

Complete each statement below with *line* or *segment*.

8. A _?_ consist of two endpoints and all the points between them. segment

9. A _?_ is made up of an infinite number of points. line

take note

Key Concept Parallel and Skew

Parallel lines are coplanar lines that do not intersect.

Skew lines are noncoplanar; they are not parallel and do not intersect.

Parallel planes are planes that do not intersect.

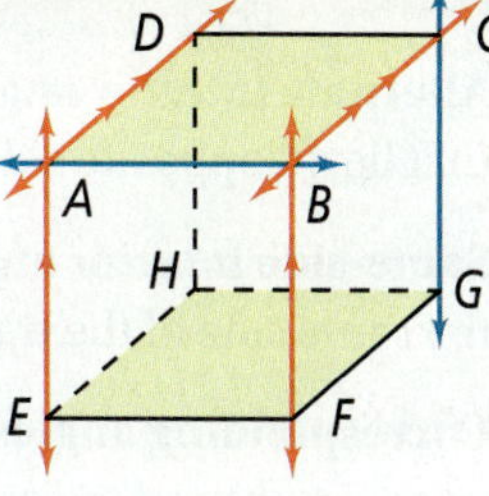

Use arrows to show $\overleftrightarrow{AE} \parallel \overleftrightarrow{BF}$ and $\overleftrightarrow{AD} \parallel \overleftrightarrow{BC}$.

10. Write each word, phrase, or symbol in the correct oval.

noncoplanar   coplanar   do not intersect

intersect $\overleftrightarrow{AE}$ and $\overleftrightarrow{CG}$ $\overleftrightarrow{CB}$ and $\overleftrightarrow{AE}$

Parallel	Skew
coplanar	noncoplanar
do not intersect	do not intersect
$\overleftrightarrow{AE}$ and $\overleftrightarrow{CG}$	$\overleftrightarrow{CB}$ and $\overleftrightarrow{AE}$

Problem 1 Identifying Nonintersecting Lines and Planes

Got It? **Use the figure at the right. Which segments are parallel to $\overline{AD}$?**

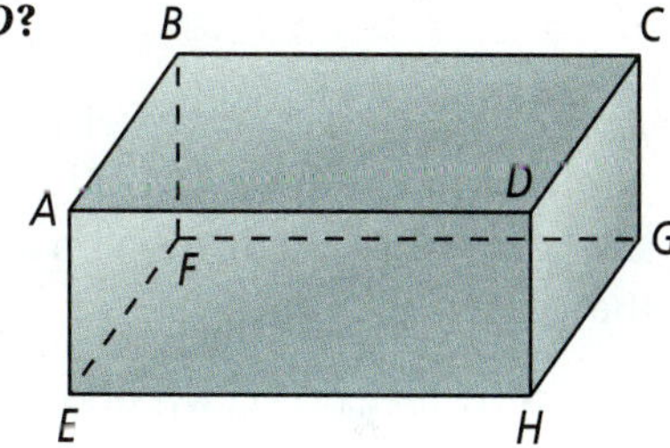

11. In plane *ADHE*, EH is parallel to $\overline{AD}$.

12. In plane *ADBC*, BC is parallel to $\overline{AD}$.

13. In plane *ADGF*, FG is parallel to $\overline{AD}$.

Got It? **Reasoning** **Explain why $\overline{FE}$ and $\overline{CD}$ are *not* skew.**

14. Cross out the words or phrases below that do NOT describe skew lines.

~~coplanar~~   do not intersect   ~~intersect~~

~~parallel~~   noncoplanar   not parallel

15. Circle the correct statement below.

Segments and rays can be skew if they lie in skew lines. (circled)

Segments and rays are never skew.

16. Underline the correct words to complete the sentence.

$\overline{FE}$ and $\overline{CD}$ are in a plane that slopes from the <u>bottom</u> / top left edge to the bottom / <u>top</u> right edge of the figure.

17. Why are $\overline{FE}$ and $\overline{CD}$ NOT skew?

Answers may vary. Sample: They are not skew segments because they are part of the plane *CDEF*. Therefore, they are coplanar.

take note

Key Concept Angle Pairs Formed by Transversals

Alternate interior angles are nonadjacent interior angles that lie on opposite sides of the transversal.

Same-side interior angles are interior angles that lie on the same side of the transversal.

Corresponding angles lie on the same side of a transversal *t* and in corresponding positions.

Alternate exterior angles are nonadjacent exterior angles that lie on opposite sides of the transversal.

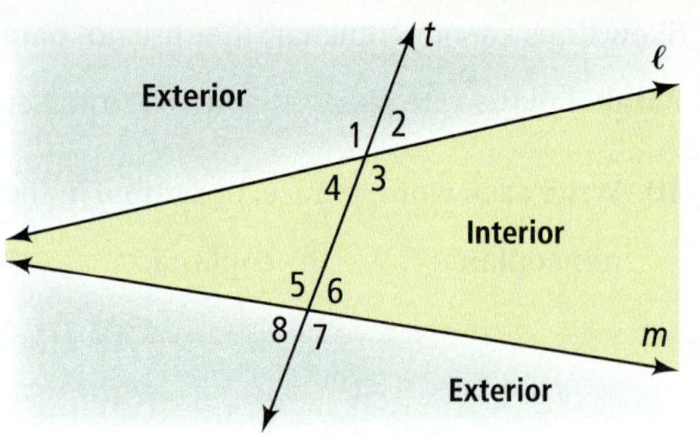

Use the diagram above. Draw a line from each angle pair in Column A to its description in Column B.

Column A	Column B
18. ∠4 and ∠6	alternate exterior angles
19. ∠3 and ∠6	same-side interior angles
20. ∠2 and ∠6	alternate interior angles
21. ∠2 and ∠8	corresponding angles

Problem 2 Identifying an Angle Pair

Got It? What are three pairs of corresponding angles in the diagram at the right?

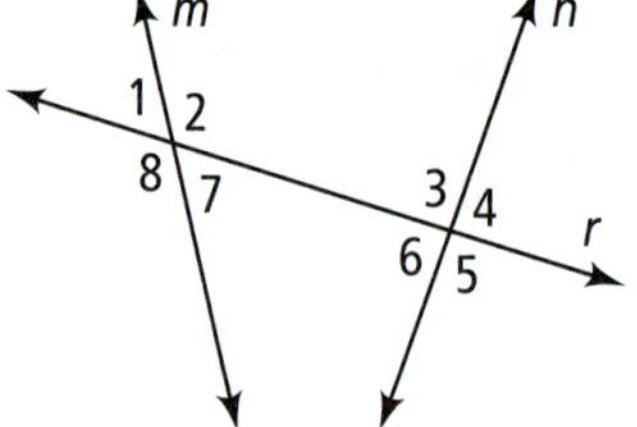

Underline the correct word(s) or letter(s) to complete each sentence.

22. The transversal is line *m* / *n* / *r*.

23. Corresponding angles are on the same side / different sides of the transversal.

24. Name three pairs of corresponding angles. Answers may vary. Accept any three of

∠ 1 and ∠ 3 ∠ 2 and ∠ 4 ∠ 8 and ∠ 6 ∠ 7 and ∠ 5

Problem 3 Classifying an Angle Pair

Got It? Are angles 1 and 3 *alternate interior angles, same-side interior angles, corresponding angles,* or *alternate exterior angles*?

25. Are ∠1 and ∠3 on the same side of the transversal? Yes / No

26. Cross out the angle types that do NOT describe ∠1 and ∠3.

~~alternate exterior~~ ~~alternate interior~~ corresponding ~~same-side interior~~

27. ∠1 and ∠3 are _?_ angles. corresponding

Lesson Check • Do you know HOW?

Name one pair of figures to match each description. Answers may vary. Samples are given.

28. parallel segments

$\overline{AB} \parallel$ $\overline{EF}$

29. skew segments

$\overline{HD}$ and $\overline{BC}$

30. parallel planes

$ABCD \parallel$ EFGH

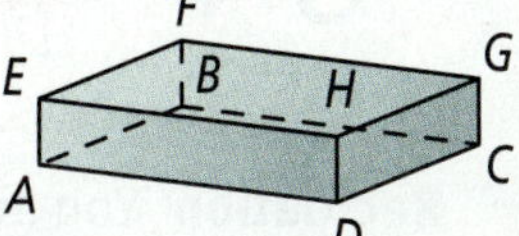

Identify one pair of each type of angles.

31. alternate interior

$\angle 8$ and $\angle$ 6

32. same-side interior

$\angle 8$ and $\angle$ 3

33. corresponding

$\angle 1$ and $\angle$ 3

34. alternate exterior

$\angle 7$ and $\angle$ 5

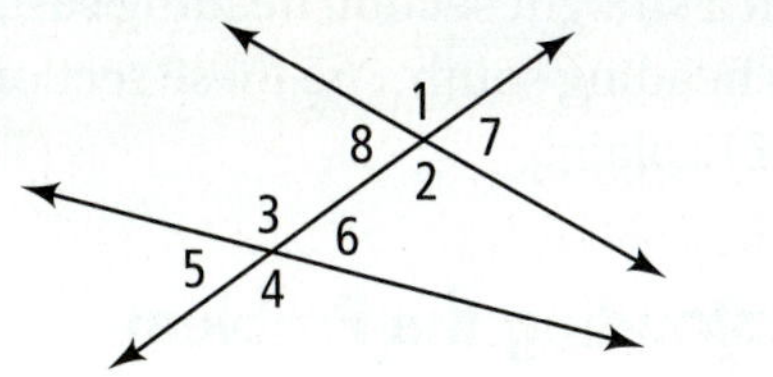

Lesson Check • Do you UNDERSTAND?

Error Analysis **In the figure at the right, lines and planes that appear to be parallel are parallel. Carly says $\overline{AB} \parallel \overline{HG}$. Juan says $\overline{AB}$ and $\overline{HG}$ are skew. Who is correct? Explain.**

D C A B G H F E

Write T for *true* or F for *false*.

T **35.** Parallel segments are coplanar.

F **36.** There are only six planes in a cube.

F **37.** No plane contains $\overline{AB}$ and $\overline{HG}$.

38. Who is correct? Explain.

Carly; Sample explanation: The segments are parallel since they do not intersect and are coplanar (plane *ABGH* contains $\overline{AB}$ and $\overline{HG}$).

Math Success

Check off the vocabulary words that you understand.

☐ angle ☐ parallel ☐ skew ☐ transversal

Rate how well you can *classify angle pairs*.

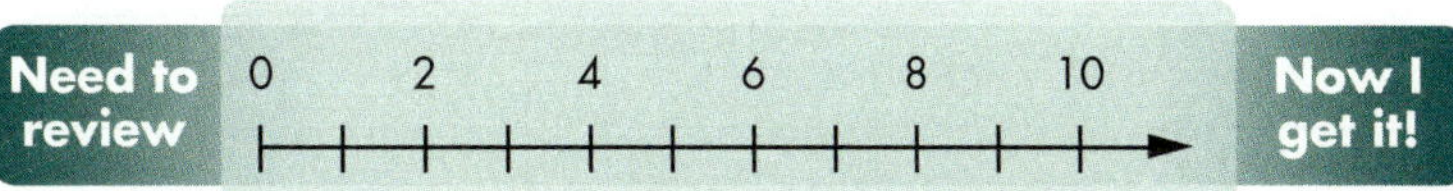

Name _______________ Class __________ Date __________

3-1 Think About a Plan

Lines and Angles

Recreation You and a friend are driving go-karts on two different tracks. As you drive on a straight section heading east, your friend passes above you on a straight section heading south. Are these sections of the two tracks *parallel, skew,* or *neither?* Explain.

Understanding the Problem

1. How are parallel lines and skew lines alike?
   They are both sets of lines that do not intersect.

2. How are parallel lines and skew lines different?
   Parallel lines are coplanar; skew lines are noncoplanar.

Planning the Solution

3. What geometric concepts do you need to find out about the tracks?
   Do the tracks intersect? Are the tracks coplanar or noncoplanar?

Getting an Answer

4. Make a sketch of the situation in the problem.

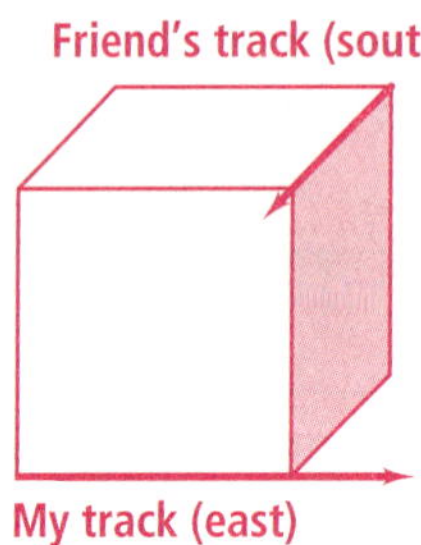

5. Would the track sections you drew intersect? no

6. Are the track sections you drew coplanar? no

7. Use what you know about the properties of parallel and skew lines to explain whether the track sections are *parallel, skew,* or *neither.*
   The tracks are skew. Because one is above the other and moves in a different direction, they are not coplanar, and so they cannot intersect.

3-1 Practice — Form K

Lines and Angles

Use the diagram to name each of the following.

1. a plane Answers may vary. Sample (one of the following): *QRSTU, VWXYZ, QRWV, RSXW, SXYT, UTYZ, QUZV*

2. a pair of parallel planes Answers may vary. Sample (one of the following): *RSWX* and *QUVZ*; *TSXY* and *QRWV*; *QRSTU* and *VWXYZ*

3. all lines that are parallel to $\overleftrightarrow{QR}$ $\overleftrightarrow{VW}$, $\overleftrightarrow{TS}$, and $\overleftrightarrow{YX}$

4. two lines that are skew to $\overleftrightarrow{ST}$ Answers may vary. Sample (two of the following): $\overleftrightarrow{UZ}$, $\overleftrightarrow{QV}$, $\overleftrightarrow{RW}$, $\overleftrightarrow{WX}$, $\overleftrightarrow{ZY}$, and $\overleftrightarrow{VZ}$

5. all lines that are parallel to plane *TSXY* $\overleftrightarrow{VW}$, $\overleftrightarrow{QR}$, $\overleftrightarrow{RW}$, $\overleftrightarrow{UZ}$, and $\overleftrightarrow{QV}$

In Exercises 6–9, describe the statement as *true* or *false*. If false, explain.

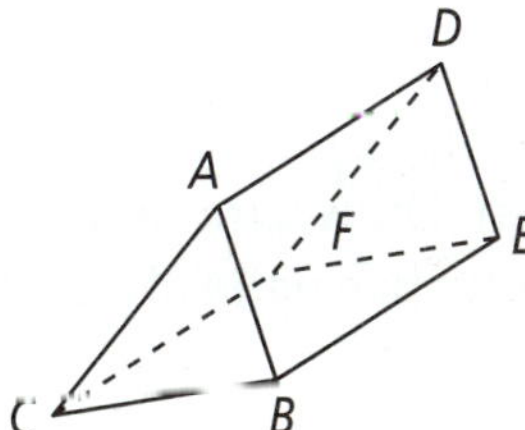

6. $\overleftrightarrow{AB} \parallel \overleftrightarrow{DE}$ true

7. plane *ABE* $\parallel$ plane *ACF* False; the planes intersect.

8. plane *ABC* $\parallel$ plane *DEF* true

9. $\overleftrightarrow{AD}$ and $\overleftrightarrow{BE}$ are skew lines. False; they are parallel.

Identify all pairs of each type of angles in the diagram. Name the two lines and the transversal that form each pair.

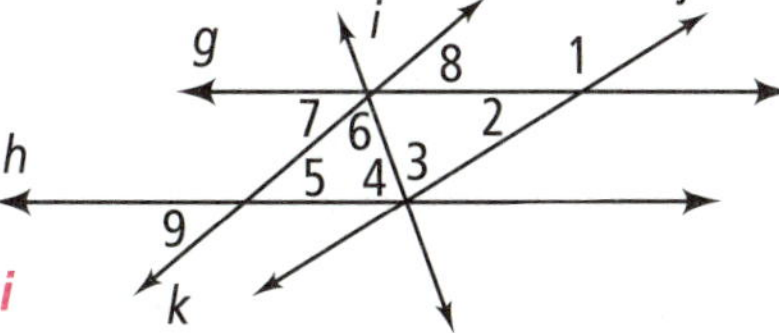

10. corresponding angles ∠8 and ∠5, lines *g* and *h* and transversal *k*; ∠7 and ∠2, lines *k* and *j* and transversal *g*; ∠7 and ∠9, lines *g* and *h* and transversal *k*

11. alternate interior angles ∠5 and ∠7, lines *g* and *h* and transversal *k*; ∠8 and ∠2, lines *k* and *j* and transversal *g*; ∠6 and ∠3, lines *k* and *j* and transversal *i*

12. same-side interior angles ∠5 and ∠4, lines *k* and *i* and transversal *h*; ∠6 and ∠4, lines *k* and *h* and transversal *i*; ∠5 and ∠6, lines *h* and *i* and transversal *k*; ∠8 and ∠1, lines *k* and *j* and transversal *g*; ∠2 and ∠3, lines *g* and *i* and transversal *j*

13. alternate exterior angles ∠8 and ∠9, lines *g* and *h* and transversal *k*

Name ______________________ Class ____________ Date ____________

3-1 Practice (continued) *Form K*

Lines and Angles

Decide whether each pair of angles labeled are *alternate interior angles, same-side interior angles, corresponding angles,* or *alternate exterior angles.*

14. 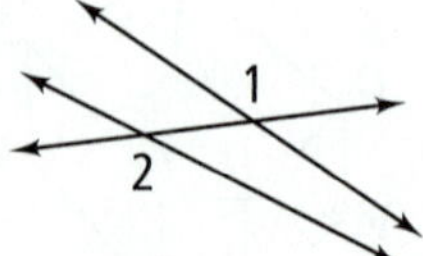

alternate exterior

15. 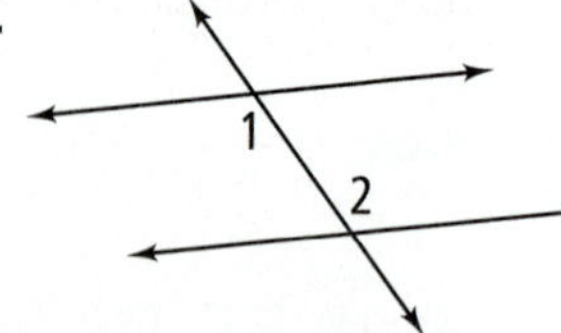

alternate interior

16. 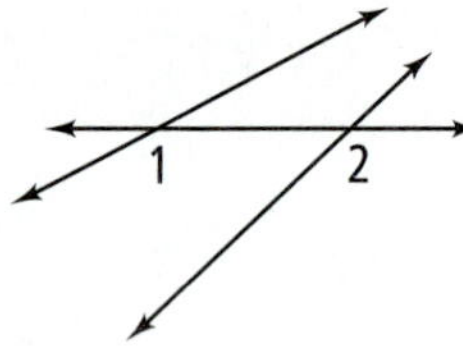

corresponding

17. 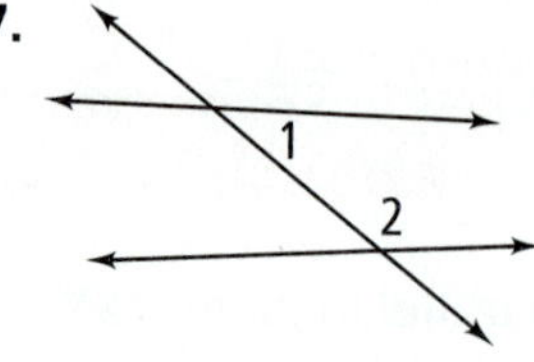

same-side interior

18. Error Analysis A student drew a square pyramid. She said the lines forming the sides of the square base of the pyramid are skew to the lines forming the triangular sides. Explain the student's error. The lines forming the sides of the square intersect the lines forming the triangular sides. Skew lines do not intersect.

19. Open-Ended Draw a three-dimensional figure with at least one pair of parallel planes, two pairs of parallel lines, and three pairs of skew lines. Check students' work.

20. Use the words *lines* and *transversal* to explain what makes an angle an interior angle or an exterior angle. Interior angles are between the two lines intersected by the transversal. Exterior angles are outside the two lines intersected by the transversal.

21. The map at the right shows the downtown area of a city. Name two pairs of locations that represent each type of angle.

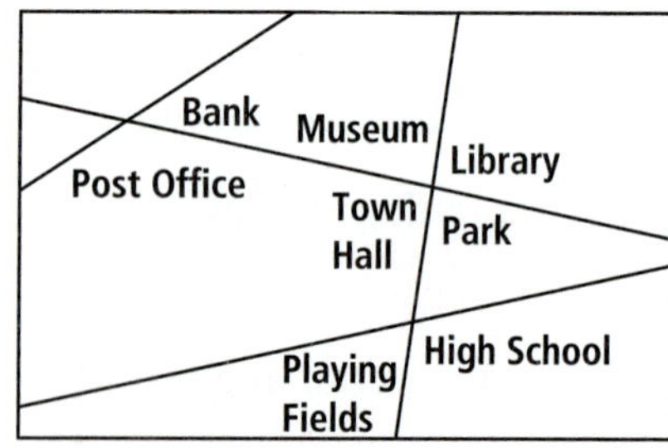

a. alternate interior angles bank and town hall; museum and post office

b. same-side interior angles post office and town hall; bank and museum

c. alternate exterior angles library and playing fields, museum and high school

d. corresponding angles Answers may vary. Sample (any two of the following pairs): post office and park, bank and library, town hall and playing fields, park and high school

Name ______________________ Class ____________ Date ____________

3-1 Standardized Test Prep

Lines and Angles

Multiple Choice

For Exercises 1–7, choose the correct letter.

For Exercises 1–3, use the figure at the right.

1. Which line segment is parallel to $\overline{GE}$? B

   A $\overline{DH}$ C $\overline{FG}$

   B $\overline{KI}$ D $\overline{HI}$

2. Which two line segments are skew? I

   F $\overline{DE}$ and $\overline{GE}$ H $\overline{EI}$ and $\overline{GK}$

   G $\overline{GK}$ and $\overline{DH}$ I $\overline{HI}$ and $\overline{DF}$

3. Which line segment is parallel to plane *FGKJ*? B

   A $\overline{FD}$ B $\overline{HI}$ C $\overline{GE}$ D $\overline{KI}$

For Exercises 4–7, use the figure at the right.

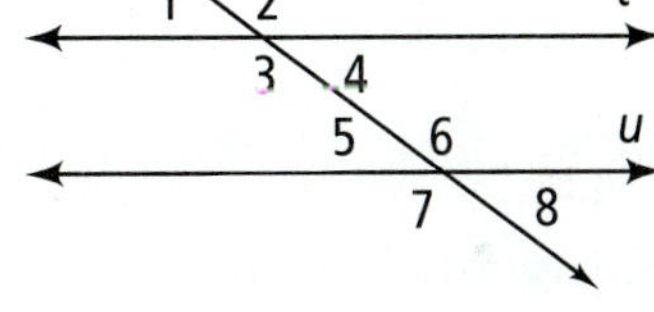

4. Which is a pair of alternate interior angles? F

   F $\angle 3$ and $\angle 6$ H $\angle 6$ and $\angle 5$

   G $\angle 2$ and $\angle 7$ I $\angle 4$ and $\angle 6$

5. Which angle corresponds to $\angle 7$? B

   A $\angle 1$ B $\angle 3$ C $\angle 4$ D $\angle 6$

6. Which pair of angles are alternate exterior angles? I

   F $\angle 1$ and $\angle 5$ G $\angle 3$ and $\angle 6$ H $\angle 5$ and $\angle 8$ I $\angle 1$ and $\angle 8$

7. Which pair of angles are same-side interior angles? D

   A $\angle 1$ and $\angle 5$ B $\angle 3$ and $\angle 6$ C $\angle 4$ and $\angle 8$ D $\angle 3$ and $\angle 5$

Short Response

8. Describe the parallel planes, parallel lines, and skew lines in a cube. Draw a sketch to illustrate your answer.

   [2] A cube has three sets of parallel planes. Each edge of the cube has three edges that are parallel to it and four edges that are skew in relation to it. [1] unclear/incomplete description or drawing OR one element missing [0] incorrect or no response

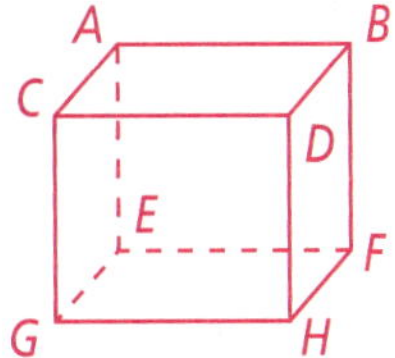

3-2 Properties of Parallel Lines

Vocabulary

Review

1. Circle the symbol for *congruent*. ≅ = ∥

(≅ is circled)

Identify each angle below as *acute, obtuse,* or *right*.

2. 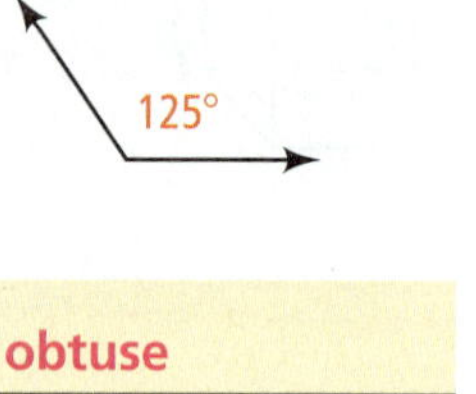

obtuse

3. right

4. 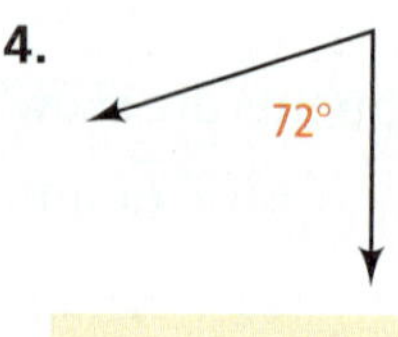

acute

Vocabulary Builder

interior (noun) **in TEER ee ur**

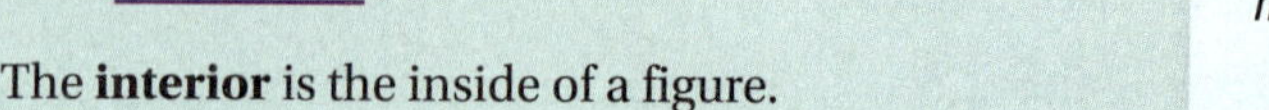

Main Idea: The **interior** is the inside of a figure.

Related Words: inside (noun), exterior (noun, antonym)

Definition: The **interior** of a pair of lines is the region between the two lines.

Example: A painter uses **interior** paint for the inside of a house.

Use Your Vocabulary

Use the diagram at the right for Exercises 5 and 6. Underline the correct point to complete each sentence.

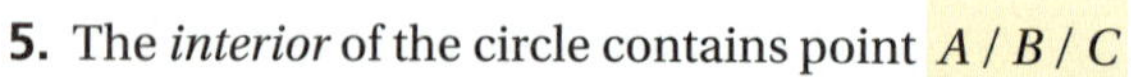

5. The *interior* of the circle contains point A / B / C. (A underlined)

6. The *interior* of the angle contains point A / B / C. (B underlined)

7. Underline the correct word to complete the sentence.

   The endpoint of an *angle* is called its ray / vertex. (vertex underlined)

8. Write two other names for $\angle ABC$ in the diagram at the right.

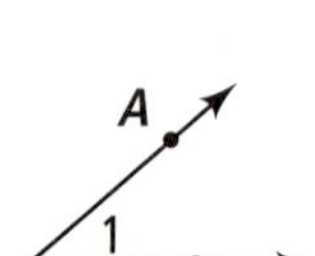

$\angle 1$ $\angle B$

take note

Postulate 3-1, Theorems 3-1, 3-2, and 3-3

If... a transversal intersects two parallel lines,

Then...

Then...	
corresponding angles are congruent.	**Postulate 3-1 Corresponding Angles Postulate**
alternate interior angles are congruent.	**Theorem 3-1 Alternate Interior Angles Theorem**
same-side interior angles are supplementary.	**Theorem 3-2 Same-Side Interior Angles Theorem**
alternate exterior angles are congruent.	**Theorem 3-3 Alternate Exterior Angles Theorem**

Use the graphic organizer and the diagram to find each congruent angle.

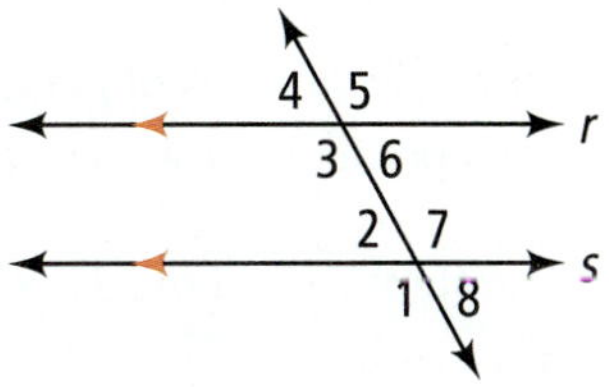

9. Postulate 3-1

$\angle 3 \cong$ ∠1

10. Theorem 3-1

$\angle 3 \cong$ ∠7

11. Theorem 3-3

$\angle 1 \cong$ ∠5

4 5 3 6 r 2 7 1 8 s

Problem 1 Identifying Congruent Angles

Got It? Reasoning One way to justify $m\angle 6 = 55$ is shown below. Can you find another way to justify $m\angle 6 = 55$? Explain.

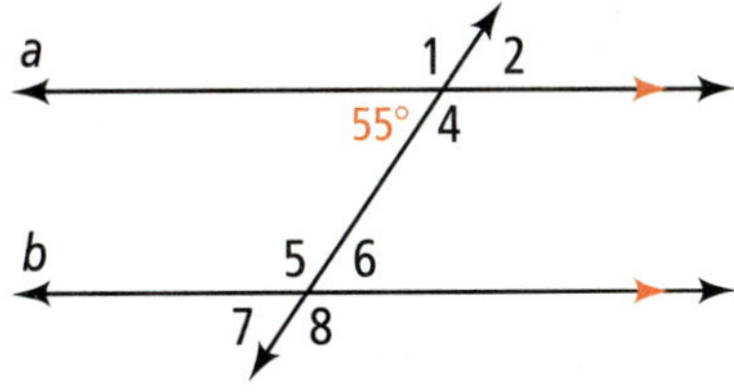

$m\angle 2 = 55$ by the Vertical Angles Theorem.

$m\angle 6 = 55$ by the Corresponding Angles Postulate because $\angle 2$ and $\angle 6$ are corresponding angles.

12. Underline the correct words to complete the sentence.

$\angle 6$ and the 55° angle form a pair of corresponding / <u>alternate interior</u> angles, so

$m\angle 6 = 55$ by Postulate / <u>Theorem</u> 3-1.

Problem 2 Proving an Angle Relationship

Got It? **Given:** $a \parallel b$

Prove: $\angle 1 \cong \angle 7$

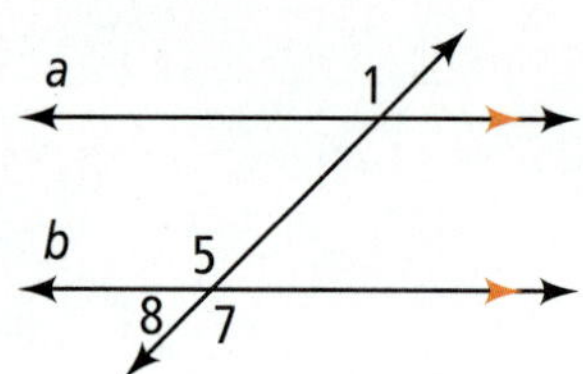

13. Use the reasons at the right to write each step of the proof.

Statements	Reasons
1) $a \parallel b$	1) Given
2) $\angle 1 \cong \angle 5$	2) If lines are $\parallel$, then corresp. angles are $\cong$.
3) $m\angle 1 = m\angle 5$	3) Congruent angles have equal measure.
4) $\angle 5 \cong \angle 7$	4) Vertical angles are congruent.
5) $m\angle 5 = m\angle 7$	5) Congruent angles have equal measure.
6) $m\angle 1 = m\angle 7$	6) Transitive Property of $\cong$
7) $\angle 1 \cong \angle 7$	7) Angles with equal measure are $\cong$.

Problem 3 Finding Measures of Angles

Got It? **Find the measure of $\angle 1$. Justify your answer.**

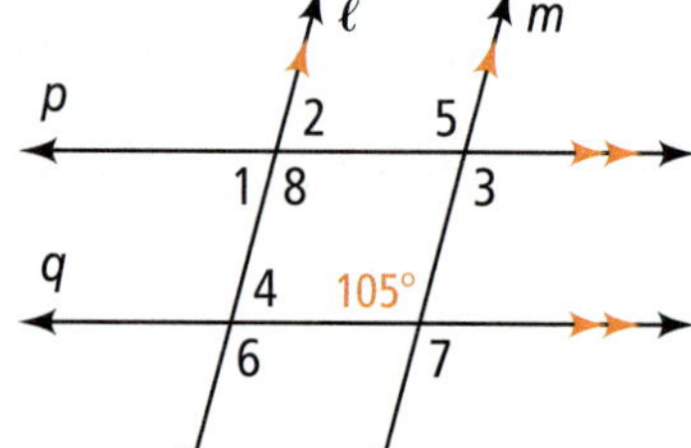

14. There are two sets of parallel lines. Each parallel line also acts as a _?_. transversal

15. The steps to find $m\angle 1$ are given below. Justify each step.

Statements	Reasons
1) $\angle 1 \cong \angle 4$	1) Alternate Interior Angles Theorem
2) $m\angle 1 = m\angle 4$	2) Congruent angles have the same measure.
3) $\angle 4$ and $\angle 6$ are supplementary.	3) Linear Pair Postulate
4) $m\angle 4 + m\angle 6 = 180$	4) Definition of supplementary angles
5) $m\angle 1 + m\angle 6 = 180$	5) Transitive Property of Equality
6) $m\angle 5 = 105$	6) Corresponding angles have the same measure.
7) $m\angle 6 = 105$	7) Alternate interior angles have the same measure.
8) $m\angle 1 + 105 = 180$	8) Substitute into Statement 5.
9) $m\angle 1 = 75$	9) Subtraction Property of Equality

Problem 4 Using Algebra to Find an Angle Measure

Got It? **In the figure at the right, what are the values of x and y?**

16. The bases of a trapezoid are parallel / perpendicular.

17. Use the Same-Side Interior Angles Theorem to complete each equation.

$2x + (x - 12) = 180$ $\qquad$ $3y + (y + 20) = 180$

18. Solve each equation.

$$2x + (x - 12) = 180$$
$$3x - 12 = 180$$
$$3x = 192$$
$$x = 64$$

$$3y + (y + 20) = 180$$
$$4y + 20 = 180$$
$$4y = 160$$
$$y = 40$$

Lesson Check • Do you UNDERSTAND?

In the diagram at the right, ∠1 and ∠8 are supplementary. What is the name for this angle pair? Explain.

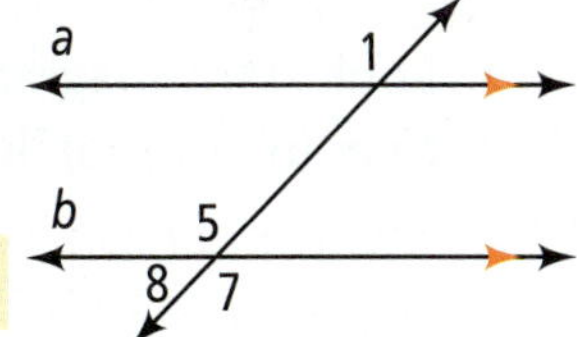

19. Circle the best name for lines a and b.

(parallel) $\quad$ perpendicular $\quad$ skew $\quad$ transversals

20. Circle the best name from the list below for ∠1 and ∠8.

alternate $\quad$ congruent $\quad$ corresponding $\quad$ (same-side)

21. Circle the best name from the list below for ∠1 and ∠8.

(exterior) $\quad$ interior

22. Use your answers to Exercises 20 and 21 to write a name for ∠1 and ∠8.

same-side exterior angles

Math Success

Check off the vocabulary words that you understand.

☐ alternate interior angles

☐ alternate exterior angles

Rate how well you can *prove angle relationships*.

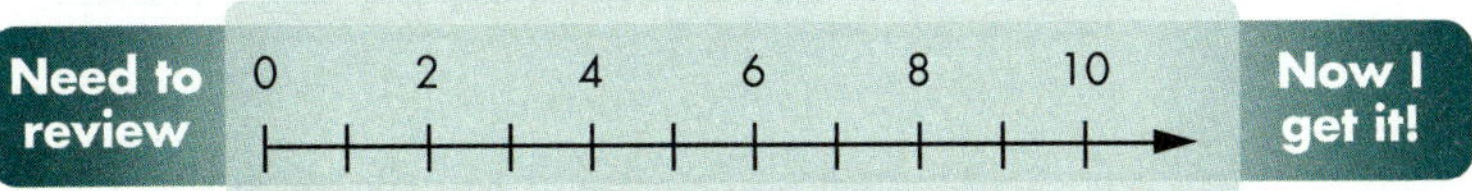

Name ______________________ Class ____________ Date ____________

3-2 Think About a Plan

Properties of Parallel Lines

Outdoor Recreation Campers often use a "bear bag" at night to avoid attracting animals to their food supply. In the bear bag system at the right, a camper pulls one end of the rope to raise and lower the food bag.

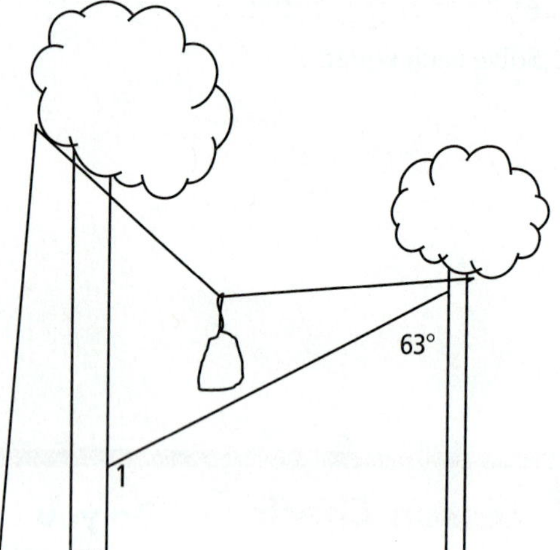

a. Suppose a camper pulls the rope taut between the two parallel trees, as shown. What is $m\angle 1$?

b. Are $\angle 1$ and the given angle *alternate interior angles, same-side interior angles,* or *corresponding angles?*

Understanding the Problem

1. Look at the diagram. How could you describe the diagonal taut rope and the trees in terms of lines and transversals?

   The trees are parallel lines intersected by a transversal (the rope).

2. What do you know about the special angle pairs formed when parallel lines are intersected by a transversal?

   They are either congruent or supplementary.

3. What strategy can you use to solve the problem?

   Answers may vary. Sample: Identify the types of angles and how they relate to each other.

Planning the Solution

4. What special angle pair do $\angle 1$ and the given angle make up? How do you know?

   Same-side interior angles; they both lie on the same side of the transversal and are both between the parallel lines.

5. What do you know about the relationship between these types of angles?

   They are supplementary.

Getting an Answer

6. What is an equation you can use to find $m\angle 1$? $m\angle 1 + 63 = 180$

7. What is the solution to the equation? 117

Name ______________________ Class ____________ Date ____________

3-2 Practice — Form K

Properties of Parallel Lines

Identify all the numbered angles that are congruent to the given angle. Justify your answers.

1.

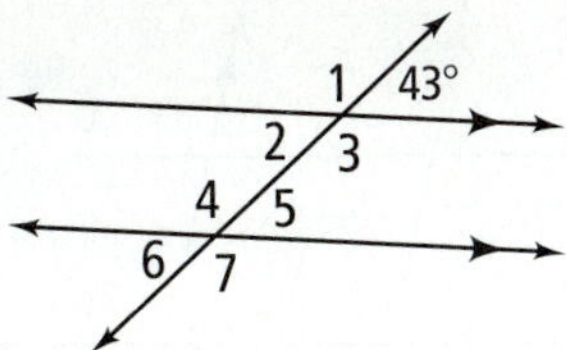

∠2; vert. ∠s are ≅; ∠5; corresp. ∠s are ≅; ∠6, alt. ext. ∠s are ≅.

2.

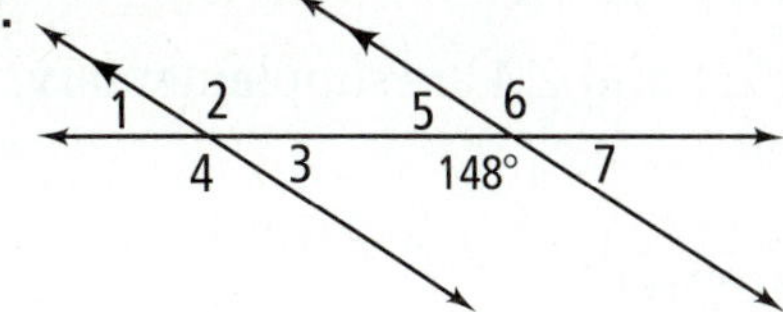

∠6; vert. ∠s are ≅; ∠4; corresp. ∠s are ≅; ∠2; alt. int. ∠s are ≅.

3.

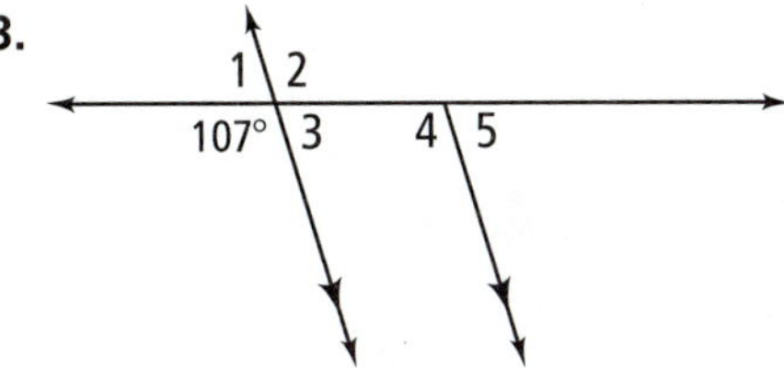

∠2; vert. ∠s are ≅; ∠4; corresp. ∠s are ≅.

4.

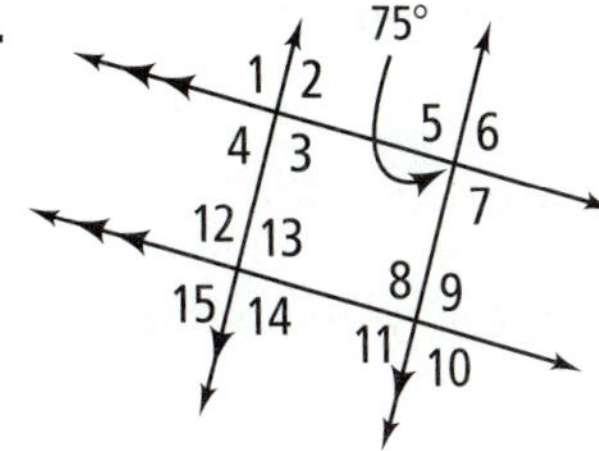

∠6; vert. ∠s are ≅; ∠4 and ∠11; corresp. ∠s are ≅; ∠2 and ∠9; alt. int. ∠s are ≅; ∠13; corresp. ∠s of alt. int. ∠s are ≅; ∠15; corresp. ∠s of corresp. ∠s are ≅.

Find $m\angle 1$ and $m\angle 2$. Justify each answer.

5.

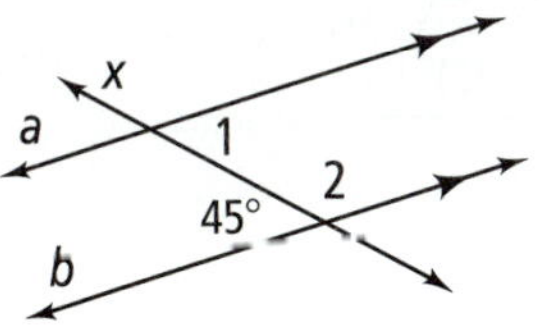

45; alt int. ∠s with 45°; 135; linear pair with 45°

6.

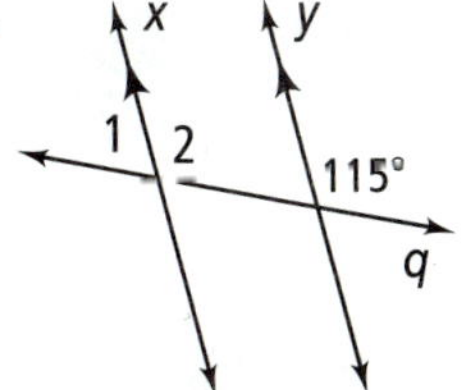

65; linear pair with ∠2; 115; corr ∠s with 115°

7.

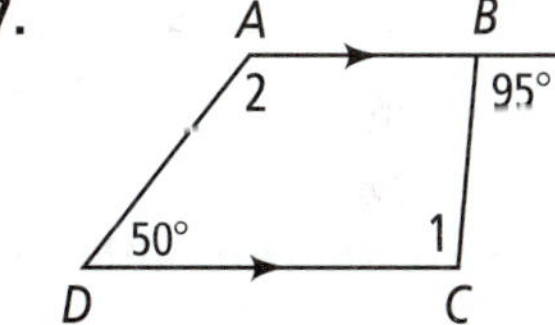

95; alt int. ∠s with 95°; 130; same-side ∠s with 50°

8. Ana made a zip line for her tree house. To do this, she attached a pulley to a cable. She then strung the cable at an angle between the tree house and another tree. She made the drawing of the zip line at the right. The two trees are parallel.

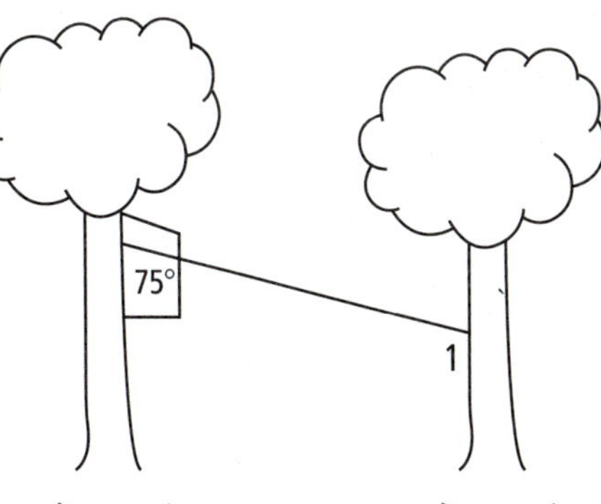

a. What is the measure of ∠1?

105

b. Are ∠1 and the given angle *same-side interior angles, alternate interior angles,* or *corresponding angles?*

same-side interior angles

Name ______________________ Class ____________ Date ____________

3-2 Practice (continued)

Form K

Properties of Parallel Lines

9. Developing Proof Supply the missing reasons in the two-column proof.

Given: $a \parallel b$, $c \parallel d$

Prove: $\angle 1$ and $\angle 4$ are supplementary.

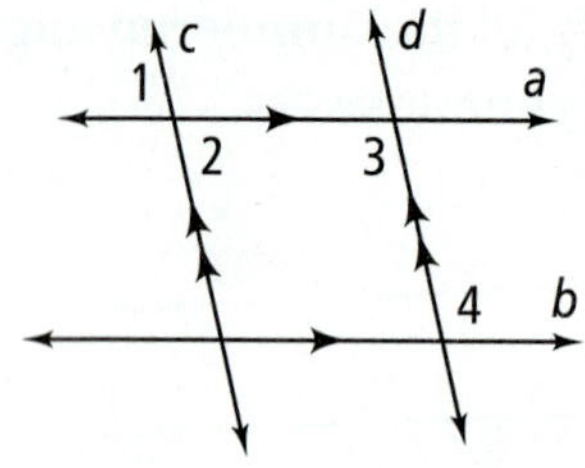

Statements	Reasons
1) $\angle 1 \cong \angle 2$	1) __?__ Vert. ∠s are ≅.
2) $c \parallel d$	2) Given
3) $\angle 2$ and $\angle 3$ are supplementary.	3) __?__ If lines are ∥, then same-side int. ∠s are suppl.
4) $a \parallel b$	4) Given
5) $\angle 3 \cong \angle 4$	5) __?__ If lines are ∥, then alt. int. ∠s are ≅.
6) $\angle 1$ and $\angle 4$ are supplementary.	6) __?__ Subst. Prop.

Algebra Find the value of x. Then find the measure of each labeled angle.

10. 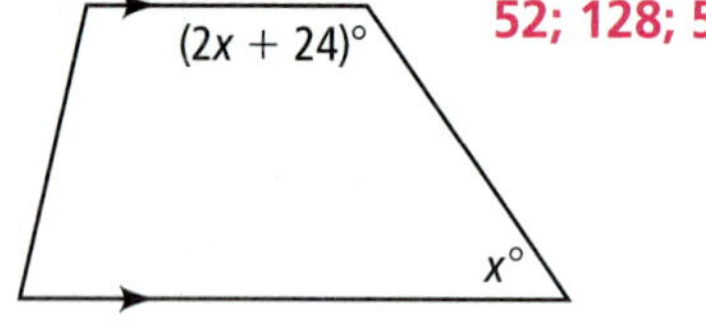

52; 128; 52

11. 18; 60; 60

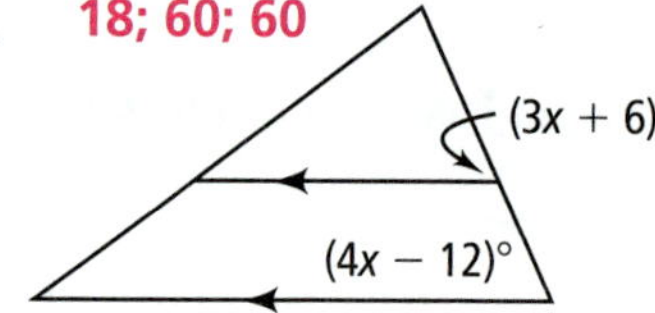

Algebra Find the values of the variables.

12. 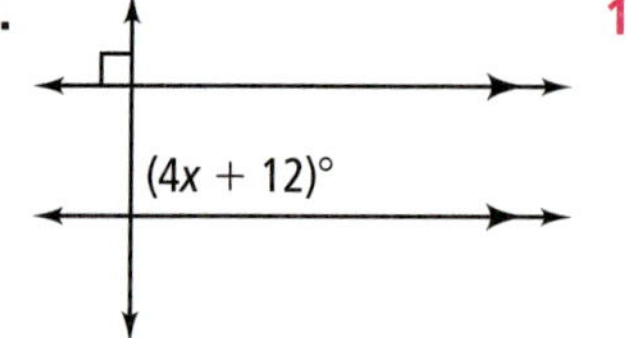

19.5

13. 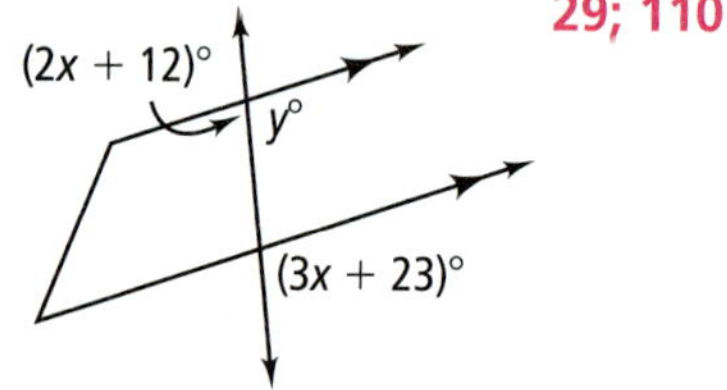

29; 110

14. Error Analysis Which solution for the value of x in the figure at the right is incorrect? Explain.

(4x − 2)°

(3x + 6)°

A.

$4x - 2 = 3x + 6$
$x = 8$

B.

$4x - 2 + 3x - 6 = 180$
$7x - 8 = 180$
$x = 24.6$

B; the marked angles are alt. int. ∠s, so they are ≅.

Name ______________________ Class ____________ Date ____________

3-2 Standardized Test Prep

Properties of Parallel Lines

Multiple Choice

For Exercises 1–6, choose the correct letter.

For Exercises 1–4, use the figure at the right.

1. Which angle is congruent to ∠1? B

(A) ∠2 (C) ∠6

(B) ∠5 (D) ∠7

2. Which angle is not supplementary to ∠6? F

(F) ∠2 (G) ∠4 (H) ∠5 (I) ∠8

3. Which can be used to prove directly that ∠1 ≅ ∠8? D

(A) Alternate Interior Angles Theorem

(B) Corresponding Angles Postulate

(C) Same-Side Interior Angles Theorem

(D) Alternate Exterior Angles Theorem

4. If $m\angle 5 = 42$, what is $m\angle 4$? F

(F) 42 (G) 48 (H) 128 (I) 138

For Exercises 5 and 6, use the figure at the right.

5. What is the value of x? C

(A) 10 (C) 30

(B) 25 (D) 120

6. What is the measure of ∠1? H

(F) 45 (G) 60 (H) 120 (I) 125

Short Response

7. Write a two-column proof of the Alternate Exterior Angles Theorem (Theorem 3-2).

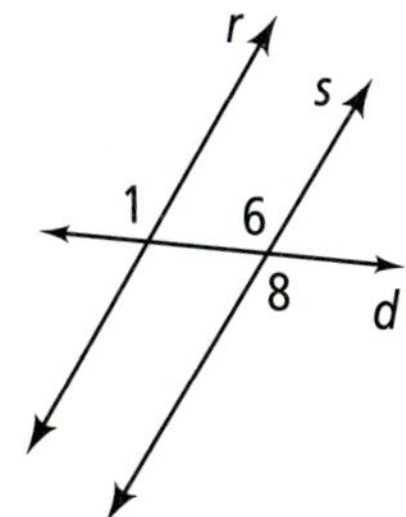

Given: $r \parallel s$

Prove: ∠1 ≅ ∠8

[2] $r \parallel s$; given; ∠1 ≅ ∠6; if lines are ∥, then corresp. ∠s are ≅; ∠6 ≅ ∠8; vert. ∠s are ≅; ∠1 ≅ ∠8; trans. prop. of ≅. [1] some steps correct [0] proof incorrect or absent

3-3 Proving Lines Parallel

Vocabulary

Review

Write the *converse* of each statement.

1. Statement: If you are cold, then you wear a sweater.

Converse: If ?, then ?.

If you wear a sweater, then you are cold.

2. Statement: If an angle is a right angle, then it measures 90°.

Converse: If an angle measures 90°, then it is a right angle.

3. The *converse* of a true statement is always / sometimes / never true.

Vocabulary Builder

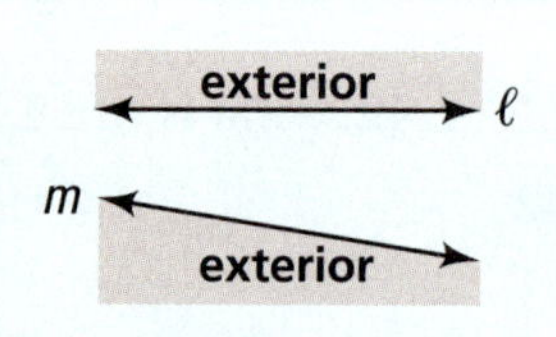

exterior (adjective) **ek** STEER **ee ur**

Related Words: **exterior** (noun), external, interior (antonym)

Definition: **Exterior** means on the outside or in an outer region.

Example: Two lines crossed by a transversal form four **exterior** angles.

Use Your Vocabulary

Underline the correct word to complete each sentence.

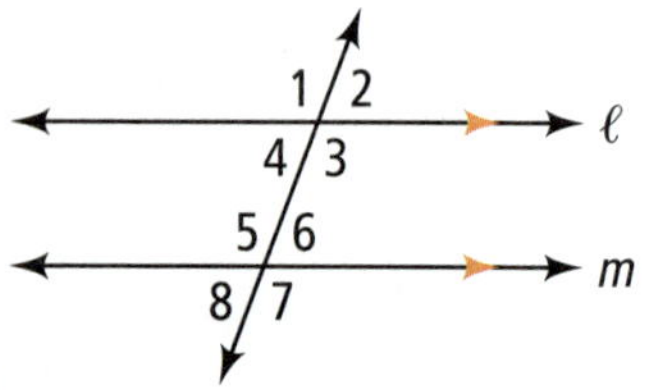

4. To paint the outside of your house, buy interior / exterior paint.

5. The protective cover prevents the interior / exterior of the book from being damaged.

6. In the diagram at the right, angles 1 and 7 are alternate interior / exterior angles.

7. In the diagram at the right, angles 4 and 5 are same-side interior / exterior angles.

Underline the *hypothesis* and circle the *conclusion* in the following statements.

8. If the lines do not intersect, then they are parallel lines.

9. If the angle measures 180°, then it is a straight angle.

take note

Postulates 3-1 and 3-2 Corresponding Angles Postulate and Its Converse

Postulate 3-1 Corresponding Angles Postulate

If a transversal intersects two parallel lines, then corresponding angles are congruent.

10. Complete the statement of Postulate 3-2.

Postulate 3-2 Converse of the Corresponding Angles Postulate

If two lines on a transversal form corresponding angles that are congruent, then the lines are _?_.

parallel

11. Use the diagram below. Place appropriate marking(s) to show that $\angle 1$ and $\angle 2$ are congruent.

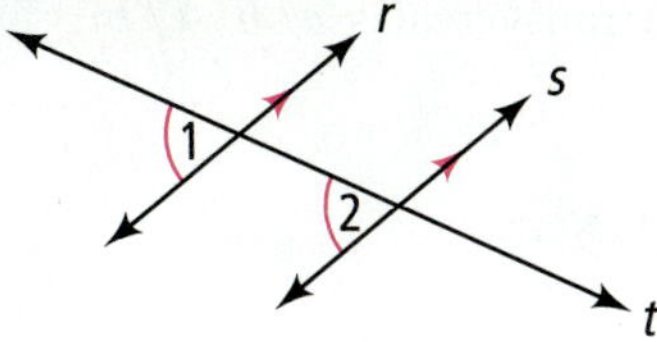

12. Circle the diagram that models Postulate 3-2.

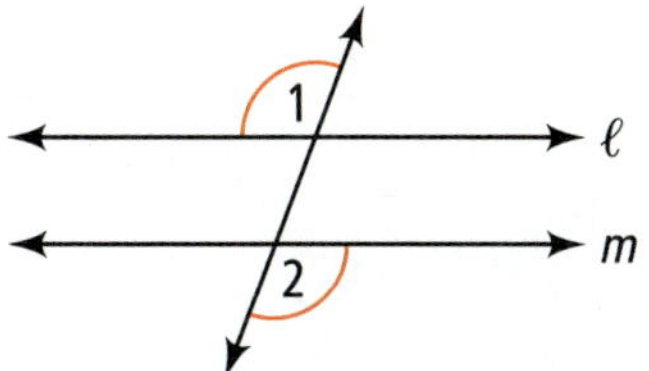

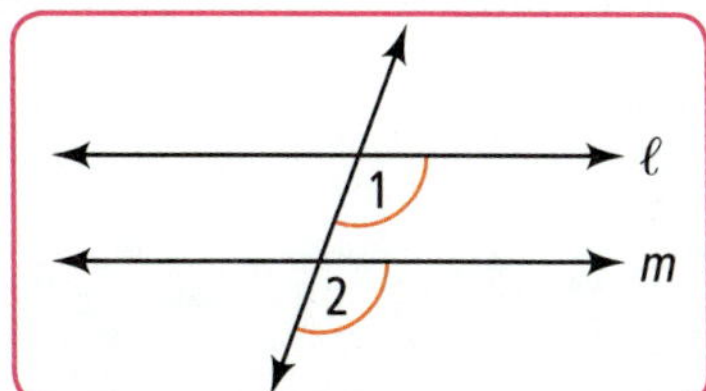

take note

Theorems 3-4, 3-5, and 3-6

Theorem 3-4 Converse of the Alternate Interior Angles Theorem

If two lines and a transversal form alternate interior angles that are congruent, then the two lines are parallel.

Theorem 3-5 Converse of the Same-Side Interior Angles Theorem

If two lines and a transversal form same-side interior angles that are supplementary, then the two lines are parallel.

Theorem 3-6 Converse of the Alternate Exterior Angles Theorem

If two lines and a transversal form alternate exterior angles that are congruent, then the two lines are parallel.

13. Use the diagram at the right to complete each example.

Theorem 3-4

If $\angle 4 \cong$ $\angle 8$, then $b \| c$.

Theorem 3-5

If $\angle 3$ and $\angle 8$ are supplementary, then $b \| c$.

Theorem 3-6

If $\angle 1 \cong$ $\angle 7$, then $b \| c$.

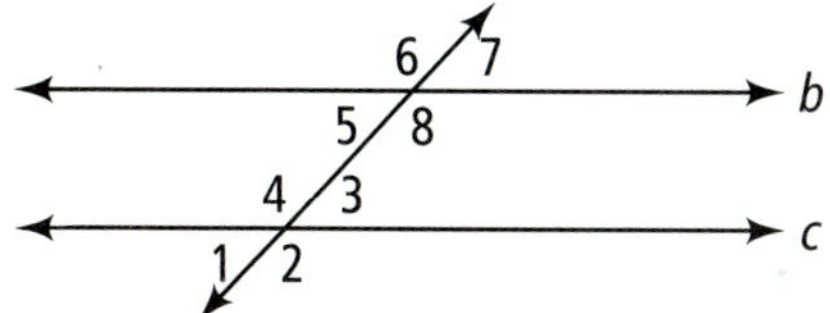

Problem 1 Identifying Parallel Lines

Got It? **Which lines are parallel if ∠6 ≅ ∠7? Justify your answer.**

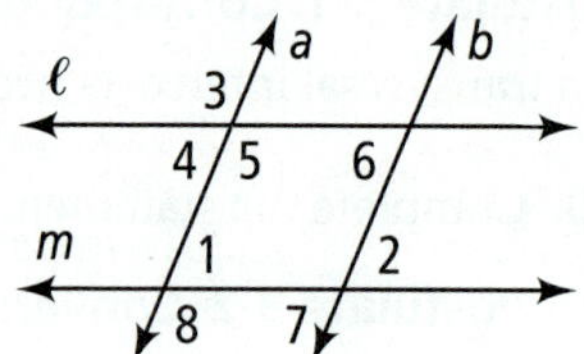

14. Underline the correct word(s) to complete each sentence.

∠6 ≅ ∠7 is given / to prove.

∠6 and ∠7 are alternate / same-side angles.

∠6 and ∠7 are corresponding / exterior / interior angles.

I can use Postulate 3-1 / Postulate 3-2 to prove the lines parallel.

Using ∠6 ≅ ∠7, lines *a* and *b* / ℓ and *m* are parallel and the transversal is *a* / *b* / ℓ / *m*.

Problem 2 Writing a Flow Proof of Theorem 3-6

Got It? **Given that ∠1 ≅ ∠7. Prove that ∠3 ≅ ∠5 using a flow proof.**

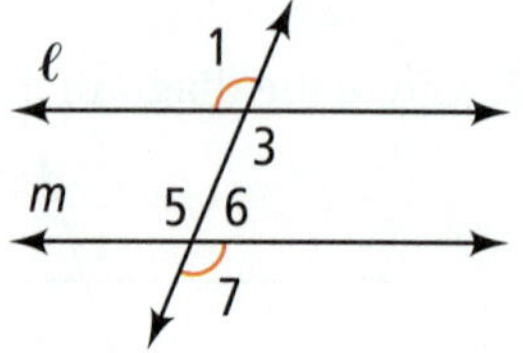

15. Use the diagram at the right to complete the flow proof below.

- ∠1 ≅ ∠7 — Given
- ∠1 ≅ ∠3 — Vertical angles are ≅.
- ∠3 ≅ ∠7 — Transitive Prop. of ≅.
- ∠7 ≅ ∠5 — Vertical angles are ≅.
- ∠3 ≅ ∠5 — Transitive Prop. of ≅.

Problem 3 Determining Whether Lines Are Parallel

Got It? **Given that ∠1 ≅ ∠2, you can use the Converse of the Alternate Exterior Angles Theorem to prove that lines *r* and *s* are parallel. What is another way to explain why *r* ∥ *s*? Justify your answer.**

r
s
t
3
2
1

16. Justify each step.

∠1 ≅ ∠2	Given
∠2 ≅ ∠3	Vertical angles are congruent.
∠1 ≅ ∠3	Transitive Property of Congruence

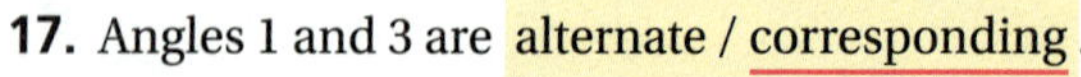

17. Angles 1 and 3 are alternate / corresponding.

18. What postulate or theorem can you now use to explain why *r* ∥ *s*?

Converse of the Corresponding Angles Postulate

Problem 4 Using Algebra

Got It? **What is the value of w for which $c \parallel d$?**

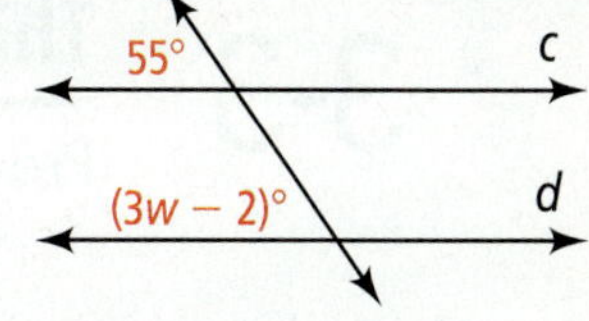

Underline the correct word to complete each sentence.

19. The marked angles are on opposite sides / the same side of the transversal.

20. By the Corresponding Angles Postulate, if $c \parallel d$ then corresponding angles are complementary / congruent / supplementary .

21. Use the theorem to solve for w.

$3w - 2 = 55$
$3w = 57$
$w = 19$

Lesson Check • Do you UNDERSTAND?

Error Analysis **A classmate says that $\overleftrightarrow{AB} \parallel \overleftrightarrow{DC}$ based on the diagram at right. Explain your classmate's error.**

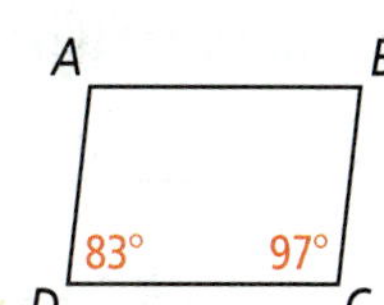

22. Circle the segments that are sides of $\angle D$ and $\angle C$. Underline the transversal.

$\overline{AB}$ $\overline{BC}$ $\overline{DC}$ $\overline{DA}$

23. Explain your classmate's error. Explanations may vary. Sample:

My classmate identified the wrong pair of parallel sides. $\angle ADC$ and $\angle BCD$ are supplementary and same-side interior angles. The transversal is $\overline{DC}$. $\overline{AD} \parallel \overline{BC}$ by the Converse of the Same-Side Interior Angles Theorem.

Math Success

Check off the vocabulary words that you understand.

☐ flow proof ☐ two-step proof ☐ parallel lines

Rate how well you can *prove that lines are parallel.*

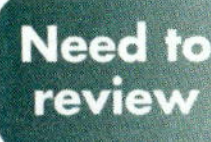

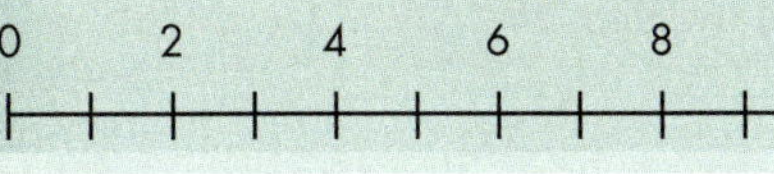

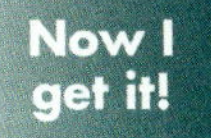

Name ______________________ Class ____________ Date ____________

3-3 Think About a Plan

Proving Lines Parallel

Algebra Determine the value of x for which $r \parallel s$. Then find $m\angle 1$ and $m\angle 2$.

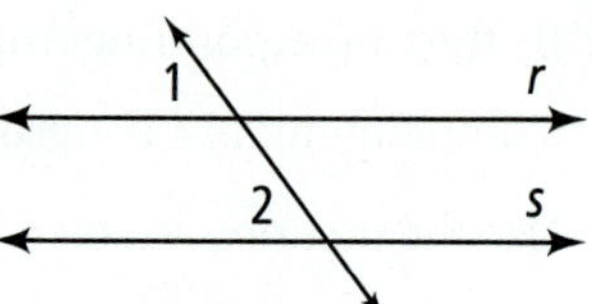

Given: $m\angle 1 = 20 - 8x$, $m\angle 2 = 30 - 16x$

1. Is $\angle 1$ an interior angle or an exterior angle? Is $\angle 2$ an interior angle or an exterior angle?

   $\angle 1$ is an exterior angle; $\angle 2$ is an interior angle.

2. Do $\angle 1$ and $\angle 2$ lie on the same side of the transversal or on opposite sides of the transversal?

   same side

3. What type of angle pair are $\angle 1$ and $\angle 2$?

   corresponding angles

4. If $r \parallel s$, and $\angle 1$ and $\angle 2$ are the type of angle pair you named above, how are the angles related?

   They are congruent.

5. What equation can you write using the given information?

   $20 - 8x = 30 - 16x$

6. What is the value of x? **1.25**

7. Substitute the value of x into each expression. What are the measures of each angle?

   $m\angle 1 = 20 - 8x =$ **10**

   $m\angle 2 = 30 - 16x =$ **10**

8. Would this value of x prove that $r \parallel s$? Explain.

   Yes; when you substitute 1.25 into each expression and simplify, you get 10 for both.

   Because the angles are congruent corresponding angles, the lines are parallel.

Name ______________________ Class ____________ Date ____________

3-3 Practice

Form K

Proving Lines Parallel

Which lines or segments are parallel? Justify your answer.

1.

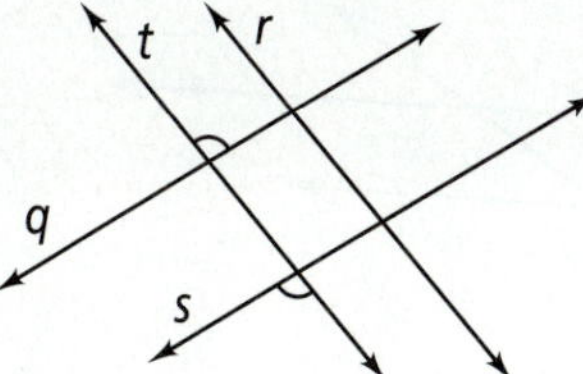

$q \parallel s$; Converse to Alt. Ext. ∠s Thm.

2.

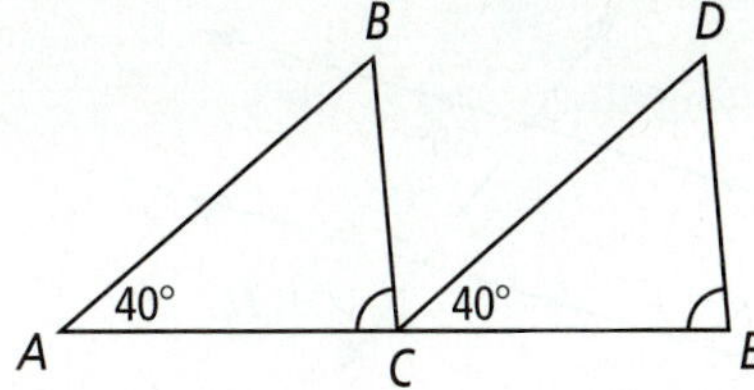

$\overline{AB} \parallel \overline{CD}$; Converse to Corresp. ∠s Thm.; $\overline{BC} \parallel \overline{DE}$; Converse to Corresp. ∠s Thm.

3.

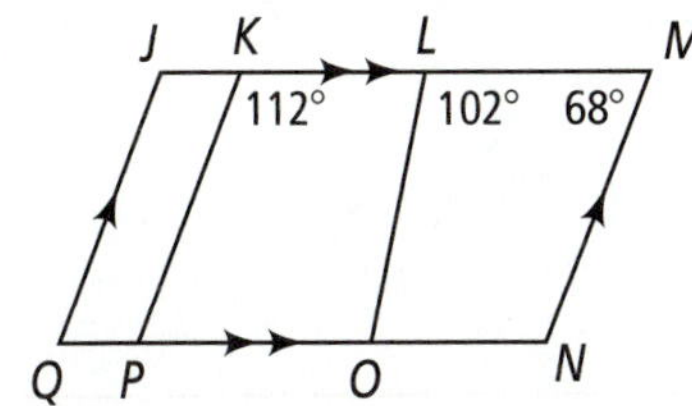

$\overline{PK} \parallel \overline{MN}$; Converse to Same-Side Int. ∠s Thm; $\overline{NM} \parallel \overline{QJ}$ and $\overline{JM} \parallel \overline{QN}$; Given

4.

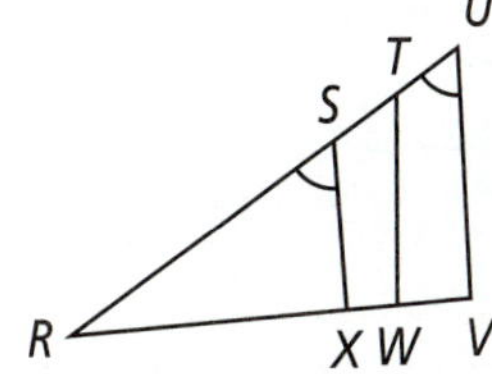

$\overline{SX} \parallel \overline{UV}$; Converse to Corresp. ∠s Thm.

5. Developing Proof Complete the flow proof below.

Given: ∠1 and ∠4 are supplementary.

Prove: $a \parallel b$

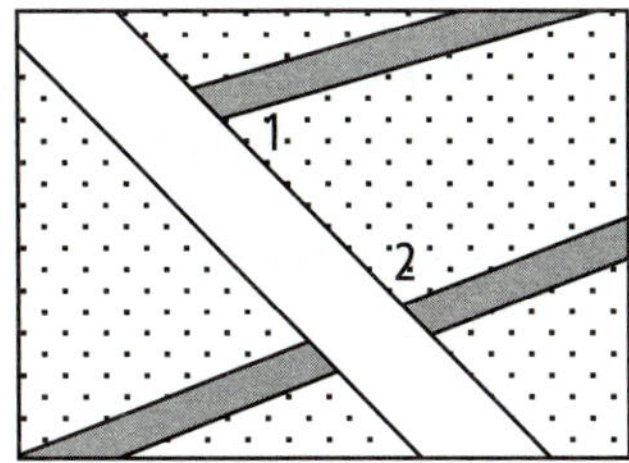

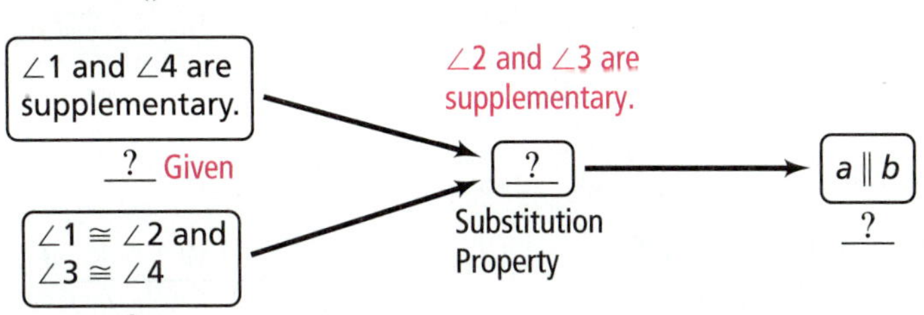

6. Mrs. Jensen made a quilt for her nephew. The pattern for one block is shown at the right. If $m\angle 1 = 60$ and $m\angle 2 = 115$, are the two gray strips of fabric parallel? Explain.

No; answers may vary. Sample: ∠1 and ∠2 are same-side int. ∠s. For the strips of fabric to be ∥, ∠1 and ∠2 must be suppl., but $115 + 60 \neq 180$.

Name ______________________ Class __________ Date __________

3-3 Practice (continued) — Form K

Proving Lines Parallel

Algebra Find the value of x for which $a \parallel b$.

7.

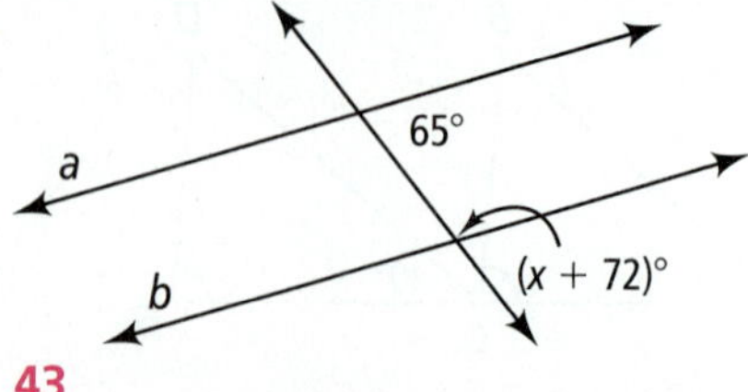

43

8.

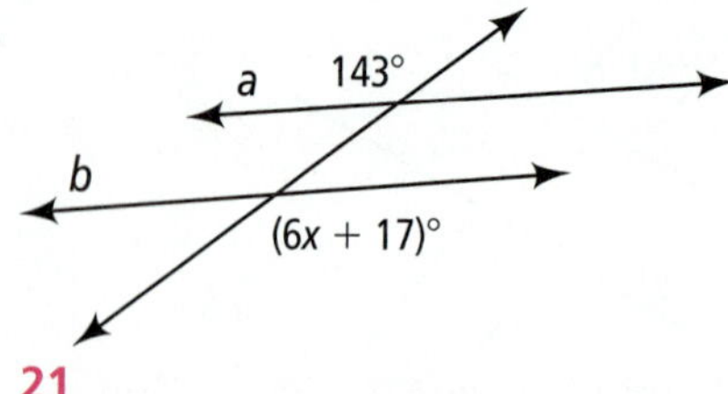

21

9.

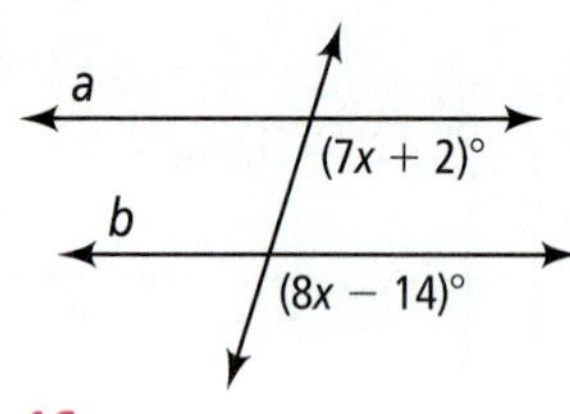

16

10.

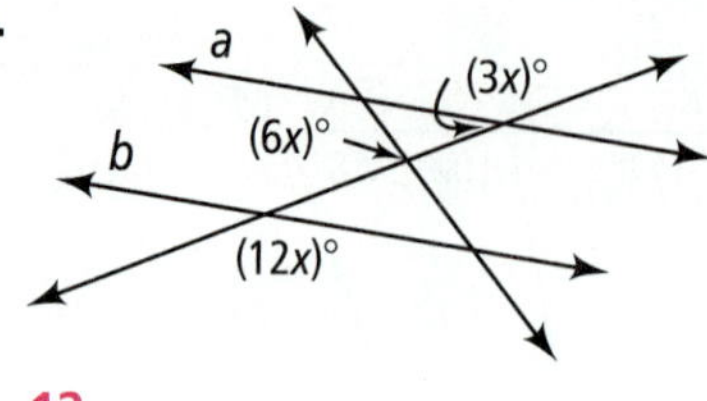

12

Developing Proof Use the given information to determine which lines, if any, are parallel. Justify each conclusion with a theorem or postulate.

x, y, s, t; angles 1–12

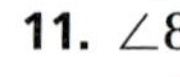

11. $\angle 8$ is supplementary to $\angle 9$.
    $x \parallel y$; Converse of Same-Side Int. ∠s Thm.

12. $\angle 7 \cong \angle 4$
    $x \parallel y$; Converse Of Alt. Ext. ∠s Thm.

13. $\angle 9$ is supplementary to $\angle 12$.
    $s \parallel t$; Converse of Same-Side Int. ∠s Thm.

14. $\angle 9 \cong \angle 11$
    $s \parallel t$; Converse Of Alt. Int. ∠s Thm.

15. **Error Analysis** A classmate said that $\overline{AB} \parallel \overline{DC}$ based on the diagram at the right. Explain your classmate's error. You can't prove that $\overline{AB} \parallel \overline{DC}$ with the information given because the congruent angles aren't formed by the same transversal.

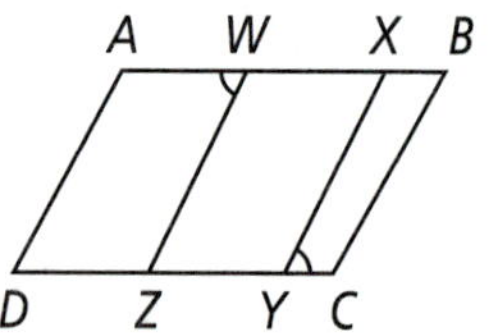

Algebra Determine the value of x for which $c \parallel d$. Then find $m\angle 1$ and $m\angle 2$.

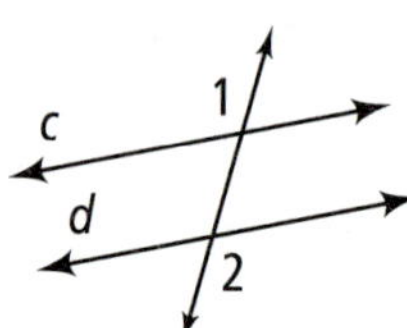

16. $m\angle 1 = 100 - x$, $m\angle 2 = 40 + 2x$
    20; 80; 80

17. $m\angle 1 = 90 - 6x$, $m\angle 2 = 100 - 8x$
    5; 60; 60

Name _______________ Class _______ Date _______

3-3 Standardized Test Prep

Proving Lines Parallel

Multiple Choice

For Exercises 1–6, choose the correct letter.

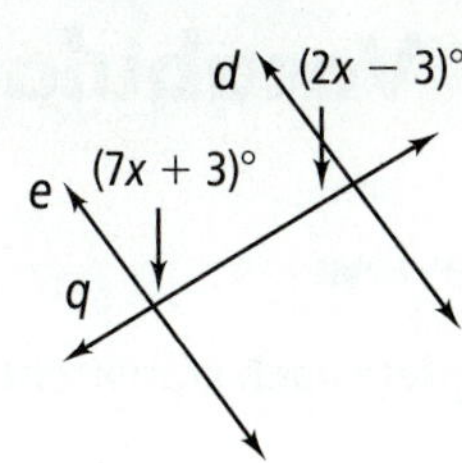

1. For what value of x is $d \parallel e$? A

   (A) 20 (B) 25 (C) 35 (D) 37

For Exercises 2 and 3, use the figure below right.

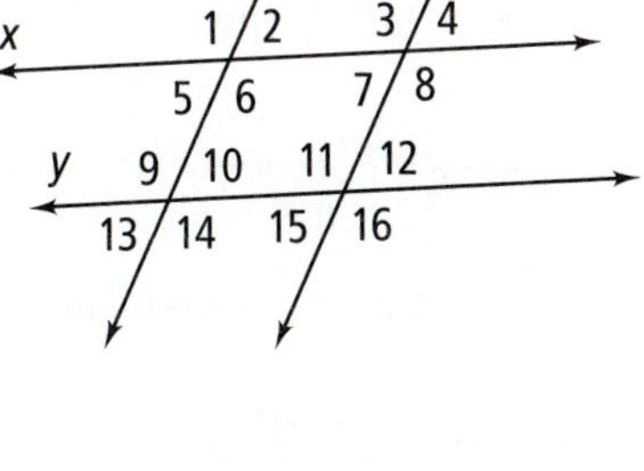

2. Which statement proves that $a \parallel b$? G

   (F) $\angle 8$ is supplementary to $\angle 12$. (H) $\angle 1 \cong \angle 6$

   (G) $\angle 10$ is supplementary to $\angle 11$. (I) $\angle 5 \cong \angle 13$

3. Which statement proves that $x \parallel y$? C

   (A) $\angle 2$ is supplementary to $\angle 3$. (C) $\angle 6 \cong \angle 9$

   (B) $\angle 14$ is supplementary to $\angle 15$. (D) $\angle 12 \cong \angle 13$

For Exercises 4–6, use the figure at the right.

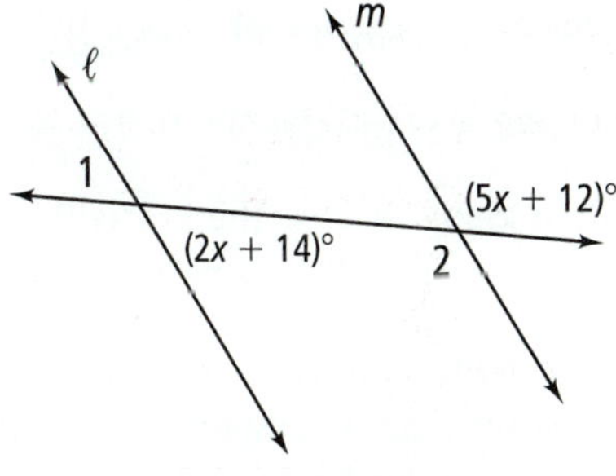

4. If $\ell \parallel m$, what is $m\angle 1$? G

   (F) 22 (G) 58 (H) 122 (I) 130

5. For what value of x is $\ell \parallel m$? A

   (A) 22 (B) 54 (C) 58 (D) 122

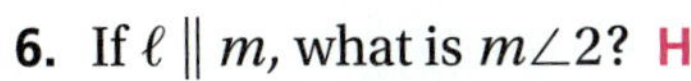

6. If $\ell \parallel m$, what is $m\angle 2$? H

   (F) 22 (G) 58 (H) 122 (I) 130

Short Response

7. Write a flow proof. [1] partly incorrect, incomplete, or disorganized proof

   Given: $\angle 2$ and $\angle 3$ are supplementary.

   Prove: $c \parallel d$ [0] incorrect or no proof

   [2]

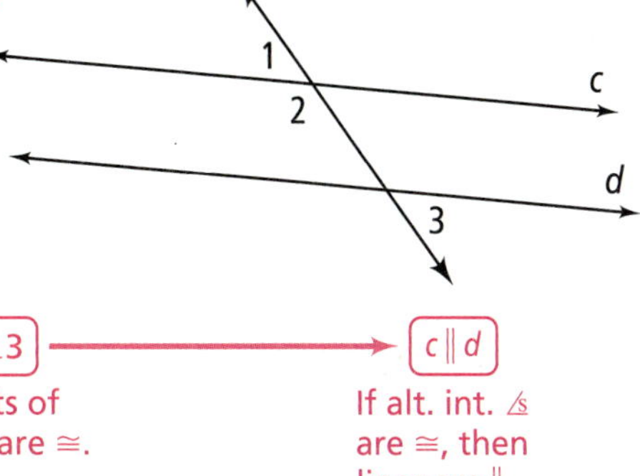

$\angle 1 \cong \angle 3$ — Supplements of the same $\angle$ are $\cong$. → $c \parallel d$ — If alt. int. $\angle$s are $\cong$, then lines are $\parallel$.

3-4 Parallel and Perpendicular Lines

Vocabulary

Review

Complete each statement with *always, sometimes* or *never*.

1. A *transversal* ? intersects at least two lines. always
2. A *transversal* ? intersects two lines at more than two points. never
3. A *transversal* ? intersects two parallel lines. sometimes
4. A *transversal* ? forms angles with two other lines. always

Vocabulary Builder

transitive (adjective) TRAN **si tiv**

Related Words: transition, transit, transitivity

Main Idea: You use the **Transitive** Property in proofs when what you know implies a statement that, in turn, implies what you want to prove.

Definition: **Transitive** describes the property where one element in relation to a second element and the second in relation to the third implies the first element is in relation to the third element.

Transitive

If $A \rightarrow B$
and $B \rightarrow C$
then $A \rightarrow C$.

Use Your Vocabulary

Complete each example of the *Transitive* Property.

5. If $a > b$ and $b > c$, then $a > c$.

6. If Joe is younger than Ann and Ann is younger than Sam, then Joe is younger than Sam.

7. If you travel from Station 2 to Station 3 and you travel from Station 3 to Station 4, then you travel from Station 2 to Station 4.

Theorem 3-7 Transitive Property of Parallel Lines and Theorem 3-8

8. Complete the table below.

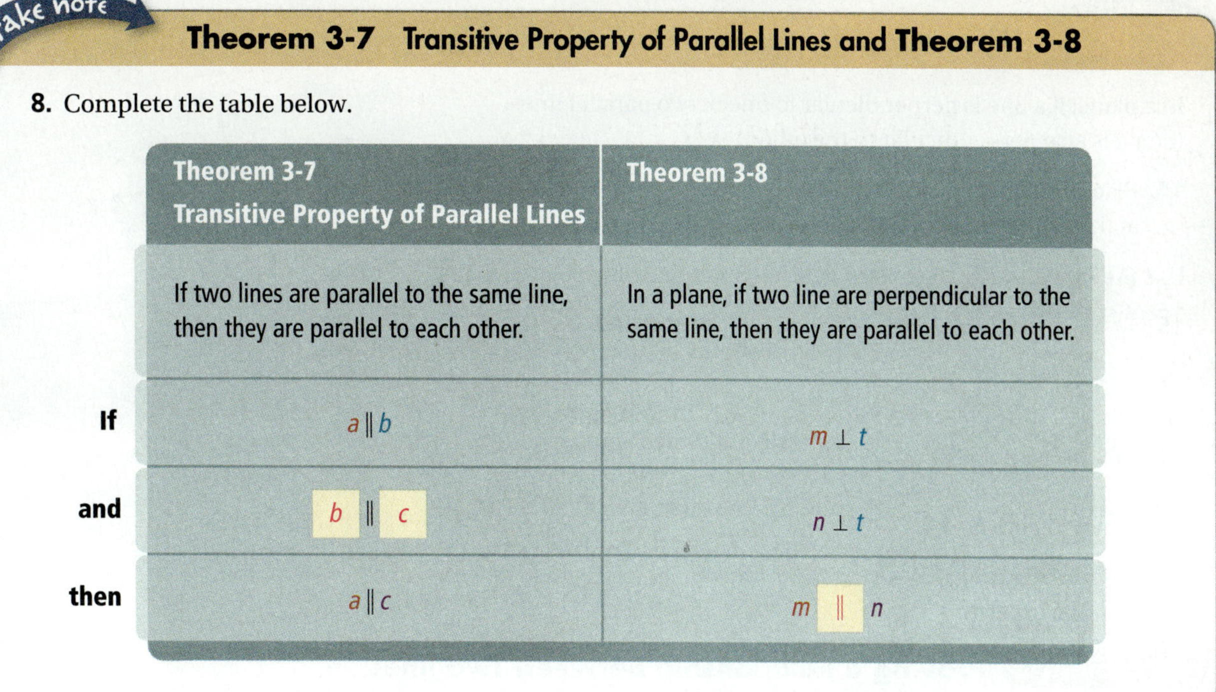

	Theorem 3-7 Transitive Property of Parallel Lines	Theorem 3-8
	If two lines are parallel to the same line, then they are parallel to each other.	In a plane, if two line are perpendicular to the same line, then they are parallel to each other.
If	$a \parallel b$	$m \perp t$
and	$b \parallel c$	$n \perp t$
then	$a \parallel c$	$m \parallel n$

Problem 1 Solving a Problem With Parallel Lines

Got It? **Can you assemble the pieces at the right to form a picture frame with opposite sides parallel? Explain.**

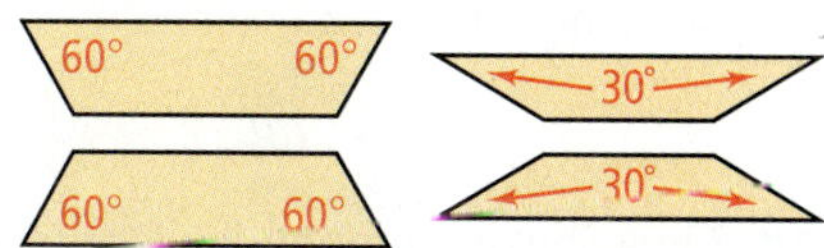

9. Circle the correct phrase to complete the sentence.

To make the picture frame, you will glue ? .

the same angle to the same angle   two different angles together

10. The angles at each connecting end measure 60 ° and 30 °.

11. When the pieces are glued together, each angle of the frame will measure 90 °.

12. Complete the flow chart below with *parallel* or *perpendicular.*

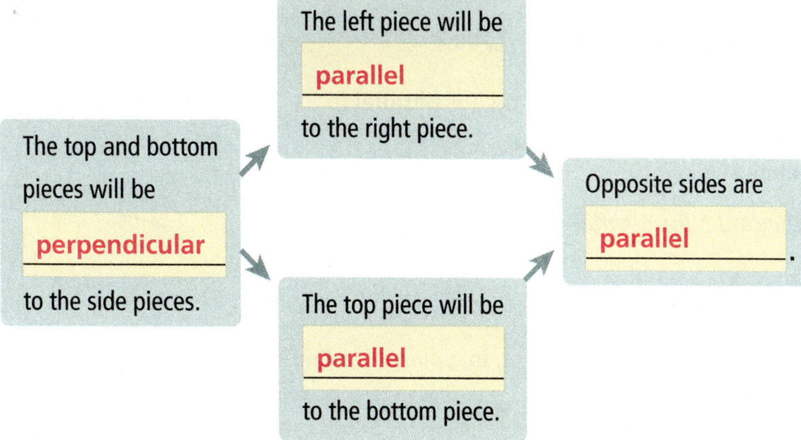

13. Underline the correct words to complete the sentence.

Yes / No , I can / cannot assemble the pieces to form a picture frame with opposite sides parallel.

take note

Theorem 3-9 Perpendicular Transversal Theorem

In a plane, if a line is perpendicular to one of two parallel lines, then it is also perpendicular to the other.

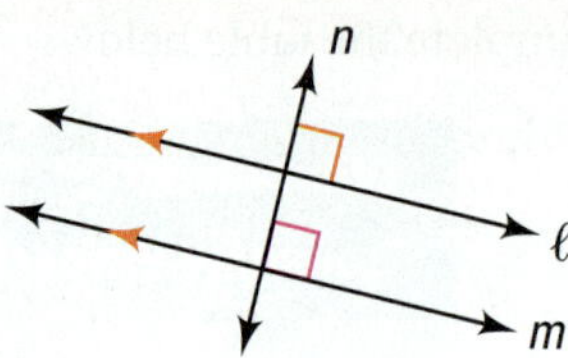

14. Place a right angle symbol in the diagram at the right to illustrate Theorem 3-9.

Use the information in each diagram to complete each statement.

15.

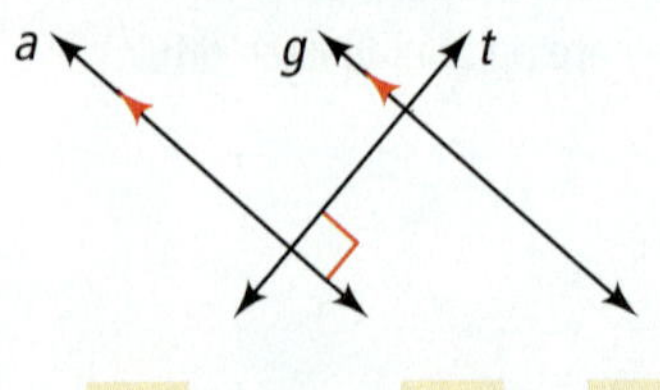

$a \parallel$ g and $a \perp$ t , so g $\perp$ t .

16.

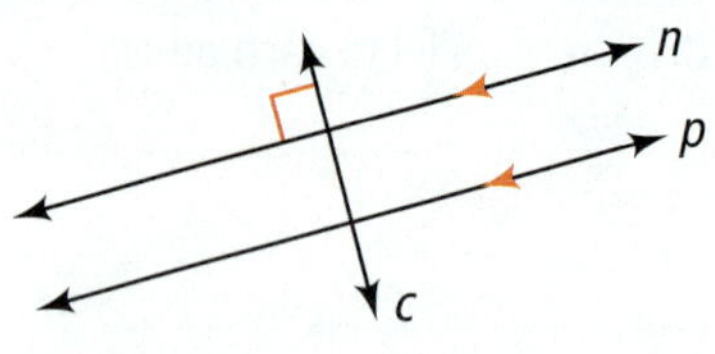

$c \perp$ n and $n \parallel$ p , so c $\perp$ p .

Problem 2 Proving a Relationship Between Two lines

Got It? **Use the diagram at the right. In a plane, $c \perp b$, $b \perp d$, and $d \perp a$. Can you conclude that $a \parallel b$? Explain.**

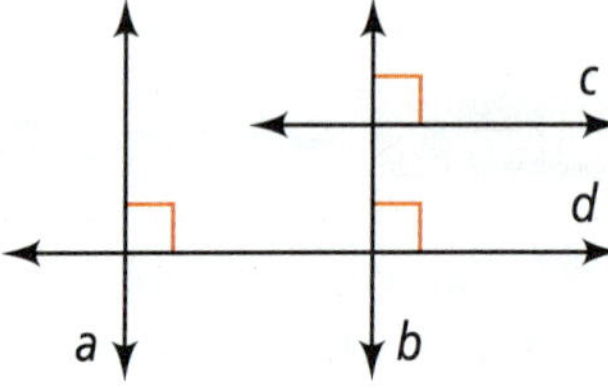

17. Circle the line(s) perpendicular to a. Underline the line(s) perpendicular to b.

a b c d

18. Lines that are perpendicular to the same line are parallel / perpendicular .

19. Can you conclude that $a \parallel b$? Explain.

Yes. Explanations may vary. Sample: Lines a and b are both perpendicular to line d, so $a \parallel b$ by Theorem 3-8.

Lesson Check • Do you know HOW?

Main Street intersects Avenue A and Avenue B. Avenue A is parallel to Avenue B. Avenue A is also perpendicular to Main Street. How are Avenue B and Main Street related? Explain.

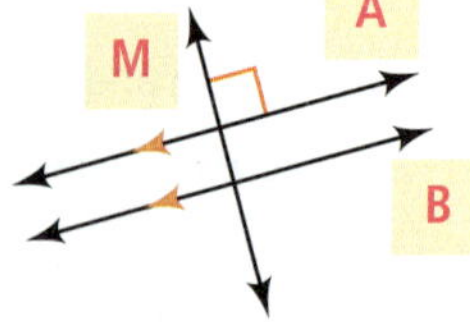

20. Label the streets in the diagram A for *Avenue A*, B for *Avenue B*, and M for *Main Street.*

21. Underline the correct word(s) to complete each sentence.

The Perpendicular Transversal Theorem states that, in a plane, if a line is parallel / perpendicular to one of two parallel / perpendicular lines, then it is also parallel / perpendicular to the other.

Avenue B and Main Street are parallel / perpendicular streets.

Lesson Check • Do you UNDERSTAND?

Which theorem or postulate from earlier in the chapter supports the conclusion in Theorem 3-8? In the Perpendicular Transversal Theorem? Explain.

Use the diagram at the right for Exercises 22 and 23.

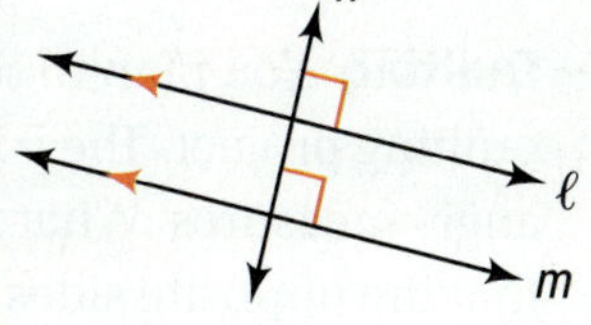

22. Complete the conclusion to Theorem 3-8.

In a plane, if two lines are perpendicular to the same line, then __?__.

they are parallel to each other

23. Complete the statement of Postulate 3-2.

If two lines and a transversal form __?__ angles that are congruent, then the lines are parallel.

corresponding

Use the diagram at the right for Exercises 24 and 25.

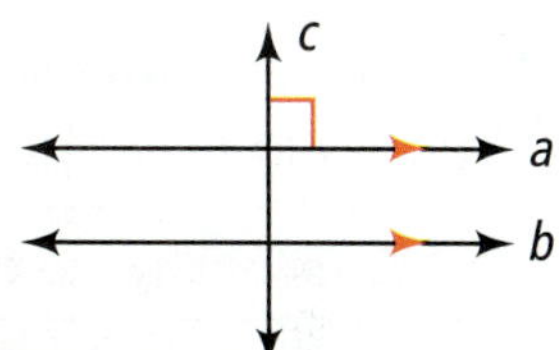

24. Complete the conclusion to the Perpendicular Transversal Theorem.

In a plane, if a line is perpendicular to one of two parallel lines, then it is also __?__.

perpendicular to the other.

25. Explain how any congruent angle pairs formed by parallel lines support the conclusion to the Perpendicular Transversal Theorem.

Answers may vary. Sample: If both alternate interior angles are right angles, then the line perpendicular to one parallel line is perpendicular to the other parallel line.

Math Success

Check off the vocabulary words that you understand.

- ☐ parallel
- ☐ perpendicular

Rate how well you can *understand parallel and perpendicular lines.*

Need to review | 0 2 4 6 8 10 | Now I get it!

Name ______________________ Class ____________ Date ____________

3-4 Think About a Plan

Parallel and Perpendicular Lines

Quilting You plan to sew two triangles of fabric together to make a square for a quilting project. The triangles are both right triangles and have the same side and angle measures. What must also be true about the triangles in order to guarantee that the opposite sides of the fabric square are parallel? Explain.

1. What do you know about the triangles? They are both right triangles.

2. What figures can you make by sewing different sides together? rectangles and squares

3. How are the triangles the same? They have the same side and angle measures.

4. In your own words, what question are you trying to answer?
What has to be true about the non-right angles of the triangle for the opposite sides of the fabric piece to be parallel?

5. Examine the drawings below. $\triangle ABC$ and $\triangle DCB$ are congruent and sides $\overline{BC}$ on each triangle are sewn together.

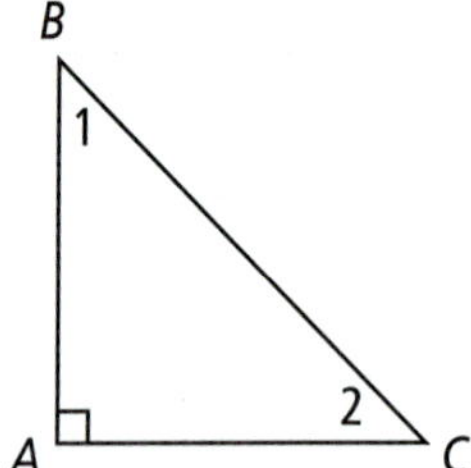

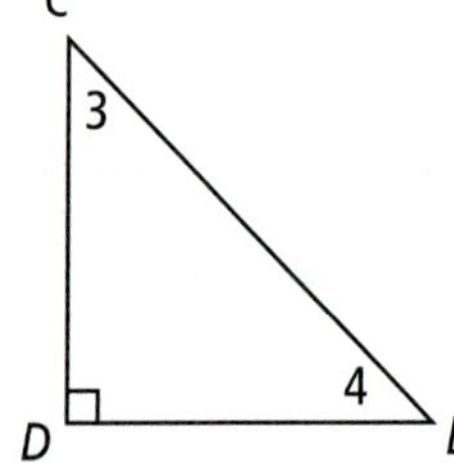

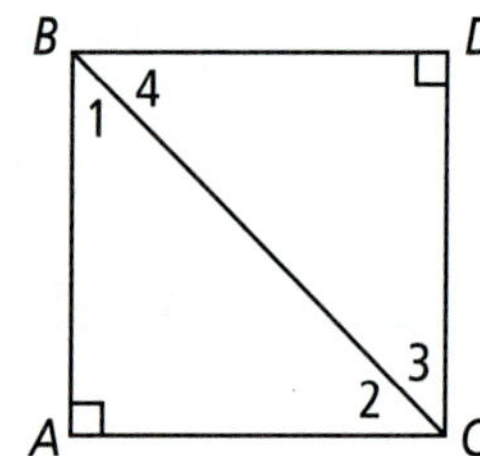

a. Which angles are congruent to each other? $\angle 1 \cong \angle 3$, $\angle 2 \cong \angle 4$

b. Is $\overline{AC} \parallel \overline{BD}$? How do you know?
Yes; by Theorem 3-4, if $\angle 2 \cong \angle 4$, then the sides are parallel.

c. Is $\overline{AB} \parallel \overline{CD}$? How do you know?
Yes; by Theorem 3-4, if $\angle 1 \cong \angle 3$, then the sides are parallel.

6. What fact about the triangles makes the opposite sides of the fabric piece parallel?
If the longest sides of the triangles are sewn together after rotating one triangle 180°, then both sets of sides will be parallel. Two sets of congruent alternate interior angles are formed.

7. How would you explain this relationship?
Both pairs of opposite sides are parallel, because they have congruent alternate interior angles when the triangles are sewn together as shown above.

Name ______________________ Class ____________ Date ____________

3-4 Practice

Form K

Parallel and Perpendicular Lines

1. A developer is planning a new housing complex. The map of the complex is shown at the right. Assume that all streets lie in a plane.

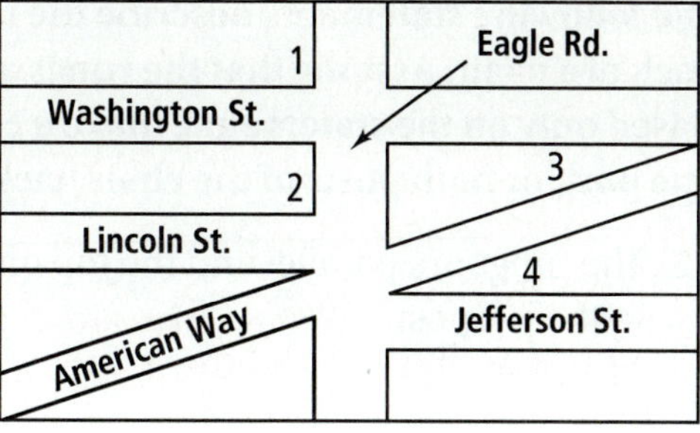

a. If Washington and Lincoln Streets are to be parallel, what must be true of $\angle 1$ and $\angle 2$?
They must be congruent.

b. Which streets must be parallel if $\angle 3 \cong \angle 4$? Justify your answer.
Washington St. and Jefferson St.

c. If $m\angle 1 = 90$ and your answers to parts (a) and (b) are true, to what roads is Eagle Road perpendicular?
Washingon St., Lincoln St., and Jefferson St.

2. **Developing Proof** Copy and complete this paragraph proof of the Perpendicular Transversal Theorem (Theorem 3-9).

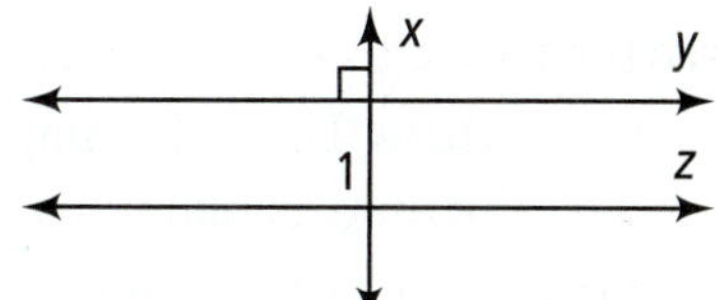

Given: In a plane, $x \perp y$ and $y \parallel z$.

Prove: $x \perp z$

Since $y \parallel z$, $m\angle 1 =$ __?__ by the __?__. 90; Corresp. ∠s Post.
By the definition of __?__ lines, $x \perp$ __?__. perpendicular; z

3. Write a paragraph proof.

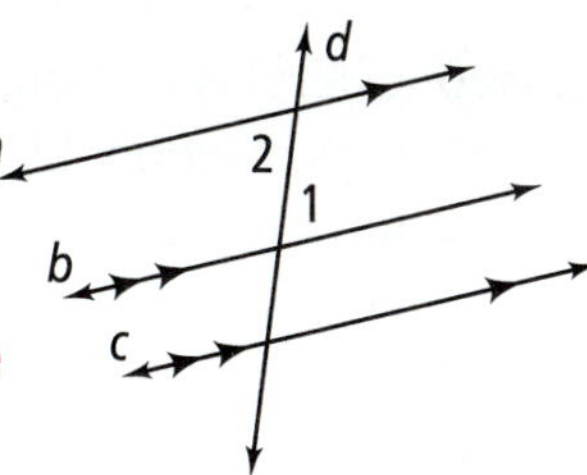

Given: $a \parallel c$; $b \parallel c$; $m\angle 2 = 65$

Prove: $m\angle 1 = 65$

Since $a \parallel c$ and $b \parallel c$, by the Transitive Property of Parallel Lines, $a \parallel b$. Since $\angle 1$ and the given angle are alternate interior angles, $m\angle 1 = 65$.

4. **Error Analysis** A classmate drew the cube at the right. He said that according to the Perpendicular Transversal Theorem, $\overline{AB} \parallel \overline{CD}$, since they are both perpendicular to $\overline{BC}$. Explain your classmate's error.

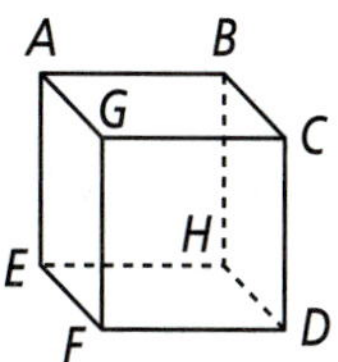

Theorem 3-8 states that the lines must be in the same plane. $\overline{AB}$ and $\overline{CD}$ are in different planes, so $\overline{AB}$ and $\overline{CD}$ are skew.

Name ______________________ Class ____________ Date ____________

3-4 Practice (continued)

Form K

Parallel and Perpendicular Lines

The following statements describe the rungs and posts that form the back of a chair. Assume that the rungs and posts all lie in a plane. Based only on the statements, make a conclusion about the rungs, one post, or both posts of the chair back. Explain.

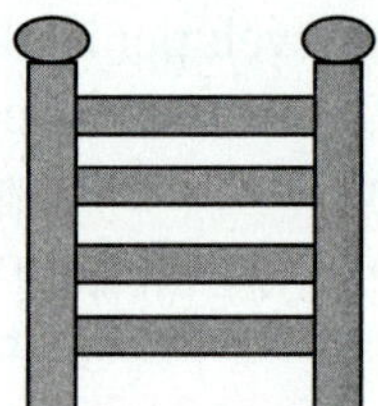

5. The rungs are parallel and the top one is perpendicular to the left post. **All the rungs are ⊥ to the left post; if a line is ⊥ to one of a set of ∥ lines, it is ⊥ to all the ∥ lines.**

6. The right post is perpendicular to all the rungs. **The rungs are all ∥; lines that are ⊥ to the same line are ∥.**

7. The rungs are parallel. The last rung is perpendicular to the right post and the first rung is perpendicular to the left post. **The rungs are ⊥ to both posts and the posts are ∥ to each other; if a line is ⊥ to one of a set of ∥ lines, it is ⊥ to all the ∥ lines.**

8. **Draw a Picture** Draw the map of a town to meet the conditions below. Based on the map, explain how each street is related to the other streets. Assume that all streets lie in a plane.
   - First Street is parallel Third Street.
   - Second Avenue is parallel to Third Street.
   - Third Street is perpendicular to Main Street.
   - Main Street is perpendicular to North Avenue.

   Check students' work; First St., Second Ave., Third St., and North Ave. ∥ to each other and ⊥ to Main St.

9. **Open-Ended** Cheryl is making a picture frame out of scraps of wood. List three pairs of values for x and y for which the sides of the frame will be parallel. Explain how you determined the values. **Answers may vary. Sample: 20 and 70, 30 and 60, 40 and 50; opposite sides are ∥ if adjacent sides are ⊥.**

10. **Reasoning** Lines a, b, c, and d are in the same plane. Line a is parallel to line c. Lines b and c are perpendicular to line d. Based on this, tell how the lines listed below are related. Justify your answers.

    a. lines a and b **$a \parallel b$; because b and c are both ⊥ to the same line, d, they are ∥ to each other. Because $a \parallel c$, by the Transitive Prop. of ∥ Lines, $a \parallel b$.**

    b. lines a and d **$a \perp d$; because $a \parallel b$ and c, and b and $c \perp d$, by the ⊥ Transversal Thm., $a \perp d$.**

Name ______________________ Class ____________ Date ____________

3-4 Standardized Test Prep

Parallel and Perpendicular Lines

Multiple Choice

For Exercises 1–5, choose the correct letter.

1. Which can be used to prove $d \perp t$? C

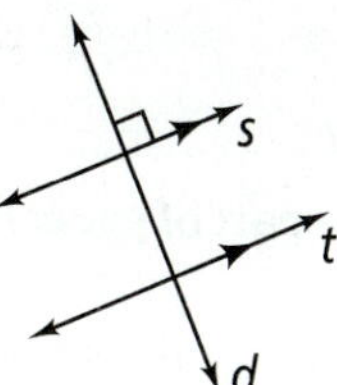

   (A) Transitive Property of Parallel Lines

   (B) Transitive Property of Congruence

   (C) Perpendicular Transversal Theorem

   (D) Converse of the Corresponding Angles Postulate

2. A carpenter is building a frame. Which values of a and b will ensure that the sides of the finished frame are parallel? H

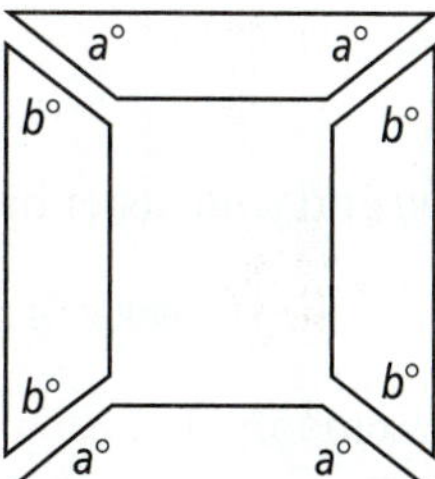

   (F) $a = 40$ and $b = 60$ (H) $a = 30$ and $b = 60$

   (G) $a = 45$ and $b = 50$ (I) $a = 40$ and $b = 40$

For Exercises 3 and 4, use the map at the right.

3. If Adam Ct. is perpendicular to Bertha Dr. and Charles St., what must be true? B

   (A) Adam Ct. $\perp$ Edward Rd. (C) Adam Ct. $\parallel$ Dana La.

   (B) Bertha Dr. $\parallel$ Charles St. (D) Dana La. $\perp$ Charles St.

4. Adam Ct. is perpendicular to Charles St. and Charles St. is parallel to Edward Rd. What must be true? F

   (F) Adam Ct. $\perp$ Edward Rd. (H) Bertha Dr. $\parallel$ Charles St.

   (G) Adam Ct. $\parallel$ Dana La. (I) Dana La. $\perp$ Charles St.

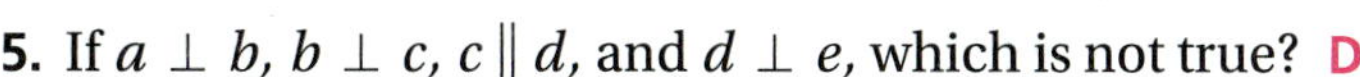

5. If $a \perp b$, $b \perp c$, $c \parallel d$, and $d \perp e$, which is not true? D

   (A) $a \perp e$ (C) $a \parallel d$

   (B) $a \parallel c$ (D) $b \parallel d$

Short Response

6. Write a paragraph proof.

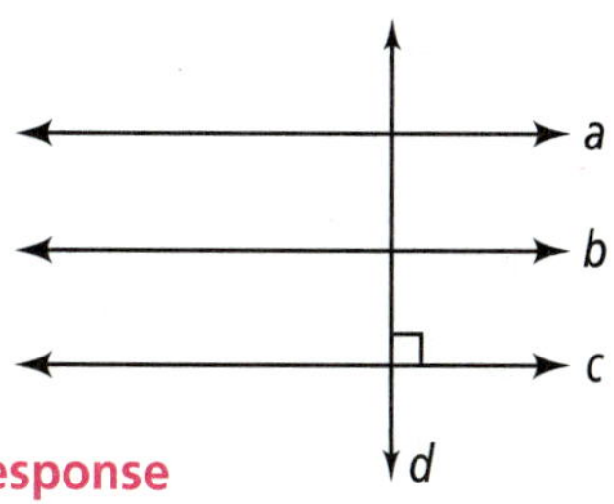

   Given: $a \parallel b$, $b \parallel c$, and $d \perp c$

   Prove: $a \perp d$

   [2] It is given that $a \parallel b$ and $b \parallel c$, so by the Transitive Property of Parallel Lines, $a \parallel c$. It is given that $d \perp c$. Then, by the Perpendicular Transversal Theorem, $a \perp d$.
   [1] one step incorrect or incomplete [0] incorrect or no response

3-5 Parallel Lines and Triangles

Vocabulary

Review

Identify the part of speech for the word *alternate* in each sentence below.

1. You vote for one winner and one *alternate*. noun

2. Your two friends *alternate* serves during tennis. verb

3. You and your sister babysit on *alternate* nights. adjective

4. Write the *converse* of the statement.

   Statement: If it is raining, then I need an umbrella.

   Converse: If I need an umbrella, then it is raining.

Vocabulary Builder

tri- (prefix) **try**

Related Word: triple

Main Idea: **Tri-** is a prefix meaning three that is used to form compound words.

Examples: triangle, tricycle, tripod

Use Your Vocabulary

Write T for *true* or F for *false*.

T **5.** A *tri*pod is a stand that has three legs.

F **6.** A *tri*angle is a polygon with three or more sides.

F **7.** A *tri*atholon is a race with two events — swimming and bicycling.

T **8.** In order to *tri*ple an amount, multiply it by three.

take note

Postulate 3-3 Parallel Postulate

Through a point not on a line, there is one and only one line parallel to the given line.

P

ℓ

9. You can draw **1** line(s) through P parallel to line ℓ.

take note

Theorem 3-10 Triangle Angle-Sum Theorem

The sum of the measures of the angles of a triangle is 180.

Find each angle measure.

10.

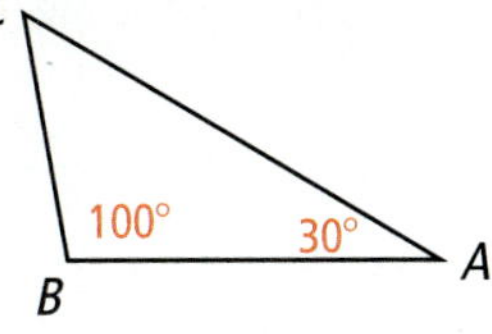

$m\angle C =$ **50**

11.

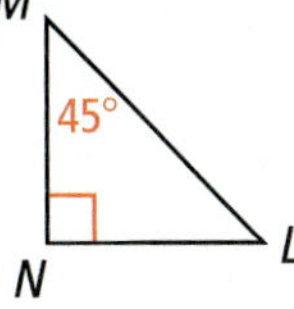

$m\angle L =$ **45**

Problem 1 Using the Triangle Angle-Sum Theorem

Got It? **Use the diagram at the right. What is the value of z?**

B, 43°, 49°, A, x°, y°, z°, C, 59°, D

Complete each statement.

12. $m\angle A =$ **59**

13. $m\angle ABC =$ **43** + **49** = **92**

14. $m\angle A + m\angle ABC + m\angle C =$ **180**

59 + **92** + z = **180**

$z =$ **180** − **59** − **92** = **29**

Check your result by solving for z another way.

15. Find $m\angle BDA$.

$m\angle A + m\angle ABD + m\angle BDA = 180$
$59 + 43 + x = 180$
$x = 180 - 102$
$= 78$

16. Then find $m\angle BDC$.

$m\angle BDA + m\angle BDC = 180$
$x + y = 180$
$y = 180 - 78$
$= 102$

17. Use your answers to Exercises 15 and 16 to find the value of z.

$z + m\angle CBD + m\angle BDC = 180$
$z + 49 + 102 = 180$
$z = 180 - (49 + 102) = 29$

take note

Theorem 3-11 Triangle Exterior Angle Theorem

An **exterior angle of a polygon** is an angle formed by a side and an extension of an adjacent side. For each exterior angle of a triangle, the two nonadjacent interior angles are its **remote interior angles.**

The measure of each exterior angle of a triangle equals the sum of the measures of its two remote interior angles.

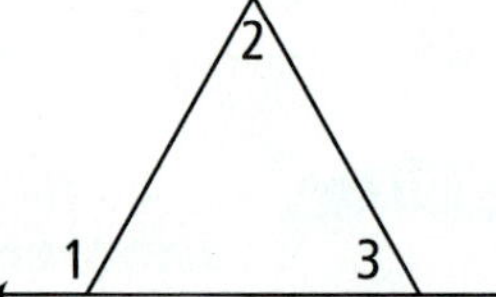

18. $m\angle 1 = m\angle 2 + m\angle 3$

Circle the number of each exterior angle and draw a box around the number of each remote interior angle.

19.

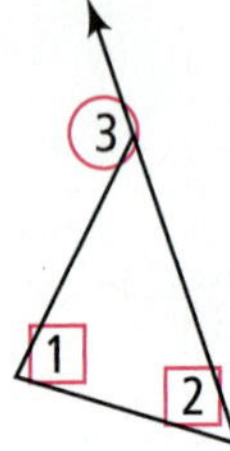

20.

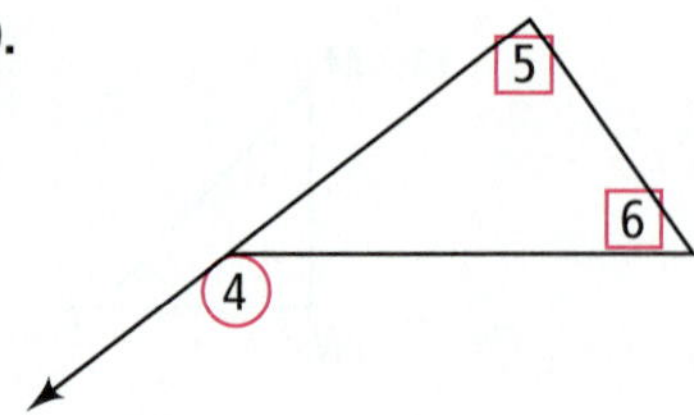

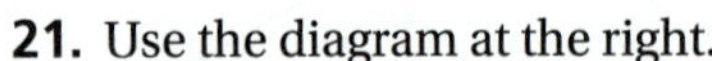

Problem 2 Using the Triangle Exterior Angle Theorem

Got It? Two angles of a triangle measure 53. What is the measure of an exterior angle at each vertex of the triangle?

21. Use the diagram at the right.

Label the interior angles 53°, 53°, and *a*.

Label the exterior angles adjacent to the 53° angles as *x* and *y*. Label the third exterior angle *z*.

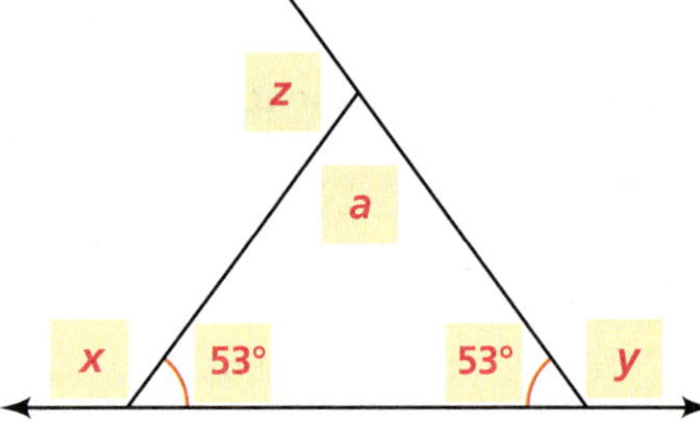

22. Complete the flow chart.

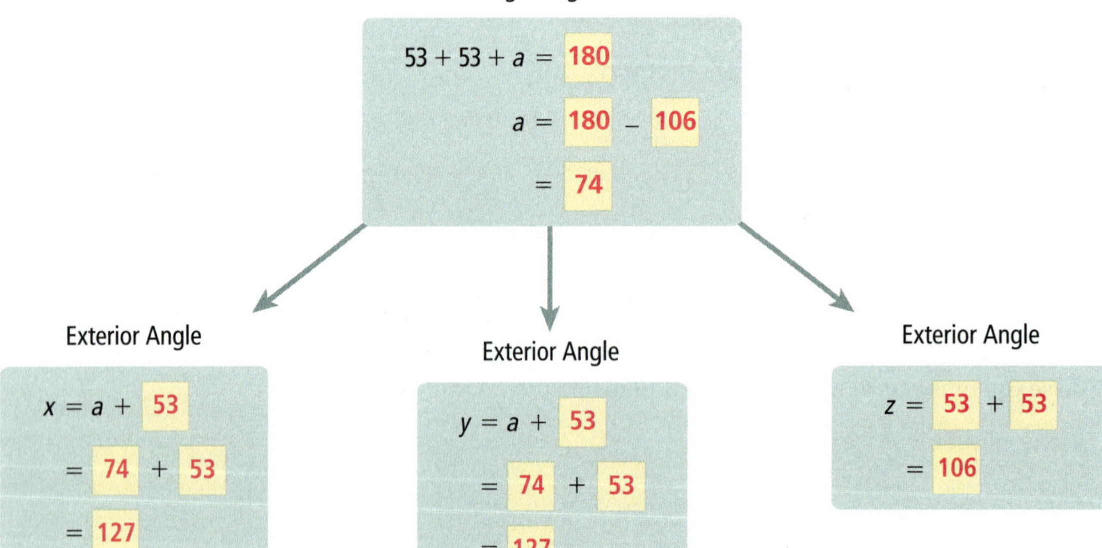

Problem 3 Applying the Triangle Theorems

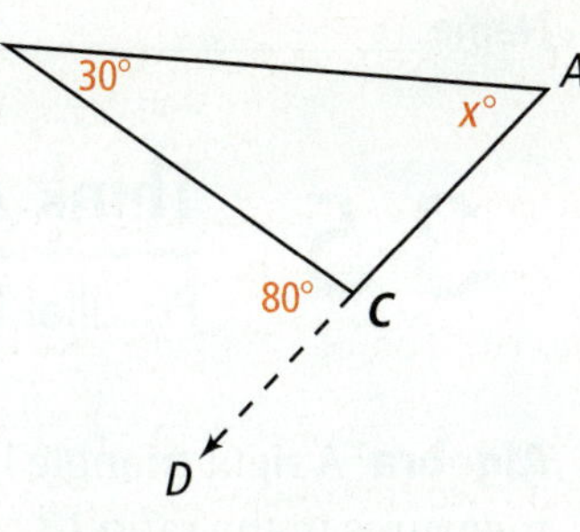

Got It? Reasoning Can you find $m\angle A$ without using the Triangle Exterior Angle Theorem? Explain.

23. $\angle ACB$ and $\angle DCB$ are complementary / <u>supplementary</u> angles.

24. Find $m\angle ACB$.

$180 - 80 = 100$

25. Can you find $m\angle A$ if you know two of the angle measures? Explain. Explanations may vary. Sample:

Yes. Use the Triangle Angle-Sum Theorem. $m\angle A = 180 - 100 - 30 = 50$

Lesson Check • Do you UNDERSTAND?

Explain how the Triangle Exterior Angle Theorem makes sense based on the Triangle Angle-Sum Theorem.

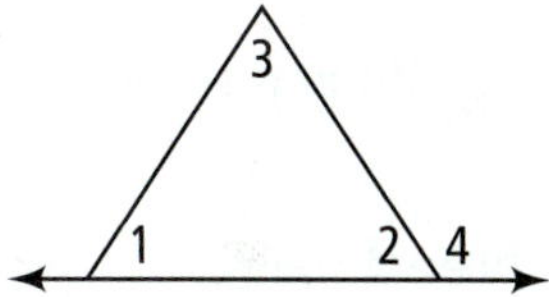

26. Use the triangle at the right to complete the diagram below.

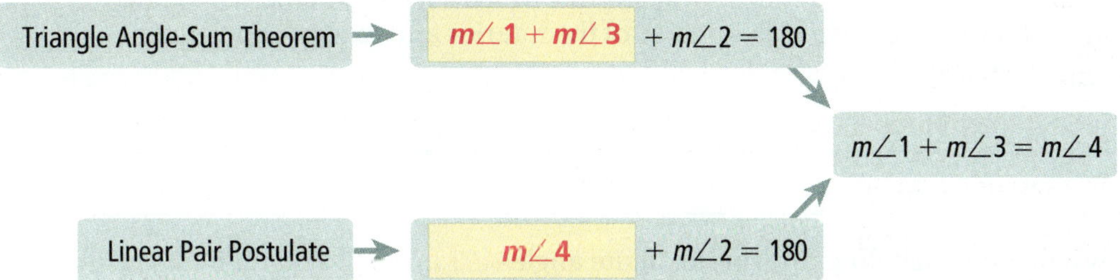

27. Explain how the Triangle Exterior Angle Theorem makes sense based on the Triangle Angle-Sum Theorem. Answers may vary. Sample:

Using the Triangle Angle-Sum Theorem, $180 - m\angle 2 = m\angle 1 + m\angle 3$. Since a linear pair is supplementary, $180 - m\angle 2 = m\angle 4$. Then by the Transitive Property, $m\angle 4 = m\angle 1 + m\angle 3$.

Math Success

Check off the vocabulary words that you understand.

☐ exterior angle ☐ remote interior angles

Rate how well you can *use the triangle theorems.*

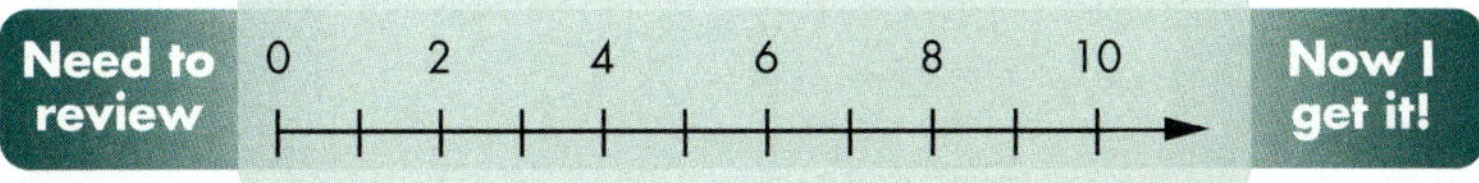

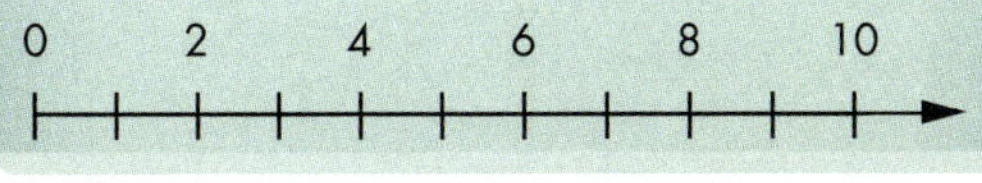

Name ______________________ Class ____________ Date ____________

3-5 Think About a Plan

Parallel Lines and Triangles

Algebra A right triangle has exterior angles at each of its acute angles with measures in the ratio 13 : 14. Find the measures of the two acute angles of the right triangle.

Know

1. What is the sum of all the interior angles in a right triangle? **180**
2. One angle in a right triangle measures 90. What is the sum of the other two angles? **90**
3. What is the sum of an interior angle and its adjacent exterior angle? **180**

Need

4. What strategy can you use to keep track of the interior and exterior angles of the triangle?

Sample: A diagram will help me keep track of the relationships between angles and what is already known.

5. Draw a diagram, labeling the interior acute angles $\angle 1$ and $\angle 2$ and their corresponding exterior angles $\angle 3$ and $\angle 4$.

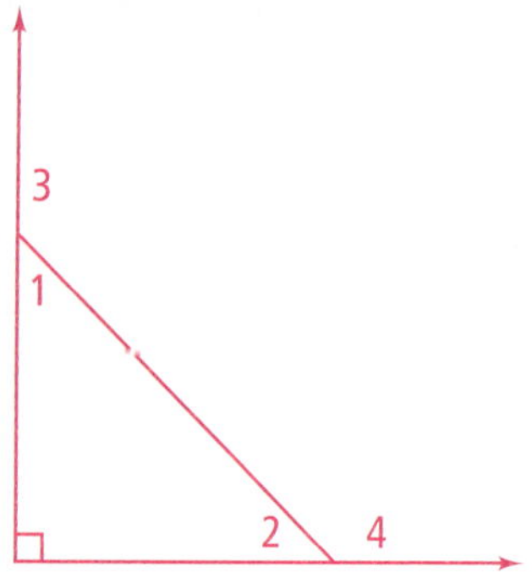

Plan

6. Use what you know to find the following sums:
   a. $m\angle 1 + m\angle 2 + m\angle 3 + m\angle 4$ **360**
   b. $m\angle 3 + m\angle 4$ **270**
7. The ratio of $m\angle 3$ to $m\angle 4$ is 13 : 14. Use this to find the measures of $\angle 3$ and $\angle 4$. Explain your work.

130; 140; Sample: I used the ratio to set up proportions: $\frac{m\angle 3}{13} = \frac{270}{13 + 14}$ **and** $\frac{m\angle 4}{14} = \frac{270}{13 + 14}$.

8. How can you use $m\angle 3$ and $m\angle 4$ to find the measures of the interior angles? What are the interior angle measures?

50; 40; Sample: I subtracted the measure of the corresponding exterior angle from 180.

Name ______________________ Class ____________ Date ____________

3-5 Practice

Form K

Parallel Lines and Triangles

Find $m\angle 1$.

1. 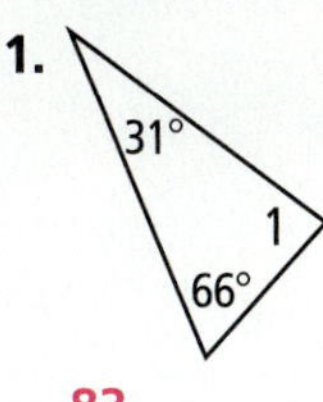

83

2. 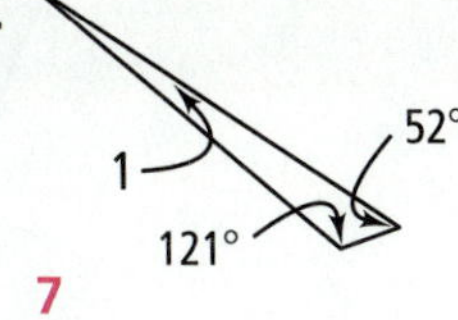

7

3. 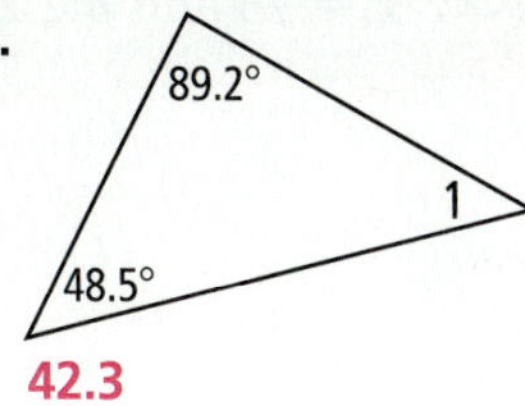

42.3

Algebra **Find the value of each variable.**

4. 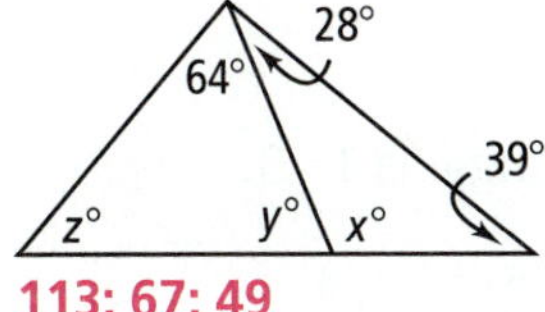

113; 67; 49

5. 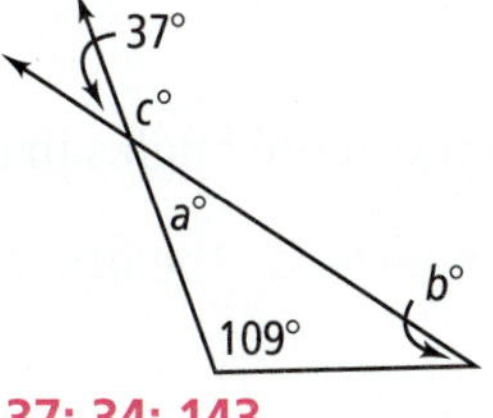

37; 34; 143

6. 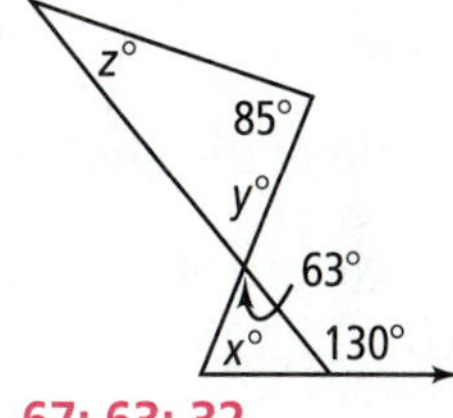

67; 63; 32

7. a. Which of the numbered angles are exterior angles?
$\angle 4$, $\angle 6$, $\angle 8$, and $\angle 10$

b. Name the remote interior angles for each exterior angle.
$\angle 4$: $\angle 2$ and $\angle 3$; $\angle 6$: $\angle 2$ and $\angle 3$; $\angle 8$: $\angle 1$ and $\angle 2$; $\angle 10$: $\angle 1$ and $\angle 3$

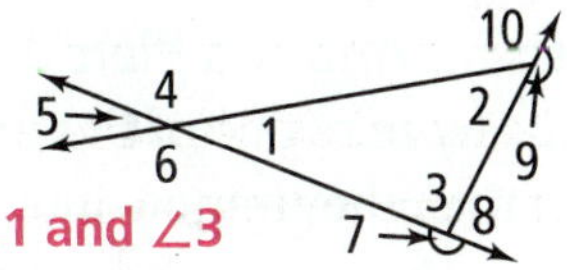

c. Which two exterior angles share the same remote interior angles? Explain.
$\angle 4$ and $\angle 6$ share the same remote interior angles because $\angle 4$ and $\angle 6$ are vertical angles.

Algebra **Find each missing angle measure.**

8. 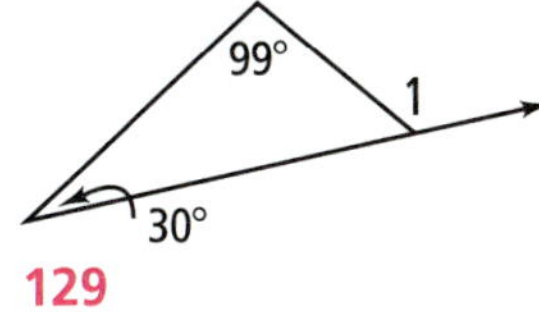

129

9. 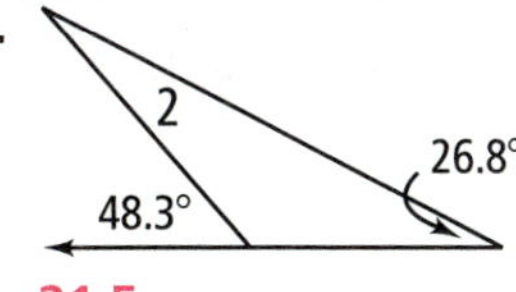

21.5

10. 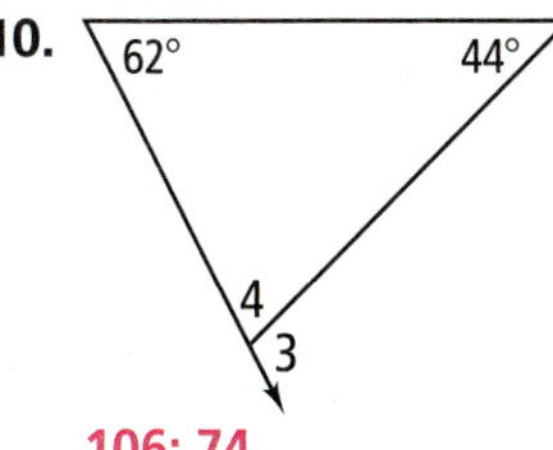

106; 74

11. What are the values of x and y in the right triangle?
124; 56

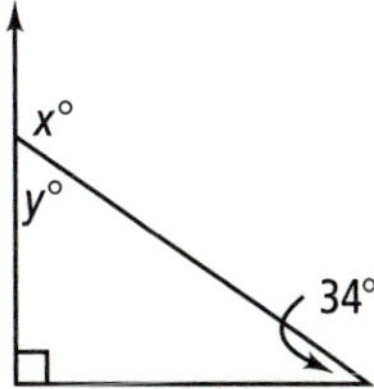

Name ______________________ Class ____________ Date ____________

3-5 Practice (continued) *Form K*

Parallel Lines and Triangles

12. A tabletop easel has different angle settings.
If $m\angle 1 = 75$ and $m\angle 2 = 40$, what is $m\angle 4$?
145

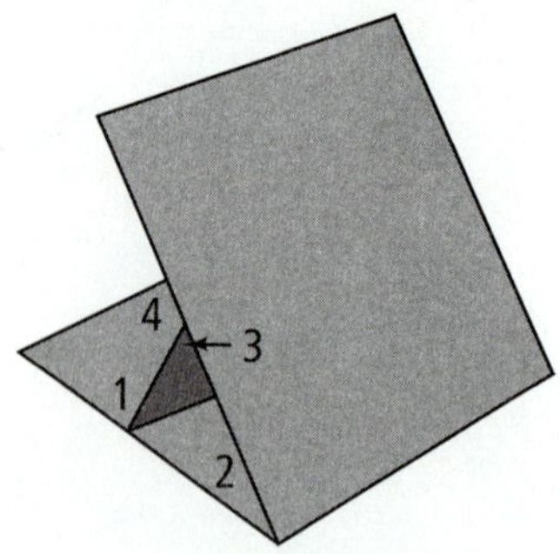

Algebra Use the given information to find the unknown angle measures in the triangle.

13. The ratio of the angle measures of the acute angles in a right triangle is 1 : 3.
22.5 and 67.5
14. The measure of one angle of a triangle is 61. The other two angles are in a ratio of 2 : 5.
34 and 85
15. The measure of the exterior angle of a triangle is 110. The measures of its remote interior angles are in a ratio of 2 : 3.
44 and 66
16. **Think About a Plan** The measure of an exterior angle of $\triangle DEF$ is $4x$. The measure of one of this angle's remote interior angles is $x + 23$. The measure of the other remote interior angle is $2x + 12$. Find the value of x, the measure of each angle of the triangle, and the measure of the exterior angle.
35; interior angles: 58, 82, and 40; exterior angle: 140
    - How can drawing a picture help you find the answers?
    A drawing can help you see how the various angles relate to each other.
    - How are the exterior angle and the third angle of the triangle related?
    They are a linear pair, so they are supplementary.

Find the values of the variables and the measures of the angles.

17. 13; 39 and 51

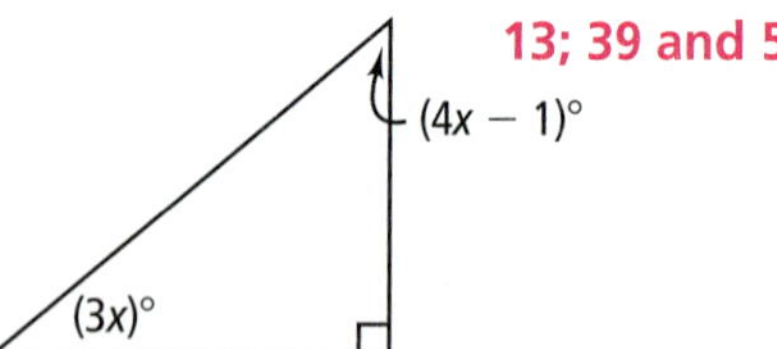

18. 21; 21, 23, and 136

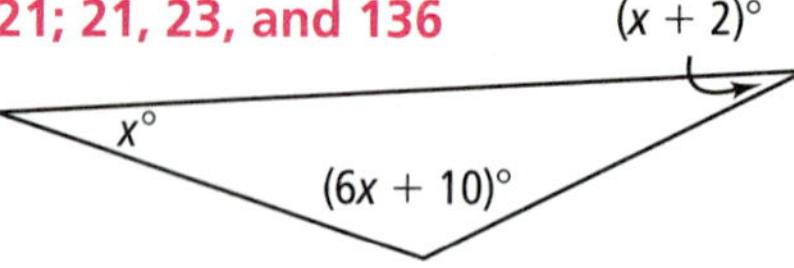

19. 29; 29; 61

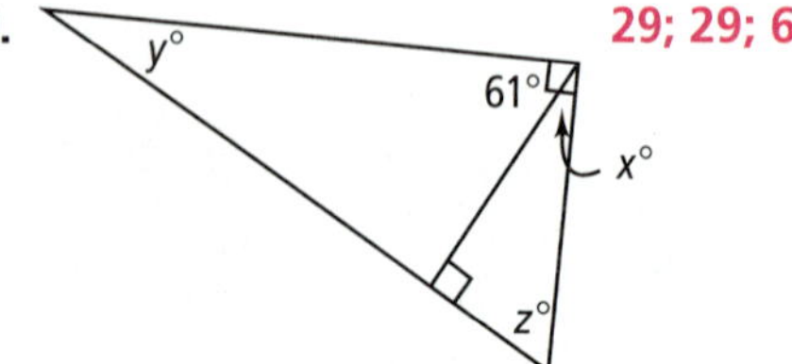

20. 52; 25; 90

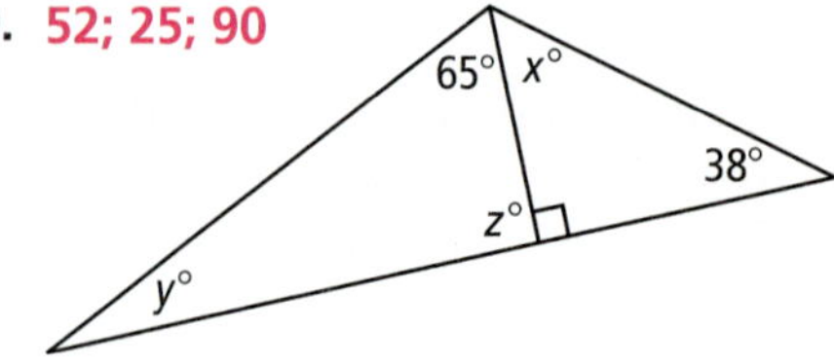

Name ______________________ Class __________ Date __________

3-5 Standardized Test Prep

Parallel Lines and Triangles

Gridded Response

1. What is the value of w?

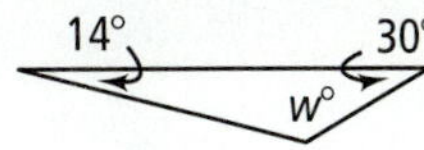

2. What is the value of z?

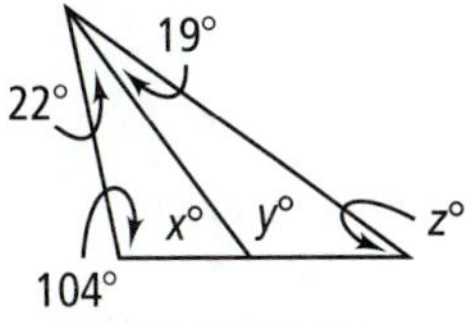

3. What is the value of s?

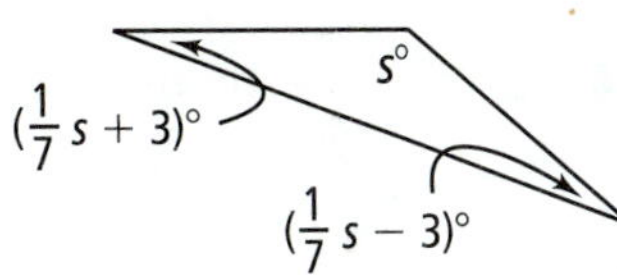

4. What is the value of e?

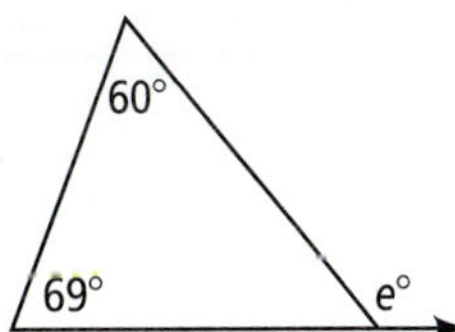

5. What is the value of t on the truss of the bridge?

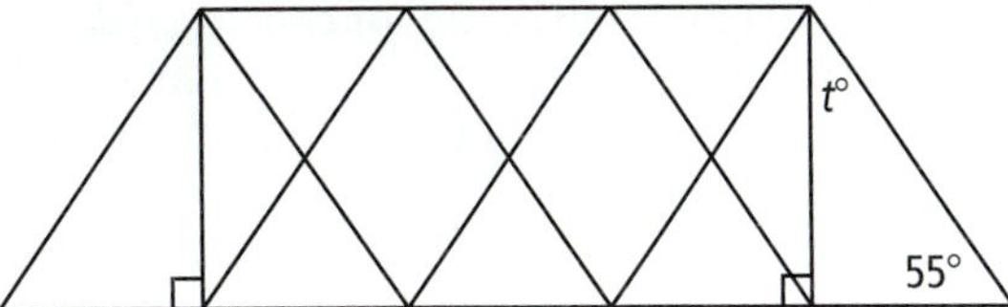

Answers

1. 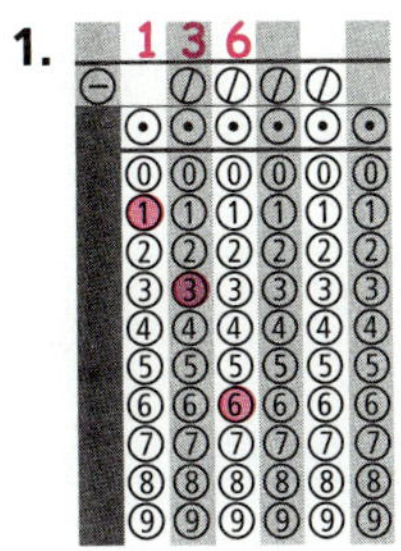

2. 

3. 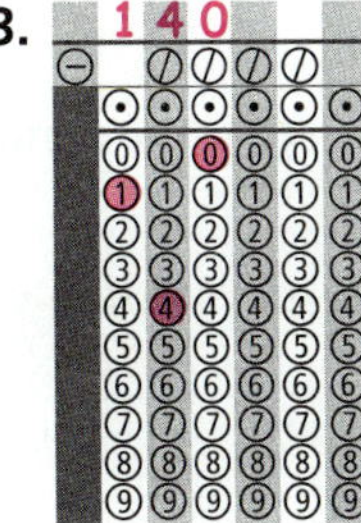

4. 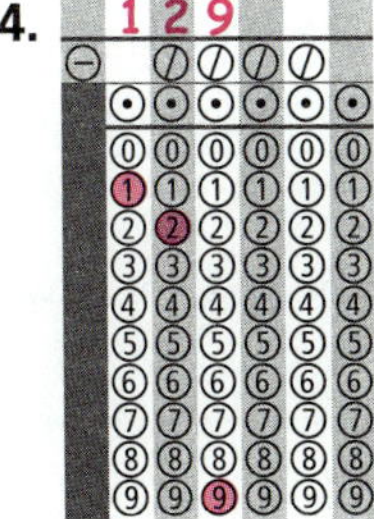

5. 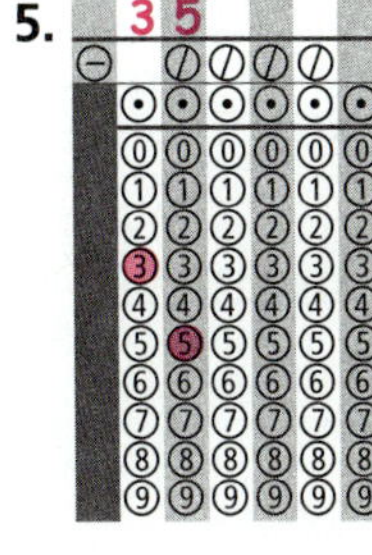

3-6 PART 1 Constructing Parallel and Perpendicular Lines

Vocabulary

Review

Write T for *true* or F for *false*.

T 1. A rectangle has two pairs of *parallel* sides.

F 2. A rectangle has two pairs of *perpendicular* sides.

Write *alternate exterior, alternate interior,* or *corresponding* to describe each angle pair.

3. 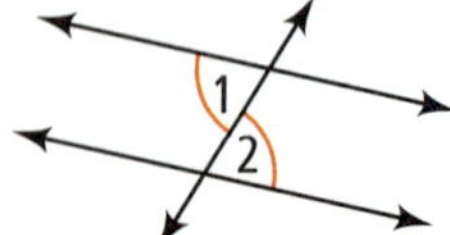

alternate interior

4. 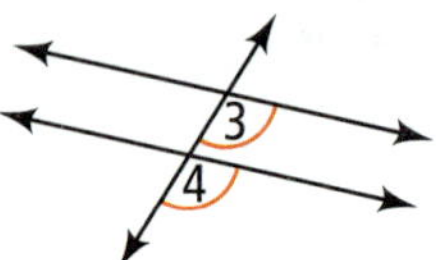

corresponding

5. 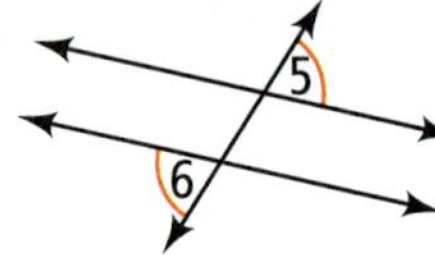

alternate exterior

Vocabulary Builder

construction (noun) **kun STRUCK shun**

Other Word Forms: construct (verb), constructive (adjective)

Main Idea: **Construction** means how something is built or *constructed.*

Math Usage: A **construction** is a geometric figure drawn using a straightedge and a compass.

Use Your Vocabulary

6. Complete each statement with the correct form of the word *construction*.

VERB	You _?_ sand castles at the beach.	construct
NOUN	The _?_ on the highway caused quite a traffic jam.	construction
ADJECTIVE	The time you spent working on your homework was _?_.	constructive

Problem 1 Constructing Parallel Lines

Got It? Reasoning **The diagram below shows the construction of line *m* through point *N* with line *m* parallel to line ℓ. Why must lines ℓ and *m* be parallel?**

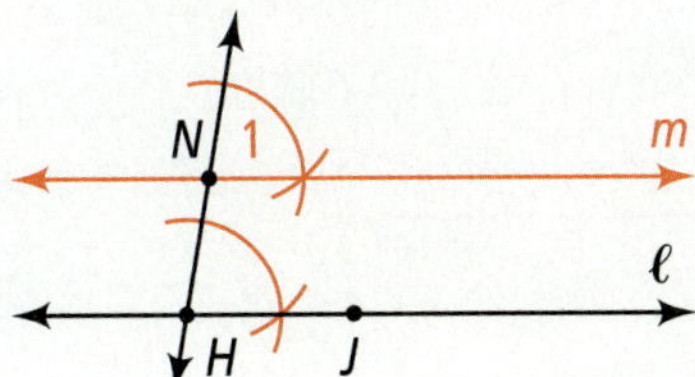

7. The diagram shows the construction of congruent angles 1 and *NHJ*.

8. Circle the description(s) of the angle pairs that were constructed.

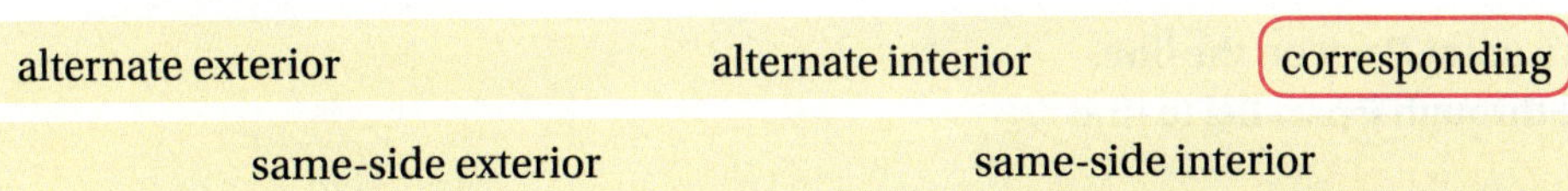

alternate exterior | alternate interior | **(corresponding)**

same-side exterior | same-side interior

9. Are the angle pairs *congruent* or *supplementary*? **(congruent)** / supplementary

10. Now explain why lines ℓ and *m* must be parallel. **Explanations may vary. Sample:**

You constructed the transversal to form congruent corresponding angles with lines ℓ and *m*, so ℓ ∥ *m* by the Converse of the Corresponding Angles Postulate.

Problem 2 Constructing a Special Quadrilateral

Got It? **Draw a segment. Label its length *m*. Construct quadrilateral *ABCD* with $\overleftrightarrow{AB} \parallel \overleftrightarrow{CD}$, so that $AB = m$ and $CD = 2m$.**

Underline the correct word or symbol to complete each step.

11. You need to construct <u>parallel</u> / perpendicular lines by constructing congruent alernate interior / <u>corresponding</u> angles.

12. Draw $\overleftrightarrow{AB}$. Draw point *D* not on $\overleftrightarrow{AB}$. Draw $\overleftrightarrow{AD}$. The length of <u>$\overline{AB}$</u> / $\overline{AD}$ is *m*.

13. At *D*, construct ∠*TDZ* perpendicular / <u>congruent</u> to ∠*DAB* so that ∠*TDZ* and ∠*DAB* are corresponding angles. Then $\overleftrightarrow{DZ} \parallel \overleftrightarrow{AB}$.

14. Now, you need a side of length $2m$. Construct *C* on $\overleftrightarrow{DZ}$ so that $DC = 2m$. Draw <u>$\overline{BC}$</u> / $\overline{BA}$.

15. Do the construction below.

Lesson Check • Do you know HOW?

Draw a line ℓ and a point *P* not on the line. Construct the line through *P* parallel to line ℓ.

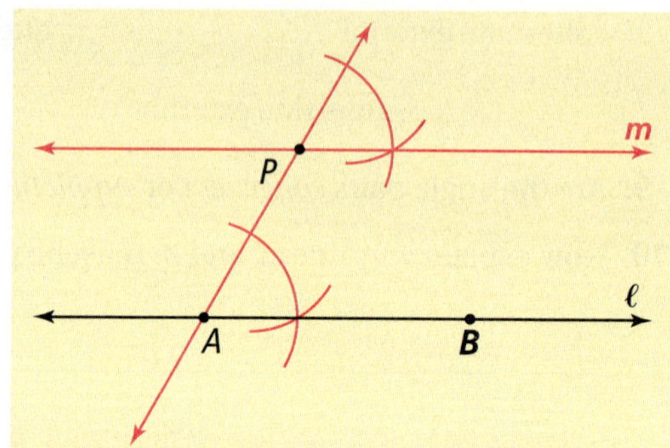

16. Line ℓ and point *P* not on the line are drawn for you. Draw $\overleftrightarrow{AP}$.

Complete each statement below and construct line *m*.

17. At *P*, construct a corresponding angle congruent to $\angle$ PAB.

18. Label the new line *m*. Line *m* is parallel to line ℓ by the _?_ Theorem.

Converse of the Corresponding Angles

Lesson Check • Do you know HOW?

Look at the diagram. What is the next step in the construction of parallel lines?

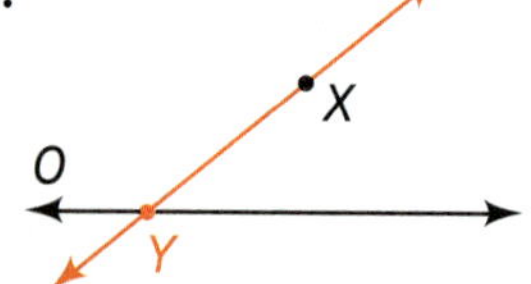

19. The steps to construct parallel lines are listed below. Place a ✔ next to each step that is already completed. Place an ✘ next to each step that has not been completed.

✔ Draw a line and a point *X* not on the line.

✔ Label point *Y* on the line.

✔ Draw $\overleftrightarrow{XY}$.

✘ At *X*, construct a corresponding angle congruent to $\angle Y$.

20. What is the next step in the construction of parallel lines?

At X, construct an angle congruent to $\angle Y$.

3-6
PART 2

Constructing Parallel and Perpendicular Lines

Vocabulary

Review

Underline the correct word to complete each sentence.

1. A polygon cannot have *parallel* / *skew* sides.
2. *Parallel* / *Skew* lines are noncoplanar.
3. A transversal intersecting two *parallel* / *skew* lines forms pairs of congruent angles.

Use the diagram at the right for Exercises 4–9. Write *parallel* or *skew* to describe each pair of segments.

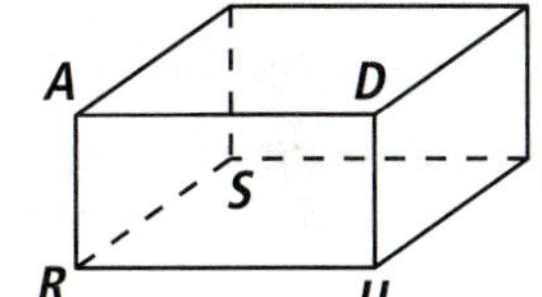

4. $\overline{BC}$ and $\overline{UT}$

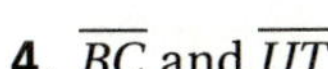

skew

5. $\overline{BC}$ and $\overline{AD}$

parallel

6. $\overline{BC}$ and $\overline{RU}$

parallel

7. $\overline{RS}$ and $\overline{UT}$

parallel

8. $\overline{RS}$ and $\overline{AD}$

skew

9. $\overline{RS}$ and $\overline{BC}$

skew

Vocabulary Builder

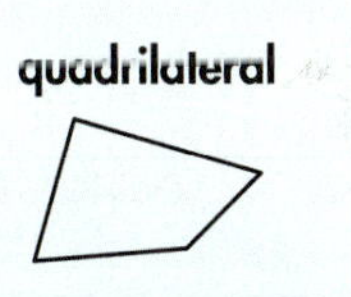

quadrilateral (noun) **kwah drih LAT ur ul**

Definition: A **quadrilateral** is a polygon with four sides and four angles.

Examples: rectangle, square, parallelogram, trapezoid

Non-Examples: triangle, octagon, circle, hexagon

Use Your Vocabulary

10. Circle the *quadrilateral(s)*.

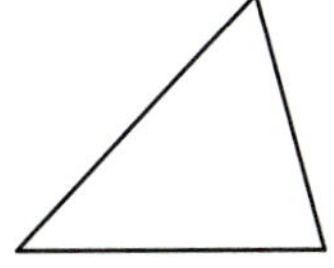

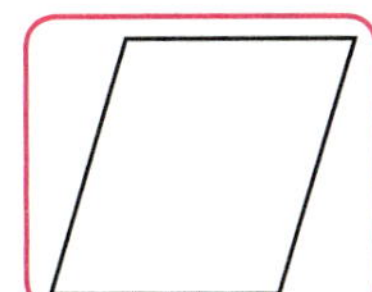

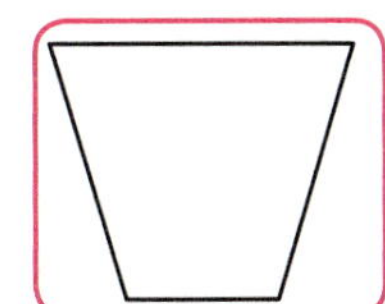

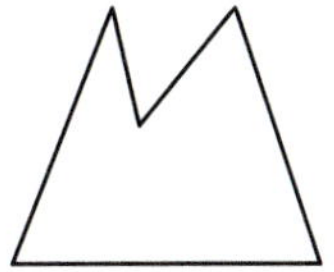

Problem 3 Perpendicular at a Point on a Line

Got It? Use a straightedge to draw $\overleftrightarrow{EF}$. Construct $\overleftrightarrow{FG}$ so that $\overleftrightarrow{FG} \perp \overleftrightarrow{EF}$ at point F.

11. Use the diagram at the right. Write each construction step.

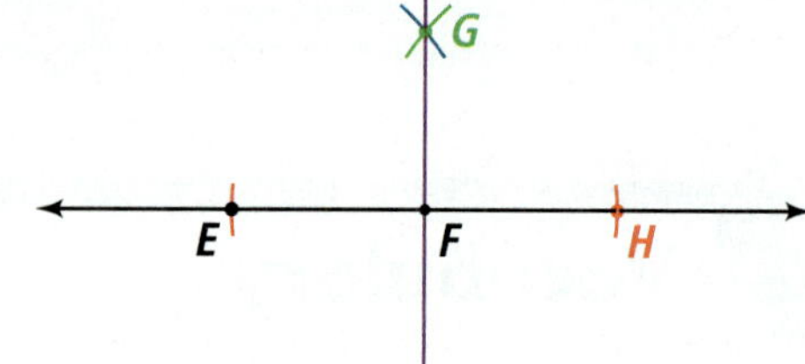

Step 1 Draw a line. Label points *E* and *F*.

Step 2 Make the compass opening *EF*. With the compass tip on point *F*, draw an arc that intersects the line twice. Mark point *H* so *EF* = *FH*.

Step 3 Make the compass opening greater than $\frac{1}{2}$ *EH*. With the compass tip on *E*, draw an arc above point *F*.

Step 4 Without changing the compass setting, place the compass tip on point *H*. Draw an arc that intersects the arc from Step 3. Label the point of intersection *G*.

Step 5 Draw $\overleftrightarrow{FG}$.

take note — Postulate 3-4 Perpendicular Postulate

Complete the statement of Postulate 3-4 below.

12. Through a point not on a line, there is one and only one line parallel / perpendicular to the given line.

13. Circle the diagram that models Postulate 3-4.

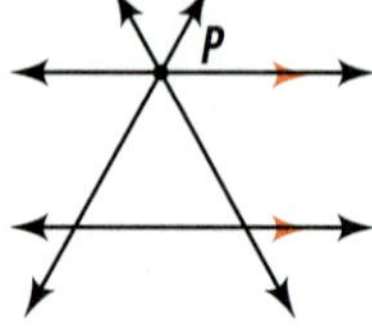

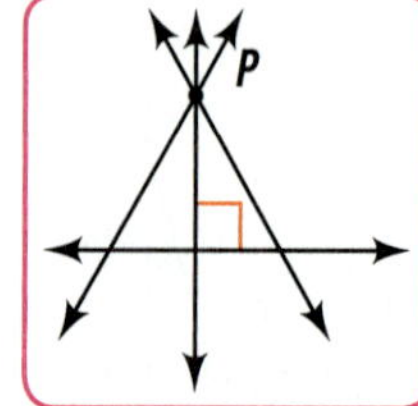

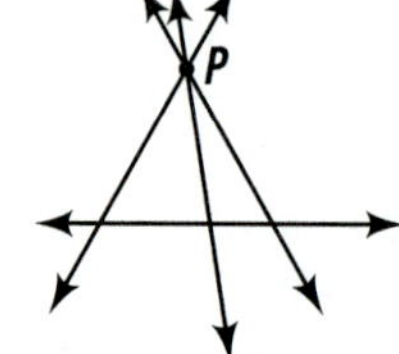

Problem 4 Perpendicular From a Point to a Line

Got It? **Draw $\overleftrightarrow{CX}$ and a point Z not on $\overleftrightarrow{CX}$. Construct $\overleftrightarrow{ZB}$ so that $\overleftrightarrow{ZB} \perp \overleftrightarrow{CX}$.**

Underline the correct word(s) to complete each sentence.

14. Open your compass to a size equal to / greater than the distance from Z to line ℓ.

15. With the compass tip on point Z, draw an arc that intersects line ℓ at one / two point(s).

16. Label the point(s) C and X / Z.

17. Place the compass point on C / Z and make an arc below line ℓ.

18. With the same opening and the compass tip on C / X, draw an arc that intersects the arc you made in Exercise 17. Label the point of intersection B.

19. Draw $\overleftrightarrow{ZB}$ / $\overleftrightarrow{CX}$.

20. Now construct a line through point Z perpendicular to line ℓ.

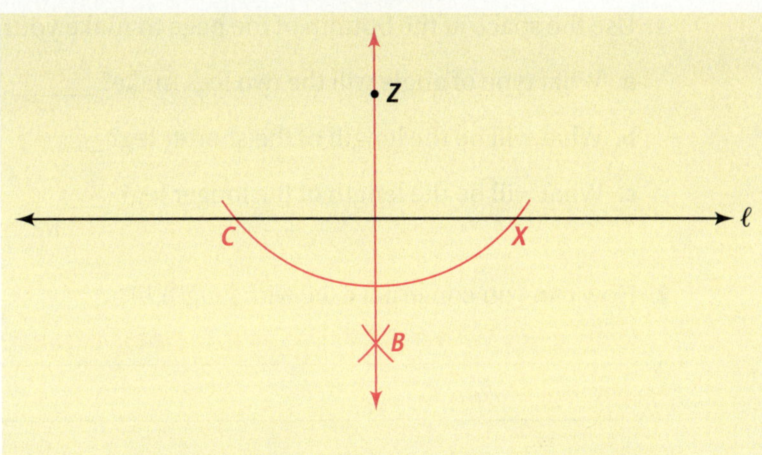

Lesson Check • Do you UNDERSTAND?

In constructing the perpendicular to $\overleftrightarrow{AB}$ at point P, is $\overline{AC}$ congruent to $\overline{BC}$? Explain.

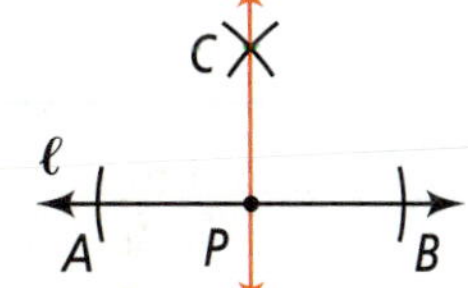

21. Are the arcs at point C made with different compass openings? Yes / No

22. Is $\overline{AC}$ congruent to $\overline{BC}$? Explain. Explanations may vary. Sample:

Yes. The same compass opening made the arcs at C, so $AC = BC$ and segments with equal length are congruent.

Math Success

Check off the vocabulary words that you understand.

☐ construction ☐ parallel ☐ perpendicular

Rate how well you can *construct parallel and perpendicular lines.*

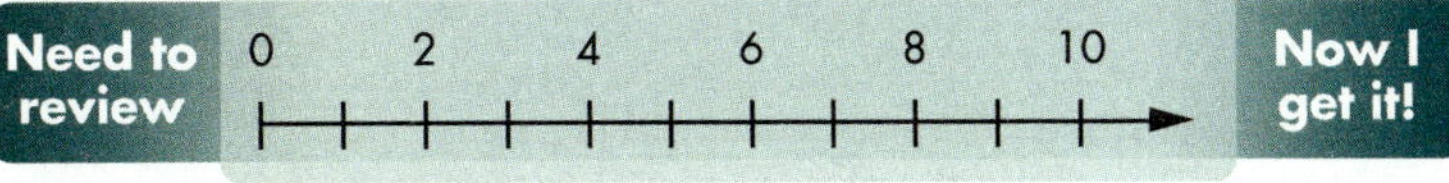

Name ______________________ Class ____________ Date ____________

3-6 Think About a Plan

Constructing Parallel and Perpendicular Lines

Construct a right triangle with legs of lengths *a* and *b*.

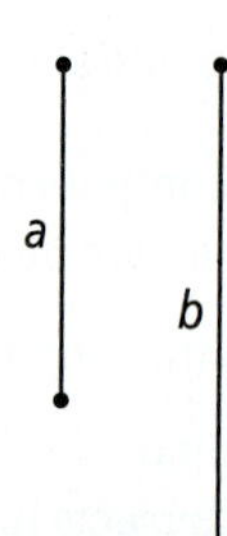

1. Use the space at the bottom of the page to make your construction.

a. What type of angle will the two legs make? right

b. What will be the length of the shorter leg? *a*

c. What will be the length of the longer leg? *b*

2. How can you construct a leg with length *b*?

Draw a line with point *X*. Use your compass to mark a point on the line that is a distance *b* from *X*.

3. How can you construct a perpendicular at one end of leg *b*? Construct leg *b* and its perpendicular according to your plan.

Use your compass to mark points *V* and *Z* on either side of *X* that are of equal distance from *X*. Open your compass to a size greater than the distance to *X*. With the compass at point *V*, draw an arc above point *X*. Without changing the compass setting, draw a similar arc from point *Z*. Draw point *W* at the place where the arcs intersect. $\overleftrightarrow{XW}$ is perpendicular to $\overleftrightarrow{XZ}$.

4. What steps do you still need to complete to finish constructing the triangle?

Mark a point on the perpendicular such that the leg's length equals *a*. Connect the distant ends of the legs.

5. Complete the construction. Check your triangle to make sure it is drawn correctly.

a. Is it a right triangle? yes

b. What is the shorter leg length? *a*

c. What is the longer leg length? *b*

Possible response:

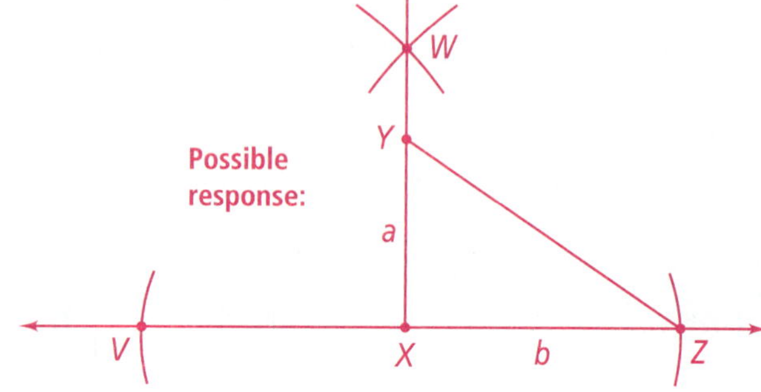

Name ______________________ Class ____________ Date ____________

3-6 Practice

Form K

Constructing Parallel and Perpendicular Lines

For Exercises 1–3, construct the line through point *D* that is parallel to $\overleftrightarrow{ST}$.

1. 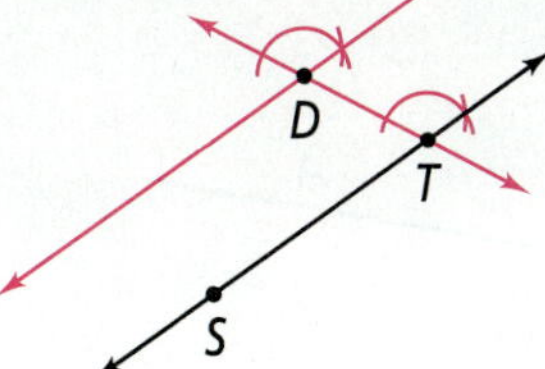

To start, draw $\overleftrightarrow{DT}$.

2. 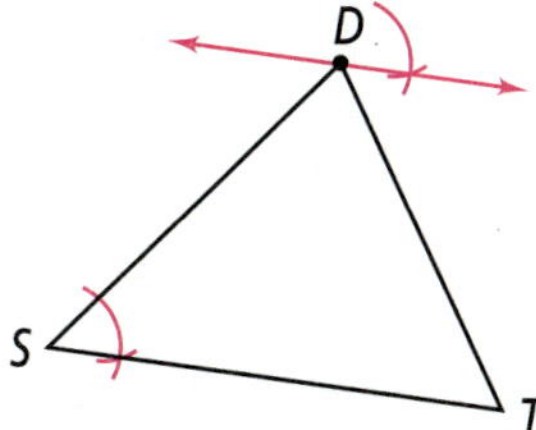

3. 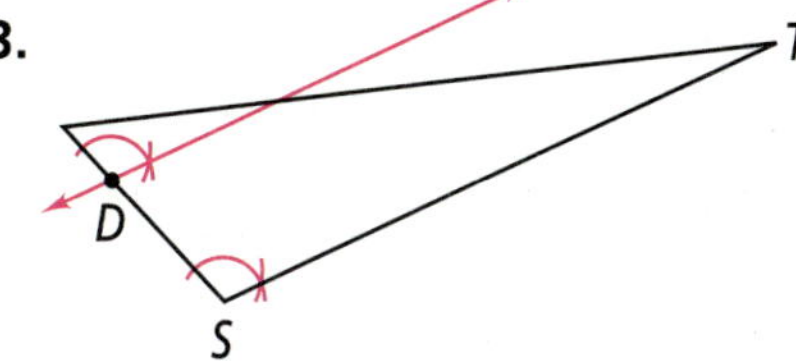

4. Use the two segments at the right. Complete the construction of quadrilateral *ABYZ* with one pair of parallel sides as described. Parallel lines have been constructed for you in the diagram at the right.

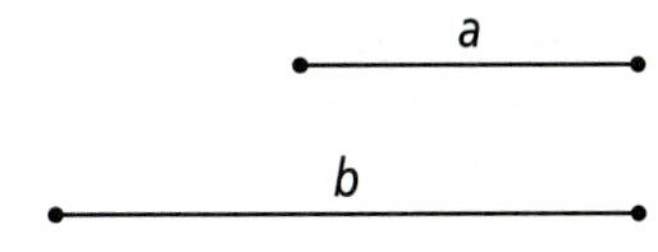

   a. Use your compass to find point *Z* at a distance *b* from *A* and point *Y* at a distance *a* from *B*.

   b. Connect *Y* and *Z* to complete quadrilateral *ABYZ*.

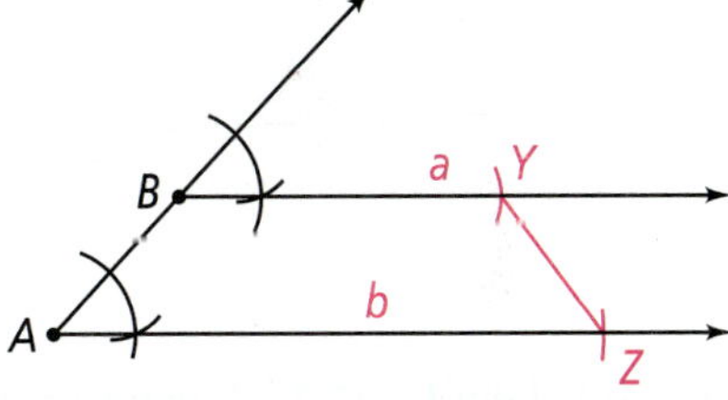

5. **Reasoning** A classmate constructs the parallel lines shown at the right. Is your classmate's method of construction accurate? Explain.
Yes; explanations may vary. Sample: Instead of constructing ≅ corresp. ∠s, the classmate has constructed ≅ alt. ext. ∠s.

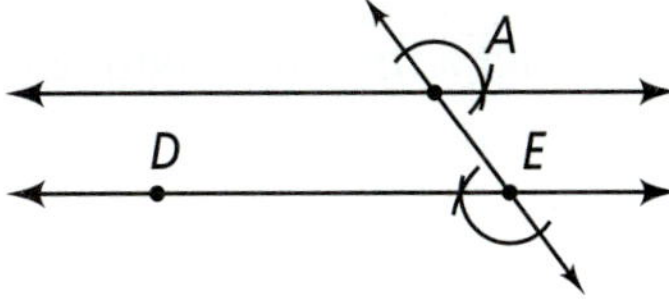

6. **Writing** Look at the diagram. What are the remaining steps in the construction of quadrilateral *ABCD* where $AB = x$ and $CD = 2x$? **Answers may vary. Sample: Place your compass point on *A* and draw an arc. Label *B* where the arc intersects the horizontal line. Keeping the same compass setting, place the compass point on *D* and draw an arc. Label point *R* where the arc intersects the horizontal line. Keeping the same compass setting, place the compass on point *R* and draw an arc. Label point C where the arc intersects the line. Draw $\overline{BC}$.**

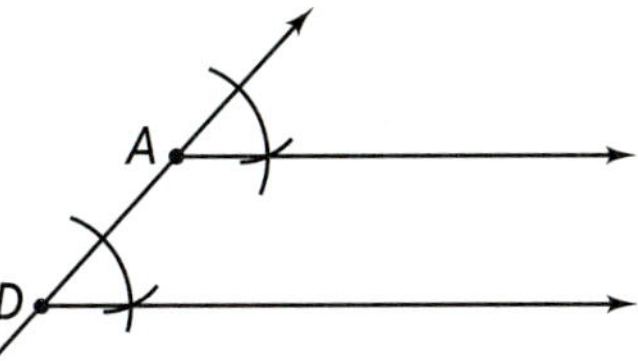

Name ______________________ Class ____________ Date ____________

3-6 Practice (continued) — Form K

Constructing Parallel and Perpendicular Lines

For Exercises 7 and 8, construct the line that is perpendicular to ℓ at point A.

7.

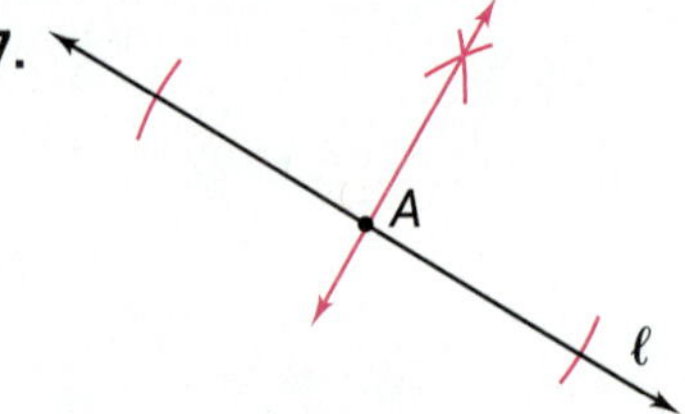

8.

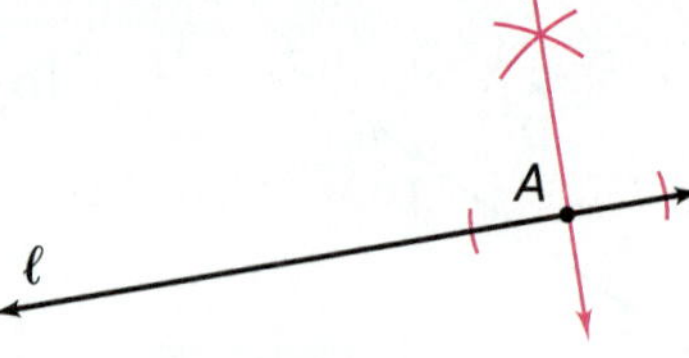

For Exercises 9 and 10, construct the line through point R that is perpendicular to $\overleftrightarrow{AB}$.

9.

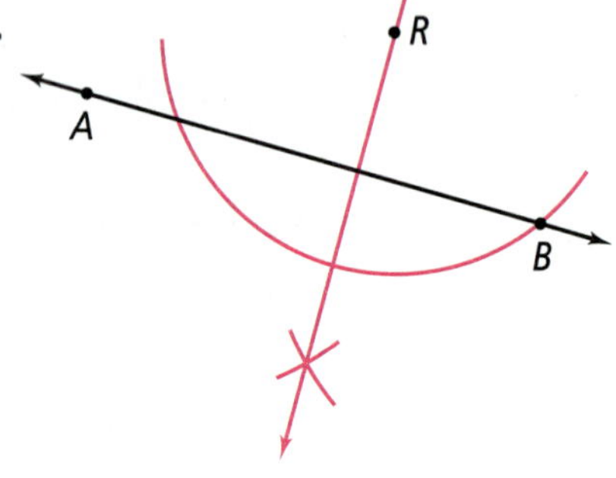

10.

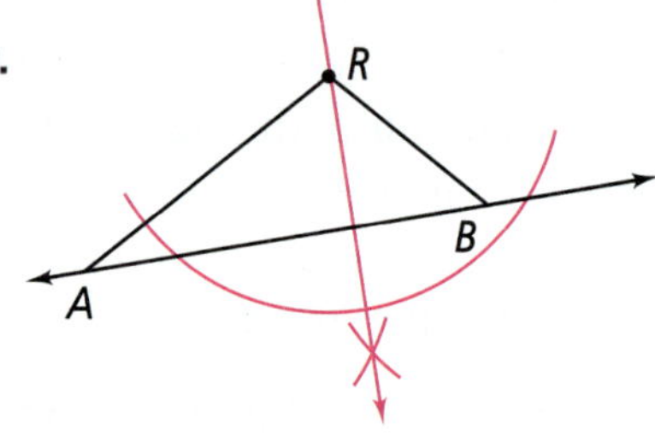

For Exercises 11 and 12, use the segments at the right.

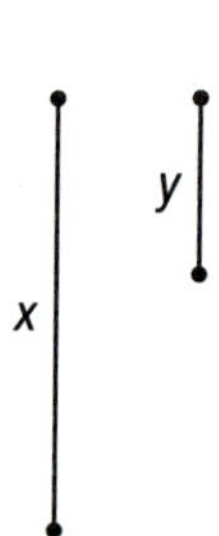

11. Construct a rectangle with a base x and height y.

Sample:

12. Construct a right triangle with one leg length y and hypotenuse length x.

Sample:

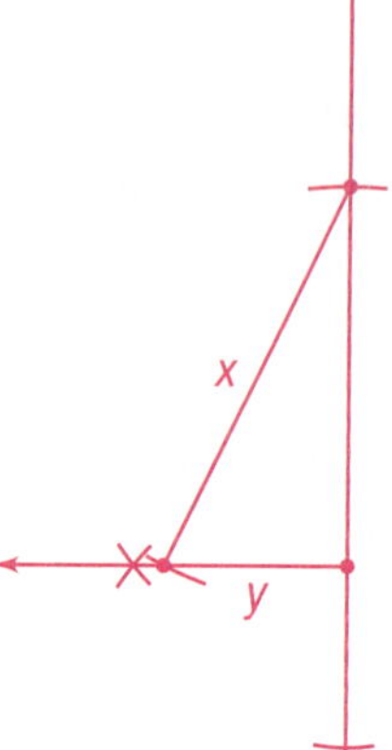

Name ______________________ Class ____________ Date ____________

3-6 Standardized Test Prep

Constructing Parallel and Perpendicular Lines

Multiple Choice

For Exercises 1–3, choose the correct letter.

1. Which diagram below shows the first step in parallel line construction on a point outside a line? B

Ⓐ
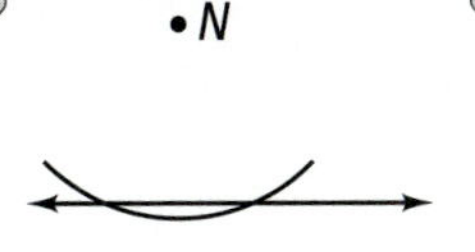

Ⓑ
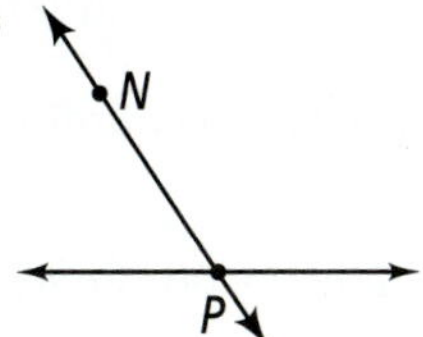

Ⓒ
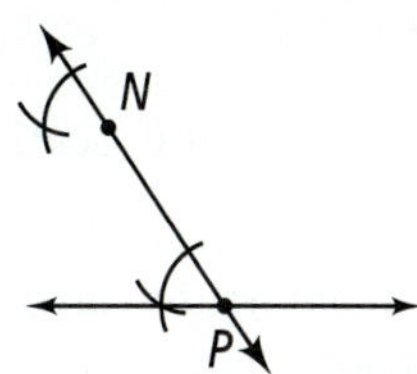

Ⓓ
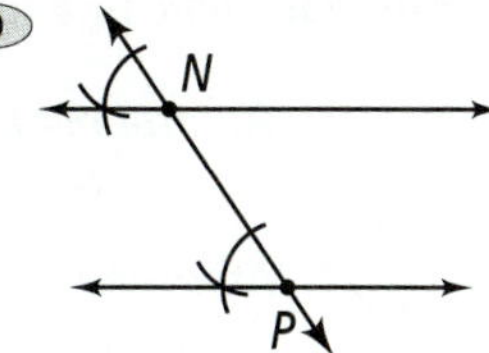

2. What kind of line is being constructed in this series of diagrams? G

Q

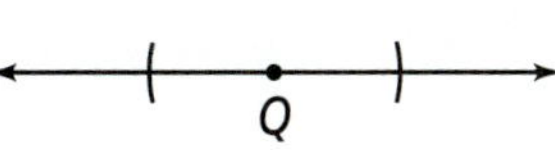

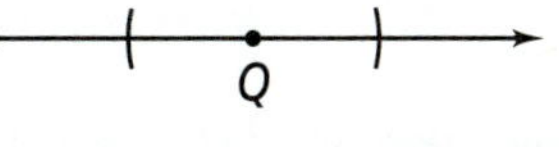

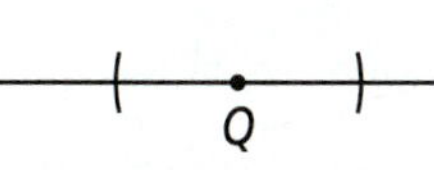

Ⓕ parallel Ⓖ perpendicular Ⓗ congruent Ⓘ similar

3. Which diagram below shows line m parallel to line n? D

Ⓐ
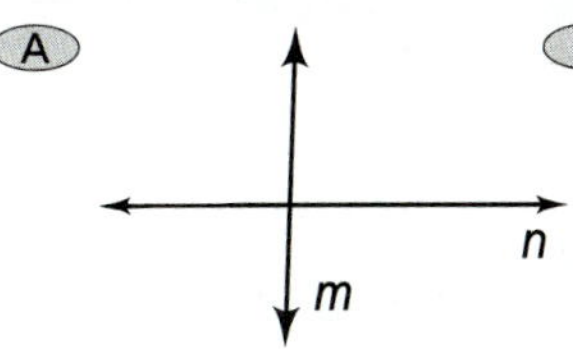

Ⓑ
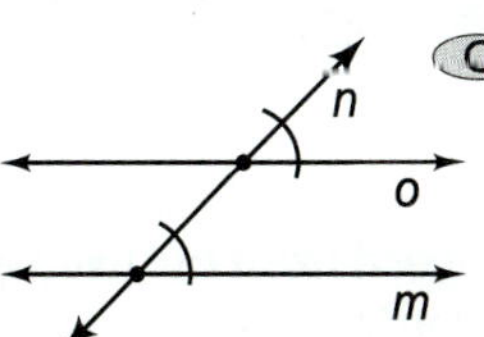

Ⓒ

P
m
n

Ⓓ
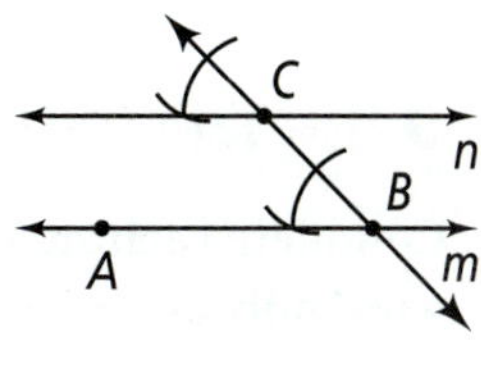

Short Response

4. **Error Analysis** Explain the error in the construction at the right. The student is attempting to draw a perpendicular line through a point not on the line.

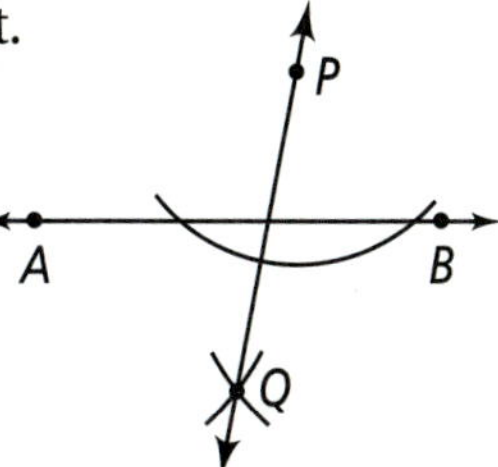

[2] Sample: The student has placed the point of the compass on the two endpoints of the line instead of the points where the arc intersects with the line. [1] Response lacks some specifics. [0] incorrect or no response

3-7 PART 1 Equations of Lines in the Coordinate Plane

Vocabulary

Review

Write T for *true* or F for *false*.

T 1. An *ordered pair* describes the location of a point in a coordinate grid.

F 2. An *ordered pair* can be written as (x-coordinate, y-coordinate) or as (y-coordinate, x-coordinate).

T 3. The *ordered pair* for the origin is (0, 0).

Vocabulary Builder

slope (noun, verb) **slohp**

Slope $= \frac{\text{rise}}{\text{run}}$

Definition: The **slope** of a line m between two points (x_1, y_1) and (x_2, y_2) on a coordinate plane is the ratio of the vertical change (rise) to the horizontal change (run). $m = \frac{\text{rise}}{\text{run}} = \frac{y_2 - y_1}{x_2 - x_1}$

Use Your Vocabulary

Complete each statement with the appropriate word from the list. Use each word only once.

slope   sloping   sloped

4. The _?_ of the hill made it difficult for bike riding. slope
5. The driveway _?_ down to the garage. sloped
6. The _?_ lawn led to the river. sloping

Draw a line from each word in Column A to its corresponding part of speech in Column B.

Column A	Column B
7. sloping	ADJECTIVE
8. slope	NOUN

Problem 1 Finding Slopes of Lines

Got It? **Use the graph at the right. What is the slope of line a?**

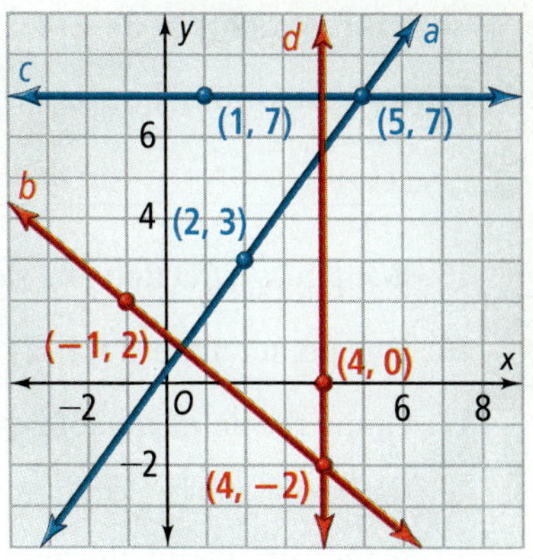

9. Complete the table below to find the slope of line a.

Think	Write
I know the slope is the ratio $\frac{\text{change in } y\text{-coordinates}}{\text{change in } x\text{-coordinates}}$.	$m = \frac{y_2 - y_1}{x_2 - x_1}$
Two points on line a are (2, 3) and (5, 7).	$= \frac{7 - 3}{5 - 2}$
Now I can simplify.	$= \frac{4}{3}$

take note Key Concept Forms of Linear Equations

Definition	Symbols
The **slope-intercept form** of an equation of a nonvertical line is $y = mx + b$, where m is the slope and b is the y-intercept.	$y = mx + b$ (m: slope; b: y-intercept)
The **point-slope form** of an equation of a nonvertical line is $y - y_1 = m(x - x_1)$, where m is the slope and (x_1, y_1) is a point on the line.	$y - y_1 = m(x - x_1)$ (y_1: y-coordinate; m: slope; x_1: x-coordinate)

10. Write *negative, positive, undefined,* or *zero* to describe the slope of each line.

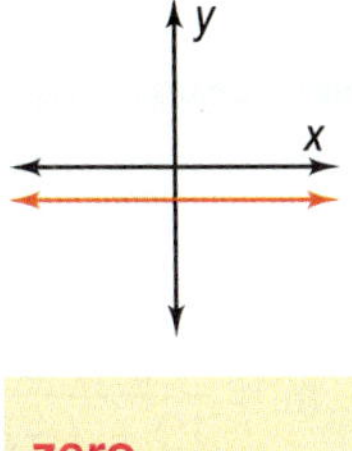

zero

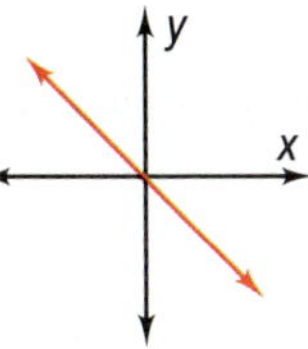

negative

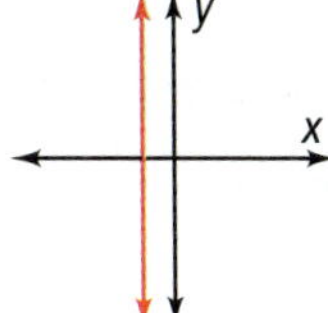

undefined

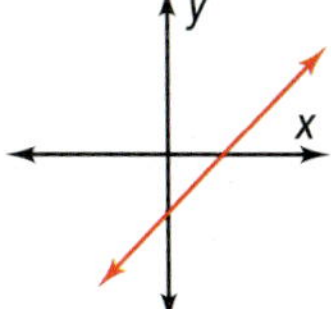

positive

Write SI if the equation is in slope-intercept form. Write PS if the equation is in point-slope form.

PS **11.** $y - 3 = 2(x + 8)$ SI **12.** $y = x - 2.6$ PS **13.** $y + 9 = x + 6$

Problem 2 Graphing Lines

Got It? Graph $y = 3x - 4$.

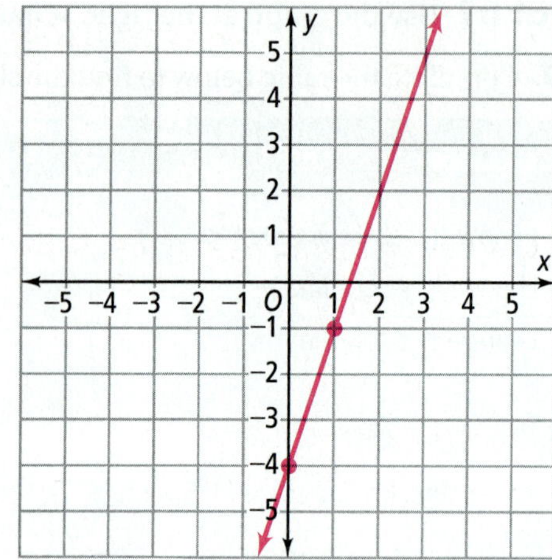

14. In what form is the given equation written?

slope-intercept form

15. Written as a fraction, the slope is $\frac{3}{1}$.

16. One point on the graph is (0 , –4).

17. Graph the point you found in Exercise 16. From that point, move 3 unit(s) *up* and 1 unit (s) *to the right*. Graph the point.

18. Draw a line through the two points to graph $y = 3x - 4$.

Lesson Check • Do you know HOW?

Find the slope of the line passing through the given points.

Underline the correct word(s) or expression to complete each sentence.

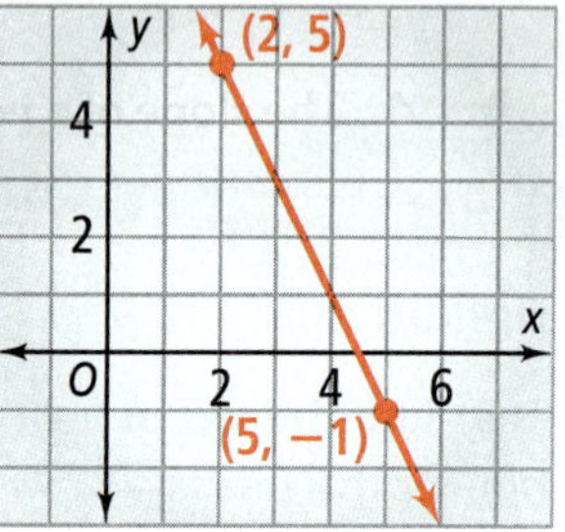

19. The slope of the line is negative / positive / zero / undefined.

20. The slope is the ratio of the horizontal / vertical change to the horizontal / vertical change.

21. If $5 - 2$ is the rise / run, then $-1 - 5$ / $5 - (-1)$ is the rise / run.

22. Now find the slope.

$m = \frac{-1 - 5}{5 - 2} = \frac{-6}{3} = -2$

Lesson Check • Do you UNDERSTAND?

Error Analysis **A classmate found the slope of the line passing through (8, –2) and (8, 10) as shown at the right. Describe your classmate's error. Then find the correct slope.**

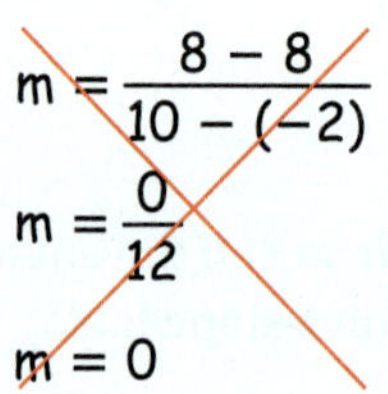

23. What is your classmate's error?

Answers may vary. Sample: Slope is rise over run, not run over rise.

24. Find the slope, m.

$m = \frac{-2 - 10}{8 - 8} = \frac{-12}{0}$

25. The run is $8 - 8 =$ 0 , so the slope is undefined.

3-7 PART 2 Equations of Lines in the Coordinate Plane

Vocabulary

Review

Write T for *true* or F for *false*.

F **1.** The x-axis is a *vertical* line.

T **2.** A line that is perpendicular to the y-axis is *horizontal.*

T **3.** A *horizontal* line has zero slope.

F **4.** The slope of a *vertical* line is positive.

Vocabulary Builder

linear (advective) LIN ee ur

Related Word: line (noun)

Definition: An object is **linear** if it is related to a line or lines.

Math Usage: A **linear** equation is the equation of a line.

Use Your Vocabulary

Complete each statement with *line, linear,* or *lines.* Use each word only once.

5. The graph of a _?_ equation is a straight line. linear

6. You use a straightedge to construct _?_. lines

7. The graph of the equation $y = 2x - 1$ is a _?_. line

8. Is the graph of a circle *linear*? Yes / No (No circled)

9. Is an equation in point-slope form a *linear* equation? Yes / No (Yes circled)

10. Is an equation in slope-intercept form a *linear* equation? Yes / No (Yes circled)

Problem 3 Writing Equations of Lines

Got It? What is an equation of the line with slope $-\frac{1}{2}$ and y-intercept 2?

11. Complete the problem-solving model below.

Know	Need	Plan
slope m = $-\frac{1}{2}$ y-intercept = 2	Write an equation of a line.	Use $y = mx + b$, the slope-intercept form of a linear equation.

12. Now write the equation.

$y = -\frac{1}{2}x + 2$

Problem 4 Using Two Points to Write an Equation

Got It? You can use the two points given on the line at the right to show that the slope of the line is $\frac{6}{5}$. So one equation of the line is $y - 5 = \frac{6}{5}(x - 3)$. What is an equation of the line if you use $(-2, -1)$ instead of $(3, 5)$ in the point-slope form of the equation?

13. The equation is found below. Write a justification for each step.

$y - y_1 = m(x - x_1)$ Write in point-slope form.

$y - (-1) = \frac{6}{5}(x - (-2))$ Substitute.

$y + 1 = \frac{6}{5}(x + 2)$ Simplify.

Got It? Use the two equations for the line shown above. Rewrite the equations in slope-intercept form and compare them. What can you conclude?

14. Write each equation in slope-intercept form.

$y - 5 = \frac{6}{5}(x - 3)$

$$y - 5 = \frac{6}{5}x - \frac{18}{5}$$
$$y = \frac{6}{5}x - \frac{18}{5} + \frac{25}{5}$$
$$y = \frac{6}{5}x + \frac{7}{5}$$

$y + 1 = \frac{6}{5}(x + 2)$

$$y + 1 = \frac{6}{5}x + \frac{12}{5}$$
$$y = \frac{6}{5}x + \frac{12}{5} - \frac{5}{5}$$
$$y = \frac{6}{5}x + \frac{7}{5}$$

15. Underline the correct word(s) to complete each sentence.

The equations are different / the same.

Choosing $(-2, -1)$ gives a different / the same equation as choosing $(3, 5)$.

The equations $y - 5 = \frac{6}{5}(x - 3)$ and $y + 1 = \frac{6}{5}(x + 2)$ are / are not equivalent.

Problem 5 Writing Equations of Horizontal and Vertical Lines

Got It? **What are the equations for the horizontal and vertical lines through (4, −3)?**

Write T for *true* or F for *false*.

T **16.** Every point on a horizontal line through (4, −3) has *y*-coordinate of −3.

F **17.** The equation of a vertical line through (4, −3) is $y = -3$.

T **18.** The equation of a vertical line through (4, −3) is $x = 4$.

19. Graph the horizontal and vertical lines through (4, −3) on the coordinate plane at the right.

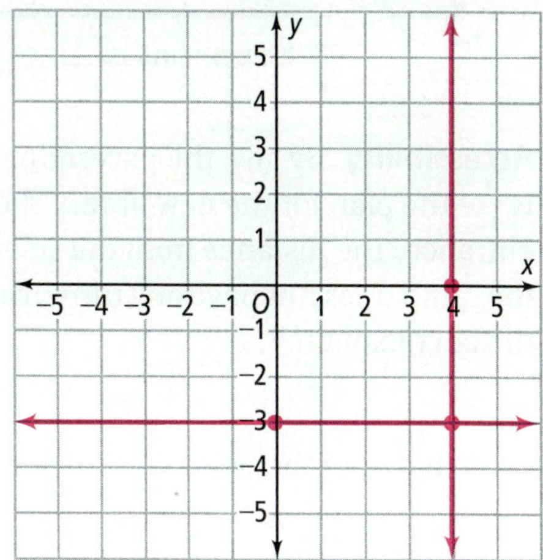

Lesson Check • Do you UNDERSTAND?

Vocabulary **Explain why you think *slope-intercept form* makes sense as a name for $y = mx + b$. Explain why you think *point-slope form* makes sense as a name for $y - y_1 = m(x - x_1)$.**

20. Is the intercept of a line a coordinate of a point on the line? Yes / No (Yes circled)

21. Is (x_1, y_1) a coordinate of a point on the line? Yes / No (No circled)

22. Explain why *slope-intercept form* makes sense as a name for $y = mx + b$ and *point-slope form* makes sense as a name for $y - y_1 = m(x - x_2)$.

Explanations may vary. Sample: $y = mx + b$ uses the slope m and y-intercept b, while $y - y_1 = m(x - x_2)$ uses the slope m and a point (x_1, y_1) on the line.

Math Success

Check off the vocabulary words that you understand.

- ☐ slope
- ☐ slope-intercept form
- ☐ point-slope form

Rate how well you can write and graph *linear equations.*

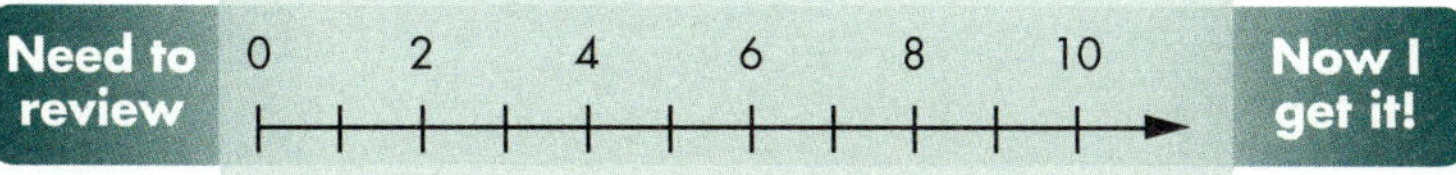

Name ______________________ Class ____________ Date ____________

3-7 Think About a Plan

Equations of Lines in the Coordinate Plane

Accessibility By law, the maximum slope of an access ramp in new construction is $\frac{1}{12}$. The plan for the new library shows a 3-ft height from the ground to the main entrance. The distance from the sidewalk to the building is 10 ft. If you assume the ramp does not have any turns, can you design a ramp that complies with the law? Explain.

1. What does the word *slope* mean in this context?

the vertical rise of the ramp divided by its horizontal length

2. What does the law require for the access ramp slope?

The rise divided by the run must be less than or equal to $\frac{1}{12}$.

3. What are the height and maximum length for the access ramp?

The ramp must be 3 ft high and 10 ft long.

4. What is the slope for that ramp? $\frac{3}{10}$

5. How does the slope compare with the required slope?

The slope of a ramp from the sidewalk to the front of the library is greater than the maximum slope allowed by law.

6. Can you design a ramp that complies with the law? Explain.

Sample: No; since $\frac{3}{10}$ is greater than $\frac{1}{12}$, you cannot design a ramp that complies with the law unless the ramp turns or starts far away from the building.

Name ______________________ Class ____________ Date ____________

3-7 Practice

Form K

Equations of Lines in the Coordinate Plane

Find the slope of the line passing through the given points.

1. (2, 0), (−6, 8) −1

2. (9, 1), (−9, −3) $\frac{2}{9}$

3. (−3, −1), (2, 8) $\frac{9}{5}$

4. (4, 6), (8, −2) −2

5. (−5, 4), (3, 6) $\frac{1}{4}$

6. (11, 2), (−1, 4) $-\frac{1}{6}$

7. $\frac{7}{6}$

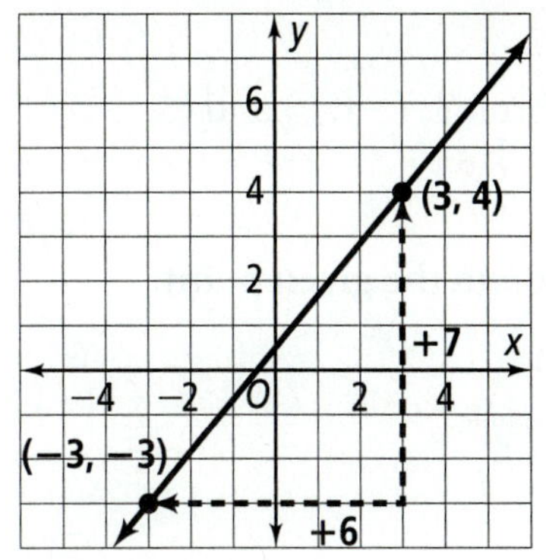

8. $-\frac{4}{3}$

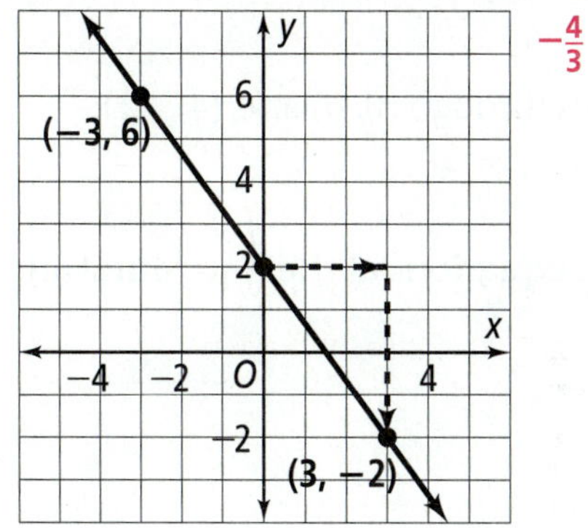

Graph each line.

9. $y = x - 4$

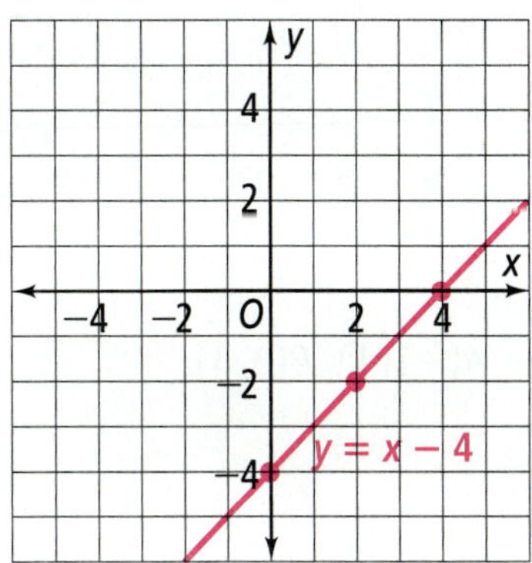

10. $y = 2x + 3$

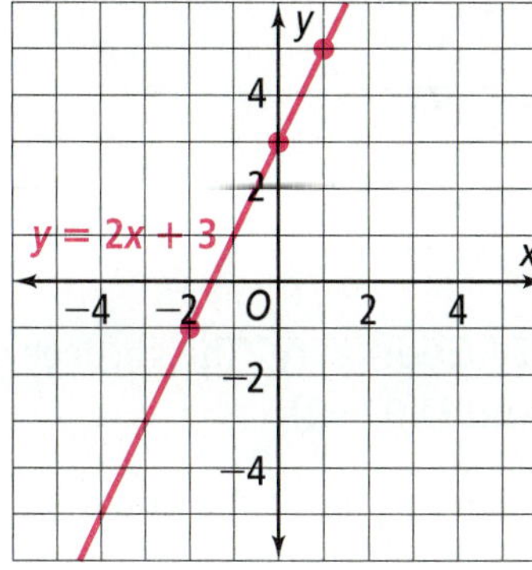

11. $y = \frac{1}{4}x$

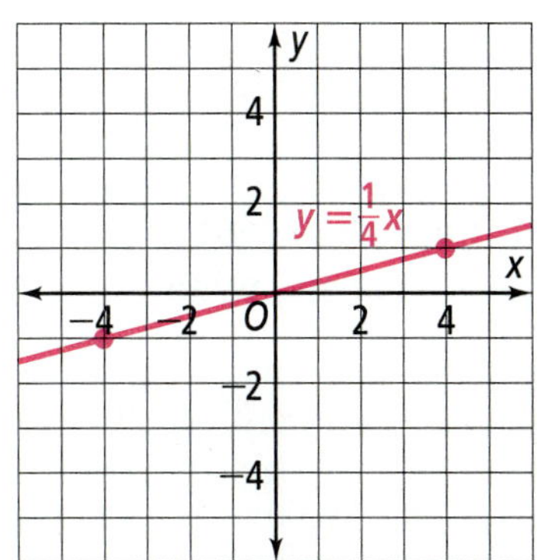

12. $y = -\frac{3}{4}x - 1$

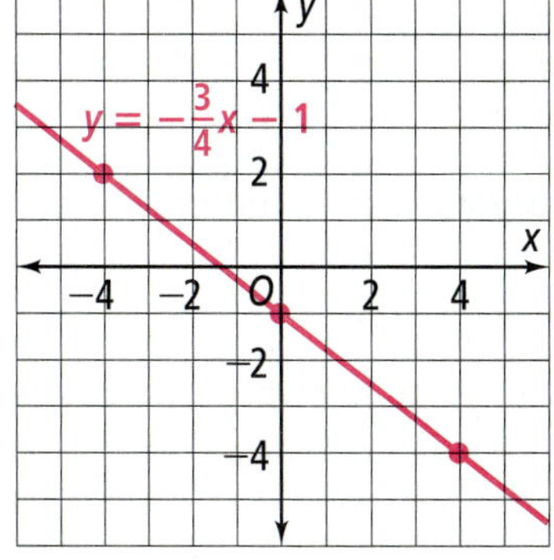

Name ______________________ Class ____________ Date ____________

3-7 Practice (continued) — Form K

Equations of Lines in the Coordinate Plane

Use the given information to write an equation of each line.

13. slope $\frac{1}{3}$, y-intercept 6
$y = \frac{1}{3}x + 6$

14. slope -10, y-intercept -3
$y = -10x - 3$

15. slope -5, passes through $(2, -3)$
$y = -5x + 7$

16. slope $\frac{3}{4}$, passes through $(-8, 2)$
$y = \frac{3}{4}x + 8$

17. passes through $(0, 6)$ and $(4, -2)$
$y = -2x + 6$

18. passes through $(-1, 8)$ and $(5, -4)$
$y = -2x + 6$

Write the equations of the horizontal and vertical lines through the given point.

19. $(5, 6)$
$y = 6$; $x = 5$

20. $(-2, -3)$
$y = -3$; $x = -2$

21. $(8, -1)$
$y = -1$; $x = 8$

22. $(10, 0)$
$y = 0$; $x = 10$

Write each equation in slope-intercept form.

23. $y - 5 = 3(x - 4)$
$y = 3x - 7$

24. $y + 2 = -5(x - 1)$
$y = -5x + 3$

25. $2x + 4y = 8$
$y = -\frac{1}{2}x + 2$

26. $10y + 16x + 4 = 2y$
$y = -2x - \frac{1}{2}$

27. Coordinate Geometry The vertices of a quadrilateral are $A(-1, 1)$, $B(2, 4)$, $C(2, -4)$, and $D(0, -2)$.

a. Write an equation for the line through A and B. $y = x + 2$

b. Write an equation for the line through C and D. $y = -x - 2$

c. Without graphing the lines, what can you tell about the lines from their slopes? **Answers may vary. Sample: The lines have the same steepness because the absolute value of *m* is the same, but they point in opposite directions because one slope is negative and the other is positive.**

28. Error Analysis A classmate says that the equation of a line through $(3, -6)$ and $(-1, -3)$ is $y - 6 = -\frac{3}{4}(x - 3)$. Explain your classmate's error and write the correct equation.

The classmate failed to subtract -6 from y. The correct equation is $y + 6 = -\frac{3}{4}(x - 3)$.

Name ______________________ Class ____________ Date ____________

3-7 Standardized Test Prep

Equations of Lines in the Coordinate Plane

Multiple Choice

For Exercises 1–4, choose the correct letter.

1. What is the slope of the line passing through the points (2, 7) and (−1, 3)? C

Ⓐ $\frac{2}{7}$ Ⓑ $\frac{3}{4}$ Ⓒ $\frac{4}{3}$ Ⓓ $\frac{1}{3}$

2. What is the correct equation of the line shown at the right? F

Ⓕ $y = \frac{3}{2}x + 3$ Ⓗ $y = \frac{2}{3}x + 3$

Ⓖ $y = -\frac{3}{2}x - 3$ Ⓘ $y = -\frac{2}{3}x - 3$

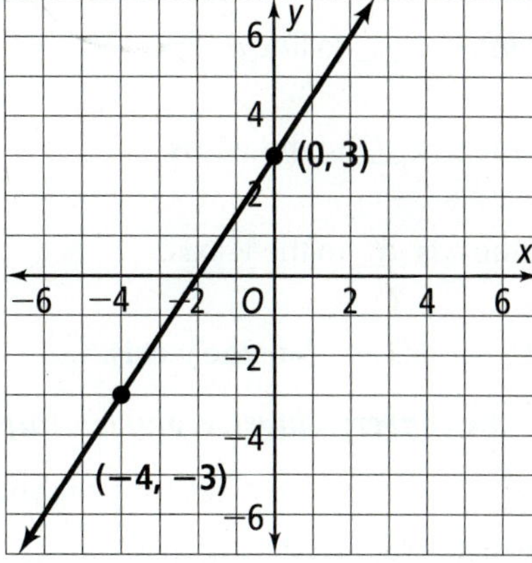

3. The x-intercept of a line is −5 and the y-intercept of the line is −2. What is the equation of the line? D

Ⓐ $y = -\frac{5}{2}x - 5$ Ⓒ $y = -\frac{5}{2}x - 2$

Ⓑ $y = \frac{2}{5}x + 2$ Ⓓ $y = -\frac{2}{5}x - 2$

4. What is the slope-intercept form of the equation $y - 7 = -\frac{5}{2}(x + 4)$? I

Ⓕ $y - 2 = -\frac{5}{2}(x + 2)$ Ⓗ $y = -\frac{4}{7}x + 2$

Ⓖ $y + 7 = -x + \frac{5}{2}$ Ⓘ $y = -\frac{5}{2}x - 3$

Short Response

5. Error Analysis A student has attempted to graph an equation that contains the point (1, −4) and has a slope of $\frac{1}{3}$.

a. What is the correct equation in slope-intercept form?

b. What is the student's error on the graph?

[2] $y = \frac{1}{3}x - 4\frac{1}{3}$; the student uses the wrong slope in the graph. The student's line has a slope of 3.
[1] wrong equation or incomplete explanation
[0] incorrect or no response

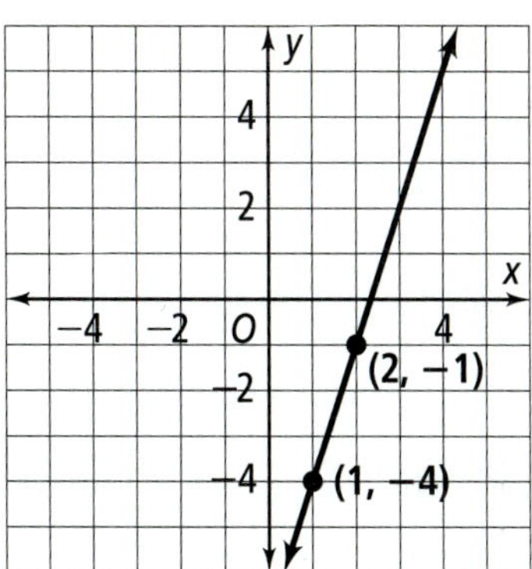

3-8 Slopes of Parallel and Perpendicular Lines

Vocabulary

Review

Use the graph at the right for Exercises 1–4. Write *parallel* or *perpendicular* to complete each sentence.

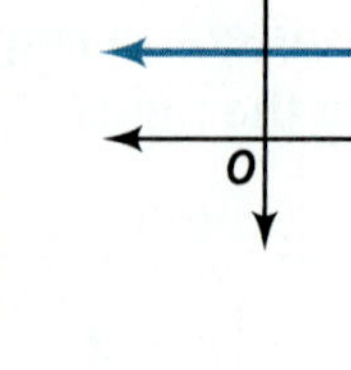

1. Line b is __?__ to line a. perpendicular

2. Line b is __?__ to the x-axis. parallel

3. Line a is __?__ to the y-axis. parallel

4. The x-axis is __?__ to the y-axis. perpendicular

Write the *converse, inverse,* and *contrapositive* of the statement below.

If a polygon is a triangle, then the sum of the measures of its angles is 180.

5. **CONVERSE** If the sum of the measures of the angles of a polygon is 180, then __?__.

   the polygon is a triangle

6. **INVERSE** If a polygon is *not* a triangle, then __?__.

   the sum of the measures of its angles is not 180

7. **CONTRAPOSITIVE** If the sum of the measures of the angles of a polygon is *not* 180, then __?__.

   the polygon is not a triangle

Vocabulary Builder

reciprocal (noun) **rih SIP ruh kul**

The **reciprocal** of x is $\frac{1}{x}$.

Other Word Forms: reciprocate (verb)

Definition: The **reciprocal** of a number is a number such that the product of the two numbers is 1. The **reciprocal** of $\frac{\text{numerator}}{\text{denominator}}$ is $\frac{\text{denominator}}{\text{numerator}}$.

Use Your Vocabulary

Complete each statement with *reciprocal* or *reciprocate*. Use each word only once.

8. VERB — After your friend helps you with your homework, you _?_ by helping your friend with his chores. **reciprocate**

9. NOUN — The _?_ of $\frac{2}{3}$ is $\frac{3}{2}$. **reciprocal**

take note

Key Concept Slopes of Parallel Lines

- If two nonvertical lines are parallel, then their slopes are equal.
- If the slopes of two distinct nonvertical lines are equal, then the lines are parallel.
- Any two vertical lines or horizontal lines are parallel.

Circle the correct statement in each exercise.

10. (circled) A vertical line is parallel to any other vertical line.

A vertical line is parallel to any horizontal line.

11. Any two nonvertical lines have the same slope.

(circled) Any two nonvertical lines that are parallel have the same slope.

Problem 1 Checking for Parallel Lines

Got It? **Line ℓ_3 contains $A(-13, 6)$ and $B(-1, 2)$. Line ℓ_4 contains $C(3, 6)$ and $D(6, 7)$. Are ℓ_3 and ℓ_4 parallel? Explain.**

12. To determine whether lines ℓ_3 and ℓ_4 are are parallel, check whether the lines have the same _?_. **slope**

13. Find the slope of each line.

slope of ℓ_3

$\frac{2-6}{-1-(-13)} = \frac{-4}{12} = -\frac{1}{3}$

slope of ℓ_4

$\frac{7-6}{6-3} = \frac{1}{3}$

14. Are the slopes equal? Yes / (No)

15. Are lines ℓ_3 and ℓ_4 parallel? Explain.

No. Explanations may vary. Sample: Since the slopes are not equal, the lines are not parallel.

Problem 2 Writing Equations of Parallel Lines

Got It? What is an equation of the line parallel to $y = -x - 7$ that contains $(-5, 3)$?

16. The slope of the line $y = -x - 7$ is -1.

17. The equation of the line parallel to $y = -x - 7$ will have slope $m = -1$.

18. Find the equation of the line using point-slope form. Complete the steps below.

$y - y_1 =$	$m(x - x_1)$	Write in point-slope form.
$y - 3 =$	$-1[x - (-5)]$	Substitute point and slope into equation.
$y - 3 =$	$-x - 5$	Simplify.
$y =$	$-x - 2$	Add 3 to both sides.

take note

Key Concept Slopes of Perpendicular Lines

- If two nonvertical lines are perpendicular, then the product of their slopes is -1.
- If the slopes of two lines have a product of -1, then the lines are perpendicular.
- Any horizontal line and vertical line are perpendicular.

Write T for *true* or F for *false*.

F **19.** The second bullet in the Take Note is the contrapositive of the first bullet.

T **20.** The product of the slopes of any horizontal line and any vertical line is -1.

Problem 3 Checking for Perpendicular Lines

Got It? Line ℓ_3 contains $A(2, 7)$ and $B(3, -1)$. Line ℓ_4 contains $C(-2, 6)$ and $D(8, 7)$. Are ℓ_3 and ℓ_4 perpendicular? Explain.

21. Find the slopes and multiply them.

$m_3 = \frac{-1-7}{3-2} = \frac{-8}{1} = -8$ $m_4 = \frac{7-6}{8-(-2)} = \frac{1}{10}$

$m_3 \times m_4 = (-8)\left(\frac{1}{10}\right) = \frac{-8}{10}$

22. Underline the correct words to complete the sentence.

Lines ℓ_3 and ℓ_4 are / <u>are not</u> perpendicular because the product of their slopes does / <u>does not</u> equal -1.

Problem 4 Writing Equations of Perpendicular Lines

Got It? What is an equation of the line perpendicular to $y = -3x - 5$ that contains $(-3, 7)$?

23. Complete the reasoning model below.

Think	Write
I can identify the slope, m_1, of the given line.	$y = -3x - 5$ is in point-slope form, so $m_1 =$ 3 .
I know that the slope, m_2, of the perpendicular line is the negative reciprocal of m_1.	m_2 is $\frac{1}{3}$ because $3 \times \frac{1}{3} = -1$.
I can use m_2 and $(-3, 7)$ to write the equation of the perpendicular line in point-slope form.	$y - y_1 = m(x - x_1)$ $y - 7 = \frac{1}{3}[x - (-3)]$ $y - 7 = \frac{1}{3}(x + 3)$

Lesson Check • Do you UNDERSTAND?

Error Analysis Your classmate tries to find an equation for a line parallel to $y = 3x - 5$ that contains $(-4, 2)$. What is your classmate's error?

slope of given line = 3
slope of parallel line = $\frac{1}{3}$
$y - y_1 = m(x - x_1)$
$y - 2 = \frac{1}{3}(x + 4)$

24. Parallel lines have the same / different slopes.

25. Show a correct solution in the box below.

slope of given line = 3; slope of parallel line = 3

$y - 2 = 3(x + 4)$

Math Success

Check off the vocabulary words that you understand.

☐ slope ☐ reciprocal ☐ parallel ☐ perpendicular

Rate how well you *understand perpendicular lines.*

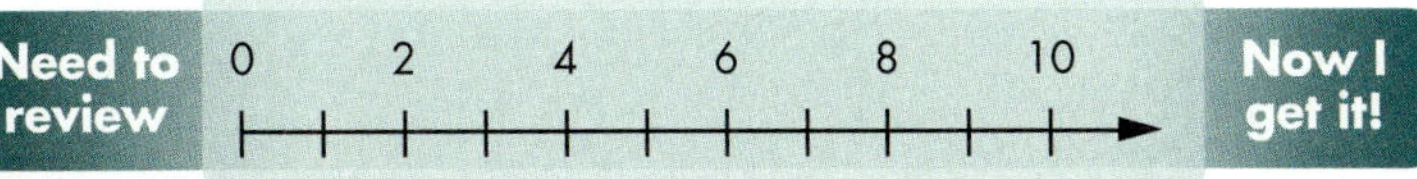

Name ______________________ Class ____________ Date ____________

3-8 Think About a Plan

Slopes of Parallel and Perpendicular Lines

Rail Trail A community recently converted an old railroad corridor into a recreational trail. The graph at the right shows a map of the trail on a coordinate grid. They plan to construct a path to connect the trail to a parking lot. The new path will be perpendicular to the recreational trail.

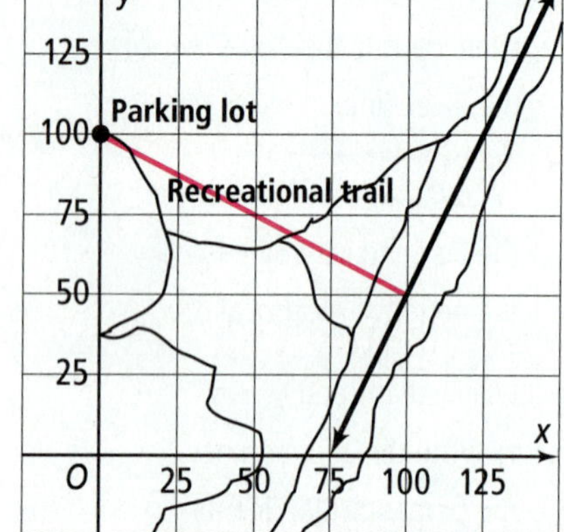

a. Write an equation of the line representing the new path.

b. What are the coordinates of the point at which the path will meet the recreational trail?

c. If each grid space is 25 yd by 25 yd, how long is the path to the nearest yard?

1. How can you tell whether two lines are perpendicular, given their equations?
The slope of one line will be the negative reciprocal of the slope of the other line.

2. What is the slope of the line representing the existing trail? 2

3. What is the slope of the line representing the new path? $-\frac{1}{2}$

4. What is the y-intercept of the line representing the new path? 100

5. Write an equation for the line representing the new path, and then graph it. $y = -\frac{1}{2}x + 100$

6. Name the point at which the path meets the recreational trail. (100, 50)

7. How long is the path in units of the coordinate grid? (*Hint:* Use the distance formula.) $2\sqrt{5}$ or about 4.47 units

8. How long is the path in yards? About 112 yd

Name ______________________ Class ____________ Date ____________

3-8 Practice

Form K

Slopes of Parallel and Perpendicular Lines

For Exercises 1 and 2, are lines ℓ_1 and ℓ_2 parallel? Explain.

1.

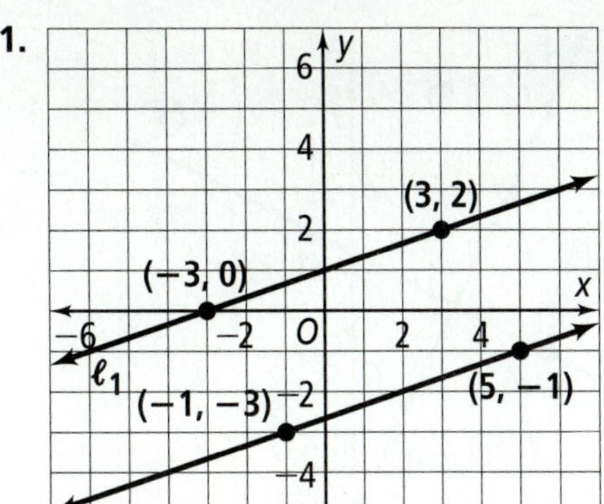

Yes; both lines have a slope of $\frac{1}{3}$.

2.

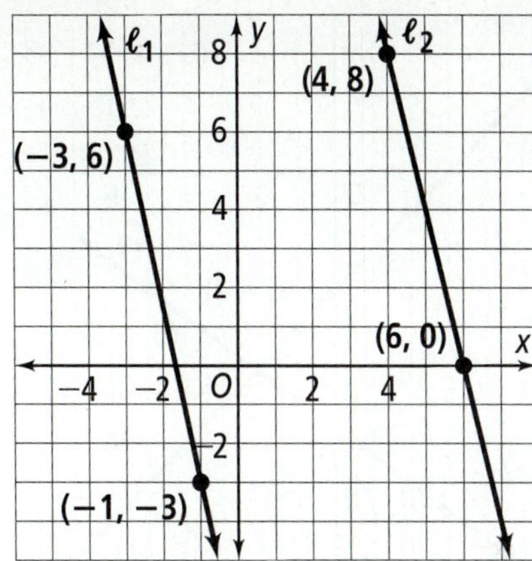

No; slope of ℓ_1 is $-\frac{9}{2}$ and slope of ℓ_2 is -4.

Write an equation of the line parallel to the given line that contains *C*.

3. $C(5, -2)$; $y = -5x + 3$

$y = -5x + 23$

4. $C(8, 1)$; $y = 2x + 6$

$y = 2x - 15$

5. $C(4, 3)$; $y = -\frac{1}{4}x + 3$

$y = -\frac{1}{4}x + 4$

6. $C(0, 6)$; $y = \frac{2}{3}x + 3$

$y = \frac{2}{3}x + 6$

Rewrite each equation in slope-intercept form, if necessary. Then determine whether the lines are parallel. Explain.

7. $y = x + 8$

$x - 2y = 4$

$y = \frac{1}{2}x - 2$; No; slope of first line is 1 and slope of second line is $\frac{1}{2}$.

8. $2y + 6x = 18$

$4y + 12x = 24$

$y = -3x + 9$; $y = -3x + 6$; yes; both lines have a slope of -3.

9. $4y - 3x = 20$

$2y = \frac{3}{2}x + 4$

$y = \frac{3}{4}x + 5$; $y = \frac{3}{4}x + 2$; yes; both lines have a slope of $\frac{3}{4}$.

Use slopes to determine whether the opposite sides of quadrilateral *WXYZ* are parallel.

10. $W(-1, -1)$, $X(-3, -1)$, $Y(-2, 4)$, $Z(2, 3)$ no

11. $W(-1, 1)$, $X(2, 4)$, $Y(4, 1)$, $Z(1, -2)$ yes; $\overline{WX} \parallel \overline{ZY}$

12. $W(3, 1)$, $X(5, -4)$, $Y(0, -4)$, $Z(-2, 0)$ no

13. $W(-1, -1)$, $X(2, -4)$, $Y(0, -5)$, $Z(-3, -2)$ yes; $\overline{WX} \parallel \overline{ZY}$ and $\overline{WZ} \parallel \overline{XY}$

Name ________________ Class ________ Date ________

3-8 Practice (continued) — Form K

Slopes of Parallel and Perpendicular Lines

For Exercises 14 and 15, are ℓ_1 and ℓ_2 perpendicular? Explain.

14. 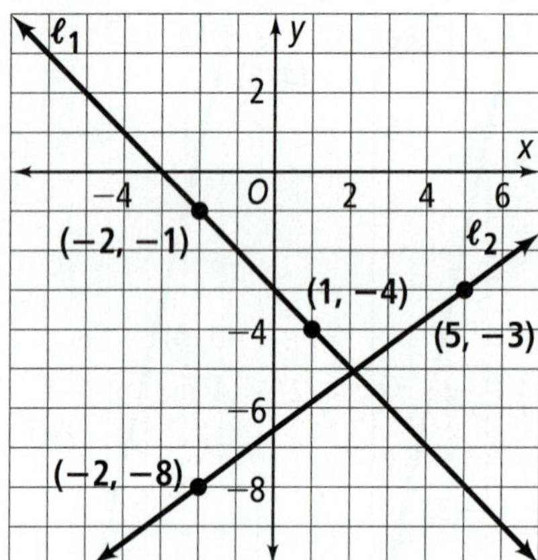

No; slope of ℓ_1 is −1 and slope of ℓ_2 is $\frac{5}{7}$.

15. 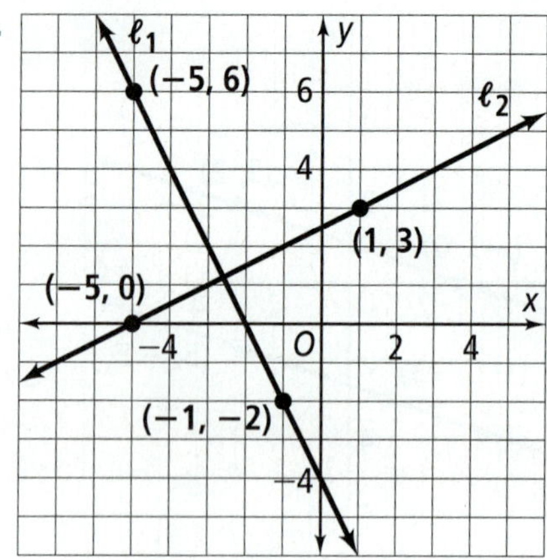

Yes; slope of ℓ_1 is −2 and slope of ℓ_2 is $\frac{1}{2}$.

Write an equation of the line perpendicular to the given line that contains *D*.

16. $D(6, 2)$; $y = -3x + 5$
$y = \frac{1}{3}x$

17. $D(0, -3)$; $y = \frac{1}{2}x - 7$
$y = -2x - 3$

18. $D(-8, 1)$; $y = -\frac{2}{3}x + 4$
$y = \frac{3}{2}x + 13$

19. $D(2, 2)$; $y = 5x + 3$
$y = -\frac{1}{5}x + 2\frac{2}{5}$

20. Think About a Plan Line ℓ_1 contains (−2, 1) and (4, 3) and line ℓ_2 contains (5, 3) and (3, *g*). What value of *g* makes ℓ_1 and ℓ_2 perpendicular? 9

- For ℓ_1 and ℓ_2 to be perpendicular, what must be true of their slopes?
  Their product must be −1.
- What equation is true if $\ell_1 \perp \ell_2$?
  $\frac{3 - 1}{4 + 2} \times \frac{g - 3}{3 - 5} = -1$

21. A classmate plotted the following points: $A(-3, 2)$, $B(-1, 4)$, and $C(1, 2)$. Where should the classmate plot point *D* so that the quadrilateral formed has perpendicular sides? (−1, 0)

22. Open-Ended Write the coordinates of a set of points which can be found on a line perpendicular to the line containing points $A(5, 3)$ and $B(8, 5)$.
Answers will vary. Check that students' lines have a slope of $\frac{-3}{2}$.

Name ______________________ Class __________ Date __________

3-8 Standardized Test Prep

Slopes of Parallel and Perpendicular Lines

Multiple Choice

For Exercises 1–4 choose the correct letter.

1. Which pair of slopes could represent perpendicular lines? C

   (A) $\frac{1}{7}, 7$ (B) $\frac{1}{2}, \frac{2}{4}$ (C) $-\frac{3}{4}, \frac{4}{3}$ (D) $\frac{1}{3}, \frac{1}{3}$

2. The lines shown in the figure at the right are F

   (F) parallel.

   (G) perpendicular.

   (H) neither parallel nor perpendicular.

   (I) both parallel and perpendicular.

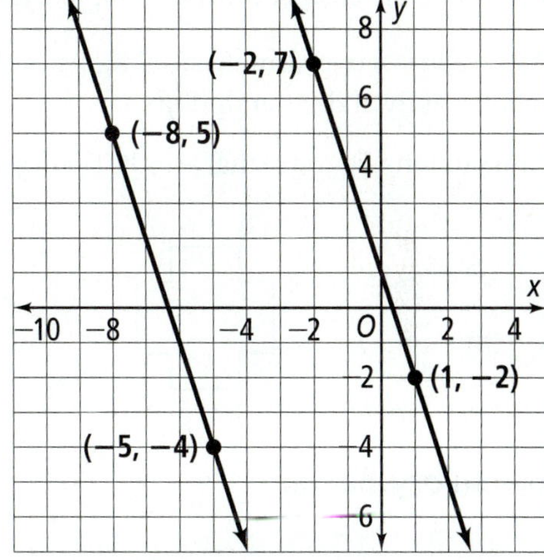

3. Two lines are perpendicular when A

   (A) the product of their slopes is −1.

   (B) the product of their slopes is greater than 0.

   (C) they have the same slope.

   (D) their slopes are undefined.

4. Which is the equation for the line perpendicular to $y = -\frac{5}{3}x + 11\frac{1}{3}$ and containing $P(-2, 3)$? I

   (F) $y - 2 = -\frac{3}{5}(x - 3)$ (G) $y = -\frac{5}{3}x + 4\frac{1}{3}$ (H) $y = -\frac{3}{5}x + 4\frac{1}{5}$ (I) $y = \frac{3}{5}x + 4\frac{1}{5}$

Extended Response

5. Graph the vertices of *ABCD* where $A(-1, 3)$, $B(-6, -2)$, $C(-1, -7)$, and $D(4, -2)$.

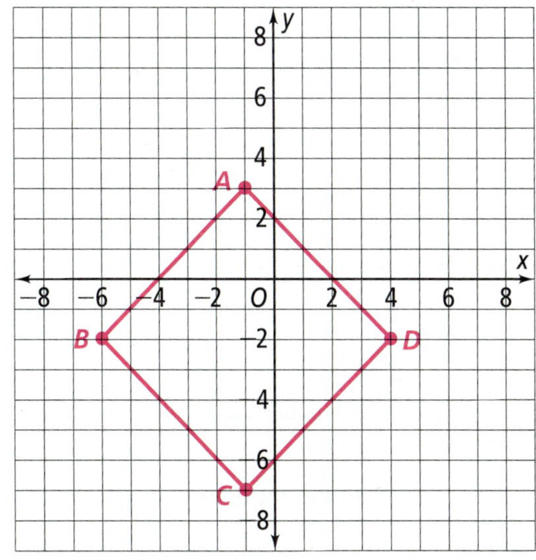

   a. Explain how you know the opposite sides of *ABCD* are parallel.
   They have the same slopes.

   b. Explain how you know the adjacent sides of *ABCD* are perpendicular.
   The product of their slopes is −1.

   c. What is the length of each side, to the nearest inch, if each grid space is equal to 2 in.?
   14 in.

   d. What kind of figure is *ABCD*?
   a square; [4] four answers correct
   [3] three correct [2] two correct
   [1] one correct [0] no answers correct

4-1 Congruent Figures

Vocabulary

Review

1. Underline the correct word to complete the sentence.

A *polygon* is a two-dimensional figure with two / three or more segments that meet exactly at their endpoints.

2. Cross out the figure(s) that are NOT *polygons*.

 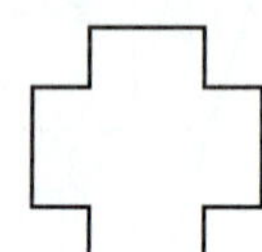 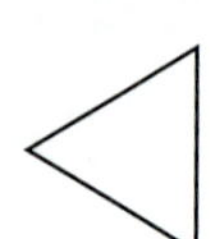  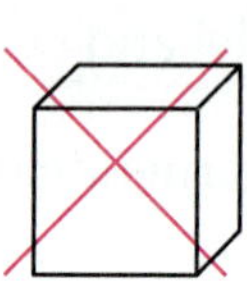

Vocabulary Builder

congruent (adjective) **kahng** GROO **unt**

Main Idea: **Congruent** figures have the same size and shape.

Related Word: congruence (noun)

Use Your Vocabulary

3. Circle the triangles that appear to be *congruent*.

Write T for *true* or F for *false*.

F **4.** *Congruent* angles have different measures.

F **5.** A prism and its net are *congruent* figures.

T **6.** The corresponding sides of *congruent* figures have the same measure.

take note Key Concept Congruent Figures

Congruent polygons have congruent corresponding parts—their matching sides and angles. When you name congruent polygons, you must list corresponding vertices in the same order.

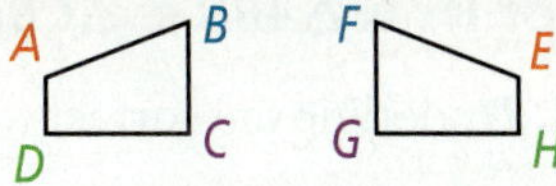

$ABCD \cong EFGH$

7. Use the figures at the right to complete each congruence statement.

$\overline{AB} \cong$ EF $\quad \overline{BC} \cong$ FG $\quad \overline{CD} \cong$ GH $\quad \overline{DA} \cong$ HE

$\angle A \cong \angle E \quad \angle B \cong \angle F \quad \angle C \cong \angle G \quad \angle D \cong \angle H$

Problem 1 Finding Congruent Parts

Got It? **If $\triangle WYS \cong \triangle MKV$, what are the congruent corresponding parts?**

8. Use the diagram at the right. Draw an arrow from each vertex of the first triangle to the corresponding vertex of the second triangle.

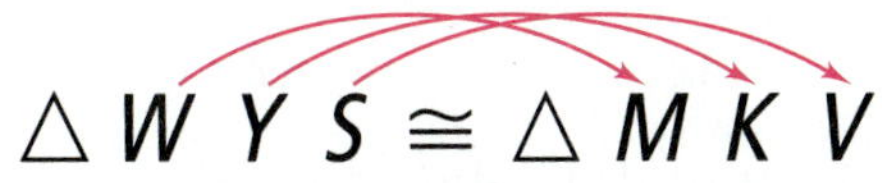

9. Use the diagram from Exercise 8 to complete each congruence statement.

Sides	$\overline{WY} \cong \overline{MK}$	$\overline{YS} \cong \overline{KV}$	$\overline{WS} \cong \overline{MV}$
Angles	$\angle W \cong \angle M$	$\angle Y \cong \angle K$	$\angle S \cong \angle V$

Problem 2 Using Congruent Parts

Got It? **Suppose that $\triangle WYS \cong \triangle MKV$. If $m\angle W = 62$ and $m\angle Y = 35$, what is $m\angle V$? Explain.**

Use the congruent triangles at the right.

10. Use the given information to label the triangles. Remember to write corresponding vertices in order.

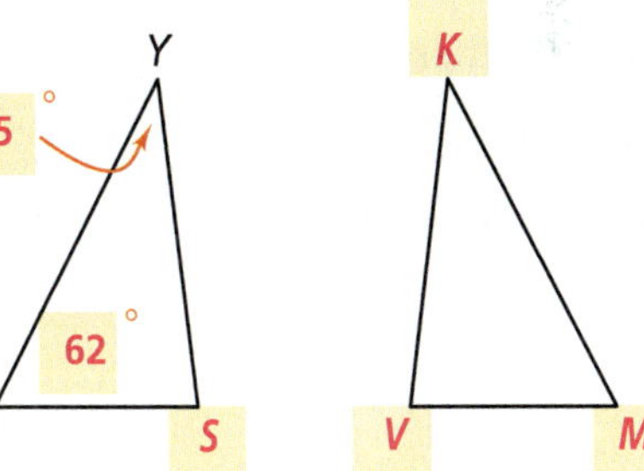

11. Complete each congruence statement.

$\angle W \cong \angle M$

$\angle Y \cong \angle K$

$\angle S \cong \angle V$

12. Use the Triangle Angle-Sum theorem.

$m\angle S + m\angle W + m\angle Y = 180$, so $m\angle S = 180 - (62 + 35)$, or 83.

13. Complete.

Since $\angle S \cong \angle V$ and $m\angle S = 83$, $m\angle V = 83$.

Problem 3 Finding Congruent Triangles

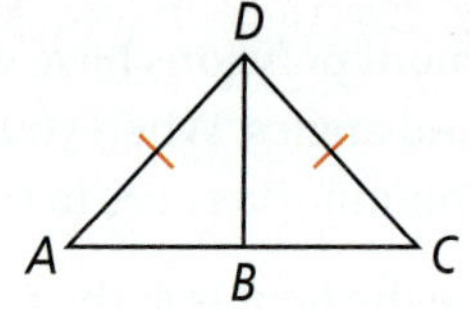

Got It? Is $\triangle ABD \cong \triangle CBD$? Justify your answer.

14. Underline the correct word to complete the sentence.

To prove two triangles congruent, show that all adjacent / corresponding parts are congruent.

15. Circle the name(s) for $\triangle ACD$.

acute   isosceles   right   scalene

16. Cross out the congruence statements that are NOT supported by the information in the figure.

$\overline{AD} \cong \overline{CD}$	$\overline{BD} \cong \overline{BD}$	~~$\overline{AB} \cong \overline{CB}$~~
$\angle A \cong \angle C$	~~$\angle ABD \cong \angle CBD$~~	~~$\angle ADB \cong \angle CDB$~~

17. You need 6 congruence statements to prove two triangles congruent, so you can / cannot prove that $\triangle ABD \cong \triangle CBD$.

Theorem 4-1 Third Angles Theorem

Theorem	If . . .	Then . . .
If two angles of one triangle are congruent to two angles of another triangle, then the third angles are congruent.	$\angle A \cong \angle D$ and $\angle B \cong \angle E$	$\angle C \cong \angle F$

Use $\triangle ABC$ and $\triangle DEF$ above.

18. If $m\angle A = 74$, then $m\angle D =$ 74.

19. If $m\angle B = 44$, then $m\angle E =$ 44.

20. If $m\angle C = 62$, then $m\angle F =$ 62.

Problem 4 Proving Triangles Congruent

Got It? **Given:** $\angle A \cong \angle D$, $\overline{AE} \cong \overline{DC}$, $\overline{EB} \cong \overline{CB}$, $\overline{BA} \cong \overline{BD}$

Prove: $\triangle AEB \cong \triangle DCB$

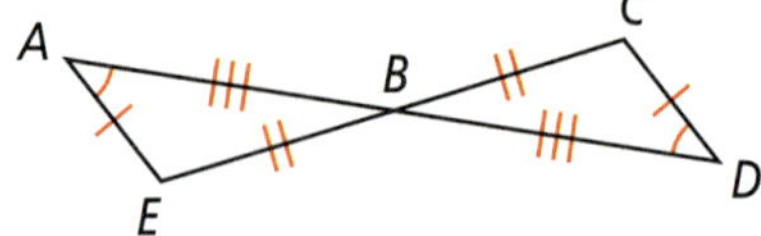

21. You are given four pairs of congruent parts. Circle the additional information you need to prove the triangles congruent.

A third pair of congruent sides   A second pair of congruent angles   A third pair of congruent angles

22. Complete the steps of the proof.

1) $\overline{AE} \cong$ DC, $\overline{EB} \cong$ CB, $\overline{BA} \cong$ BD	1) Given
2) $\angle A \cong$ $\angle D$	2) Given
3) $\angle ABE \cong$ $\angle DBC$	3) Vertical angles are congruent.
4) $\angle E \cong$ $\angle C$	4) Third Angles Theorem
5) $\triangle AEB \cong$ $\triangle DCB$	5) Definition of $\cong$ triangles

Lesson Check • Do you UNDERSTAND?

Error Analysis **Walter sketched the diagram at the right. He claims it shows that the two polygons are congruent. What information is missing to support his claim?**

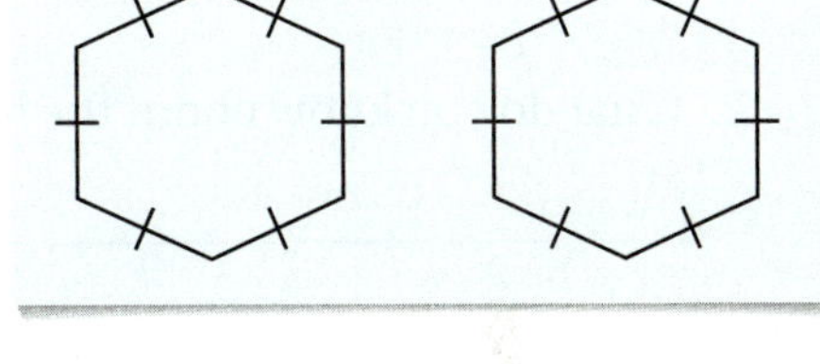

23. Underline the correct word(s) to complete the sentence.

Two polygons are congruent if they have congruent corresponding angles / sides / angles and sides.

24. Does the diagram show six pairs of congruent corresponding sides? Yes / No

25. Does the diagram show six pairs of congruent corresponding angles? Yes / No

26. What other information is needed to show that the two polygons are congruent?

Answers may vary. Sample: The diagram also needs to show that six pairs of corresponding angles are congruent.

Math Success

Check off the vocabulary words that you understand.

☐ congruent ☐ polygons

Rate how well you can ***identify congruent polygons.***

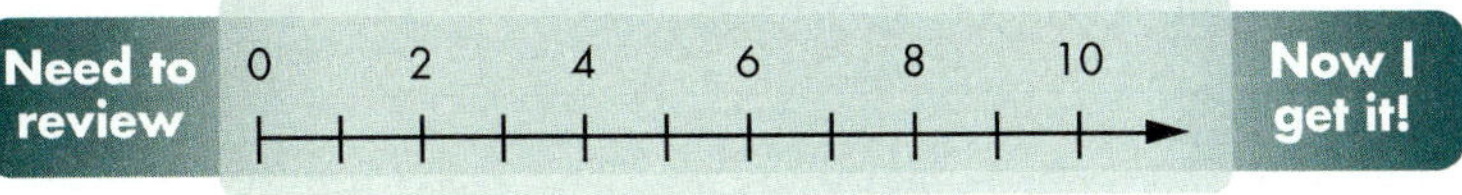

Name ______________________ Class ____________ Date ____________

4-1 Think About a Plan

Congruent Figures

Algebra Find the values of the variables.

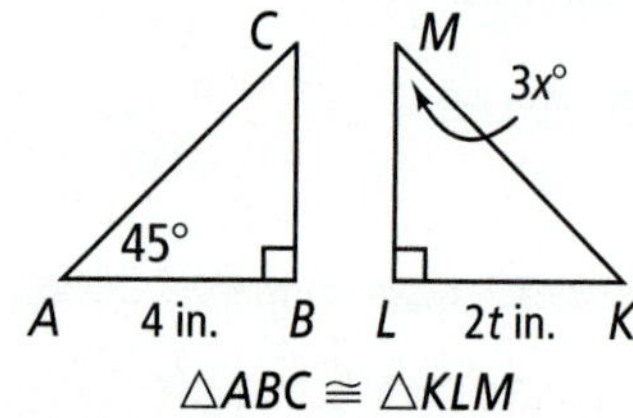

Know

1. What do you know about the measure of each of the non-right angles?

   The measure of each of the non-right angles are complementary.

2. What do you know about the length of each of the legs?

   All of the legs are equal in length.

3. What types of triangles are shown in the figure?

   isosceles right triangles

Need

4. What information do you need to know to find the value of x?

   You need to know that the measure of each of the non-right angles is 45.

5. What information do you need to know to find the value of t?

   You need to know that the length of each of the legs is 4 in.

Plan

6. How can you find the value of x? What is its value?

   Answers may vary. Sample: Set $3x$ equal to 45. So, $3x = 45$; $x = 15$.

7. How do you find the value of t? What is its value?

   Answers may vary. Sample: Set $2t$ equal to 4. So, $2t = 4$; $t = 2$.

Name _______________ Class _______ Date _______

4-1 Practice

Form K

Congruent Figures

Each pair of polygons is congruent. Find the measures of the numbered angles.

1. 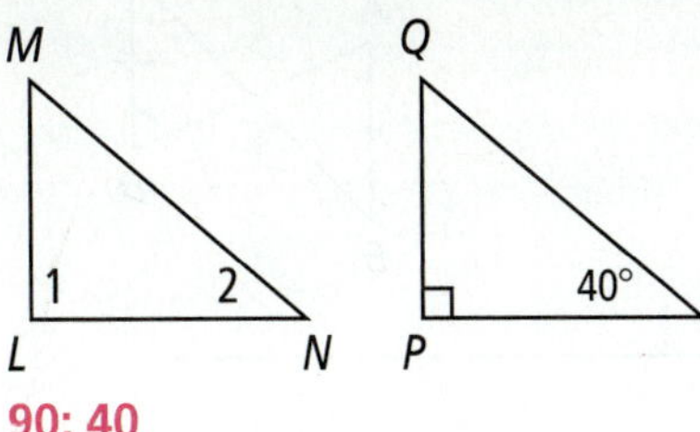

90; 40

2. 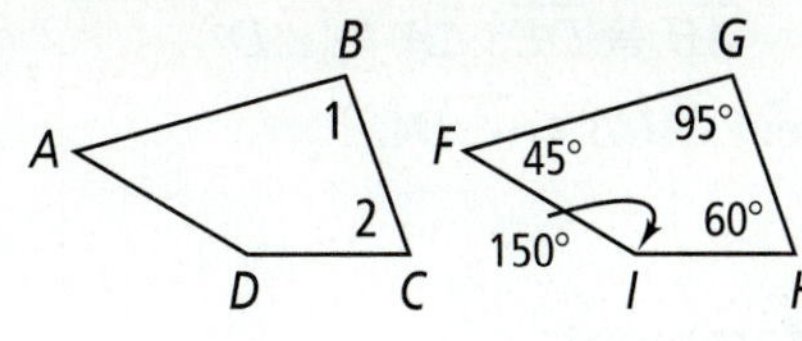

95; 60

Use the diagram at the right for Exercises 3–7. $\triangle ABC \cong \triangle XYZ$. Complete the congruence statements.

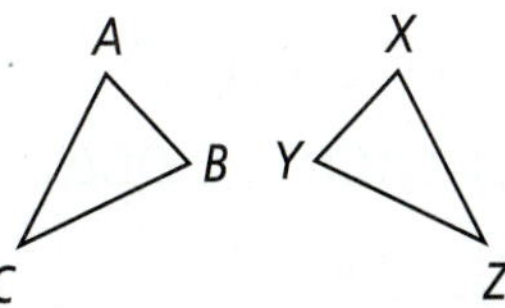

3. $\overline{AB} \cong$ $\overline{XY}$

To start, use the congruence statement to identify the points that correspond to A and B.

A corresponds to X. B corresponds to Y.

4. $\overline{ZY} \cong$ $\overline{CB}$

5. $\angle Z \cong$ $\angle C$

6. $\angle BAC \cong$ $\angle YXZ$

7. $\angle B \cong$ $\angle Y$

***FOUR* $\cong$ *MANY*. List each of the following.**

8. four pairs of congruent angles $\angle F \cong \angle M$; $\angle O \cong \angle A$; $\angle U \cong \angle N$; $\angle R \cong \angle Y$

9. four pairs of congruent sides $\overline{FO} \cong \overline{MA}$; $\overline{OU} \cong \overline{AN}$; $\overline{UR} \cong \overline{NY}$; $\overline{RF} \cong \overline{YM}$

For Exercises 10 and 11, can you conclude that the figures are congruent? Justify your answers.

10. $\triangle SRT$ and $\triangle PRQ$

S R Q T P

No; $\angle SRT \cong \angle PRQ$ because vert. ∠s are ≅, and $\angle RST \cong \angle RPQ$ by Third Angles Thm., but none of the sides are necessarily congruent.

11. $\triangle ABC$ and $\triangle FGH$

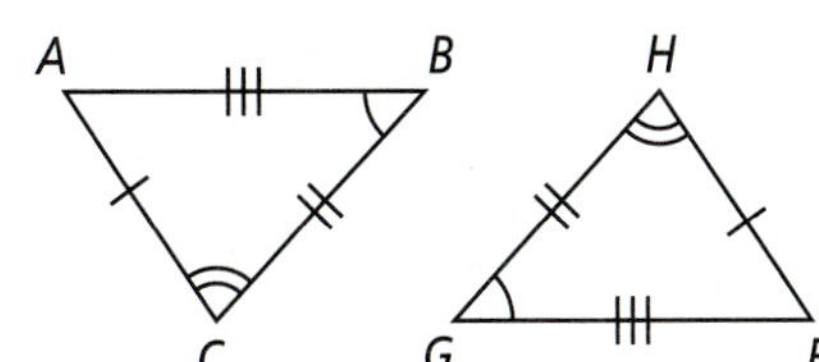

Yes; $\angle BAC \cong \angle GFH$ by Third Angles Thm. Therefore, $\triangle ABC \cong \triangle FGH$ by the def. of ≅ triangles.

Name ______________________ Class ____________ Date ____________

4-1 Practice (continued)

Form K

Congruent Figures

12. Given: $\overline{AD}$ and $\overline{BE}$ bisect each other.

$\overline{AB} \cong \overline{DE}$; $\angle A \cong \angle D$

Prove: $\triangle ACB \cong \triangle DCE$

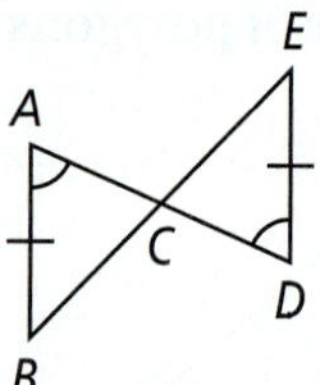

Statements	Reasons
1) $\overline{AD}$ and $\overline{BE}$ bisect each other. $\overline{AB} \cong \overline{DE}$, $\angle A \cong \angle D$	1) Given
2) $\overline{AC} \cong \overline{CD}$, $\overline{BC} \cong \overline{CE}$	2) _?_ Definition of bisect
3) $\angle ACB \cong \angle DCE$	3) _?_ Vertical angles are ≅.
4) $\angle B \cong \angle E$	4) _?_ Third Angles Theorem
5) $\triangle ACB \cong \triangle DCE$	5) _?_ Definition of ≅ Triangles

13. If $\triangle ABC \cong \triangle JKL$, which of the following must be a correct congruence statement? C

A $\angle A \cong \angle L$

C $\angle B \cong \angle K$

B $\overline{AB} \cong \overline{JL}$

D $\triangle BAC \cong \triangle LKJ$

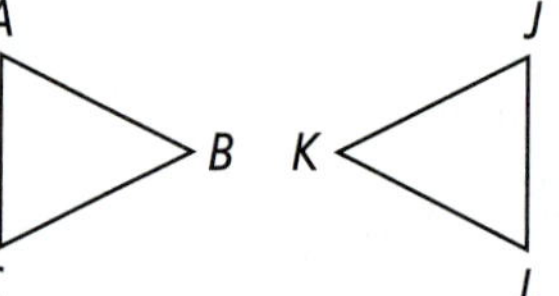

14. Reasoning A student says she can use the information in the figure to prove $\triangle ACB \cong \triangle ACD$. Is she correct? Explain.

No; explanations may vary. Sample: Corresponding parts are not congruent. The figure can be used to prove $\triangle ACB \cong \triangle CAD$.

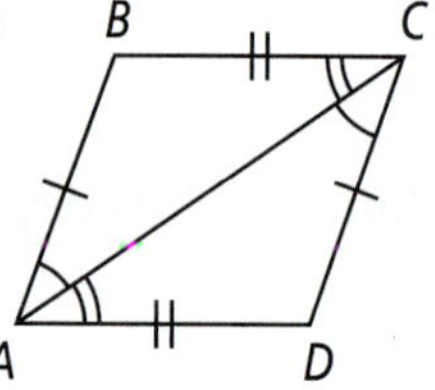

Algebra **Find the values of the variables.**

15. $\triangle XYZ \cong \triangle FED$ 3; 15

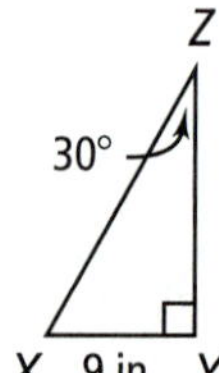

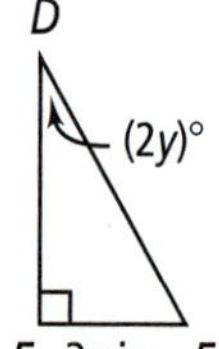

16. $\triangle ABD \cong \triangle CDB$ 15

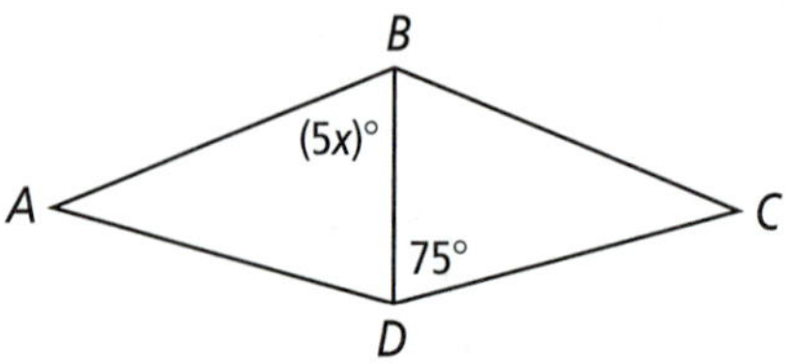

Algebra **$\triangle FGH \cong \triangle QRS$. Find the measures of the given angles or the lengths of the given sides.**

17. $m\angle F = x + 24$; $m\angle Q = 3x$ 36; 36

18. $\overline{GH} = 3x - 2$; $\overline{RS} = x + 6$ 10; 10

Name ____________________ Class ____________ Date ____________

4-1 Standardized Test Prep

Congruent Figures

Multiple Choice

For Exercises 1–6, choose the correct letter.

1. The pair of polygons at the right is congruent. What is $m\angle J$? **A**

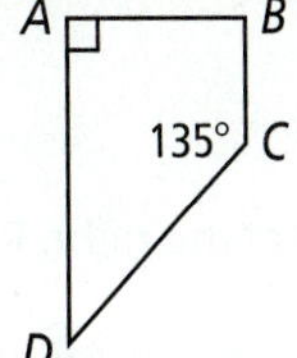

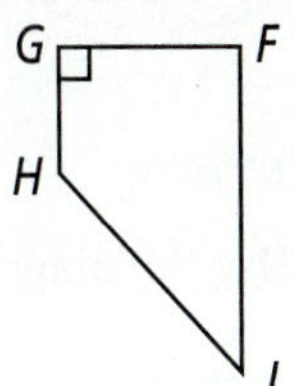

 45   (C) 135

 90   (D) 145

2. The triangles at the right are congruent. Which of the following statements must be true? **I**

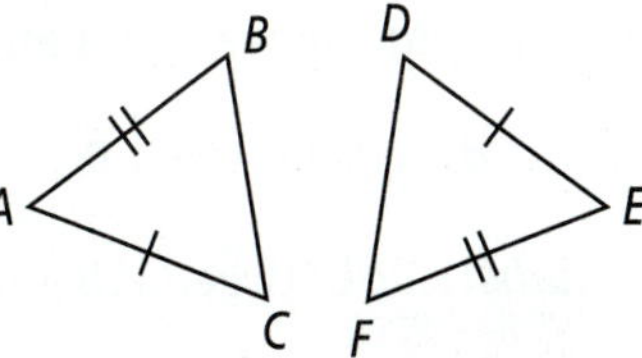

(F) $\angle A \cong \angle D$ (H) $\overline{AB} \cong \overline{DE}$

(G) $\angle B \cong \angle E$ (I) $\overline{BC} \cong \overline{FD}$

3. Given the diagram at the right, which of the following must be true? **B**

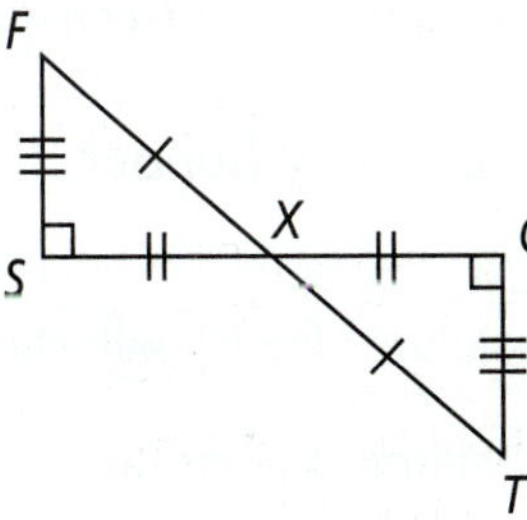

(A) $\triangle XSF \cong \triangle XTG$ (C) $\triangle FXS \cong \triangle XGT$

(B) $\triangle SXF \cong \triangle GXT$ (D) $\triangle FXS \cong \triangle GXT$

4. If $\triangle RST \cong \triangle XYZ$, which of the following need not be true? **I**

(F) $\angle R \cong \angle X$ (G) $\angle T \cong \angle Z$ (H) $\overline{RT} \cong \overline{XZ}$ (I) $\overline{SR} \cong \overline{YZ}$

5. If $\triangle ABC \cong \triangle DEF$, $m\angle A = 50$, and $m\angle E = 30$, what is $m\angle C$? **C**

(A) 30   (B) 50   (C) 100   (D) 120

6. If $ABCD \cong QRST$, $m\angle A = x - 10$, and $m\angle Q = 2x - 30$, what is $m\angle A$? **F**

(F) 10   (G) 20   (H) 30   (I) 40

Short Response

[2] $\angle ABD \cong \angle CDB$ and $\angle ADB \cong \angle CBD$, both by the Alt. Int Angles Thm. So, by Third Angles Thm., $\angle A \cong \angle C$. Because $\overline{DB} \cong \overline{BD}$ by the Refl. Prop. of Congruence, and we know $\overline{AB} \cong \overline{CD}$ and $\overline{AD} \cong \overline{CB}$, then all the corresponding parts are congruent and $\triangle ABD \cong \triangle CDB$.
[1] incomplete proof **[0]** no proof or incorrect proof

7. Given: $\overline{AB} \parallel \overline{DC}$, $\overline{AD} \parallel \overline{BC}$, $\overline{AB} \cong \overline{CD}$, $\overline{AD} \cong \overline{CB}$

Prove: $\triangle ABD \cong \triangle CDB$

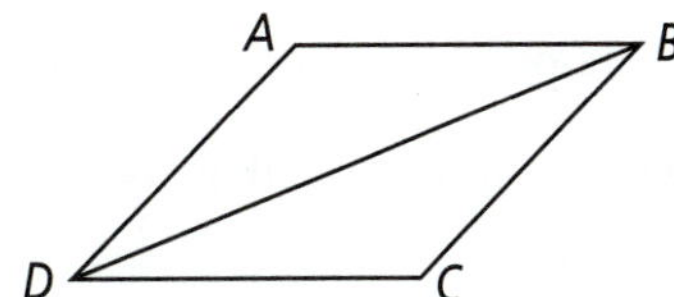

4-2 Triangle Congruence by SSS and SAS

Vocabulary

Review

1. Use the diagram at the right. Find each.

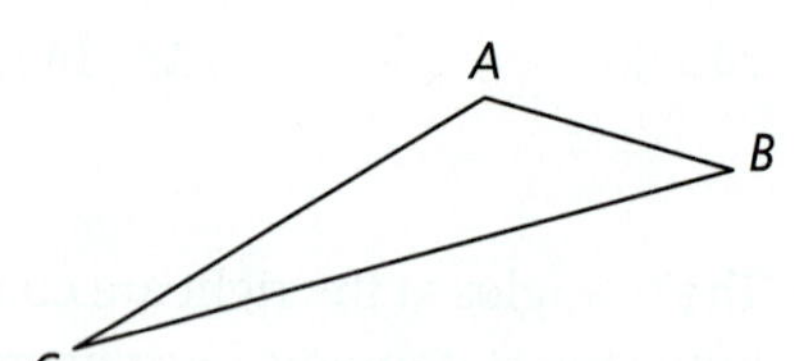

included angle between $\overline{AB}$ and $\overline{CA}$ $\angle A$

included side between $\angle A$ and $\angle C$ $\overline{AC}$

included angle between $\overline{BC}$ and $\overline{CA}$ $\angle C$

included side between $\angle B$ and $\angle C$ $\overline{BC}$

included angle between $\overline{BC}$ and $\overline{AB}$ $\angle B$

included side between $\angle B$ and $\angle A$ $\overline{AB}$

Vocabulary Builder

postulate (noun) PAHS chuh lit

Definition: A **postulate** is a statement that is accepted as true without being proven true.

Main Idea: In geometry, you use what you know to be true to prove new things true. The statements that you accept as true without proof are called **postulates** or axioms.

Use Your Vocabulary

2. Underline the correct word to complete the sentence.

You can use properties, *postulates*, and previously proven theorems as reasons / statements in a proof.

3. **Multiple Choice** What is a *postulate*?

(A) a convincing argument using deductive reasoning

(B) a conjecture or statement that you can prove true

(C) a statement accepted as true without being proven true

(D) a conclusion reached by using inductive reasoning

take note

Postulate 4-1 Side-Side-Side (SSS) Postulate

Postulate 4-1 Side-Side-Side (SSS) Postulate

If the three sides of one triangle are congruent to the three sides of another triangle, then the two triangles are congruent.

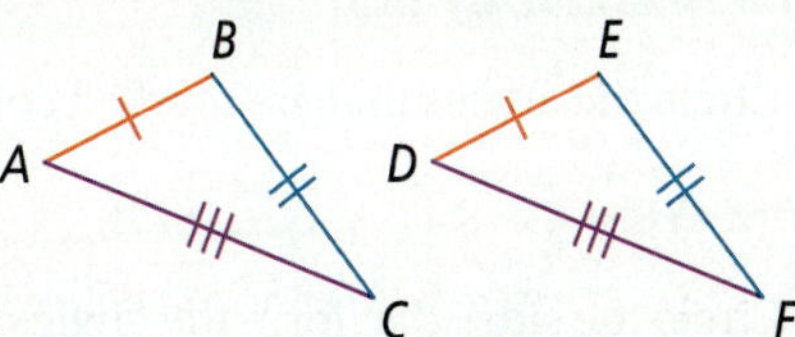

4. Use the figures at the right to complete the sentence.

If $\overline{AB} \cong \overline{DE}$, $\overline{BC} \cong \overline{EF}$, and $\overline{AC} \cong$ $\overline{DF}$, then $\triangle ABC \cong \triangle$ DEF.

Problem 1 Using SSS

Got It? Given: $\overline{BC} \cong \overline{BF}$, $\overline{CD} \cong \overline{FD}$

Prove: $\triangle BCD \cong \triangle BFD$

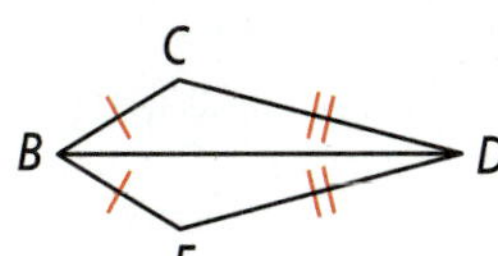

5. You know two pairs of sides that are congruent. What else do you need to prove the triangles congruent by SSS?

a third pair of congruent sides

6. The triangles share side BD .

7. Complete the steps of the proof.

Statement	Reason
1) $\overline{BC} \cong$ $\overline{BF}$	1) Given
2) $\overline{CD} \cong$ $\overline{FD}$	2) Given
3) $\overline{BD} \cong$ $\overline{BD}$	3) Reflexive Property of $\cong$
4) $\triangle BCD \cong$ $\triangle BFD$	4) SSS

take note

Postulate 4-2 Side-Angle-Side (SAS) Postulate

Postulate 4-2 Side-Angle-Side (SAS) Postulate

If two sides and the included angle of one triangle are congruent to two sides and the included angle of another triangle, then the two triangles are congruent.

Use the figures below to complete each statement.

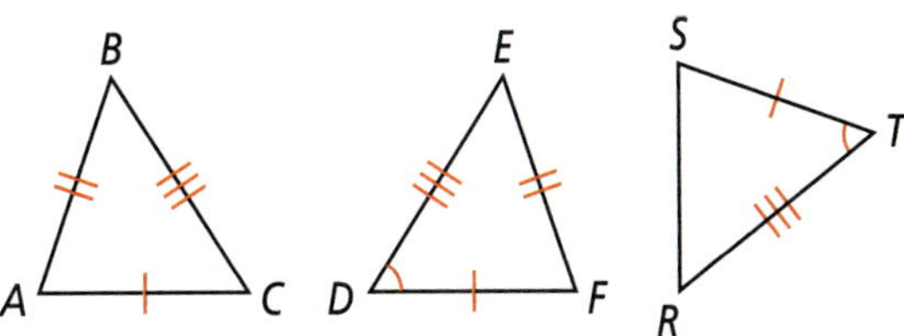

8. $\triangle DEF \cong$ $\triangle TRS$ by SAS.

9. $\triangle ABC \cong$ $\triangle FED$ by SSS.

Problem 2 Using SAS

Got It? **What other information do you need to prove $\triangle LEB \cong \triangle BNL$ by SAS?**

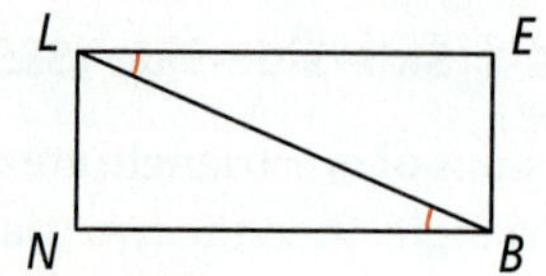

10. Circle the angles that are marked congruent in the diagram.

$\angle EBL$ $\angle ELB$ $\angle NBL$ $\angle NLB$

11. Circle the sides that form the angles that are marked congruent in the diagram.

$\overline{BE}$ $\overline{BL}$ $\overline{BN}$ $\overline{LB}$ $\overline{LE}$ $\overline{LN}$

12. Complete each congruence statements.

$\overline{LB} \cong$ $\overline{LB}$ $\angle BLE \cong$ $\angle LBN$

Underline the correct word(s) to complete each sentence.

13. Proving $\triangle LEB \cong \triangle BNL$ by SAS requires one / two pair(s) of congruent sides and one / two pair(s) of congruent angles.

14. The diagram shows congruency of zero / one / two pair(s) of congruent sides and zero / one / two pair(s) of congruent angles.

15. To prove the triangles congruent by SAS, you still need zero / one / two pair(s) of congruent sides and zero / one / two pair(s) of congruent angles .

16. To prove the triangles congruent, you need to prove $\overline{NB}$ and $\overline{EL}$ congruent.

Problem 3 Identifying Congruent Triangles

Got It? **Would you use SSS or SAS to prove the triangles below congruent? Explain.**

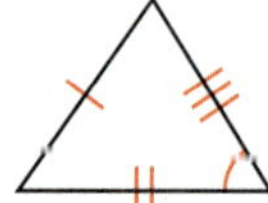

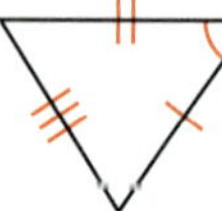

Complete each statement with *SSS* or *SAS*.

17. Use _?_ if you have three pairs of sides congruent. SSS

18. Use _?_ if you have two pairs of sides and the included angle congruent. SAS

Write T for *true* or F for *false*.

T **19.** The diagram shows congruence of three sides.

T **20.** In the triangle on the left, the marked angle is the included angle of the side with two marks and the side with three marks.

F **21.** In the triangle on the right, the marked angle is the included angle of the side with two marks and the side with three marks.

22. Would you use SSS or SAS to prove the triangles congruent? Explain.

SSS. Explanations may vary. Sample:

You can't use SAS because the included angles aren't

between congruent sides.

Lesson Check • Do you UNDERSTAND?

Error Analysis **Your friend thinks that the triangles shown below are congruent by SAS. Is your friend correct? Explain.**

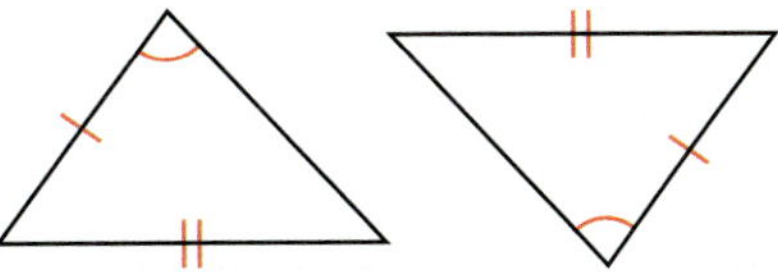

23. Are two pairs of corresponding sides congruent? Yes / No (Yes circled)

24. Is there a pair of congruent angles? Yes / No (Yes circled)

25. Are the congruent angles the included angles between the corresponding congruent sides? Yes / No (No circled)

26. Are the triangles congruent by SAS? Explain.

No. Explanations may vary. Sample: They cannot be proven congruent by SAS because the congruent angles are not included angles.

Math Success

Check off the vocabulary words that you understand.

☐ congruent ☐ corresponding

Rate how well you can *use SSS and SAS to prove triangles congruent.*

Need to review 0 2 4 6 8 10 Now I get it!

Name ______________________ Class ____________ Date ____________

4-2 Think About a Plan

Triangle Congruence by SSS and SAS

Use the Distance Formula to determine whether $\triangle ABC$ and $\triangle DEF$ are congruent. Justify your answer.

$A(1, 4), B(5, 5), C(2, 2)$

$D(-5, 1), E(-1, 0), F(-4, 3)$

Understanding the Problem

1. You need to determine if $\triangle ABC \cong \triangle DEF$. What are the three ways you know to prove triangles congruent?

   If all corresponding parts are congruent, if all three sides are congruent, or, if two sides and the included angle are congruent, then the triangles are congruent.

2. What information is given in the problem?

   the coordinates for each vertex of each triangle

Planning the Solution

3. If you use the SSS Postulate to determine whether the triangles are congruent, what information do you need to find?

   the lengths of the three sides of each triangle

4. How can you find distances on a coordinate plane without measuring?

   Use the Distance Formula.

5. In an ordered pair, which number is the x-coordinate? Which is the y-coordinate?

   The x-coordinate is the first number and the y-coordinate is the second number.

Getting an Answer

6. Find the length of each segment using the Distance Formula, $D = \sqrt{(y_1 - y_2)^2 + (x_1 - x_2)^2}$. Your answers may be in simplest radical form.

   $\overline{AB}$ $\sqrt{17}$ $\overline{BC}$ $3\sqrt{2}$ $\overline{CA}$ $\sqrt{5}$

   $\overline{DE}$ $\sqrt{17}$ $\overline{EF}$ $3\sqrt{2}$ $\overline{FD}$ $\sqrt{5}$

7. Using the SSS Postulate, are the triangles congruent? Explain.

   Yes; the triangles are congruent, because three pairs of sides are congruent.

Name ______________________________ Class ______________ Date ______________

4-2 Practice

Form K

Triangle Congruence by SSS and SAS

1. Developing Proof Copy and complete the flow proof.

Given: $\overline{RX} \cong \overline{SX}$, $\overline{QX} \cong \overline{TX}$

Prove: $\triangle QXR \cong \triangle TXS$

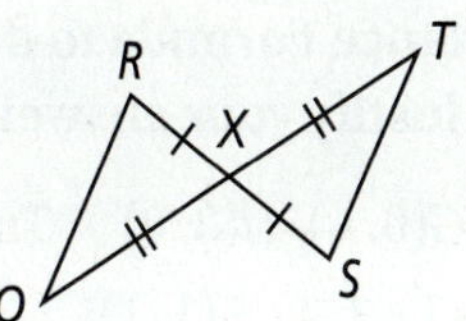

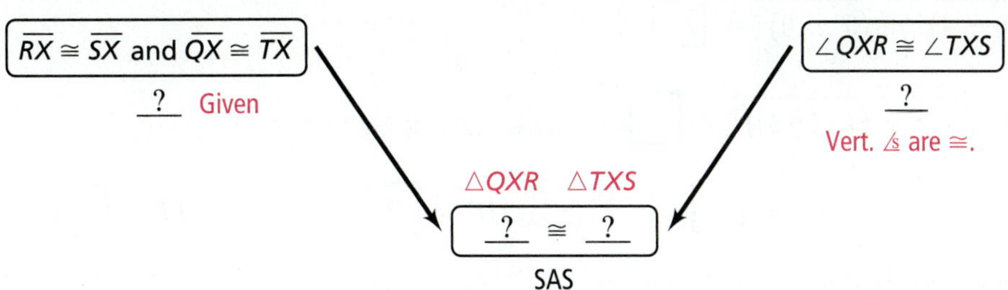

What other information, if any, do you need to prove the two triangles congruent by SAS? Explain. To start, list the pairs of congruent, corresponding parts you already know.

2.

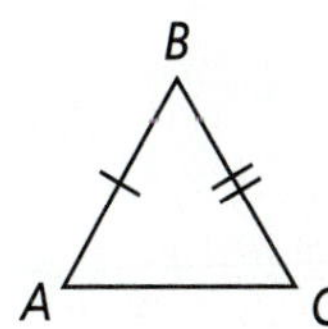

$\overline{AB} \cong$ $\overline{HG}$ and $\overline{BC} \cong$ $\overline{GF}$

Need $\angle B \cong \angle G$; these are the included ∠s.

3.

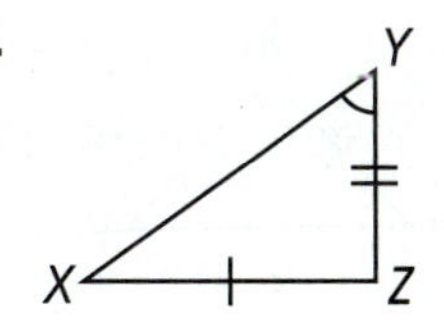

$\overline{XZ} \cong \overline{RT}$ and $\overline{ZY} \cong \overline{TS}$ and $\angle Y \cong \angle S$

need $\angle Z \cong \angle T$ or $\overline{XY} \cong \overline{RS}$

Would you use SSS or SAS to prove these triangles congruent? If there is not enough information to prove the triangles congruent by SSS or SAS, write *not enough information.* Explain your answer.

4.

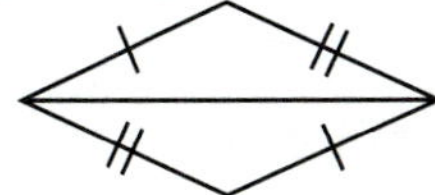

SSS; third side is shared by both ∆s and is ≅ to itself by Refl. Prop. of ≅.

5.

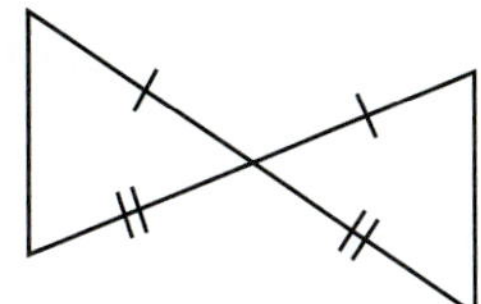

SAS; vertical ∠s are ≅.

Name ______________________ Class ____________ Date ____________

4-2 Practice (continued) Form K

Triangle Congruence by SSS and SAS

Use the Distance Formula to determine whether $\triangle FGH$ and $\triangle JKL$ are congruent. Justify your answer.

6. $F(0, 0)$, $G(0, 4)$, $H(3, 0)$ To start, find the lengths of the corresponding sides.
$J(1, 4)$, $K(-3, 4)$, $L(1, 1)$

$FG = \sqrt{(0-4)^2 + (0-0)^2} = \boxed{4}$

$JK = \sqrt{(4-4)^2 + (1-(-3))^2} = \boxed{4}$ Yes; they are ≅ by SSS.

$GH = \boxed{5}$ $KL = \boxed{5}$ $HF = \boxed{3}$ $LJ = \boxed{3}$

7. $F(-2, 5)$, $G(4, -3)$, $H(4, 3)$
$J(2, 1)$, $K(-6, 7)$, $L(-6, 1)$ No; they are not ≅ because $\overline{FH}$ and $\overline{JL}$ have different lengths.

Can you prove the triangles congruent? If so, write the congruence statement and name the postulate you would use. If not, write *not enough information* and tell what other information you would need.

8.

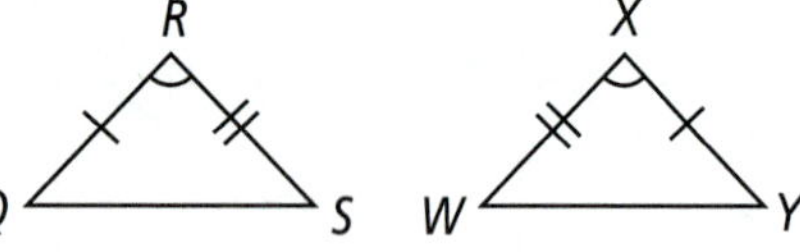

Yes; $\triangle QRS \cong \triangle YXW$ by SAS.

9.

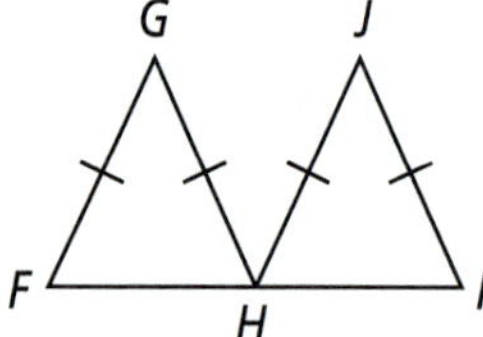

not enough information; need $\overline{FH} \cong \overline{HK}$ to apply SSS or $\angle G \cong \angle J$ to apply SAS

10. Reasoning Suppose $\overline{AB} \cong \overline{DE}$, $\angle B \cong \angle E$, and $\overline{AB} \cong \overline{BC}$. Is $\triangle ABC$ congruent to $\triangle DEF$? Explain. Not necessarily; $\overline{EF}$ may not be ≅ to $\overline{BC}$.

11. Given: $\overline{BD}$ is the perpendicular bisector of $\overline{AC}$.

Prove: $\triangle BAD \cong \triangle BCD$

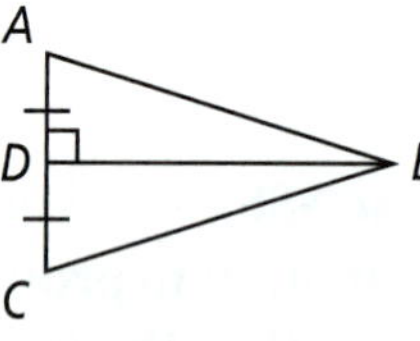

Statements	Reasons
1) $\overline{BD}$ is the perpendicular bisector of $\overline{AC}$.	1) Given
2) $\overline{AD} \cong \overline{CD}$	2) Definition of segment bisector
3) $\angle ADB$ and $\angle CDB$ are right ∠s.	3) Definition of perpendicular
4) ? $\angle ADB \cong \angle CDB$	4) ? All right angles are ≅.
5) ? $\overline{BD} \cong \overline{BD}$	5) ? Reflexive Property of ≅
6) ? $\triangle BAD \cong \triangle BCD$	6) ? SAS

Name ______________________________ Class ____________ Date ____________

4-2 Standardized Test Prep

Triangle Congruence by SSS and SAS

Multiple Choice

For Exercises 1–4, choose the correct letter.

1. Which pair of triangles can be proved congruent by SSS? C

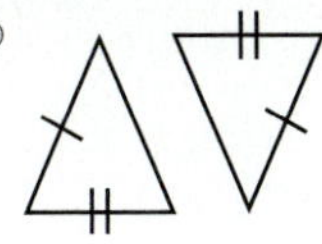
B
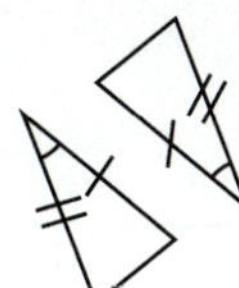
C

D
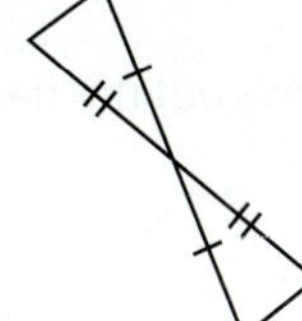

2. Which pair of triangles can be proved congruent by SAS? G

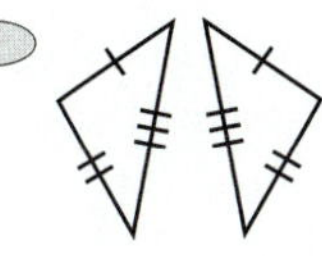
G
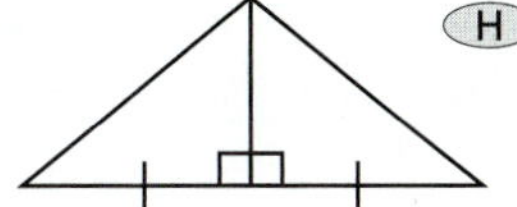

I

3. What additional information do you need to prove $\triangle NOP \cong \triangle QSR$? D

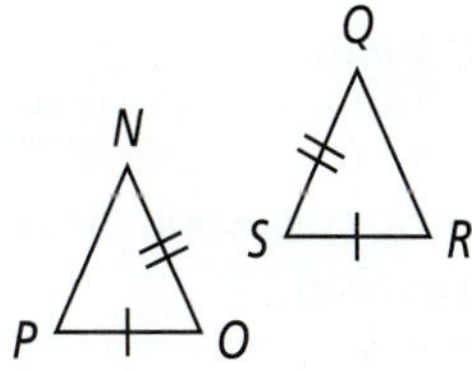

A. $\overline{PN} \cong \overline{SQ}$ C. $\angle P \cong \angle S$

B. $\overline{NO} \cong \overline{QR}$ D. $\angle O \cong \angle S$

4. What additional information do you need to prove $\triangle GHI \cong \triangle DEF$? F

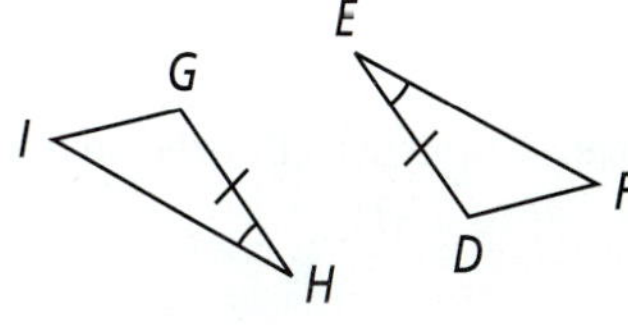

F. $\overline{HI} \cong \overline{EF}$ H. $\angle F \cong \angle G$

G. $\overline{HI} \cong \overline{ED}$ I. $\overline{GI} \cong \overline{DF}$

Short Response

5. Write a two-column proof.

Given: M is the midpoint of $\overline{LS}$, $\overline{PM} \cong \overline{QM}$.

Prove: $\triangle LMP \cong \triangle SMQ$

L, M, Q, P, S

[2] Statements: 1) M is the midpoint of $\overline{LS}$; 2) $\overline{LM} \cong \overline{SM}$;

3) $\angle LMP \cong \angle SMQ$; 4) $\overline{PM} \cong \overline{QM}$; 5) $\triangle LMP \cong \triangle SMQ$; Reasons:
1) Given; 2) Def. of a midpoint; 3) Vert. ∠s are ≅; 4) Given;
5) SAS [1] incomplete proof [0] incorrect or no proof

4-3 PART 1 Triangle Congruence by ASA and AAS

Vocabulary

1. Cross out the figure(s) that are NOT *triangle*(s).

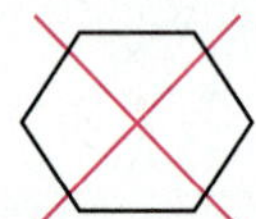 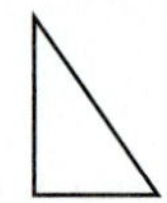 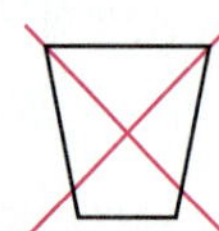 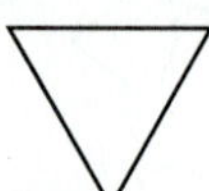 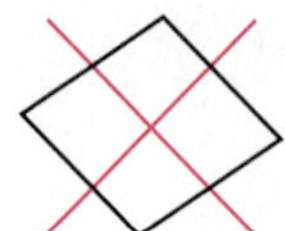

2. A *triangle* is a polygon with 3 sides.

3. A *triangle* with a right angle is called a(n)
obtuse / right / scalene *triangle*.

Vocabulary Builder

corresponding (adjective) **kawr uh SPAHN ding**

Other Word Forms: correspond (verb), correspondence (noun)

Definition: **Corresponding** means similar in position, purpose, or form.

Math Usage: Congruent figures have congruent **corresponding** parts.

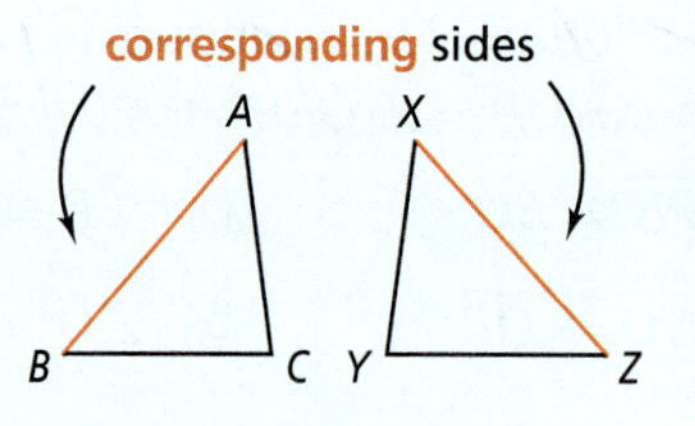

Use Your Vocabulary

Draw a line from each part of $\triangle ABC$ in Column A to the *corresponding* part of $\triangle XYZ$ in Column B.

Column A	Column B
4. $\overline{BC}$	$\angle Z$
5. $\angle A$	$\angle Y$
6. $\overline{AB}$	$\overline{YZ}$
7. $\angle C$	$\angle X$
8. $\overline{AC}$	$\overline{XY}$
9. $\angle B$	$\overline{XZ}$

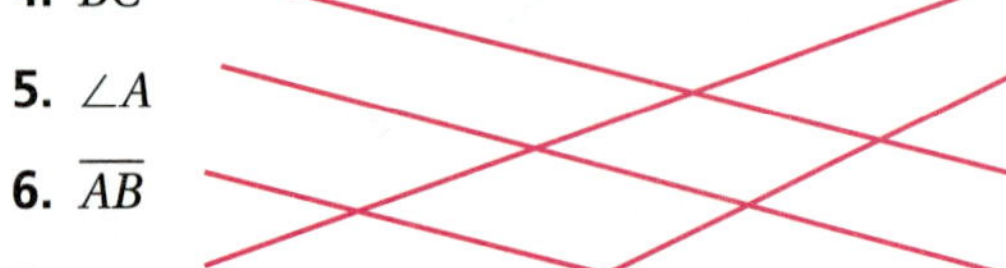

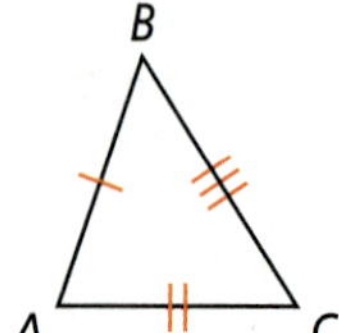

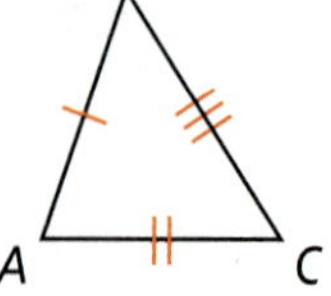

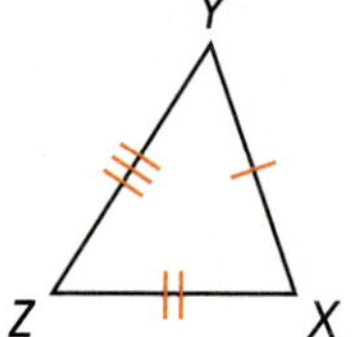

take note

Postulate 4–3 Angle-Side-Angle (ASA) Postulate

Postulate	If . . .	Then . . .
If two angles and the included side of one triangle are congruent to two angles and the included side of another triangle, then the two triangles are congruent.	$\angle A \cong \angle D$, $\overline{AC} \cong \overline{DF}$, $\angle C \cong \angle F$	$\triangle ABC \cong \triangle DEF$

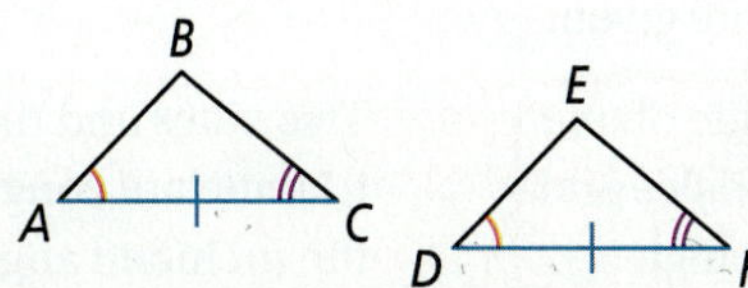

10. Explain how the ASA Postulate is different from the SAS Postulate.

Explanations may vary. Sample: The ASA Postulate uses two angles and an included side and the SAS Postulate uses two sides and an included angle.

Problem 1 Using ASA

Got It? **Which two triangles are congruent by ASA? Explain.**

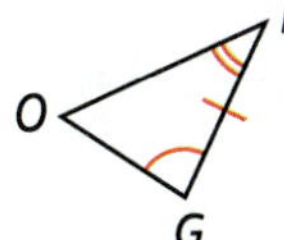

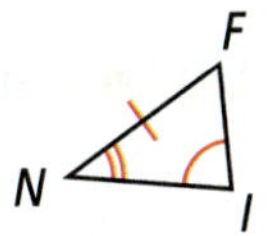

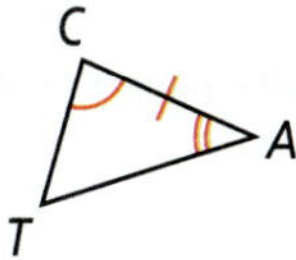

11. Name the triangles. List the vertices in corresponding order: list the vertex with the one arc first, the vertex with the two arcs second, and the third vertex last.

$\triangle GHO$ $\triangle INF$ $\triangle CAT$

12. $\angle G \cong \angle$ I $\cong \angle$ C

13. $\angle H \cong \angle$ N $\cong \angle$ A

14. $\overline{HG} \cong$ $\overline{NF}$ $\cong$ $\overline{AC}$

15. The congruent sides that are included between congruent angles are $\overline{HG}$ and $\overline{AC}$.

16. Write a congruence statement. Justify your reasoning.

$\triangle$ GHO $\cong \triangle$ CAT

Answers may vary. Sample: $\triangle GHO$ and $\triangle CAT$ have two pairs of congruent angles and a pair of included congruent sides.

Problem 2 Writing a Proof Using ASA

Got It? **Given:** $\angle CAB \cong \angle DAE$, $\overline{BA} \cong \overline{EA}$, $\angle B$ and $\angle E$ are right angles

Prove: $\triangle ABC \cong \triangle AED$

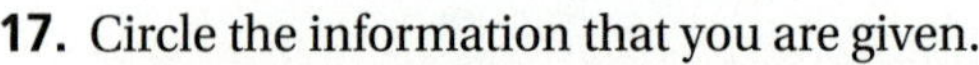

17. Circle the information that you are given.

Two angles and the included side of one triangle are congruent to two angles and the included side of another triangle. (circled)	Two sides and the included angle of one triangle are conguent to two sides and the included angle of another triangle.

18. Complete the flow chart to prove $\triangle ABC \cong \triangle AED$.

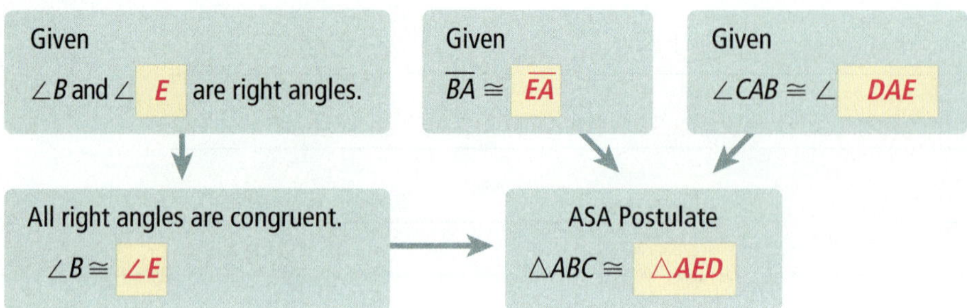

Lesson Check • Do you UNDERSTAND?

Error Analysis **Your friend asks you for help on a geometry exercise. Below is your friend's paper. What error did your friend make? Explain.**

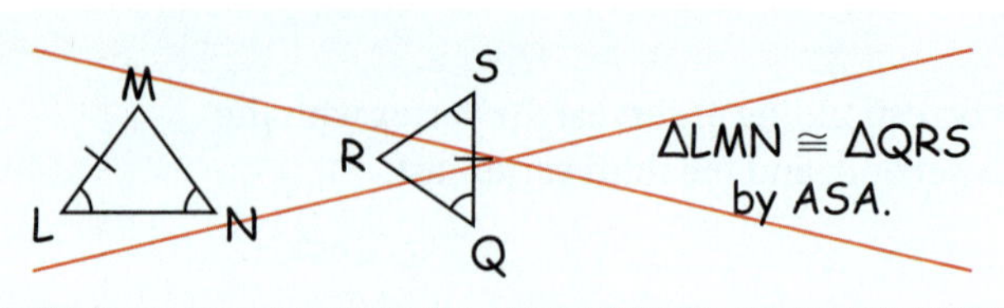

19. Circle the side in $\triangle LMN$ that is included between $\angle L$ and $\angle N$.

$\overline{LM}$	$\overline{LN}$ (circled)	$\overline{MN}$

20. Circle the side in $\triangle QRS$ that is included between side of $\angle Q$ and $\angle S$.

$\overline{QR}$	$\overline{QS}$ (circled)	$\overline{RS}$

21. Do you know whether the included sides you circled in Exercises 19 and 20 are congruent? Yes / No (circled)

22. What error did your friend make? Explain.

Answers may vary. Sample: My friend said the triangles were congruent by ASA, but the diagram does not show that the included sides $\overline{LN}$ and $\overline{QS}$ are congruent.

4-3 PART 2 Triangle Congruence by ASA and AAS

Vocabulary

Review

Write T for *true* or F for *false*.

T 1. *Congruent* angles have the same measure.

F 2. A triangle and a square are *congruent* figures.

T 3. All *congruent* figures are similar.

4. Circle the pair(s) of triangles that appear to be *congruent*.

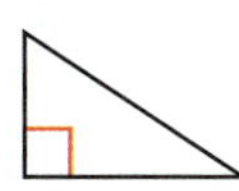

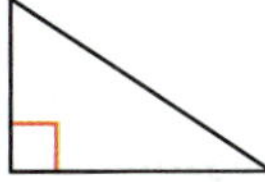

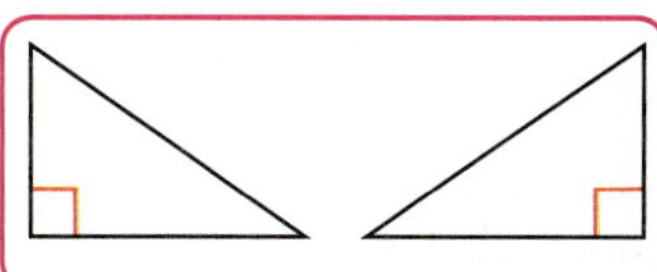

Vocabulary Builder

nonincluded (adjective) nahn in KLOO did

Definition: **Nonincluded** means not contained between or within.

Math Usage: In $\triangle ABC$, $\overline{AC}$ is a **nonincluded** side of $\angle A$ and $\angle B$ because it is not between $\angle A$ and $\angle B$.

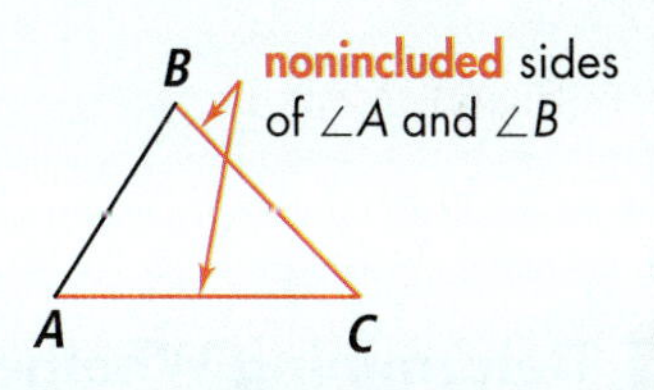

Use Your Vocabulary

Use the triangle at the right. Circle the nonincluded sides of each pair of angles.

S
R
T

5. $\angle R$ and $\angle S$

$\overline{RS}$ $\overline{RT}$ $\overline{ST}$

6. $\angle R$ and $\angle T$

$\overline{RS}$ $\overline{RT}$ $\overline{ST}$

7. $\angle T$ and $\angle S$

$\overline{RS}$ $\overline{RT}$ $\overline{ST}$

take note

Theorem 4-2 Angle-Angle-Side (AAS) Theorem

Theorem	If . . .	Then . . .
If two angles and a nonincluded side of one triangle are congruent to two angles and the corresponding nonincluded side of another triangle, then the two triangles are congruent.	$\angle A \cong \angle D$, $\angle B \cong \angle E$, $\overline{AC} \cong \overline{DF}$	$\triangle ABC \cong \triangle DEF$

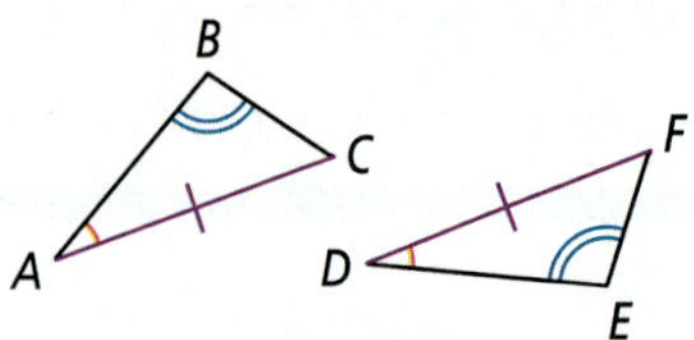

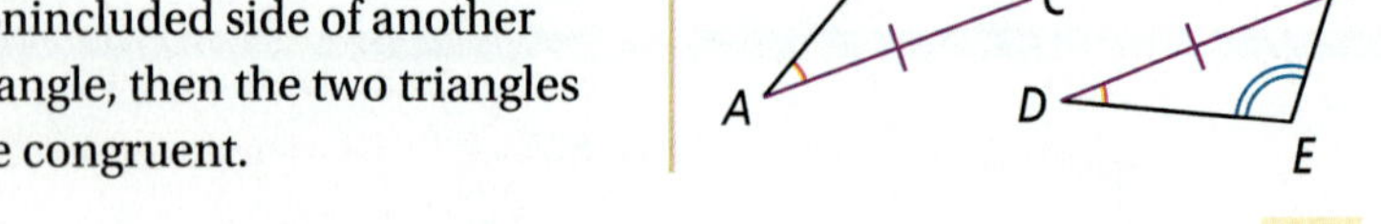

8. The nonincluded congruent sides of $\triangle ABC$ and $\triangle DEF$ are $\overline{AC}$ and $\overline{DF}$.

Problem 3 Writing a Proof Using AAS

Got It? **Given:** $\angle S \cong \angle Q$, $\overline{RP}$ bisects $\angle SRQ$

Prove: $\triangle SRP \cong \triangle QRP$

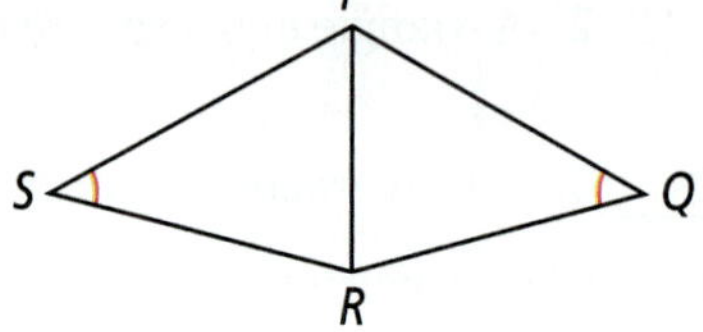

9. Complete the statements to prove $\triangle SRP \cong \triangle QRP$.

Statements	Reasons
1) $\angle S \cong$ $\angle Q$	1) Given
2) $\overline{RP}$ bisects $\angle SRQ$	2) Given
3) $\angle SRP \cong$ $\angle QRP$	3) Definition of an angle bisector
4) $\overline{RP} \cong$ $\overline{RP}$	4) Reflexive Property of Congruence
5) $\triangle SRP \cong$ $\angle QRP$	5) AAS

Problem 4 Determining Whether Triangles Are Congruent

Got It? Are $\triangle PAR$ and $\triangle SIR$ congruent? Explain.

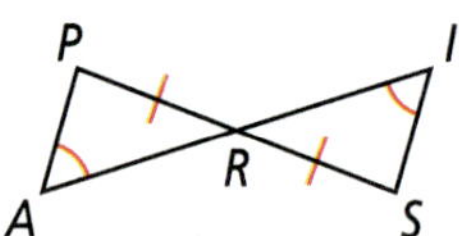

10. The congruence marks show that $\angle A \cong$ $\angle I$ and $\overline{PR} \cong$ $\overline{SR}$.

11. What other corresponding congruent parts exist? Explain.

$\angle PRA \cong \angle SRI$ because they are vertical angles.

12. Are $\triangle PAR$ and $\triangle SIR$ congruent? Explain.

$\triangle PAR$ and $\triangle SIR$ are congruent by AAS because two pairs of corresponding angles and one pair of corresponding nonincluded sides are congruent.

Lesson Check • Do you know HOW?

Which postulate or theorem could you use to prove $\triangle ABC \cong \triangle DEF$?

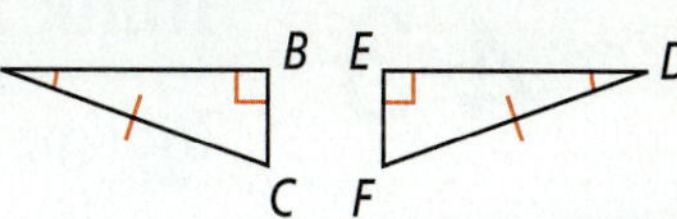

Underline the correct word(s) to complete each sentence.

13. The diagram shows that zero / one / two pair(s) of angles are congruent and zero / one / two pair(s) of sides are congruent.

14. $\overline{AC}$ is a(n) included / nonincluded side of $\angle A$ and $\angle B$.

15. $\overline{DF}$ is a(n) included / nonincluded side of $\angle D$ and $\angle E$.

16. To prove $\triangle ABC \cong \triangle DEF$, you can use ASA / AAS.

Lesson Check • Do you UNDERSTAND?

Reasoning **Suppose $\angle E \cong \angle I$ and $\overline{FE} \cong \overline{GI}$. What else must you know in order to prove $\triangle FDE \cong \triangle GHI$ by ASA? By AAS?**

17. Label the diagram at the right.

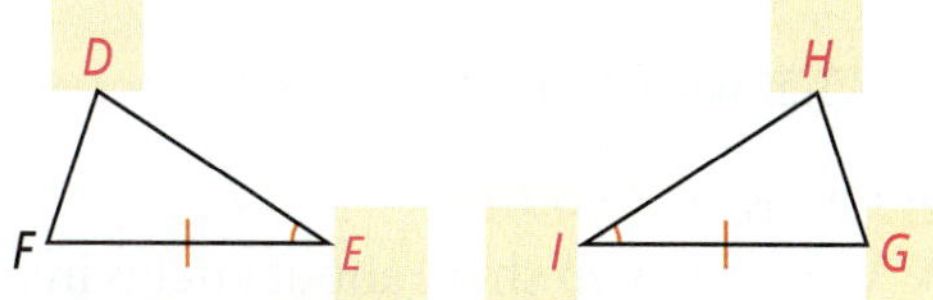

18. Circle what you need to prove the triangles congruent by ASA. Underline what you need to prove the triangles congruent by AAS.

two pairs of congruent angles and a pair of nonincluded congruent sides

two pairs of congruent angles and a pair of included congruent sides

19. If you want to use ASA, $\angle$ F and $\angle$ G must also be congruent.

20. If you want to use AAS, $\angle$ D and $\angle$ H must also be congruent.

Math Success

Check off the vocabulary words that you understand.

☐ included ☐ nonincluded ☐ corresponding

Rate how well you can *use ASA and AAS.*

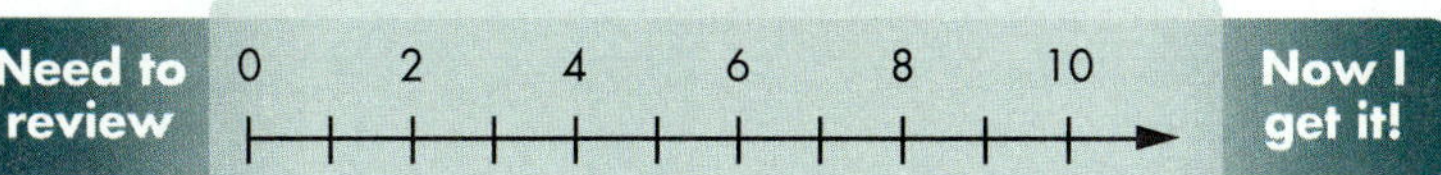

Name ______________________ Class ____________ Date ____________

4-3 Think About a Plan

Triangle Congruence by ASA and AAS

Given: $\overline{AB} \parallel \overline{CD}$, $\overline{AD} \parallel \overline{CB}$

Prove: $\triangle ABC \cong \triangle CDA$

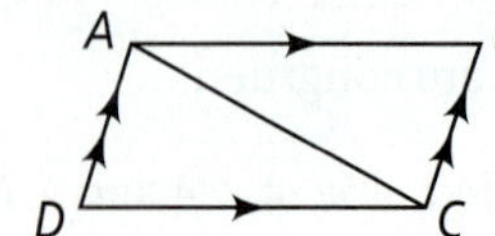

1. What do you need to find to solve the problem?

   Sample: at least three corresponding pairs of sides or angles that I can prove to be congruent

2. What are the corresponding parts of the two triangles?

   $\angle CAB$ and $\angle ACD$; $\angle D$ and $\angle B$; $\angle DAC$ and $\angle BCA$; $\overline{AC}$ and $\overline{CA}$; $\overline{AB}$ and $\overline{CD}$; and $\overline{BC}$ and $\overline{DA}$

3. What word would you use to describe $\overline{AC}$? transversal

4. What can you show about angles in the triangles that can indicate congruency?

   I can find congruent angles using alternate interior angles of the transversal $\overline{AC}$.

5. What do you know about a side or sides of the triangles that can be used to show congruency?

   The transversal is part of both triangles, so it is congruent to itself by the Reflexive Property of Congruence.

6. Write a proof in paragraph form.

   Answers may vary. Sample: $\overline{AB} \parallel \overline{DC}$ and $\overline{AD} \parallel \overline{BC}$ are given. Therefore $\overline{AC}$ is a transversal. $\angle CAB \cong \angle ACD$ and $\angle DAC \cong \angle BCA$ by the Alternate Interior Angles Theorem. The transversal is part of both triangles, so $\overline{AC} \cong \overline{CA}$ by the Reflexive Property of Congruence. $\triangle ABC \cong \triangle CDA$ by the ASA Postulate.

Name ______________________ Class __________ Date __________

4-3 Practice

Form K

Triangle Congruence by ASA and AAS

Name the two triangles that are congruent by ASA.

1. 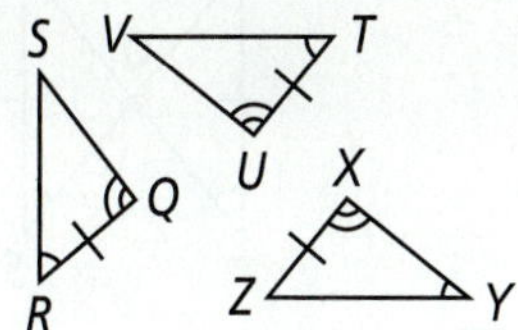

$\triangle RQS \cong \triangle TUV$

2. 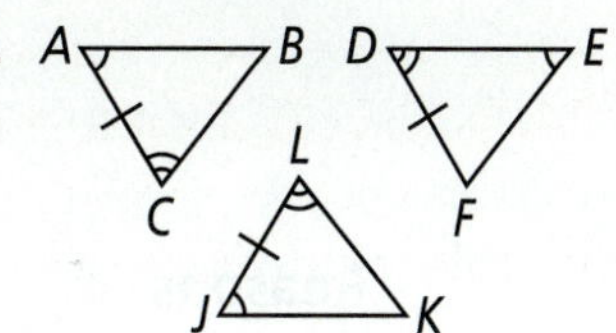

$\triangle ABC \cong \triangle JKL$

3. 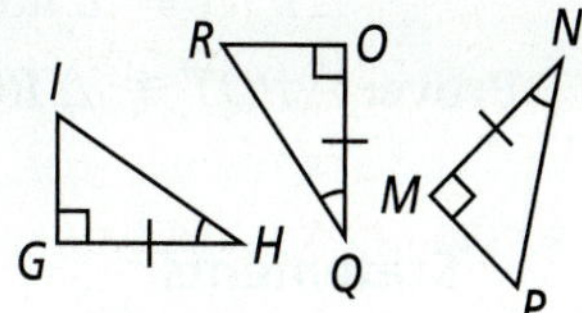

$\triangle GHI \cong \triangle MNP \cong \triangle OQR$

4. Developing Proof Complete the two-column proof by filling in the blanks.

Given: $\overline{BD} \perp \overline{AC}$, $\overline{BD}$ bisects $\angle ABC$

Prove: $\triangle ABD \cong \triangle CBD$

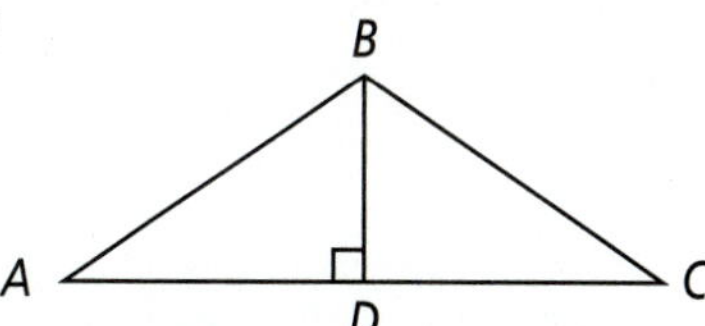

Statements	Reasons
1) $\overline{BD} \perp \overline{AC}$, $\overline{BD}$ bisects $\angle ABC$	1) Given
2) ? $\angle ADB$ and $\angle CDB$ are right ∆s	2) Def. of perpendicular
3) $\angle ADB \cong \angle CDB$	3) ? All right angles are $\cong$.
4) $\angle ABD \cong \angle CBD$	4) ? Definition of $\angle$ bisector
5) ? $\overline{BD} \cong \overline{BD}$	5) Reflexive Property of $\cong$
6) ? $\triangle ABD \cong \triangle CBD$	6) ASA

5. Given: $\overline{KJ} \cong \overline{MN}$, $\angle KJL \cong \angle MNL$

Prove: $\triangle JKL \cong \triangle NML$

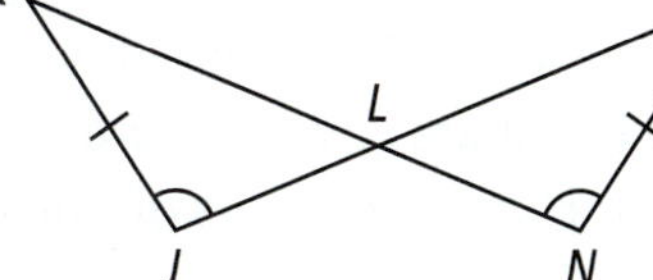

Statements	Reasons
1) $\overline{KJ} \cong \overline{MN}$, $\angle KJL \cong \angle MNL$	1) Given
2) $\angle KLJ \cong \angle MLN$	2) ? Vertical ∆ are $\cong$.
3) ? $\angle LKJ \cong \angle LMN$	3) Third Angles Theorem
4) ? $\triangle JKL \cong \triangle NML$	4) ASA

4-3 Practice (continued) — Form K

Triangle Congruence by ASA and AAS

6. Given: $\overline{PT} \cong \overline{RS}$

$\angle PTR \cong \angle RSP$

Prove: $\triangle PQT \cong \triangle RQS$

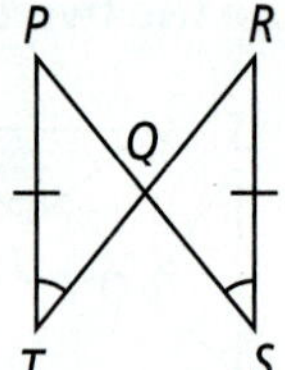

Statements	Reasons
1) ? $\overline{PT} \cong \overline{RS}$, $\angle PTR \cong \angle RSP$	1) Given
2) $\angle PQT \cong \angle RQS$	2) ? Vertical ∠s are ≅.
3) ? $\triangle PQT \cong \triangle RQS$	3) AAS

7. Given: $\overline{BD}$ is the angle bisector of $\angle ABC$ and $\angle ADC$.

Prove: $\triangle ABD \cong \triangle CBD$

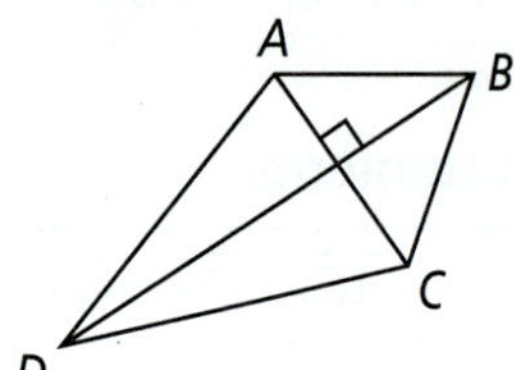

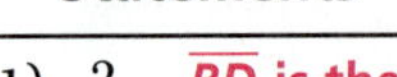

Statements	Reasons
1) ? $\overline{BD}$ is the angle bisector of $\angle ABC$ and $\angle ADC$.	1) ? Given
2) ? $\angle ABD \cong \angle CBD$, $\angle ADB \cong \angle CDB$	2) Definition of ∠ bisector
3) $\angle BAD \cong \angle BCD$	3) ? Third Angles Theorem
4) $\overline{BD} \cong \overline{BD}$	4) ? Reflexive Property of ≅
5) ? $\triangle ABD \cong \triangle CBD$	5) AAS

8. Reasoning A student tells you that he can prove the AAS Theorem using the SAS Postulate and the Third Angles Theorem. Do you agree with him? Explain. (*Hint:* How many pairs of sides does the SAS Postulate use?)

Answers may vary. Sample: No; the SAS Postulate requires two pairs of corresp. ≅ sides.

9. Reasoning Can you prove the triangles congruent? Justify your answer.

Answers may vary. Sample. No; there are no included sides or included ∠s that correspond in both △s, and you cannot use the Third Angles Theorem.

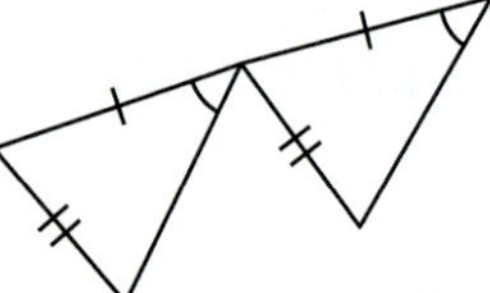

Name ______________________ Class __________ Date __________

4-3 Standardized Test Prep

Triangle Congruence by ASA and AAS

Multiple Choice

For Exercises 1–4, choose the correct letter.

1. Which pair of triangles can be proven congruent by the ASA Postulate? C

(A) 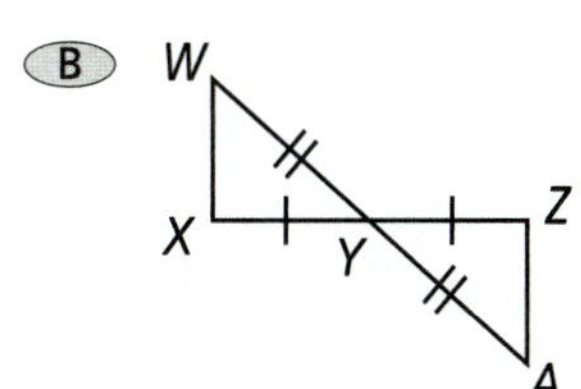

(C) 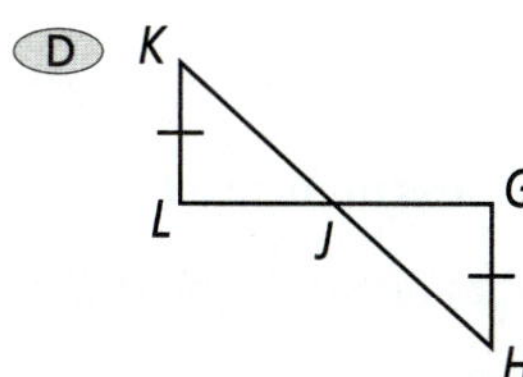

(B) W X Y Z A

(D) K L J G H

2. For the ASA Postulate to apply, which side of the triangle must be known? F

(F) the included side
(H) the shortest side
(G) the longest side
(I) a non-included side

3. Which pair of triangles can be proven congruent by the AAS Theorem? D

(A) A C D B F E

(C) 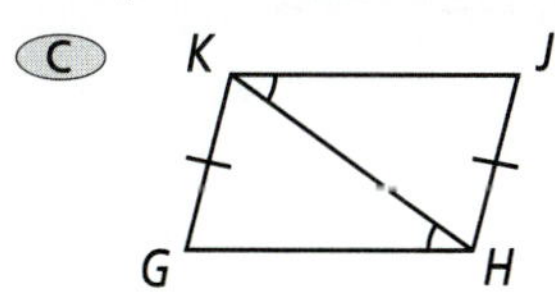

(B) 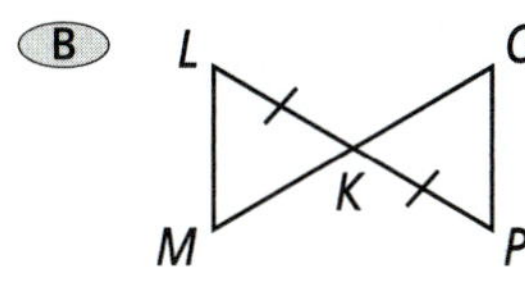

(D) 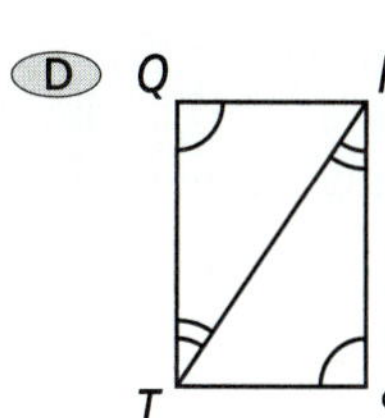

4. For the AAS Theorem to apply, which side of the triangle must be known? I

(F) the included side
(H) the shortest side
(G) the longest side
(I) a non-included side

Short Response

5. Write a paragraph proof.

Given: $\angle 3 \cong \angle 5, \angle 2 \cong \angle 4$

Prove: $\triangle VWX \cong \triangle VYX$

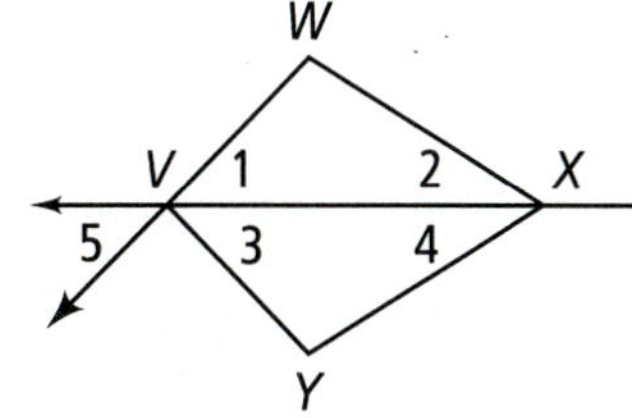

[2] $\angle 3 \cong \angle 5$ is given. $\angle 1 \cong \angle 5$ because vert. ∠s are ≅. $\angle 3 \cong \angle 1$ by the Trans. Prop. of ≅. $\angle 2 \cong \angle 4$ is given. $\overline{VX} \cong \overline{VX}$ by the Refl. Prop. of ≅. $\triangle VWX \cong \triangle VYX$ by ASA.
[1] incomplete proof
[0] incorrect or no proof

4-4 Using Corresponding Parts of Congruent Triangles

Vocabulary

Review

Underline the correct word(s) to complete each sentence.

1. The *Reflexive* Property of Congruence states that any geometric figure is congruent / similar to itself.

2. The *Reflexive* Property of Equality states that any quantity is equal to / greater than / less than itself.

3. Circle the expressions that illustrate the *Reflexive* Property of Equality.

$a = a$ If $AB = 2$, then $2 = AB$.

$3(x + y) = 3x + 3y$ $5 + c = 5 + c$

4. Circle the expressions that illustrate the *Reflexive* Property of Congruence.

If $\angle A \cong \angle B$, then $\angle B \cong \angle A$.   If $\overline{CD} \cong \overline{LM}$ and $\overline{LM} \cong \overline{XY}$, then $\overline{CD} \cong \overline{XY}$.

$\angle ABC \cong \angle ABC$ $\overline{CD} \cong \overline{CD}$

Vocabulary Builder

proof (noun) proof

Related Word: prove (verb)

Definition: A **proof** is convincing evidence that a statement or theory is true.

Math Usage: A **proof** is a convincing argument that uses deductive reasoning.

Use Your Vocabulary

Complete each statement with *proof* or *prove*.

5. In geometry, a _?_ uses definitions, postulates, and theorems to prove theorems. proof

6. No one can _?_ how our universe started. prove

7. He can _?_ when he bought the computer because he has a receipt. prove

8. Complete the steps in the *proof.*

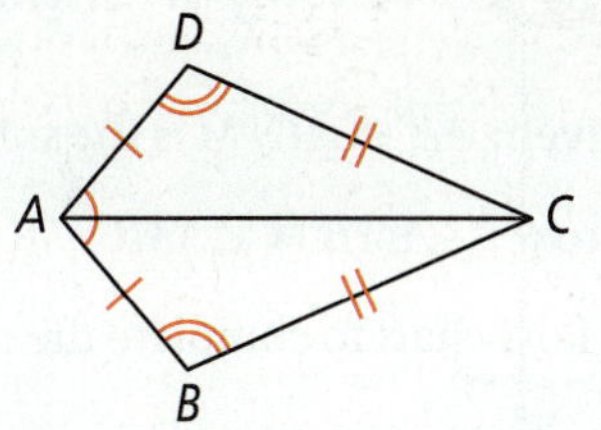

Given: $\overline{AB} \cong \overline{AD}$, $\overline{BC} \cong \overline{DC}$,
$\angle D \cong \angle B$, $\angle DAC \cong \angle BAC$

Prove: $\triangle ABC \cong \triangle ADC$

Statements	Reasons
1) $\overline{AB} \cong$ $\overline{AD}$ $\overline{BC} \cong$ $\overline{DC}$	1) Given
2) $\overline{AC} \cong$ $\overline{AC}$	2) Reflexive Property of $\cong$
3) $\angle D \cong$ $\angle B$ $\angle DAC \cong$ $\angle BAC$	3) Given
4) $\angle DCA \cong$ $\angle BCA$	4) Third Angles Theorem
5) $\triangle ABC \cong$ $\triangle ADC$	5) Definition of $\cong$ triangles

Problem 1 Proving Parts of Triangles Congruent

Got It? **Given:** $\overline{BA} \cong \overline{DA}$, $\overline{CA} \cong \overline{EA}$

Prove: $\angle C \cong \angle E$

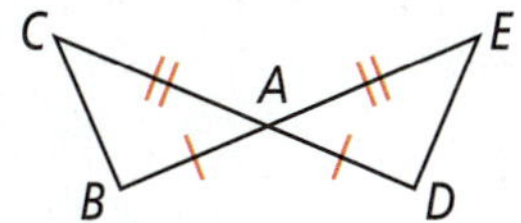

9. Name four ways you can use congruent parts of two triangles to prove that the triangles are congruent.

SSS ASA

SAS AAS

10. To prove triangles are congruent when you know two pairs of congruent corresponding sides, you can use SSS or SAS .

Underline the correct word to complete the sentence.

11. The *Given* states and the diagram shows that there are one / two / three pairs of congruent sides.

12. Give a reason for each statement of the proof.

Statements	Reasons
1) $\overline{BA} \cong \overline{DA}$	1) Given
2) $\overline{CA} \cong \overline{EA}$	2) Given
3) $\angle CAB \cong \angle EAD$	3) Vertical angles are congruent.
4) $\triangle CAB \cong \triangle EAD$	4) SAS
5) $\angle C \cong \angle E$	5) Corresponding parts of congruent triangles are congruent.

Problem 2 Proving Triangle Parts Congruent to Measure Distance

Got It? **Given:** $\overline{AB} \cong \overline{AC}$, M is the midpoint of $\overline{BC}$

Prove: $\angle AMB \cong \angle AMC$

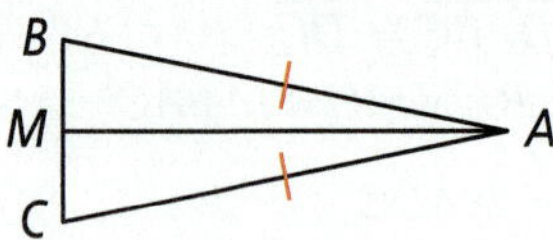

13. Use the flow chart to complete the proof.

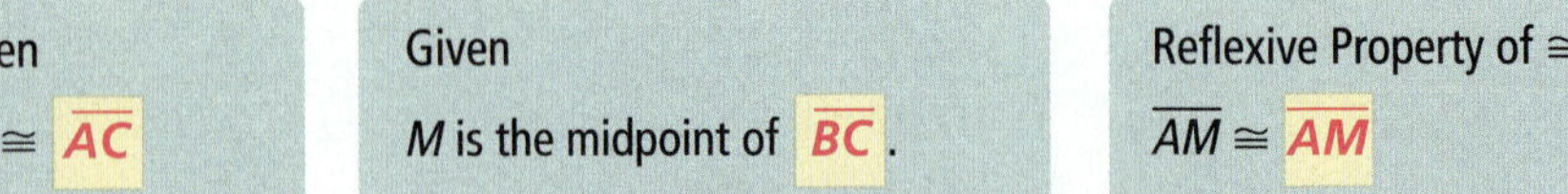

Definition of midpoint

$\overline{BM} \cong \overline{CM}$

SSS Theorem

$\triangle AMB \cong \triangle AMC$

Corresponding parts of ≅ triangles are ≅.

$\angle AMB \cong \angle AMC$

Lesson Check • Do you know HOW?

Name the postulate or theorem that you can use to show the triangles are congruent. Then explain why $\overline{EA} \cong \overline{MA}$.

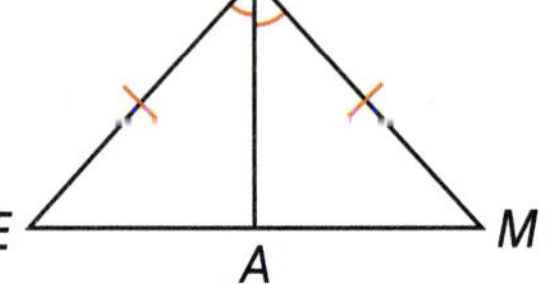

14. Circle the angles that are marked congruent.

$\angle E$ ($\angle ETA$) $\angle M$ $\angle EAT$ ($\angle MTA$)

15. Circle the sides that are marked congruent.

($\overline{ET}$)   ($\overline{MT}$) $\overline{EA}$ $\overline{MA}$ $\overline{AT}$

16. Circle the sides that are congruent by the Reflexive Property of Congruence.

$\overline{ET}$ and $\overline{MT}$ $\overline{EA}$ and $\overline{MA}$ ($\overline{AT}$ and $\overline{AT}$)

17. Underline the correct postulate or theorem to complete the sentence.

$\triangle EAT \cong \triangle MAT$ by <u>SAS</u> / AAS / ASA / SSS.

18. Now explain why $\overline{EA} \cong \overline{MA}$.

Corresponding parts of congruent triangles are congruent.

Lesson Check • Do you UNDERSTAND?

Error Analysis **Find and correct the error(s) in the proof.**

Given: $\overline{KH} \cong \overline{NH}$, $\angle L \cong \angle M$ **Prove:** H is the midpoint of $\overline{LM}$.

Proof: $\overline{KH} \cong \overline{NH}$ because it is given. $\angle L \cong \angle M$ because it is given. $\angle KHL \cong \angle NHM$ because vertical angles are congruent. So, $\triangle KHL \cong \triangle MHN$ by ASA Postulate. Since corresponding parts of congruent triangles are congruent, $\overline{LH} \cong \overline{MH}$. By the definition of midpoint, H is the midpoint of $\overline{LM}$.

K H M L N

Place a ✓ in the box if the statement is correct. Place an ✗ if it is incorrect.

✓ **19.** $\angle KHL \cong \angle NHM$ because vertical angels are congruent.

✗ **20.** $\triangle KHL \cong \triangle MHN$ by ASA Postulate.

Underline the correct word to complete each sentence.

21. When you name congruent triangles, you must name corresponding vertices in a different / the same order.

22. To use the ASA Postulate, you need two pairs of congruent angles and a pair of included / nonincluded congruent sides.

23. To use the AAS Theorem, you need two pairs of congruent angles and a pair of included / nonincluded congruent sides.

24. Identify the error(s) in the proof.

$\triangle KHL$ is not congruent to $\triangle MHN$. The ASA Postulate cannot be used to prove the triangles congruent.

25. Correct the error(s) in the proof.

$\triangle KHL \cong \triangle NHM$ by the AAS Theorem.

Math Success

Check off the vocabulary words that you understand.

☐ congruent ☐ corresponding ☐ proof

Rate how well you can *use congruent triangles.*

Need to review

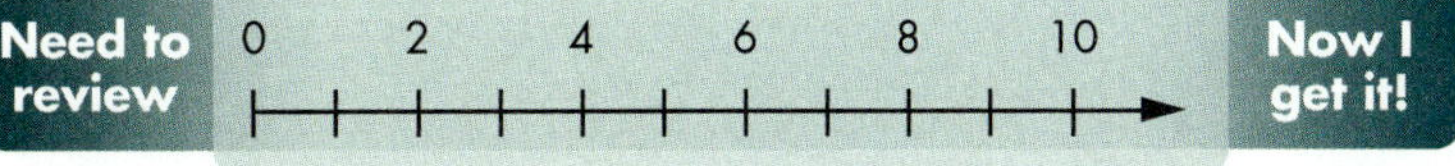

Now I get it!

Name ______________________ Class ____________ Date ____________

4-4 Think About a Plan

Using Corresponding Parts of Congruent Triangles

Constructions The construction of $\angle B$ congruent to given $\angle A$ is shown. $\overline{AD} \cong \overline{BF}$ because they are the radii of the same circle. $\overline{DC} \cong \overline{FE}$ because both arcs have the same compass settings. Explain why you can conclude that $\angle A \cong \angle B$.

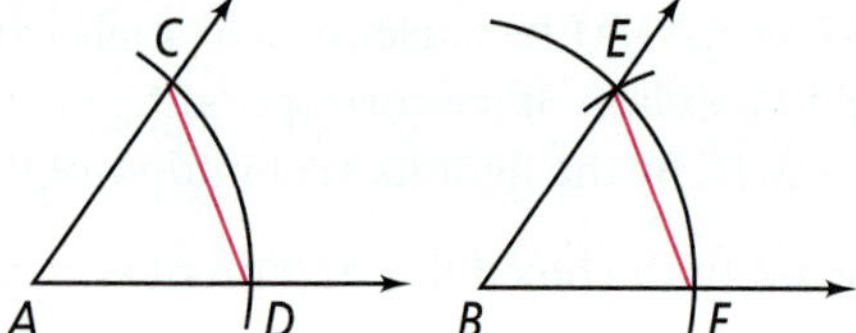

Understanding the Problem

1. What is the problem asking you to prove?

   $\angle A \cong \angle B$

2. Segments $\overline{DC}$ and $\overline{FE}$ are not drawn on the construction. Draw them in. What figures are formed by drawing these segments?

   two triangles

3. What information do you need to be able to use corresponding parts of congruent triangles?

   $\overline{AC}$ needs to be shown as congruent to $\overline{BE}$.

Planning the Solution

4. To use corresponding parts of congruent triangles, which two triangles do you need to show to be congruent?

   $\triangle ACD$ and $\triangle BEF$

5. What reason can you use to state that $\overline{AC} \cong \overline{BE}$?

   They are congruent because they are radii of the same circle by construction.

Getting an Answer

6. Write a paragraph proof that uses corresponding parts of congruent triangles to prove that $\angle A \cong \angle B$.

   $\overline{AC} \cong \overline{BE}$ and $\overline{AD} \cong \overline{BF}$ because they are both radii of the same circle. $\overline{DC} \cong \overline{FE}$ because they both have the same compass settings. Therefore, $\triangle ACD \cong \triangle BEF$ by SSS and $\angle A \cong \angle B$ by CPCTC.

Name ______________________ Class ____________ Date ____________

4-4 Practice

Form K

Using Corresponding Parts of Congruent Triangles

1. Developing Proof State why the two triangles are congruent. Then list all other corresponding parts of the triangles that are congruent.

AAS; $\triangle QRS \cong \triangle TWX$; $\angle Q \cong \angle T$, $\overline{RS} \cong \overline{WX}$

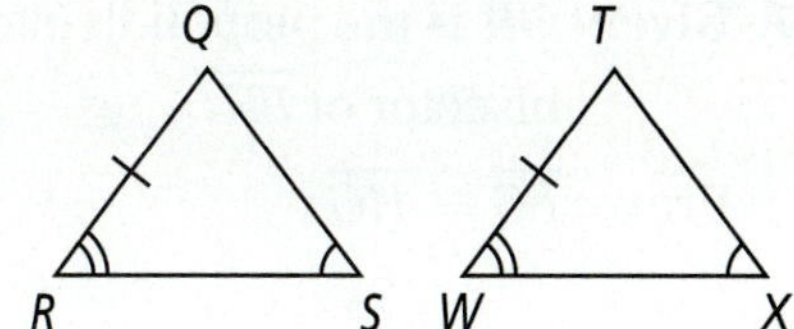

2. Developing Proof State why $\triangle AXY$ and $\triangle CYX$ are congruent. Then list all other corresponding parts of the triangles that are congruent.

Answers may vary. Sample: SAS; $\angle AYX \cong \angle CXY$, $\overline{AY} \cong \overline{CX}$

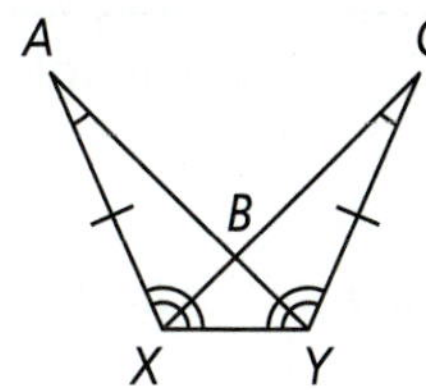

3. Given: $\overline{QS} \parallel \overline{RT}$, $\angle R \cong \angle S$

Prove: $\angle QTS \cong \angle TQR$

To start, determine how you can prove the triangles are congruent.

The triangles share a side and have a pair of congruent angles.

Because $\overline{QS} \parallel$ **$\overline{RT}$**, alternate interior angles $\angle SQT$ and **$\angle RTQ$** are congruent. The triangles can be proven congruent by AAS.

Statements	Reasons
1) ? **$\overline{QS} \parallel \overline{RT}$, $\angle R \cong \angle S$**	1) Given
2) ? **$\angle SQT \cong \angle RTQ$**	2) Alternate interior ∠s are ≅.
3) ? **$\overline{QT} \cong \overline{TQ}$**	3) Reflexive Property of Congruence
4) ? **$\triangle STQ \cong \triangle RQT$**	4) AAS
5) ? **$\angle QTS \cong \angle TQR$**	5) Corresp. parts of ≅ △ are ≅.

Reasoning Copy and mark the figure to show the given information. Explain how you would prove $\overline{AB} \cong \overline{DE}$.

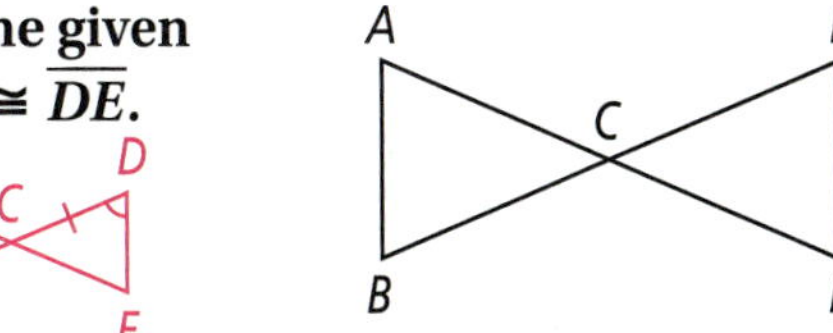

4. Given: $\overline{AC} \cong \overline{DC}$, $\angle B \cong \angle D$

AAS and Corresp. parts of ≅ △ are ≅.

5. Given: $\overline{AE}$ bisects $\overline{BD}$, $\overline{DB}$ bisects $\overline{AE}$

SAS and Corresp. parts of ≅ △ are ≅.

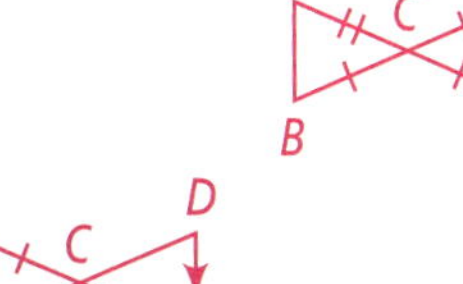

6. Given: $\overline{AB} \parallel \overline{DE}$, $AC = EC$

Answers may vary. Sample: AAS and Corresp. parts of ≅ △ are ≅.

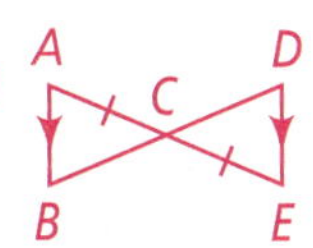

Name ______________________ Class ____________ Date ____________

4-4 Practice (continued) Form K

Using Corresponding Parts of Congruent Triangles

7. Given: $\overline{GK}$ is the perpendicular bisector of $\overline{FH}$.

Prove: $\overline{FG} \cong \overline{HG}$

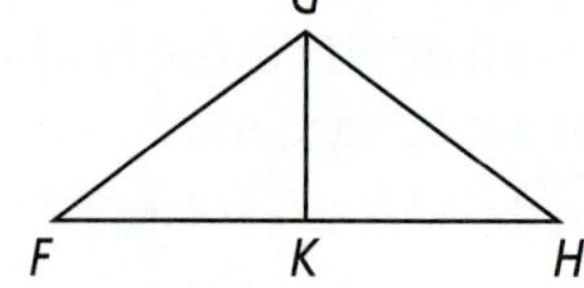

Statements	Reasons
1) $\overline{GK}$ is the perpendicular bisector of $\overline{FH}$.	1) ? **Given**
2) ? **$\overline{KF} \cong \overline{KH}$**	2) Definition of perpendicular bisector
3) $\angle GKF \cong \angle GKH$	3) Definition of perpendicular bisector; all right angles are congruent.
4) ? **$\overline{GK} \cong \overline{GK}$**	4) Reflexive Property of Congruence
5) $\triangle FGK \cong \triangle HGK$	5) ? **SAS**
6) ? **$\overline{FG} \cong \overline{HG}$**	6) Corresp. parts of ≅ ▲s are ≅.

8. Given: *ABCE* is a rectangle, *D* is the midpoint of $\overline{CE}$

Prove: $\overline{AD} \cong \overline{BD}$

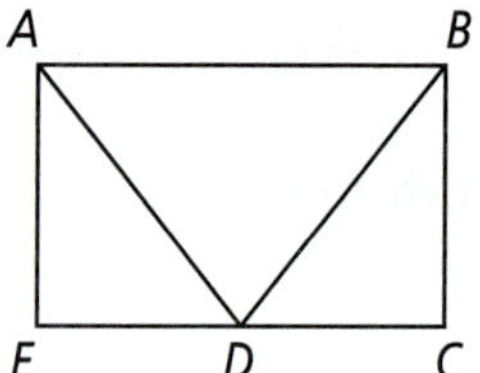

Statements	Reasons
1) *ABCE* is a rectangle, *D* is the midpoint of $\overline{CE}$	1) Given
2) $\angle AED \cong \angle BCD$	2) Definition of rectangle
3) $\overline{AE} \cong \overline{BC}$	3) Definition of rectangle
4) ? **$\overline{ED} \cong \overline{CD}$**	4) ? **Definition of midpoint**
5) ? **$\triangle AED \cong \triangle BCD$**	5) ? **SAS**
6) ? **$\overline{AD} \cong \overline{BD}$**	6) ? **Corresp. parts of ≅ ▲s are ≅.**

Name ______________________ Class ____________ Date ____________

4-4 Standardized Test Prep

Using Corresponding Parts of Congruent Triangles

Multiple Choice

For Exercises 1–6, choose the correct letter.

1. Based on the given information in the figure at the right, how can you justify that $\triangle JHG \cong \triangle HJI$? B

   (A) ASA (C) AAS
   (B) SSS (D) ASA

2. In the figure at the right the following is true: $\angle ABD \cong \angle CDB$ and $\angle DBC \cong \angle BDA$. How can you justify that $\triangle ABD \cong \triangle CDB$? H

   (F) SAS (H) ASA
   (G) SSS (I) CPCTC

3. $\triangle BRM \cong \triangle KYZ$. How can you justify that $\overline{YZ} \cong \overline{RM}$? A

   (A) CPCTC (B) SAS (C) ASA (D) SSS

4. Which statement *cannot* be justified given only that $\triangle PBJ \cong \triangle TIM$? I

   (F) $\overline{PB} \cong \overline{TI}$ (G) $\angle B \cong \angle I$ (H) $\angle BJP \cong \angle IMT$ (I) $\overline{JP} \cong \overline{MI}$

5. In the figure at the right, which theorem or postulate can you use to prove $\triangle ADM \cong \triangle ZMD$? C

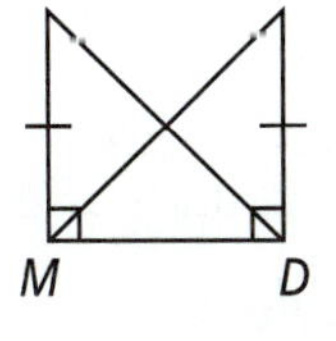

   (A) ASA (C) SAS
   (B) SSS (D) AAS

6. In the figure at the right, which theorem or postulate can you use to prove $\triangle KGC \cong \triangle FHE$? H

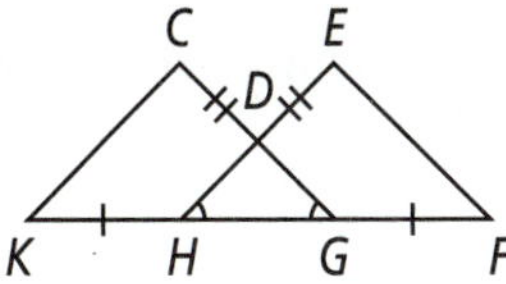

   (F) ASA (H) SAS
   (G) SSS (I) AAS

Short Response

7. What would a brief plan for the following proof look like?

   Given: $\overline{AB} \cong \overline{DC}$, $\angle ABC \cong \angle DCB$

   Prove: $\overline{AC} \cong \overline{DB}$

   [2] $\overline{CB} \cong \overline{BC}$ by the Reflexive Property. $\triangle CBD \cong \triangle BCA$ by SAS. $\overline{AC} \cong \overline{DB}$ by CPCTC; [1] one step missing or one reason incorrect [0] incorrect or no response

4-5 Isosceles and Equilateral Triangles

Vocabulary

Review

Underline the correct word to complete each sentence.

1. An *equilateral* triangle has two/ three congruent sides.
2. An *equilateral* triangle has acute / obtuse angles.
3. Circle the *equilateral* triangle.

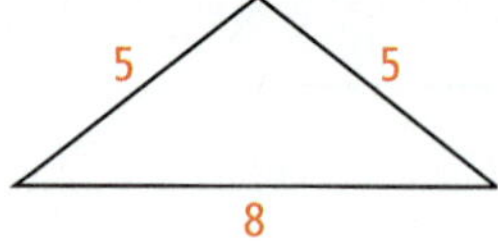

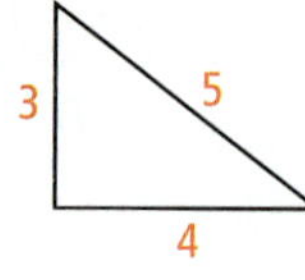

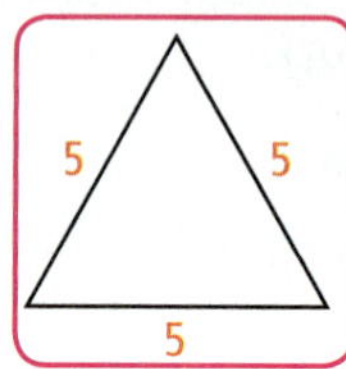

Vocabulary Builder

isosceles (adjective) eye SAHS uh leez

Related Words: equilateral, scalene

Definition A triangle is **isosceles** if it has two congruent sides.

Main Idea: The angles and sides of **isosceles** triangles have special relationships.

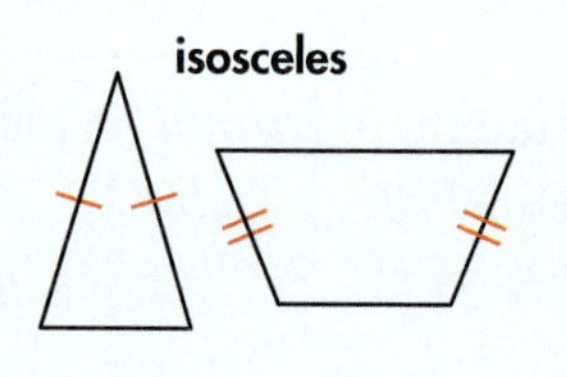

Use Your Vocabulary

4. Use the triangles below. Write the letter of each triangle in the correct circle(s) at the right.

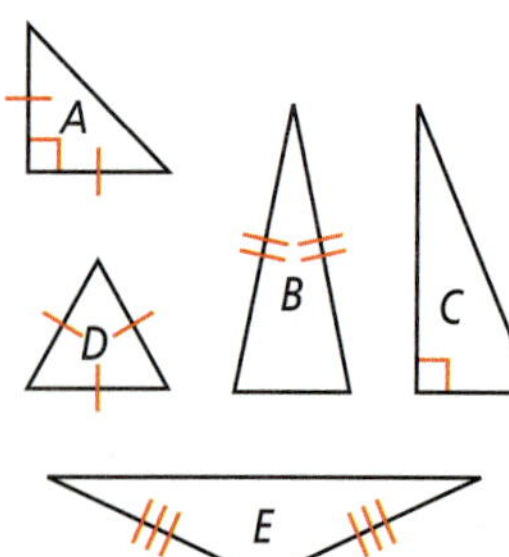

Equilateral	Isosceles	Right
D	A, B, D, E	A, C

take note

Theorems 4-3, 4-4, 4-5

Theorem 4-3 Isosceles Triangle Theorem

If two sides of a triangle are congruent, then the angles opposite those sides are congruent.

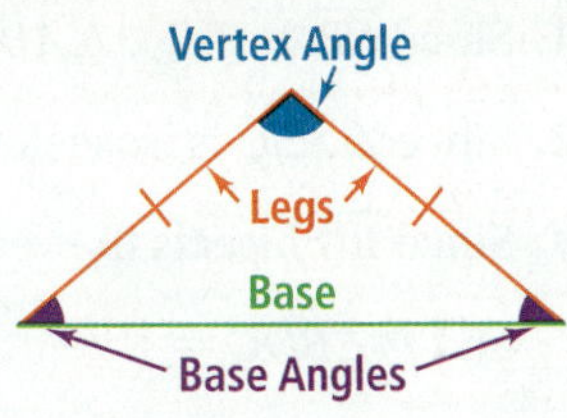

Theorem 4-4 Converse of Isosceles Triangle Theorem

If two angles of a triangle are congruent, then the sides opposite those angles are congruent.

Theorem 4-5

If a line bisects the vertex angle of an isosceles triangle, then the line is also the perpendicular bisector of the base.

5. If $\overline{PQ} \cong \overline{RQ}$ in $\triangle PQR$, then $\angle$ **P** $\cong \angle$ **R**.

6. Underline the correct theorem number to complete the sentence.

The theorem illustrated below is Theorem 4-3 / 4-4 / 4-5.

If . . .

Then . . .

Problem 1 Using the Isosceles Triangle Theorems

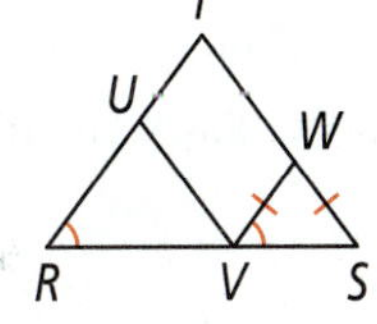

Got It? Is $\angle WVS$ congruent to $\angle S$? Is $\overline{TR}$ congruent to $\overline{TS}$? Explain.

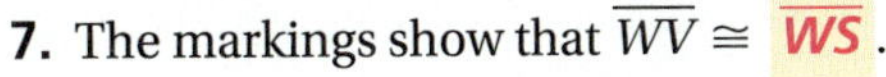

7. The markings show that $\overline{WV} \cong$ **$\overline{WS}$**.

8. Is $\angle WVS \cong \angle S$? Explain.

Yes. Explanations may vary. Sample: Since $\overline{WV} \cong \overline{WS}$, $\angle WVS \cong \angle S$ by the Isosceles Triangle Theorem.

9. Is $\angle R \cong \angle S$? Explain.

Yes. Explanations may vary. Sample: $\angle R \cong \angle WVS$ and $\angle WVS \cong \angle S$, so $\angle R \cong \angle S$ by the Transitive Property of Congruence.

10. Is $\overline{TR} \cong \overline{TS}$? Explain.

Yes. Explanations may vary. Sample: Since $\angle R \cong \angle S$, $\overline{TR} \cong \overline{TS}$ by the Converse of the Isosceles Triangle Theorem.

Problem 2 Using Algebra

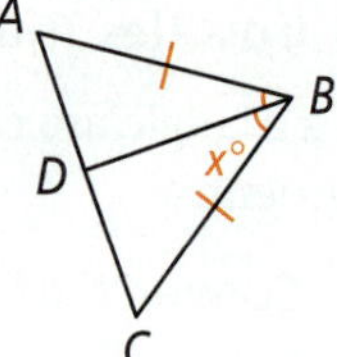

Got It? Suppose $m\angle A = 27$. What is the value of x?

11. Since $\overline{CB} \cong$ $\overline{AB}$, $\triangle ABC$ is isosceles.

12. Since $\triangle ABC$ is isosceles, $m\angle A = m\angle$ C $=$ 27.

13. Since $\overline{BD}$ bisects the vertex of an isosceles triangle, $\overline{BD} \perp$ $\overline{AC}$

and $m\angle BDC =$ 90.

14. Use the justifications below to find the value of x.

$m\angle C + m\angle BDC + x = 180$	Triangle Angle-Sum Theorem
$27 + 90 + x = 180$	Substitute.
$117 + x = 180$	Simplify.
$x = 63$	Subtract 117 from each side.

take note

Corollaries to Theorems 4-3 and 4-4

Corollary to Theorem 4-3

If a triangle is equilateral, then the triangle is equiangular.

Corollary to Theorem 4-4

If a triangle is equiangular, then the triangle is equilateral.

15. Underline the correct number to complete the sentence.

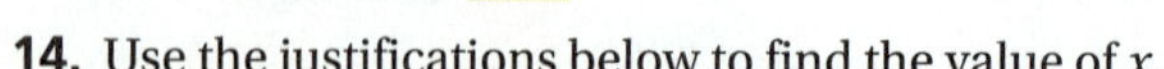

The corollary illustrated below is Corollary to Theorem 4-3 / 4-4.

If . . .

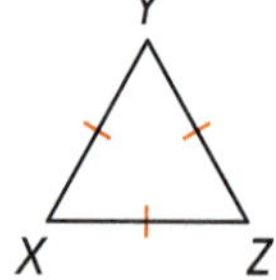

Then . . .

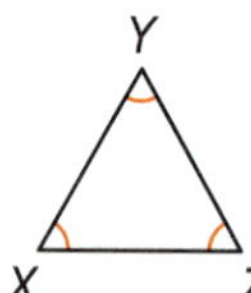

Problem 3 Finding Angle Measures

Got It? Suppose the triangles at the right are isosceles triangles, where $\angle ADE$, $\angle DEC$, and $\angle ECB$ are vertex angles. If the vertex angles each have a measure of 58, what are $m\angle A$ and $m\angle BCD$?

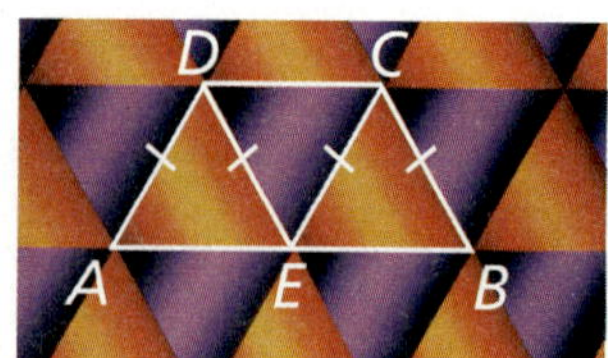

16. Which triangles are congruent by the Side-Angle-Side Theorem?

$\triangle ADE$, $\triangle DEC$, $\triangle ECB$

17. Which angles are congruent by the Isosceles Triangle Theorem?

$\angle A$, $\angle DEA$, $\angle EDC$, $\angle ECD$, $\angle CEB$, $\angle B$

18. By the Triangle Angle-Sum Theorem, $m\angle A + 58 + m\angle DEA =$ 180.

19. Solve for $m\angle A$.

$2m\angle A + 58 = 180$

$2m\angle A = 122$

$m\angle A = 61$

20. Since $\angle A \cong \angle ECD$, $m\angle ECD =$ 61.

21. Using the Angle Addition Postulate, $m\angle BCD = 58 + m\angle ECD =$ 119.

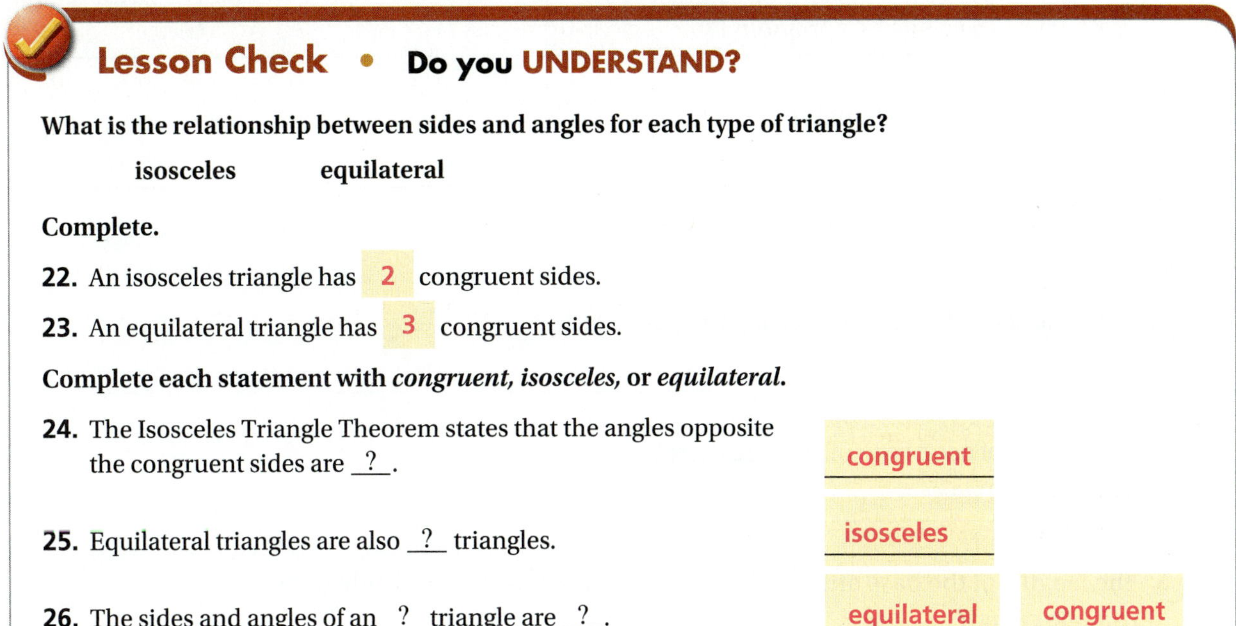

Lesson Check • Do you UNDERSTAND?

What is the relationship between sides and angles for each type of triangle?

isosceles **equilateral**

Complete.

22. An isosceles triangle has 2 congruent sides.

23. An equilateral triangle has 3 congruent sides.

Complete each statement with *congruent, isosceles,* or *equilateral.*

24. The Isosceles Triangle Theorem states that the angles opposite the congruent sides are _?_. congruent

25. Equilateral triangles are also _?_ triangles. isosceles

26. The sides and angles of an _?_ triangle are _?_. equilateral congruent

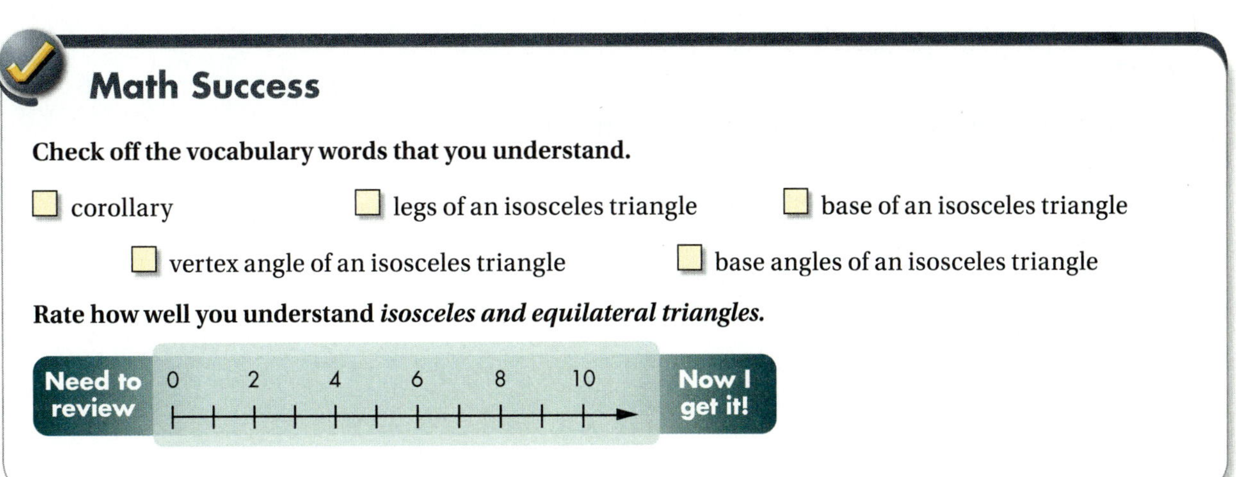

Math Success

Check off the vocabulary words that you understand.

- ☐ corollary
- ☐ legs of an isosceles triangle
- ☐ base of an isosceles triangle
- ☐ vertex angle of an isosceles triangle
- ☐ base angles of an isosceles triangle

Rate how well you understand *isosceles and equilateral triangles.*

Name ______________________ Class ____________ Date ____________

4-5 Think About a Plan

Isosceles and Equilateral Triangles

Algebra The length of the base of an isosceles triangle is x. The length of a leg is $2x - 5$. The perimeter of the triangle is 20. Find x.

Know

1. What is the perimeter of a triangle?

   the sum of the sides of a triangle

2. What is an isosceles triangle?

   a triangle with two sides the same length

Need

3. What are the sides of an isosceles triangle called?

   base and leg

4. How many of each type of side are there?

   1 base and 2 legs

5. The lengths of the base and one leg are given. What is the third side of the triangle called?

   leg

Plan

6. Write an expression for the length of the third side. $2x - 5$

7. Write an equation for the perimeter of this isosceles triangle.

   $x + (2x - 5) + (2x - 5) = 20$

8. Solve the equation for x. Show your work.

   $5x - 10 = 20$

   $5x = 30$

   $x = 6$

Name ______________________________ Class ____________ Date ____________

4-5 Practice

Form K

Isosceles and Equilateral Triangles

Complete each statement. Explain why it is true.

1. $\overline{AB} \cong$ __?__ Answers may vary. Sample: $\overline{AC}$; the legs of an isosceles triangle are congruent.

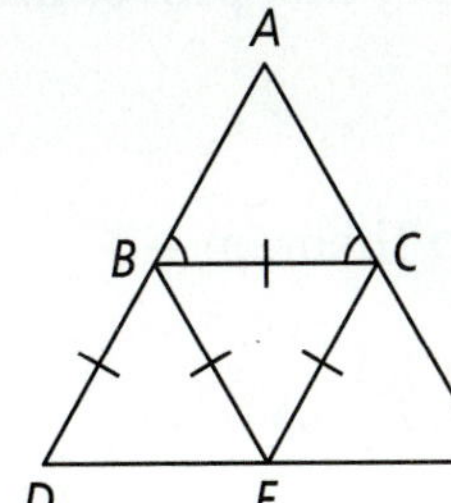

2. $\angle BDE \cong$ __?__ Answers may vary. Sample: $\angle BED$; the base angles of an isosceles triangle are congruent.

3. $\angle CBE \cong$ __?__ $\cong \angle BCE$ Answers may vary. Sample: $\angle BEC$; all the angles of an equilateral triangle are congruent.

Algebra Find the values of x and y.

4. 90; 30

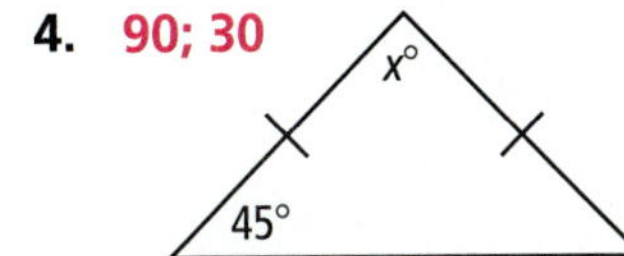

To start, determine what types of triangles are shown in the diagram. Then use an equation to find x.

Because two sides are marked congruent in both triangles, the triangles are both __?__. isosceles

$45 + \boxed{45} + x = \boxed{180}$

5. 15; 120

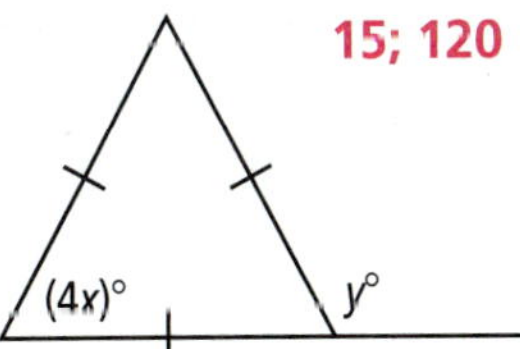

6. 69; 37

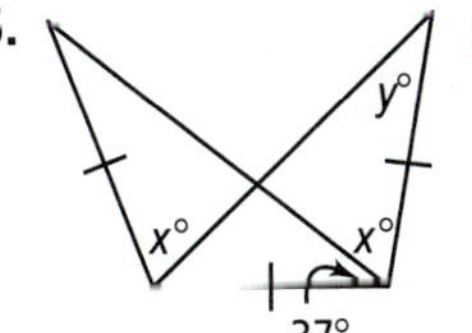

Use the properties of isosceles triangles to complete each statement.

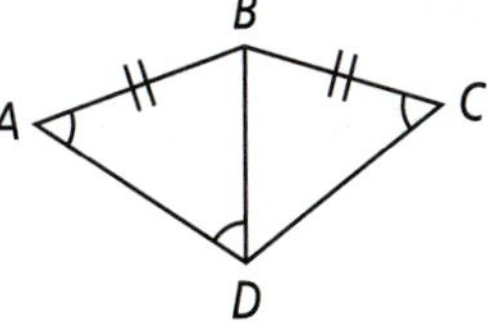

7. If $m\angle ADB = 54$, then $m\angle CBD =$ __?__. 72

8. If $AB = 8$, then $BD =$ __?__. 8

9. You are asked to put a V-shaped roof on a house. The slope of the roof is 40°. What is the measure of the angle needed at the vertex of the roof? 100

10. **Reasoning** The measure of one angle of a triangle is 30. Of the two remaining angles, the larger angle is four times the size of the smaller angle. Is the triangle isosceles? Explain. Yes, because the measure of the smaller angle is 30.

Name ______________________ Class ____________ Date ____________

4-5 Practice (continued) Form K

Isosceles and Equilateral Triangles

For Exercises 11 and 12, use the diagram to complete each congruence statement. Then list the theorem or corollary that proves the statement. The first one has been done for you.

$\angle B \cong$?

Answer: $\angle BAC$ (or $\angle ACB$); Corollary to Theorem 4-3

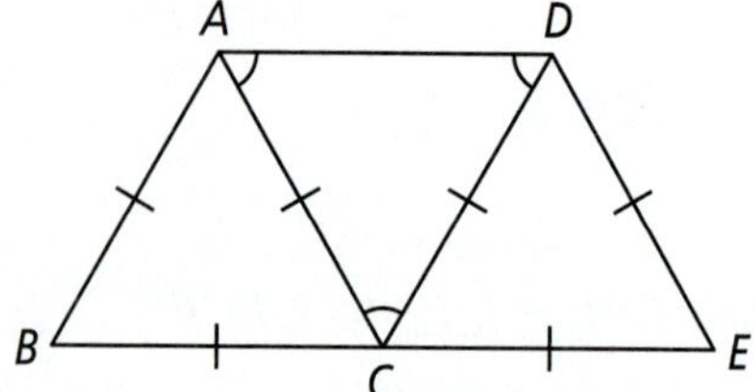

11. $\overline{AD} \cong$? Answers may vary. Sample: $\overline{AC}$ or $\overline{DC}$; Corollary to Theorem 4-4

12. $\angle E \cong$? Answers may vary. Sample: $\angle DCE$ or $\angle CDE$; Corollary to Theorem 4-3

For Exercises 13–15, use the diagram to complete each congruence statement. Then list the theorem or corollary that proves the statement.

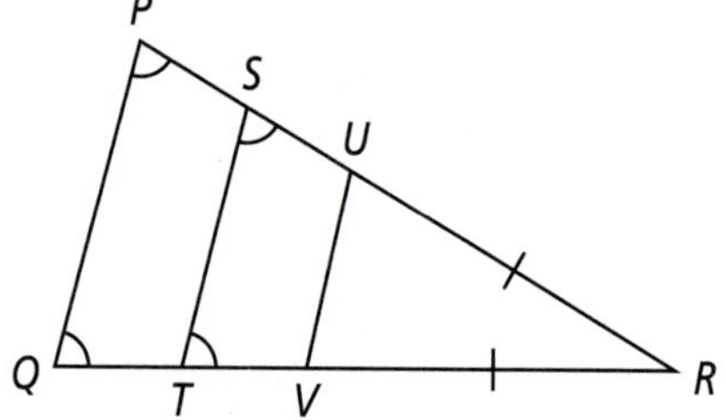

13. $\overline{PR} \cong$? $\overline{QR}$; Converse of the Isosceles Triangle Theorem

14. $\angle RUV \cong$? $\angle RVU$; Isosceles Triangle Theorem

15. $\overline{SR} \cong$? $\overline{TR}$; Converse of the Isosceles Triangle Theorem

16. Reasoning An equilateral triangle and an isosceles triangle share a common side as shown at the right. What is the measure of the vertex angle? Explain.

120; the congruent angles in the diagram both have a measure of 60. The base angles of the isosceles triangle have a measure of 30 because one is the other angle in a right triangle. The vertex angle must measure 120 if the base angles both measure 30.

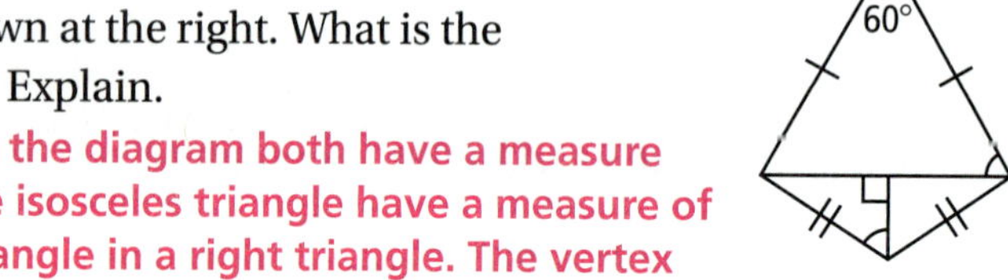

Algebra Find the values of *m* and *n*.

17.

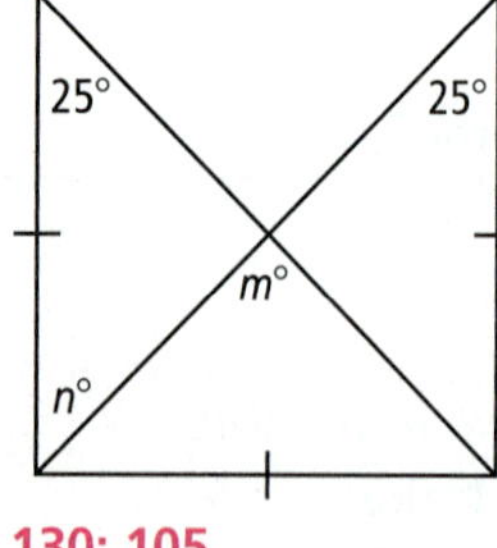

130; 105

18.

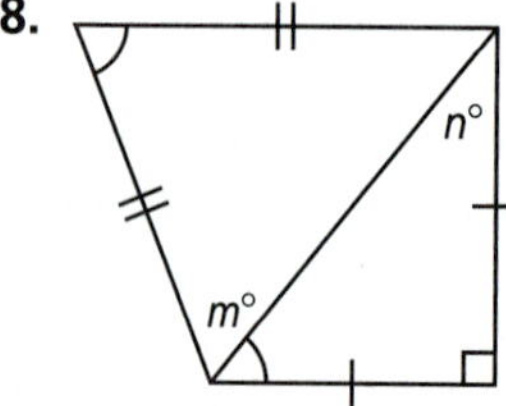

67.5; 45

Name ______________________ Class ____________ Date ____________

4-5 Standardized Test Prep

Isosceles and Equilateral Triangles

Gridded Response

Solve each exercise and enter your answer on the grid provided.

Refer to the diagram for Exercises 1–3.

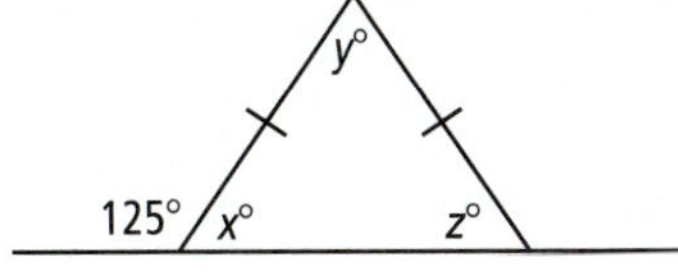

1. What is the value of x?

2. What is the value of y?

3. What is the value of z?

4. The measures of two of the sides of an equilateral triangle are $3x + 15$ in. and $7x - 5$ in. What is the measure of the third side in inches?

5. In $\triangle GHI$, $HI = GH$, $m\angle IHG = 3x + 4$, and $m\angle IGH = 2x - 24$. What is $m\angle HIG$?

Answers

1. 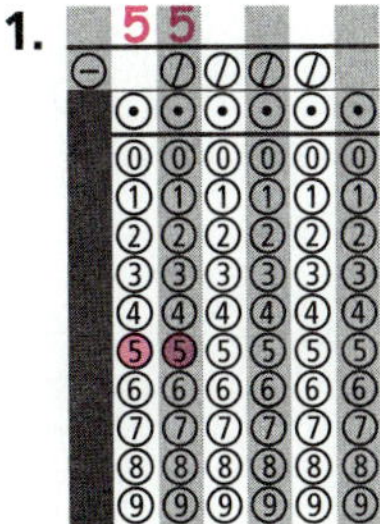

2. 

3. 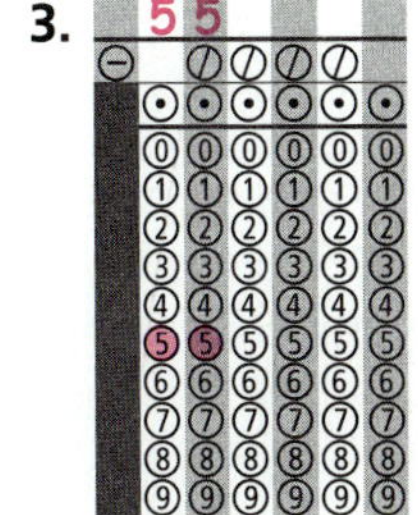

4. 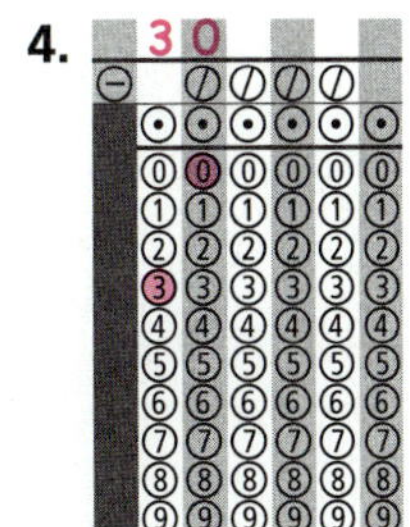

5. 

4-6 Congruence in Right Triangles

Vocabulary

Review

Write T for *true* or F for *false*.

T **1.** Segments that are *congruent* have the same length.

F **2.** Polygons that are *congruent* have the same shape but are not always the same size.

T **3.** In *congruent* figures, corresponding angles have the same measure.

Vocabulary Builder

hypotenuse
leg
leg

hypotenuse (noun) **hy** PAH **tuh noos**

Related Word: leg

Definition: The **hypotenuse** is the side opposite the right angle in a right triangle.

Main Idea: The **hypotenuse** is the longest side in a right triangle.

Use Your Vocabulary

Underline the correct word(s) to complete each sentence.

4. One side of a right triangle is / is not a *hypotenuse*.

5. A right triangle has one / two / three *legs*.

6. The length of the *hypotenuse* is always equal to / greater than / less than the lengths of the *legs*.

Use the triangles at the right for Exercises 7 and 8.

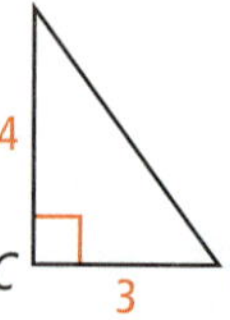

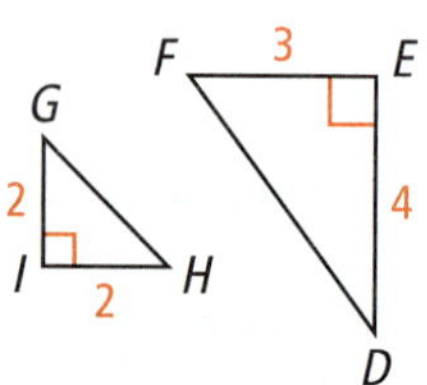

7. Cross out the side that is NOT a *hypotenuse*.

~~$\overline{BC}$~~	$\overline{AB}$	$\overline{GH}$	$\overline{FD}$

8. Circle the *leg(s)*.

($\overline{AC}$)	$\overline{AB}$	($\overline{HI}$)	($\overline{ED}$)

You can prove that two triangles are congruent without having to show that *all* corresponding parts are congruent. In this lesson, you will prove right triangles congruent by using one pair of right angles, a pair of hypotenuses, and a pair of legs.

take note

Theorem 4-6 Hypotenuse-Leg (HL) Theorem and Conditions

Theorem	If . . .	Then . . .
If the hypotenuse and a leg of one right triangle are congruent to the hypotenuse and leg of another right triangle, then the triangles are congruent.	$\triangle PQR$ and $\triangle XYZ$ are right triangles, $\overline{PR} \cong \overline{XZ}$, and $\overline{PQ} \cong \overline{XY}$	$\triangle PQR \cong \triangle XYZ$

P Q R X Y Z

9. To use the HL Theorem, the triangles must meet three conditions. Complete each sentence with *right* or *congruent.*

There are two _?_ triangles. **right**

The triangles have _?_ hypotenuses. **congruent**

There is one pair of _?_ legs. **congruent**

Use the information in the Take Note for Exercises 10–12.

10. How do the triangles in the Take Note meet the first condition in Exercise 9? Explain.

$\angle PQR$ and $\angle XYZ$ are right angles.

11. How do the triangles in the Take Note meet the second condition in Exercise 9? Explain.

The hypotenuses $\overline{PR}$ and $\overline{XZ}$ are marked congruent on the diagram.

12. How do the triangles in the Take Note meet the third condition in Exercise 9? Explain.

Legs $\overline{PQ}$ and $\overline{XY}$ are marked congruent on the diagram.

Problem 1 Using the HL Theorem

Got It? **Given:** $\angle PRS$ and $\angle RPQ$ are right angles, $\overline{SP} \cong \overline{QR}$
Prove: $\triangle PRS \cong \triangle RPQ$

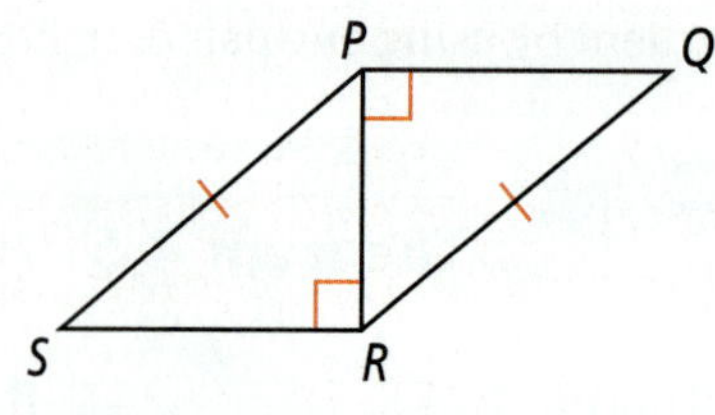

13. Complete each step of the proof.

Given
$\angle PRS$ and $\angle$ RPQ are right angles.

Given
$\overline{SP} \cong$ $\overline{QR}$

Reflexive Prop. of $\cong$
$\overline{PR} \cong$ $\overline{RP}$

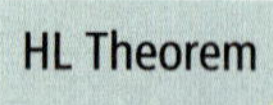

Definition of right triangle
$\triangle PRS$ and $\triangle$ RPQ are right triangles.

HL Theorem
$\triangle PRS \cong \triangle$ RPQ

Problem 2 Writing a Proof Using the HL Theorem

Got It? **Given:** $\overline{CD} \cong \overline{EA}$, $\overline{AD}$ is the perpendicular bisector of $\overline{CE}$
Prove: $\triangle CBD \cong \triangle EBA$

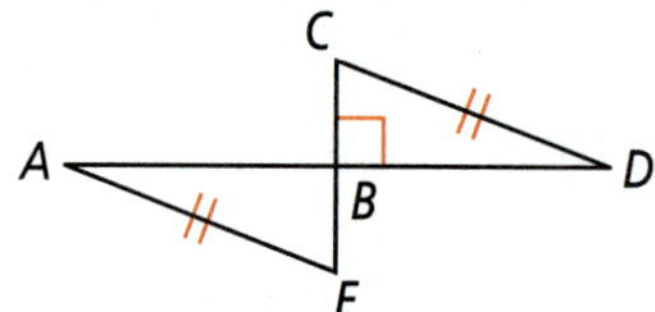

14. Circle what you know because $\overline{AD}$ is the perpendicular bisector of $\overline{CE}$.

(circled) $\angle CBD$ and $\angle EBA$ are right angles.	$\angle CBD$ and $\angle EBA$ are acute angles.
B is the midpoint of $\overline{AD}$.	(circled) B is the midpoint of $\overline{CE}$.

15. Circle the congruent legs.

$\overline{AB}$	(circled) $\overline{CB}$	$\overline{DB}$	(circled) $\overline{EB}$

16. Write the hypotenuse of each triangle.

$\triangle CBD$ $\overline{CD}$ $\qquad$ $\triangle EBA$ $\overline{EA}$

17. Complete the proof.

Statements	**Reasons**
1) $\overline{CD} \cong$ $\overline{EA}$	1) Given
2) $\angle CBD$ and $\angle$ EBA are right $\angle$s.	2) Definition of $\perp$ bisector
3) $\triangle CBD$ and $\triangle$ EBA are right $\triangle$s.	3) Definition of right $\triangle$
4) $\overline{CB} \cong$ $\overline{EB}$	4) Definition of $\perp$ bisector
5) $\triangle CBD \cong$ EBA	5) HL Theorem

Lesson Check • Do you UNDERSTAND?

Error Analysis **Your classmate says that there is not enough information to determine whether the two triangles at the right are congruent. Is your classmate correct? Explain.**

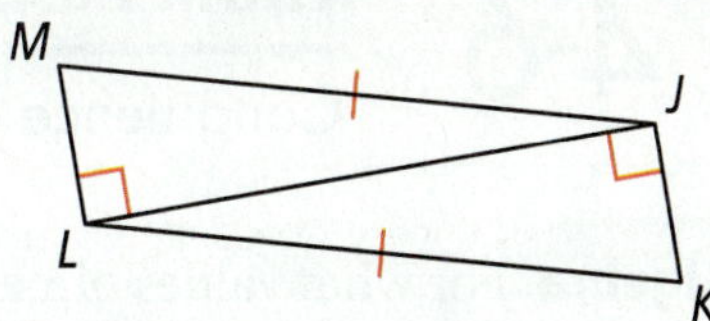

Write T for *true* or F for *false*.

F **18.** There are three right angles.

T **19.** There are two right triangles.

T **20.** There are two congruent hypotenuses.

F **21.** There are no congruent legs.

T **22.** You need to use the Reflexive Property of Congruence.

F **23.** $\overline{LJ} \cong \overline{LJ}$ is given.

24. Do you always need three congruent corresponding parts to prove triangles congruent? Explain. **Explanations may vary. Sample:**

No. You usually need three congruent corresponding parts, but not if the triangles are right triangles.

25. Is your classmate correct? Explain. **Explanations may vary. Sample:**

No. Since the hypotenuse and the shared leg of one right triangle are congruent to the hypotenuse and the shared leg ofanother right triangle, the triangles are congruent by the HL Theorem.

Math Success

Check off the vocabulary words that you understand.

☐ hypotenuse ☐ legs of a right triangle

Rate how well you can *use the Hypotenuse-Leg (HL) Theorem.*

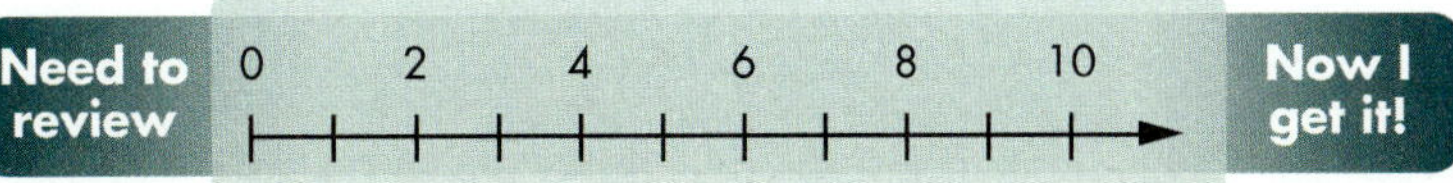
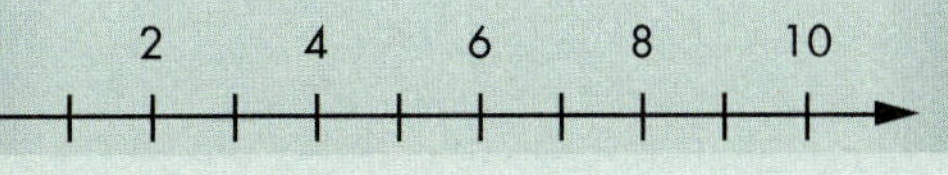

Name ______________________ Class ____________ Date ____________

4-6 Think About a Plan

Congruence in Right Triangles

Algebra For what values of x and y are the triangles congruent by HL?

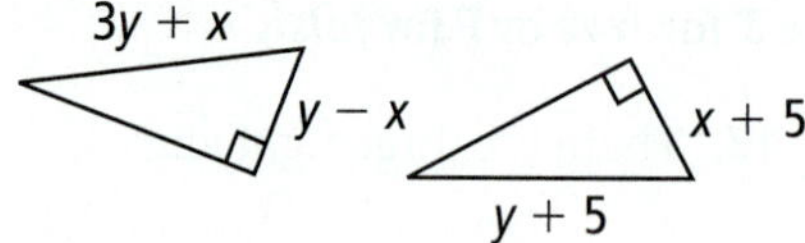

Know

1. For two triangles to be congruent by the Hypotenuse-Leg Theorem, there must be a pair of right angles, and the lengths of the hypotenuses and one of the legs of each triangle must be equal.

2. The length of the hypotenuse of the triangle on the left is $3y + x$ and the hypotenuse of the triangle on the right is $y + 5$.

3. The length of the leg of the triangle on the left is $y - x$ and the length of the leg of the triangle on the right is $x + 5$.

Need

4. To solve the problem you need to find the values of x and y.

Plan

5. What system of equations can you use to find the values of x and y?
   $3y + x = y + 5$; $y - x = x + 5$

6. What method(s) can you use to solve the system of equations?
   Sample: Solve one equation for y and substitute into the other equation; graph both equations.

7. What is the value of y? What is the value of x? 3; -1

Name ______________________ Class ____________ Date ____________

4-6 Practice — Form K

Congruence in Right Triangles

1. **Developing Proof** Complete the proof.

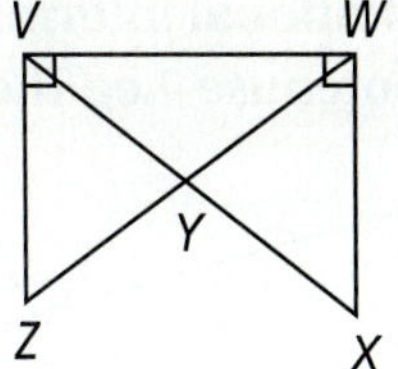

Given: $\angle WVZ$ and $\angle VWX$ are right angles.

$\overline{WZ} \cong \overline{VX}$

Prove: $\triangle WVZ \cong \triangle VWX$

To prove that right triangles $\triangle WVZ$ and $\triangle VWX$ are congruent, you must prove that the hypotenuses are congruent and that one __?__ is congruent.
leg

Statements	Reasons
1) __?__ **$\angle WVZ$ and $\angle VWX$ are right ∠s.**	1) Given
2) __?__ **$\overline{WZ} \cong \overline{VX}$**	2) Given
3) __?__ **$\overline{WV} \cong \overline{VW}$**	3) Reflexive Property of Congruence
4) __?__ **$\triangle WVZ \cong \triangle VWX$**	4) HL Theorem

2. Look at Exercise 1. If $m\angle X = 54$, what is $m\angle Z$? **54**

3. Look at Exercise 1. If $m\angle X = 54$, what is $m\angle VWZ$? **36**

4. Study Exercise 1. Can you prove that $\triangle WVZ$ and $\triangle VWX$ are congruent without using the HL Theorem? Explain.
Yes; answers may vary. Sample: by using the Pythagorean Theorem to find another pair of congruent sides

Algebra For what values of x and y are the triangles congruent by HL?

5.

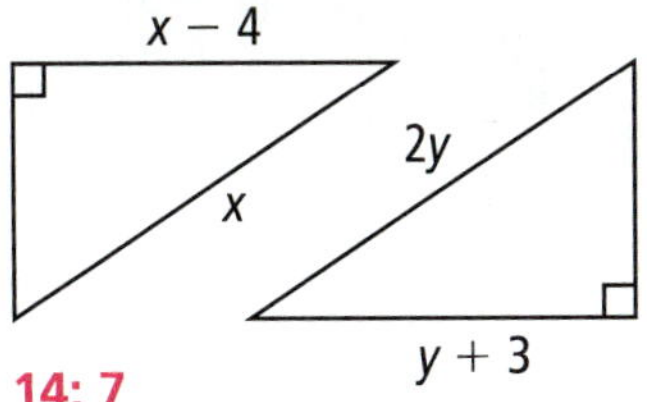

14; 7

6.

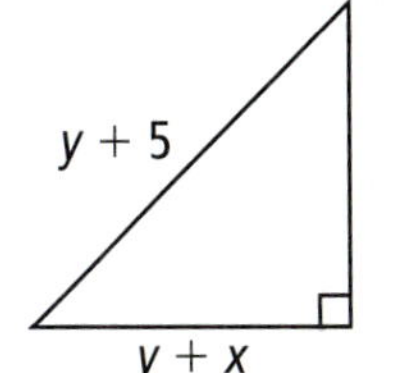

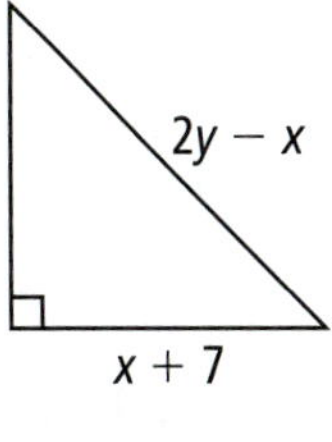

2; 7

7. **Reasoning** The LL Theorem says that two right triangles are congruent if both pairs of legs are congruent. What theorem or postulate could be used to prove that the LL Theorem is true? Explain.
Answers may vary. Sample: The SAS Postulate could be used to prove the LL Theorem because the two right triangles would have two pairs of congruent legs and the included right angles would also be congruent.

Name ______________________________ Class ______________ Date ______________

4-6 Practice (continued) — Form K

Congruence in Right Triangles

What additional information would prove each pair of triangles congruent by the Hypotenuse-Leg Theorem?

8.

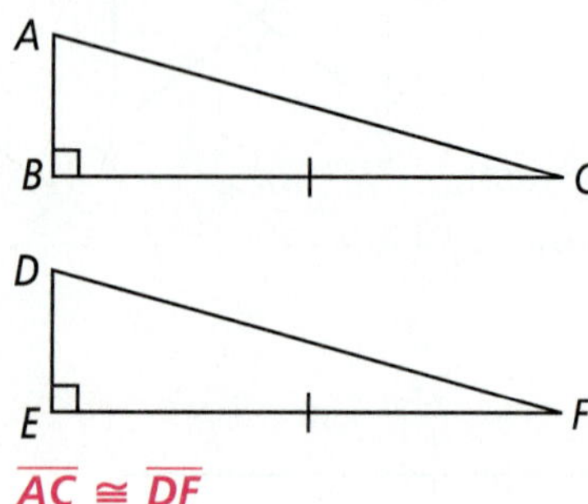

$\overline{AC} \cong \overline{DF}$

9.

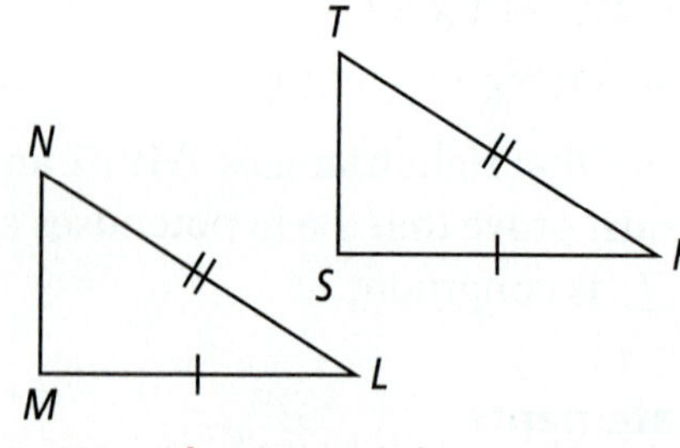

$\angle M$ and $\angle S$ are right angles.

10.

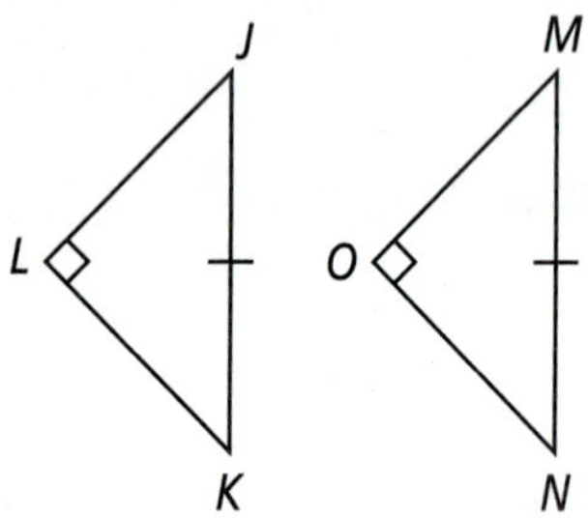

$\overline{JL} \cong \overline{MO}$ or $\overline{KL} \cong \overline{NO}$

11.

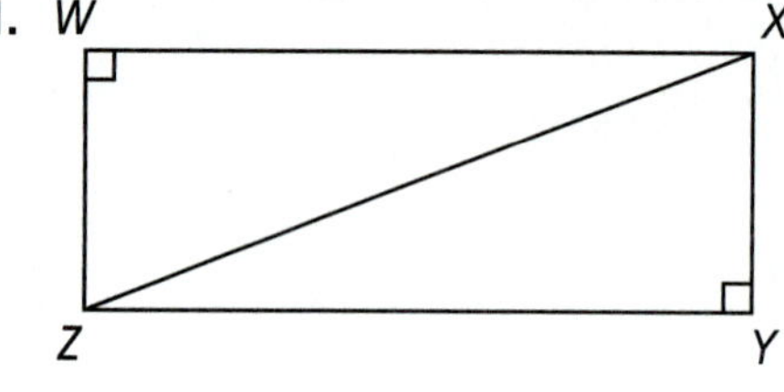

$\overline{WZ} \cong \overline{YX}$ or $\overline{WX} \cong \overline{YZ}$

Coordinate Geometry **Use the figure at the right for Exercises 12–14.**

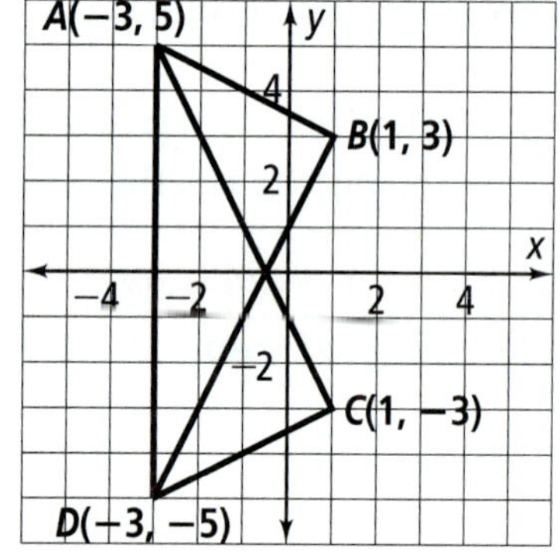

12. Complete the paragraph proof that shows that $\overline{AC}$ and $\overline{CD}$ are perpendicular.

The slope of $\overline{AC}$ is [−2]. The slope of $\overline{CD}$ is [0.5]. The product of the two slopes is [−1]. Therefore the line segments are __?__. perpendicular

13. How do you know that $AB = CD$?

The Distance Formula shows that both line segments have length $2\sqrt{5}$.

14. Complete the paragraph proof below that shows that $\triangle ACD \cong \triangle DBA$.

$\angle ACD$ is a __?__ (right angle) from Exercises 12. You can also use the product of slopes to show that $\angle ABD$ is a right angle. $\triangle ACD$ and $\triangle ABD$ share the same hypotenuse. You can use the __?__ to show that $AB = CD$. Therefore, by the __?__, $\triangle ACD \cong \triangle DBA$. Distance Formula

HL Theorem

Name ______________________ Class __________ Date __________

4-6 Standardized Test Prep

Congruence in Right Triangles

Multiple Choice

For Exercises 1–4, choose the correct letter.

1. Which additional piece of information would allow you to prove that the triangles are congruent by the HL theorem? C

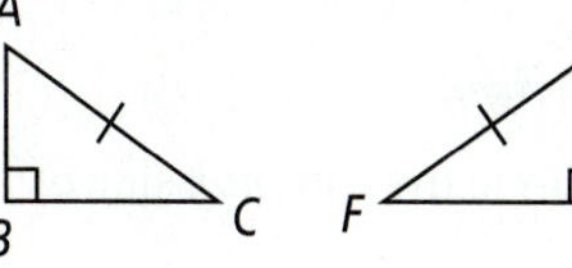

Ⓐ $m\angle DFE = 40$

Ⓒ $\overline{AB} \cong \overline{DE}$

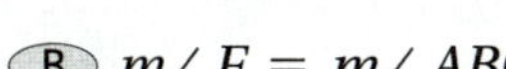
Ⓑ $m\angle F = m\angle ABC$

Ⓓ $\overline{AC} \cong \overline{DF}$

2. For what values of x and y are the triangles shown congruent? F

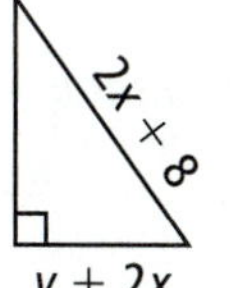

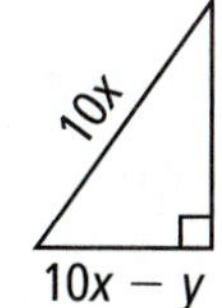

Ⓕ $x = 1, y = 4$

Ⓗ $x = 4, y = 1$

Ⓖ $x = 2, y = 4$

Ⓘ $x = 1, y = 3$

3. Two triangles have two pairs of corresponding sides that are congruent. What else must be true for the triangles to be congruent by the HL Theorem? D

Ⓐ The included angles must be right angles.

Ⓑ They have one pair of congruent angles.

Ⓒ Both triangles must be isosceles.

Ⓓ There are right angles adjacent to just one pair of congruent sides.

4. Which of the following statements is true? H

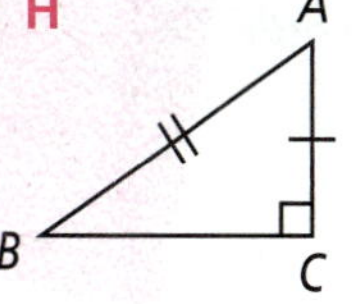

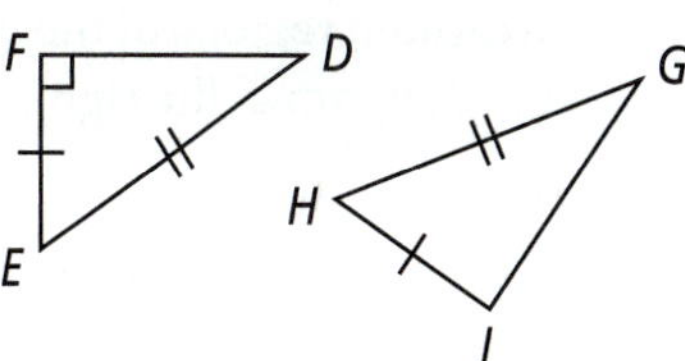

Ⓕ $\triangle BAC \cong \triangle GHI$ by SAS.

Ⓖ $\triangle DEF \cong \triangle GHI$ by SAS.

Ⓗ $\triangle BAC \cong \triangle DEF$ by HL.

Ⓘ $\triangle DEF \cong \triangle GHI$ by HL.

Extended Response

5. Are the given triangles congruent by the HL Theorem? Explain.

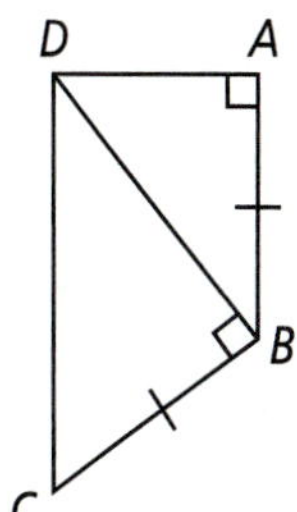

[4] No; they are right triangles, and have a pair of congruent legs ($\overline{AB} \cong \overline{BC}$), but the hypotenuses, $\overline{DB}$ and $\overline{DC}$, are not congruent. So, the triangles only meet two of the three conditions for congruence by the HL Theorem.
[3] appropriate response plus a discussion of two of the three criteria for congruence [2] recognition only that the hypotenuses are not congruent [1] recognition that the triangles are not congruent [0] incorrect or no response

4-7 Congruence in Overlapping Triangles

Vocabulary

Review

1. Circle the *common* side of $\triangle ABC$ and $\triangle ADC$.

$\overline{AB}$	$\overline{AC}$	$\overline{AD}$	$\overline{BC}$

2. Circle the *common* side of $\triangle XWZ$ and $\triangle YWZ$.

$\overline{WZ}$	$\overline{WX}$	$\overline{WY}$	$\overline{ZY}$

3. Circle the *common* side of $\triangle RST$ and $\triangle RPT$.

$\overline{RP}$	$\overline{RS}$	$\overline{RT}$	$\overline{ST}$

Vocabulary Builder

overlapping (adjective) **oh vur LAP ing**

Other Word Form: overlap (noun)

Definition: **Overlapping** events or figures have parts in common.

Math Usage: Two or more figures with common regions are **overlapping** figures.

Use Your Vocabulary

Circle the common regions of the *overlapping* figures in the diagram at the right.

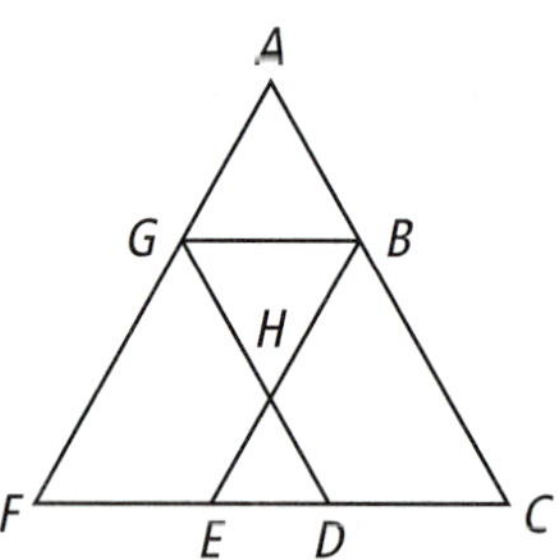

4. $\triangle FGD$ and $\triangle CBE$

$\triangle ABG$	$\triangle ACF$	$\triangle EHD$	$\triangle GHB$

5. $\triangle BEC$ and $\triangle HED$

$\triangle BEC$	$\triangle GBH$	$\triangle GDF$	$\triangle HED$

6. $\triangle ACF$ and $\triangle ABG$

$\triangle ABG$	$\triangle ACF$	$\triangle GBH$	$\triangle EHD$

7. $\triangle ACF$ and $\triangle GBH$

$\triangle ABG$	$\triangle ACF$	$\triangle GBH$	$\triangle HED$

Problem 1 Identifying Common Parts

Got It? What is the common side in $\triangle ABD$ and $\triangle DCA$?

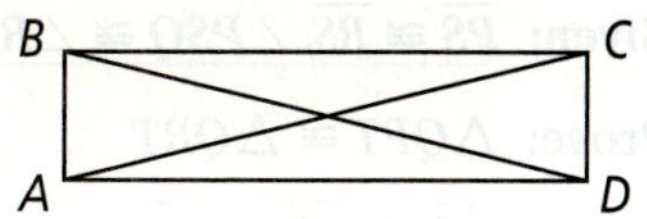

8. Separate and redraw $\triangle ABD$ and $\triangle DCA$.

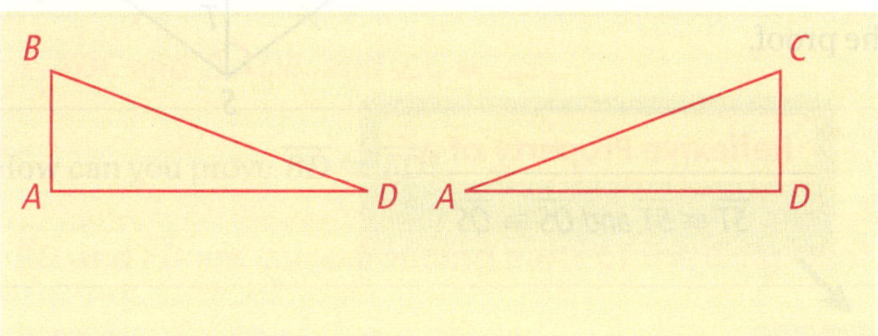

9. You drew $\overline{AD}$ twice, so the common side is $\overline{AD}$.

Problem 2 Using Common Parts

Got It? Given: $\triangle ACD \cong \triangle BDC$

Prove: $\overline{CE} \cong \overline{DE}$

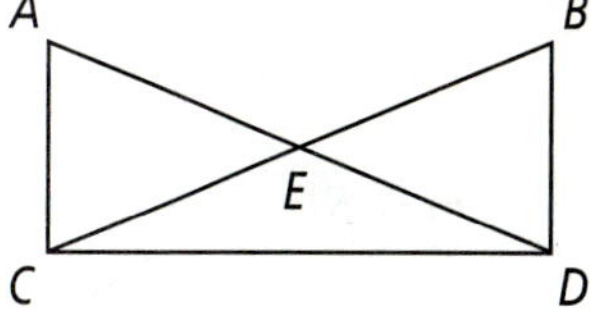

10. Use the information in the problem to complete the problem-solving model below.

Know	Need	Plan
$\triangle ACD \cong \triangle BDC$; $\triangle ACD$ and $\triangle BDC$ are overlapping triangles.	Common parts of $\triangle ACD$ and $\triangle BDC$.	Show $\triangle ACE \cong \triangle BED$. Then use corresponding parts to prove $\overline{CE} \cong \overline{DE}$.

11. Use the justifications below to complete each statement.

Statements	Reasons
1) $\triangle ACD \cong \triangle BDC$	1) Given
2) $\overline{AC} \cong \overline{BD}$	2) Corresponding parts of $\cong$ triangles are $\cong$.
3) $\angle A \cong \angle B$	3) Corresponding parts of $\cong$ triangles are $\cong$.
4) $\angle AEC \cong \angle BED$	4) Vertical angles are congruent.
5) $\triangle AEC \cong \triangle BED$	5) Angle-Angle-Side (AAS) Theorem
6) $\overline{CE} \cong \overline{DE}$	6) Corresponding parts of $\cong$ triangles are $\cong$.

12. How could you use the Converse of the Isosceles Triangle Theorem to prove $\overline{CE} \cong \overline{DE}$? Answers may vary. Sample:

$\angle BCD$ and $\angle ADC$ are corresponding parts of congruent triangles, so $\angle BCD \cong \angle ADC$. $\overline{CE}$ is opposite $\angle ADC$ and $\overline{DE}$ is opposite $\angle BCD$, so $\overline{CE} \cong \overline{DE}$ by the converse of Isosceles Triangle Theorem.

Name ______________________ Class __________ Date __________

4-7 Think About a Plan

Congruence in Overlapping Triangles

Given: $\overline{QT} \perp \overline{PR}$, $\overline{QT}$ bisects $\overline{PR}$, $\overline{QT}$ bisects $\angle VQS$

Prove: $\overline{VQ} \cong \overline{SQ}$

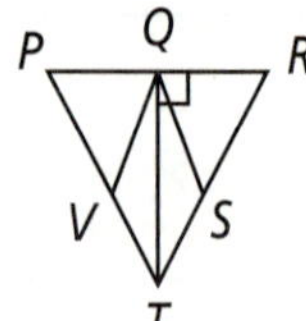

Know

1. What information are you given? What else can you determine from the given information and the diagram?

   $\overline{QT} \perp \overline{PR}$, $\overline{QT}$ bisects $\overline{PR}$, $\overline{QT}$ bisects $\angle VQS$; $\angle PQT$ and $\angle RQT$ are right angles, $PQ = QR$, $\angle VQT \cong \angle SQT$

2. To solve the problem, what will you need to prove?

   $\overline{VQ} \cong \overline{SQ}$

Need

3. For which two triangles are $\overline{VQ}$ and $\overline{SQ}$ corresponding parts?

   $\triangle PQV$ and $\triangle RQS$ or $\triangle VQT$ and $\triangle SQT$

4. You need to use corresponding parts to prove the triangles from Exercise 3 congruent. Which two triangles should you prove congruent first, using the given information? Which theorem or postulate should you use?

   $\triangle PQT$ and $\triangle RQT$ by SAS

5. Which corresponding parts should you then use to prove that the triangles in Exercise 3 are congruent?

   Answers may vary. Sample: $\angle P$ and $\angle R$

Plan

6. Use the space below to write the proof.

   Statements: 1) $\overline{QT} \perp \overline{PR}$; $\overline{QT}$ bisects $\overline{PR}$, $\overline{QT}$ bisects $\angle VQS$; 2) $m\angle PQT = m\angle RQT = 90$; 3) $PQ = QR$; 4) $QT = QT$; 5) $\triangle PQT \cong \triangle RQT$; 6) $\angle P \cong \angle R$; 7) $\angle PQV$ and $\angle VQT$ are compl. $\angle RQS$ and $\angle SQT$ are compl.; 8) $\angle VQT \cong \angle SQT$; 9) $\angle PQV \cong \angle RQS$; 10) $\triangle PQV \cong \triangle RQS$; 11) $\overline{VQ} \cong \overline{SQ}$; Reasons: 1) Given; 2) Definition of perpendicular lines; 3) Definition of bisector; 4) Reflexive Property of Congruence; 5) SAS; 6) CPCTC; 7) Definition of complementary angles; 8) Definition of angle bisector; 9) Complements of ≅ ∡ are ≅; 10) ASA; 11) CPCTC

Name ______________________ Class ____________ Date ____________

4-7 Practice

Form K

Congruence in Overlapping Triangles

In each diagram, the stated triangles are congruent. Identify their common side or angle.

1. $\triangle BAE \cong \triangle ABC$ $\overline{AB}$

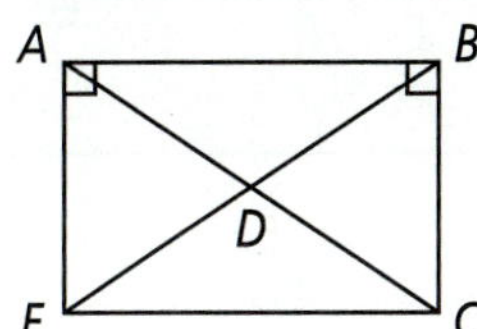

2. $\triangle SUV \cong \triangle WUT$ $\angle U$

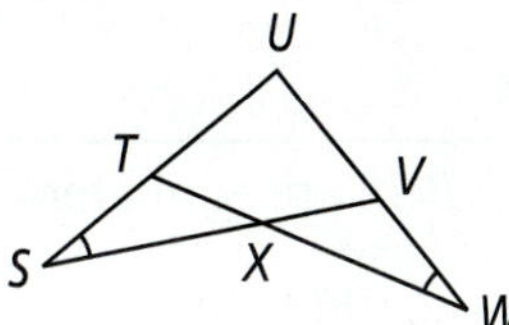

Separate and redraw the indicated triangles. Identify any common angles or sides.

3. $\triangle ACF$ and $\triangle AEB$ $\angle A$

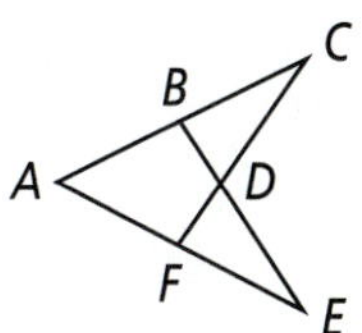

To start, redraw each triangle separately:

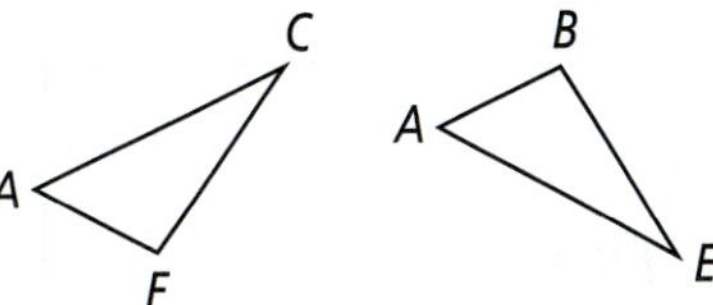

4. $\triangle FKJ$ and $\triangle HJK$ $\overline{JK}$

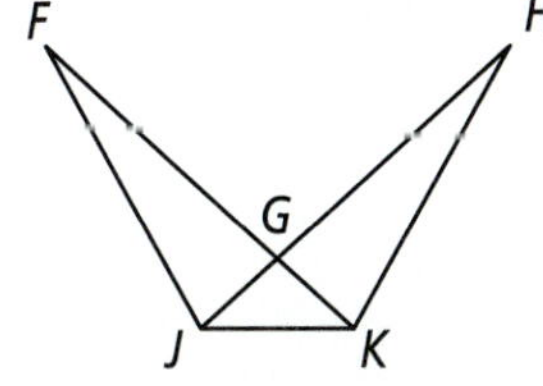

Complete the drawing to separate the triangles:

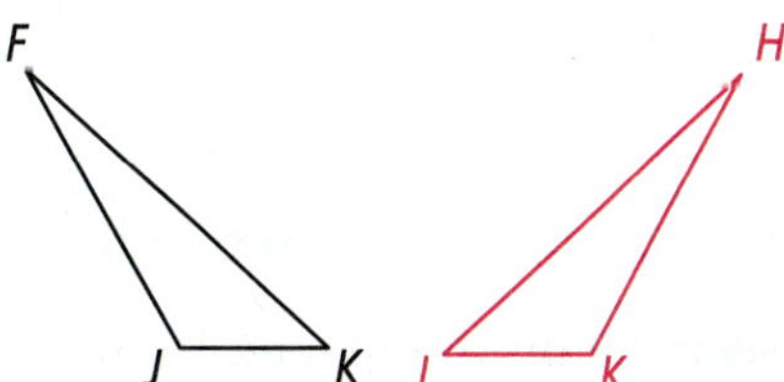

5. Developing Proof Complete the two-column proof.

Given: $m\angle FEH = m\angle GFE = 90$, $\overline{EH} \cong \overline{FG}$

Prove: $\overline{HF} \cong \overline{EG}$

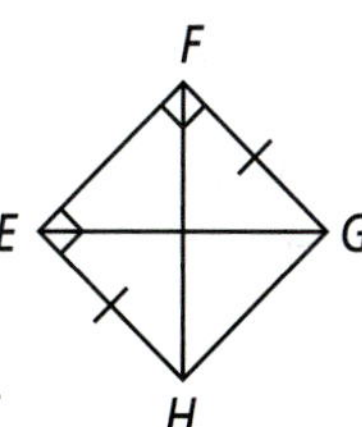

Statements	Reasons
1) $m\angle FEH = m\angle GFE = 90$, $\overline{EH} \cong \overline{GF}$	1) Given
2) $\angle FEH \cong \angle EFG$	2) ? All right ∠s are ≅.
3) $\overline{FE} \cong \overline{FE}$	3) ? Reflexive Prop. of ≅
4) ? $\triangle FEH \cong \triangle GFE$	4) SAS
5) $\overline{HF} \cong \overline{EG}$	5) ? Corresp. parts of ≅ △s are ≅.

Name ______________________ Class ______________ Date ______________

4-7 Practice (continued)

Form K

Congruence in Overlapping Triangles

6. Given: $\triangle AFD$ and $\triangle BGE$ are equilateral triangles.
$\angle A \cong \angle B$, $\overline{DE} \cong \overline{FG}$

Prove: $\overline{AD} \cong \overline{BE}$

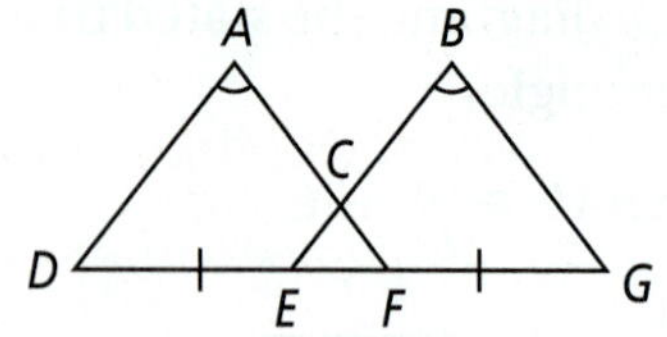

Statements	Reasons
1) $\triangle AFD$ and $\triangle BGE$ are equilateral ⚠s.	1) Given
2) $\angle A \cong \angle D \cong \angle AFD$	2) _?_ **Corollary to Theorem 4-3**
3) $\angle B \cong \angle G \cong \angle BEG$	3) _?_ **Corollary to Theorem 4-3**
4) $\angle A \cong \angle B$	4) Given
5) $\angle A \cong \angle D \cong \angle B \cong \angle G$	5) _?_ **Transitive Prop. of ≅**
6) $\overline{EF} \cong \overline{EF}$	6) _?_ **Reflexive Prop. of ≅**
7) $\overline{DE} \cong \overline{FG}$	7) Given
8) $DE + EF = EF + FG$	8) _?_ **Addition Prop. of =**
9) _?_ $\overline{DF} \cong \overline{EG}$	9) Definition of ≅
10) _?_ $\triangle AFD \cong \triangle BGE$	10) AAS
11) $\overline{AD} \cong \overline{BE}$	11) _?_ **Corresp. parts of ≅ ⚠s are ≅.**

Open-Ended Draw the diagram described.

7. Draw a line segment on your paper. Then draw two overlapping, congruent triangles that share the segment as a common side.
Check students' work.

8. Draw two right triangles that share a common angle that is not a right angle.
Check students' work.

9. The pattern at the right has been designed for a square floor tile. Both $\triangle ACF$ and $\triangle DBG$ are 30°-60°-90° right triangles. Write a paragraph proof to prove that $\triangle FGE$ is an equilateral triangle.
Answers may vary. Sample: $ADGF$ is a square, so $m\angle AFG = m\angle DGF = 90$. $m\angle EFG = m\angle EGF = 60$ because they are complements of 30° angles; $m\angle GEF = 60$ by the △ Angle-Sum Thm., so $\triangle FGE$ is equilateral by Thm. 4-3.

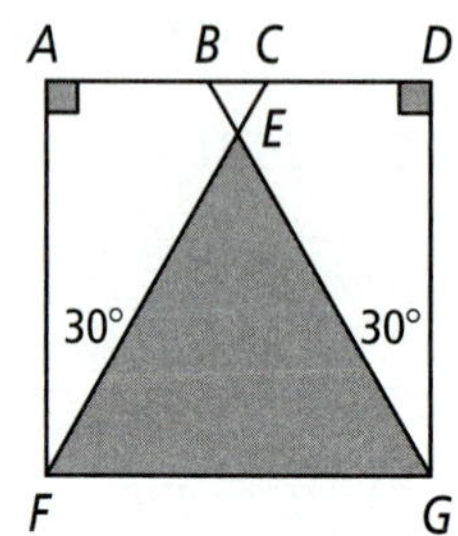

Name ______________________ Class ____________ Date ____________

4-7 Standardized Test Prep

Congruence in Overlapping Triangles

Multiple Choice

For Exercises 1–5, choose the correct letter.

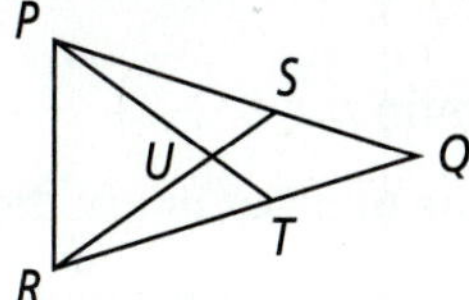

1. What is the common angle of $\triangle PQT$ and $\triangle RSQ$? A

   A. $\angle PQT$　　C. $\angle SRQ$

   B. $\angle SPT$　　D. $\angle SUT$

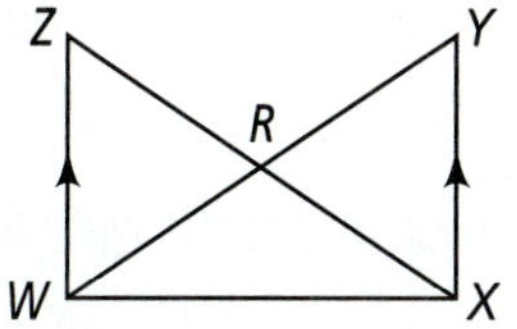

Use the following information for Exercises 2–5.

Given: $\triangle ZWX \cong \triangle YXW$, $\overline{ZW} \parallel \overline{YX}$

Prove: $\triangle ZWR \cong \triangle YRX$

2. Which corresponding parts statement is needed to prove $\triangle ZWR \cong \triangle YRX$? H

   F. $\angle ZWR \cong \angle YXR$　　H. $ZW = YX$

   G. $\angle Z \cong \angle R$　　I. $WX = WX$

3. A classmate writes the statement $\angle ZRW \cong \angle YRX$ to help prove the congruence of the triangles. What reason should the classmate give? D

   A. Given

   B. Angles cut by a bisector are congruent.

   C. Base angles of an isosceles triangle are congruent.

   D. Vertical angles are congruent.

4. After using the congruence statements from Exercises 2 and 3, which statement can be used to prove the triangles congruent? F

   F. $\angle Z \cong \angle Y$　　H. $\overline{WX} \cong \overline{WX}$

   G. $\angle ZWR \cong \angle RYX$　　I. $\overline{WR} \cong \overline{RX}$

5. Which theorem or postulate will prove $\triangle ZWR \cong \triangle YRX$? D

   A. SAS　　B. SSS　　C. ASA　　D. AAS

Short Response

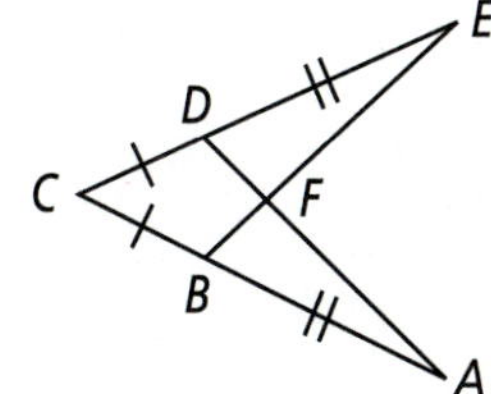

6. In the diagram at the right, which two triangles should be proved congruent first to help prove $\triangle ABF \cong \triangle EDF$?
   [2] $\triangle ACD$ and $\triangle ECB$ [1] Correct △ named but vertices do not correspond. [0] incorrect △ named

5-1 Midsegments of Triangles

Vocabulary

Review

Use the number line at the right for Exercises 1–3.

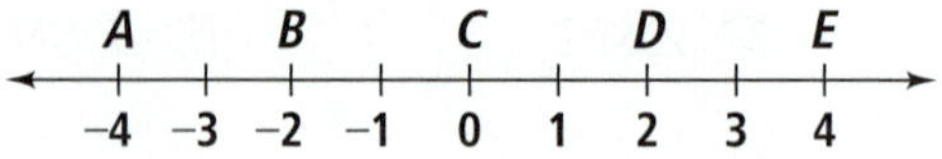

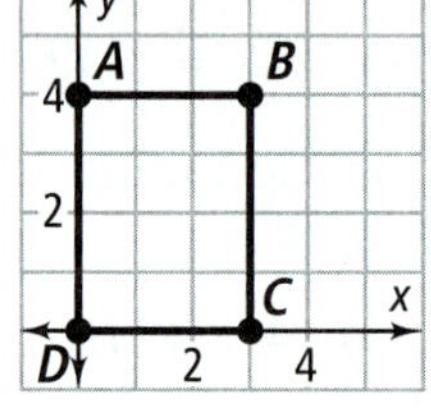

1. Point C is the *midpoint* of $\overline{AE}$.
2. Point D is the *midpoint* of $\overline{CE}$.
3. Point B is the *midpoint* of $\overline{AC}$.

Use the graph at the right for Exercises 4–6. Name each *segment*.

4. a *segment* that lies on the *x*-axis

   $\overline{DC}$ or $\overline{CD}$

5. a *segment* that contains the point (0, 4)

   $\overline{DA}$, $\overline{AD}$, $\overline{AB}$, or $\overline{BA}$

6. a *segment* whose endpoints both have *x*-coordinate 3

   $\overline{BC}$ or $\overline{CB}$

Vocabulary Builder

midsegment (noun) MID seg munt

Related Words: midpoint, segment

Definition: A **midsegment** of a triangle is a segment connecting the midpoints of two sides of the triangle.

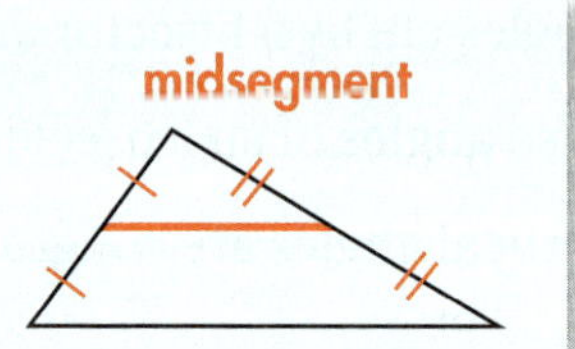

Use Your Vocabulary

Circle the correct statement in each pair.

7. (A *midsegment* connects the midpoints of two sides of a triangle.) [circled]

   A *midsegment* connects a vertex of a triangle to the midpoint of the opposite side.

8. A triangle has exactly one *midsegment*. (A triangle has three *midsegments*.) [circled]

take note

Theorem 5-1 Triangle Midsegment Theorem

If a segment joins the midpoints of two sides of a triangle, then the segment is parallel to the third side and is half as long.

9. Use the triangle at the right to complete the table below.

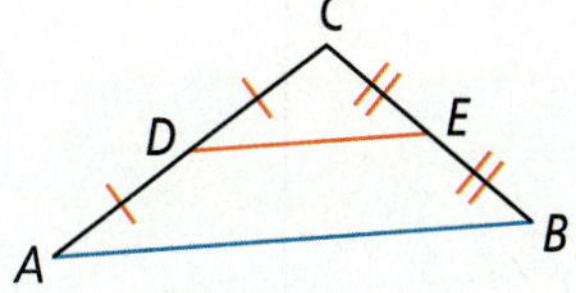

If	Then
D is the midpoint of $\overline{CA}$ and	$\overline{DE} \parallel \overline{AB}$
E is the midpoint of $\overline{CB}$	$DE = \frac{1}{2}AB$

Use the graph at the right for Exercises 10–11.

10. Draw $\overline{RS}$. Then underline the correct word or number to complete each sentence below.

$\overline{RS}$ is a midsegment of / parallel to $\triangle ABC$.

$\overline{RS}$ is a midsegment of / parallel to $\overline{AC}$.

11. Use the Triangle Midsegment Theorem to complete.

$RS = \frac{1}{2} AC$

12. Draw $\overline{ST}$. What do you know about $\overline{ST}$?

Sample: It is a midsegment of $\triangle ABC$; it is parallel to and half the length of $\overline{BC}$.

Problem 1 Identifying Parallel Segments

Got It? **In $\triangle XYZ$, A is the midpoint of $\overline{XY}$, B is the midpoint of $\overline{YZ}$, and C is the midpoint of $\overline{ZX}$. What are the three pairs of parallel segments?**

13. Draw a diagram to illustrate the problem.

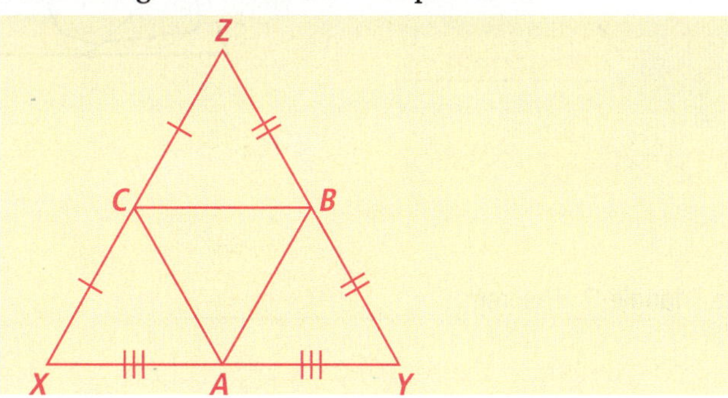

14. Write the segment parallel to each given segment.

$\overline{AB} \parallel$ ZX $\overline{CB} \parallel$ XY $\overline{CA} \parallel$ YZ

Problem 2 Finding Lengths

Got It? In the figure below, $AD = 6$ and $DE = 7.5$. What are the lengths of $\overline{DC}$, $\overline{AC}$, $\overline{EF}$, and $\overline{AB}$?

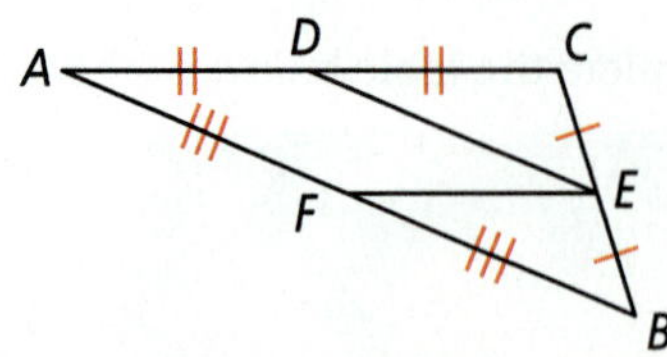

15. Complete the problem-solving model below.

Know	Need	Plan
$AD = 6$ and $DE = 7.5$. $CE = EB$, $AD = DC$, $BF =$ FA	The lengths of $\overline{DC}$, $\overline{AC}$, $\overline{EF}$, and $\overline{AB}$	Use the Triangle Midsegment Theorem to find DC, AC, EF, and AB.

16. The diagram shows that $\overline{EF}$ and $\overline{DE}$ join the midpoints of two sides of $\triangle$ ABC.

By the Triangle Midsegment Theorem, $EF = \frac{1}{2} \cdot$ AC and $DE = \frac{1}{2} \cdot$ AB.

Complete each statement.

17. $DC = AD =$ 6

18. $AC = AD +$ DC $=$ 6 $+$ 6 $=$ 12

19. $EF =$ $\frac{1}{2}$ $\cdot AC =$ $\frac{1}{2}$ $\cdot$ 12 $= 6$

20. $AB =$ 2 $\cdot DE =$ 2 $\cdot$ 7.5 $= 15$

Problem 3 Using a Midsegment of a Triangle

Got It? $\overline{CD}$ is a bridge being built over a lake, as shown in the figure at the right. What is the length of the bridge?

21. Complete the flow chart to find the length of the bridge.

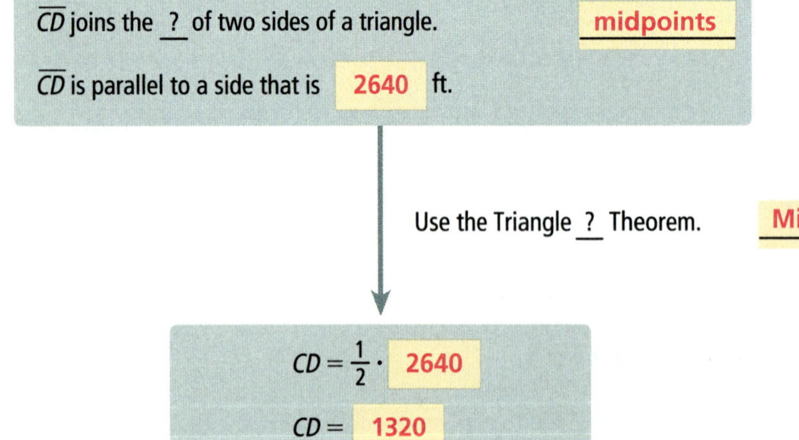

$\overline{CD}$ joins the ? of two sides of a triangle. midpoints

$\overline{CD}$ is parallel to a side that is 2640 ft.

Use the Triangle ? Theorem. Midsegment

$CD = \frac{1}{2} \cdot$ 2640

$CD =$ 1320

22. The length of the bridge is 1320 ft.

Lesson Check • Do you know HOW?

If $JK = 5x + 20$ and $NO = 20$, what is the value of x?

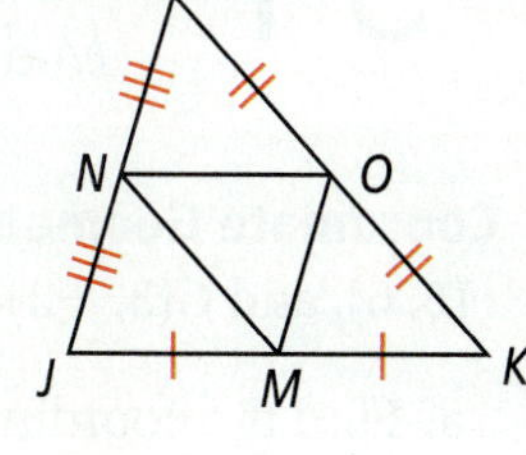

Complete each statement.

23. N is the midpoint of $\overline{LJ}$.

24. O is the midpoint of $\overline{LK}$.

25. $\overline{NO}$ is a __?__ of $\triangle JKL$, so $NO = \frac{1}{2}JK$. midsegment

26. Substitute the given information into the equation in Exercise 25 and solve for x.

$NO = \frac{1}{2}JK$

$20 = \frac{1}{2}(2x + 20)$

$40 = (2x + 20)$

$20 = 5x$

$x = 4$

Lesson Check • Do you UNDERSTAND?

Reasoning **If two noncollinear segments in the coordinate plane have slope 3, what can you conclude?**

27. Place a ✓ in the box if the response is correct. Place an ✗ if it is incorrect.

✓ If two segments in a plane are parallel, then they have the same slope.

✗ If two segments lie on the same line, they are parallel.

28. Now answer the question. Answers may vary. Sample:

The segments do not lie on the same line,

so they are parallel lines.

Math Success

Check off the vocabulary words that you understand.

☐ midsegment ☐ midpoint ☐ segment

Rate how well you can *use properties of midsegments.*

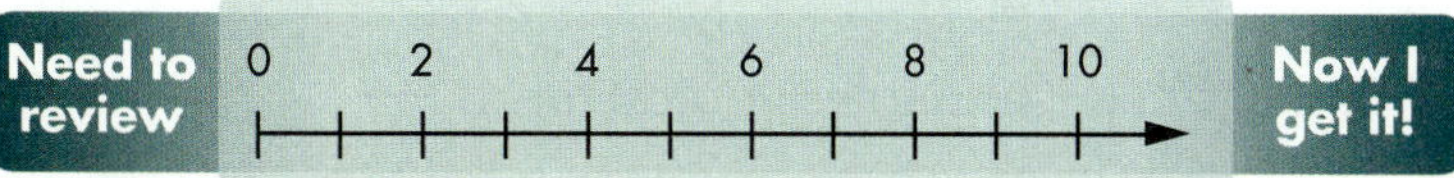

Name ______________________ Class ____________ Date ____________

5-1 Think About a Plan

Midsegments of Triangles

Coordinate Geometry The coordinates of the vertices of a triangle are $E(1, 2)$, $F(5, 6)$, and $G(3, -2)$.

a. Find the coordinates of H, the midpoint of $\overline{EG}$, and J, the midpoint of $\overline{FG}$.

b. Show that $\overline{HJ} \parallel \overline{EF}$.

c. Show that $HJ = \frac{1}{2}EF$.

1. In part (a), what formula would you use to find the midpoints of $\overline{EG}$ and $\overline{FG}$? Write this formula. **Midpoint Formula; $\left(\frac{x_1 + x_2}{2}, \frac{y_1 + y_2}{2}\right)$**

2. Substitute the x- and y-coordinates of E and G into the formula. $\left(\frac{1 + 3}{2}, \frac{2 + (-2)}{2}\right)$

3. Solve to find the coordinates of H, the midpoint of $\overline{EG}$. **(2, 0)**

4. Use the coordinates of F and G to find the coordinates of J, the midpoint of $\overline{FG}$. **(4, 2)**

5. In part (b), what information do you need to show $\overline{HJ} \parallel \overline{EF}$? Write the formula you would use. **need to show the slopes are equal; $m = \frac{y_2 - y_1}{x_2 - x_1}$**

6. Substitute the x- and y-coordinates of H and J into the formula. $m = \frac{2 - 0}{4 - 2}$

7. Solve to find the slope of $\overline{HJ}$. **1**

8. Use the coordinates of E and F to find the slope of $\overline{EF}$. **1**

9. Is $\overline{HJ} \parallel \overline{EF}$? Explain. **Yes; both segments have the same slope.**

10. In part (c), what formula would you use to find HJ and EF? Write this formula.
Distance Formula; $d = \sqrt{(x_2 - x_1)^2 + (y_2 - y_1)^2}$

11. Substitute the x- and y-coordinates of H and J into the formula.
$d = \sqrt{(4 - 2)^2 + (2 - 0)^2}$

12. Solve to find HJ. Keep in simplest radical form. $2\sqrt{2}$

13. Use the coordinates of E and F to find EF. Keep in simplest radical form.
$d = \sqrt{(5 - 1)^2 + (6 - 2)^2} = 4\sqrt{2}$

14. What is the relationship between HJ and EF? $HJ = \frac{1}{2}EF$

Name ______________________ Class ____________ Date ____________

5-1 Practice — Form K
Midsegments of Triangles

Identify three pairs of parallel sides in the diagram.

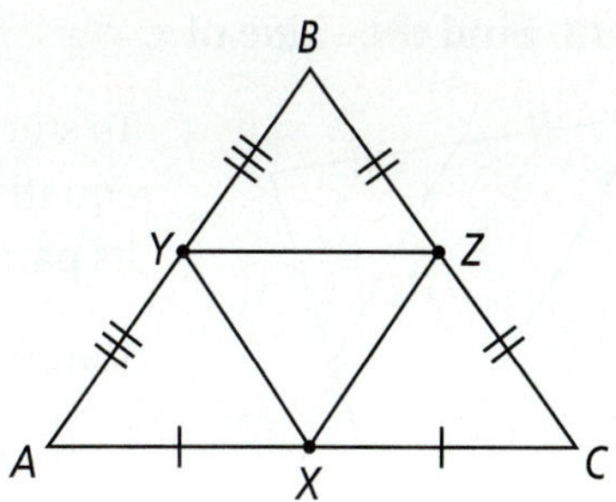

1. $\overline{AB} \parallel$ _?_ $\overline{XZ}$

2. $\overline{BC} \parallel$ _?_ $\overline{YX}$

3. $\overline{AC} \parallel$ _?_ $\overline{YZ}$

Name the side that is parallel to the given side.

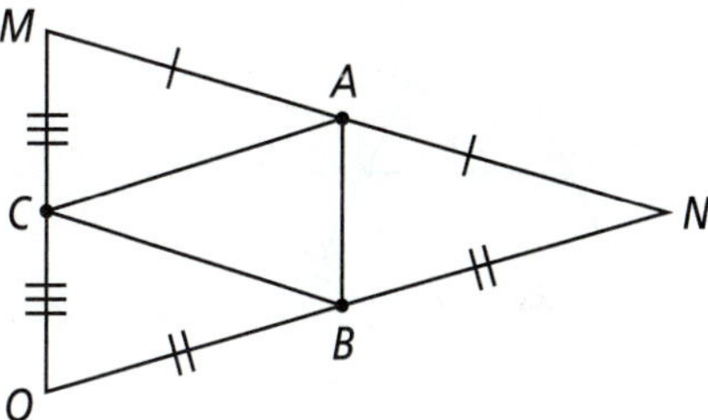

4. $\overline{MN}$ $\overline{BC}$

5. $\overline{ON}$ $\overline{AC}$

6. $\overline{AB}$ $\overline{MO}$

7. $\overline{CB}$ $\overline{MN}$

8. $\overline{OM}$ $\overline{AB}$

9. $\overline{AC}$ $\overline{ON}$

Points *J*, *K*, and *L* are the midpoints of the sides of $\triangle XYZ$.

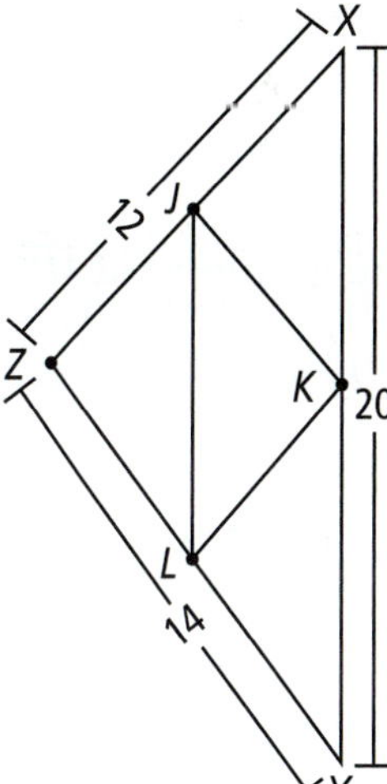

10. Find *LK*. 6

    To start, identify what kind of segment $\overline{LK}$ is. Then identify which relationship in the Triangle Midsegment Theorem will help you find the length.

    $\overline{LK}$ is a midsegment of $\triangle XYZ$.

    $\overline{LK}$ is parallel to $\overline{ZX}$.

11. Find *YK*. 10

12. Find *JK*. 7

13. Find *XK*. 10

14. Find *JL*. 10

15. Find *YL*. 7

16. Find *KL*. 6

17. Draw a triangle and label it *ABC*. Draw all the midpoints and label them. Identify pairs of parallel sides and congruent angles in your triangle.
    Check students' work.

Name ______________________ Class ____________ Date ____________

5-1 Practice (continued) — Form K

Midsegments of Triangles

Algebra **Find the value of *x*.**

18. 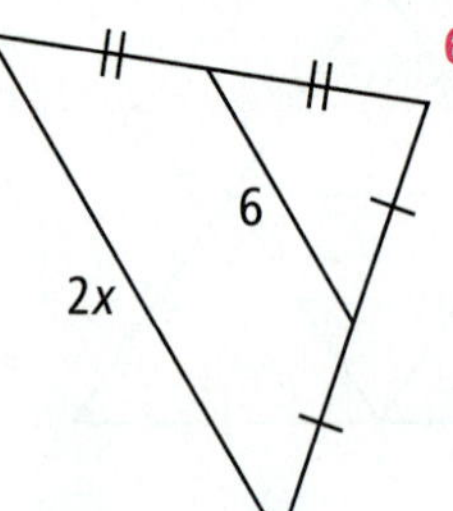

6

To start, identify the midsegment. Then write an equation to show that its length is half the length of its parallel segment.

The segment with length [6] is the midsegment.

$\boxed{6} = \frac{1}{2} \cdot \boxed{2x}$

19. 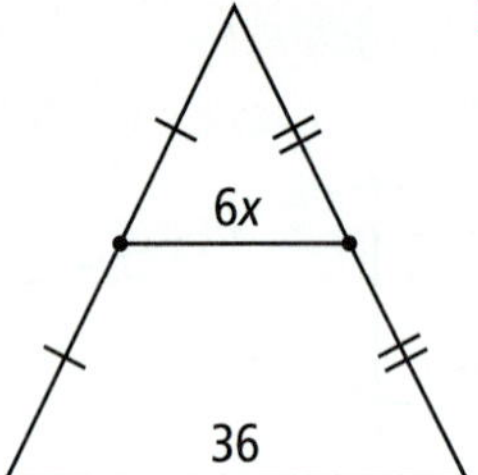

3

20. 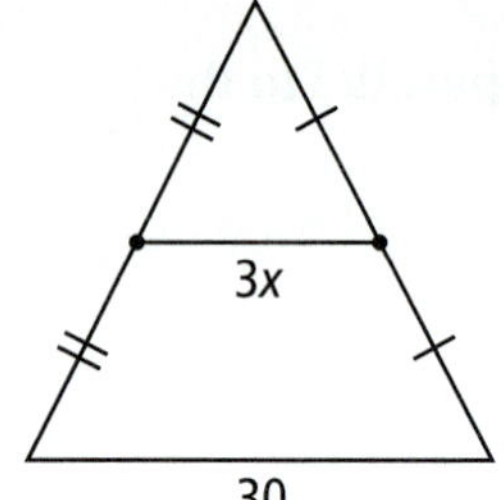

5

21. 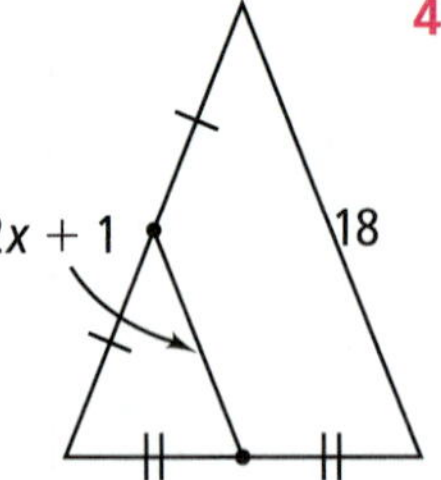

4

22. 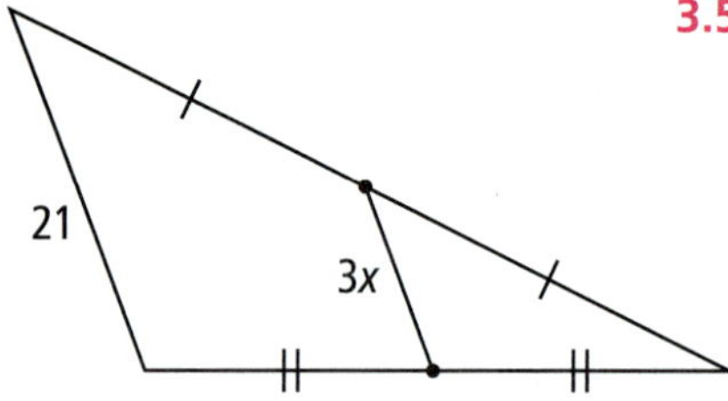

3.5

***X* is the midpoint of $\overline{MN}$. *Y* is the midpoint of $\overline{ON}$.**

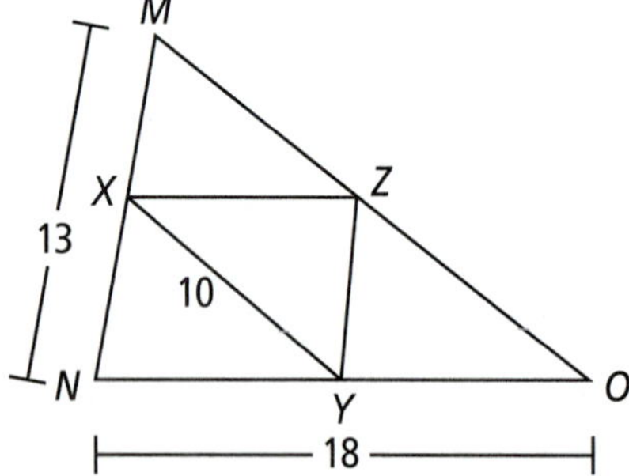

23. Find *XZ*. 9

24. If $XY = 10$, find *MO*. 20

25. If $m\angle M$ is 64, find $m\angle XYZ$. 64

Use the diagram at the right for Exercises 26 and 27.

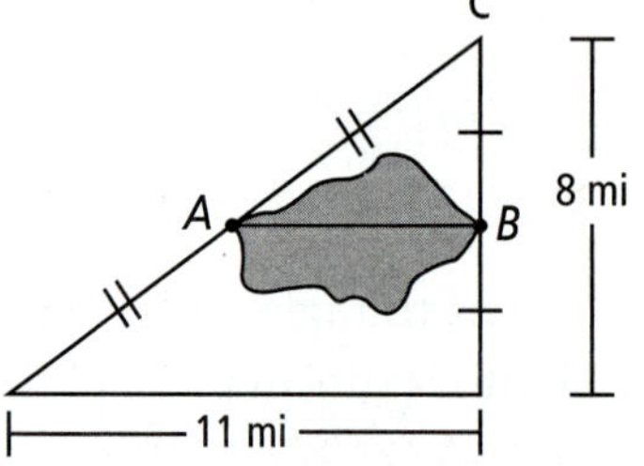

26. What is the distance across the lake?
5.5 mi

27. Is it a shorter distance from *A* to *B* or from *B* to *C*? Explain.
B to C is shorter; *BC* is half of 8 mi, while *AB* is half of 11 mi.

Name ______________________ Class ____________ Date ____________

5-1 Standardized Test Prep

Midsegments of Triangles

Gridded Response

Solve each exercise and enter your answer on the grid provided.

In $\triangle RST$, U is the midpoint of $\overline{RS}$, V is the midpoint of $\overline{ST}$, and W is the midpoint of $\overline{TR}$.

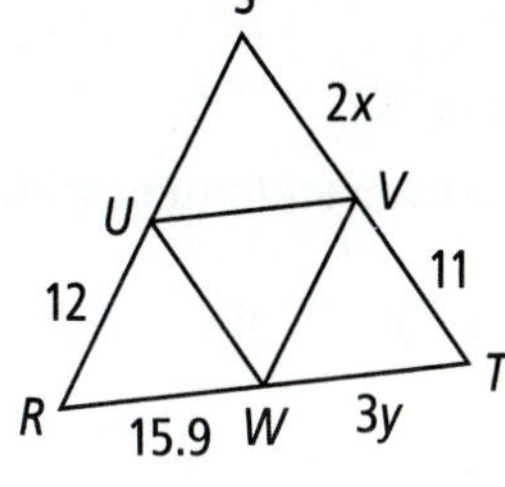

1. What is the length of $\overline{RS}$?

2. What is the value of x?

3. What is the value of y?

4. What is the length of $\overline{UW}$?

5. What is the length of $\overline{UV}$?

Answers

1. 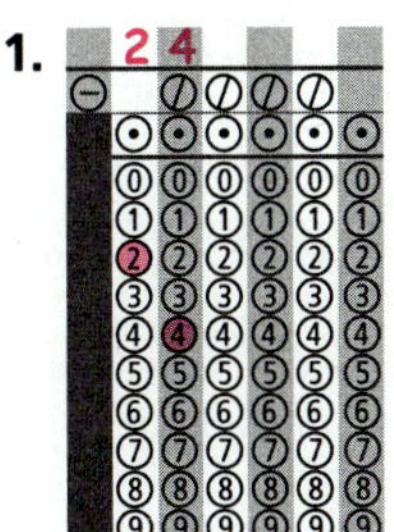

2. 5 . 5

3. 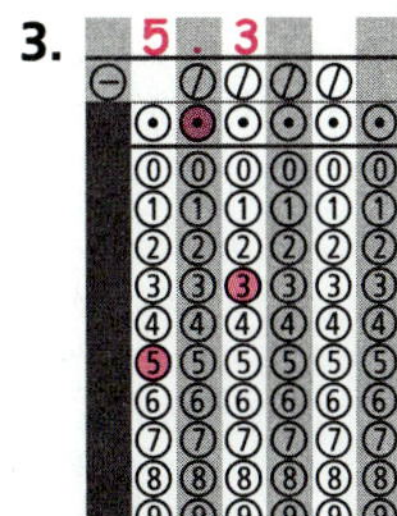

4. 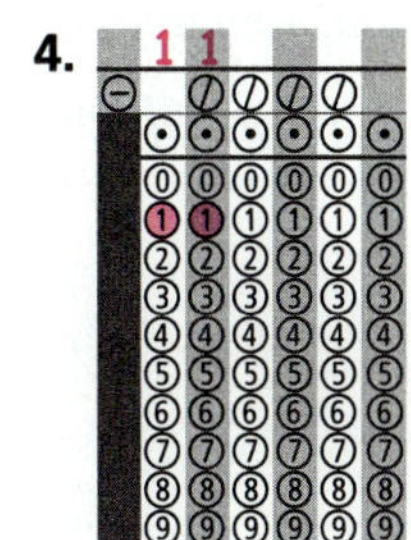

5. 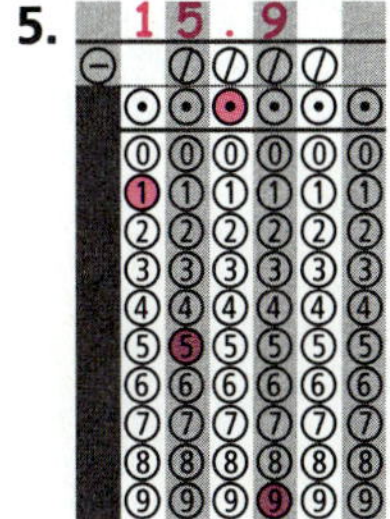

Perpendicular and Angle Bisectors

Vocabulary

Review

Complete each statement with *bisector* or *bisects*.

1. $\overrightarrow{BD}$ is the __?__ of $\angle ABC$. bisector

2. BD __?__ $\angle ABC$. bisects

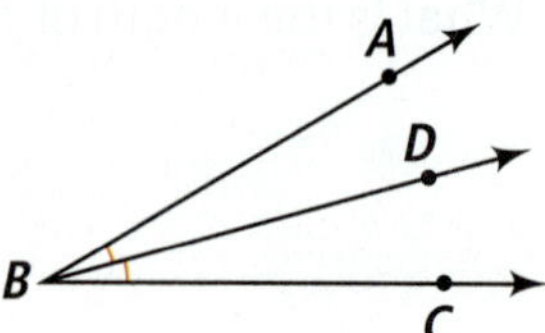

Write T for *true* or F for *false*.

T 3. Two *perpendicular* segments intersect to form four right angles.

F 4. You can draw more than one line *perpendicular* to a given line through a point not on the line.

Vocabulary Builder

equidistant (adjective) **ee kwih DIS tunt**

Related Words: equal, distance

Definition: **Equidistant** means at an equal distance from a single point or object.

equidistant

Use Your Vocabulary

Use to the number line at the right for Exercises 5 and 6.

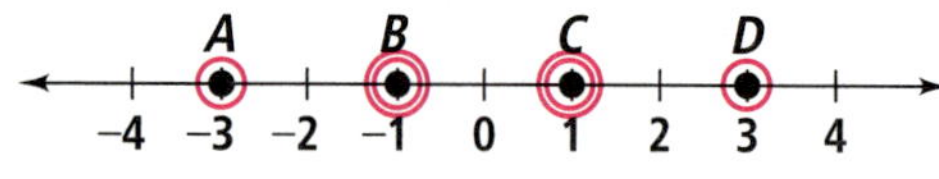

5. Circle two points *equidistant* from zero.

6. Name points that are *equidistant* from point *C*.

   B and D

Use to the diagram at the right for Exercises 7 and 8.

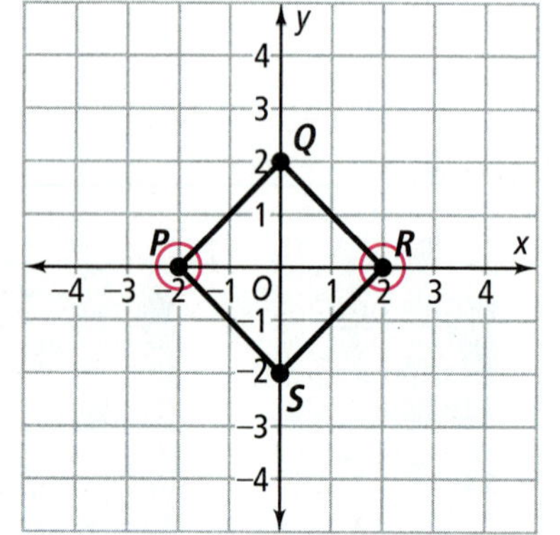

7. Circle two points *equidistant* from point *Q*.

8. Name four segments that are *equidistant* from the origin.

   $\overline{PQ}$ $\overline{QR}$ $\overline{RS}$ $\overline{SP}$

Theorem 5-2 Perpendicular Bisector Theorem

take note

If a point is on the perpendicular bisector of a segment, then it is equidistant from the endpoints of the segment.

9. Use the diagrams below to complete the hypothesis and the conclusion.

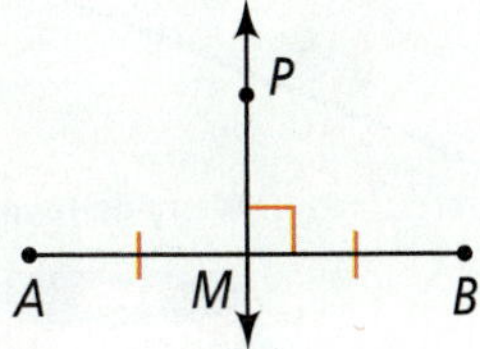

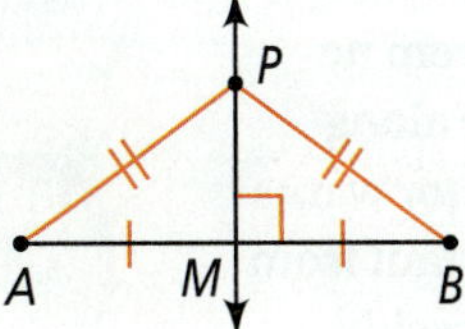

If
$\overleftrightarrow{PM} \perp \overline{AB}$ and $AM =$ **MB**

Then
$PA =$ **PB**

Theorem 5-3 Converse of the Perpendicular Bisector Theorem

take note

10. Complete the converse of Theorem 5-2.

If a point is equidistant from the endpoints of a segment, then it is on the __?__ of the segment.

perpendicular bisector

11. Complete the diagram at the right to illustrate Theorem 5-3.

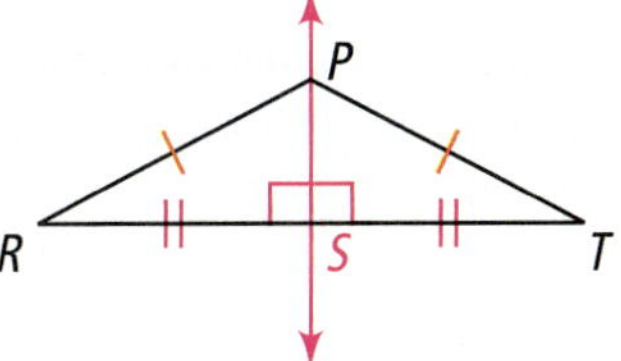

Problem 1 Using the Perpendicular Bisector Theorem

Got It? Use the diagram at the right. What is the length of $\overline{QR}$?

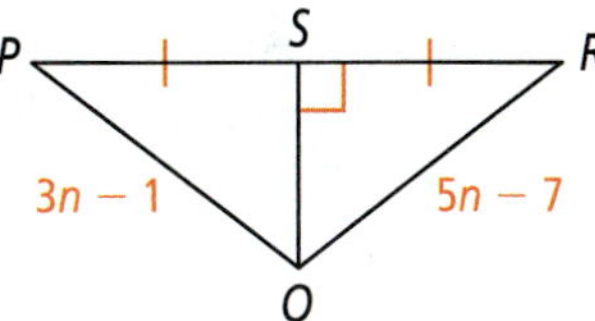

12. Complete the reasoning model below.

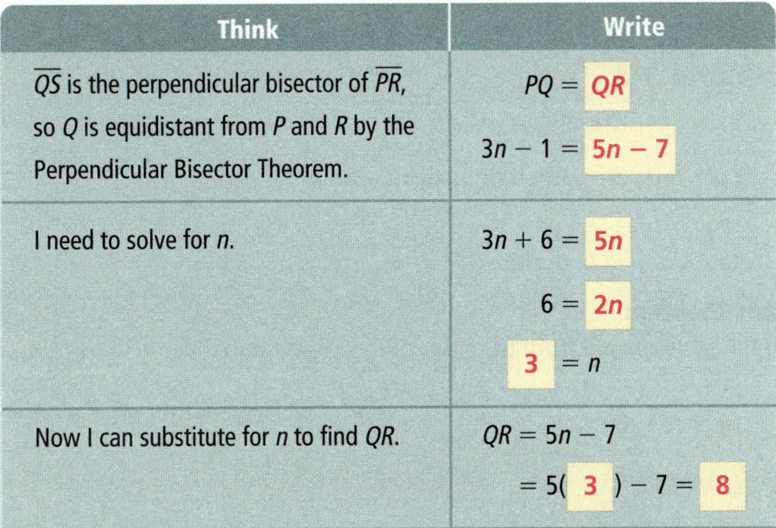

Think	Write
$\overline{QS}$ is the perpendicular bisector of $\overline{PR}$, so Q is equidistant from P and R by the Perpendicular Bisector Theorem.	$PQ =$ **QR** $3n - 1 =$ **5n − 7**
I need to solve for n.	$3n + 6 =$ **5n** $6 =$ **2n** **3** $= n$
Now I can substitute for n to find QR.	$QR = 5n - 7$ $= 5($ **3** $) - 7 =$ **8**

Problem 2 Using a Perpendicular Bisector

Got It? **If the director of the park at the right wants a T-shirt stand built at a point equidistant from the Spaceship Shoot and the Rollin' Coaster, by the Perpendicular Bisector Theorem he can place the stand anywhere along line ℓ. Suppose the park director wants the T-shirt stand to be equidistant from the paddle boats and the Spaceship Shoot. What are the possible locations?**

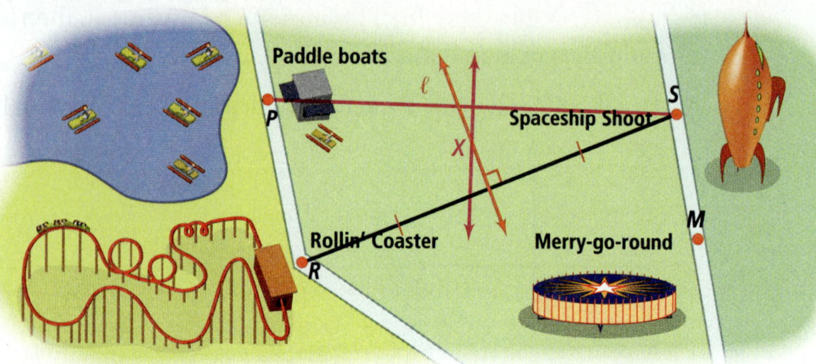

13. On the diagram, draw $\overline{PS}$.

14. On the diagram, sketch the points that are equidistant from the paddle boats and the Spaceship Shoot. Describe these points.

    the points on the perpendicular bisector of $\overline{PS}$

Got It? **Reasoning** **Can you place the T-shirt stand so that it is equidistant from the paddle boats, the Spaceship Shoot, and the Rollin' Coaster? Explain.**

15. Does the line you drew in Exercise 14 intersect line ℓ? Yes / No (Yes circled)

16. Where should the T-shirt stand be placed so that it is equidistant from the paddle boats, the Spaceship Shoot, and the Rollin Coaster? Explain. Answers may vary.

    Sample: Place the stand at the intersection point X of the perpendicular bisectors of $\overline{RS}$ and $\overline{PS}$. By the Perpendicular Bisector Theorem, $XR = XS$ and $XS = XP$, so $XR = XS = XP$ by the Transitive Property.

The **distance from a point to a line** is the length of the perpendicular segment from the point to the line. This distance is also the length of the shortest segment from the point to the line.

take note

Theorems 5-4 and 5-5

Angle Bisector Theorem

If a point is on the bisector of an angle, then the point is equisdistant from the sides of the angle.

17. If point S is on the angle bisector of $\angle$ PQR, then $SP =$ SR.

Converse of the Angle Bisector Theorem

If a point in the interior of an angle is equidistant from the sides of the angle, then the point is on the angle bisector.

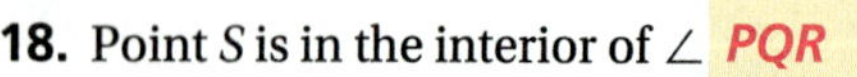

18. Point S is in the interior of $\angle$ PQR.

19. If $SP = SR$, then S is on the __?__ of $\angle PQR$. angle bisector

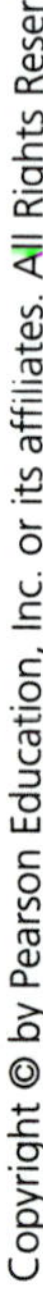

Problem 3 Using the Angle Bisector Theorem

Got It? What is the length of $\overline{FB}$?

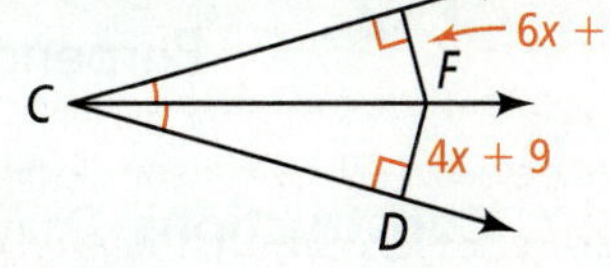

20. The problem is solved below. Justify each step.

$FB = FD$	Angle Bisector Theorem
$6x + 3 = 4x + 9$	Substitute.
$6x = 4x + 6$	Subtract 3 from each side.
$2x = 6$	Subtract 4x from each side.
$x = 3$	Divide each side by 2.
$FB = 6x + 3$	Given
$= 6(3) + 3 = 21$	Substitute 3 for x and simplify.

Lesson Check • Do you know HOW?

Use the figure at the right. What is the relationship between $\overline{AC}$ and $\overline{BD}$?

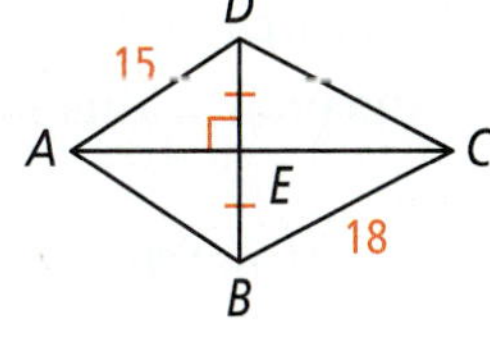

21. Underline the correct word or symbol to complete each sentence.

$\overline{AC}$ is parallel / perpendicular to $\overline{BD}$.

$\overline{AC}$ divides $\overline{BD}$ into two congruent / noncongruent segments.

$\overline{BD}$ divides $\overline{AC}$ into two congruent / noncongruent segments.

$\overline{AC}$ / $\overline{BD}$ is the perpendicular bisector of $\overline{AC}$ / $\overline{BD}$.

Math Success

Check off the vocabulary words that you understand.

☐ perpendicular bisector ☐ equidistant ☐ distance from a point to a line

Rate how well you can *understand bisectors.*

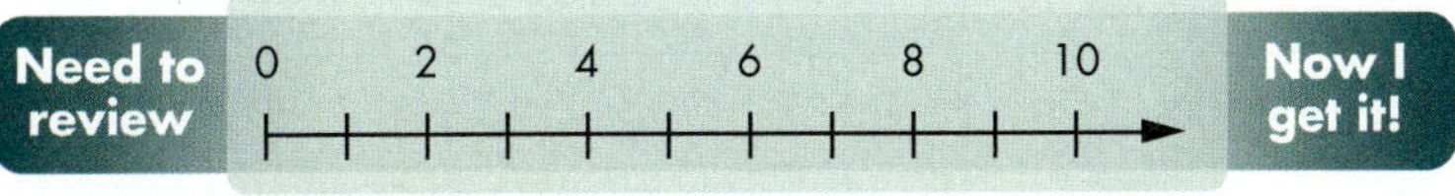

Name ______________________ Class ____________ Date ____________

5-2 Think About a Plan

Perpendicular and Angle Bisectors

a. Constructions Draw a large acute scalene triangle, $\triangle PQR$. Construct the perpendicular bisectors of each side.

b. Make a Conjecture What appears to be true about the perpendicular bisectors?

c. Test your conjecture with another triangle.

1. For part (a), what is an acute scalene triangle?

a triangle in which all angles are acute and no side lengths are equal

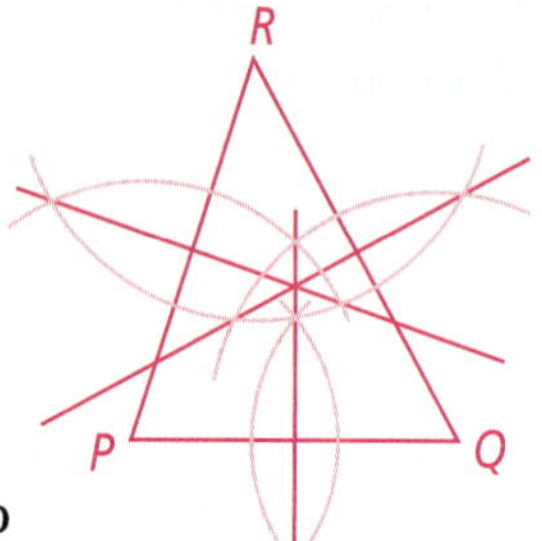

2. Sketch a large acute scalene triangle. Use a protractor to make sure each angle is less than 90°. Label the vertices *P*, *Q*, and *R*. Check to make sure the triangle is scalene by comparing the side lengths.

3. To construct the perpendicular bisector for $\overline{PQ}$, set the compass to greater than **$\frac{1}{2}QP$**. Draw two arcs, one from *P* and one from *Q*. The arcs **intersect** at two points. Draw a segment connecting the points. This segment is the **perpendicular bisector**.

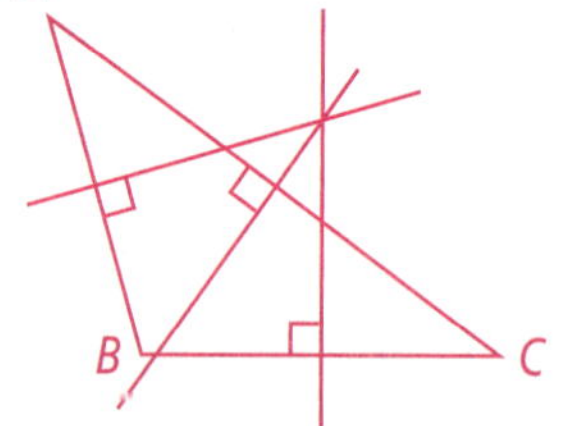

4. Construct the perpendicular bisectors of $\overline{QR}$ and $\overline{RP}$.

5. For part (b), examine the three perpendicular bisectors. Write a conjecture about the perpendicular bisectors in all triangles.

Answers may vary. Sample: The perpendicular bisectors of any triangle intersect at one point inside the triangle.

6. For part (c), repeat Steps 1–4 for an obtuse, equilateral, or isosceles triangle. Does the conjecture appear to be true for this triangle?

Answers may vary. Sample: No; for an obtuse triangle, the intersection of the perpendicular bisectors lies outside the triangle.

Name ______________________ Class ____________ Date ____________

5-2 Practice

Form K

Perpendicular and Angle Bisectors

Use the figure at the right for Exercises 1–3.

1. What is the value of x? 4

To start, determine the relationship between $\overline{AC}$ and $\overline{BD}$.
Then write an equation to show the relationships of the sides.

$\overline{BD}$ is the __?__ bisector of $\overline{AC}$. Therefore, point B is equidistant from points A and [C]. perpendicular

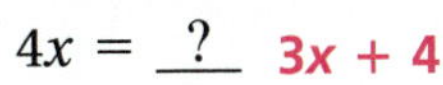

$4x =$ __?__ $3x + 4$

2. Find AB. 16

3. Find BC. 16

Use the figure at the right for Exercises 4–7.

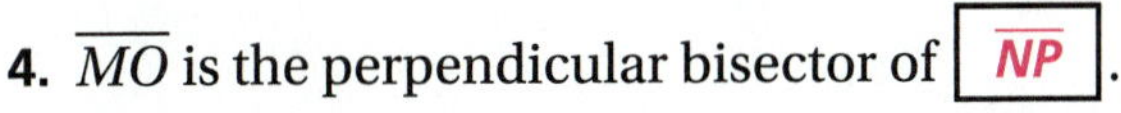

4. $\overline{MO}$ is the perpendicular bisector of [$\overline{NP}$].

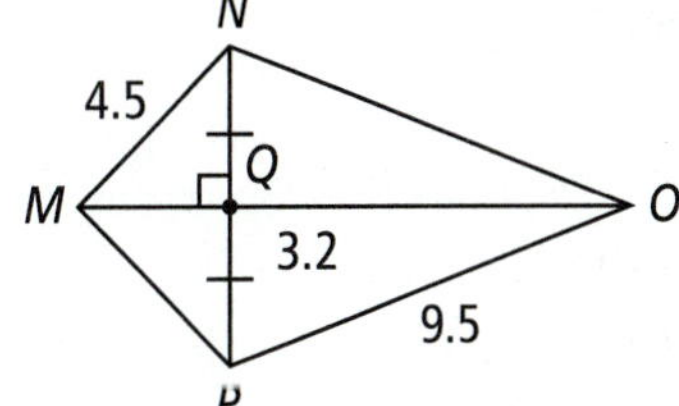

5. Find MP. 4.5

6. Find NO. 9.5

7. Find NP. 6.4

Use the figure at the right for Exercises 8–13.

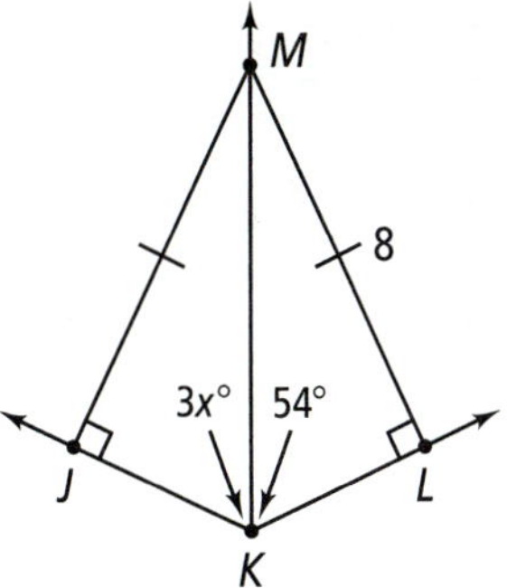

8. How far is M from $\overline{KL}$? 8

9. How far is M from $\overline{JK}$? 8

10. How is $\overline{KM}$ related to $\angle JKL$? $\overline{KM}$ bisects $\angle JKL$.

11. Find the value of x. 18

12. Find $m\angle MKL$. 54

13. Find $m\angle JMK$ and $m\angle LMK$. 36; 36

Name ______________________ Class ____________ Date ____________

5-2 Practice (continued) Form K

Perpendicular and Angle Bisectors

Use the figure at the right for Exercises 14–16.

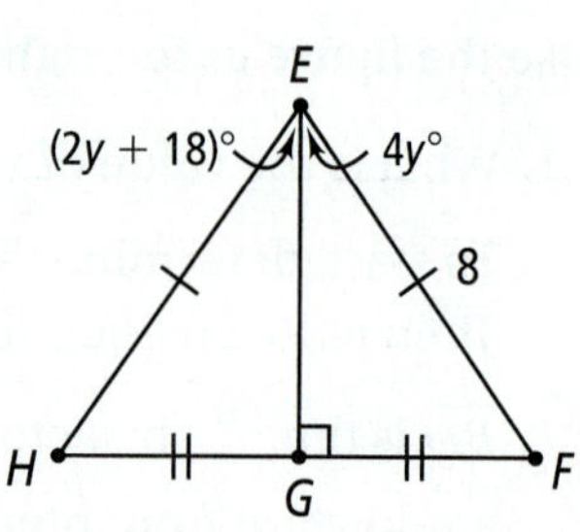

14. What are the lengths of $\overline{EF}$ and $\overline{EH}$? 8; 8

15. Find the value of y. 9

16. Find $m\angle GEH$ and $m\angle GEF$. 36; 36

Algebra **Find the indicated values of the variables and measures.**

17. x, BA, BC 6; 16; 16

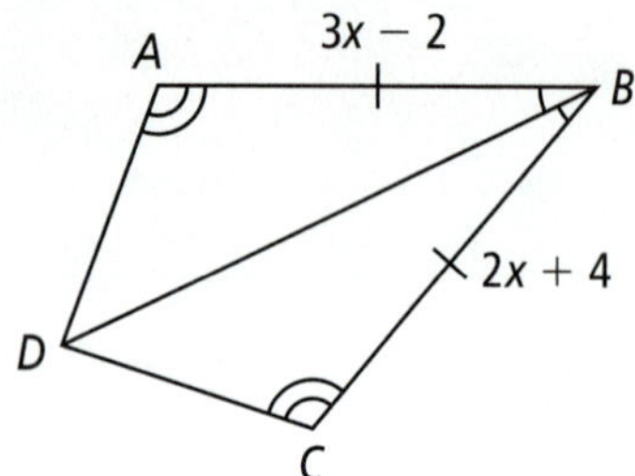

18. x, EH, EF 2; 13; 13

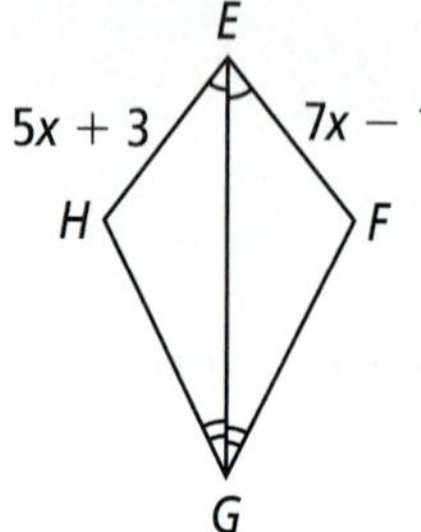

19. x, IK 3; 18

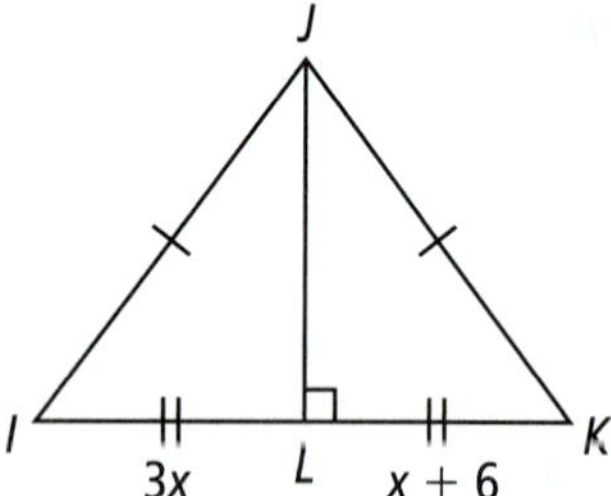

20. x, $m\angle UWV$, $m\angle UWT$ 4; 20; 20

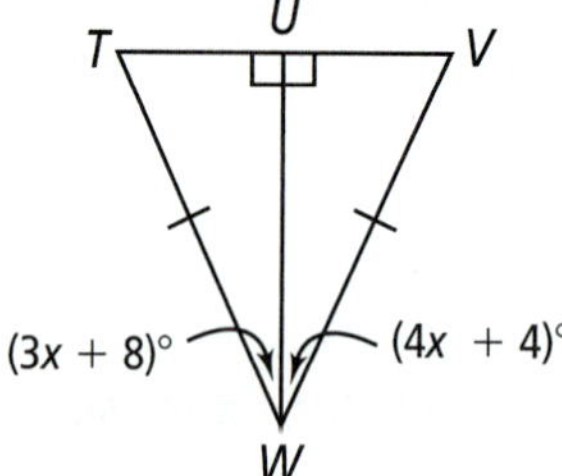

21. x, $m\angle TPS$, $m\angle RPS$ 19; 32; 32

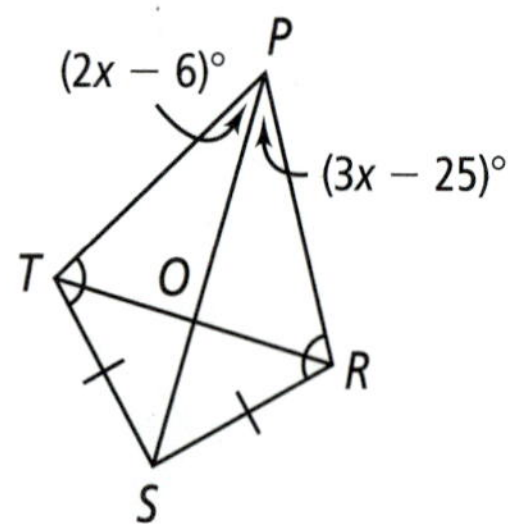

22. a, b 6; 20

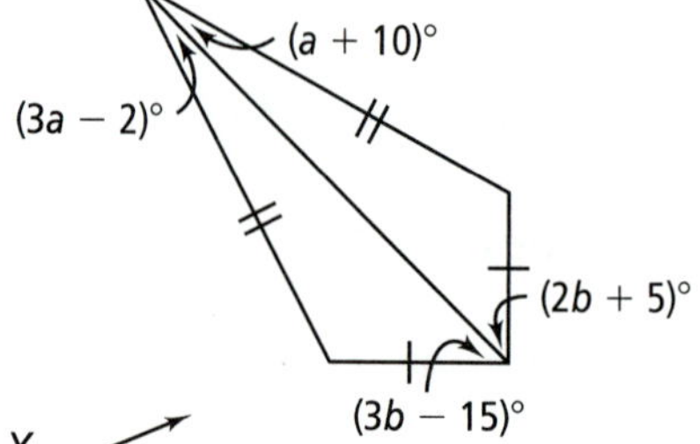

23. **Writing** Is A on the angle bisector of $\angle XYZ$? Explain.
Yes; A is equidistant from both rays of the angle, so A must be on the bisector.

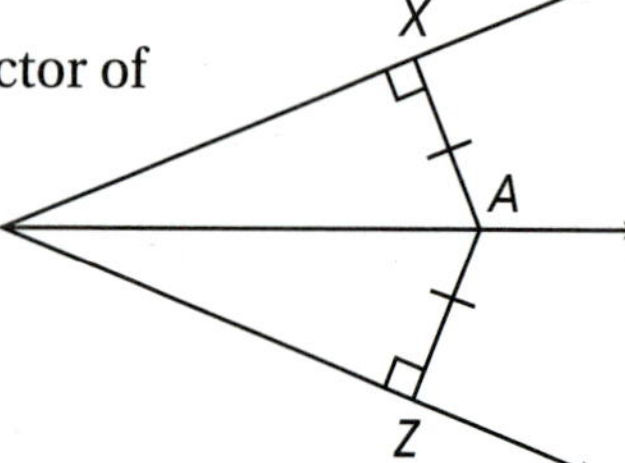

Name ________________________ Class ____________ Date ____________

5-2 Standardized Test Prep

Perpendicular and Angle Bisectors

Multiple Choice

For Exercises 1–6, choose the correct letter. Use the figure at the right.

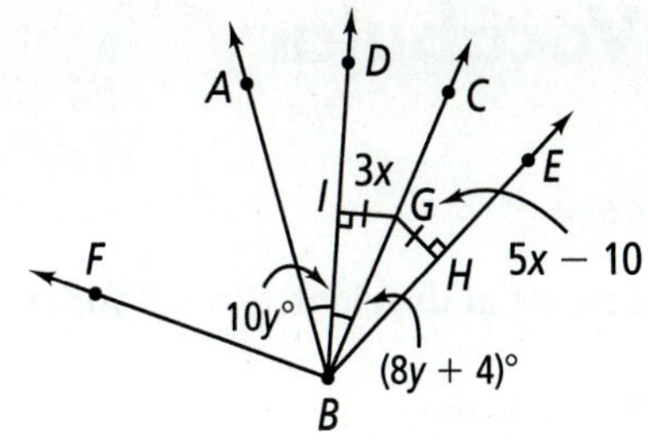

1. Which ray is a bisector of $\angle ABC$? B

Ⓐ $\overrightarrow{BC}$ Ⓒ $\overrightarrow{BA}$

Ⓑ $\overrightarrow{BD}$ Ⓓ $\overrightarrow{BF}$

2. What is GH? H

Ⓕ 5 Ⓖ 10 Ⓗ 15 Ⓘ 25

3. What is the value of y? A

Ⓐ 2 Ⓑ 4 Ⓒ 16 Ⓓ 20

4. What is $m\angle DBE$? H

Ⓕ 20 Ⓖ 30 Ⓗ 40 Ⓘ 50

5. What is $m\angle ABE$? D

Ⓐ 20 Ⓑ 30 Ⓒ 40 Ⓓ 60

6. If $m\angle FBA = 7x + 6y$, what is $m\angle FBA$? H

Ⓕ 40 Ⓖ 44 Ⓗ 47 Ⓘ 60

Short Response

7. Construct the bisector of $\angle ABC$. Answers may vary. Sample:

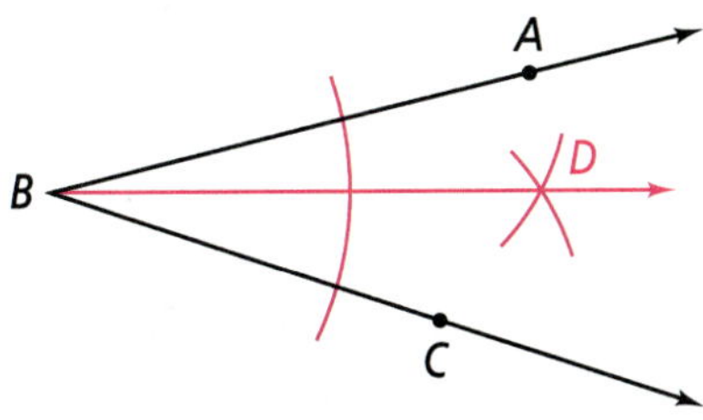

[2] Student construction is accurate and complete, including three arcs and a bisector labeled with two points. [1] The construction is incorrect or there are key elements, such as one of the arcs, missing. [0] There is no ray added to the diagram.

Bisectors in Triangles

Vocabulary

Review

Use the figure at the right. Write T for *true* or F for *false*.

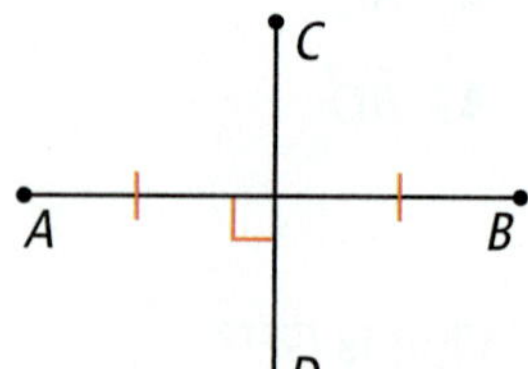

F 1. $\overline{AB}$ is the *perpendicular bisector* of $\overline{CD}$.

T 2. $\overline{CD}$ is a *perpendicular bisector*, so it intersects $\overline{AB}$ at its midpoint.

T 3. Any point on $\overline{CD}$ is *equidistant* from points A and B.

Vocabulary Builder

concurrent (adjective) **kun KUR unt**

Main Idea: Concurrent means occurring or existing at the same time.

Math Usage: When three or more lines intersect in one point, they are **concurrent.**

concurrent lines

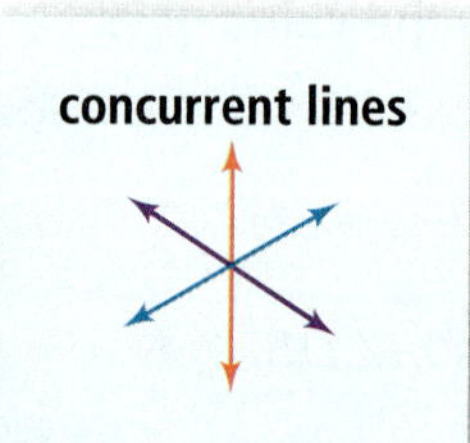

Use Your Vocabulary

Complete each statement with *concurrency, concurrent,* or *concurrently.*

4. Two classes are _?_ when they meet at the same time. concurrent

5. The point of _?_ of three streets is the intersections of the streets. concurrency

6. A person may go to school and hold a job _?_. concurrently

Label each diagram below *concurrent* or *not concurrent.*

7. 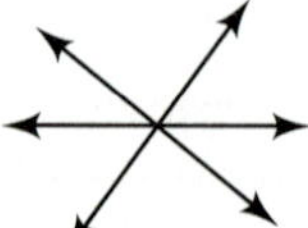

concurrent

8. 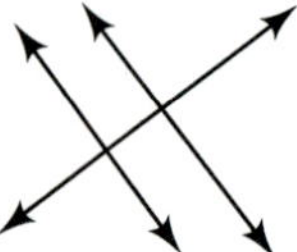

not concurrent

9. 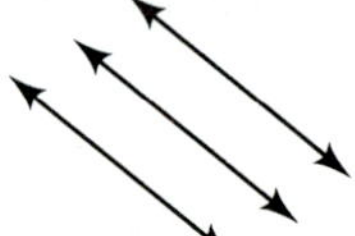

not concurrent

Theorem 5-6 Concurrency of Perpendicular Bisectors Theorem

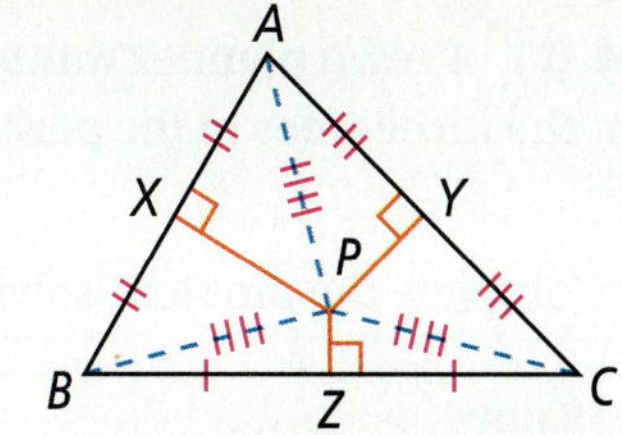

The perpendicular bisectors of the sides of a triangle are concurrent at a point equidistant from the vertices.

Perpendicular bisectors $\overline{PX}$, $\overline{PY}$ and $\overline{PZ}$ are concurrent at P.

10. Mark $\triangle ABC$ to show all congruent segments.

The point of concurrency of the perpendicular bisectors of a triangle is called the *circumcenter* of the triangle. The circumcenter of a triangle can be inside, on, or outside a triangle.

Underline the correct word to complete each sentence.

11. The circumcenter is equidistant from each side / vertex of a triangle.

12. The circumcenter of a triangle is the center of a circle that contains each midpoint / vertex of the triangle.

13. The circumcenter P of $\triangle LMN$ is shown below. Use a compass and your answers to Exercises 11–12 to construct a circle that circumscribes $\triangle LMN$.

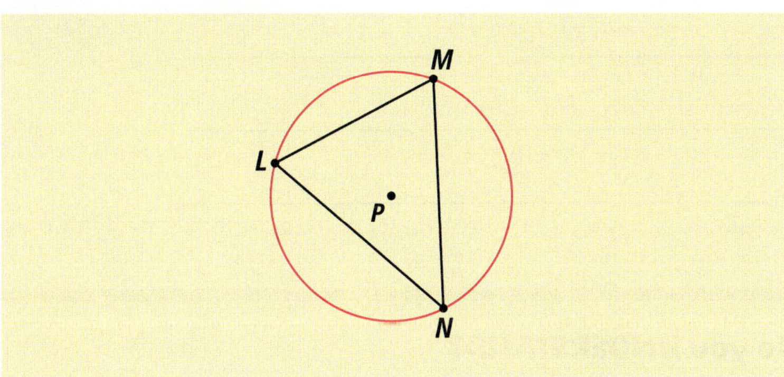

Problem 1 Finding the Circumcenter of a Triangle

Got It? **What are the coordinates of the circumcenter of the triangle with vertices $A(2, 7)$, $B(10, 7)$, and $C(10, 3)$?**

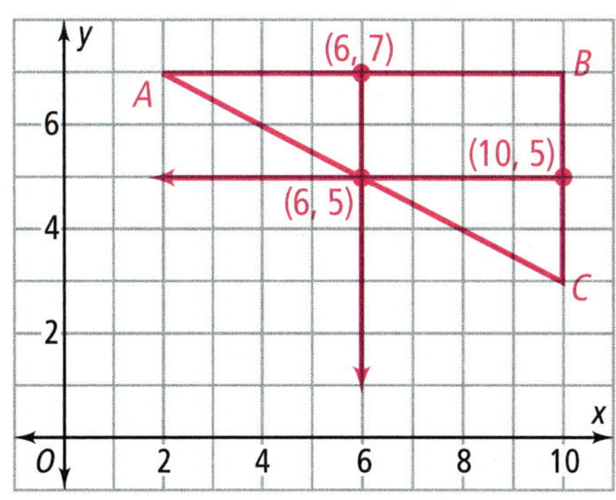

14. Draw $\triangle ABC$ on the coordinate plane.

15. Label the coordinates of the midpoint of $\overline{AB}$ and the midpoint of $\overline{BC}$.

16. Draw the perpendicular bisector of $\overline{AB}$.

17. Draw the perpendicular bisector of $\overline{BC}$.

18. Label the coordinates of the point of intersection of the bisectors.

19. The circumcenter of $\triangle ABC$ is (6 , 5).

20. A circle circumscribed about $\triangle ABC$ has center (6 , 5).

Problem 2 Using a Circumcenter

Got It? **A town planner wants to place a bench equidistant from the three trees in the park. Where should he place the bench?**

A, B, C

21. Complete the problem-solving model below.

Know	Need	Plan
The trees form the ___?___ of a triangle.	Find the point of concurrency of the ___?___ of the sides.	Find the ___?___ of the triangle, which is equidistant from the three trees.
vertices	perpendicular bisectors	circumcenter

22. How can the town planner determine where to place the bench? Explain.

Explanations may vary. Sample: The town planner can place the bench at the circumcenter of the triangle formed by the three trees.

Lesson Check • Do you UNDERSTAND?

Vocabulary **A triangle's circumcenter is outside the triangle. What type of triangle is it?**

23. Draw an example of each type of triangle on a coordinate plane below. Answers may vary. Samples are given.

acute

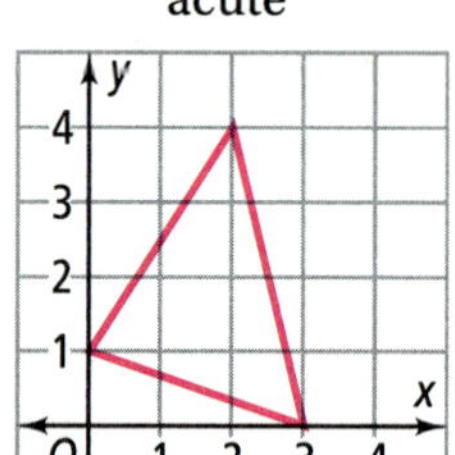

obtuse

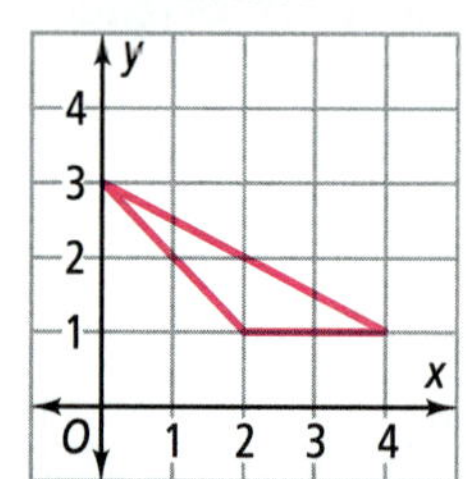

right

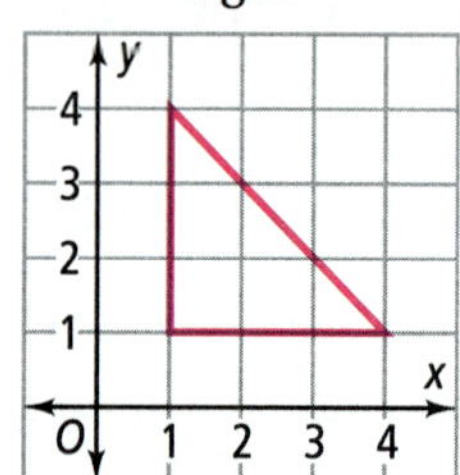

Underline the correct word to complete each sentence.

24. The circumcenter of a triangle is the intersection of the perpendicular bisectors of each angle / <u>side</u> of the triangle.

25. You need three / <u>two</u> lines to find one point of intersection.

26. When a triangle's circumcenter is outside the triangle, the triangle is acute / <u>obtuse</u> / right.

5-3 PART 2 Bisectors in Triangles

Vocabulary

Review

1. Circle the drawing(s) that show an angle bisector.

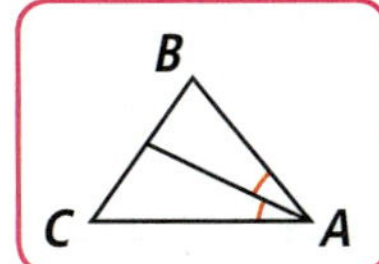

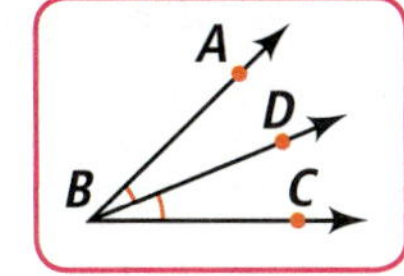

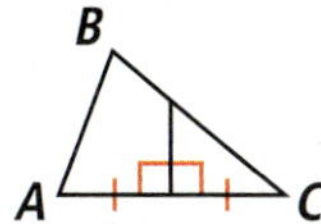

Vocabulary Builder

circum- (prefix) SUR cum

Related words: *circumcenter* (noun), *circumference* (noun)

Definition: **Circum-** is a prefix that means *around, about, surrounding,* or *on all sides.*

Use Your Vocabulary

Complete each statement with the correct word from the list below. Use each word only once.

circumcenter circumference circumscribe

2. To _?_ means to draw a line around or encircle. circumscribe

3. The _?_ is the center of a circumscribed circle. circumcenter

4. The _?_ is the distance around a circular figure. circumference

take note

Theorem 5-7 Concurrency of Angle Bisectors Theorem

The bisectors of the angles of a triangle are concurrent at a point equidistant from the sides of the triangle.

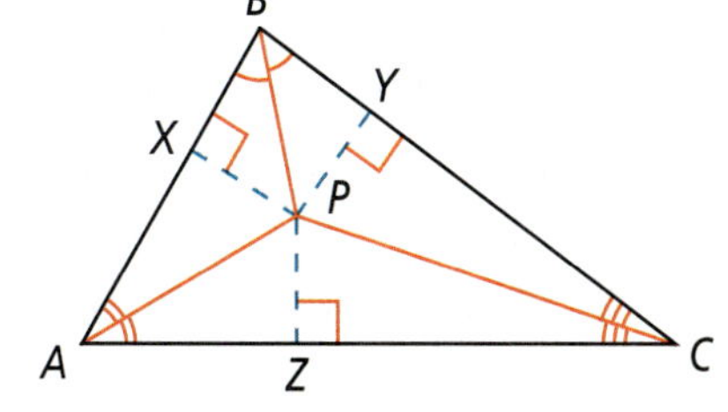

Complete.

5. Angle bisectors $\overline{AP}$, $\overline{BP}$, and $\overline{CP}$ are concurrent at P.

6. $PX =$ PY $=$ PZ

The point of concurrency of the angle bisectors of a triangle is called the *incenter* of the triangle.

7. Label the incenter P of each triangle.

acute

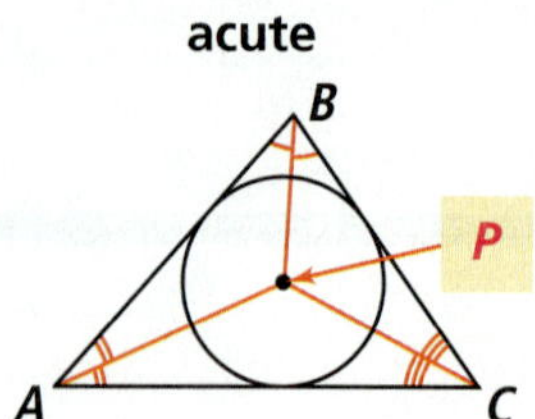

obtuse

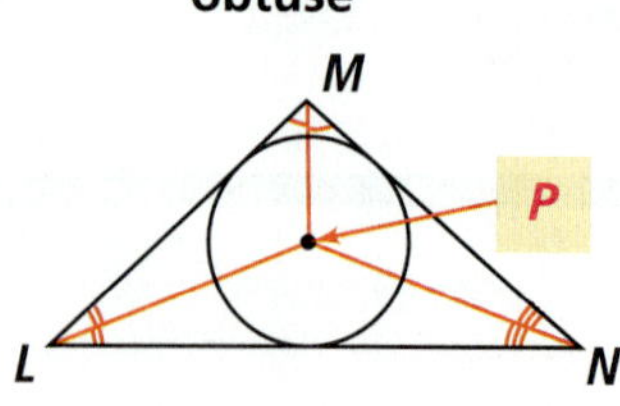

right

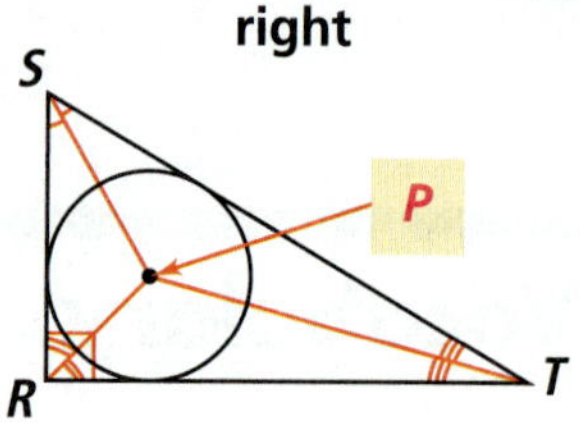

Complete each sentence with *inside, incenter*, or *inscribed*.

8. The point of concurrency of the angle bisectors of a triangle is the __?__ of the triangle.

9. The point of concurrency of the angle bisectors of a triangle is always __?__ the triangle.

10. In the diagram at the right, the circle is __?__ in $\triangle TUV$.

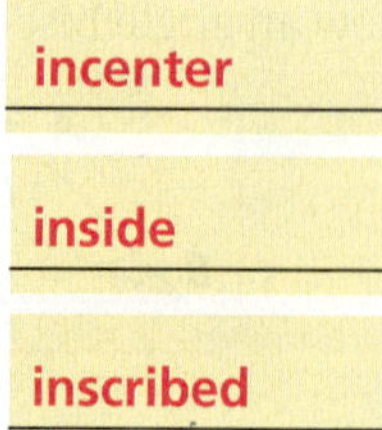

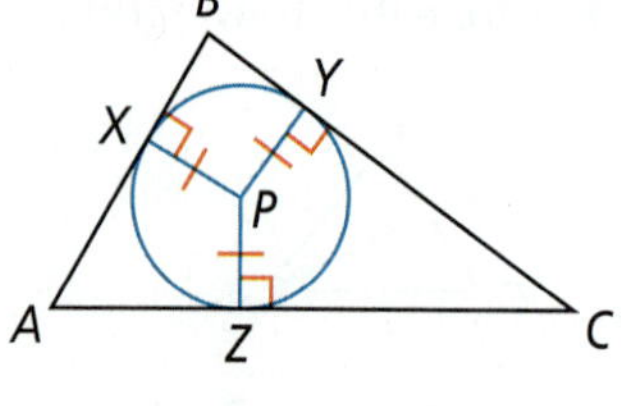

Problem 3 Identifying and Using the Incenter of a Triangle

Got It? $QN = 5x + 36$ **and** $QM = 2x + 51$**. What is** QO**?**

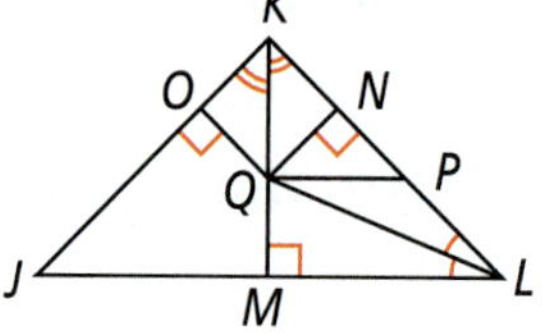

11. Complete the reasoning model below.

Think	Write
I know that Q is the point of concurrency of the angle bisectors.	Q is the incenter / midpoint of $\triangle JKL$.
And I know that	the distance from Q to each side of $\triangle JKL$ is equal / unequal.
I can write an equation and solve for x.	$QN = QM$ $5x + 36 = 2x + 51$ $5x = 2x + 15$ $3x = 15$ $x = 5$
I can use the value of x to find QO.	$QO = 5 \cdot 5 + 36$ $= 61$

Got It? Reasoning **Is it possible for QP to equal 50? Explain.**

12. Drawn an inscribed circle in the diagram at the right.

13. Cross out the segment that is NOT a radius of the circle you drew.

$\overline{QM}$ $\qquad$ $\overline{QN}$ $\qquad$ $\overline{QO}$ $\qquad$ ~~$\overline{QP}$~~

14. Circle the correct relationship between QO and QP.

($QO < QP$) $\qquad$ $QO = QP$ $\qquad$ $QO > QP$

15. Is it possible for QP equal to equal 50? Explain. **Answers may vary. Sample:**

No. The radii measure 61, since $\overline{QO}$ is one of the radii.

$\overline{QP}$ is longer than the radius of the circle, so its

length cannot be 50.

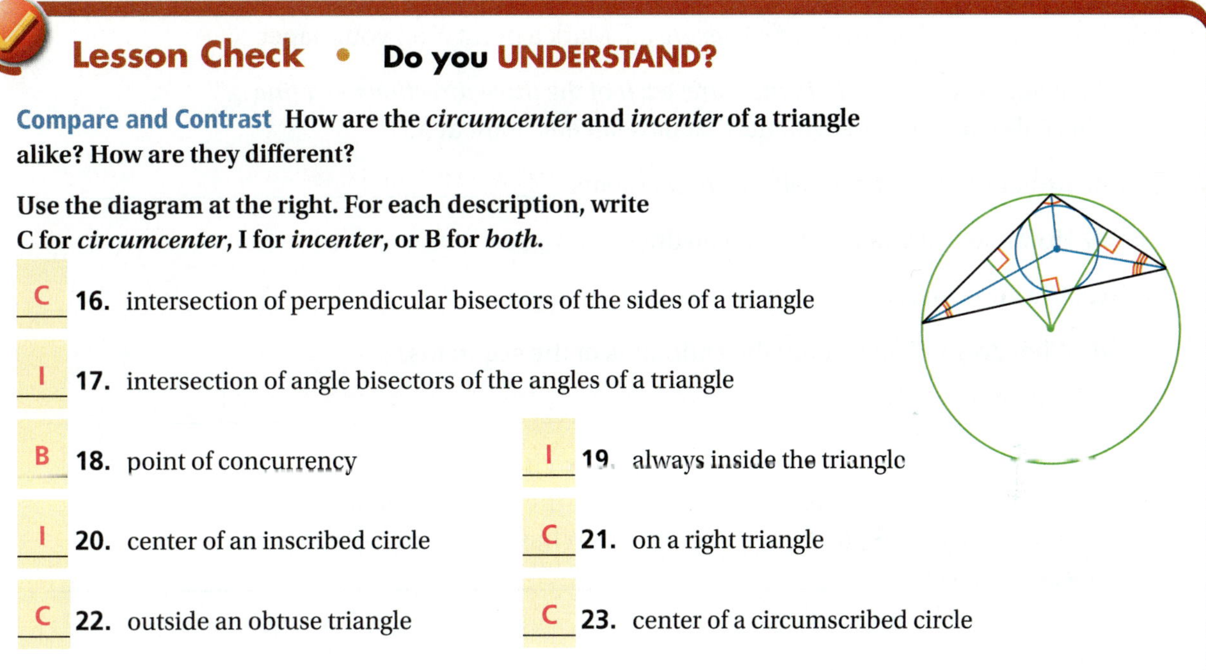

Lesson Check • Do you UNDERSTAND?

Compare and Contrast **How are the *circumcenter* and *incenter* of a triangle alike? How are they different?**

Use the diagram at the right. For each description, write C for *circumcenter*, I for *incenter*, or B for *both*.

C **16.** intersection of perpendicular bisectors of the sides of a triangle

I **17.** intersection of angle bisectors of the angles of a triangle

B **18.** point of concurrency

I **19.** always inside the triangle

I **20.** center of an inscribed circle

C **21.** on a right triangle

C **22.** outside an obtuse triangle

C **23.** center of a circumscribed circle

Math Success

Check off the vocabulary words that you understand.

☐ concurrent ☐ circumscribed about ☐ incenter ☐ inscribed in ☐ bisector

Rate how well you can *use bisectors in triangles.*

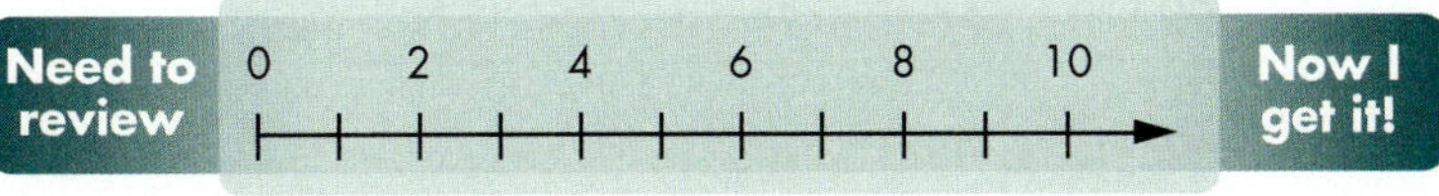

Name ______________________ Class __________ Date __________

5-3 Think About a Plan

Bisectors in Triangles

Writing Ivars found an old piece of paper inside an antique book. It read:

From the spot I buried Olaf's treasure, equal sets of paces did I measure; each of three directions in a line, there to plant a seedling Norway pine. I could not return for failing health; now the hounds of Haiti guard my wealth. —Karl

After searching Caribbean islands for five years, Ivars found an island with three tall Norway pines. How might Ivars find where Karl buried Olaf's treasure?

Know

1. Make a sketch as you answer the questions. **Check students' drawings.**
2. "*From the spot I buried Olaf's treasure ...*" Mark a point *X* on your paper.
3. "*... equal sets of paces I did measure; each of the three directions in a line ...*" This tells you to draw segments that have an endpoint at *X*.
   a. Explain how you know these are segments. **the words "in a line"**
   b. How many segments should you draw? **3**
   c. What do you know about the length of the segments? **They are equal.**
   d. What do you know about the endpoints of the segments?
   Each segment has an endpoint at *X* and an endpoint at a Norway pine.
4. You do not know in which direction to draw each segment, but you can choose three directions for your sketch. Mark the locations of the trees. Draw a triangle with the trees at its vertices. What is the name of the point where *X* is located? **circumcenter**

Need

5. Look at your sketch. What do you need to find? **point *X*, the location of the circumcenter**

Plan

6. Describe how to find the treasure. The first step is done for you.

   Step 1 Find the midpoints of each side of the triangle.

   Step 2 **Use the midpoints to draw perpendicular bisectors for each side.**

   Step 3 **Find the point of concurrency of the perpendicular bisectors. This is the circumcenter, where point *X* is located.**

Name ______________________________ Class ____________ Date ____________

5-3 Practice

Form K

Bisectors in Triangles

Coordinate Geometry **Find the coordinates of the circumcenter of each triangle.**

1. 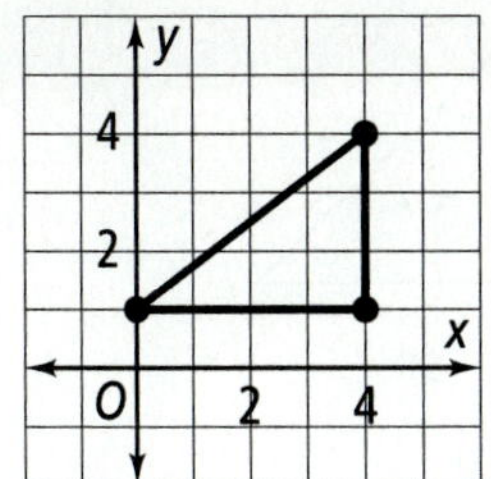 **(2, 2.5)**

2.  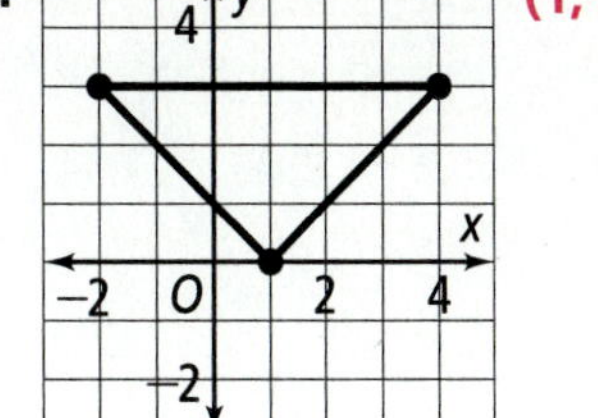 **(1, 3)**

Coordinate Geometry **Find the circumcenter of $\triangle PQR$.**

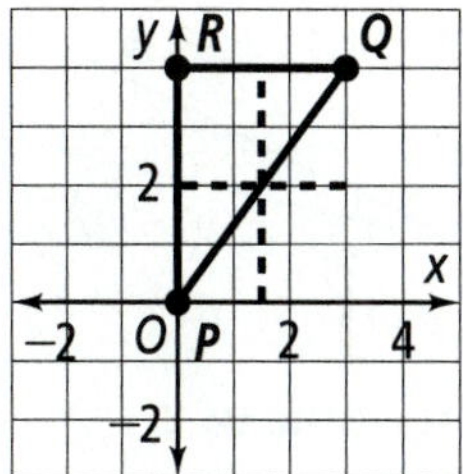

3. $P(0, 0)$ **(1.5, 2)**
$Q(3, 4)$
$R(0, 4)$

To start, graph the vertices and connect them on a coordinate plane. Then draw two perpendicular bisectors.

4. $P(1, -5)$ **(2.5, −3.5)**
$Q(4, -5)$
$R(1, -2)$

5. $P(-3, -5)$ **(−1, −1.5)**
$Q(-3, 2)$
$R(1, -5)$

6. $P(-6, 6)$ **(−1.5, 4)**
$Q(3, 6)$
$R(-6, 2)$

7. $P(4, 6)$ **(2.5, 2)**
$Q(1, 6)$
$R(1, -2)$

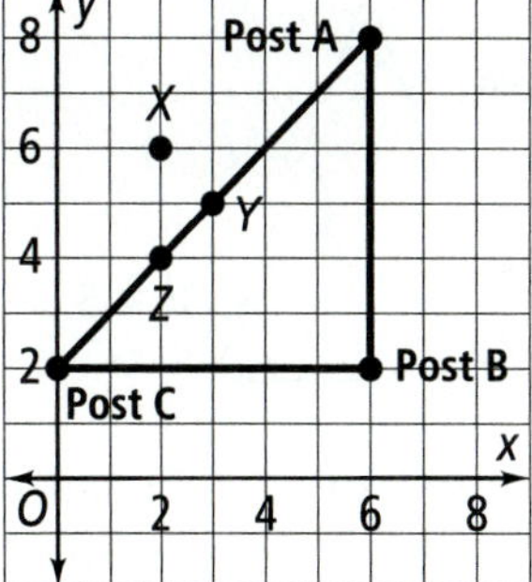

8. a. Which point is equidistant from the three posts? ***Y***

b. Where are the coordinates of this point? **(3, 5)**

9. Construction Construct three perpendicular bisectors for $\triangle ABC$. Then use the point of concurrency to construct the circumscribed circle.

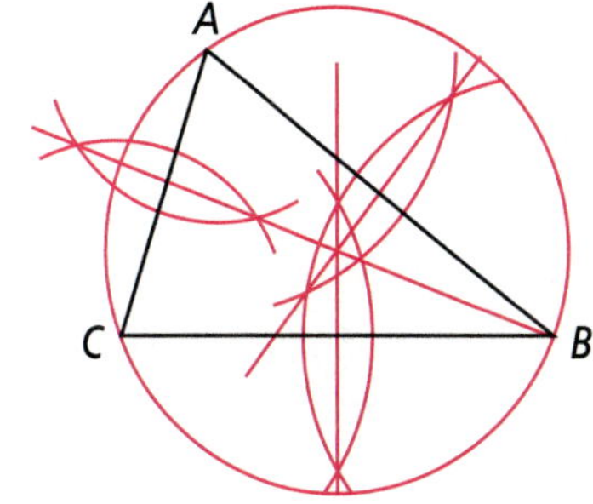

Name ____________________ Class ____________ Date ____________

5-3 Practice (continued) Form K

Bisectors in Triangles

Name the point of concurrency of the angle bisectors.

10. Q

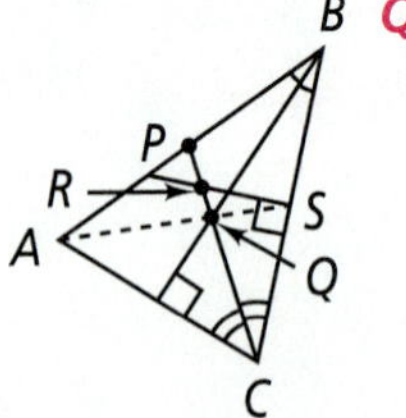

11. U

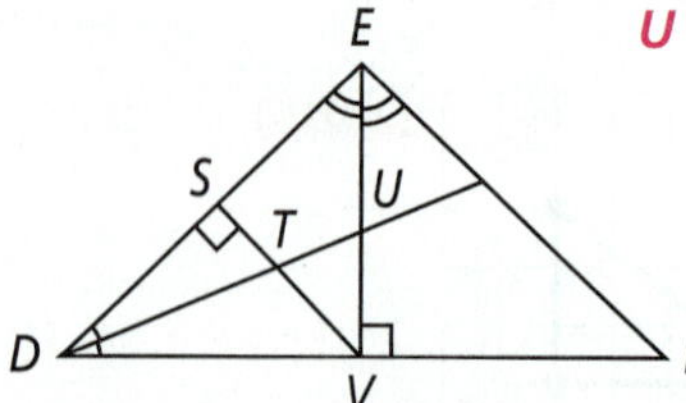

12. X

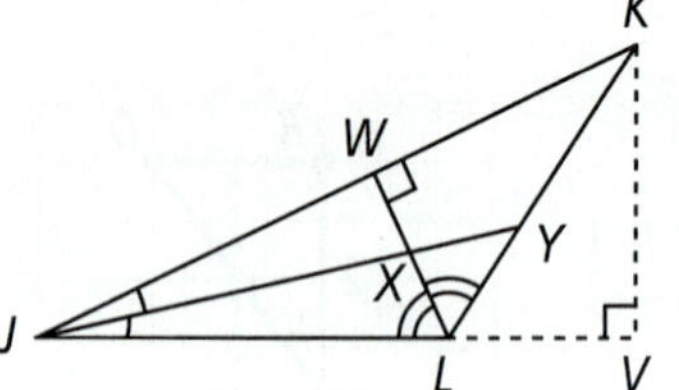

13. Z

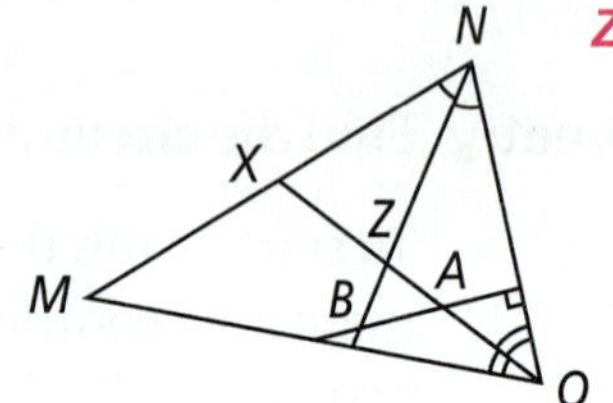

Find the value of *x*.

14. To start, identify the relationship between the line segments that are labeled.

Because the segments meet at the point where the __?__ meet, the segments are __?__.

angle bisectors; congruent

Then write an equation to find *x*:

[3x] = [2x] + [4]

4

15. 2

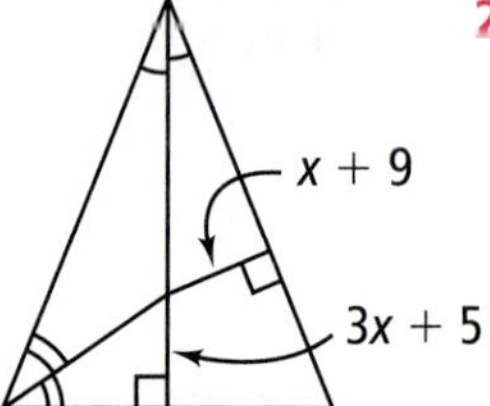

16. 11

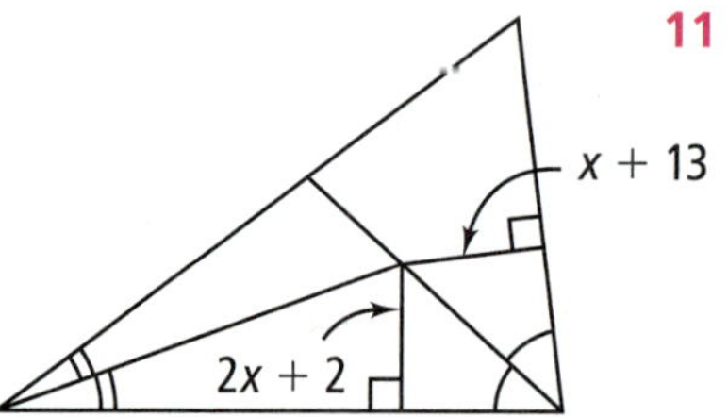

17. **Construction** Construct two angle bisectors for $\triangle XYZ$. Then use the point of concurrency to construct the inscribed circle.

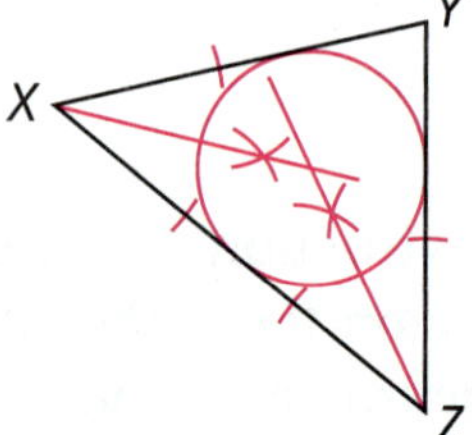

Name ______________________________ Class ____________ Date ____________

5-3 Standardized Test Prep

Bisectors in Triangles

Multiple Choice

For Exercises 1–5, choose the correct letter. Use the figure below.

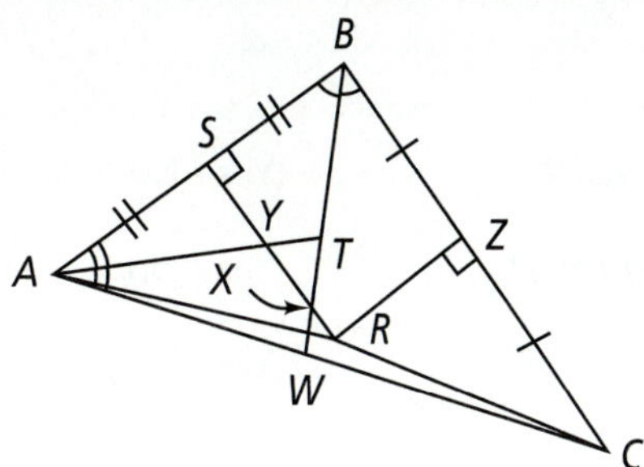

1. Which point is the incenter of $\triangle ABC$? B

   (A) X (B) T (C) R (D) Y

2. Which point is the circumcenter of $\triangle ABC$? H

   (F) X (G) T (H) R (I) Y

3. Which segment is an angle bisector of $\triangle ABC$? A

   (A) $\overline{BX}$ (B) $\overline{SX}$ (C) $\overline{AS}$ (D) $\overline{RZ}$

4. Which segment is a perpendicular bisector of $\triangle ABC$? I

   (F) $\overline{BW}$ (G) $\overline{SB}$ (H) $\overline{AS}$ (I) $\overline{RZ}$

5. If $RC = x + 3$ and $RA = 3x - 3$, what is the value of x? A

   (A) 3 (B) 6 (C) 7 (D) 9

Extended Response

6. Draw $\triangle ABC$. Construct three angle bisectors. Use the point of concurrency to construct the inscribed circle.
   [4] Student draws $\triangle ABC$, constructs three angle bisectors, and constructs the inscribed circle. [3] Student draws $\triangle ABC$, constructs two angle bisectors and the inscribed circle. [2] Student submits an incomplete but accurate drawing. [1] Student drawing is inaccurate. [0] Student fails to submit a drawing or constructs no angle bisectors.

Medians and Altitudes

Vocabulary

Review

1. Are three diameters of a circle *concurrent*? Yes / No (Yes circled)

2. Are two diagonals of a rectangle *concurrent*? Yes / No (No circled)

3. Is point *C* at the right a point of *concurrency*? Yes / No (Yes circled)

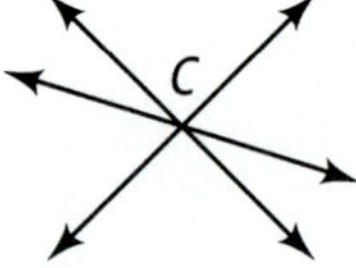

Vocabulary Builder

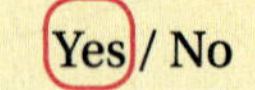

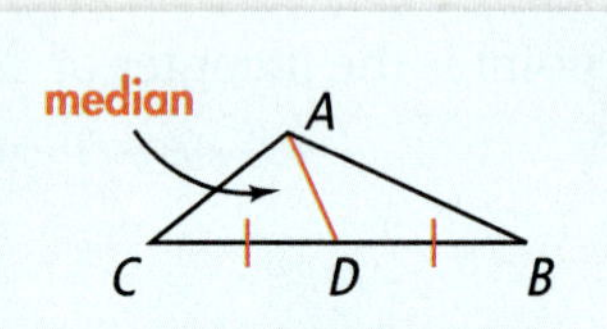

median (noun) MEE **dee un**

Related Words: median (adjective), middle (noun), midpoint (noun)

Definition: A **median** of a triangle is a segment whose endpoints are a vertex and the midpoint of the opposite side.

Use Your Vocabulary

Write T for *true* or F for *false*.

F 4. The *median* of a triangle is a segment that connects the midpoint of one side to the midpoint of an adjacent side.

T 5. The point of concurrency of the *medians* of a triangle is where they intersect.

F 6. A triangle has one *median*.

7. Circle the drawing that shows *median* $\overline{AD}$ of $\triangle ABC$.

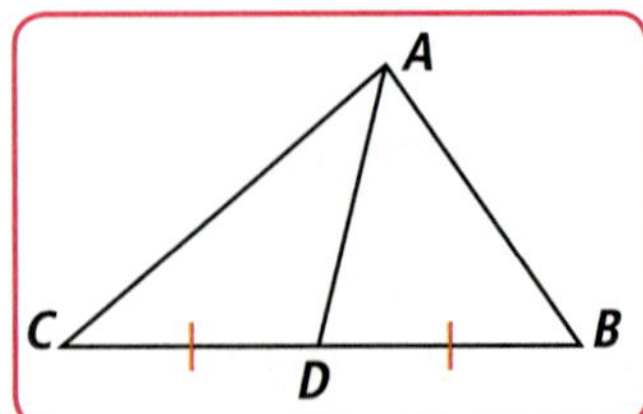

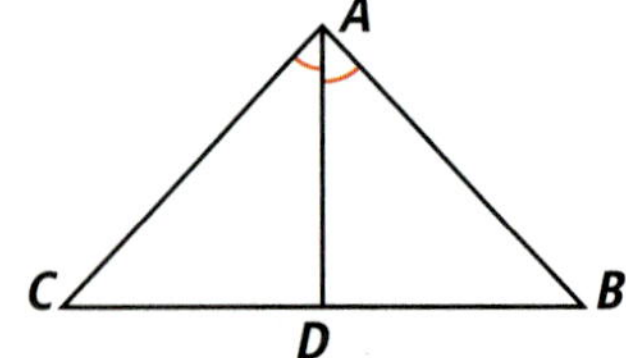

take note

Theorem 5-8 Concurrency of Medians Theorem

The medians of a triangle are concurrent at a point (the *centroid* of the triangle) that is two thirds the distance from each vertex to the midpoint of the opposite side.

For any triangle, the centroid is always inside the triangle.

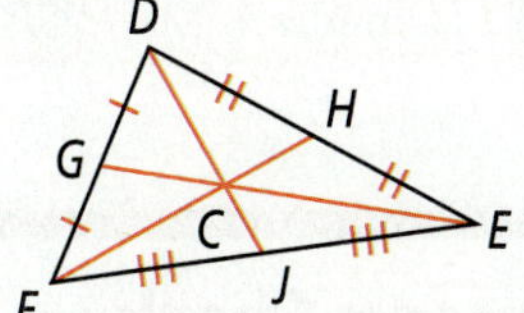

8. Complete each equation.

$DC = \frac{2}{3}$ **DJ** $\qquad EC = \frac{2}{3}$ **EG** $\qquad FC =$ $\frac{2}{3}FH$

Problem 1 Finding the Length of a Median

Got It? **In the diagram at the right, $ZA = 9$. What is the length of $\overline{ZC}$?**

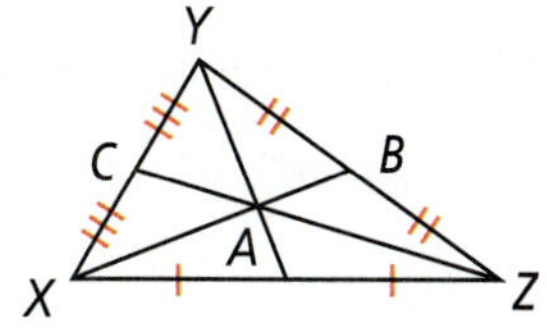

9. Point **A** is the centroid of $\triangle XYZ$.

10. Use the justifications at the right to solve for ZC.

$ZA = \frac{2}{3} \cdot ZC$	Concurrency of Medians Theorem
$9 = \frac{2}{3} \cdot ZC$	Substitute for ZA.
$9\left(\frac{3}{2}\right) = \left(\frac{3}{2}\right)\frac{2}{3} \cdot ZC$	Multiply each side by $\frac{3}{2}$.
$\frac{27}{2} = ZC$	Simplify.

11. ZC is $\frac{27}{2}$, or $13\frac{1}{2}$.

An *altitude* of a triangle is the perpendicular segment from a vertex of the triangle to the line containing the opposite side. An altitude can be inside or outside the triangle, or it can be a side of the triangle.

Problem 2 Identifying Medians and Altitudes

Got It? **For $\triangle ABC$, is each segment, $\overline{AD}$, $\overline{EG}$, and $\overline{CF}$, a *median*, an *altitude*, or *neither*? Explain.**

12. Read each statement. Then cross out the words that do NOT describe $\overline{AD}$.

$\overline{AD}$ is a segment that extends from vertex A to $\overline{CB}$, which is opposite A.

$\overline{AD}$ meets $\overline{CB}$ at point D, which is the midpoint of $\overline{CB}$ since $\overline{CD} \cong \overline{DB}$.

$\overline{AD}$ is not perpendicular to $\overline{CB}$.

~~altitude~~ median 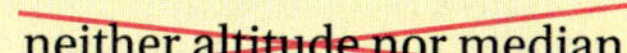 ~~neither altitude nor median~~

13. Circle the correct statement below.

($\overline{AD}$ is a median.) [circled] $\qquad \overline{AD}$ is an altitude. $\qquad \overline{AD}$ is neither a median nor an altitude.

14. Read the statement. Then circle the correct description of $\overline{EG}$.

$\overline{EG}$ does not extend from a vertex.

$\overline{EG}$ is a median. $\qquad \overline{EG}$ is an altitude. $\qquad$ ($\overline{EG}$ is neither a median nor an altitude.) [circled]

15. Read each statement. Then circle the correct description of $\overline{CF}$.

$\overline{CF}$ is a segment that extends from vertex C to $\overline{AB}$, which is opposite C.

$\overline{CF} \perp \overline{AB}$

$\overline{CF}$ is a median. | ($\overline{CF}$ is an altitude.) [circled] | $\overline{CF}$ is neither a median nor an altitude.

Lesson Check • Do you know HOW?

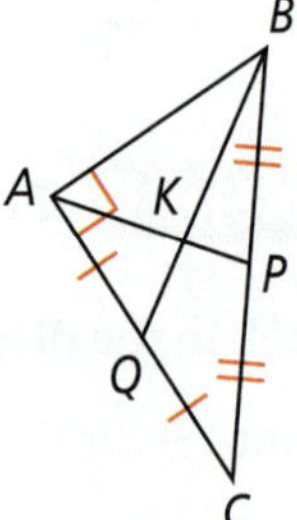

In $\triangle ABC$, is $\overline{AP}$ a *median* or an *altitude*?

16. Cross out the incorrect statement.

~~$\overline{AP} \perp \overline{BC}$~~ | $\overline{AP}$ bisects $\overline{BC}$

17. Circle the statement that is correct.

($\overline{AP}$ is a median.) [circled] | $\overline{AP}$ is an altitude.

Lesson Check • Do you know HOW?

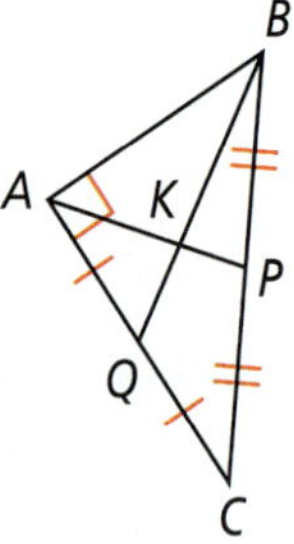

In $\triangle ABC$, if $AP = 18$, what is KP?

Underline the correct word to complete each sentence.

18. $\overline{AP}$ is a(n) altitude / <u>median</u>.

19. $\overline{BQ}$ is a(n) altitude / <u>median</u>.

20. $\overline{BQ}$ and $\overline{AP}$ intersect at the <u>centroid</u> / orthocenter of $\triangle ABC$.

21. $AP = 18$, so $KP = \frac{1}{3} \cdot 18 = 6$.

Lesson Check • Do you UNDERSTAND?

Error Analysis **Your classmate says she drew $\overline{HJ}$ as an altitude of $\triangle ABC$. What error did she make?**

22. Did your classmate draw a segment perpendicular to a side?

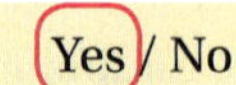

(Yes) [circled] / No

23. Is your classmate's segment between a vertex and an opposite side?

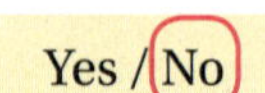

Yes / (No) [circled]

24. What error did she make?

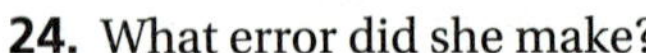

Answers may vary. Sample: My classmate did not draw a perpendicular segment from a vertex of the triangle, so the segment is not an altitude.

5-4 PART 2 Medians and Altitudes

Vocabulary

Review

Underline the correct word(s) to complete each sentence.

1. The measure of a *right angle* is less than / equal to / greater than 90 degrees.
2. Two intersecting perpendicular lines form two / four *right angles.*
3. A right triangle has one / two / three *right angle*(s).

Use the diagram at the right for Exercises 4–5.

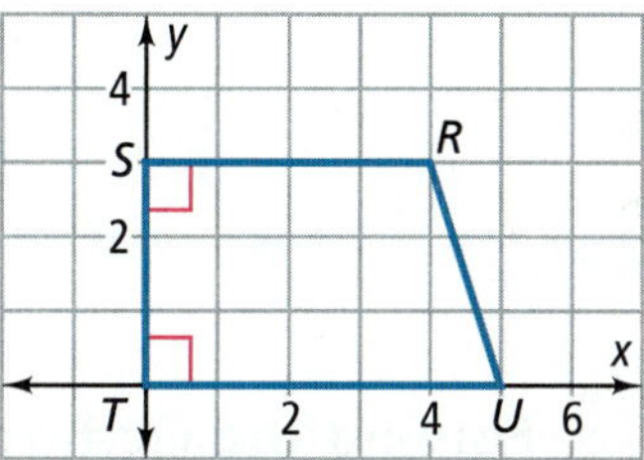

4. Which segment pairs form *right angles*?

$\overline{SR}$ and $\overline{ST}$ $\overline{ST}$ and $\overline{TU}$

5. Insert a *right-angle* symbol at each *right angle.*

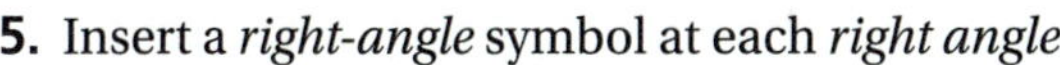

Vocabulary Builder

altitude (noun) AL tuh tood

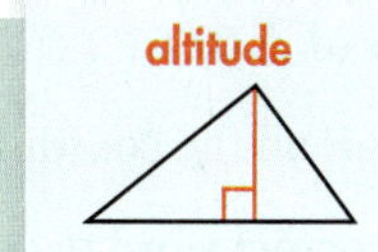

Definition: An **altitude** is the perpendicular segment from a vertex of a figure to the line containing the opposite side.

Main Idea: An **altitude** of a triangle is a perpendicular segment from a vertex to the opposite side.

Use Your Vocabulary

In each triangle, draw the named *altitude*. Mark each right angle.

6. $\overline{BR}$ 7. $\overline{CS}$ 8. $\overline{BT}$

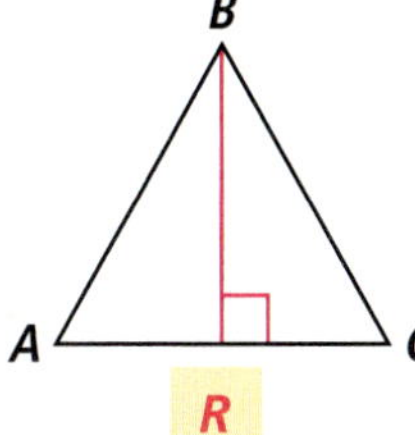

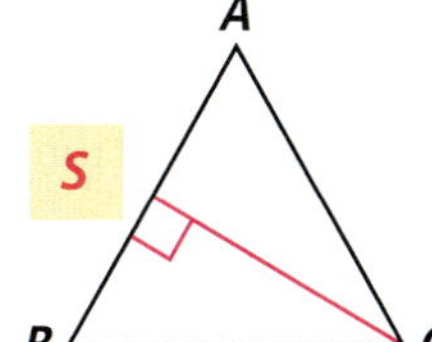

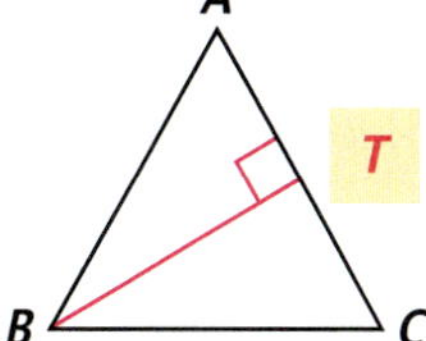

take note

Theorem 5-9 Concurrency of Altitudes Theorem

The lines that contain the altitudes of a triangle are concurrent.

9. Draw an example of each type of triangle on a coordinate plane. Answers may vary. Samples are given.

acute

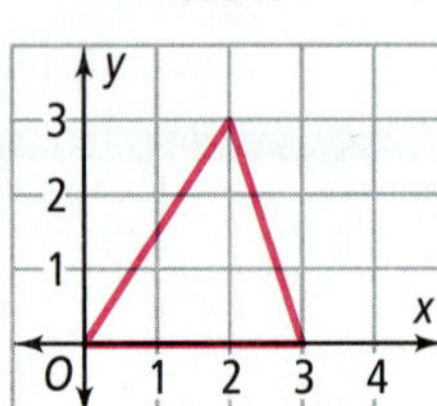

obtuse

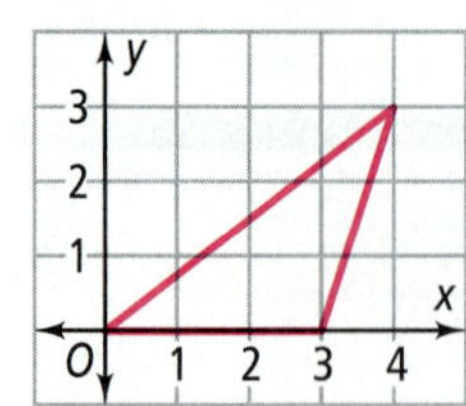

right

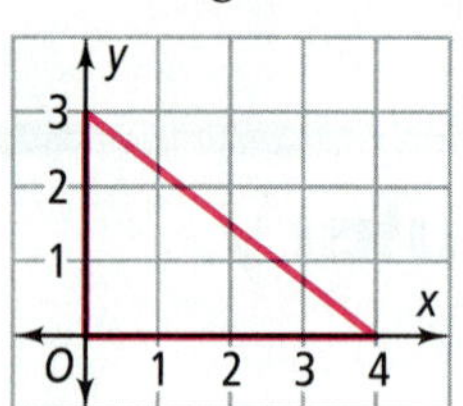

The point of concurrency of the altitudes of a triangle is the *orthocenter* of the triangle. The orthocenter of a triangle can be inside, on, or outside the triangle.

Draw a line from the type of triangle in Column A to the location of its orthocenter in Column B.

Column A	Column B
10. acute	outside the triangle
11. right	inside the triangle
12. obtuse	at a vertex of the triangle

Problem 3 Finding the Orthocenter

Got It? **$\triangle DEF$ has vertices $D(1, 2)$, $E(1, 6)$, and $F(4, 2)$. What are the coordinates of the orthocenter of $\triangle DEF$?**

13. Graph $\triangle DEF$ on the coordinate plane.

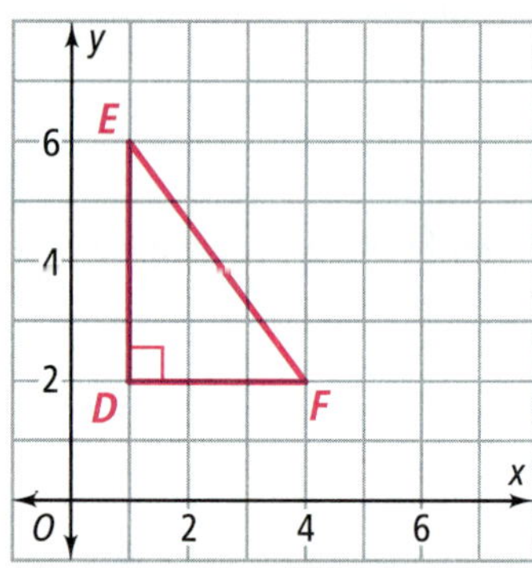

Underline the correct word to complete each sentence.

14. $\triangle DEF$ is a(n) acute / obtuse / right triangle.

15. The orthocenter of this kind of triangle is inside / on / outside the triangle.

16. You need to find the intersection of one / two / three altitudes.

17. The altitude to $\overline{DF}$ is horizontal / slanted / vertical.

18. The altitude to $\overline{DE}$ is horizontal / slanted / vertical.

19. The altitude to $\overline{EF}$ is horizontal / slanted / vertical.

20. For which two altitudes do you already know the coordinates of the intersection point? Explain.

The altitudes to $\overline{DF}$ and $\overline{DE}$. They intersect at $D(1, 2)$.

21. The altitudes intersect at (1 , 2).

22. The orthocenter of $\triangle DEF$ is (1 , 2).

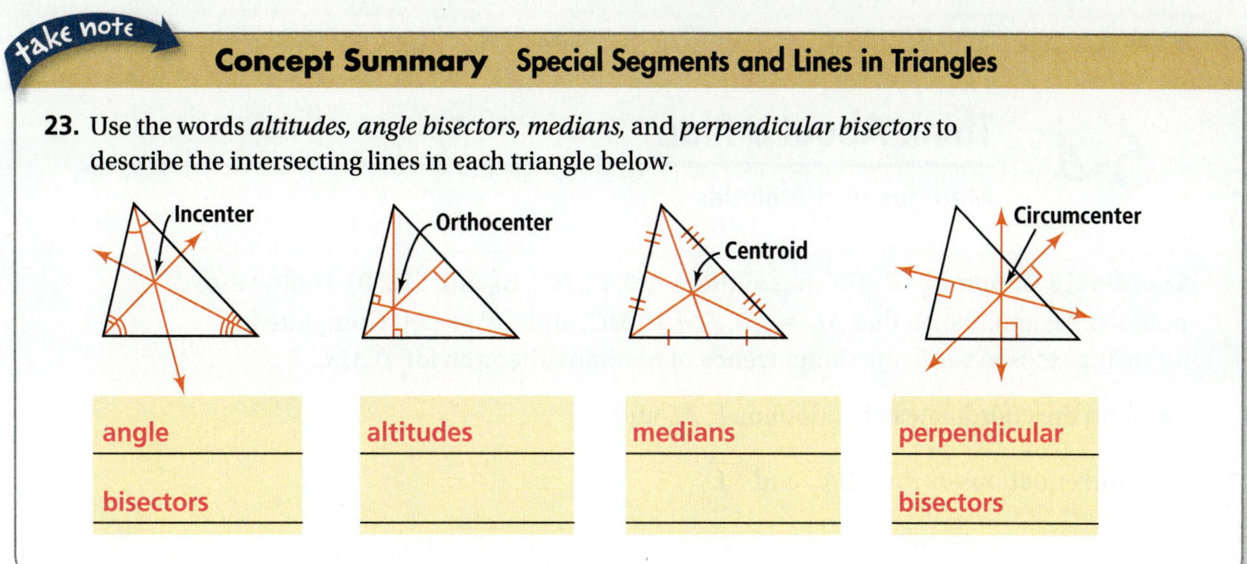

take note

Concept Summary Special Segments and Lines in Triangles

23. Use the words *altitudes, angle bisectors, medians,* and *perpendicular bisectors* to describe the intersecting lines in each triangle below.

angle bisectors	altitudes	medians	perpendicular bisectors

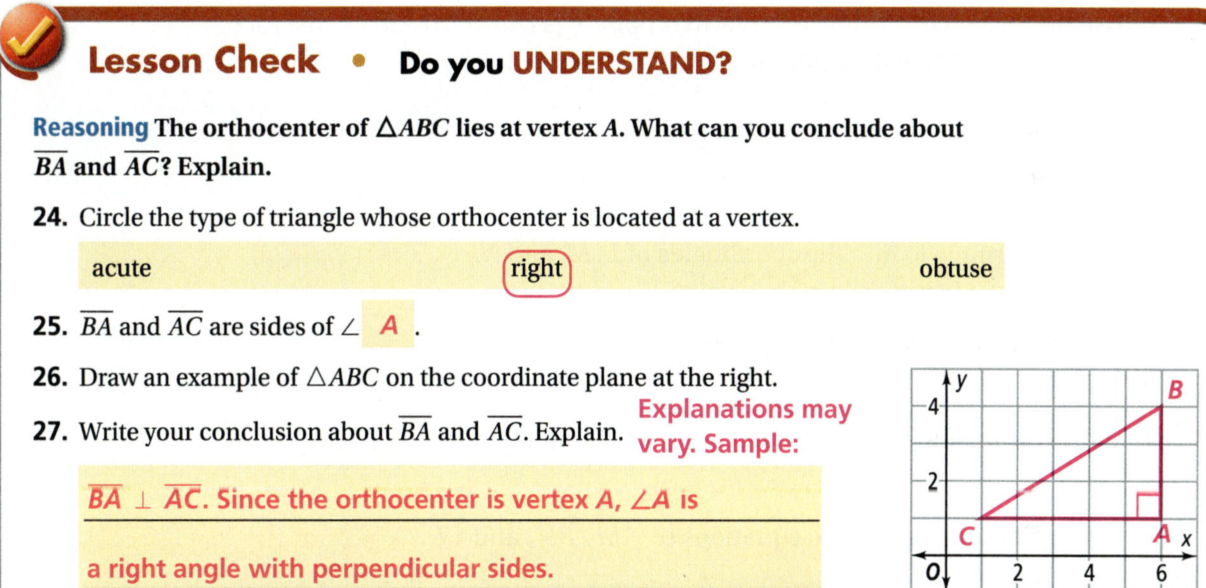

Lesson Check • Do you UNDERSTAND?

Reasoning **The orthocenter of $\triangle ABC$ lies at vertex A. What can you conclude about $\overline{BA}$ and $\overline{AC}$? Explain.**

24. Circle the type of triangle whose orthocenter is located at a vertex.

acute   (right)   obtuse

25. $\overline{BA}$ and $\overline{AC}$ are sides of $\angle$ A .

26. Draw an example of $\triangle ABC$ on the coordinate plane at the right.

27. Write your conclusion about $\overline{BA}$ and $\overline{AC}$. Explain. Explanations may vary. Sample:

$\overline{BA} \perp \overline{AC}$. Since the orthocenter is vertex A, $\angle A$ is a right angle with perpendicular sides.

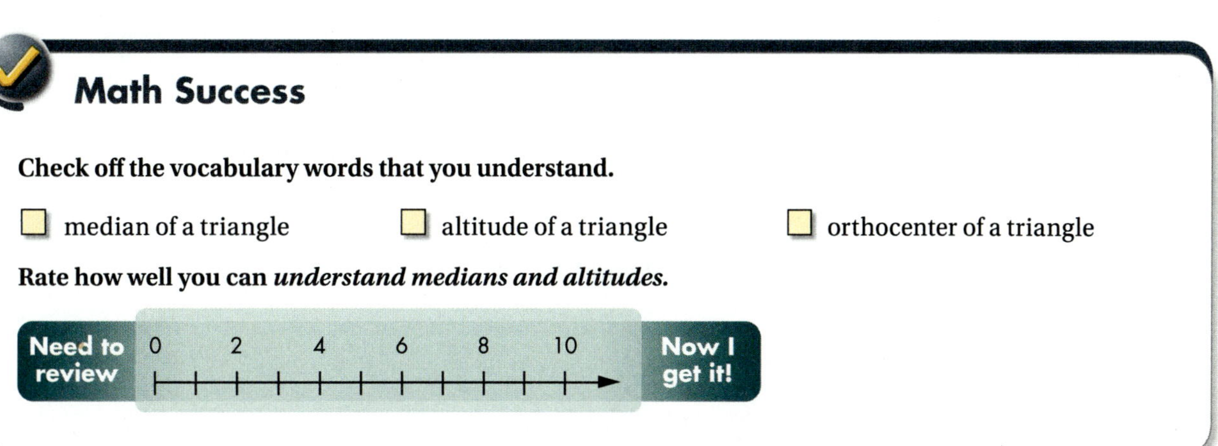

Math Success

Check off the vocabulary words that you understand.

☐ median of a triangle ☐ altitude of a triangle ☐ orthocenter of a triangle

Rate how well you can *understand medians and altitudes.*

Name ______________________ Class ____________ Date ____________

5-4 Think About a Plan

Medians and Altitudes

Coordinate Geometry $\triangle ABC$ has vertices $A(0, 0)$, $B(2, 6)$, and $C(8, 0)$. Define the points L, M, and N such that $AL = LB$, $BM = MC$, and $CN = NA$. Complete the following steps to verify the Concurrency of Medians Theorem for $\triangle ABC$.

a. Find the coordinates of midpoints L, M, and N.

b. Find equations of $\overleftrightarrow{AM}$, $\overleftrightarrow{BN}$, and $\overleftrightarrow{CL}$.

c. Find the coordinates of P, the intersection of $\overleftrightarrow{AM}$ and $\overleftrightarrow{BN}$. This is the centroid.

d. Show that point P is on $\overleftrightarrow{CL}$.

e. Use the Distance Formula to show that point P is two-thirds of the distance from each vertex to the midpoint of the opposite side.

1. Write the midpoint formula. $\left(\frac{x_1 + x_2}{2}, \frac{y_1 + y_2}{2}\right)$

2. Use the formula to find the coordinates of L, M, and N. (1, 3); (5, 3); (4, 0)

3. Find the slopes of $\overleftrightarrow{AM}$, $\overleftrightarrow{BN}$, and $\overleftrightarrow{CL}$. $\frac{3}{5}$; -3; $-\frac{3}{7}$

4. Write the general point-slope form of a linear equation. $y - y_1 = m(x - x_1)$

5. Write the point-slope form equations of $\overleftrightarrow{AM}$, $\overleftrightarrow{BN}$, and $\overleftrightarrow{CL}$. $y = \frac{3}{5}x$ or $y - 3 = \frac{3}{5}(x - 5)$; $y = -3(x - 4)$ or $y - 6 = -3(x - 2)$; $y = -\frac{3}{7}(x - 8)$ or $y - 3 = -\frac{3}{7}(x - 1)$

6. Solve the system of equations for $\overleftrightarrow{AM}$ and $\overleftrightarrow{BN}$ to find the point of intersection. $(3\frac{1}{3}, 2)$

7. Show that the coordinates of point P satisfy the equation of $\overleftrightarrow{CL}$. $2 = -\frac{3}{7}(3\frac{1}{3} - 8)$

8. Use the distance formula to find AM, BN, and CL. Use a calculator and round to the nearest hundredth. 5.83; 6.32; 7.62

9. Use the distance formula to find AP, BP, and CP. 3.89; 4.22; 5.08

10. Check to see that $AP = \frac{2}{3}AM$, $BP = \frac{2}{3}BN$, and $CP = \frac{2}{3}CL$.
$5.83 \times \frac{2}{3} = 3.89$; $6.32 \times \frac{2}{3} = 4.21$; $7.62 \times \frac{2}{3} = 5.08$

Name ______________________ Class ____________ Date ____________

5-4 Practice

Form K

Medians and Altitudes

In $\triangle XYZ$, A is the centroid.

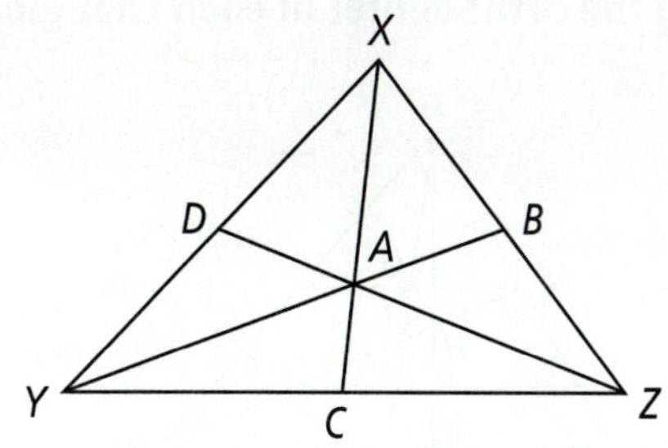

1. If $DZ = 12$, find ZA and AD. 8; 4

To start, write an equation relating the distance between the vertex and centroid to the length of the median.

$ZA = \boxed{\frac{2}{3}} DZ$

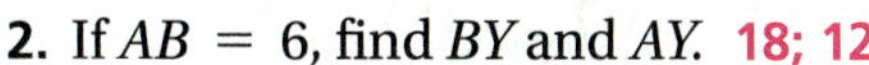

2. If $AB = 6$, find BY and AY. 18; 12

3. If $AC = 3$, find CX and AX. 9; 6

Is $\overline{MN}$ a *median*, an *altitude*, or *neither*? Explain.

4.

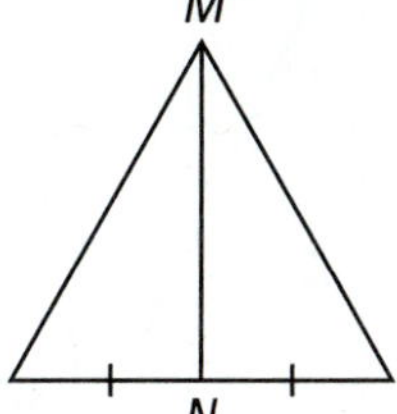

To start, identify the relationship between $\overline{MN}$ and the side it intersects.

$\overline{MN}$ _?_ the side of the triangle it intersects. bisects

Median; $\overline{MN}$ bisects the opposite side.

5.

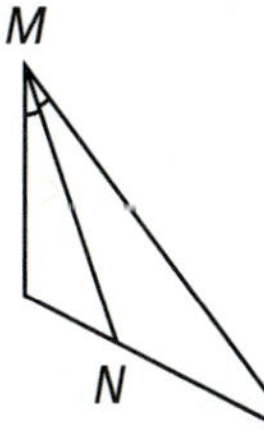

Neither; $\overline{MN}$ is not perpendicular to nor does it bisect the opposite side.

6.

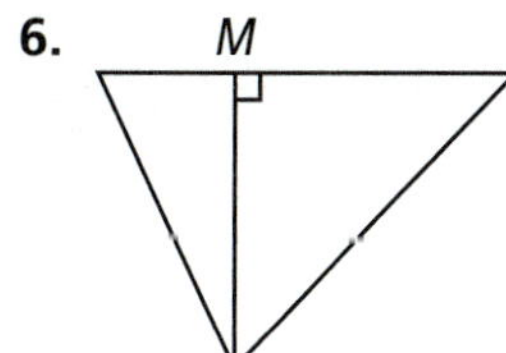

Altitude; $\overline{MN}$ is perpendicular to the opposite side.

In Exercises 7–10, name each segment.

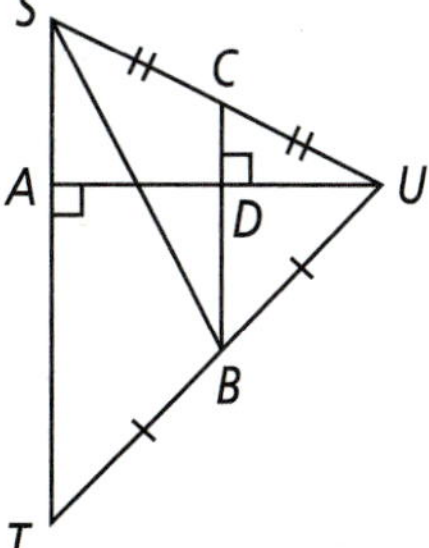

7. a median in $\triangle STU$ $\overline{SB}$

8. an altitude in $\triangle STU$ $\overline{AU}$

9. a median in $\triangle SBU$ $\overline{CB}$

10. an altitude in $\triangle CBU$ $\overline{DU}$

11. Q is the centroid of $\triangle JKL$. $PK = 9x + 21y$. Write expressions to represent PQ and QK.
$PQ = 3x + 7y$, $QK = 6x + 14y$

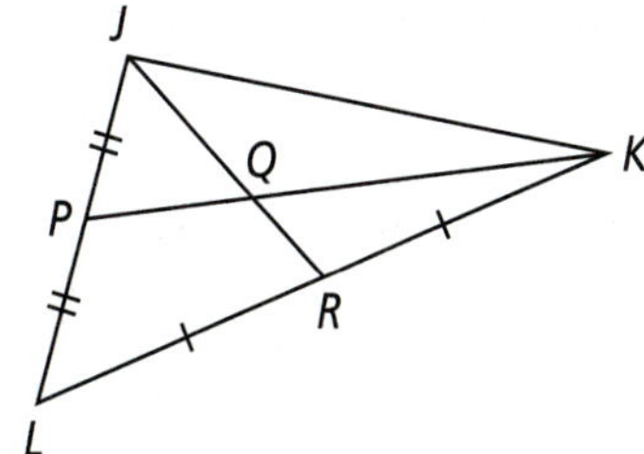

Name ______________________ Class ____________ Date ____________

5-4 Practice (continued) Form K

Medians and Altitudes

Find the orthocenter of each triangle.

12. *H*

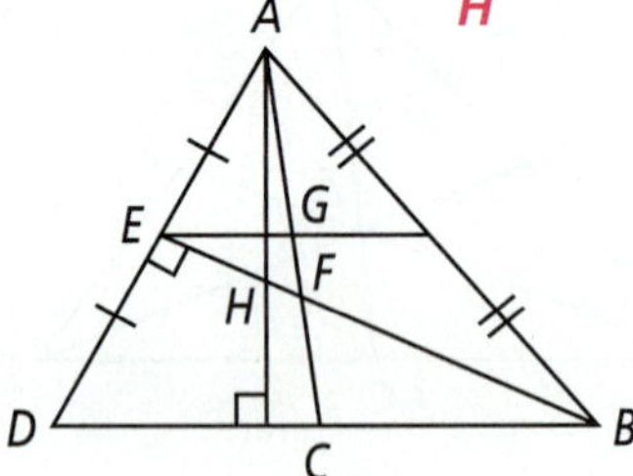

13. *Y*

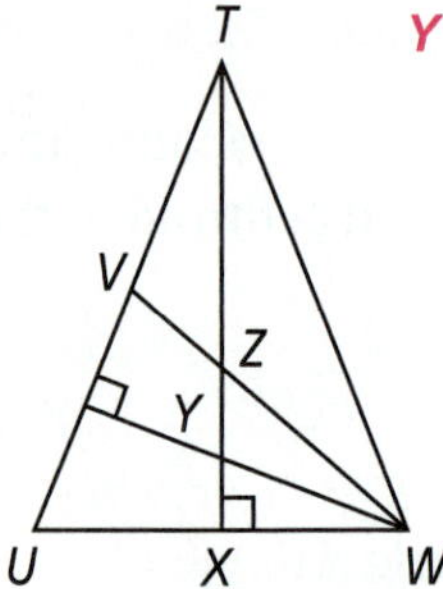

Coordinate Geometry **Find the coordinates of the orthocenter of △ABC.**

14. $A(6, 10)$, $B(2, 2)$, $C(10, 2)$ **(6, 4)**

To start, graph the vertices of the triangle in a coordinate plane.

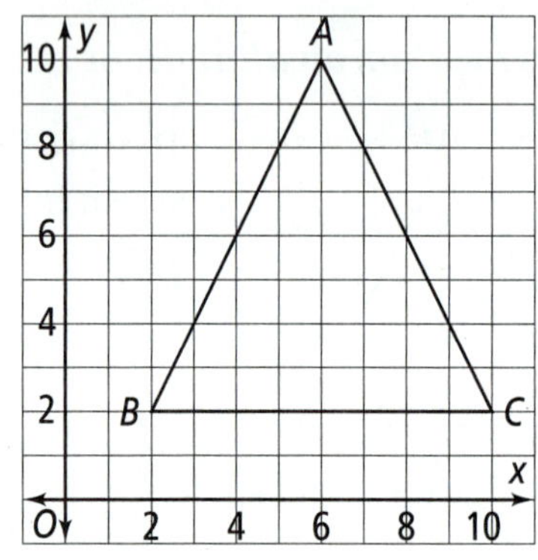

15. $P(1, 7)$, $Q(1, 2)$, $R(11, 2)$ **(1, 2)**

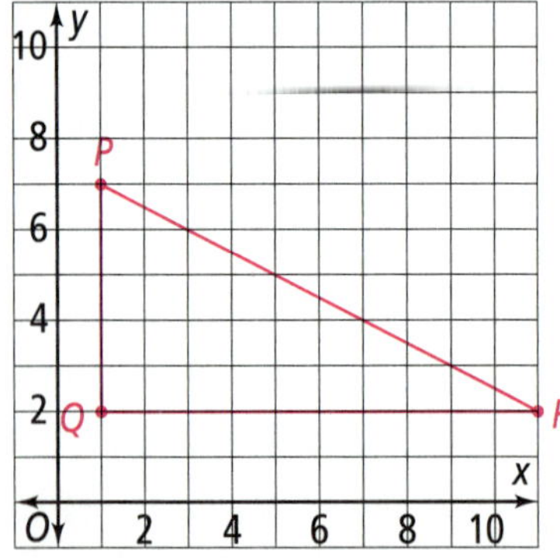

16. $D(5, 11)$, $E(2, 5)$, $F(11, 5)$ **(5, 8)**

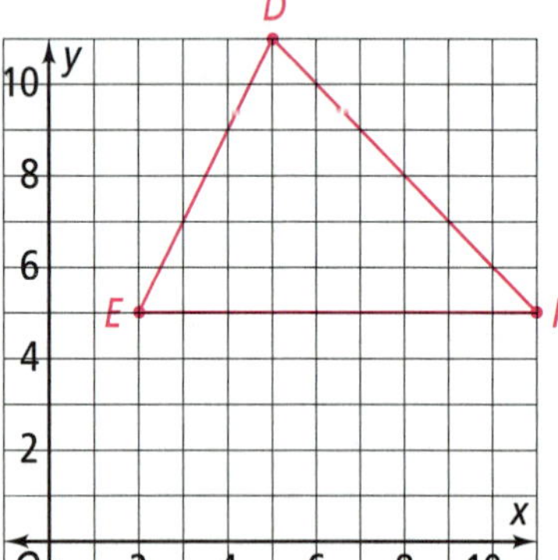

17. Which triangle has a centroid at the same point as the orthocenter?
△GHI

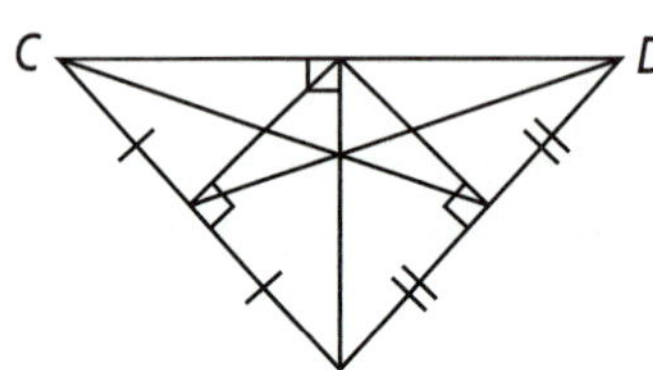

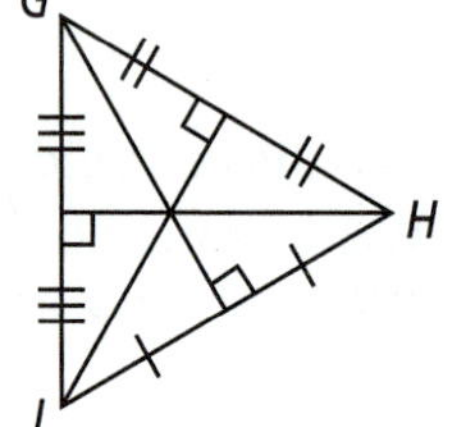

Name ______________________ Class ____________ Date ____________

5-4 Standardized Test Prep

Medians and Altitudes

Multiple Choice

For Exercises 1–5, choose the correct letter.

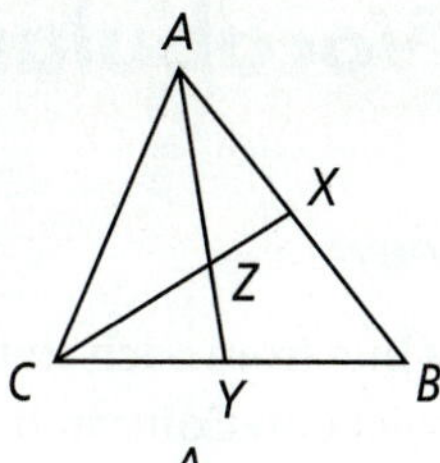

1. Z is the centroid of $\triangle ABC$. If $AZ = 12$, what is ZY? A

   (A) 6 (C) 12

   (B) 9 (D) 18

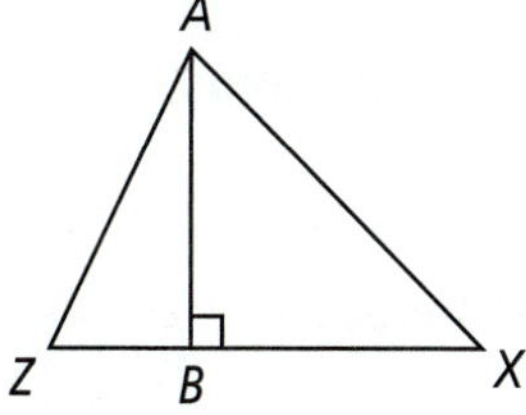

2. What is the best description of $\overline{AB}$? F

   (F) altitude

   (G) perpendicular bisector

   (H) median

   (I) angle bisector

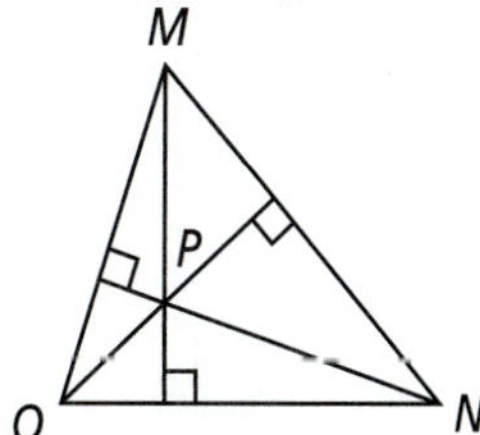

3. What is the best description of P? D

   (A) incenter

   (B) centroid

   (C) circumcenter

   (D) orthocenter

Use $\triangle XYZ$ for Exercises 4 and 5.

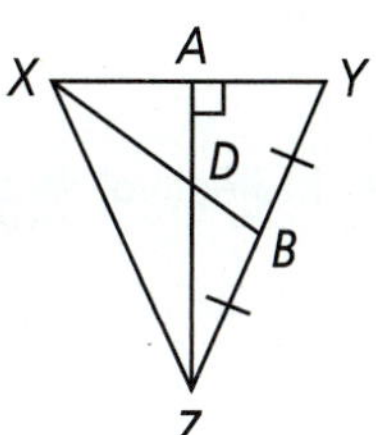

4. Which is an altitude of $\triangle XYZ$? F

   (F) $\overline{AZ}$ (H) $\overline{XB}$

   (G) $\overline{XY}$ (I) $\overline{ZY}$

5. Which is a median of $\triangle XYZ$? B

   (A) $\overline{AZ}$ (C) $\overline{XY}$

   (B) $\overline{BX}$ (D) $\overline{YZ}$

Short Response

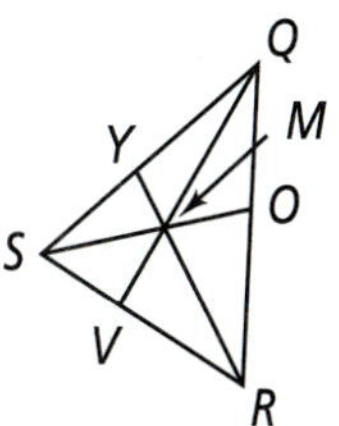

6. M is the centroid of $\triangle QRS$, and $QM = 22x + 10y$. What expressions can you write for MV and QV?
   [2] $MV = 11x + 5y$ AND $QV = 33x + 15y$
   [1] $MV = 11x + 5y$ OR $QV = 33x + 15y$
   [0] No correct response is given.

5-5 Indirect Proof

Vocabulary

Review

Draw a line from each statement in Column A to one or more pictures that contradict it in Column B.

Column A	Column B
1. $x < y$	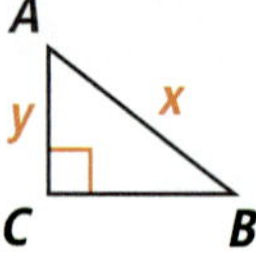
2. $x = y$	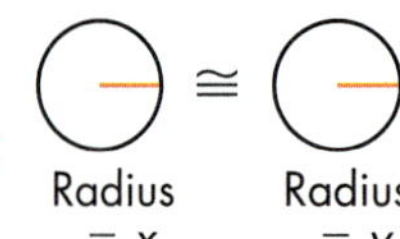 Radius $= x$ ≅ Radius $= y$
3. $x > y$	Ordered pair (3, 3)

Vocabulary Builder

indirect (adjective) **in duh** REKT

Definition: **Indirect** means not direct in course or action, taking a roundabout route to get to a point or idea.

Math Usage: In **indirect** reasoning, all possibilities are considered and then all but one are proved false. The remaining possibility must be true.

Use Your Vocabulary

Write *indirect* or *indirectly* to complete each sentence.

4. The _?_ way home from school takes a lot more time. indirect

5. By finding the negation of a statement false, you _?_ prove the statement true. indirectly

Key Concept Writing an Indirect Proof

Step 1
State as a temporary assumption the opposite (negation) of what you want to prove.

Step 2
Show that this temporary assumption leads to a contradiction.

Step 3
Conclude that the temporary assumption must be false and what you want to prove must be true.

Problem 1 Writing the First Step of an Indirect Proof

Got It? **Suppose you want to write an indirect proof of the statement. As the first step of the proof, what would you assume?**

At least one of the items costs more than $25.

6. What do you want to prove?

At least one of the items costs more than $25.

For Exercises 7–8, use <, >, ≤, ≥, or = to complete each statement. Let n = the cost of the items.

7. What do you want to prove?

n > 25

8. What is the opposite of what you want to prove?

n ≤ 25

9. The first step in the indirect proof is to write the following:

At least one of the items costs _?_ $25.

at most

Got It? **Suppose you want to write an indirect proof of the statement. As the first step of the proof, what would you assume?**

$\triangle BOX$ is not acute.

10. What do you want to prove?

$\triangle BOX$ is not acute.

11. What is the opposite of what you want to prove?

$\triangle BOX$ is acute.

12. The first step in the indirect proof is to write the following:

$\triangle BOX$ is _?_.

acute

Write the first step of the indirect proof of each statement.

13. Prove: $AB = CD$

Assume temporarily that $AB \neq CD$

14. Prove: The sun is shining.

Assume temporarily that the sun is not shining.

Problem 2 Identifying Contradictions

Got It? Which two statements contradict each other?

I. $\triangle XYZ$ is acute. II. $\triangle XYZ$ is scalene III. $\triangle XYZ$ is equiangular

15. Use the words in the box at the right to complete the flow chart below.

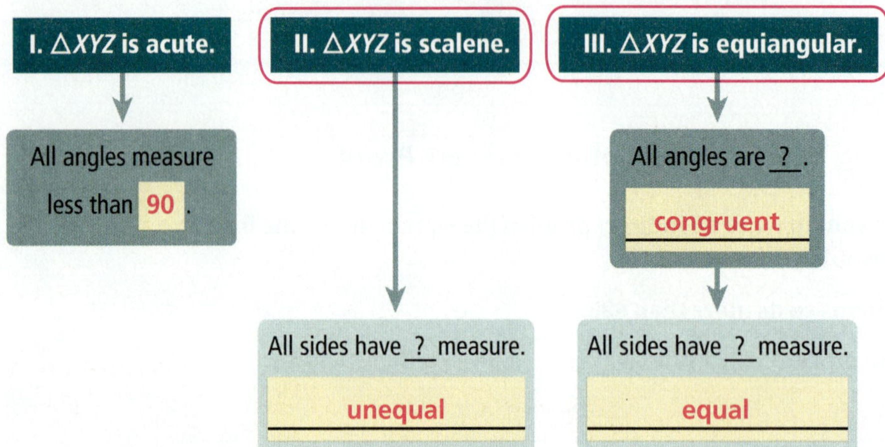

90
congruent
equal
unequal

16. In the first row of the flow chart above, circle the two statements that contradict one another.

Problem 3 Writing an Indirect Proof

Got It? Given: $7(x + y) = 70$ and $x \neq 4$.

Prove: $y \neq 6$

17. Give the reason for each statement of the proof. Answers may vary. Samples are given.

Statements	Reasons
1) Assume $y = 6$.	1) Assume the opposite of what you want to prove.
2) $7(x + y) = 70$	2) Given
3) $7(x + 6) = 70$	3) Substitute 6 for y.
4) $7x + 42 = 70$	4) The Distributive Property.
5) $7x = 28$	5) Subtract 42 from each side.
6) $x = 4$	6) Divide each side by 7.
7) $x \neq 4$	7) Given
8) $y \neq 6$	8) Statements (6) and (7) contradict each other. Reaching a contradiction means the assumption was wrong.

Lesson Check • Do you know HOW?

Suppose you want to write an indirect proof of the following statement. As the first step of the proof, what would you assume?

Quadrilateral *ABCD* has four right angles.

18. Place a ✓ if the statement is the correct assumption to make as the first step in the indirect proof. Place an ✗ if it is not.

✗ Quadrilateral *ABCD* is a rectangle.

✗ Quadrilateral *ABCD* has four non-right angles.

✓ Quadrilateral *ABCD* does *not* have four right angles.

Lesson Check • Do you UNDERSTAND?

Error Analysis **A classmate began an indirect proof as shown at the right. Explain and correct your classmate's error.**

~~Given: △ABC~~
~~Prove: ∠A is obtuse.~~
~~Assume temporarily that ∠A is acute.~~

19. Complete the flow chart.

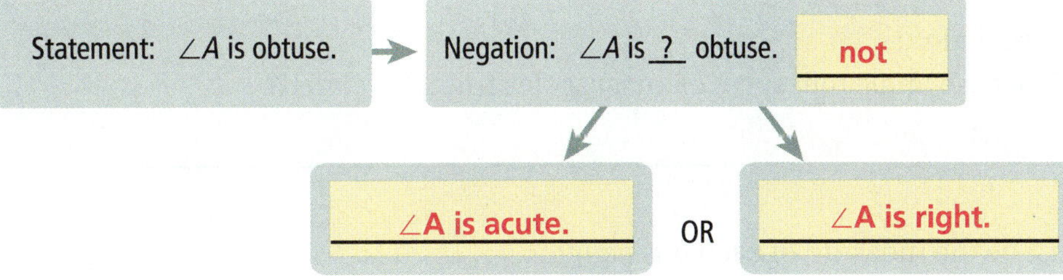

20. Underline the correct words to complete the sentence.

The indirect proof has an incorrect conclusion / <u>assumption</u> because the opposite of "∠A is obtuse" is "∠A is acute / <u>not obtuse</u> / right."

Math Success

Check off the vocabulary words that you understand.

☐ indirect reasoning ☐ indirect proof ☐ contradiction

Rate how well you can *use indirect reasoning.*

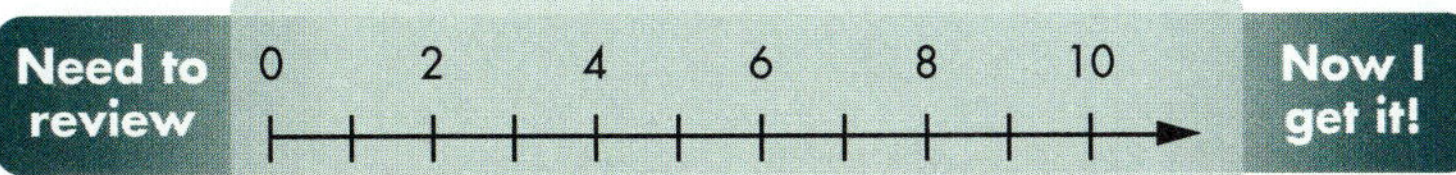

Name ______________________ Class ____________ Date ____________

5-5 Think About a Plan

Indirect Proof

Write an indirect proof.

Given: $\triangle XYZ$ is isosceles.

Prove: Neither base angle is a right angle.

1. What is the first step in writing an indirect proof?

   State the opposite of what you want to prove as a temporary assumption.

2. Write the first step for this indirect proof.

   Assume temporarily that at least one of the base angles is a right angle.

3. What is the second step in writing an indirect proof?

   Show that the temporary assumption leads to a contradiction.

4. Find the contradiction:

   a. How are the base angle measures of an isosceles triangle related?

      The base angles have equal measures.

   b. What must be the measure of each base angle?

      90; 90

   c. What is the sum of the angle measures in a triangle? 180

   d. If both base angles of $\triangle XYZ$ are right angles, and the non-base angle has a measure greater than 0, what must be true of the sum of the angle measures?

      The sum of the angle measures must be greater than 180.

   e. What does your assumption contradict?

      the Triangle Angle-Sum Theorem

5. What is your conclusion?

   The assumption is false. Therefore, neither base angle in an isosceles triangle is a right angle.

Name ______________________ Class ____________ Date ____________

5-5 Practice

Form K

Indirect Proof

Complete the first step of an indirect proof of the given statement.

1. There are fewer than 11 pencils in the box.
Assume temporarily that there are __?__ pencils in the box. **11 or more**

2. If a number ends in 0, then it is not divisible by 3.
Assume temporarily that a number that ends in 0 __?__. **is divisible by 3**

3. $4x + 3 > 12$
Assume temporarily that $4x + 3$ [$\leq$] 12.

4. $\triangle RST$ is not an isosceles triangle.
Assume temporarily that __?__. **$\triangle RST$ is an isosceles triangle**

Write the first step of an indirect proof of the given statement.

5. There are more than 20 apples in a box.
Assume temporarily that there are 20 or fewer apples in a box.

6. If a number ends in x, then it is a multiple of 5.
Assume temporarily that a number that ends in x is not a multiple of 5.

7. $m\angle XYZ < 100$
Assume temporarily that $m\angle XYZ \geq 100$.

8. $\triangle DEF$ is a right triangle.
Assume temporarily that $\triangle DEF$ is not a right triangle.

Identify the two statements that contradict each other.

9. **I.** $\overleftrightarrow{MN} \parallel \overleftrightarrow{GH}$
II. $\overleftrightarrow{MN}$ and $\overleftrightarrow{GH}$ do not intersect.
III. $\overleftrightarrow{MN}$ and $\overleftrightarrow{GH}$ are skew. **I and III**

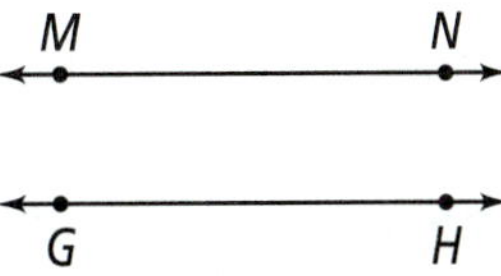

To start, identify two conditions that cannot be true at the same time.

__?__ lines must be in the same plane. **Parallel**
__?__ lines must not be in the same plane. **Skew**
Therefore, two lines cannot be both __?__ and __?__. **parallel; skew**

5-5 Practice (continued) Form K

Indirect Proof

Identify the two statements that contradict each other.

10. I. $\triangle CDE$ is equilateral.

II. $\angle C$ and $\angle E$ have the same measure.

III. $m\angle C > 60$ **I and III**

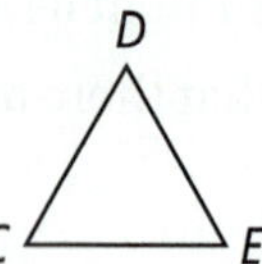

11. I. $\triangle JKL$ is scalene.

II. $\triangle JKL$ is obtuse.

III. $\triangle JKL$ is isosceles. **I and III**

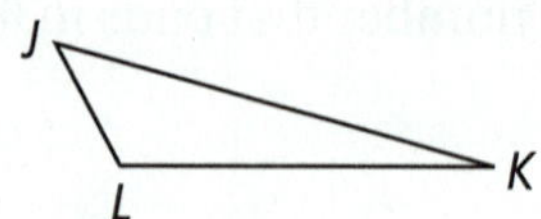

12. I. The orthocenter of $\triangle CDE$ is point G.

II. The centroid and orthocenter of $\triangle CDE$ are both point G.

III. $\triangle CDE$ is scalene. **II and III**

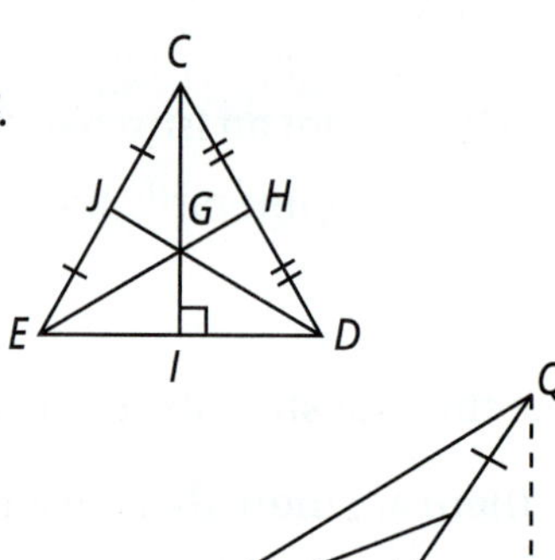

13. I. An altitude of $\triangle PQR$ is outside the triangle.

II. $\triangle PQR$ is acute.

III. An median of $\triangle PQR$ is inside the triangle. **I and II**

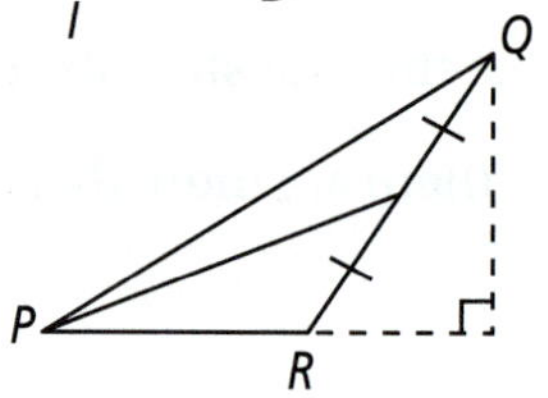

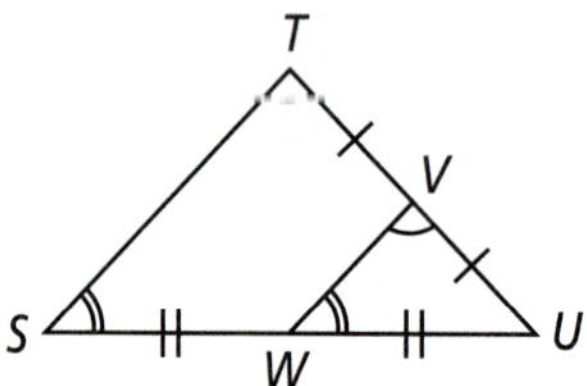

Complete the indirect proof.

14. Given: $\angle S \cong \angle VWU$
$\angle T \cong \angle WVU$

Prove: $\overline{TS} \parallel \overline{VW}$

Assume temporarily that ? . **$\overline{TS}$ is not parallel to $\overline{VW}$**

Then by the Converse of the ? , $\angle S$ and $\angle VWU$ cannot be ? . **congruent**
Corresp. ∠s Thm.

This contradicts the given information that ? . **$\angle S \cong \angle VWU$**

Therefore, $\overline{TS}$ must be ? $\overline{VW}$. **is parallel to**

Name ______________________ Class __________ Date __________

5-5 Standardized Test Prep

Indirect Proof

Multiple Choice

For Exercises 1–5, choose the correct letter.

1. Which two statements contradict each other? A

I. $\triangle ABC$ is scalene.

II. $\triangle ABC$ is isosceles.

III. $\triangle ABC$ is right.

IV. $\triangle ABC$ is acute.

(A) I and II (B) I and IV (C) II and III (D) II and IV

2. $\triangle MNO$ is equilateral. Which is a contradiction to this statement? H

(F) $\triangle MON$ is equilateral.

(G) $\triangle MNO$ is acute.

(H) $m\angle M = 120$

(I) $m\angle M = 60$

3. What is the first step of the following indirect proof? A

Given: The side lengths of a triangle are 4, 4, and 6.

Prove: The triangle is not a right triangle.

(A) Assume the triangle is a right triangle.

(B) Assume the triangle is obtuse.

(C) Assume the side lengths are not 4, 4, and 6.

(D) Assume the side lengths are 4, 5, and 6.

4. $MN = PQ$. Which is a contradiction to this statement? I

(F) $\overline{MN} \parallel \overline{PQ}$

(G) $\overline{MN} \perp \overline{PQ}$

(H) $\overline{MN} \cong \overline{PQ}$

(I) $\overline{MN}$ is not congruent to $\overline{PQ}$.

5. What is the first step of an indirect proof of the statement: A number x is not divisible by 5? B

(A) Assume x is not divisible by 5.

(B) Assume x is divisible by 5.

(C) Assume x is divisible by 2.

(D) Assume x is prime.

Short Response

6. What is the first step of an indirect proof of the following statement? Explain.

If a number ends in 0, then it is divisible by 5.

[2] Assume a number that ends in 0 is not divisible by 5. This is the opposite of what I want to prove. [1] Assume the opposite of what I want to prove OR Assume a number that ends in 0 is not divisible by 5. [0] No assumption or explanation is given.

5-6 PART 1 Inequalities in One Triangle

Vocabulary

Review

1. Circle the labeled *exterior angle.*

2. Write the *Exterior Angle* Theorem as it relates to the diagram.

   $m\angle$ 4 $= m\angle$ 1 $+ m\angle$ 2

3. Draw an *exterior angle* adjacent to $\angle 1$ and label it $\angle 5$.

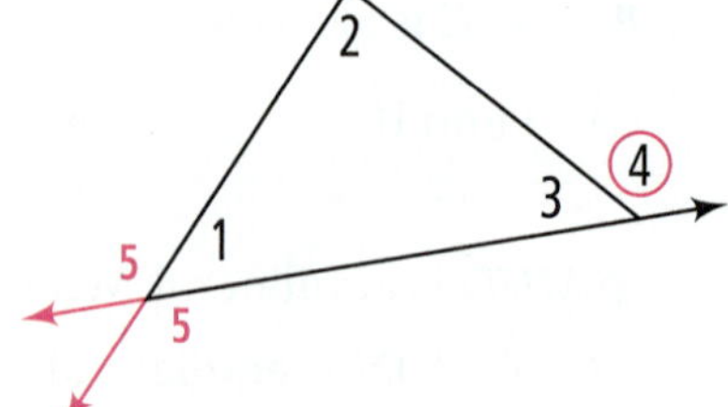

Vocabulary Builder

inequality (noun) in ee KWAL uh tee

Related Words: equal (adjective), unequal (adjective)

Math Usage: An **inequality** is a statement relating two quantities that are not equal ($\neq$), where one quantity may be greater than ($>$), greater than or equal to ($\geq$), less than ($<$), or less than or equal to ($\leq$) another quantity.

inequality symbols

$<, >, \leq, \geq$ and $\neq$

Use Your Vocabulary

Circle the statement that represents an *inequality* in each pair below.

4. $x \neq 32$

   $x = 32$

5. The number of votes is equal to 10,000.

   The number of votes is greater than 10,000.

Complete each statement with an inequality symbol.

6. y is less than or equal to z.

   $y \leq z$

7. The temperature t is at least 80 degrees.

   $t \geq 80°$

take note

Property Comparison Property of Inequality

If $a = b + c$ and $c > 0$, then $a > b$.

8. Circle the group of values that satisfies the Comparison Property of Inequality.

   $a = 5, b = 5$, and $c = 0$ $\quad$ $a = 5, b = 2$, and $c = 3$ $\quad$ $a = 8, b = 6$, and $c = 1$

take note

Corollary — Corollary to the Triangle Exterior Angle Theorem

The measure of an exterior angle of a triangle is greater than the measure of each of its remote interior angles.

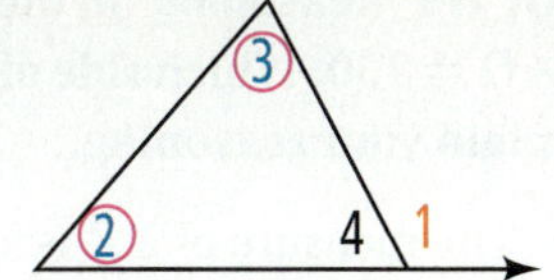

9. Circle the angles whose measures are always less than the measure of $\angle 1$.

Problem 1 Applying the Corollary

Got It? **Use the figure at the right. Why is $m\angle 5 > m\angle C$?**

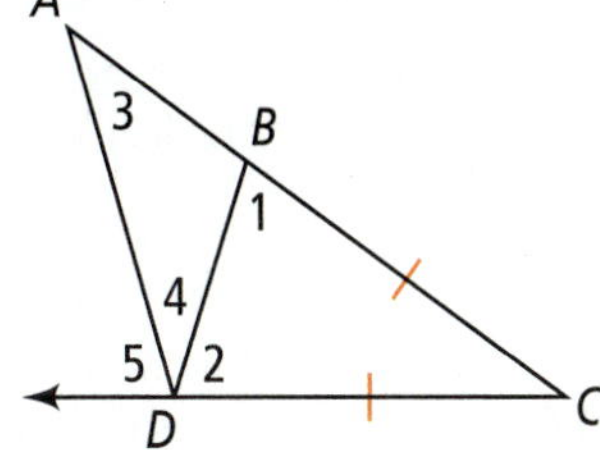

10. $\angle 5$ is an exterior angle of $\triangle$ADC.

11. Explain why $m\angle 5 > m\angle C$.

Corollary to the Triangle Exterior Angle Theorem

take note

Theorem 5-10 and Theorem 5-11

Theorem 5-10 If two sides of a triangle are not congruent, then the larger angle lies opposite the longer side.

If $XZ > XY$, then $m\angle Y > m\angle Z$.

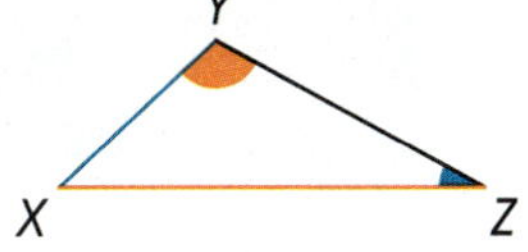

12. Theorem 5-11 is related to Theorem 5-10. Write the text of Theorem 5-11 by exchanging the words "larger angle" and "longer side."

Theorem 5-11 If two sides of a triangle are not congruent, then the longer side lies opposite the larger angle.

13. Write the side of $\triangle ABC$ that is opposite the given angle.

$\angle A$ $\overline{BC}$ $\angle B$ $\overline{AC}$ $\angle C$ $\overline{AB}$

Problem 2 Using Theorem 5-10

Got It? **Suppose a landscape architect wants to place a drinking fountain at the corner with the second-largest angle. Which two streets form the corner with the second-largest angle?**

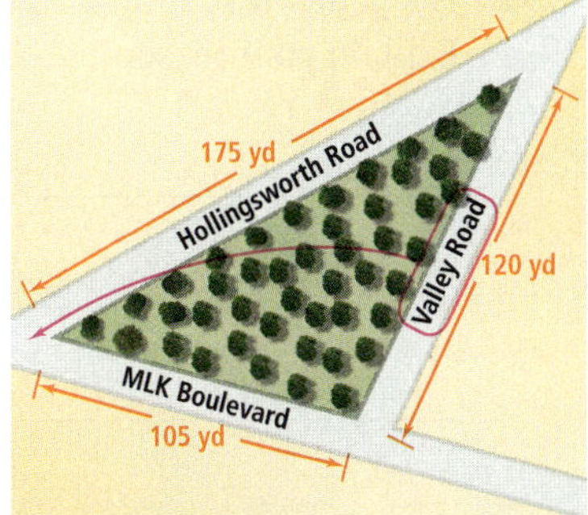

14. Circle the name of second-longest street in the diagram. Then draw an arrow from the second-longest street to the angle opposite it.

15. The second-largest angle is formed by ? and ? .

Hollingworth Rd. MLK Boulevard

Problem 3 Using Theorem 5-11

Got It? Reasoning **In the figure at the right, $m\angle S = 24$ and $m\angle O = 130$. Which side of $\triangle SOX$ is the shortest side? Explain your reasoning.**

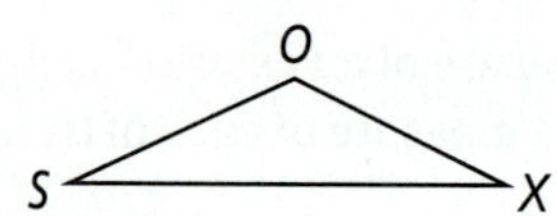

16. The measure of $\angle X$ is found below. Write a justification for each step.

$m\angle S = 24$ and $m\angle O = 130$	Given
$m\angle S + m\angle O + m\angle X = 180$	Triangle Angle-Sum Theorem
$24 + 130 + m\angle X = 180$	Substitute.
$m\angle X + 154 = 180$	Simplify.
$m\angle X = 26$	Subtract 154 from each side.

17. Complete the table below.

angle	$\angle O$	$\angle X$	$\angle S$
angle measure	130	26	24
opposite side	$\overline{SX}$	$\overline{SO}$	$\overline{OX}$

18. The shortest side is $\overline{OX}$ because it is opposite the smallest angle, $\angle$ S .

Lesson Check • Do you UNDERSTAND?

Reasoning **Is it possible to draw a right triangle with an exterior angle measuring 88? Explain your reasoning.**

19. A supplement of an 88° angle measures 92 .

20. A right angle measures 90 .

21. By the Triangle Angle-Sum Theorem, the sum of the measures of the angles of a triangle is 180 .

22. Is it possible to draw a right triangle with an exterior angle measuring 88? Explain your reasoning. Explanations may vary. Sample:

No. Its supplementary interior angle would measure 92, and the right angle measures 90. Then the sum of the measures of the angles of the triangle would be greater than 180, which contradicts the Triangle Angle-Sum Theorem.

5-6 PART 2 Inequalities in One Triangle

Vocabulary

Review

Underline the correct word to complete each sentence.

1. An *inequality* / equation is a statement relating two quantities that are not equal.
2. Use the symbol = to write an *inequality* / equation.
3. Several different symbols show an *inequality* / equation.
4. You can write an *inequality* / equation when two quantities are the same.

Use the diagram at the right. Use < or > to complete each *inequality*.

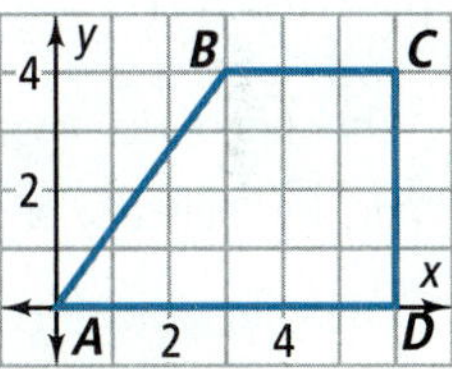

5. AD > BC
6. BC < CD
7. AB < AD
8. AD > CD
9. BC < BA
10. AB > CD

Vocabulary Builder

compare (verb) **kum PEHR**

Other Word Form: comparison (noun)

There are more letters in the word *comparison* than in the word *compare*.

Definition: To **compare** is to examine two or more items, noting similarities and differences.

Math Usage: Use inequalities to **compare** amounts.

Use Your Vocabulary

11. Complete each statement with the appropriate form of the word *compare*.

NOUN By _?_, a spider has more legs than a beetle. comparison

VERB You can _?_ products before deciding which to buy. compare

VERB To _?_ quantities, you can write an equation or an inequality. compare

NOUN A price _?_ can help a buyer choose between two car models. comparison

take note

Theorem 5-12 Triangle Inequality Theorem

The sum of the lengths of any two sides of a triangle is greater than the length of the third side.

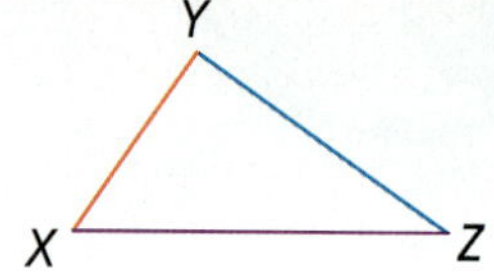

12. Complete each inequality.

$XY + YZ >$ XZ $\qquad YZ + ZX >$ YX $\qquad ZX + XY >$ ZY

13. Use Theorem 5-12 to write three inequalities about $\triangle ABC$

$AB + BC >$ AC $\qquad BC + AC >$ AB $\qquad AC + AB >$ BC

Problem 4 Using the Triangle Inequality Theorem

Got It? Can a triangle have sides with lengths 2 m, 6 m, and 9 m? Explain.

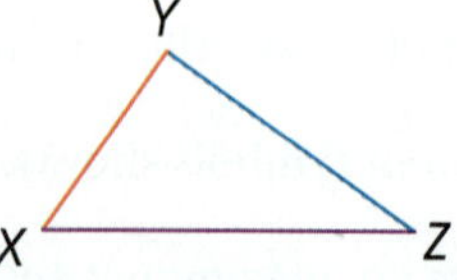

14. Complete the reasoning model below.

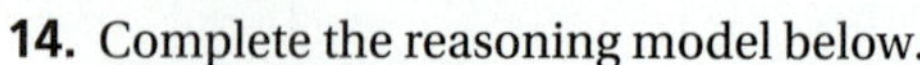

Think	Write		
The sum of the lengths of any two sides must be greater than the length of the third side.	2 + 6 = 8	6 + 9 = 15	2 + 9 = 11
I need to write three sums and three inequalities.	8 < 9	15 > 2	11 > 6
One of those sums is greater / not greater than the length of the third side.	It is / is not possible for a triangle to have sides with lengths 2 m, 6 m, and 9 m.		

Problem 5 Finding Possible Side Lengths

Got It? A triangle has side lengths of 4 in. and 7 in. What is the range of possible lengths for the third side?

15. Let x = the length of the third side. Use the Triangle Inequality Theorem to write and solve three inequalities.

$x + 4 >$ 7 $\qquad x + 7 >$ 4 $\qquad 7 + 4 >$ x

$x >$ 3 $\qquad x >$ −3 $\qquad 11 >$ x

16. Underline the correct word to complete each sentence.

Length is always / sometimes / never positive.

The first / second / third inequality pair is invalid in this situation.

17. Write the remaining two inequalities as one compound inequality.

3 $< x <$ 11

18. The third side must be longer than 3 in. and shorter than 11 in.

Lesson Check • Do you know HOW?

Can a triangle have sides of lengths 4, 5, and 10? Explain.

19. Write the sum of the lengths of two sides. Below each equation, write the length of the side you will compare to the sum.

$4 + 5 =$ 9 $4 +$ 10 $=$ 14   5 $+$ 10 $=$ 15

10   5   4

20. Write three inequalities to compare the sum of the lengths of two sides to the length of the third side.

$9 < 10$ $14 > 5$ $15 > 4$

21. Can a triangle have sides of lengths 4, 5, and 10? Explain. **Explanations may vary. Sample:**

No. The sum $4 + 5$ is not greater than 10.

Lesson Check • Do you UNDERSTAND?

Error Analysis **A friend tells you that she drew a triangle with perimeter 16 and one side of length 8. How do you know she made an error in her drawing?**

22. If one side length is 8 and the perimeter is 16, then the sum of the lengths of the two remaining sides must be $16 - 8 =$ 8 .

Underline the correct words or number to complete each sentence.

23. By the Triangle Inequality Theorem, the sum of the lengths of two sides of a triangle must be equal to / greater than / less than the length of the third side.

24. By the Triangle Inequality Theorem, the sum of the lengths of the two unknown sides must be equal to / greater than / less than the length 8 / 16 .

25. But 8 is *not* equal to / greater than 8, so there must be an error in the drawing.

Math Success

Check off the vocabulary words that you understand.

- ☐ exterior angle
- ☐ comparison property of inequality

Rate how well you can *use the Triangle Inequality Theorem.*

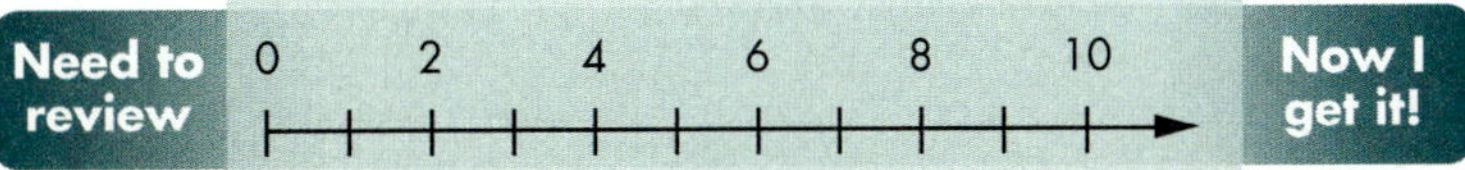

Name ______________________ Class ____________ Date ____________

5-6 Think About a Plan

Inequalities in One Triangle

Prove this corollary to Theorem 5-11: The perpendicular segment from a point to a line is the shortest segment from the point to the line.

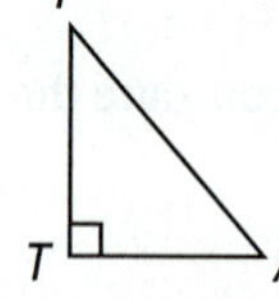

Given: $\overline{PT} \perp \overline{TA}$

Prove: $PA > PT$

1. What is $m\angle T$? Explain how you know this.

   90; two perpendicular line segments form right angles, and right angles are 90°.

2. What is $m\angle P + m\angle A + m\angle T$? Explain how you know this.

   180; the Triangle Angle-Sum Theorem

3. What is $m\angle P + m\angle A$? Explain how you know this.

   90; I subtracted the value of $m\angle T$ from both sides of the equation

   $m\angle P + m\angle A + m\angle T = 180$.

4. Write an inequality to show $m\angle A$. **$0 < m\angle A < 90$**

5. Write an inequality to show the relationship between $m\angle A$ and $m\angle T$. **$m\angle A < m\angle T$**

6. Which side lies opposite $\angle A$ and which side lies opposite $\angle T$?

   $\overline{PA}$ lies opposite $\angle T$, and $\overline{PT}$ lies opposite $\angle A$.

7. What is Theorem 5-11?

   If two angles of a triangle are not congruent, then the longer side lies opposite the larger angle.

8. What can you conclude about PA and PT?

   $PA > PT$

Name ______________________ Class __________ Date __________

5-6 Practice

Form K

Inequalities in One Triangle

1. Explain the relationship of $m\angle 1$, $m\angle 2$, and $m\angle 3$.

The measure of an exterior angle of a triangle is __?__ than the measure of each of its remote __?__ angles. **greater; interior**

$\angle 1$ is an __?__ angle of the triangle, so $m\angle 1 >$ __?__ and $m\angle 1 >$ __?__. **exterior; $m\angle 2$; $m\angle 3$**

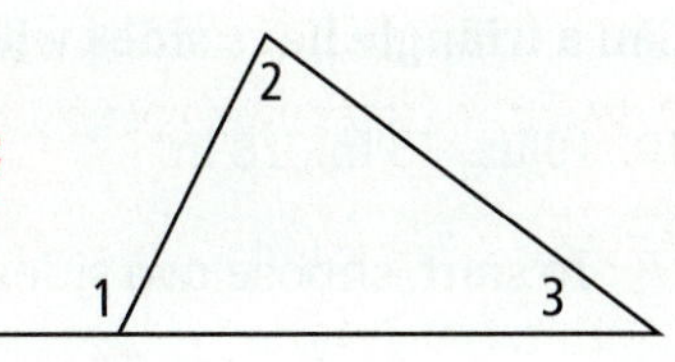

For Exercises 2–5, list the angles of each triangle in order from smallest to largest.

2. **$\angle C$, $\angle B$, $\angle A$**

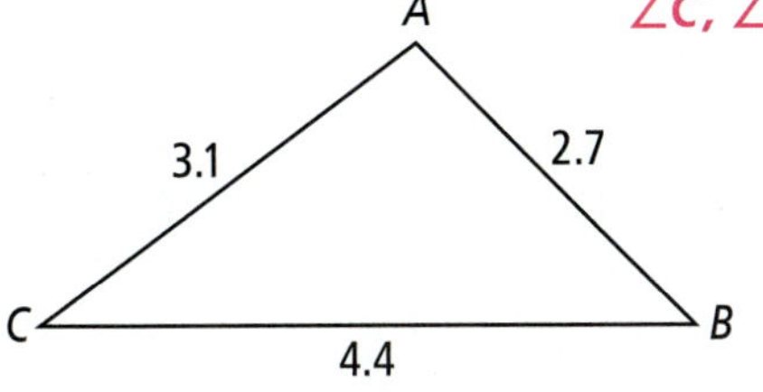

To start, order the side lengths from least to greatest.

[2.7] < [3.1] < [4.4]

3. **$\angle E$, $\angle D$, $\angle F$**

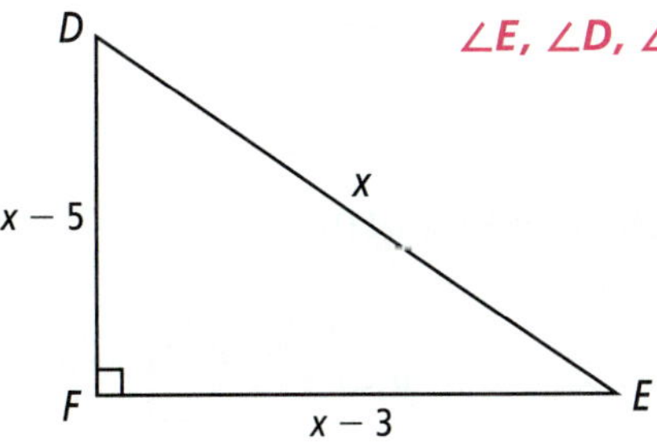

4. **$\angle G$, $\angle I$, $\angle H$**

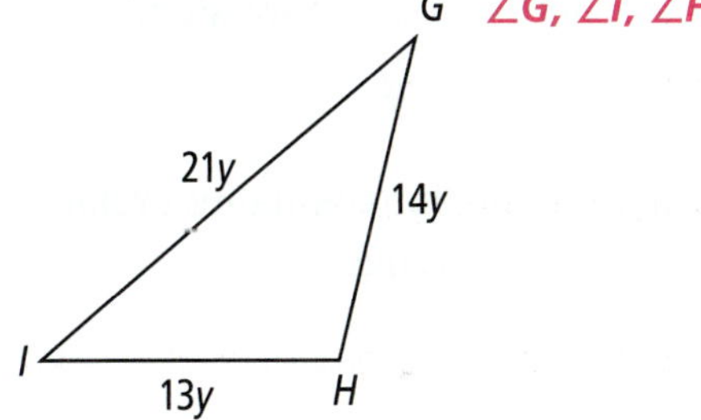

5. $\triangle XYZ$, where $XY = 25$, $YZ = 11$, and $XZ = 15$ **$\angle X$, $\angle Y$, $\angle Z$**

For Exercises 6–8, list the sides of each triangle in order from shortest to longest.

6. **$\overline{PQ}$, $\overline{QR}$, $\overline{PR}$**

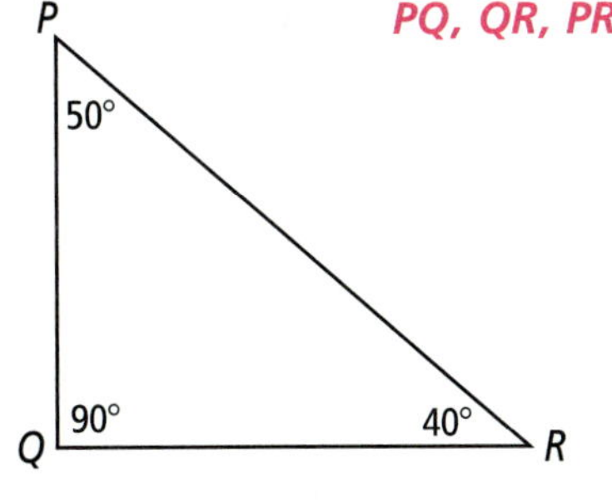

7. **$\overline{UV}$, $\overline{UW}$, $\overline{WV}$**

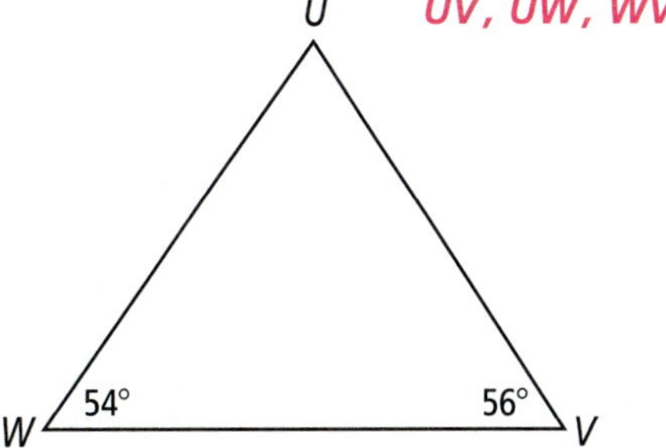

8. $\triangle MNO$, where $m\angle M = 56$, $m\angle N = 108$, and $m\angle O = 16$ **$\overline{MN}$, $\overline{NO}$, $\overline{MO}$**

9. **Algebra** List the sides in order from shortest to longest in $\triangle XYZ$, with $m\angle X = 50$, $m\angle Y = 5x + 10$, and $m\angle Z = 5x$. **$\overline{YZ}$, $\overline{XY}$, $\overline{XZ}$**

Name ______________________ Class ____________ Date ____________

5-6 Practice (continued) — Form K

Inequalities in One Triangle

Can a triangle have sides with the given lengths? Explain.

10. 10 in., 13 in., 18 in.

To start, choose two sides and see if their sum exceeds the third side.

$10 + 13 \; [\overset{?}{>}] \; 18$ (yes) / no (Circle the correct answer.)

Check the other two sums. Yes; the sum of the lengths of the two shorter sides is always greater than the length of the third side.

11. 6 m, 5 m, 12 m No; the sum of the lengths of the two shorter sides is less than the length of the third side; $6 + 5 < 12$.

12. 11 ft, 8 ft, 18 ft Yes; the sum of the lengths of the two shorter sides is always greater than the length of the third side.

Algebra The lengths of two sides of a triangle are given. Find the range of possible lengths for the third side.

13. 4, 8 any length that is greater than 4 and less than 12

To start, write the inequalities relating the known side lengths and the unknown side length.

$x + 4 > 8$ $\quad$ $x + 8 > \boxed{4}$ $\quad$ $8 + 4 > \boxed{x}$

14. 13, 8 any length that is greater than 5 and less than 21

15. 10, 15 any length that is greater than 5 and less than 25

16. Error Analysis A student draws a triangle with a perimeter of 12 in. The student says that the longest side measures 7 in. How do you know that the student is incorrect? Explain. If one side measures 7 in., the other two side measures must sum to 5 in., but the Triangle Inequality Theorem says that the sum of the measures must be greater than 7 in.

17. Algebra $\triangle XYZ$ has the side lengths shown at the right. What values of x result in side lengths that could be the sides of a triangle. (*Hint:* Write and solve three inequalities.) $x > \frac{10}{3}$

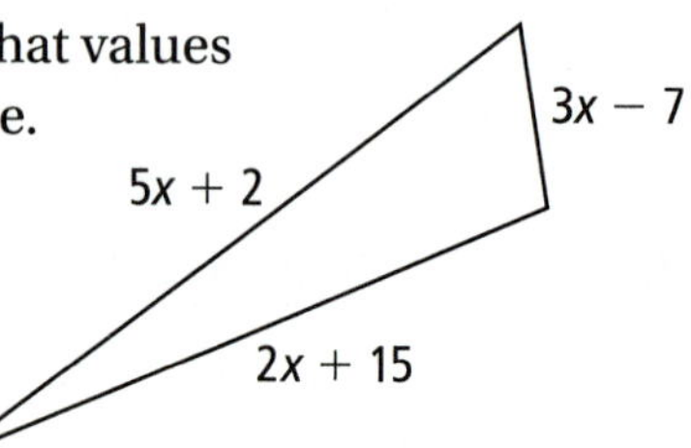

Name ______________________ Class ____________ Date ____________

5-6 Standardized Test Prep

Inequalities in One Triangle

Multiple Choice

For Exercises 1–6, choose the correct letter.

1. Which of the following could be lengths of sides of a triangle? C

Ⓐ 11, 15, 27 Ⓑ 13, 14, 32 Ⓒ 16, 19, 34 Ⓓ 33, 22, 55

2. $\triangle ABC$ has the following angle measures: $m\angle A = 120$, $m\angle B = 40$, and $m\angle C = 20$. Which lists the sides in order from shortest to longest? G

Ⓕ $\overline{CB}, \overline{BA}, \overline{AC}$ Ⓗ $\overline{AC}, \overline{BA}, \overline{CB}$

Ⓖ $\overline{BA}, \overline{AC}, \overline{CB}$ Ⓘ $\overline{CB}, \overline{AC}, \overline{BA}$

3. $\triangle RST$ has the following side lengths: $RS = 7$, $ST = 13$, and $RT = 19$. Which lists the angles in order from smallest to largest? D

Ⓐ $\angle R, \angle S, \angle T$ Ⓒ $\angle S, \angle T, \angle R$

Ⓑ $\angle T, \angle S, \angle R$ Ⓓ $\angle T, \angle R, \angle S$

4. A triangle has side lengths 21 and 17. Which is a possible length for the third side? H

Ⓕ 2 Ⓖ 4 Ⓗ 25 Ⓘ 39

5. Look at $\triangle LMN$. Which lists the angles in order from the smallest to the largest? D

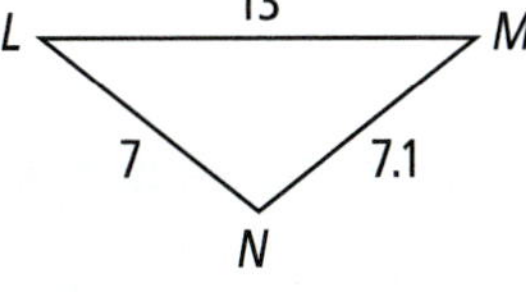

Ⓐ $\angle L, \angle M, \angle N$ Ⓒ $\angle N, \angle M, \angle L$

Ⓑ $\angle M, \angle N, \angle L$ Ⓓ $\angle M, \angle L, \angle N$

6. **Algebra** What are the possible lengths for x, the third side of a triangle, if two sides are 13 and 7? F

Ⓕ $6 < x < 20$ Ⓖ $7 < x < 13$ Ⓗ $6 \leq x \leq 20$ Ⓘ $7 \leq x \leq 13$

Short Response

7. What is the relationship between a and y? Explain.

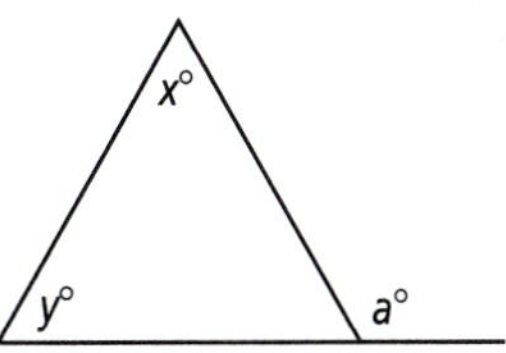

[2] $a > y$; the measure of an exterior angle of a triangle is greater than the measure of a remote interior angle (Corollary to the Triangle Exterior Angle Theorem).
[1] $a > y$ OR the measure of an exterior angle of a triangle is greater than the measure of a remote interior angle (Corollary to the Triangle Exterior Angle Theorem).
[0] No relationship is stated nor explanation given.

5-7 Inequalities in Two Triangles

Vocabulary

Review

Circle the *included angles* in each diagram.

1.

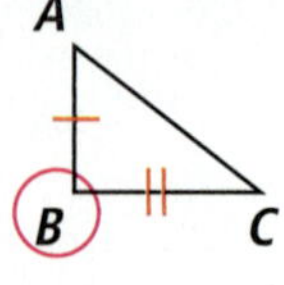

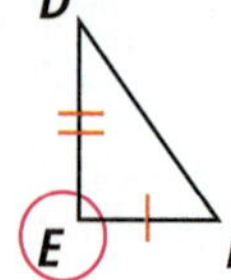

2.

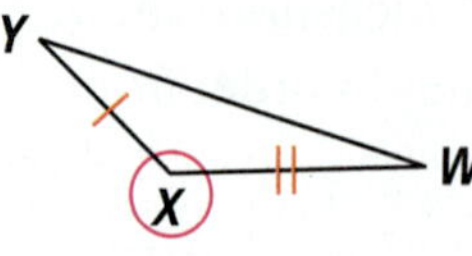

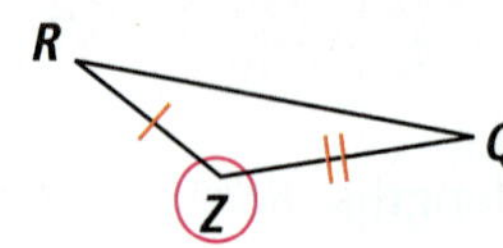

In Exercises 3–5, cross out the group of values that does not satisfy the *Comparison Property of Inequality*.

3. ~~$a = 3, b = 3, c = 0$~~

$a = 6, b = 4, c = 2$

4. $a = 11, b = 3, c = 8$

~~$a = 1, b = 2, c = 3$~~

5. $a = 8, b = 3, c = 5$

~~$a = 8, b = 5, c = 4$~~

Write a number so that each group satisfies the *Comparison Property of Inequality*.

6. $a =$ 2 $, b = 0, c = 2$

7. $a = 9, b =$ 8 $, c = 1$

8. $a = 3, b =$ 1 $, c = 2$

Vocabulary Builder

hinge (noun, verb) hinj

Definition (noun): A **hinge** is a device on which something else depends or turns.

Definition (verb): To **hinge** upon means to depend on.

Use Your Vocabulary

Circle the correct form of the word *hinge*.

9. Everything *hinges* on his decision. Noun / Verb

10. The *hinge* on a gate allows it to swing open or closed. Noun / Verb

11. Your plan *hinges* on your teacher's approval. Noun / Verb

12. The lid was attached to the jewelry box by two *hinges*. Noun / Verb

take note

Theorems 5-13 and 5-14 The Hinge Theorem and its Converse

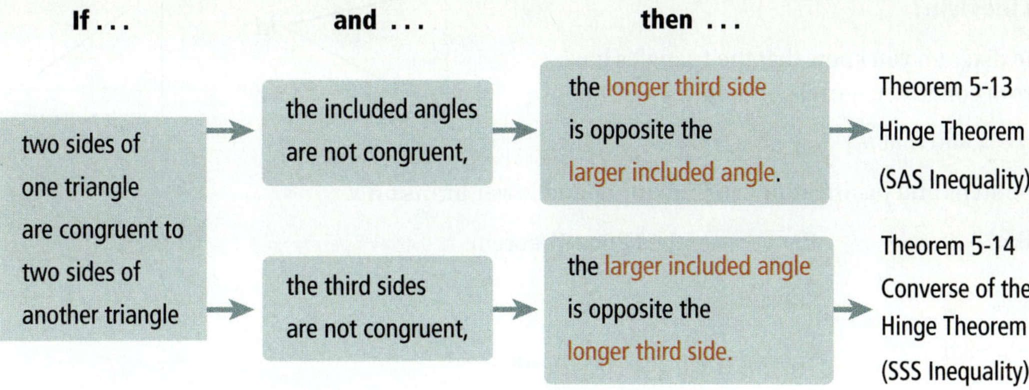

13. Use the triangles at the right to complete the table.

Theorem	If...	Then...
5-13: Hinge Theorem	$m\angle A > m\angle X$	BC > YZ
5-14: Converse of the Hinge Theorem	$BC > YZ$	$m\angle A > m\angle X$

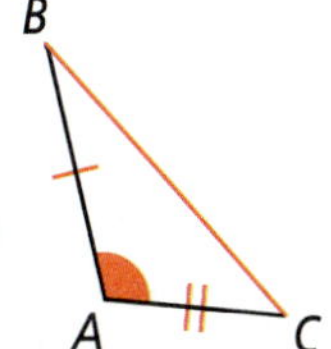

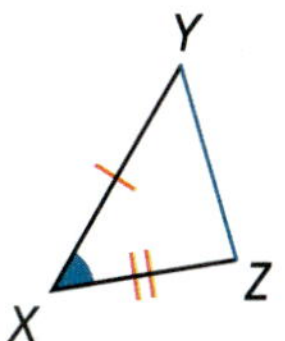

14. Explain why Theorems 5-13 and 5-14 are also called the SAS and SSS Inequality Theorems. **Answers may vary. Sample:**

Theorem 5-13 compares two pairs of sides and the pair of included angles (SAS).

Theorem 5-14 compares three pairs of sides (SSS).

Problem 1 Using the Hinge Theorem

Got It? **What inequality relates *LN* and *OQ* in the figure at the right?**

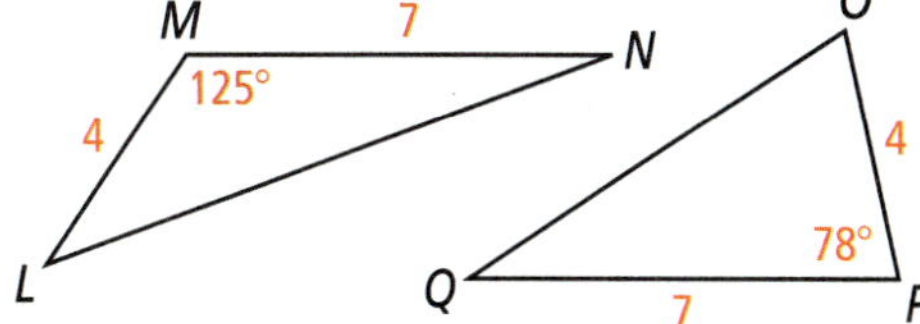

15. Use information in the diagram to complete each statement.

The included angle in $\triangle LMN$ is $\angle$ **M**.

The included angle in $\triangle OPQ$ is $\angle$ **P**.

16. Circle the side opposite the included angle in $\triangle LMN$. Underline the side opposite the included angle in $\triangle OPQ$.

$\overline{LM}$ ($\overline{LN}$) $\overline{MN}$

<u>$\overline{QO}$</u> $\overline{QP}$ $\overline{OP}$

17. Use the Hinge Theorem to complete the statement below.

$m\angle$ **M** $> m\angle$ **P**, so $LN >$ **OQ**.

Problem 3 Using the Converse of the Hinge Theorem

Got It? What is the range of possible values for x in the figure at the right?

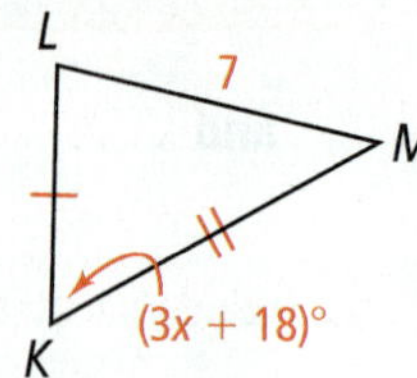

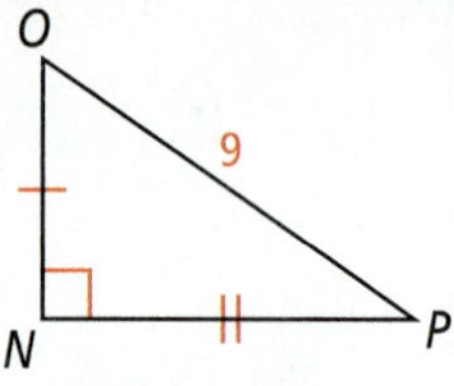

18. From the diagram you know that the triangles have two pairs of congruent corresponding sides, that $LM <$ **OP**, and that $m\angle N =$ **90**.

Complete the steps and justifications to find upper and lower limits on x.

19. $m\angle K <$ **$m\angle N$** Converse of the Hinge Theorem

$3x + 18 <$ **90** Substitute.

$3x <$ **72** Subtract **18** from each side.

$x <$ **24** Divide each side by **3**.

20. $m\angle K >$ **0** The measure of an angle of a triangle is greater than 0.

$3x + 18 >$ **0** Substitute.

$3x >$ **−18** Subtract **18** from each side.

$x >$ **−6** Divide each side by **3**.

21. Write the two inequalities as the compound inequality **−6** $< x <$ **24**.

Problem 4 Proving Relationships in Triangles

Got It? **Given:** $m\angle MON = 80$; O is the midpoint of $\overline{LN}$.

Prove: $LM > MN$

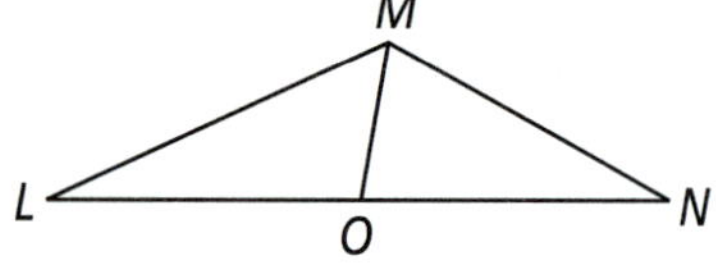

22. Write a justification for each statement.

Statements	Reasons
1) $m\angle MON = 80$	1) Given
2) $m\angle MON + m\angle MOL = 180$	2) Supplementary Angles
3) $80 + m\angle MOL = 180$	3) Substitute 80 for $m\angle MON$.
4) $m\angle MOL = 100$	4) Subtract 80 from each side.
5) $\overline{LO} \cong \overline{ON}$	5) O is the midpoint of $\overline{LN}$.
6) $\overline{MO} \cong \overline{MO}$	6) Reflexive Property of Congruence
7) $m\angle MOL > m\angle MON$	7) 100 > 80
8) $LM > MN$	8) Hinge Theorem

Lesson Check • Do you know HOW?

Write an inequality relating FD and BC.

In Exercises 23–26, circle the correct statement in each pair.

23. $\overline{AC} \cong \overline{EF}$ $AC > EF$ **24.** $AB > ED$ $\overline{AB} \cong \overline{ED}$

25. $m\angle BAC > m\angle FED$ $m\angle BAC < m\angle FED$

26. By the Hinge Theorem, you can relate FD and BC.

By the Converse of Hinge Theorem, you can relate FD and BC.

27. Write an inequality relating FD and BC.

FD > BC

Lesson Check • Do you UNDERSTAND?

Error Analysis **From the figure at the right, your friend concludes that $m\angle BAD > m\angle BCD$. How would you correct your friend's mistake?**

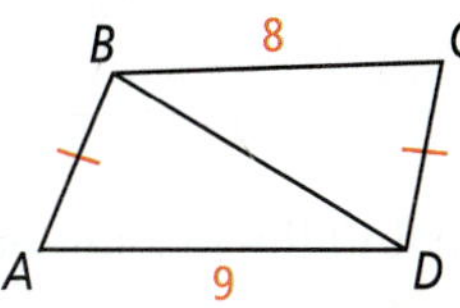

Write T for *true* or F for *false*.

T **28.** $AB = CD$

F **29.** $AD = CB$

T **30.** $BD = BD$

31. Your friend should compare AD and CB.

32. The longer of the two sides your friend should compare is AD.

33. How would you correct your friend's mistake? Explain.

Answers may vary. Sample: $AD > CB$, so use the Converse of the Hinge Theorem to conclude that $m\angle ABD > m\angle CDB$.

Math Success

Check off the vocabulary words that you understand.

☐ exterior angle ☐ comparison property of inequality ☐ Hinge Theorem

Rate how well you can *use triangle inequalities.*

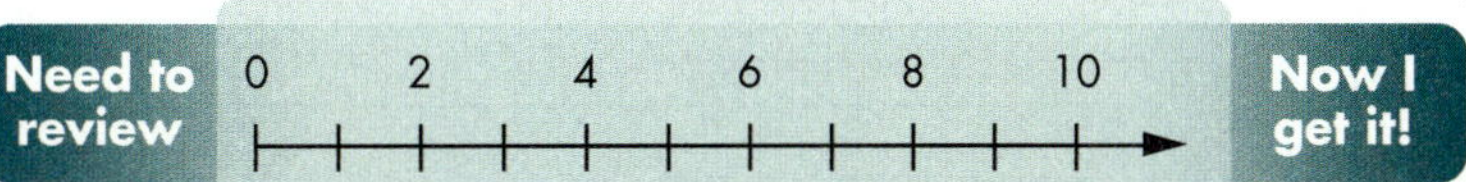

Name ______________________ Class ____________ Date ____________

5-7 Think About a Plan

Inequalities in Two Triangles

Reasoning The legs of a right isosceles triangle are congruent to the legs of an isosceles triangle with an 80° vertex angle. Which triangle has a greater perimeter? How do you know?

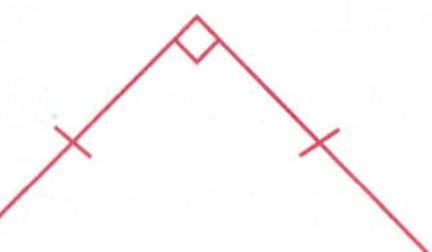

1. How can you use a sketch to help visualize the problem? Draw a sketch.

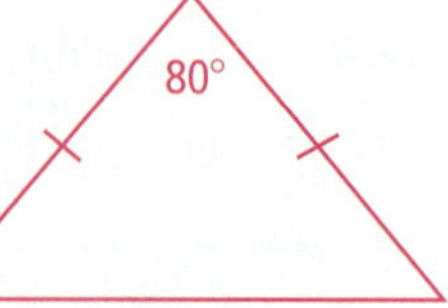

2. The triangles have two pairs of congruent sides. For the right triangle, what is the measure of the included angle? How do you know this?

   90; it is a right angle.

3. For the second triangle, what is the measure of the included angle? How do you know this?

   80; it is given that the vertex angle, the angle between the legs, or congruent sides, is 80°.

4. How could you find the perimeter of each triangle?

   Add the lengths of the legs and the base.

5. How does the sum of the lengths of the legs in the right triangle compare to the sum of the lengths of the legs in the other triangle?

   They are the same.

6. Write formulas for the perimeters of each triangle. Use the variable ℓ for leg length, b_1 for base length of the right triangle, and b_2 for base length of the second triangle.

   $P(\text{right triangle}) = \ell + \ell + b_1$; $P(\text{second triangle}) = \ell + \ell + b_2$

7. What values do you need to compare to find the triangle with the greater perimeter?

   base lengths, or b_1 and b_2

8. How can you use the Hinge Theorem to find which base length is longer?

   The longer base length will be opposite the larger included angle.

9. Which base length is longer? b_1, or the base length of the right triangle

10. Which triangle has the greater perimeter? the right isosceles triangle

Name ______________________ Class ____________ Date ____________

5-7 Practice

Form K

Inequalities in Two Triangles

Write an inequality relating the given side lengths. If there is not enough information to reach a conclusion, write *no conclusion*.

1. *AB* and *CB* **AB < CB**

To start, determine whether the triangles have two pairs of congruent sides.

$\overline{AD} \cong \overline{CD}$

$\overline{DB} \cong$? $\overline{DB}$

Then compare the hinge angles.

$m\angle CDB =$ 100

$m\angle$ ADB $=$ 80

2. *JL* and *MO* **JL > MO**

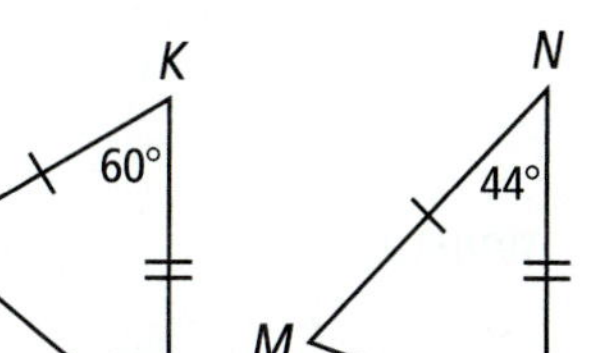

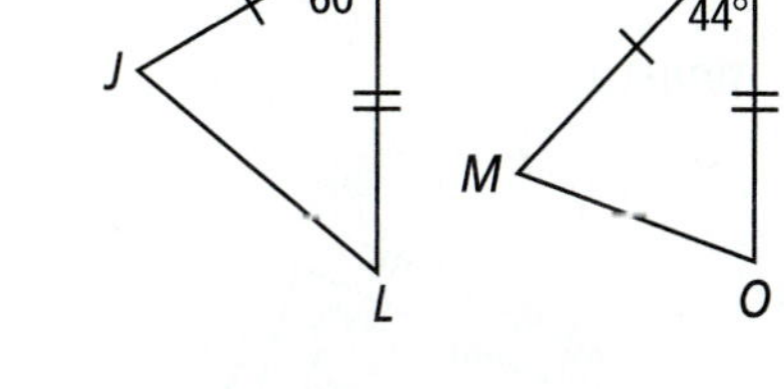

3. *ST* and *BT* **no conclusion**

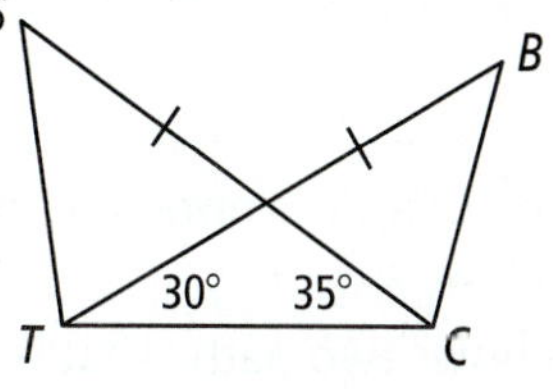

4. Two identical laptops are shown at the right. In which laptop is the distance from the top edge of the screen to the front edge of the keyboard greater? Explain.

Laptop B; the lengths of the laptops' keyboards and screens are the same. Laptop B is open wider, so the hinge angle is greater than it is for Laptop A.

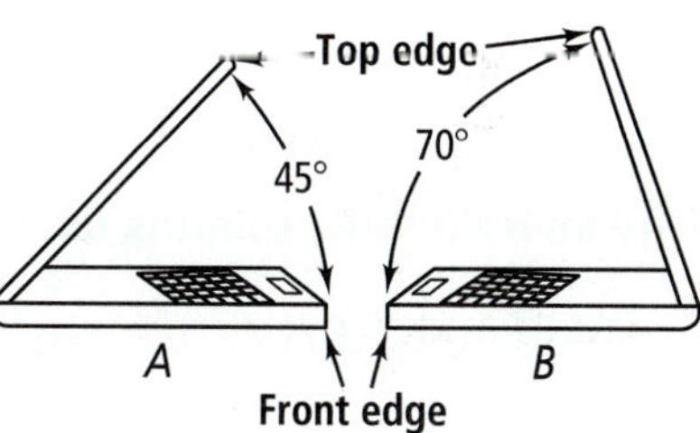

Algebra **Find the range of possible values for each variable.**

5.

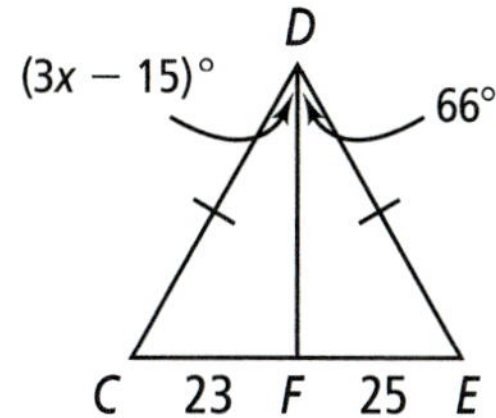

$m\angle CDF < m\angle EDF$ $\quad$ $m\angle CDE > 0$

$x <$ 27 $\quad$ $x >$ 5

6.

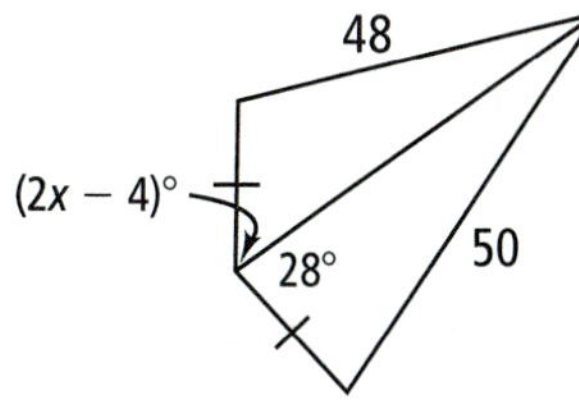

2 $< x <$ 16

Name ______________________ Class ____________ Date ____________

5-7 Practice (continued) Form K

Inequalities in Two Triangles

Use the diagram at the right for Exercises 7–9. Complete each comparison with < or >. Then complete the explanation.

A C D
46° 90°
45° 45°
B E

7. $m\angle ACB$ [>] $m\angle DCE$

[$\angle DCE$] forms a straight angle with [$\angle BCE$] and [$\angle ACB$].

The measure of $\angle DCE$ is [44].

8. AB [>] DE

Because $\triangle BCE$ is an isosceles triangle, [BC] = [CE].

[$\triangle ACB$] and [$\triangle DCE$] have two pairs of congruent sides.

So, by the _?_ Theorem, AB [>] DE.
Hinge

9. BE [>] CE

The longest side of a $\triangle$ is opposite the angle with the _?_ measure.
greatest

10. The diagram shows two paths that lead through a park. Would a jogger run a greater distance on Path A or Path B? Explain.

Path A; the paths have two pairs of congruent sides, but Path A angles off at 26°, while Path B angles off at 25°. The longer side is the one opposite the greater angle.

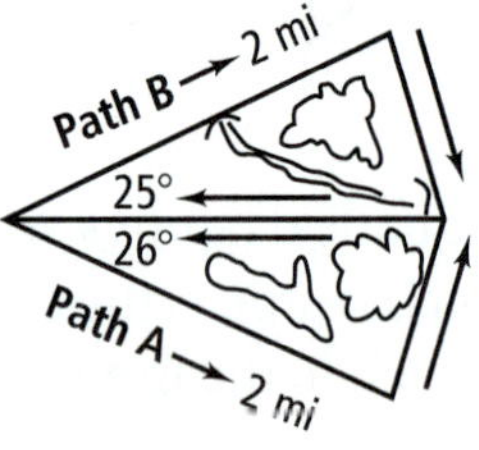

Write an inequality relating the given angle measures.

11. $m\angle M$ and $m\angle R$ $m\angle M > m\angle R$

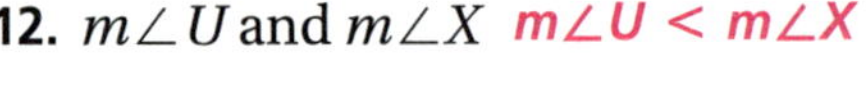

12. $m\angle U$ and $m\angle X$ $m\angle U < m\angle X$

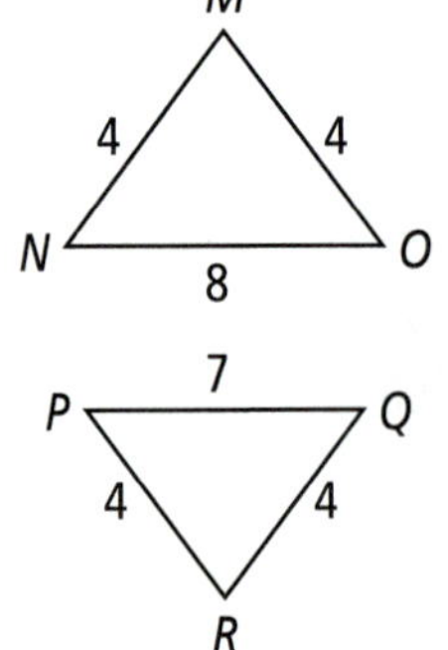

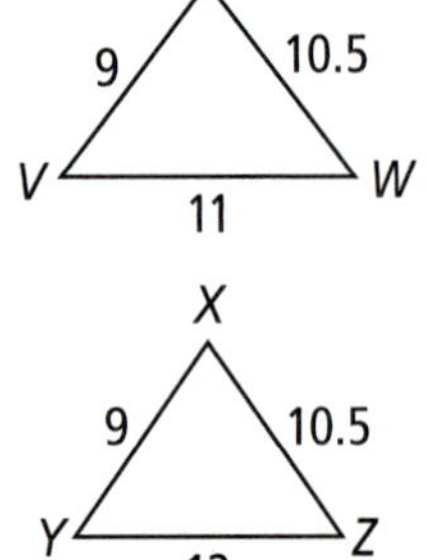

$\overline{MN}$, $\overline{MO}$, $\overline{PR}$, and $\overline{QR}$ are _?_. congruent

NO [>] PQ

Name ______________________ Class ____________ Date ____________

5-7 Standardized Test Prep

Inequalities in Two Triangles

Multiple Choice

For Exercises 1–5, choose the correct letter.

1. At which time is the distance between the tip of the hour hand and the tip of the minute hand on a clock the greatest? C

(A) 12:00 (B) 12:10 (C) 1:30 (D) 5:25

2. What is the range of possible values for x? G

(F) $\frac{2}{3} < x < 24$ (H) $0 < x < 48$

(G) $\frac{3}{2} < x < 24$ (I) $x > 24$

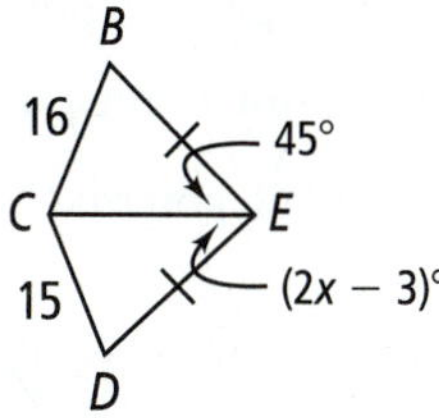

3. Which inequality relates BC and XY? A

(A) $BC < XY$ (C) $BC = XY$

(B) $BC > XY$ (D) $BC \geq XY$

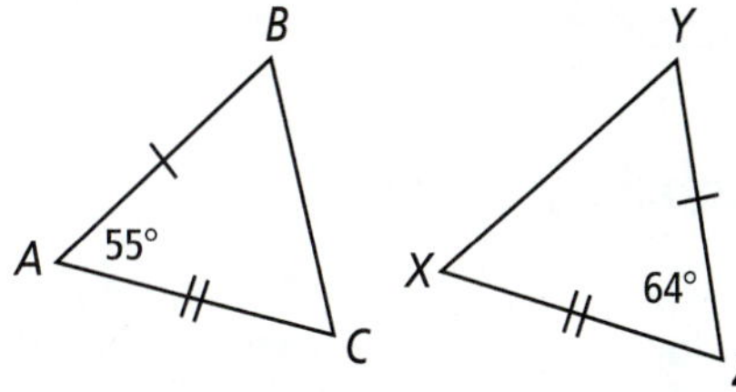

4. Four pairs of identical scissors lie on a table. Scissors 1 is opened 30°, scissors 2 is opened 29°, scissors 3 is opened 59°, and scissors 4 is opened 74°. In which pair of scissors is the distance between the tips of the scissor blades greatest? I

(F) scissors 1 (G) scissors 2 (H) scissors 3 (I) scissors 4

5. In $\triangle ABC$ and $\triangle DEF$, $AB = DE$, $CA = FD$, and $BC < EF$. Which of the following must be true? B

(A) $m\angle B < m\angle E$ (C) $m\angle C < m\angle F$

(B) $m\angle A < m\angle D$ (D) $m\angle B = m\angle E$

Short Response

6. What value must x be greater than, and what value must x be less than?

[2] x must be greater than 3 AND x must be less than 17.
[1] x must be greater than 3 OR x must be less than 17.
[0] No correct value for x is given.

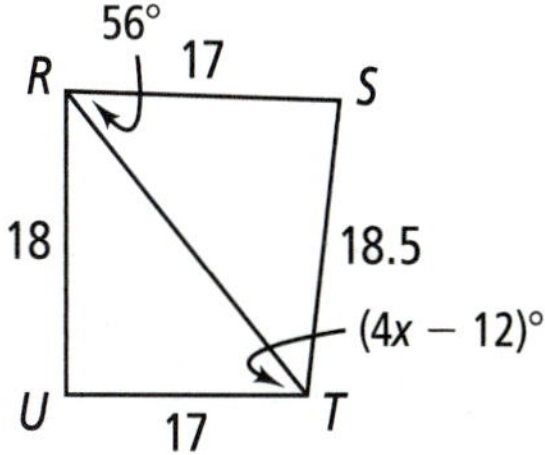

6-1 The Polygon Angle-Sum Theorems

Vocabulary

Review

1. Underline the correct word to complete the sentence.

   In a *convex* polygon, no point on the lines containing the sides of the polygon is in the interior / exterior of the polygon.

2. Cross out the polygon that is NOT *convex*.

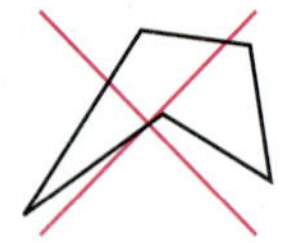

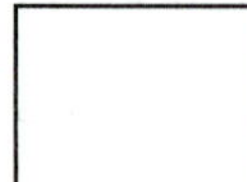

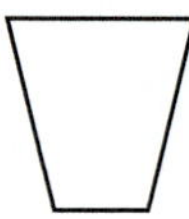

Vocabulary Builder

regular polygon (noun) REG yuh lur PAHL ih gahn

Definition: A **regular polygon** is a polygon that is both equilateral and equiangular.

Example: An equilateral triangle is a **regular polygon** with three congruent sides and three congruent angles.

Use Your Vocabulary

Underline the correct word(s) to complete each sentence.

3. The sides of a *regular polygon* are congruent / scalene .

4. A right triangle is / is not a *regular polygon.*

5. An isosceles triangle is / is not always a *regular polygon.*

Write *equiangular, equilateral,* or *regular* to identify each hexagon. Use each word once.

6. 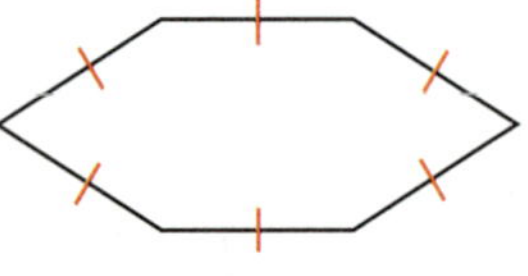

equilateral

7. 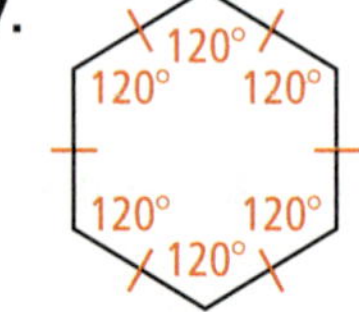

regular

8. 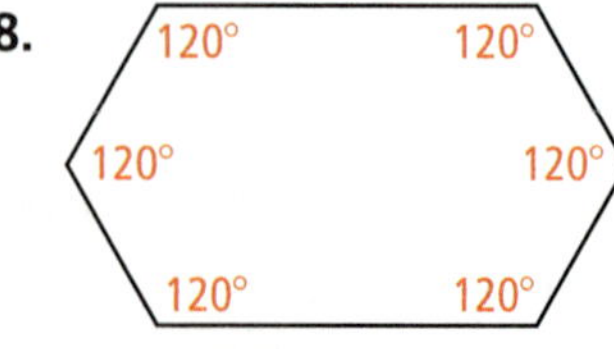

equiangular

Theorem 6-1 Polygon Angle-Sum Theorem and Corollary

Theorem 6-1 The sum of the measures of the interior angles of an n-gon is $(n - 2)180$.

Corollary The measure of each interior angle of a regular n-gon is $\frac{(n-2)180}{n}$.

9. When $n - 2 = 1$, the polygon is a(n) _?_. triangle

10. When $n - 2 = 2$, the polygon is a(n) _?_. quadrilateral

Problem 1 Finding a Polygon Angle Sum

Got It? **What is the sum of the interior angle measures of a 17-gon?**

11. Use the justifications below to find the sum.

sum $= (n - 2)180$	Polygon Angle-Sum Theorem
$= (17 - 2)180$	Substitute for n.
$= 15 \cdot 180$	Subtract.
$= 2700$	Simplify.

12. Draw diagonals from vertex A to check your answer.

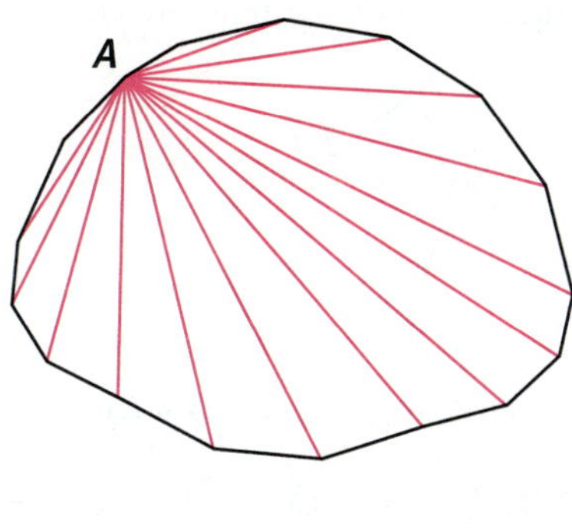

13. The sum of the interior angle measures of a 17-gon is 2700.

Problem 2 Using the Polygon Angle-Sum Theorem

Got It? **What is the measure of each interior angle in a regular nonagon?**

Underline the correct word or number to complete each sentence.

14. The interior angles in a regular polygon are congruent / different.

15. A regular nonagon has 7 / 8 / 9 congruent sides.

16. Use the Corollary to the Polygon Angle-Sum Theorem to find the measure of each interior angle in a regular nonagon.

$$\text{Measure of an angle} = \frac{(9 - 2)180}{9}$$

$$= \frac{(7)180}{9}$$

$$= 140$$

17. The measure of each interior angle in a regular nonagon is 140.

Problem 3 Using the Polygon Angle-Sum Theorem

Got It? What is $m\angle G$ in quadrilateral $EFGH$?

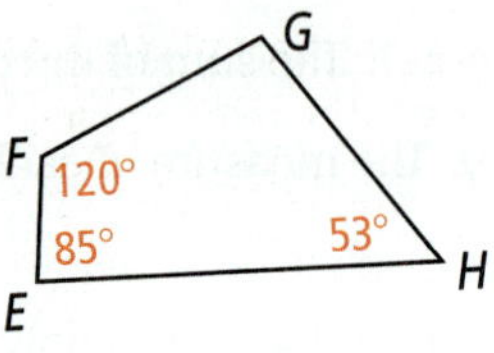

18. Use the Polygon Angle-Sum Theorem to find $m\angle G$ for $n = 4$.

$$m\angle E + m\angle F + m\angle G + m\angle H = (n - 2)180$$

$$m\angle E + m\angle F + m\angle G + m\angle H = (4 - 2)180$$

$$85 + 120 + m\angle G + 53 = 2 \cdot 180$$

$$m\angle G + 258 = 360$$

$$m\angle G = 102$$

19. $m\angle G$ in quadrilateral $EFGH$ is 102.

take note

Theorem 6-2 Polygon Exterior Angle-Sum Theorem

The sum of the measures of the exterior angles of a polygon, one at each vertex, is 360.

20. In the pentagon below, $m\angle 1 + m\angle 2 + m\angle 3 + m\angle 4 + m\angle 5 =$ 360.

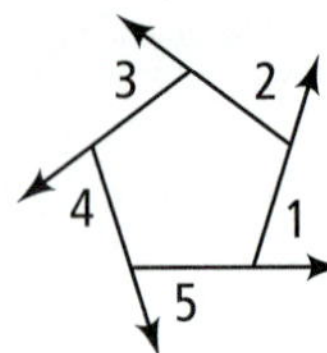

Use the Polygon Exterior Angle-Sum Theorem to find each measure.

21.

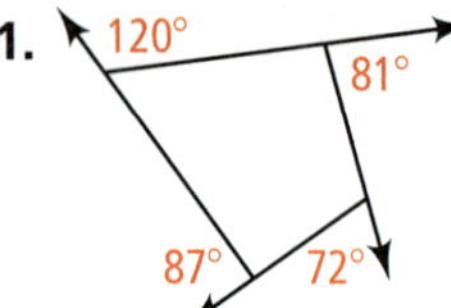

$120 + 81 + 72 + 87 = 360$

22.

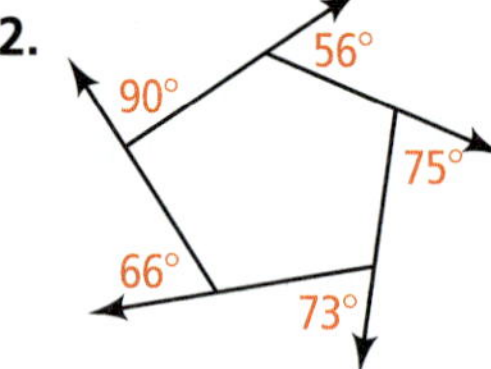

$90 + 56 + 75 + 73 + 66 = 360$

Problem 4 Finding an Exterior Angle Measure

Got It? What is the measure of an exterior angle of a regular nonagon?

Underline the correct number or word to complete each sentence.

23. Since the nonagon is regular, its interior angles are congruent / right.

24. The exterior angles are complements / supplements of the interior angles.

25. Since the nonagon is regular, its exterior angles are congruent / right.

26. The sum of the measures of the exterior angles of a polygon is 180 / 360.

27. A regular nonagon has 7 / 9 / 12 sides.

28. What is the measure of an exterior angle of a regular nonagon? Explain.

40°. Explanations may vary. Sample: Divide 360 by 9, the number of sides in a nonagon.

Lesson Check • Do you UNDERSTAND?

Error Analysis Your friend says that she measured an interior angle of a regular polygon as 130. Explain why this result is impossible.

29. Use indirect reasoning to find a contradiction.

Assume temporarily that a regular n-gon has a 130° interior angle.

angle sum	$= 130 \cdot n$	A regular n-gon has n congruent angles.
angle sum	$= (n - 2)180$	Polygon Angle-Sum Theorem
$130n$	$= (n - 2)180$	Use the Transitive Property of Equality.
$130n$	$= 180n - 360$	Use the Distributive Property.
$-50n$	$= -360$	Subtract $180n$ from each side.
n	$= 7.2$	Divide each side by -50.
n	$\neq 7.2$	The number of sides in a polygon is a whole number ≥ 3.

30. Explain why your friend's result is impossible.

Answers may vary. Sample: If each interior angle measures 130, then the regular polygon would have 7.2 sides. This is impossible because the number of sides is an integer greater than 2. So, each angle cannot be 130.

Math Success

Check off the vocabulary words that you understand.

☐ equilateral polygon ☐ equiangular polygon ☐ regular polygon

Rate how well you can *find angle measures of polygons.*

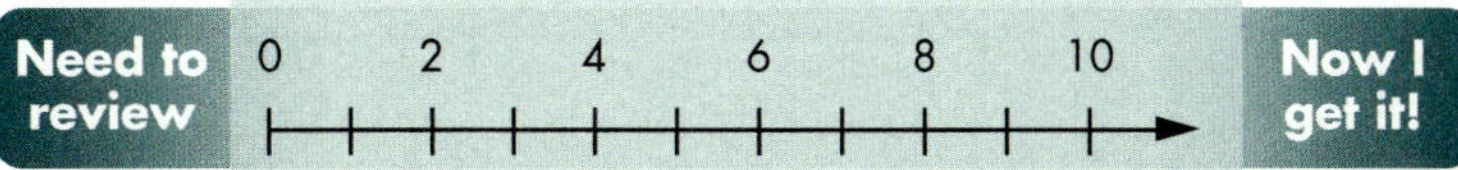

Name ______________________ Class ____________ Date ____________

6-1 Think About a Plan

The Polygon Angle-Sum Theorems

Reasoning Your friend says she has another way to find the sum of the angle measures of a polygon. She picks a point inside the polygon, draws a segment to each vertex, and counts the number of triangles. She multiplies the total by 180, and then subtracts 360 from the product. Does her method work? Explain.

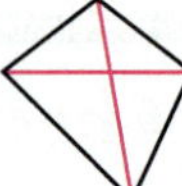

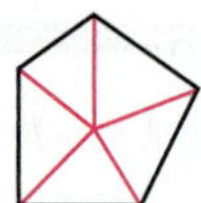

Understanding the Problem

1. According to the Polygon Angle-Sum Theorem, what is the relationship between the number of sides of a polygon and the sum of the measures of the interior angles of a polygon?

   The sum is always 180 times two less than the number of sides.

2. How can you write this relationship as an expression in which n is the number of sides? **$(n - 2)180$**

Planning the Solution

3. Mark a point near the center of each figure. Then draw a segment from that point to each vertex as described in the problem.

4. What is the relationship between the number of sides in a polygon and the number of triangles in that polygon?

   The number of triangles is the same as the number of sides.

5. What expression can you write to represent multiplying the number of triangles by 180 and then subtracting 360? Let n represent the number of sides. Explain how this expression relates to the picture you drew.

   $180n - 360$; the sum of the angles in the triangles is 180 times n, and this is always 360 (the degrees around the point in the center) more than the sum of the angles in the polygon.

Getting an Answer

6. Can you show that the two expressions you wrote are equal? Explain.

   Yes; if you apply the Distributive Property, the expressions become the same.

Name ______________________ Class ______________ Date ____________

6-1 Practice
Form K

The Polygon Angle-Sum Theorems

Find the sum of the angle measures of each polygon.

1. 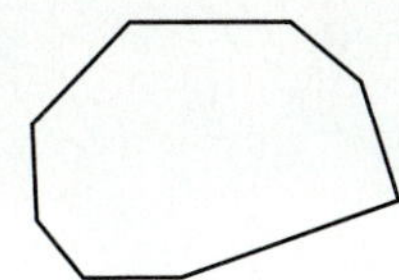

To start, determine the sum of the angles using the Polygon Angle-Sum Theorem.

Sum $= (n - 2)180$

$= (\boxed{8} - 2)180 = \boxed{1080}$

2. 21-gon **3420**

3. 42-gon **7200**

4. 50-gon **8640**

5. 205-gon **36,540**

Find the measure of one angle in each regular polygon.

6. 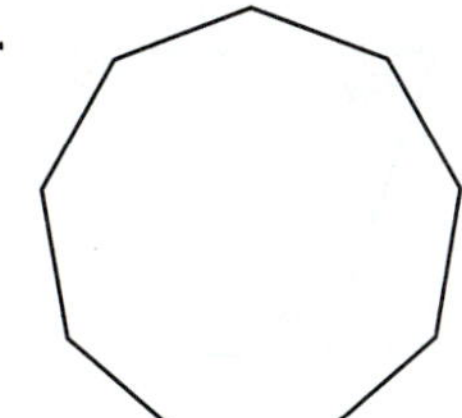

To start, write the formula used to calculate the measure of an angle of a regular polygon. Then substitute $n = 9$ into the formula.

$$\frac{(n - 2)180}{n} = \frac{(\boxed{9} - 2)180}{\boxed{9}} = \boxed{140}$$

7.  **120**

8.  **108**

Pentagon, Washington, D.C.

Find the missing angle measures.

9. To start, determine the sum of the angles using the Polygon Angle-Sum Theorem.

Sum $= (n - 2)180 = (6 - 2)180 = 720$

Write an equation relating each interior angle to the sum of the angles.

$n + 156 + 122 + 143 + 108 + 110 = 720$ **81**

10. 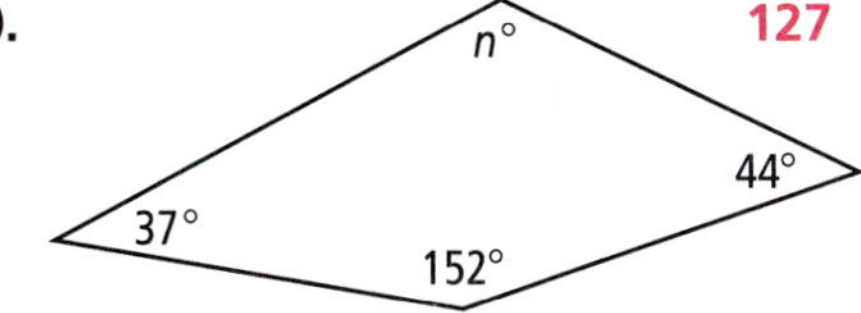

127

11. 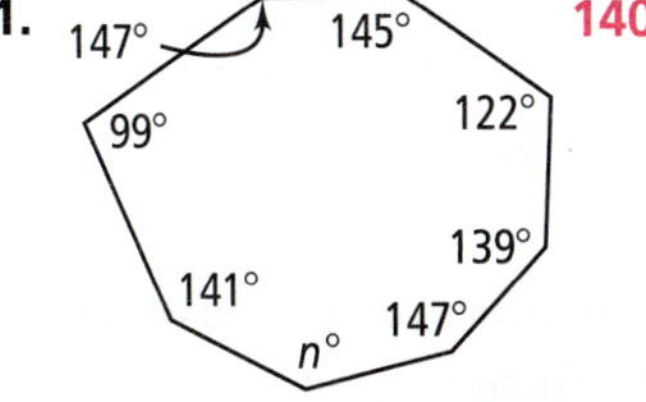

140

Name ______________________ Class ____________ Date ____________

6-1 Practice (continued) — Form K

The Polygon Angle-Sum Theorems

Find the measure of an exterior angle of each regular polygon.

12. 12-gon **30** **13.** 24-gon **15** **14.** 45-gon **8**

The sum of the angle measures of a polygon with *n* sides is given. Find *n*.

15. 900 **7** **16.** 1440 **10** **17.** 2340 **15**

18. Carly built a Ferris wheel using her construction toys. The frame of the wheel is a regular 16-gon. Find the sum of the angle measures of the Ferris wheel and the measure of one angle. **2520; 157.5**

Algebra Find the value of each variable.

19. 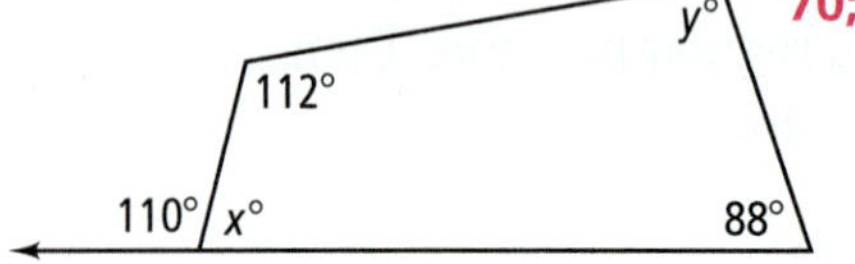

70; 90

20. 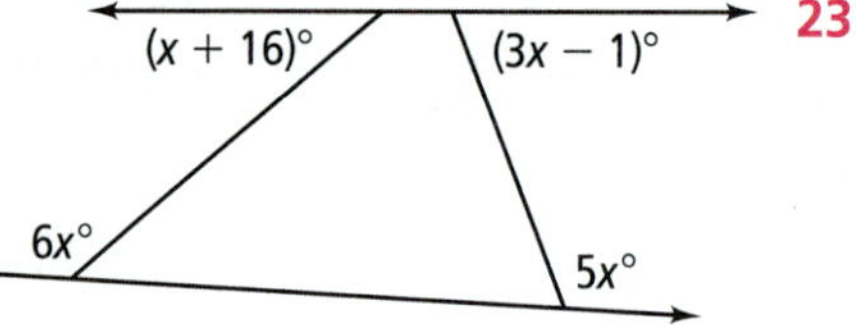

23

21. Your friend wants to build the picture frame shown at the right.

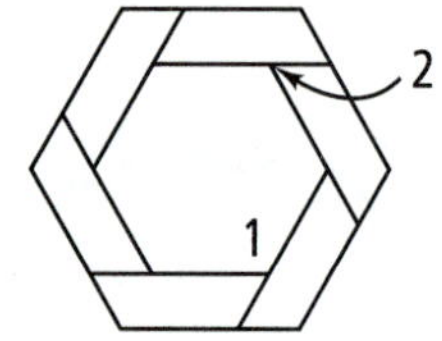

a. What regular polygon is the inside of the frame? **hexagon**

b. Find the measure of each numbered angle. **120; 60**

c. Reasoning If you extended one of the exterior sides of the outside of the frame, would the measure of the exterior angle be the same as the measure of ∠2? Explain.
Yes; they are both exterior angles of regular hexagons.

22. Caning chair seats first became popular in England in the 1600s. This method of weaving natural materials produces a pattern that contains several polygons. Identify the outlined polygon. Then, assuming that the polygon is regular, find the measure of each numbered angle. **octagon; 45; 135**

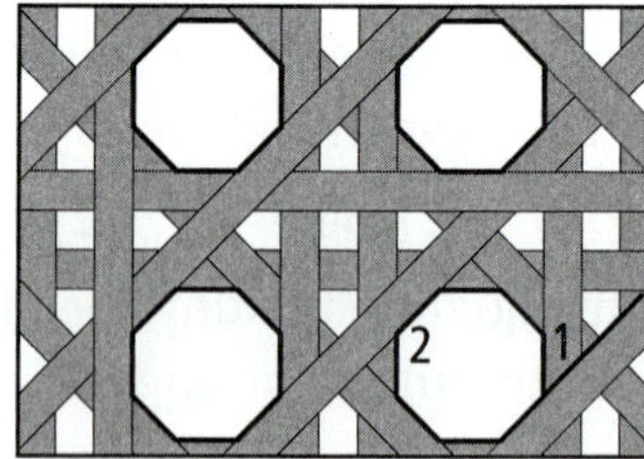

23. Algebra The measure of an interior angle of a regular polygon is four times the measure of an exterior angle of the same polygon. What is the name of the polygon? **decagon**

24. Reasoning The measure of the exterior angle of a regular polygon is 30. What is the measure of an interior angle of the same polygon? Explain.
150; interior and exterior angles are supplementary

Name ______________________ Class ____________ Date ____________

6-1 Standardized Test Prep

The Polygon Angle-Sum Theorems

Gridded Response

Solve each exercise and enter your answer on the grid provided.

1. What is the sum of the interior angle measures of a regular octagon?

2. What is the measure of one interior angle of a regular 12-gon?

3. What is the value of x in the regular polygon at the right?

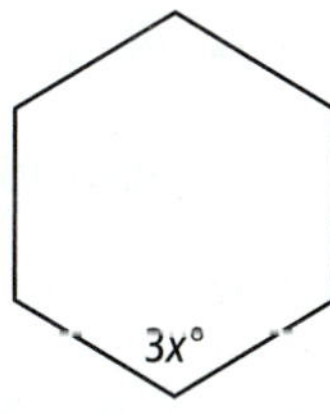

4. What is the measure of an exterior angle of a regular octagon?

5. If the measure of an exterior angle of a regular polygon is 24, how many sides does the polygon have?

Answers

1. 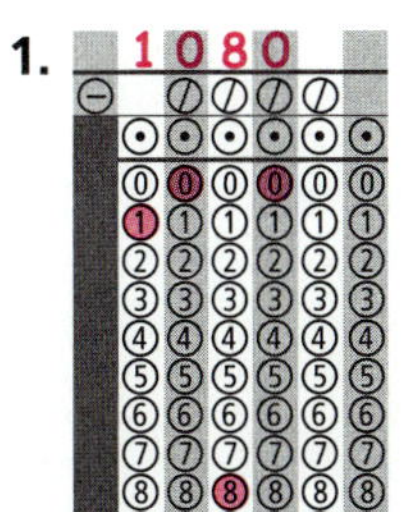

2. 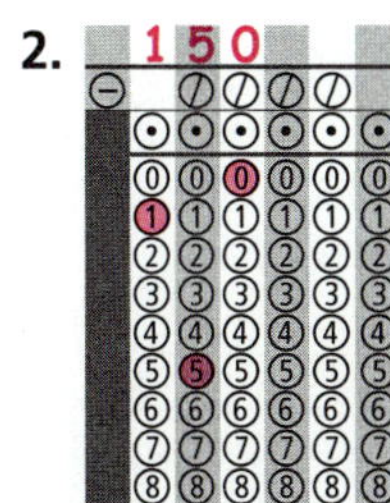

3. 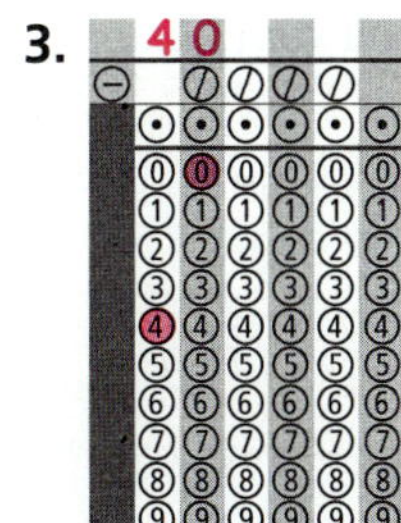

4. 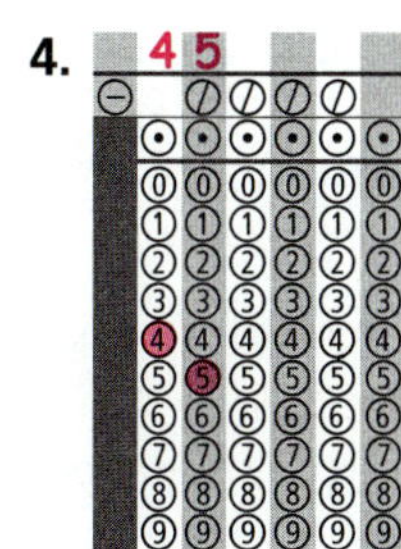

5. 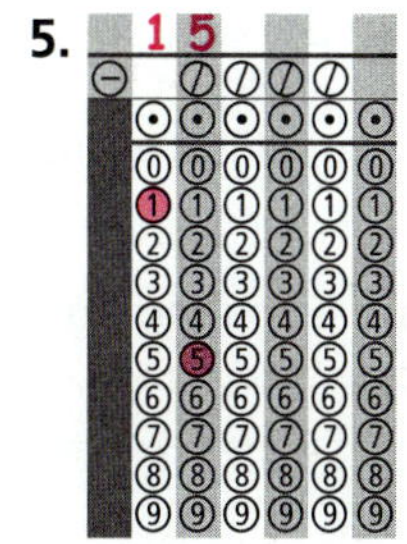

6-2 PART 1 Properties of Parallelograms

Vocabulary

Review

1. *Supplementary* angles are two angles whose measures sum to 180.
2. Suppose $\angle X$ and $\angle Y$ are *supplementary*. If $m\angle X = 75$, then $m\angle Y =$ 105.

Underline the correct word to complete each sentence.

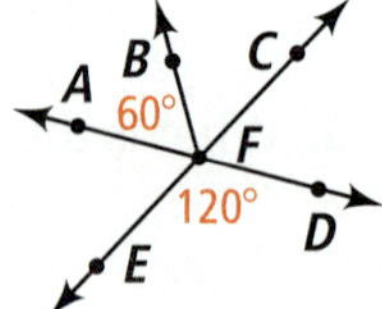

3. A linear pair is complementary / *supplementary*.
4. $\angle AFB$ and $\angle EFD$ at the right are complementary / *supplementary*.

Vocabulary Builder

consecutive (adjective) **kun** SEK **yoo tiv**

Definition: **Consecutive** items follow one after another in uninterrupted order.

Math Usage: **Consecutive** angles of a polygon share a common side.

Examples: The numbers −3, −2, −1, 0, 1, 2, 3, . . . are **consecutive** integers.

Non-Example: The letters A, B, C, F, P, . . . are NOT **consecutive** letters of the alphabet.

Use Your Vocabulary

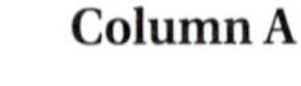

Use the diagram at the right. Draw a line from each angle in Column A to a *consecutive* angle in Column B.

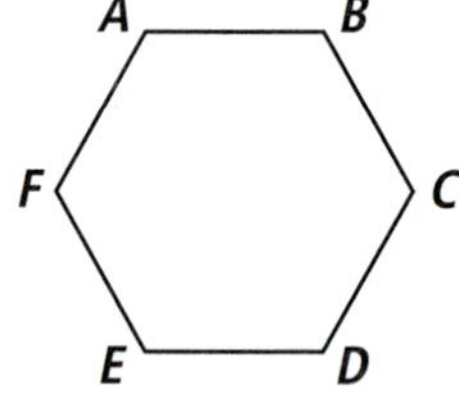

	Column A	Column B
5.	$\angle A$	$\angle F$
6.	$\angle C$	$\angle E$
7.	$\angle D$	$\angle D$

Write the next two *consecutive* months in each sequence.

8. January, February, March, April, May, June
9. December, November, October, September, August, July

take note

Theorems 6-3, 6-4, and 6-5

Theorem 6-3 If a quadrilateral is a parallelogram, then its opposite sides are congruent.

Theorem 6-4 If a quadrilateral is a parallelogram, then its consecutive angles are supplementary.

Theorem 6-5 If a quadrilateral is a parallelogram, then its opposite angles are congruent.

Use the diagram at the right for Exercises 10 and 11.

10. Mark parallelogram *ABCD* to model Theorem 6-3 and Theorem 6-5.

11. Circle the angle pairs that are supplementary.

$\angle A$ and $\angle B$	$\angle A$ and $\angle C$	$\angle A$ and $\angle D$
$\angle B$ and $\angle C$	$\angle B$ and $\angle D$	$\angle C$ and $\angle D$

Problem 1 Using Consecutive Angles

Got It? **Suppose you adjust the lamp so that $m\angle S = 86$. What is $m\angle R$ in $\square PQRS$?**

Underline the correct word or number to complete each statement.

12. $\angle R$ and $\angle S$ are adjacent / consecutive angles, so they are supplementary.

13. $m\angle R + m\angle S =$ 90 / 180

14. Now find $m\angle R$.

$m\angle R + 86 = 180$
$m\angle R = 180 - 86$
$m\angle R = 94$

15. $m\angle R =$ 94 .

Problem 2 Using Properties of Parallelograms in a Proof

Got It? **Use the diagram at the right.**

Given: $\square ABCD$, $\overline{AK} \cong \overline{MK}$ **Prove:** $\angle BCD \cong \angle CMD$

16. Circle the classification of $\triangle AKM$.

equilateral isosceles right

17. Complete the proof. The reasons are given.

Statements	Reasons
1) $\overline{AK} \cong \overline{MK}$	1) Given
2) $\angle DAB \cong \angle CMD$	2) Angles opposite congruent sides of a triangle are congruent.
3) $\angle BCD \cong \angle DAB$	3) Opposite angles of a parallelogram are congruent.
4) $\angle BCD \cong \angle CMD$	4) Transitive Property of Congruence

Lesson Check • Do you know HOW?

Use the diagram of ▱$ABCD$ to find the value of x.

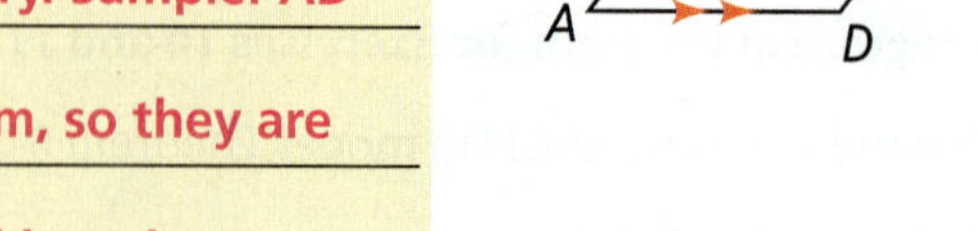

18. What do you know about the lengths of $\overline{AB}$ and $\overline{CD}$? Explain.

The lengths are equal. Explanations may vary. Sample: $\overline{AB}$ and $\overline{CD}$ are opposite sides of a parallelogram, so they are congruent. Congruent segments have equal lengths.

19. Use the expressions for the lengths of $\overline{AB}$ and $\overline{CD}$ to write an equation.

$2x - 3 = x + 2$

20. Use your equation from Exercise 19 to find the value of x.

$2x - 3 = x + 2$

$x - 3 = 2$

$x = 5$

21. The value of x is 5.

Lesson Check • Do you UNDERSTAND?

Reasoning **If you know one angle measure of a parallelogram, how do you find the other three angle measures? Explain.**

Underline the correct word to complete each sentence.

22. If a quadrilateral is a parallelogram, then its consecutive angles are complementary / <u>supplementary</u>.

23. If a quadrilateral is parallelogram, then its consecutive / <u>opposite</u> angles are congruent.

24. Look at ▱$QRST$ at the right. Suppose you know $m\angle Q$. Explain how you can find the other three angle measures.

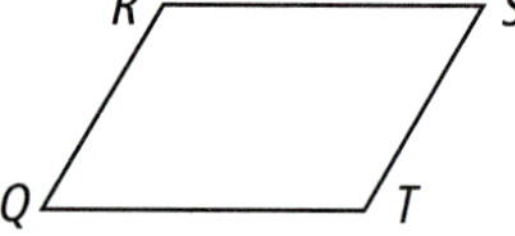

Explanations may vary. Sample: $m\angle S = m\angle Q$ because they are opposite angles. $m\angle R = 180 - m\angle Q$ because they are consecutive and supplementary angles. $m\angle T = m\angle R$ because they are opposite angles.

6-2 PART 2 Properties of Parallelograms

Vocabulary

Review

1. **Multiple Choice** What does *bisect* mean?

   (A) to cross at a point
   (C) to divide into two equal parts
   (B) to reflect across a line
   (D) to form a right angle

Use the diagram at the right for Exercises 2 and 3.

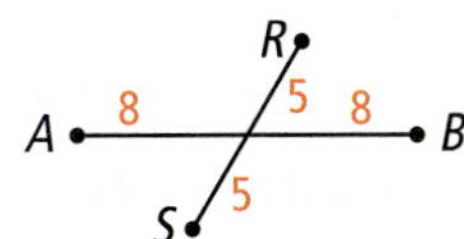

2. $\overline{AB}$ *bisects* $\overline{RS}$.

3. $\overline{RS}$ is a *bisector* of $\overline{AB}$.

Vocabulary Builder

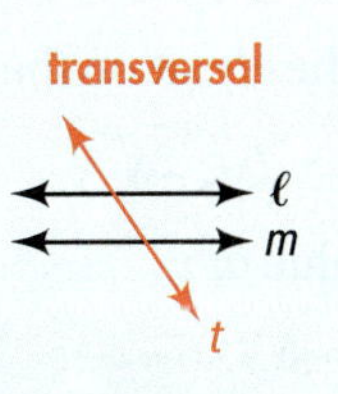

transversal (noun) **trans VUR sul**

Definition: A **transversal** is a line that intersects two or more coplanar lines at distinct points.

Main Idea: If three (or more) parallel lines cut off congruent segments on one **transversal,** then they cut off congruent segments on every **transversal.**

Use Your Vocabulary

4. Underline the correct word(s) to complete the sentence.

   A *transversal* intersects / is parallel to two or more coplanar lines.

Use the diagram at the right for Exercises 5 and 6.

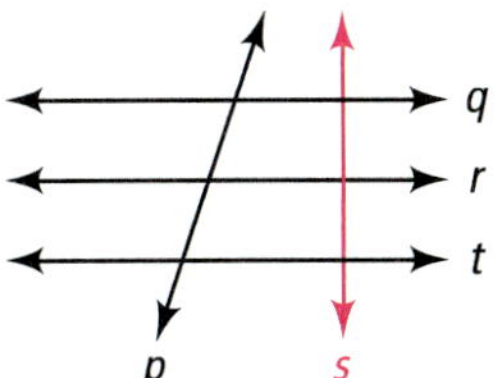

5. Circle *the transversal(s).*

   p q r t

6. Draw another *transversal.* Label it s. Answers may vary. Sample:

Complete each sentence with the number of angles formed.

7. A transversal that intersects two lines forms 8 angles.

8. A transversal that intersects four lines forms 16 angles.

take note: Theorems 6-6 and 6-7

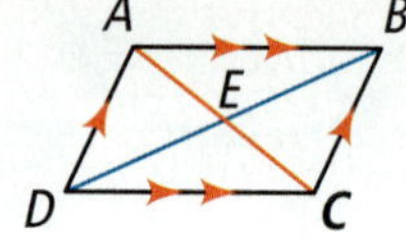

Theorem 6-6 If a quadrilateral is a parallelogram, then its diagonals bisect each other.

9. Use the diagram at the right. If $ABCD$ is a $\square$, then $\overline{AE} =$ **$\overline{CE}$** and $\overline{BE} \cong$ **$\overline{DE}$**.

Theorem 6-7 If three (or more) parallel lines cut off congruent segments on one transversal, then they cut off congruent segments on every transversal.

Use the diagram at the right for Exercises 10 and 11.

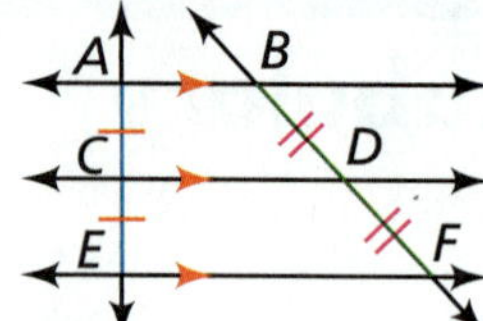

10. If $\overleftrightarrow{AB} \parallel \overleftrightarrow{CD} \parallel \overleftrightarrow{EF}$ and $\overline{AC} \cong \overline{CE}$, then $\overline{BD} \cong$ **$\overline{DF}$**.

11. Mark the diagram to show your answer to Exercise 10.

Problem 3 Using Algebra to Find Lengths

Got It? **Find the values of x and y in $\square PQRS$ at the right. What are PR and SQ?**

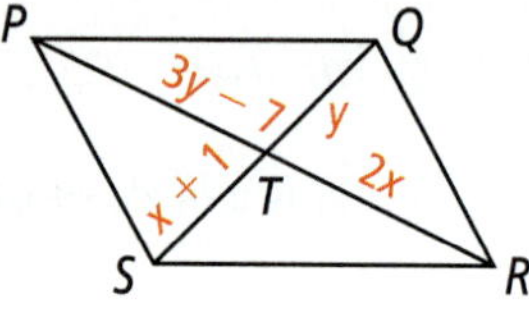

12. Circle the reason $\overline{PT} \cong \overline{TR}$ and $\overline{ST} \cong \overline{TQ}$.

(circled) Diagonals of a parallelogram bisect each other.	Opposite sides of a parallelogram are congruent.	$\overline{PR}$ is the perpendicular bisector of $\overline{QS}$.

13. Cross out the equation that is NOT true.

$3(x + 1) - 7 = 2x$ $y = x + 1$ ~~$3y - 7 = x + 1$~~ $3y - 7 = 2x$

14. Find the value of x.

$$3(x + 1) - 7 = 2x$$
$$3x + 3 - 7 = 2x$$
$$3x - 4 = 2x$$
$$x = 4$$

15. Find the value of y.

$$y = x + 1$$
$$y = 4 + 1$$
$$y = 5$$

16. Find PT.

$PT = 3($ **5** $) - 7$

$=$ **15** $- 7$

$=$ **8**

17. Find ST.

$ST =$ **4** $+ 1$

$=$ **5**

18. Find PR.

$PR = 2($ **8** $)$

$=$ **16**

19. Find SQ.

$SQ = 2($ **5** $)$

$=$ **10**

20. Explain why you do not need to find TR and TQ after finding PT and ST.

Answers may vary. Sample: The diagonals of a parallelogram bisect each other, so $PT = TR$ and $ST = TQ$.

Problem 4 Using Parallel Lines and Transversals

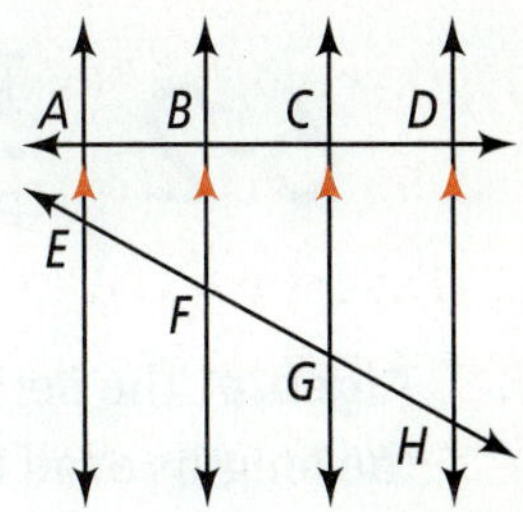

Got It? **In the figure at the right, $\overleftrightarrow{AE} \parallel \overleftrightarrow{BF} \parallel \overleftrightarrow{CG} \parallel \overleftrightarrow{DH}$. If $EF = FG = GH = 6$ and $AD = 15$, what is CD?**

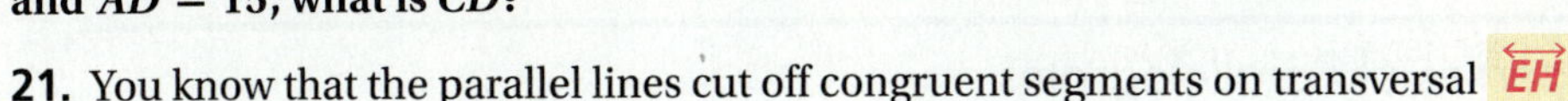

21. You know that the parallel lines cut off congruent segments on transversal $\overleftrightarrow{EH}$.

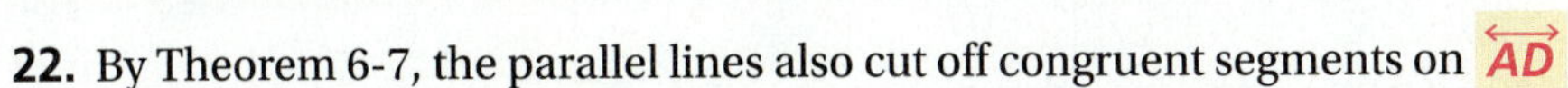

22. By Theorem 6-7, the parallel lines also cut off congruent segments on $\overleftrightarrow{AD}$.

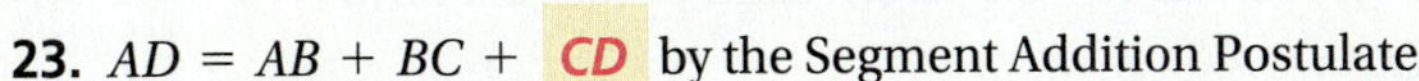

23. $AD = AB + BC + CD$ by the Segment Addition Postulate.

24. $AB = BC = CD$, so $AD = 3 \cdot CD$. Then $CD = \frac{1}{3} \cdot AD$.

25. You know that $AD = 15$, so $CD = \frac{1}{3} \cdot 15 = 5$.

Lesson Check • Do you UNDERSTAND?

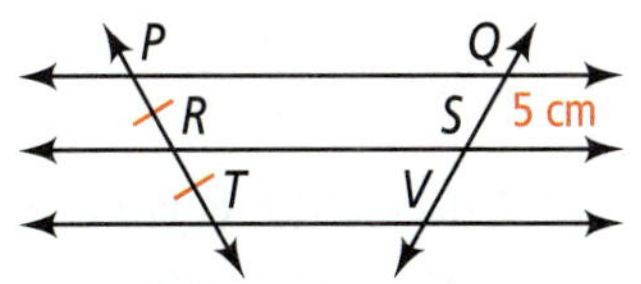

Error Analysis **Your classmate says that $QV = 10$. Explain why the statement may not be correct.**

26. Place a ✓ in the box if you are given the information. Place an ✗ if you are not given the information.

- ✓ three lines cut by two transversals
- ✗ three parallel lines cut by two transversals
- ✓ congruent segments on one transversal

27. What needs to be true for QV to equal 10?

The lines cut by transversals need to be parallel.

28. Explain why your classmate's statement may not be correct.

Answers may vary. Sample: The lines may not be parallel.

Math Success

Check off the vocabulary words that you understand.

☐ parallelogram ☐ opposite sides ☐ opposite angles ☐ consecutive angles

Rate how well you *understand parallelograms.*

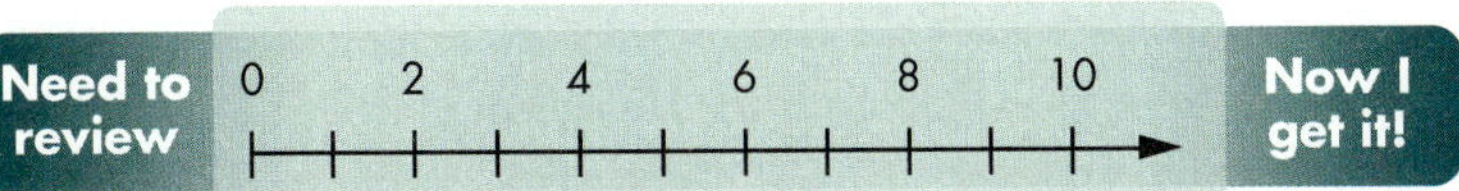

Name ______________________ Class ____________ Date ____________

6-2 Think About a Plan

Properties of Parallelograms

Algebra The perimeter of ▱*ABCD* is 92 cm. *AD* is 7 cm more than twice *AB*. Find the lengths of all four sides of ▱*ABCD*.

1. What is perimeter? **the sum of the measures of the outside edges of the figure**

2. Write a formula to find the perimeter of ▱*ABCD* with side lengths *AB, BC, CD,* and *DA*. **$P = AB + BC + CD + DA$**

3. What is the relationship between opposite sides of a parallelogram?

They are congruent.

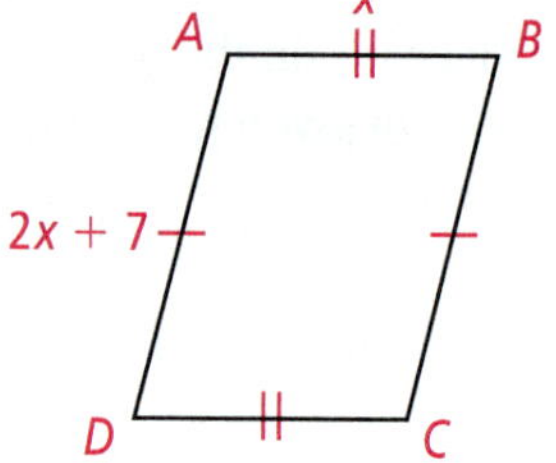

4. Mark the vertices of the parallelogram at the right so it is ▱*ABCD*. Then mark the appropriate sides congruent.

5. How could you use the relationship between opposite sides of a parallelogram to rewrite the formula you wrote in Step 2?

Since opposite sides are congruent, $P = 2AD + 2AB$.

6. Now look back at the relationship between the sides as described in the problem. Let *x* represent *AB*. What expression can you write to represent *AD*? **$2x + 7$**

7. Write the side lengths from Step 6 on the parallelogram above.

8. How can you use these expressions in the perimeter formula you wrote in Step 5?

Substitute $2x + 7$ for *AD*, and x for *AB*.

9. Rewrite the perimeter formula using the expressions and the value of the perimeter given in the problem. **$92 = 2(2x + 7) + 2x$**

10. What property can you use to simplify the equation? Rewrite the simplified equation and then solve for *x*.

Distributive Property; $92 = 4x + 14 + 2x$; $x = 13$

11. Now substitute the value of *x* back into the expression to find *AD*. What is the length of each of the four sides of *ABCD*?

$AB = 13$ cm; $BC = 33$ cm; $CD = 13$ cm; $AD = 33$ cm

Name ______________________ Class ____________ Date ____________

6-2 Practice — Form K

Properties of Parallelograms

Find the value of *x* in each parallelogram.

1. $x°$ $51°$ **129**

To start, identify the relationship between the marked angles in the diagram.

The marked angles are consecutive angles. By Theorem 6-4, the angles are supplementary.

Then write an equation: $\boxed{x}$ + 51 = 180

2. **104**

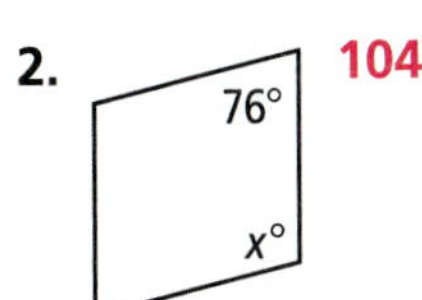

3. $x°$ $154°$ **26**

4. **98**

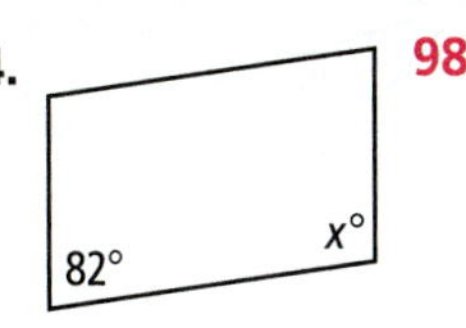

Algebra Find the values of the variables in ▱*DEFG*.

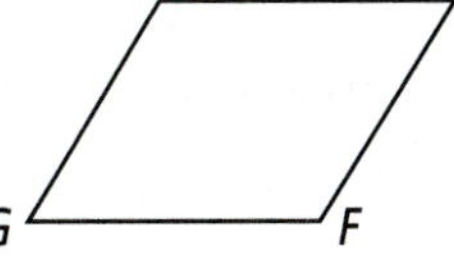

5. $DG = 2x + 2$, $EF = 3x - 3$, $DE = 3x + 1$, $GF = 2x + 6$ **5**

6. $DG = 4a$, $EF = 5a - 6$, $DE = 3a + 2$, $GF = 2a + 8$ **6**

7. $DG = 2r + 3$, $EF = 3r - 3$, $DE = 2r + 6$, $GF = 4r - 6$ **6**

8. $DG = 2t - 10$, $EF = t + 5$, $DE = t + 15$, $GF = 2t$ **15**

Algebra Find the value of *b* in each parallelogram. Then find each side length or angle measure.

9. **6; 20.5; 11.7** **10.** **15; 55; 125**

11. Developing Proof Complete this two-column proof.

Given: ▱*QRST*, ▱*TSVU*

Prove: $\overline{RQ} \cong \overline{VU}$

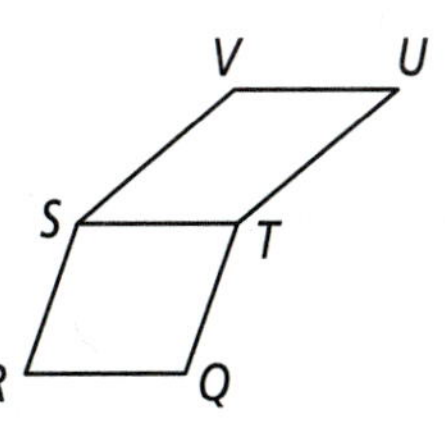

Statements	Reasons
1) ▱*QRST*, ▱*TSVU*	1) _?_ **Given**
2) $\overline{RQ} \cong \overline{ST}$, _?_ **$\overline{ST} \cong \overline{VU}$**	2) Theorem 6-3 Opposite sides of ▱
3) $\overline{RQ} \cong \overline{VU}$	3) _?_ **Trans. Prop. of ≅**

Name ______________________ Class ____________ Date ____________

6-2 Practice (continued)

Form K

Properties of Parallelograms

Algebra Find the value of each variable in each parallelogram.

12. 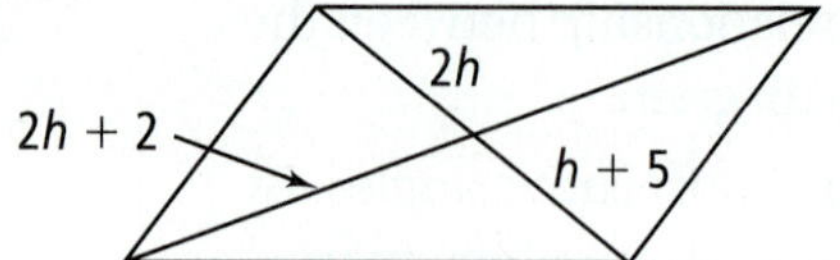

5

13. 3d
d + 3
2d + 1
2

14. 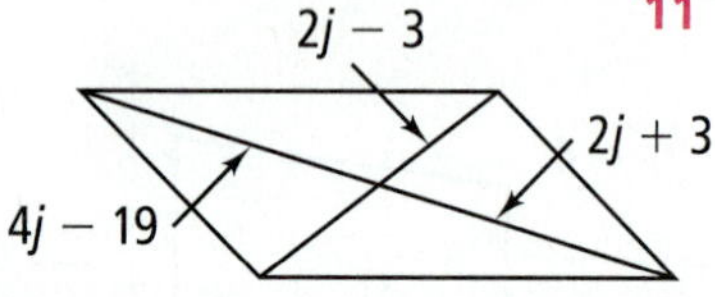

11

15. 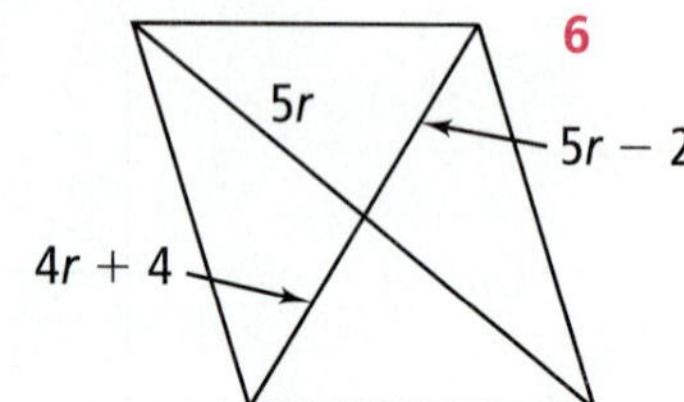

6

In the figure, $GH = HI = IJ$. Find each length.

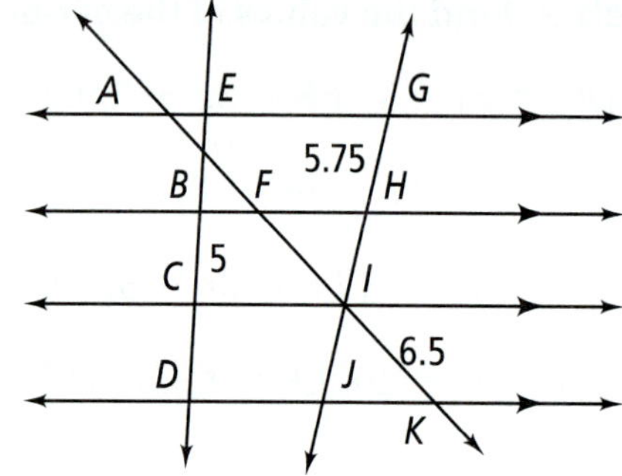

16. EB 5

17. BD 10

18. AF 6.5

19. AK 19.5

20. CD 5

21. GJ 17.25

Find the value of a in each parallelogram.

22. 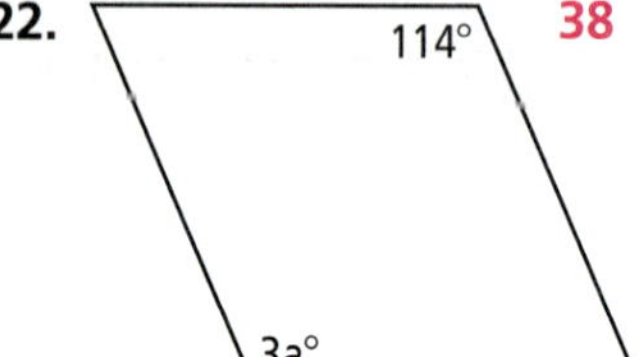

38

23. 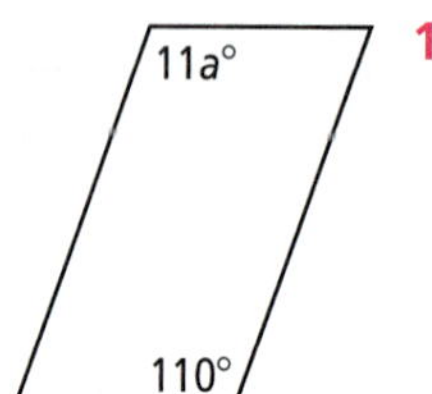

10

24. 15 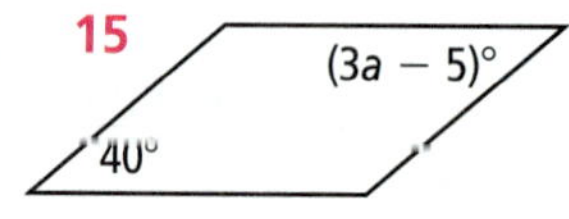

25. The length of one side of a parallelogram is 3 more than twice the length of the adjacent side. The perimeter of the parallelogram is 30 cm. Find the lengths of the two adjacent sides of the parallelogram. 4 cm and 11 cm

26. **Reasoning** A classmate draws a parallelogram for which one side is twice as long as the other. If one side is 26 units, what are all the possible lengths of the perimeter? 78 units or 156 units

Name ______________________ Class ____________ Date ____________

6-2 Standardized Test Prep

Properties of Parallelograms

Multiple Choice

For Exercises 1–5, choose the correct letter.

1. In $\square ABCD$, $m\angle A = 53$. What is $m\angle C$? **B**

Ⓐ 37 Ⓑ 53 Ⓒ 127 Ⓓ 307

2. What is the value of x in $\square QRST$? **I**

Ⓕ 16 Ⓗ 8

Ⓖ 12 Ⓘ 4

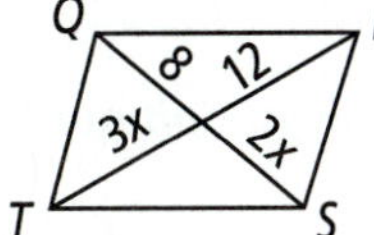

3. What is the value of y in $\square LMNO$? **C**

Ⓐ 4 Ⓒ 12

Ⓑ 6 Ⓓ 24

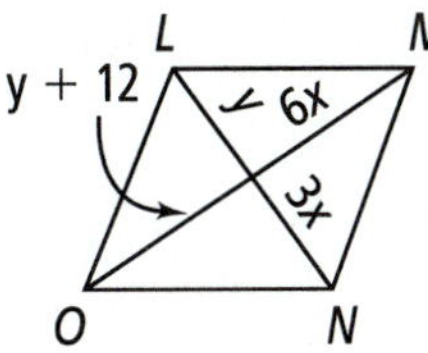

4. What is $m\angle 1$ in this parallelogram? **H**

Ⓕ 20 Ⓗ 80

Ⓖ 60 Ⓘ 100

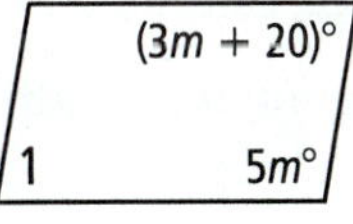

5. What is $m\angle 2$ in this parallelogram? **C**

Ⓐ 115 Ⓒ 15

Ⓑ 50 Ⓓ 2

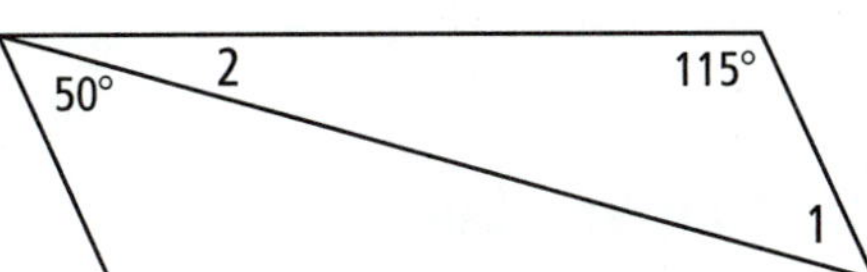

Extended Response

6. Figure $ABCD$ is a parallelogram. What are four geometric attributes you know because $ABCD$ is a parallelogram?

[4] Student lists four attributes from the following list of seven attributes: $\overline{AB} \cong \overline{CD}$, $\overline{BC} \cong \overline{DA}$, $\angle A \cong \angle C$, $\angle B \cong \angle D$, $\overline{AB} \parallel \overline{CD}$, $\overline{BC} \parallel \overline{DA}$, and diagonals bisect each other. [3] Student lists three attributes. [2] Student lists two attributes. [1] Student lists one attribute. [0] Student gives no answer or wrong answer based on an inappropriate plan.

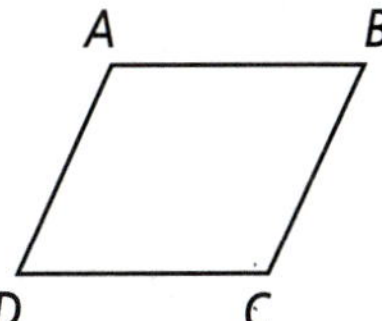

6-3 Proving That a Quadrilateral Is a Parallelogram

Vocabulary

Review

1. Does a pentagon have *opposite sides*? Yes / No (circled: No)

2. Does an n-gon have *opposite sides* if n is an odd number? Yes / No (circled: No)

Draw a line from each side in Column A to the *opposite side* in Column B.

	Column A	Column B
3.	$\overline{AB}$	$\overline{BC}$
4.	$\overline{AD}$	$\overline{DC}$

(Lines drawn: $\overline{AB}$ — $\overline{DC}$; $\overline{AD}$ — $\overline{BC}$)

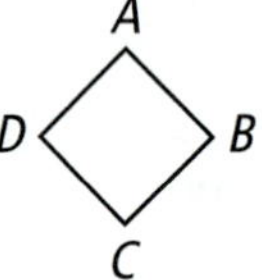

Vocabulary Builder

parallelogram (noun) pa ruh LEL uh gram

Definition: A **parallelogram** is a quadrilateral with two pairs of opposite sides parallel. Opposite sides may include arrows to show the sides are parallel.

Related Words: square, rectangle, rhombus

parallelogram

P S Q R

Use Your Vocabulary

Write P if the statement describes a *parallelogram* or NP if it does not.

NP **5.** octagon

NP **6.** five congruent sides

P **7.** regular quadrilateral

Write P if the figure appears to be a *parallelogram* or NP if it does not.

P **8.** 

NP **9.** 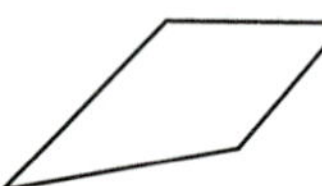

P **10.** 

take note

Theorems 6-8 through 6-12

Theorem 6-8 If both pairs of opposite sides of a quadrilateral are congruent, then the quadrilateral is a parallelogram.

Theorem 6-9 If an angle of a quadrilateral is supplementary to both of its consecutive angles, then the quadrilateral is a parallelogram.

Theorem 6-10 If both pairs of opposite angles of a quadrilateral are congruent, then the quadrilateral is a parallelogram.

Theorem 6-11 If the diagonals of a quadrilateral bisect each other, then the quadrilateral is a parallelogram.

Theorem 6-12 If one pair of opposite sides of a quadrilateral is both congruent and parallel, then the quadrilateral is a parallelogram.

Use the diagram at the right and Theorems 6-8 through 6-12 for Exercises 11–16.

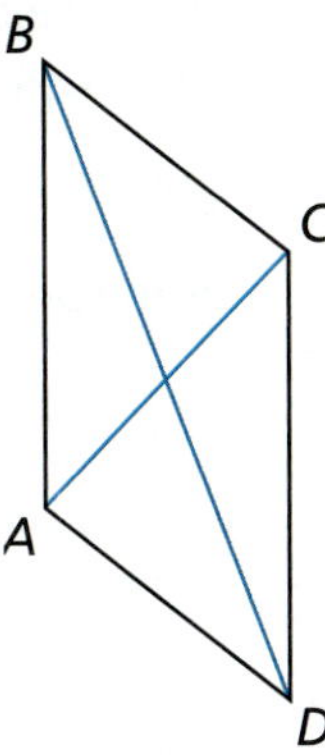

11. If $\overline{AB} \cong$ **CD**, and $\overline{BC} \cong$ **DA**, then *ABCD* is a ▱.

12. If $m\angle A + m\angle B =$ **180** and $m\angle$ **A** $+ m\angle D = 180$, then *ABCD* is a ▱.

13. If $\angle A \cong \angle$ **C** and $\angle$ **B** $\cong \angle D$, then *ABCD* is a ▱.

14. If $\overline{AE} \cong$ **CE** and $\overline{BE} \cong$ **DE**, then *ABCD* is a ▱.

15. If $\overline{BC} \cong$ **DA** and $\overline{BC} \parallel$ **DA**, then *ABCD* is a ▱.

16. If $\overline{CD} \cong$ **BA** and $\overline{CD} \parallel$ **BA**, then *ABCD* is a ▱.

Problem 1 Finding Values for Parallelograms

Got It? **Use the diagram at the right. For what values of *x* and *y* must *EFGH* be a parallelogram?**

E F G H
$(3y - 2)°$
$(4x + 13)°$
$(y + 10)°$
$(12x + 7)°$

17. Circle the equation you can use to find the value of *y*. Underline the equation you can use to find the value of *x*.

$y + 10 = 3y - 2$ $\qquad$ $y + 10 = 4x + 13$ (underlined) $\qquad$ $(y + 10) + (3y - 2) = 180$ (circled)

18. Find *y*.

$(y + 10) + (3y - 2) = 180$
$4y + 8 = 180$
$4y = 172$
$y = 43$

19. Find *x*.

$y + 10 = 4x + 13$
$43 + 10 = 4x + 13$
$40 = 4x$
$10 = x$

20. What equation could you use to find the value of *x* first? $(4x + 13) + (12x + 7) = 180$

21. *EFGH* must be a parallelogram for $x =$ **10** and $y =$ **43**.

Problem 2 Deciding Whether a Quadrilateral Is a Parallelogram

Got It? **Can you prove that the quadrilateral is a parallelogram based on the given information? Explain.**

D E G F

Given: $\overline{EF} \cong \overline{GD}$, $\overline{DE} \parallel \overline{FG}$

Prove: *DEFG* is a parallelogram.

22. Circle the angles that are consecutive with $\angle G$.

 $\angle D$ $\angle E$ 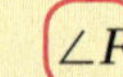 $\angle F$

23. Underline the correct word to complete the sentence.

Same-side interior angles formed by parallel lines cut by a transversal are complementary / congruent / supplementary.

24. Circle the interior angles on the same side of transversal $\overline{DG}$. Underline the interior angles on the same side of transversal $\overline{EF}$.

 $\angle D$ $\angle E$  $\angle F$ 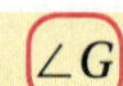 $\angle G$

25. Can you prove *DEFG* is a parallelogram? Explain.

No. Explanations may vary. Sample: An angle of *DEFG* is not supplementary to both of its consecutive angles, so Theorem 6-9 does not apply.

Problem 3 Identifying Parallelograms

Got It? **Reasoning** **A truck sits on the platform of a vehicle lift. Two moving arms raise the platform. What is the maximum height that the vehicle lift can elevate the truck? Explain.**

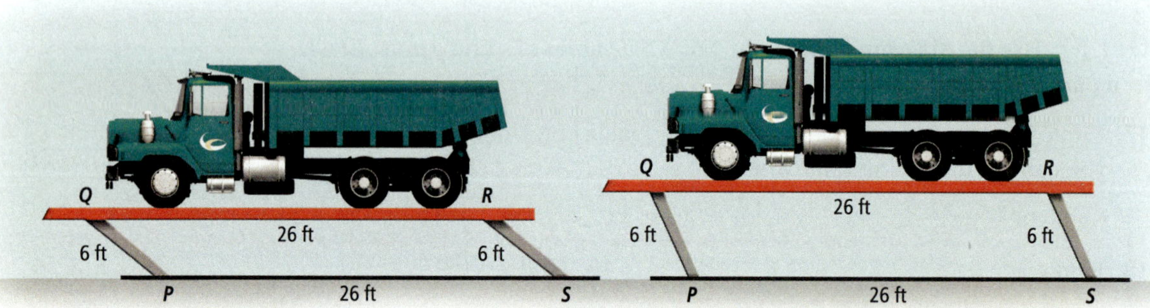

26. Do the lengths of the opposite sides change as the truck is lifted? Yes / No

27. The least and greatest possible angle measures for $\angle P$ and $\angle Q$ are 0 and 90.

28. The greatest possible height is when $m\angle P$ and $m\angle Q$ are 90.

29. What is the maximum height that the vehicle lift can elevate the truck? Explain.

6 ft. Explanations may vary. Sample: The maximum height occurs when the angles are 90° and *PQRS* is a rectangle.

Lesson Check • Do you UNDERSTAND?

Compare and Contrast **How is Theorem 6-11 in this lesson different from Theorem 6-6 in the previous lesson? In what situations should you use each theorem? Explain.**

For each theorem, circle the hypothesis and underline the conclusion.

30. Theorem 6-6

If a quadrilateral is a parallelogram, then its diagonals bisect each other.

31. Theorem 6-11

If the diagonals of a quadrilateral bisect each other, then the quadrilateral is a parallelogram.

Draw a line from each statement in Column A to the corresponding diagram in Column B.

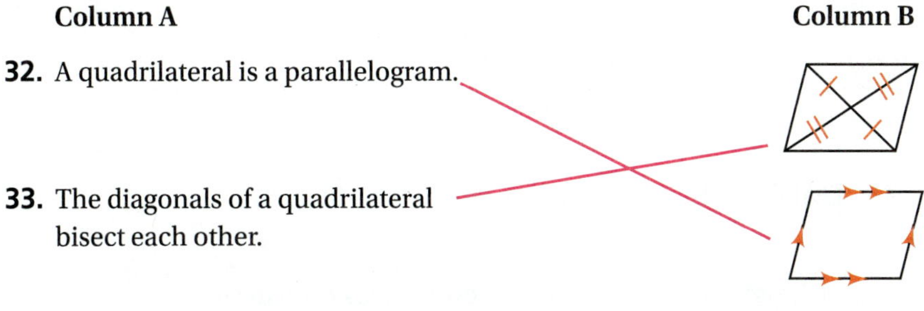

Column A	Column B
32. A quadrilateral is a parallelogram.	
33. The diagonals of a quadrilateral bisect each other.	

34. Circle the word that describes how Theorem 6-6 and Theorem 6-11 are related.

contradiction contrapositive converse inverse

35. In which situations should you use each theorem? Explain.

Answers may vary. Sample: Use Theorem 6-6 to use properties of parallelograms. Use Theorem 6-11 to prove a quadrilateral is a parallelogram.

Math Success

Check off the vocabulary words that you understand.

☐ diagonal ☐ parallelogram ☐ quadrilateral

Rate how well you can ***prove that a quadrilateral is a parallelogram.***

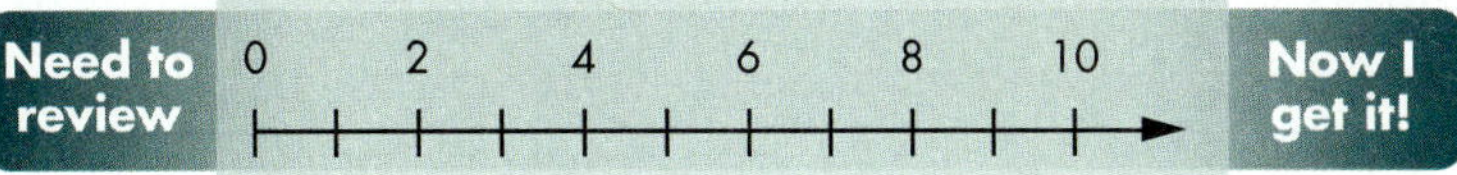

Name ______________________ Class __________ Date __________

6-3 Think About a Plan

Proving That a Quadrilateral Is a Parallelogram

Prove Theorem 6-8.

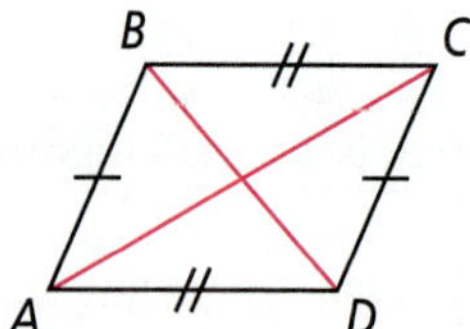

Given: $\overline{AB} \cong \overline{CD}$ and $\overline{BC} \cong \overline{DA}$

Prove: *ABCD* is a parallelogram.

1. What is the definition of a parallelogram?
   A parallelogram is a quadrilateral in which both pairs of opposite sides are parallel.

2. What are some of the ways that you can prove that two lines are parallel using a transversal?
   You can prove that alternate interior, alternate exterior, or corresponding angles are congruent, or that same-side interior angles are supplementary.

3. Draw a transversal on *ABCD* above. This will help you prove that $\overline{BC} \parallel \overline{AD}$.
   Check students' work.

4. How can you prove that the triangles formed by the diagonal are congruent?
   Because $\overline{BD} \cong \overline{DB}$ by the Reflexive Property, and it is given that $\overline{AB} \cong \overline{CD}$ and $\overline{BC} \cong \overline{DA}$, then $\triangle ABD \cong \triangle CDB$ by SSS.

5. If $\overline{BD}$ is a transversal between lines $\overline{BC}$ and $\overline{AD}$, which angles represent the alternate interior angles? **$\angle CBD$ and $\angle ADB$**

6. How can you prove $\angle CBD \cong \angle ADB$? **CPCTC**

7. What can you conclude about $\overline{BC}$ and $\overline{AD}$?
   They are parallel.

8. Draw a transversal to help prove that $\overline{AB} \parallel \overline{DC}$. **Check students' work.**

9. How can you prove that $\angle BAC \cong \angle DCA$?
   Because $\overline{CA} \cong \overline{AC}$ by the Reflexive Property, and it is given that $\overline{AB} \cong \overline{CD}$ and $\overline{BC} \cong \overline{DA}$, $\triangle ABC \cong \triangle CDA$ by SSS. So $\angle BAC \cong \angle DCA$ by CPCTC.

10. What can you conclude about $\overline{AB}$ and $\overline{CD}$? Why?
    They are parallel; $\angle BAC$ and $\angle DCA$ are congruent alternate interior angles.

11. How can you conclude that *ABCD* is a parallelogram?
    Its opposite sides are parallel, which is the definition of a parallelogram.

Name ____________________ Class ____________ Date ____________

6-3 Practice

Form K

Proving That a Quadrilateral Is a Parallelogram

Algebra For what values of x and y must $ABCD$ be a parallelogram?

1. 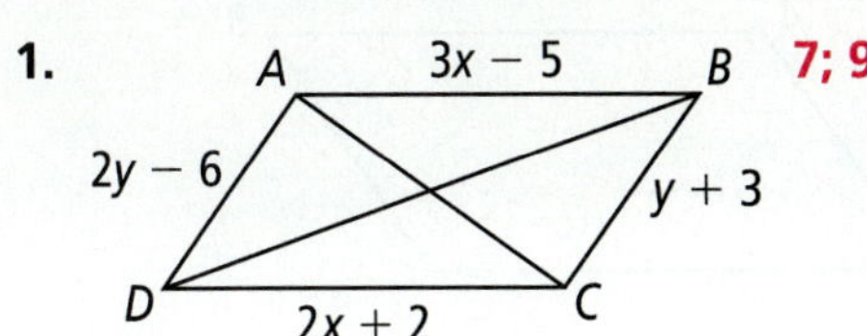

7; 9

To start, write an equation that relates the lengths of opposite sides that have algebraic expressions with the same variable.

$3x - 5 = \underline{\ ?\ }$ **2x + 2**

2. 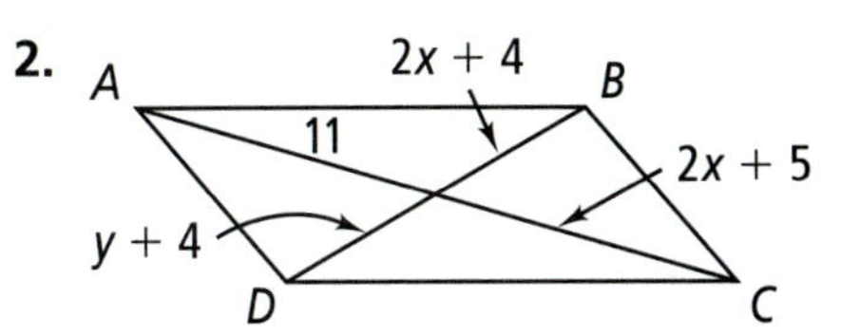

3; 6

3. 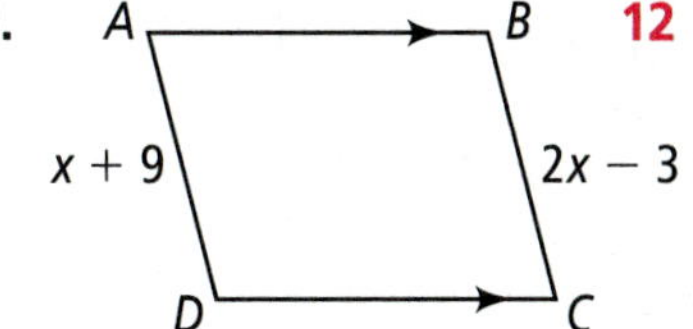

12

4. 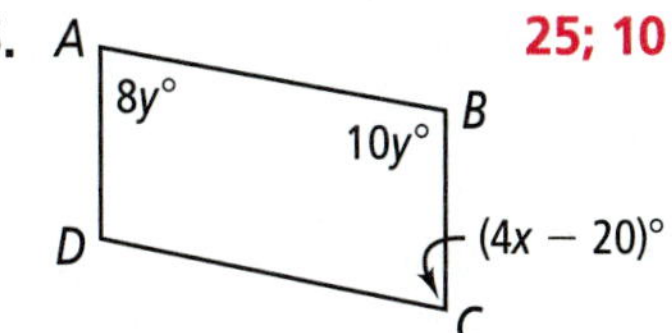

8; 29

5. A B D C, $8y°$, $10y°$, $(4x - 20)°$
25; 10

Can you prove the quadrilateral is a parallelogram based on the given information? Explain.

6. 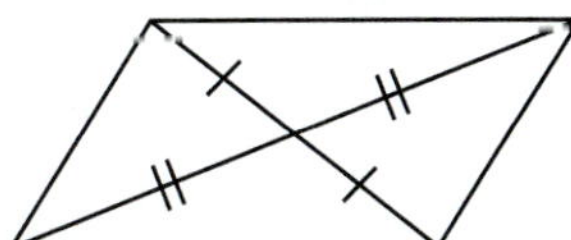

Yes; the diagonals bisect each other.

7. 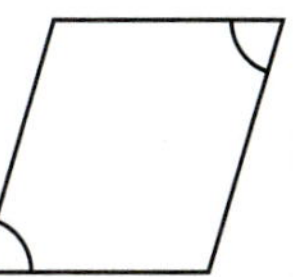

No; both sets of opposite angles need to be congruent.

8. 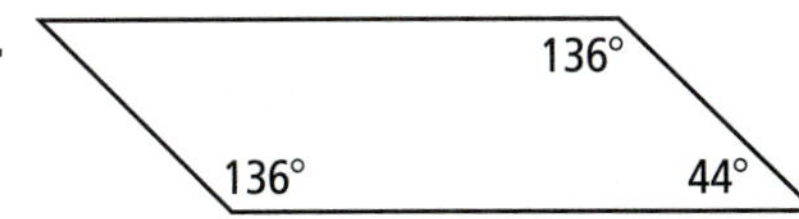

Yes; an angle is supplementary to both of its consecutive angles.

9. 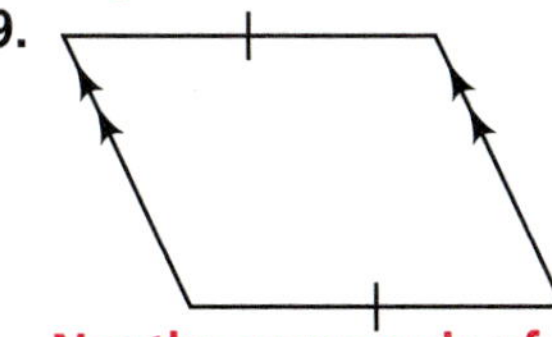

No; the same pair of sides needs to be both congruent and parallel.

10. **Reasoning** A classmate drew a quadrilateral with two diagonals. This divided the figure into four isosceles triangles. Is the quadrilateral a parallelogram? Use a drawing to justify your answer.

Yes; since all the sections of the diagonals are congruent, the diagonals bisect each other and the figure is a parallelogram.

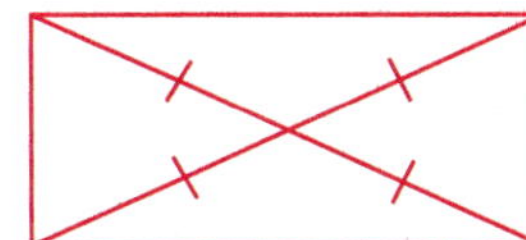

Name ______________________ Class ____________ Date ____________

6-3 Practice (continued)

Form K

Proving That a Quadrilateral Is a Parallelogram

11. Developing Proof Complete this two-column proof of Theorem 6-8.

Given: $\overline{AB} \cong \overline{CD}$ and $\overline{BC} \cong \overline{DA}$

Prove: $ABCD$ is a parallelogram.

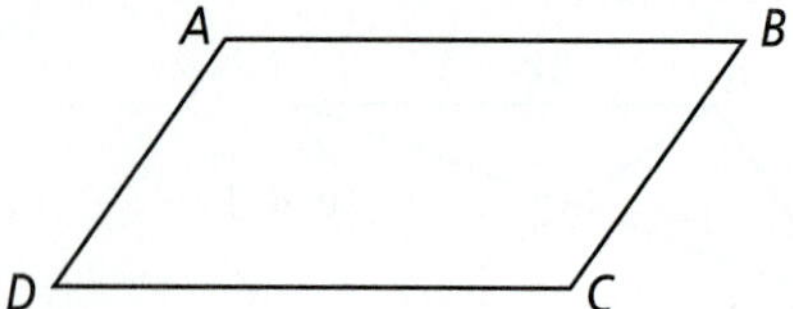

Statements	Reasons
1) Draw diagonal $\overline{AC}$.	1) Definition of a diagonal
2) $\overline{AB} \cong \overline{CD}$ and $\overline{BC} \cong \overline{DA}$	2) ? Given
3) $\overline{AC} \cong \overline{AC}$	3) ? Reflexive Prop. of ≅
4) $\triangle ABC \cong$? $\triangle CDA$	4) ? SSS
5) $\angle B \cong$? $\angle D$	5) ? CPCTC
6) Draw diagonal $\overline{BD}$.	6) Definition of a diagonal
7) $\overline{BD} \cong \overline{BD}$	7) ? Reflexive Prop. of ≅
8) $\triangle BCD \cong$? $\triangle DAB$	8) ? SSS
9) $\angle A \cong$? $\angle C$	9) ? CPCTC
10) $ABCD$ is a parallelogram.	10) ? Theorem 6-10

12. Error Analysis A classmate said that a quadrilateral is a parallelogram only if one angle is supplementary to all the others. What is your classmate's error? Explain. One ∠ must be suppl. to both of its consecutive ∠s. The classmate is describing a rectangle, which is one type of parallelogram.

For what values of the variables must *ABCD* be a parallelogram?

13. 12; 14

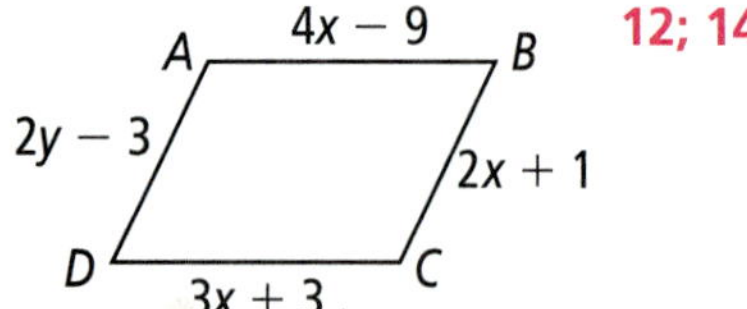

14. 9; 18

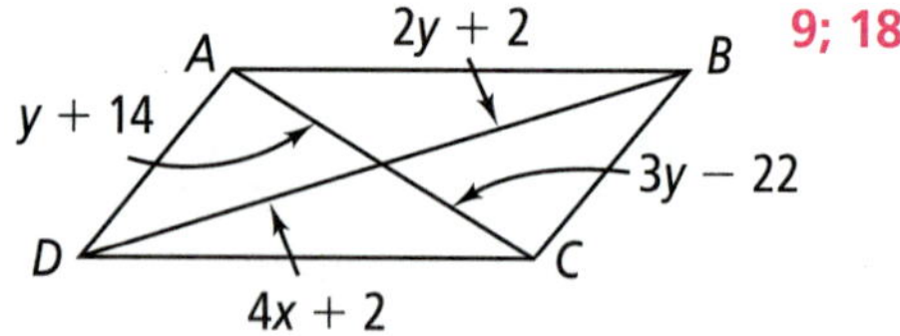

15. 21.5; 39

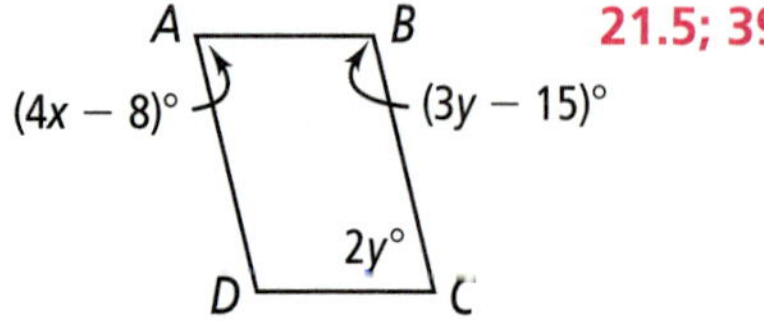

16. 7; 3

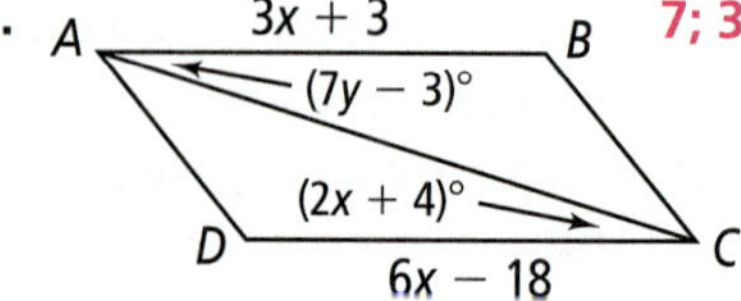

Name ______________________ Class ____________ Date ____________

6-3 Standardized Test Prep

Proving That a Quadrilateral Is a Parallelogram

Multiple Choice

For Exercises 1–4, choose the correct letter.

1. For what value of x must $ABCD$ be a parallelogram? A

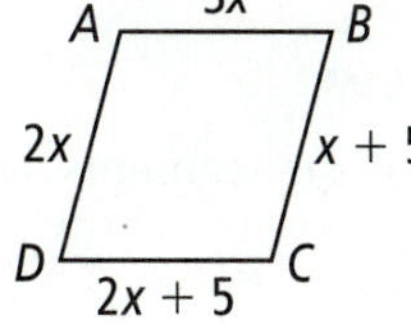

Ⓐ 5 Ⓒ 15

Ⓑ 10 Ⓓ 20

2. For what value of y must $QRST$ be a parallelogram? G

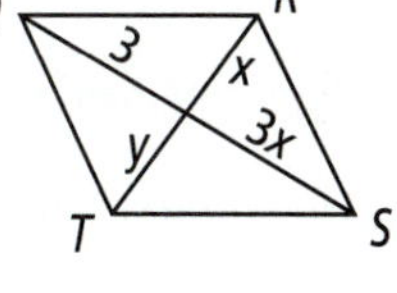

Ⓕ 0.5 Ⓗ 2

Ⓖ 1 Ⓘ 3

3. Which reason can be used to conclude that $DFGH$ is a parallelogram? C

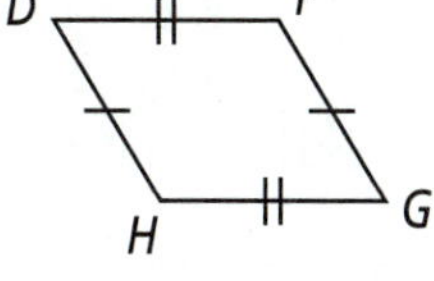

Ⓐ There are two pairs of congruent opposite angles.

Ⓑ The diagonals bisect each other.

Ⓒ There are two pairs of congruent opposite sides.

Ⓓ There are two pairs of opposite parallel sides.

4. Which reason can be used to conclude that $LMNO$ is a parallelogram? I

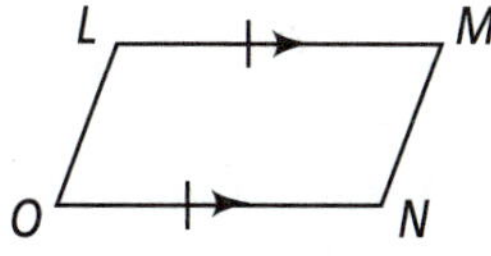

Ⓕ There are two pairs of congruent opposite angles.

Ⓖ There are two pairs of congruent opposite sides.

Ⓗ There are two pairs of opposite parallel sides.

Ⓘ There is one pair of congruent and parallel sides.

Short Response

5. What additional pieces of information could be supplied to make $ABCD$ a parallelogram?

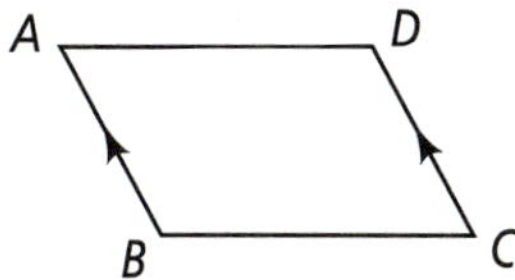

[2] Answers may vary. Sample: $\overline{AD} \parallel \overline{BC}$ or $\overline{AB} \cong \overline{DC}$
[1] Only one piece of information is listed. [0] no answer or wrong answer based on an inappropriate plan

6-4 Properties of Rhombuses, Rectangles, and Squares

Vocabulary

Review

1. Circle the segments that are *diagonals*.

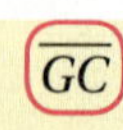
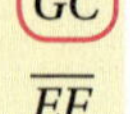

$\overline{AG}$	$\overline{AC}$	$\overline{HD}$	$\overline{GC}$ (circled)
$\overline{BF}$	$\overline{AE}$ (circled)	$\overline{EG}$	$\overline{EF}$

2. Is a *diagonal* ever a line or a ray? Yes / No (No circled)

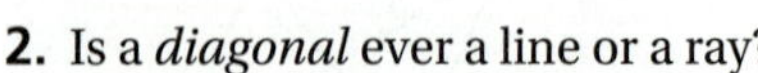

3. The *diagonals* of quadrilateral *JKLM* are $\overline{JL}$ and $\overline{KM}$.

Vocabulary Builder

rhombus (noun) RAHM **bus**

Definition: A **rhombus** is a parallelogram with four congruent sides.

Main Idea: A **rhombus** has four congruent sides but not necessarily four right angles.

Examples: diamond, square

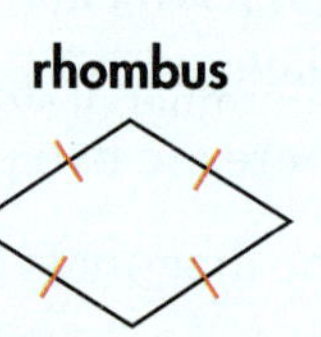

Use Your Vocabulary

Complete each statement with *always, sometimes,* or *never*.

4. A *rhombus* is __?__ a parallelogram. always

5. A parallelogram is __?__ a *rhombus.* sometimes

6. A rectangle is __?__ a *rhombus.* sometimes

7. A square is __?__ a *rhombus.* always

8. A *rhombus* is __?__ a square. sometimes

9. A *rhombus* is __?__ a hexagon. never

take note Key Concept Special Parallelograms

A *rhombus* is a parallelogram with four congruent sides.

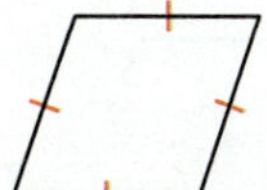

A *rectangle* is a parallelogram with four right angles.

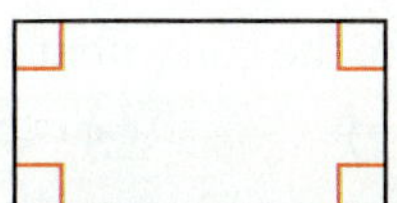

A *square* is a parallelogram with four congruent sides and four right angles.

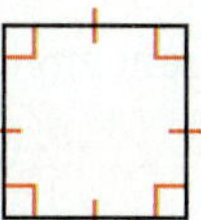

10. Write the words *rectangles, rhombuses,* and *squares* in the Venn diagram below to show that one special parallelogram has the properties of the other two.

Special Parallelograms

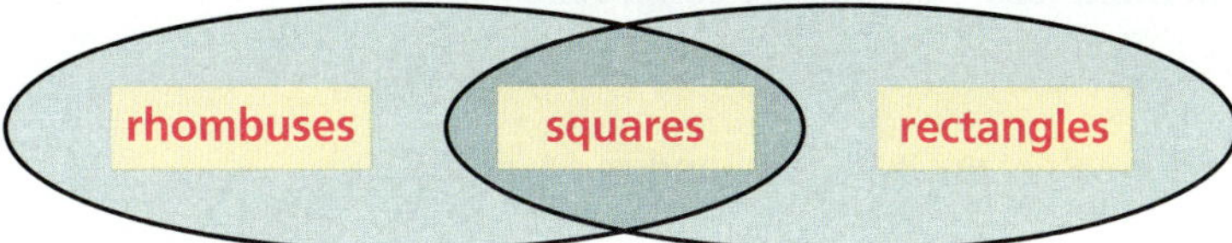

Problem 1 Classifying Special Parallograms

Got It? **Is ▱*EFGH* a *rhombus*, a *rectangle*, or a *square*? Explain.**

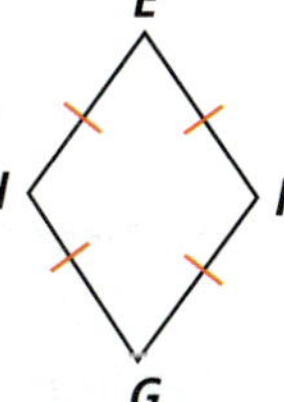

11. Circle the number of sides marked congruent in the diagram.

12. Are any of the angles right angles? Yes / No

13. Is ▱*EFGH* a rhombus, a rectangle, or a square? Explain.

Rhombus. Explanations may vary. Sample: ▱*EFGH* has four congruent sides and no right angles.

take note Theorems 6-13 and 6-14

Theorem 6-13 If a parallelogram is a rhombus, then its diagonals are perpendicular.

Theorem 6-14 If a parallelogram is a rhombus, then each diagonal bisects a pair of opposite angles.

Use the diagram at the right for Exercises 14–18.

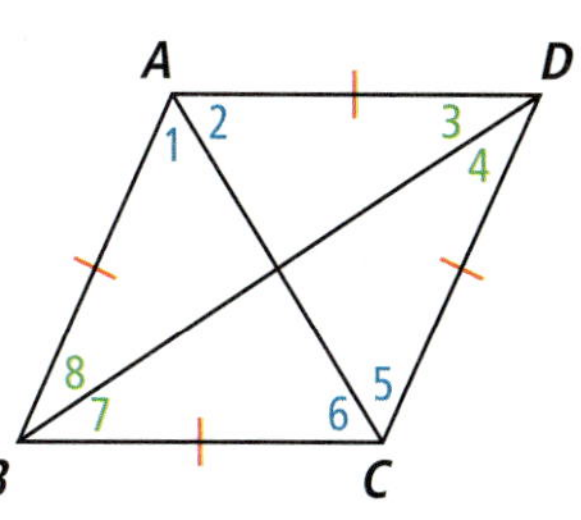

14. If *ABCD* is a rhombus, then $\overline{AC} \perp$ 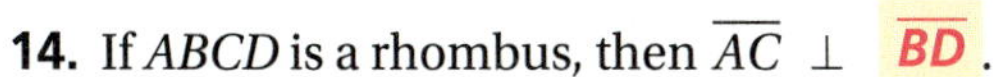 $\overline{BD}$.

15. If *ABCD* is a rhombus, then $\overline{AC}$ bisects ∠ BAD and ∠ BCD.

16. If *ABCD* is a rhombus, then ∠1 ≅ ∠2 ≅ ∠ 5 ≅ ∠ 6.

17. If *ABCD* is a rhombus, then $\overline{BD}$ bisects ∠ ADC and ∠ ABC.

18. If *ABCD* is a rhombus, then ∠3 ≅ ∠ 4 ≅ ∠ 7 ≅ ∠ 8.

Problem 2 Finding Angle Measures

Got It? **What are the measures of the numbered angles in rhombus $PQRS$?**

19. Circle the word that describes $\triangle PQR$ and $\triangle RSP$.

equilateral | (isosceles) | right

20. Circle the congruent angles in $\triangle PQR$. Underline the congruent angles in $\triangle RSP$.

($\angle 1$) | <u>$\angle 2$</u> | ($\angle 3$) | <u>$\angle 4$</u> | $\angle Q$ | $\angle S$

21. $m\angle 1 + m\angle 2 + 104 =$ 180 **22.** $m\angle 1 + m\angle 2 =$ 76 **23.** $m\angle 1 =$ 38

24. Each diagonal of a rhombus _?_ a pair of opposite angles. bisects

25. Circle the angles in rhombus $PQRS$ that are congruent.

($\angle 1$) | ($\angle 2$) | ($\angle 3$) | ($\angle 4$)

26. $m\angle 1 =$ 38 , $m\angle 2 =$ 38 , $m\angle 3 =$ 38 , and $m\angle 4 =$ 38 .

Theorem 6-15

Theorem 6-15 If a parallelogram is a rectangle, then its diagonals are congruent.

27. If $RSTU$ is a rectangle, then $\overline{RT} \cong$ $\overline{SU}$.

Problem 3 Finding Diagonal Length

Got It? **If $LN = 4x - 17$ and $MO = 2x + 13$, what are the lengths of the diagonals of rectangle $LMNO$?**

Underline the correct word to complete each sentence.

28. $LMNO$ is a <u>rectangle</u> / rhombus .

29. The diagonals of this figure are <u>congruent</u> / parallel .

30. Complete.

$LN =$ MO, so $4x - 17 =$ $2x + 13$.

31. Write and solve an equation to find the value of x.

$4x - 17 = 2x + 13$
$2x - 17 = 13$
$2x = 30$
$x = 15$

32. Use the value of x to find the length of $\overline{LN}$.

$4x - 17 = 4(15) - 17 = 60 - 17 = 43$

33. The diagonals of a rectangle are congruent, so the length of each diagonal is 43 .

Lesson Check • Do you UNDERSTAND?

Error Analysis **Your class needs to find the value of *x* for which ▱*DEFG* is a rectangle. A classmate's work is shown below. What is the error? Explain.**

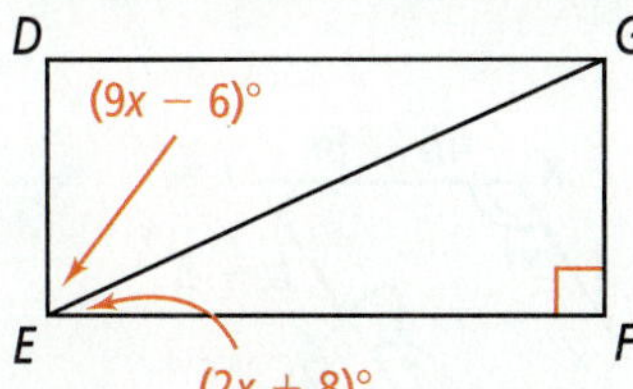

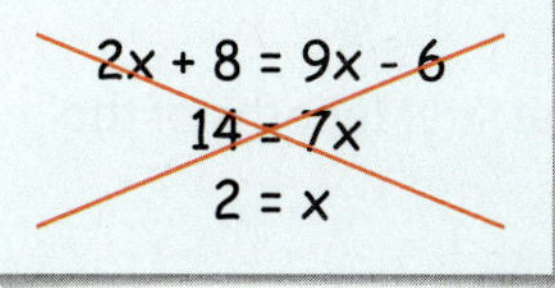

Write T for *true* or F for *false*.

F **34.** If a parallelogram is a rectangle, then each diagonal bisects a pair of opposite angles.

T **35.** If a parallelogram is a rhombus, then each diagonal bisects a pair of opposite angles.

36. If *DEFG* is a rectangle, $m\angle D = m\angle$ E $= m\angle$ F $= m\angle$ G.

37. $m\angle F =$ 90.

38. What is the error? Explain.

Answers may vary. Sample: The diagonals of a rhombus bisect a pair of opposite angles, but the diagonals of a rectangle do not. The expressions should be added and set equal to 90.

39. Find the value of *x* for which ▱*DEFG* is a rectangle.

$$2x + 8 + 9x - 6 = 90$$
$$11x + 2 = 90$$
$$11x = 88$$
$$x = 8$$

40. The value of *x* for which ▱*DEFG* is a rectangle is 8.

Math Success

Check off the vocabulary words that you understand.

☐ parallelogram ☐ rhombus ☐ rectangle ☐ square ☐ diagonal

Rate how well you can *find angles and diagonals of special parallelograms.*

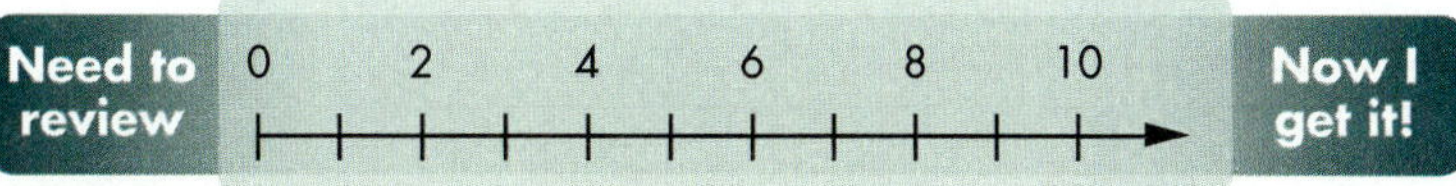

Name ______________________ Class ____________ Date ____________

6-4 Think About a Plan

Properties of Rhombuses, Rectangles, and Squares

Algebra Find the angle measures and the side lengths of the rhombus at the right.

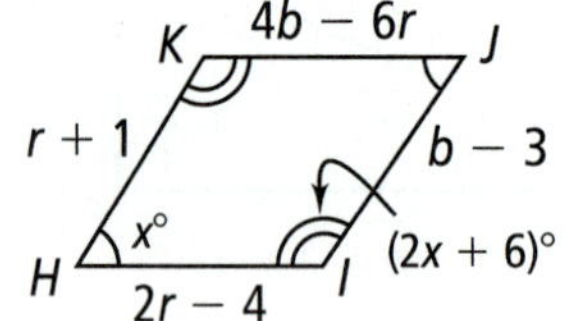

1. What do you know about the sum of the angle measures of a quadrilateral?

   The sum is always equal to 360°.

2. Write an equation to represent the sum of the measures of each angle in this rhombus. **$m\angle K + m\angle I + m\angle J + m\angle H = 360$**

3. Based on the diagram, which pairs of angles are congruent? **$\angle K$ and $\angle I$; $\angle J$ and $\angle H$**

4. What is the value of $m\angle H$ given in the diagram? Explain how you can use this value to rewrite the equation from Step 2. Rewrite the equation using this value.

   x; replace $m\angle H$ and $m\angle J$ with x because the ∠s are ≅; $m\angle I + m\angle K + x + x = 360$

5. What is the value of $m\angle I$ given in the diagram? Explain how you can use this value to rewrite the equation from Step 4. Rewrite the equation using this value.

   $2x + 6$; replace $m\angle K$ and $m\angle I$ with $2x + 6$ because the angles are congruent;

   $(2x + 6) + (2x + 6) + x + x = 360$

6. In the space at the right, simplify and solve the equation. **$6x + 12 = 360$; 58**

7. $m\angle H = m\angle J = x =$ **58**

8. $m\angle I = m\angle K = 2x + 6 =$ **122**

9. How can you check that your answer is correct?

   The sum of the measures of the four angles should be 360: $58 + 58 + 122 + 122 = 360$.

10. What do you know about the sides of a rhombus? **They are congruent.**

11. What does your answer to Step 10 tell you about the expressions for the sides of the rhombus shown in the diagram? **They are all equal to each other.**

12. Which two expressions in the figure contain the same variable? **$r + 1$ and $2r - 4$**

13. How do these expressions relate to each other? Explain how you can use this relationship to find the value of r. Find the value of r.

    They are equal. Set them equal to each other and solve for r; $r + 1 = 2r - 4$; $r = 5$

14. How can you find the length of each side of the rhombus? What is the length of each side? **Substitute 5 into an expression and simplify; 6**

Name ______________________ Class ____________ Date ____________

6-4 Practice

Form K

Properties of Rhombuses, Rectangles, and Squares

Decide whether the parallelogram is a rhombus, a rectangle, or a square. Explain.

1.

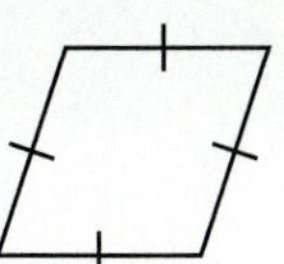

rhombus; four congruent sides, no right angles

2.

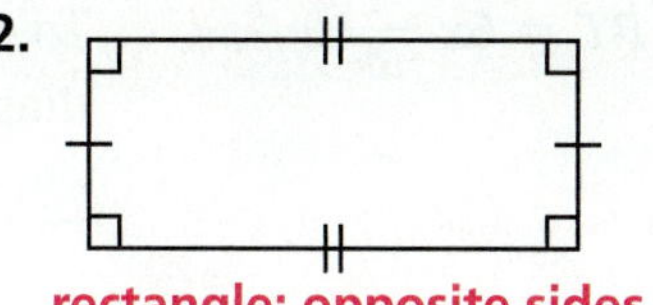

rectangle; opposite sides congruent, four right angles

3.

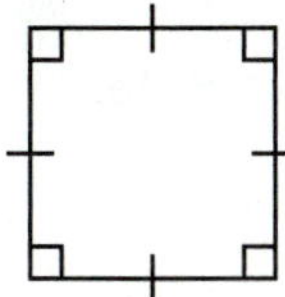

square; four right angles and four congruent sides

4.

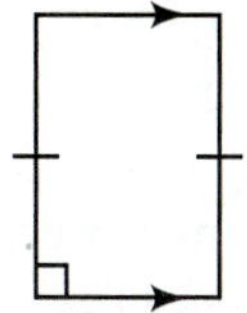

rectangle; right angles, opposite sides congruent

Find the measures of the numbered angles in each rhombus.

5.

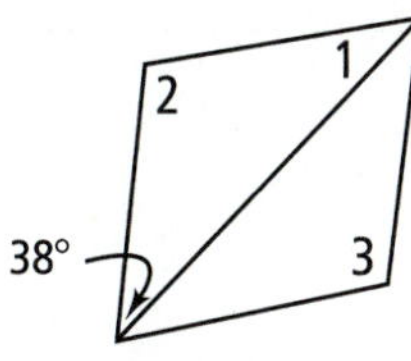

38; 104; 104

To start, a diagonal of a rhombus forms an isosceles triangle with congruent base angles.

So, $m\angle$ 1 = 38.

6.

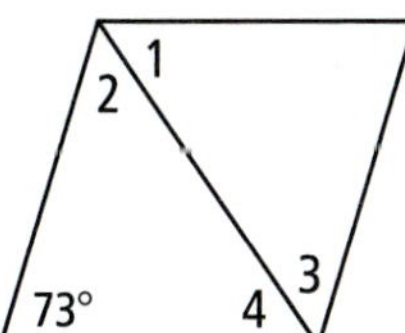

53.5; 53.5; 53.5; 53.5

7.

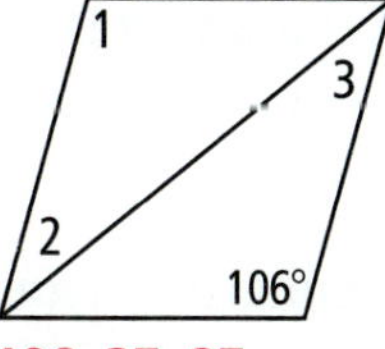

106; 37; 37

8.

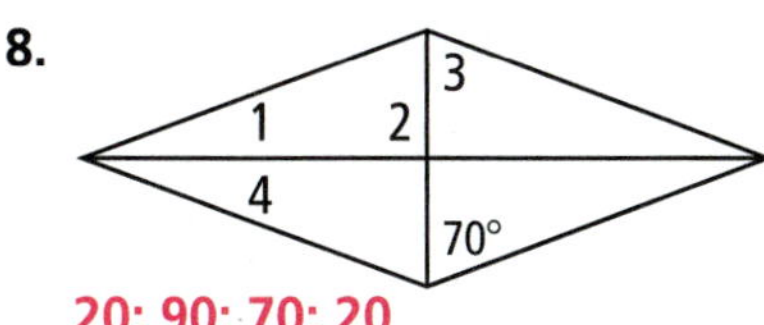

20; 90; 70; 20

To start, the diagonals of a rhombus are perpendicular.

So, $m\angle$ 2 = 90.

9.

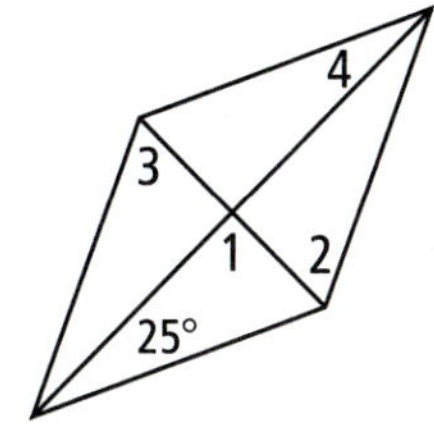

90; 65; 65; 25

10.

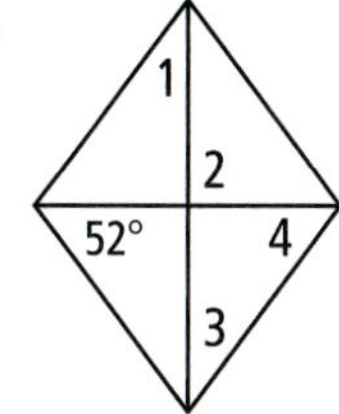

38; 90; 38; 52

Name ______________________ Class ____________ Date ____________

6-4 Practice (continued) Form K

Properties of Rhombuses, Rectangles, and Squares

Algebra ***QRST*** **is a rectangle. Find the value of** ***x*** **and the length of each diagonal.**

11. $QS = x$ and $RT = 6x - 10$ **2; 2**

    To start, write an equation to show the diagonals are congruent.

    _?_ = _?_ **x; 6x − 10**

12. $QS = 4x - 7$ and $RT = 2x + 11$
    9; 29

13. $QS = 5x + 12$ and $RT = 6x - 2$
    14; 82

14. $QS = 6x - 3$ and $RT = 4x + 19$
    11; 63

15. $QS = x + 45$ and $RT = 4x - 45$
    30; 75

Determine the most precise name for each quadrilateral.

16. 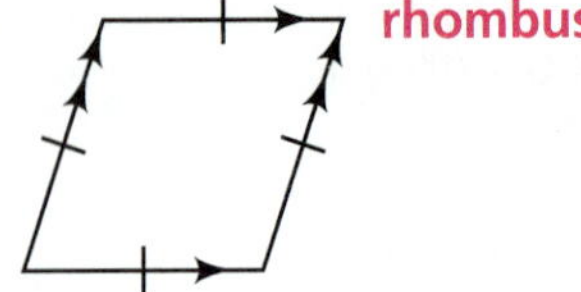 **rhombus**

17. 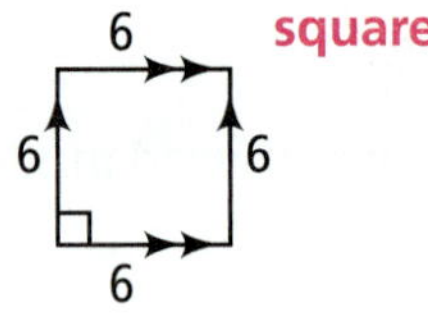

square

18. 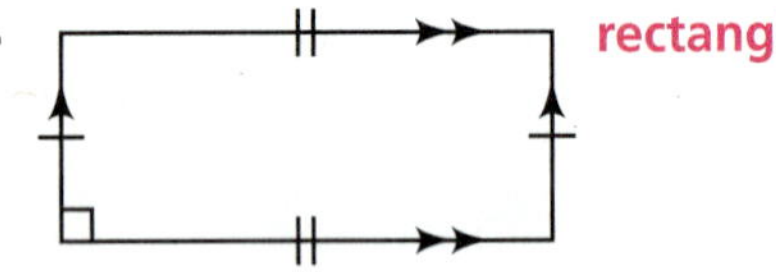 **rectangle**

19. 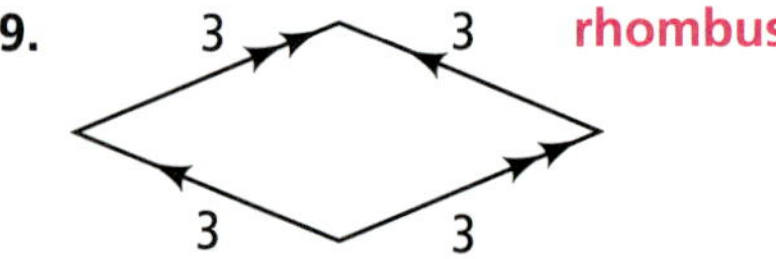

rhombus

Determine whether each statement is ***true*** **or** ***false.*** **If it is false, rewrite the sentence to make it true. If it is true, list any other quadrilaterals for which the sentence would be true.**

20. Rhombuses have four congruent sides. **true; squares**

21. Rectangles have four congruent angles. **true; squares**

22. The diagonals of a rectangle bisect the opposite angles. **False; the diagonals of a rhombus bisect the opposite angles.**

23. The diagonals of a rhombus are always congruent. **False; the diagonals of rectangles or squares are congruent, but not all rhombuses are rectangles or squares.**

Algebra Find the values of the variables. Then find the side lengths.

24. 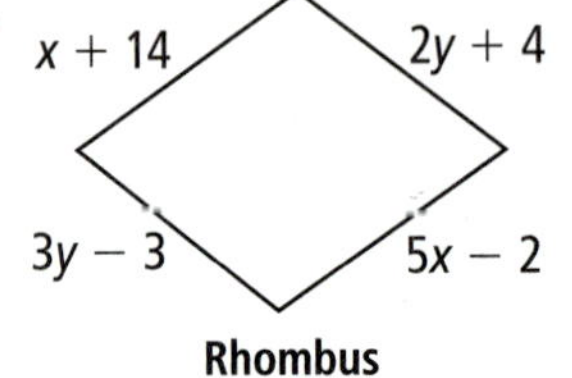

4; 7; 18

25. 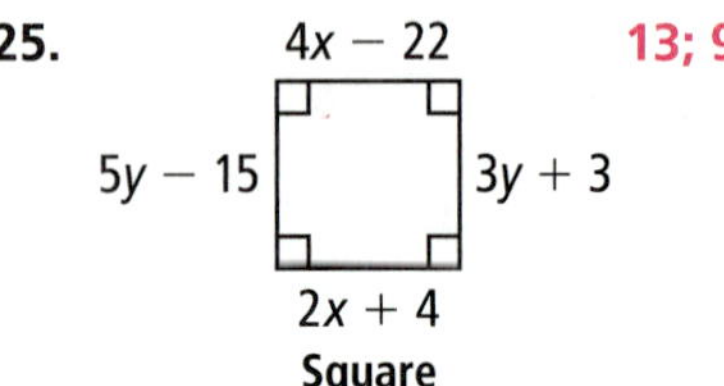

13; 9; 30

Name ______________________ Class ____________ Date ____________

6-4 Standardized Test Prep

Properties of Rhombuses, Rectangles, and Squares

Multiple Choice

For Exercises 1–6, choose the correct letter.

Use rhombus *TQRS* for Exercises 1–4.

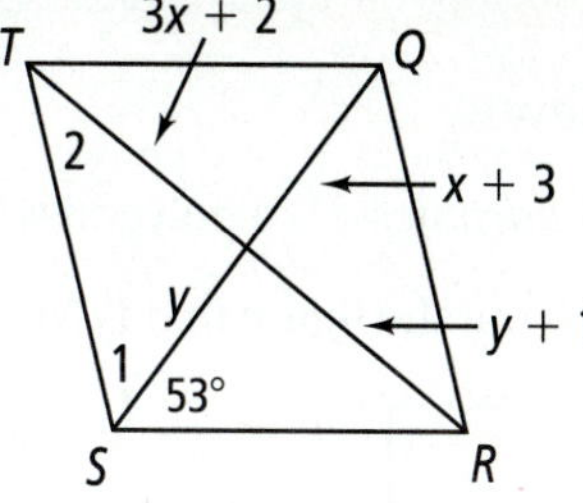

1. What is the measure of $\angle 1$? D

   (A) 47 (C) 74

   (B) 37 (D) 53

2. What is the measure of $\angle 2$? H

   (F) 47 (G) 74 (H) 37 (I) 53

3. What is the value of x? B

   (A) 2 (B) 1 (C) 5 (D) 4

4. What is the value of y? F

   (F) 4 (G) 3 (H) 2 (I) 1

5. What statement would be sufficient to prove that a quadrilateral is a rhombus? C

   (A) The quadrilateral has four congruent angles.

   (B) The quadrilateral has two pairs of parallel sides.

   (C) The quadrilateral has four congruent sides.

   (D) The quadrilateral has two pairs of congruent angles.

6. *EFGH* is a kite. To prove that the diagonals of a kite are perpendicular, which pair of angles must you prove congruent using CPCTC? H

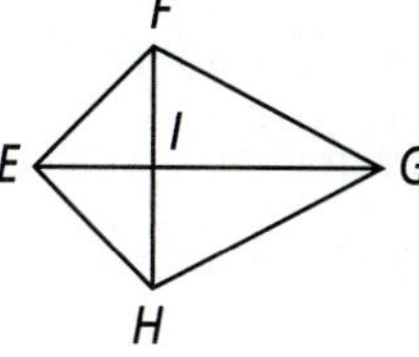

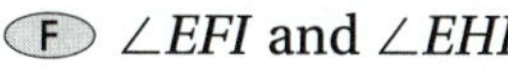

   (F) $\angle EFI$ and $\angle EHI$ (H) $\angle EIF$ and $\angle EIH$

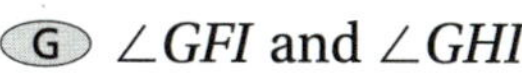

   (G) $\angle GFI$ and $\angle GHI$ (I) $\angle FIE$ and $\angle HIG$

Short Response

7. Why is it that the statement "all rhombuses are squares" is false, but the statement "all squares are rhombuses" is true? Explain.

   [2] A square has all the properties of a rhombus, plus the additional property of four congruent angles. Not all rhombuses have four congruent angles, so they cannot all be categorized as squares. [1] Student only provides a description of the properties of a square or a rhombus but does not compare the properties of squares and rhombuses. [0] Student does not describe squares and rhombuses or compare their properties.

6-5 Conditions for Rhombuses, Rectangles, and Squares

Vocabulary

Review

1. A *quadrilateral* is a polygon with 4 sides.

2. Cross out the figure that is NOT a *quadrilateral*.

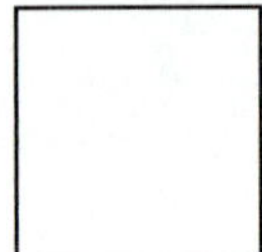 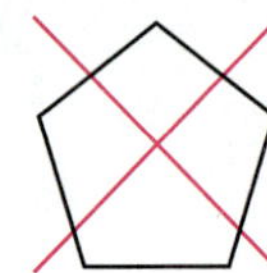  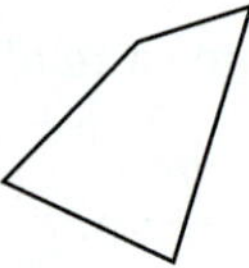

Vocabulary Builder

diagonal (noun) dy AG uh nul

Definition: A **diagonal** is a segment with endpoints at two nonadjacent vertices of a polygon.

Word Origin: The word **diagonal** comes from the Greek prefix *dia-*, which means "through," and *gonia*, which means "angle" or "corner."

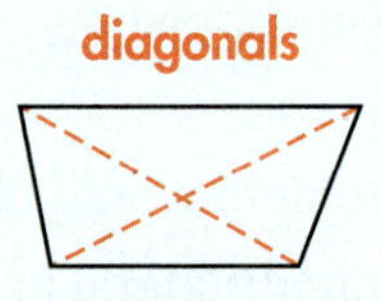

Use Your Vocabulary

3. Circle the polygon that has no *diagonal*.

triangle quadrilateral pentagon hexagon

4. Circle the polygon that has two *diagonals*.

triangle quadrilateral pentagon hexagon

5. Draw the *diagonals* from one vertex in each figure.

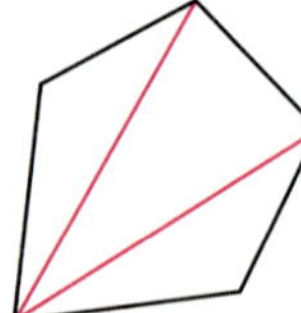 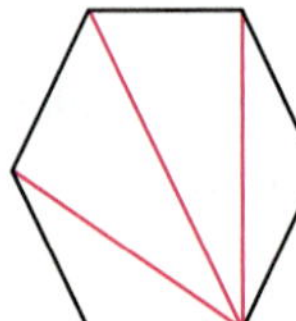 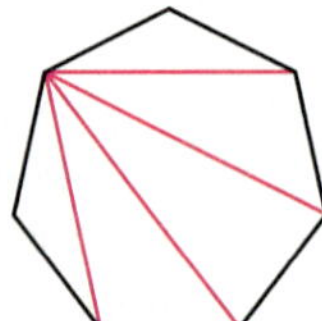

6. Write the number of diagonals you drew in each of the figures above.

pentagon: 2 hexagon: 3 heptagon: 4

take note

Theorems 6-16, 6-17, and 6-18

Theorem 6-16 If the diagonals of a parallelogram are perpendicular, then the parallelogram is a rhombus.

Theorem 6-17 If one diagonal of a parallelogram bisects a pair of opposite angles, then the parallelogram is a rhombus.

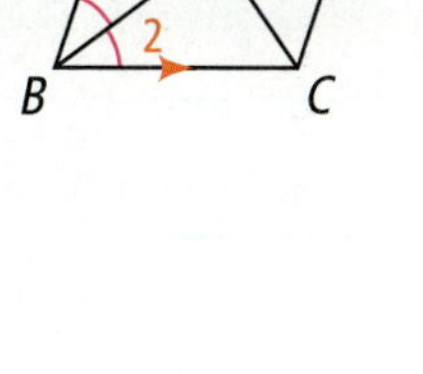

7. Insert a right angle symbol in the parallelogram at the right to illustrate Theorem 6-16. Insert congruent marks to illustrate Theorem 6-17.

Use the diagram from Exercise 7 to complete Exercises 8 and 9.

8. If *ABCD* is a parallelogram and $\overline{AC} \perp$ $\overline{BD}$, then *ABCD* is a rhombus.

9. If *ABCD* is a parallelogram, $\angle 1 \cong$ $\angle 2$, and $\angle 3 \cong$ $\angle 4$, then *ABCD* is a rhombus.

Theorem 6-18 If the diagonals of a parallelogram are congruent, then the parallelogram is a rectangle.

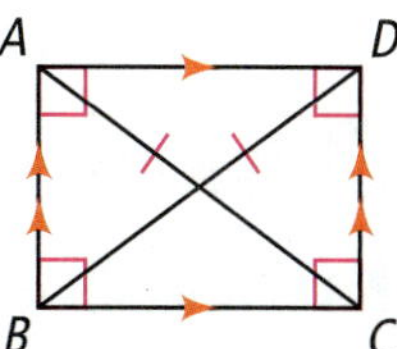

10. Insert congruent marks and right angle symbols in the parallelogram to the right to illustrate Theorem 6-18.

11. Use the diagram from Exercise 10 to complete the statement.

If *ABCD* is a parallelogram, and $\overline{BD} \cong$ $\overline{AC}$ then *ABCD* is a rectangle.

12. Circle the parallelogram that has diagonals that are both perpendicular and congruent.

parallelogram rectangle rhombus square

Problem 1 Identifying Special Parallelograms

Got It? **A parallelogram has angle measures of 20, 160, 20, and 160. Can you conclude that it is a rhombus, a rectangle, or a square? Explain.**

13. Draw a parallelogram in the box below. Label the angles with their measures. Use a protractor to help you make accurate angle measurements.

Parallelograms may vary. Sample is given.

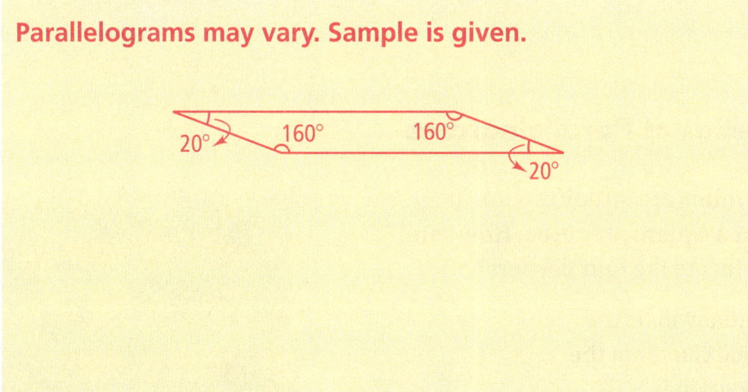

Underline the correct word or words to complete each sentence.

14. You do / do not know the lengths of the sides of the parallelogram.

15. You do / do not know the lengths of the diagonals.

16. The angles of a rectangle are all acute / obtuse / right angles.

17. The angles of a square are all acute / obtuse / right angles.

18. Can you conclude that the parallelogram is a rhombus, a rectangle, or a square? Explain.

No. Explanations may vary. Sample: The parallelogram cannot be a rectangle or square because it does not have four right angles. There is not enough information to tell whether it is a rhombus.

Problem 2 Using Properties of Special Parallelograms

Got It? For what value of y is $\square DEFG$ a rectangle?

19. For $\square DEFG$ to be a parallelogram, the diagonals must _?_ each other. bisect

20. $EG = 2(5y + 3)$

$= 10y + 6$

21. $DF = 2(7y - 5)$

$= 14y - 10$

22. For $\square DEFG$ to be a rectangle, the diagonals must be _?_. congruent

23. Now write an equation and solve for y.

$$10y + 6 = 14y - 10$$
$$10y - 14y = -10 - 6$$
$$-4y = -16$$
$$y = 4$$

24. $\square DEFG$ is a rectangle for $y = 4$.

Problem 3 Using Properties of Parallelograms

Got It? Suppose you are on the volunteer building team at the right. You are helping to lay out a square play area. How can you use properties of diagonals to locate the four corners?

25. You can cut two pieces of rope that will be the diagonals of the square play area. Cut them the same length because a parallelogram is a _?_ if the diagonals are congruent. rectangle

26. You join the two pieces of rope at their midpoints because a quadrilateral is a _?_ if the diagonals bisect each other. parallelogram

27. You move so the diagonals are perpendicular because a parallelogram is a _?_ if the diagonals are perpendicular. rhombus

28. Explain why the polygon is a square when you pull the ropes taut.

Answers may vary. Sample: Congruent diagonals bisect each other, so you formed a rectangle. Diagonals are perpendicular, so you formed a rhombus. A rectangle that is a rhombus is a square.

Lesson Check • Do you UNDERSTAND?

Name all of the special parallelograms that have each property.

A. Diagonals are perpendicular. **B. Diagonals are congruent.** **C. Diagonals are angle bisectors.**

D. Diagonals bisect each other. **E. Diagonals are perpendicular bisectors of each other.**

29. Place a ✓ in the box if the parallelogram has the property. Place an ✗ if it does not.

Property	Rectangle	Rhombus	Square
A	✗	✓	✓
B	✓	✗	✓
C	✗	✓	✓
D	✓	✓	✓
E	✗	✓	✓

Math Success

Check off the vocabulary words that you understand.

☐ rhombus ☐ rectangle ☐ square ☐ diagonal

Rate how well you can *use properties of parallelograms.*

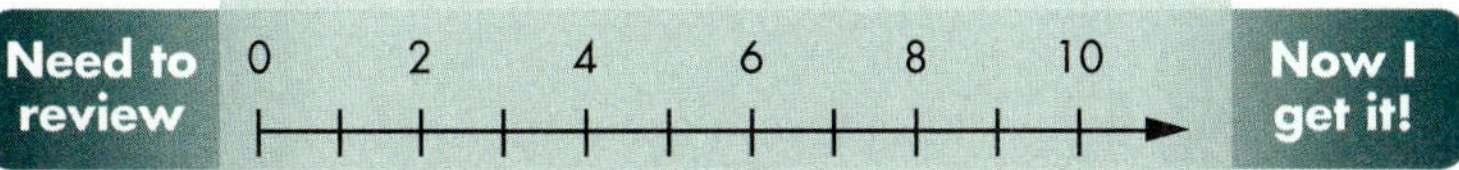

Name _______________ Class _______________ Date _______________

6-5 Think About a Plan

Conditions for Rhombuses, Rectangles, and Squares

Prove Theorem 6-18.

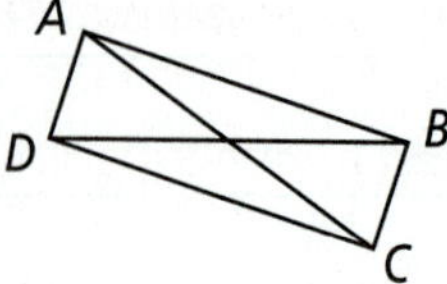

Given: $\square ABCD$, $\overline{AC} \cong \overline{DB}$

Prove: *ABCD* is a rectangle.

Understanding the Problem

1. What must you prove in order to show that parallelogram *ABCD* is a rectangle?
All four angles are right angles.

Planning the Solution

2. Using the properties of parallelograms, prove $\triangle BAD \cong \triangle CDA$. Show the steps of this proof below.

Statement	Reason
$\overline{AD} \cong \overline{DA}$	Reflexive Property of Congruence
$\overline{AC} \cong \overline{DB}$	Given
$\overline{AB} \cong \overline{DC}$	Opposite sides of a parallelogram are congruent.
$\triangle BAD \cong \triangle CDA$	SSS Theorem

3. If $\triangle BAD \cong \triangle CDA$, which angles are congruent?
$\angle BAD \cong \angle CDA$, $\angle DBA \cong \angle ACD$, $\angle ADB \cong \angle DAC$

4. To prove that the angles are right angles you need to use the properties of parallel lines. When a transversal intersects parallel lines, which angles are supplementary?
same-side interior angles

5. Given that $\overline{AB} \parallel \overline{CD}$, which angles in $\triangle BAD$ and $\triangle CDA$ are supplementary?
$\angle BAD$ and $\angle CDA$

6. If these angles are both congruent and supplementary, what must the measure of each angle be? 90°

7. How can you prove that the other angles of the parallelogram are right angles?
Opposite angles in a parallelogram are congruent.

Name ______________________ Class ____________ Date ____________

6-5 Practice

Form K

Conditions for Rhombuses, Rectangles, and Squares

Can you conclude that the parallelogram is a rhombus, a rectangle, or a square? Explain.

1. To start, identify the congruent figures marked in the diagram.

The diagonals bisect each other.

The diagonals intersect at right angles.

Rhombus; the diagonals are perpendicular.

2. 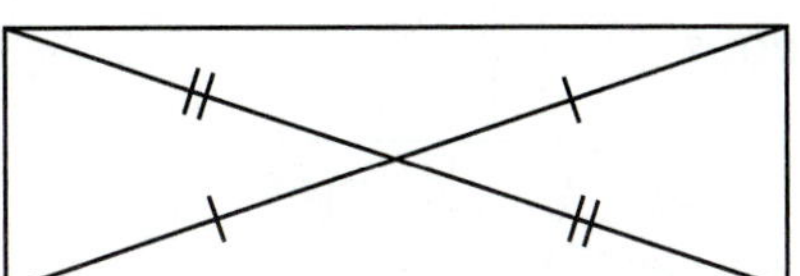

Neither; the figure could be a ▱ that is neither a rectangle nor a rhombus

3. 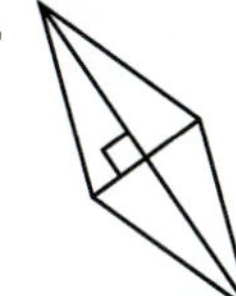

Rhombus; the diagonals are perpendicular.

4. A parallelogram has two pairs of adjacent sides that are congruent. rhombus

5. A parallelogram's diagonals form eight congruent angles at the vertices. square

Algebra **For what value of x is the figure the given special parallelogram?**

6. rectangle 12

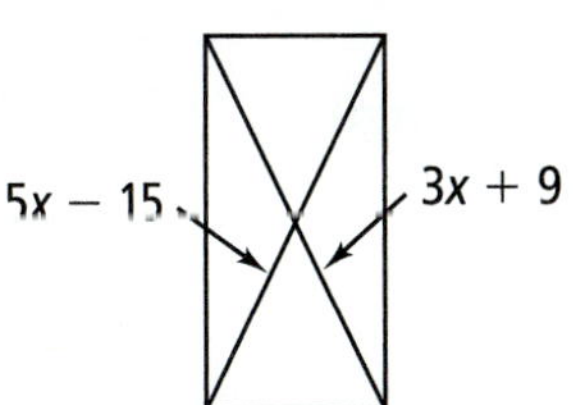

To start, write an equation for the congruent segments.

$\underline{\ ?\ } = \underline{\ ?\ }$ $5x - 15$; $3x + 9$

7. rhombus 19.25

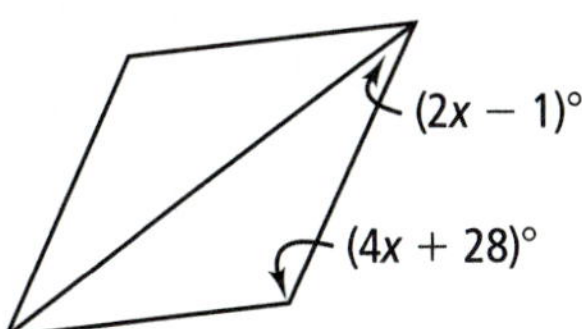

8. square 6

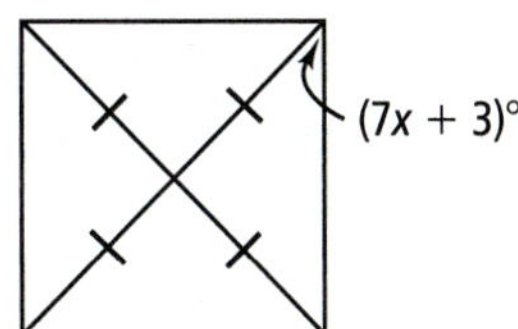

9. rectangle 5

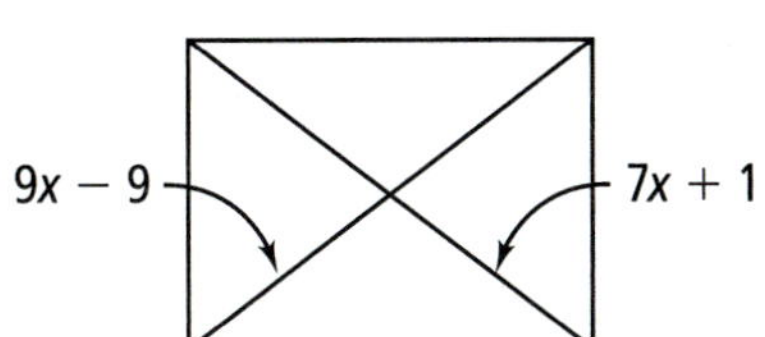

10. rectangle 24

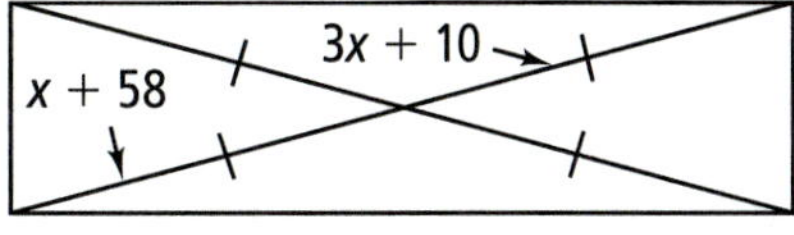

Name ______________________ Class ____________ Date ____________

6-5 Practice (continued) Form K

Conditions for Rhombuses, Rectangles, and Squares

Algebra **For what value of x is the figure the given special parallelogram?**

11. rhombus 18

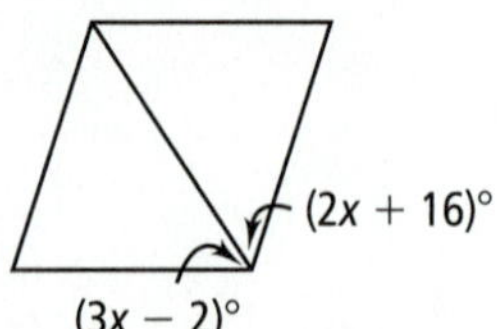

12. rhombus 14

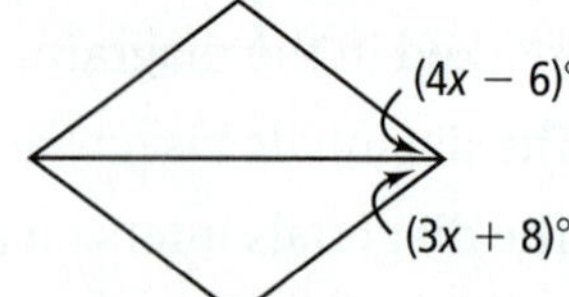

13. rectangle 20

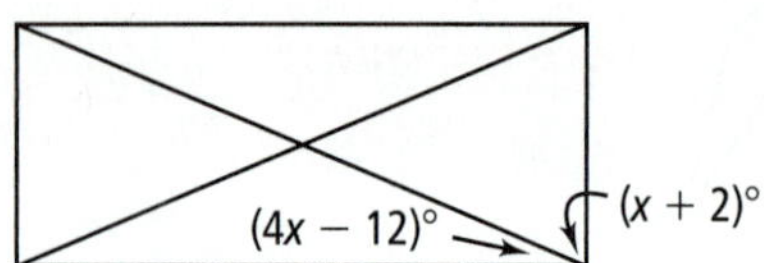

14. rhombus 12

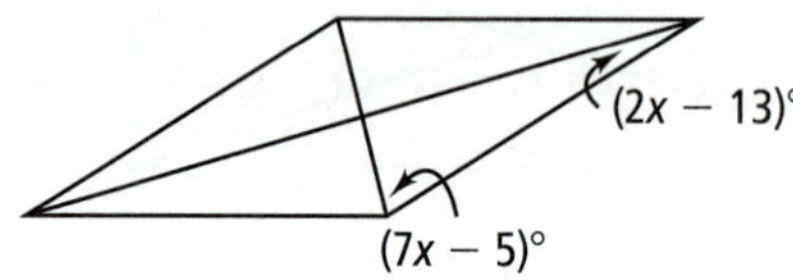

15. rectangle 7

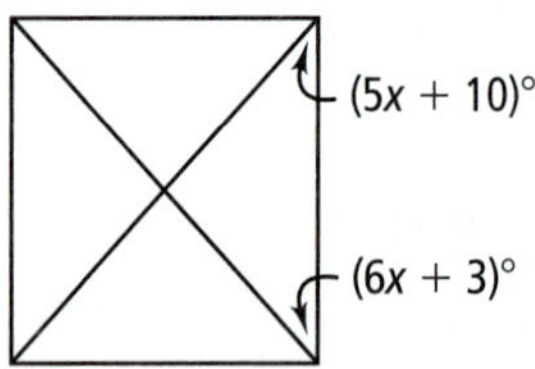

16. rhombus 15

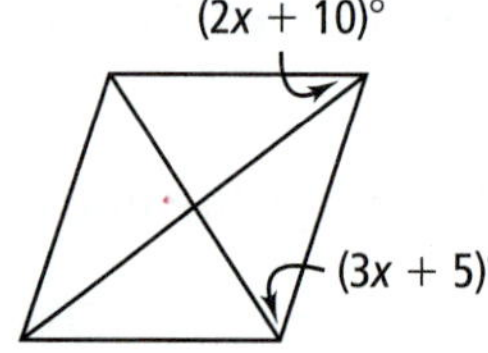

17. Reasoning Your friend draws a parallelogram with diagonals the length of x and y. Which special type of parallelograms could your friend draw if $x = y$? Which special type of parallelogram could your friend draw if $x \neq y$?

If $x = y$, the figure is definitely a rectangle and possibly a square.
If $x \neq y$, the figure could only be a rhombus.

18. Error Analysis A classmate draws the figure at the right and says that it is a square because its diagonals are both perpendicular and congruent. What is your classmate's error?

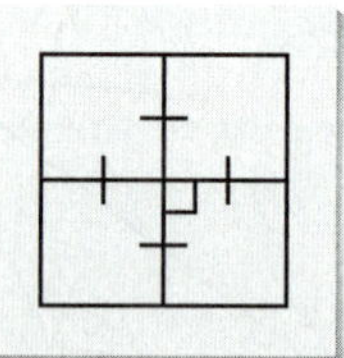

The lines drawn are not diagonals so they cannot be used to prove the figure is a square.

19. Students are planning a courtyard garden. They want the garden to be a square. How can the students use ropes to check that the garden is square? Justify your answer and name any theorems you used.

The ropes should be the same length because the diagonals of rectangles are congruent (Theorem 6-18). They should join the ropes at their midpoints because diagonals of parallelograms bisect each other (Theorem 6-11). They need to pull the ropes so they are perpendicular because diagonals of rhombuses are perpendicular (Theorem 6-16). The ends of the ropes will mark the vertices of a square.

Name ______________________ Class ____________ Date ____________

6-5 Standardized Test Prep

Conditions for Rhombuses, Rectangles, and Squares

Multiple Choice

For Exercises 1–4, choose the correct letter.

1. Which is the most precise name of this figure? B

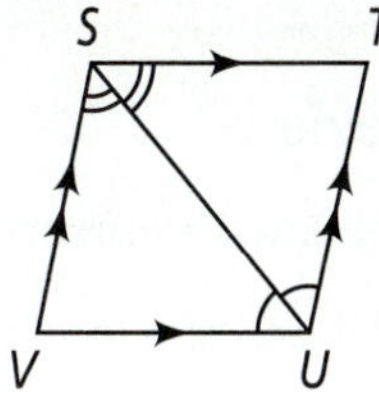

   (A) parallelogram (C) rectangle

   (B) rhombus (D) square

2. Which of the following conditions or set of conditions must be met for a parallelogram to be a rectangle? G

   (F) Diagonals are perpendicular.

   (G) Diagonals are congruent.

   (H) All sides are congruent.

   (I) The length of a diagonal is equal to the length of a side.

3. Which of the following conditions or set of conditions is sufficient for a parallelogram to be a square? A

   (A) Diagonals are perpendicular and diagonals are congruent.

   (B) Diagonals are congruent.

   (C) All sides are congruent.

   (D) The length of a diagonal is equal to the length of a side.

4. For what value of x is $\square XYZA$ a rectangle? H

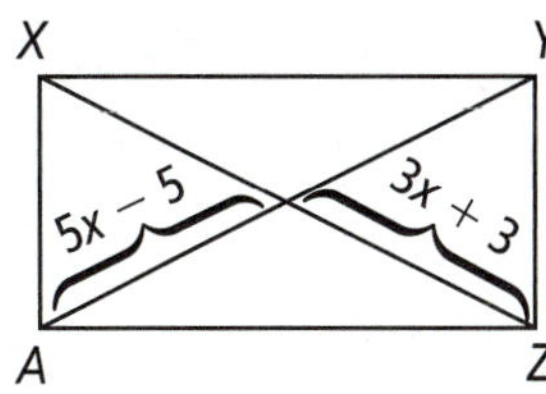

   (F) 2 (H) 4

   (G) 3 (I) 5

Short Response

5. The diagonals of a parallelogram are 2.3 cm and 3.2 cm long. Can you tell if the parallelogram is a rhombus? Explain.

   [2] No; no information is given to indicate the diagonals are perpendicular, and no information is given to indicate that a diagonal bisects opposite angles.
   [1] Student offers half the explanation. [0] no answer or wrong answer based on an inappropriate plan

Trapezoids and Kites

Vocabulary

Review

Underline the correct word to complete each sentence.

1. An *isosceles* triangle always has two / three congruent sides.
2. An equilateral triangle is also a(n) *isosceles* / right triangle.
3. Cross out the length(s) that could NOT be side lengths of an *isosceles* triangle.

3, 4, 5	8, 8, 10	3.6, 5, 3.6	7, 11, 11

Vocabulary Builder

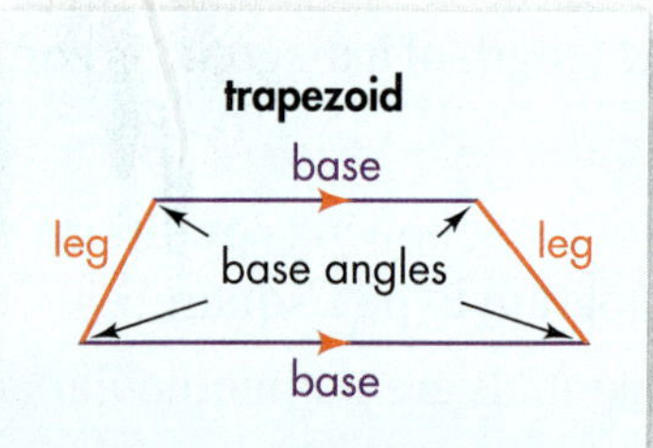

trapezoid (noun) TRAP ih zoyd

Related Words: base, leg

Definition: A **trapezoid** is a quadrilateral with exactly one pair of parallel sides.

Main Idea: The parallel sides of a **trapezoid** are called *bases*. The nonparallel sides are called *legs*. The two angles that share a base of a **trapezoid** are called *base angles*.

Use Your Vocabulary

4. Cross out the figure that is NOT a *trapezoid*.

 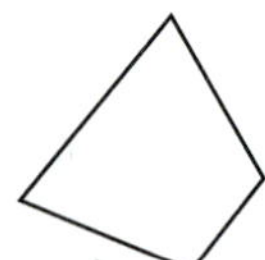 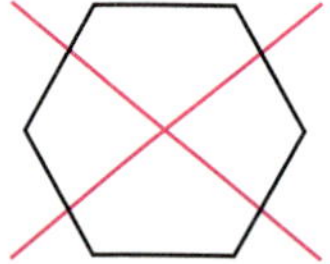 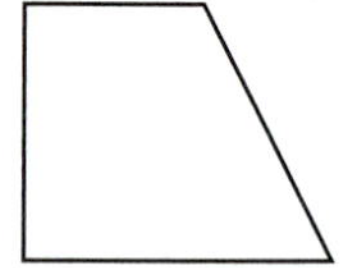

5. Circle the figure(s) than can be divided into two *trapezoids*. Then divide each figure that you circled into two *trapezoids*.

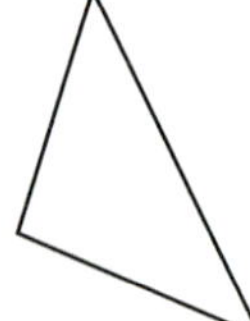 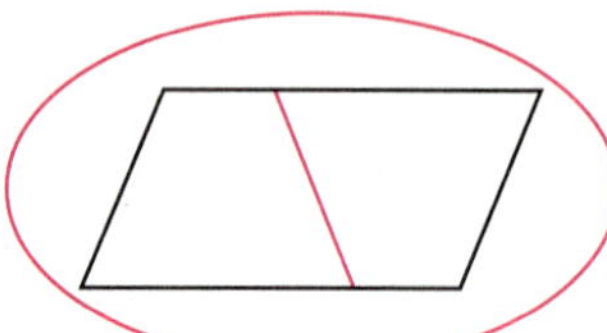 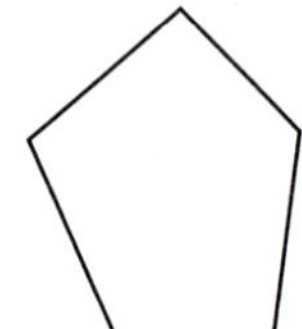 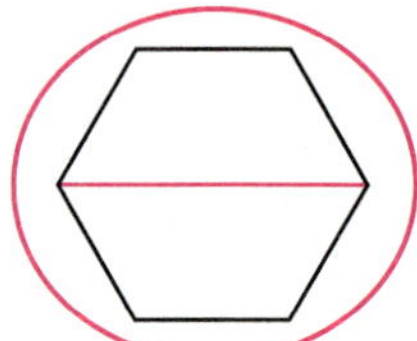

take note — Theorems 6-19, 6-20, and 6-21

Theorem 6-19 If a quadrilateral is an isosceles trapezoid, then each pair of base angles is congruent.

Theorem 6-20 If a quadrilateral is an isosceles trapezoid, then its diagonals are congruent.

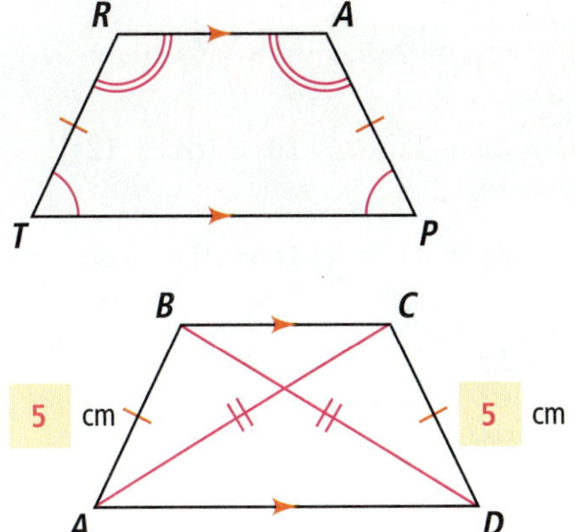

6. If *TRAP* is an isosceles trapezoid with bases $\overline{RA}$ and $\overline{TP}$, then $\angle T \cong \angle$ P and $\angle R \cong \angle$ A .

7. Use Theorem 6-19 and your answers to Exercise 6 to draw congruence marks on the trapezoid at the right.

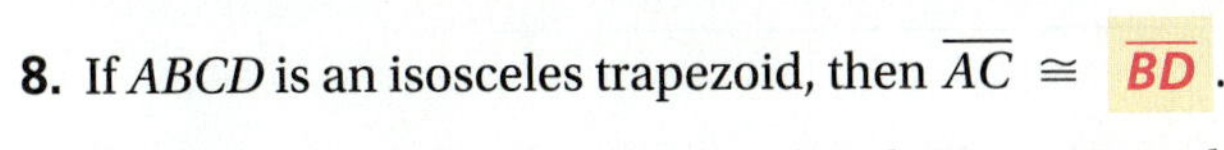

8. If *ABCD* is an isosceles trapezoid, then $\overline{AC} \cong$ $\overline{BD}$.

9. If *ABCD* is an isosceles trapezoid and $AB = 5$ cm, then $CD =$ 5 cm.

10. Use Theorem 6-20 and your answer to Exercises 8 and 9 to label the diagram at the right.

Theorem 6-21 Trapezoid Midsegment Theorem If a quadrilateral is a trapezoid, then

(1) the midsegment is parallel to the bases, and

(2) the length of the midsegment is half the sum of the lengths of the bases.

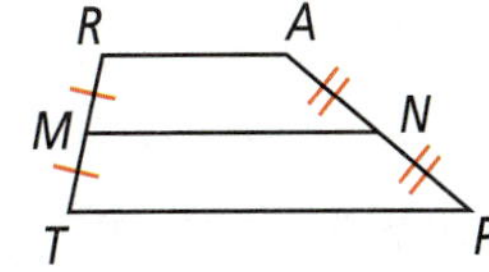

11. If *TRAP* is a trapezoid with midsegment $\overline{MN}$, then

(1) $\overline{MN} \parallel$ $\overline{TP}$ $\parallel$ $\overline{RA}$ (2) $MN = \frac{1}{2}($ TP + RA $)$

Problem 2 Finding Angle Measures in Isosceles Trapezoids

Got It? **A fan has 15 angles meeting at the center. What are the measures of the base angles of the congruent isosceles trapezoids in its second ring?**

Use the diagram at the right for Exercises 12–16.

12. Circle the number of isosceles triangles in each wedge. Underline the number of isosceles trapezoids in each wedge.

one two three four

13. $a = 360 \div$ 15 = 24

14. $b = \dfrac{180 - \boxed{24}}{2} =$ 78

15. $c = 180 -$ 78 = 102

16. $d = 180 -$ 102 = 78

17. The measures of the base angles of the isosceles trapezoids are 102 and 78 .

Problem 3 Using the Midsegment of a Trapezoid

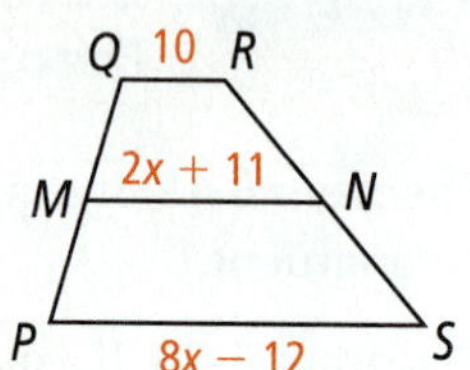

Got It? Algebra $\overline{MN}$ is the midsegment of trapezoid $PQRS$. What is x? What is MN?

18. The value of x is found below. Write a reason for each step.

$MN = \frac{1}{2}(QR + PS)$	Trapezoid Midsegment Theorem
$2x + 11 = \frac{1}{2}[10 + (8x - 12)]$	Substitute.
$2x + 11 = \frac{1}{2}(8x - 2)$	Simplify.
$2x + 11 = 4x - 1$	Distributive Property
$2x + 12 = 4x$	Add 1 to each side.
$12 = 2x$	Subtract $2x$ from each side.
$6 = x$	Divide each side by 2.

19. Use the value of x to find MN.

$MN = 2x + 11 = 2(6) + 11 = 12 + 11 = 23$

Lesson Check • Do you UNDERSTAND?

Error Analysis Since a parallelogram has two pairs of parallel sides, it certainly has one pair of parallel sides. Therefore, a parallelogram must also be a trapezoid. What is the error in this reasoning? Explain.

A trapezoid is a quadrilateral with exactly one pair of parallel sides.

A parallelogram is a quadrilateral with both pairs of opposite sides parallel.

20. Look at the definitions at the right. Circle the total number of pairs of parallel sides that a quadrilateral with *exactly* one pair of parallel sides must have.

(one pair) two pairs three pairs

21. Circle the total number of pairs of parallel sides that a quadrilateral with *both* pairs of opposite sides parallel must have.

one pair (two pairs) three pairs

22. Explain why a parallelogram is NOT a trapezoid.

Explanations may vary. Sample: "Exactly one" means no more than one. A parallelogram must have two pairs of parallel sides, so it cannot be a trapezoid.

Trapezoids and Kites

Vocabulary

Review

1. Underline the correct word to complete the sentence.

Perpendicular lines meet at acute / obtuse / right angles.

2. Circle the pairs(s) of lines that are *perpendicular*.

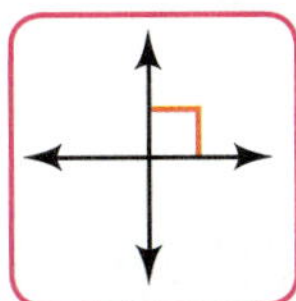
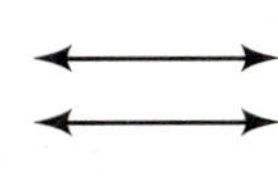
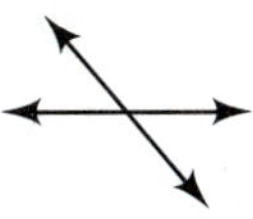
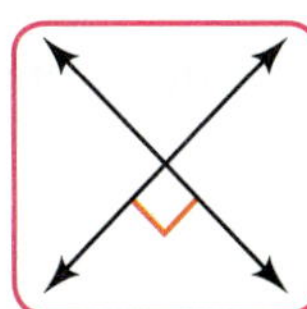

Vocabulary Builder

kite (noun) **kyt**

Definition: A **kite** is a quadrilateral with two pairs of consecutive sides congruent and no opposite sides congruent.

Main Idea: The diagonals of a **kite** are perpendicular.

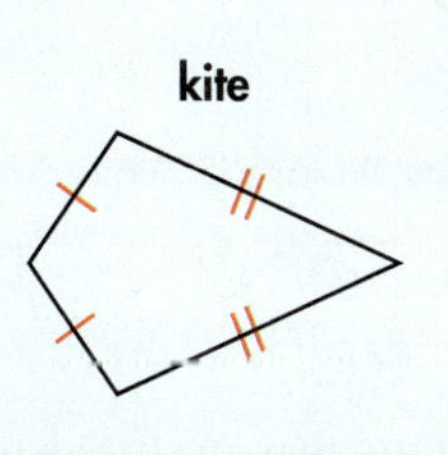

Use Your Vocabulary

3. Cross out the figure(s) that are not *kites*.

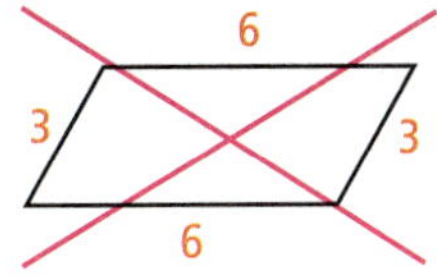

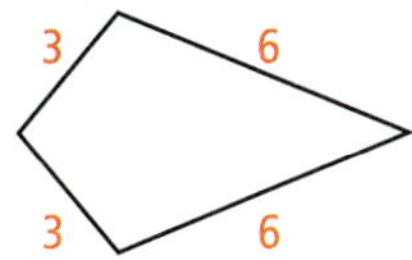

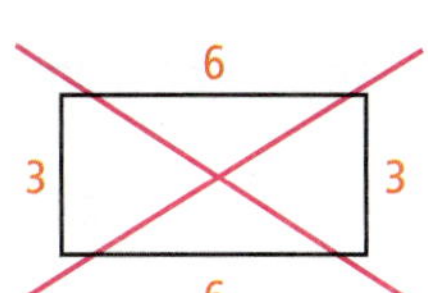

The lengths of three sides of a *kite* are given. Write the length of the fourth side.

4. 6, 10, 10, 6 **5.** 5.5, 5.5, 9, 9 **6.** 24, 15, 15, 24

Divide each *kite* into two isosceles triangles.

7.

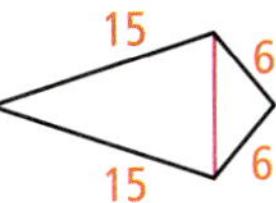

8.

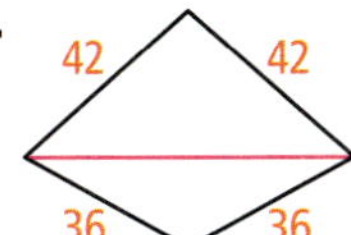

9.

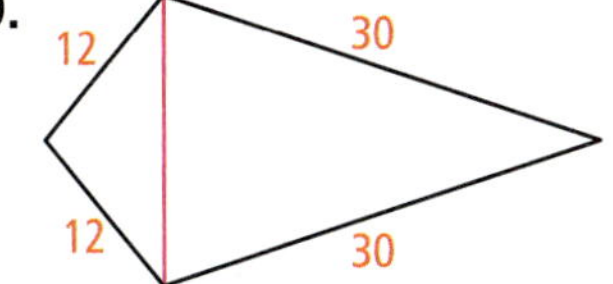

take note

Theorem 6-22

Theorem 6-22 If a quadrilateral is a kite, then its diagonals are perpendicular.

10. If $ABCD$ is a kite, then $\overline{AC} \perp$ $\overline{BD}$.

11. Use Theorem 6-22 and Exercise 10 to draw congruence marks and right angle symbol(s) on the kite at the right.

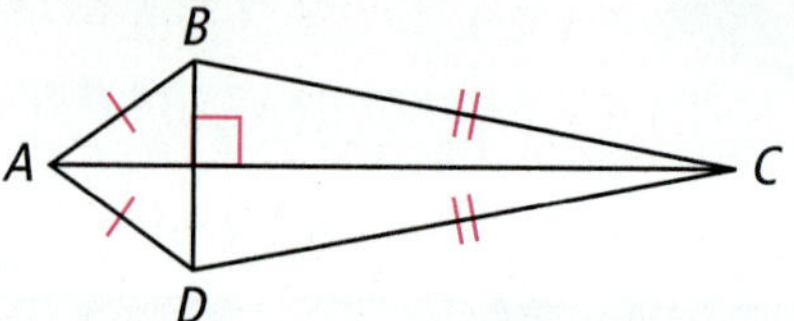

Problem 4 Finding Angle Measures in Kites

Got It? **Quadrilateral $KLMN$ is a kite. What are $m\angle 1$, $m\angle 2$, and $m\angle 3$?**

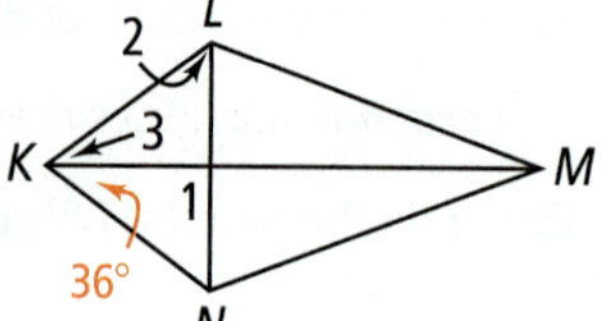

12. Diagonals of a kite are perpendicular, so $m\angle 1 =$ 90.

13. $\triangle KNM \cong \triangle KLM$ by SSS, so $m\angle 3 = m\angle NKM =$ 36.

14. $m\angle 2 = m\angle 1 - m\angle$ 3 by the Triangle Exterior Angle Theorem.

15. Solve for $m\angle 2$.

$m\angle 2 = 90 - 36 = 54$

16. $m\angle 1 =$ 90, $m\angle 2 =$ 54, and $m\angle 3 =$ 36.

Lesson Check • Do you know HOW?

What are the measures of the numbered angles?

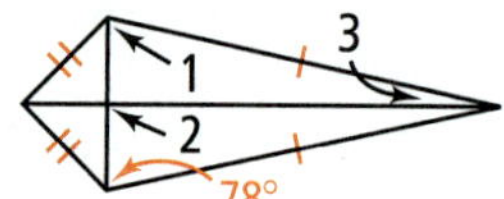

17. Use one of the reasons in the list below to justify each step.

Diagonals of a kite are ⊥.
Isosceles Triangle Theorem
Subtraction Property of Equality.
Substitute.
Triangle Exterior Angle Theorem.

$m\angle 1 = 78$	Isosceles Triangle Theorem
$m\angle 2 = 90$	Diagonals of a kite are ⊥.
$m\angle 2 = m\angle 1 + m\angle 3$	Triangle Exterior Angle Theorem.
$90 = 78 + m\angle 3$	Substitute.
$12 = m\angle 3$	Subtraction Property of Equality

18. $m\angle 1 =$ 78, $m\angle 2 =$ 90, and $m\angle 3 =$ 12.

Lesson Check • Do you UNDERSTAND?

Compare and Contrast **How is a kite similar to a rhombus? How is it different? Explain.**

19. Place a ✓ in the box if the description fits the figure. Place an ✗ if it does not.

Kite	Description	Rhombus
✓	Quadrilateral	✓
✓	Perpendicular diagonals	✓
✗	Each diagonal bisects a pair of opposite angles.	✓
✗	Congruent opposite sides	✓
✓	Two pairs of congruent consecutive sides	✓
✗	Two pairs of congruent opposite angles	✓
✗	Supplementary consecutive angles	✓

20. How is a kite similar to a rhombus? How is it different? Explain.

Answers may vary. Sample: Similar: Both are quadrilaterals with perpendicular diagonals, two pairs of congruent consecutive sides and one pair of congruent opposite angles. Different: Kites have no congruent opposite sides, only one pair of congruent opposite angles, and no supplementary consecutive angles.

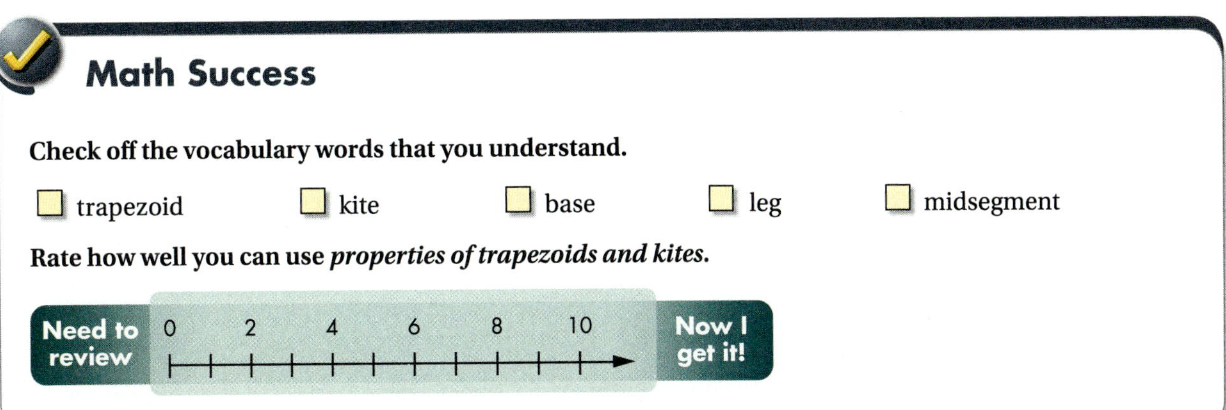

Math Success

Check off the vocabulary words that you understand.

☐ trapezoid ☐ kite ☐ base ☐ leg ☐ midsegment

Rate how well you can use *properties of trapezoids and kites.*

Name ______________________ Class ____________ Date ____________

6-6 Think About a Plan

Trapezoids and Kites

Prove the converse of Theorem 6-19: If a trapezoid has a pair of congruent base angles, then the trapezoid is isosceles.

Understanding the Problem

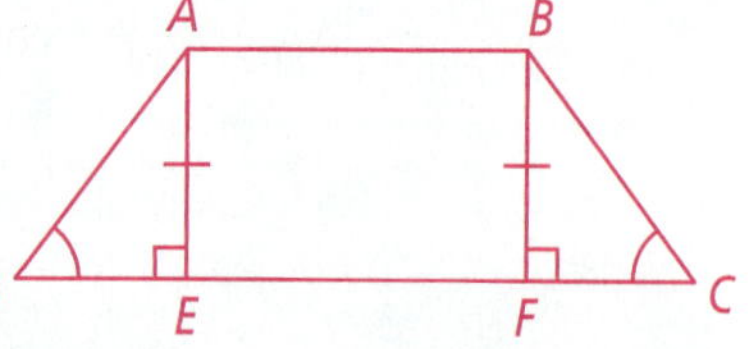

1. To help you solve this problem, draw trapezoid $ABCD$ in the space to the right. Mark the base angles congruent and label the vertices so that $\overline{AB} \parallel \overline{CD}$.

2. Which two sides of the trapezoid do you need to prove congruent? **$\overline{AD}$ and $\overline{BC}$**

Planning the Solution

3. What type of polygons can you construct inside the trapezoid to prove that $\overline{AD} \cong \overline{BC}$? **a rectangle and right triangles**

4. What makes a set of lines parallel? Describe the relationship between two segments that are perpendicular to a pair of parallel lines and have endpoints on the lines.

   Parallel lines are always the same distance apart. The segments must be the same length.

5. In your diagram draw $\overline{AE} \perp \overline{DC}$ and $\overline{BF} \perp \overline{DC}$. What must be true about the length of these segments? Mark the diagram appropriately.

   They must be congruent because they are perpendicular to the same set of parallel lines and have endpoints on the lines.

6. What must be true of $\angle AED$ and $\angle BFC$? Explain your answer, and then mark the diagram appropriately.

   They are congruent because they are both 90° angles.

Getting an Answer

7. How can you prove that $\triangle AED \cong \triangle BFC$? Explain.

   AAS Theorem: It is given that $\angle D \cong \angle C$; $\angle AED \cong \angle BFC$ because they are both right angles, and $\overline{AE} \cong \overline{BF}$ because both are perpendicular to the same set of parallel lines with endpoints on the lines.

8. How does this allow you to prove that $\overline{AD} \cong \overline{BC}$? **CPCTC**

Name ______________________ Class ____________ Date ____________

6-6 Practice

Form K

Trapezoids and Kites

Find the measures of the numbered angles in each isosceles trapezoid.

1. 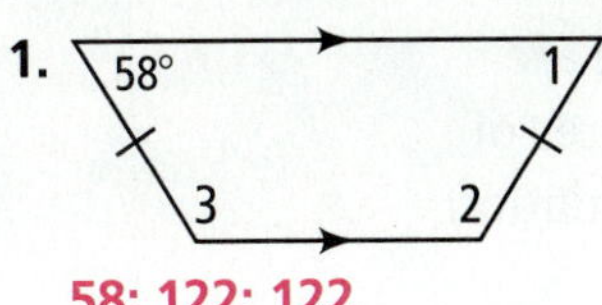

58; 122; 122

To start, identify which angles are congruent to and supplementary to the known angle.

∠ [1] is congruent to the 58° angle.

∠ [2] and ∠ [3] are supplementary to the 58° angle.

2. 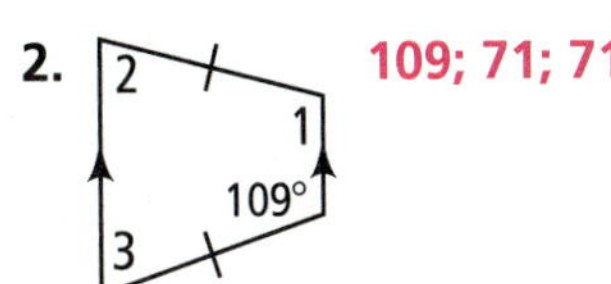

109; 71; 71

3. 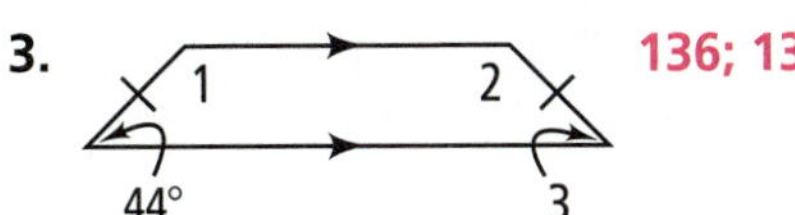

136; 136; 44

Find *GH* in each trapezoid.

4. 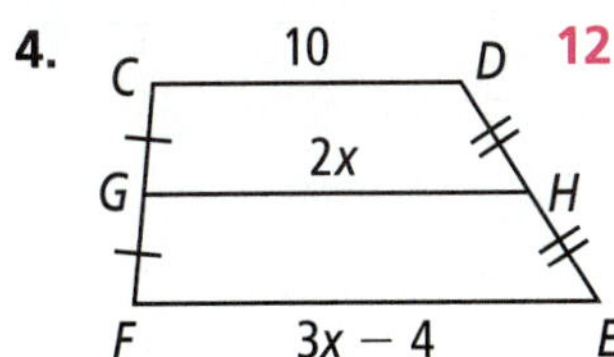 12

5. C 10 D 13

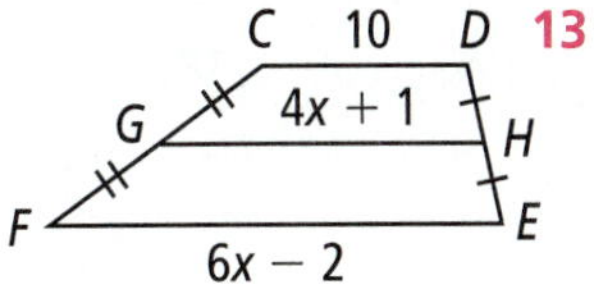

6. 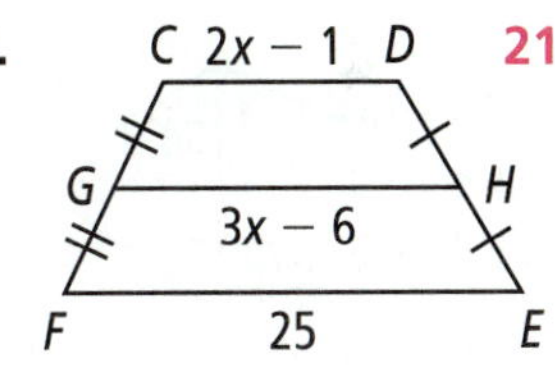 21

Algebra Find the value of the variable in each isosceles trapezoid.

7. 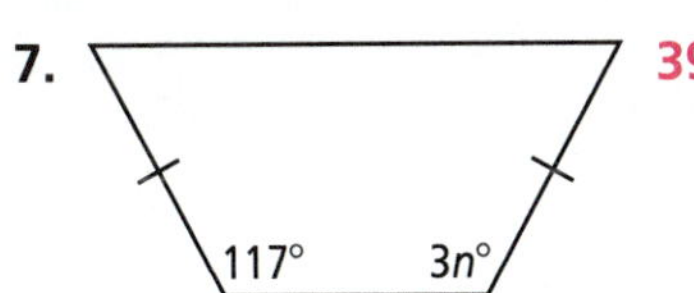

39

8. 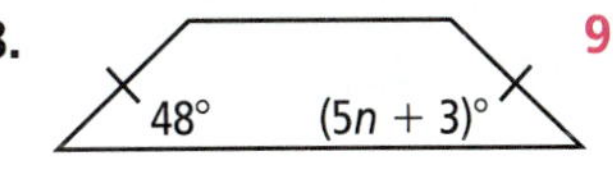

9

9. $AC = x + 5$ 7

$BD = 2x - 2$

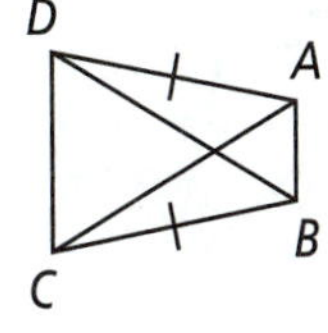

Algebra Find the lengths of the segments with variable expressions.

10. x − 6

x

2x − 9

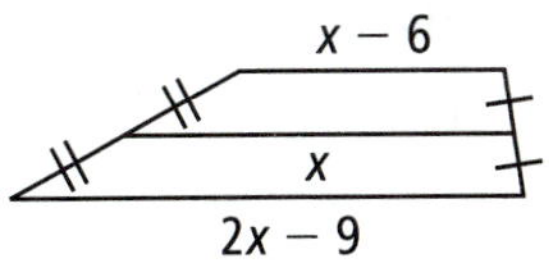

9; 15; 21

11. 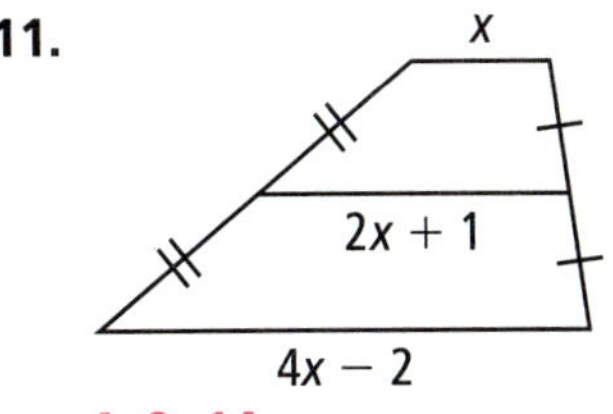

4; 9; 14

12. 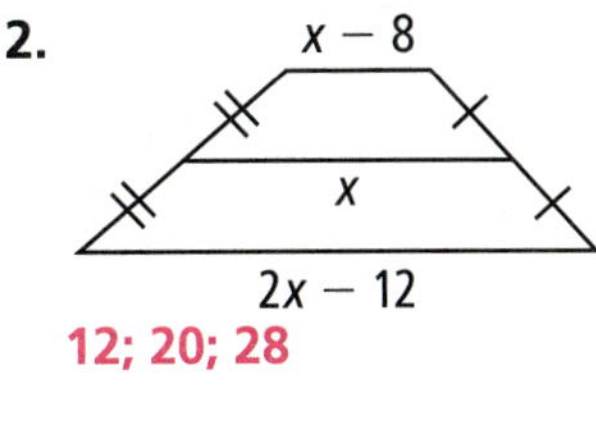

12; 20; 28

13. **Open-Ended** The midsegment of a trapezoid is 16 in. List three possible pairs of lengths for the bases of the trapezoid.

Answers may vary. Accept any pair of lengths that have a sum of 32.

Name ______________________ Class ____________ Date ____________

6-6 Practice (continued)

Form K

Trapezoids and Kites

Find the measures of the numbered angles in each kite.

14. 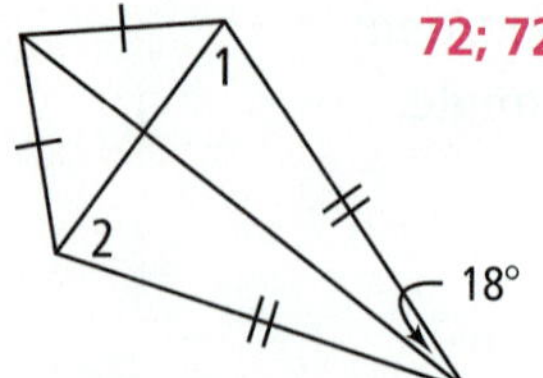

72; 72

To start, since the diagonals of a kite are perpendicular and the angle measures of a triangle add up to 180, write an equation with $m\angle 1$.

$m\angle 1 + \boxed{90} + \boxed{18} = 180$

15. 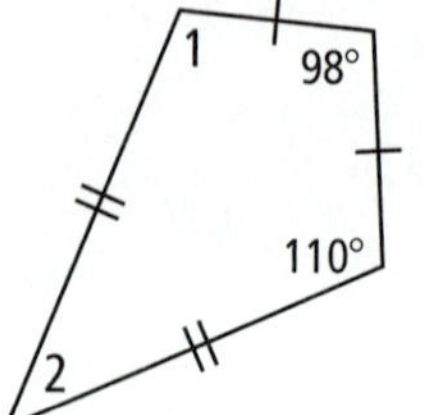

110; 42

16. 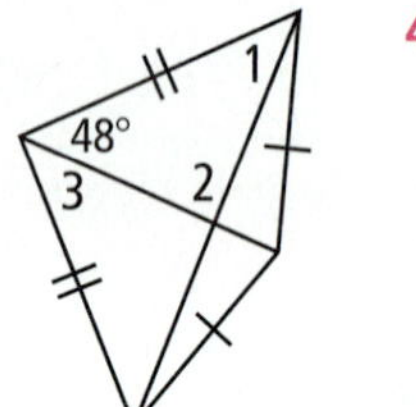

42; 90; 48

17. 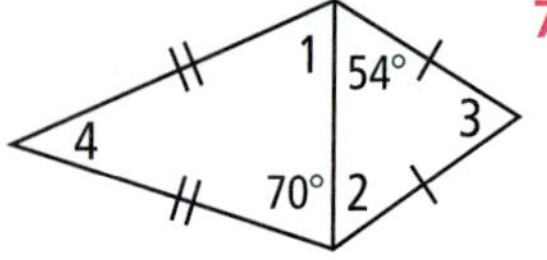

70; 54; 72; 40

18. 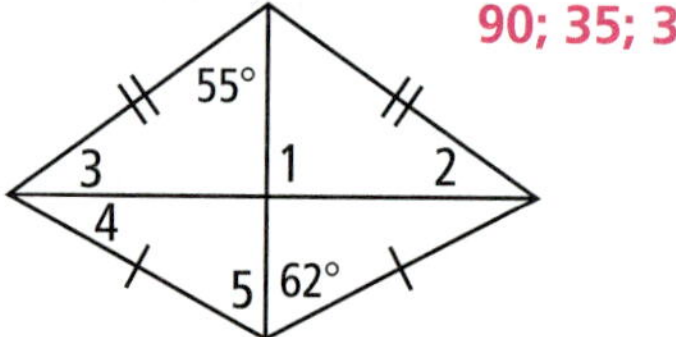

90; 35; 35; 28; 62

Algebra Find the value(s) of the variable(s) in each kite.

19. 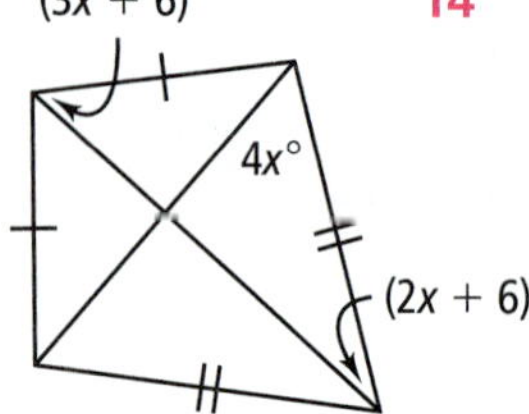

14

20. 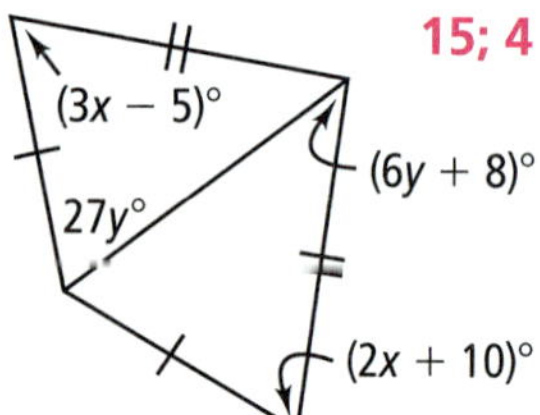

15; 4

21. 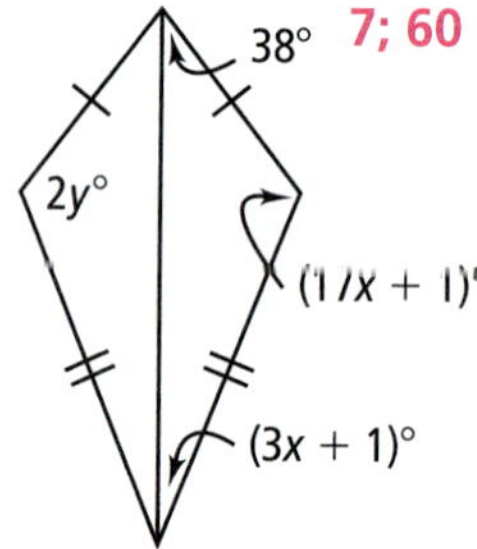

7; 60

Determine whether each statement is *true* or *false*. Justify your response.

22. All kites are quadrilaterals. True; all kites have four sides.

23. A kite is a parallelogram. False; the opposite sides of a kite are not ∥.

24. A kite can have congruent diagonals. True; a kite may have congruent diagonals as long as only one diagonal is bisected.

25. Both diagonals of a kite bisect angles at the vertices.
False; one diagonal bisects angles at the vertices but the other diagonal does not.

Name ______________________ Class ____________ Date ____________

6-6 Standardized Test Prep

Trapezoids and Kites

Multiple Choice

For Exercises 1–5, choose the correct letter.

1. In the isosceles trapezoid at the right, what is the measure of $\angle L$? C

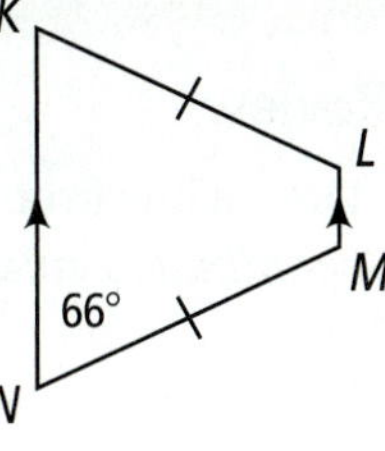

(A) 24 (C) 114

(B) 66 (D) 132

2. What is true about the diagonals in an isosceles trapezoid? F

(F) They are congruent.

(G) They are perpendicular.

(H) They are congruent and perpendicular.

(I) The length of each diagonal is equal to half the sum of the bases.

3. $\overline{LM}$ is the midsegment of trapezoid *RSXY*. What is *LM*? C

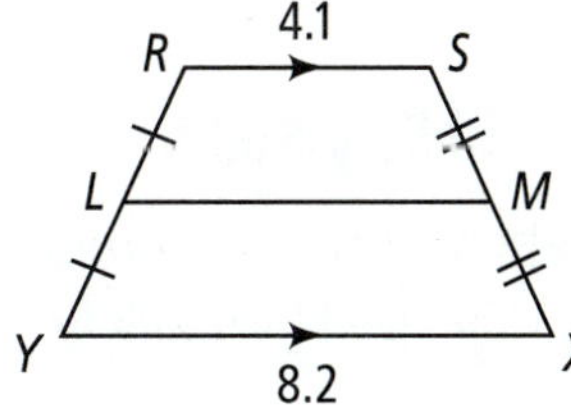

(A) 4.1 (C) 6.15

(B) 6 (D) 12.3

4. For which value of x is *ABCD* a kite? I

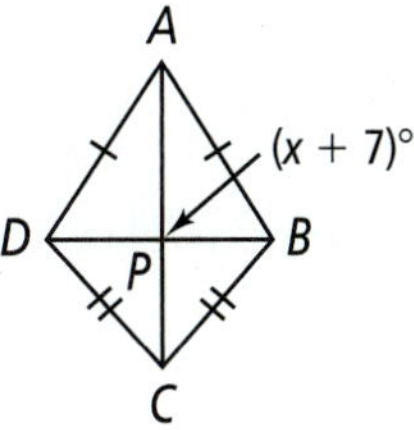

(F) 23 (H) 73

(G) 33 (I) 83

5. Algebra What is the value of x in kite *ABCD* at the right? B

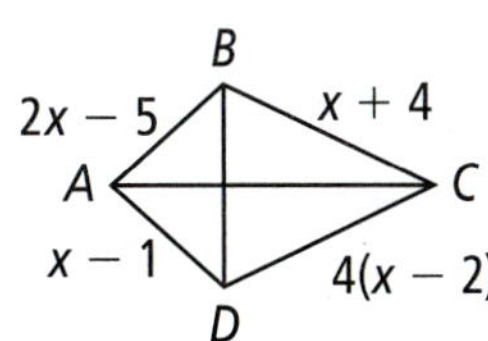

(A) 2 (C) 8

(B) 4 (D) 16

Short Response

6. A quadrilateral has diagonals that are congruent and bisect opposite pairs of angles. Could this quadrilateral be a kite? Explain. [2] No; it is a square, and in squares there are four congruent sides rather than two pairs of adjacent congruent sides. [1] correct answer with no explanation [0] no answer or wrong answer based on an inappropriate plan

6-7 Polygons in the Coordinate Plane

Vocabulary

Review

1. Draw a line from each item in Column A to the corresponding part of the *coordinate plane* in Column B.

Column A

origin
Quadrant I
Quadrant II
Quadrant III
Quadrant IV
x-axis
y-axis

Column B

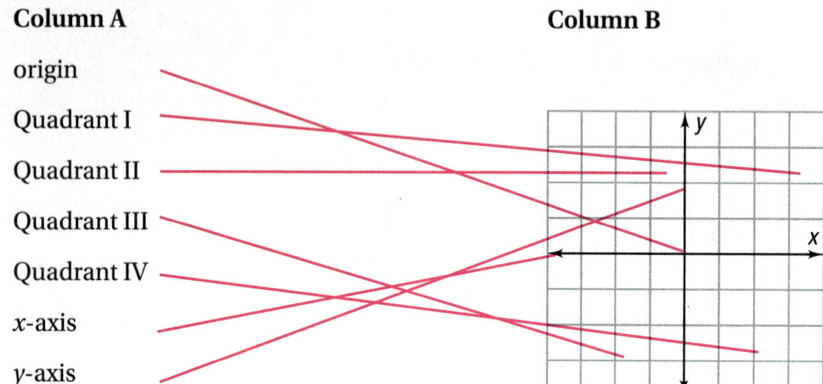

Vocabulary Builder

classify (verb) KLAS uh fy

Definition: To **classify** is to organize by category or type.

Math Usage: You can **classify** figures by their properties.

Related Words: classification (noun), classified (adjective)

Example: Rectangles, squares, and rhombuses are **classified** as parallelograms.

Use Your Vocabulary

Complete each statement with the correct word from the list. Use each word only once.

classification classified classify

2. Trapezoids are _?_ as quadrilaterals. classified

3. Taxonomy is a system of _?_ in biology. classification

4. Schools _?_ children by age. classify

take note

Key Concept Formulas on the Coordinate Plane

	Distance Formula	Midpoint Formula	Slope Formula
Formula	$d = \sqrt{(x_2 - x_1)^2 + (y_2 - y_1)^2}$	$M = \left(\frac{x_1 + x_2}{2}, \frac{y_1 + y_2}{2}\right)$	$m = \frac{y_2 - y_1}{x_2 - x_1}$
When to Use It	To determine whether • sides are congruent • diagonals are congruent	To determine • the coordinates of the midpoint of a side • whether diagonals bisect each other	To determine whether • opposite sides are parallel • diagonals are perpendicular • sides are perpendicular

Decide when to use each formula. Write D for *Distance Formula,* M for *Midpoint Formula,* or S for *Slope Formula.*

M **5.** You want to know whether diagonals bisect each other.

S **6.** You want to find whether opposite sides of a quadrilateral are parallel.

D **7.** You want to know whether sides of a polygon are congruent.

Problem 1 Classifying a Triangle

Got It? $\triangle DEF$ **has vertices** $D(0, 0)$, $E(1, 4)$, **and** $F(5, 2)$. **Is** $\triangle DEF$ ***scalene, isosceles,*** **or *equilateral*?**

8. Graph $\triangle DEF$ on the coordinate plane at the right.

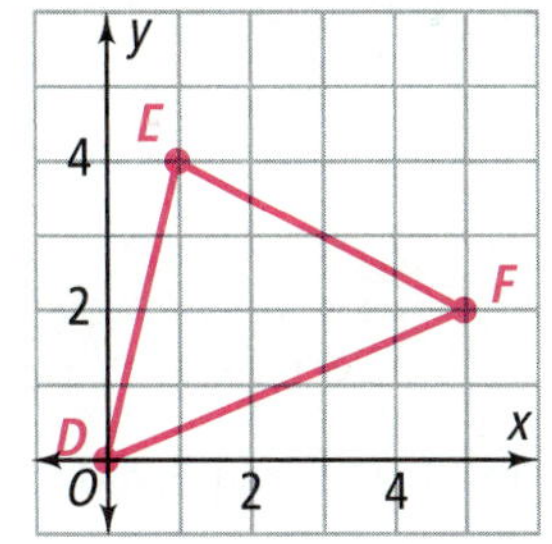

Use the Distance Formula to find the length of each side.

9. $EF = \sqrt{(5 - 1)^2 + (2 - 4)^2}$

$= \sqrt{16 + 4}$

$= \sqrt{20}$

10. $DE = \sqrt{(1 - 0)^2 + (4 - 0)^2}$

$= \sqrt{1 + 16}$

$= \sqrt{17}$

11. $DF = \sqrt{(5 - 0)^2 + (2 - 0)^2}$

$= \sqrt{25 + 4}$

$= \sqrt{29}$

12. What type of triangle is $\triangle DEF$? Explain. Answers may vary. Sample:

No side lengths are equal, so $\triangle DEF$ is scalene.

Problem 2 Classifying a Parallelogram

Got It? **$\square MNPQ$ has vertices $M(0, 1)$, $N(-1, 4)$, $P(2, 5)$, and $Q(3, 2)$. Is $\square MNPQ$ a rectangle? Explain.**

13. Find MP and NQ to determine whether the diagonals $\overline{MP}$ and $\overline{NQ}$ are congruent.

$$MP = \sqrt{(2 - 0)^2 + (5 - 1)^2} \qquad NQ = \sqrt{(3 - (-1))^2 + (2 - 4)^2}$$

$$= \sqrt{4 + 16} \qquad = \sqrt{16 + 4}$$

$$= \sqrt{20} \qquad = \sqrt{20}$$

14. Is $\square MNPQ$ a rectangle? Explain.

Yes. Explanations may vary. Sample: The diagonals are congruent.

Problem 3 Classifying a Quadrilateral

Got It? **An isosceles trapezoid has vertices $A(0, 0)$, $B(2, 4)$, $C(6, 4)$, and $D(8, 0)$. What special quadrilateral is formed by connecting the midpoints of the sides of $ABCD$?**

15. Draw the trapezoid on the coordinate plane at the right.

16. Find the coordinates of the midpoints of each side.

$\overline{AB}$

$$\left(\frac{0 + 2}{2}, \frac{0 + 4}{2}\right) = (1, 2)$$

$\overline{CD}$

$$\left(\frac{6 + 8}{2}, \frac{4 + 0}{2}\right) = (7, 2)$$

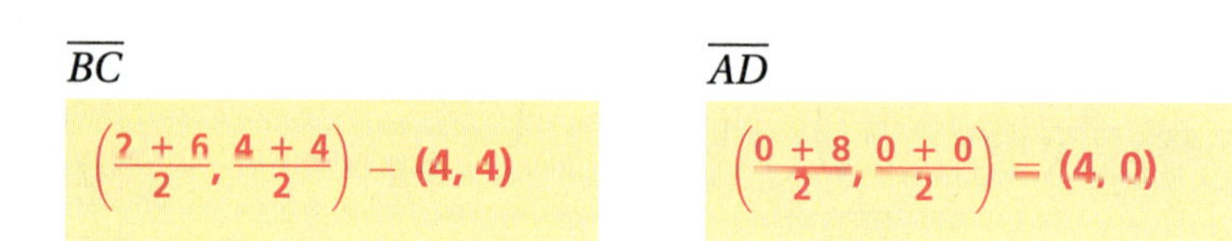

$\overline{BC}$

$$\left(\frac{2 + 6}{2}, \frac{4 + 4}{2}\right) = (4, 4)$$

$\overline{AD}$

$$\left(\frac{0 + 8}{2}, \frac{0 + 0}{2}\right) = (4, 0)$$

17. Draw the midpoints on the trapezoid and connect them. Judging by appearance, what type of special quadrilateral did you draw? Circle the most precise answer.

kite   parallelogram   (rhombus)   trapezoid

18. To verify your answer to Exercise 17, find the slopes of the segments.

connecting midpoints of $\overline{AB}$ and $\overline{BC}$: $\frac{2}{3}$

connecting midpoints of $\overline{BC}$ and $\overline{CD}$: $-\frac{2}{3}$

connecting midpoints of $\overline{CD}$ and $\overline{AD}$: $\frac{2}{3}$

connecting midpoints of $\overline{AD}$ and $\overline{AB}$: $-\frac{2}{3}$

19. Are the slopes of opposite segments equal? (Yes) / No

20. Are consecutive segments perpendicular? Yes / (No)

21. The special quadrilateral is a __?__. rhombus

Lesson Check • Do you UNDERSTAND?

Error Analysis A student says that the quadrilateral with vertices $D(1, 2)$, $E(0, 7)$, $F(5, 6)$, and $G(7, 0)$ is a rhombus because its diagonals are perpendicular. What is the student's error?

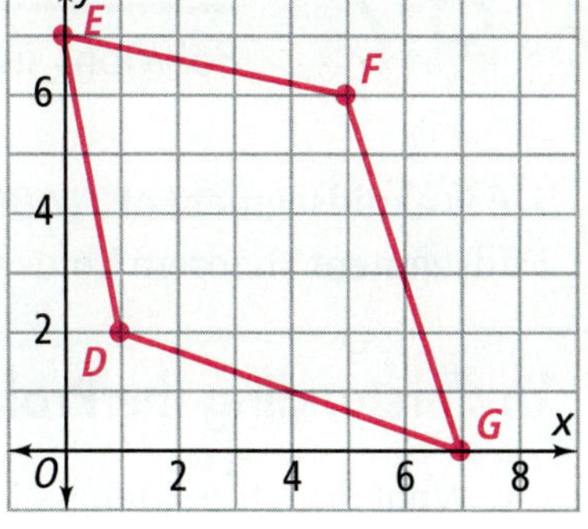

22. Draw *DEFG* on the coordinate plane at the right.

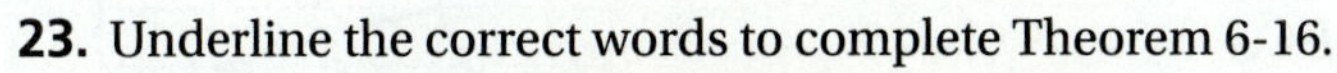

23. Underline the correct words to complete Theorem 6-16.

If the diagonals of a parallelogram / polygon are perpendicular, then the parallelogram / polygon is a rhombus.

24. Check whether *DEFG* is a parallelogram.

slope of $\overline{DE}$: $\frac{7 - 2}{0 - 1} = -5$ slope of $\overline{FG}$: $\frac{0 - 6}{7 - 5} = -3$

slope of $\overline{DG}$: $\frac{0 - 2}{7 - 1} = -\frac{1}{3}$ slope of $\overline{EF}$: $\frac{6 - 7}{5 - 0} = -\frac{1}{5}$

25. Are both pairs of opposite sides parallel? Yes / No (circled: No)

26. Find the slope of diagonal $\overline{DF}$.

$m = \frac{y_2 - y_1}{x_2 - x_1}$

$m = \frac{6 - 2}{5 - 1}$

$m = \frac{4}{4}$

$m = 1$

27. Find the slope of diagonal $\overline{EG}$.

$m = \frac{y_2 - y_1}{x_2 - x_1}$

$m = \frac{0 - 7}{7 - 0}$

$m = \frac{-7}{7}$

$m = -1$

28. Are the diagonals perpendicular? Yes / No (circled: Yes)

29. Explain the student's error. Answers may vary. Sample:

Although the quadrilateral has perpendicular diagonals, it is not a parallelogram, so it cannot be a rhombus.

Math Success

Check off the vocabulary words that you understand.

☐ distance ☐ midpoint ☐ slope

Rate how well you can *classify quadrilaterals in the coordinate plane.*

Need to review 0 2 4 6 8 10 Now I get it!

Name ______________________ Class ____________ Date ____________

6-7 Think About a Plan

Polygons in the Coordinate Plane

$\overline{DE}$ is a midsegment of $\triangle ABC$ at the right. Show that the Triangle Midsegment Theorem holds true for $\triangle ABC$.

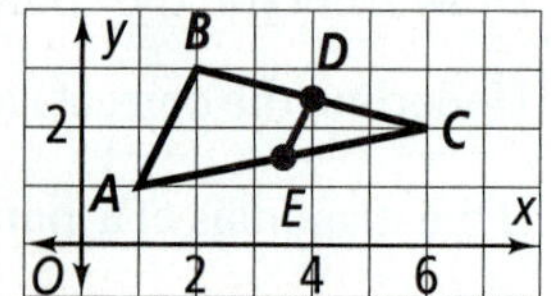

Understanding the Problem

1. What does the Triangle Midsegment Theorem state?
   If a segment joins the midpoints of two sides of a triangle, the segment is parallel to the third side and is one-half its length.

2. What do you need to prove to show that the Triangle Midsegment Theorem holds true for $\triangle ABC$? You must prove that $\overline{DE} \parallel \overline{BA}$ and that $2DE = BA$.

Planning the Solution

3. What is always true of the slope of parallel lines? the slopes are equal

4. Which formula can you use to find the length of a segment on the coordinate plane? Distance Formula

5. What are the coordinates for D and E? $D(4, 2.5)$ and $E(3.5, 1.5)$

Getting an Answer

6. Find the slope of segments $\overline{DE}$ and $\overline{BA}$ below.

   Slope of $\overline{DE}$: $m = \dfrac{2.5 - 1.5}{4 - 3.5} = \dfrac{1}{.5} = 2$

   Slope of $\overline{BA}$: $m = \dfrac{3 - 1}{2 - 1} = \dfrac{2}{1} = 2$

7. Are segments $\overline{DE}$ and $\overline{BA}$ parallel? yes

8. Find the length of segments $\overline{DE}$ and $\overline{BA}$ below.

   Length of $\overline{DE}$: $\sqrt{(\square - \square)^2 + (\square - \square)^2} = \square$

   $\sqrt{(4 - 3.5)^2 + (2.5 - 1.5)^2} = \sqrt{1.25}$

   Length of $\overline{BA}$: $\sqrt{(\square - \square)^2 + (\square - \square)^2} = \square$

   $\sqrt{(2 - 1)^2 + (3 - 1)^2} = \sqrt{5} = \sqrt{4 \times 1.25} = 2\sqrt{1.25}$

9. Does the Triangle Midsegment Theorem hold true for $\triangle ABC$? Explain.
   Yes; $\overline{DE} \parallel \overline{BA}$ and the length of $\overline{DE}$ is one-half the length of $\overline{BA}$.

Name ______________________ Class ____________ Date ____________

6-7 Practice

Form K

Polygons in the Coordinate Plane

Determine whether △*ABC* is *scalene, isosceles,* or *equilateral.* Explain.

1. 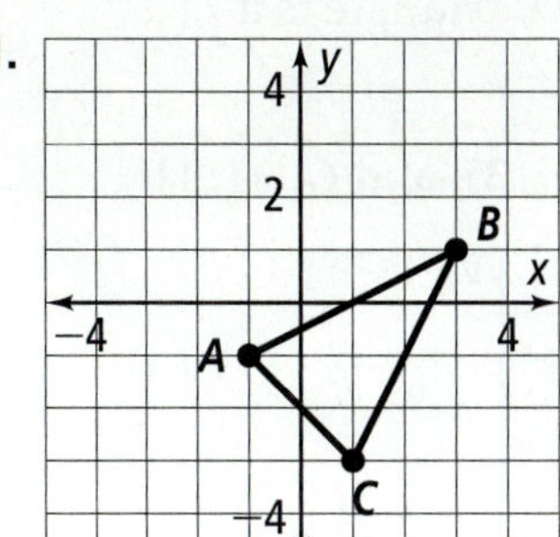

To start, determine the vertices of the triangle. Then use the Distance Formula to find the length of each side.

$A(-1, -1)$, $B(3, 1)$, $C(\boxed{1}, \boxed{-3})$

isosceles; $AB = CB$

2. 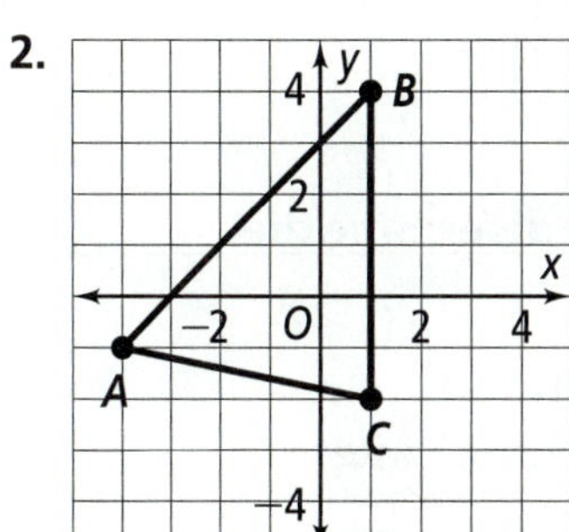

Scalene; no sides are congruent.

3. 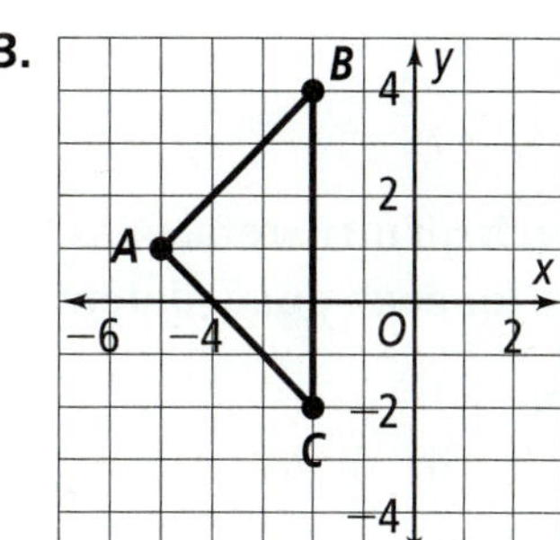

isosceles; $AC = AB$

Determine whether the parallelogram is a *rhombus, rectangle, square,* or *none.* Explain.

4. $(-3, -1)$, $(-3, 2)$, $(1, 1)$, $(1, -2)$
none

5. $(-5, 2)$, $(-3, 4)$, $(-3, 0)$, $(-1, 2)$
Square; diagonals are ≅ and ⊥.

6. $(-2, -1)$,$(-3, -3)$, $(1, -5)$, $(2, -3)$
Rectangle; sides are perpendicular, diagonals are ≅, opposite sides are ≅.

7. $(-6, -3)$, $(0, 5)$, $(10, 5)$, $(4, -3)$
Rhombus; diagonals are ⊥ and sides are ≅ but not ⊥.

What is the most precise classification of the quadrilateral formed by connecting in order the midpoints of each figure below?

8. ▱ *JKLM* parallelogram

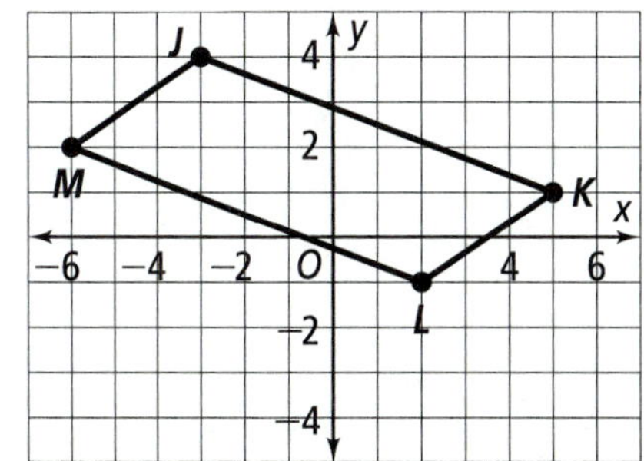

9. kite *WXYZ* rectangle

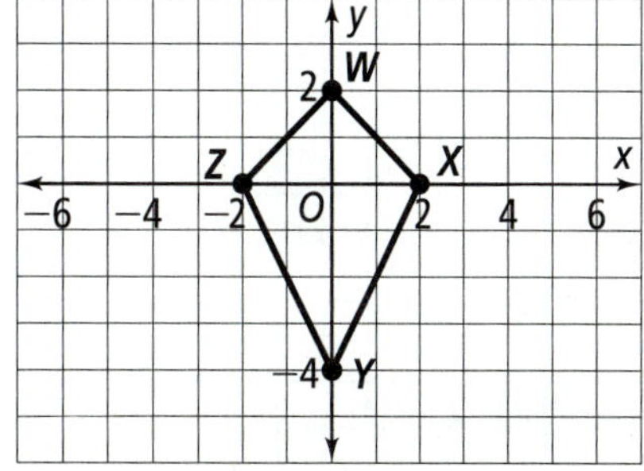

Name ______________________ Class ____________ Date ____________

6-7 Practice (continued)

Form K

Polygons in the Coordinate Plane

Graph and label each triangle with the given vertices. Determine whether each triangle is *scalene, isosceles,* or *equilateral.* Then tell whether each triangle is a right triangle.

10. $V(-3, -2)$, $W(3, -2)$, and $X(0, 3)$

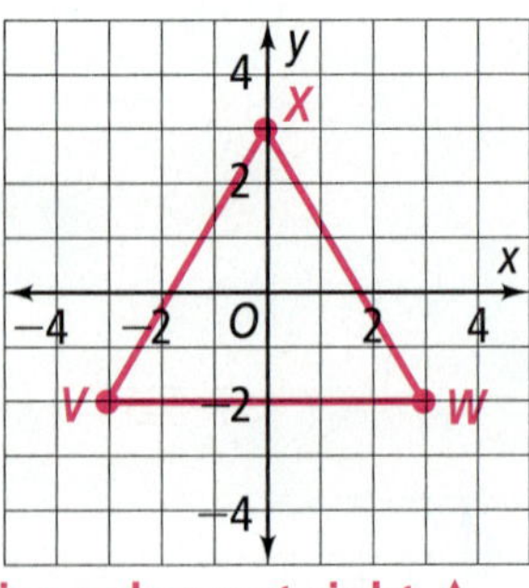

isosceles; not right △

11. $A(-6, 3)$, $B(-1, 3)$, and $C(-1, 1)$

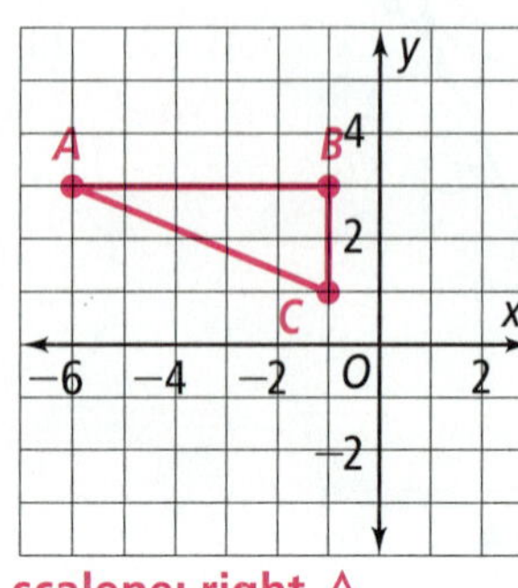

scalene; right △

Graph and label each quadrilateral with the given vertices. Then determine the most precise name for each quadrilateral.

12. $Q(-5, 1)$, $R(-1, -2)$, $S(-1, -7)$, $T(-5, -4)$ rhombus

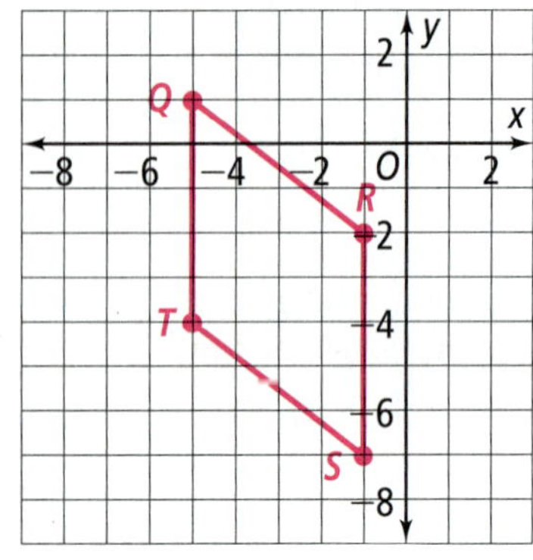

13. $G(-4, 4)$, $H(-1, -2)$, $I(-4, -5)$, $J(-7, -2)$ kite

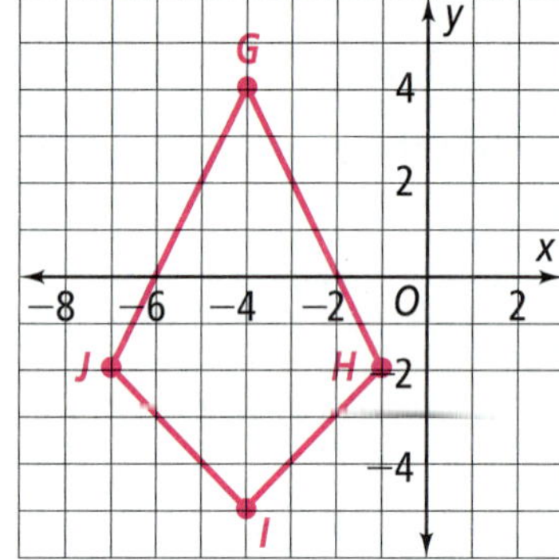

14. $A(2, 0)$, $B(-1, 3)$, $C(2, 6)$, $D(5, 3)$ square

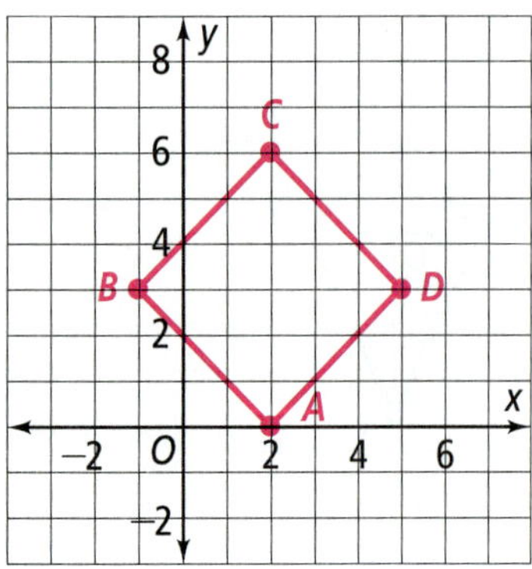

15. $J(-1, 8)$, $K(1, 6)$, $L(-5, 0)$, $M(-7, 2)$ rectangle

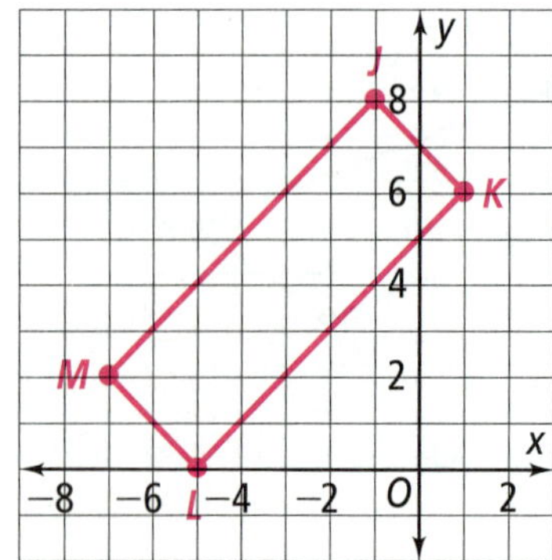

Name ______________________ Class __________ Date __________

6-7 Standardized Test Prep

Polygons in the Coordinate Plane

Multiple Choice

For Exercises 1–4, choose the correct letter.

1. What kind of triangle is this? D

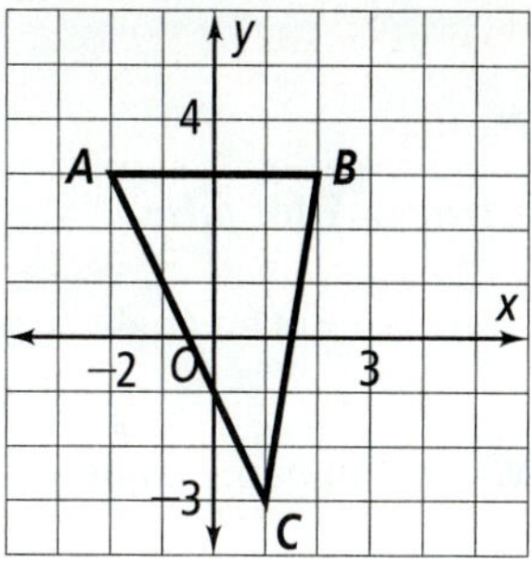

Ⓐ right

Ⓑ equilateral

Ⓒ isosceles

Ⓓ scalene

2. What is the most accurate description of the polygon at the right? F

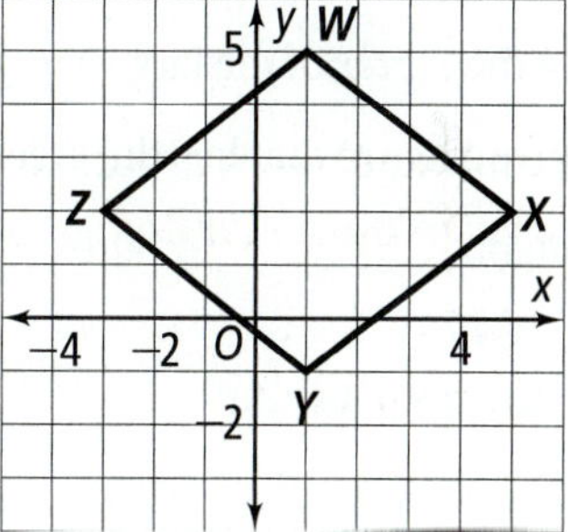

Ⓕ rhombus

Ⓖ square

Ⓗ rectangle

Ⓘ parallelogram

3. What is the most accurate description of the polygon at the right? D

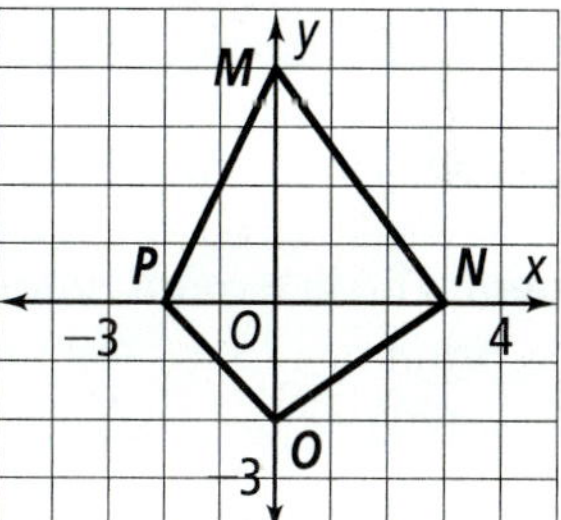

Ⓐ rhombus Ⓒ kite

Ⓑ trapezoid Ⓓ quadrilateral

4. What kind of triangle is made by connecting the points $A(0, -6)$, $B(3, -6)$, and $C(3, -2)$? G

Ⓕ equilateral Ⓗ isosceles

Ⓖ right Ⓘ right and isosceles

Short Response

5. What type of quadrilateral is formed by connecting the points (0, 9), (3, 6), (0, 1), and (−3, 6)? Explain. [2] Kite; two pairs of consecutive sides are congruent and no side is congruent to the side opposite it. [1] Kite; student explains that two pairs of consecutive sides are congruent or that no side is congruent to the side opposite it. [0] no answer or wrong answer based on an inappropriate plan

6-8 Applying Coordinate Geometry

Vocabulary

Review

Write T for *true* or F for *false*.

T 1. The *vertex* of an angle is the endpoint of two rays.

F 2. When you name angles using three points, the *vertex* gets named first.

T 3. A polygon has the same number of sides and *vertices*.

4. Circle the *vertex* of the largest angle in $\triangle ABC$ at the right.

5. Circle the figure that has the greatest number of *vertices*.

hexagon kite rectangle trapezoid

Vocabulary Builder

coordinates (noun) koh AWR din its

Definition: *Coordinates* are numbers or letters that specify the location of an object.

Math Usage: The *coordinates* of a point on a plane are an ordered pair of numbers.

Main Idea: The first *coordinate* of an ordered pair is the *x-coordinate*. The second is the *y-coordinate*.

coordinates

(−1, 3)

x-coordinate y-coordinate

Use Your Vocabulary

Draw a line from each point in Column A to its *coordinates* in Column B.

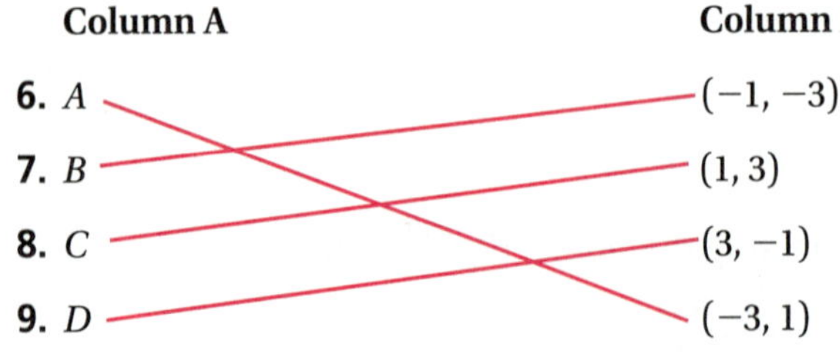

Column A	Column B
6. *A*	(−1, −3)
7. *B*	(1, 3)
8. *C*	(3, −1)
9. *D*	(−3, 1)

Problem 1 Naming Coordinates

Got It? ***RECT* is a rectangle with height *a* and length 2*b*. The *y*-axis bisects $\overline{EC}$ and $\overline{RT}$. What are the coordinates of the vertices of *RECT*?**

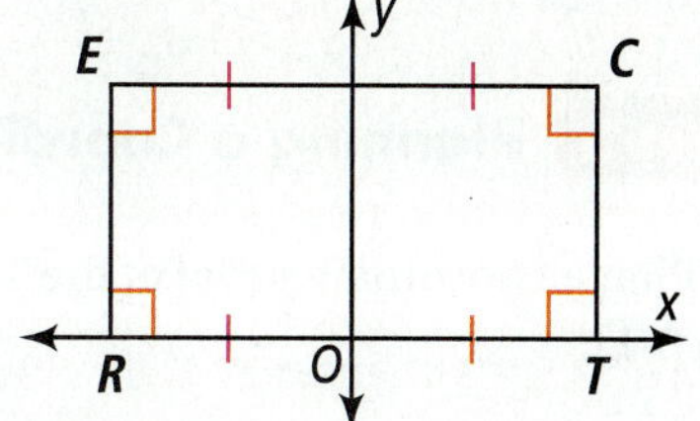

10. Use the information in the problem to mark all segments that are congruent to $\overline{OT}$.

11. Rectangle *RECT* has length 2*b*,

so $RT =$ 2*b* and $RO = OT =$ *b*.

12. The coordinates of *O* are (0 , 0), so the coordinates of *T* are (*b* , 0), and the coordinates of *R* are (− *b* , 0).

13. Rectangle *RECT* has height *a*, so $TC = RE =$ *a*.

14. The coordinates of *C* are (*b* , *a*), so the coordinates of *E* are (−*b* , *a*).

15. Why is it helpful that one side of rectangle *RECT* is on the *x*-axis and the figure is centered on the *y*-axis.

Answers may vary. Sample: The only variables the coordinates contain are *a* and *b*.

Problem 2 Using Variable Coordinates

Got It? Reasoning **The diagram at the right shows a general parallelogram with a vertex at the origin and one side along the *x*-axis. Explain why the *x*-coordinate of *B* is the sum of 2*a* and 2*b*.**

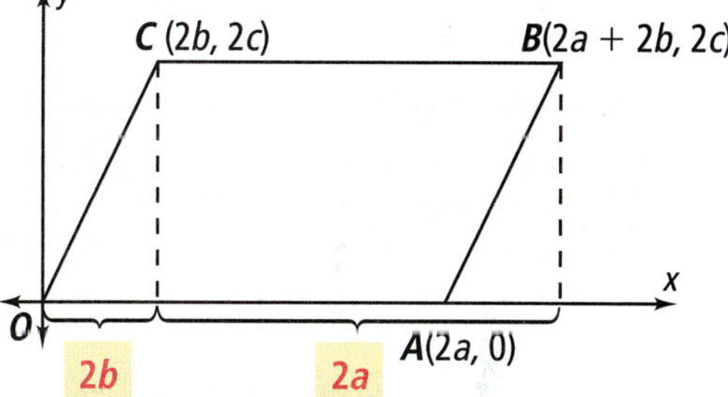

16. Complete the diagram.

17. Complete the reasoning model below.

Think	Write
Opposite sides of a parallelogram are congruent.	$OA =$ *BC* = 2*a*
The *x*-coordinate is the sum of the lengths in the brackets.	The *x*-coordinate of *B* is 2*b* + 2*a* = 2*a* + 2*b*.

18. Explain why the *x*-coordinate of *B* is the sum of $2a + 2b$.

Answers may vary. Sample: Since opposite sides of a parallelogram are congruent, *BC* = 2*a*. The *x*-coordinate of *C* is 2*b*, so the *x*-coordinate of *B* is 2*a* + 2*b*.

You can use coordinate geometry and algebra to prove theorems in geometry. This kind of proof is called a *coordinate proof.*

Problem 3 Planning a Coordinate Proof

Got It? **Plan a coordinate proof of the Triangle Midsegment Theorem (Theorem 5-1).**

19. Underline the correct words to complete Theorem 5-1.

If a segment joins the vertices / midpoints of two sides of a triangle, then the segment is perpendicular / parallel to the third side, and is half its length.

20. Write the coordinates of the vertices of $\triangle ABC$ on the grid below. Use multiples of 2 to name the coordinates.

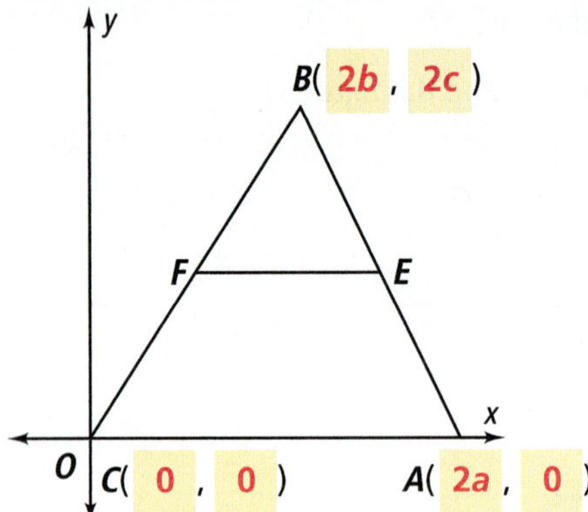

21. **Reasoning** Why should you make the coordinates of A and B multiples of 2? Answers may vary. Sample:

Make the coordinates of A and B multiples of 2 so the coordinates of the midpoints will not be fractions.

22. Complete the *Given* and *Prove.*

Given: E is the _?_ of $\overline{AB}$ and F is the _?_ of $\overline{BC}$. midpoint midpoint

Prove: $\overline{EF} \parallel \overline{AC}$, and $EF = \frac{1}{2}AC$

23. Circle the formula you need to use to prove $\overline{EF} \parallel \overline{AC}$. Underline the formula you need to use to prove $EF = \frac{1}{2}AC$.

Distance Formula   Midpoint Formula   Slope Formula

Underline the correct word to complete each sentence.

24. If the slopes of $\overline{EF}$ and $\overline{AC}$ are equal, then $\overline{EF}$ and $\overline{AC}$ are congruent / parallel.

25. If you know the lengths of $\overline{EF}$ and $\overline{AC}$, then you can add / compare them.

26. Write three steps you must do before writing the plan for a coordinate proof.

Accept reasonable answers. Sample: Draw and label a figure, state the Given and Prove, and determine the formulas you will need.

Lesson Check • Do you know HOW?

In ▱*KLMO*, *OM* = 2*a*. What are the coordinates of *K* and *M*?

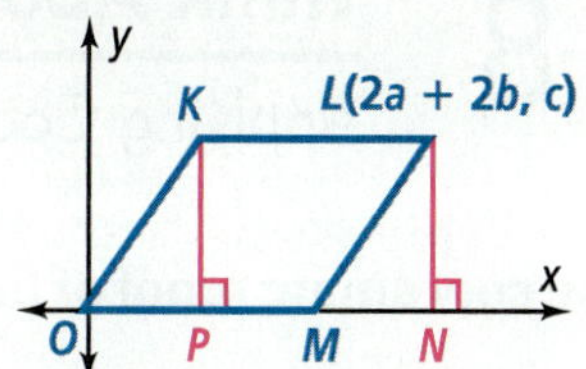

Complete.

27. The x-coordinate of O is 0 and $OM = 2a$, so the x-coordinate of M is $2a$.

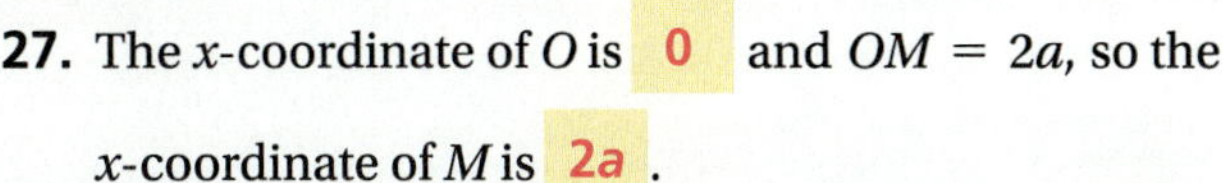

28. M is on the x-axis, so the y-coordinate of M is 0.

29. The coordinates of M are ($2a$, 0).

30. On the diagram, draw segments $\overline{KP}$ and $\overline{LN}$ that join K and L to the x-axis.

Use Exercises 31–32 to find an expression for *OP*, the *x*-coordinate of *K*.

31. You can show $\triangle KOP \cong \triangle$ LMN, so $OP =$ MN.

32. Complete the steps to find an expression for MN. Write a justification for each step.

$ON = OM + MN$	Segment Addition Postulate
$2a + 2b = 2a + MN$	Substitute the expressions for ON and OM.
$2b = MN$	Subtract $2a$ from each side.

Complete.

33. $OP = MN$, so the x-coordinate of K is $2b$.

34. The y-coordinate of K is the same as the y-coordinate of L, so the y-coordinate of K is k.

35. The coordinates of K are ($2b$, k).

Math Success

Check off the vocabulary words that you understand.

☐ coordinate geometry ☐ coordinate proof ☐ variable coordinates

Rate how well you can *use properties of special figures*.

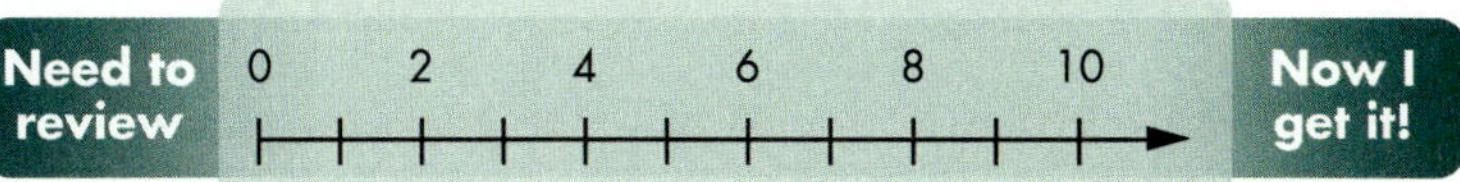

Name ______________________ Class ____________ Date ____________

6-8 Think About a Plan

Applying Coordinate Geometry

Plan the coordinate proof of the statement.

The diagonals of a rectangle bisect each other.

Know

1. What does it mean when we say that the diagonals bisect each other?

   They divide each other in half.

2. If the diagonals do bisect each other, what should the point of intersection be for each diagonal?

   the midpoint of that diagonal

Need

3. Which formula will you need to use to prove that the diagonals bisect each other?

   Midpoint Formula

4. Based on the formula you need to use, what type of number should you use for the coordinates of the vertices?

   multiples of 2

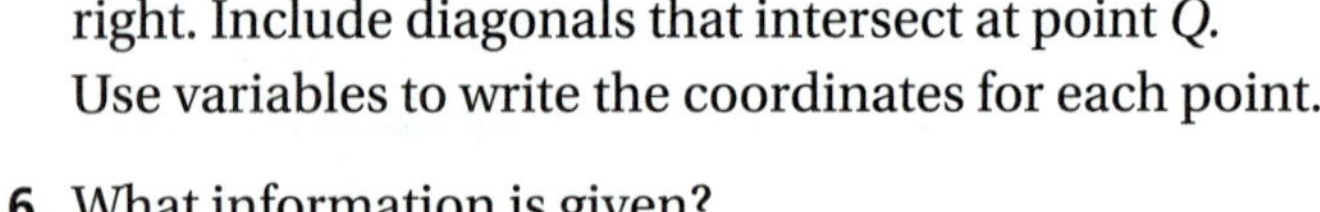

5. Draw rectangle *WXYZ* on the coordinate plane at the right. Include diagonals that intersect at point *Q*. Use variables to write the coordinates for each point.

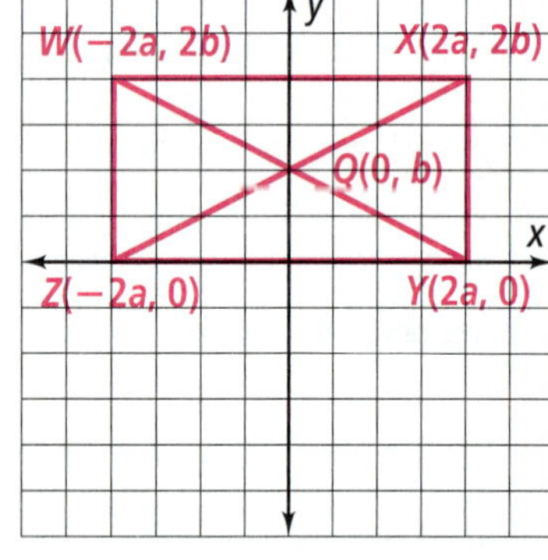

6. What information is given?

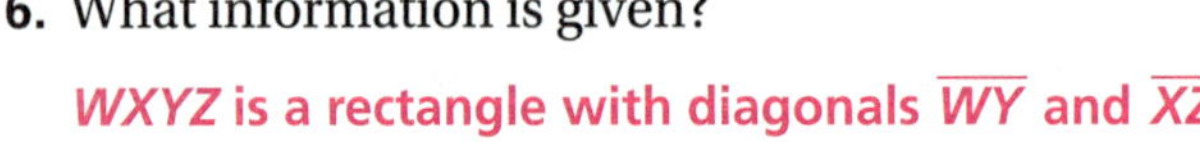

   WXYZ is a rectangle with diagonals $\overline{WY}$ and $\overline{XZ}$.

7. What must you prove?

   Q is the midpoint of both $\overline{WY}$ and $\overline{XZ}$.

Plan

8. How will you go about proving this?

   Use the Midpoint Formula to find the midpoints of $\overline{WY}$ and $\overline{XZ}$. If the coordinates of the midpoint of both lines are the coordinates of Point *Q*, the statement is proven.

Name ______________________ Class ____________ Date ____________

6-8 Practice

Form K

Applying Coordinate Geometry

Algebra What are the coordinates of the vertices of each figure?

1. rectangle with base $2b$ and height h **$A(-b, h)$, $B(b, h)$, $C(b, 0)$, $D(-b, 0)$**

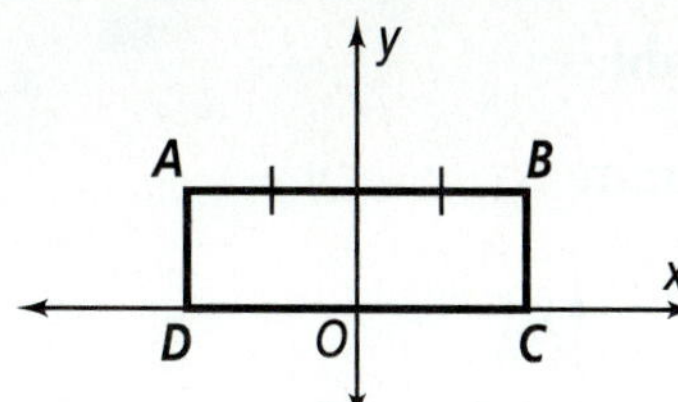

To start, identify the coordinates of C.
Because $CD = 2b$, the x-coordinate of C is $\frac{2b}{2}$, or [**b**]. C is on the x-axis, so its y-coordinate is [**0**].

2. parallelogram with height a, and point P distance b from the origin

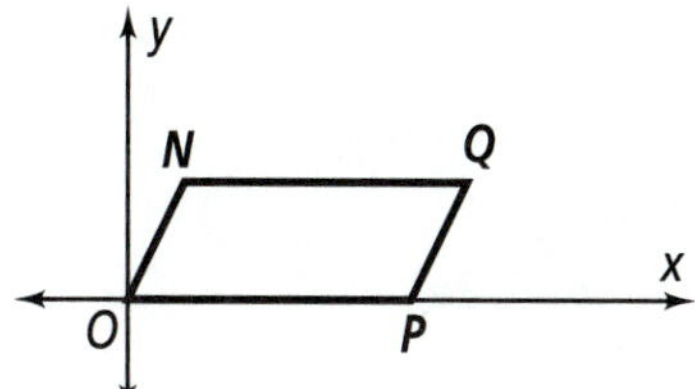

$N(c, a)$, $O(0, 0)$, $P(b, 0)$, $Q(b + c, a)$

3. isosceles trapezoid with base centered at the origin, with bases $4a$ and $2b$, and height c

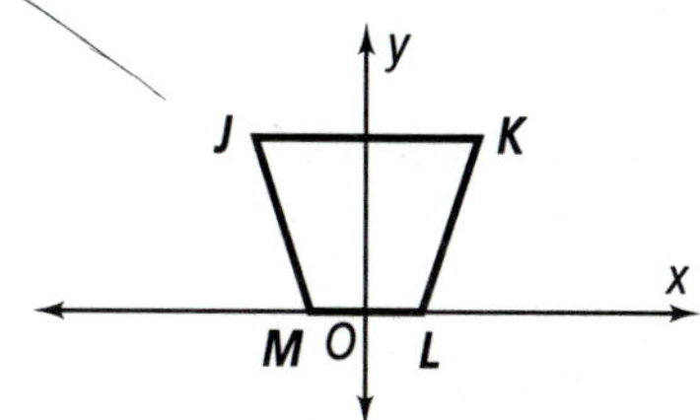

$J(-2a, c)$, $K(2a, c)$, $L(b, 0)$, $M(-b, 0)$

4. The diagram shows a rectangle with base a and height b. What are the coordinates of D, the point of intersection of the diagonals of rectangle $GHIJ$? Explain.
$\left(\frac{a}{2}, \frac{b}{2}\right)$; these are the x-coordinate of the midpoint of $\overline{GH}$ and the y-coordinate of the midpoint of $\overline{HI}$.

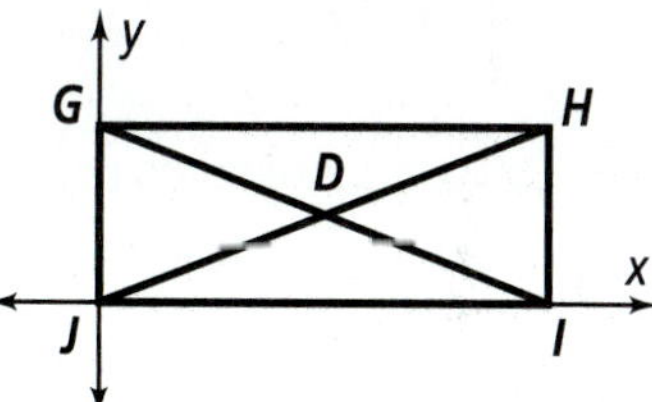

5. Plan a coordinate proof to show that a parallelogram is a rectangle.

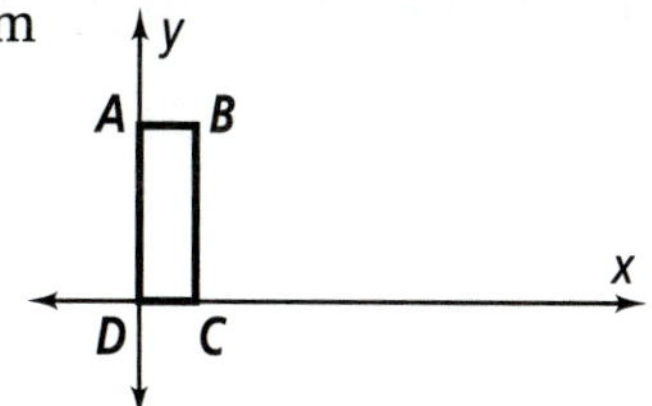

a. Name the coordinates of ▱ $ABCD$ at the right with base b and height h.
$A(0, h)$, $B(b, h)$, $C(b, 0)$, $D(0, 0)$

b. Write the *Given* and *Prove* Statements.
Given: ▱ $ABCD$; Prove: $ABCD$ is a rectangle.

c. What information do you need to prove that the parallelogram is a rectangle?
Answers may vary. Sample: You need to prove that the adjacent sides are perpendicular. To do this, you need to show that the slopes of the lines of the adjacent sides are negative reciprocals.

6. Open-Ended Place a kite in the coordinate plane.
Check students' work. Kite could be placed so that the diagonals are the x- and y-axes.

6-8 Practice (continued) — Form K

Applying Coordinate Geometry

7. **Reasoning** A rhombus $QRST$ is centered at the origin with $QS = 4r$ and $RT = 4t$. What are the coordinates of each vertex?
$Q(-2r, 0)$, $R(0, 2t)$, $S(2r, 0)$, $T(0, -2t)$ or $Q(0, -2r)$, $R(2t, 0)$, $S(0, 2r)$, $T(-2t, 0)$

Give the coordinates for point D without using any new variables.

8. isosceles triangle $(a, 0)$

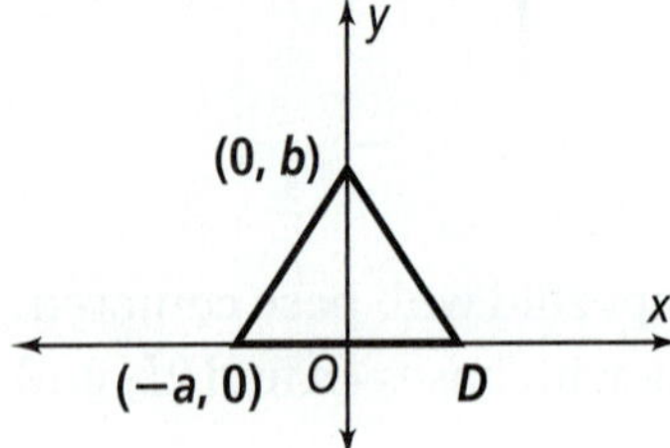

9. parallelogram $(b + a, c)$

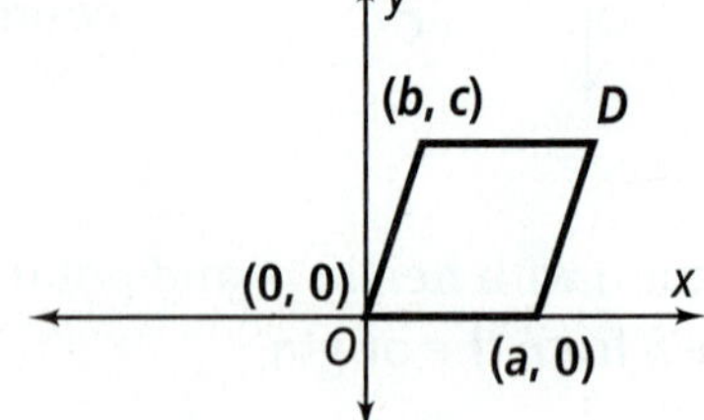

10. square $(a, 2a)$

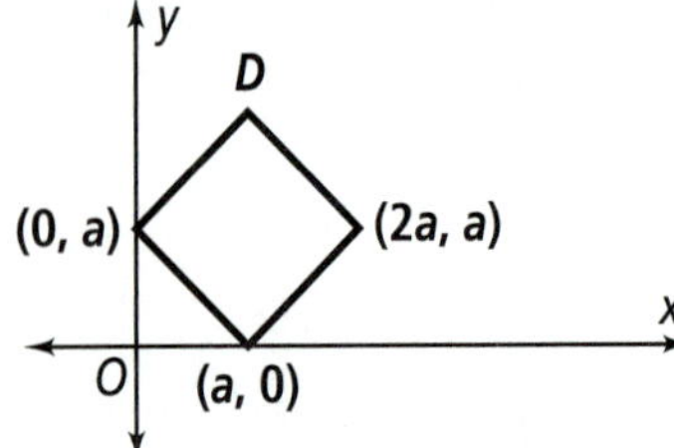

11. rhombus $(0, -2a)$

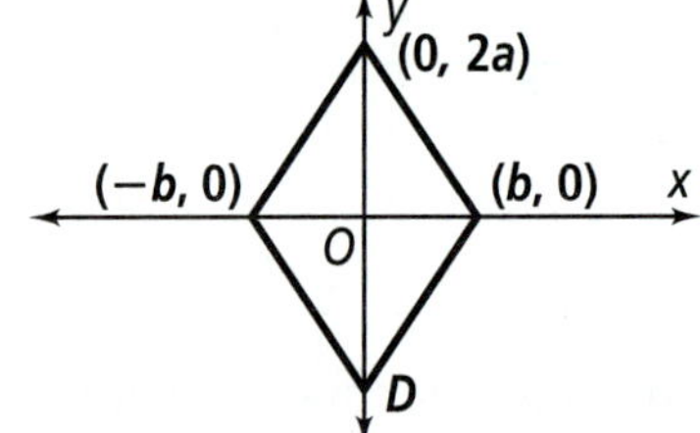

12. a. Draw an isosceles trapezoid with height $2h$ and bases $2a$ and $2b$ so that the origin is the midpoint of the base with length $2b$.

y
(−a, 2h) (a, 2h)
x
(−b, 0) O (b, 0)

b. Give the coordinates of the vertices of the trapezoid.

c. Compute the length of the legs of the trapezoid.
$\sqrt{(a - b)^2 + (2h)^2}$

d. Find the slopes of the two legs of the trapezoid.
$\frac{2h}{a - b}$ and $\frac{2h}{-a + b}$

e. Find the midpoints of the legs of the trapezoid.
$(\frac{a + b}{2}, h)$; $(\frac{-a + (-b)}{2}, h)$

13. **Reasoning** Is the triangle at the right an isosceles triangle with base $\overline{GI}$? How can you tell without using the Distance Formula?
No; answers may vary. Sample: the points G and I are different distances from the origin.

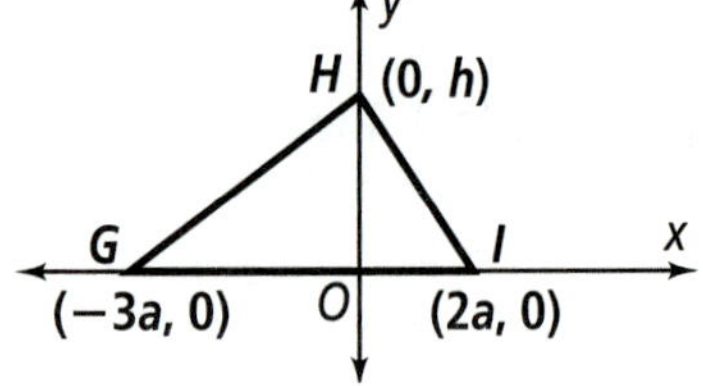

Name ______________________ Class __________ Date __________

6-8 Standardized Test Prep

Applying Coordinate Geometry

Multiple Choice

For Exercises 1–5, choose the correct letter.

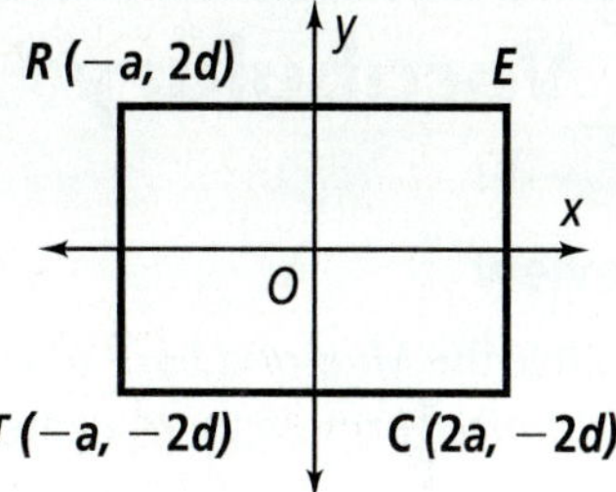

1. Rectangle *RECT* is shown at the right. What are the coordinates of point *E*? D

   A $(2a, d)$ C $(-2a, d)$

   B $(a, 2d)$ D $(2a, 2d)$

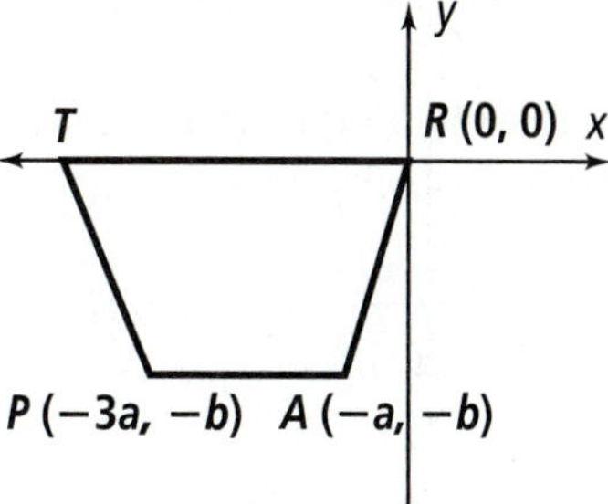

2. Isosceles trapezoid *TRAP* is shown at the right. What are the coordinates of point *T*? F

   F $(-4a, 0)$ H $(0, -4a)$

   G $(-b, 0)$ I $(-3b, 0)$

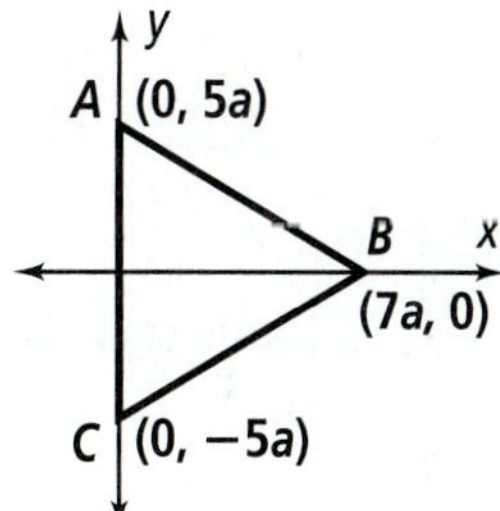

3. What type of triangle is shown at the right? C

   A equilateral C isosceles

   B right D scalene

4. What is the most precise description of a quadrilateral with coordinates $A(-a, b)$, $B(3a, b)$, $C(3a, -b)$, $D(-a, -b)$? G

   F kite G rectangle H rhombus I square

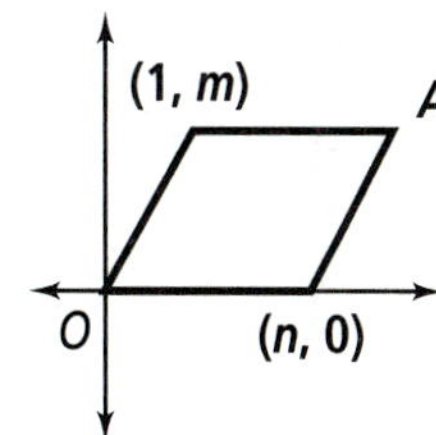

5. What coordinates for point *A* can you write without using any new variables? B

   A (n, m) C $(n + m, 1)$

   B $(1 + n, m)$ D $(m, n + 1)$

Short Response

6. What type of quadrilateral is formed by connecting the points $(0, 0)$, $(3x, b)$, $(18x, b)$, and $(15x, 0)$? Explain.

   [2] Sample: A parallelogram; opposite sides are ≅ and parallel, but diagonals are not ≅ and adjacent sides are not ≅. [1] Student proves it is a parallelogram, but not that it is not a special parallelogram. [0] no answer or wrong answer based on an inappropriate plan

6-9 Proofs Using Coordinate Geometry

Vocabulary

Review

1. Circle the *Midpoint Formula* for a segment in the coordinate plane. Underline the *Distance Formula* for a segment in the coordinate plane.

$M = \left(\frac{x_1 + x_2}{2}, \frac{y_1 + y_2}{2}\right)$ $\qquad d = \sqrt{(x_2 - x_1)^2 + (y_2 - y_1)^2}$ $\qquad m = \frac{y_2 - y_1}{x_2 - x_1}$

2. Circle the *Midpoint Formula* for a segment on a number line. Underline the *Distance Formula* for a segment on a number line.

$M = \frac{x_1 + x_2}{2}$ $\qquad d = |x_1 - x_2|$ $\qquad m = \frac{x_1 - x_2}{2}$

Vocabulary Builder

variable (noun) VEHR ee uh bul

Related Words: vary (verb), variable (adjective)

Definition: A **variable** is a symbol (usually a letter) that represents one or more numbers.

Math Usage: A **variable** represents an unknown number in equations and inequalities.

x and *y* are often used as **variables**.

Use Your Vocabulary

Underline the correct word to complete each sentence.

3. An interest rate that can change is a *variable* / vary interest rate.

4. You can *variable* / vary your appearance by changing your hair color.

5. The amount of daylight *variables* / varies from summer to winter.

6. Circle the *variable(s)* in each expression below.

$3n$ $\qquad 4 + x$ $\qquad p^2 - 2p$ $\qquad \frac{4}{y}$

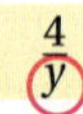

7. Cross out the expressions that do NOT contain a *variable*.

$2 + m$ $\qquad 36 \div (2 \cdot 3)$ $\qquad 9a^2 - 4a$ $\qquad 8 - (15 \div 3)$

Problem 1 Writing a Coordinate Proof

Got It? **Reasoning** **You want to prove that the midpoint of the hypotenuse of a right triangle is equidistant from the three vertices. What is the advantage of using coordinates $O(0, 0)$, $E(0, 2b)$, and $F(2a, 0)$ rather than $O(0, 0)$, $E(0, b)$, and $F(a, 0)$?**

8. Label each triangle.

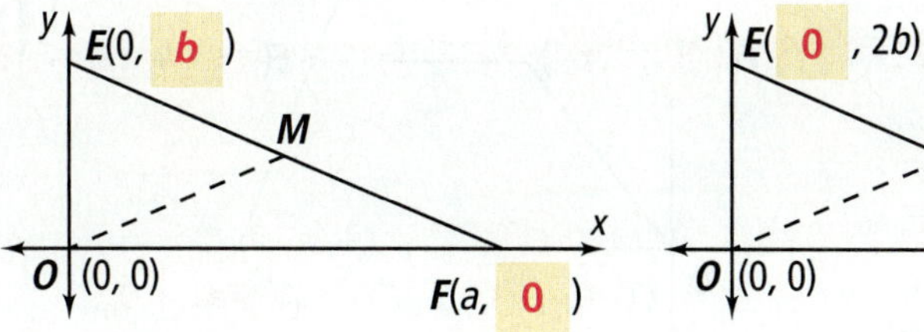

9. Use the Midpoint Formula $M = \left(\frac{x_1 + x_2}{2}, \frac{y_1 + y_2}{2}\right)$ to find the coordinates of M in each triangle.

Fisrt Triangle

$$\left(\frac{a + 0}{2}, \frac{0 + b}{2}\right) = \left(\frac{a}{2}, \frac{b}{2}\right)$$

Second Triangle

$$\left(\frac{2a + 0}{2}, \frac{0 + 2b}{2}\right) = (a, b)$$

10. Use the Distance Formula, $d = \sqrt{(x_2 - x_1)^2 + (y_2 - y_1)^2}$ and your answers to Exercise 9 to verify that $EM = FM = OM$ for the first triangle.

EM

$$\sqrt{\left(0 - \frac{a}{2}\right)^2 + \left(b - \frac{b}{2}\right)^2} = \sqrt{\left(\frac{-a}{2}\right)^2 + \left(\frac{b}{2}\right)^2} = \sqrt{\frac{a^2}{4} + \frac{b^2}{4}}$$

FM

$$\sqrt{\left(a - \frac{a}{2}\right)^2 + \left(0 - \frac{b}{2}\right)^2} = \sqrt{\left(\frac{a}{2}\right)^2 + \left(\frac{-b}{2}\right)^2} = \sqrt{\frac{a^2}{4} + \frac{b^2}{4}}$$

OM

$$\sqrt{\left(0 - \frac{a}{2}\right)^2 + \left(0 - \frac{b}{2}\right)^2} = \sqrt{\left(\frac{-a}{2}\right)^2 + \left(\frac{-b}{2}\right)^2} = \sqrt{\frac{a^2}{4} + \frac{b^2}{4}}$$

11. Use the Distance Formula, $d = \sqrt{(x_2 - x_1)^2 + (y_2 - y_1)^2}$ and your answers to Exercise 9 to verify that $EM = FM = OM$ for the second triangle.

EM

$$\sqrt{(0 - a)^2 + (2b - b)^2} = \sqrt{a^2 + b^2}$$

FM

$$\sqrt{(2a - a)^2 + (0 - b)^2} = \sqrt{a^2 + b^2}$$

OM

$$\sqrt{(0 - a)^2 + (0 - b)^2} = \sqrt{a^2 + b^2}$$

12. Which set of coordinates is easier to use? Explain. **Answers may vary. Sample:**

Coordinates $O(0, 0)$, $E(0, 2b)$, and $F(2a, 0)$ are easier to use because I don't have fractions in the Distance Formula.

Problem 2 Writing a Coordinate Proof

Got It? **Write a coordinate proof of the Triangle Midsegment Theorem (Theorem 5-1).**

Given: E is the midpoint of $\overline{AB}$ and

F is the midpoint of $\overline{BC}$

Prove: $\overline{EF} \parallel \overline{AC}$, $EF = \frac{1}{2}AC$

Use the diagram at the right.

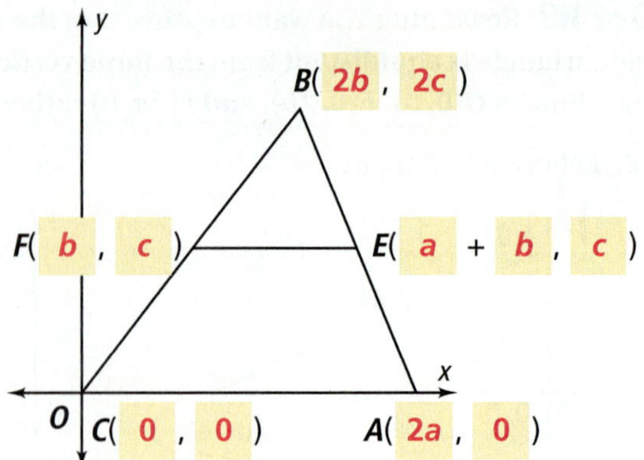

13. Label the coordinates of point C.

14. **Reasoning** Why should you make the coordinates of A and B multiples of 2?

Answers may vary. Sample: Make the coordinates of A and B multiples of 2 so the coordinates of the midpoints are not fractions.

15. Label the coordinates of A and B in the diagram.

16. Use the Midpoint Formula to find the coordinates of E and F. Label the coordinates in the diagram.

coordinates of E

$$\left(\frac{2a + 2b}{2}, \frac{0 + 2c}{2}\right) = (a + b, c)$$

coordinates of F

$$\left(\frac{0 + 2b}{2}, \frac{0 + 2c}{2}\right) = (b, c)$$

17. Use the Slope Formula to determine whether $\overline{EF} \parallel \overline{AC}$.

$$\text{slope of } \overline{EF} = \frac{c - c}{a + b - b} = 0$$

$$\text{slope of } \overline{AC} = \frac{0 - 0}{2a - 0} = 0$$

18. Is $\overline{EF} \parallel \overline{AC}$? Explain.

Yes. Explanations may vary but should state that $\overline{EF} \parallel \overline{AC}$ because the slopes of $\overline{EF}$ and $\overline{AC}$ are equal.

19. Use the Distance Formula to determine whether $EF = \frac{1}{2}AC$.

$$EF = \sqrt{(a + b - b)^2 + (c - c)^2} = \sqrt{(a)^2 + (0)^2} = a$$

$$AC = \sqrt{(2a - 0)^2 + (0 - 0)^2} = \sqrt{(2a)^2 + (0)^2} = 2a$$

20. $\frac{1}{2}AC = \frac{1}{2} \cdot 2a = a = EF$

Lesson Check • Do you know HOW?

Use coordinate geometry to prove that the diagonals of a rectangle are congruent.

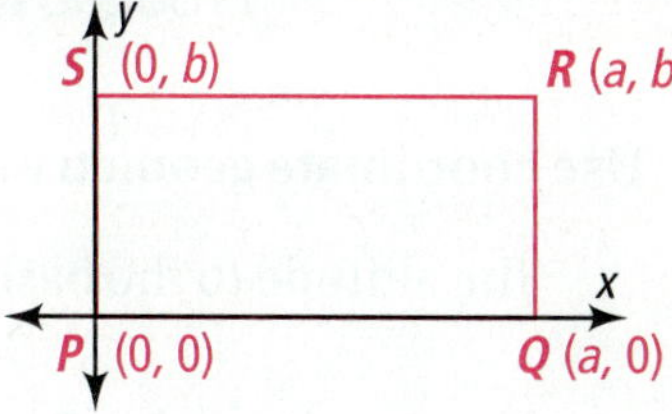

21. Draw rectangle *PQRS* with *P* at (0, 0).

22. Label $Q(a,$ 0 $)$, $R($ a $, b)$, and $S($ 0 , b $)$.

23. Complete the *Given* and *Prove* statements.

Given: *PQRS* is a rectangle . **Prove:** $\overline{PR} \cong$ $\overline{QS}$

24. Use the Distance Formula to find the length of eatch diagonal.

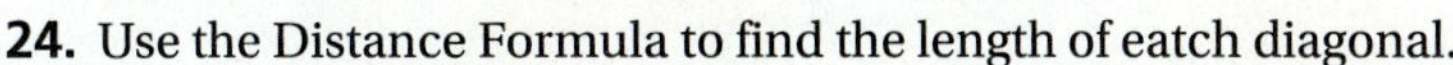

$$PR = \sqrt{(a - 0)^2 + (b - 0)^2} = \sqrt{a^2 + b^2}$$

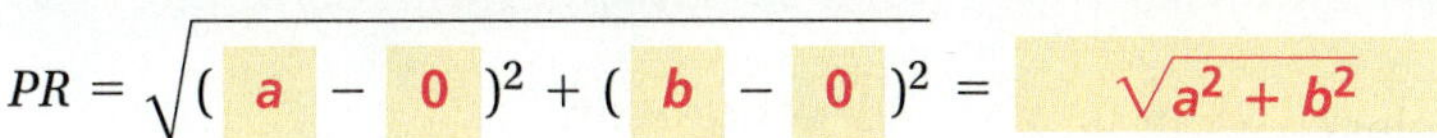

$$QS = \sqrt{(a - 0)^2 + (0 - b)^2} = \sqrt{a^2 + b^2}$$

25. $PR =$ QS , so $\overline{PR} \cong$ $\overline{QS}$.

Lesson Check • Do you UNDERSTAND?

Error Analysis **Your classmate places a trapezoid on the coordinate plane. What is the error?**

y
P(b, c) Q(a − b, c)
x
O
R(a, 0)

26. Check whether the coordinates are for an isosceles trapezoid.

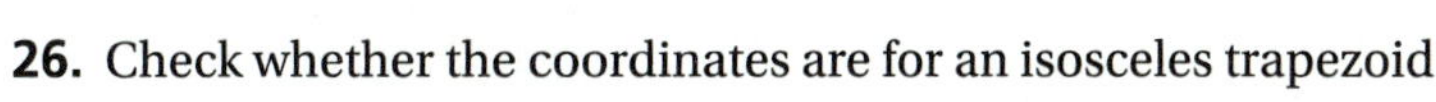

$$OP = \sqrt{(b - 0)^2 + (c - 0)^2} = \sqrt{b^2 + c^2}$$

$$QR = \sqrt{(a - (a - b))^2 + (0 - c)^2} = \sqrt{b^2 + c^2}$$

27. Does the trapezoid look like an isosceles triangle? Yes / (No)

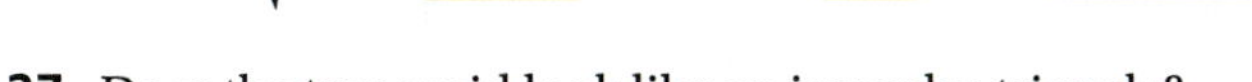

28. Describe your classmate's error. Answers may vary. Sample:

The *x*-coordinate of *Q* is for an isosceles trapezoid.

Math Success

Check off the vocabulary words that you understand.

☐ proof ☐ theorem ☐ coordinate plane ☐ coordinate geometry

Rate how well you can *prove theorems using coordinate geometry*.

Need to review 0 2 4 6 8 10 Now I get it!

Name ______________________ Class ____________ Date ____________

6-9 Think About a Plan

Proofs Using Coordinate Geometry

Use coordinate geometry to prove the following statement.

The altitude to the base of an isosceles triangle bisects the base.

Understanding the Problem

1. What makes a triangle isosceles? Two of its sides are congruent.

2. What is an altitude?

   the perpendicular segment that connects one vertex of a triangle to the opposite side

3. What does it mean when we say that the altitude bisects the base?

   The altitude divides the base into two congruent halves.

4. If the altitude bisects the base, what should the point of intersection between the altitude and the base represent? the midpoint of the base

Planning the Solution

5. Which formula will you need to use to prove that the altitude bisects the base?

   Midpoint Formula

6. Based on the formula you chose, what type of numbers should the coordinates be? multiples of 2

7. Think about how you can draw the triangle on the coordinate plane so that the altitude will intersect $\overline{YZ}$ at (0, 0). Draw isosceles triangle XYZ such that $\overline{XY} \cong \overline{XZ}$. Draw altitude $\overline{XP}$. Use variables to write the coordinates for each point.

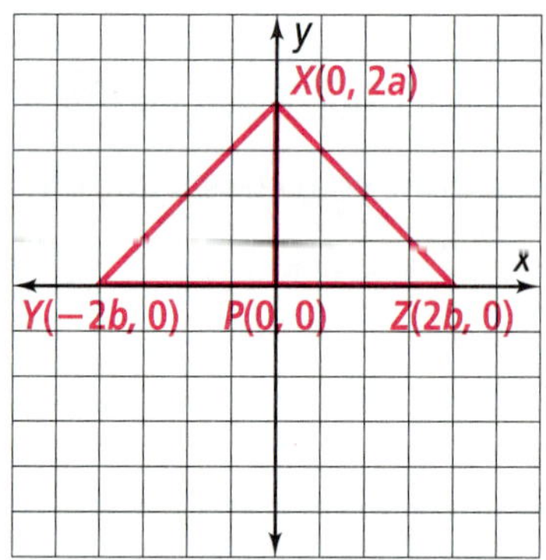

Getting an Answer

8. Use the Midpoint Formula to find the midpoint of $\overline{YZ}$.

   $M = \left(\frac{? + ?}{2}, \frac{? + ?}{2}\right)$ $\left(\frac{-2b + 2b}{2}, \frac{0 + 0}{2}\right) = (0, 0)$

9. Does the altitude to the base of an isosceles triangle bisect the base? Explain.

   Yes; the coordinates of the midpoint of the base are the same as the coordinates of the intersection of the altitude and the base.

Name ______________________ Class ____________ Date ____________

6-9 Practice — Form K

Proofs Using Coordinate Geometry

Developing Proof **Complete the following coordinate proofs.**

1. Triangle Midsegment Theorem

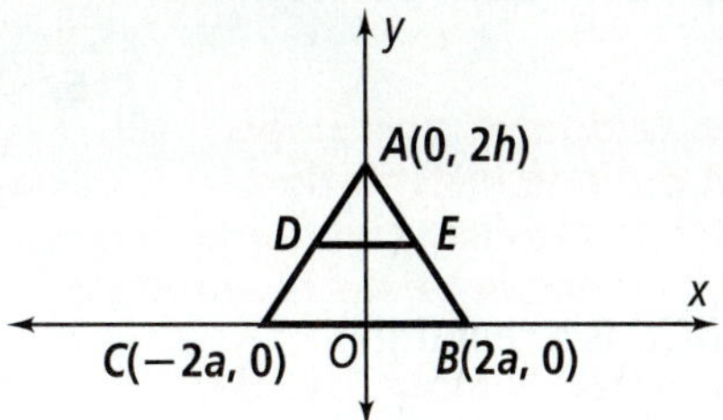

Given: $\triangle ABC$

D is the midpoint of $\overline{AC}$.

E is the midpoint of $\overline{AB}$.

Prove: $DE = \frac{1}{2}CB$ and $\overline{DE} \parallel \overline{CB}$.

a. Find the coordinates of D and E.

To start, use the Midpoint Formula.

$D\left(\frac{-2a + 0}{2}, \frac{2h + 0}{2}\right)$ or $D(\boxed{-a}, \boxed{h})$

$E\left(\frac{2a + 0}{2}, \frac{2h + 0}{2}\right)$ or $E(\boxed{a}, \boxed{h})$

b. Find DE and CB. **The length of the midsegment is half the length of the base.**

To start, use the Distance Formula.

$DE = \sqrt{(-a - a)^2 + (h - h)^2} = \boxed{2a}$

$CB = \sqrt{(-2a - 2a)^2 + (0 - 0)^2} = \boxed{4a}$

c. Find the slope of $\overline{DE}$ and the slope of $\overline{BC}$. Explain.
0; 0; the midsegment is ∥ to the base. The Triangle Midsegment Theorem is proved: The midsegment is ∥ to the base and half its length.

2. Reasoning In Exercise 1, explain why is it easier to use the coordinates $(0, 2h)$, $(2a, 0)$, and $(-2a, 0)$, rather than $(0, h)$, $(a, 0)$, and $(-a, 0)$.
When you use the Midpoint Formula to find the coordinates of *D* and *E*, you need to divide by 2. Using coordinates that are multiples of 2 makes this easier.

3. A parallelogram is a square.

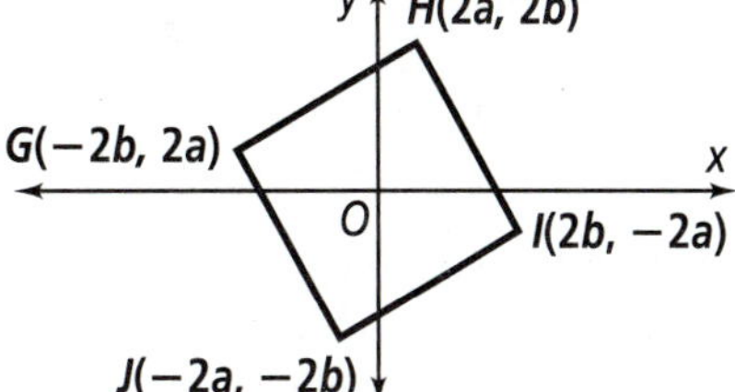

Given: ▱ $GHIJ$

Prove: $GHIJ$ is a square.

a. Find GI and HJ. **$\sqrt{(4a)^2 + (4b)^2}$; $\sqrt{(4a)^2 + (4b)^2}$; The diagonals are ≅.**

b. Find the slopes of GI and HJ.
$-\frac{a}{b}$; $\frac{b}{a}$; the slopes are negative reciprocals, so the diagonals are ⊥. Therefore, *GHIJ* is a square because the diagonals are ≅ and ⊥.

Name _______________ Class _______________ Date _______________

6-9 Practice (continued) Form K

Proofs Using Coordinate Geometry

Tell whether you can reach each type of conclusion below using coordinate methods. Give a reason for each answer.

4. $m\angle A = m\angle G$
No; the Distance, Midpoint, and Slope Formulas do not provide information about angle measures unless additional information is given or can be determined.

5. $\triangle ABC \cong \triangle GHI$
Yes; use the Distance Formula to prove the △s are ≅ by SSS.

6. Quadrilateral *ABCD* is a rectangle.
Yes; answers may vary. Sample: Use the Slope Formula to show that consecutive sides are ⊥.

7. $\triangle HIJ$ is equiangular.
Yes; use the Distance Formula to prove the △ is equilateral.

8. The base angles of an isosceles trapezoid are congruent.
Yes; answers may vary. Sample: draw diagonals and use the Distance Formula to prove the triangles are congruent.

9. Quadrilateral *WXYZ* is a parallelogram.
Yes; answers may vary. Sample: use the Midpoint Formula to show that the diagonals bisect each other.

10. **Think About a Plan** If the diagonals of a quadrilateral are perpendicular but do not bisect each other, then the quadrilateral is a kite.

- How will you place the quadrilateral in the coordinate plane?
so its diagonals are on the *x*- and *y*-axes
- What formula(s) will you use?
Distance Formula
- What are the coordinates of the vertices?
Answers may vary. Sample: $J(-2b, 0)$, $G(0, 2a)$, $H(2c, 0)$, $I(0, -2a)$

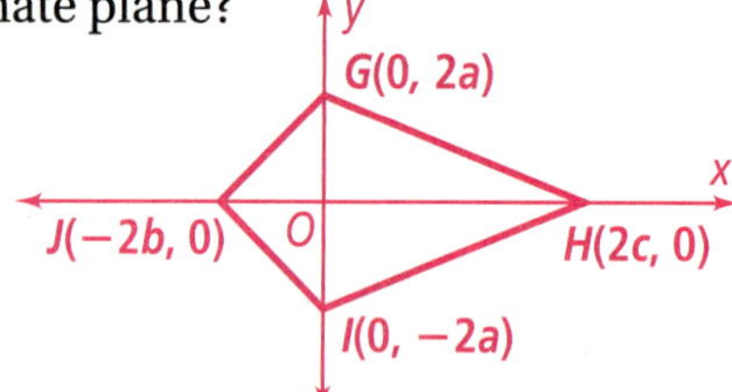

Use coordinate geometry to prove each statement.

11. The vertex of an isosceles triangle is on the perpendicular bisector of the base.
Place base of △ on *x*-axis with $A(-a, 0)$ and $B(a, 0)$. For the △ to be isosceles, *C* must be equidistant from *A* and *B*. The line containing all points equidistant from *A* and *B* is the *y*-axis. This line is the perpendicular bisector $A(-a, 0)$ and $B(a, 0)$.

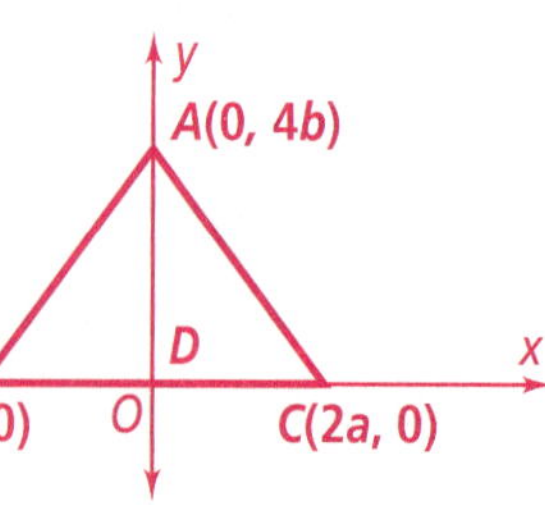

12. $\triangle ABC$ is a right, isosceles triangle.

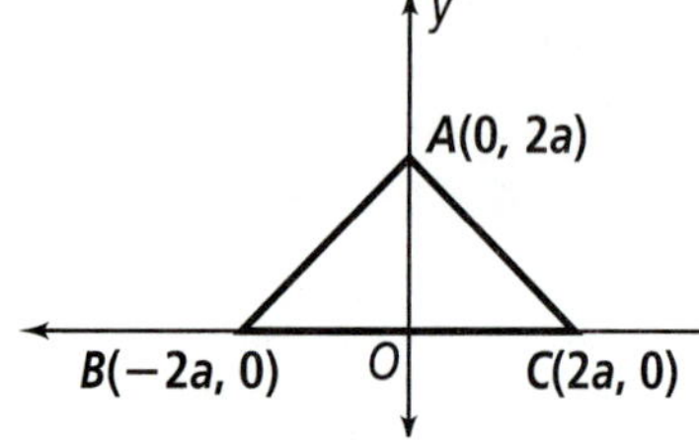

The slope of $\overline{AB} = \frac{2a - 0}{0 - (-2a)} = 1$ and the slope of $\overline{AC} = \frac{0 - 2a}{2a - 0} = -1$. Since the product of these slopes is -1, $\overline{AB} \perp \overline{AC}$, meaning that $\angle A$ is a right angle, so $\triangle ABC$ a right triangle; $AB = \sqrt{(2a)^2 + (-2a)^2} = \sqrt{8a^2}$ and $AC = \sqrt{(-2a)^2 + (2a)^2} = \sqrt{8a^2}$. Since $AB = AC$, $\triangle ABC$ is an isosceles triangle.

Name ______________________ Class ____________ Date ____________

6-9 Standardized Test Prep

Proofs Using Coordinate Geometry

Multiple Choice

For Exercises 1–4, choose the correct letter.

1. Which of the following could you conclude using coordinate geometry? A

- (A) $\triangle EFG$ is an equilateral triangle.
- (B) $m\angle E = 60$
- (C) $m\angle F = 99$
- (D) $m\angle E = m\angle F$

2. Quadrilateral *TRAP* is shown at the right. Which of the following could you use to show that *TRAP* is a trapezoid? H

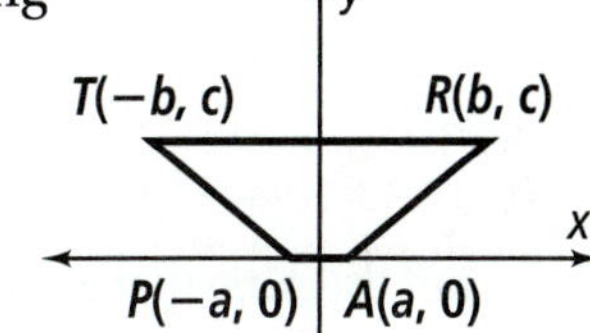

- (F) Prove $RA = TP$.
- (G) Prove $\overline{RA} \perp \overline{AP}$.
- (H) Prove $\overline{TR} \parallel \overline{PA}$.
- (I) Prove that there are no right angles formed by the line segments.

3. Which formula or formulas do you need to use to prove that if the segments connecting the midpoints of a trapezoid are joined they form a parallelogram? D

- (A) Slope Formula
- (B) Distance Formula
- (C) Distance Formula and Slope Formula
- (D) Slope Formula and Midpoint Formula

4. Which formula or formulas do you need to use to prove that a quadrilateral is an isosceles trapezoid? H

- (F) Slope Formula
- (G) Distance Formula
- (H) Distance Formula and Slope Formula
- (I) Slope Formula and Midpoint Formula

Short Response

5. How would you use coordinate geometry to prove that two line segments are perpendicular?

[2] Find the slopes of the line segments, and show that the product of the slopes is −1. [1] Find the slopes of the line segments. [0] no answer or wrong answer based on an inappropriate plan

7-1 Ratios and Proportions

Vocabulary

Review

1. Write a *ratio* to compare 9 red marbles to 16 blue marbles in three ways.

9 to 16 $\frac{9}{16}$ 9 : 16

In simplest form, write the *ratio* of vowels to consonants in each word below.

2. comparison $\frac{2}{3}$
3. geometry 1 to 1
4. ratio 3 : 2

5. Cross out the *ratio* that is NOT equivalent to 12 to 8.

~~6 : 2~~ 9 to 6 $\frac{24}{16}$ 48 : 32

Vocabulary Builder

proportion (noun) pruh PAWR shun

Other Word Form: proportional (adjective)

Definition: A **proportion** is an equation stating that two ratios are equal.

Examples: $\frac{2}{3} = \frac{8}{12}$ and $\frac{1}{2} = \frac{5}{10}$ are **proportions.**

A **proportion** always includes an **equal** sign, =.

Use Your Vocabulary

6. Write 3 or 6 to make each *proportion* true.

$\frac{2}{3} = \frac{6}{9}$ $\frac{3}{4} = \frac{6}{8}$ $\frac{1}{3} = \frac{2}{6}$ $\frac{5}{3} = \frac{10}{6}$

Underline the correct word to complete each sentence.

7. Distance on a map is proportion / <u>proportional</u> to the actual distance.

8. The number of ounces in 3 lb is in <u>proportion</u> / proportional to the number of ounces in 1 lb.

take note

Key Concept Properties of Proportions

Cross Products Property In a proportion $\frac{a}{b} = \frac{c}{d}$, where $b \neq 0$ and $d \neq 0$, the product of the extremes a and d equals the product of the means b and c.

$$\frac{a}{b} = \frac{c}{d}$$

$$a \cdot d = b \cdot \boxed{c}$$

$$\boxed{ad} = \boxed{bc}$$

Equivalent Forms of Proportions

Property 1	Property 2	Property 3
$\frac{a}{b} = \frac{c}{d}$ is equivalent to	$\frac{a}{b} = \frac{c}{d}$ is equivalent to	$\frac{a}{b} = \frac{c}{d}$ is equivalent to
$\frac{b}{a} = \frac{d}{c}$.	$\frac{a}{c} = \frac{b}{d}$.	$\frac{a+b}{b} = \frac{c+d}{d}$.

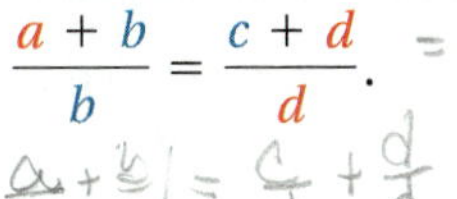

9. Identify the *means* and *extremes* in the proportion $\frac{2}{3} = \frac{4}{x}$.

Means 3 and 4 **Extremes** 2 and x

Identify the *Property of Proportions* each statement illustrates.

10. If $\frac{3}{12} = \frac{1}{4}$, then $\frac{3}{1} = \frac{12}{4}$. Property 2

11. If $\frac{4}{5} = \frac{8}{10}$, then $4(10) = 5(8)$. Cross Products Property

12. If $\frac{1}{3} - \frac{3}{9}$, then $\frac{3}{1} = \frac{9}{3}$. Property 1

13. If $\frac{3}{4} = \frac{x}{y}$, then $\frac{7}{4} = \frac{x+y}{y}$. Property 3

Problem 1 Writing a Ratio

Got It? **A bonsai tree is 18 in. wide and stands 2 ft tall. What is the ratio of the width of the bonsai to its height?**

14. The bonsai is 18 in. wide and 24 in. tall.

15. Write the same ratio three different ways.

width of bonsai to height of bonsai

Write using the word "to."	Write as a fraction.	Write using a colon.
18 to 24	$\frac{18}{24}$	18 : 24

Problem 3 Using an Extended Ratio

Got It? **The lengths of the sides of a triangle are in the extended ratio 4 : 7 : 9. The perimeter is 60 cm. What are the lengths of the sides?**

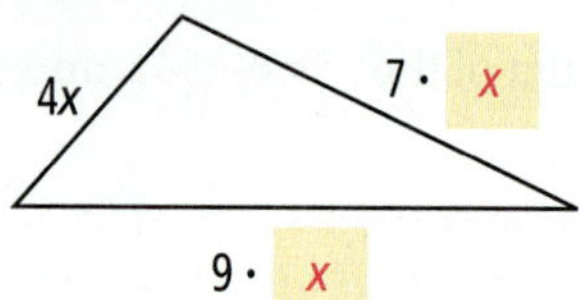

perimeter = 60

16. Label the triangle at the right. Use the extended ratio to write an expression for each side length.

17. Complete the model to write an equation.

Relate	the sum of the side lengths	is	the perimeter
Write	$4x + 7x + 9x$	=	60

18. Use the justifications below to find the value of x.

$4x + x + 9x = 60$	Write the equation.
$20 \cdot x = 60$	Combine like terms.
$\frac{20 \cdot x}{20} = \frac{60}{20}$	Divide each side by 20.
$x = 3$	Simplify.

19. Use the value of x to find each side length.

$4x = 4 \cdot 3$
$= 12$

$7x = 7 \cdot 3$
$= 21$

$9x = 9 \cdot 3$
$= 27$

20. The lengths of the sides of the triangle are 12 cm, 21 cm, and 27 cm.

Problem 4 Solving a Proportion

Got It? **Algebra** **What is the solution of the proportion $\frac{9}{2} = \frac{a}{14}$?**

21. Write a justification for each statement below.

$\frac{9}{2} = \frac{a}{14}$	Write a proportion.
$9(14) = 2a$	Cross Products Property
$126 = 2a$	Multiply.
$\frac{126}{2} = \frac{2a}{2}$	Divide each side by 2.
$a = 63$	Simplify.

Problem 5 Writing Equivalent Proportions

Got It? **Use the proportion $\frac{x}{6} = \frac{y}{7}$. What ratio completes the equivalent proportion $\frac{6}{x} = \frac{\blacksquare}{\blacksquare}$? Justify your answer.**

22. Use the diagram at the right. Draw arrows from the x and the 6 in the original proportion to the x and the 6 in the new proportion.

$$\frac{x}{6} = \frac{y}{7} \qquad \frac{6}{x} = \frac{\blacksquare}{\blacksquare}$$

23. Circle the proportion equivalent to $\frac{a}{b} = \frac{c}{d}$ that you can use.

$\frac{b}{a} = \frac{d}{c}$ (circled) $\qquad \frac{a}{c} = \frac{b}{d} \qquad \frac{a+b}{b} = \frac{c+d}{d}$

24. Complete: $\frac{x}{6} = \frac{y}{7}$ is equivalent to $\frac{6}{x} = \frac{7}{y}$.

Lesson Check • Do you UNDERSTAND?

Error Analysis **What is the error in the solution of the proportion at the right?**

$$\frac{7}{3} = \frac{4}{x}$$
$$28 = 3x$$
$$\frac{28}{3} = x$$

25. Circle the means of the proportion. Then underline the extremes.

3 (circled)  4 (circled) $\qquad$ 7 (underlined) $\qquad$ x (underlined)

26. Write each product.

Means $3 \cdot 4 = 12$ $\qquad$ **Extremes** $7 \cdot x = 7x$

27. What is the error in the solution of the proportion? Answers may vary. Sample:

The cross products are $7x$ and 12, not 28 and $3x$.

28. Now solve the proportion correctly.

$$\frac{7}{3} = \frac{4}{x}$$
$$7x = 12$$
$$x = \frac{12}{7}$$

Math Success

Check off the vocabulary words that you understand.

☐ proportion ☐ means ☐ extremes ☐ Cross Products Property

Rate how well you can *solve proportions*.

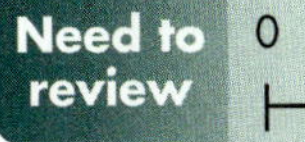

Name ________________ Class ________ Date ________

7-1 Think About a Plan

Ratios and Proportions

Reasoning The means of a proportion are 4 and 15. List all possible pairs of positive integers that could be the extremes of the proportion.

Understanding the Problem

1. What is a proportion? an equation that states two ratios are equal

2. What are some of the forms in which a proportion can be written?

   Answers may vary. Samples: $a : b = c : d$ or $\frac{a}{b} = \frac{c}{d}$

3. Explain the difference between the means and the extremes of a proportion. Use an example in your explanation.

   When you write a proportion in the form $a : b = c : d$, the first and last numbers are the extremes and the middle numbers are the means. In this example a and d are the extremes and b and c are the means.

Planning the Solution

4. How can you write the proportion described in the problem, using variables for the extremes? Should you use the same variable for the extremes or different variables?

   $a : 4 = 15 : b$; use different variables because the extremes may be different numbers.

5. How can you rewrite the proportion as equivalent fractions? $\frac{a}{4} = \frac{15}{b}$

6. How do you solve for variables in a proportion? Apply this to the proportion you wrote in Step 5. Find the cross-products; $ab = 60$.

Getting an Answer

7. Look at the equation you wrote in Step 6. How do the two variables on the one side of the equation relate to the value on the other side?

   The value is the product of the two variables.

8. How can you use factoring to find all the positive integers that could represent the values of the variables?

   List all factor pairs for 60. These are the possible values for the extremes.

9. Find the solution to the problem.

   1 and 60; 2 and 30; 3 and 20; 4 and 15; 5 and 12; 6 and 10

Name ______________________ Class ____________ Date ____________

7-1 Practice — Form K

Ratios and Proportions

Write the ratio of the first measurement to the second measurement.

1. length of car: 14 ft 10 in.
   length of model car: 8 in.

   $\frac{14 \text{ ft } 10 \text{ in.}}{8 \text{ in.}} = \frac{\boxed{178} \text{ in.}}{8 \text{ in.}} = \frac{\boxed{89}}{\boxed{4}}$

2. weight of car: 2900 lb
   weight of model car: 8 oz

   $\frac{2900 \text{ lb}}{8 \text{ oz}} = \frac{2900 \text{ lb}}{\boxed{} \text{ lb}} = \frac{\boxed{1}}{\boxed{\frac{1}{2}}}$ 5800

3. diameter of car tire: 40 cm
   diameter of toy car tire: 18 mm 200 : 9

4. height of car: 4 ft 8 in.
   height of toy car: 3 in. 56 : 3

5. There are 238 juniors at a high school. The ratio of girls to boys in the junior class is 3 : 4. How many juniors are girls? How many are boys? 102; 136

6. The sides of a rectangle are in the ratio 2 : 5. The perimeter of the rectangle is 70 cm. What is the width of the rectangle? 10 cm

7. The measures of the angles of a triangle are in the extended ratio 6 : 1 : 5. What is the measure of the largest angle? 90

Algebra Solve each proportion. To start, use the Cross Products Property.

8. $\frac{3}{5} = \frac{x}{25}$ 15

9. $\frac{x}{4} = \frac{9}{2}$ 18

10. $\frac{x - 2}{8} = \frac{3}{4}$ 8

11. $\frac{y}{3} = \frac{y + 6}{8}$ 3.6

In the diagram, $\frac{a}{b} = \frac{2}{3}$. Complete each statement. Justify your answer.

12. $\frac{b}{a} = \frac{\boxed{3}}{\boxed{2}}$

    Prop. of Proportions (1)

13. $\frac{\boxed{a}}{\boxed{2}} = \frac{b}{3}$

    Prop. of Proportions (2)

14. $\frac{a + b}{b} = \frac{\boxed{5}}{\boxed{3}}$

    Prop. of Proportions (3)

15. $\frac{b}{\boxed{a}} = \frac{3}{\boxed{2}}$

    Prop. of Proportions (1)

Name ______________________ Class ____________ Date ____________

7-1 Practice (continued)

Form K

Ratios and Proportions

Coordinate Geometry **Use the graph. Write each ratio in simplest form.**

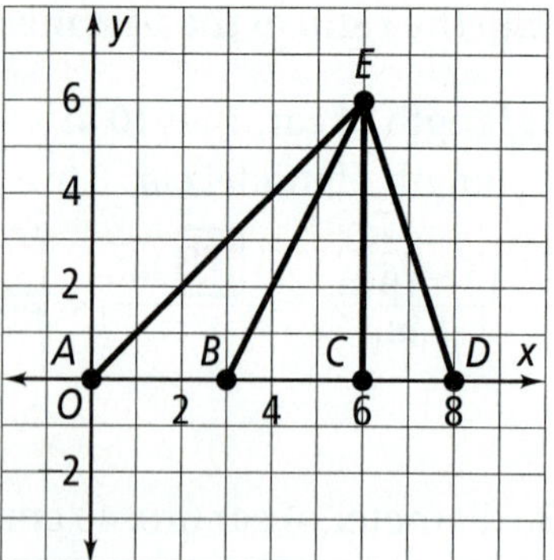

16. $\frac{AC}{AD} = \frac{\boxed{6}}{\boxed{8}}$; simplified to $\frac{\boxed{3}}{\boxed{4}}$.

17. $\frac{AB}{EC}$ $\frac{1}{2}$

18. slope of $\overline{ED}$ -3

19. You are helping to hang balloons in the gym for a school dance. There are a total of 175 balloons. Some of the balloons are gold and the rest are silver. If the ratio of gold to silver is 3 : 2, how many gold balloons are there? **105**

20. The ratio of the width to the height of a window is 2 : 7. The width of the window is 3 ft. Write and solve a proportion to find the height.
$\frac{2}{7} = \frac{3}{x}$; 10.5 ft

21. The sides of a triangle are in the extended ratio of 3 : 4 : 10. If the length of the shortest side is 9 in., what is the perimeter of the triangle? **51 in.**

22. Write a proportion that has means 4 and 15 and extremes 6 and 10.
Answers may vary. Sample: $\frac{6}{4} = \frac{15}{10}$

Algebra **Solve each proportion.**

23. $\frac{x}{4} = \frac{77}{28}$ **11**

24. $\frac{3}{4y} = \frac{9}{138}$ **11.5**

25. $\frac{6}{d+5} = \frac{3}{d+1}$ **3**

26. $\frac{8}{2y-3} = \frac{6}{y+4}$ **12.5**

27. Writing Explain how the Cross Products Property can be used to show that $\frac{2}{x-3} = \frac{4}{2x+1}$ is not a true proportion.
Answers may vary. Sample: When you multiply the means and the extremes and simplify, you get $2 = -12$, which is not true.

Name ____________________ Class ____________ Date ____________

7-1 Standardized Test Prep

Ratios and Proportions

Gridded Response

Solve each exercise and enter your answer on the grid provided.

Use the graph at the right for Exercises 1 and 2.

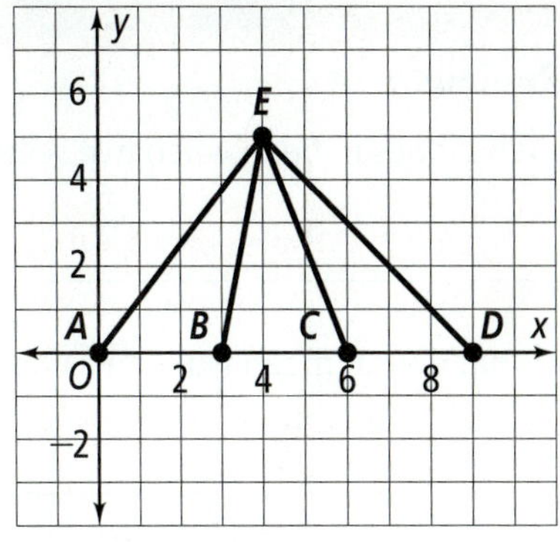

1. What is $\frac{AD}{AB}$ in simplest form?

2. What is $\frac{\text{slope of } \overline{BE}}{\text{slope of } \overline{AE}}$ in simplest form?

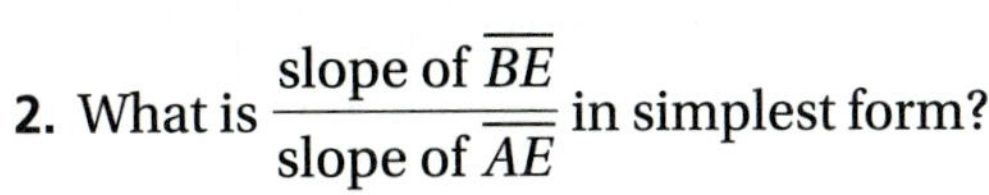

3. What is the value of x in the proportion $\frac{(x - 1)}{5} = \frac{(4x + 2)}{35}$?

4. What is the value of x in the proportion $\frac{x + 1}{x + 3} = \frac{15}{21}$?

5. The lengths of the sides of a triangle are in the extended ratio 3 : 10 : 12. The perimeter is 400 cm. What is the length of the longest side in centimeters?

Answers

1. 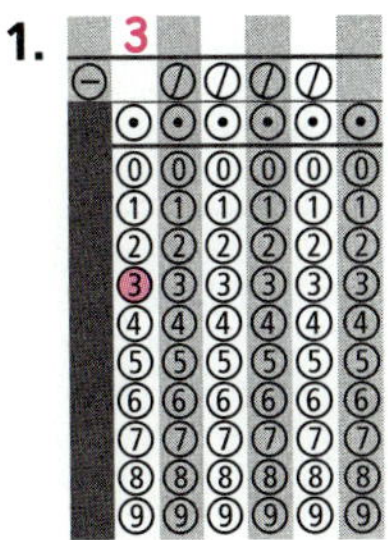

2. 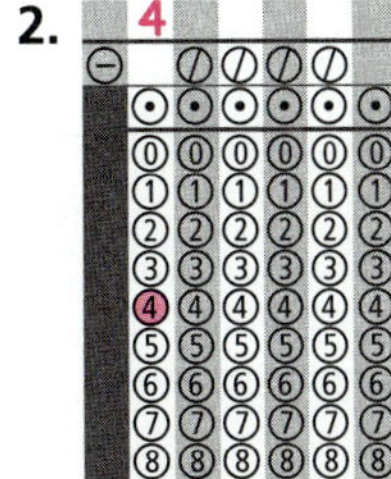

3. 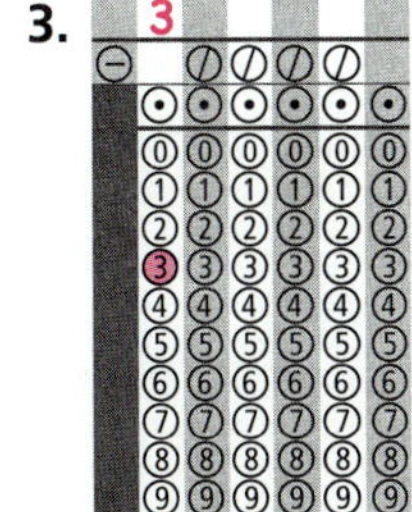

4. 

5. 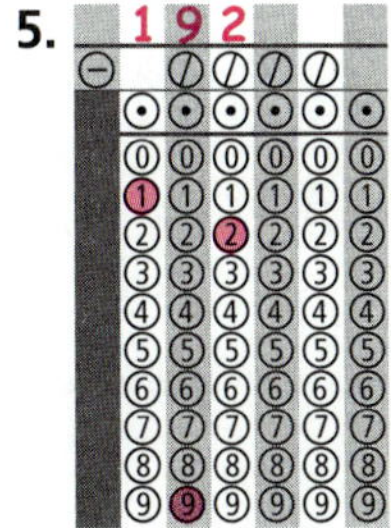

7-2 Similar Polygons

Vocabulary

Review

1. What does it mean when two segments are *congruent*?

They have the same length.

2. What does it mean when two angles are *congruent*?

They have the same measure.

3. Measure each segment. Then circle the congruent segments.

Vocabulary Builder

The symbol for **similar** is ~.

similar (adjective) SIM uh lur

Other Word Forms: similarity (noun), similarly (adverb)

Definition: Things that are **similar** are alike, but not identical.

Math Usage: Figures that have the same shape but not necessarily the same size are **similar.**

Use Your Vocabulary Answers may vary. Samples are given.

4. How are the two squares at the right *similar*?

They have the same shape.

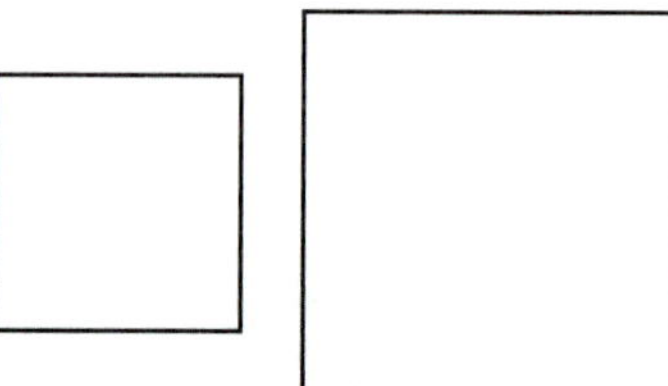

5. How are the two squares NOT *similar*?

They are not the same size.

Key Concept Similar Polygons

Two polygons are **similar polygons** if corresponding angles are congruent and if the lengths of corresponding sides are proportional.

***ABCD* ~ *GHIJ*. Draw a line from each angle in Column A to its corresponding angle in Column B.**

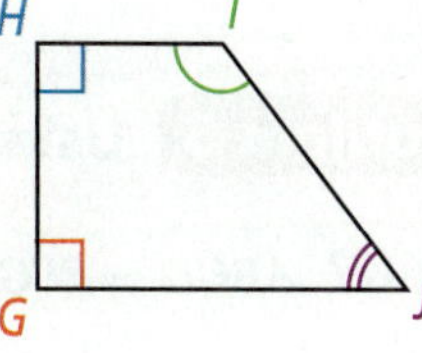

Column A	Column B
6. $\angle A$	$\angle H$
7. $\angle B$	$\angle J$
8. $\angle C$	$\angle G$
9. $\angle D$	$\angle I$

10. Complete the extended proportion to show that corresponding sides of *ABCD* and *GHIJ* are proportional.

$$\frac{AB}{GH} = \frac{BC}{HI} = \frac{CD}{IJ} = \frac{AD}{GJ}$$

Problem 1 Understanding Similarity

Got It? ***DEFG* ~ *HJKL*. What are the pairs of congruent angles? What is the extended proportion for the ratios of the lengths of corresponding sides?**

11. Complete each congruence statement.

$\angle D \cong \angle H$

$\angle E \cong \angle J$

$\angle K \cong \angle F$

$\angle L \cong \angle G$

12. Complete the extended proportion.

$$\frac{DE}{HJ} = \frac{EF}{JK} = \frac{FG}{KL} = \frac{DG}{HL}$$

A *scale factor* is the ratio of the lengths of corresponding sides of similar triangles.

Problem 2 Determining Similarity

Got It? **Are the polygons similar? If they are, write a similarity statement and give the scale factor.**

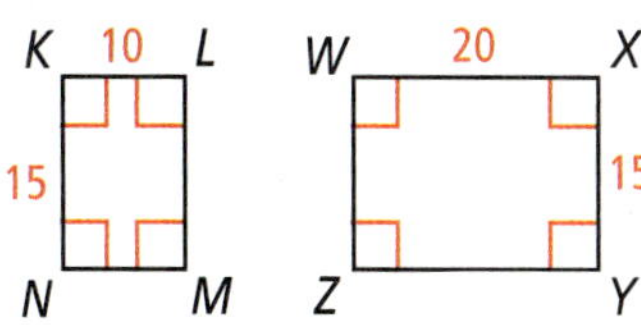

13. Circle the short sides of each rectangle. Underline the long sides.

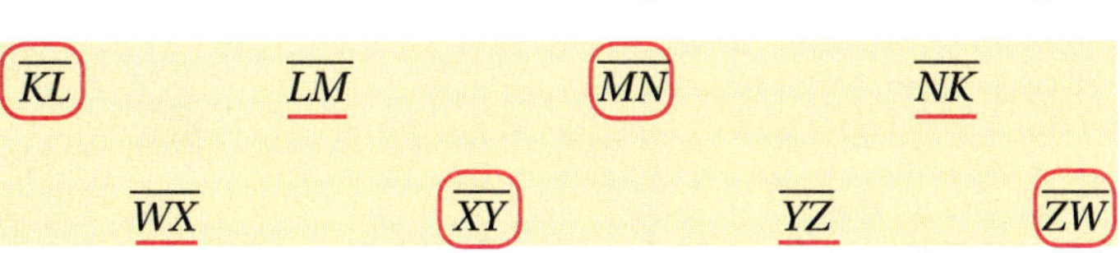

14. Write the ratios of corresponding sides in simplest form.

$\frac{KL}{XY} = \frac{10}{15} = \frac{2}{3}$ $\quad \frac{LM}{YZ} = \frac{15}{20} = \frac{3}{4}$ $\quad \frac{MN}{ZW} = \frac{10}{15} = \frac{2}{3}$ $\quad \frac{NK}{WX} = \frac{15}{20} = \frac{3}{4}$

15. Place a ✓ in the box if the statement is correct. Place an ✗ if it is incorrect.

✗ $KLMN \sim XYZW$ and the scale factor is $\frac{2}{3}$.

✗ $KLMN \sim XYZW$ and the scale factor is $\frac{3}{4}$.

✓ The polygons are not similar.

Problem 3 Using Similar Polygons

Got It? $ABCD \sim EFGD$. **What is the value of** y**?**

16. Circle the side of $ABCD$ that corresponds to $\overline{EF}$.

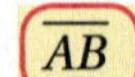

$\overline{AB}$ $\overline{BC}$ $\overline{CD}$ $\overline{AD}$

17. Use the justifications at the right to find the value of y.

$\frac{EF}{AB} = \frac{ED}{AD}$ Corresponding sides of similar polygons are proportional.

$\frac{y}{5} = \frac{6}{9}$ Substitute.

$9y = 30$ Cross Products Property

$y = 3\frac{1}{3}$ Divide each side by 9.

Problem 4 Using Similarity

Got It? **A rectangular poster's design is 6 in. high by 10 in. wide. What are the dimensions of the largest complete poster that will fit in a space 3 ft high by 4 ft wide?**

18. Determine how many times the design can be enlarged.

Height: 3 ft = 36 in.

36 in. ÷ 6 in. = 6

Width: 4 ft = 48 in.

48 in. ÷ 10 in. = 4.8

The design can be enlarged at most 4.8 times.

19. Let x represent the height of the poster. Write a proportion and solve for x.

$\frac{10}{48} = \frac{6}{x}$

$10x = 288$

$x = 28.8$

20. The largest complete poster that will fit is 28.8 in. by 48 in.

Problem 5 Using a Scale Drawing

Got It? **Use the scale drawing of the bridge. What is the actual height of the towers above the roadway?**

0.8 cm

21. Use a centimeter ruler to measure the height of the towers above the roadway in the scale drawing. Label the drawing with the height.

22. Identify the variable.

Let h = the _?_ of the towers.

actual height

23. Use the information on the scale drawing to write a proportion. Then solve to find the value of the variable.

$\left(\textit{Hint: } \frac{1}{200} = \frac{\text{tower height in drawing (cm)}}{\text{actual height (m)}}\right)$

$\frac{1}{200} = \frac{0.8}{h}$

$h = 160$

24. The actual height of the towers above the roadway is 160 m.

Lesson Check • Do you UNDERSTAND?

The triangles at the right are similar. What are three similarity statements for the triangles?

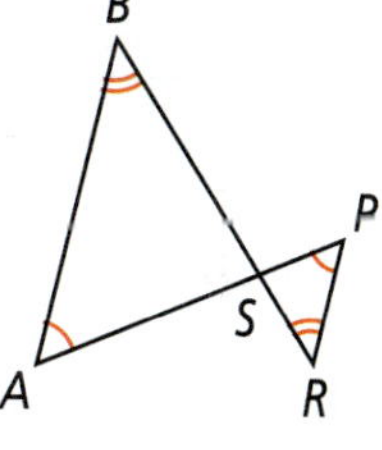

25. The triangles are △ *ABS* and △ *PRS*.

26. $\angle A \cong \angle P$ $\angle B \cong \angle R$ $\angle S \cong \angle S$

27. $\triangle ABS \sim \triangle PRS$ $\triangle BSA \sim \triangle RSP$ $\triangle SAB \sim \triangle SPR$

Math Success

Check off the vocabulary words that you understand.

☐ similar ☐ extended proportion ☐ scale factor ☐ scale drawing

Rate how well you can *identify and apply similar polygons.*

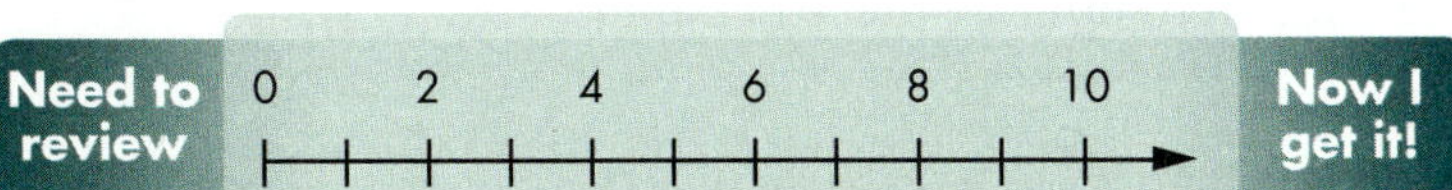

Name ______________________________ Class ____________ Date ____________

7-2 Think About a Plan

Similar Polygons

Sports Choose a scale and make a scale drawing of a rectangular soccer field that is 110 yd by 60 yd.

1. What is a scale drawing? How does a figure in a scale drawing relate to an actual figure?
   Answers may vary. Sample: A scale drawing is enlarged or reduced proportionally to the actual figure. A figure in a scale drawing and the actual figure are similar figures.

2. What is a scale? What will the scale of your drawing compare? Write a ratio to represent this.
   Answers may vary. Sample: a ratio of the actual size to the size in the drawing; the soccer field's actual length to the length in the drawing; actual length : length of drawing

3. To select a scale you need to choose a unit for the drawing. Assuming you are going to make your drawing on a typical sheet of paper, which customary unit of length should you use? **inches**

4. You have to choose how many yards each unit you chose in Step 3 will represent. The soccer field is 110 yd long. What is the least number of yards each unit can represent and still fit on an 8.5-in.-by-11-in. sheet of paper? Explain. Does this scale make sense for your scale drawing?
   The least number of yards each inch can represent is 10 yd. If the scale is 1 in. = 10 yd, the scale drawing will be 11 in. long, which is the length of the paper. It might make sense to use a scale that makes the drawing smaller.

5. Choose the scale of your drawing. **Answers may vary. Sample: 1 in. = 20 yd**

6. How can you use the scale to write a proportion to find the length of the field in the scale drawing? Write and solve a proportion to find the length of the soccer field in the scale drawing.
   Answers may vary. Sample: Make a proportion using the actual length of the soccer field, the length in the drawing, and the scale factor. $\frac{110 \text{ yd}}{\ell \text{ in.}} = \frac{20 \text{ yd}}{1 \text{ in.}}$; **5.5 in.**

7. Write and solve a proportion to find the width of the soccer field in the scale drawing. **Answers may vary. Sample:** $\frac{60 \text{ yd}}{w \text{ in.}} = \frac{20 \text{ yd}}{1 \text{ in.}}$; **3 in.**

8. Use a ruler to create the scale drawing on a separate piece of paper.
   Check students' work.

Name ______________________ Class ____________ Date ____________

7-2 Practice

Form K

Similar Polygons

List the pairs of congruent angles and the extended proportion that relates the corresponding sides for the similar polygons.

1. $ABCD \sim WXYZ$

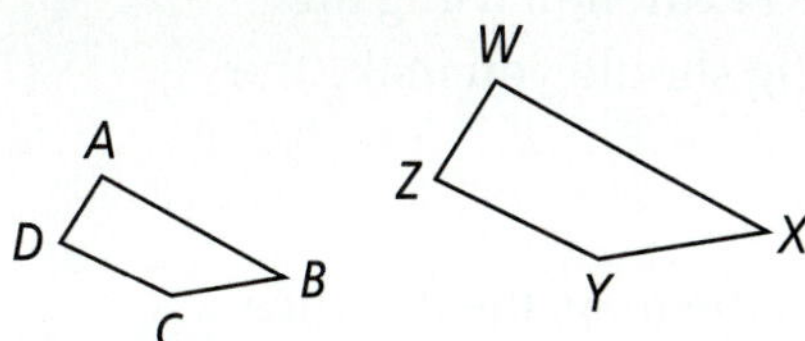

$\angle A \cong \angle W$ $\angle B \cong$ ∠X

$\angle C \cong$ ∠Y $\angle D \cong$ ∠Z

$\frac{AB}{WX} = \frac{BC}{XY} = \frac{CD}{YZ} = \frac{DA}{ZW}$

2. $\triangle GHI \sim \triangle KJL$

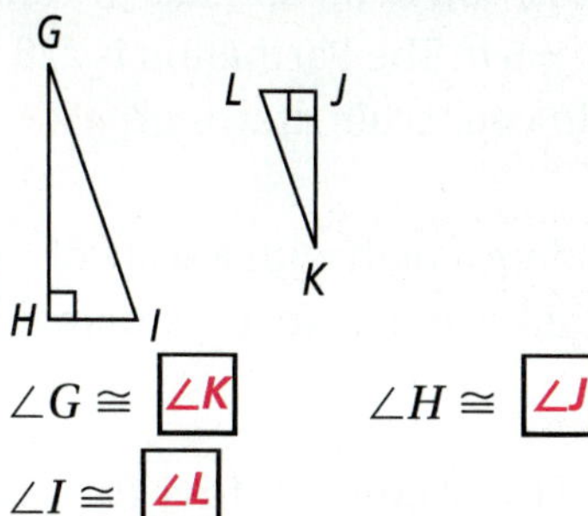

$\angle G \cong$ ∠K $\angle H \cong$ ∠J

$\angle I \cong$ ∠L

$\frac{GH}{KJ} = \frac{HI}{JL} = \frac{IG}{LK}$

Determine whether the polygons are similar. If so, write a similarity statement and give the scale factor. If not, explain.

3.

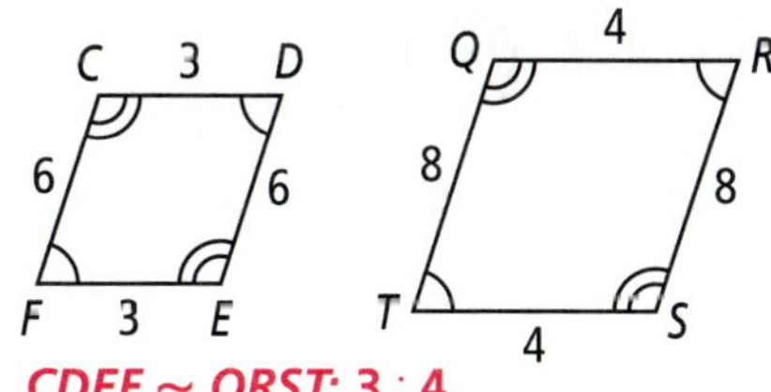

CDEF ~ QRST; 3 : 4

4.

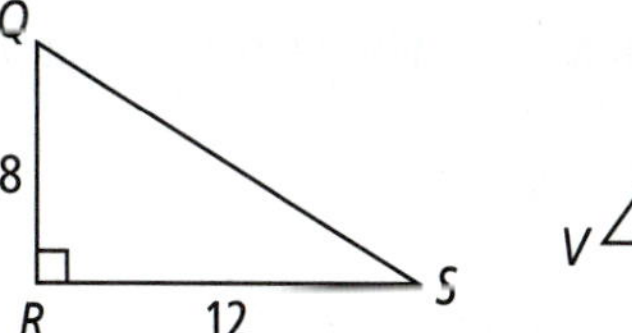

no; corresponding sides not proportional

5.

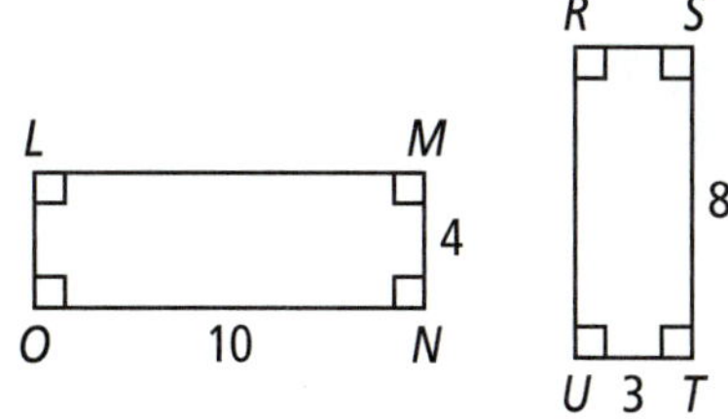

no; corresponding sides not proportional

6.

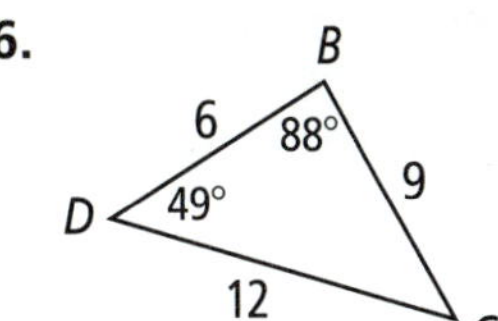

$\triangle DBC \sim \triangle JHI$; 3 : 2

Algebra **The polygons are similar. Find the value of each variable.**

7.

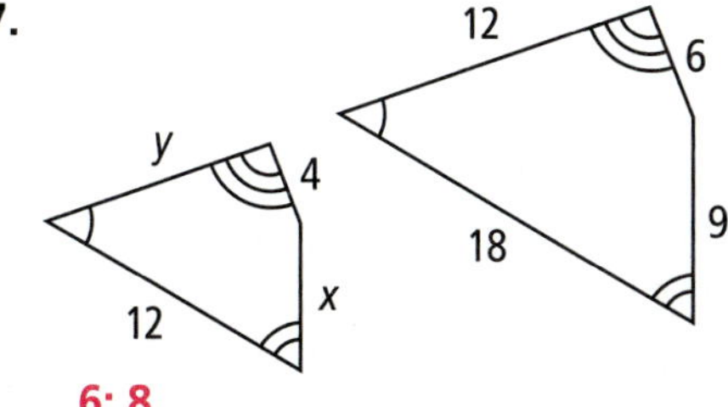

6; 8

8.

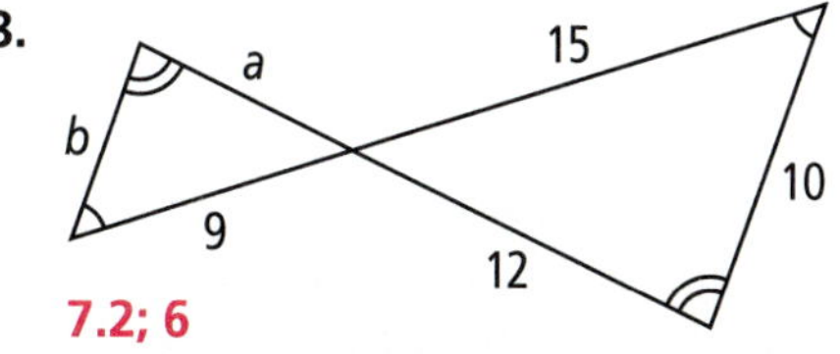

7.2; 6

7-2 Practice (continued)

Form K

Similar Polygons

9. You want to enlarge a 3 in-by-5 in. photo. The paper you will print on is 8.5 in.-by-14 in. What is the largest size the photo can be? **8.4 in.-by-14 in.**

10. For art class, you need to make a scale drawing of the Parthenon using the scale 1 in. = 5 ft. The Parthenon is 228 ft long. How long should you make the building in your scale drawing? **45.6 in.**

11. Ella is reading a map with a scale of 1 in. = 20 mi. On the map, the distance Ella must drive is 4.25 in. How many miles is this? **85 mi**

Algebra Find the value of *z*. Give the scale factor of the polygons.

12. $\triangle JKL \sim \triangle QRS$ **2; 1 : 3**

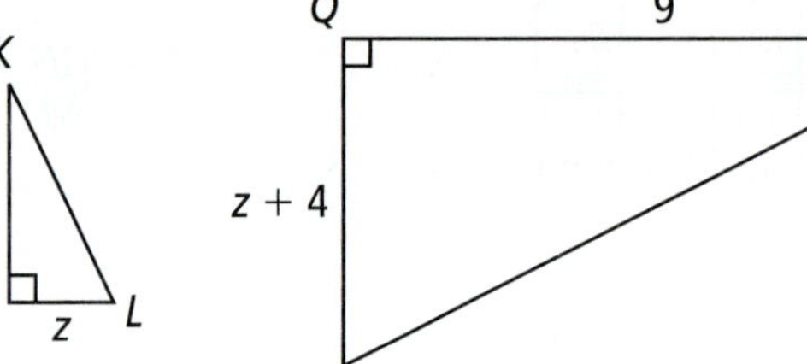

13. The scale factor of *ABCD* to *EFGH* is 7 : 20. What is the scale factor of *EFGH* to *ABCD*? **20 : 7**

In the diagram below, $\triangle NOP \sim \triangle WXY$. Find each of the following.

14. the scale factor of $\triangle NOP$ to $\triangle WXY$ **2 : 5**

15. $m\angle X$ **58**

16. $m\angle Y$ **73**

17. $\frac{NP}{WY}$ **$\frac{2}{5}$**

18. WX **15**

19. NP **4.8**

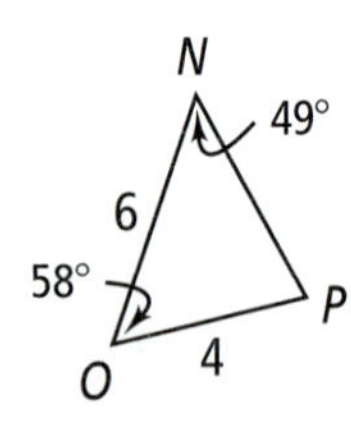

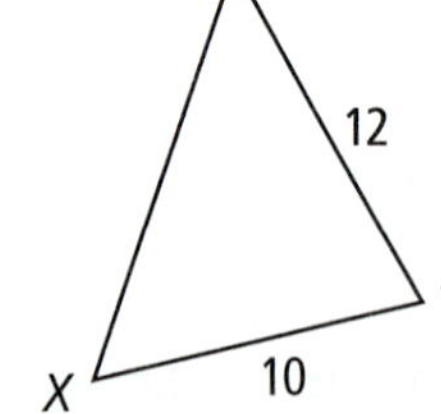

20. A company makes rugs. Their smallest rug is a 2 ft-by-3 ft rectangle. Their largest rug is a similar rectangle. If one side of their largest rug is 18 ft, what are the possible dimensions of their largest rug? **18 ft-by-27 ft or 12 ft-by-18 ft**

Name ______________________ Class ____________ Date ____________

7-2 Standardized Test Prep

Similar Polygons

Multiple Choice

For Exercises 1–5, choose the correct letter.

1. You make a scale drawing of a tree using the scale 5 in. = 27 ft. If the tree is 67.5 ft tall, how tall is the scale drawing? **D**

A 10 in. B 11.5 in. C 12 in. D 12.5 in.

2. You make a scale drawing of a garden plot using the scale 2 in. = 17 ft. If the length of a row of vegetables on the drawing is 3 in., how long is the actual row? **G**

F 17 ft G 25.5 ft H 34 ft I 42.5 ft

3. The scale factor of $\triangle RST$ to $\triangle DEC$ is 3 : 13. What is the scale factor of $\triangle DEC$ to $\triangle RST$? **D**

A 3 : 13 B 1 : 39 C 39 : 1 D 13 : 3

4. $\triangle ACB \sim \triangle FED$. What is the value of x? **I**

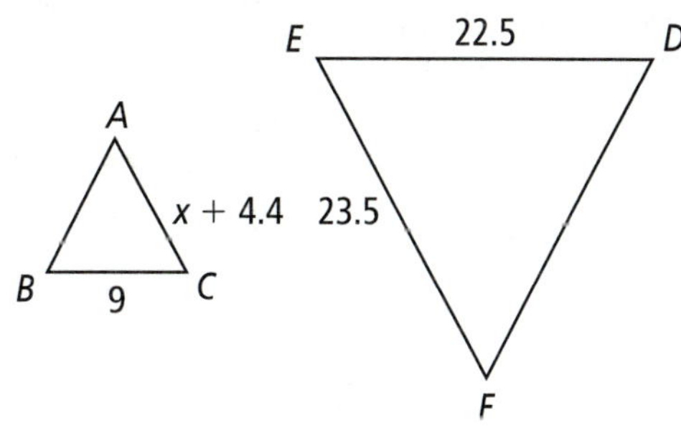

F 4 G 4.2 H 4.5 I 5

5. $MNOP \sim QRST$ with a scale factor of 5 : 4. MP = 85 mm. What is the value of QT? **B**

A 60 mm B 68 mm C 84 mm D 106.25 mm

Short Response

6. Are the triangles at the right similar? Explain.

[2] Yes; corresponding angles are congruent and lengths of corresponding sides are proportional. [1] recognition that corresponding angles are congruent or corresponding side lengths are proportional. [0] No explanation given.

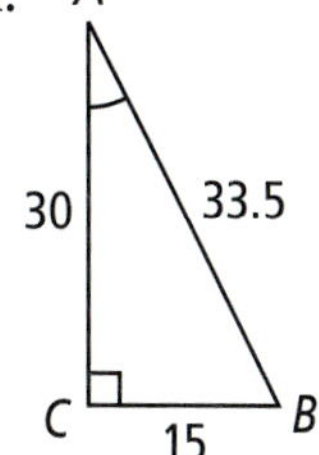

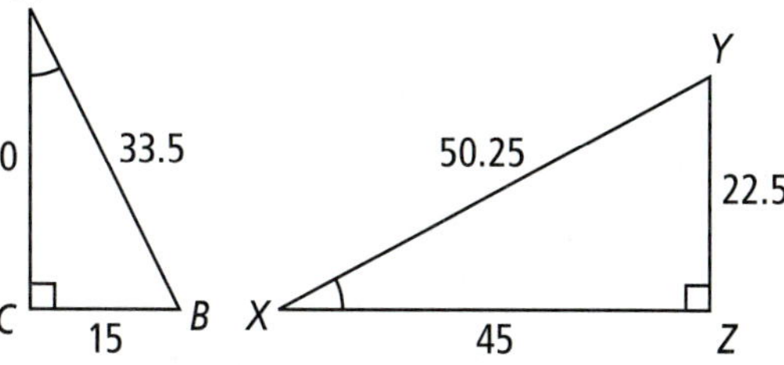

7-3 Proving Triangles Similar

Vocabulary

Review

Write the converse of each *theorem*.

1. If the diagonals of a parallelogram are perpendicular, then the parallelogram is a rhombus.

If a parallelogram is a rhombus,

then its diagonals are perpendicular.

2. If a point is on the perpendicular bisector of a segment, then it is equidistant from the endpoints of the segment.

If a point is equidistant from the endpoints of a segment,

then it is on the perpendicular bisector of the segment.

Vocabulary Builder

verify (verb) VEHR uh fy

Related Word: proof (noun)

Definition: To **verify** something means to find the truth or accuracy of it.

Math Usage: A proof is a way to **verify** a conjecture or statement.

Use Your Vocabulary

Write T for *true* or F for *false*.

F **3.** You can *verify* that two triangles are similar by showing that corresponding angles are proportional.

T **4.** You can use properties, postulates, and previously proven *theorems* to *verify* steps in a proof.

take note

Key Concept Postulate 7-1, Theorem 7-1, Theorem 7-2

Postulate 7-1 Angle-Angle Similarity (AA ~) Postulate If two angles of one triangle are congruent to two angles of another triangle, then the triangles are similar.

Theorem 7-1 Side-Angle-Side Similarity (SAS ~) Theorem If an angle of one triangle is congruent to an angle of a second triangle, and the sides that include the two angles are proportional, then the triangles are similar.

Theorem 7-2 Side-Side-Side Similarity (SSS ~) Theorem If the corresponding sides of two triangles are proportional, then the triangles are similar.

5. Write the postulate or theorem that proves the triangles similar.

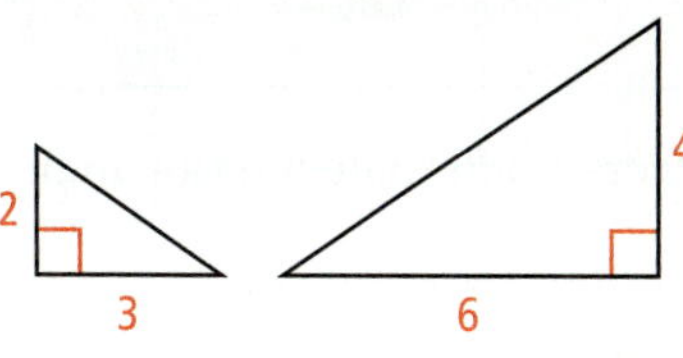

SAS ~ Theorem

Problem 1 Using the AA ~ Postulate

Got It? **Are the two triangles similar? How do you know?**

6. Complete the diagram.

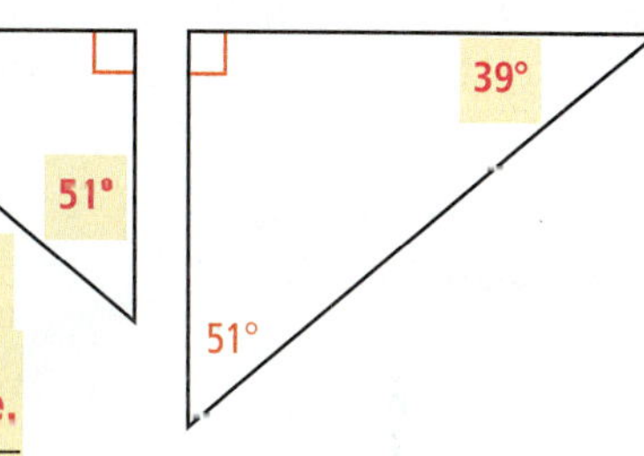

7. Are the triangles similar? Explain. Explanations may vary.

Sample: Yes. Three pairs of corresponding angles are congruent, so the triangles are similar by the AA ~ Postulate.

Problem 2 Verifying Triangle Similarity

Got It? **Are the triangles similar? If so, write a similarity statement for the triangles and explain how you know the triangles are similar.**

8. Write ratios for each pair of corresponding sides.

$\frac{AB}{EF} = \frac{9}{12} = \frac{3}{4}$ $\frac{AC}{EG} = \frac{6}{8} = \frac{3}{4}$ $\frac{BC}{FG} = \frac{6}{8} = \frac{3}{4}$

9. Circle the postulate or theorem you can use to verify that the triangles are similar.

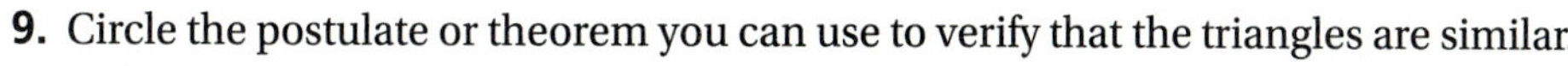

AA ~ Postulate SAS ~ Theorem **(SSS ~ Theorem)**

10. Complete the similarity statement.

$\triangle ABC \sim \triangle$ EFG

Problem 3 Proving Triangles Similar

Got It? **Given:** $\overline{AC} \parallel \overline{MP}$ **Prove:** $\triangle ABC \sim \triangle PBM$

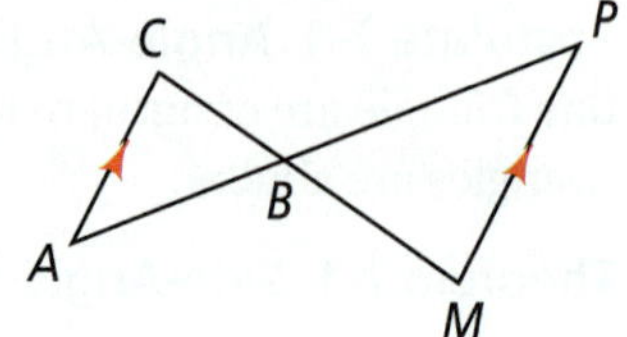

11. The proof is shown below. Write a reason from the box for each statement.

AA ~ Postulate
Given
Vertical angles are congruent.

Statements	Reasons
1) $\overline{AC} \parallel \overline{MP}$	1) Given
2) $\angle A \cong \angle P$	2) If parallel lines are cut by a transversal, alternate interior angles are congruent.
3) $\angle ABC \cong \angle PBM$	3) Vertical angles are congruent.
4) $\triangle ABC \sim \triangle PBM$	4) AA ~ Postulate

Problem 4 Finding Lengths in Similar Triangles

Got It? Reasoning **Why is it important that the ground be flat to use the method of indirect measurement illustrated in the problem below? Explain.**

Before rock climbing, Darius wants to know how high he will climb. He places a mirror on the ground and walks backward until he can see the top of the cliff in the mirror.

12. If the ground is NOT flat, will $\angle HTV$ and $\angle JSV$ be right angles? Yes / No (circled: No)

13. If the ground is NOT flat, will you be able to find congruent angles? Yes / No (circled: No)

14. Why is it important that the ground be flat? Explain.

Answers may vary. Sample: If the ground is flat, $\angle HTV$ and $\angle JSV$ will be right angles and $\angle HVT$ and $\angle JVS$ will be congruent.

Lesson Check • Do you UNDERSTAND?

Error Analysis **Which solution for the value of x in the figure at the right is correct? Explain.**

A.

$$\frac{4}{8} = \frac{8}{x}$$
$$4x = 72$$
$$x = 18$$

B.

$$\frac{8}{x} = \frac{4}{6}$$
$$48 = 4x$$
$$12 = x$$

15. Write the side lengths of the triangles.

Triangle	Shortest Side	Longest Side	Third Side
Smaller	4	8	6
Larger	6	x	9

16. Write ratios to compare the lengths of the corresponding sides.

shortest sides: $\frac{4}{6}$ longest sides: $\frac{8}{x}$ third sides: $\frac{6}{9}$

17. Circle the proportions that show ratios of corresponding sides.

$\frac{6}{9} = \frac{4}{6}$ (circled) $\frac{4}{9} = \frac{8}{x}$ $\frac{8}{x} = \frac{4}{6}$ (circled) $\frac{8}{x} = \frac{6}{9}$ (circled)

18. Circle the solution that shows ratios of corresponding sides.

Solution A   Solution B (circled)

19. Explain why the solution you circled shows the correct value of x. Explanations may vary. Sample:

Only Solution B uses ratios of corresponding sides.

Math Success

Check off the vocabulary words that you understand.

☐ indirect measurement   ☐ similar triangles

Rate how well you can *prove triangles similar.*

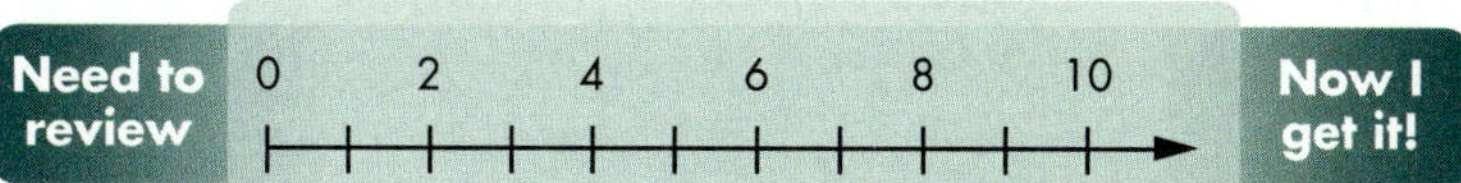

Name _______________ Class _______________ Date _______________

7-3 Think About a Plan

Proving Triangles Similar

Indirect Measurement A 2-ft vertical post casts a 16-in. shadow at the same time a nearby cell phone tower casts a 120-ft shadow. How tall is the cell phone tower?

Answers may vary. Sample:

Know

1. Draw a sketch of the situation described in the problem. Label the sketch with information from the problem and assign a variable to represent the unknown.

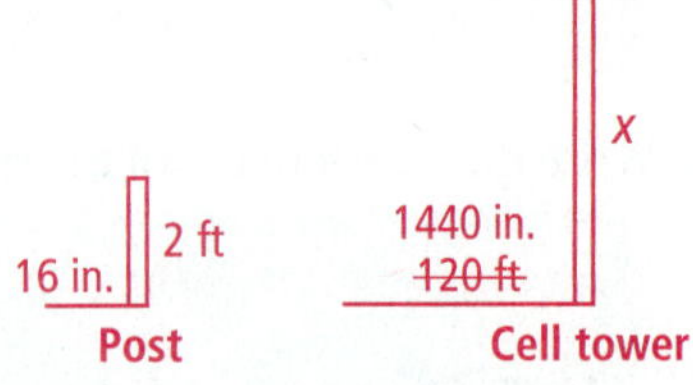

2. If you connect the top of each figure to the end of its shadow, what kind of polygons have you formed? How are these polygons related?
   right triangles; they are similar.

3. Which parts of the polygons are corresponding?
   Answers may vary. Sample: the lengths of the shadows are corresponding and the heights of the objects are corresponding.

Need

4. In your diagram, which corresponding parts have different units?
   the lengths of the post's shadow and the cell phone tower's shadow

5. What must you do so that corresponding parts have the same units? Which unit does it make the most sense to change? Explain.
   Answers may vary. Sample: convert in. to ft or ft to in.; change 120 ft to inches; easier because you don't need to use fractions or decimals.

6. Change the units and update your diagram.
   Check students' work.

Plan

7. Write a proportion in words that compares the corresponding parts.
   $\frac{\text{height of post}}{\text{length of post's shadow}} = \frac{\text{height of tower}}{\text{length of tower's shadow}}$

8. Use information from the diagram to write and solve a numerical proportion. What is the height of the cell phone tower?
   $\frac{2\text{ ft}}{16\text{ in.}} = \frac{x}{1440\text{ in.}}$; 180 ft

Name ______________________ Class ____________ Date ____________

7-3 Practice

Form K

Proving Triangles Similar

Determine whether the triangles are similar. If so, write a similarity statement and name the postulate or theorem you used. If not, explain.

1.

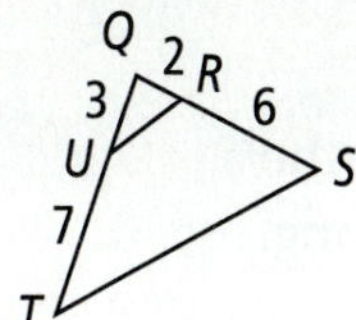

not similar; corresp. sides not proportional

2.

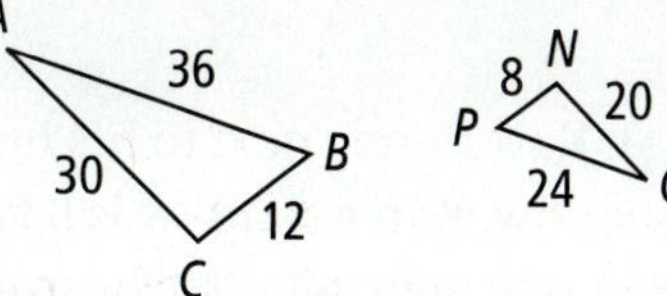

$\triangle ABC \sim \triangle OPN$; SSS ~ Thm.

3.

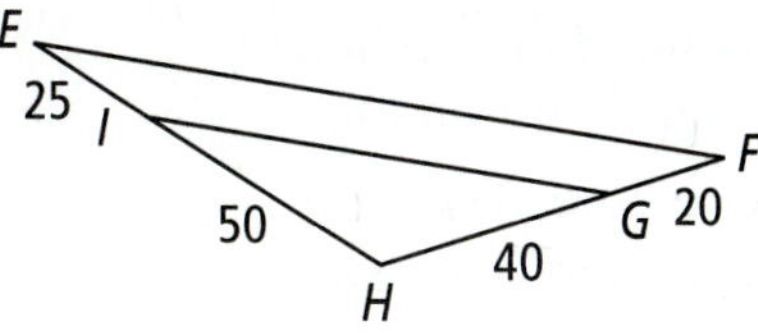

$\triangle EFH \sim \triangle IGH$; SAS ~ Thm.

4.

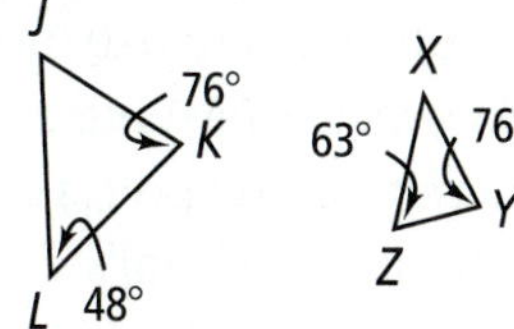

not similar; corresp. angles not ≅

5. Given: $PQ = \frac{3}{4}PR$, $PT = \frac{3}{4}PS$

Prove: $\triangle PQT \sim \triangle PRS$

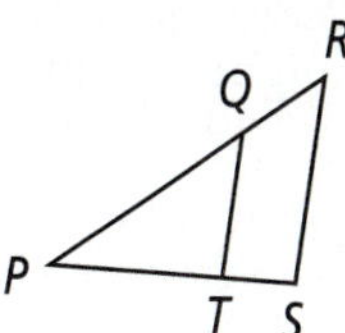

Statements	Reasons
1) $PQ = \frac{3}{4}PR$ and $PT = \frac{3}{4}PS$	1) ? Given
2) $\frac{PQ}{PR} = \frac{3}{4}$ and $\frac{PT}{PS} = \frac{3}{4}$	2) ? Division Property of =
3) $\frac{PQ}{PR} = \frac{PT}{PS}$	3) ? Transitive Property of =
4) $\angle P \cong \angle P$	4) ? Reflexive Property of ≅
5) ? $\triangle PQT \sim \triangle PRS$	5) ? SAS ~ Theorem

Explain why the triangles are similar. Then find the distance represented by *x*.

6.

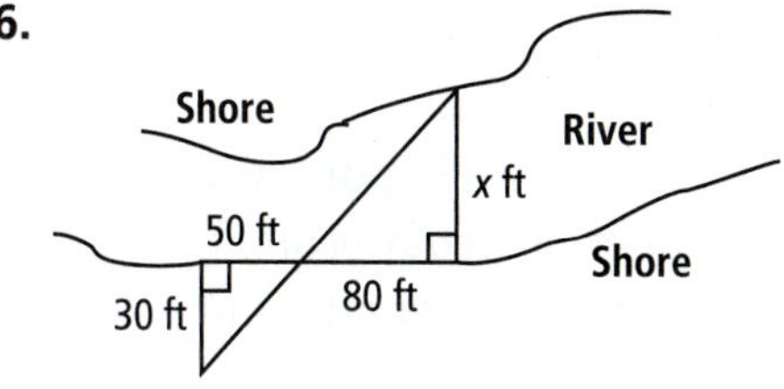

AA ~ Post.; 48 ft

7.

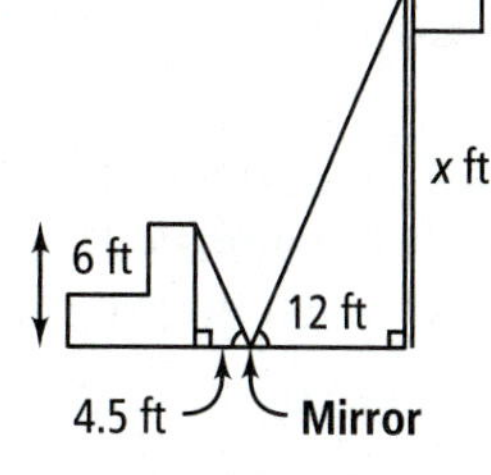

AA ~ Post.; 16 ft

7-3 Practice (continued) — Form K

Proving Triangles Similar

8. A 1.6-m-tall woman stands next to the Eiffel Tower. At this time of day, her shadow is 0.5 m long. At the same time, the tower's shadow is 93.75 m long. How tall is the Eiffel Tower? **300 m**

9. At 4:00 P.M. Karl stands next to his house and measures his shadow and the house's shadow. Karl's shadow is 8 ft long. The house's shadow is 48 ft long. If Karl is 6 ft tall, how tall is his house? **36 ft**

10. Error Analysis Jacob wants to use indirect measurement to find the height of his school. He knows the basketball pole next to the school is 13 ft high. He measures the length of the pole's shadow. At the same time of day, he measures the length of the school's shadow. Then he writes a proportion:

$$\frac{13 \text{ ft}}{\text{school height}} = \frac{\text{school shadow}}{\text{pole shadow}}.$$

What error has Jacob made?
The proportion should compare corresp. sides of ~ △s: $\frac{\text{pole height}}{\text{school height}} = \frac{\text{pole shadow}}{\text{school shadow}}$.

11. Reasoning Explain why there is an AA Similarity Postulate but not an AA Congruence Postulate. **Answers may vary. Sample: If two pairs of ∠s in two △s are ≅, the third pair of ∠s are determined, so you can prove the △s are ~. But to prove △s are ≅, you must show at least one pair of corresp. sides are ≅.**

Algebra **Explain why the triangles are similar. Then find the value of *x*.**

12.

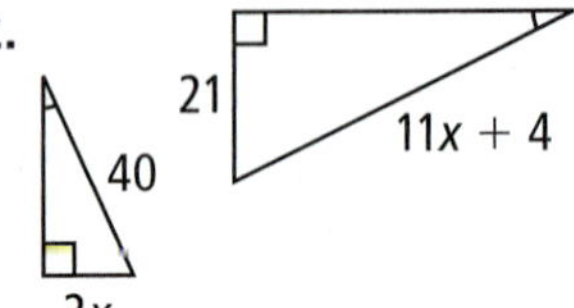

AA ~ Post.; 6

13.

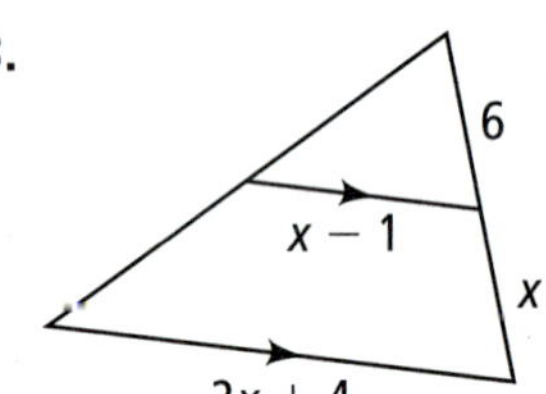

AA ~ Post.; 10

14.

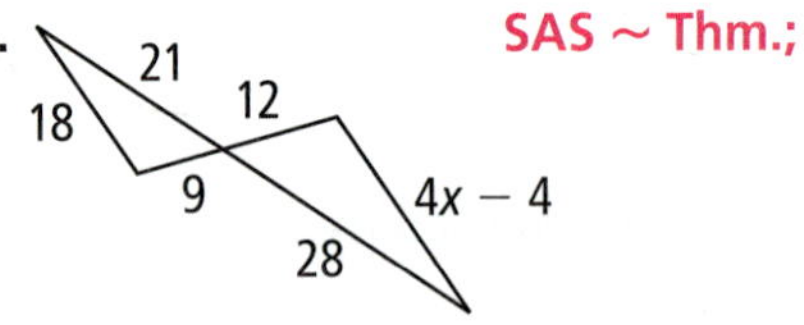

SAS ~ Thm.; 7

15.

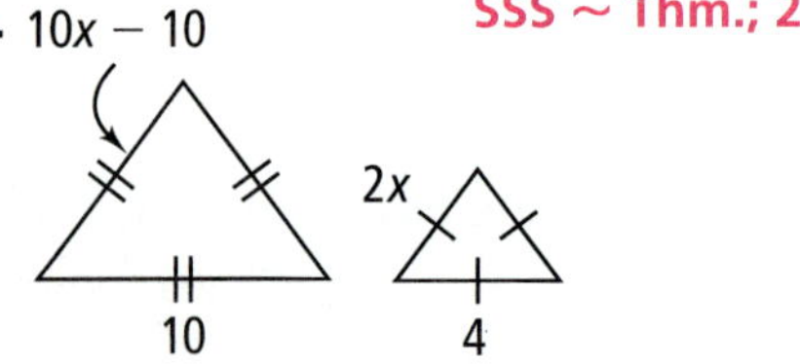

SSS ~ Thm.; 2

16. Think About a Plan A right triangle has legs 3 cm and 4 cm and a hypotenuse 5 cm. Another right triangle has a 12-cm leg. Find all the possible lengths of the second leg that would make the triangles similar. For each possible length, find the corresponding length of the hypotenuse. **9 cm and 15 cm; 16 cm and 20 cm**

- To which measures must you compare the 12-cm leg? **to the 3-cm leg and 4-cm leg**
- How can you find the measure of the hypotenuse? **Use a proportion.**

Name ______________________ Class ____________ Date ____________

7-3 Standardized Test Prep

Proving Triangles Similar

Multiple Choice

For Exercises 1–3, choose the correct letter.

1. Which pair of triangles can be proven similar by the AA ~ Postulate? C

Ⓐ 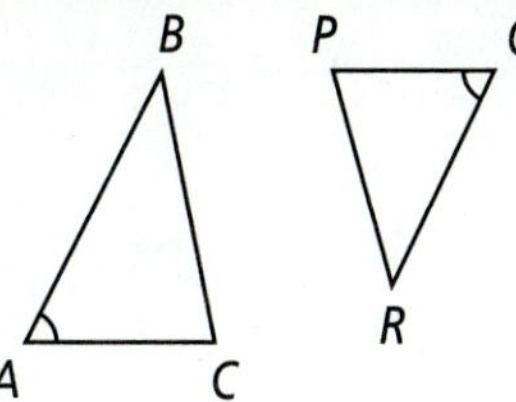

Ⓒ 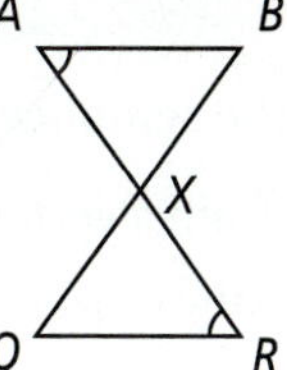

Ⓑ 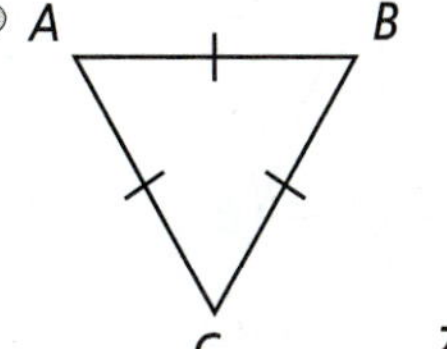

Ⓓ 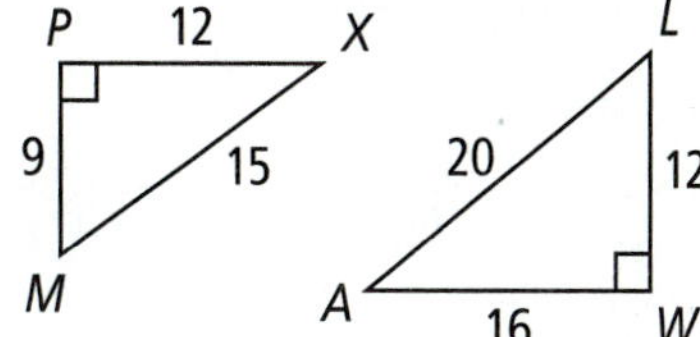

2. $\triangle AXY \sim \triangle ABC$. What is the value of x? I

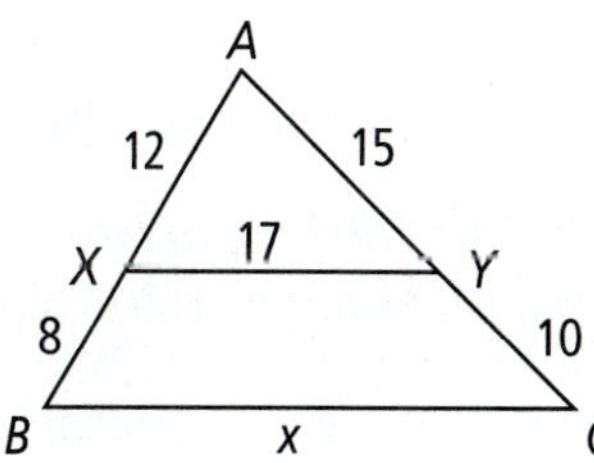

Ⓕ $10\frac{1}{5}$ Ⓗ $11\frac{1}{3}$

Ⓖ 19 Ⓘ $28\frac{1}{3}$

3. $\triangle LMN \sim \triangle PON$. What is the value of x? A

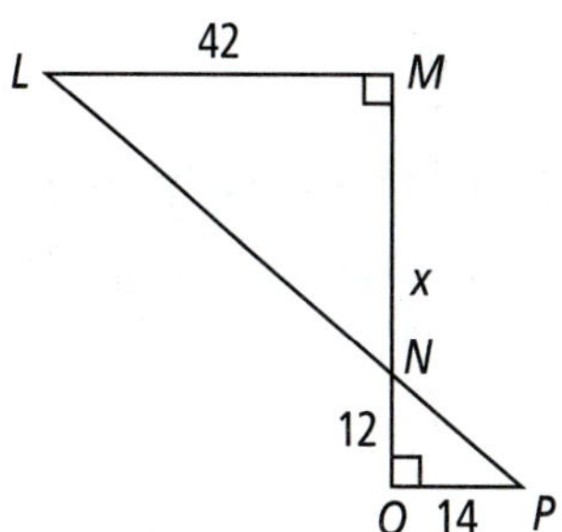

Ⓐ 36 Ⓒ 25

Ⓑ 20 Ⓓ $28\frac{1}{3}$

Short Response

4. Irene places a mirror on the ground 24 ft from the base of an oak tree. She walks backward until she can see the top of the tree in the middle of the mirror. At that point, Irene's eyes are 5.5 ft above the ground, and her feet are 4 ft from the mirror. How tall is the oak tree? Explain.

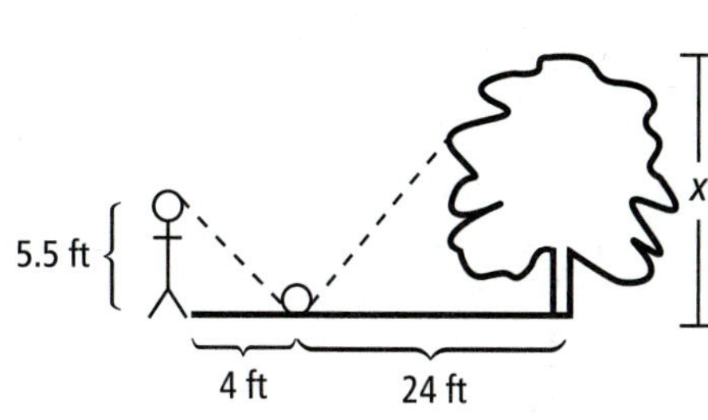

[2] Set up the extended proportion: $\frac{5.5}{x} = \frac{4}{24}$. Solve for x. The oak tree is 33 ft tall. [1] incorrect proportion or error in calculation [0] incorrect proportion and error in calculation

7-4 Similarity in Right Triangles

Vocabulary

Review

Underline the correct word to complete the sentence.

1. The *altitude* of a triangle is a segment from a vertex to the opposite side that is parallel / perpendicular to the opposite side.

2. In an isosceles triangle, the *altitude* to the base divides the triangle into two congruent / isosceles triangles.

3. Circle the *altitude* of $\triangle ABC$..

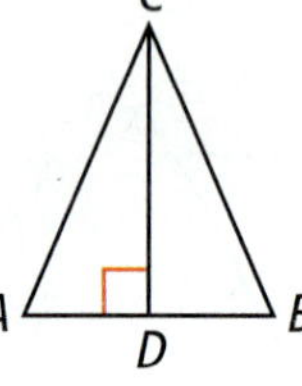

$\overline{AB}$ $\overline{AC}$ $\overline{BC}$ $\overline{CD}$

Vocabulary Builder

geometric mean (noun) **jee uh MEH trik meen**

Definition: For any two positive numbers a and b, the **geometric mean** of a and b is the positive number x such that $\frac{a}{x} = \frac{x}{b}$.

Example: The **geometric mean** of 4 and 10 is the value of x in $\frac{4}{x} = \frac{x}{10}$, or $x = 2\sqrt{10}$.

Use Your Vocabulary

4. **Multiple Choice** Which proportion can you use to find the *geometric mean* of 5 and 15?

Ⓐ $\frac{x}{5} = \frac{x}{15}$ Ⓑ $\frac{5}{x} = \frac{15}{x}$ Ⓒ $\frac{5}{x} = \frac{x}{15}$ Ⓓ $\frac{5}{15} = \frac{x}{x}$

Underline the correct equation to complete each sentence.

5. The *geometric mean* x of a and b is $x = \sqrt{ab}$ / $x = ab$.

6. The *geometric mean* x of 3 and 7 is $x = \sqrt{21}$ / $x = 21$.

7. Circle the *geometric mean* of $\sqrt{3}$ and $\sqrt{3}$.

$\sqrt{3}$ 3 $3\sqrt{3}$ $\sqrt{33}$

take note

Key Concept Theorem 7-3 and Corollaries 1 and 2

Theorem 7-3 The altitude to the hypotenuse of a right triangle divides the triangle into two triangles that are similar to the original triangle and to each other.

If . . .

$\triangle ABC$ is a right triangle with right $\angle ACB$, and $\overline{CD}$ is the altitude to the hypotenuse

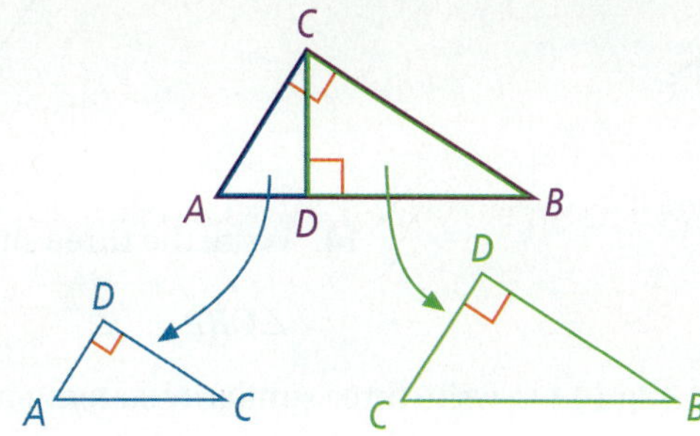

Then . . .

$\triangle ABC \sim \triangle ACD$

$\triangle ABC \sim \triangle CBD$

$\triangle ACD \sim \triangle CBD$

Corollary 1 to Theorem 7-3

The length of the altitude to the hypotenuse of a right triangle is the geometric mean of the lengths of the segments of the hypotenuse.

If . . .

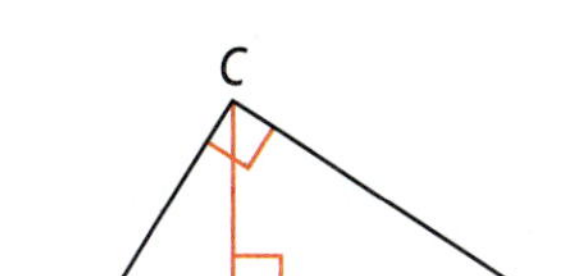

Then . . .

$\frac{AD}{CD} = \frac{CD}{DB}$

Corollary 2 to Theorem 7-3

The altitude to the hypotenuse of a right triangle separates the hypotenuse so that the length of each leg of the triangle is the geometric mean of the length of the hypotenuse and the length of the segment of the hypotenuse adjacent to the leg.

If . . .

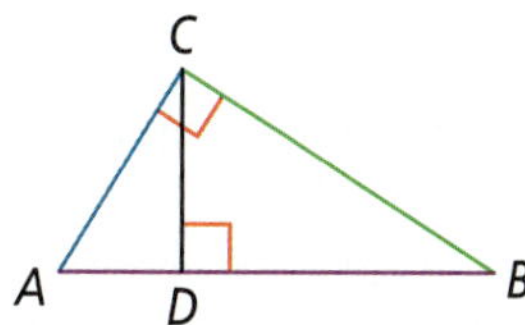

Then . . .

$\frac{AB}{AC} = \frac{AC}{AD}$

$\frac{AB}{CB} = \frac{CB}{DB}$

8. $\triangle LMN$ is a right triangle with right $\angle LMN$. $\overline{NP}$ is the altitude to the hypotenuse. Complete the similarity statements.

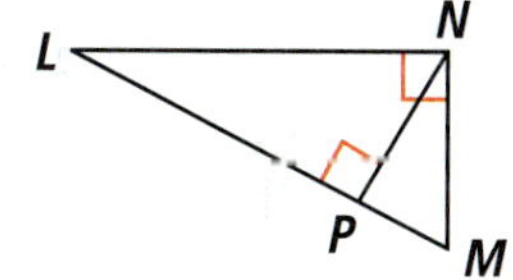

$\triangle LMN \sim \triangle$ LNP

$\triangle LMN \sim \triangle$ NMP

$\triangle LNP \sim \triangle$ NMP

Use the triangle at the right. Write *Corollary 1* or *Corollary 2* for each proportion.

9. $\frac{c}{a} = \frac{a}{x}$ Corollary 2

10. $\frac{x}{m} = \frac{m}{y}$ Corollary 1

11. $\frac{c}{b} = \frac{b}{y}$ Corollary 2

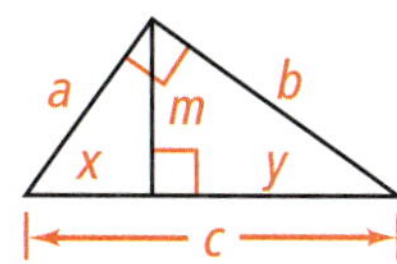

Problem 1 Identifying Similar Triangles

Got It? **What similarity statement can you write relating the three triangles in the diagram?**

12. Write the names of the triangles.

$\triangle RPQ$ $\quad \triangle$ PQS $\quad \triangle$ PRS

13. Write the three right angles.

$\angle RPQ$ $\quad \angle$ QSP $\quad \angle$ PSR

14. Write the three smallest angles.

$\angle QRP$ $\quad \angle$ SPQ $\quad \angle$ SRP

15. Use your answers to Exercises 13 and 14 to write three similarity statements beginning with the vertex of the smallest angle in each triangle and ending with the vertex of the right angle.

$\triangle RQP \sim \triangle$ PQS $\qquad \triangle RQP \sim \triangle$ RPS $\qquad \triangle$ PQS $\sim \triangle$ RSP

Problem 2 Finding the Geometric Mean

Got It? **What is the geometric mean of 4 and 18?**

16. Use the justifications below to find the geometric mean.

$\frac{4}{x} = \frac{x}{18}$	Definition of geometric mean
$x^2 = 72$	Cross Products Property
$x = \sqrt{72}$	Take the positive square root of each side.
$x = 6\sqrt{2}$	Write in simplest radical form.

Problem 3 Using the Corollaries

Got It? **What are the values of x and y?**

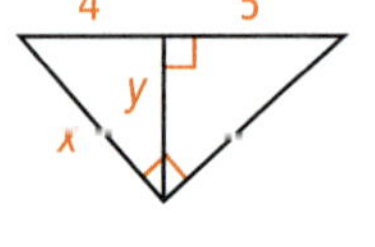

Underline the correct word to complete each sentence.

17. x is the length of a leg of the largest triangle, so use Corollary 1 / Corollary 2 to find the value of x.

18. y is the length of the altitude of the largest triangle, so use Corollary 1 / Corollary 2 to find the value of y.

19. The values of x and y are found below. Write a justification for each step.

$\frac{4}{x} = \frac{x}{4 + 5}$	Write a proportion.	$\frac{4}{y} = \frac{y}{5}$
$x^2 = 36$	Cross Products Property	$y^2 = 20$
$x = \sqrt{36}$	Take the positive square root.	$y = \sqrt{20}$
$x = 6$	Simplify.	$y = 2\sqrt{5}$

Problem 4 Finding a Distance

Got It? **Points A, B, and C are located so that $AB = 20$ in., and $\overline{AB} \perp \overline{BC}$. Point D is located on $\overline{AC}$ so that $\overline{BD} \perp \overline{AC}$ and $DC = 9$ in. You program a robot to move from A to D and to pick up a plastic bottle at D. From point D, the robot must turn right and move to point B to put the bottle in a recycling bin. How far does the robot travel from D to B?**

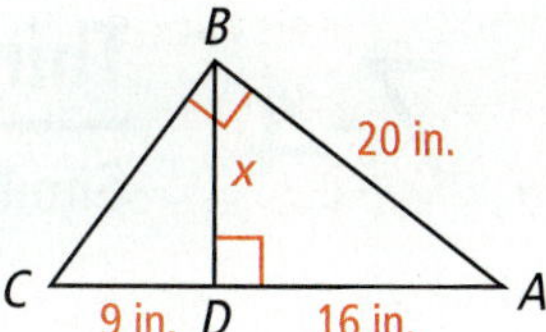

20. Place a ✓ in the box if the statement is correct. Place an ✗ if it is incorrect.

- ✓ I know the length of the hypotenuse of $\triangle ABC$.
- ✓ I know the lengths of the segments of the hypotenuse of $\triangle ABC$.
- ✗ I know the length of the altitude of $\triangle ABC$.
- ✓ I can use Corollary 1 to solve the problem.

21. Find the length of $\overline{BD}$.

$$\frac{9}{x} = \frac{x}{16}$$
$$x^2 = 144$$
$$x = \sqrt{144}$$
$$x = 12$$

22. The robot travels 12 in. from D to B.

Lesson Check • Do you UNDERSTAND?

Vocabulary Identify the following in $\triangle RST$.

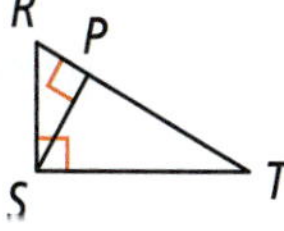

23. The hypotenuse is $\overline{RT}$.

24. The segments of the hypotenuse are $\overline{RP}$ and $\overline{TP}$.

25. The segment of the hypotenuse adjacent to leg $\overline{ST}$ is $\overline{TP}$.

Math Success

Check off the vocabulary words that you understand.

- ☐ geometric mean
- ☐ altitude
- ☐ similarity

Rate how well you understand *similar right triangles.*

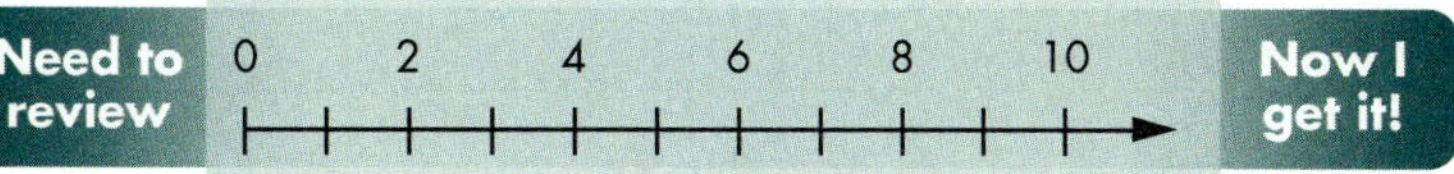

Name ______________________ Class ____________ Date ____________

7-4 Think About a Plan

Similarity in Right Triangles

Coordinate Geometry $\overline{CD}$ is the altitude to the hypotenuse of right $\triangle ABC$. The coordinates of *A*, *D*, and *B* are (4, 2), (4, 6), and (4, 15), respectively. Find all possible coordinates of point *C*.

Understanding the Problem

1. What is an altitude? a segment from a vertex to the opposite side, ⊥ to the opposite side

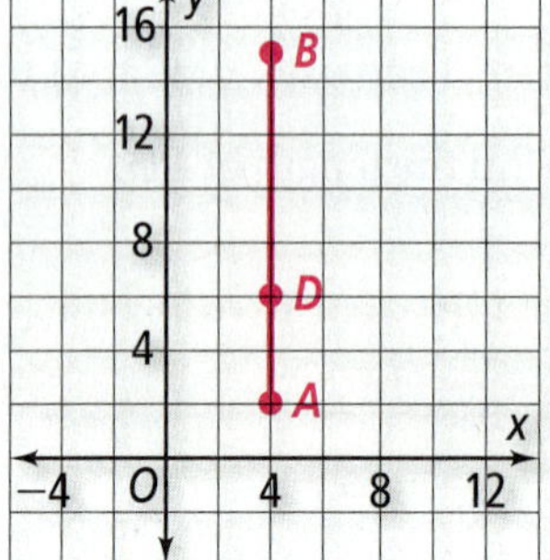

2. Plot the points given in the problem on the grid. Which side of the triangle must $\overline{AB}$ be? Explain.

$\overline{AB}$ is the hypotenuse because $\overline{CD}$ is the altitude to the hypotenuse, and C lies opposite $\overline{AB}$.

3. What is the special relationship between the altitude to a hypotenuse of a right triangle and the lengths of the segments it creates? The length of the altitude is the geometric mean of the lengths of the segments of the hypotenuse it creates.

4. What does the phrase "Find all possible coordinates of point *C*" tell you about the problem? There may be more than one correct answer.

Planning the Solution

5. How can you find the geometric mean of a pair of numbers?

Write a proportion in which the geometric mean is each mean of the proportion, and the known pair of numbers are the extremes, or vice versa.

6. For which numbers or lengths are you finding the geometric mean? How can you determine the geometric mean? 4 and 9; you can determine the geometric mean by setting up and solving the proportion $\frac{4}{x} = \frac{x}{9}$.

Getting an Answer

7. Find the geometric mean. $\frac{4}{x} = \frac{x}{9}$; $x^2 = 36$; $x = 6$

8. What does your answer represent? *CD*

9. Why is there more than one possible correct answer?

The altitude can extend 6 units to the right of *D* or 6 units to the left of *D*.

10. What are the possible coordinates of point *C*? (−2, 6) and (10, 6)

Name ______________________ Class __________ Date __________

7-4 Practice

Form K

Similarity in Right Triangles

Identify the following in right $\triangle XYZ$.

1. the hypotenuse $\overline{XY}$

2. the segments of the hypotenuse $\overline{XR}$ and $\overline{RY}$

3. the altitude to the hypotenuse $\overline{ZR}$

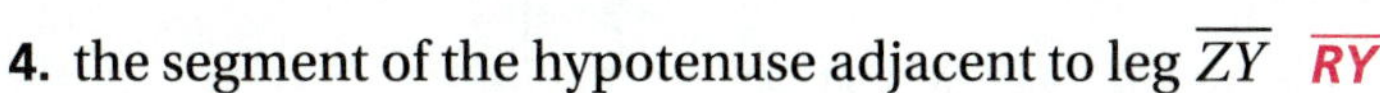

4. the segment of the hypotenuse adjacent to leg $\overline{ZY}$ $\overline{RY}$

Write a similarity statement relating the three triangles in each diagram.

5.

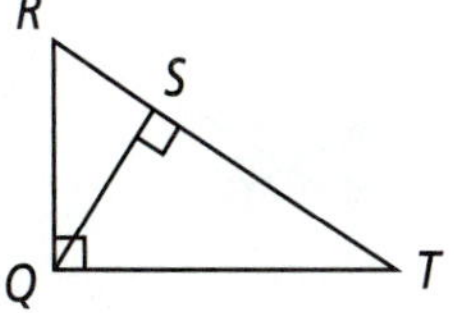

$\triangle QRT \sim \triangle SQT \sim \triangle SRQ$

6.

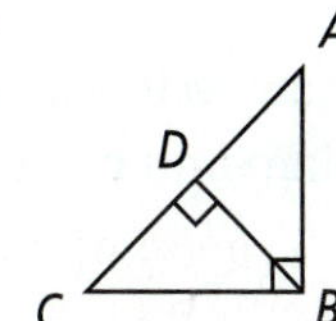

$\triangle ABC \sim \triangle BDC \sim \triangle ADB$

7.

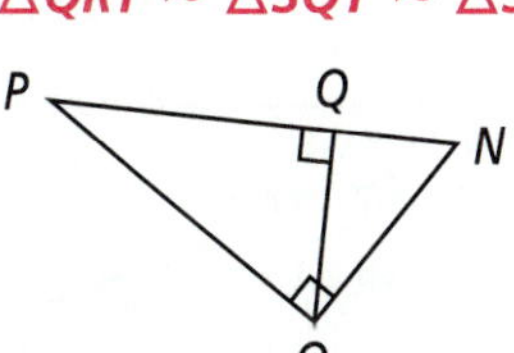

$\triangle PNO \sim \triangle POQ \sim \triangle ONQ$

8.

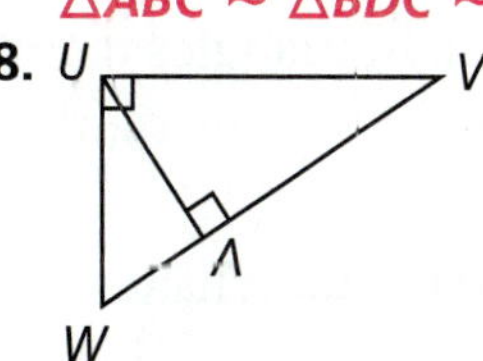

$\triangle WVU \sim \triangle WUA \sim \triangle UVA$

Algebra Find the geometric mean of each pair of numbers.

9. 4 and 9 $\quad \frac{4}{x} = \frac{\boxed{x}}{9} \rightarrow x^2 = \boxed{36} \rightarrow x = \boxed{6}$

10. 6 and 12 $\quad \frac{6}{y} = \frac{y}{\boxed{12}} \rightarrow y^2 = \boxed{72} \rightarrow y = \boxed{}$ $6\sqrt{2}$

11. 14 and 12 $2\sqrt{42}$

12. 6 and 500 $10\sqrt{30}$

13. 4.2 and 10 $\sqrt{42}$

14. $\sqrt{50}$ and $\sqrt{2}$ 10

Use the figure at the right to complete each proportion.

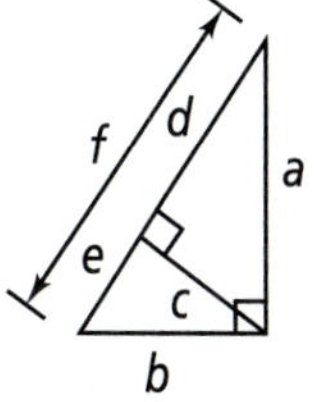

15. $\frac{d}{c} = \frac{c}{\boxed{e}}$

16. $\frac{\boxed{f}}{b} = \frac{b}{e}$

17. $\frac{f}{\boxed{a}} = \frac{\boxed{a}}{d}$

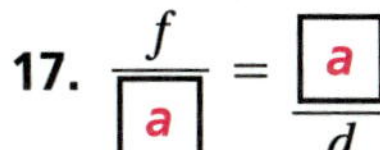

18. $\frac{f}{b} = \frac{b}{\boxed{e}}$

Name ______________________ Class ____________ Date ____________

7-4 Practice (continued) — Form K

Similarity in Right Triangles

Algebra **Solve for *x* and *y*.**

19. 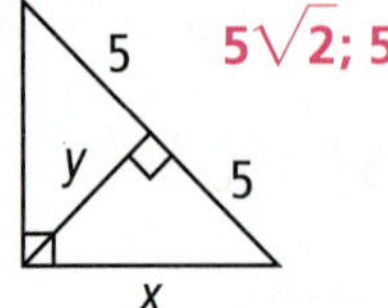

$5\sqrt{2}$; 5

20. 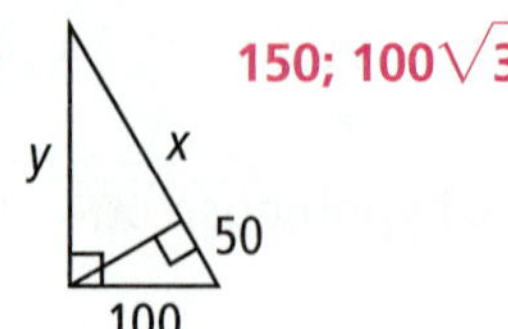

150; $100\sqrt{3}$

21. 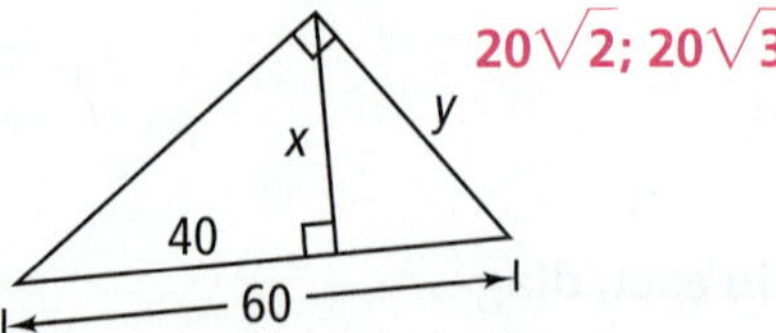

$20\sqrt{2}$; $20\sqrt{3}$

22. 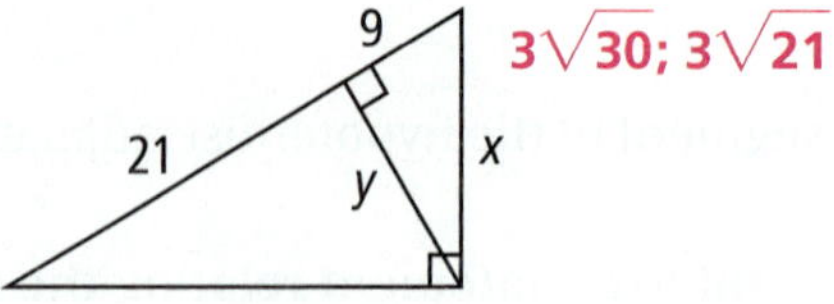

$3\sqrt{30}$; $3\sqrt{21}$

23. Error Analysis A classmate writes an incorrect proportion to find *x*. Explain and correct the error.

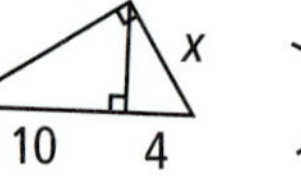

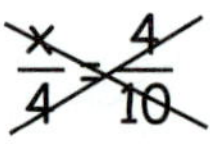

Find *x* using the geometric mean of the hypotenuse and the segment of the hypotenuse adjacent to the leg; $\frac{4}{x} = \frac{x}{14}$.

24. A quilter sews three right triangles together to make the rectangular quilt block at the right. What is the area of the rectangle? $72\sqrt{2}$ cm^2

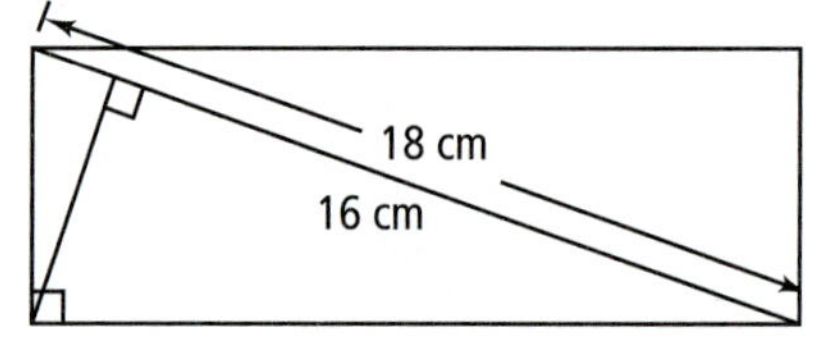

- How can you find the dimensions of the rectangle? Use Corollary 1 to Theorem 7-3 and Corollary 2 to Theorem 7-3.
- What is the formula for the area of a rectangle? $A = bh$

25. The altitude to the hypotenuse of a right triangle divides the hypotenuse into segments 9 in. and 12 in. long. Find the length of the altitude to the hypotenuse. $6\sqrt{3}$ in.

26. The altitude to the hypotenuse of a right triangle divides the hypotenuse into segments 4 in. long and 12 in. long. What are the lengths of the other legs of the triangle? $8\sqrt{3}$ in.; 8 in.

27. A carpenter is framing a roof for a shed. What is the length of the longer slope of the roof? 12 ft

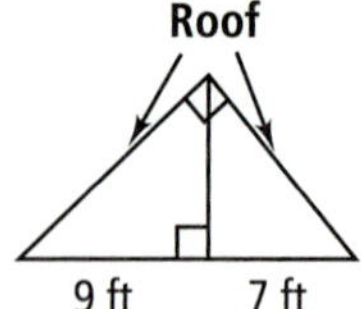

Name ______________________ Class ____________ Date ____________

7-4 Standardized Test Prep

Similarity in Right Triangles

Multiple Choice

For Exercises 1–5, choose the correct letter.

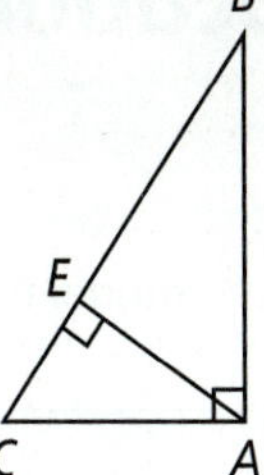

1. Which segment of the hypotenuse is adjacent to $\overline{AB}$? D

   (A) $\overline{EC}$ (B) $\overline{AC}$ (C) $\overline{AE}$ (D) $\overline{BE}$

2. What is the geometric mean of 7 and 12? H

   (F) $1\frac{5}{7}$ (G) 9.5 (H) $2\sqrt{21}$ (I) $4\sqrt{21}$

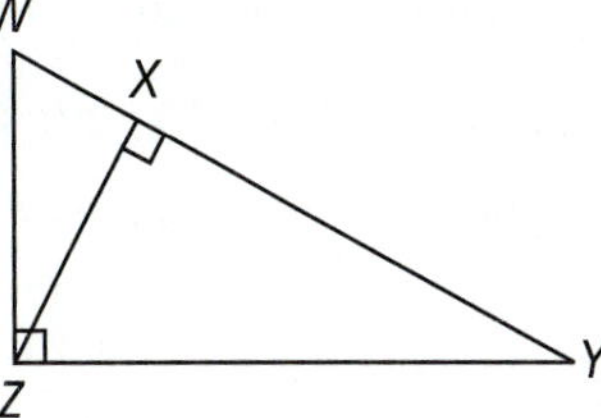

3. Which similarity statement is true? B

   (A) $\triangle WYZ \sim \triangle XZW \sim \triangle XYZ$

   (B) $\triangle WYZ \sim \triangle WZX \sim \triangle ZYX$

   (C) $\triangle YZW \sim \triangle XZW \sim \triangle XZY$

   (D) $\triangle YZW \sim \triangle ZXW \sim \triangle ZYX$

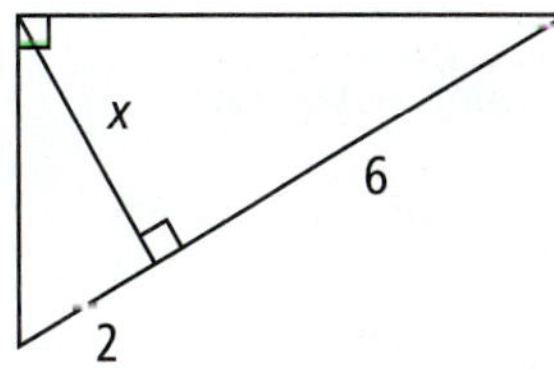

4. What is the value of x? F

   (F) $2\sqrt{3}$ (H) 4

   (G) $4\sqrt{3}$ (I) 6

5. The altitude of the hypotenuse of a right triangle divides the hypotenuse into segments of lengths 14 and 8. What is the length of the altitude? B

   (A) $2\sqrt{77}$ (B) $4\sqrt{7}$ (C) $4\sqrt{11}$ (D) 11

Extended Response

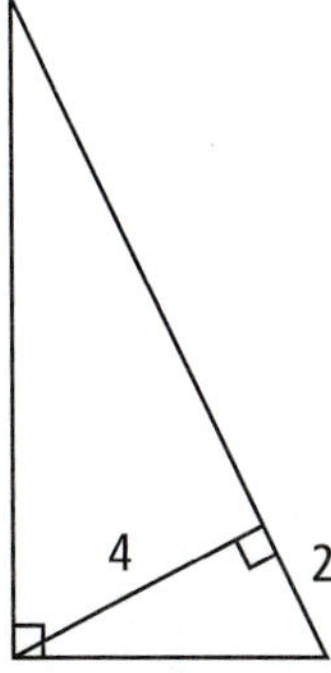

6. What is the perimeter of the large triangle shown at the right? Show your work.

   [4] $10 + 6\sqrt{5}$; $h_2 = \frac{2}{4} = \frac{4}{x} = 8$; $\ell_1 : \frac{2}{x} = \frac{x}{10}$, so $x^2 = \sqrt{20} = 2\sqrt{5}$; $\ell_2 : \frac{8}{x} = \frac{x}{10}$; $x^2 = \sqrt{80} = 4\sqrt{5}$; perimeter $= 8 + 2 + 2\sqrt{5} = 10 + 6\sqrt{5}$

   [3] appropriate methods, but with one computational error

   [2] appropriate methods, but with several computational errors

   [1] correct perimeter only [0] inappropriate methods, several computational errors, and incorrect perimeter

7-5 Proportions in Triangles

Vocabulary

Review

1. Circle the model that can form a *proportion* with $\frac{10}{15}$.

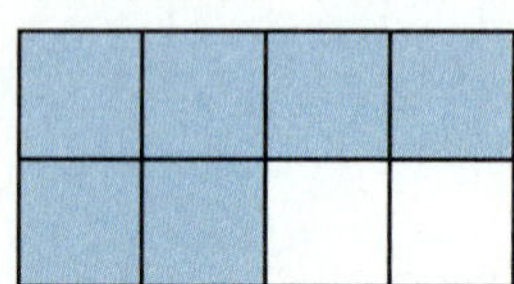

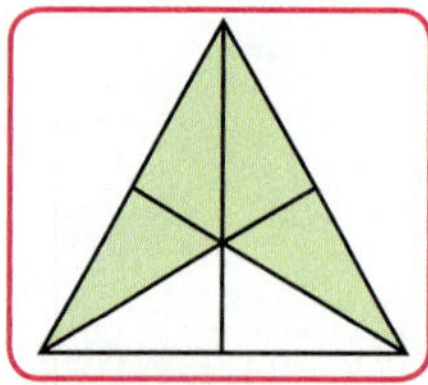

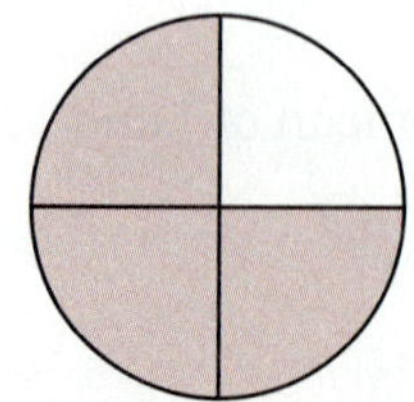

2. Circle the ratios that you can use to form a *proportion*.

$\frac{1}{2}$	$\frac{3}{4}$	$\frac{25}{100}$	$\frac{75}{100}$

3. Cross out the *proportion* that does NOT have the same solution as the others.

$\frac{12}{17} = \frac{n}{20}$	$\frac{12}{n} = \frac{17}{20}$	$\frac{n}{17} = \frac{20}{12}$	$\frac{20}{n} = \frac{17}{12}$

Vocabulary Builder

bisector (noun) **BY sek tur**

Other Word Form: bisect (verb)

Definition: A **bisector** divides a whole into two equal parts.

Math Usage: A **bisector** is a point, segment, ray, or line that divides an angle or a segment into two congruent angles or segments.

Use Your Vocabulary

Use the diagram at the right. Complete each statement with the correct word from the list below. Use each word only once.

bisects bisector bisected

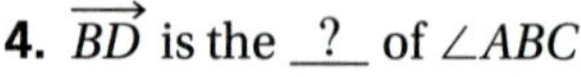

4. $\overrightarrow{BD}$ is the _?_ of $\angle ABC$. bisector

5. $\angle ABC$ is _?_ by $\overrightarrow{BD}$. bisected

6. $\overrightarrow{BD}$ _?_ $\angle ABC$. bisects

take note

Theorem 7-4 Side-Splitter Theorem and Its Corollary

Side-Splitter Theorem

If a line is parallel to one side of a triangle and intersects the other two sides, then it divides those sides proportionally.

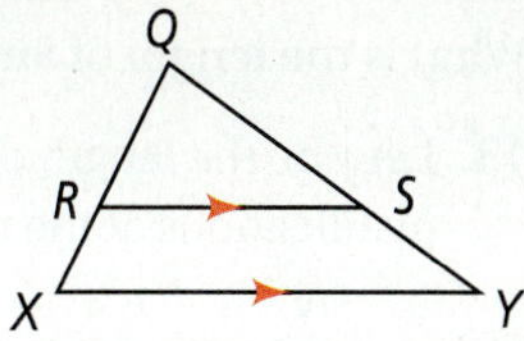

If $\overleftrightarrow{RS} \parallel \overleftrightarrow{XY}$, then $\frac{XR}{RQ} = \frac{YS}{SQ}$.

7. If $XR = 4$, $RQ = 4$, and $YS = 5$, then $SQ = $ 5 .

8. If $XR = 3$, $RQ = 6$, and $YS = 4$, then $SQ = $ 8 .

Corollary to the Side-Splitter Theorem

If three parallel lines intersect two transversals, then the segments intercepted on the transversals are proportional.

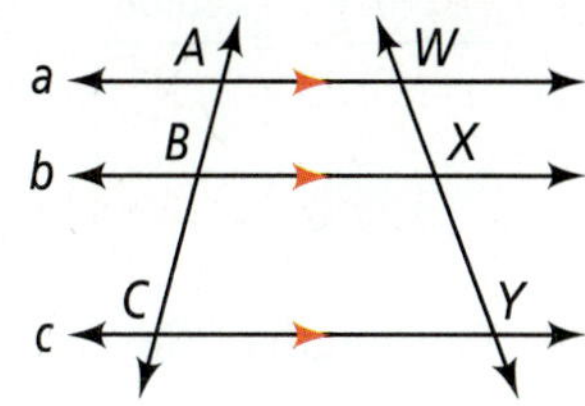

If $a \parallel b \parallel c$, then $\frac{AB}{BC} = \frac{WX}{XY}$.

Complete each proportion.

9. $\frac{BC}{AB} = \frac{XY}{WX}$ **10.** $\frac{CB}{BA} = \frac{YX}{XW}$ **11.** $\frac{AC}{AB} = \frac{WY}{WX}$

Problem 1 Using the Side-Splitter Theorem

Got It? What is the value of a in the diagram at the right?

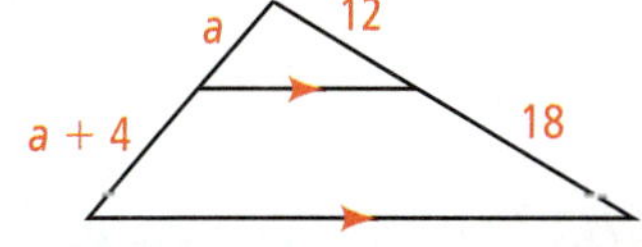

12. The value of a is found below. Use one of the reasons in the box to justify each step.

Cross Products Property	Divide each side by 6.
Side-Splitter Theorem	Simplify.
Subtract 12a from each side.	

$\frac{a}{a + 4} = \frac{12}{18}$ Side-Splitter Theorem

$18a = 12a + 48$ Cross Products Property

$18a - 12a = 12a - 12a + 48$ Subtract 12a from each side.

$6a = 48$ Simplify.

$\frac{6a}{6} = \frac{48}{6}$ Divide each side by 6.

$a = 8$ Simplify.

Problem 2 Finding a Length

Got It? **Camping** **Three campsites are shown in the diagram. What is the length of Site C along the road?**

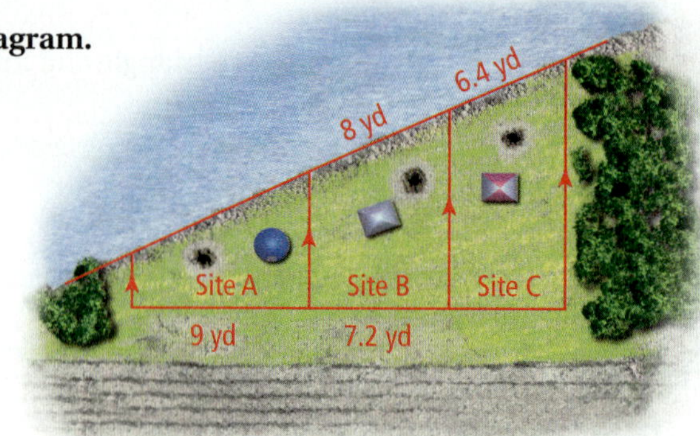

13. Let y be the length of Site C along the road. Use the justifications at the right to find the value of y.

$\frac{y}{7.2} = \frac{6.4}{8}$	Corollary to Side-Splitter Theorem
$8 \cdot y = 46.08$	Cross Products Property
$\frac{8 \cdot y}{8} = \frac{46.08}{8}$	Divide each side by the coefficient of y.
$y = 5.76$	Simplify.

14. The length of Site C along the road is 5.76 yd.

take note

Theorem 7-5 Triangle-Angle-Bisector Theorem

Triangle-Angle-Bisector Theorem

If a ray bisects an angle of a triangle, then it divides the opposite side into two segments that are proportional to the other two sides of the triangle.

If $\overrightarrow{AD}$ bisects $\angle CAB$, then $\frac{CD}{DB} = \frac{CA}{BA}$.

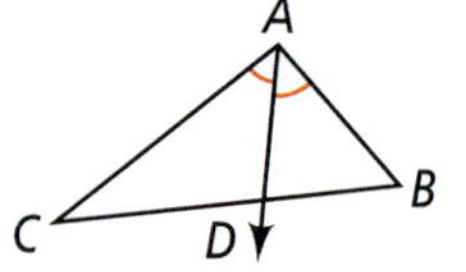

Problem 3 Using the Triangle-Angle-Bisector Theorem

Got It? **What is the value of y in the diagram at the right?**

y 24
9.6 16

15. Complete the reasoning model below.

Think	Write
I can use the Triangle-Angle-Bisector Theorem to write a proportion.	$\frac{9.6}{16} = \frac{y}{24}$
Then I can use the Cross-Products Property.	$230.4 = 16y$
Now I divide each side by 16 and simplify.	$\frac{230.4}{16} = \frac{16}{16}y$ $y = 14.4$

16. The value of y is 14.4.

Lesson Check • Do you know HOW?

What is the value of x in the figure at the right?

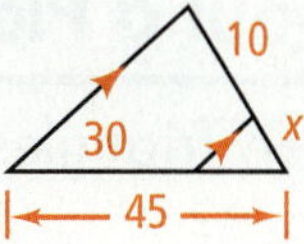

17. Circle the proportion you can use to solve the problem.

$\frac{10}{30} = \frac{x}{45}$ $\frac{x}{10} = \frac{30}{45}$ $\frac{x}{x + 10} = \frac{30}{45}$ **(circled)** $\frac{10}{x + 10} = \frac{30}{45}$

18. Solve the proportion.

$$\frac{10}{x + 10} = \frac{30}{45}$$
$$10(45) = 30(x + 10)$$
$$45 = 3x + 30$$
$$15 = 3x$$
$$5 = x$$

Lesson Check • Do you UNDERSTAND?

Error Analysis **A classmate says you can use the Side-Splitter Theorem to find both x and y in the diagram. Explain what is wrong with the statement.**

19. Cross out the lengths that are NOT parts of the sides intersected by the parallel line.

2 2.4 3 ~~7~~ ~~x~~ y

20. Can you use the Side-Splitter Theorem to find x? Yes / **(No)**

21. Can you use the Side-Splitter Theorem to find y? **(Yes)** / No

22. Explain what is wrong with your classmate's statement.

Explanations may vary. Sample: x is not part of the transversal so I cannot use the Side-Splitter Theorem to find x.

Math Success

Check off the vocabulary words that you understand.

☐ bisector ☐ proportion ☐ Side-Splitter Theorem

Rate how well you understand *side and angle bisectors.*

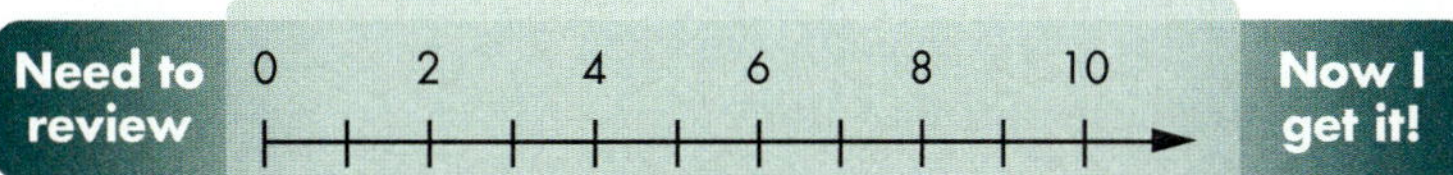

Name ______________________ Class ____________ Date ____________

7-5 Think About a Plan

Proportions in Triangles

An angle bisector of a triangle divides the opposite side of the triangle into segments 5 cm and 3 cm long. A second side of the triangle is 7.5 cm long. Find all possible lengths for the third side of the triangle.

1. What is the Triangle-Angle-Bisector Theorem? What relationships does it specifically describe?

   It states that the angle bisector of a triangle divides the opposite side of the triangle into proportional segments. So the ratio of one segment and its adjacent side is proportional to the ratio of the second segment and its adjacent side.

2. What information is given in this problem? What information is not given?

   You know that the lengths of the two segments created by the angle bisector are 5 cm and 3 cm long. You know the length of the second side is 7.5 cm, but you don't know to which segment this side is adjacent.

3. What does the phrase "all possible lengths" tell you about the problem?

   There may be more than one answer.

4. In the space below, draw all the possible representations of the triangle described in the problem.

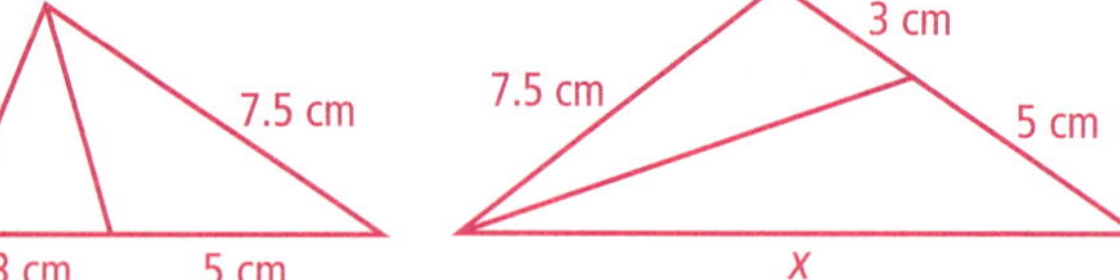

5. How can proportions be used to solve this problem?

   Write a proportion comparing the ratio of each segment to its adjacent side.

6. How many proportions will you need to set up? Explain.

   You will need to set up two proportions because you don't know the segment that is adjacent to the 7.5 cm side.

7. Use the space below to write and solve the proportions.

   $\frac{3}{7.5} = \frac{5}{x}$ $\quad$ $\frac{3}{x} = \frac{5}{7.5}$

   $3x = 37.5$ $\quad$ $5x = 22.5$

   $x = 12.5$ $\quad$ $x = 4.5$

8. What are the possible lengths for the third side of the triangle?

   12.5 cm or 4.5 cm

Name ______________________ Class ____________ Date ____________

7-5 Practice — Form K

Proportions in Triangles

Use the figure at the right to complete each proportion.

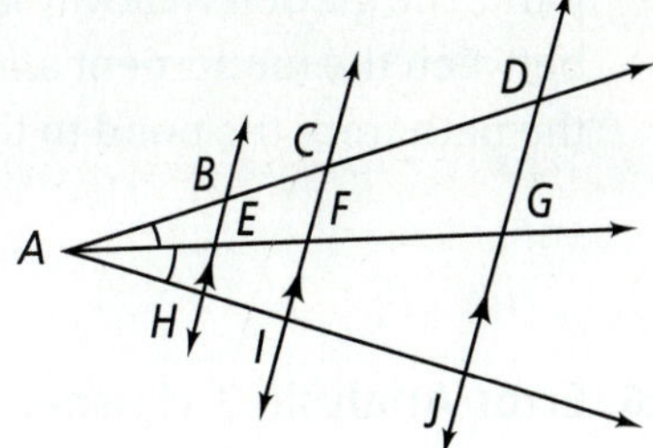

1. $\frac{CF}{FI} = \frac{AC}{AI}$

2. $\frac{AB}{BC} = \frac{AH}{HI}$

3. $\frac{CD}{IJ} = \frac{BC}{HI}$

4. $\frac{JG}{AJ} = \frac{GD}{AD}$

5. $\frac{FG}{EF} = \frac{CD}{BC}$

6. $\frac{AC}{AI} = \frac{CD}{IJ}$

Algebra **Solve for *x*.**

7. 3

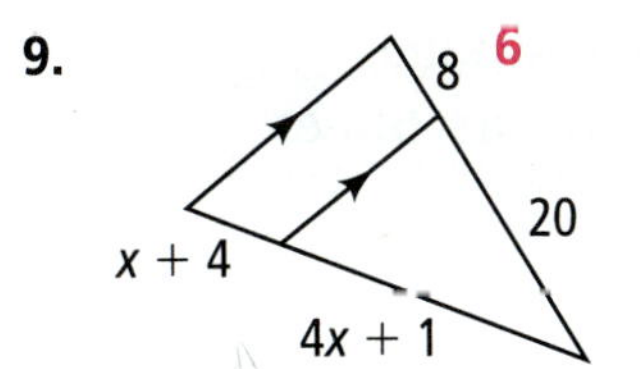

8. 8.5

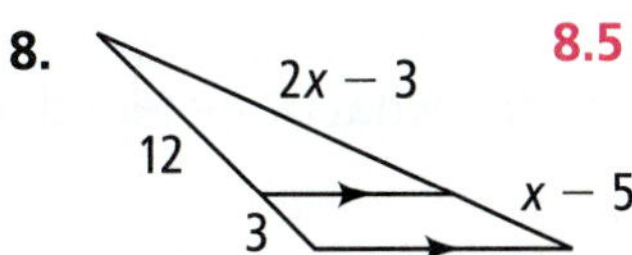

9. 6

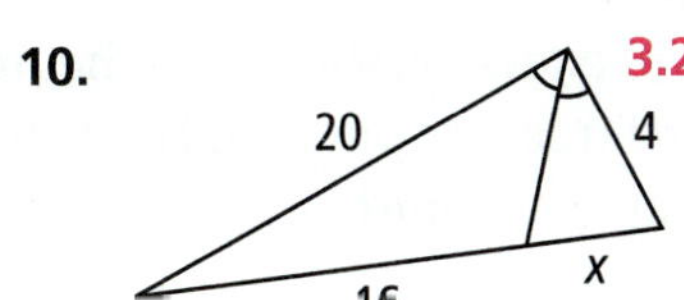

10. 3.2

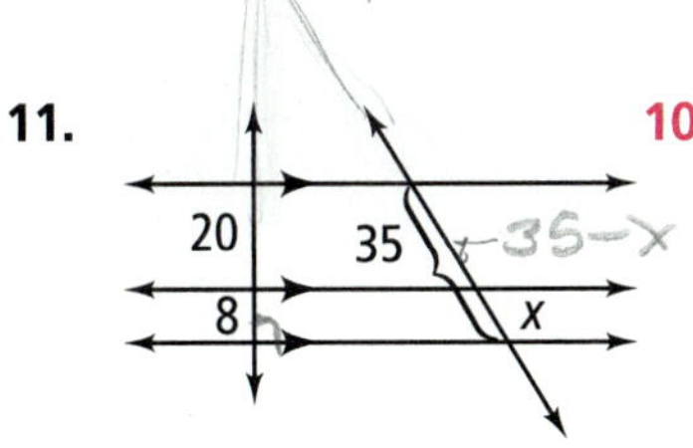

11. 10

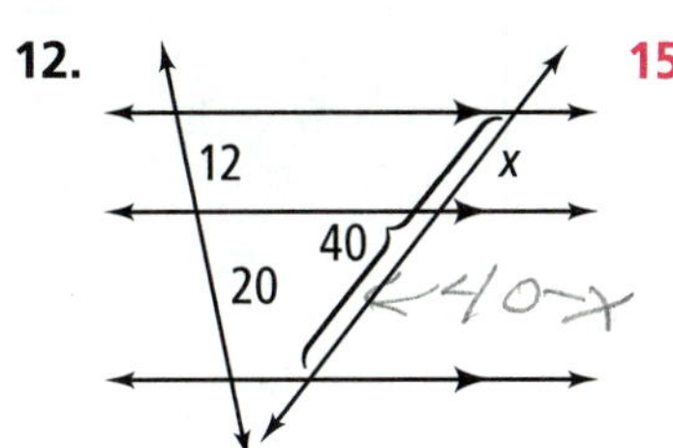

12. 15

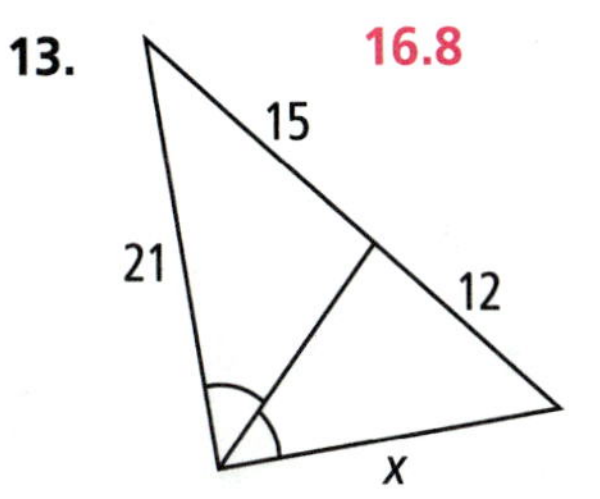

13. 16.8

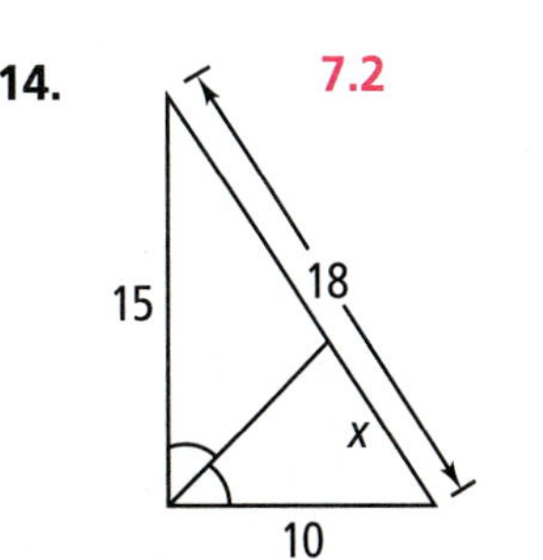

14. 7.2

15 18 x 10

Name ______________________ Class ____________ Date ____________

7-5 Practice (continued)

Form K

Proportions in Triangles

15. The map at the right shows the walking paths at a local park. The garden walkway is parallel to the walkway between the monument and the pond. How long is the path from the pond to the playground? 70 yd

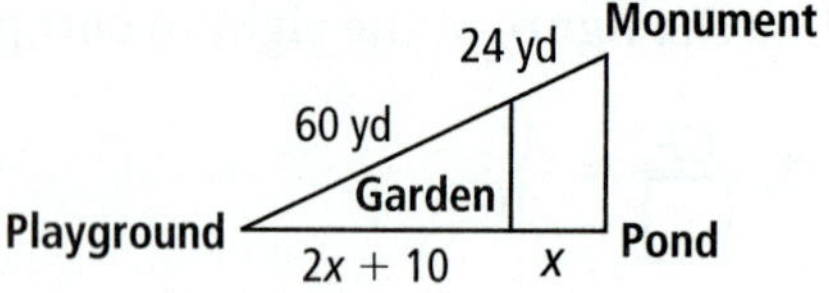

16. **Error Analysis** A classmate says you can use the Triangle-Angle-Bisector Theorem to find the length of *GI*. Explain what is wrong with your classmate's statement.
Answers may vary. Sample: The Triangle-Angle-Bisector Thm. states that the segments formed when the bisector divides a side are proportional to the other sides. It cannot be used to find the length of the bisector.

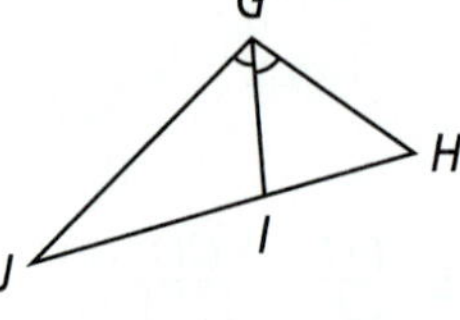

17. Triangle *QRS* has line *XY* parallel to side *RS*. The length of *QY* is 12 in. The length of *QX* is 8 in.
    a. Draw a picture to represent the problem.
    Answers may vary. Sample:
    b. If the length of *XR* is 5 in., what is the length of *QS*? 19.5 in.

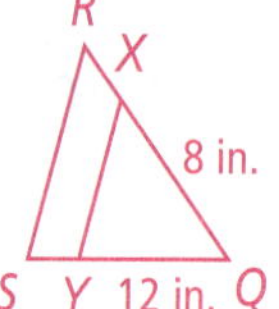

18. The business district of a town is shown on the map below. Maple Avenue, Oak Avenue, and Elm Street are parallel. How long is the section of First Street from Elm Street to Maple Avenue? 2275 ft

Algebra Solve for *x*.

19.

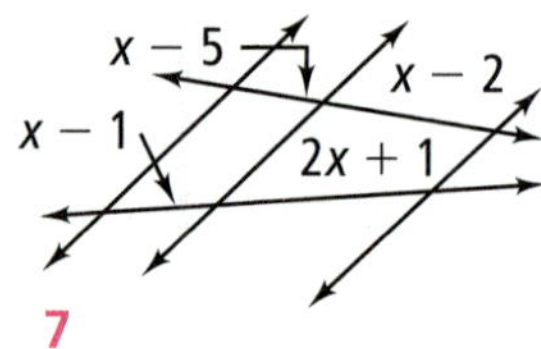

7

20.

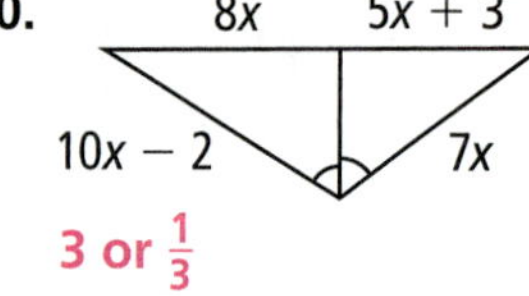

3 or $\frac{1}{3}$

21.

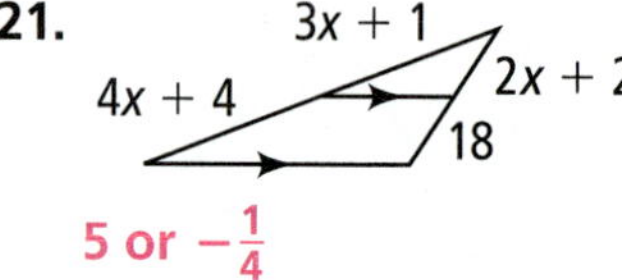

5 or $-\frac{1}{4}$

Name ______________________ Class ____________ Date ____________

7-5 Standardized Test Prep

Proportions in Triangles

Multiple Choice

For Exercises 1–5, choose the correct letter.

For Exercises 1 and 2, use the diagram at the right.

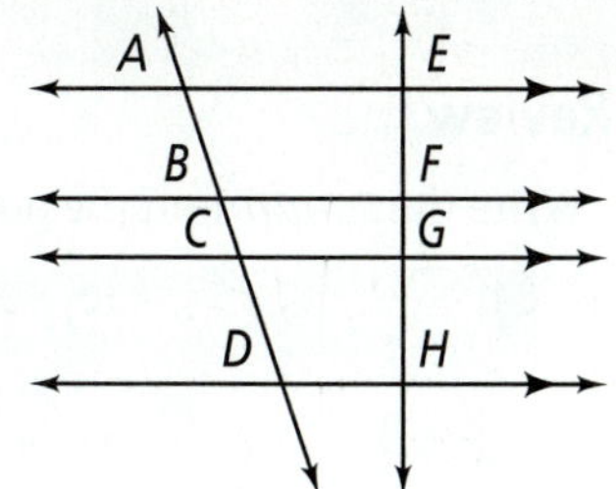

1. Which makes the proportion true? $\frac{AB}{\square} = \frac{EF}{GH}$ C

   (A) AD (C) CD

   (B) DH (D) BC

2. Which proportion is *not* true? I

   (F) $\frac{BC}{CD} = \frac{FG}{GH}$ (G) $\frac{AC}{CD} = \frac{EG}{GH}$ (H) $\frac{BD}{FH} = \frac{AD}{EH}$ (I) $\frac{AB}{AE} = \frac{EF}{BF}$

3. What is the value of y? A

   (A) 2 (C) 3

   (B) 4 (D) 6

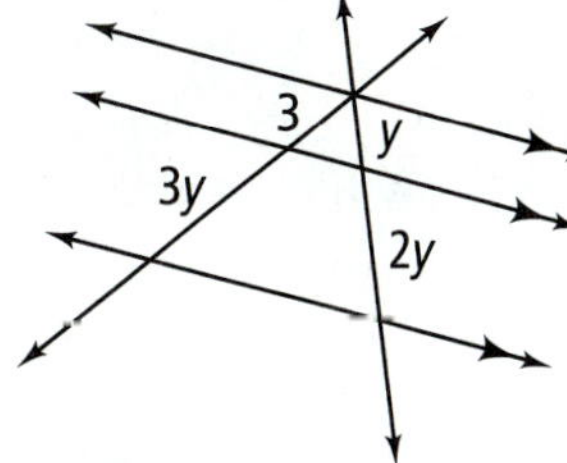

4. What is the value of x? G

   (F) 3 (H) 6

   (G) 8 (I) 12

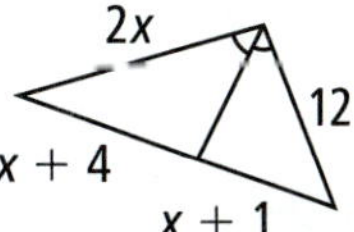

5. In $\triangle DEF$, the bisector of $\angle F$ divides the opposite sides into segments that are 4 and 9 in. long. The side of the triangle adjacent to the 4 in. segment is 6 in. long. To the nearest tenth of an inch, how long is the third side of the triangle? D

   (A) 2.7 in. (B) 6 in. (C) 13 in. (D) 13.5 in.

Short Response

6. In $\triangle QRS$, $\overline{XY} \parallel \overline{SR}$. $\overline{XY}$ divides $\overline{QR}$ and $\overline{QS}$ into segments as follows: $\overline{SX} = 3$, $\overline{XQ} = 2x$, $\overline{RY} = 4.5$, and $\overline{YQ} = 7.5$. Write a proportion to find x. What is the length of $\overline{QS}$? [2] $\frac{7.5}{4.5} = \frac{2x}{3}$; $x = 2.5$; 8 [1] incorrect proportion or error in calculation [0] incorrect proportion and error in calculation

8-1 PART 1 The Pythagorean Theorem and Its Converse

Vocabulary

Review

1. Write the *square* and the positive *square root* of each number.

Number	Square	Positive Square Root
9	81	3
1	1	1
$\frac{1}{4}$	$\frac{1}{16}$	$\frac{1}{2}$
0.81	0.6561	0.9

Vocabulary Builder

leg (noun) leg

Related Word: hypotenuse

Definition: In a right triangle, the sides that the right angle are the legs.

Main Idea: The **legs** of a right triangle are perpendicular. The hypotenuse is the side opposite the right angle.

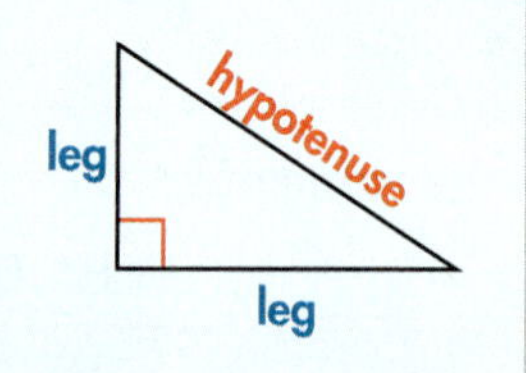

Use Your Vocabulary

Underline the correct word to complete each sentence.

2. The *hypotenuse* is the longest / shortest side in a right triangle.

3. The *legs* of a right triangle form a(n) acute / obtuse / right angle.

Write T for *true* or F for *false*.

F 4. The *hypotenuse* of a right triangle can be any one of the three sides.

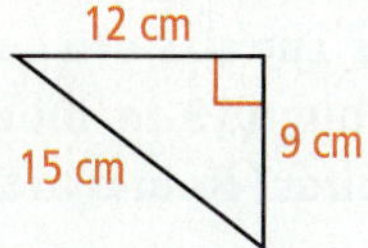

T 5. One *leg* of the triangle at the right has length 9 cm.

F 6. The sum of the lengths of the *legs* of the triangle is 36 cm.

T 7. The *hypotenuse* of the triangle at the right has length 15 cm.

take note

Theorem 8-1 Pythagorean Theorem

If a triangle is a right triangle, then the sum of the squares of the lengths of the legs is equal to the square of the length of the hypotenuse.

If $\triangle ABC$ is a right triangle, then $a^2 + b^2 = c^2$.

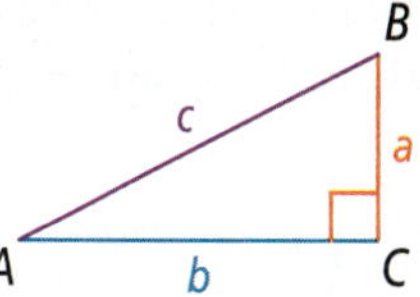

8. Circle the equation that shows the correct relationship among the legs and the hypotenuse of a right triangle.

$13^2 + 5^2 = 12^2$ $\quad$ $5^2 + 12^2 = 13^2$ (circled) $\quad$ $12^2 + 13^2 = 5^2$

Problem 1 Finding the Length of the Hypotenuse

Got It? **The legs of a right triangle have lengths 10 and 24. What is the length of the hypotenuse?**

9. Label the triangle at the right.

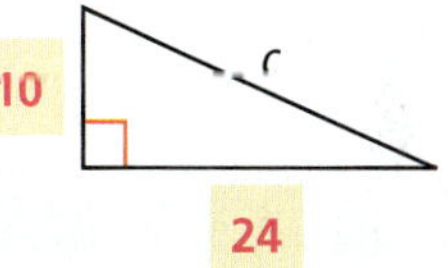

10. Complete the steps below to find the length of the hypotenuse.

$a^2 + b^2 = c^2$	Pythagorean Theorem
$10^2 + 24^2 = c^2$	Substitute for *a* and *b*.
$100 + 576 = c^2$	Simplify.
$676 = c^2$	Add.
$26 = c$	Take the positive square root.

11. The length of the hypotenuse is 26.

12. One Pythagorean triple is 5, 12, and 13. If you multiply each number by 2, what numbers result? How do the numbers that result compare to the lengths of the sides of the triangle in Exercises 9–11?

10, 24, 26. Answers may vary. Sample: The numbers are the same as the lengths of the sides of the triangle in Exercises 9–11.

Problem 3 Finding Distance

Got It? **The size of a computer monitor is the length of its diagonal. You want to buy a 19-in. monitor that has a height of 11 in. What is the width of the monitor? Round to the nearest tenth of an inch.**

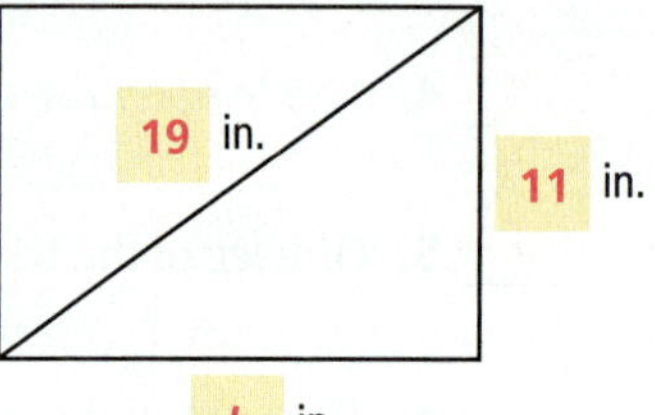

13. Label the diagram of the computer monitor at the right.

14. The equation is solved below. Write a justification for each step.

$a^2 + b^2 = c^2$	Pythagorean Theorem
$11^2 + b^2 = 19^2$	Substitute.
$121 + b^2 = 361$	Simplify.
$121 - 121 + b^2 = 361 - 121$	Subtract 121 from each side.
$b^2 = 240$	Simplify.
$b = \sqrt{240}$	Take the positive square root.
$b \approx 15.49193338$	Use a calculator.

15. To the nearest tenth of an inch, the width of the monitor is 15.5 in.

Lesson Check • Do you UNDERSTAND?

Vocabulary **Describe the conditions that a set of three numbers must meet in order to form a Pythagorean triple.**

16. The table below shows three Pythagorean triples a, b, c. Complete the table.

a	b	c	a^2	b^2	c^2	$a^2 + b^2$
3	4	5	9	16	25	25
5	12	13	25	144	169	169
8	15	17	64	225	289	289

17. Describe the characteristics of a set of three numbers that form a Pythagorean triple.

Answers may vary. Sample: The three numbers must be positive integers. The square of the greatest number must equal the sum of the squares of the other two numbers.

8-1 PART 2 The Pythagorean Theorem and Its Converse

Vocabulary

Review

Circle the *converse* of each statement.

1. If your state bird is the cactus wren, then your state is Arizona.

If your state is Arizona, then your state bird is the cactus wren. (circled)	If your state bird is not the cactus wren, then your state is not Arizona.

2. If it is raining, then you use an umbrella.

If you do not use an umbrella, then it is not raining.	If you use an umbrella, then it is raining. (circled)

Vocabulary Builder

classify (verb) KLAS uh fy

Other Word Forms: classification (noun), classified (adjective)

Main Idea: When you **classify** numbers or geometric figures, you put them into groups based on a property that they have.

Use Your Vocabulary

Complete each statement with the correct word from the list below.

classification classified classify

3. Polygons are _?_ by their number of sides. classified

4. You can _?_ triangles by the lengths of their sides. classify

5. One _?_ of counting numbers is by odd and even. classification

6. *Classify* each angle as *right*, *acute*, or *obtuse*.

120°	90°	55°
obtuse	right	acute

Theorem 8-2 Converse of the Pythagorean Theorem

If the sum of the squares of the lengths of two sides of a triangle is equal to the square of the length of the third side, then the triangle is a right triangle.

If $a^2 + b^2 = c^2$, then $\triangle ABC$ is a right triangle.

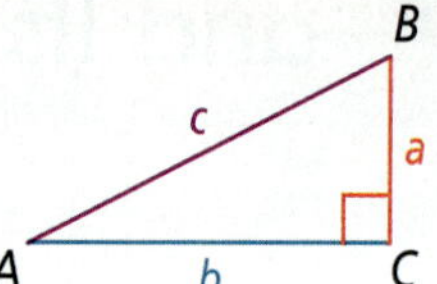

Underline the correct words to complete each sentence.

7. A triangle with side lengths 3, 4, and 5 is / is not a right triangle because $3^2 + 4^2$ is equal / not equal to 5^2.

8. A triangle with side lengths 4, 5, and 6 is / is not a right triangle because $4^2 + 5^2$ is equal / not equal to 6^2.

Problem 4 Identifying a Right Triangle

Got It? A triangle has side lengths 16, 48, and 50. Is the triangle a right triangle? Explain.

9. Circle the equation you will use to determine whether the triangle is a right triangle.

$16^2 + 48^2 \stackrel{?}{=} 50^2$ $\qquad$ $16^2 + 50^2 \stackrel{?}{=} 48^2$ $\qquad$ $48^2 + 50^2 \stackrel{?}{=} 16^2$

10. Simplify your equation from Exercise 9.

$$16^2 + 48^2 \stackrel{?}{=} 50^2$$
$$256 + 2304 \stackrel{?}{=} 2500$$
$$2560 \neq 2500$$

11. Underline the correct words to complete the sentence.

The equation is true / false, so the triangle is / is not a right triangle.

Theorems 8-3 and 8-4

Theorem 8-3 If the square of the length of the longest side of a triangle is greater than the sum of the squares of the lengths of the other two sides, then the triangle is obtuse.

Theorem 8-4 If the square of the length of the longest side of a triangle is less than the sum of the squares of the lengths of the other two sides, then the triangle is acute.

Use the figures at the right. Complete each sentence with *acute* or *obtuse*.

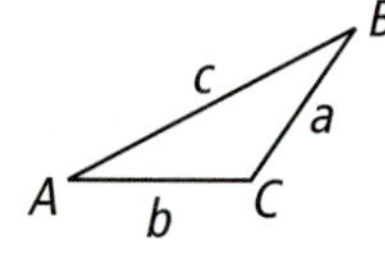

12. In $\triangle ABC$, $c^2 > a^2 + b^2$, so $\triangle ABC$ is __?__. obtuse

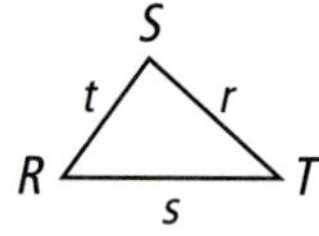

13. In $\triangle RST$, $s^2 < r^2 + t^2$, so $\triangle RST$ is __?__. acute

Problem 5 Classifying a Triangle

Got It? Is a triangle with side lengths 7, 8, and 9 *acute, obtuse,* or *right*?

14. Circle the length of the longest side, c. Underline the lengths of the other two sides, a and b.

7 8 9

15. Complete.

$a^2 + b^2 =$ 49 + 64 = 113 $c^2 =$ 81

16. Underline the correct words to complete the sentence.

Since c^2 is equal to / greater than / less than $a^2 + b^2$, the triangle is acute / obtuse / right .

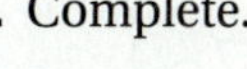

Lesson Check • Do you UNDERSTAND?

Error Analysis **A triangle has side lengths 16, 34, and 30. Your friend says it is not a right triangle. Describe your friend's error.**

$16^2 + 34^2 \stackrel{?}{=} 30^2$
$256 + 1156 \stackrel{?}{=} 900$
$1412 \neq 900$

17. The length of the longest side of the triangle is 34 .

18. Circle the length that your friend used as the longest side, c, in the comparison.

16 30 34

19. Write the comparison that your friend should have used to determine whether the triangle is a right triangle.

$16^2 + 30^2 \stackrel{?}{=} 34^2$

20. Describe the error in your friend's work. Answers may vary. Sample:

My friend used the wrong length for c in the comparison.

The comparison should be $16^2 + 30^2 \stackrel{?}{=} 34^2$.

Math Success

Check off the vocabulary words that you understand.

☐ hypotenuse ☐ leg ☐ Pythagorean Theorem ☐ Pythagorean triple

Rate how well you can *use the Pythagorean Theorem and its converse.*

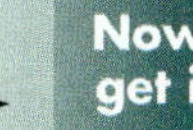

Need to review 0 2 4 6 8 10 Now I get it!

Name ______________________ Class ____________ Date ____________

8-1 Think About a Plan

The Pythagorean Theorem and Its Converse

Astronomy The Hubble Space Telescope orbits 600 km above Earth's surface. Earth's radius is about 6370 km. Use the Pythagorean Theorem to find the distance x from the telescope to Earth's horizon. Round your answer to the nearest ten kilometers. (Diagram is not to scale.)

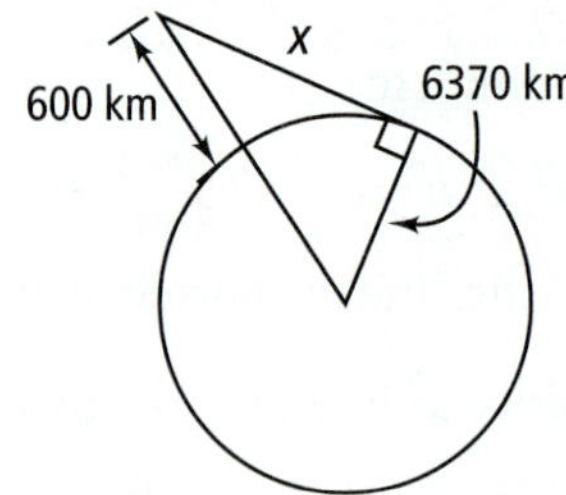

Know

1. Write the Pythagorean Theorem. $a^2 + b^2 = c^2$

2. Look at the diagram. What could replace a and b in the Pythagorean Theorem?
   x, the distance from the telescope to the horizon, and the radius of Earth, 6370 km

Need

3. How can you find the value of c, the hypotenuse of the right triangle?
   Add the radius, 6370 km, and the distance from the telescope to Earth's surface, 600 km.

4. What is the value of c? 6970 km

5. Substitute the known and unknown values for a, b, and c. $6370^2 + x^2 = 6970^2$

Plan

6. How can you find the value of x^2?
   Subtract 6370^2 from 6970^2.

7. What is the value of x^2? 8,004,000 km^2

8. How can you find the value of x?
   Find the square root of 8,004,000 km^2.

9. What is the value of x, to the nearest 10 kilometers? 2830 km

10. Is your answer reasonable? Explain.
    Yes; Sample: The distance makes sense in this situation.

Name ______________________ Class ____________ Date ____________

8-1 Practice

Form K

The Pythagorean Theorem and Its Converse

Algebra **Find the value of** x**.**

1. 12, x, 9

To start, use the Pythagorean Theorem. Then substitute 9 for a, 12 for b, and x for c.

$\square^2 + \square^2 = \square^2$ **9; 12; x; 15**

2. **51**

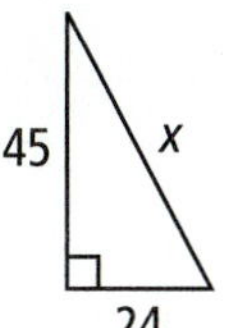

3. **50**

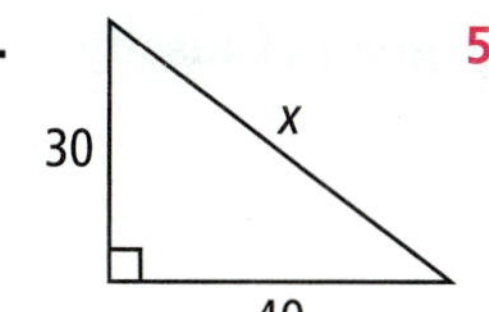

4. **82**

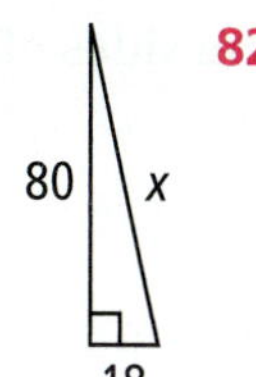

Does each set of numbers form a Pythagorean triple? Explain.

5. 6, 8, 10 **yes; $6^2 + 8^2 = 36 + 64 = 100 = 10^2$**

6. 7, 16, 18 **no; $7^2 + 16^2 = 49 + 256 = 305 \neq 18^2$**

7. 16, 30, 34 **yes; $16^2 + 30^2 = 256 + 900 = 1156 = 34^2$**

Algebra **Find the value of** x**. Express your answer in simplest radical form.**

8. 4, 18, x **$2\sqrt{77}$**

9. **$\sqrt{39}$**

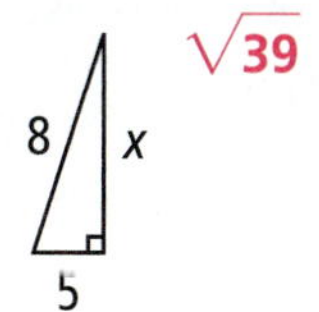

10. **$2\sqrt{19}$**

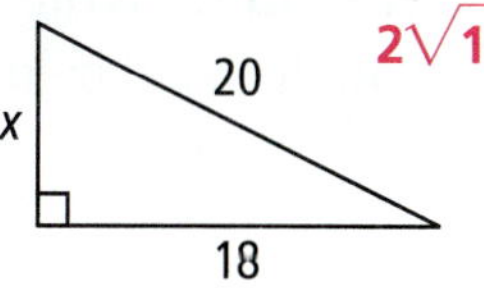

11. **$2\sqrt{154}$**

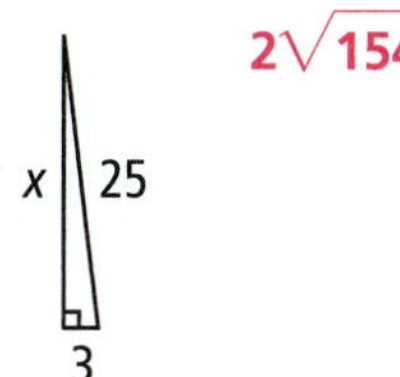

12. **$3\sqrt{3}$**

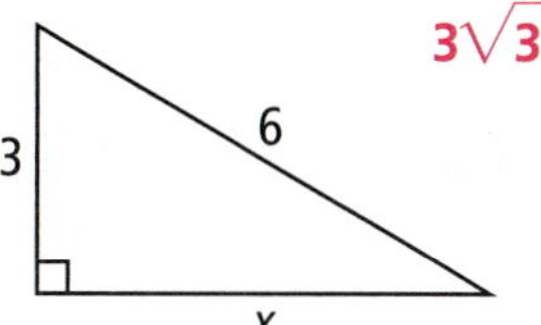

13. **$6\sqrt{13}$**

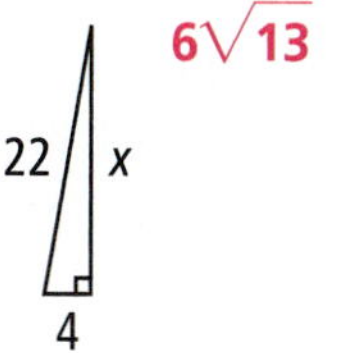

14. A window washer has an 18-ft ladder. He needs to reach the bottom of a window 16 feet off the ground. How far out from the building should the base of the ladder be? Round to the nearest tenth of a foot. **8.2 ft**

To start, use the Pythagorean Theorem. Then substitute 16 for a and 18 for $\boxed{c}$.

15. **Reasoning** A square has a diagonal of 12 cm. What is the perimeter of the square? Express in simplest radical form. **$24\sqrt{2}$**

8-1 Practice (continued) Form K

The Pythagorean Theorem and Its Converse

Is each triangle a right triangle? Explain.

16. 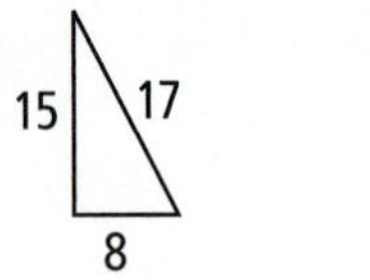

yes; $8^2 + 15^2 = 17^2$

17. 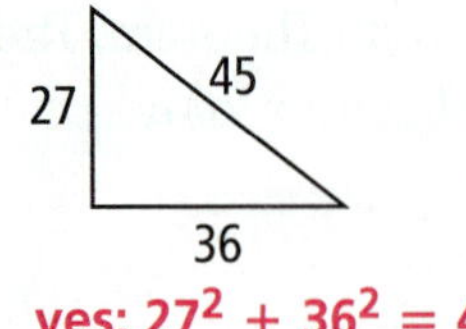

yes; $27^2 + 36^2 = 45^2$

18. 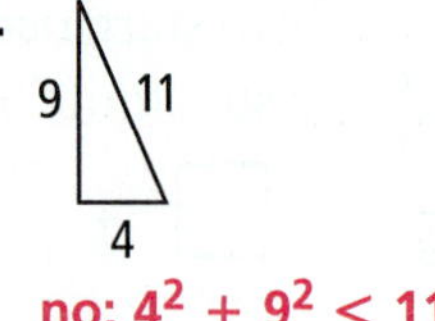

no; $4^2 + 9^2 < 11^2$

The lengths of the sides of a triangle are given. Classify each triangle as *acute*, *right*, or *obtuse*.

19. 3, 4, 6 obtuse

To start, compare c^2 to $a^2 + b^2$. Substitute the greatest length for c.

20. 9, 11, 16 obtuse

21. 4, 6, 7 acute

22. 6, 8, 12 obtuse

23. 24, 70, 74 right

24. 10, 12, 14 acute

25. 20, 25, 31 acute

26. Reasoning In parallelogram $ABCD$, $AB = 20$, $BC = 15$, and $AC = 22$. Is $ABCD$ a rectangle? Explain.
It is not a rectangle. If $ABCD$ were a rectangle, then $\triangle ABC$ would be a right $\triangle$, then $AB^2 + BC^2 = AC^2$, but $15^2 + 20^2 > 22^2$.

27. Open-Ended Write a set of three numbers to represent the sides of each type of triangle listed below. Then draw each triangle.

a. acute Check students' work. The square of the greatest number must be less than the sum of the squares of the other two numbers.

b. obtuse Check students' work. The square of the greatest number must be greater than the sum of the squares of the other two numbers.

c. right Check students' work. The square of the greatest number must be equal to the sum of the squares of the other two numbers.

Open-Ended Find integers *j* and *k* such that (a) the two given integers and *j* represent the side lengths of an acute triangle, and (b) the two given integers and *k* represent the side lengths of an obtuse triangle.

28. 33, 55 Answers may vary. $45 \le j \le 64$; $23 \le k \le 43$ or $65 \le k \le 87$

29. 60, 65 Answers may vary. $26 \le j \le 88$; $6 \le k \le 24$ or $89 \le k \le 124$

30. Reasoning A classmate drew an acute triangle with sides 9 in. and 12 in. What is the greatest possible whole number that can be the length of the longest side of the triangle in inches? 14

Name ____________________ Class ____________ Date ____________

8-1 Standardized Test Prep

The Pythagorean Theorem and Its Converse

Gridded Response

Solve each exercise and enter your answer on the grid provided. What is the value of *x*?

1.

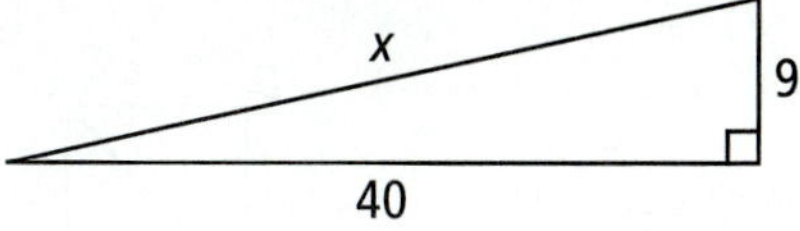

2.

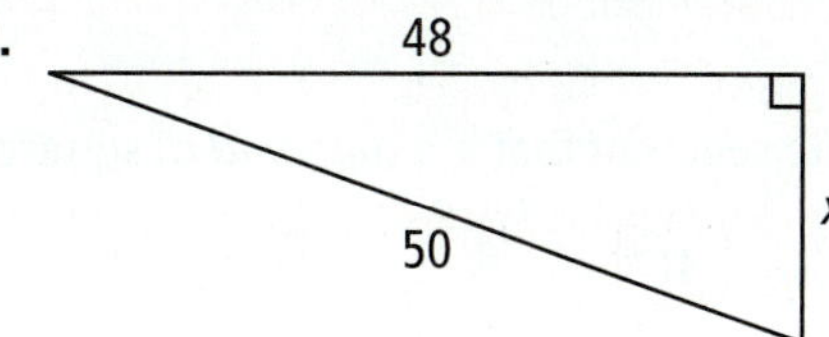

3.

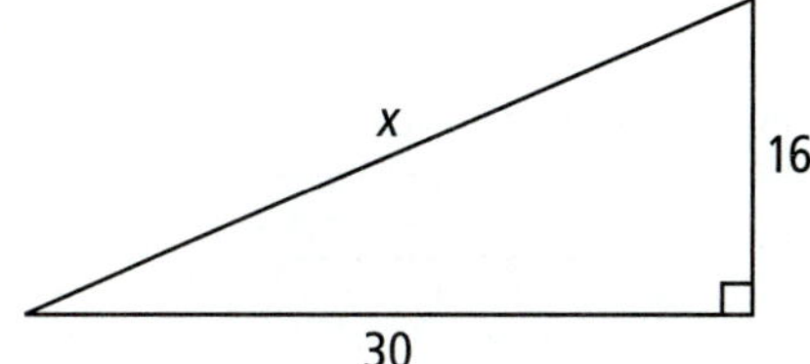

4.

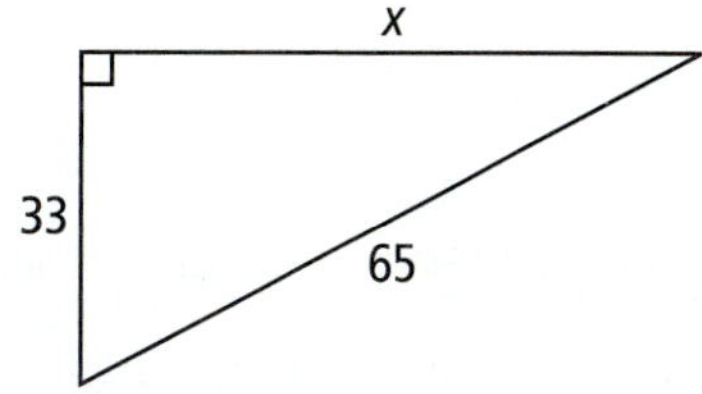

5. An acute triangle has sides that are 14 mm and 97 mm long, respectively. The third side of the triangle must be greater than what whole number of millimeters?

Answers

1. 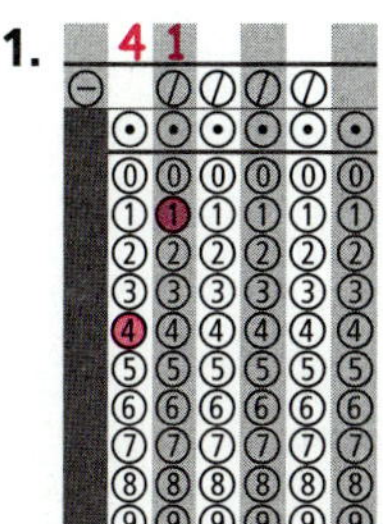

2. 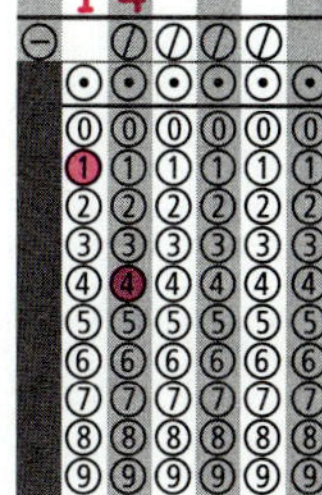

3. 

4. 

5. 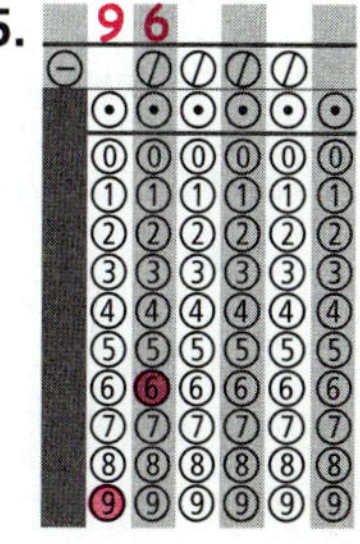

8-2 Special Right Triangles

Vocabulary

Review

1. Circle the segment that is a *diagonal* of square *ABCD*.

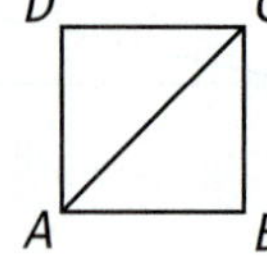

$\overline{AB}$ 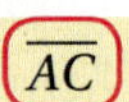 $\overline{AC}$ 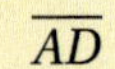 $\overline{AD}$ $\overline{BC}$ 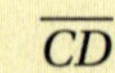 $\overline{CD}$

2. Underline the correct word to complete the sentence.

   A *diagonal* is a line segment that joins two sides / vertices of a polygon.

Vocabulary Builder

complement (noun) KAHM pluh munt

Other Word Form: complementary (adjective)

Math Usage: When the measures of two angles have a sum of 90, each angle is a **complement** of the other.

Nonexample: Two angles whose measures sum to 180 are supplementary.

Use Your Vocabulary

Complete each statement with the word *complement* or *complementary*.

3. If $m\angle A = 40$ and $m\angle B = 50$, the angles are _?_. complementary

4. If $m\angle A = 30$ and $m\angle B = 60$, $\angle B$ is the _?_ of $\angle A$. complement

5. $\angle P$ and $\angle Q$ are _?_ because the sum of their measures is 90. complementary

Complete.

6. If $\angle R$ has a measure of 35, then the *complement* of $\angle R$ has a measure of 55.

7. If $\angle X$ has a measure of 22, then the *complement* of $\angle X$ has a measure of 68.

8. If $\angle C$ has a measure of 65, then the *complement* of $\angle C$ has a measure of 25.

9. Circle the *complementary* angles.

60°

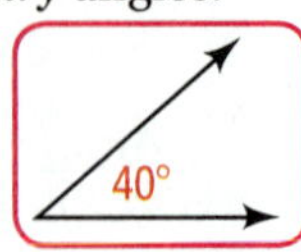

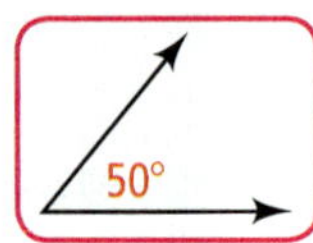

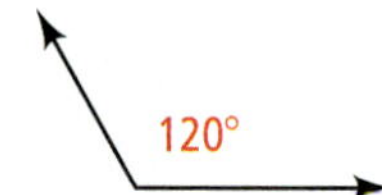

take note

Theorem 8-5 45°-45°-90° Triangle Theorem

In a 45°-45°-90° triangle, both legs are congruent and the length of the hypotenuse is $\sqrt{2}$ times the length of a leg.

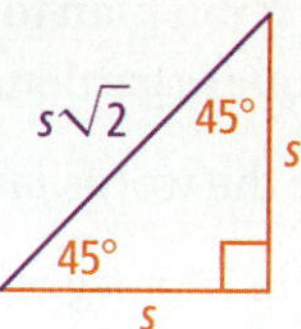

Complete each statement for a 45° – 45° – 90° triangle.

10. hypotenuse = $\sqrt{2}$ · leg

11. If leg = 10, then hypotenuse = $\sqrt{2}$ · 10 .

Problem 1 Finding the Length of the Hypotenuse

Got It? What is the length of the hypotenuse of a 45°-45°-90° triangle with leg length $5\sqrt{3}$?

12. Use the justifications to find the length of the hypotenuse.

hypotenuse = $\sqrt{2}$ · leg	45°-45°-90° Triangle Theorem
= $\sqrt{2} \cdot 5\sqrt{3}$	Substitute.
= $5\sqrt{2} \cdot \sqrt{3}$	Commutative Property of Multiplication.
= $5\sqrt{6}$	Simplify.

Problem 2 Finding the Length of a Leg

Got It? The length of the hypotenuse of a 45°-45°-90° triangle is 10. What is the length of one leg?

13. Will the length of the leg be *greater than* or *less than* 10? Explain.

Less than. Explanations may vary. Sample: The hypotenuse is the longest side.

14. Use the justifications to find the length of one leg.

hypotenuse = $\sqrt{2}$ · leg	45°-45°-90° Triangle Theorem
10 = $\sqrt{2}$ · leg	Substitute.
$\frac{10}{\sqrt{2}} = \frac{\sqrt{2}}{\sqrt{2}} \cdot$ leg	Divide each side by $\sqrt{2}$.
leg = $\frac{10}{\sqrt{2}}$	Simplify.
leg = $\frac{10}{\sqrt{2}} \cdot \frac{\sqrt{2}}{\sqrt{2}}$	Multiply by a form of 1 to rationalize the denominator.
leg = $\frac{10\sqrt{2}}{2}$	Simplify.
leg = $5\sqrt{2}$	Divide by 2.

Problem 3 Finding Distance

Got It? **You plan to build a path along one diagonal of a 100 ft-by-100 ft square garden. To the nearest foot, how long will the path be?**

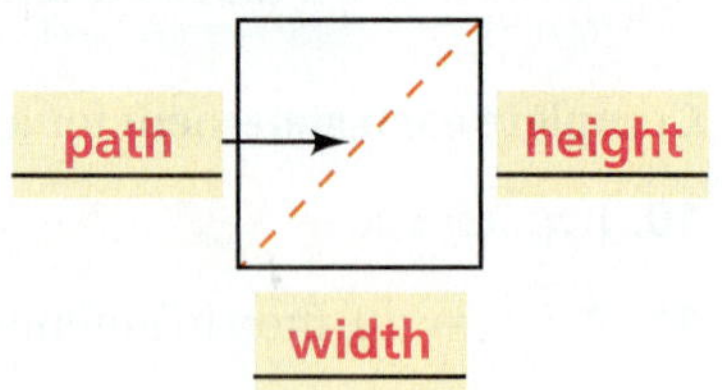

15. Use the words *path, height,* and *width* to complete the diagram.

16. Write L for *leg* or H for *hypotenuse* to identify each part of the right triangle in the diagram.

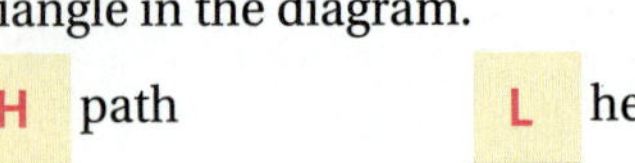
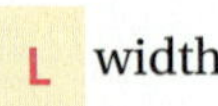

H path L height L width

17. Substitute for hypotenuse and leg. Let h = the length of the hypotenuse.

$$\text{hypotenuse} = \sqrt{2} \cdot \text{leg}$$

$$h = \sqrt{2} \cdot 100$$

18. Solve the equation. Use a calculator to find the length of the path.

$h = \sqrt{2} \cdot 100$
$h \approx 141.4213562$

19. To the nearest foot, the length of the path will be 141 feet.

take note

Theorem 8-6 30°-60°-90° Triangle Theorem

In a 30°-60°-90° triangle, the length of the hypotenuse is twice the length of the shorter leg. The length of the longer leg is $\sqrt{3}$ times the length of the shorter leg.

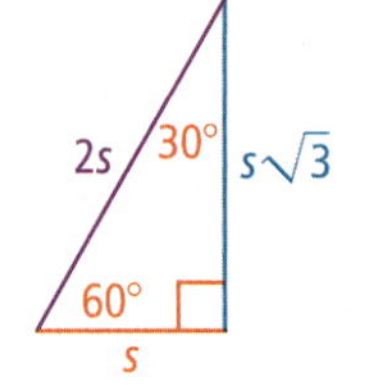

Complete each statement for a 30°-60°-90° triangle.

20. hypotenuse = 2 · shorter leg

21. longer leg = $\sqrt{3}$ · shorter leg

Problem 4 Using the Length of One Side

Got It? **What is the value of f in simplest radical form?**

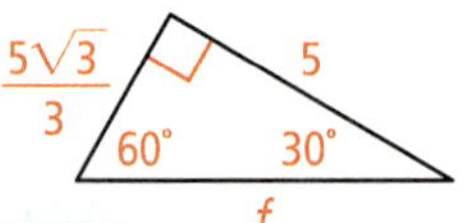

22. Complete the reasoning model below.

Think	Write
f is the length of the hypotenuse. I can write an equation relating the hypotenuse and the shorter leg $\frac{5\sqrt{3}}{3}$ of the 30°-60°-90° triangle.	hypotenuse = 2 · shorter leg $f = 2 \cdot \frac{5\sqrt{3}}{3}$
Now I can solve for f.	$f = \frac{10\sqrt{3}}{3}$

Problem 5 Applying the 30°-60°-90° Triangle Theorem

Got It? Jewelry Making An artisan makes pendants in the shape of equilateral triangles. Suppose the sides of a pendant are 18 mm long. What is the height of the pendant to the nearest tenth of a millimeter?

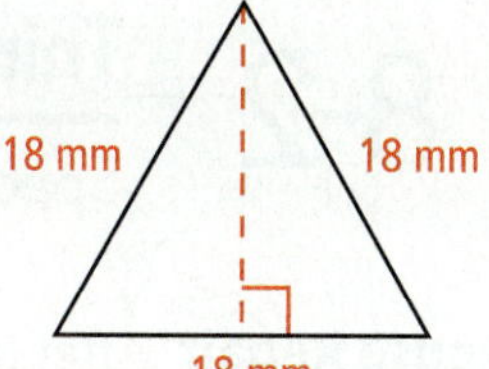

23. Circle the formula you can use to find the height of the pendant.

hypotenuse $= 2 \cdot$ shorter leg | longer leg $= \sqrt{3} \cdot$ shorter leg

24. Find the height of the pendant.

longer leg $= \sqrt{3} \cdot$ shorter leg
$= \sqrt{3} \cdot 9$
≈ 15.58845727

25. To the nearest tenth of a millimeter, the height of the pendant is 15.6 mm.

Lesson Check • Do you UNDERSTAND?

Reasoning A test question asks you to find two side lengths of a 45°-45°-90° triangle. You know that the length of one leg is 6, but you forgot the special formula for 45°-45°-90° triangles. Explain how you can still determine the other side lengths. What are the other side lengths?

26. Underline the correct word(s) to complete the sentence. In a 45°-45°-90° triangle, the lengths of the legs are different / the same.

27. Use the Pythagorean Theorem to find the length of the longest side.

longest side: $c^2 = 6^2 + 6^2$
$c^2 = 36 + 36$
$c^2 = 72$
$c = \sqrt{72} = 6\sqrt{2}$

28. The other two side lengths are 6 and $6\sqrt{2}$.

Math Success

Check off the vocabulary words that you understand.

☐ leg ☐ hypotenuse ☐ right triangle ☐ Pythagorean Theorem

Rate how well you can *use the properties of special right triangles.*

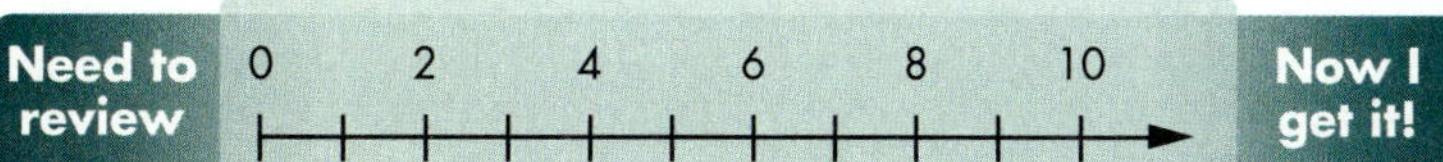

Name ______ Class ______ Date ______

8-2 Think About a Plan

Special Right Triangles

House Repair After heavy winds damaged a house, workers placed a 6-m brace against its side at a 45° angle. Then, at the same spot on the ground, they placed a second, longer brace to make a 30° angle with the side of the house.

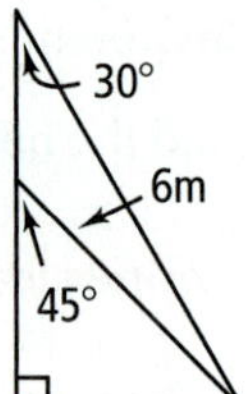

a. How long is the longer brace? Round to the nearest tenth of a meter.

b. About how much higher does the longer brace reach than the shorter brace?

1. In a 45°-45°-90° triangle, how is the length of the hypotenuse related to the length of each leg? Write this information in an equation. The hypotenuse is $\sqrt{2}$ times the length of a leg; hypotenuse = $\sqrt{2}$ × leg.

2. What is the distance from the bottom of the brace to the house? Round to the nearest tenth of a meter. 4.2 m

3. In a 30°-60°-90° triangle, how are the hypotenuse and leg lengths related? Write this information in two equations. hypotenuse = 2 × shorter leg; longer leg = $\sqrt{3}$ × shorter leg

4. What do the legs and hypotenuse of the 30°-60°-90° triangle represent with respect to the brace, the house, and the ground? Which of these lengths do you know? The hypotenuse is the longer brace, the shorter leg is the distance from the bottom of the brace to the house, and the longer leg is the distance from the top of the brace to the ground; the shorter leg, 4.2 m.

5. What is the length of the longer brace? Round to the nearest tenth of a meter. 8.5 m

6. What is the distance from the top of the shorter brace to the ground? Round to the nearest tenth of a meter. 4.2 m

7. How can you find the distance from the top of the longer brace to the ground? What is this distance? Round to the nearest tenth of a meter. This is the longer leg of the triangle. Multiply the length of the shorter leg by $\sqrt{3}$ to find its length; 7.3 m.

8. How can you find how much higher the longer brace reaches than the shorter brace? What is this distance? Subtract the distance from the top of the shorter brace to the ground from the distance from the top of the longer brace to the ground; 3.1 m.

Name ______________________ Class ____________ Date ____________

8-2 Practice

Form K

Special Right Triangles

Find the value of each variable. If your answer is not an integer, express it in simplest radical form.

1. 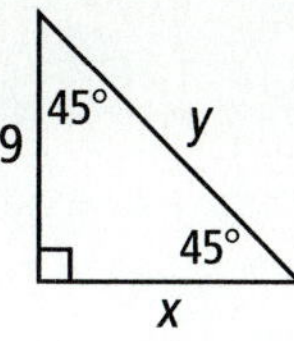

To start, use the 45°-45°-90° Triangle Theorem to find x.

Because the legs are __?__, $x = \boxed{9}$.

congruent

9; $9\sqrt{2}$

2. 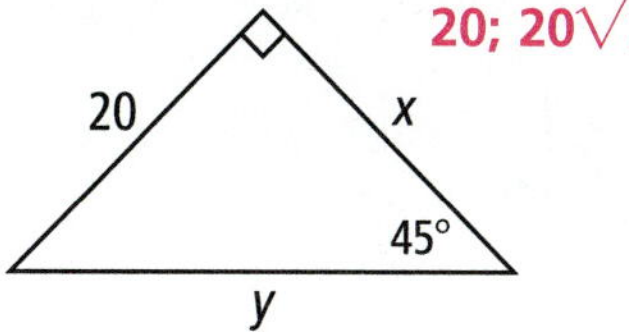

20; $20\sqrt{2}$

3. 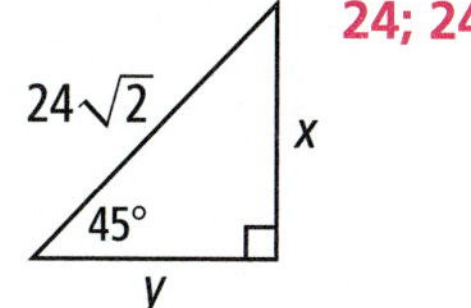

24; 24

4. 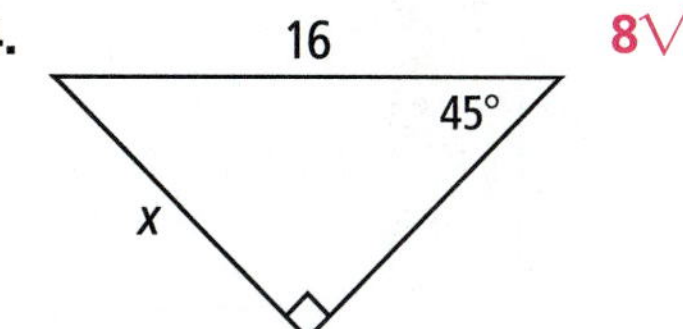

$8\sqrt{2}$

5. 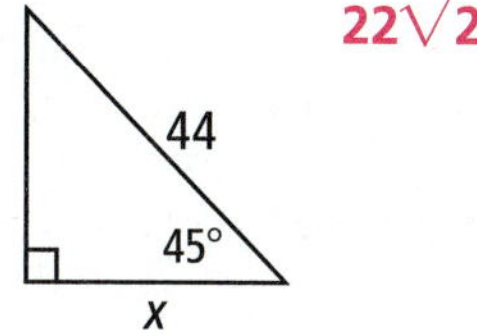

$22\sqrt{2}$

6. An architect is planning a new town square. The square has sides that are 20 ft long. A walkway will also cut diagonally through the square. How long will the walkway be? Round to the nearest tenth of a foot. 28.3 ft

7. Charlene made a square quilt block by piecing together four congruent isosceles right triangles. The diagonal of the square is 6 in. What is the perimeter of the square in simplest radical form? $12\sqrt{2}$ in.

8. A square has a side length of $11\sqrt{2}$ meters. What is the length of the diagonal of the square? 22 m

9. A square has a diagonal of 15 cm. What is the length of a side? Express in simplest radical form. $\frac{15\sqrt{2}}{2}$

10. **Reasoning** A classmate said that the perimeter of an isosceles right triangle can never be a whole number. Is this true? Explain.
No; there is always an isosceles triangle that can be made with a given perimeter. To show this, make an isosceles triangle from a piece of string with a whole number length.

Name ______________________ Class ____________ Date ____________

8-2 Practice (continued)

Form K

Special Right Triangles

Find the value of each variable. If your answer is not an integer, express it in simplest radical form.

11.

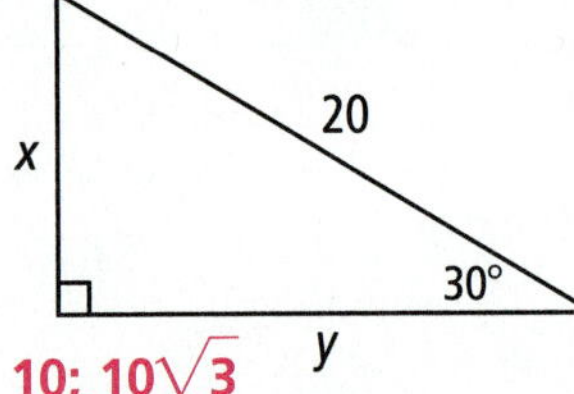

$10; 10\sqrt{3}$

To start, find the length of the leg.

Use the 30°-60°-90° Triangle Theorem to write an equation in terms of x.

$\boxed{20} = 2 \cdot \boxed{x}$

12.

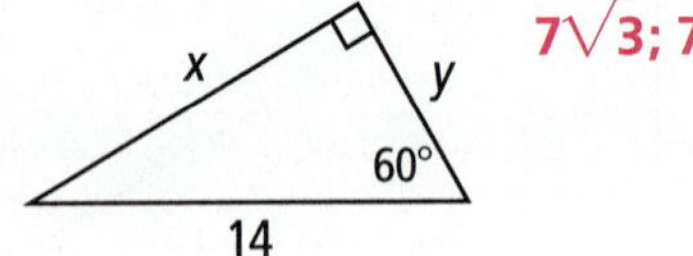

$7\sqrt{3}; 7$

13.

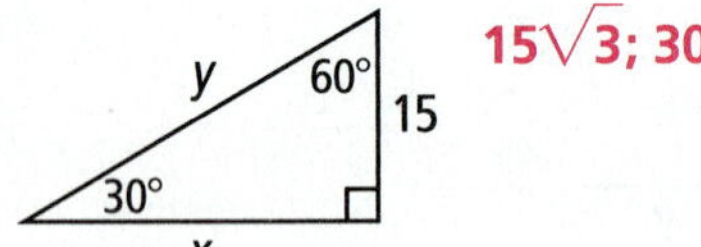

$15\sqrt{3}; 30$

14.

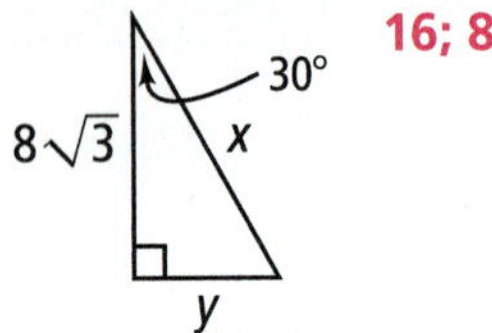

16; 8

15.

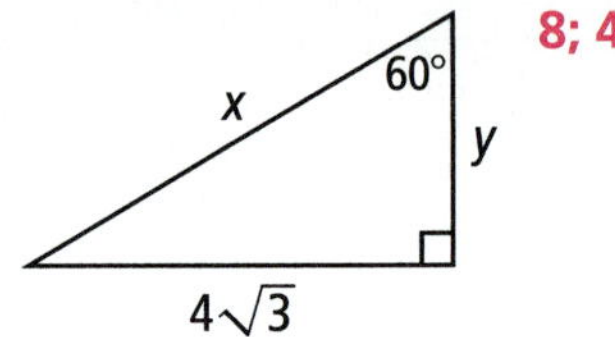

8; 4

16. The top of a giant slide is 30 ft off the ground. The slide rises at a 30° angle. To the nearest whole foot, what is the distance down the slide?
60 ft

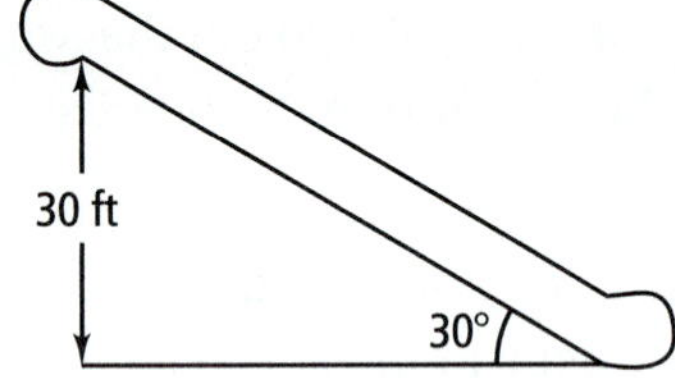

17. The frame for a garage roof is shown at the right. How long is each of the top pieces? Round to the nearest tenth of a foot. 6.9

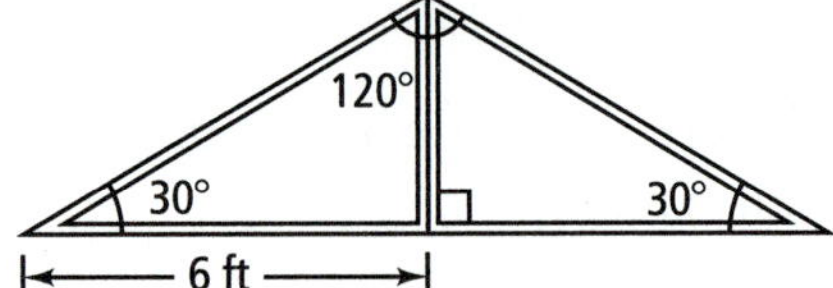

Algebra Find the value of each variable. If your answer is not an integer, express it in simplest radical form.

18.

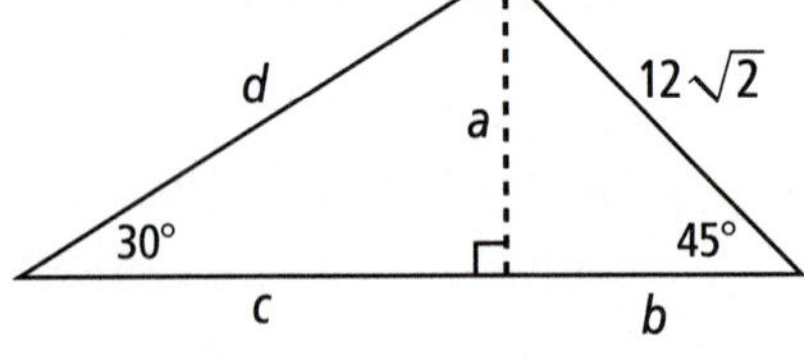

$a = 12; b = 12; c = 12\sqrt{3}; d = 24$

19.

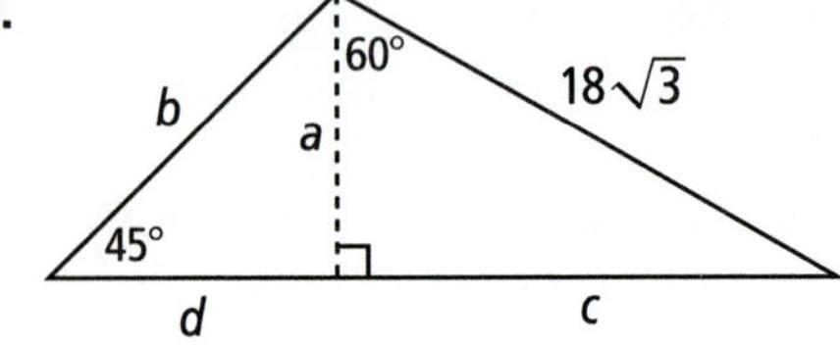

$a = 9\sqrt{3}; b = 9\sqrt{6}; c = 27; d = 9\sqrt{3}$

Name ______________________ Class __________ Date __________

8-2 Standardized Test Prep

Special Right Triangles

Multiple Choice

For Exercises 1–5, choose the correct letter.

1. What is the value of *s*? D

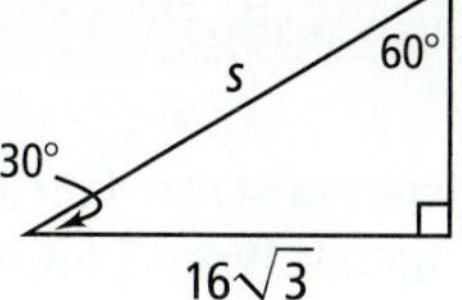

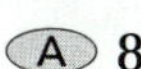

A 8 C $16\sqrt{2}$

B 16 D 32

2. What are the angle measures of the triangle? F

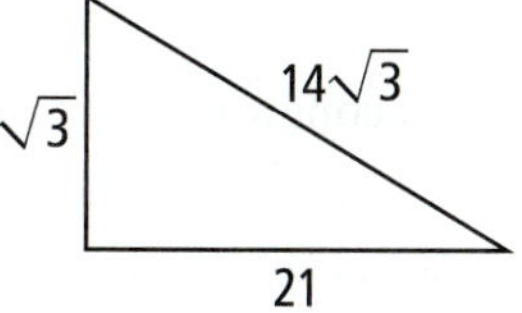

F 30°, 60°, and 90° H 60°, 60°, and 60°

G 45°, 45°, and 90° I They cannot be determined.

3. What is the value of *p*? B

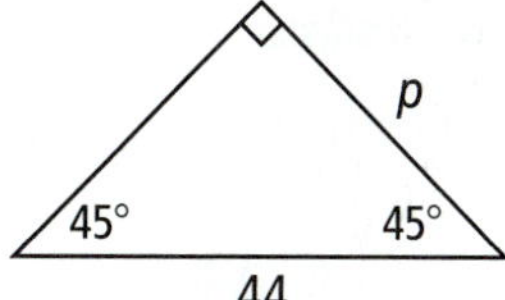

A 22 C 44

B $22\sqrt{2}$ D $44\sqrt{3}$

4 In the center of town there is a square park with side length 30 ft. If a person walks from one corner of the park to the opposite corner, how far does the person walk? Round to the nearest foot. G

F 21 ft G 42 ft H 52 ft I 60 ft

5. An equilateral triangle has an altitude of 15 m. What is the perimeter of the triangle? C

A $30\sqrt{2}$ m B 45 m C $30\sqrt{3}$ m D $60\sqrt{3}$ m

Short Response

6. The hypotenuse of a 30°-60°-90° triangle is 24.2 ft. Explain how to find the lengths of the legs of the triangle.

[2] Answers may vary. Sample: The hypotenuse is twice the length of the shorter leg, so to find the length of the shorter leg, divide the hypotenuse by 2. To find the longer leg, multiply the length of the shorter leg by $\sqrt{3}$. [1] explanation for finding either the length of the shorter leg OR the length of the longer leg [0] no response or incorrect response

8-3 PART 1 Trigonometry

Vocabulary

Review

The Venn diagram at the right shows the relationship between *similar* and congruent figures. Write T for *true* or F for *false*.

Similar Figures

Congruent Figures

F 1. All *similar* figures are congruent figures.

T 2. All congruent figures are *similar* figures.

T 3. Some *similar* figures are congruent figures.

4. Circle the postulate or theorem you can use to verify that the triangles at the right are *similar*.

 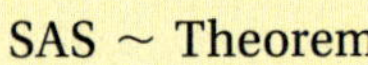

AA ~ Postulate (circled) SAS ~ Theorem SSS ~ Theorem

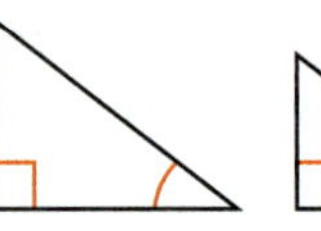 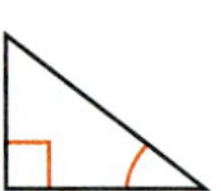

Vocabulary Builder

ratio (noun) RAY shee oh

Related Words: rate, rational

Definition: A **ratio** is the comparison of two quantities by division.

Example: If there are 6 triangles and 5 squares, the **ratio** of triangles to squares is $\frac{6}{5}$ and the **ratio** of squares to triangles is $\frac{5}{6}$.

Use Your Vocabulary

Use the triangle at the right for Exercises 5 and 6.

5 13 12

5. Circle the *ratio* of the length of the longer leg to the length of the shorter leg.

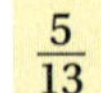

$\frac{5}{13}$ $\frac{5}{12}$ $\frac{12}{13}$ $\frac{13}{12}$ $\frac{12}{5}$ (circled) $\frac{13}{5}$

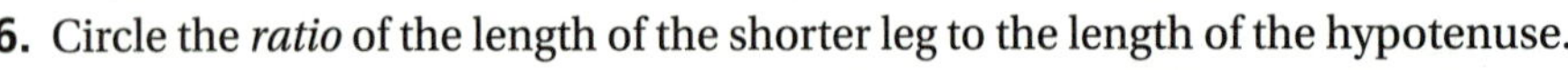

6. Circle the *ratio* of the length of the shorter leg to the length of the hypotenuse.

$\frac{5}{13}$ (circled) $\frac{5}{12}$ $\frac{12}{13}$ $\frac{13}{12}$ $\frac{12}{5}$ $\frac{13}{5}$

take note

Key Concept The Trigonometric Ratios

sine of $\angle A = \dfrac{\text{length of leg opposite } \angle A}{\text{length of hypotenuse}} = \dfrac{a}{c}$

cosine of $\angle A = \dfrac{\text{length of leg adjacent to } \angle A}{\text{length of hypotenuse}} = \dfrac{b}{c}$

tangent of $\angle A = \dfrac{\text{length of leg opposite } \angle A}{\text{length of leg adjacent to } \angle A} = \dfrac{a}{b}$

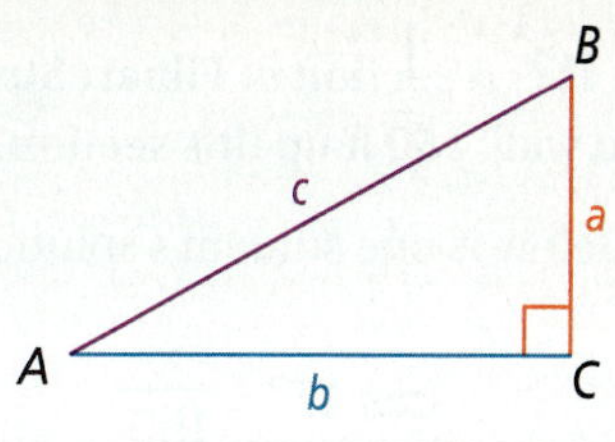

Draw a line from each trigonometric ratio in Column A to its corresponding ratio in Column B.

Column A	Column B
7. $\sin B$	$\frac{a}{c}$
8. $\cos B$	$\frac{b}{a}$
9. $\tan B$	$\frac{b}{c}$

10. Reasoning Suppose $\triangle ABC$ is a right isosceles triangle. What would the tangent of $\angle B$ equal? Explain.

1. Explanations may vary. Sample: The legs would be congruent, so $\frac{b}{a}$ would equal 1.

Problem 1 Writing Trigonometric Ratios

Got It? **What are the sine, cosine, and tangent ratios for $\angle G$?**

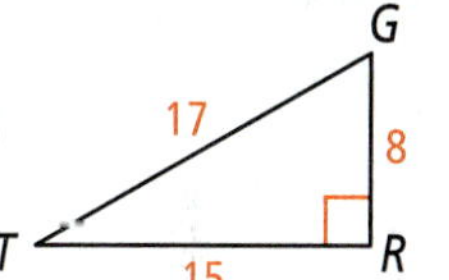

11. Circle the measure of the leg opposite $\angle G$.

8 (15) 17

12. Circle the measure of the hypotenuse.

8 15 (17)

13. Circle the measure of the leg adjacent to $\angle G$.

(8) 15 17

14. Write each trigonometric ratio.

$\sin G = \dfrac{\text{opposite}}{\text{hypotenuse}} = \dfrac{15}{17}$

$\cos G = \dfrac{\text{adjacent}}{\text{hypotenuse}} = \dfrac{8}{17}$

$\tan G = \dfrac{\text{opposite}}{\text{adjacent}} = \dfrac{15}{8}$

Problem 2 Using a Trigonometric Ratio to Find Distance

Got It? **A section of Filbert Street in San Francisco rises at an angle of about 17°. If you walk 150 ft up this section, what is your vertical rise? Round to the nearest foot.**

Below is one student's solution and diagram.

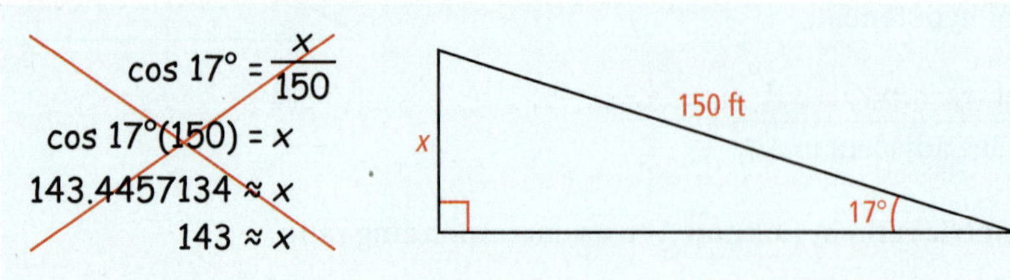

15. What error did the student make?

Answers may vary. Sample: The student wrote $\cos 17° = \frac{x}{150}$ rather than $\sin 17° = \frac{x}{150}$.

16. Find the vertical rise correctly.

$$\sin 17° = \frac{x}{150}$$
$$\sin 17°(150) = x$$
$$43.85575571 \approx x$$
$$44 \approx x$$

17. The vertical rise is about 44 feet.

Lesson Check • Do you know HOW?

Use the triangle at the right. Write each ratio.

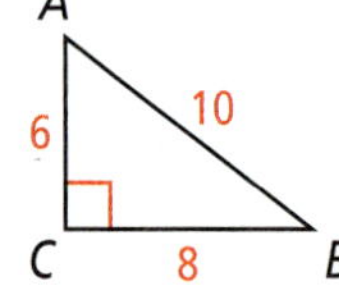

18. sin A

$\frac{8}{10} = \frac{4}{5}$

19. cos A

$\frac{6}{10} = \frac{3}{5}$

20. tan A

$\frac{8}{6} = \frac{4}{3}$

21. sin B

$\frac{6}{10} = \frac{3}{5}$

22. cos B

$\frac{8}{10} = \frac{4}{5}$

23. tan B

$\frac{6}{8} = \frac{3}{4}$

8-3 PART 2 Trigonometry

Vocabulary

Review

Complete each sentence with the word *hypotenuse* or *leg(s)*.

1. The longest side in a right triangle is the _?_. hypotenuse

2. In a right triangle, the _?_ is opposite the right angle. hypotenuse

3. The sum of the squares of the _?_ of a right triangle is equal to the square of the _?_. legs hypotenuse

Vocabulary Builder

inverse (noun) IN vurs

Related Word: opposite

Definition: The **inverse** of something is the opposite.

Main Idea: If you know the sine, cosine, or tangent ratio for an angle, you can use an **inverse** ($\sin^{-1}$, $\cos^{-1}$, or $\tan^{-1}$) to find the measure of the angle.

Examples: Sin^{-1} is the **inverse** of the sine ratio.

Use Your Vocabulary

Underline the correct word to complete each sentence.

4. Multiplication and addition / division / subtraction are *inverse* operations.

5. Tan^{-1} is the *inverse* of the cosine / sine / tangent ratio.

Identify the *inverse* of the operation used in the equation. Write *addition, division, multiplication,* or *subtraction*.

6. $3x = 45$ division

7. $a - 4.2$ addition

8. $27 = \frac{x}{3}$ multiplication

9. $15 + b = -2$ subtraction

Problem 3 Using Inverses

Got It? **Use the figure below. What is $m\angle Y$ to the nearest degree?**

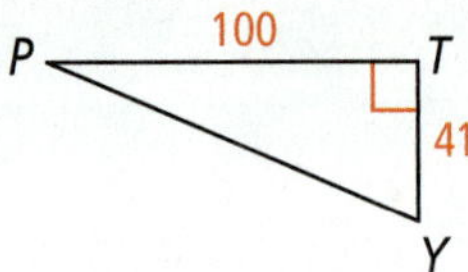

10. Circle the lengths that you know.

hypotenuse   (side adjacent to $\angle Y$)   (side opposite $\angle Y$)

11. Cross out the ratios that you will NOT use to find $m\angle Y$.

~~sine~~   ~~cosine~~   tangent

12. Underline the correct word to complete the sentence.

If you know the sine, cosine, or tangent ratio of an angle, you can use the (inverse) / ratio to find the measure of the angle.

13. Follow the steps to find $m\angle Y$.

1. Write the ratio.
   $\tan Y = \frac{100}{41}$
2. Use the inverse.
   $Y = \tan^{-1}\left(\frac{100}{41}\right)$
3. Use a calculator.
   $Y \approx 67.70637084$

14. To the nearest degree, $m\angle Y = 68$.

Lesson Check • Do you know HOW?

What is the value of x? Round to the nearest tenth.

15. Circle the equation you can use to find the value of x.

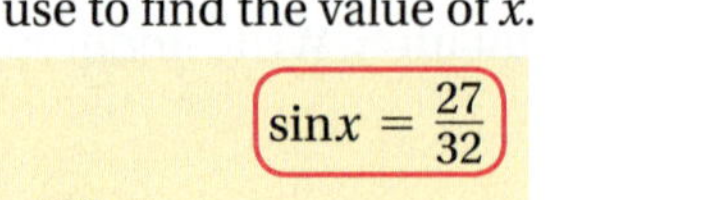

$\cos x = \frac{27}{32}$ $\tan x = \frac{27}{32}$ ($\sin x = \frac{27}{32}$)

16. Solve your equation from Exercise 15.

$\sin x = \frac{27}{32}$

$x = \sin^{-1}\left(\frac{27}{32}\right)$

$x = 57.53825503$

17. To the nearest tenth, the value of x is 57.5 .

Lesson Check • Do you UNDERSTAND?

Error Analysis **A student states that $\sin A > \sin X$ because the lengths of the sides of $\triangle ABC$ are greater than the lengths of the sides of $\triangle XYZ$. What is the student's error? Explain.**

Underline the correct word(s) to complete each sentence.

18. $\triangle ABC$ and $\triangle XYZ$ are / are not similar.

19. $\angle A$ and $\angle X$ are / are not congruent.

20. Sin 35° is / is not equal to sin 35°.

21. What is the student's error? Explain.

Answers may vary. Sample: The student did not look at the measures of $\angle A$ and $\angle X$. Congruent angles have equal sine ratios.

Math Success

Check off the vocabulary words that you understand.

☐ trigonometric ratios ☐ sine ☐ cosine ☐ tangent

Rate how well you can *use trigonometric ratios*.

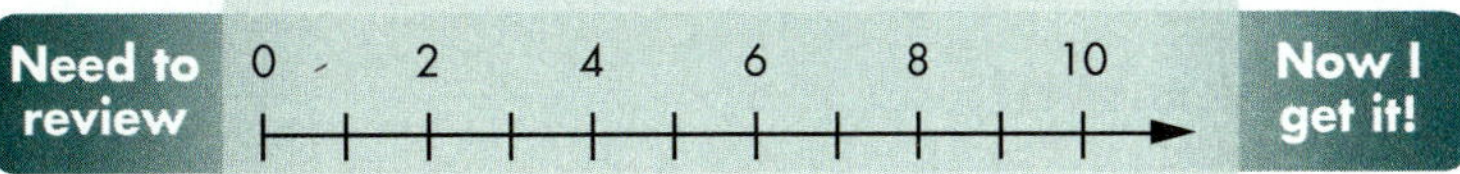

Name ______________________ Class ____________ Date ____________

8-3 Think About a Plan

Trigonometry

Find the values of *w* and then *x*. Round lengths to the nearest tenth and angle measures to the nearest degree.

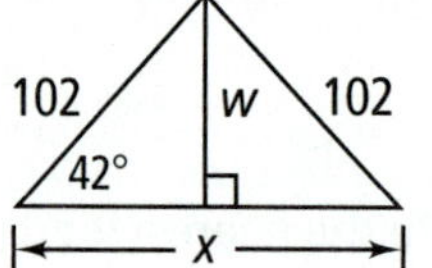

1. What type of triangle is the largest triangle? Explain.

   An isosceles triangle; two legs are the same length.

2. The measure of one of the base angles is given. What is the measure of the other base angle? Explain.

   42; the base angles of an isosceles triangle have the same measure.

3. What is the sine of an angle? $\frac{\text{length of leg opposite}}{\text{length of hypotenuse}}$

4. Focus on one of the smaller triangles. Write an equation relating sin 42° and *w*. $\sin 42^\circ = \frac{w}{102}$

5. How can you find the value of *w*? What is this value? Round to the nearest tenth.

   Multiply sin 42° by 102; $w \approx 68.3$.

6. Look at one of the smaller triangles. What is the measure of the angle between side *w* and the side with length 102? Explain.

   48; the sum of the measures of the angles of a triangle is equal to 180. For one of the small triangles, $48 + 90 + 42 = 180$.

7. What is the length of the third side (the base) of one of the small triangles in terms of *x*? Explain.

   $\frac{1}{2}x$; the third side lengths of the two small triangles are equal and sum to *x*.

8. Focus on one of the smaller triangles. Write an equation for the length of the third side, in terms of *x*, using the sine function. $\sin 48^\circ = \frac{\frac{1}{2}x}{102}$

9. How can you find the value of *x*? What is this value? Round to the nearest tenth.

   First multiply 102 by sin 48°. This value is approximately 75.8. Next, multiply this value by 2 to find *x*; $x \approx 151.6$.

10. How could you use tan 48° to check your answer?

    $\tan 48^\circ = \frac{\text{length of leg opposite } 48^\circ}{\text{length of leg adjacent to } 48^\circ} \approx 1.11$ and $\frac{75.8}{68.3} \approx 1.11$. The value for $\frac{1}{2}x$ is correct, so the value for *x* is correct.

Name ______________________ Class ____________ Date ____________

8-3 Practice — Trigonometry

Form K

Write the ratios for sin *D*, cos *D*, and tan *D*.

1. $\frac{4}{5}, \frac{3}{5}, \frac{4}{3}$

To start, write the ratio of sin *D*. Then determine the length of the side __?__ $\angle D$ and the length of the hypotenuse. **opposite**

$$\sin D = \frac{\text{opposite}}{\text{hypotenuse}} = \frac{4}{5}$$

2. $\frac{8}{17}, \frac{15}{17}, \frac{8}{15}$

3. $\frac{\sqrt{3}}{2}; \frac{1}{2}; \sqrt{3}$

Find the value of *x*. Round to the nearest tenth.

4. To start, identify how the sides relate to the given angle.

Side *x* is __?__ to the given angle. **adjacent**

The given side is the hypotenuse. **6.6**

5. **5.2**

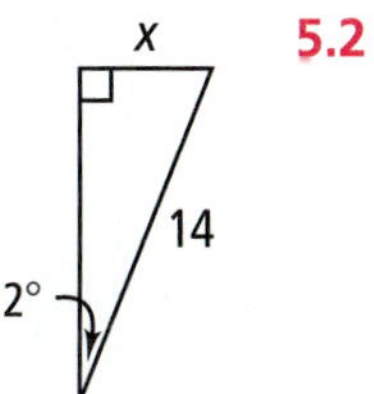

6. **18.6**

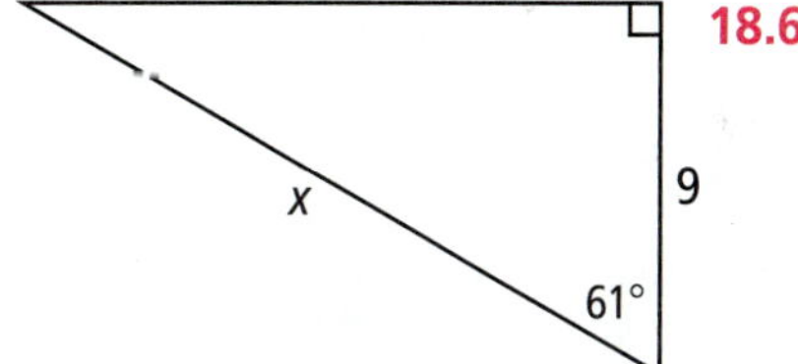

7. **34.0**

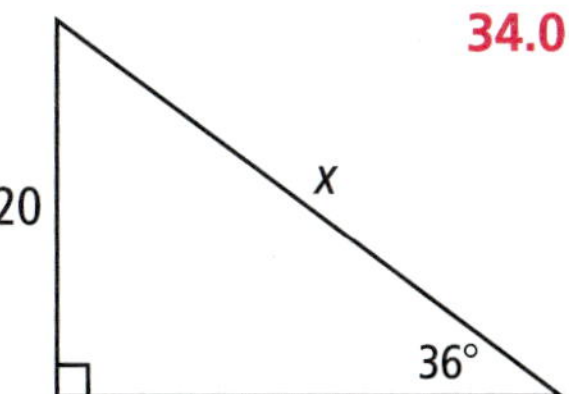

8. **2.4**

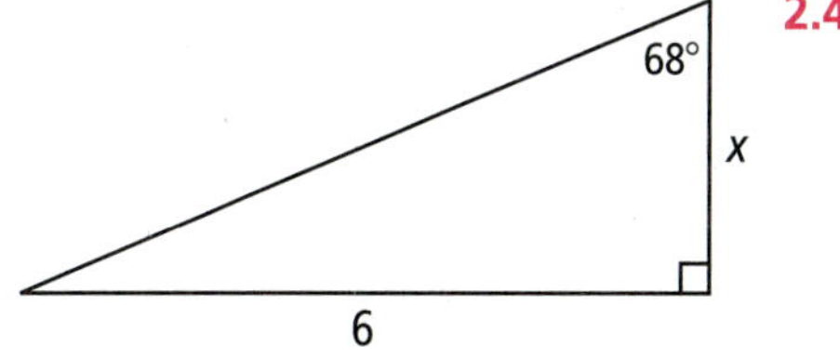

9. The ramp on the back of a moving van is 3 ft high and rises at an angle of 25°. How long is the ramp? Round to the nearest foot. **7 ft**

10. A rope attached to the top of a tent is staked into the ground. The rope is 4.5 ft long. The angle formed by the rope and the ground is 46°. How far from the center of the base of the tent is the rope staked? Round to the nearest tenth of a foot. **3.1 ft**

Name ______________________ Class ____________ Date ____________

8-3 Practice (continued) Form K

Trigonometry

Find the value of *x*. Round to the nearest degree.

11.

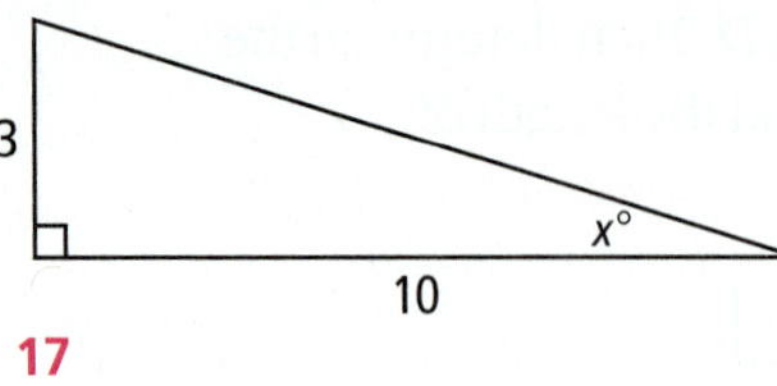

17

To start, identify the given sides in relation to *x*.
Then write the trigonometric ratio.
The given sides are the side opposite

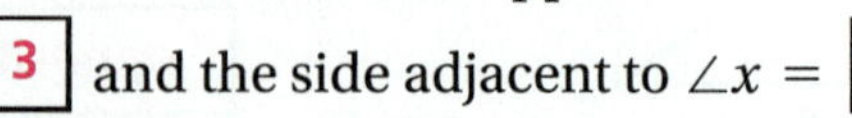

$\angle x =$ [3] and the side adjacent to $\angle x =$ [10].

$\tan x° = \frac{[3]}{[10]}$

12.

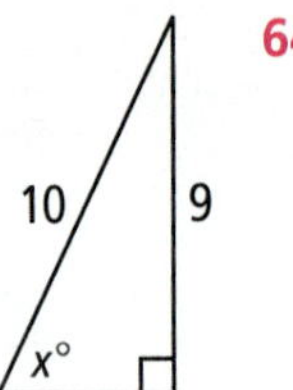

64

13.

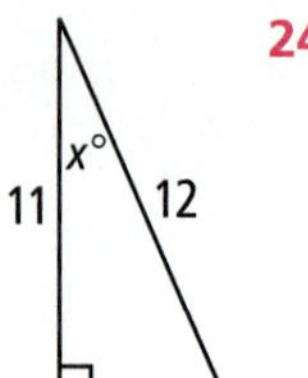

24

14.

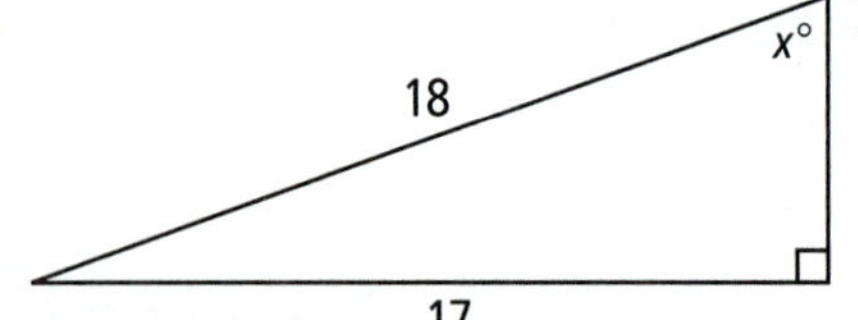

71

15.

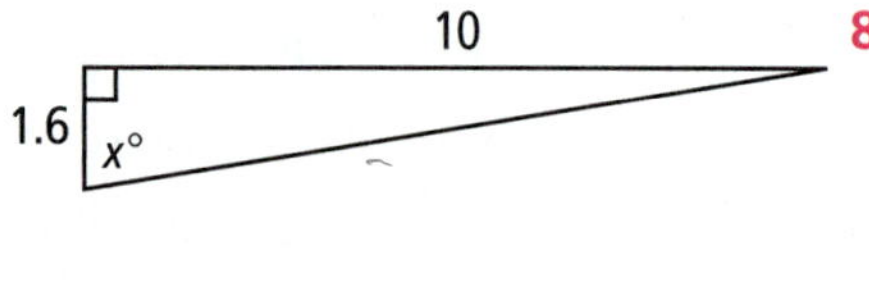

81

Find the values of *w* and then *x*. Round lengths to the nearest tenth and angle measures to the nearest degree.

16.

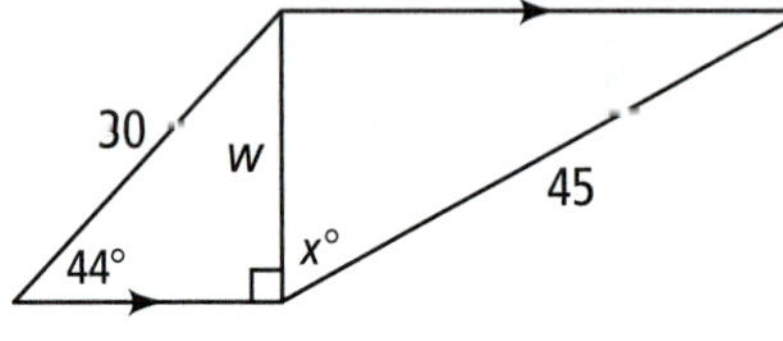

20.8; 62

17.

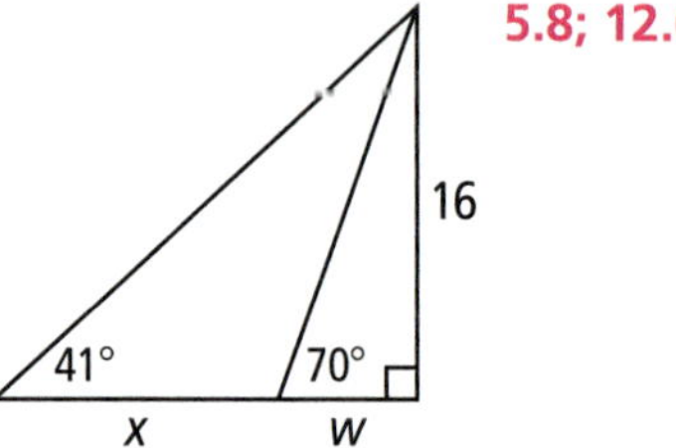

5.8; 12.6

18. Jed is building a roof for his shed. The highest point of the roof will be 3 ft higher than the top of the shed. The slanted roof will be 7 ft long. What is the measure of the angle formed by the top of the shed and the slanted roof? 25°

The sine, cosine, and tangent ratios each have a reciprocal ratio. The reciprocal ratios are cosecant (csc), secant (sec), and cotangent (cot). Use $\triangle DEF$ and the definitions below to write each ratio.

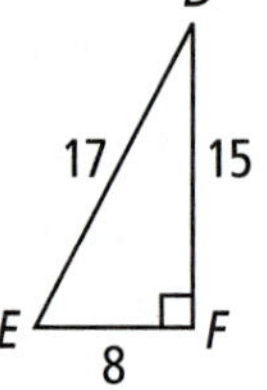

$\csc X = \frac{1}{\sin X}$ $\sec X = \frac{1}{\cos X}$ $\cot X = \frac{1}{\tan X}$

19. $\csc D$ $\frac{17}{8}$

20. $\sec D$ $\frac{17}{15}$

21. $\cot D$ $\frac{15}{8}$

Name ______________________ Class ____________ Date ____________

8-3 Standardized Test Prep

Trigonometry

Multiple Choice

For Exercises 1–6, choose the correct letter.

1. What is the value of sin N? C

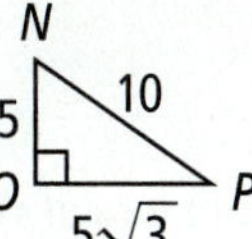

A 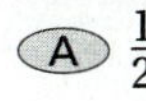 $\frac{1}{2}$ C $\frac{\sqrt{3}}{2}$

B 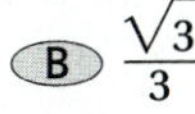 $\frac{\sqrt{3}}{3}$ D $\sqrt{3}$

2. What is the value of x to the nearest tenth? I

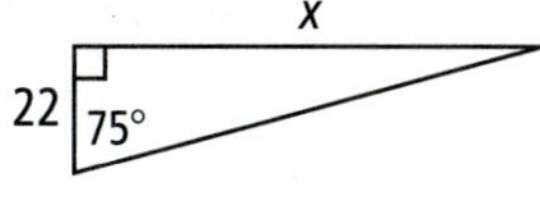

F 5.7 H 30.3

G 21.2 I 82.1

3. What is the value of x to the nearest degree? A

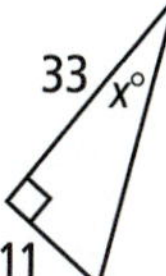

A 18 C 71

B 19 D 72

4. A 14-ft-long ramp rises at an angle of 22.2°. How long is the base of the ramp to the nearest foot? G

F 11 ft G 13 ft H 17 ft I 22 ft

5. What is the value of w to the nearest degree? C

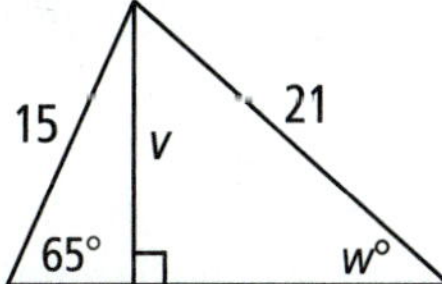

A 25 C 40

B 35 D 45

6. A right triangle has an angle that measures 34 and the adjacent side measures 17. What is the length of the hypotenuse to the nearest tenth? F

F 20.5 G 25.2 H 30.4 I 34

Short Response

7. A 12-ft-long ladder is leaning against a wall and makes an 80° angle with the ground. How high up the wall does the ladder reach, and how far is the base of the ladder from the base of the wall? Round to the nearest inch.

[2] The ladder reaches 11 ft 10 in. up the wall, and the base of the ladder is 2 ft 1 in. away from the base of the wall. [1] The ladder reaches 11 ft 10 in. up the wall OR the base of the ladder is 2 ft 1 in. away from the base of the wall. [0] no correct response given

8-4 Angles of Elevation and Depression

Vocabulary

Review

Underline the correct word(s) or number to complete each sentence.

1. The measure of a *right angle* is greater / less than the measure of an acute angle and greater / less than the measure of an obtuse angle.
2. A *right angle* has a measure of 45 / 90 / 180 .
3. Lines that intersect to form four *right angles* are parallel / perpendicular lines.
4. Circle the *right angle*(s) in the figure.

∠ACB	∠ADB	∠BAC
∠BAD	∠CBA	∠DBA

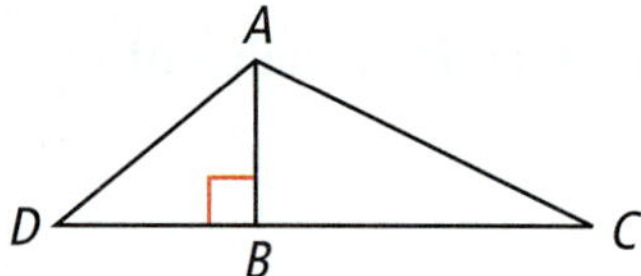

Vocabulary Builder

elevation (noun) **el uh VAY shun**

Related Word: depression

Definition: The **elevation** of an object is its height above a given level, such as eye level or sea level.

Math Usage: Angles of **elevation** and **depression** are acute angles of right triangles formed by a horizontal distance and a vertical height.

Use Your Vocabulary

Complete each statement with the correct word from the list below. Use each word only once.

elevate elevated elevation

5. John _?_ his feet on a footstool. elevated
6. The _?_ of Mt McKinley is 20,320 ft. elevation
7. You _?_ an object by raising it to a higher position. elevate

Problem 1 Identifying Angles of Elevation and Depression

Got It? **What is a description of ∠2 as it relates to the situation shown?**

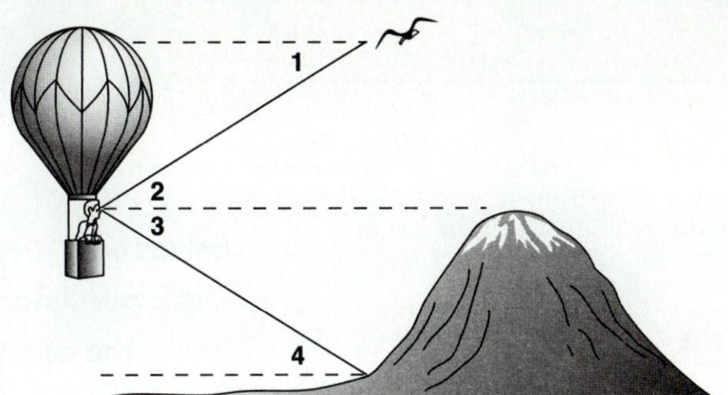

Write T for *true* or F for *false*.

T 8. ∠2 is above the horizontal line.

T 9. ∠2 is the *angle of elevation* from the person in the hot-air balloon to the bird.

F 10. ∠2 is the *angle of depression* from the person in the hot-air balloon to the bird.

F 11. ∠2 is the *angle of elevation* from the top of the mountain to the person in the hot-air balloon.

12. Describe ∠2 as it relates to the situation shown.

Answers may vary. Sample: ∠2 is the angle of elevation from the person in the hot-air balloon to the bird.

Problem 2 Using the Angle of Elevation

Got It? **You sight a rock climber on a cliff at a 32° angle of elevation. Your eye level is 6 ft above the ground and you are 1000 feet from the base of the cliff. What is the approximate height of the rock climber from the ground?**

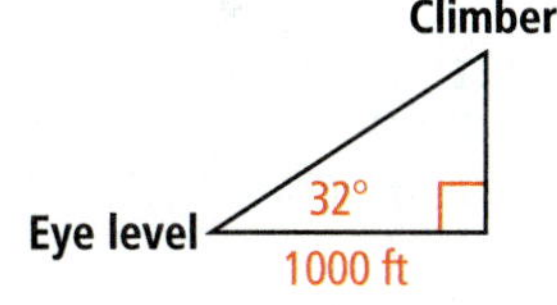

13. Use the information in the problem to complete the problem-solving model below.

Know
Angle of elevation is 32°.
Distance to the cliff is 1000 ft.
Eye level is 6 ft above the ground.

Need
Height of climber from the ground

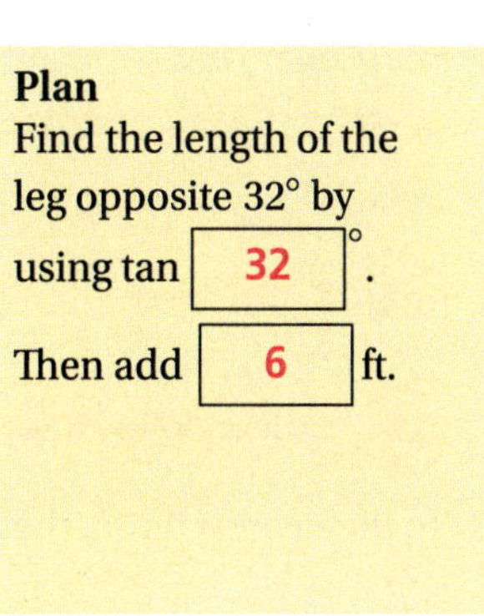

Plan
Find the length of the leg opposite 32° by using tan 32°.
Then add 6 ft.

14. Explain why you use tan 32° and not sin 32° or cos 32°. **Answers may vary. Sample:**

The sine ratio involves two unknowns. The cosine ratio involves the hypotenuse and 1000, but I do not want to know the hypotenuse. The ratio that uses the unknown height and 1000 is the tangent ratio.

15. The problem is solved below. Use one of the reasons from the list at the right to justify each step.

Solve for *d*.
Use a calculator.
Write the equation.

$\tan 32° = \frac{d}{1000}$	**Write the equation.**
$(\tan 32°)\,1000 = d$	**Solve for *d*.**
$d \approx 624.8693519$	**Use a calculator.**

16. The height from your eye level to the climber is about **625** ft.

17. The height of the rock climber from the ground is about **631** ft.

Problem 3 Using the Angle of Depression

Got It? **An airplane pilot sights a life raft at a 26° angle of depression. The airplane's altitude is 3 km. What is the airplane's horizontal distance *d* from the raft?**

18. Label the diagram below.

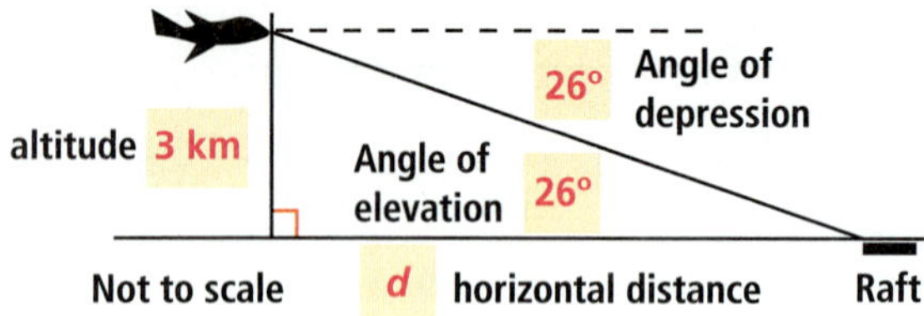

19. Circle the equation you could use to find the horizontal distance *d*.

$\sin 26° = \frac{3}{d}$ $\qquad$ $\cos 26° = \frac{3}{d}$ $\qquad$ $\tan 26° = \frac{3}{d}$ (circled)

20. Solve your equation from Exercise 19.

$\tan 26° = \frac{3}{d}$

$d = \frac{3}{\tan 26°}$

$d = 6.150911525$

21. To the nearest tenth, the airplane's horizontal distance from the raft is **6.2** km.

Lesson Check • Do you UNDERSTAND?

Vocabulary **How is an angle of elevation formed?**

Underline the correct word(s) to complete each sentence.

22. The angle of elevation is formed above / below a horizontal line.

23. The angle of depression is formed above / below a horizontal line.

24. The measure of an angle of elevation is equal to / greater than / less than the measure of the angle of depression.

Lesson Check • Do you UNDERSTAND?

Error Analysis **A homework question says that the angle of depression from the bottom of a house window to a ball on the ground is 20°. At the right is your friend's sketch of the situation. Describe your friend's error.**

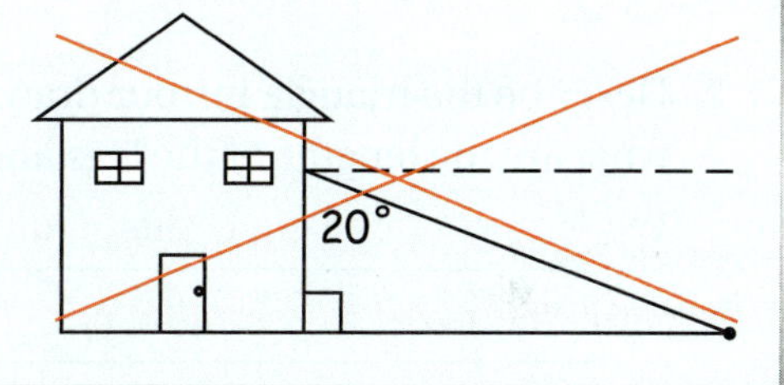

25. Is the angle that your friend identified as the angle of depression formed by the horizontal and the line of sight? Yes / No

26. Is the correct angle of depression *adjacent to* or *opposite* the angle identified by your friend? adjacent to / opposite

27. Describe your friend's error.

Answers may vary. Sample: My friend identified the wrong angle. The correct angle of depression is below the horizontal line.

Math Success

Check off the vocabulary words that you understand.

☐ angle of elevation ☐ angle of depression ☐ trigonometric ratios

Rate how well you can *use angles of elevation and depression.*

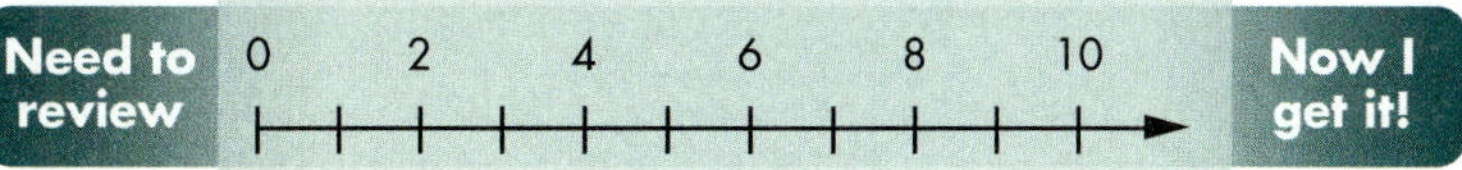

Name ______________________ Class ____________ Date ____________

8-4 Think About a Plan

Angles of Elevation and Depression

The world's tallest unsupported flagpole is a 282-ft-tall steel pole in Surrey, British Columbia. The shortest shadow cast by the pole during the year is 137 ft long. To the nearest degree, what is the angle of elevation of the sun when casting the flagpole's shortest shadow?

Know

1. Draw a sketch using the information given in the problem. Draw an arrow pointing to the angle of elevation.

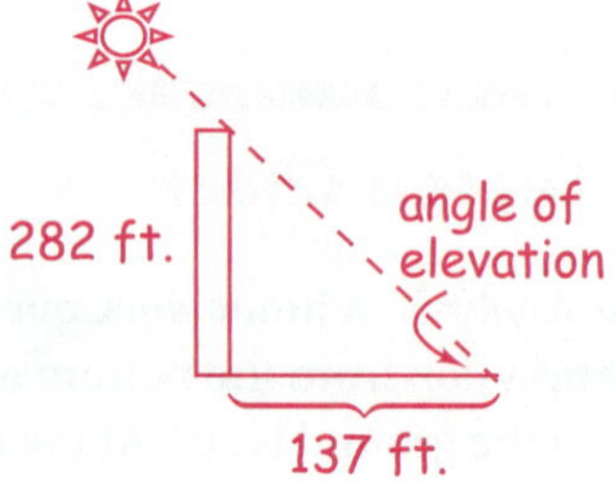

2. Describe the triangle in your drawing. In general terms, what are the lengths of the legs and the hypotenuse?

   The length of one leg is the height of the pole (282 ft) and the length of the second leg is the length of the shadow (137 ft); the hypotenuse is the distance between the top of the pole and the end of the shadow.

Need

3. Where is the angle of elevation?

   between the hypotenuse and the shadow

4. What is the tangent ratio? $\tan x = \frac{\text{length of leg opposite } x}{\text{length of leg adjacent to } x}$

Plan

5. Assign the variable x to the angle of elevation. What is the tangent of the angle of elevation?

   $\tan x = \frac{282 \text{ ft}}{137 \text{ ft}} \approx 2.06$

6. How can you use the inverse tangent to find the angle of elevation?

   Take the inverse tangent of 2.06. Because $\tan x = 2.06$, $x = \tan^{-1}(2.06) \approx 64°$.

Name ______________________ Class ____________ Date ____________

8-4 Practice

Form K

Angles of Elevation and Depression

Describe each angle as it relates to the the diagrams below.

1. $\angle 1$ angle of depression from person on cliff to person in boat
2. $\angle 2$ angle of elevation from person in boat to person on cliff
3. $\angle 3$ angle of depression from person in boat to scuba diver
4. $\angle 4$ angle of elevation from scuba diver to person in boat
5. $\angle 5$ angle of depression from bird to person
6. $\angle 6$ angle of elevation from person to bird
7. $\angle 7$ angle of depression from person to car
8. $\angle 8$ angle of elevation from car to person

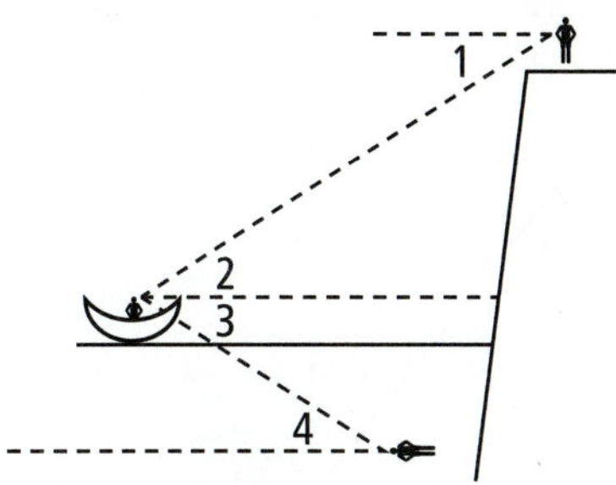

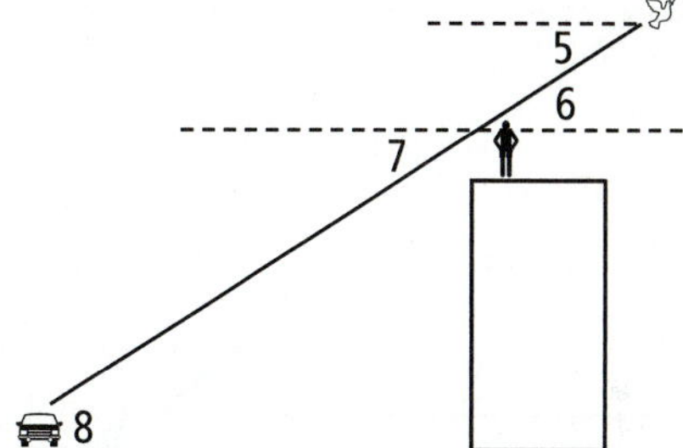

Find the value of *x*. Round to the nearest tenth of a unit.

9. 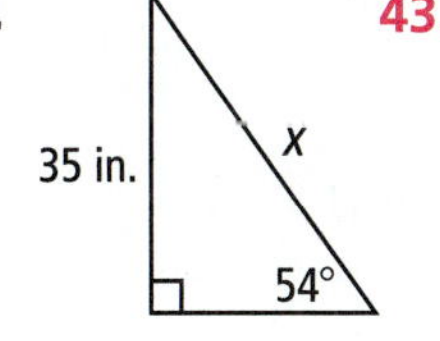

43.3 in.

10. 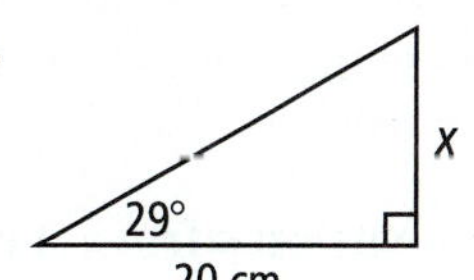

11.1 cm

11. 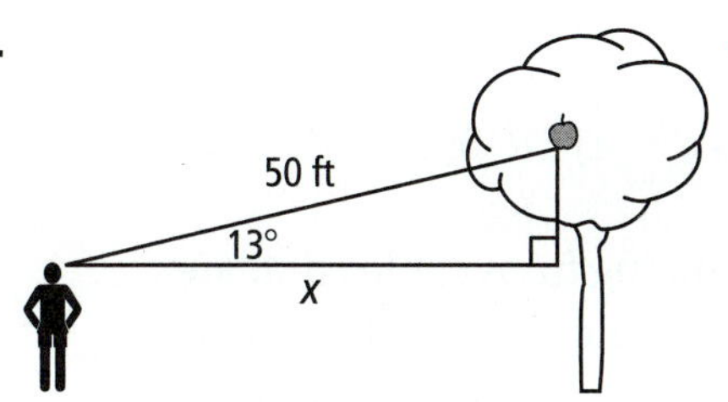

48.7 ft

12. 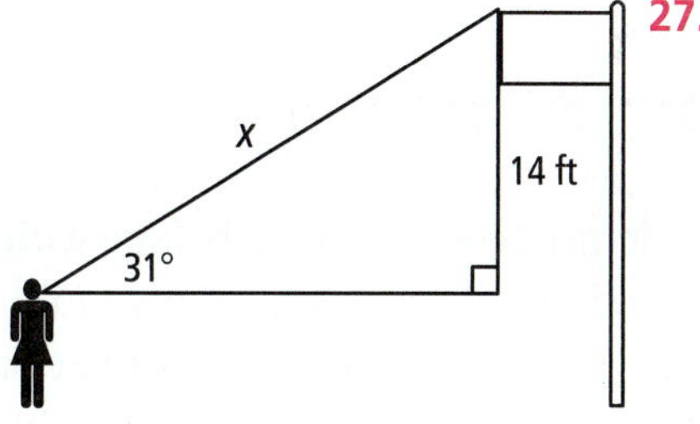

27.2 ft

13. A child is standing across the street from his apartment. His mother is on their balcony. The angle of elevation between the child's eyes and his mother's eyes is 22°. If the distance between their eyes is 32 ft, how far is the child standing from his apartment building? Round to the nearest foot. 30 ft

14. A woman looks down from a hot air balloon. She sees a sheep below and measures the angle of depression as 35°. If the sheep is 125 ft from where the woman is looking down from the balloon, how high off the ground is the balloon? Round to the nearest foot. 72 ft

Name ______________________ Class ____________ Date ____________

8-4 Practice (continued)

Form K

Angles of Elevation and Depression

Find the value of x. Round to the nearest tenth of a unit.

15. 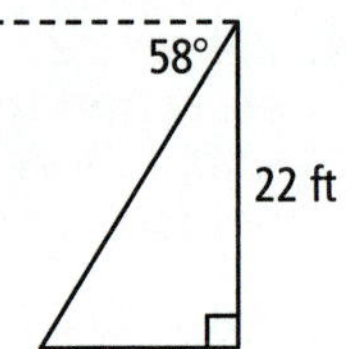

To start, use alternate interior angles to help you get an angle measure inside the triangle.

The angle of __?__ is 58°. Since alternate interior angles are __?__, the angle adjacent to x is 58°. depression congruent

16. 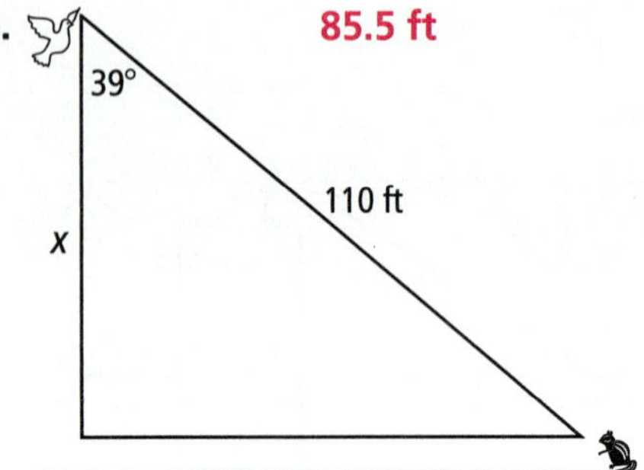

85.5 ft

17. 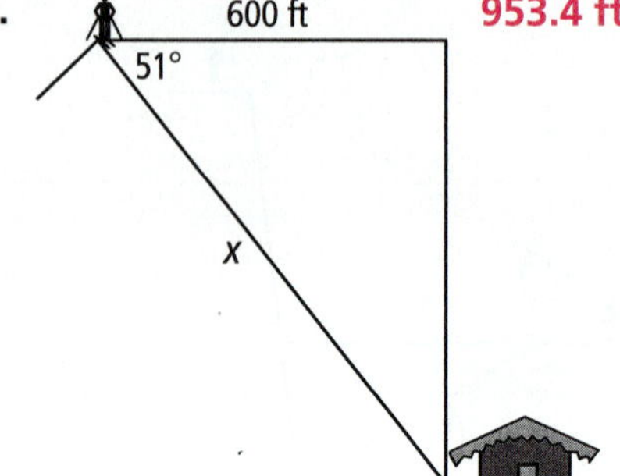

953.4 ft

18. Indirect Measurement You are 55 ft from a tree. The angle of elevation from your eyes, which are 4.5 ft off the ground, to the top of the tree is 61°. To the nearest foot, how tall is the tree? 104 ft

Algebra The angle of elevation e from A to B and the angle of depression d from B to A are given. Find the measure of each angle.

19. e: $(3x - 16)°$; d: $2(x + 2)°$ 44°; 44°

20. e: $(5x - 2)°$; d: $6(x - 3)°$ 78°; 78°

21. e: $(3x + 8)°$; d: $5(x - 2)°$ 35°; 35°

22. e: $(4x - 4)°$; d: $5(x - 4)°$ 60°; 60°

23. The picture below shows a bridge with a roadway hanging from cables that are attached to towers. Assume you could measure the distances along the bridge as well as the angles formed by the cables and the roadway. Explain how you could estimate the length of each cable.

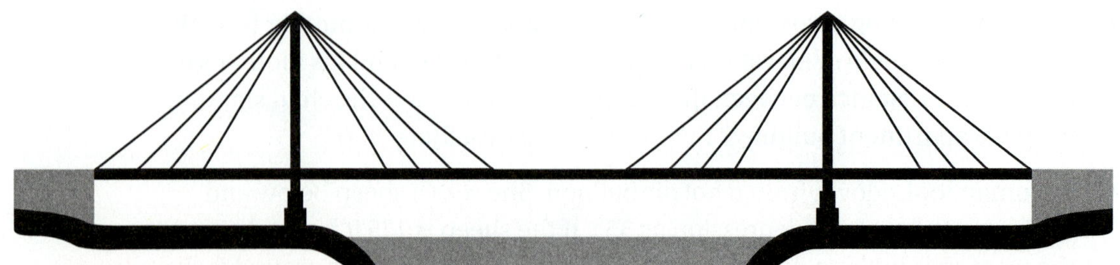

To find the length of each cable, divide the distance from the bottom of the tower to the bottom of the cable by the cosine of the angle formed by the cable and the roadway.

Name ______________________ Class ____________ Date ____________

8-4 Standardized Test Prep

Angles of Elevation and Depression

Multiple Choice

For Exercises 1–5, choose the correct letter.

1. A person can see the top of a building at an angle of 65°. The person is standing 50 ft away from the building and has an eye level of 5 ft. How tall is the building to the nearest tenth of a foot? D

(A) 26.1 ft (B) 50.3 ft (C) 107.2 ft (D) 112.2 ft

2. A fire ranger on a 150-ft-tall tower spots a fire at a 30° angle of depression. How many feet away from the tower is the fire to the nearest tenth? H

(F) 86.6 ft (G) 129.9 ft (H) 259.8 ft (I) 300 ft

3. What is the value of x to the nearest foot? B

(A) 6713 ft (C) 10,443 ft

(B) 9534 ft (D) 12,445 ft

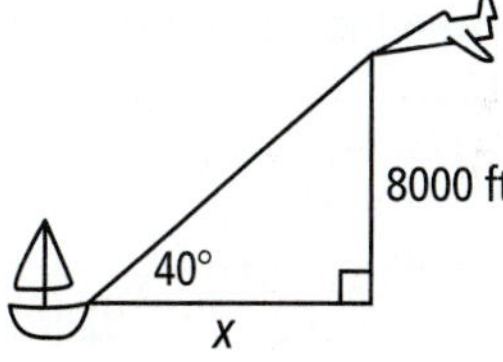

4. What is the value of x to the nearest foot? F

(F) 2097 ft (H) 3108 ft

(G) 2529 ft (I) 6706 ft

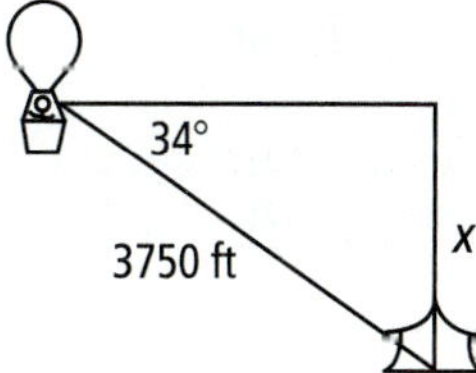

5. A wildlife biologist looks up at a 78° angle of elevation to see a flock of geese in the air. The biologist is standing 200 ft away from a place directly underneath the geese. How high are the geese flying, to the nearest tenth of a foot? C

(A) 195.6 ft (B) 204.5 ft (C) 940.9 ft (D) 961.9 ft

Extended Response

6. Two buildings stand 90 ft apart at their closest points. At those points, the angle of depression from the top of the taller building to the top of the shorter building is 12°. How much taller is the taller building? Draw a diagram to support your answer. Round your answer to the nearest foot. Explain.

19 ft; $\tan 12° = \frac{x}{90}$, so $x = 90 \tan 12° \approx 19.1$; check students' drawings. [4] Student provides correct answer and reasoning and sufficient drawing. [3] Student provides correct answer with minor error in reasoning. [2] Student provides correct answer and no reasoning or incorrect drawing. [1] Student provides correct drawing but incorrect response. [0] incorrect or no response

8-5 Vectors

Vocabulary

Review

1. Circle the drawing that shows only *segment AB*.

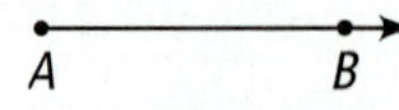

Use the number line below to find the length of each *segment*.

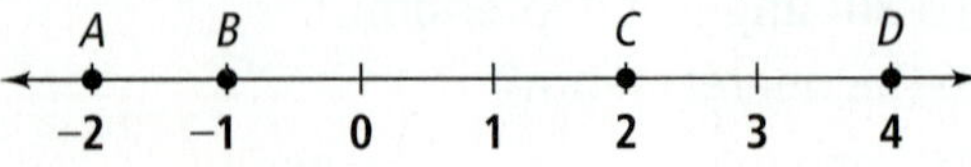

2. $AB =$ 1 **3.** $AC =$ 4 **4.** $BC =$ 3 **5.** $BD =$ 5

6. Explain how a line *segment* is different from a line.

Explanations may vary. Sample: A line segment has endpoints. A line does not have endpoints and extends without end.

Vocabulary Builder

vector (noun) VEK tur

Related Words: magnitude, direction

Definition: A **vector** is any quantity with magnitude (size) and direction.

Main Idea: You can use **vectors** to model motion and direction.

Example: A car's speed and direction together represent a **vector**.

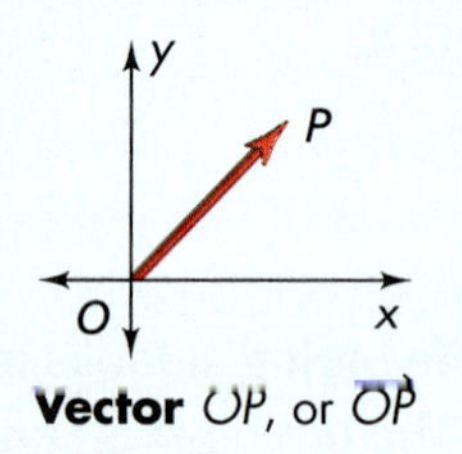

Vector OP, or $\overrightarrow{OP}$

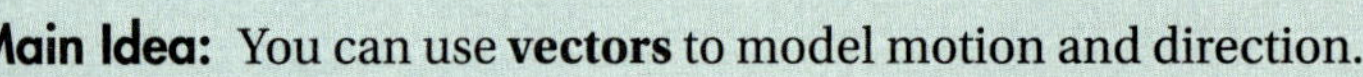

Use Your Vocabulary

Write T for *true* or F for *false*.

T **7.** A *vector* has an initial point and a terminal point.

F **8.** The terminal point of the *vector* at the right is point O.

T **9.** In symbols, *vector OB* is written as $\overrightarrow{OB}$.

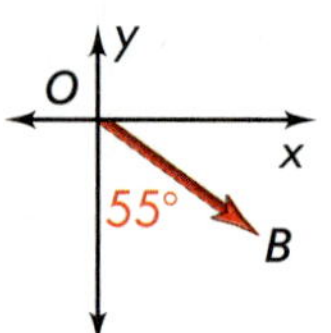

Problem 1 Describing a Vector

Got It? **How can you describe the vector at the right as an ordered pair? Round the coordinates to the nearest tenth.**

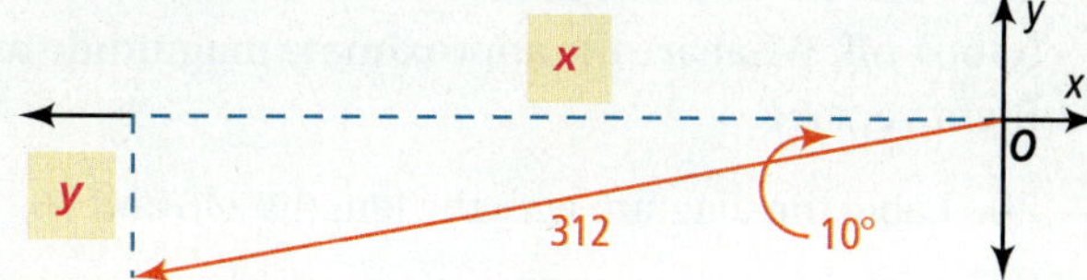

10. Label the diagram with the lengths x and y.

11. Circle the part of the triangle that has a length of 312.

leg opposite 10°-angle	leg adjacent to 10°-angle	hypotenuse (circled)

12. Circle the part of the triangle that has length x.

leg opposite 10°-angle	leg adjacent to 10°-angle (circled)	hypotenuse

13. Circle the part of the triangle that has length y.

leg opposite 10°-angle (circled)	leg adjacent to 10°-angle	hypotenuse

14. Use the justifications below to find the values of x and y.

$\cos 10° = \dfrac{x}{51}$	Write the ratios.	$\sin 10° = \dfrac{y}{312}$
$312 \cdot \cos 10° = x$	Solve for x and y.	$312 \cdot \sin 10° = y$
$307.2600189 \approx x$	Use a calculator.	$54.17823143 \approx y$
$307.3 \approx x$	Round to the nearest tenth.	$54.2 \approx y$

15. Decide whether each coordinate is *positive* or *negative*.

x-coordinate: ? negative

y-coordinate: ? negative

16. Written as an ordered pair, the vector is $\langle -307.3, -54 \rangle$.

Problem 2 Describing a Vector Direction

Got It? **What is the direction of the vector at the right?**

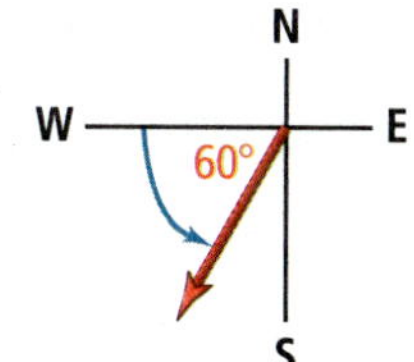

17. Is the angle above (north) or below (south) the west-east line? above / below (circled)

18. Is the angle to the left (west) or to the right (east) of the north-south line? left (circled) / right

19. Circle the direction of the vector.

60° south of east	60° north of east	60° south of west (circled)	60° north of west

Problem 3 Finding the Magnitude and Direction of a Vector

Got It? An airplane lands 246 mi east and 76 mi north from where it took off. What are the approximate magnitude and direction of its flight vector?

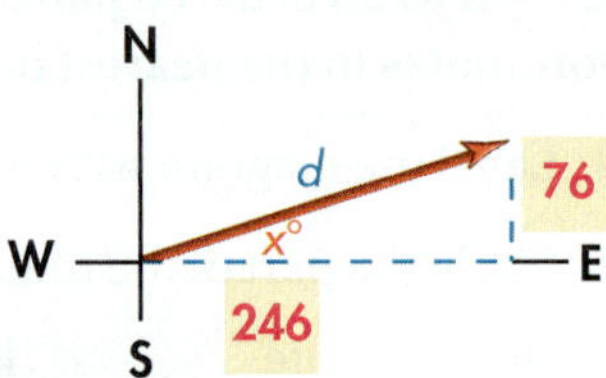

20. Label the diagram with the lengths 246 and 76.

21. The vector ⟨ 246 , 76 ⟩ describes the result of the trip.

22. Complete the reasoning model below.

Think	Write
The magnitude is the distance from the initial point to the terminal point. I can use the Distance Formula to find the distance between (0, 0) and (246, 76).	$d = \sqrt{(246-0)^2 + (76-0)^2}$ $= \sqrt{60{,}516 + 5776}$ $= \sqrt{66{,}292}$ $= 257.4723286$
The vector is $x°$ north of east. I can use the tangent ratio to find this angle formed by the vector. Then I can use a calculator to find the inverse tangent.	$\tan x° = \frac{76}{246}$ $x = \tan^{-1}\frac{76}{246}$ $x \approx 17.16817244$

23. The magnitude is about 257 mi and the direction is about 17° north of east.

take note

Property Adding Vectors

For $\vec{a} = \langle x_1, y_1 \rangle$ and $\vec{c} = \langle x_2, y_2 \rangle$, $\vec{a} + \vec{c} = \langle x_1 + x_2, y_1 + y_2 \rangle$.

Problem 4 Adding Vectors

Got It? What is the resultant of ⟨2, 3⟩ and ⟨ −4 , −2 ⟩ as an ordered pair?

24. The sum is found below. Use one of the reasons in the list to justify each step.

Step	Reason
$\vec{e} = \vec{a} + \vec{c}$	Write the sum.
$\vec{e} = \langle 2, 3 \rangle + \langle -4, -2 \rangle$	Substitute.
$\vec{e} = \langle 2 + (-4), 3 + (-2) \rangle$	Add the coordinates.
$\vec{e} = \langle -2, 1 \rangle$	Simplify.

Substitute.
Write the sum.
Simplify.
Add the coordinates.

Problem 5 Applying Vectors

Got It? Reasoning **The speed of a powerboat in still water is 35 mi/h. The river flows directly south at 8 mi/h. At what angle should the powerboat head up river in order to travel directly west?**

25. Label the sides of the triangle in the diagram.

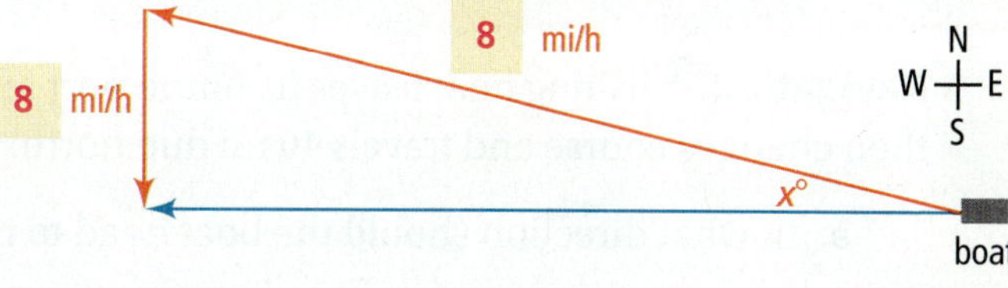

26. Use trigonometry to find x.

$\sin x = \frac{8}{35}$

$x = \sin^{-1}\left(\frac{8}{35}\right)$

$x \approx 13.21298036$

27. The angle at which the powerboat should head up river is about 13.2° .

Lesson Check • Do you UNDERSTAND?

Error Analysis **Your friend says that the magnitude of vector $\langle 10, 7 \rangle$ is greater than that of vector $\langle -10, -7 \rangle$ because the coordinates of $\langle 10, 7 \rangle$ are positive and the coordinates of $\langle -10, -7 \rangle$ are negative. Explain why your friend's statement is incorrect.**

28. Complete to find the magnitude of each vector.

$d_1 = \sqrt{(10 - 0)^2 + (7 - 0)^2}$

$= \sqrt{10^2 + 7^2}$

$= \sqrt{100 + 49}$

$= \sqrt{149}$

$d_2 = \sqrt{(-10 - 0)^2 + (-7 - 0)^2}$

$= \sqrt{(-10)^2 + (-7)^2}$

$= \sqrt{100 + 49}$

$= \sqrt{149}$

29. Explain why your friend's statement is incorrect. Explanations may vary.

Sample: When using the Distance Formula to find magnitude, you square the coordinates. $10^2 + 7^2 = (-10)^2 + (-7)^2$, so the magnitudes are equal.

Math Success

Check off the vocabulary words that you understand.

☐ vector ☐ magnitude ☐ initial point ☐ terminal point ☐ resultant

Rate how well you can *use and describe vectors.*

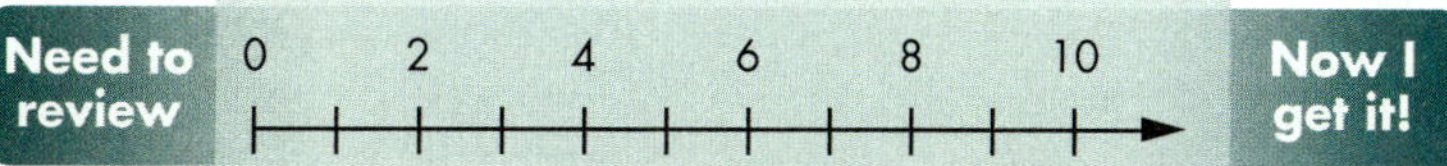

Name ______________________ Class ____________ Date ____________

8-5 Think About a Plan

Vectors

Navigation A fishing boat leaves its home port and travels 150 mi directly east. It then changes course and travels 40 mi due north.

a. In what direction should the boat head to return to its home port?

b. If the boat averages 23 mi/h, how long will the return trip take?

1. Make a sketch that will help you describe the vector for the return trip as an ordered pair. Begin by putting the start and endpoint of the boat at the center of a coordinate grid.

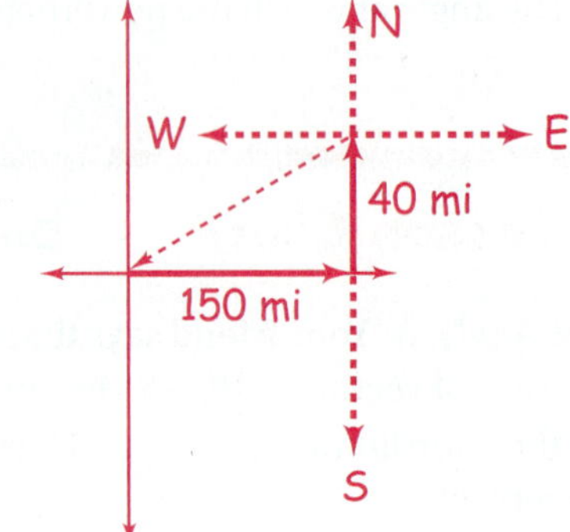

2. What is the ordered pair for the initial point of the vector for the return trip? **(150, 40)**

3. Overlay a west-east line and a north-south line onto your drawing. Put the intersection of these lines at the point where the boat turns to head for home. In general, what is the direction of the return trip?

south of west, or west of south

4. What type of triangle is formed by the paths of the boat? **right triangle**

5. Which could you use to find the angle formed between the return trip and the 40-mi-northward path: sine, cosine, or tangent? Explain.

Tangent; both the opposite and adjacent sides to this angle are given.

6. What is the measure of this angle, to the nearest degree? **75°**

7. What is the direction of the vector of the return trip?

15° south of west, or 75° west of south

8. How can you use the distance formula to find the magnitude of this vector? (*Think:* what are the coordinates of the home port on the grid?)

Find the distance between (0, 0) (home port) and (150, 40).

9. What is the magnitude of this vector, or the distance of the return trip? Round to the nearest mile. **155 mi**

10. What formula describes the relationship between distance, rate, and time? $d = rt$

11. What information do you have about the return trip? **distance, 155 mi; rate, 23 mi/h**

12. How long does the return trip take? **6.74 h**

Name ______________________ Class __________ Date __________

8-5 Practice

Form K

Vectors

Describe each vector as an ordered pair. Round the coordinates to the nearest tenth.

1.

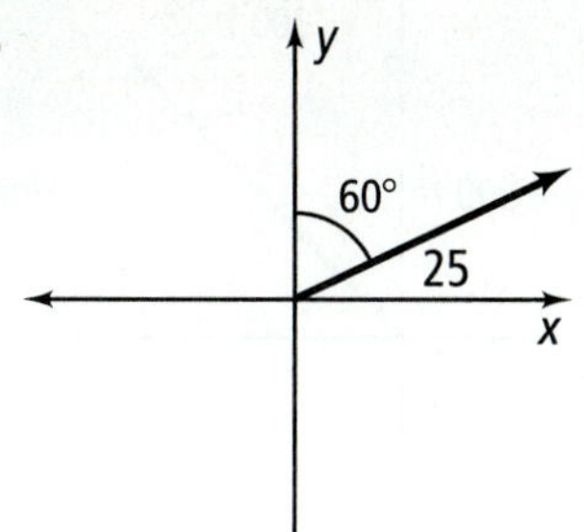

To start, use the sine ratio to find the value of x.

$$\sin 60^\circ = \frac{x}{25}$$

Then use the cosine ratio to find the value of y.

$$\cos 60^\circ = \frac{y}{25}$$

⟨21.7, 12.5⟩

2.

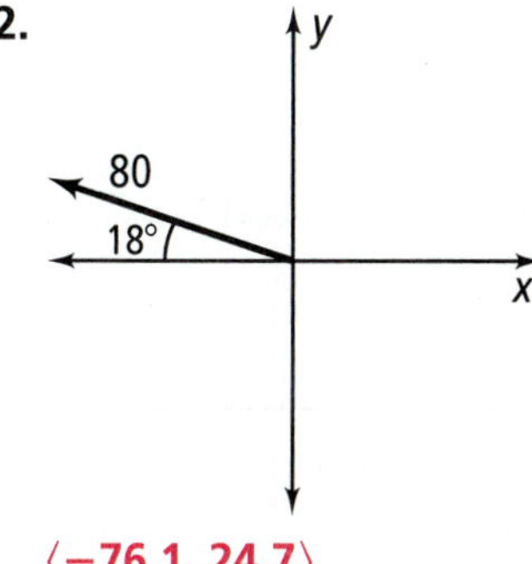

⟨−76.1, 24.7⟩

3.

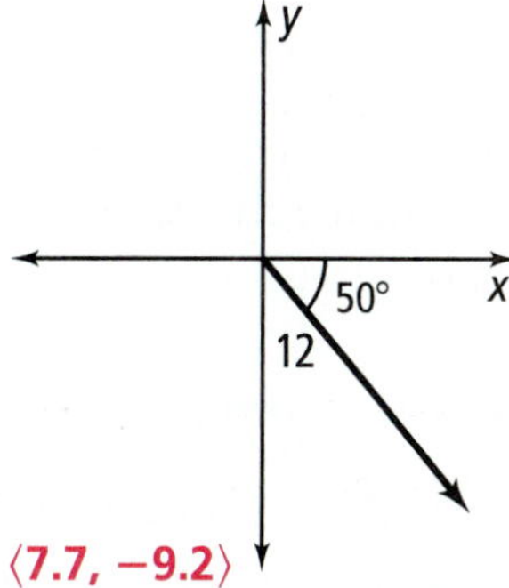

⟨7.7, −9.2⟩

4.

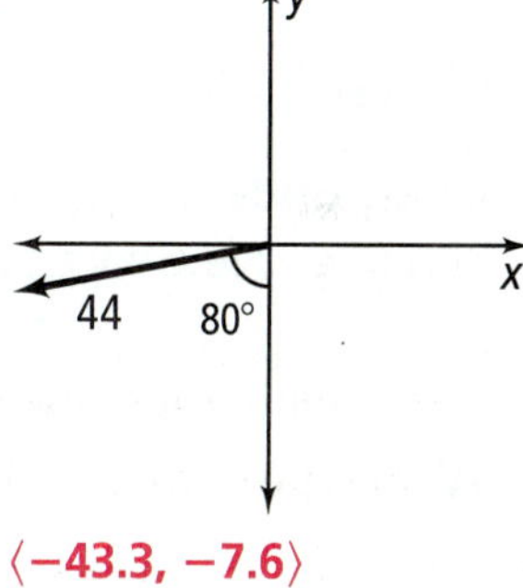

⟨−43.3, −7.6⟩

Use compass directions to describe the direction of each vector.

5.

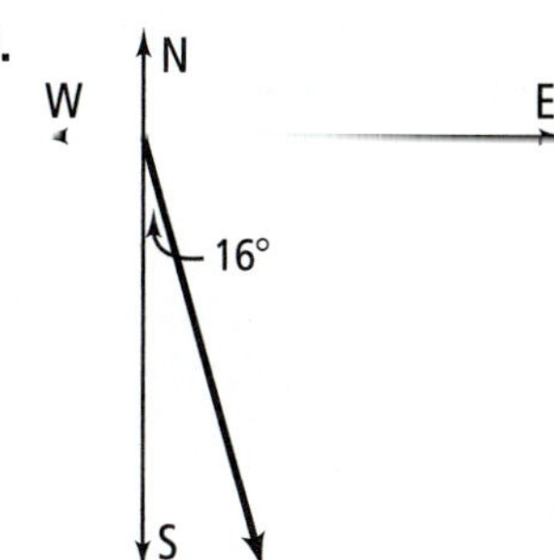

16° east of south

6.

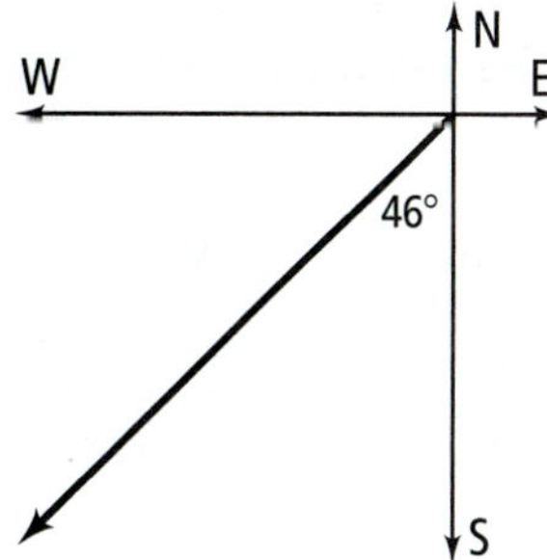

46° west of south

7.

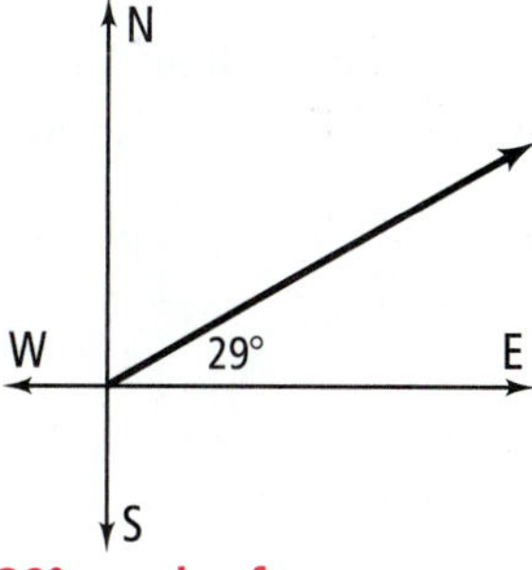

29° north of east

Sketch a vector that has the given direction.

8. 84° north of west

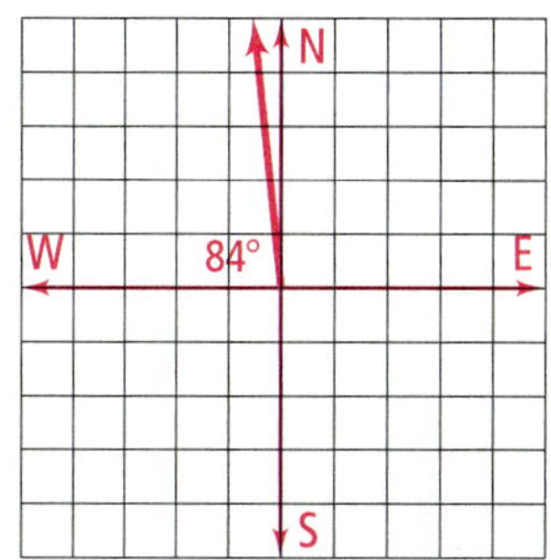

9. 23° east of south

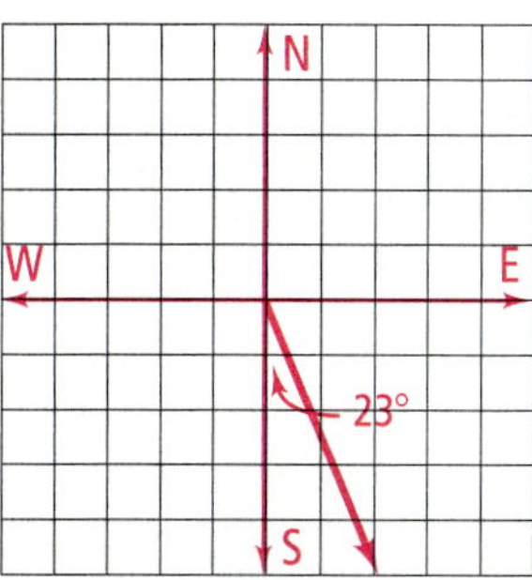

10. 66° west of south

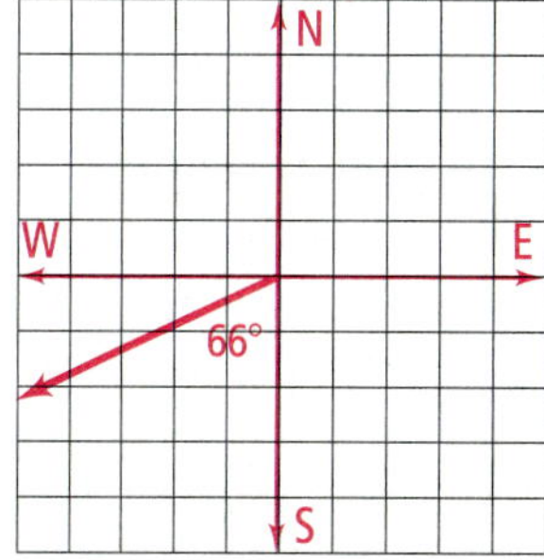

Name ______________________ Class ____________ Date ____________

8-5 Practice (continued)

Vectors

Form K

Find the magnitude and direction of each vector.

11.

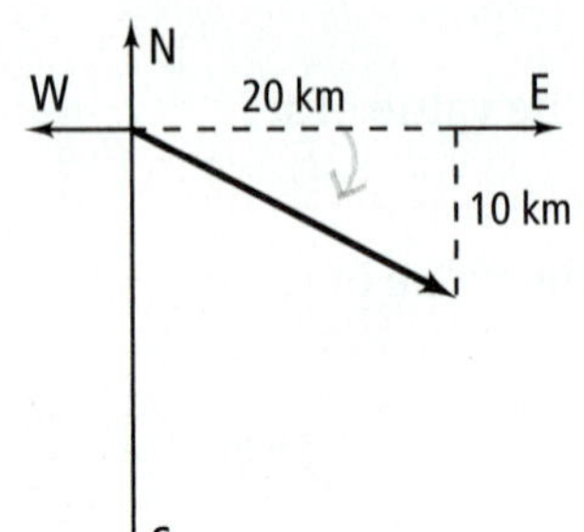

22.4 km; 27° south of east

12.

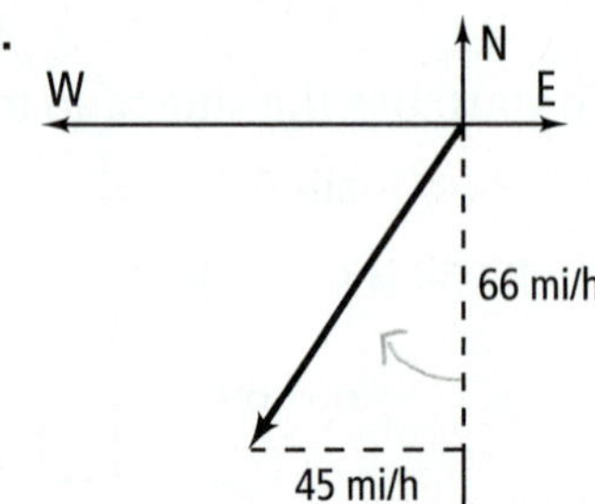

79.9 mi/h; 34° west of south

13.

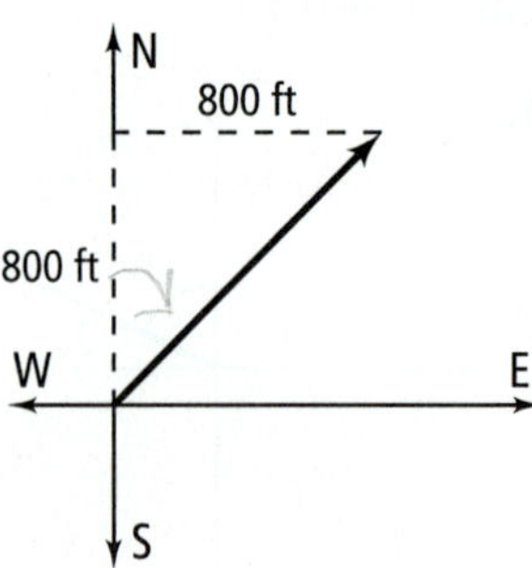

1131 ft; 45° east of north

14. After takeoff, a helicopter heads 14 mi due west, then 25 mi due south. What are the distance and direction of the helicopter's flight? Round each to the nearest tenth. 28.7 mi; 60.8° south of west

15. **Open-Ended** Write a word problem involving a vector that can be described by a negative *x*-coordinate and a positive *y*-coordinate. Check students' work.

Write the resultant of the two vectors as an ordered pair.

16. $\langle 4, 5\rangle$ and $\langle 9, -7\rangle$ To start, add the *x*-coordinates, then the *y*-coordinates.
$\langle 13, -2\rangle$

17. $\langle -3, -10\rangle$ and $\langle 8, 2\rangle$ $\langle 5, -8\rangle$

18. $\langle 0, 6\rangle$ and $\langle -4, 7\rangle$ $\langle -4, 13\rangle$

For Exercises 18 and 19, (a) write the resultant of the two vectors as an ordered pair and (b) draw the resultant.

19.

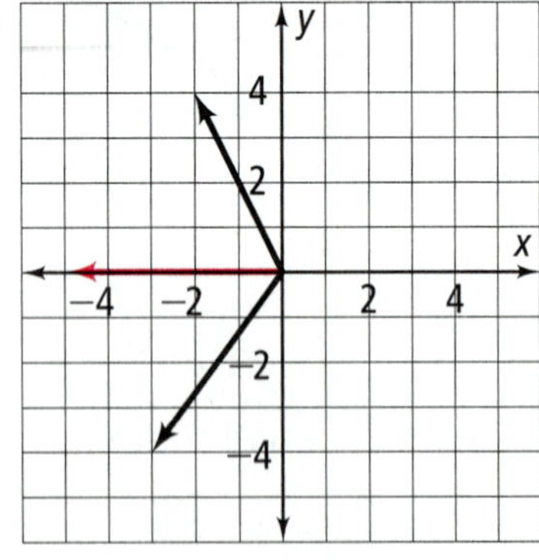

$\langle -5, 0\rangle$

20.

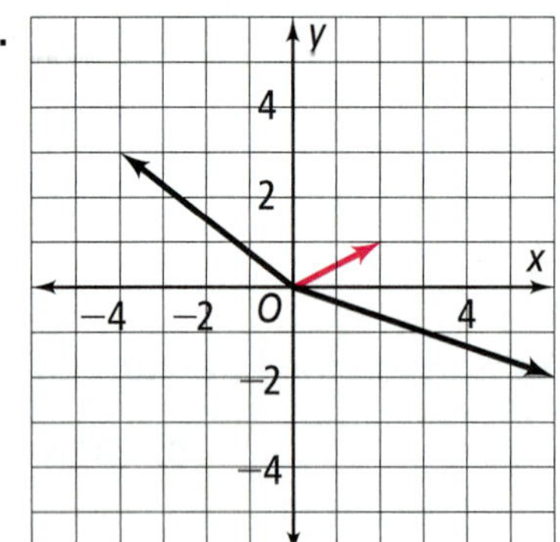

$\langle 2, 1\rangle$

21. You are traveling by boat heading due east at a rate of 15 mi/h. The current flows south at a rate of 6 mi/h. What are the resulting speed and direction of the boat? Round to the nearest unit.
16 mi/h; 22° south of east

Name ______________________ Class ____________ Date ____________

8-5 Standardized Test Prep

Vectors

Multiple Choice

For Exercises 1–6, choose the correct letter.

1. Which choice shows the sum of the two vectors $\langle -2, 0\rangle$ and $\langle 4, -5\rangle$ written as an ordered pair? B

A $\langle 4, -5\rangle$ B $\langle 2, -5\rangle$ C $\langle -2, 0\rangle$ D $\langle -6, 5\rangle$

2. The ordered pairs $\langle -8, 2\rangle$ and $\langle 5, -6\rangle$ represent two vectors. What is the magnitude of the resultant? H

F 1 G 2 H 5 I 15

3. The ordered pairs $\langle 5, 2\rangle$ and $\langle 3, -2\rangle$ represent two vectors. What is the magnitude of the resultant? D

A 2 B 4.5 C 6 D 8

4. Jill rides her horse 5 miles due north and then 3 miles due east. What is the magnitude and direction of Jill's ride? Round to the nearest tenth. H

F 5 mi; 45° northeast
H 5.8 mi; 31° east of north
G 4 mi; 31° east of north
I 8 mi; 60° east of north

5. An airplane has a speed of 350 mi/h in still air. It is heading due north and encounters a 25 mi/h wind blowing due west. What is the resulting speed and direction of the plane? Round to the nearest unit. A

A 351 mi/h; 4° west of north
C 349 mi/h; 4° west of north
B 349 mi/h; 4° north of west
D 351 mi/h; 4° north of west

6. A boat heads directly across a river at 12 mi/h. The river is 3 mi wide. After reaching the other side, the boat is 1 mi downstream from where the captain had intended to land. What is the speed of the river's current? I

F 1 mi/h G 2 mi/h H 3 mi/h I 4 mi/h

Short Response

7. Sketch a vector that is 35° south of east with a magnitude of 40.

[2] Drawing is accurate and correctly labeled.
[1] Direction is incorrect OR magnitude is not labeled.
[0] incorrect vector or no response

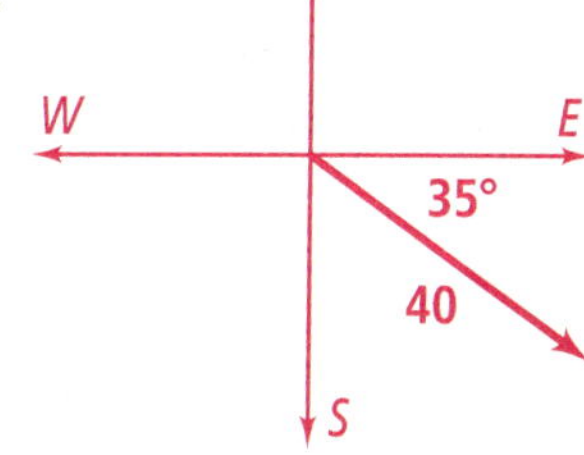

9-1 Translations

Vocabulary

Review

1. Underline the correct word to complete the sentence.

A *transformation* of a geometric figure is a change in the position, shape, or color / <u>size</u> of the figure.

2. Cross out the word that does NOT describe a *transformation*.

~~erase~~	flip	rotate	slide	turn

Vocabulary Builder

isometry (noun) **eye SAHM uh tree**

Definition: An **isometry** is a transformation in which the preimage and the image of a geometric figure are congruent.

Example:

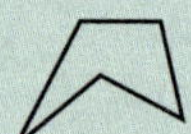

Preimage

Image

Non-Example:

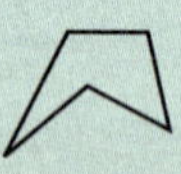

Preimage

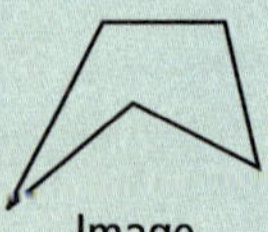

Image

Use Your Vocabulary

Complete each statement with *congruent, image* or *preimage.*

3. In an *isometry* of a triangle, each side of the __?__ is congruent to each side of the preimage. image

4. In an *isometry* of a trapezoid, each angle of the image is congruent to each angle of the __?__. preimage

5. An *isometry* maps a preimage onto a(n) __?__ image. congruent

Problem 1 Identifying an Isometry

Got It? Does the transformation below appear to be an isometry? Explain.

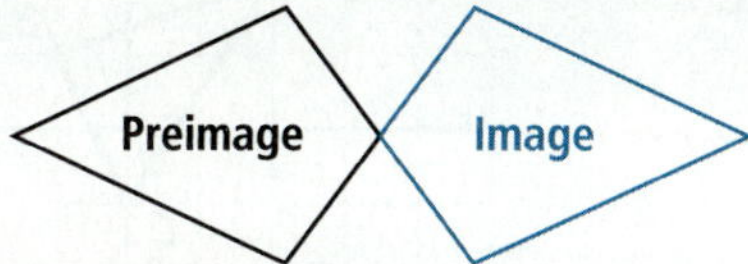

6. Name the polygon that is the preimage.

kite

7. Name the polygon that is the image.

kite

8. Do the preimage and image appear congruent? Yes / No

9. Does the transformation appear to be an isometry? Explain.

Yes. Explanations may vary. Sample: The preimage and the image appear congruent, so the transformation appears to be an isometry.

Problem 2 Naming Images and Corresponding Parts

Got It? In the diagram, $\triangle NID \rightarrow \triangle SUP$. What are the images of $\angle I$ and point D?

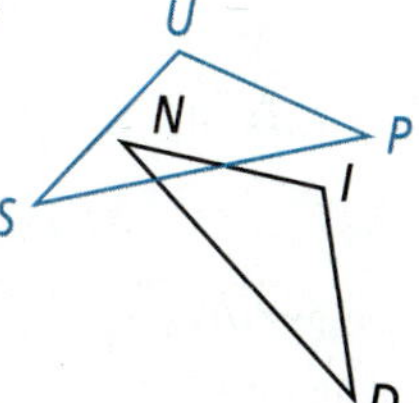

10. The arrow ($\rightarrow$) shows that $\triangle$ SUP is the image of $\triangle NID$, so $\triangle NID \cong \triangle$ SUP .

11. Describe how to list corresponding parts of the preimage and image.

List corresponding parts of the preimage and image in the same order.

12. Circle the image of $\angle I$.

$\angle I$ $\angle S$ $\angle P$ $\angle U$

13. Circle the image of point D.

I S P U

take note

Key Concept Translation

A **translation** is a transformation that maps all points of a figure the same distance in the same direction.

A translation is an isometry. Prime notation (′) identifies image points.

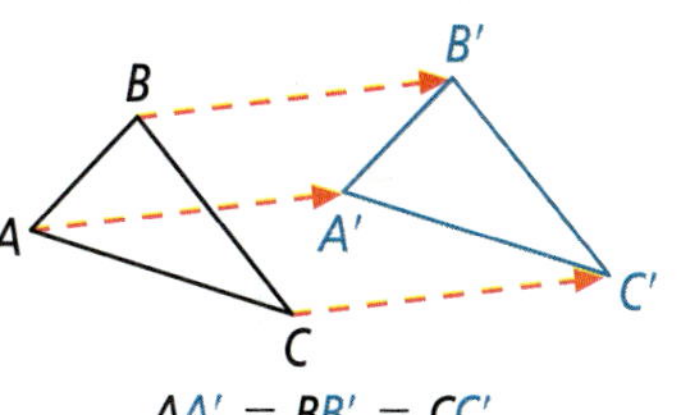

$AA' = BB' = CC'$

14. If $\square PQRS$ is translated right 2 units, then every point on $\square P'Q'R'S'$ is 2 units to the right of its preimage point.

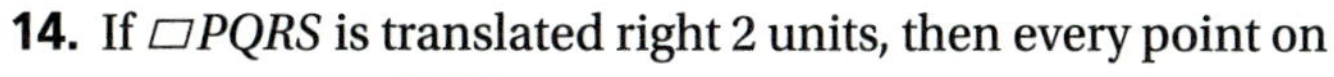

Problem 3 Finding the Image of a Translation

Got It? What are the images of the vertices of $\triangle ABC$ for the translation $(x, y) \rightarrow (x + 1, y - 4)$? Graph the image of $\triangle ABC$.

15. Identify the coordinates of each vertex.

$A(-2, 2)$

$B(1, 1)$

$C(0, -1)$

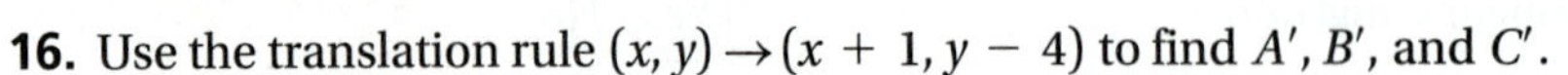

16. Use the translation rule $(x, y) \rightarrow (x + 1, y - 4)$ to find A', B', and C'.

$A'(-2 + 1, 2 - 4) = A'(-1, -2)$

$B'(1 + 1, 1 - 4) = B'(2, -3)$

$C'(0 + 1, -1 - 4) = C'(1, -5)$

17. Circle how each point is translated.

1 unit to the right and 4 units up | **(1 unit to the right and 4 units down)** | 1 unit to the left and 4 units up | 1 unit to the left and 4 units down

18. Graph the image of $\triangle ABC$ on the coordinate plane above.

Problem 4 Writing a Rule to Describe a Translation

Got It? The translation image of $\triangle LMN$ is $\triangle L'M'N'$ with $L'(1, -2)$, $M'(3, -4)$, and $N'(6, -2)$. What is a rule that describes the translation?

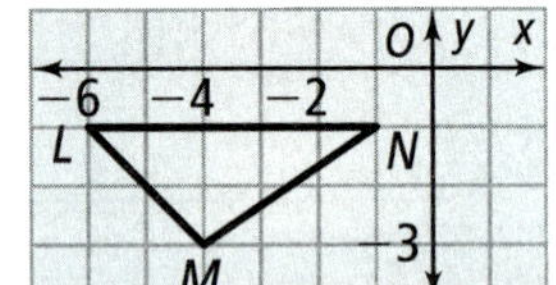

19. Circle the coordinates of point L.

$(6, -1)$ | $(-1, -6)$ | **($(-6, -1)$)** | $(-1, 6)$

20. Circle the coordinates of point M.

($(-4, -3)$) | $(-3, -4)$ | $(-4, 3)$ | $(-3, 4)$

21. Circle the coordinates of point N.

$(-1, 1)$ | $(1, -1)$ | $(-1, 0)$ | **($(-1, -1)$)**

22. Find the horizontal change from L to L'.

$1 - (-6) = 7$

23. Find the vertical change from L to L'.

$-2 - (-1) = -1$

Underline the correct word to complete each sentence.

24. From $\triangle LMN$ to $\triangle L'M'N'$, each value of x <u>increases</u> / decreases.

25. From $\triangle LMN$ to $\triangle L'M'N'$, each value of y increases / <u>decreases</u>.

26. A rule that describes the translation is? $(x, y) \rightarrow (x + 7, y - 1)$.

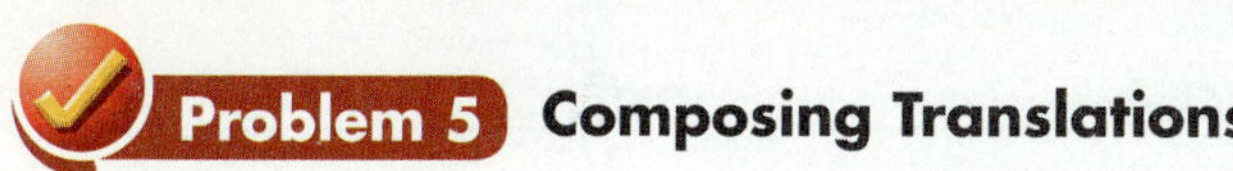

Problem 5 Composing Translations

Got It? **The diagram at the right shows a chess game with the black bishop 6 squares right and 2 squares down from its original position after two moves. The bishop next moves 3 squares left and 3 squares down. Where is the bishop in relation to its original position?**

27. If (0, 0) represents the bishop's original position, the bishop is now at the point (6 , −2).

28. Write the translation rule that represents the bishop's next move.

$(x, y) \rightarrow (x - 3, y - 3)$

29. Substitute the point you found in Exercise 27 into the rule you wrote in Exercise 28.

$(6, -2) \rightarrow (6 - 5, 3 - 3)$

30. In relation to (0, 0), the bishop is at (3 , −5).

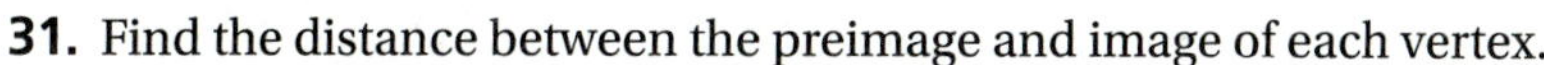

Lesson Check • Do you UNDERSTAND?

Error Analysis **Your friend says the transformation $\triangle ABC \rightarrow \triangle PQR$ is a translation. Explain and correct her error.**

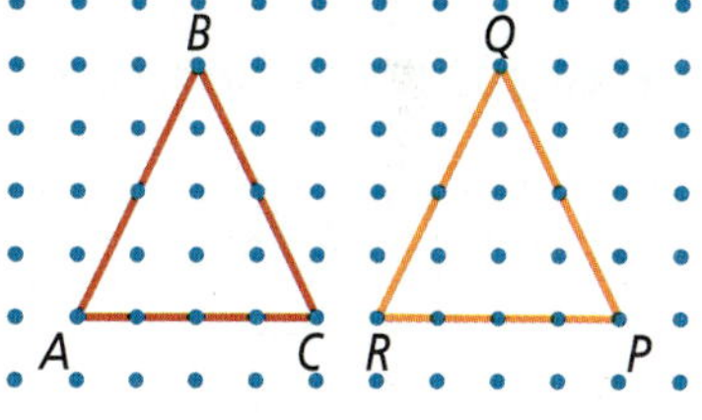

31. Find the distance between the preimage and image of each vertex.

$BQ =$ 5 $AP =$ 9 $CR =$ 1

32. Does this transformation map all points the same distance? Yes / No (circled: No)

33. Is $\triangle ABC \rightarrow \triangle PQR$ a translation? Explain. **Explanations may vary. Sample:**

No. The distances between preimage and image vertices are not equal.

34. Correct your friend's error. **Answers may vary. Sample:**

The transformation is a flip.

Math Success

Check off the vocabulary words that you understand.

☐ transformation ☐ preimage ☐ image ☐ isometry ☐ translation

Rate how well you can *find transformation images.*

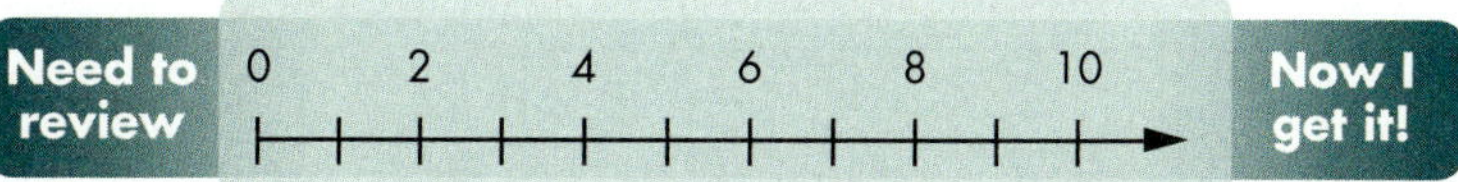

Name ______________________ Class __________ Date __________

9-1 Think About a Plan

Translations

Coordinate Geometry Quadrilateral *PLAT* has vertices $P(-2, 0)$, $L(-1, 1)$, $A(0, 1)$, and $T(-1, 0)$. Quadrilateral $P'L'A'T'$ is the image of quadrilateral *PLAT* for the translation $(x, y) \rightarrow (x + 2, y - 3)$. Show that $\overline{PP'}$, $\overline{LL'}$, $\overline{AA'}$, and $\overline{TT'}$ are all parallel.

Understanding the Problem

1. How can you use the three sentences of the problem to help you break the problem down into manageable pieces?

   Answers may vary. Sample: The first sentence contains the given information. The second contains the operation I can use to obtain the coordinates of the image. The third directs me toward what I need to prove.

Planning the Solution

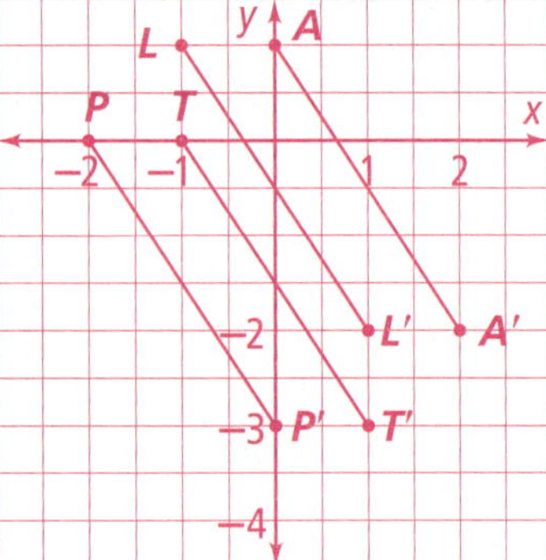

2. How can you use a diagram to help you solve the problem?

   Plot the given points and the points of the image on a coordinate grid.

3. Use the given translation to find the image points.

   $P'(0, -3)$, $L'(1, -2)$, $A'(2, -2)$, $T'(1, -3)$

4. Graph $\overline{PP'}$, $\overline{LL'}$, $\overline{AA'}$, and $\overline{TT'}$. What theorems about parallel lines come to mind when you look at the graph?

   If the slopes of two lines are equal, then the lines are parallel.

Getting an Answer

5. Find the slopes of the lines that connect each original point to its image.

   $-\frac{3}{2}; -\frac{3}{2}; -\frac{3}{2}; -\frac{3}{2}$

6. How can you use the slopes to establish that $\overline{PP'}$, $\overline{LL'}$, $\overline{AA'}$, and $\overline{TT'}$ are all parallel?

   The lines are parallel because the lines all have the same slope.

Name ______________________ Class ____________ Date ____________

9-1 Practice — Form K

Translations

Tell whether the transformation appears to be an isometry. Explain.

1. 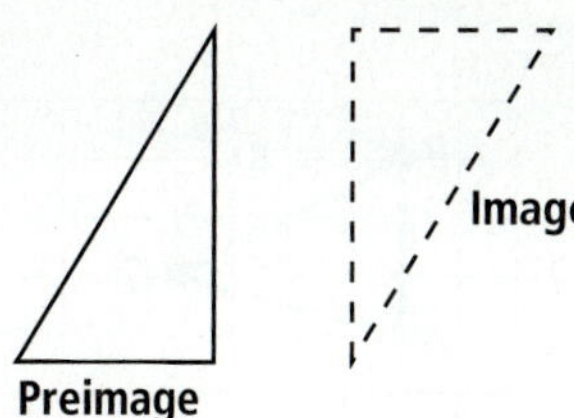

yes; image and preimage congruent

2. 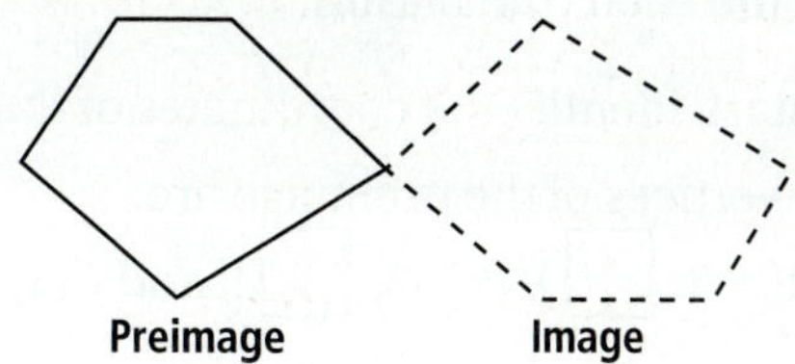

no; image and preimage not congruent

In each diagram, the dashed-line figure is an image of the solid-line figure.
(a) Choose an angle or point from the preimage and name its image.
(b) List all pairs of corresponding sides.

3. 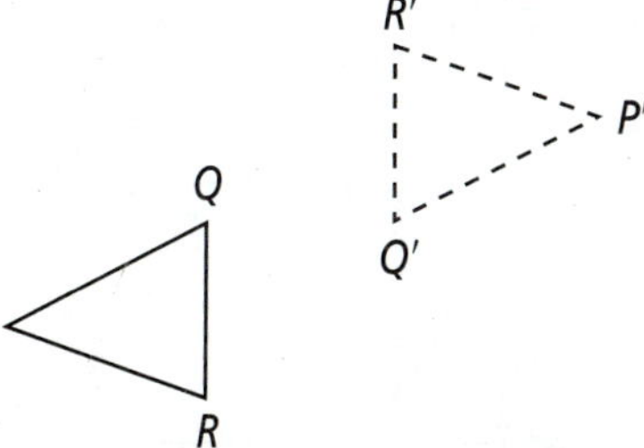

Answers may vary. Sample: $P \rightarrow P'$;
$\overline{PQ} \rightarrow \overline{P'Q'}$; $\overline{QR} \rightarrow \overline{Q'R'}$; $\overline{PR} \rightarrow \overline{P'R'}$

4. 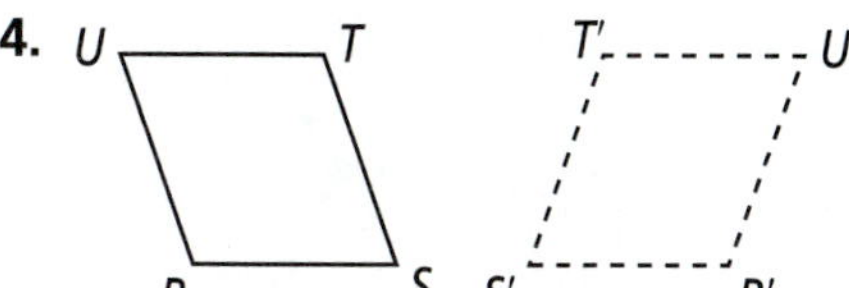

Answers may vary. Sample: $\angle U \rightarrow \angle U'$;
$\overline{RS} \rightarrow \overline{R'S'}$; $\overline{ST} \rightarrow \overline{S'T'}$; $\overline{TU} \rightarrow \overline{T'U'}$; $\overline{UR} \rightarrow \overline{U'R'}$

Copy each graph. Graph the image of each figure under the given translation.

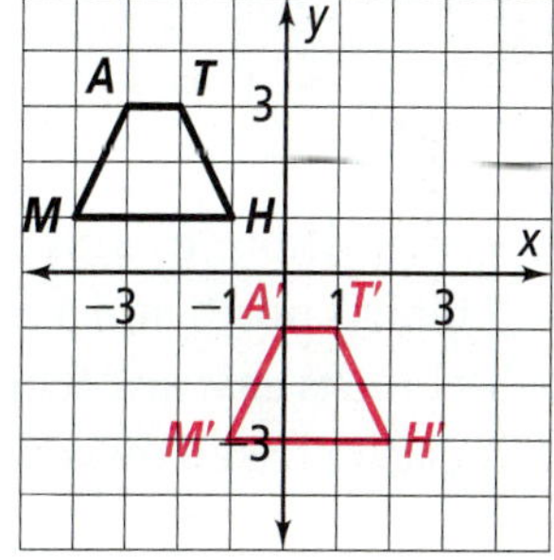

5. to the right 3 units and down 4 units

To start, identify the coordinates of each vertex.

The vertices are:

$M($ −4 $, 1)$, $A($ −3 $, 3)$, $T(-2,$ 3 $)$, and $H(-1,$ 1 $)$.

6. $(x, y) \rightarrow (x - 2, y + 3)$

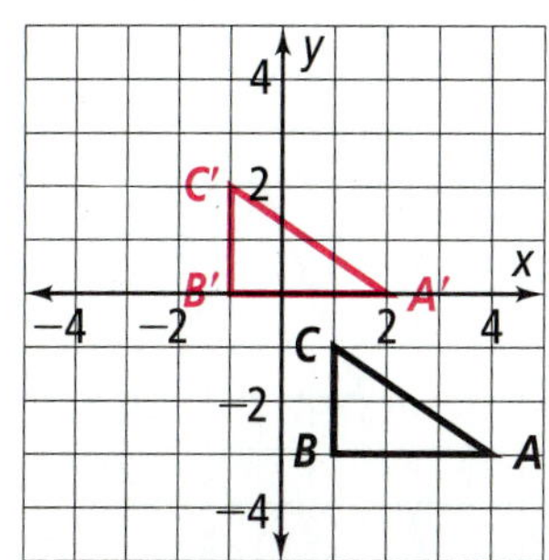

7. $(x, y) \rightarrow (x + 2, y - 3)$

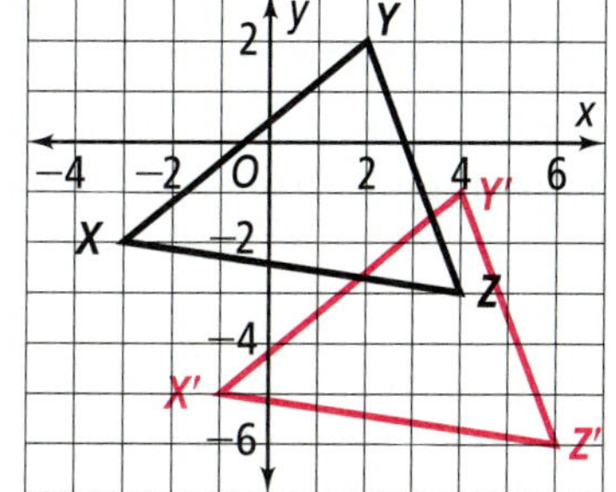

Name ______________________ Class ____________ Date ____________

9-1 Practice (continued) — Form K

Translations

The dashed-line figure is a translation image of the solid-line figure. Write a rule to describe each translation.

8. To start, identify the coordinates of the vertices of both figures.

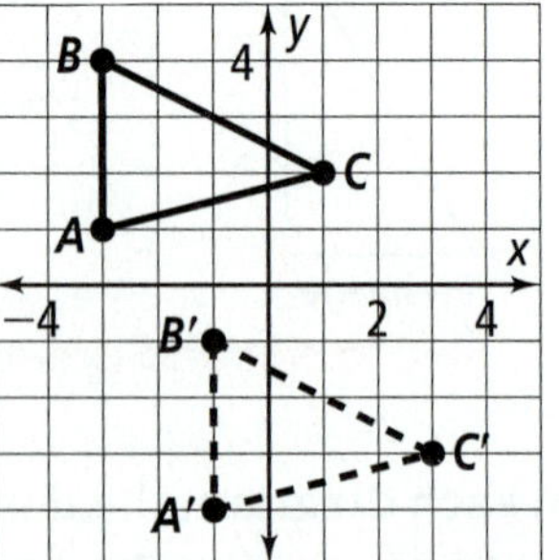

The vertices of the preimage are:

$A(-3, \boxed{1})$, $B(-3, \boxed{4})$, and $C(1, \boxed{2})$.

The vertices of the image are:

$A'(\boxed{-1}, -4)$, $B'(\boxed{-1}, -1)$, and $C'(3, \boxed{-3})$.

The translation rule is _?_. $(x, y) \rightarrow (x + 2, y - 5)$

9.

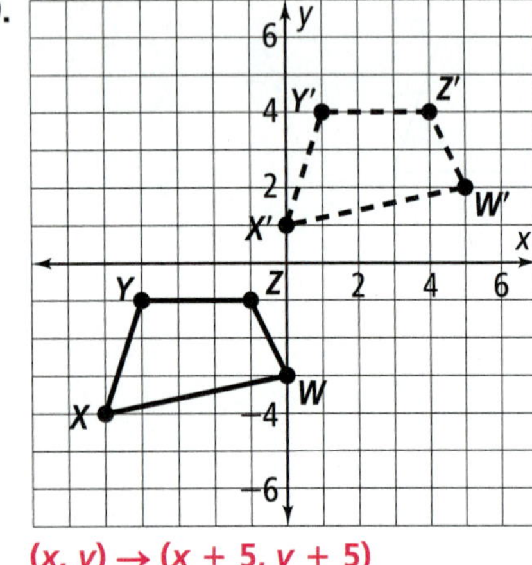

$(x, y) \rightarrow (x + 5, y + 5)$

10.

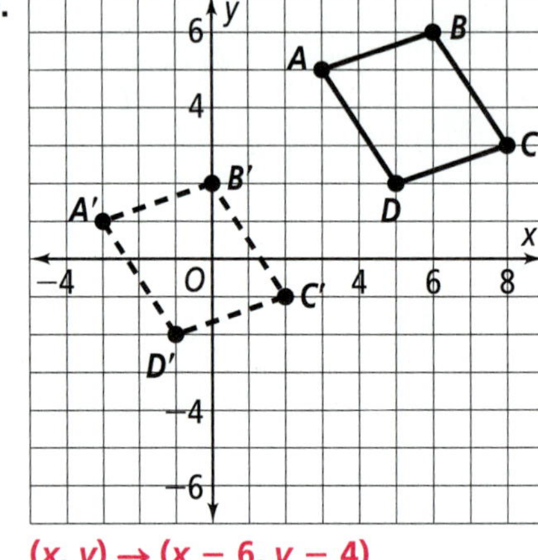

$(x, y) \rightarrow (x - 6, y - 4)$

11. You and your friends are visiting a city with blocks laid out in a grid. You walk 7 blocks north and 3 blocks west to a restaurant. After you eat, you then walk 10 blocks east and 3 blocks south to meet up with a friend. Describe your final location based on your starting point.
4 blocks north and 7 blocks east

12. $\triangle ABC$ has coordinates $A(2, 3)$, $B(4, -2)$, and $C(3, 0)$. After a translation the coordinates of A' are $(6, -1)$. What are the coordinates of B' and C'?
$B'(8, -6)$, $C'(7, -4)$

13. Use the graph to the right. Write three different translation rules for which the image of $\triangle RST$ has a vertex at the origin.
$(x, y) \rightarrow (x - 3, y - 2)$; $(x, y) \rightarrow (x - 5, y - 6)$;
$(x, y) \rightarrow (x - 7, y - 2)$

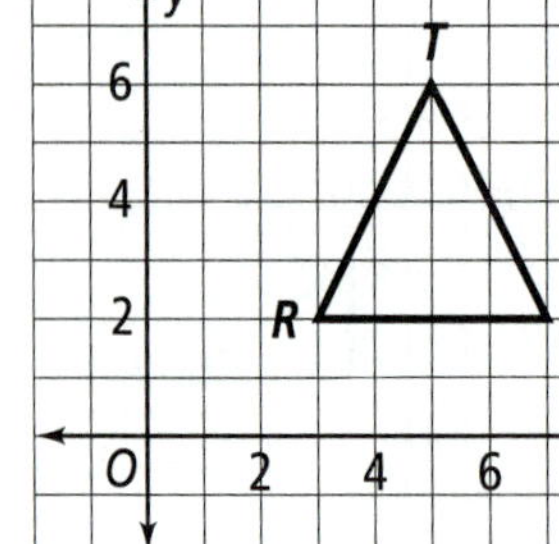

Name ______________________ Class ____________ Date ____________

9-1 Standardized Test Prep

Translations

Multiple Choice

For Exercises 1–4, choose the correct letter.

1. In the diagram, $\triangle A'B'C'$ is an image of $\triangle ABC$. Which rule describes this translation? **B**

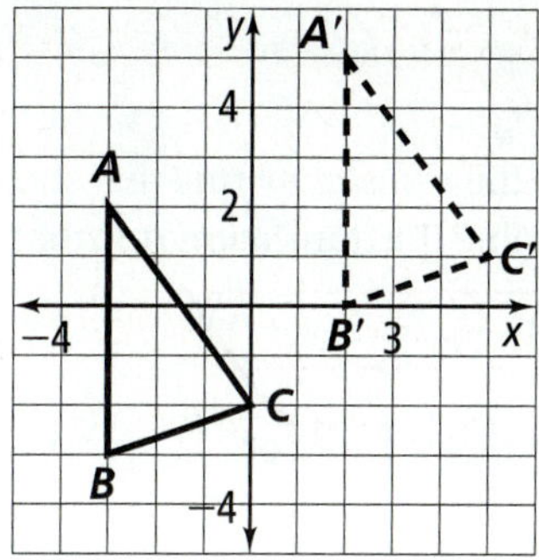

Ⓐ $(x, y) \rightarrow (x - 5, y - 3)$

Ⓑ $(x, y) \rightarrow (x + 5, y + 3)$

Ⓒ $(x, y) \rightarrow (x - 3, y - 5)$

Ⓓ $(x, y) \rightarrow (x + 3, y + 5)$

2. The translation $(x, y) \rightarrow (x + 3, y - 7)$ maps $TUVW$ onto $T'U'V'W'$. What translation maps $T'U'V'W'$ onto $TUVW$? **I**

Ⓕ $(x, y) \rightarrow (x + 3, y - 7)$

Ⓖ $(x, y) \rightarrow (x - 7, y + 3)$

Ⓗ $(x, y) \rightarrow (x + 7, y - 3)$

Ⓘ $(x, y) \rightarrow (x - 3, y + 7)$

3. Which of the following is true for an isometry? **A**

Ⓐ The preimage and the image are congruent.

Ⓑ The preimage is larger than the image.

Ⓒ The preimage is smaller than the image.

Ⓓ The preimage is in the same position as the image.

4. $\triangle RSV$ has coordinates $R(2, 1)$, $S(3, 2)$, and $V(2, 6)$. A translation maps point R to R' at $(-4, 8)$. What are the coordinates for S' for this translation? **H**

Ⓕ $(-6, -4)$ Ⓖ $(-3, 2)$ Ⓗ $(-3, 9)$ Ⓘ $(-4, 13)$

Short Response

5. $\triangle LMP$ has coordinates $L(3, 4)$, $M(6, 6)$, and $P(5, 5)$. A translation maps point L to L' at $(7, -4)$. What are the coordinates for M' and for P' for this translation?

[2] *M*′(10, −2) and *P*′(9, −3) [1] one correct coordinate given
[0] no correct coordinates given

9-2 Reflections

Vocabulary

Review

1. Circle the *translation* rule that shows a mapping 2 units left and 1 unit up.
Underline the translation rule that shows a mapping 2 units right and 1 unit down.

$(x, y) \rightarrow (x - 2, y + 1)$ $\qquad$ $(x, y) \rightarrow (x + 2, y - 1)$ $\qquad$ $(x, y) \rightarrow (x - 2, y - 1)$

Vocabulary Builder

reflection (noun) rih FLEK shun

Related Words: line of **reflection**

Definition: A **reflection** is a mirror image of an object that has the same size and shape but an opposite orientation.

Math Usage: A **reflection** is a transformation where each point on the preimage is the same distance from the line of reflection as its **reflection** image.

Use Your Vocabulary

Write T for *true* or F for *false*.

T 2. A *reflection* is the same shape as the original figure.

F 3. A *reflection* makes a figure larger.

take note

Key Concept Reflection Across a Line

Reflection across a line *r*, called the **line of reflection,** is a transformation with these two properties:

- If a point A is on line r, then the image of A is itself (that is, $A' = A$).
- If a point B is not on line r, then r is the perpendicular bisector of $\overline{BB'}$.

A reflection across a line is an isometry.

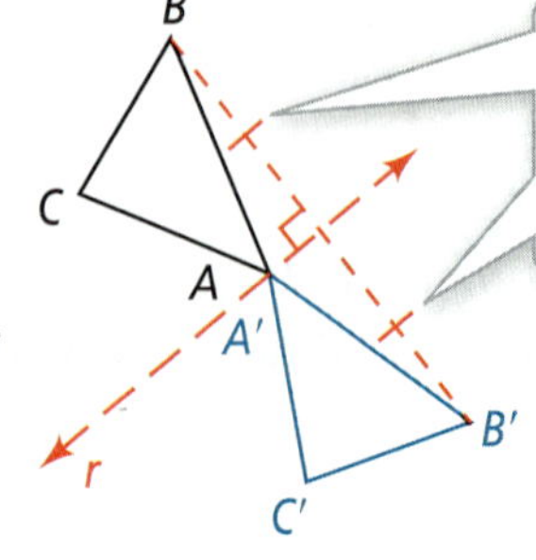

4. Line r is the perpendicular bisector of $\overline{CC'}$.

Problem 1 Reflecting a Point Across a Line

Got It? **What is the image of $P(3, 4)$ reflected across the line $x = -1$?**

5. Graph P on the coordinate plane at the right.

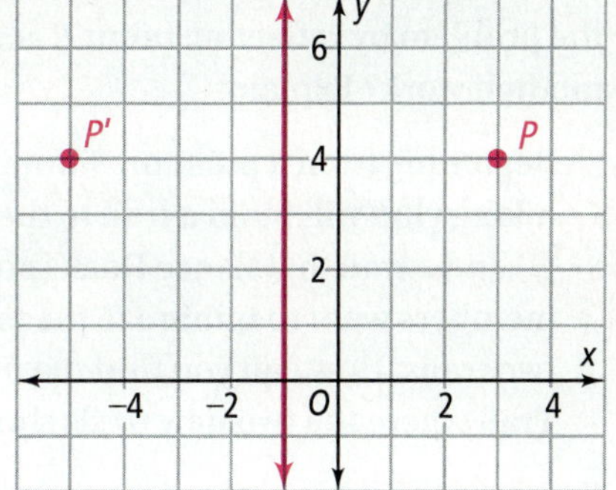

6. Describe the line of reflection. Then graph the line of reflection.

Answers may vary. Sample: $x = -1$ is a vertical line.

7. The distance from point P to the line of reflection is 4 units.

Underline the correct word(s) to complete each sentence.

8. The x-coordinates of P and P' are different / the same.

9. The y-coordinates of P and P' are different / the same.

10. Point P is reflected to the left / right across the line of reflection.

11. Graph the image of $P(3, 4)$ and label it P'.

12. The coordinates of P' are (−5 , 4).

Problem 2 Graphing a Reflection Image

Got It? **Graph points $A(-3, 4)$, $B(0, 1)$, and $C(4, 2)$. What is the image of $\triangle ABC$ reflected across the x-axis?**

13. The x-axis is the line $y =$ 0.

14. Circle the distance in units from point A to the x-axis. Underline the distance from point B to the x-axis. Put a square around the distance from point C to the x-axis.

0   1   2   3   4

15. Point B' is 1 unit(s) below the x-axis.

16. Point C' is 2 unit(s) below the x-axis.

17. The arrow shows how to find vertex A'. Graph the image of $\triangle ABC$ and label vertices B' and C' on the coordinate plane below.

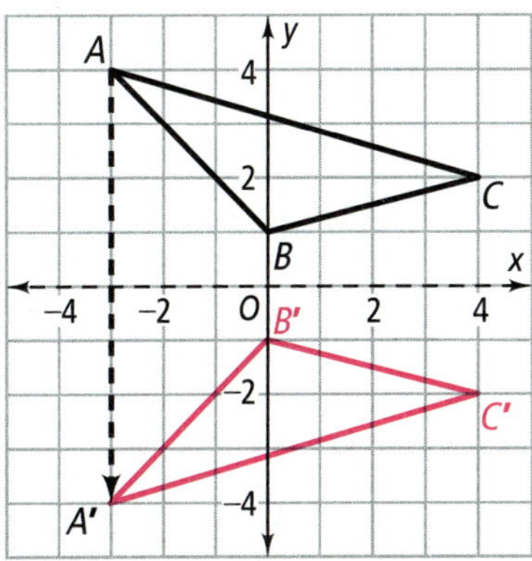

Problem 3 Minimizing a Distance

Got It? Reasoning The diagram shows one solution of the problem below. Your classmate began to solve the problem by reflecting point *R* across line *t*. Will her method work? Explain.

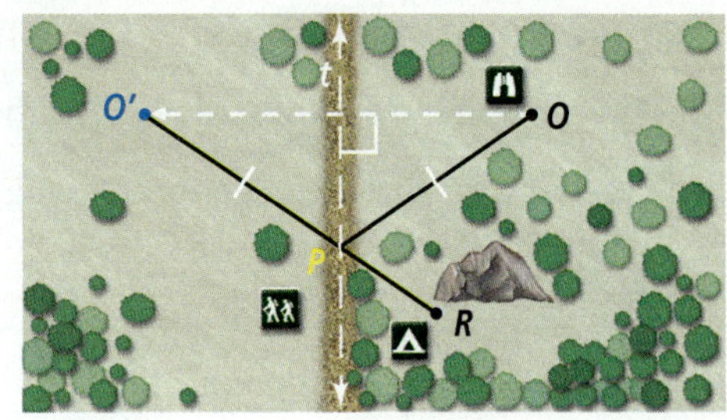

Beginning from a point on Summit Trail (line *t*), a hiking club will build a trail to the Overlook (point *O*) and a trail to Balance Rock (point *R*). The club members want to minimize the total length of the two trails. How can you find the point on Summit Trail where the two new trails should start?

You need to find the point *P* on line *t* such that the distance $OP + PR$ is as small as possible. In the diagram, the problem was solved by locating O', the reflection image of *O* across *t*. Because *t* is the perpendicular bisector of $\overline{OO'}$, $PO = PO'$, and $OP + PR = O'P + PR$. By the Triangle Inequality Theorem, the sum $O'P + PR$ is least when *R*, *P*, and O' are collinear. So, the trails should start at the point *P* where $\overline{RO'}$ intersects line *t*.

Place a ✓ in the box if the response is correct. Place an ✗ if it is incorrect.

✓ **18.** When point *R* is reflected across line *t*, *t* is the perpendicular bisector of $\overline{RR'}$.

✗ **19.** $PR \neq PR'$

✓ **20.** $RP + PO = R'P + PO$

✗ **21.** Points *O*, *P*, and R' are NOT collinear.

✓ **22.** The trails should start at the point *P* where $\overline{OR'}$ intersects *t*.

23. Reflect *R* across line *t* in the diagram at the right. Label the reflection R'.

24. Draw $\overline{RR'}$.

25. Draw $\overline{R'O}$.

26. Label the point where $\overline{R'O}$ intersects line *t* as point *P*. Draw $\overline{PR}$.

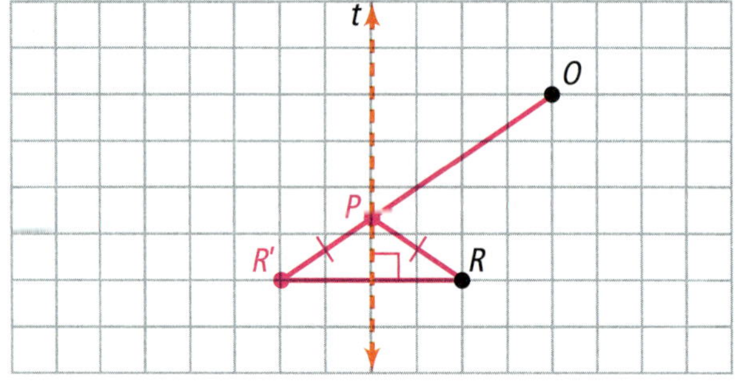

27. What do you notice about point *P* after reflecting *R* across line *t*?

Answers may vary. Sample: Reflecting point *R* across line *t* locates the same point *P* as found in the solution shown in the diagram.

28. Will your classmate's method work? Explain.

Yes. Explanations may vary. Sample: Her method works because both methods locate the point at the same place on line *t*.

Lesson Check • Do you UNDERSTAND?

What are the coordinates of a point $P(x, y)$ reflected across the y-axis? Across the x-axis?

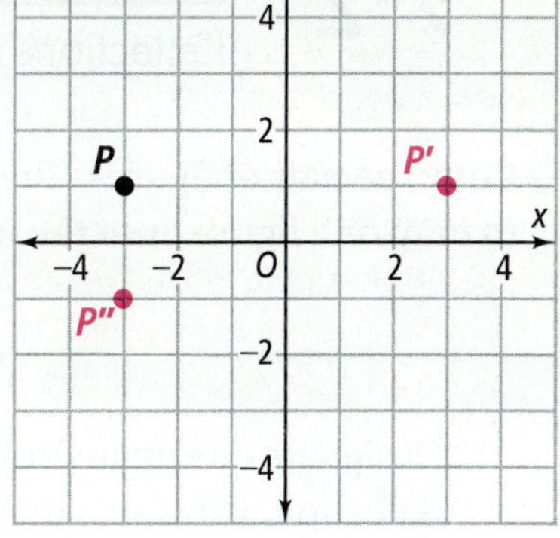

29. Reflect point P across the y-axis. Label the image P'.

30. Circle the coordinates of point P.

(3, 1) (−3, −1) (−3, 1) (3, −1)

31. Circle the coordinates of point P'.

(3, 1) (−3, −1) (−3, 1) (3, −1)

32. Describe how the coordinates of P' are different from the coordinates of P.

The x-coordinates are opposites. The y-coordinates do not change.

33. Reflect point P across the x-axis. Label the image P''. The coordinates of P'' are (−3 , −1).

34. Describe how the coordinates of P'' are different from the coordinates of P.

The x-coordinates do not change. The y-coordinates are opposites.

35. Complete the model below to find the coordinates of $P(x, y)$ reflected across the y-axis and across the x-axis.

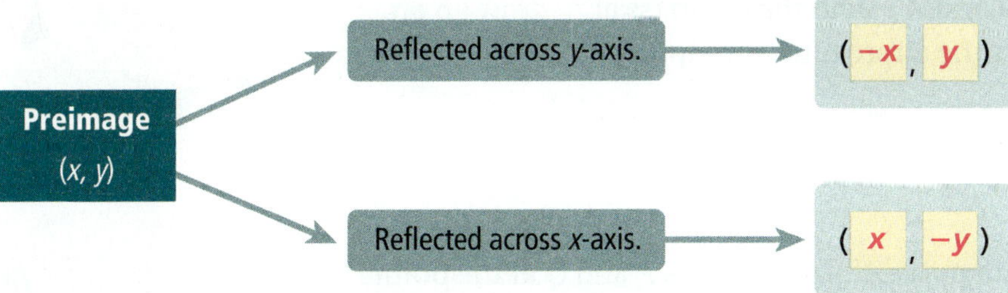

Math Success

Check off the vocabulary words that you understand.

☐ reflection ☐ line of reflection

Rate how well you can *find reflection images of figures*.

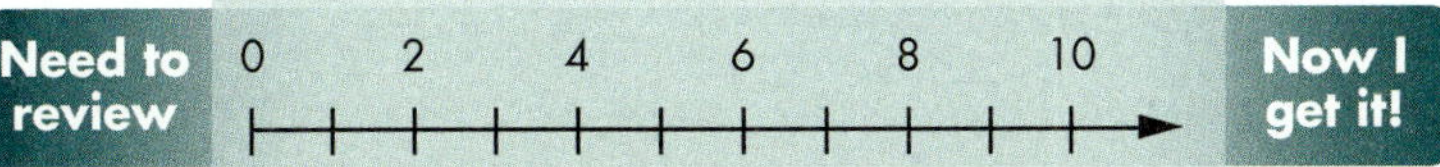

Name ______________________ Class ____________ Date ____________

9-2 Think About a Plan

Reflections

Copy the pair of figures. Then draw the line of reflection you can use to map one figure onto the other. Answers may vary. Samples:

1. Designate one figure to be the preimage and one to be its reflection. Label two points A and B on the preimage and label their images (A' and B') on the reflection.

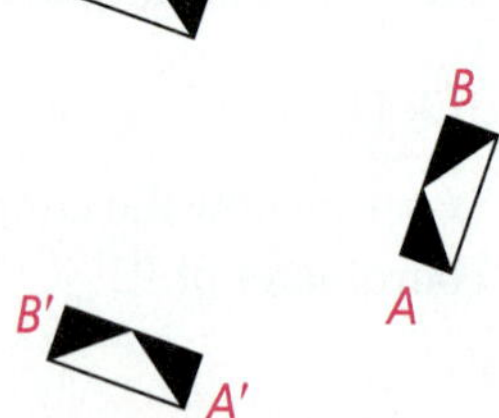

2. Sketch $\overline{AA'}$ and $\overline{BB'}$. This step is optional, but provides a frame of reference for later steps.

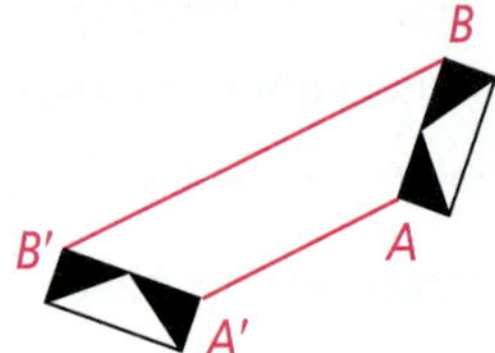

3. Open your compass to a size greater than half the distance between point A and A'. With the compass at A, draw an arc above and below the approximate midpoint of $\overline{AA'}$.

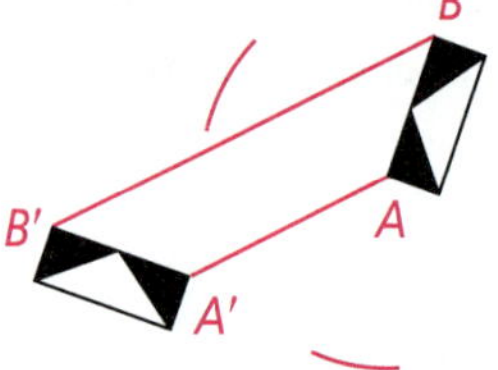

4. Do the same from point A'. Label points P and Q at the points where the arcs intersect.

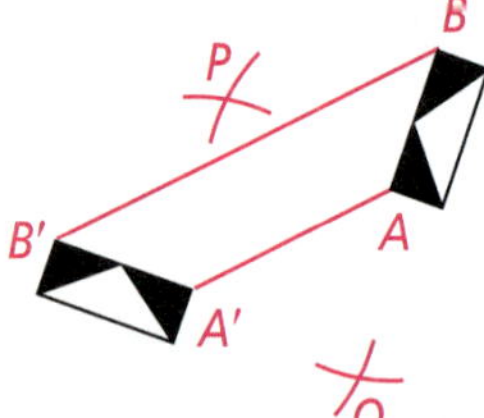

5. Draw $\overline{PQ}$. To check your work, do the same from points B and B'.

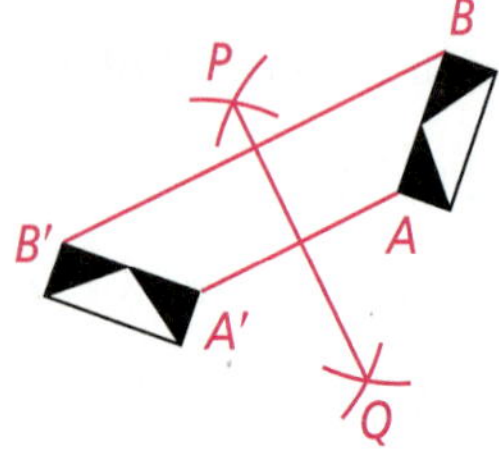

Name ______________________ Class ____________ Date ____________

9-2 Practice
Reflections

Form K

Find the coordinates of each image.

1. $R_{x\text{-axis}}(A)$ (4, −2)
2. $R_{y\text{-axis}}(B)$ (−3, −3)
3. $R_{y=1}(C)$ (−2, −1)
4. $R_{x=-1}(D)$ (2, −3)
5. $R_{y=-3}(E)$ (1, −5)
6. $R_{x=-2}(F)$ (−6, 3)

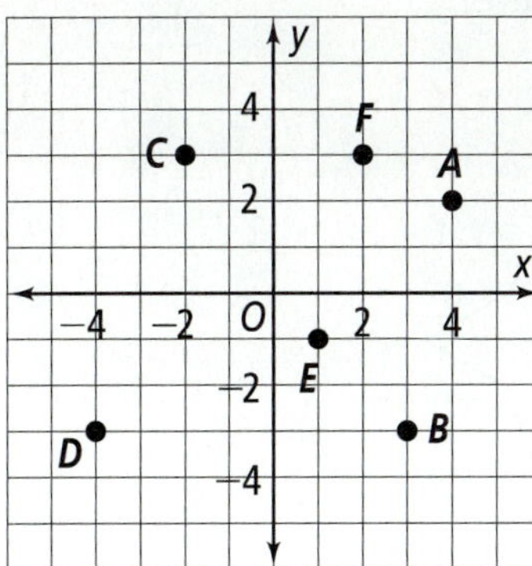

Coordinate Geometry **Given points $S(1, -2)$, $T(4, -1)$, and $V(4, -4)$, graph $\triangle STV$ and its reflection image as indicated.**

7. $R_{y\text{-axis}}$

   To start, draw the triangle and show the *y*-axis as the dashed line of refection.

   Then locate S' so that the *y*-axis is the perpendicular bisector of $\overline{SS'}$.

   Repeat to find T' and V'.

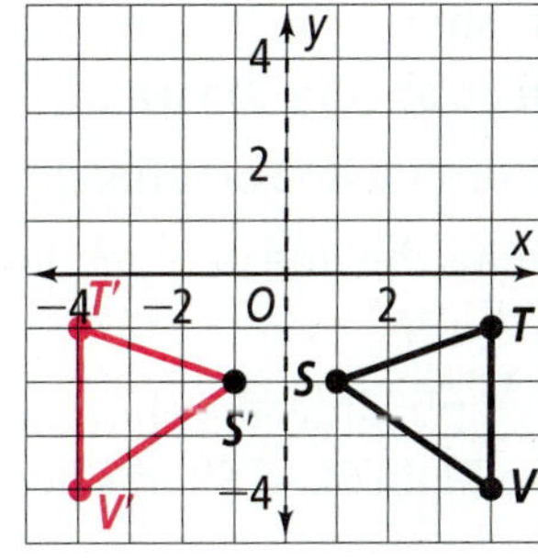

8. $R_{x\text{-axis}}$

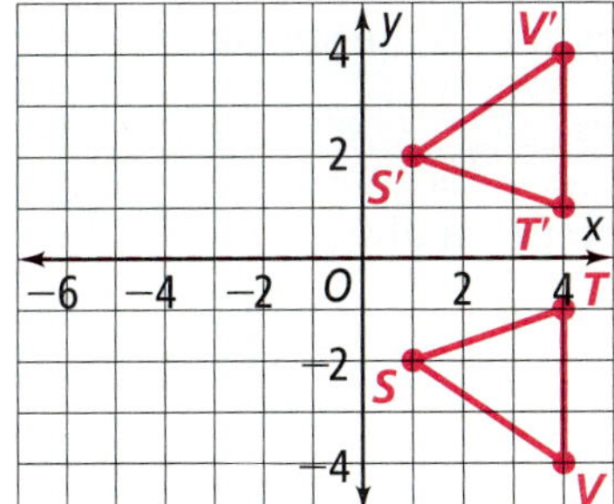

9. $R_{x=-1}$

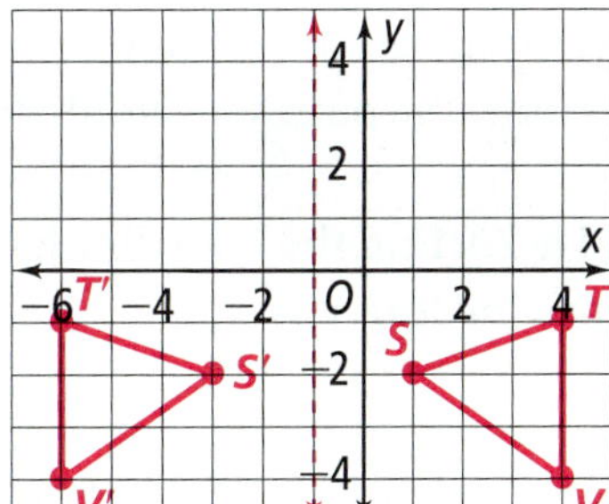

Copy each figure and line ℓ. Draw each figure's reflection image across line ℓ.

10.

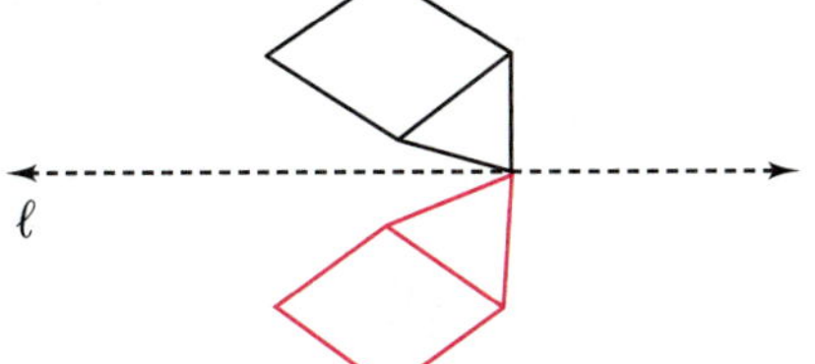

11.

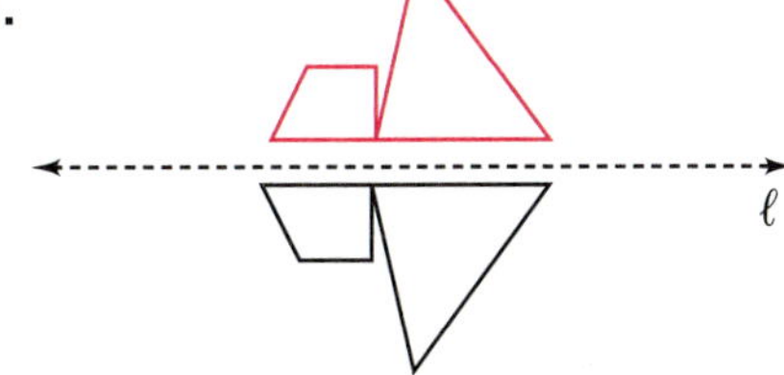

Name _________________________ Class _____________ Date _____________

9-2 Practice (continued)

Form K

Reflections

Copy each pair of figures. Then draw the line of reflection you can use to map one figure onto the other.

12.

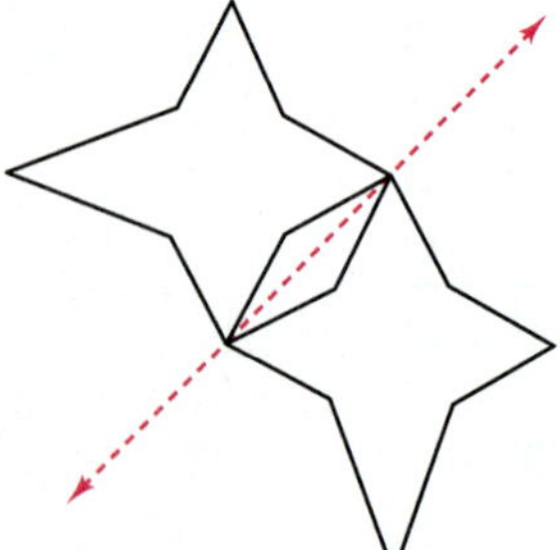

13.

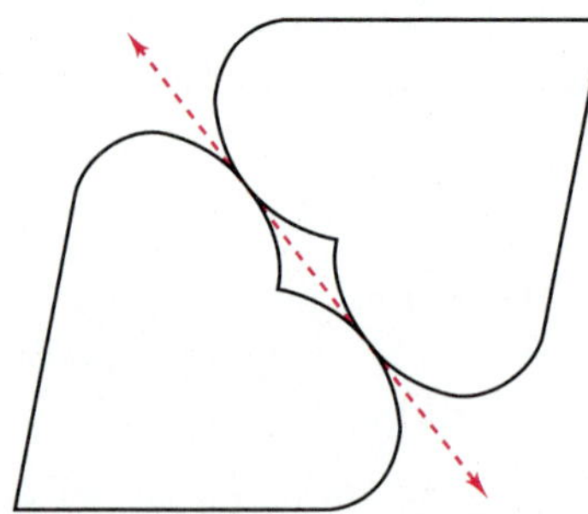

Use the figure at the right to help you solve Exercises 14 and 15.

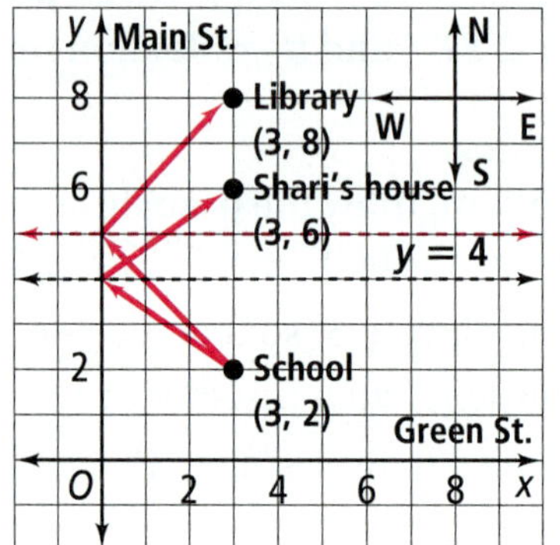

14. Shari wants to start at school, walk to Main St., then continue on to her house. She wants the whole trip to be the shortest distance possible. To which point on Main St. should she walk?

To start, draw a line of reflection $y = 4$.

Where does the line of reflection intersect Main St.? **at (0, 4)**

On the graph, draw the shortest route from school to Main St. to Shari's house.

15. Shari decides instead to walk to the library. She wants to walk the shortest possible total distance, starting from school, walking to Main St., and then to the library. On the graph, draw a line of reflection to help you find the shortest path. Then draw the path she should take to the library.

For Exercises 16–20, find the coordinates of the image of each point after reflection across the line $y = x$.

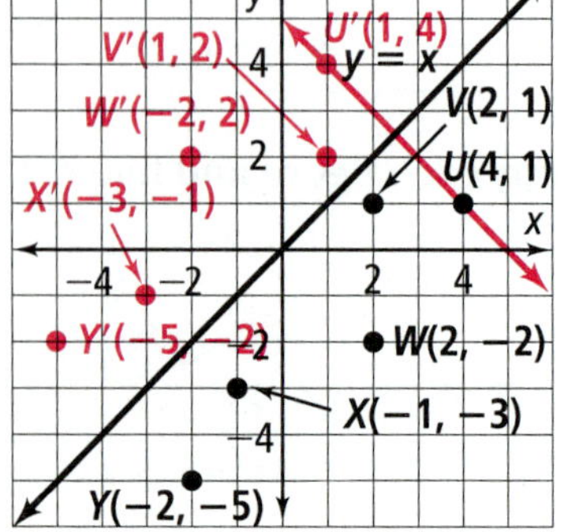

16. $U(4, 1)$ **U′(1, 4)**

To start, draw line ℓ_1 through U perpendicular to $y = x$. The slope of $y = x$ is _?_, so the slope of line ℓ_1 is _?_.

What are the coordinates of U' so that $\overline{UU'}$ is bisected by $y = x$? **1; −1; U′(1, 4)**

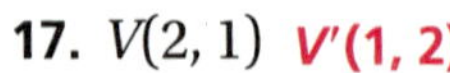

17. $V(2, 1)$ **V′(1, 2)**

18. $W(2, -2)$ **W′(−2, 2)**

19. $X(-1, -3)$ **X′(−3, −1)**

20. $Y(-2, -5)$ **Y′(−5, −2)**

Name ______________________ Class ____________ Date ____________

9-2 Standardized Test Prep

Reflections

Multiple Choice

For Exercises 1–5, choose the correct letter.

1. In the graph at the right, point D is reflected across the y-axis. What are the coordinates of its image? **C**

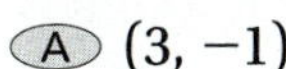

A $(3, -1)$ C $(-3, -1)$

B $(3, 1)$ D $(-3, 1)$

2. The coordinates of the vertices of $\triangle CDE$ are $C(1, 4)$, $D(3, 6)$, and $E(7, 4)$. If the triangle is reflected over the line $y = 3$, what are the coordinates of the image of D? **H**

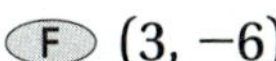

F $(3, -6)$ G $(3, -3)$ H $(3, 0)$ I $(3, 9)$

3. What is true for an image and a preimage in a reflection? **D**

A The image is larger than the preimage.

B The image is smaller than the preimage.

C The image and the preimage have the same orientation.

D The image and the preimage have different orientations.

4. In the graph at the right, what is the line of reflection for $\triangle XYZ$ and $\triangle X'Y'Z'$? **H**

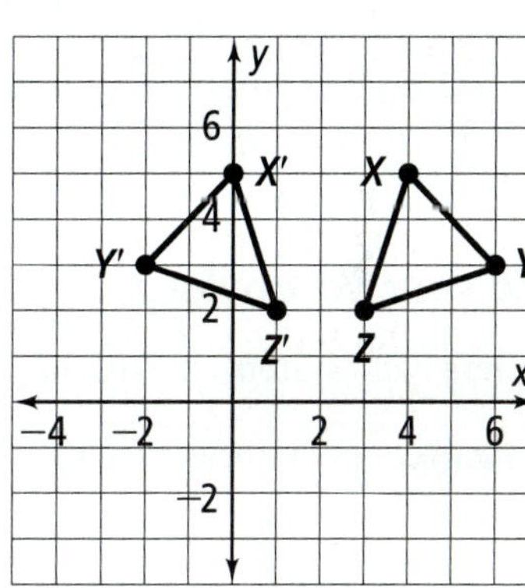

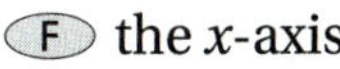

F the x-axis

G the y-axis

H $x = 2$

I $y = 2$

5. What is the image of $A(3, -1)$ after a reflection, first across the line $y = 3$, and then across the line $x = -1$? **A**

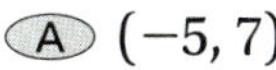

A $(-5, 7)$ C $(-5, -1)$

B $(3, -1)$ D $(1, -5)$

Extended Response

6. $RSTU$ has coordinates $R(0, 0)$, $S(2, 3)$, $T(6, 3)$, and $U(4, 0)$. If the parallelogram is reflected over the line $y = x$, what will the coordinates of the image be?
[4] $R'(0, 0)$, $S'(3, 2)$, $T'(3, 6)$, and $U'(0, 4)$ [3] Any three of the four coordinates are correct. [2] Any two of the four coordinates are correct. [1] Any one of the four coordinates is correct. [0] No correct coordinates are given.

9-3 Rotations

Vocabulary

Review

1. The diagram at the right shows the reflection of point A across a *line of reflection*. Draw the *line of reflection*.

2. Circle the equation of the *line of reflection* in the diagram above.

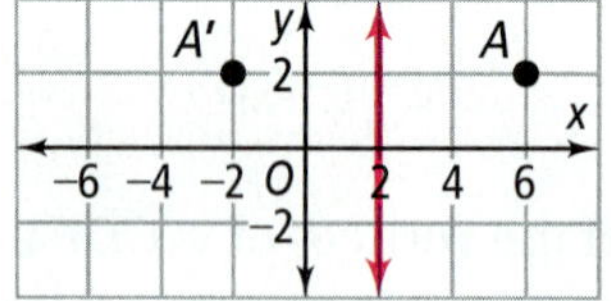

$x = 1$ $y = 1$ $x = 2$ $y = 2$

Vocabulary Builder

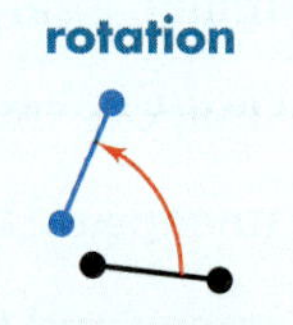

rotation (noun) **roh** TAY **shun**

Definition: A **rotation** is a spinning motion that turns a figure about a point or a line.

Related Words: center of **rotation**, axis of **rotation**

Math Usage: A **rotation** about a point is a transformation that turns a figure clockwise or counterclockwise a given number of degrees.

Use Your Vocabulary

Complete each statement with *always, sometimes,* or *never*.

3. The *rotation* of the moon about Earth _?_ takes a year. never

4. A *rotation* image _?_ has the same orientation as the preimage. always

5. A transformation is _?_ a *rotation*. sometimes

6. A *rotation* is _?_ a transformation. always

7. A 110° counterclockwise *rotation* is the same as a 250° clockwise *rotation* about the same point. always

take note

Key Concept Rotation About a Point

A **rotation** of $x°$ about a point R, called the **center of rotation,** is a transformation with these two properties:

- The image of R is itself (that is, $R' =$ R).
- For any other point V, $RV' = RV$ and $m\angle VRV' = x$.

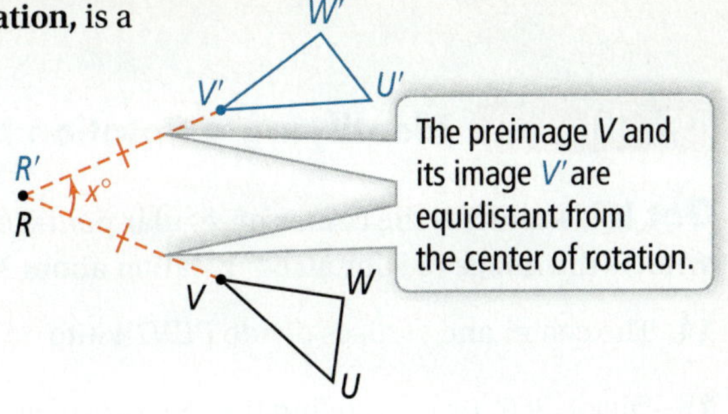

The positive number of degrees a figure rotates is the **angle of rotation.**

A rotation about a point is an isometry.

Use the diagram above for Exercises 8–10.

8. The preimage is $\triangle$ UVW and the image is $\triangle$ U'V'W' .

9. $RW' =$ RW and $m\angle WRW' =$ x .

10. $RU' =$ RU and $m\angle URU' =$ x .

Problem 1 Drawing a Rotation Image

Got It? What is the image of $\triangle LOB$ for a 60° rotation about C?

C • O L B

11. You know that O and O' must be equidistant from C .

12. Follow the steps below to draw the rotation image in the space provided.

Step 1 Use a protractor to draw a 60° counterclockwise angle with vertex C and side $\overline{CO}$.

Step 2 Use a compass to locate O' so that $\overline{CO'} \cong \overline{CO}$.

Step 3 Use a protractor to draw a 60° angle with vertex C and side $\overline{CL}$.

Step 4 Use a compass to Locate L' so that $\overline{CL'} \cong \overline{CL}$.

Step 5 Use a protractor to draw a 60° angle with vertex C and side $\overline{CB}$.

Step 6 Use a compass to locate B' so that $\overline{CB'} \cong \overline{CB}$.

Step 7 Draw $\triangle L'O'B'$.

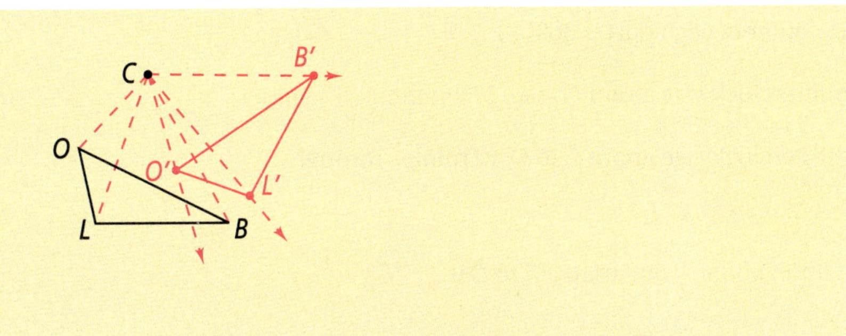

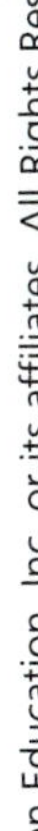

The **center of a regular polygon** is the point that is equidistant from its vertices. The center and the vertices of a regular n-gon determine n congruent triangles.

13. The center and the vertices of a square determine 4 congruent triangles.

Problem 2 Identifying a Rotation Image

Got It? Point X is the center of regular pentagon $PENTA$. What is the image of E for a 144° rotation about X?

14. The center and vertices divide $PENTA$ into 5 congruent triangles.

15. Divide 360° by 5 to find the measure of each central angle.

16. Each central angle measures 72°.

Underline the correct word to complete each sentence.

17. A 144° rotation is one / two / three times the rotation of the measure in Exercise 16.

18. A 144° rotation moves each vertex counterclockwise two / three vertices.

19. Circle the image of E for a 144° rotation about X.

P	E	N	T	A

Problem 3 Finding an Angle of Rotation

Got It? Hubcaps of car wheels often have interesting designs that involve rotation. What is the angle of rotation about C that maps M to Q?

20. The hubcap design has 9 spokes that divide the circle into 9 congruent parts.

21. The angle at the center of each part is 360° ÷ 9 = 40°.

22. As M rotates counterclockwise about C to Q, M touches 6 spokes.

23. As M rotates counterclockwise about C to Q, M rotates through

6 · 40°, or 240°.

24. The angle of rotation about C that maps M to Q is 240°.

Problem 4 Finding a Composition of Rotations

Got It? **What are the coordinates of the image of point $A(-2, 3)$ for a composition of two 90° rotations about the origin?**

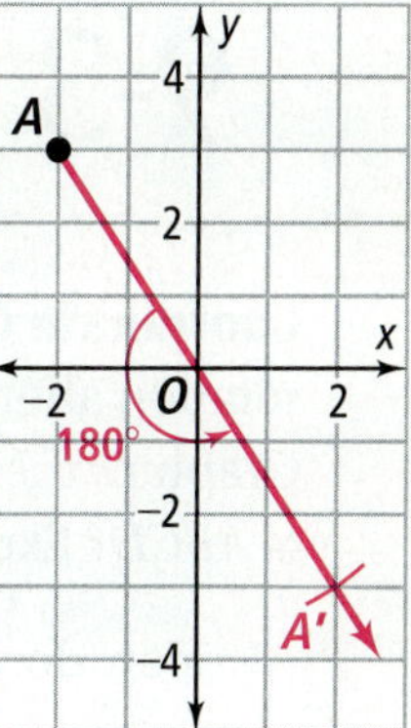

25. The composition of two 90° rotations is one 90° + 90°, or 180° rotation.

26. Complete each step to locate point A' on the diagram at the right.

Step 1 Draw $\overline{AO}$.

Step 2 Use a protractor to draw a 180° angle with the vertex at O and side $\overline{OA}$.

Step 3 Use a compass to construct $\overline{OA'} \cong \overline{OA}$. Graph point A'.

27. The coordinates of A' are (2 , −3).

Lesson Check • Do you UNDERSTAND?

Compare and Contrast **Compare rotating a figure about a point to reflecting the figure across a line. How are the transformations alike? How are they different?**

28. Rotate $\triangle RST$ 90° about the origin.

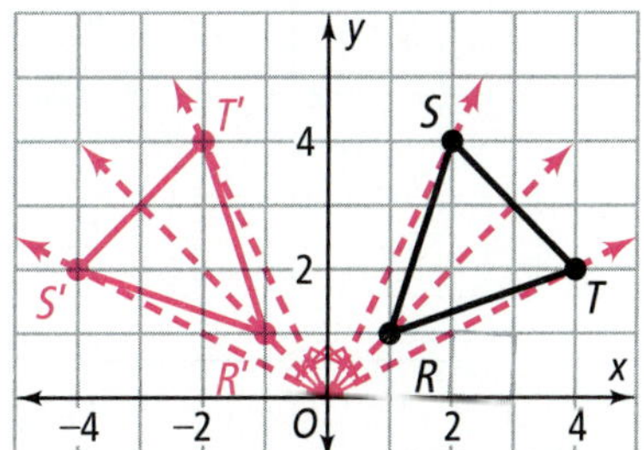

29. Reflect $\triangle RST$ across the y-axis.

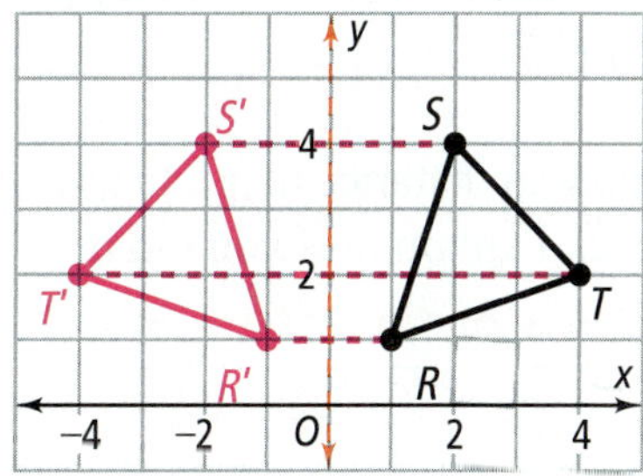

30. Circle the transformation(s) that preserve the size and shape of the preimage. Underline the transformation(s) that preserve the orientation of the preimage.

reflection across a line rotation about a point

31. How are rotating and reflecting a figure alike? How are they different? Answers may vary. Sample:

The size and shape of the figure are the same. A reflection reverses the orientation.

Math Success

Check off the vocabulary words that you understand.

☐ rotation ☐ center of rotation ☐ angle of rotation ☐ center of a regular polygon

Rate how well you can *draw and identify rotation images*.

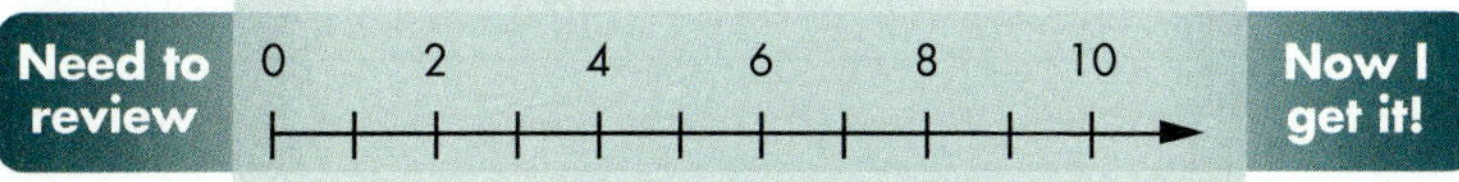

Name ______________________ Class ______________ Date ______________

9-3 Think About a Plan

Rotations

Coordinate Geometry Graph $A(5, 2)$. Graph B, the image of A for a 90° rotation about the origin O. Graph C, the image of A for a 180° rotation about O. Graph D, the image of A for a 270° rotation about O. What type of quadrilateral is $ABCD$? Explain.

1. How do you know that $\overline{AO}$, $\overline{BO}$, $\overline{CO}$, and $\overline{DO}$ will be congruent?

   A, B, C, and D are the same distance from O because the image and preimage are the same distance from the center of rotation.

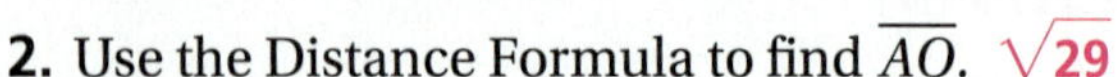

2. Use the Distance Formula to find $\overline{AO}$. $\sqrt{29}$

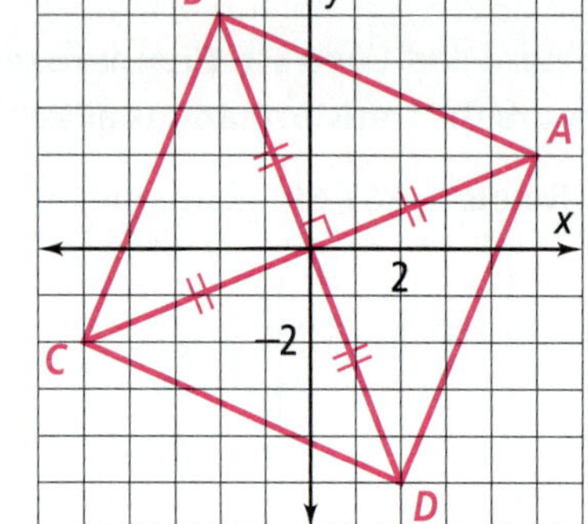

3. Graph A and O. What is the slope of $\overline{AO}$? $\frac{2}{5}$

4. $\overline{BO}$ is perpendicular to $\overline{AO}$. Use the slope of $\overline{AO}$ to find the slope of $\overline{BO}$. $-\frac{5}{2}$

5. Using the slope and distance to guide you, find the coordinates of B. Explain how you did it.

   $B(-2, 5)$; B must lie on the line $y = -\frac{5}{2}x$, so substitute $y = -\frac{5}{2}x$ into $\sqrt{x^2 + y^2} = \sqrt{29}$; $\sqrt{x^2 + (\frac{-5x}{2})^2} = \sqrt{29}$; $x = 2$ or -2

6. Graph B, C, and D. **Check student graphs for $B(-2, 5)$, $C(-5, -2)$, and $D(2, -5)$.**

7. The figure looks like a square. How can you prove it is a square?

   Answers may vary. Sample: Show $AB = BC = CD = DA$ and $m\angle ABC = m\angle BCD = m\angle CDA = m\angle DAC = 90$.

8. How can you use the SAS Congruence Postulate to establish that the sides of $ABCD$ are congruent?

   By Step 1 above, $\overline{AO}$, $\overline{BO}$, $\overline{CO}$, and $\overline{DO}$ are ≅. $m\angle AOB = m\angle BOC = m\angle COD = m\angle DOA = 90$, and so are ≅. Since $\triangle AOB$, $\triangle BOC$, $\triangle COD$, and $\triangle DOA$ are ≅ by SAS ≅, $\overline{AB}$, $\overline{BC}$, $\overline{CD}$, and $\overline{DA}$ are ≅.

9. How can you use what you know about right triangles to show that $ABCD$ must be a square?

   $\triangle AOB$, $\triangle BOC$, $\triangle COD$, and $\triangle DOA$ are isosceles right △, so they must be 45°-45°-90° △. Each 45° ∠ is adjacent to another 45° ∠, so each corner of the quadrilateral is a right angle. A quadrilateral with four 90° angles and sides of equal lengths is a square.

Name ______________________ Class ____________ Date ____________

9-3 Practice

Form K

Rotations

Copy each figure and point *R*. Draw the image of each figure for the given rotation about *R*. Use prime notation to label the vertices of the image.

1. 30°

To start, draw a 30° angle with *R* as the vertex and $\overline{RA}$ as one side.

Locate A' so that $\overline{RA'} \cong$ _?_. $\overline{RA}$

Continue to find B' and C'.

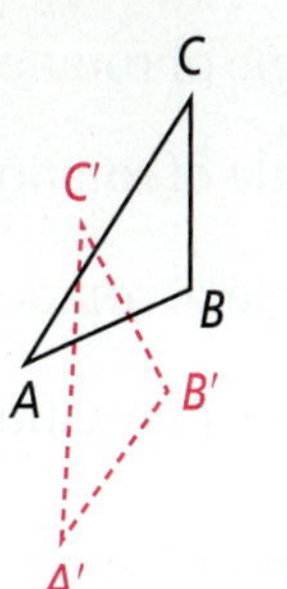

2. 60°

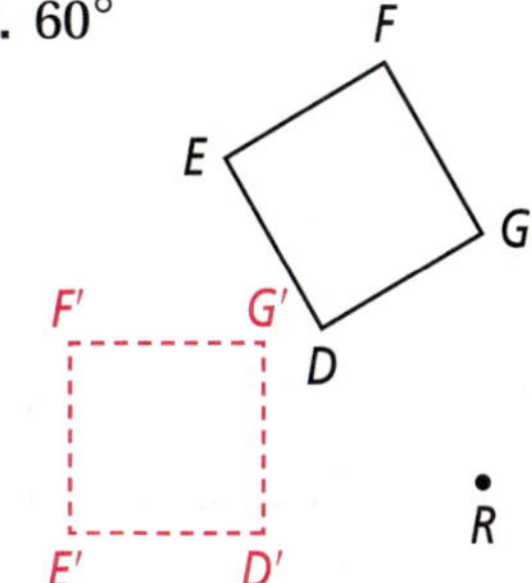

3. 90°

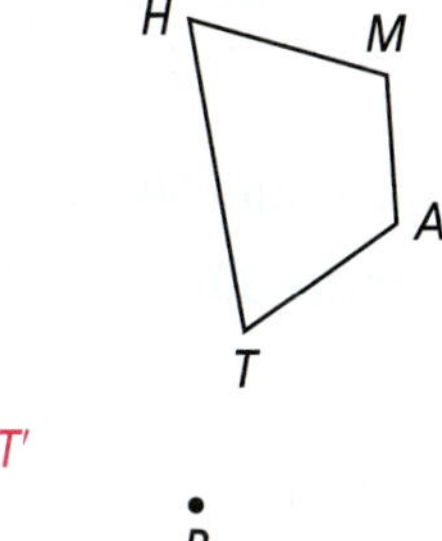

Copy each figure and point *R*. Then draw the image of $\overline{XY}$ for a 120° rotation about *R*. Use prime notation to label the vertices of the image.

4.

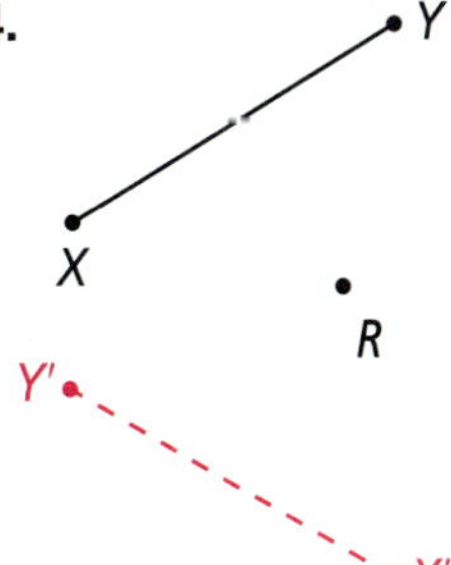

5.

Point *R* is the center of regular quadrilateral *MATH*. Find the image of the given point or segment for the given rotation.

6. 90° rotation of *H* about *R* **T**

7. 180° rotation of *M* about *R* **T**

8. 270° rotation of $\overline{AT}$ about *R* $\overline{TH}$

9. 360° rotation of $\overline{HM}$ about *R* $\overline{HM}$

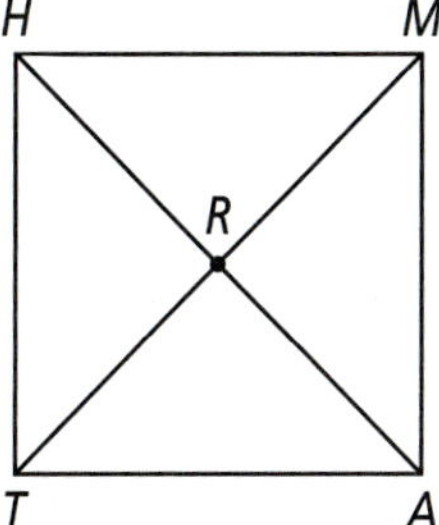

Name ______________________ Class ____________ Date ____________

9-3 Practice (continued) Form K

Rotations

Use the figure at the right for Exercises 10–13. Point M is the center of the regular hexagon.

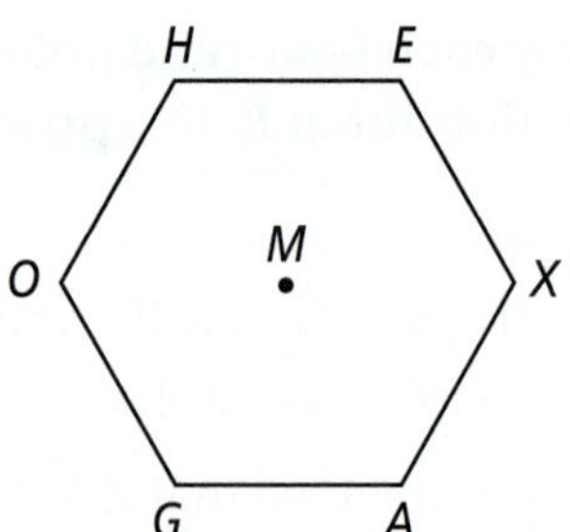

10. What is the angle of rotation that maps H to X? 240°

11. What is the angle of rotation that maps E to G? 180°

12. What is the angle of rotation that maps $\overline{HE}$ to $\overline{AG}$? 180°

13. What is the angle of rotation that maps $\overline{HE}$ to $\overline{GO}$? 120°

For Exercises 14 and 15, copy $\triangle ABC$. Draw the image of $\triangle ABC$ for the given composition of rotations about the given point.

14. 60°, then 30°; R

To start, rotate the figure 60° about R.

Then rotate the figure 30° about R.

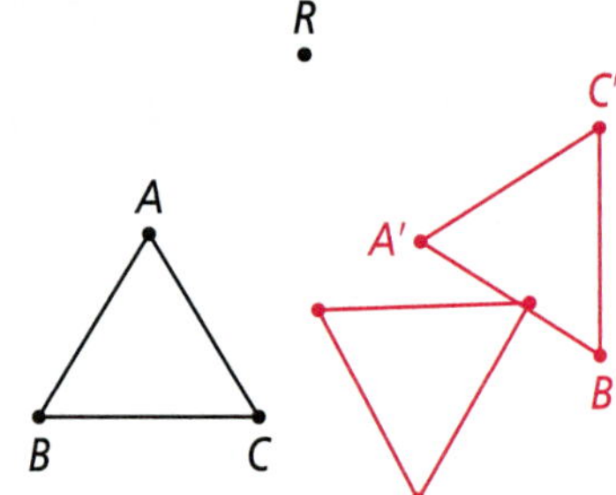

15. 30°, then 135°; P

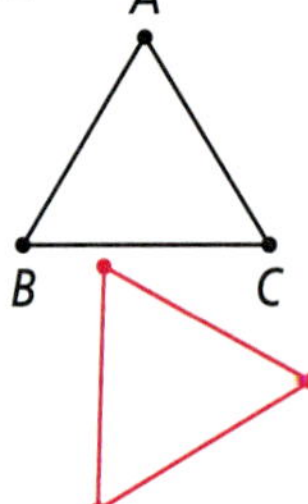

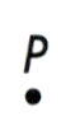

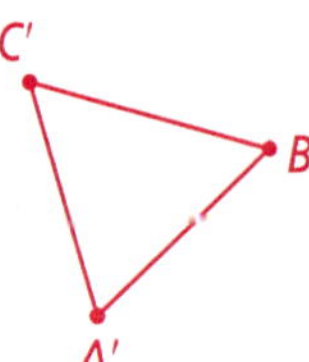

Find the angle of rotation about B that maps the solid-line figure to the dashed-line figure.

16. 270°

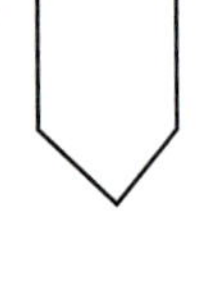

B

17. 135°

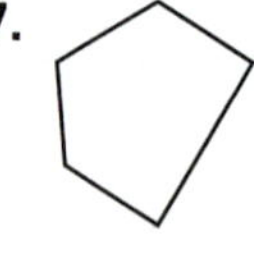

• B

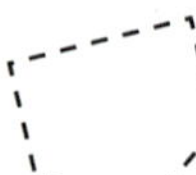

18. $\triangle XYZ$ has vertices at $X(2, 0)$, $Y(0, 0)$, and $Z(0, 5)$. Find the coordinates of the vertices after a 180° rotation about Y.

$X(-2, 0)$, $Y(0, 0)$, $Z(0, -5)$

Name ______________________ Class ____________ Date ____________

9-3 Standardized Test Prep

Rotations

Multiple Choice

In Exercises 1–5, choose the correct letter. Use the figure at the right for Exercises 1 and 2.

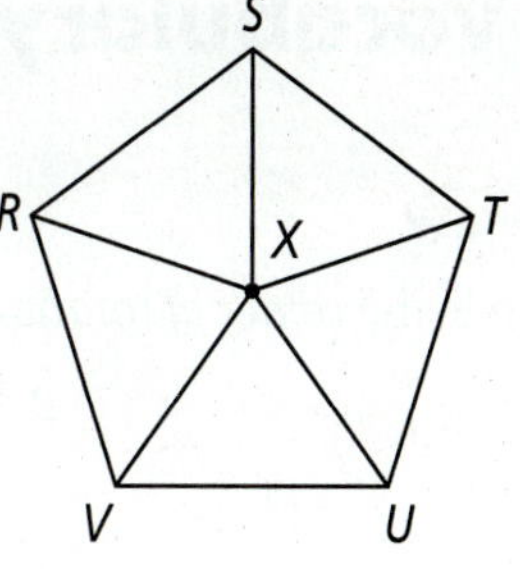

1. Point *X* is the center of regular pentagon *RSTUV*. What is the measure of the angle of rotation that will map *S* onto *U*? **D**

(A) 70 (C) 144

(B) 72 (D) 216

2. Point *X* is the center of regular pentagon *RSTUV*. What is the image of $\overline{RS}$ after a 144° rotation about *X*? **H**

(F) $\overline{ST}$ (G) $\overline{TU}$ (H) $\overline{UV}$ (I) $\overline{VR}$

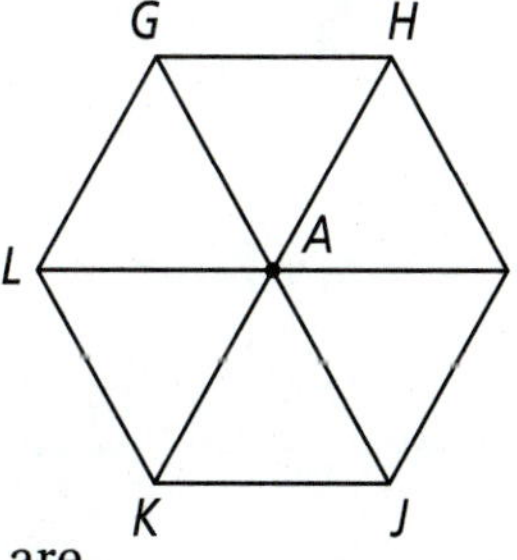

3. Point *A* is the center of regular hexagon *GHIJKL*. What is the image of *I* after a 300° rotation about *A*? **A**

(A) *J* (C) *L*

(B) *K* (D) *M*

4. A Ferris wheel has 16 cars spaced equal distances apart. The cars are numbered 1–16 clockwise. What is the measure of the angle of rotation that will map the position of car 16 onto the position of car 13? **H**

(F) 22.5 (G) 45 (H) 67.5 (I) 90

5. What are the coordinates of (2, −5) after a 90° rotation about the origin? **A**

(A) (5, 2) (B) (−5, 2) (C) (5, −2) (D) (−2, −5)

Short Response

6. △*ABC* has coordinates *A*(3, 3), *B*(0, 0), and *C*(3, 0). If the triangle is rotated 180° about point *B*, what will be the coordinates of the images of *A* and *C* (*A*′ and *C*′)?

[2] *A*′(−3, −3) and *C*′(−3, 0) [1] one correct coordinate given [0] no correct coordinates given

9-4 Symmetry

Vocabulary

Review

1. Circle the *center of rotation* for the transformation at the right.

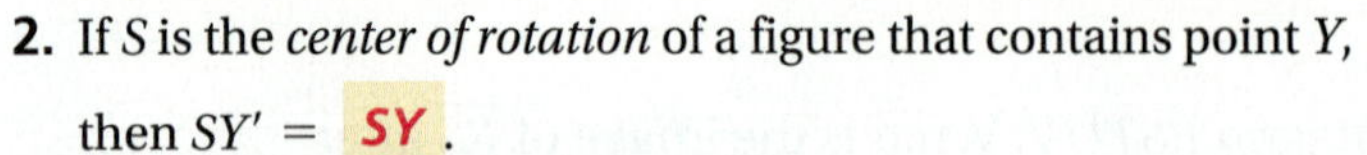

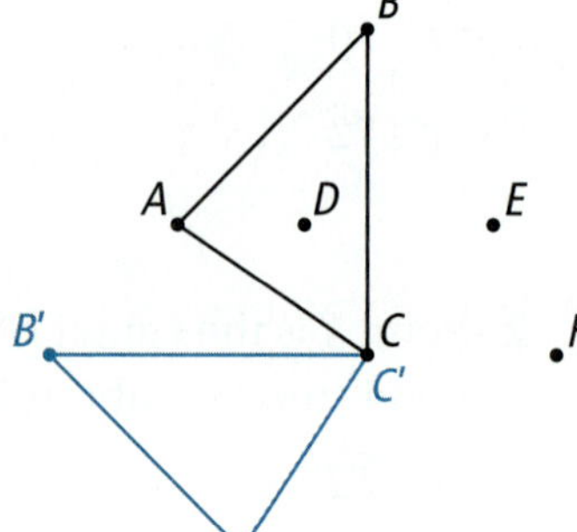

2. If S is the *center of rotation* of a figure that contains point Y, then $SY' =$ **SY**.

3. Cross out the figure(s) for which point A is NOT the *center of rotation*.

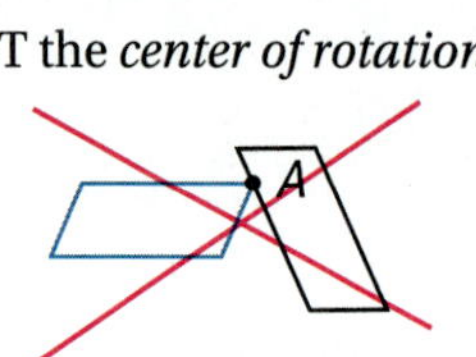

Vocabulary Builder

symmetry (noun) SIM uh tree

Related Word: symmetrical (adjective)

Math Usage: A figure has **symmetry** if there is an isometry that maps the figure onto itself. Figures having **symmetry** are symmetrical.

Use Your Vocabulary

4. Complete each statement with the appropriate form of the word *symmetry*.

NOUN Some figures have rotational _?_. **symmetry**

ADJECTIVE A figure that maps onto itself is _?_. **symmetrical**

Underline the correct word to complete each sentence.

5. A figure that is its own image is symmetrical / *symmetry*.

6. A line of reflection is a line of symmetrical / *symmetry*.

7. A butterfly's wings are symmetrical / *symmetry*.

Key Concept Types of Symmetry

A figure has **line symmetry** or **reflectional symmetry** if there is a reflection for which the figure is its own image. The line of reflection is called a *line of symmetry*. It divides the figure into congruent halves.

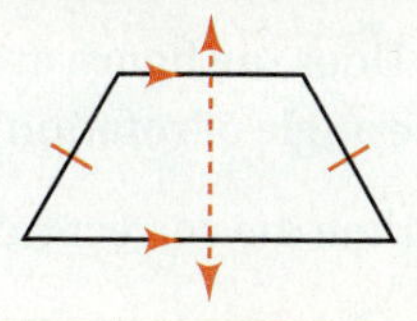

8. Does the trapezoid at the right have a horizontal line of symmetry? Yes / No (circled: No)

A figure has **rotational symmetry** if there is a rotation of 180° or less for which the figure is its own image. The angle of rotation for rotational symmetry is the smallest angle needed for the figure to rotate onto itself.

9. Is the measure of the angle of rotation for an equilateral triangle 60°? Yes / No (circled: No)

A figure with 180° rotational symmetry also has **point symmetry**. Each segment joining a point and its 180° rotation image passes through the center of rotation.

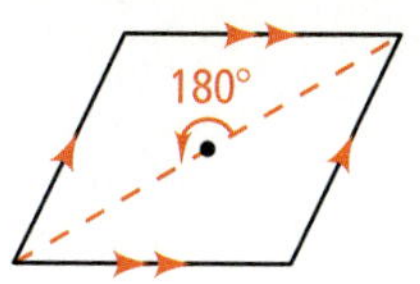

A square, which has both 90° and 180° rotational symmetry, also has point symmetry.

10. Is the center of rotation of the parallelogram at the right equidistant from all vertices? Yes / No (circled: No)

Problem 1 Identifying Lines of Symmetry

Got It? **Draw a rectangle that is not a square. How many lines of symmetry does your rectangle have?**

11. Circle the figure that is a rectangle but not a square.

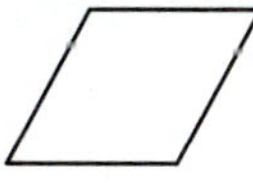 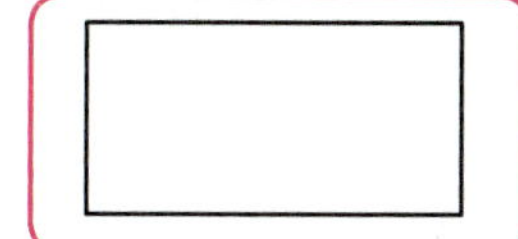 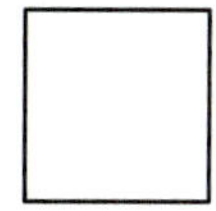

12. Draw a rectangle that is not a square on the grid at the right.

13. Lines of symmetry divide a figure into 2 congruent parts.

14. Draw the line(s) of symmetry on your rectangle.

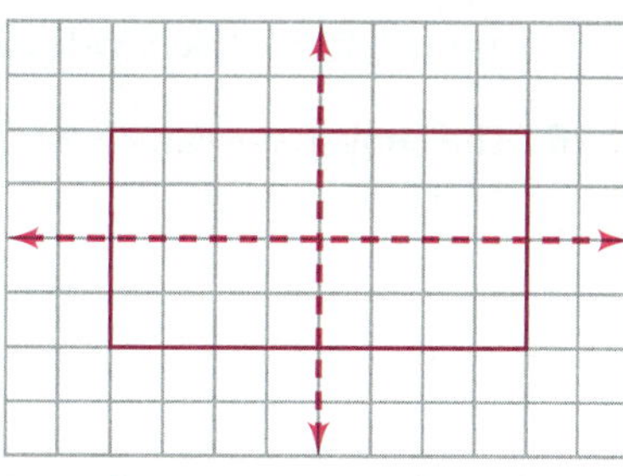

Drawings may vary, but should have one vertical and one horizontal line of symmetry.

15. Does your rectangle have a vertical line of symmetry?

Yes / No (circled: Yes)

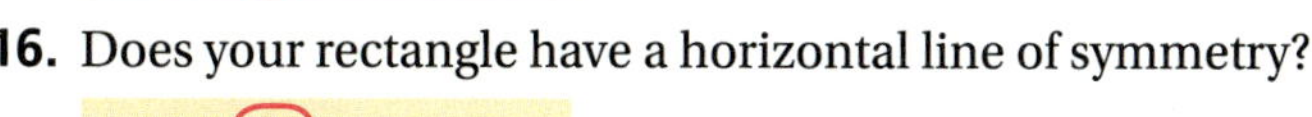

16. Does your rectangle have a horizontal line of symmetry?

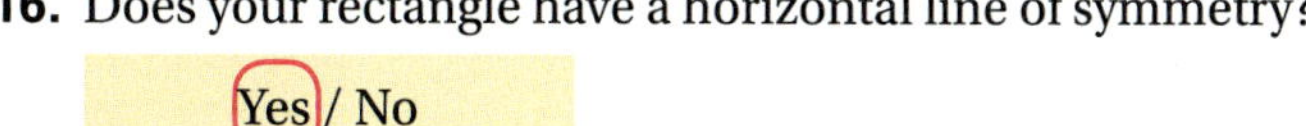

Yes / No (circled: Yes)

17. Does your rectangle have a diagonal line of symmetry?

Yes / No (circled: No)

18. A rectangle that is not a square has 2 line(s) of symmetry.

Problem 2 Identifying Rotational Symmetry

Got It? **Does the figure at the right have rotational symmetry? If so, what is the angle of rotation?**

19. Underline the correct word to complete the sentence.

Each / No side is horizontal or vertical.

20. To keep the same orientation of the sides, the angle of rotation must be a multiple of 90°.

21. Draw the image after a 90° rotation about point *P*. Two sides are drawn for you.

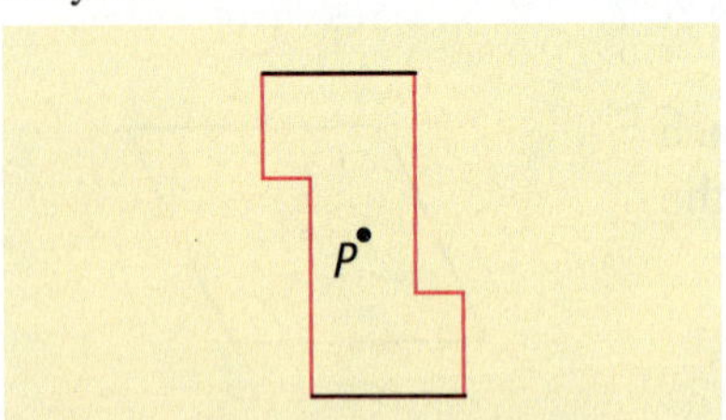

22. Draw the figure after a 180° rotation about point *P*. Two sides are drawn for you.

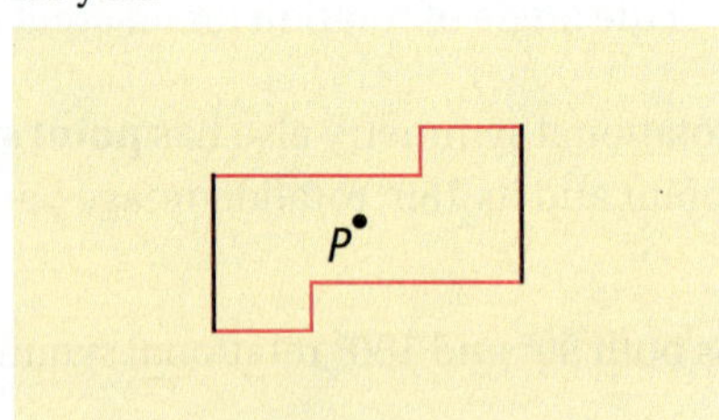

23. Does the figure have rotational symmetry? If so, what is the angle of rotation?

Yes; 180°

Problem 3 Identifying Symmetry in a Three-Dimensional Object

Got It? **Does the lampshade have *reflectional symmetry in a plane*, *rotational symmetry about a line*, or *both*?**

Write T for *true* or F for *false*.

F **24.** A plane that is parallel to the top of the lampshade and passes through its middle divides the lampshade into two congruent parts.

T **25.** A plane that is perpendicular to the top of the lampshade and passes through its middle divides the lampshade into two congruent parts.

F **26.** The lampshade can be rotated about a horizontal line so that it matches perfectly.

T **27.** The lampshade can be rotated about a vertical line so that it matches perfectly.

28. Does the lampshade have *reflectional symmetry in a plane*, *rotational symmetry about a line*, or *both*? Explain.

Both. Explanations may vary. Sample: The lampshade has reflectional symmetry in a vertical plane and rotational symmetry about a vertical line.

Lesson Check • Do you UNDERSTAND?

Error Analysis **Your friend thinks that the regular pentagon in the diagram at the right has 10 lines of symmetry. Explain and correct your friend's error.**

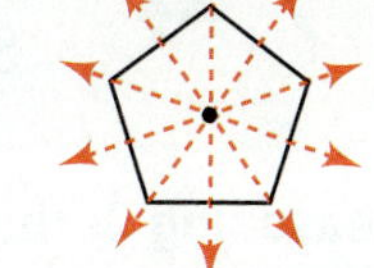

29. Place a ✓ in the box if the response is correct. Place an ✗ if it is incorrect.

- ✓ Each line of symmetry bisects an angle of the pentagon.
- ✓ Each line of symmetry bisects a side of the pentagon.
- ✗ Each line of symmetry is parallel to another line of symmetry.
- ✗ The pentagon has 10 congruent angles.
- ✗ The pentagon has 10 congruent sides.
- ✓ The pentagon has 5 congruent angles.
- ✓ The pentagon has 5 lines of symmetry.

30. Explain your friend's error.

Answers may vary. Sample: Your friend counted each arrow, not each line.

31. Use the regular pentagon below. Draw each line of symmetry in a different color.

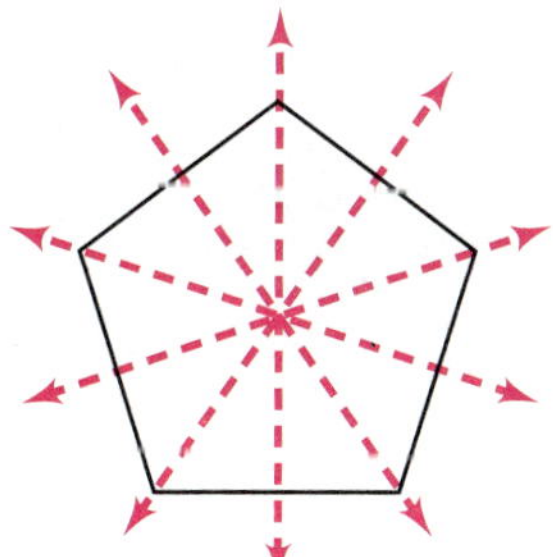

Math Success

Check off the vocabulary words that you understand.

☐ symmetry ☐ line of symmetry

Rate how well you can *identify symmetry in a figure.*

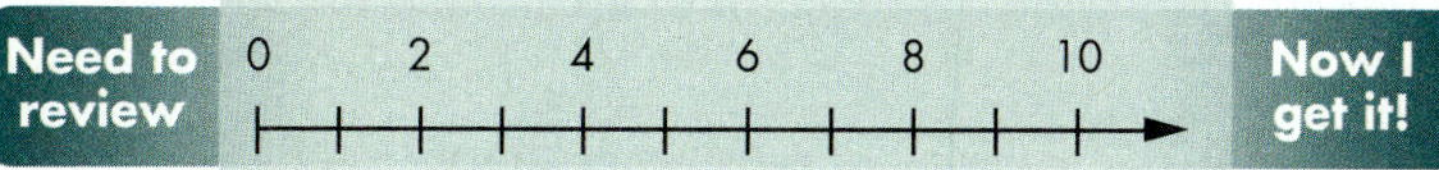

Name ______________________ Class ____________ Date ____________

9-4 Think About a Plan

Symmetry

Reasoning Is the line that contains the bisector of an angle also a line of symmetry of the angle? Explain.

Know

1. What are the properties of an angle bisector?

   An angle bisector is a line that divides the angle into two equal halves.

2. A figure has a line of symmetry if there is a reflection for which the figure is its own image.

3. On the figure at the right, mark information that you already have. For example, line m is an angle bisector, so $m\angle ABC$ = $m\angle A'BD$; check students' work.

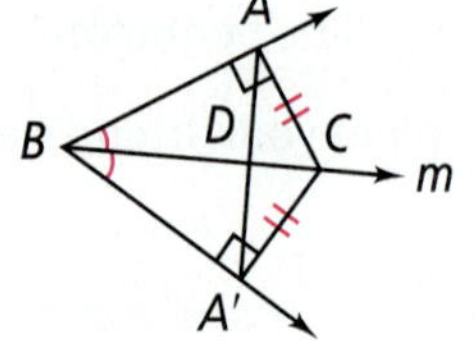

4. By the Angle Bisector Theorem, point C is equidistant from the sides of $\angle ABA'$. What segments can you mark as congruent on your diagram?

   $\overline{AC}$ and $\overline{A'C}$

Need

5. To prove that two points, A and A', are reflections about line m, you need to show that Answers may vary. Sample: $AD = A'D$ and $m\angle ADC = 90$.

Plan

6. Which triangles do you need to prove congruent? How can you prove these triangles are congruent? Answers may vary. Sample: $\triangle ACD$ and $\triangle A'CD$; the sum of $\angle$ measures in a $\triangle$ is 180, so $m\angle ACB = 90 - m\angle ABC$ and $m\angle A'CB = 90 - m\angle A'BC$. Line m is the $\angle$ bisector, so $m\angle ABC = m\angle A'BC$, and therefore $m\angle ACB = m\angle A'CB$. $\overline{DC} \cong \overline{DC}$ by the Refl. Prop. of $\cong$, and $\overline{AC} \cong \overline{A'C}$, so $\triangle ACD \cong \triangle A'CD$ by SAS $\cong$.

7. How can you prove that $AD = A'D$ and $m\angle ADC = m\angle A'DC = 90$?

   $\triangle ADC \cong \triangle A'DC$, so $AD = A'D$ and $\angle ADC \cong \angle A'DC$ by corresp. parts of $\cong$ ⚠ are $\cong$.

   $\angle ADC$ and $\angle A'DC$ are suppl. ⦞, so by Thm. 2-5, $m\angle ADC = m\angle A'DC = 90$.

8. Explain how you know that the line that contains the bisector of an angle is a line of symmetry of the angle.

   Answers may vary. Sample: For any point on $\overline{BA}$, I can show that its corresponding point on $\overline{BA'}$ is a reflection across the angle bisector, line m.

Name ______________________________ Class ____________ Date ____________

9-4 Practice

Form K

Symmetry

Tell what type(s) of symmetry each figure has. If it has line symmetry, sketch the line(s) of symmetry. If it has rotational symmetry, tell the angle of rotation.

1. To start, look for the ways that the figure will reflect across a line onto itself.
line symmetry

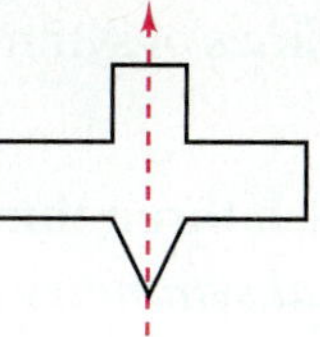

2. Look for a possible center point.
Think about angles formed by joining image-preimage pairs to the center. All these angles must be _?_ for a figure to have rotational symmetry.
congruent; rotational symmetry; 90°

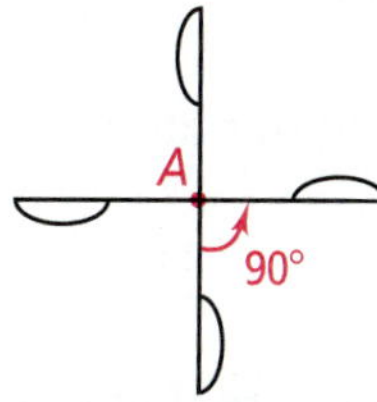

3. line symmetry

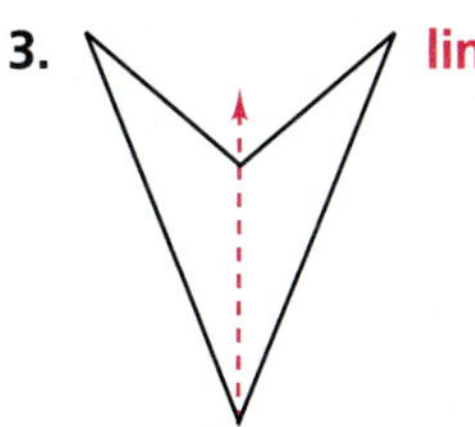

4. none

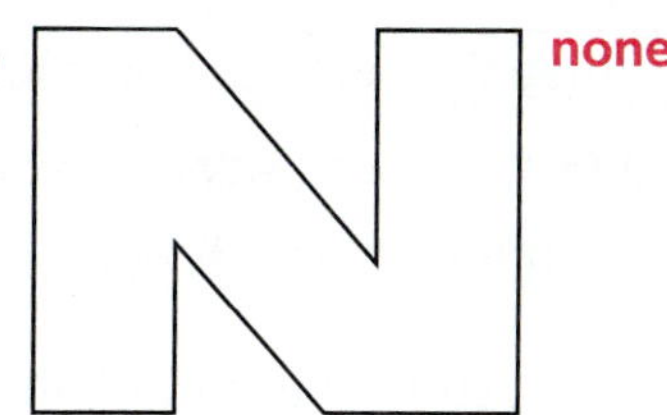

5. line, rotational, and point symmetry; 90°

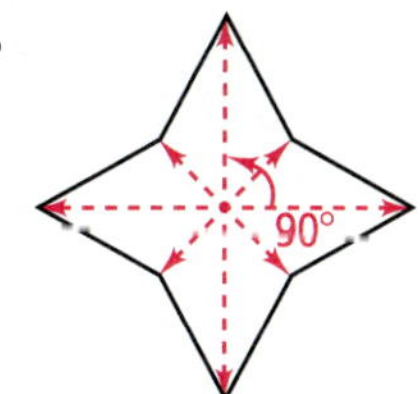

6. point symmetry; rotational symmetry; 180°

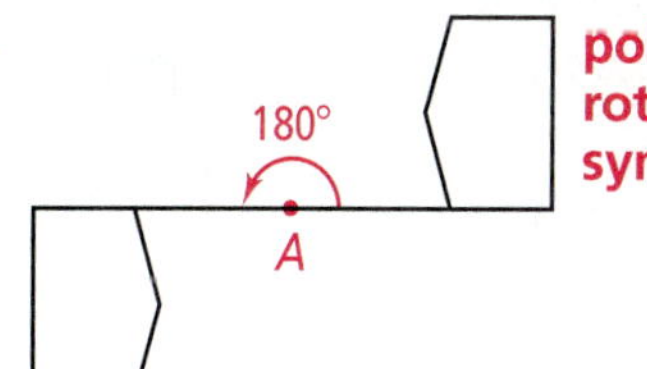

Determine how many lines of symmetry each type of polygon has. Include a sketch to support your answer.

7. equilateral triangle 3

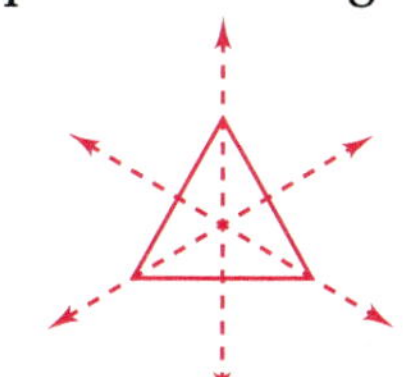

8. square 4

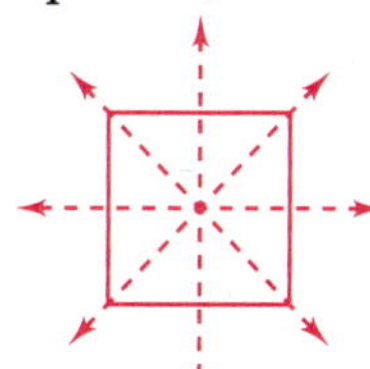

9. regular pentagon 5

10. regular octagon 8

Name ______________________ Class ____________ Date ____________

9-4 Practice (continued) — Form K

Symmetry

11. **Make a Conjecture** What is the relationship between the number of sides of a regular polygon and the number of lines of symmetry? **The number of lines of symmetry of a regular polygon is the same as the number of sides.**

12. How many lines of symmetry are found in a regular polygon with 40 sides? **40**

Tell whether each three-dimensional object has *reflectional symmetry in a plane, rotational symmetry about a line,* or *both.*

13. a light bulb **both**

14. a pair of pants **reflectional symmetry in a plane**

15. a rectangular table **both**

16. a round table **both**

17. a sand dollar **both**

18. butterfly **reflectional symmetry in a plane**

19. Draw a figure that has:

 a. point symmetry **Check students' work.**

 b. line symmetry **Check students' work.**

 c. rotational symmetry **Check students' work.**

20. A club uses the secret code words below. Describe the types of symmetry, if any, of each code word.

A
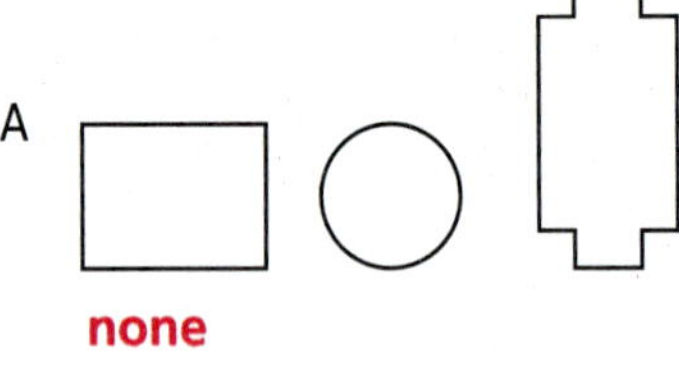
none

B
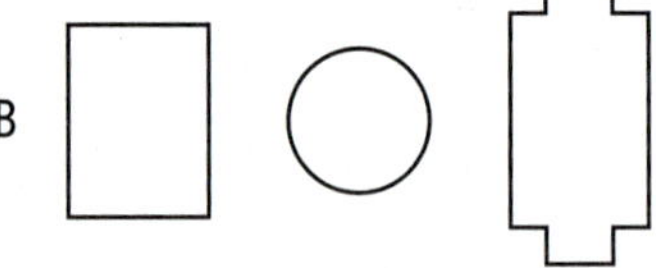
line symmetry

C

rotational symmetry, point symmetry

D
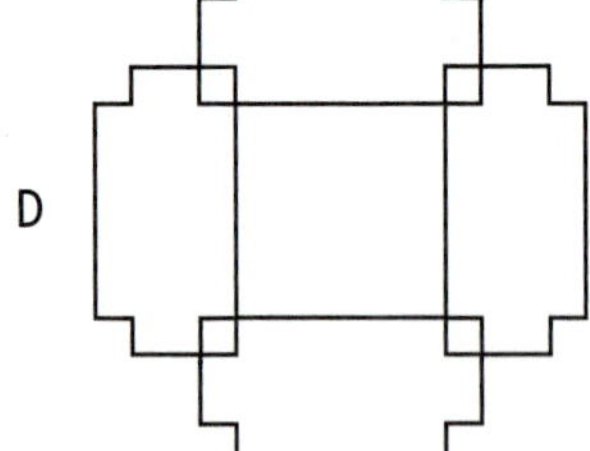
line symmetry, rotational symmetry, point symmetry

E

line symmetry

F
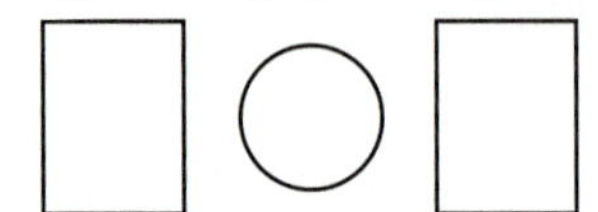
line symmetry, rotational symmetry, point symmetry

Name ______________________ Class __________ Date __________

9-4 Standardized Test Prep

Symmetry

Multiple Choice

For Exercises 1–5, choose the correct letter.

1. Which type(s) of symmetry does the uppercase letter N have? C

A reflectional symmetry
C rotational and point symmetry
B rotational symmetry
D reflectional and rotational symmetry

2. Which type of symmetry is shown by the lowercase letter w? F

F reflectional symmetry
H no symmetry
G point symmetry
I rotational symmetry

3. What type(s) of symmetry is shown in the figure below? C

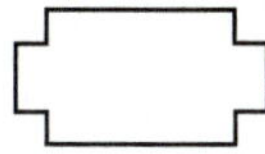

A reflectional symmetry
C reflectional, rotational, and point symmetry
B point symmetry
D rotational symmetry

4. Which of the following three-dimensional objects has rotational symmetry about a line? H

F a car
H a rolling pin
G a set of rectangular stairs
I a stapler

5. How many lines of symmetry are there in a regular decagon? C

A 0
C 10
B 5
D 20

Short Response

6. Does the figure have point symmetry, rotational symmetry, or both? Explain.

[2] Rotational symmetry only; it can be rotated onto itself but the angle of rotation is less than or greater than 180°. [1] Student gives correct answer but incomplete explanation. [0] Student incorrectly identifies type of symmetry.

9-5 Dilations

Vocabulary

Review

Complete each statement with *ratio* or *similar*.

1. The __?__ of corresponding parts of similar figures is the *scale factor*. **ratio**

2. You can use a *scale factor* to make a larger or smaller copy that is __?__ to the original figure. **similar**

3. Circle the *scale factor* that makes an image larger than the preimage.

$\frac{2}{3}$	$\frac{4}{3}$ (circled)	$\frac{7}{8}$	$\frac{1}{10}$

4. Circle the *scale factor* that makes an image smaller than the preimage.

$\frac{5}{2}$	$\frac{9}{2}$	$\frac{1}{4}$ (circled)	3

Vocabulary Builder

dilation (noun) dy LAY shun

Definition: A **dilation** is the widening of an object such as the pupil of an eye or a blood vessel.

Math Usage: A **dilation** is a transformation that reduces or enlarges a figure so that the image is similar to the preimage.

Related Words: reduction, enlargement, scale factor, center of dilation

Examples: an enlargement of a photograph, a model of the solar system

Use Your Vocabulary

5. Underline the correct word to complete the sentence.

A *dilation* is an enlargement if the figure decreases / increases (underlined) in size.

6. Cross out the transformation that does NOT have a center.

~~reflection~~	rotation	dilation

7. Circle the transformations that are isometries.

reflection (circled)	rotation (circled)	dilation

take note

Key Concept Dilation

A **dilation** with center C and **scale factor** n, $n > 0$, is a transformation with these two properties:

- The image of C is itself (that is, $C' = C$).
- For any other point R, R' is on $\overrightarrow{CR}$ and $CR' = n \cdot CR$, or $n = \frac{CR'}{CR}$.

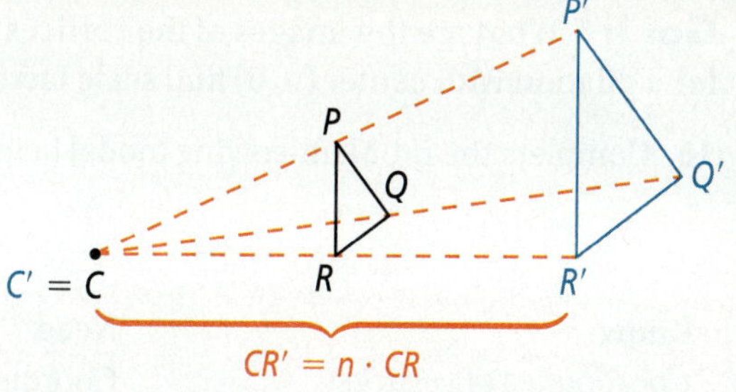

The image of a dilation is similar to its preimage.

8. For a dilation of $\triangle PQR$ with scale factor 2, $CR' =$ 2 $\cdot CR$.

Problem 1 Finding a Scale Factor

Got It? $J'K'L'M'$ **is a dilation image of** $JKLM$**. The center of dilation is** O**. Is the dilation an** ***enlargement*** **or a** ***reduction*****? What is the scale factor of the dilation?**

Underline the correct word to complete each sentence.

9. The image is larger / <u>smaller</u> than preimage.

10. The dilation is a(n) enlargement / <u>reduction</u>.

11. How can you tell which segments are corresponding sides of $JKLM$ and $J'K'L'M'$?

Answers may vary. Sample: Corresponding sides have the same letters as endpoints and are listed in the same order.

12. Circle the side that corresponds to $\overline{JK}$.

($\overline{J'K'}$) $\overline{J'M'}$ $\overline{L'K'}$

13. Find the length of each side.

$$JK = \sqrt{(6 - 0)^2 + (0 - 2)^2} = \sqrt{40}$$

$$J'K' = \sqrt{(3 - 0)^2 + (0 - 1)^2} = \sqrt{10}$$

14. Find the scale factor.

$$\frac{J'K'}{JK} = \frac{\sqrt{10}}{\sqrt{40}} = \sqrt{\frac{1}{4}} = \frac{1}{2}$$

15. The scale factor is $\frac{1}{2}$.

Problem 2 Finding a Dilation Image

Got It? **What are the images of the vertices of $\triangle PZG$ for a dilation with center (0, 0) and scale factor $\frac{1}{2}$?**

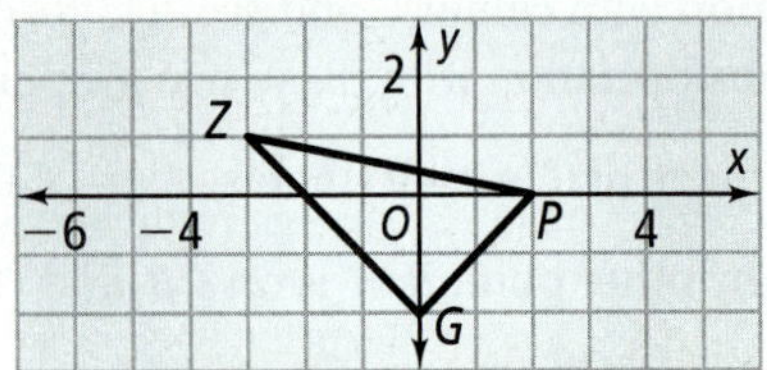

16. Complete the problem-solving model below.

Know
Coordinates of vertices:
$P(2, 0)$, $Z(-3, 1)$,
and $G(0, -2)$
Center of dilation:

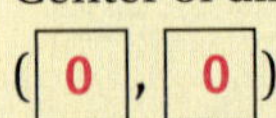

(0, 0)

Scale factor: $\frac{1}{2}$

Need
Coordinates of the images of the vertices

Plan
Substitute the coordinates of the vertices into the dilation rule: $(x, y) \rightarrow$
$\left(\frac{1}{2} \cdot x, \frac{1}{2} \cdot y\right)$

17. Use the dilation rule to find the coordinates of the images of the vertices.

$P(2, 0) \rightarrow P'(1, 0)$

$Z(-3, 1) \rightarrow Z'\left(-\frac{3}{2}, \frac{1}{2}\right)$

$G(0, -2) \rightarrow G'(0, -1)$

18. Graph the images of the vertices of $\triangle PZG$ on the coordinate plane. Graph $\triangle P'Z'G'$.

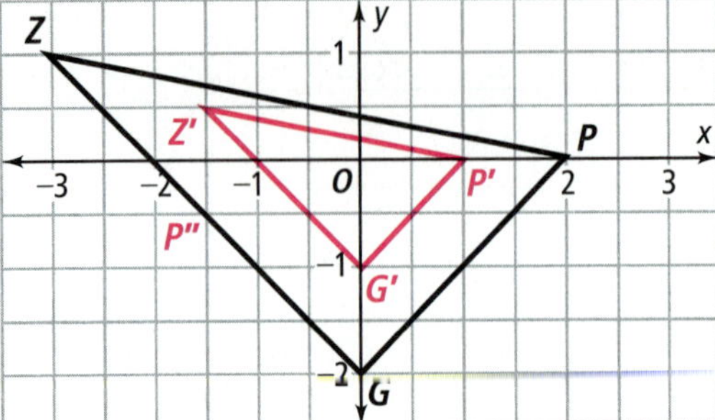

Problem 3 Using a Scale Factor to Find a Length

Got It? **The height of a document on your computer screen is 20.4 cm. When you change the zoom setting on your screen from 100% to 25%, the new image of your document is a dilation of the previous image with scale factor 0.25. What is the height of the new image?**

19. Underline the correct word to complete the sentence.

The scale factor 0.25 is less than 1, so the dilation is a(n) enlargement / reduction.

20. Image length = scale factor · original length, so image height = 0.25 · 20.4,

or 5.1 cm.

Lesson Check • Do you UNDERSTAND?

Error Analysis **The blue figure is a dilation image of the black figure for a dilation with center *A*.**

Two students made errors when asked to find the scale factor. Explain and correct their answers.

A.

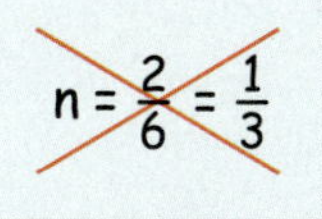

B.

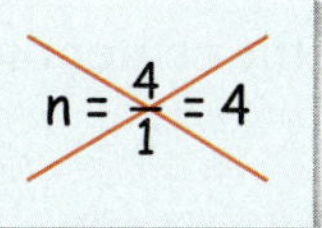

Write T for *true* or F for *false*.

F 21. The dilation is an enlargement.

F 22. The side lengths of the black triangle are 6 and 3.

T 23. The side lengths of the blue triangle are 2 and 1.

T 24. The scale factor is between 0 and 1.

25. Explain the error the student made in solution A.

Answers may vary. Sample: The student did not use the length 8 of the black triangle.

26. Explain the error the student made in solution B.

Answers may vary. Sample: The student didn't write the image length in the numerator.

27. The correct scale factor is $\frac{1}{4}$.

Math Success

Check off the vocabulary words that you understand.

- ☐ dilation
- ☐ center of dilation
- ☐ scale factor of a dilation
- ☐ enlargement
- ☐ reduction

Rate how well you *understand dilation images of figures.*

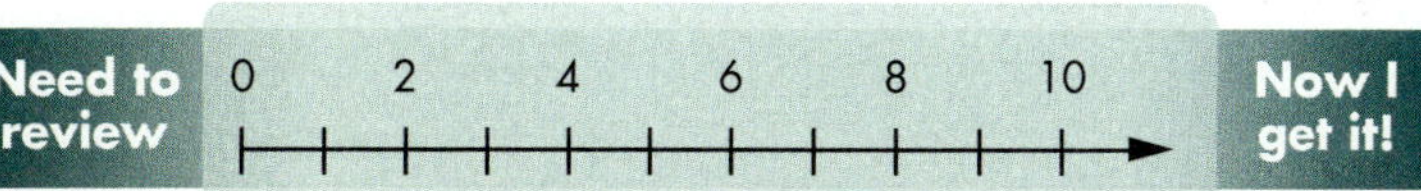
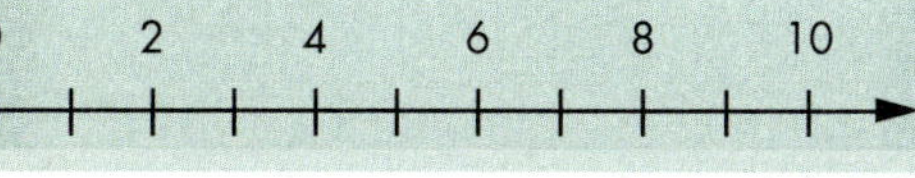

Name ______________________ Class ____________ Date ____________

9-5 Think About a Plan

Dilations

Reasoning You are given $\overline{AB}$ and its dilation image $\overline{A'B'}$ with A, B, A', and B' noncollinear. Explain how to find the center of dilation and scale factor.

Know

1. What do you know about the relationship of A, A', and C, the center of dilation?

   They are collinear.

2. Is this true also of B, B', and C? **yes**

3. What relationship exists between the lengths of the segments $\overline{A'B'}$ and $\overline{AB}$?

   Their ratio is the scale factor.

Need

4. Is it possible to answer this question using a specific point C and a specific scale factor? Explain.

   No; there is not enough information given. The answer can only be given in general terms.

Plan

5. How do you find the center of dilation?

   Draw a line connecting A and A' and a second line connecting B and B'. Point C will be at the point where the two intersect.

6. How do you find the scale factor?

   Simplify the ratio of $\frac{\text{length of image}}{\text{length of preimage}}$, or $\frac{A'B'}{AB}$.

Name ______________________ Class ____________ Date ____________

9-5 Practice

Form K

Dilations

The dashed-line figure is a dilation image of the solid-line figure. The labeled point is the center of dilation. Tell whether the dilation is an enlargement or a reduction. Then find the scale factor of the dilation.

1. To start, identify whether the image is larger or smaller than the preimage.

Next, find the scale factor:

$$\frac{\text{image length}}{\text{preimage length}} = \frac{\boxed{1}}{\boxed{2}}$$ reduction

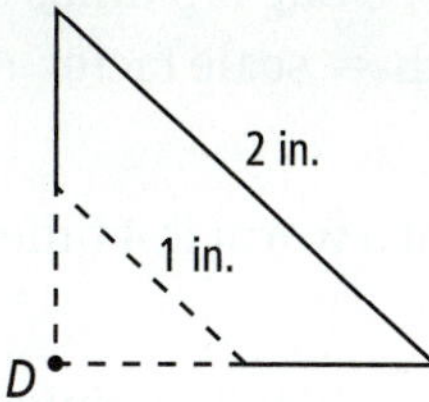

2.

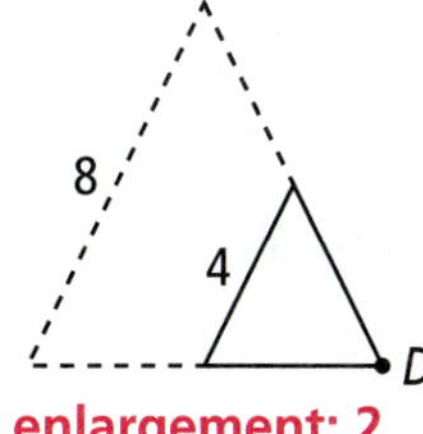

enlargement; 2

3.

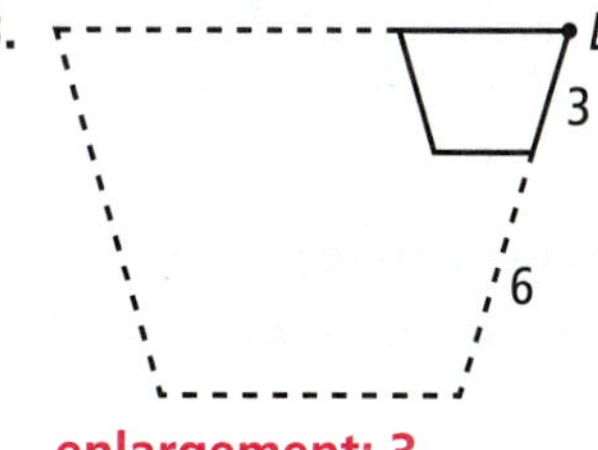

enlargement; 3

4.

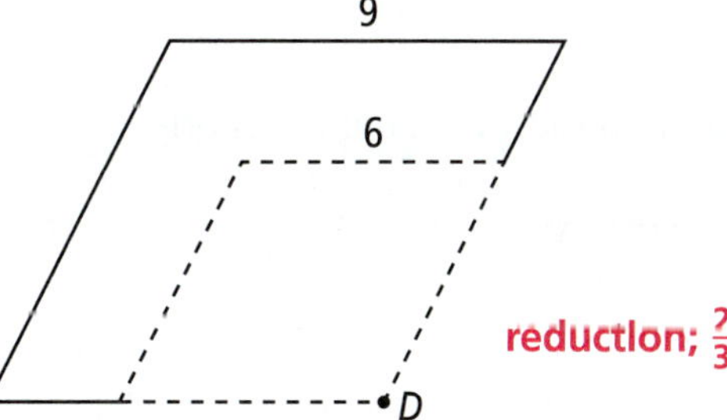

reduction; $\frac{2}{3}$

5.

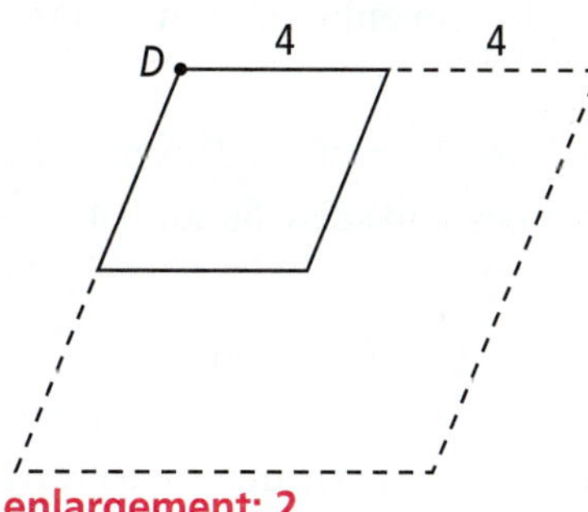

enlargement; 2

A dilation has center (0, 0). Find the image of each point for the given scale factor.

6. $B(2, 3)$; 6 (12, 18)

To start, multiply each coordinate by the scale factor.

$(2 \cdot \boxed{6}, 3 \cdot \boxed{6}) \rightarrow (\boxed{12}, \boxed{18})$

7. $D(7, 2)$; 3 (21, 6)

8. $U(-3, -2)$; 3 (−9, −6)

9. $A(0, -5)$; $\frac{2}{5}$ (0, −2)

10. $G(3, 1)$; −4 (−12, −4)

11. $R(-3, 5)$; $\frac{1}{4}$ $\left(-\frac{3}{4}, 1\frac{1}{4}\right)$

12. $X\left(\frac{1}{2}, -3\right)$; −2 (−1, 6)

Name ______________________ Class ____________ Date ____________

9-5 Practice (continued) — Form K

Dilations

You look at each object described in Exercises 13–15 under a magnifying glass. Find the actual dimension of each object.

13. The image of a bug is 5 times its actual size and has a width of 1.5 cm.
image length = scale factor · actual length = __?__ · __?__ = __?__ 1.5 cm; 5; *x*; 0.3 cm

14. The image of a worm is 4 times its actual size and has a length of 7 cm. $\frac{7}{4}$ cm

15. The image of a hair is 10 times its actual size and has a length of 0.4 cm. 0.04 cm

16. A dilation maps $\triangle QRS$ to $\triangle Q'R'S'$. $QR = 10$ in. and $Q'R' = 12$ in. If $RS = 12$ in., what is $R'S'$? 14.4 in.

17. A dilation on a coordinate grid has center (0, 0) and scale factor 2.5. Point *A* is at (3, 7). What is the *y*-coordinate of the image of *A*? 17.5

18. $\triangle A'B'C'$ is a dilation image of $\triangle ABC$. The scale factor for the dilation is 1.25. Is the dilation an enlargement or a reduction? enlargement

19. A square has 12-cm sides. Describe its image for a dilation with center at one of the vertices and scale factor 0.4. The dilation image will be a square with 4.8-cm sides that shares the vertex that is the dilation center with the original square. The sides will be parallel to or along the original sides.

20. Graph pentagon *PENTA* and its image $P'E'N'T'A'$ for a dilation with center (0, 0) and scale factor 0.5. The vertices of *PENTA* are: $P(0, 4)$, $E(6, 6)$, $N(4, 0)$, $T(0, -4)$, $A(-2, 0)$.

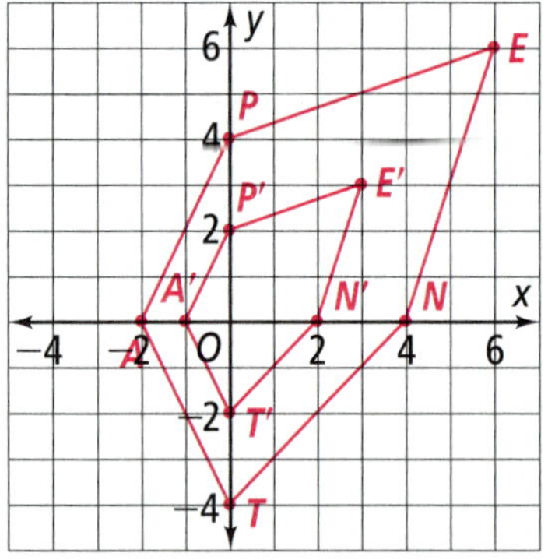

A dilation maps ΔMNO onto $\Delta M'N'O'$. Find the missing values.

21. $MN = 2$ in., $M'N' = 3.5$ in.

$NO = 3$ in., $N'O' =$ [5.25] in.

$MO = 4$ in., $M'O' =$ [7.0] in.

22. $MN = 2$ cm, $M'N' = 1.6$ cm

$NO = 5$ cm, $N'O' =$ [4.0] cm

$MO = 6$ cm, $M'O' =$ [4.8] cm

Name ______________________ Class __________ Date __________

9-5 Standardized Test Prep

Dilations

Gridded Response

The solid-line figure is a dilation of the dashed-line figure. The labeled point is the center of dilation. Find the scale factor for each dilation. Use whole numbers or decimals. Enter your responses on the grid provided.

1. 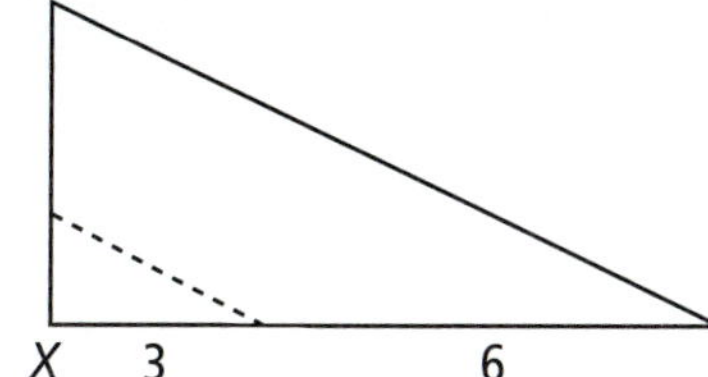

2. 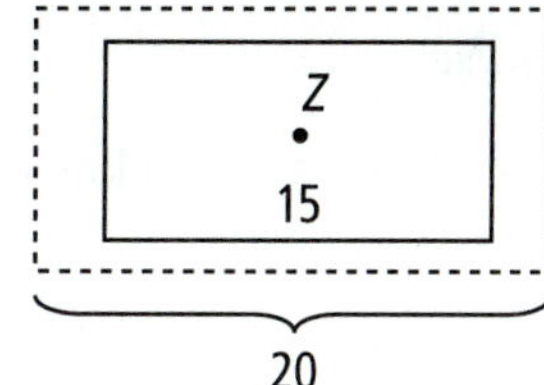

Solve the problem and enter your response on the grid provided.

3. The image of an eraser in a magnifying glass is three times the eraser's actual size and has a width of 14.4 cm. What is the actual width in cm?

4. A square on a transparency is 1.7 in. long. The square's image on the screen is 11.05 in. long. What is the scale factor of the dilation?

5. A dilation maps $\triangle LMN$ to $\triangle L'M'N'$. $MN = 14$ in. and $M'N' = 9.8$ in. If $LN = 13$ in., what is $L'N'$?

Answers

1. 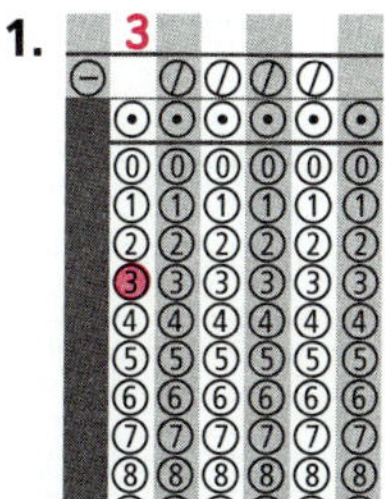

2. 0.75

3. 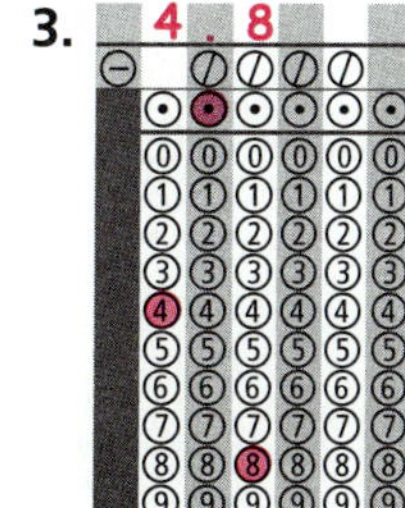

4. 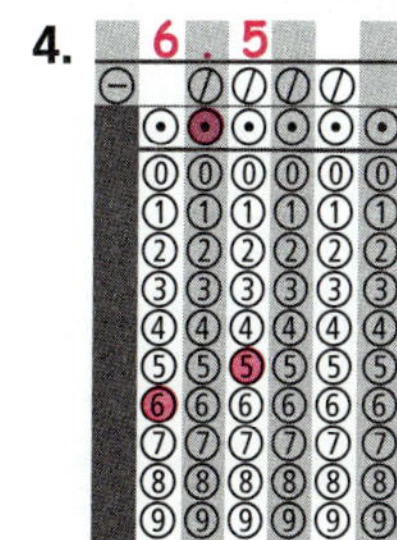

5. 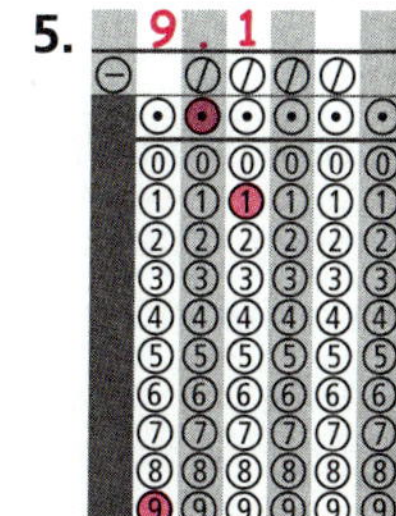

9-6 Compositions of Reflections

Vocabulary

Review

Write T for *true* or F for *false*.

T 1. A *reflection* flips a figure across a line of *reflection*.

F 2. A *reflection* turns a figure about a point.

T 3. A *reflection* preimage and image are congruent.

T 4. The orientation of a figure reverses after a *reflection*.

F 5. A line of *reflection* is either horizontal or vertical.

Vocabulary Builder

composition (noun) **kahm puh ZISH un**

Other Word Forms: compose (verb), composite (adjective), composite (noun)

Definition: A **composition** combines parts.

Math Usage: A **composition** of transformations combines two or more transformations in a given order.

Use Your Vocabulary

Complete each statement with the appropriate word from the list. Use each word only once.

reflections rotation symmetry

6. A *composition* of reflections has at least one line of ? . symmetry

7. You can map any congruent figure onto another using a *composition* of ? . reflections

8. A *composition* of rotations is always a ? . rotation

Theorem 9-1 and Theorem 9-2

Theorem 9-1 A translation or rotation is a composition of two reflections.

Theorem 9-2

A composition of reflections across parallel lines is a translation.

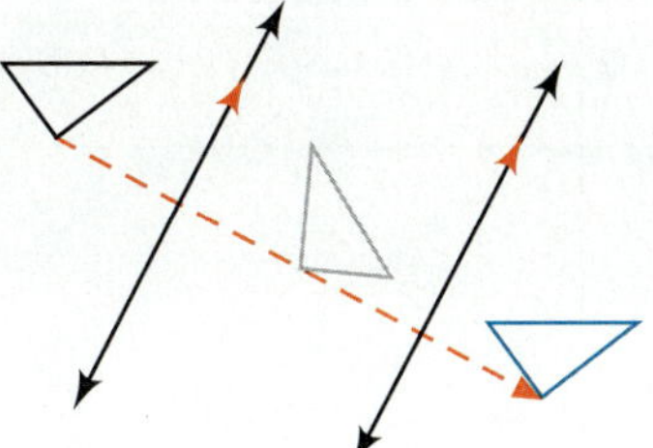

A composition of reflections across two intersecting lines is a rotation.

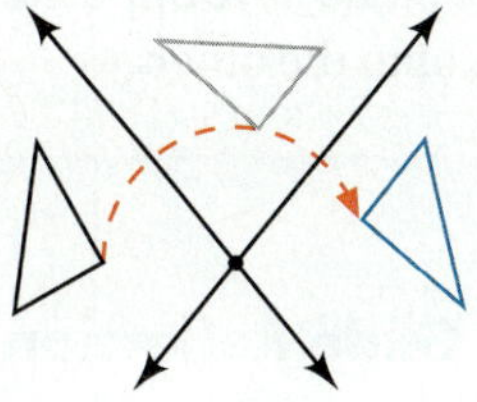

Problem 1 Composing Reflections Across Parallel Lines

Got It? **Lines ℓ and m are parallel. R is between ℓ and m. What is the image of R reflected first across line ℓ and then across line m? What are the direction and distance of the resulting translation?**

9. The diagram shows a dashed line perpendicular to ℓ and m that intersects ℓ at point A, m at point B, and R only at point P. Complete each step to show the composition of the reflections.

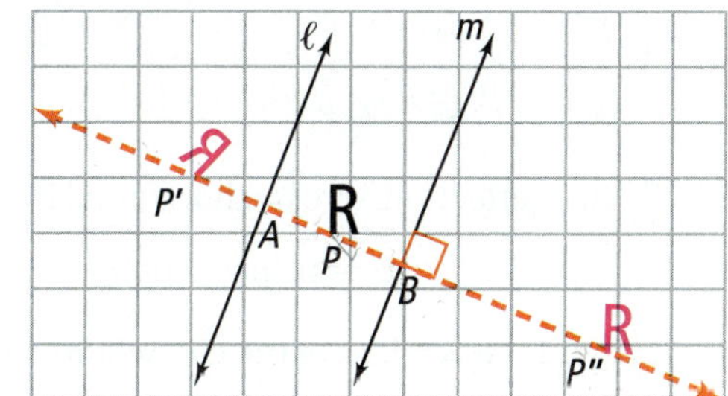

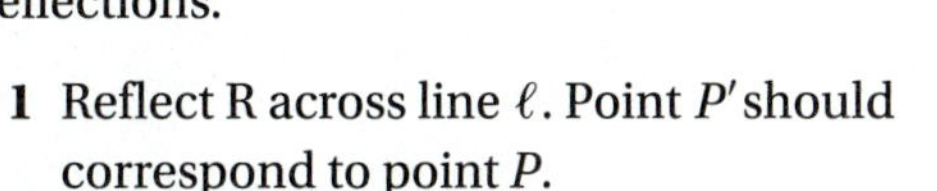

Step 1 Reflect R across line ℓ. Point P' should correspond to point P.

Step 2 Reflect the image across line m. Point P'' should correspond to point P'.

10. Underline the correct word to complete each sentence.

The translation is to the <u>right</u> / left along the dashed line.

The direction of the translation is parallel / <u>perpendicular</u> to lines ℓ and m.

11. Use the justifications at the right to find the distance PP'' of the resulting translation.

$PP'' = PB + BP''$	Segment Addition Postulate
$= PB + BP'$	Definition of reflection across line m
$= PB + (BP + PA + AP')$	Segment Addition Postulate
$= PB + BP + 2PA$	Definition of reflection across line ℓ
$= 2 \cdot BP + 2PA$	Simplify.
$= 2 \cdot (BP + PA)$	Use the Distributive Property.
$= 2 \cdot AB$	Segment Addition Postulate

12. The resulting translation moved R a distance of $2AB$.

take note

Theorem 9-3 Fundamental Theorem of Isometries

In a plane, one of two congruent figures can be mapped onto the other by a composition of at most three reflections.

13. Underline the correct word to complete the sentence.

If two congruent figures in a plane have opposite orientations, an even / odd number of reflections maps one figure onto the other.

Problem 3 Finding a Glide Reflection Image

Got It? **What is the image of $\triangle TEX$ for a glide reflection where the translation is $(x, y) \rightarrow (x + 1, y)$ and the line of reflection is $y = -2$?**

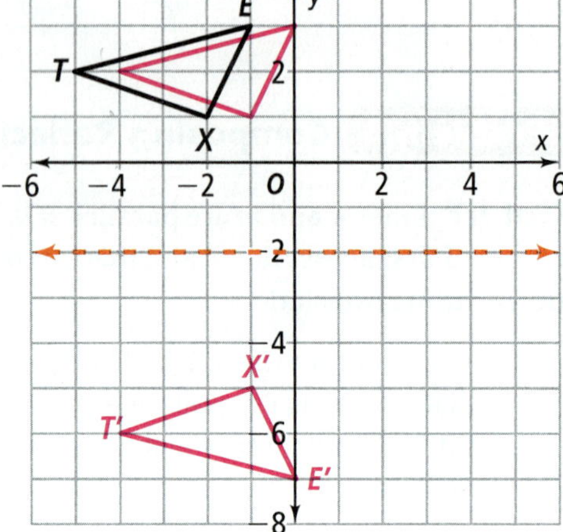

Use the coordinate plane at the right for Exercises 14–17.

14. Find the vertices of the translation image. Then graph the translation image.

$T(-5, 2) \rightarrow (-5 +$ 1, 2 $) = ($ −4, 2 $)$

$E(-1, 3) \rightarrow (-1 +$ 1, 3 $) = ($ 0, 3 $)$

$X(-2, 1) \rightarrow (-2 +$ 1, 1 $) = ($ −1, 1 $)$

15. In a reflection across a horizontal line, only the y -coordinate changes.

16. Find the vertices of the triangle you graphed in Exercise 14 after reflection across the line $y = -2$.

(−4, 2) $\rightarrow T'($ −4, −6 $)$

(0, 3) $\rightarrow E'($ 0, −7 $)$

(−1, 1) $\rightarrow X'($ −1, −5 $)$

17. The image of $\triangle TEX$ for the given glide reflection is the triangle with vertices $T'($ −4, −6 $)$, $E'($ 0, −7 $)$, and $X'($ −1, −5 $)$. Graph $\triangle T'E'X'$.

take note

Theorem 9-4 Isometry Classification Theorem

There are only four isometries.

Translation	Rotation	Reflection	Glide Reflection
			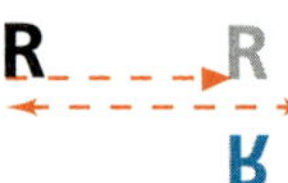

Orientations are the same. Orientations are opposite.

Problem 4 Classifying Isometries

Got It? **Each figure is an isometry image of the figure at the right. Are the orientations of the preimage and image the *same* or *opposite*? What type of isometry maps the preimage to the image?**

A. 

B.

C.

Choose the correct words from the list to complete each sentence.

Word list
opposite
same
translation
rotation
reflection
glide reflection

18. Image A has the _?_ orientation and is a _?_.

same | rotation

19. Image B has the _?_ orientation and is a _?_.

same | translation

20. Image C has the _?_ orientation and is a _?_.

opposite | glide reflection

Lesson Check • Do you UNDERSTAND?

Error Analysis **You reflect $\triangle DEF$ first across line m and then across line n. Your friend says you can get the same result by reflecting $\triangle DEF$ first across line n and then across line m. Explain your friend's error.**

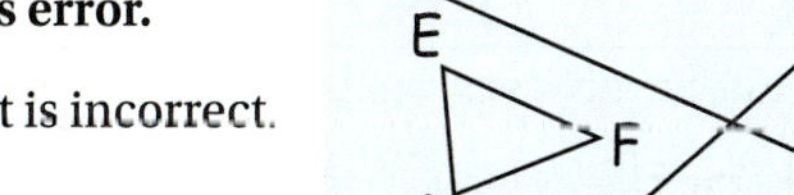

21. Place a ✓ in the box if the response is correct. Place an ✗ if it is incorrect.

✗ Lines m and n are perpendicular.

✗ A clockwise or counterclockwise rotation has the same image.

22. Explain your friend's error. Answers may vary. Sample:

The resulting rotation is not in the same direction.

Math Success

Check off the vocabulary words that you understand.

☐ composition of reflections ☐ glide reflection ☐ isometry

Rate how well you can *find compositions of reflections*.

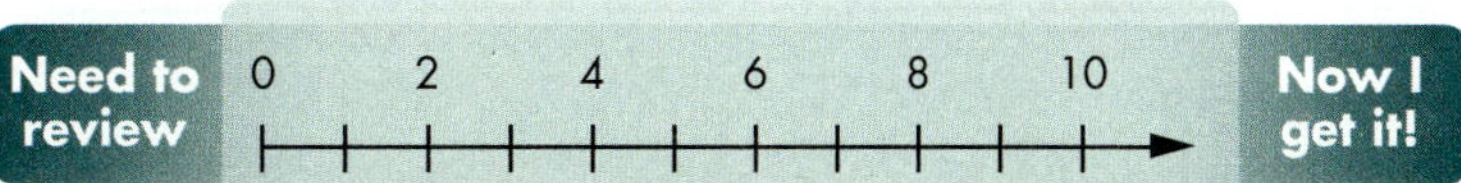

Name ______________________ Class ____________ Date ____________

9-6 Think About a Plan

Compositions of Reflections

Identify the mapping $\triangle EDC \rightarrow \triangle PQM$ as a translation, reflection, rotation, or glide reflection. Find the translation rule, reflection line, center of rotation and angle of rotation, or translation rule and reflection line.

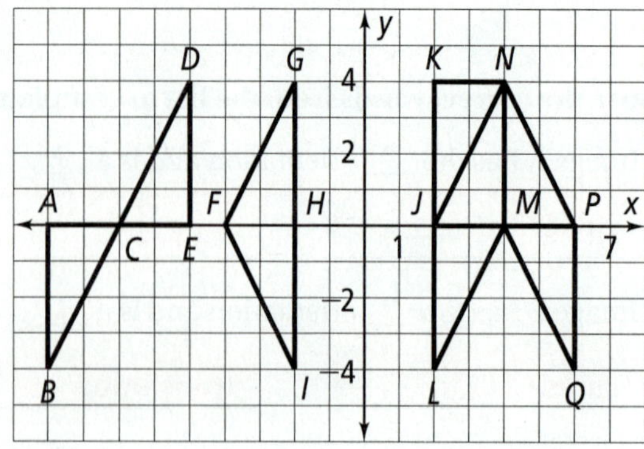

Know

1. What strategy could you use to isolate the figures with which you are working?

   Draw a diagram of $\triangle EDC$ and $\triangle PQM$ only.

2. What kind of mapping appears to have happened here? Explain.

   a glide reflection; $\triangle EDC$ is translated from Quadrant II to Quadrant I, and then reflected into Quadrant IV on to $\triangle PQM$

Need

3. What more do we need to know to have a complete answer?

   the translation rule and the reflection line

Plan

4. Find the translation rule for $\triangle EDC \rightarrow \triangle PQM$.

   $(x, y) \rightarrow (x + 11, y)$

5. What is the line of reflection for $\triangle EDC \rightarrow \triangle PQM$?

   the x-axis

Name ______________________ Class ______________ Date ______________

9-6 Practice

Form K

Compositions of Reflections

Find the image of each figure for a reflection first across line ℓ and then across line *m*. Is the resulting transformation a translation or a rotation? For a translation, describe the direction and distance. For a rotation, tell the center of rotation and the angle of rotation.

1. To start, if the lines ℓ and m are parallel, then it is a __?__. translation

If ℓ and m intersect, then it is a __?__. rotation

translation; directly right; twice the distance between the two lines.

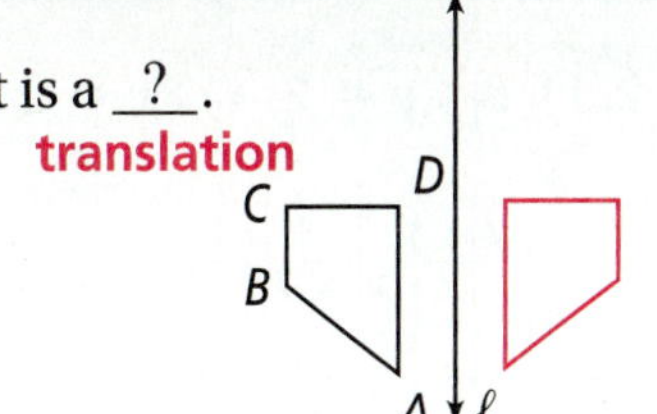

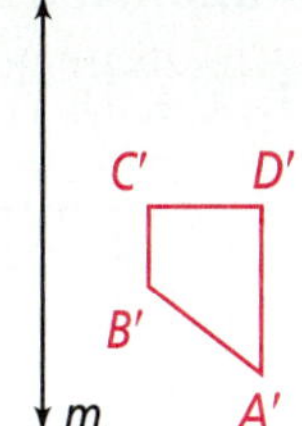

2.

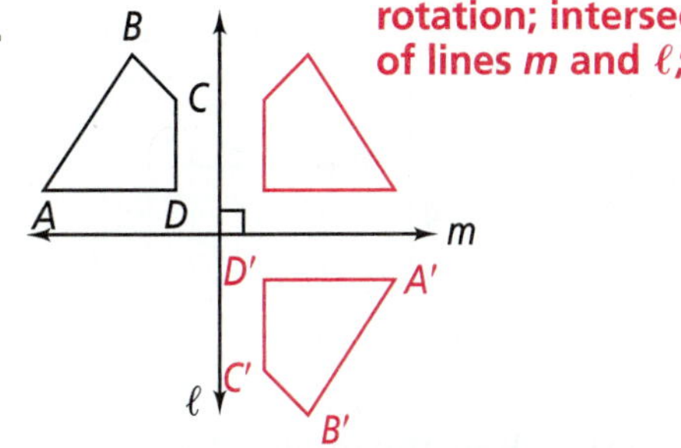

rotation; intersection of lines m and ℓ; 180°

3.

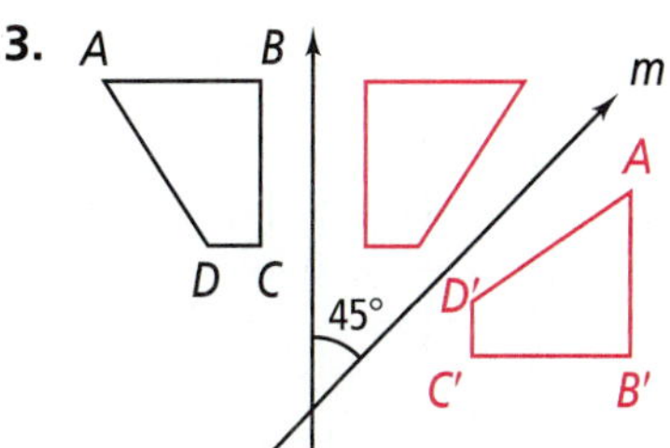

rotation; intersection of lines m and ℓ; 90° clockwise

Graph $\triangle ABC$ and its glide reflection image for the given translation and reflection line.

4. $(x, y) \rightarrow (x - 2, y)$; $y = 0$

To start, translate the vertices of $\triangle ABC$ to:

A'(3, 5), B'(5, 1), C'(1, 1).

Then, reflect $\triangle A'B'C'$ across ☐. $y = 0$

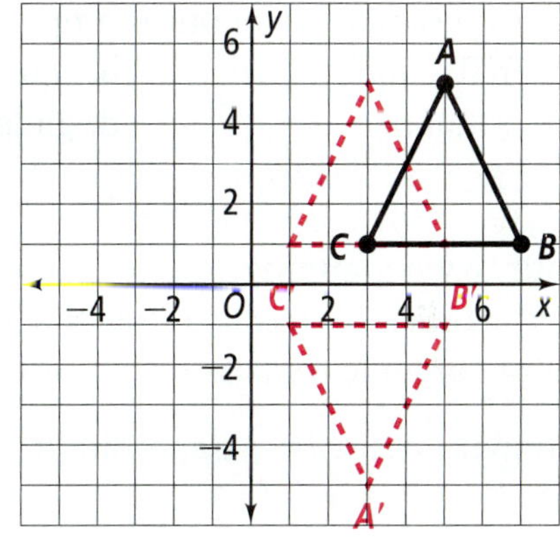

5. $(x, y) \rightarrow (x, y - 3)$; $x = 0$

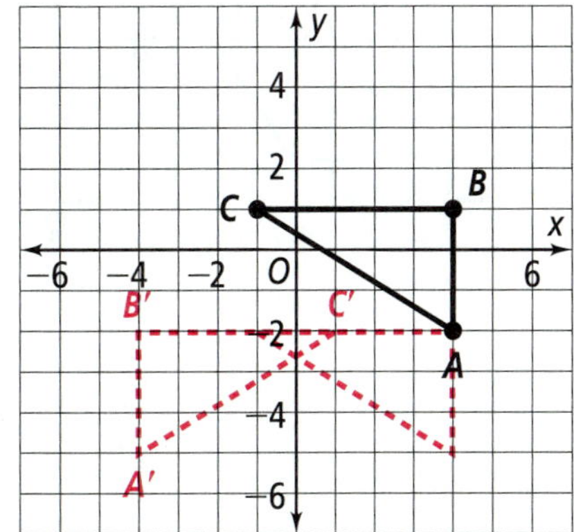

6. $(x, y) \rightarrow (x + 1, y - 1)$; $y = -1$

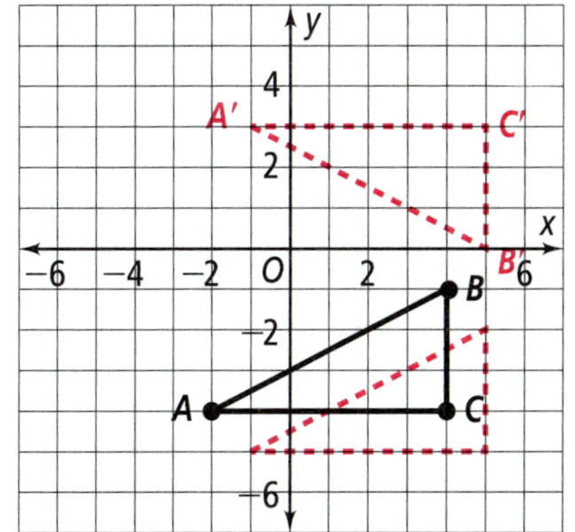

9-6 Practice (continued) Form K

Compositions of Reflections

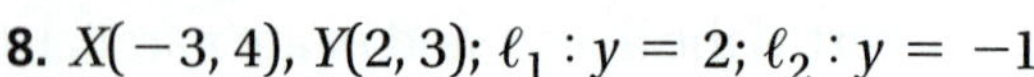

Use the given points and lines. Graph $\overline{XY}$ and its image $\overline{X'Y'}$ after a reflection first across ℓ_1 and then across ℓ_2. Is the resulting transformation a translation or a rotation? For a translation, describe the distance and direction. For a rotation, tell the center of rotation and the angle of rotation.

7. $X(4, 3)$, $Y(-2, 1)$; $\ell_1 : y = 2$; $\ell_2 : x = 2$

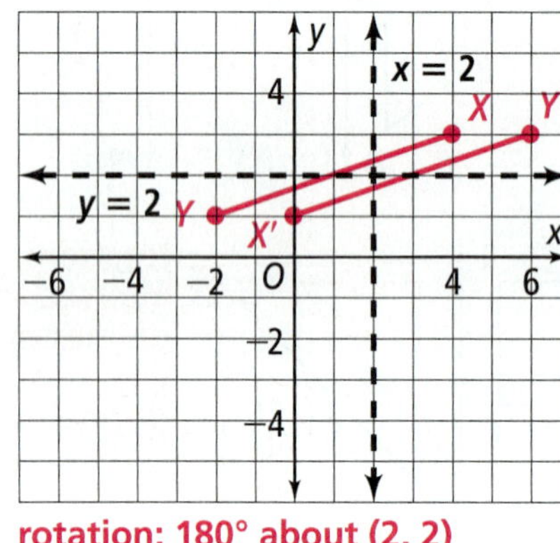

rotation; 180° about (2, 2)

8. $X(-3, 4)$, $Y(2, 3)$; $\ell_1 : y = 2$; $\ell_2 : y = -1$

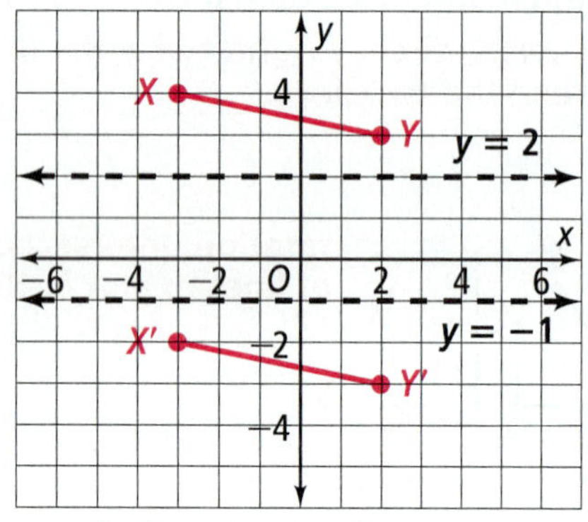

translation; 6 units down

9. **Open-Ended** Draw a quadrilateral on a coordinate grid. Draw the image of the quadrilateral for one example of each transformation. Check students' work.
   a. reflection
   b. translation
   c. rotation
   d. glide reflection

Identify each mapping as a translation, reflection, rotation, or glide reflection. Find the translation rule, reflection line, center of rotation and angle of rotation, or glide translation rule and reflection line.

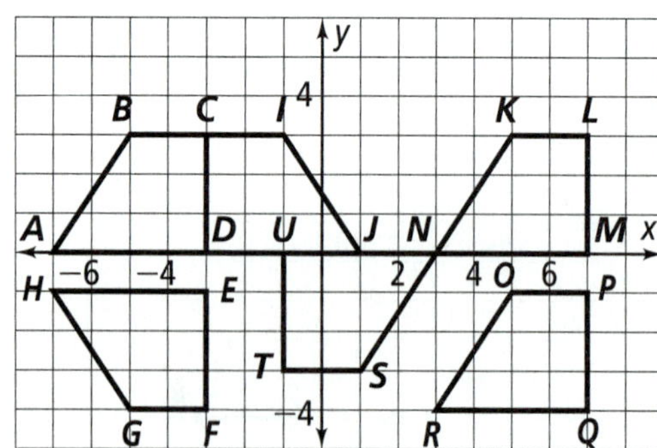

10. trapezoid $ABCD \rightarrow$ trapezoid $JICD$
    reflection; $x = -3$

11. trapezoid $ABCD \rightarrow$ trapezoid $NKLM$
    translation; $(x, y) \rightarrow (x + 10, y)$

12. trapezoid $CIJD \rightarrow$ trapezoid $LKNM$
    reflection; $x = 2$

13. trapezoid $CIJD \rightarrow$ trapezoid $TSNU$
    glide reflection; $(x, y) \rightarrow (x + 2, y)$, $y = 0$

14. trapezoid $KLMN \rightarrow$ trapezoid $STUN$
    rotation; 180° around point N

Name ______________________ Class ____________ Date ____________

9-6 Standardized Test Prep

Compositions of Reflections

Multiple Choice

For Exercises 1–5, choose the correct letter.

1. For which transformations are the image and the preimage in opposite orientations? D

   (A) translations and rotations
   (B) translations and reflections
   (C) rotations and reflections
   (D) reflections and glide reflections

2. What type of transformation maps $\triangle ABC$ onto $\triangle DEF$? F

   (F) translation
   (G) rotation
   (H) reflection
   (I) glide reflection

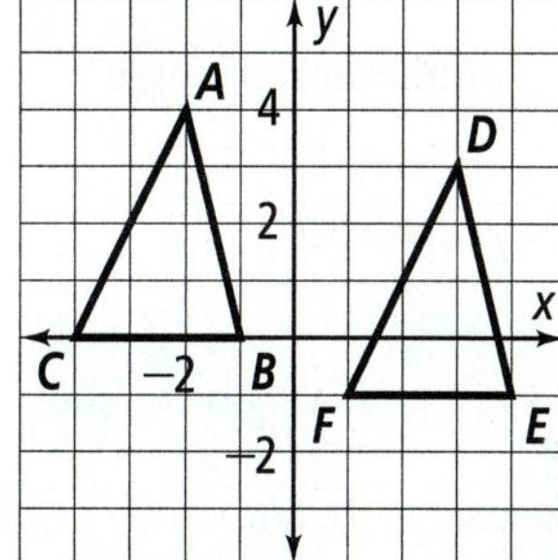

3. A triangle is reflected across line ℓ and then across line m. If the lines intersect, what kind of isometry is this composition of reflections? B

   (A) translation (B) rotation (C) reflection (D) glide reflection

4. What type of isometry is shown at the right? H

   (F) translation (H) reflection
   (G) rotation (I) glide reflection

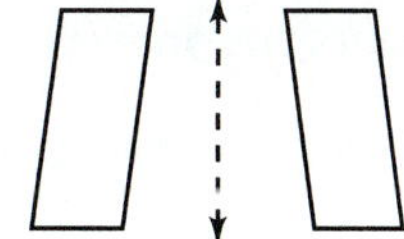

5. $X \rightarrow X'(3, -2)$ by a glide reflection. The translation is $(x, y) \rightarrow (x, y + 3)$ and the line of reflection is $y = -1$. What are the coordinates of X? D

   (A) $(-5, -2)$ (B) $(-2, -2)$ (C) $(-2, -5)$ (D) $(3, -3)$

Short Response

6. What type of transformation is shown? Give the translation rule, reflection line, center and angle of rotation, or translation rule and reflection line.

   Answers may vary. Sample: [2] glide reflection; $(x, y) \rightarrow (x, y - 4)$; line of reflection $x = 0$
   [1] Student identifies transformation or identifies rule.
   [0] incorrect or no transformation type given

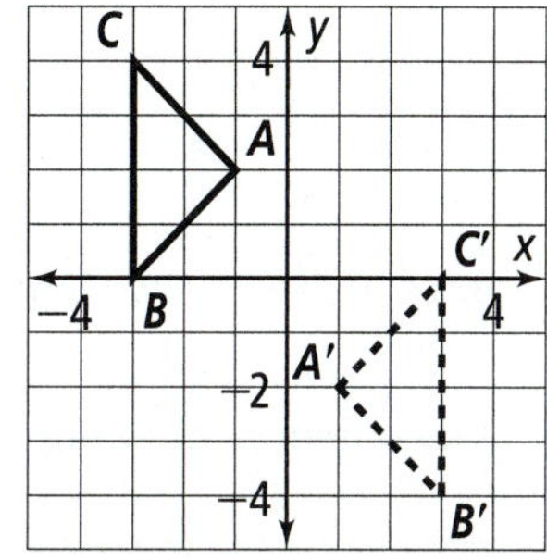

9-7 Tessellations

Vocabulary

Review

1. Underline the correct word to complete the sentence.

A square has two / <u>four</u> lines of *symmetry*.

2. Circle the figure that has exactly two lines of *symmetry*.

circle   equilateral triangle   isosceles triangle   (rectangle)   square

Vocabulary Builder

tessellation (noun) **tes uh LAY shun**

Related Words: tessellate (verb), tiling (noun)

Definition: A **tessellation** is a repeated pattern of figures that completely covers a plane, without gaps or overlaps.

tessellation

Main Idea: You can identify the transformations and symmetries in **tessellations**.

Example: Squares make a **tessellation** because laying them side by side completely covers the plane without gaps or overlaps.

Non-Example: Circles cannot make a **tessellation** because they leave gaps when placed so they touch but do not overlap.

Use Your Vocabulary

Write T for *true* or F for *false*.

F **3.** A *tessellation* of two figures may overlap.

T **4.** You can make a *tessellation* with translations.

F **5.** You cannot make a *tessellation* with reflections.

F **6.** You can use any two figures to make a *tessellation*.

T **7.** A tiled floor is an example of a *tessellation*.

Problem 1 Describing Tessellations

Got It? **What is the repeating figure in the tessellation? What transformation does the tessellation use?**

8. Underline the correct word to complete the sentence.

The repeating figure in the tessellation is a lizard / bird / turtle .

9. Describe the orientation of repeating figures in the tessellation. Answers may vary. Sample:

Repeating figures all look to the right, so they have the same orientation.

10. Circle the transformation used in the tessellation.

glide reflection   reflection   rotation   translation

Problem 2 Determining Whether a Figure Tessellates

Got It? **Does a regular hexagon tessellate? Explain.**

11. Place a ✓ in the box if the statement is correct. Place an ✗ if it is incorrect.

✓ If the measure of one interior angle of a regular polygon is a factor of 360°, the polygon tessellates.

✓ If the sum of the measures of n angles of a regular polygon is less than 360°, there are gaps when n copies of the polygon are placed around a vertex.

✗ If the sum of the measures of n angles of a regular polygon is greater than 360°, there are gaps when n copies of the polygon are placed around a vertex.

12. The sum of the measures of the interior angles of a regular hexagon is 720°.

13. The measure of each interior angle of a regular hexagon is 120°.

14. Does a regular hexagon tessellate? Explain.

Yes. Explanations may vary. Sample: The measure of each angle is 120° so 3 copies of the hexagon will exactly fill the 360° around any vertex.

Problem 3 Identifying Symmetries in a Tessellation

Got It? What types of symmetry does the tessellation at the right have?

Draw a line from the type of symmetry in Column A to its description in Column B.

	Column A	Column B
15.	glide reflectional symmetry	A figure maps onto itself after a turn.
16.	reflectional symmetry	A figure is its own image after moving a given distance.
17.	rotational symmetry	A line of symmetry divides the figure into two congruent halves.
18.	translational symmetry	A figure maps onto itself after a translation and a reflection.

Use the diagrams below for Exercises 19–23.

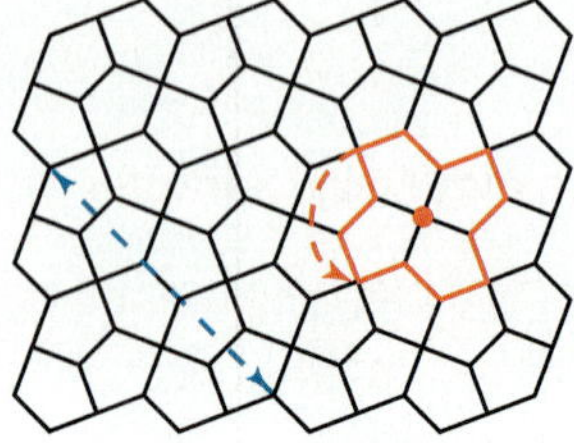

Tessellation A

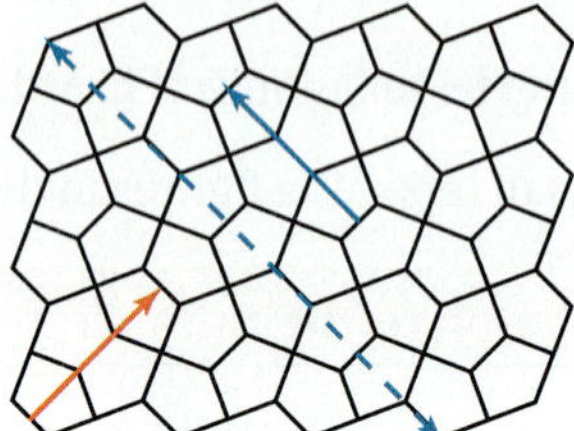

Tessellation B

19. Circle the type of symmetry shown by the red point and arc in Tessellation A.

glide reflectional   reflectional   (rotational)   translational

20. Circle the type of symmetry shown by the blue line in Tessellation A.

glide reflectional   (reflectional)   rotational   translational

21. Circle the type of symmetry shown by the red arrow in Tessellation B.

glide reflectional   reflectional   rotational   (translational)

22. Circle the type of symmetry shown by the blue arrow and dashed line in Tessellation B.

(glide reflectional)   reflectional   rotational   translational

23. What types of symmetry does the tessellation have?

The tessellation has glide reflectional symmetry, reflectional symmetry, rotational symmetry, and translational symmetry.

Lesson Check • Do you UNDERSTAND?

Reasoning **If you arrange three regular octagons so that they meet at one vertex, will they leave a gap or will they overlap? Explain.**

24. Complete the reasoning model below.

Think	Write
I know that all angles of a regular polygon have the same measure.	Let a = the measure of one angle.
I can use the Polygon Angle-Sum Theorem to find a.	$a = \dfrac{180(n - 2)}{n}$
I know that a regular octagon has 8 sides. I can substitute 8 for n.	$a = \dfrac{180(8 - 2)}{8}$
Now I can simplify.	$a = 135$
Finally, I should find the total measure of 3 angles.	$3 \cdot 135 = 405$

25. If you arrange three regular octagons so that they meet at one vertex, will they leave a gap or will they overlap? Explain.

They will overlap. Explanations may vary. Sample: The sum of the measures of the three angles is 405, which is greater than 360.

Math Success

Check off the vocabulary words that you understand.

☐ tessellation ☐ tiling

Rate how well you can *identify figures that tessellate.*

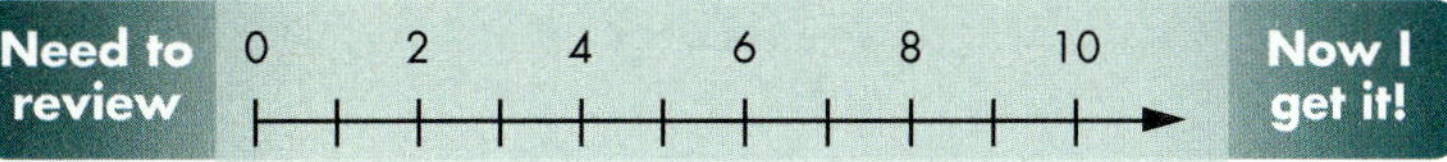

Name ______________________ Class ____________ Date ____________

9-7 Think About a Plan

Tessellations

Can the set of polygons be used to make a tessellation? If so, draw a sketch.

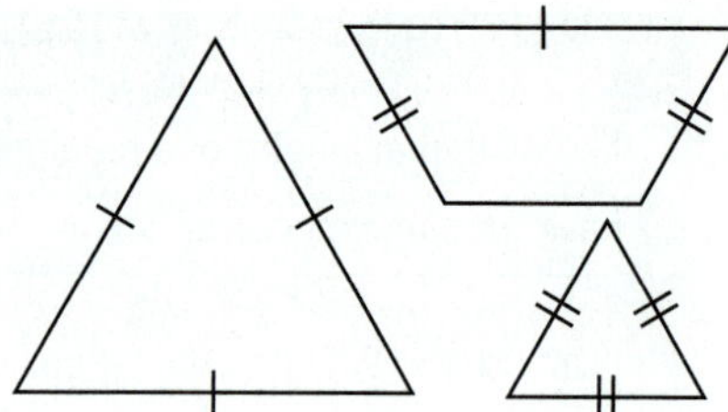

Know

1. What strategies might be useful for this problem?
   make a model; guess and check

Need

2. Sketch the large equilateral triangle on a piece of paper. Cut out this triangle.

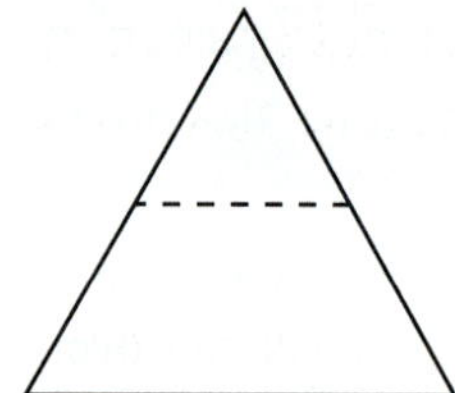

3. Sketch and cut out another identical triangle.

4. To make the trapezoid and the smaller triangle, cut parallel to the base of the triangle, exactly halfway between the base and the angle opposite the base.

Plan

5. Try to arrange the figures so that they could tessellate. If it helps, cut out a second set of models.

6. Sketch your tessellation.
   Answers may vary. Sample:

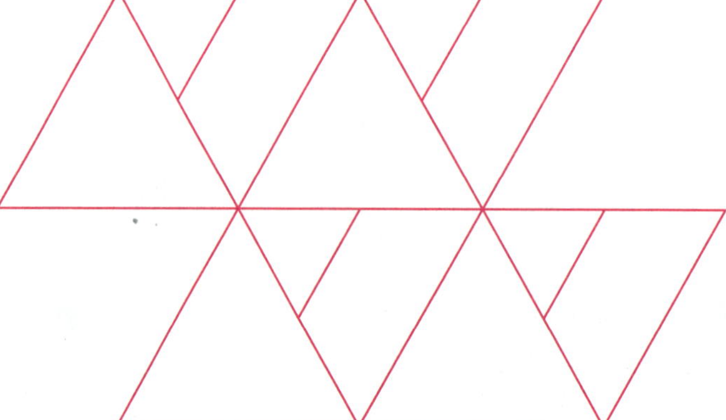

Name ____________________ Class ____________ Date ____________

9-7 Practice

Form K

Tessellations

Does the picture show a tessellation of a repeating figure? If so, identify the repeating figure and the transformation used.

1.

yes; fish; translational symmetry

2. 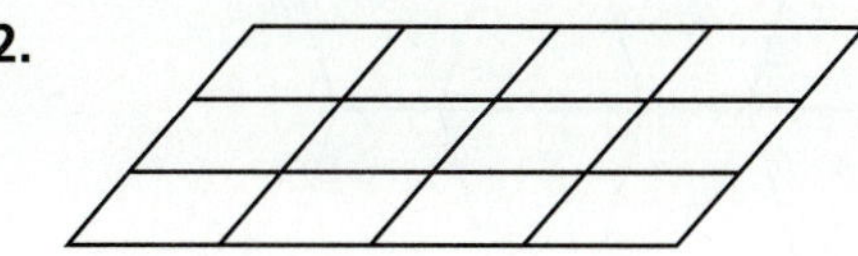

yes; parallelogram; translational symmetry

3. A pure tessellation is made up of congruent copies of one figure. Make a tessellation of your own. Draw a sketch.
Check students' work.

Determine whether each figure will tessellate a plane. Explain.

4. a regular decagon

To start, use the Polygon Angle-Sum Theorem to find the measure of one interior angle. $\frac{180(10 - 2)}{10} = \boxed{144}$

No, 360 is not a multiple of the measure of one interior angle.

5. a trapezoid
Yes; every quadrilateral tessellates.

6. an equilateral triangle
Yes; every triangle tessellates.

7. a scalene triangle
Yes; every triangle tessellates.

8. a regular hexagon
Yes; the measure of one angle is 120, which can be multiplied by 3 to get 360.

List the type(s) of symmetry each tessellation has.

9. Can you translate the figure? yes

Can you rotate the figure? yes

Can you reflect the figure? yes

translational, reflectional, rotational, and glide reflectional symmetry

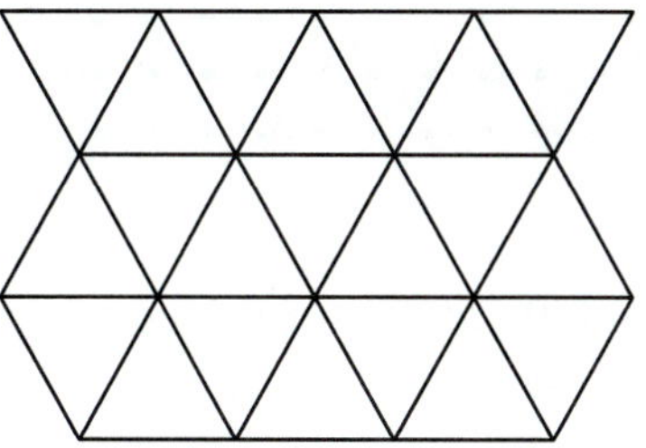

10. 

translational symmetry

11. 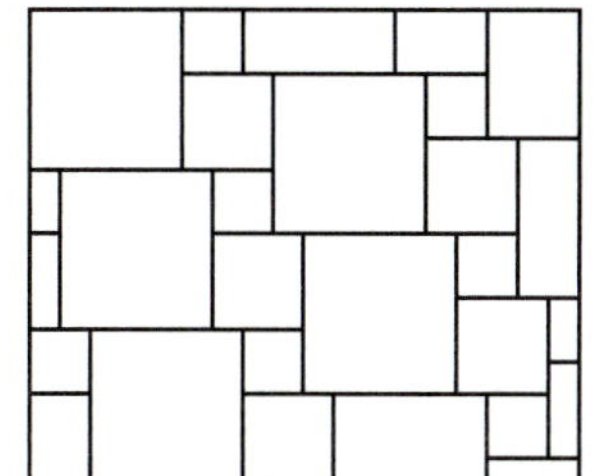

translational and rotational symmetry

Name ______________________ Class ____________ Date ____________

9-7 Practice (continued) — Form K

Tessellations

List the types of symmetry each tessellation has.

12.

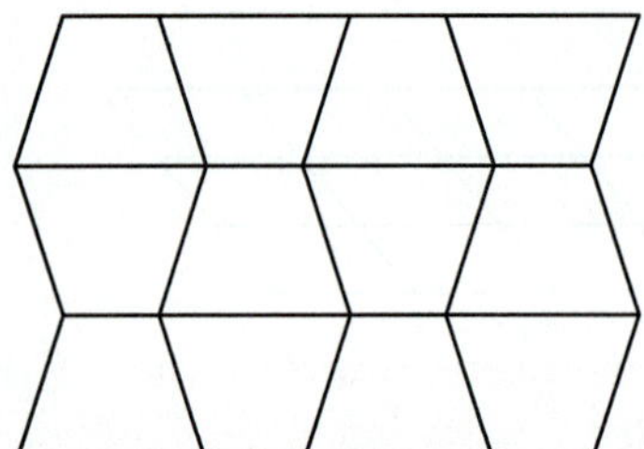

reflectional, translational, rotational, and glide reflectional symmetry

13.

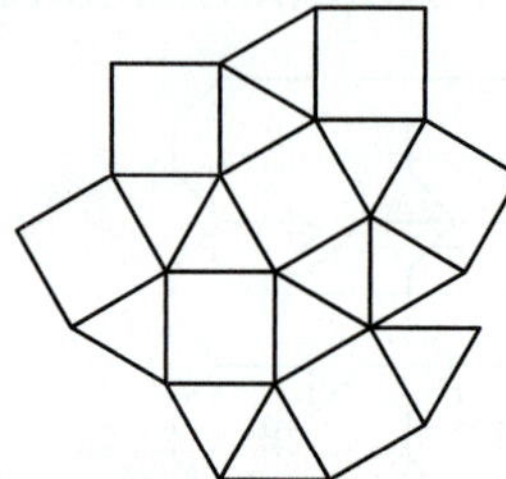

rotational and translational symmetry

Use each figure to make a tessellation on dot paper.

14. To start, copy the figure on your own paper. Next, match up the various parts to complete the picture.

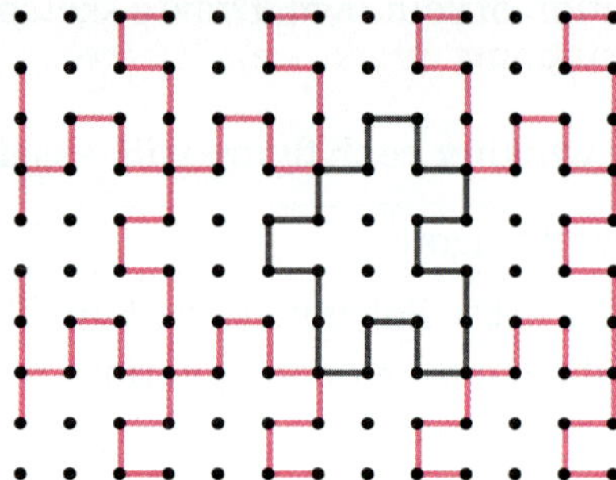

15.

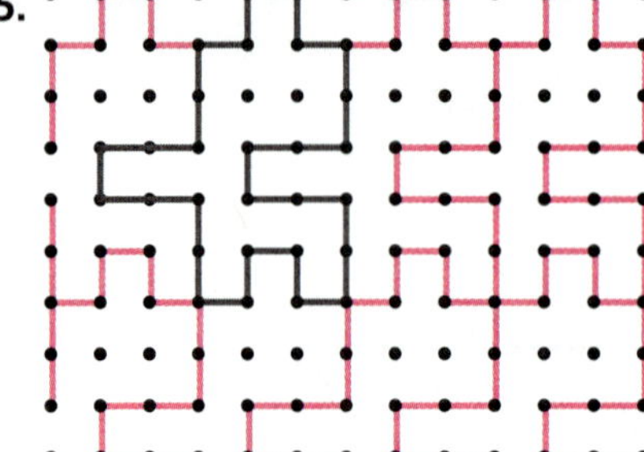

16.

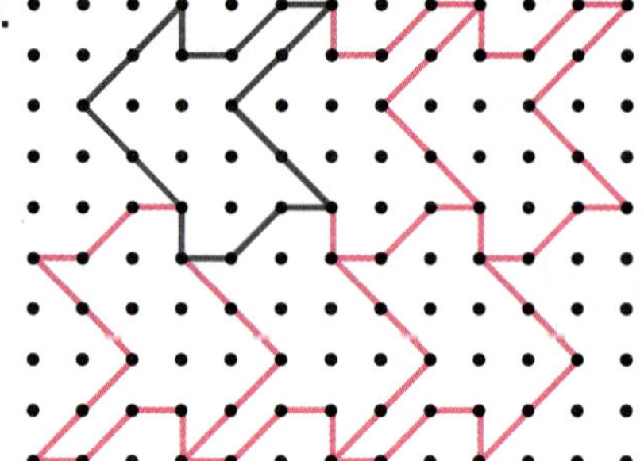

Can each set of polygons be used to make a tessellation? If so, draw a sketch.

17.

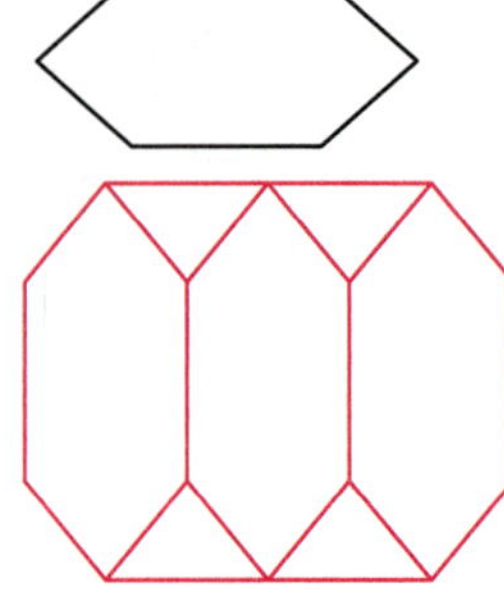

yes

18.

no

Name ______________________ Class ____________ Date ____________

9-7 Standardized Test Prep

Tessellations

Multiple Choice

For Exercises 1–4, choose the correct letter.

1. For which type of symmetry does a linear movement of a tessellation in one direction map the tessellation onto itself? **D**

(A) glide reflectional symmetry
(B) reflectional symmetry
(C) rotational symmetry
(D) translational symmetry

2. Which of the following figures can tessellate in a plane? **H**

 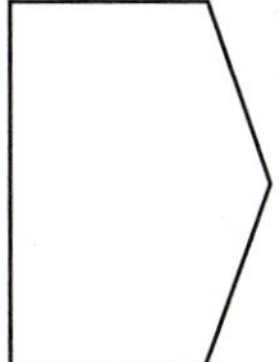
(G) 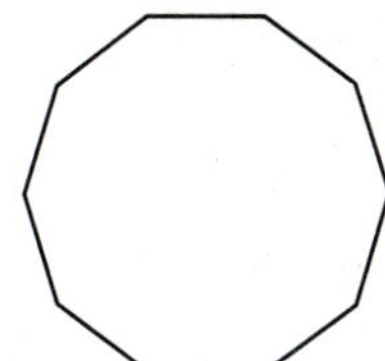
(H) 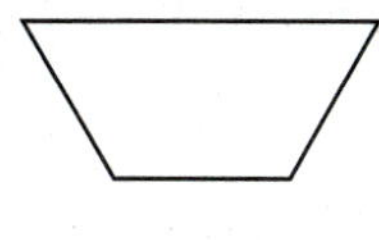
(I) 

3. What type(s) of symmetry is shown in the tessellation below? **D**

(A) glide reflectional symmetry
(B) reflectional and rotational symmetry
(C) rotational and translational symmetry
(D) translational symmetry

4. Which of the following figures will tessellate a plane? **G**

(F) a regular pentagon
(G) a regular hexagon
(H) a regular octagon
(I) a regular decagon

Short Response

5. What type(s) of symmetry does the tessellation within the box have?

[2] translational and rotational symmetry
[1] translational or rotational symmetry
[0] no correct response given

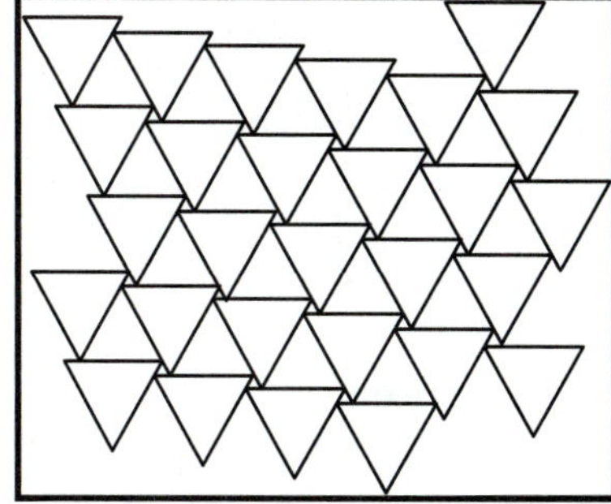

Areas of Parallelograms and Triangles

Vocabulary

Review

The diagram below shows the different types of *parallelograms*.

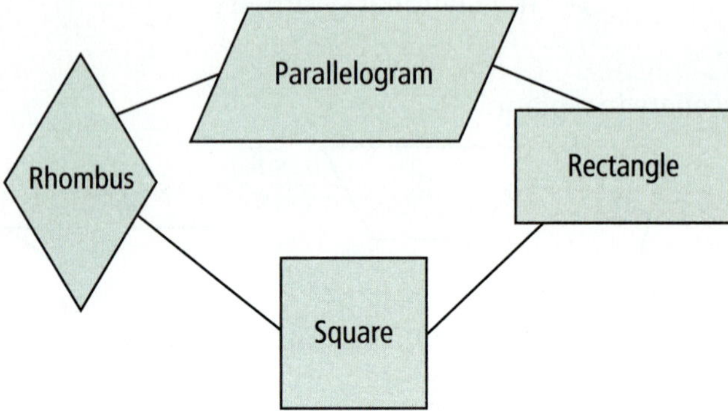

Underline the correct word to complete each sentence.

1. All *parallelograms* are quadrilaterals / rectangles .
2. All *parallelograms* have opposite sides parallel / perpendicular .
3. Some *parallelograms* are trapezoids / rectangles .

Vocabulary Builder

area (noun) EHR ee uh

Definition: **Area** is the number of square units needed to cover a given surface.

Main Idea: You can find the **area** of a parallelogram or a triangle when you know the length of its base and its height.

Use Your Vocabulary

Find the area of each figure.

4. 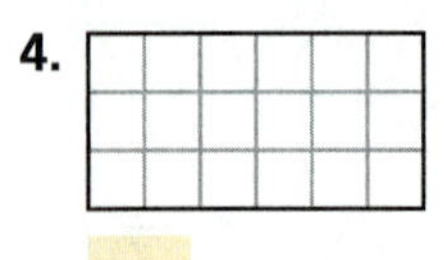

18 square units

5. 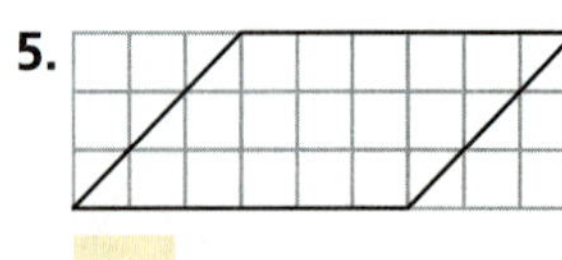

18 square units

6. 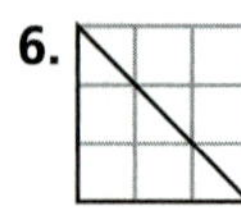

4.5 square units

take note

Theorems 10-1 and 10-2 Area of a Rectangle and of a Parallelogram

Theorem 10-1 Area of a Rectangle
The area of a rectangle is the product of its base and height.

$A = bh$

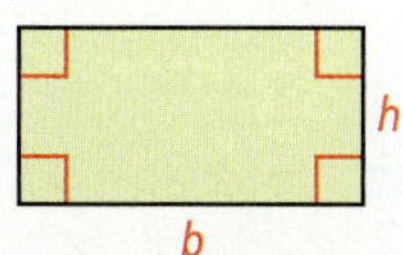

Theorem 10-2 Area of a Parallelogram
The area of a parallelogram is the product of a base and the corresponding height.

$A = bh$

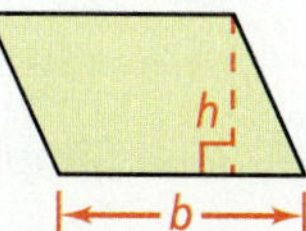

7. Explain how finding the area of a parallelogram and finding the area of a rectangle are alike. **Explanations may vary. Sample:**

For each figure, you find the product of the base and its corresponding height.

Problem 1 Finding the Area of a Parallelogram

Got It? **What is the area of a parallelogram with base length 12 m and height 9 m?**

8. Label the parallelogram at the right.

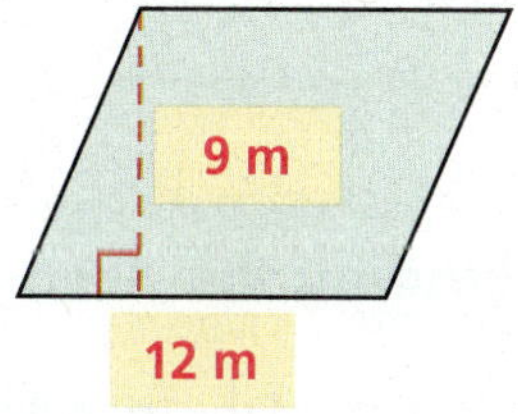

9. Find the area.

$A = bh$	Write the formula.
$= 12(9)$	Substitute.
$= 108$	Simplify.

10. The area of the parallelogram is 108 m^2.

Problem 2 Finding a Missing Dimension

Got It? **A parallelogram has sides 15 cm and 18 cm. The height corresponding to a 15-cm base is 9 cm. What is the height corresponding to an 18-cm base?**

11. Label the parallelogram at the right. Let h represent the height corresponding to the 18-cm base.

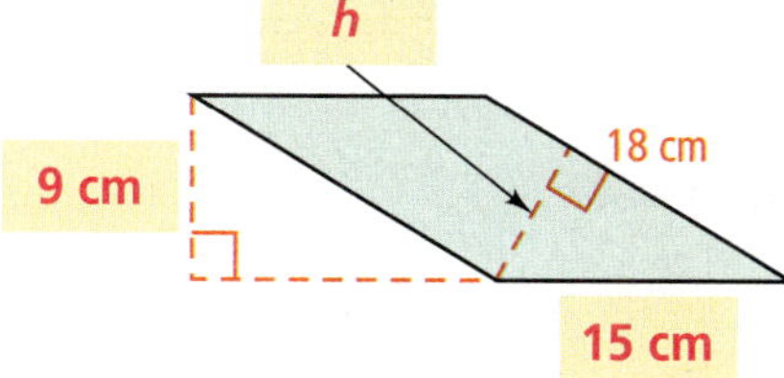

12. Find the area.

$A = bh$
$= 15 \cdot 9$
$= 135$

13. The area of the parallelogram is 135 cm^2.

14. Use the area of the parallelogram to find the height corresponding to an 18-cm base.

$A = bh$ Write the formula.

$135 = (18)h$ Substitute.

$\frac{135}{18} = \frac{(18)h}{18}$ Divide each side by the length of the base.

$7.5 = h$ Simplify.

15. The height corresponding to an 18-cm base is 7.5 cm.

take note

Theorem 10-3 Area of a Triangle

The area of a triangle is half the product of a base and the corresponding height.

$A = \frac{1}{2}bh$

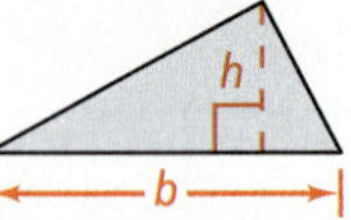

16. Explain how finding the area of a triangle is different from finding the area of a rectangle. Explanations may vary. Sample:

For a triangle, find half the product of the base and height. For a rectangle, find the product of the base and height.

Problem 3 Finding the Area of a Triangle

Got It? What is the area of the triangle?

5 in.
1 ft 1 in.
1 ft

17. Circle the formula you can use to find the area of the triangle.

$A = bh$ $A = \frac{1}{2}bh$ (circled)

18. Convert the lengths of the base and the hypotenuse to inches.

base: 1 ft = 12 in.

hypotenuse: 1 ft 1 in. = 13 in.

19. Find the area of the triangle.

$A = \frac{1}{2}bh$
$= \frac{1}{2}(12)(5)$
$= \frac{1}{2}(60)$
$= 30$

20. The area of the triangle is 30 in.^2.

Problem 4 Finding the Area of an Irregular Figure

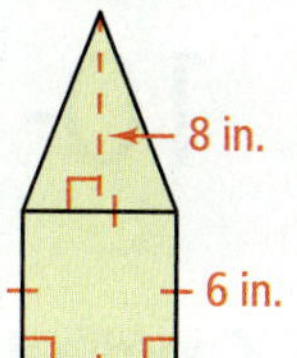

Got It? Reasoning Suppose the base lengths of the square and triangle in the figure are doubled to 12 in., but the height of each polygon remains the same. How is the area of the figure affected?

21. Complete to find the area of each irregular figure.

Area of Original Irregular Figure

$A = 6(6) + \frac{1}{2}(6)(8)$

$= \boxed{36} + 24$

$= \boxed{60}$

Area of New Irregular Figure

$A = (2)(6)(6) + \frac{1}{2}(2)(6)(8)$

$= (2)(36) + (2)(\boxed{24})$

$= (2)(\boxed{36} + \boxed{24}) = (2)(\boxed{60}) = \boxed{120}$

22. How is the area affected?

The area is doubled.

Lesson Check • Do you UNDERSTAND?

$\square ABCD$ is divided into two triangles along diagonal $\overline{AC}$. If you know the area of the parallelogram, how do you find the area of $\triangle ABC$?

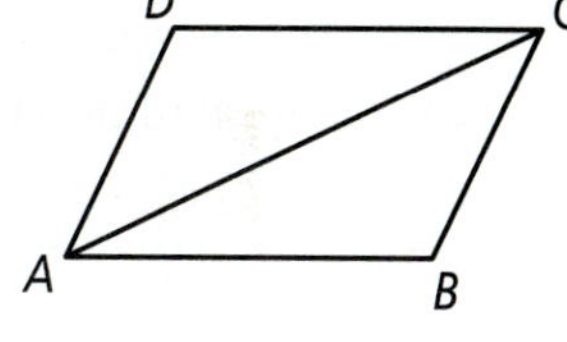

Write T for *true* or F for *false*.

T **23.** Since $\overline{AC}$ is a diagonal of $\square ABCD$, $\triangle ABC$ is congruent to $\triangle CDA$.

F **24.** The area of $\triangle ABC$ is greater than the area $\triangle CDA$.

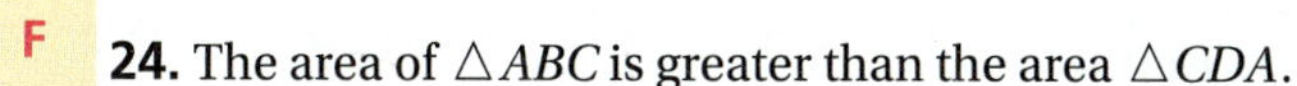

T **25.** The area of $\triangle ABC$ is half the area of $\square ABCD$.

26. If you know the area of the parallelogram, how do you find the area of $\triangle ABC$?

Divide the area of the parallelogram by 2.

Math Success

Check off the vocabulary words that you understand.

☐ base of a parallelogram ☐ height of a parallelogram

☐ base of a triangle ☐ height of a triangle

Rate how well you can *find the area of parallelograms and triangles.*

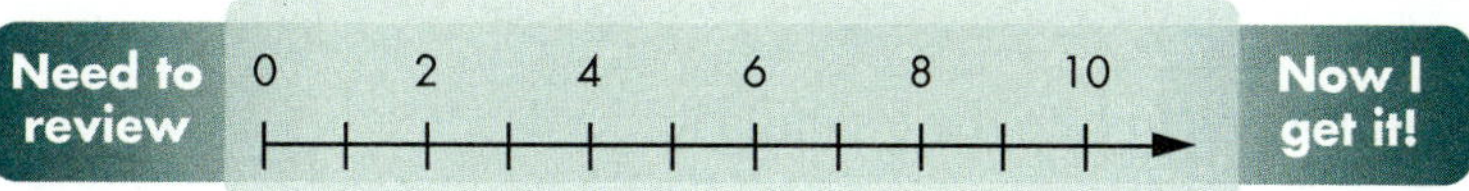

Name ______________________ Class ____________ Date ____________

10-1 Think About a Plan

Areas of Parallelograms and Triangles

Coordinate Geometry Find the area of a polygon with the given vertices.

$A(3, 9)$, $B(8, 9)$, $C(2, -3)$, $D(-3, -3)$

Understanding the Problem

1. What is the first thing you need to know about the polygon to find its area?

   the type of polygon

2. What is the simplest way to determine this?

   Draw the polygon on a coordinate grid.

Planning the Solution

3. Plot the points on the coordinate grid. What type of polygon is it? How can you tell?

   Parallelogram; its opposite sides are congruent and parallel.

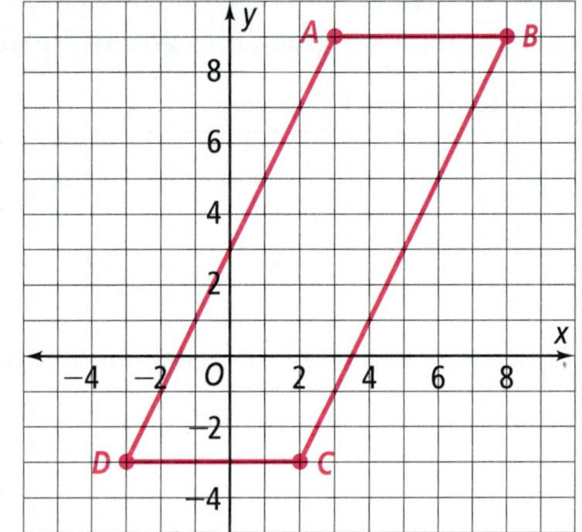

4. What is the formula for finding the area of this type of polygon? $A = bh$

5. Which segment will you use as the base?

   Answers may vary. Sample: either $\overline{AB}$ or $\overline{DC}$

6. How can you add to the figure to find the height?

   Answers may vary. Sample: Use $\overline{DC}$ as the base and extend $\overline{DC}$ so you can draw an altitude from B to the line containing $\overline{DC}$.

7. How can you find the measure of the base and height? What are the base and the height?

   Either use the Distance Formula or just count on the grid; $b = 5$; $h = 12$.

Getting an Answer

8. Substitute the values for the base and height into the formula and solve. $A = 5 \times 12$; 60

9. What unit should you use for your answer? What is the area?

   square units; 60 square units

Name ______________________ Class ____________ Date ____________

10-1 Practice

Form K

Areas of Parallelograms and Triangles

Find the area of each parallelogram.

1. 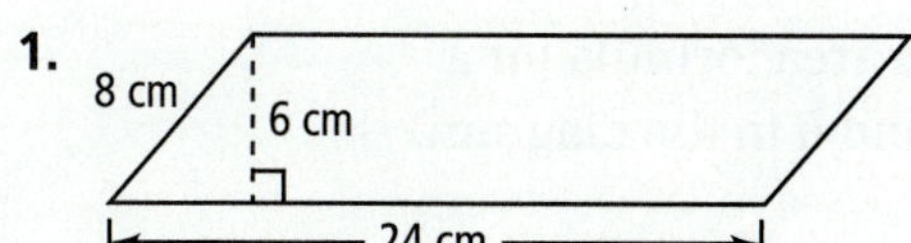

144 cm^2

2. 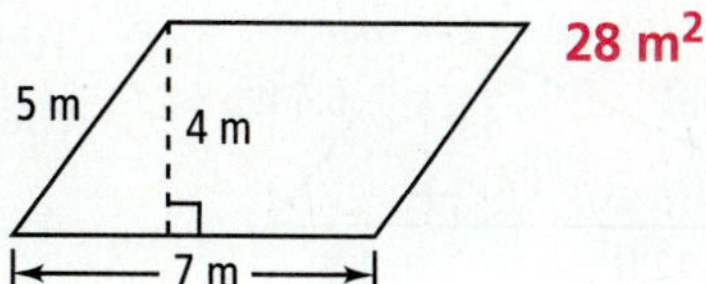

28 m^2

3. 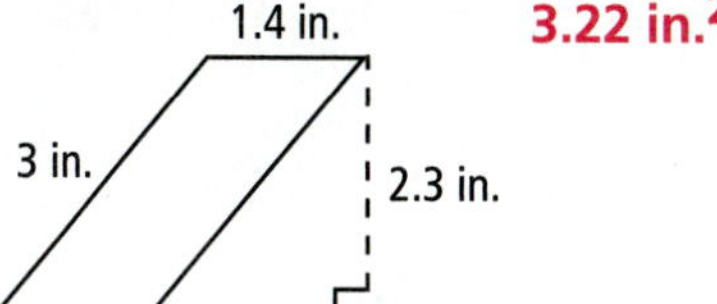

3.22 $in.^2$

4. 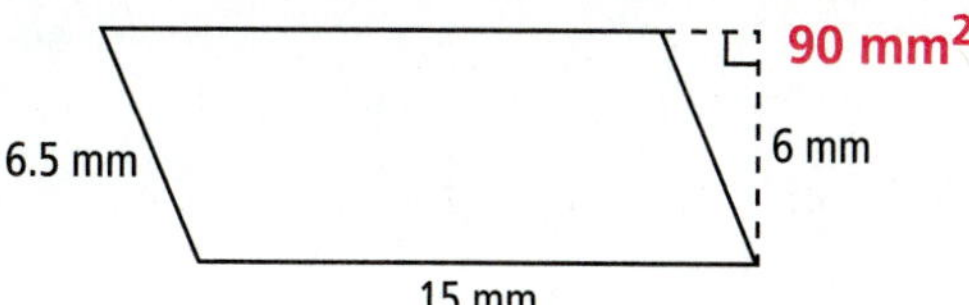

90 mm^2

Find the value of *h* for each parallelogram.

5. 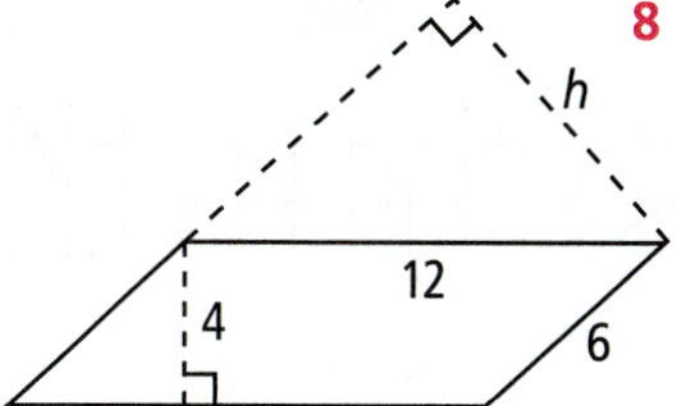

8

To start, write the area formula for a parallelogram. Substitute 12 for *b* and 4 for *h*.

$A = bh$

$= \underline{\ ?\ } \cdot \underline{\ ?\ }$ 12; 4

6. 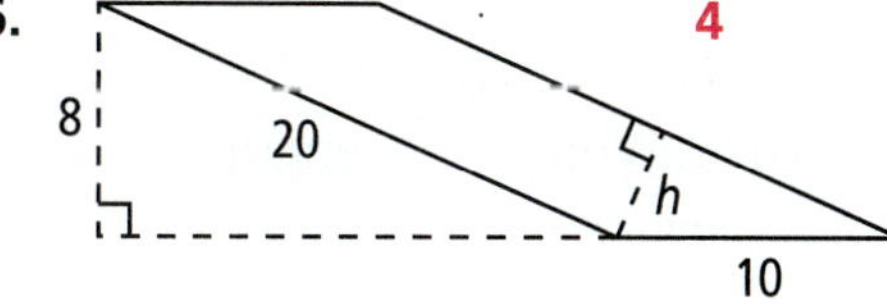

4

7. 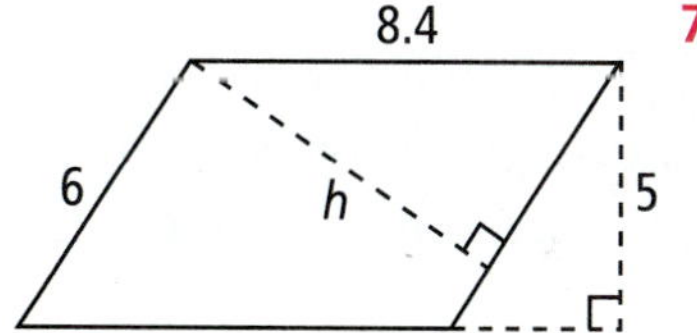

7

8. The area of a triangle is 36 m^2 and the height is 9 m. Find the length of the corresponding base. 8 m

9. **Algebra** In a parallelogram, a base and a corresponding height are in the ratio 5 : 2. The area is 250 cm^2. Find the lengths of the base and the corresponding height. (*Hint:* Use $5x$ for the base and $2x$ for the height of the parallelogram.) 25 cm; 10 cm

10. A triangle has area 16 m^2. List all the possible positive integers that could represent the lengths of its base and height. 1 m and 32 m, 2 m and 16 m, 4 m and 8 m, 8 m and 4 m, 16 m and 2 m, 32 m and 1 m

11. A classmate drew a rectangle with a height of 8 units and a base of 10 units. What is the area of each figure formed when the rectangle is divided along one of its diagonals? 40 $units^2$

Name ______________________ Class ____________ Date ____________

10-1 Practice (continued) — Form K

Areas of Parallelograms and Triangles

Find the area of each triangle.

12.

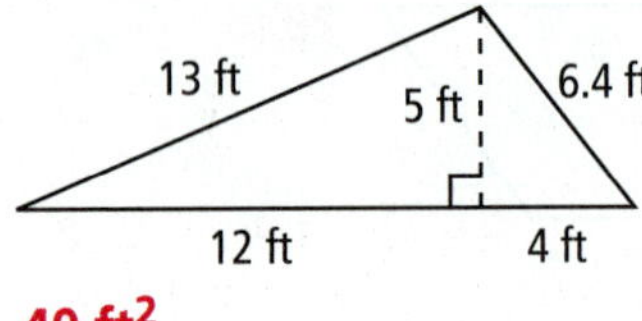

40 ft²

To start, write the area formula for a triangle. Find b and h in the diagram.

$A = \frac{1}{2}bh$

The height h is perpendicular to the base b so $h = 5$ and $b = \underline{\ ?\ } + \underline{\ ?\ } = \underline{\ ?\ }$. **12; 4; 16**

13.

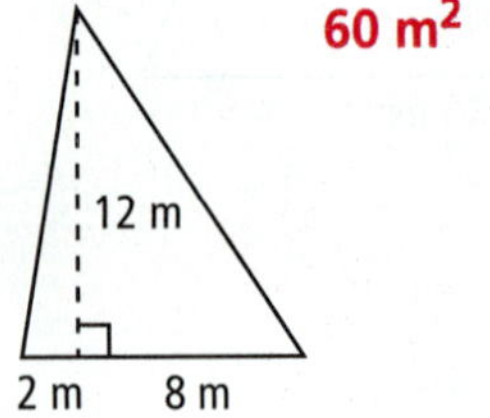

60 m²

14.

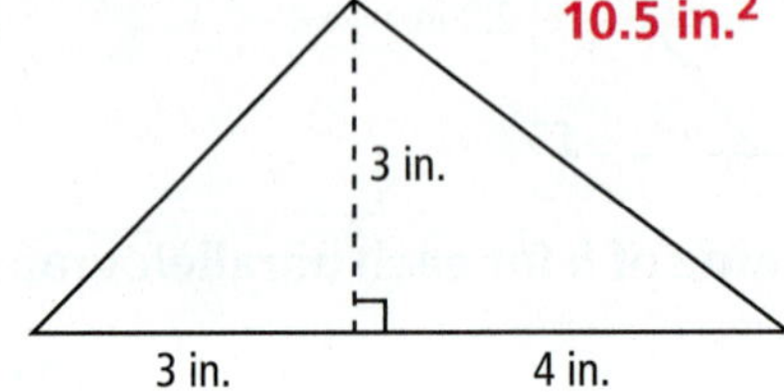

10.5 in.²

15.

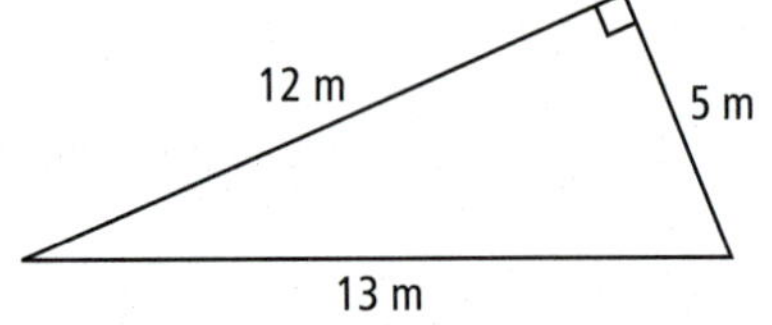

30 m²

16.

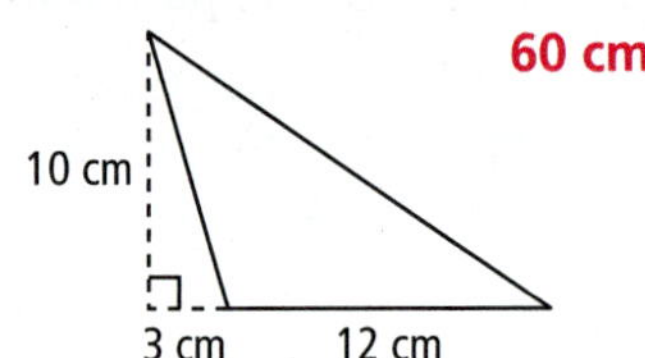

60 cm²

17. Reasoning A parallelogram has sides that are 30 in. and 12 in. long. The length of the height corresponding to the 30-in. base is 8 in. What is the length of the height corresponding to the 12-in. base? **20 in.**

Coordinate Geometry Find the area of a polygon with the given vertices.

18. $A(-3, 1)$, $B(-3, 4)$, $C(7, 1)$, $D(7, 4)$
30 units²

19. $A(\ \ 1, 1)$, $B(-1, 6)$, $C(2, 6)$
7.5 units²

20. $A(2, 2)$, $B(5, 5)$, $C(5, 0)$, $D(2, -3)$
15 units²

21. $A(-5, -2)$, $B(-3, 0)$, $C(-3, -4)$
4 units²

Find the area of each figure.

22.

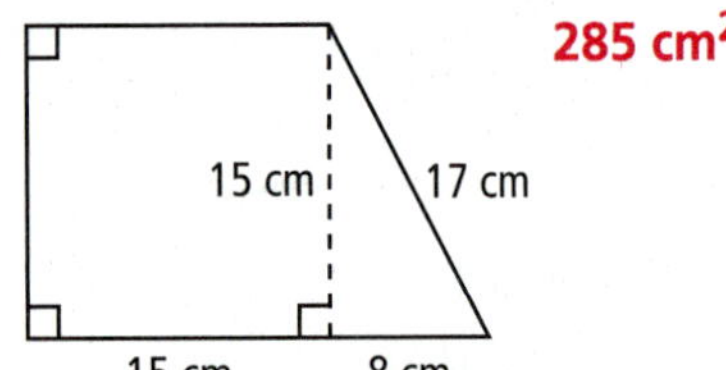

285 cm²

23.

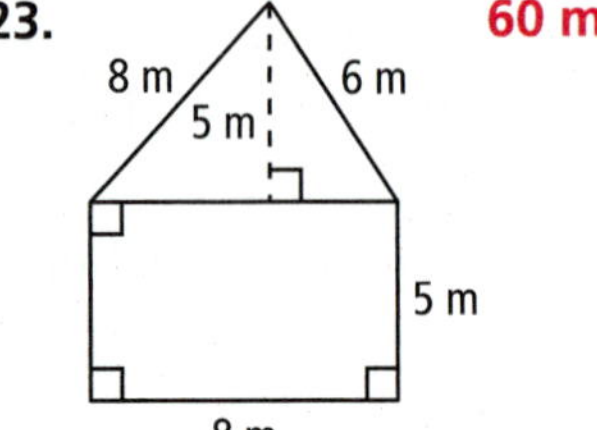

60 m²

Name ______________________ Class ____________ Date ____________

10-1 Standardized Test Prep

Areas of Parallelograms and Triangles

Multiple Choice

For Exercises 1–6, choose the correct letter.

1. What is the area of the parallelogram at the right? C

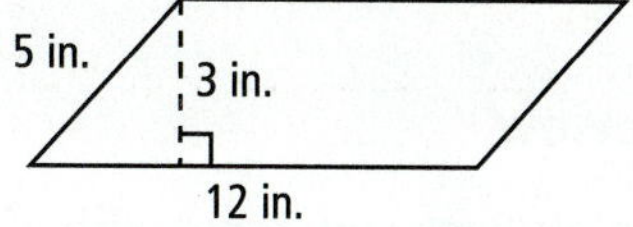

(A) 18 in.^{2} (C) 36 in.^{2}

(B) 30 in.^{2} (D) 60 in.^{2}

2. What is the area of the parallelogram at the right? G

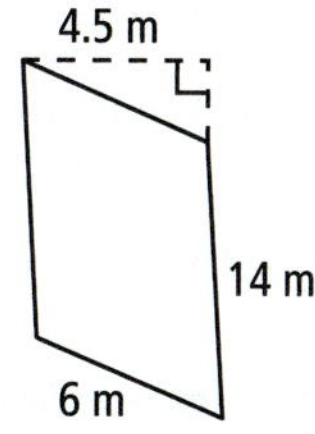

(F) 31.5 m^2 (H) 84 m^2

(G) 63 m^2 (I) 126 m^2

3. What is the value of h for the parallelogram at the right? A

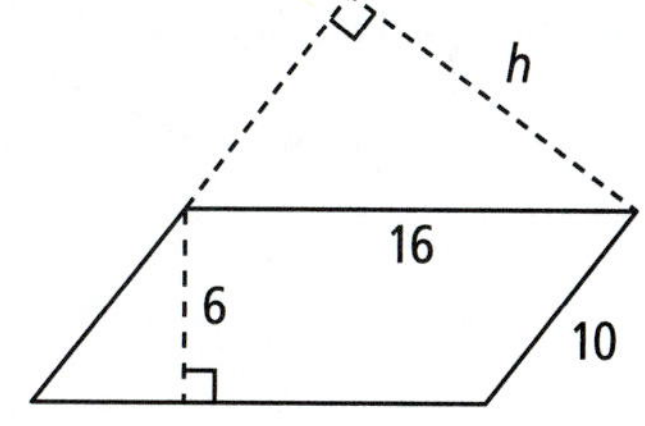

(A) 9.6 units (C) 48 units

(B) 26.7 units (D) 96 units

4. What is the area of the figure at the right? F

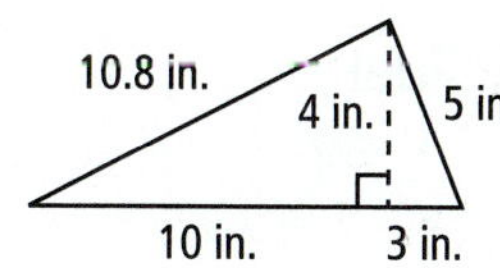

(F) 26 in.^{2} (H) 52 in.^{2}

(G) 27 in.^{2} (I) 54 in.^{2}

5. A parallelogram has sides 8 ft and 6 ft and an area of 54 ft^2. What is the length of the altitude to the 8-ft base? A

(A) 6.75 ft (B) 9 ft (C) 24 ft (D) 27 ft

6. What is the area of the figure at the right? I

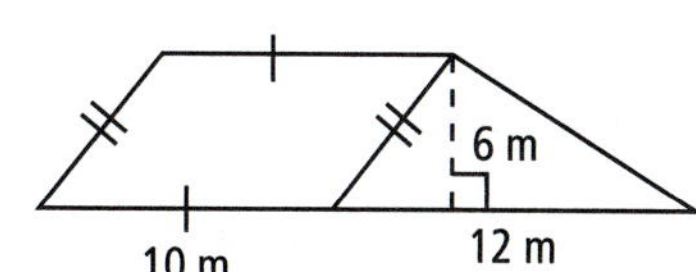

(F) 36 m^2 (H) 72 m^2

(G) 60 m^2 (I) 96 m^2

Short Response

7. In a triangle, a base and a corresponding height are in the ratio 5 : 2. The area is 80 ft^2. What is the base and the corresponding height? Show your work.

[2] $\frac{1}{2}5x(2x) = 80$; $5x^2 = 80$; $x = 4$ ft; base $= 5(4) = 20$ ft; height $= 2(4) = 8$ ft [1] error in calculation or incorrect work [0] error in calculation and no work provided

10-2 PART 1 Areas of Trapezoids, Rhombuses, and Kites

Vocabulary

Review

Complete each statement with *always*, *sometimes*, or *never*.

1. A *trapezoid* is _?_ a quadrilateral. always

2. A *trapezoid* _?_ has two pairs of parallel sides. never

3. The legs of a *trapezoid* are _?_ congruent. sometimes

4. Label each side of the *trapezoid* at the right with the word *leg* or *base*.

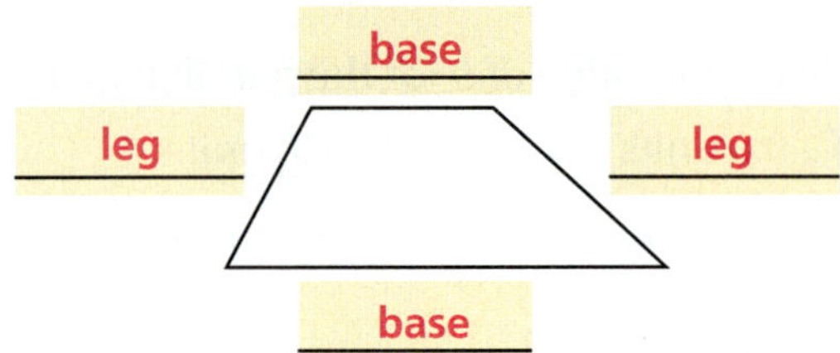

base

Vocabulary Builder

height (noun) hyt

Related Word: altitude (noun)

Definition: **Height** is the perpendicular distance between the bottom and the top of an object.

Math Usage: In a polygon, the length of the altitude is the **height**.

Use Your Vocabulary

Use the figure at the right for Exercises 5 and 6.

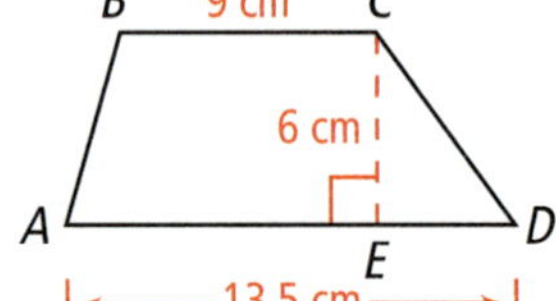

5. Circle the *height* of the trapezoid.

6 cm (circled)	9 cm	13.5 cm

6. Circle the altitude of the trapezoid.

$\overline{AB}$	$\overline{AD}$	$\overline{BC}$	$\overline{CD}$	$\overline{CE}$ (circled)

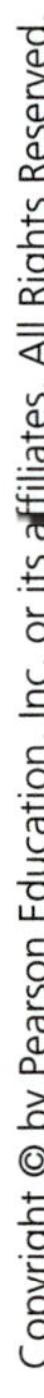

take note

Theorem 10-4 Area of a Trapezoid

The area of a trapezoid is half the product of the height and the sum of the bases.

$$A = \frac{1}{2}h(b_1 + b_2)$$

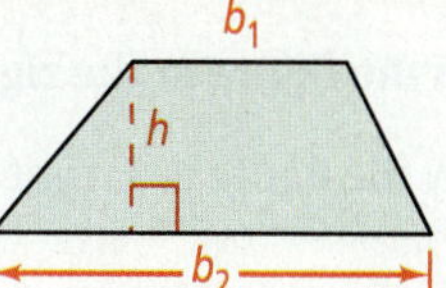

Underline the correct word to complete each sentence.

7. The bases of a trapezoid are parallel / perpendicular .

8. The height / width of a trapezoid is the perpendicular distance between the bases.

Problem 1 Area of a Trapezoid

Got It? What is the area of a trapezoid with height 7 cm and bases 12 cm and 15 cm?

9. Use the justifications below to find the area of the trapezoid.

$A = \frac{1}{2}h(b_1 + b_2)$	Use the formula for area of a trapezoid.
$= \frac{1}{2}(\ 7\ )(\ 12\ + 15)$	Substitute.
$= \frac{1}{2}(\ 7\ )(\ 27\ )$	Add.
$=$ 94.5	Simplify.

10. The area of the trapezoid is 94.5 cm^2.

Problem 2 Finding Area Using a Right Triangle

Got It? Reasoning Suppose *h* decreases in trapezoid *PQRS* so that $m\angle P = 45$ while angles *R* and *Q* and the bases stay the same. What is the area of trapezoid *PQRS*?

11. If $m\angle P = 45$, is the triangle still a 30°-60°-90° triangle?

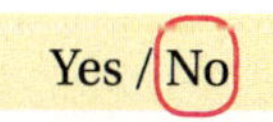

12. Is the triangle a 45°-45°-90° triangle?

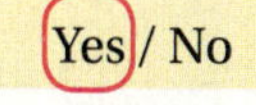

13. Are the legs of a 45°-45°-90° triangle congruent?

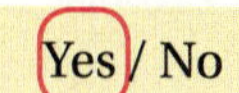

14. The height of the triangle is 2 m.

15. The area is found below. Write a justification for each step.

$A = \frac{1}{2}h(b_1 + b_2)$	Use the trapezoid area formula.
$= \frac{1}{2}(2)(5 + 7)$	Substitute.
$= \frac{1}{2}(2)(12)$	Add.
$= 12$	Simplify.

16. The area of trapezoid *PQRS* is 12 m^2.

Lesson Check • Do you know HOW?

Find the area of the figure at the right.

17. Explain why the figure is a trapezoid. Answers may vary. Sample:

A quadrilateral with two noncongruent, parallel sides is a trapezoid.

18. Complete.

$b_1 = 10$ $b_2 = $ 4 $h = $ 6

19. Use the formula for the area of trapezoid to find the area of the figure.

$A = \frac{1}{2}h(b_1 + b_2)$

$= \frac{1}{2}(6)(10 + 4) = \frac{1}{2}(84) = 42$

20. The area of the figure is 42 m^2.

Lesson Check • Do you UNDERSTAND?

Vocabulary Can a trapezoid and a parallelogram with the same base and height have the same area? Explain.

21. **Reasoning** Let b_1 = the length of the top base of the trapezoid shown at the right. Circle the equation that would be true if the trapezoid and the parallelogram had the same area.

$h(b_1 + b) = \frac{1}{2}bh$ $\frac{1}{2}h(b_1 + b) = bh$ (circled) $\frac{1}{2}h(b_1)(b) = 2bh$

22. Solve your equation from Exercise 21 for b_1.

$\frac{1}{2}h(b_1 + b) = bh$ $b_1 + b = 2b$

$\frac{1}{2}(b_1 + b) = b$ $b_1 = b$

23. Explain how your result in Exercise 22 shows that the trapezoid is a parallelogram.

Answers may vary. Sample: $b_1 = b$ means that the parallel bases of the trapezoid are also congruent. A quadrilateral with a pair of congruent parallel sides is a parallelogram.

24. Underline the correct word(s) to complete each sentence.

A trapezoid can / <u>cannot</u> also be a parallogram.

Assuming that a trapezoid and a parallelogram with the same base and height have the same area <u>leads</u> / does not lead to a contradiction, so the trapezoid and the parallelogram can / <u>cannot</u> have the same area.

10-2 PART 2 Areas of Trapezoids, Rhombuses, and Kites

Vocabulary

Review

1. Is a *rhombus* a parallelogram? Yes / No (Yes circled)

2. Are all *rhombuses* squares? Yes / No (No circled)

3. Are all squares *rhombuses*? Yes / No (Yes circled)

4. Cross out the figure that is NOT a *rhombus*.

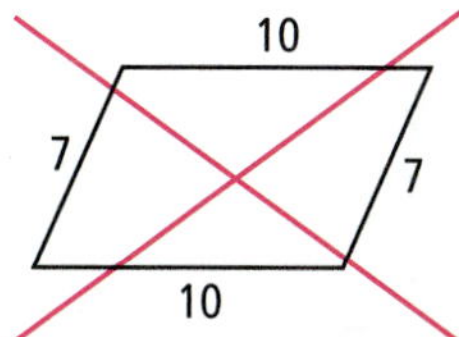

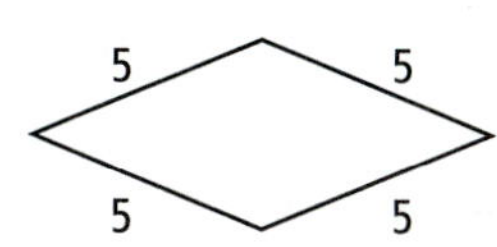

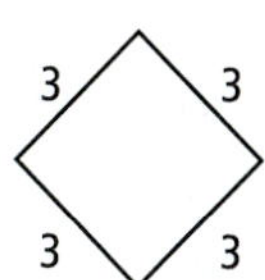

Vocabulary Builder

kite (noun) kyt

Definition: A **kite** is a quadrilateral with two pairs of congruent adjacent sides.

Main Idea: You can find the area of a **kite** when you know the lengths of its diagonals.

Word Origin: The name for this quadrilateral is taken from the name of the flying toy that it looks like.

Use Your Vocabulary

5. Circle the *kite*.

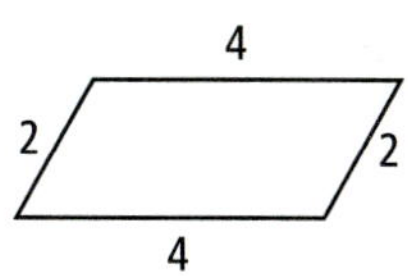

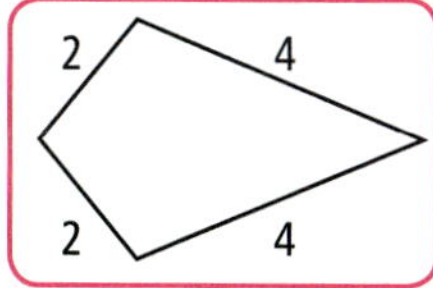

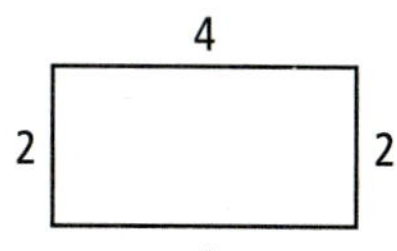

6. The figure at the right is a *kite*. What is the value of x? Explain.

Explanations may vary. Sample:

5; a kite has two pairs of congruent adjacent sides.

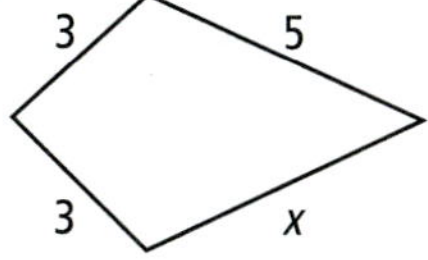

take note

Theorem 10-5 Area of a Rhombus or a Kite

The area of a rhombus or a kite is half the product of the lengths of its diagonals.

$A = \frac{1}{2}(d_1 d_2)$

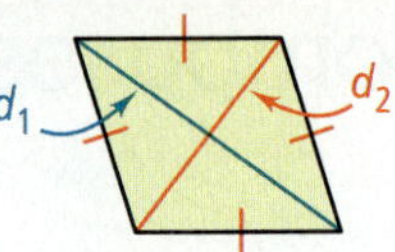

Rhombus

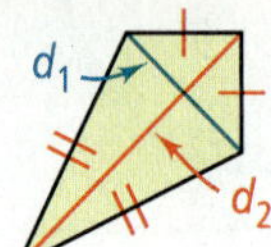

Kite

7. Describe one way that finding the area of rhombus or a kite is *different* from finding the area of a trapezoid.

Answers may vary. Sample: Instead of using the height and the lengths of the bases, you use the lengths of the diagonals.

Problem 3 Finding the Area of a Kite

Got It? **What is the area of a kite with diagonals that are 12 in. and 9 in. long?**

8. **Error Analysis** Below is one student's solution. What error did the student make?

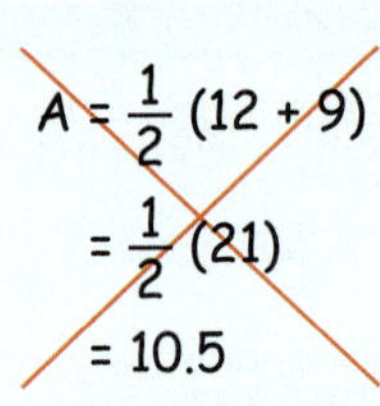

Answers may vary. Sample: The student added the lengths of the diagonals instead of multiplying them.

9. Find the area of the kite.

$A = \frac{1}{2}(12)(9)$

$= \frac{1}{2}(108)$

$= 54$

10. The area of the kite is 54 in.^{2}.

Problem 4 Finding the Area of a Rhombus

Got It? **A rhombus has sides 10 cm long. If the longer diagonal is 16 cm, what is the area of the rhombus?**

Underline the correct words to complete the sentence.

11. The diagonals of a rhombus bisect each other / side and are parallel / perpendicular .

12. Label the rhombus at the right.

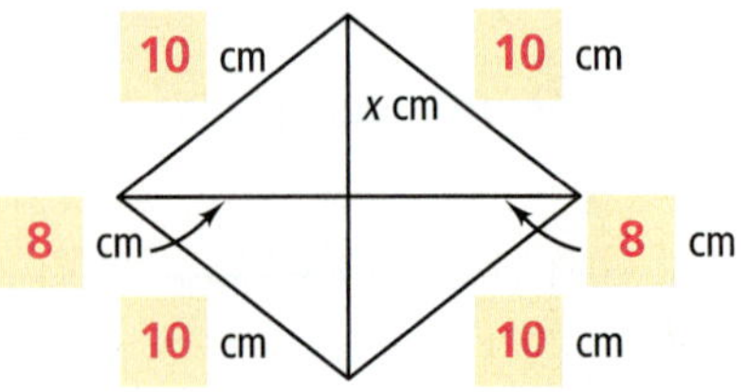

13. The shorter diagonal is x + x , or $2x$.

14. Use the Pythagorean Theorem to find the value of x.

$x^2 + 8^2 = 10^2$
$x^2 + 64 = 100$
$x^2 = 36$
$x = 6$

15. Find the area of the rhombus.

$A = \frac{1}{2}(6 + 6)(16)$
$= \frac{1}{2}(12)(16)$
$= \frac{1}{2}(192)$
$= 96$

16. The area of the rhombus is 96 cm^2.

Lesson Check • Do you know HOW?

Find the area of the figure at the right.

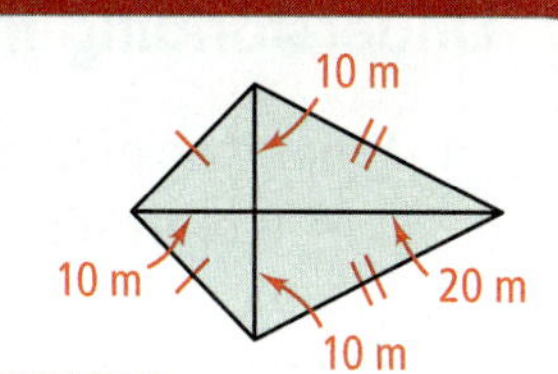

17. Circle the name of the figure.

(kite) parallelogram rhombus trapezoid

18. Circle the lengths you know.

lengths of sides lengths of bases height (lengths of diagonals)

19. Circle the formula you can use to find the area of the figure.

$A = bh$ $A = \frac{1}{2}bh$ ($A = \frac{1}{2}(d_1d_2)$) $A = \frac{1}{2}h(b_1 + b_2)$

20. Use your formula from Exercise 20 to find the area.

$A = \frac{1}{2}(d_1d_2)$
$= \frac{1}{2}(10 + 10)(10 + 20)$
$= \frac{1}{2}(20)(30)$
$= 300$

21. The area of the figure is 300 m^2.

Math Success

Check off the vocabulary words that you understand.

☐ kite ☐ rhombus ☐ trapezoid ☐ height of a trapezoid

Rate how well you can *find the area of a trapezoid, rhombus, or kite.*

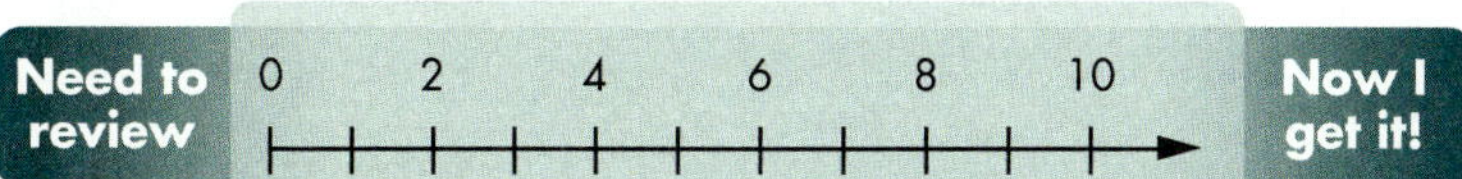

Name ______________________ Class ____________ Date ____________

10-2 Think About a Plan

Areas of Trapezoids, Rhombuses, and Kites

a. **Coordinate Geometry** Graph the lines $x = 0, x = 6, y = 0$, and $y = x + 4$.

b. What type of quadrilateral do the lines form?

c. Find the area of the quadrilateral.

Understanding the Problem

1. What type of line does $x = 0$ and $x = 6$ represent? What type of line does $y = 0$ represent?
   vertical line; horizontal line

2. What can you tell about the relationships among the lines $x = 0$, $x = 6$, and $y = 0$?
   parallel: $x = 0$ and $x = 6$; perpendicular: $x = 0$ and $y = 0$, $x = 6$ and $y = 0$

3. How do you graph a line in the form $y = mx + b$?
   Answers may vary. Sample: The y-intercept is b, so you can plot $(0, b)$. You can use the value of m, the slope, to graph other points near the y-intercept.

Planning the Solution

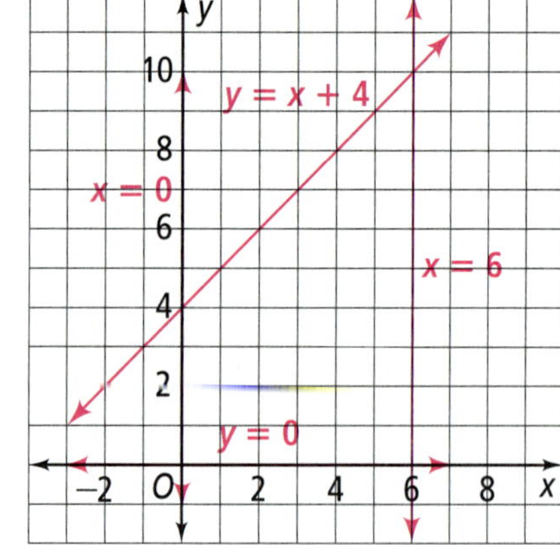

4. Graph the lines on the coordinate grid. What type of quadrilateral is formed? How can you tell?
   Trapezoid; one pair of opposite sides is parallel, but the other pair is not.

5. What is the formula for finding the area of this type of quadrilateral? $A = \frac{1}{2}h(b_1 + b_2)$

6. Which lines contain the bases? Explain.
   $x = 0$ and $x = 6$; they are parallel.

7. How can you find the lengths of the bases?
   Use the Distance Formula or count on the grid.

8. Which line contains the height? How can you find the length of the height?
   $y = 0$; use the Distance Formula or count on the grid.

Getting an Answer

9. Substitute the values for the bases and height into the formula and solve for the area. 42 square units

Name ______________________ Class ____________ Date ____________

10-2 Practice
Form K

Areas of Trapezoids, Rhombuses, and Kites

Find the area of each trapezoid.

1. 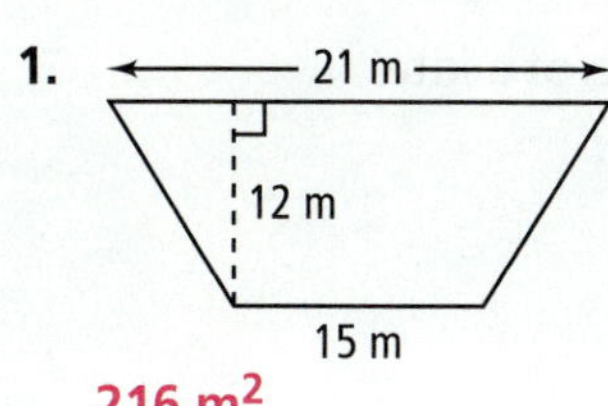

216 m^2

To start, write the formula for the area of a trapezoid. Find h, b_1, and b_2 in the diagram.

$A = \frac{1}{2}h(b_1 + b_2)$

The height h is perpendicular to the bases, so $h = \underline{\ ?\ }$, $b_1 = \underline{\ ?\ }$, and $b_2 = \underline{\ ?\ }$. 12 m; 21 m; 15 m

2. 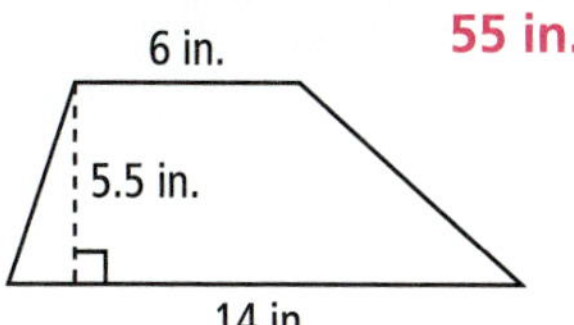

55 $in.^2$

3. 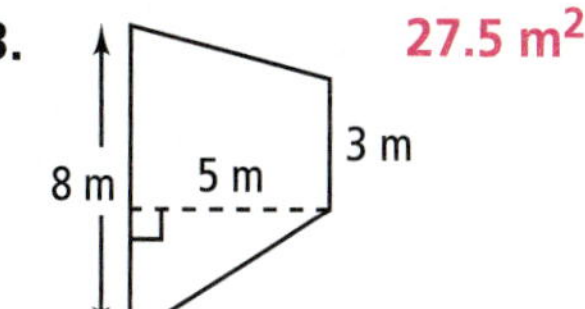

27.5 m^2

4. Find the area of a trapezoid with bases 16 in. and 7 in. and height 9 in. 103.5 $in.^2$

5. Find the area of a trapezoid with bases 5 ft and 11 ft and height 7.4 ft. 59.2 ft^2

Find the area of each trapezoid. If your answer is not an integer, leave it in simplest radical form.

6. 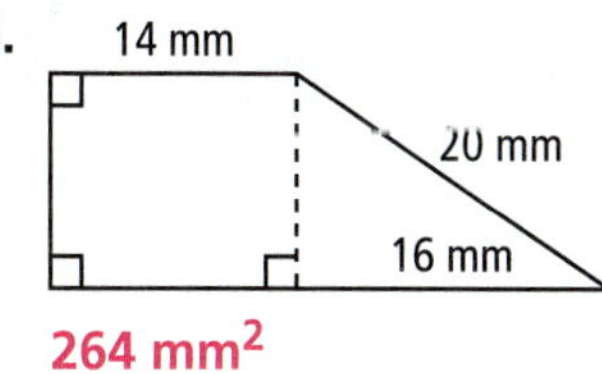

264 mm^2

To start, find the height of the trapezoid using the Pythagorean Theorem, $a^2 + b^2 = c^2$.

The height is the other leg of the right triangle with leg 16 mm and hypotenuse 20 mm.

$h^2 + 16^2 = 20^2$

$h^2 + 256 = 400$

$h^2 = \underline{\ ?\ }$ 144 mm^2

$h = \underline{\ ?\ }$ 12 mm

7. 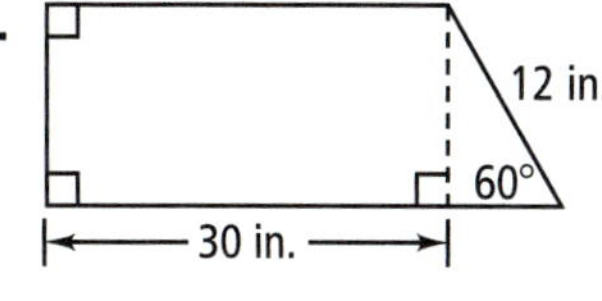

$198\sqrt{3}$ $in.^2$

8. 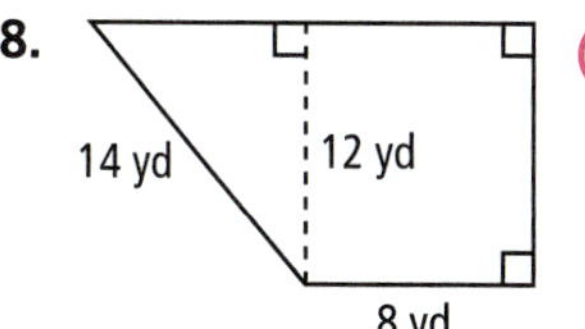

$(96 + 12\sqrt{13})$ yd^2

Find the area of each trapezoid to the nearest tenth.

9. 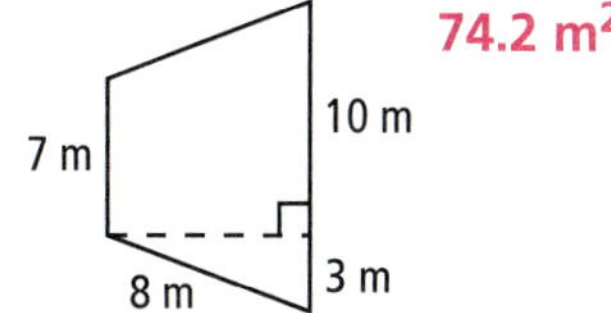

74.2 m^2

10. 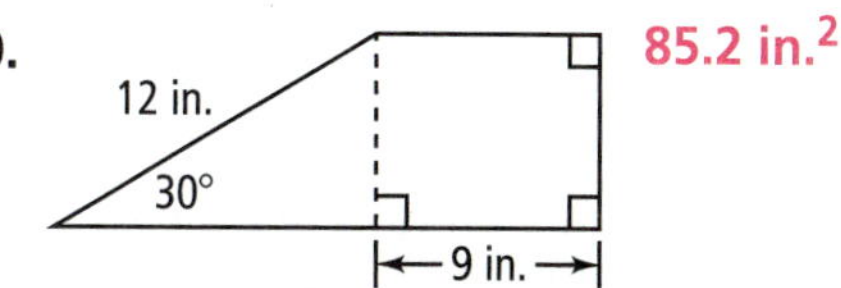

85.2 $in.^2$

Name ____________________ Class ____________ Date ____________

10-2 Practice (continued) Form K

Areas of Trapezoids, Rhombuses, and Kites

Find the area of each kite.

11. 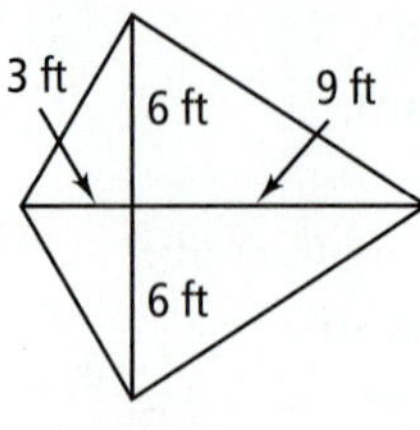

To start, write the formula for the area of a kite. Find the lengths of the two diagonals.

$A = \frac{1}{2}d_1d_2$

$d_1 = 6 + 6 = \underline{\ ?\ }$ 12 ft

$d_2 = \underline{\ ?\ } + \underline{\ ?\ } = \underline{\ ?\ }$ 3; 9; 12 ft

72 ft^2

12. 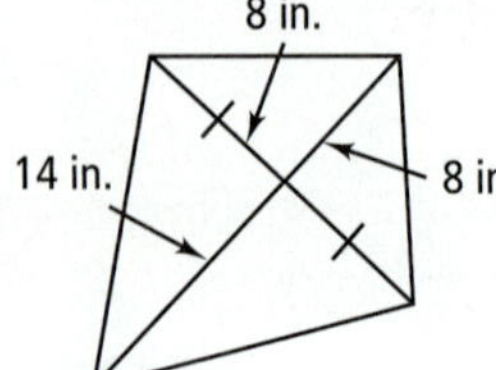

176 in.^{2}

13. 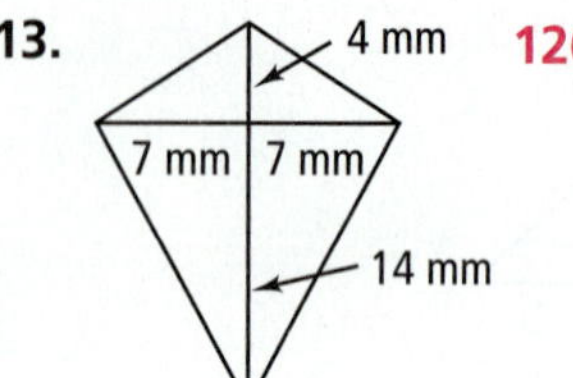

126 mm^2

14. **Algebra** The diagonals of a kite are in the ratio 3 : 2. The area of the kite is 27 cm^2. Find the length of both diagonals. (*Hint:* Let the lengths of the diagonals be $3x$ and $2x$.) 9 cm and 6 cm

Find the area of each rhombus.

15. 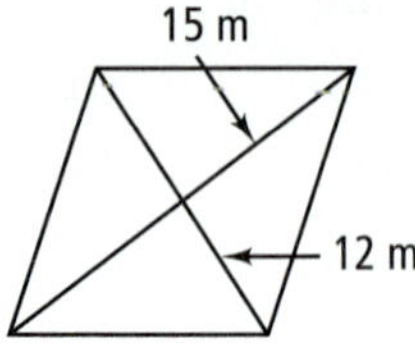

To start, write the formula for the area of a rhombus. Find the lengths of the two diagonals.

$A = \frac{1}{2}d_1d_2$

$d_1 = \underline{\ ?\ } \cdot 2 = \underline{\ ?\ }$ 12; 24 m

$d_2 = \underline{\ ?\ } \cdot 2 = \underline{\ ?\ }$ 15; 30 m

360 m^2

16. 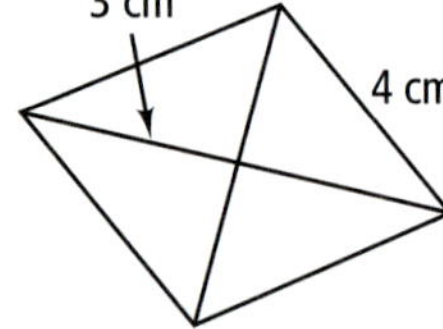

$6\sqrt{7}$ cm^2

17. 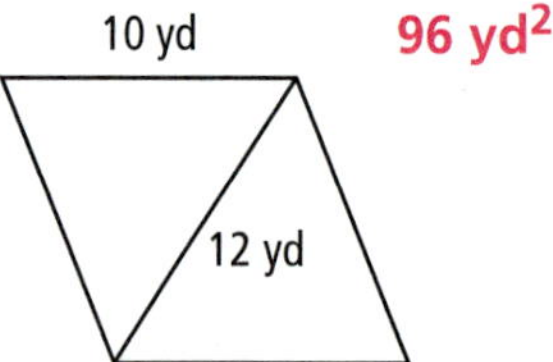

96 yd^2

Find the area of each rhombus. Leave your answer in simplest radical form.

18. 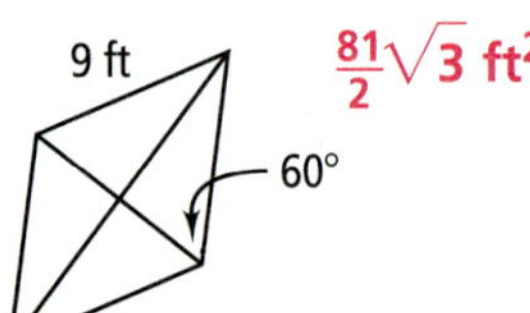

$\frac{81}{2}\sqrt{3}$ ft^2

19. 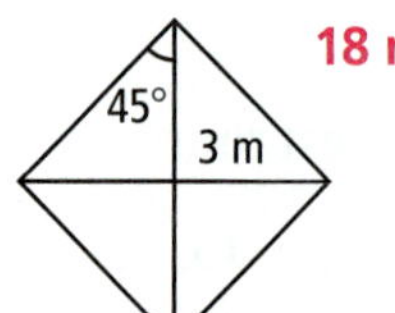

18 m^2

20. 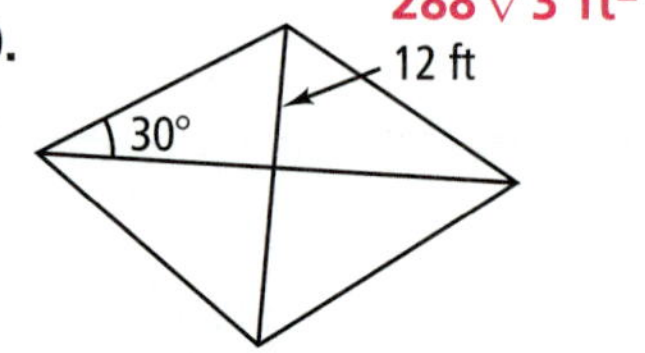

$288\sqrt{3}$ ft^2

Name ______________________ Class ____________ Date ____________

10-2 Standardized Test Prep

Areas of Trapezoids, Rhombuses, and Kites

Multiple Choice

For Exercises 1–6, choose the correct letter.

1. What is the area of a trapezoid with height 5 m and bases 8 m and 1 m? B

(A) 6.5 m^2 (B) 22.5 m^2 (C) 24 m^2 (D) 45 m^2

2. What is the area of the figure at the right? G

(F) 45 $in.^2$ (H) 135 $in.^2$

(G) 90 $in.^2$ (I) 180 $in.^2$

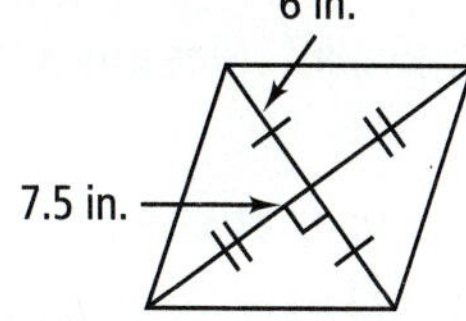

3. What is the area of the kite at the right? C

(A) 30 ft^2 (C) 96 ft^2

(B) 60 ft^2 (D) 120 ft^2

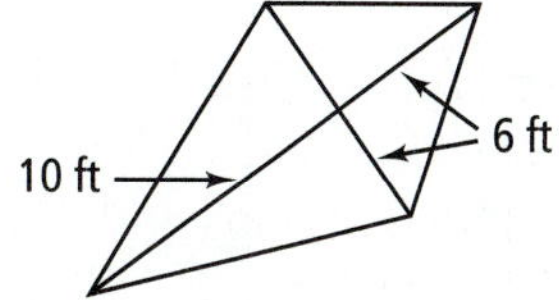

4. What is the area of the trapezoid at the right? F

(F) $36\sqrt{3}$ cm^2 (H) 65 cm^2

(G) $44\sqrt{3}$ cm^2 (I) 88 cm^2

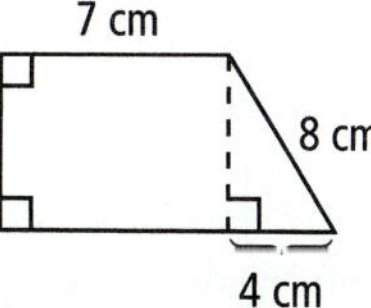

5. What is the area of the figure at the right? C

(A) 7.5 m^2 (C) 21.25 m^2

(B) 15 m^2 (D) 42.5 m^2

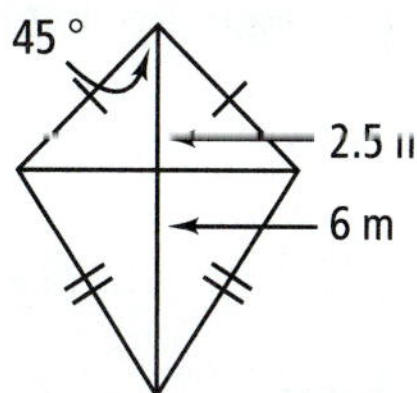

6. A trapezoid has an area of 166.5 $in.^2$, height 9 in., and one base 15 in. What is the length of the other base? I

(F) 3.5 in. (H) 18.5 in.

(G) 7 in. (I) 22 in.

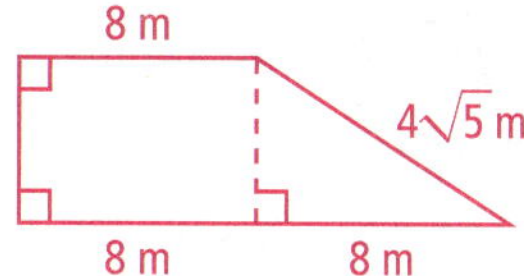

Extended Response

7. A trapezoid has two right angles and bases that measure 16 m and 8 m. The right triangle formed by an altitude has a hypotenuse of $4\sqrt{5}$ m. Sketch the trapezoid. What are its perimeter and area? Show your work.

[4] $(4\sqrt{5})^2 = 8^2 + h^2$; $h = 4$; $A = 0.5(4)(16 + 8) = 48$ m^2; $p = 4 + 8 + 4\sqrt{5} + 16 = 36.9$ m [3] appropriate methods, but with one computational error [2] appropriate methods, but with multiple computational errors [1] drawing or work not shown [0] no progress made

10-3 Areas of Regular Polygons

Vocabulary

Review

Write T for *true* or F for *false*.

T **1.** In a *regular polygon,* all sides are congruent.

F **2.** In a *regular polygon,* all angles are acute.

3. Cross out the figure that is NOT a *regular polygon.*

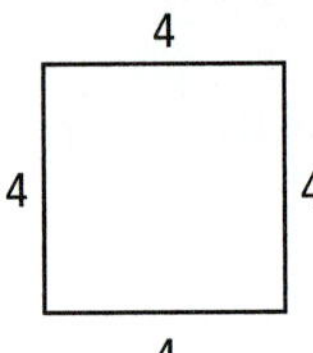

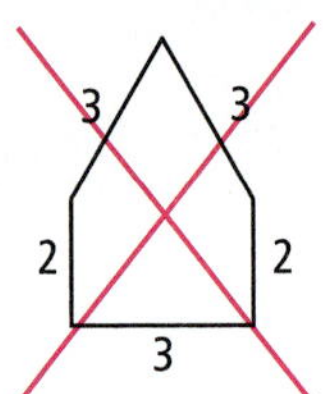

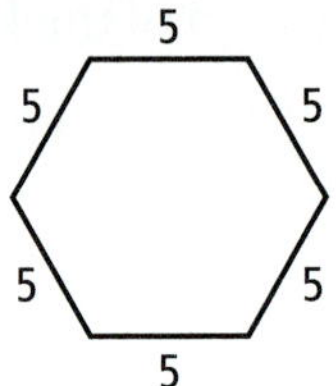

Vocabulary Builder

apothem (noun) **AP uh them**

Related Words: center, regular polygon

Definition: The **apothem** is the perpendicular distance from the center of a regular polygon to one of its sides.

Use Your Vocabulary

4. Underline the correct word to complete the statement.

In a regular polygon, the *apothem* is the perpendicular distance from the center to a(n) angle / side.

5. Label the regular polygon below using *apothem, center,* or *side.*

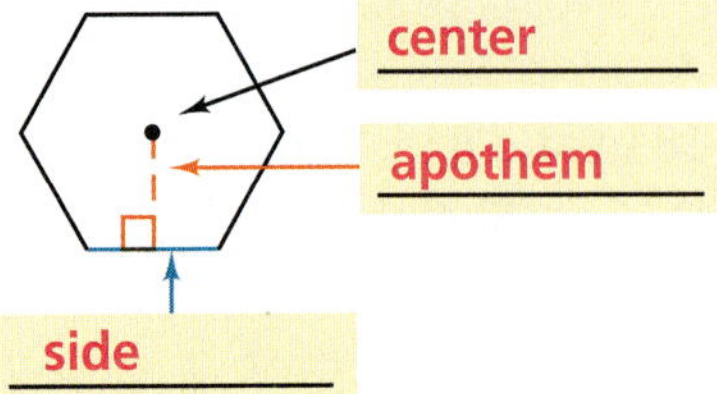

Problem 1 Finding Angle Measures

Got It? **At the right, a portion of a regular octagon has radii and an apothem drawn. What is the measure of each numbered angle?**

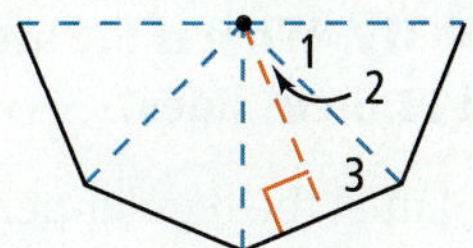

6. A regular octagon has 8 sides.

7. Circle the type of triangles formed by the radii of the regular octagon.

equilateral   (isosceles)   right

8. Use the justifications below to find the measure of each numbered angle.

$m\angle 1 = \frac{360}{8} = 45$	Divide 360 by the number of sides.
$m\angle 2 = \frac{1}{2}(m\angle 1)$ $= \frac{1}{2}(45) = 22.5$	The apothem bisects the vertex angle of the triangle formed by the radii.
$90 + m\angle 2 + m\angle 3 = 180$	Triangle Angle-Sum Theorem
$90 + 22.5 + m\angle 3 = 180$	Substitute.
$112.5 + m\angle 3 = 180$	Simplify.
$m\angle 3 = 67.5$	Subtraction Property of Equality

9. Write the measure of each numbered angle.

$m\angle 1 = 45$ $m\angle 2 = 22.5$ $m\angle 3 = 67.5$

take note

Postulate 10-1 and Theorem 10-6

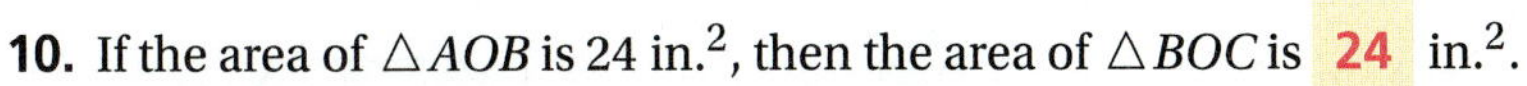

Postulate 10-1 If two figures are congruent, then their areas are equal.

The isosceles triangles in the regular hexagon at the right are congruent. Complete each statement.

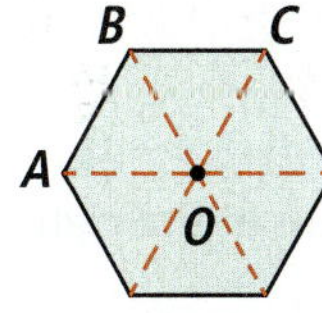

10. If the area of $\triangle AOB$ is 24 in.^{2}, then the area of $\triangle BOC$ is 24 in.^{2}.

11. If the area of $\triangle BOC$ is 8 cm^2, then the area of $\triangle AOC$ is 16 cm^2.

Theorem 10-6 Area of a Regular Polygon

The area of a regular polygon is half the product of the apothem and the perimeter.

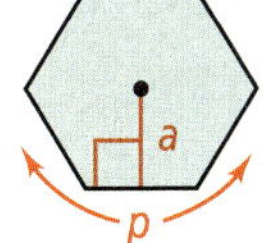

$$A = \frac{1}{2}ap$$

Complete.

12. apothem: 10   perimeter: 80   area: $\frac{1}{2}(10) \cdot 80$

13. apothem: 5   perimeter: $30\sqrt{3}$ area: $\frac{1}{2} \cdot 5 \cdot 30\sqrt{3}$

14. apothem: $5\sqrt{3}$ perimeter: 60   area: $\frac{1}{2} \cdot 5\sqrt{3} \cdot 60$

Problem 2 Finding the Area of a Regular Polygon

Got It? **What is the area of a regular pentagon with an 8-cm apothem and 11.6-cm sides?**

15. Label the regular pentagon with the lengths of the apothem and the sides.

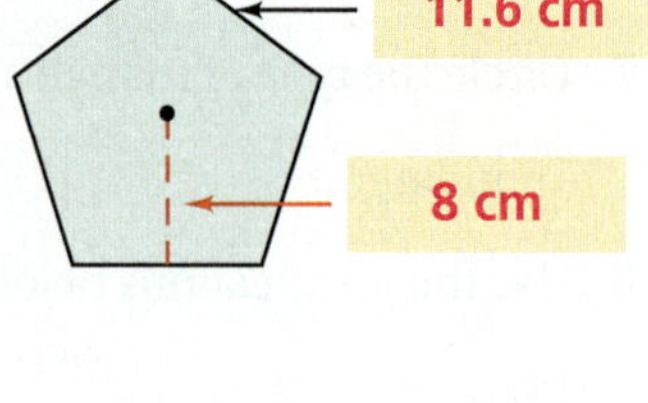

16. Use the justifications below to find the perimeter.

$p = ns$	Use the formula for the perimeter of an n-gon.
$= 5\ (11.6)$	Substitute for n and for s.
$= 58$	Simplify.

17. Use the justifications below to find the area.

$A = \frac{1}{2}ap$	Use the formula for the area of a regular polygon.
$= \frac{1}{2} \cdot 8 \cdot 58$	Substitute for a and for p.
$= 232$	Simplify.

18. The regular pentagon has an area of 232 cm^2.

Problem 3 Using Special Triangles to Find Area

Got It? **The side of a regular hexagon is 16 ft. What is the area of the hexagon? Round your answer to the nearest square foot.**

19. Use the information in the problem to complete the problem-solving model below.

Know	Need	Plan
I know that the length of each side of the regular hexagon is 16 ft.	The apothem and the perimeter	Draw a diagram to help find the apothem. Then use the perimeter and area formulas.

Use the diagram at the right.

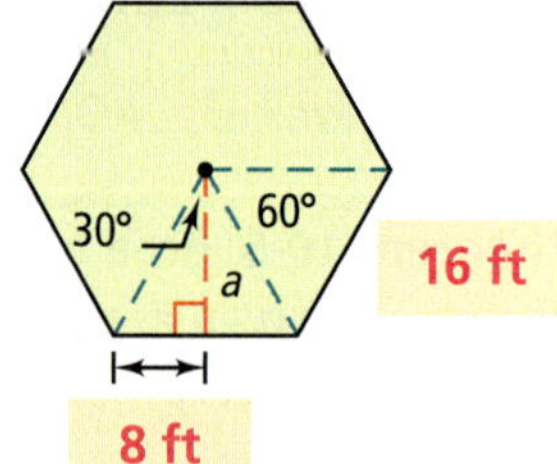

20. Label the diagram.

21. Circle the relationship you can use to find the apothem.

hypotenuse = 2 · shorter leg　　longer leg = $\sqrt{3}$ · shorter leg

22. Complete.

length of shorter leg = 8 ft

length of longer leg (apothem) = $8\sqrt{3}$ ft

23. Use the formula $p = ns$ to find the perimeter of the hexagon.

$p = ns$
$= 6(16)$
$= 96$

24. Now use the perimeter and the formula $A = \frac{1}{2}ap$ to find the area of the hexagon.

$A = \frac{1}{2}ap$
$= \frac{1}{2}(8\sqrt{3})(96)$
$= 665.1075101$

25. To the nearest square foot, the area of the hexagon is 665 ft^2.

Lesson Check • Do you UNDERSTAND?

What is the relationship between the side length and the apothem in each figure?

square

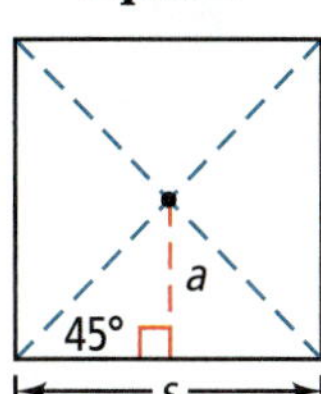

regular hexagon

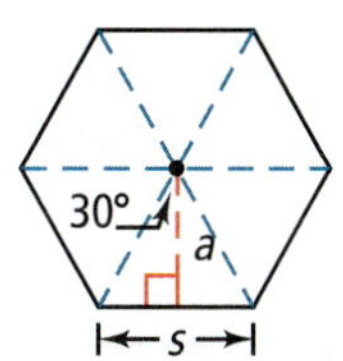

equilateral triangle

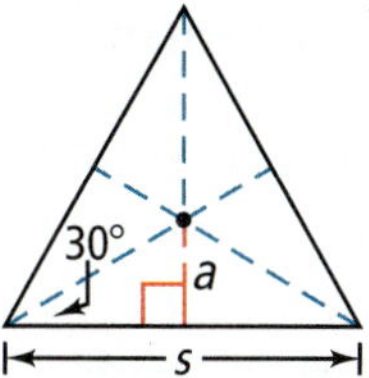

26. The radius and apothem form what type of triangle in each figure?

square

45°-45°-90° triangle

regular hexagon

30°-60°-90° triangle

equilateral triangle

30°-60°-90° triangle

27. Complete to show the relationship between the side length and the apothem.

square

leg = leg

$a = \frac{1}{2}s$

regular hexagon

longer leg = $\sqrt{3}$ · shorter leg

$a = \sqrt{3} \cdot \frac{1}{2}s$

$a = \frac{\sqrt{3}}{2}s$

equilateral triangle

longer leg = $\sqrt{3}$ · shorter leg

$\frac{1}{2}s = \sqrt{3} \cdot a$

$s = 2\sqrt{3}a$

Math Success

Check off the vocabulary words that you understand.

☐ radius of a regular polygon

☐ apothem

Rate how well you can *find the area of a regular polygon.*

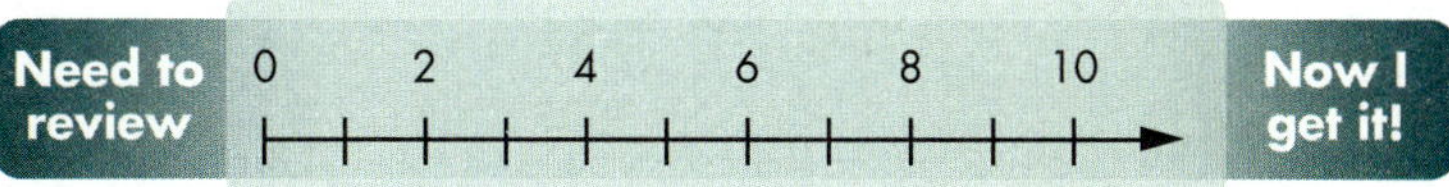

Name ______________________ Class ____________ Date ____________

10-3 Think About a Plan

Areas of Regular Polygons

A regular hexagon has perimeter 120 m. Find its area.

Understanding the Problem

1. What is the formula for the area of a regular polygon? $A = \frac{1}{2}ap$

2. What information is given? What information do you need?
The perimeter is given; you need to find the length of the apothem.

Planning the Solution

3. Divide the hexagon into six congruent triangles. What type of triangle are these? Explain how you know.
Equilateral; answers may vary. Sample: In a regular hexagon, the central angle measures $360 \div 6 = 60$. The base angles are congruent because the legs are congruent radii, so all three angles measure 60.

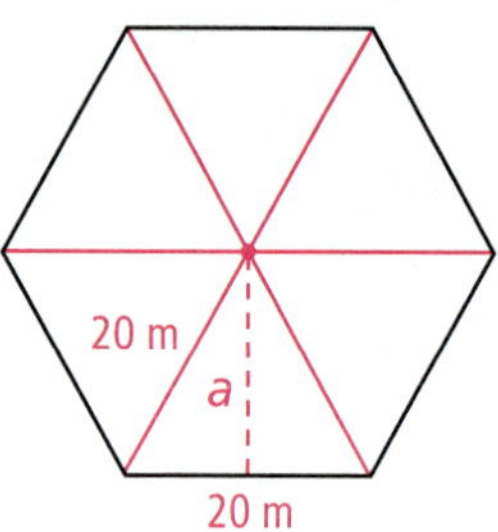

4. What is the length of the radius? Explain.
20 m; each side of the hexagon is $120 \div 6 = 20$ m. The sides of an equilateral triangle are congruent. Two sides are radii, so each radius is 20 m.

5. Draw an apothem. What type of triangle is formed by one radius, half of one side, and the apothem? What are the angles in this polygon?
right triangle; 30°-60°-90°

6. What relationships exist among the sides of this type of triangle?
The length of the shorter leg is half the length of the hypotenuse. The length of the longer leg is $\frac{\sqrt{3}}{2}$ times the length of the hypotenuse.

7. How can you find the length of the apothem? Find its length.
Answers may vary. Sample: Multiply the radius by $\frac{\sqrt{3}}{2}$; $10\sqrt{3}$ m.

Getting an Answer

8. Substitute the values for the apothem and the perimeter into the formula and solve. $A = \frac{1}{2}(10\sqrt{3})(120)$; $600\sqrt{3}\ \text{m}^2$

Name ______________________ Class ____________ Date ____________

10-3 Practice

Form K

Areas of Regular Polygons

Each regular polygon has radii and apothem as shown. Find the measure of each numbered angle.

1. 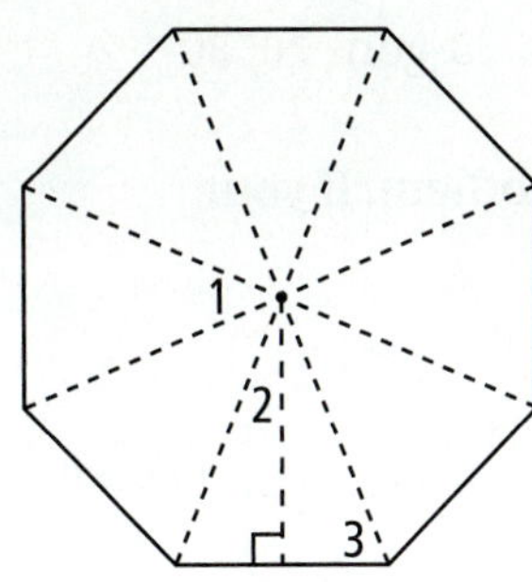

45; 22.5; 67.5

2. 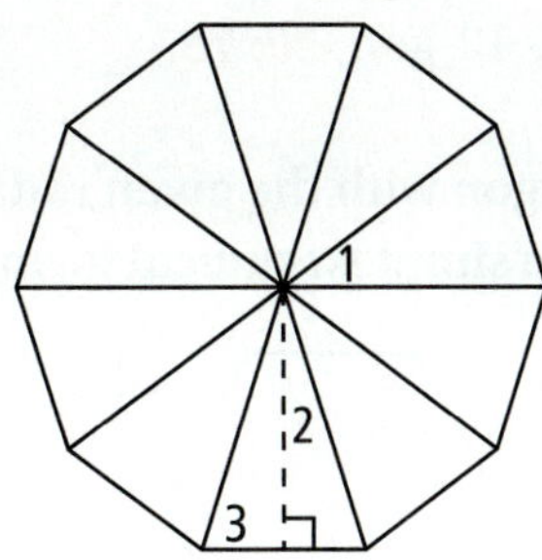

36; 18; 72

3. 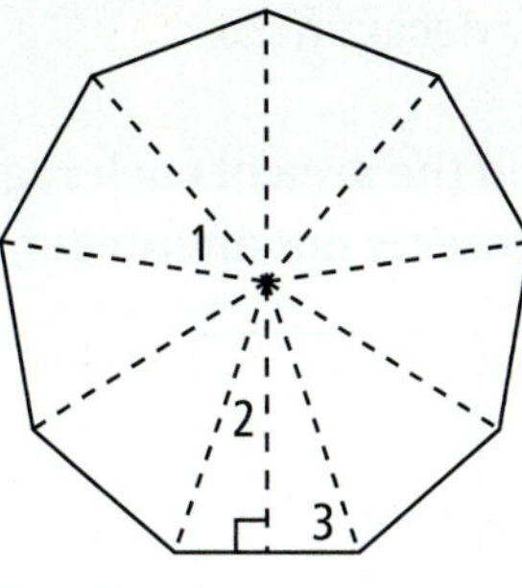

40; 20; 70

Find the area of each regular polygon with the given apothem *a* and side length *s*.

4. pentagon, $a = 1.6$ in., $s = 2.4$ in. 9.6 in.^{2}

   To start, write the area formula for a regular polygon. $A = \frac{1}{2}ap$

   Find the perimeter p of the polygon. $p = ns = 5 \cdot \underline{\ ?\ } = \underline{\ ?\ }$ 2.4; 12 in.

5. hexagon, $a = 2.6$ ft, $s = 3$ ft
   23.4 ft^2

6. decagon, $a = 3.8$ in., $s = 2.5$ in.
   47.5 in.^{2}

7. octagon, $a = 9.3$ cm, $s = 7.7$ cm
   286.44 cm^2

8. nonagon, $a = 5.6$ mm, $s = 4.1$ mm
   103.32 mm^2

Find the area of each regular polygon. Round your answer to the nearest tenth.

9. 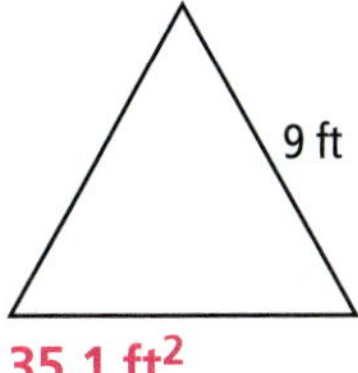

35.1 ft^2

   To start, write the area formula for a regular polygon. Find the length of the apothem.

   $A = \frac{1}{2}ap$

   The radii form three 120° angles at the center. You can use a 30°-60°-90° triangle to find the apothem.

   $a = \text{shorter leg} = \frac{\text{longer leg}}{\sqrt{3}} = \frac{4.5}{\sqrt{3}} = \underline{\ ?\ }$ $1.5\sqrt{3}$ ft

10. 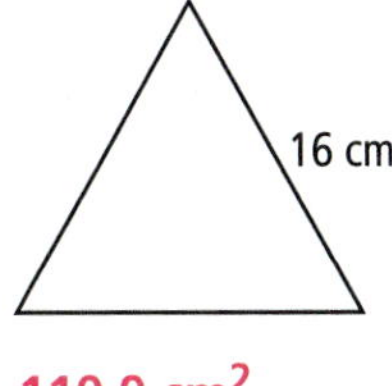

110.9 cm^2

11. 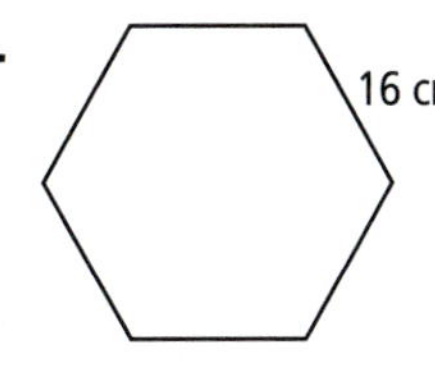

665.1 cm^2

12. 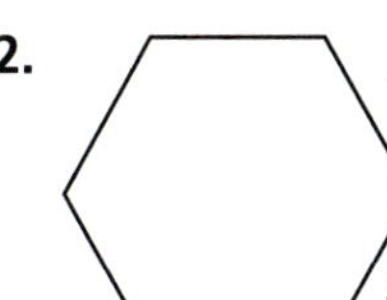

23.4 in.^{2}

Name ______________________________ Class ____________ Date ____________

10-3 Practice (continued)

Form K

Areas of Regular Polygons

Find the measures of the angles formed by (a) two consecutive radii and (b) a radius and a side of the given regular polygon.

13. decagon 36; 72

14. 12-gon 30; 75

15. 18-gon 20; 80

Find the area of each regular polygon with the given radius or apothem. If your answer is not an integer, leave it in simplest radical form.

16. 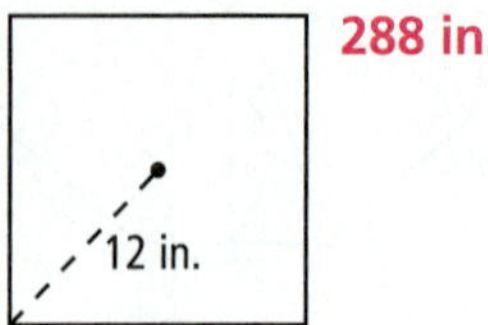

288 in.^{2}

17. 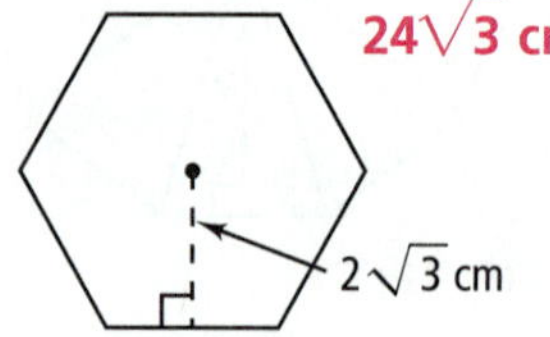

$24\sqrt{3}$ cm^2

18. 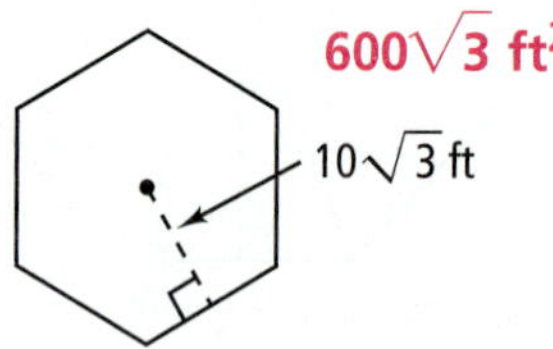

$600\sqrt{3}$ ft^2

19. 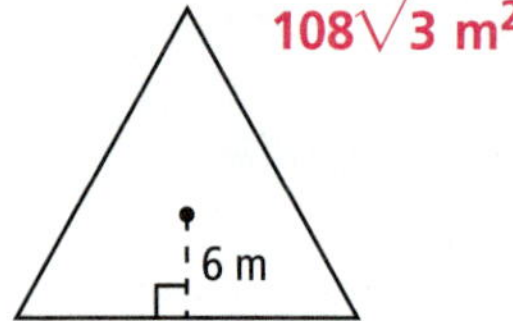

$108\sqrt{3}$ m^2

20. 

$48\sqrt{3}$ in.^{2}

21. 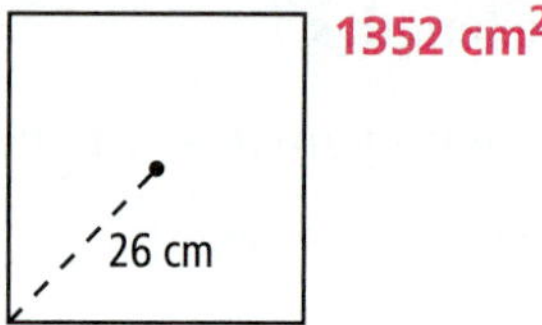

1352 cm^2

22. Your friend printed a picture of a regular 18-gon. She wants to cut the 18-gon into right triangles. If she divides the figure into 36 right triangles, what are the measures of the non-right angles of each triangle? 10; 80

23. A math teacher draws an equilateral triangle with radius 6 in. and a square with the same radius. Which figure has a greater area? To the nearest tenth, how much greater is the area? square; 25.2 in.^{2}

24. A family wants to put the tiles shown at the right in their bathroom. Each tile is a regular hexagon with a radius of 1 in. They need to cover an area that is 48 square ft. About how many tiles do they need? Round to the nearest whole tile. 2660 tiles

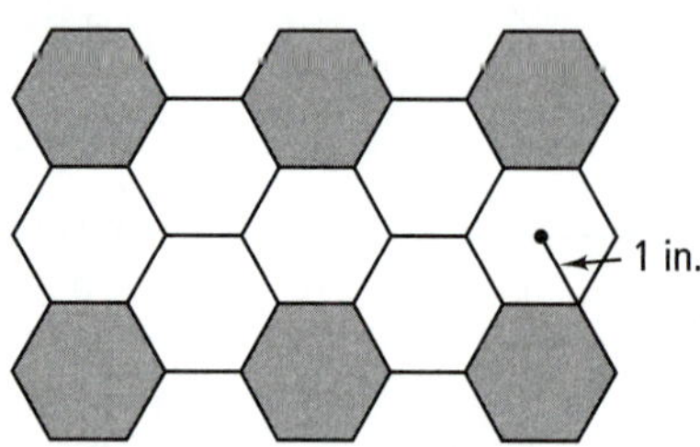

25. An equilateral triangle has a perimeter of 18 cm. Find its area to the nearest tenth. 15.6 cm^2

26. The logo for a company is a regular hexagon inscribed inside a circle. The logo will be painted on the side of the company's office building. The radius of the circle will be 8 ft. Find the area of the hexagon to the nearest whole foot. 166 ft^2

Name ______________________ Class ____________ Date ____________

10-3 Standardized Test Prep

Areas of Regular Polygons

Multiple Choice

For Exercises 1–6, choose the correct letter.

For Exercises 1 and 2, use the diagram at the right.

1. The figure at the right is a regular octagon with radii and an apothem drawn. What is $m\angle 1$? **B**

(A) 22.5 (C) 60

(B) 45 (D) 67.5

2. What is $m\angle 2$? **I**

(F) 22.5 (G) 45 (H) 60 (I) 67.5

3. A regular pentagon has an apothem of 3.2 m and an area of 37.2 m^2. What is the length of one side of the pentagon? **B**

(A) 3.96 m (B) 4.65 m (C) 11.875 m (D) 23.75 m

4. What is the area of the square at the right? **I**

(F) 16.97 cm^2 (H) 144 cm^2

(G) 72 cm^2 (I) 288 cm^2

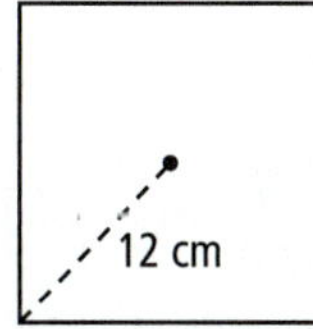

5. A regular hexagon has perimeter 60 in. What is the hexagon's area? **B**

(A) $75\sqrt{3}$ in.^{2} (B) $150\sqrt{3}$ in.^{2} (C) $300\sqrt{3}$ in.^{2} (D) $600\sqrt{3}$ in.^{2}

6. For which regular polygon can you *not* use special triangles to find the apothem? **F**

(F) pentagon (G) triangle (H) square (I) hexagon

Short Response

7. The area of an equilateral triangle is $108\sqrt{3}$ ft^2. What is the length of a side and the apothem in simplest radical form? Draw a diagram and show your work.

[2] Substitute values into the area formula and solve: $A = \frac{1}{2}ap$; $108\sqrt{3} = \frac{1}{2}(x)(3)(2x\sqrt{3})$; $x = 6$; $s = 2\sqrt{3}(6) = 12\sqrt{3}$ ft; $a = 6$ ft; [1] correct procedure with some calculation errors [0] drawing and work not shown.

10-4 Perimeters and Areas of Similar Figures

Vocabulary

Review

1. What does it mean when two figures are *similar*?

   Answers may vary. Sample: The figures have the same shape.

2. Are the corresponding angles of *similar* figures always congruent? Yes / No

3. Are the corresponding sides of *similar* figures always proportional? Yes / No

4. Circle the pairs of *similar* figures.

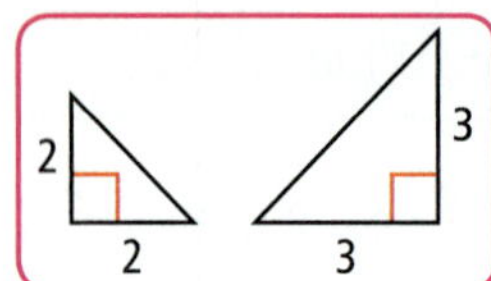

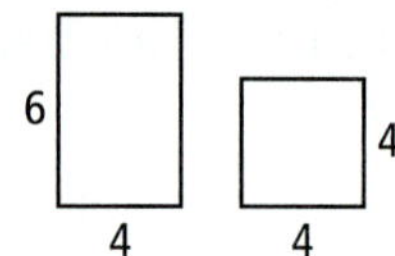

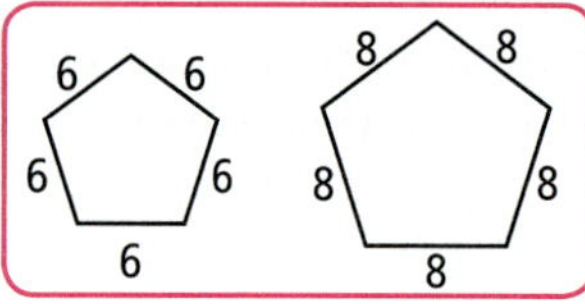

Vocabulary Builder

radius (noun) RAY dee us (plural radii)

Related Words: apothem, center

Definition: The **radius** of a regular polygon is the distance from the center to a vertex.

Main Idea: The **radii** of a regular polygon divide the polygon into congruent triangles.

Use Your Vocabulary

5. Cross out the segment that is NOT a *radius* of regular pentagon *ABCDE.*

   $\overline{OA}$ $\overline{OD}$ $\overline{OB}$ $\overline{OE}$ $\overline{OC}$ $\overline{OF}$

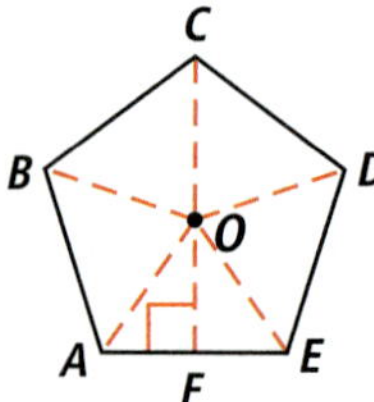

Underline the correct word(s) to complete each sentence.

6. The *radii* of a regular polygon are / are not congruent.

7. The triangles formed by the *radii* and sides of regular pentagon *ABCDE* are / are not congruent.

Theorem 10-7 Perimeters and Areas of Similar Figures

If the scale factor of two similar figures is $\frac{a}{b}$, then

(1) the ratio of their perimeters is $\frac{a}{b}$ and

(2) the ratio of their areas is $\frac{a^2}{b^2}$.

8. The name for the ratio of the length of one side of a figure to the length of the corresponding side of a similar figure is the _?_. **scale factor**

9. If the scale factor of two figures is $\frac{1}{2}$, then the ratio of their perimeters is $\frac{1}{2}$.

10. If the scale factor of two figures is $\frac{3}{x}$, then the ratio of their perimeters is $\frac{3}{x}$.

11. If the scale factor of two figures is $\frac{3}{5}$, then the ratio of their areas is $\frac{3^2}{5^2}$.

12. If the scale factor of two figures is $\frac{1}{x}$ then the ratio of their areas is $\frac{1^2}{x^2}$.

Problem 1 Finding Ratios in Similar Figures

Got It? **Two similar polygons have corresponding sides in the ratio 5 : 7. What is the ratio (larger to smaller) of their perimeters? What is the ratio (larger to smaller) of their areas?**

13. Circle the similar polygons that have corresponding sides in the ratio 5 : 7.

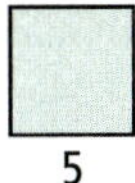

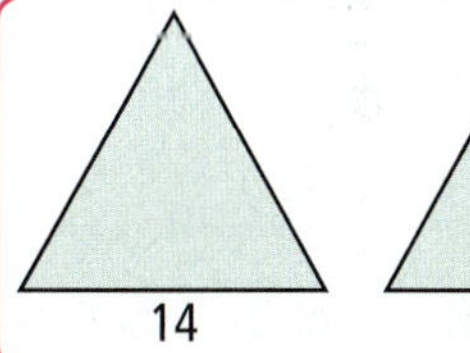

Underline the correct word to complete each sentence.

14. In similar figures, the ratio of the areas / <u>perimeters</u> equals the ratio of corresponding sides.

15. In similar figures, the ratio of the <u>areas</u> / perimeters equals the ratio of the squares of corresponding sides.

16. Complete.

ratio (larger to smaller) of corresponding sides	ratio (larger to smaller) of perimeters	ratio (larger to smaller) of areas
$\frac{7}{5}$	$\frac{7}{5}$	$\frac{7^2}{5^2} = \frac{49}{25}$

Problem 2 Finding Areas Using Similar Figures

Got It? **The scale factor of two similar parallelograms is $\frac{3}{4}$. The area of the larger parallelogram is 96 in.^{2}. What is the area of the smaller parallelogram?**

Write T for *true* or F for *false*.

F **17.** The ratio of the areas is $\frac{3}{4}$.

T **18.** The ratio of the areas is $\frac{9}{16}$.

19. Use the justifications below to find the area A of the smaller parallelogram.

$\frac{9}{16} = \frac{A}{96}$	Write a proportion.
$16A = 96 \cdot 9$	Cross Products Property
$16A = 864$	Multiply.
$\frac{16A}{16} = \frac{864}{16}$	Divide each side by 16.
$A = 54$	Simplify.

20. The area of the smaller parallelogram is 54 in.^{2}.

Problem 3 Applying Area Ratios

Got It? **The scale factor of the dimensions of two similar pieces of window glass is 3 : 5. The smaller piece costs \$2.50. How much should the larger piece cost?**

21. Use the information in the problem to complete the reasoning model below.

Think	Write
The ratio of areas is the square of the scale factor.	Ratio of areas $= 3^2 : 5^2$ $= 9 : 25$
I can use a proportion to find the cost c of the larger piece to the nearest hundredth.	$\frac{9}{25} = \frac{2.50}{c}$ $9 \cdot c = 2.50 \cdot 25$ $9 \cdot c = 62.5$ $\frac{9 \cdot c}{9} = \frac{62.5}{9}$ $c \approx 6.94$

22. The larger piece of glass should cost about \$ 6.94.

Problem 4 Finding Perimeter Ratios

Got It? **The areas of two similar rectangles are 1875 ft^2 and 135 ft^2. What is the ratio of their perimeters?**

23. The scale factor is found below. Use one of the reasons listed in the blue box to justify each step.

Step	Reason
$\frac{a^2}{b^2} = \frac{135}{1875}$	Write a proportion.
$\frac{a^2}{b^2} = \frac{9}{125}$	Simplify.
$\frac{a}{b} = \frac{3}{5\sqrt{5}}$	Take the positive square root of each side.
$\frac{a}{b} = \frac{3}{5\sqrt{5}} \cdot \frac{\sqrt{5}}{\sqrt{5}}$	Rationalize the denominator.
$\frac{a}{b} = \frac{3\sqrt{5}}{25}$	Simplify.

Rationalize the denominator.
Simplify.
Simplify.
Take the positive square root of each side.
Write a proportion.

24. The ratio of the perimeters equals the scale factor $3\sqrt{5}$: 25 .

Lesson Check • Do you UNDERSTAND?

Reasoning **The area of one rectangle is twice the area of another. What is the ratio of their perimeters? How do you know?**

25. Let x and y be the sides of the smaller rectangle. Complete.

area of smaller rectangle	area of larger rectangle	ratio of larger to smaller areas
xy	$2 \cdot xy$	$2xy$: xy

26. Find the square root of the ratio of larger to smaller areas to find the scale factor.

$$\frac{\sqrt{2xy}}{\sqrt{xy}} = \sqrt{\frac{2xy}{xy}} = \sqrt{\frac{2}{1}} = \frac{\sqrt{2}}{1}$$

27. The ratio of perimeters is $\sqrt{2}$: 1 because the scale factor is $\sqrt{2}$: 1 .

Math Success

Check off the vocabulary words that you understand.

☐ similar polygons ☐ radius ☐ perimeter ☐ area

Rate how well you can ***find the perimeters and areas of similar polygons.***

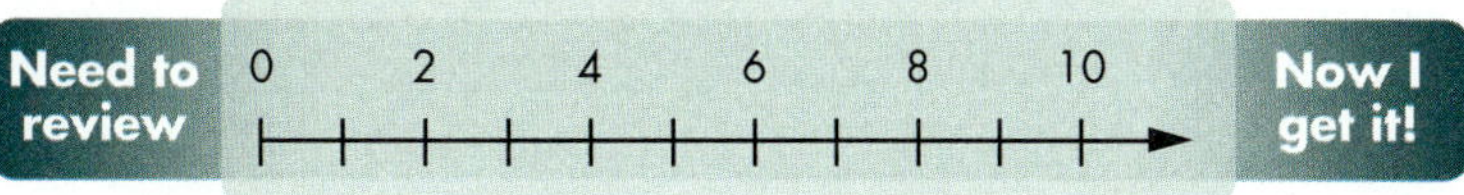

Name ______________________ Class ____________ Date ____________

10-4 Think About a Plan

Perimeters and Areas of Similar Figures

The shorter sides of a parallelogram are 5 m. The shorter sides of a similar parallelogram are 15 m. The area of the smaller parallelogram is 28 m^2. What is the area of the larger parallelogram?

Understanding the Problem

1. How are the lengths of corresponding sides of similar figures related?
   They are proportional.

2. How can you represent this relationship mathematically?
   Write a proportion comparing corresponding side lengths.

3. How can you use this relationship to find the scale factor of the figures?
   Reduce one of the ratios in the proportion to lowest terms.

4. How are the areas of two similar figures related to the scale factor?
   The ratio of the areas is proportional to the square of the scale factor.

Planning the Solution

5. Write the mathematical relationship that relates the lengths of corresponding sides in the two parallelograms. $\frac{5}{15}$

6. Use this relationship to find the scale factor for the parallelograms. $\frac{1}{3}$

7. Use the scale factor to find the relationship between the areas of the parallelograms. $\frac{A_{smaller}}{A_{larger}} = \frac{1^2}{3^2} = \frac{1}{9}$

Getting an Answer

8. Substitute the known quantities in the relationship you wrote in Step 7. Then solve. $\frac{28}{A_{larger}} = \frac{1}{9}$; 252

9. What is the larger parallelogram's area? Be sure to use correct units. 252 m^2

Name ______________________ Class ______________ Date ______________

10-4 Practice

Form K

Perimeters and Areas of Similar Figures

The figures in each pair are similar. Compare the first figure to the second. Give the ratio of the perimeters and the ratio of the areas.

1. 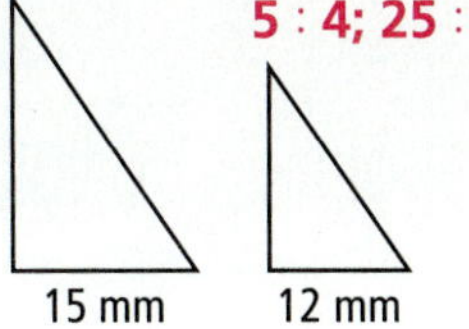

5 : 4; 25 : 16

To start, find the scale factor. The scale factor is the ratio of the lengths of corresponding sides.

scale factor $\frac{15}{12} = \frac{5}{4}$

2. 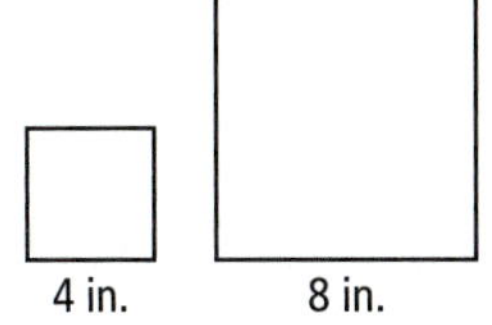

1 : 2 and 1 : 4

3. 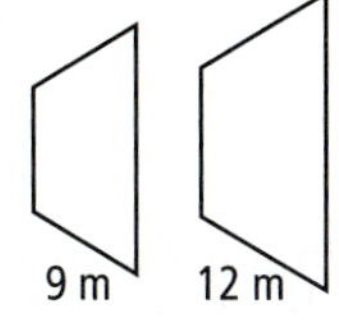

3 : 4 and 9 : 16

4. 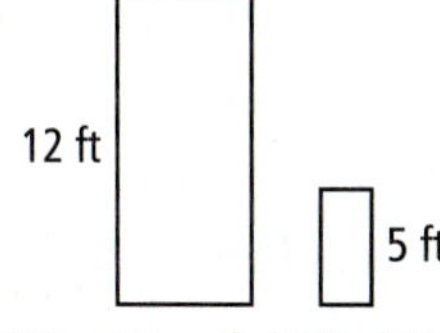

12 : 5 and 144 : 25

The figures in each pair are similar. The area of one figure is given. Find the area of the other figure to the nearest whole number.

5. 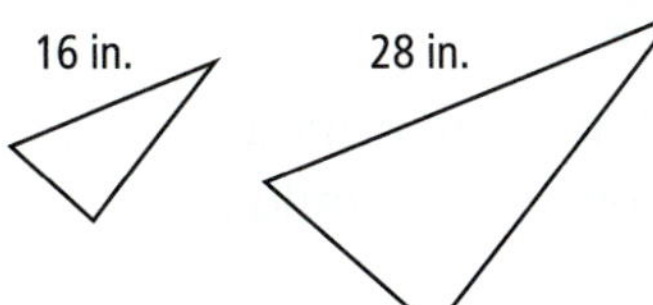

Area of smaller triangle = 54 in.^{2}

165 in.^{2}

To start, find the scale factor. Then find the ratio of the areas.

scale factor $\frac{16}{28} = \frac{4}{7}$

area ratio $\frac{4^2}{7^2} = \frac{16}{49}$

6. 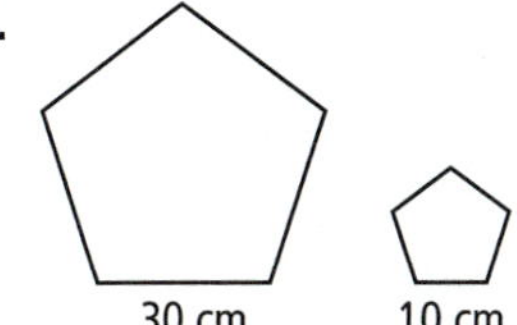

Area of larger pentagon = 100 cm^2

11 cm^2

7. 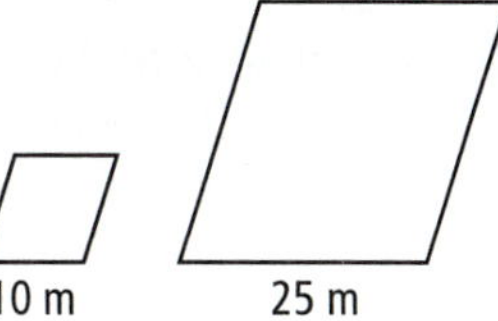

Area of larger rhombus = 500 m^2

80 m^2

The scale factor of two similar polygons is given. Find the ratio of their perimeters and the ratio of their areas.

8. 9 : 3
3 : 1; 9 : 1

9. 10 : 4
5 : 2; 25 : 4

10. $\frac{8}{12}$
2 : 3; 4 : 9

11. $\frac{4}{20}$
1 : 5; 1 : 25

Name ______________________ Class ____________ Date ____________

10-4 Practice (continued) *Form K*

Perimeters and Areas of Similar Figures

Find the scale factor and the ratio of perimeters for each pair of similar figures.

12. two regular pentagons with areas 50 in.^{2} and 162 in.^{2} 5 : 9; 5 : 9

13. two rectangles with areas 8 m^2 and 98 m^2 2 : 7; 2 : 7

14. two regular pentagons with areas 45 ft^2 and 20 ft^2 3 : 2; 3 : 2

15. two equilateral triangles with areas $8\sqrt{3}$ cm^2 and $128\sqrt{3}$ cm^2 1 : 4; 1 : 4

16. two circles with areas 27π in.^{2} and 48π in.^{2} 3 : 4; 3 : 4

17. The area of a regular octagon is 120 ft^2. What is the area of a regular octagon with sides $\frac{1}{4}$ the length of the sides of the larger octagon? 7.5 ft^2

18. It takes 12 h to paint a 10-ft-by-18-ft mural. At this rate, how long will it take the same number of people to paint the same mural on a 15-ft-by-27-ft wall? 27 h

19. It costs $3.95 to print a 12-in.-by-16-in. color page. A friend needs to print a poster that is twice as long and twice as wide. At this rate, how much would he expect to pay for the poster? $15.80

20. The longer base of a trapezoid is 8 ft. The longer base of a similar trapezoid is 13 ft. The area of the smaller trapezoid is 240 ft^2. What is the area of the larger trapezoid? 633.75 ft^2

21. Two similar parallelograms have areas 72 m^2 and 32 m^2. The height of the larger parallelogram is 12 m. What are the lengths of the bases of both parallelograms? 6 m and 4 m

22. Reasoning How would increasing the length and width of a rectangle by a scale factor of 4 affect the area of the new figure? Explain.
The area would be 16 times greater; the area ratio equals the scale factor squared.

23. Error Analysis A parking garage is expanding. The old garage can hold 300 cars. The new garage will hold 900 cars. The old garage has an area of 21,000 ft^2. A classmate says the new garage will have an area of 189,000 ft^2. Explain the error your classmate has made and give the correct area for the new garage.
A certain number of cars fit in a given area. Tripling the area will triple the number of cars, so all that is needed is the area ratio (3 : 1). The area of the new garage will be 63,000 ft^2.

Name ______________________ Class ____________ Date ____________

10-4 Standardized Test Prep

Perimeters and Areas of Similar Figures

Gridded Response

Solve each exercise and enter your answer on the grid provided.

For Exercises 1 and 2, use the diagram at the right.

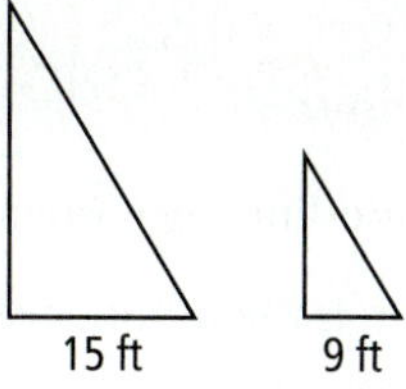

1. The triangles at the right are similar. What is the ratio (larger to smaller) of the perimeters?

2. The triangles at the right are similar. What is the ratio (larger to smaller) of the areas?

3. The pentagons at the right are similar. The area of the smaller pentagon is 30 m^2. What is the area of the larger pentagon in m^2?

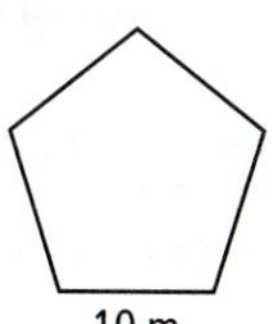

4. It costs \$350 to carpet an 8 ft by 10 ft room. At this rate, how many dollars would it cost to put the same carpeting in a 24 ft by 30 ft room?

5. The areas of two similar octagons are 112 $in.^2$ and 63 $in.^2$. What is the ratio (larger to smaller) of their perimeters?

Answers

1. 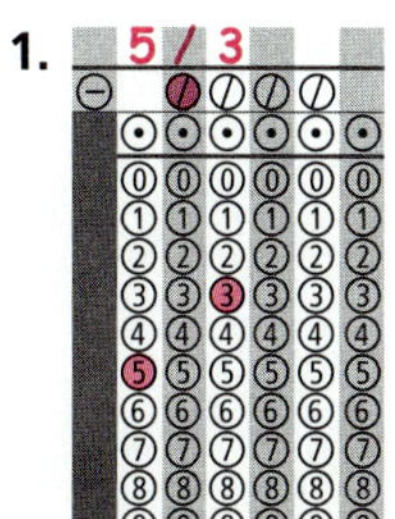

2. 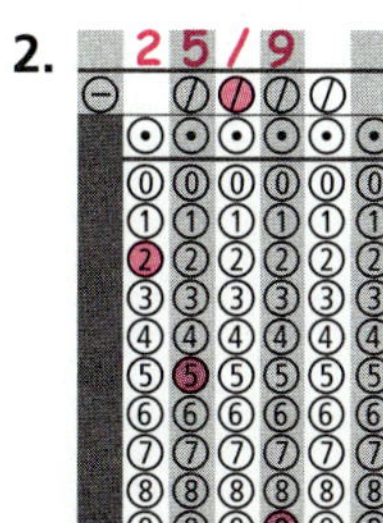

3. 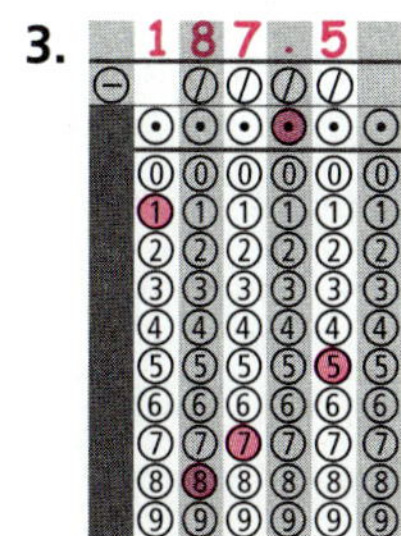

4. 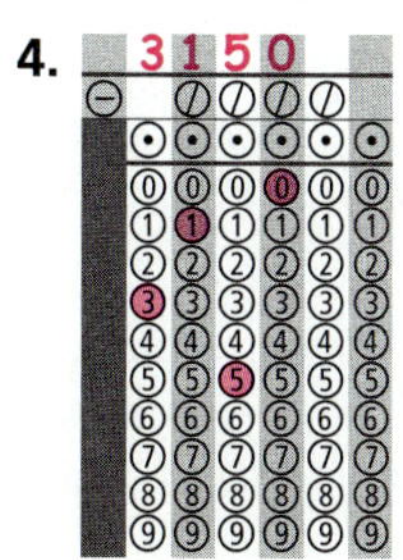

5. 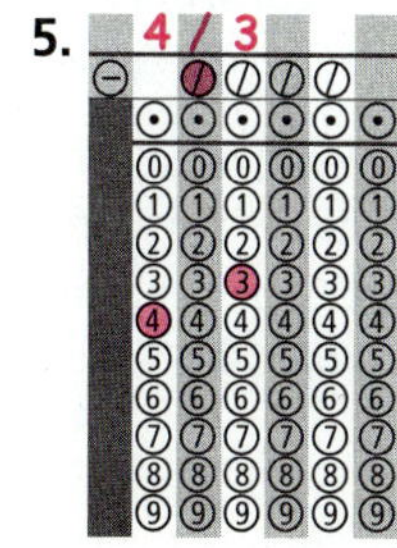

10-5 Trigonometry and Area

Vocabulary

Review

1. Underline the correct word to complete the sentence.

   Area is the number of cubic / square units needed to cover a given surface.

2. Circle the formula for the *area* of a triangle.

   $A = bh$ $\qquad A = \frac{1}{2}bh \qquad A = \frac{1}{2}h(b_1 + b_2) \qquad A = \frac{1}{2}d_1d_2$

Vocabulary Builder

trigonometry (noun) **trig uh NAHM uh tree**

Other Word Form: trigonometric (adjective)

Related Words: cosine, sine, tangent

Definition: **Trigonometry** is the study of the relationships among two sides and an angle in a right triangle.

Main Idea: You can use **trigonometry** to find the area of a regular polygon.

Use Your Vocabulary

Complete each sentence with the word *trigonometry* or *trigonometric*.

3. The sine, cosine, and tangent ratios are _?_ ratios. trigonometric

4. This year I am studying _?_ in math. trigonometry

Draw a line from each *trigonometric ratio* in Column A to its name in Column B.

	Column A	Column B
5.	$\frac{\text{length of opposite leg}}{\text{length of hypotenuse}}$	cosine
6.	$\frac{\text{length of adjacent leg}}{\text{length of hypotenuse}}$	sine
7.	$\frac{\text{length of opposite leg}}{\text{length of adjacent leg}}$	tangent

Answers: 5 — sine; 6 — cosine; 7 — tangent

Got It? **What is the area of a regular pentagon with 4-in. sides? Round your answer to the nearest square inch.**

8. Underline the correct words to complete the sentence.

To find the area using the formula $A = \frac{1}{2}ap$, you need to know the apothem / radius and the perimeter / width of the pentagon.

9. In the regular pentagon at the right, label center C, apothem $\overline{CR}$, and radii $\overline{CD}$ and $\overline{CE}$.

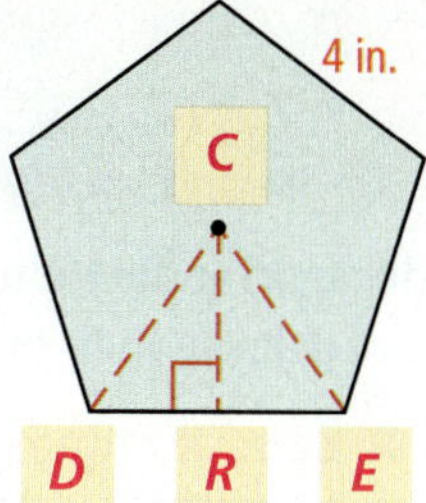

10. The perimeter of the pentagon is 5 · 4 in., or 20 in.

11. The measure of central angle DCE is $\frac{360}{5}$, or 72.

Complete Exercises 12 and 13.

12. $m\angle DCR = \frac{1}{2}m\angle DCE$

$= \frac{1}{2} \cdot 72$

$= 36$

13. $DR = \frac{1}{2}DE$

$= \frac{1}{2} \cdot 4$

$= 2$

14. Use your results from Exercises 12 and 13 to label the diagram below.

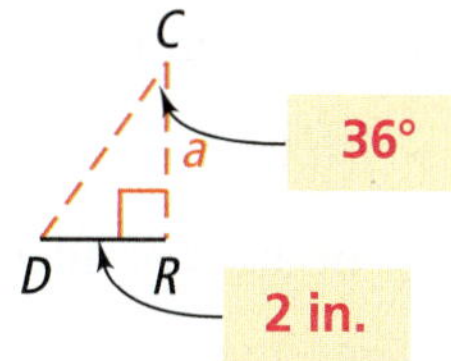

15. Circle the equation you can use to find the apothem a.

$\tan 72° = \frac{36}{a}$ $\quad$ $\tan 36° = \frac{2a}{a}$ $\quad$ $\tan 36° = \frac{2}{a}$ (circled)

$\tan 36° = \frac{a}{2}$ $\quad$ $\tan 72° = \frac{2}{a}$

16. Use the justifications below to find the apothem and the area.

$\tan 72° = \frac{2}{a}$	Use the tangent ratio.
$a \cdot \tan 36° = 2$	Multiply each side by a.
$a = \frac{2}{\tan 36°}$	Divide each side by tan 36°.
$A = \frac{1}{2}ap$	Write the formula for the area of a regular polygon.
$= \frac{1}{2} \cdot \frac{2}{\tan 36°} \cdot 20$	Substitute for a and p.
≈ 27.52763841	Use a calculator.

17. To the nearest square inch, the area of the regular pentagon is 28 in.^{2}.

Problem 2 Finding Area

Got It? A tabletop has the shape of a regular decagon with a radius of 9.5 in. What is the area of the tabletop to the nearest square inch?

18. Complete the problem-solving model below.

Know	Need	Plan
The radius and number of sides of the decagon	The apothem and the length of a side	Use trigonometric ratios to find the apothem and the length of a side.

19. Look at the decagon at the right. Explain why the measure of each central angle of a decagon is 36 and $m\angle C$ is 18.

There are 10 central angles and $\frac{360}{10} = 36$. The apothem bisects a central angle, so $m\angle C = \frac{1}{2}(36)$, or 18.

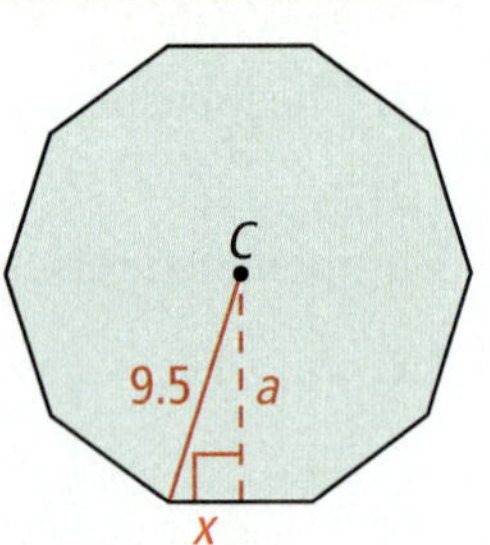

20. Use the cosine ratio to find the apothem a.

$$\cos 18^\circ = \frac{a}{9.5}$$

$$9.5 \cdot \cos 18^\circ = a$$

21. Use the sine ratio to find x.

$$\sin 18^\circ = \frac{x}{9.5}$$

$$9.5 \cdot \sin 18^\circ = x$$

22. Use the justifications below to find the perimeter.

$p = 10 \cdot$ length of one side	perimeter = number of sides times length of one side
$= 10 \cdot 2 \cdot x$	The length of each side is $2x$.
$= 10 \cdot 2 \cdot 9.5(\sin 18^\circ)$	Substitute for x.
$= 190 \cdot \sin 18^\circ$	Simplify.

23. Find the area. Use a calculator.

$$A = \frac{1}{2}ap$$

$$= \frac{1}{2} \cdot 9.5(\cos 18^\circ) \cdot 190(\sin 18^\circ) \approx 265.2380947$$

24. To the nearest square inch, the area of the tabletop is 265 in.^{2}.

take note

Theorem 10-8 Area of a Triangle Given SAS

The area of a triangle is half the product of the lengths of two sides and the sine of the included angle.

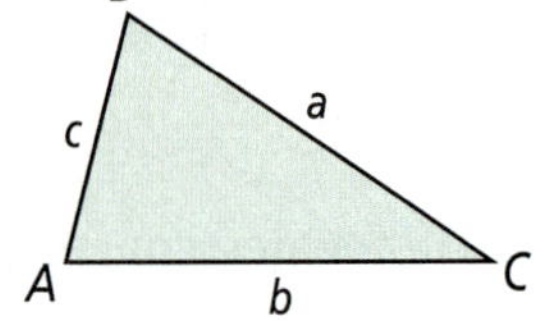

25. Complete the formula below.

Area of $\triangle ABC = \frac{1}{2}bc(\sin A)$

Problem 3 Finding Area

Got It? **What is the area of the triangle? Round your answer to the nearest square inch.**

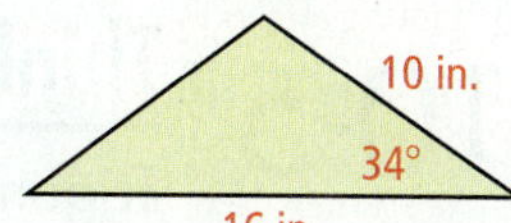

26. Complete the reasoning model below.

Think	Write
I know the lengths of two sides and the measure of the included angle.	Side lengths: 10 in. and 16 in. Angle measure: 34
I can use the formula for the area of a triangle given SAS.	$A = \frac{1}{2} \cdot 10 \cdot 16 \cdot \sin 34$ $\approx$ 44.73543228

27. To the nearest square inch, the area of the triangle is 45 in.^{2}.

Lesson Check • Do you UNDERSTAND?

Error Analysis **Your classmate needs to find the area of a regular pentagon with 8-cm sides. To find the apothem, he sets up and solves a trigonometric ratio. What error did he make? Explain.**

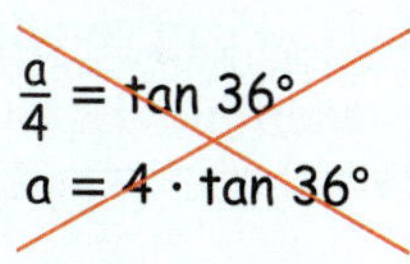

28. The lengths of the legs of the triangle in the regular pentagon are a and 4 cm.

29. The tangent of the 36° angle is $\frac{\text{length of opposite leg}}{\text{length of adjacent leg}}$, or $\frac{4}{a}$.

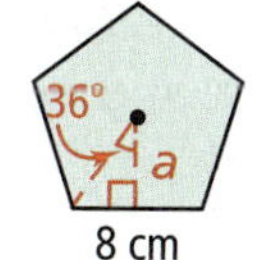

30. Explain the error your classmate made.

He used $\frac{a}{4}$ instead of $\frac{4}{a}$ for the tangent ratio.

Math Success

Check off the vocabulary words that you understand.

☐ area ☐ trigonometry

Rate how well you can use *trigonometry to find area.*

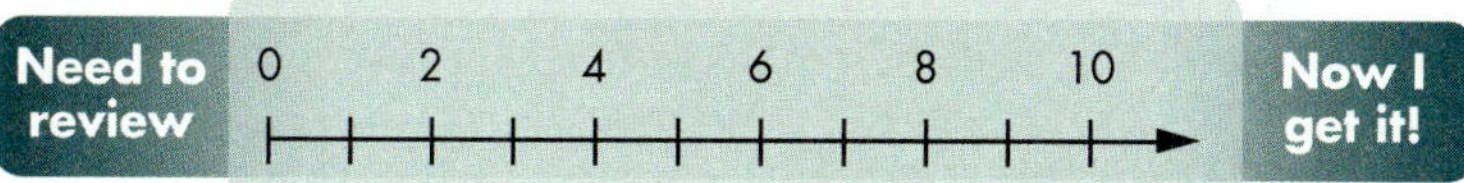

Name ______________________ Class ____________ Date ____________

10-5 Think About a Plan

Trigonometry and Area

Architecture The Pentagon in Arlington, Virginia, is one of the world's largest office buildings. It is a regular pentagon, and the length of each of its sides is 921 ft. What is the area of land the Pentagon covers to the nearest thousand square feet?

Understanding the Problem

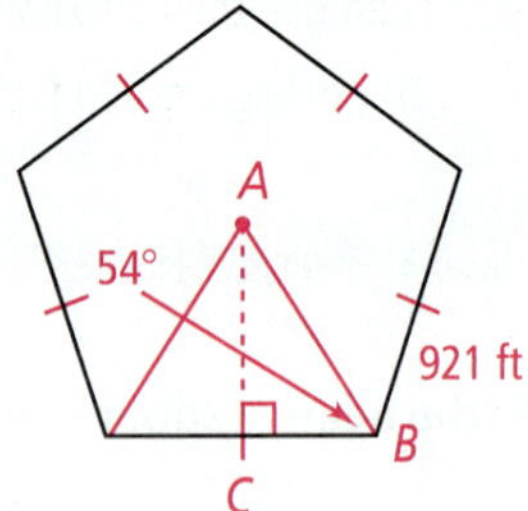

1. The figure at the right is a regular pentagon. Label the side length with the information given in the problem.

2. The formula for the area of a regular polygon is $A = \frac{1}{2}ap$. Which measures do you need to solve the problem?

   perimeter and apothem length

Planning the Solution

3. How can you find the perimeter?

   Multiply the side length by the number of sides.

4. Draw an apothem and radius on the figure. Label the center A, and draw right $\triangle ABC$ formed by the apothem and radius, where $\overline{AB}$ is the hypotenuse.

   Check students' work.

5. How can you find $m\angle ABC$? Write this measure on the diagram.

   Answers may vary. Sample: Find the central angle: 360 ÷ 5 = 72. Because the apothem bisects the central angle, $m\angle BAC = 36$. So, $m\angle ABC = 90 - m\angle BAC = 90 - 36 = 54$.

6. Which trigonometric ratio can you use to find the apothem? Explain.

   The tangent ratio; you know the length of the side adjacent to the 54° angle and you want to find the length of the side opposite that angle.

Getting an Answer

7. Complete the equation below. Then solve for a, the apothem.

   $\boxed{\tan 54°} = \frac{a}{\boxed{460.5}}$; $a \approx \boxed{633.8}$ ft

8. Use the formula for the area of a regular polygon to find the area.

   $A \approx 1{,}459{,}000 \text{ ft}^2$

Name ______________________ Class ____________ Date ____________

10-5 Practice

Form K

Trigonometry and Area

Find the area of each regular polygon. Round your answers to the nearest tenth.

1. pentagon with side length 8 in. **110.1 in.^{2}**

To start, find the measure of a central angle.
Then use trigonometry to find a.
The measure of the central angle of the regular pentagon is $\frac{360}{5} = \boxed{72}$ so, $m\angle C = \frac{1}{2} \cdot \boxed{72} = \boxed{36}$.

$\tan 36^\circ = \frac{4}{a}$; $a = \frac{4}{\tan 36^\circ} = \frac{4}{?} = \underline{\ ?\ }$ **0.7265; 5.5055 in.**

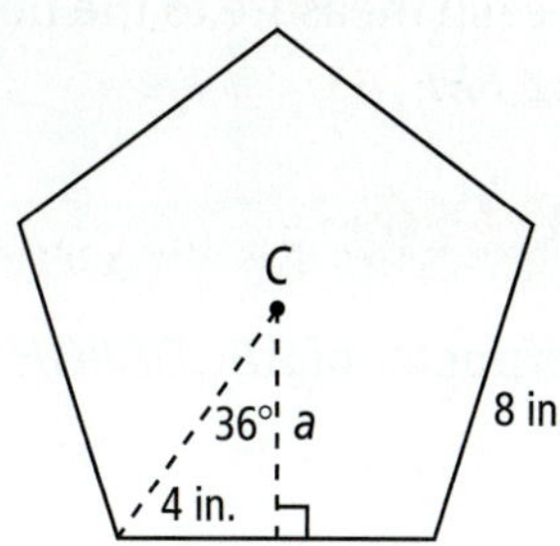

2. hexagon with side length 9 m **210.4 m^2**

3. decagon with radius 4 mm **47.0 mm^2**

4. octagon with radius 10 cm **282.8 cm^2**

5. 20-gon with radius 5 in. **77.3 in.^{2}**

6. 15-gon with perimeter 90 ft **635.1 ft^2**

7. 18-gon with perimeter 126 m **1250.5 m^2**

Find the area of each triangle. Round your answers to the nearest tenth.

8.

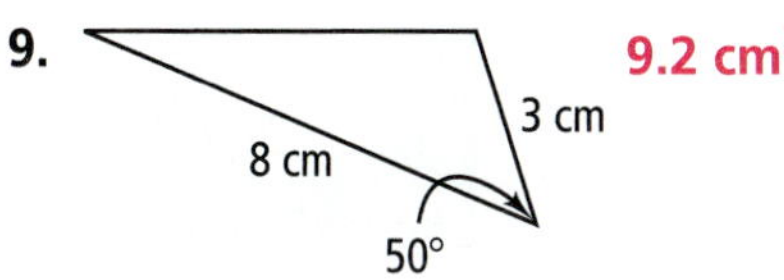

60.0 in.^{2}

To start, write the SAS formula, then substitute given values into the formula.

$A = \frac{1}{2}bc(\sin A)$

$= \frac{1}{2}(\boxed{8})(\boxed{15})(\sin 92^\circ)$

9. **9.2 cm^2**

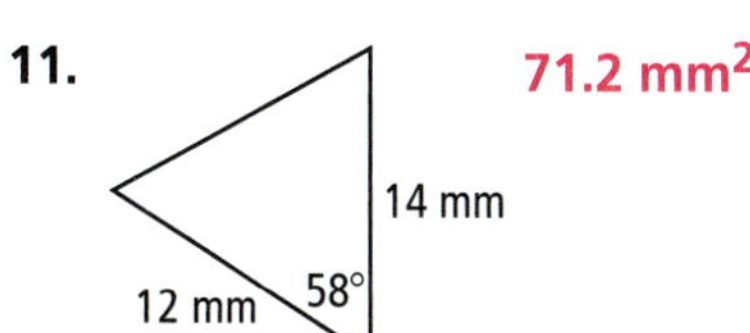

10. **81.6 ft^2**

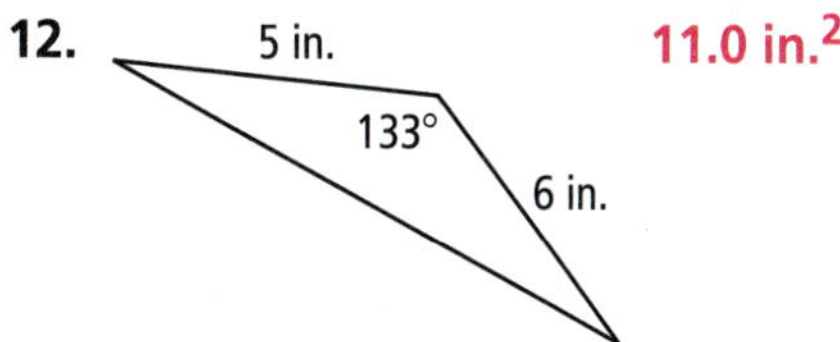

11. **71.2 mm^2**

14 mm
12 mm
58°

12. **11.0 in.^{2}**

5 in.
133°
6 in.

Name ____________________ Class ____________ Date ____________

10-5 Practice (continued)

Form K

Trigonometry and Area

13. *ABCDEFGH* is a regular octagon with center *X* and radius 5 cm. Find each measure to the nearest tenth.

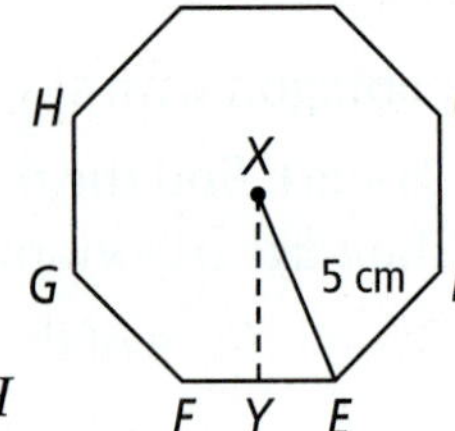

a. $m\angle FXE$ 45

b. $m\angle YXE$ 22.5

c. XY 4.6 cm

d. FE 3.8 cm

e. perimeter of *ABCDEFGH* 30.6 cm

f. area of *ABCDEFGH* 70.7 cm^2

Find the perimeter and area of each regular polygon to the nearest tenth.

14.

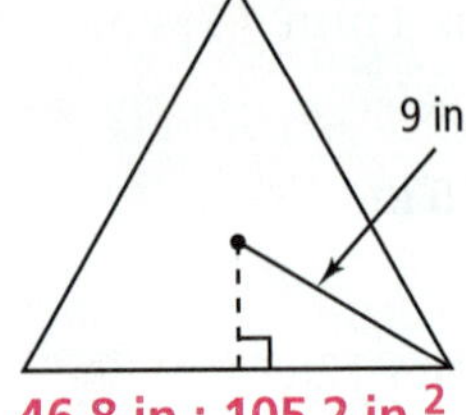

46.8 in.; 105.2 $in.^2$

15.

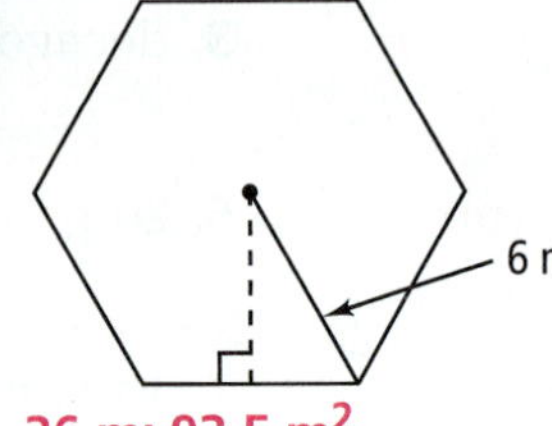

36 m; 93.5 m^2

16.

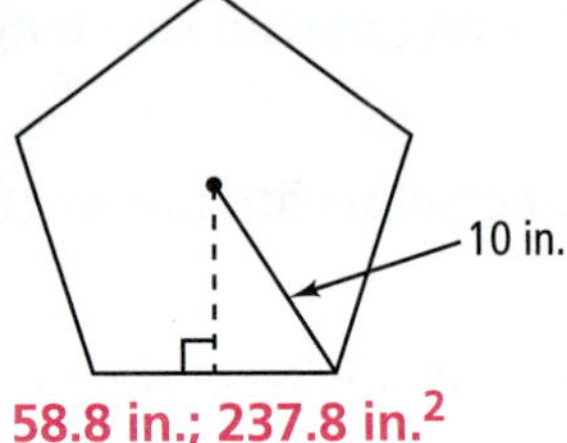

58.8 in.; 237.8 $in.^2$

17. The Rileys are replacing the carpet on their outdoor deck. The deck is a regular hexagon with radius 9 ft. The cost for carpet and installation is $3.75/$ft^2$. What will it cost to replace the carpet? $789.17

The polygons are regular polygons. Find the area of the shaded region to the nearest tenth.

18.

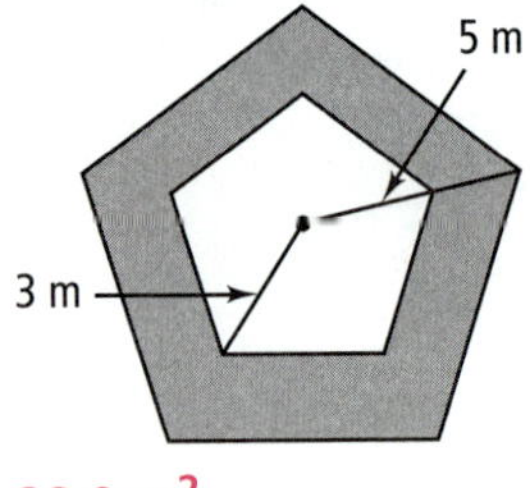

38.0 m^2

19.

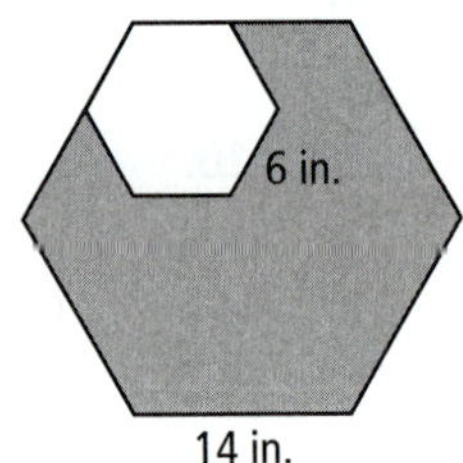

415.7 $in.^2$

20.

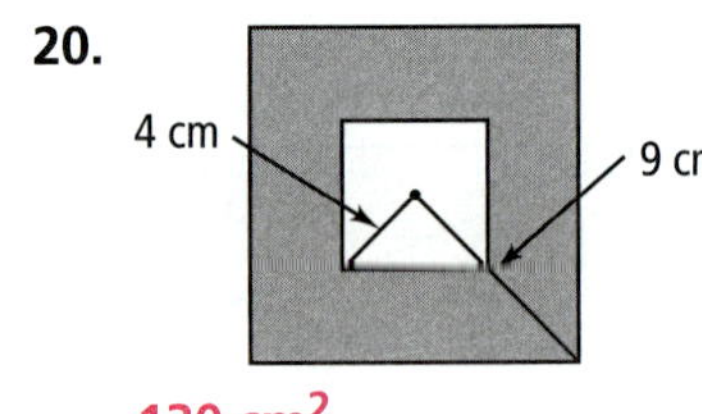

130 cm^2

21. Which has the greater area, a regular octagon with side length 10 ft, or a regular nonagon with side length 10 ft? Justify your answer. nonagon; octagon's area is 482.8 ft^2; nonagon's area is 618.2 ft^2

22. Several streets intersect to form triangles near Dupont Circle in Washington, D.C. One such triangle is formed by New Hampshire Avenue, Massachusetts Avenue, and 16th Street. The section of New Hampshire Avenue is about 3100 ft long. The section of 16th Street is about 3500 ft long. The angle enclosed by the two streets has a measure of about 35. What is the area of this triangle, to the nearest 100 ft^2? 3,111,700 ft^2

Name ______________________ Class ____________ Date ____________

10-5 Standardized Test Prep

Trigonometry and Area

Multiple Choice

For Exercises 1–6, choose the correct letter.

1. What is the area of the regular pentagon at the right? A

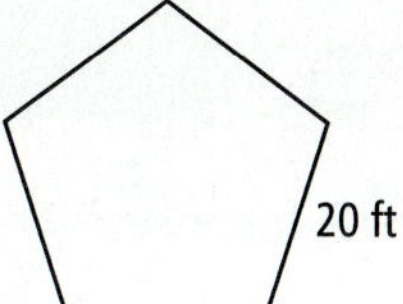

Ⓐ 688.2 ft^2 Ⓒ 951.1 ft^2

Ⓑ 850.7 ft^2 Ⓓ 1376.4 ft^2

2. What is the area of the regular octagon at the right? G

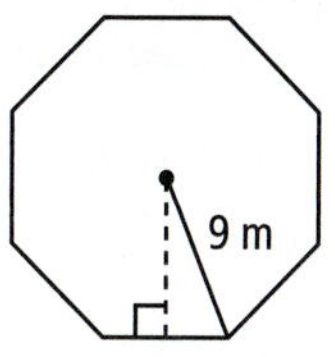

Ⓕ 114.5 m^2 Ⓗ 391.1 m^2

Ⓖ 229.1 m^2 Ⓘ 458.2 m^2

3. What is the area of a regular hexagon with sides 8 cm? B

Ⓐ 110.1 cm^2 Ⓑ 166.3 cm^2 Ⓒ 309.0 cm^2 Ⓓ 332.6 cm^2

4. What is the area of a regular nonagon with a radius of 14 in.? H

Ⓕ 70.9 $in.^2$ Ⓖ 141.7 $in.^2$ Ⓗ 566.9 $in.^2$ Ⓘ 1211.6 $in.^2$

5. What is the area of a 15-gon with a perimeter of 90 m? B

Ⓐ 528.2 m^2 Ⓑ 635.1 m^2 Ⓒ 1270.3 m^2 Ⓓ 142,903.1 m^2

6. What is the area of the triangle at the right? G

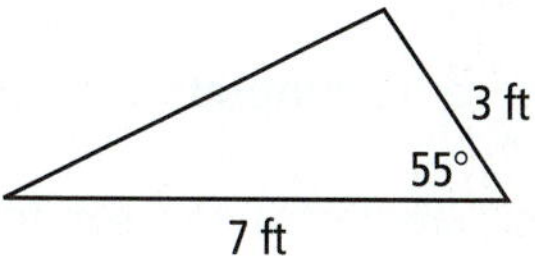

Ⓕ 6.0 ft^2 Ⓗ 15.0 ft^2

Ⓖ 8.6 ft^2 Ⓘ 17.2 ft^2

Short Response

7. What is the area of the triangle shown at the right? Show your work and explain how you got your answer.

[2] $\frac{1}{2}(5)(5)(\sin 118) \approx 11.04$ $in.^2$; because the base angles are equal, the triangle is isosceles and the sides opposite the base angles are congruent. The vertex angle is equal to $180 - 31 - 31 = 118$. To find the area, multiply the lengths of the congruent sides and the sine of the included 118° angle and divide by 2. [1] appropriate methods, but with one computational error or work not shown [0] incorrect answer with no work shown

10-6 PART 1 Circles and Arcs

Vocabulary

Review

1. Is a *circle* a two-dimensional figure? Yes / No

2. Is a *circle* a polygon? Yes / No

3. Is every point on a *circle* the same distance from the center? Yes / No

4. Circle the figure that is a *circle*.

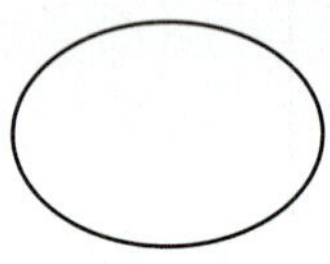 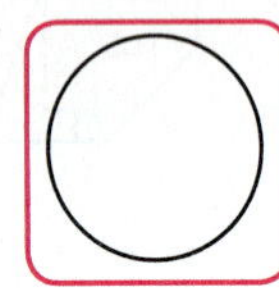 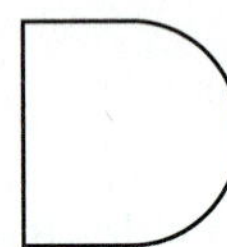 

Vocabulary Builder

arc (noun) **ahrk**

Definition: An **arc** is part of a circle.

Related Words: minor arc, major arc, semicircle

Example: Semicircle *AB* is an **arc** of the circle.

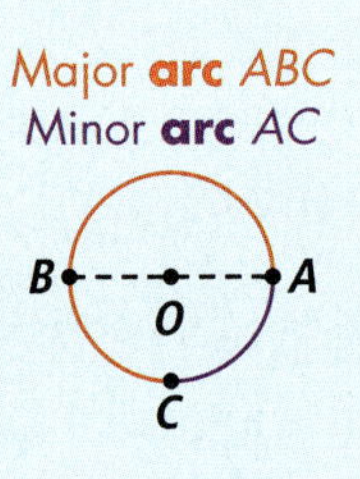

Use Your Vocabulary

Underline the correct word to complete each sentence.

5. A *minor arc* is larger / smaller than a semicircle.

6. A *major arc* is larger / smaller than a semicircle.

7. You use two / three points to name a *major arc*.

8. You use two / three points to name a *minor arc*.

9. Circle the name of the red *arc*.

$\overset{\frown}{JK}$ $\overset{\frown}{KL}$ $\overset{\frown}{LJK}$ $\overset{\frown}{LKJ}$

10. Circle the name of the blue *arc*.

$\overset{\frown}{JK}$ $\overset{\frown}{KL}$ $\overset{\frown}{LJK}$ $\overset{\frown}{LKJ}$

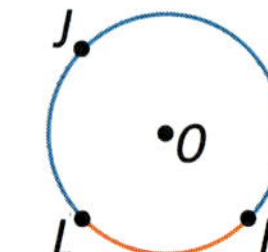

Problem 1 Naming Arcs

Got It? What are the minor arcs of $\odot A$?

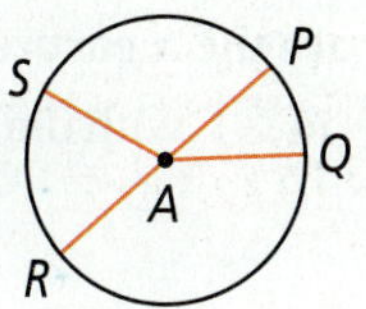

Draw a line from each central angle in Column A to its corresponding minor arc in Column B.

Column A	Column B
11. $\angle PAQ$	$\overset{\frown}{RS}$
12. $\angle QAR$	$\overset{\frown}{SP}$
13. $\angle RAS$	$\overset{\frown}{PQ}$
14. $\angle SAP$	$\overset{\frown}{QR}$
15. $\angle SAQ$	$\overset{\frown}{SQ}$

16. Is $\overset{\frown}{PR}$ a minor arc of $\odot A$? Explain.

No. Explanations may vary. Sample: $\overset{\frown}{PR}$ is a diameter of $\odot A$, so $\overset{\frown}{PR}$ is a semicircle.

17. The minor arcs of $\odot A$ are $\overset{\frown}{PQ}$, $\overset{\frown}{QR}$, $\overset{\frown}{RS}$, $\overset{\frown}{SP}$, and $\overset{\frown}{SQ}$.

take note

Key Concepts Arc Measure and Postulate 10-2

Arc Measure

The measure of a minor arc is equal to the measure of its corresponding central angle.

The measure of a major arc is the measure of the related minor arc subtracted from 360.

The measure of a semicircle is 180.

Use $\odot S$ at the right for Exercises 18 and 19.

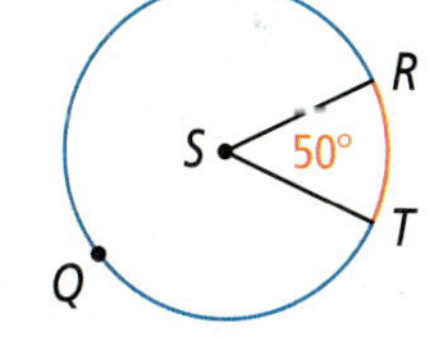

18. $m\overset{\frown}{RT} = m\angle RST =$ 50

19. $m\overset{\frown}{TQR} = 360 - m\overset{\frown}{RT} = 360 -$ 50 $=$ 310

Adajacent arcs are arcs of the same circle that have exactly one point in common. In the circle below, $\overset{\frown}{AB}$ is adjacent to $\overset{\frown}{BC}$. $\overset{\frown}{AB}$ and $\overset{\frown}{BC}$ have only point B in common.

Postulate 10-2 Arc Addition Postulate

The measure of the arc formed by two adjacent arcs is the sum of the measures of the two arcs.

$$m\overset{\frown}{ABC} = m\overset{\frown}{AB} + m\overset{\frown}{BC}$$

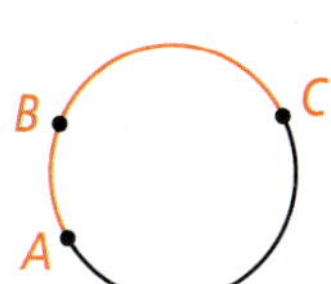

Use the circle at the right for Exercises 20 and 21.

20. If $m\overset{\frown}{AB} = 40$ and $m\overset{\frown}{BC} = 100$, then $m\overset{\frown}{ABC} =$ 140.

21. If $m\overset{\frown}{ABC} = 160$ and $m\overset{\frown}{BC} = 110$, then $m\overset{\frown}{AB} =$ 50.

Problem 2 Finding the Measures of Arcs

Got It? What are the measures of $\overset{\frown}{PR}$, $\overset{\frown}{RS}$, $\overset{\frown}{PRQ}$, and $\overset{\frown}{PQR}$ in $\odot C$ with diameter $\overline{PS}$?

Complete.

22. $m\angle PCR =$ 77, so $m\overset{\frown}{PR} =$ 77.

23. $m\angle RCS = m\angle PCS - m\angle PCR$

$= 180 -$ 77

$=$ 103

24. $m\angle RCS =$ 103, so $m\overset{\frown}{RS} =$ 103.

25. $m\overset{\frown}{PRQ} = m\overset{\frown}{PR} + m\overset{\frown}{RS} + m\overset{\frown}{SQ}$

$=$ 77 $+$ 103 $+$ 28

$=$ 208

26. $m\overset{\frown}{PQR} = 360 - m\overset{\frown}{PR}$

$= 360 -$ 77

$=$ 283

Lesson Check • Do you know HOW?

Use $\odot P$ at the right to write the name of each of the following.

a minor arc **a major arc** **a semicircle**

27. Do you use *two* or *three* points to name a minor arc? Two / Three

28. Do you use *two* or *three* points to name a major arc? Two / Three

29. Do you use *two* or *three* points to name a semicircle? Two / Three

30. Circle the minor arc(s) of $\odot P$. Underline the major arc(s). Cross out the semicircle(s).

$\overset{\frown}{AB}$ $\overset{\frown}{BC}$ $\overset{\frown}{BD}$ $\overset{\frown}{CA}$ $\overset{\frown}{DA}$ $\overset{\frown}{DC}$

$\overset{\frown}{ABD}$ $\overset{\frown}{ABC}$ $\overset{\frown}{BDA}$ $\overset{\frown}{BDC}$ $\overset{\frown}{DCA}$

Lesson Check • Do you UNDERSTAND?

Vocabulary **What is the difference between a major arc and a minor arc?**

Underline the correct word to comlete each sentence.

31. A major arc is larger / smaller than a semicircle.

32. A minor arc is larger / smaller than a semicircle.

33. A major arc is larger / smaller than a minor arc.

Circle and Arcs

Vocabulary

Review

Use the figure at the right for Exercises 1 and 2.

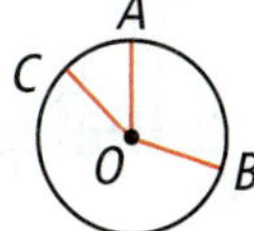

1. The vertex of the *central angles* in ⊙*O* is O.
2. Name the *central angle* that corresponds to each arc.

$\overset{\frown}{AB}$ $\angle AOB$ $\overset{\frown}{AC}$ $\angle AOC$ $\overset{\frown}{BC}$ $\angle BOC$

3. Underline the correct words to complete the sentence.

The measure of a minor arc is equal to / greater than / less than the measure of its corresponding *central angle*.

Vocabulary Builder

circumference (noun) sur KUM fur uns

Related Words: perimeter, diameter, radius, pi

Definition: The **circumference** of a circle is the distance around the circle.

Main Idea: The **circumference** of a circle is π times the diameter.

Use Your Vocabulary

Complete each statement with the correct word from the list below. Use each word only once.

circumference diameter pi radius

4. A _?_ is a segment that has one endpoint at the center of the circle and the other endpoint on the circle. radius
5. A _?_ is a segment that contains the center of a circle and has both endpoints on the circle. diameter
6. The _?_ of a circle is the distance around the circle. circumference
7. The number _?_ is the ratio of the circumference of a circle to its diameter. pi

Theorem 10-9 Circumference of a Circle

The circumference of a circle is π times the diameter.

$C = \pi d$ or $C = 2\pi r$

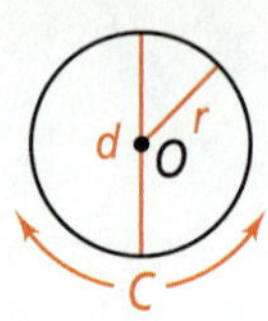

8. Explain why you can use either $C = \pi d$ or $C = 2\pi r$ to find the circumference of a circle.

Explanations may vary. Sample: The length of the diameter is twice the length of the radius.

Problem 3 Finding a Distance

Got It? **A car has a circular turning radius of 16.1 ft. The distance between the two front tires is 4.7 ft. How much farther does a tire on the outside of the turn travel than a tire on the inside?**

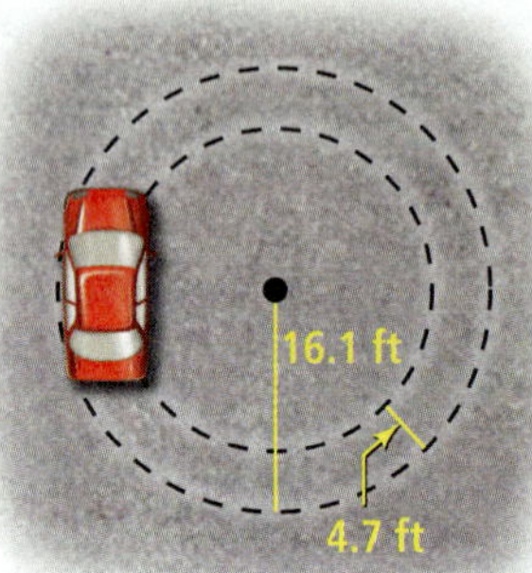

9. The two circles have the same center. To find the radius of the inner circle, do you *add* or *subtract*?

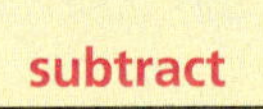

Complete.

10. radius of outer circle = 16.1

radius of inner circle = 16.1 − 4.7 = 11.4

11. circumference of outer circle $= 2\pi r = 2\pi \cdot$ 16.1 = 32.2 $\cdot \pi$

circumference of inner circle $= 2\pi r = 2\pi \cdot$ 11.4 = 22.8 $\cdot \pi$

12. Find the differences in the two distances traveled. Use a calculator.

32.2 $\cdot \pi -$ 22.8 $\cdot \pi =$ 9.4 $\cdot \pi$

$\approx$ 29.53097094

13. To the nearest tenth, a tire on the outer circle travels 29.5 ft farther.

Theorem 10-10 Arc Length

The length of an arc of a circle is the product of the ratio $\frac{\text{measure of the arc}}{360}$ and the circumference of the circle.

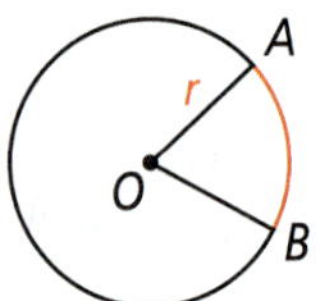

14. Complete the formula below.

length of $\widehat{AB}$ $= \frac{m\widehat{AB}}{360} \cdot 2\pi r = \frac{m\widehat{AB}}{360} \cdot \pi d$

15. Is the *length* of an arc the same as the *measure* of the arc? Yes / No (circled: No)

Problem 4 Finding Arc Length

Got It? **What is the length of a semicircle with radius 1.3 m? Leave your answer in terms of π.**

16. The measure of a semicircle is 180.

17. Use the justifications below to find the length of the semicircle.

length of semicircle	$= \frac{\text{measure of semicircle}}{360} \cdot 2\pi r$	Use the formula for arc length.
	$= \frac{180}{360} \cdot 2\pi \cdot 1.3$	Substitute.
	$= 1.3 \cdot \pi$	Simplify.

18. The length of the semicircle is 1.3π.

Lesson Check • Do you UNDERSTAND?

Error Analysis **Your class must find the length of $\overset{\frown}{AB}$. A classmate submits the following solution. What is the error?**

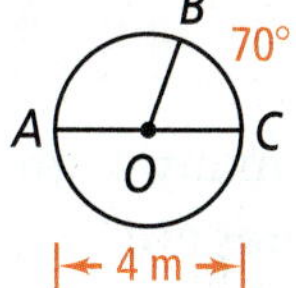

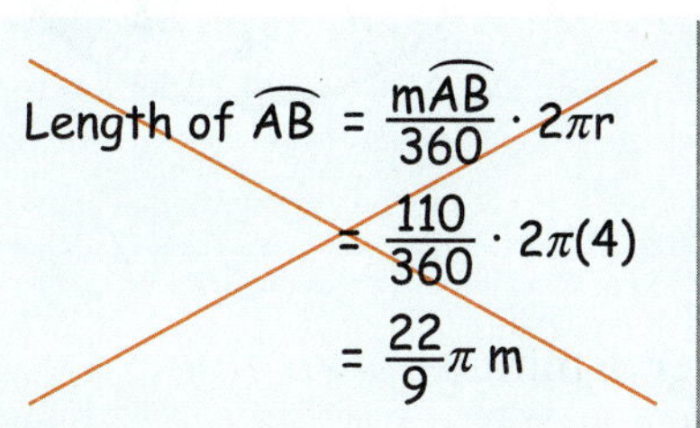

19. Is $\overset{\frown}{AC}$ a semicircle? Yes / No (Yes circled)

20. Does $m\overset{\frown}{AB} = 180 - 70 = 110$? Yes / No (Yes circled)

21. Is the length of the radius 4? Yes / No (No circled)

22. What is the error? Answers may vary. Sample:

The student substituted the diameter instead of the radius for r.

Math Success

Check off the vocabulary words that you understand.

☐ circle ☐ minor arc ☐ major arc ☐ circumference

Rate how well you can *use central angles, arcs, and circumference.*

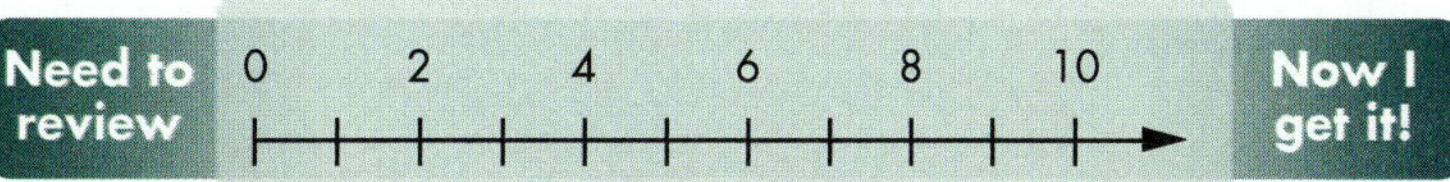

Name ________________________ Class ____________ Date ____________

10-6 Think About a Plan

Circles and Arcs

Time Hands of a clock suggest an angle whose measure is continually changing. How many degrees does a minute hand move through during each time interval?

a. 1 min **b.** 5 min **c.** 20 min

Understanding the Problem

1. Draw the minute hand pointing to 12. Then draw the minute hand where it would be 5 min later.

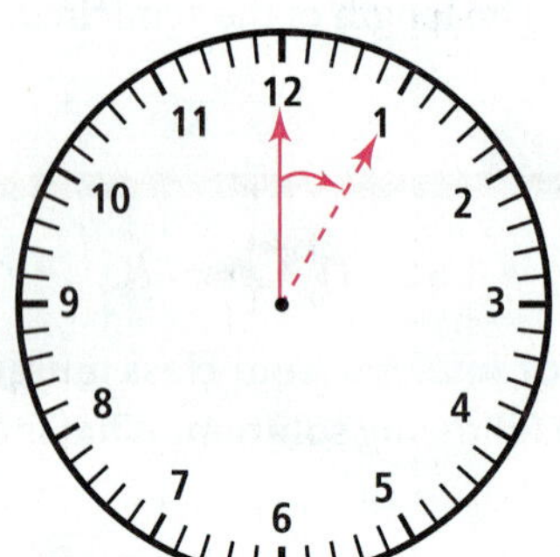

2. What type of angle is formed by the hand in these two positions?
   a central angle or an acute angle

3. How many degrees are in a complete circle? How many minutes are in an hour? 360; 60

Planning the Solution

4. How can you show the relationship between the number of minutes in an hour and the total number of degrees in a circle? Write a ratio.

5. Use words to write a proportion that can be used to find the number of degrees represented by any time interval.
   $\frac{\text{minutes in 1 hour}}{\text{degrees in a circle}} = \frac{\text{number of minutes}}{\text{number of degrees}}$

6. Which part of this proportion will be represented by a variable?
   the number of degrees

7. What is the ratio of the minutes in one hour to the degrees in a circle in simplest form? 1 : 6

Getting an Answer

8. Write and solve a proportion to find the number of degrees the minute hand moves through in a 1-min interval. $\frac{1}{6} = \frac{1}{x}$; 6°

9. Write and solve proportions to find the number of degrees the minute hand moves through in 5-min and 20-min intervals.
   $\frac{1}{6} = \frac{5}{x}$; 30°; $\frac{1}{6} = \frac{20}{x}$; 120°

Name ______________________ Class ____________ Date ____________

10-6 Practice — Circles and Arcs

Form K

Name the following in ⊙*A*.

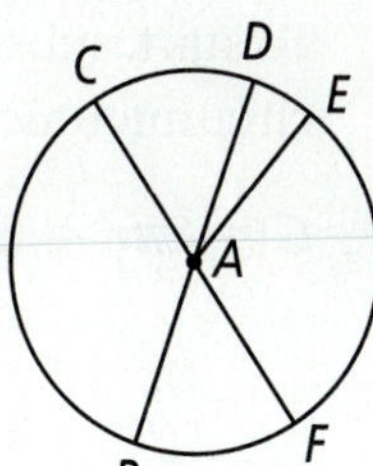

1. the minor arcs $\overset{\frown}{CD}$; $\overset{\frown}{CE}$; $\overset{\frown}{CB}$; $\overset{\frown}{DE}$; $\overset{\frown}{DF}$; $\overset{\frown}{EF}$; $\overset{\frown}{EB}$; $\overset{\frown}{FB}$

2. the major arcs $\overset{\frown}{BFC}$; $\overset{\frown}{BCF}$; $\overset{\frown}{CBE}$; $\overset{\frown}{CBD}$; $\overset{\frown}{DBF}$; $\overset{\frown}{DBE}$; $\overset{\frown}{ECF}$; $\overset{\frown}{EDB}$;

3. the semicircles $\overset{\frown}{CBF}$; $\overset{\frown}{CEF}$; $\overset{\frown}{DEB}$; $\overset{\frown}{DCB}$

Find the measure of each arc in ⊙*R*.

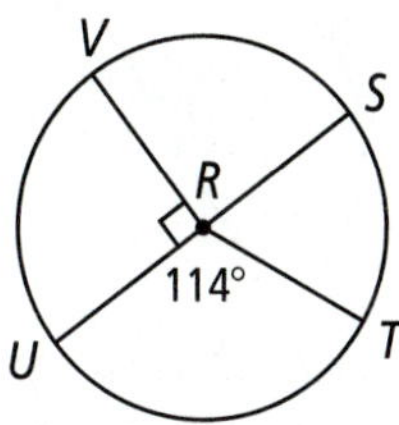

4. $\overset{\frown}{UT}$ 114

To start, identify the central angle that intercepts $\overset{\frown}{UT}$.

The central angle that intercepts $\overset{\frown}{UT}$ has a measure of [114].

5. $\overset{\frown}{ST}$ 66
6. $\overset{\frown}{SV}$ 90
7. $\overset{\frown}{VST}$ 156
8. $\overset{\frown}{UV}$ 90
9. $\overset{\frown}{VUT}$ 204
10. $\overset{\frown}{SVT}$ 294
11. $\overset{\frown}{USV}$ 270
12. $\overset{\frown}{UTS}$ 180
13. $\overset{\frown}{UVT}$ 246
14. $\overset{\frown}{TUS}$ 294
15. $\overset{\frown}{TSU}$ 246
16. $\overset{\frown}{VUS}$ 270

Find each indicated measure for ⊙*D*.

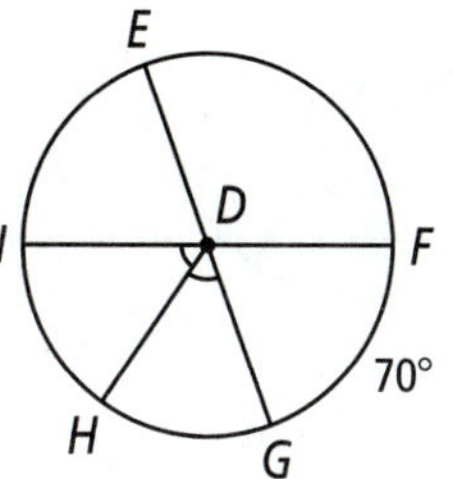

17. $m\angle EDI$ 70
18. $m\overset{\frown}{EF}$ 110
19. $m\overset{\frown}{GI}$ 110
20. $m\angle IDH$ 55
21. $m\overset{\frown}{FHE}$ 250
22. $m\overset{\frown}{GIF}$ 290

Algebra **Find the value of each variable.**

23. 75

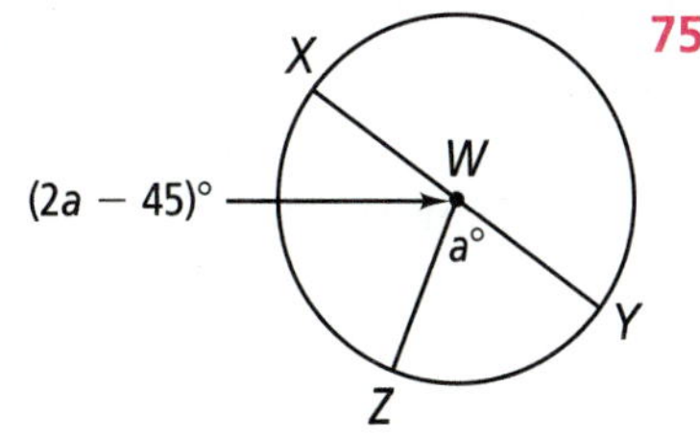

24. 15

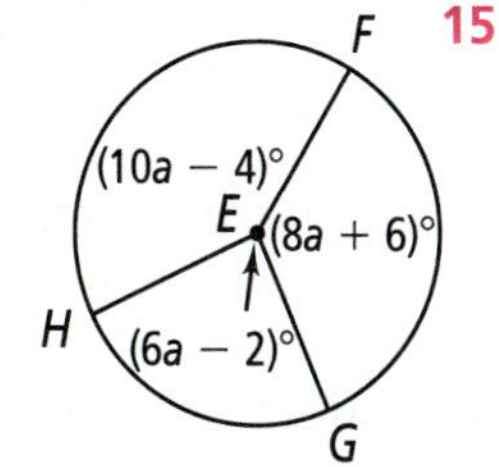

Name ________________________ Class ____________ Date ____________

10-6 Practice (continued)

Form K

Circles and Arcs

Find the circumference of each circle. Leave your answer in terms of π.

25.

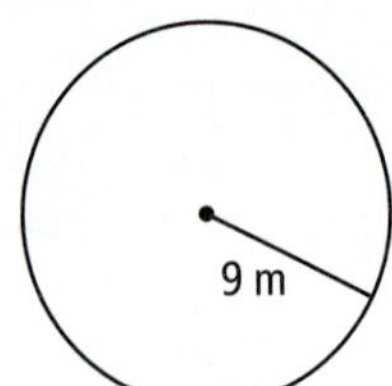

To start, substitute values into the formula for the circumference of a circle.

$C = 2\pi r = 2\pi \cdot$ [9] $=$ [18π] m

26. 15π cm

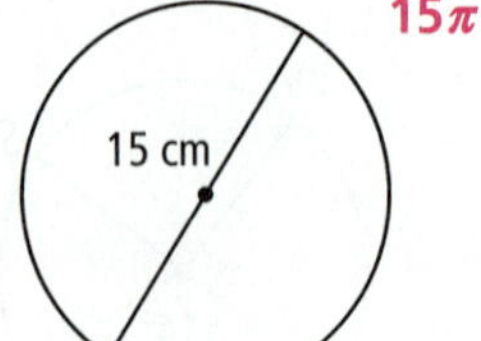

27. 11.6π in.

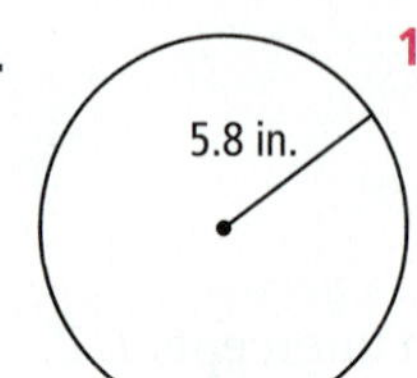

28. 6.3π ft

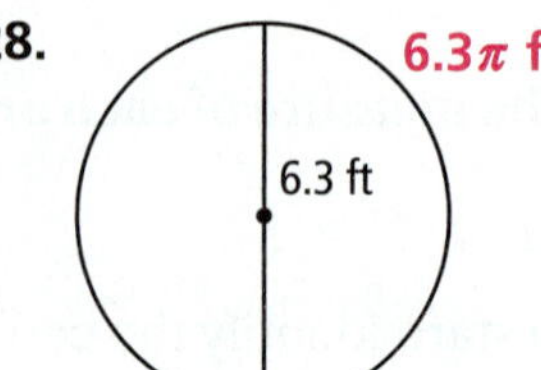

Find the length of each darkened arc. Leave your answer in terms of π.

29.

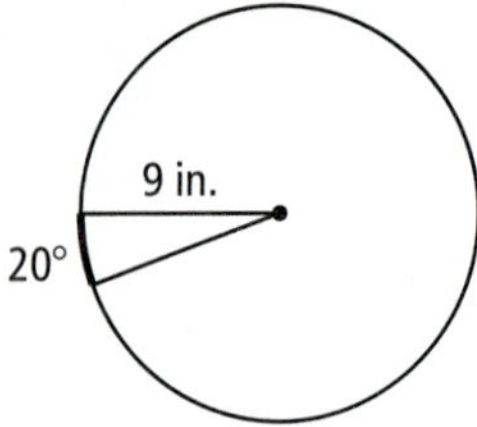

To start, find the ratio for the measure of the arc to 360.

$\frac{20}{360} = \frac{[1]}{[18]}$

π in.

30. 5π cm

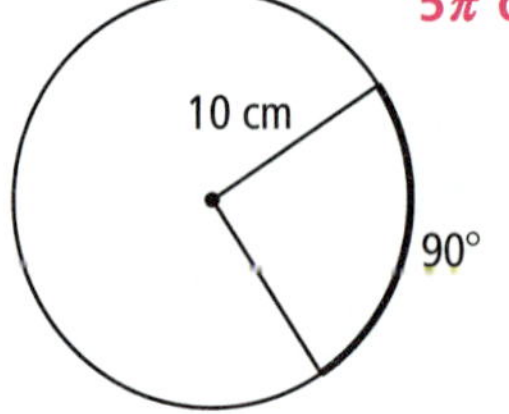

31. 5π ft

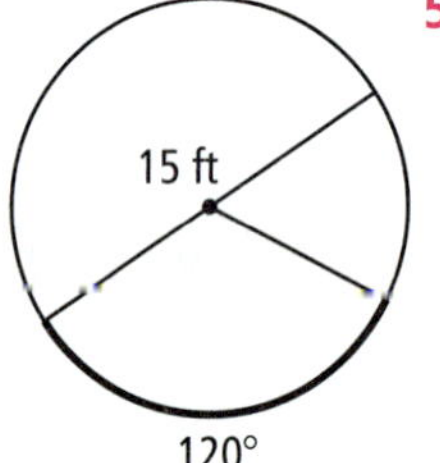

32. 11π m

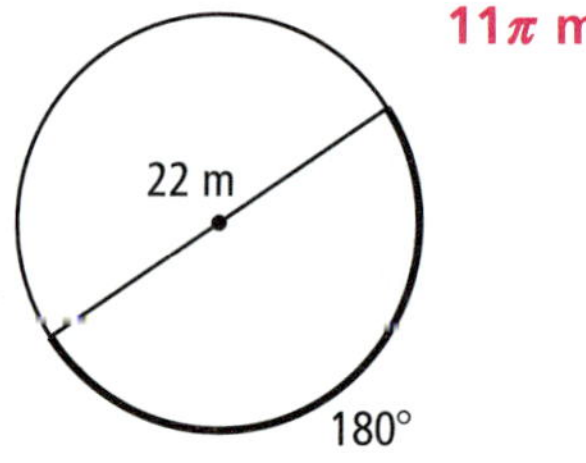

33. A motorcycle has tires with a 25-in. diameter. A monster truck has tires with a 66-in. diameter. To the nearest inch, how much farther does a monster truck tire travel in one revolution than a motorcycle tire? **129 in.**

34. Hands of a clock suggest an angle whose measure is continually changing. How many degrees does a minute hand move through during each time interval?

a. 9 min **54°** **b.** 35 min **210°** **c.** 45 min **270°**

35. A bicycle tire has a diameter of 21 in. How many inches will the bike travel after 100 revolutions of the wheel? Round your answer to the nearest inch. **6597 in.**

10-6 Standardized Test Prep

Circles and Arcs

Multiple Choice

For Exercises 1–6, choose the correct letter.

For Exercises 1–3, use the figure at the right.

1. Which is a minor arc in $\odot L$? **B**

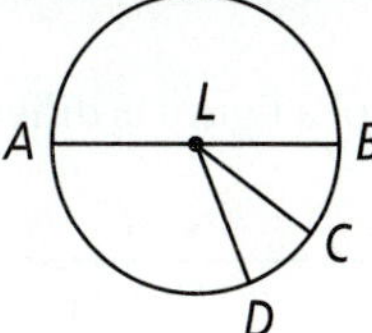

Ⓐ $\overset{\frown}{AB}$ Ⓒ $\overset{\frown}{ABD}$

Ⓑ $\overset{\frown}{DB}$ Ⓓ $\overset{\frown}{CBD}$

2. Which is a major arc in $\odot L$? **G**

Ⓕ $\overset{\frown}{ADB}$ Ⓖ $\overset{\frown}{DBA}$ Ⓗ $\overset{\frown}{AD}$ Ⓘ $\overset{\frown}{CA}$

3. Which is a semicircle in $\odot L$? **A**

Ⓐ $\overset{\frown}{ADB}$ Ⓑ $\overset{\frown}{BCD}$ Ⓒ $\overset{\frown}{BC}$ Ⓓ $\overset{\frown}{ADC}$

4. What is the degree measure of $\overset{\frown}{TUR}$? **H**

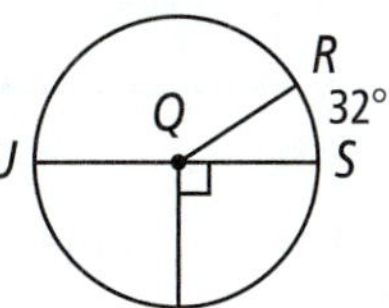

Ⓕ 32 Ⓗ 238

Ⓖ 122 Ⓘ 248

5. Which shows the circumference of $\odot Z$? **C**

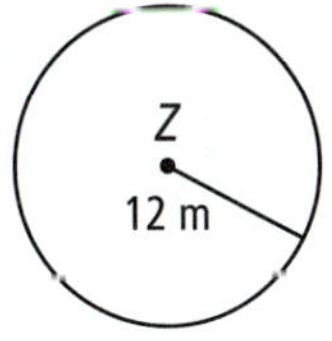

Ⓐ 6π Ⓒ 24π

Ⓑ 12π Ⓓ 144π

6. Which shows the length of the darkened arc? **I**

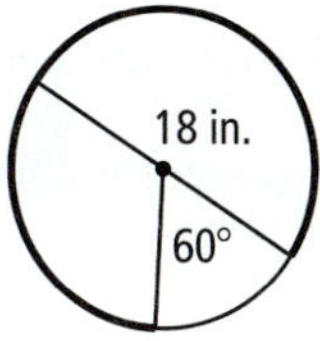

Ⓕ 1.5π Ⓗ 7.5π

Ⓖ 3π Ⓘ 15π

Short Response

7. The wheel of one car has a diameter of 20 in. The wheel of another car has a diameter of 24 in. About how many more revolutions must the smaller wheel make than the larger wheel to travel 100 ft?

[2] three more revolutions; smaller wheel $C = 20\pi \approx 62.8$; larger wheel $C = 24\pi \approx 75.36$; 100 feet = 1200 in.; number of revolutions for smaller wheel = $1200 \div 62.8 \approx 19.1$; number of revolutions for larger wheel = $1200 \div 75.36 \approx 15.9$; $19 - 16 = 3$
[1] appropriate methods, but with computational errors or work missing
[0] incorrect answer with no work shown

10-7 Areas of Circles and Sectors

Vocabulary

Review

1. Explain how the *area* of a figure is different from the perimeter of the figure.

   Area is the measure of the space inside a figure while perimeter is the distance around the figure.

2. Circle the formula for the *area* of a parallelogram.

   $A = bh$ (circled) $\qquad A = \frac{1}{2}bh \qquad A = \frac{1}{2}h(b_1 + b_2) \qquad A = \frac{1}{2}d_1d_2$

3. Find the *area* of each figure.

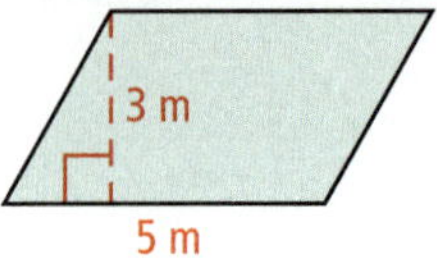

$A =$ **15** m^2

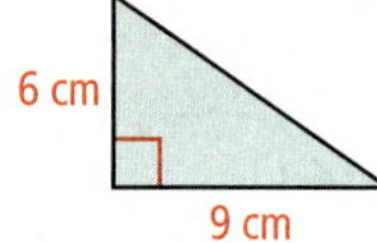

$A =$ **27** cm^2

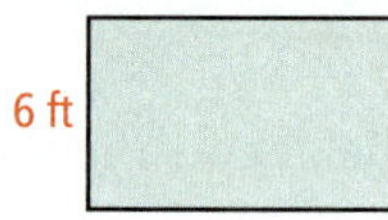

$A =$ **60** ft^2

Vocabulary Builder

sector (noun) SEK tur

Definition: A **sector** of a circle is a region bounded by an arc of the circle and the two radii to the arc's endpoints.

Main Idea: The area of a **sector** is a fractional part of the area of a circle.

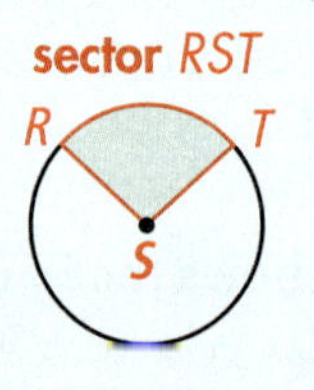

Use Your Vocabulary

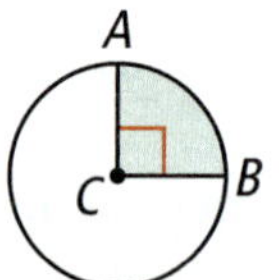

4. Name the arc and the radii that are the boundaries of the shaded *sector.*

   arc **AB** radii **CA** and **CB**

5. Circle the name of the shaded *sector.*

   sector *ABC* sector *ACB* (circled) sector *BAC*

6. The shaded *sector* is what fractional part of the area of the circle? Explain.

   $\frac{1}{4}$; $\widehat{AB}$ is a 90° arc and $\frac{90}{360} = \frac{1}{4}$.

take note

Theorem 10-11 Area of a Circle

The area of a circle is the product of π and the square of the radius.

$A = \pi r^2$

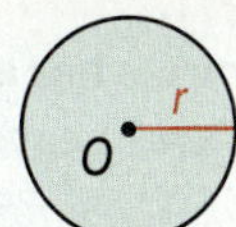

Complete each statement.

7. If the radius is 5 ft, then $A = \pi \cdot$ 5 $\cdot$ 5 , or 25 $\cdot \pi$ ft^2.

8. If the diameter is 1.8 cm, then $A = \pi \cdot$ 0.9 $\cdot$ 0.9 , or 0.81π cm^2.

Problem 1 Finding the Area of a Circle

Got It? **What is the area of a circular wrestling region with a 42-ft diameter?**

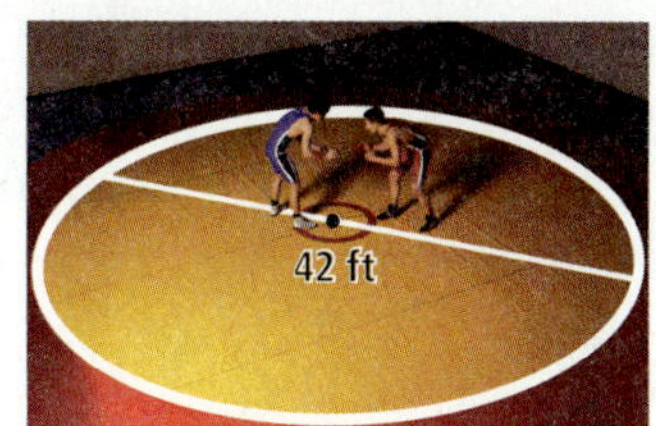

9. The radius of the wrestling region is 21 ft.

10. Complete the reasoning model below.

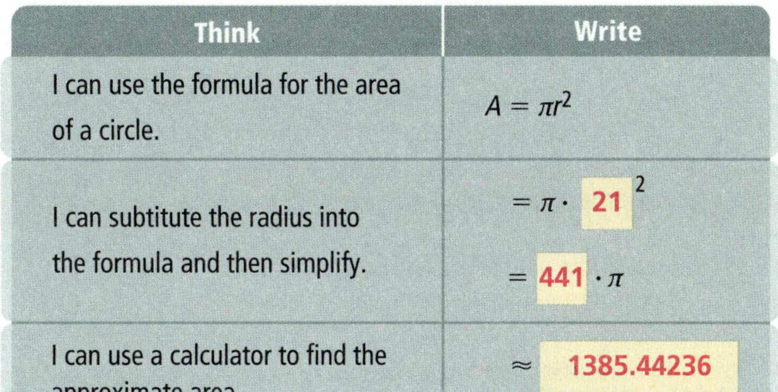

Think	Write
I can use the formula for the area of a circle.	$A = \pi r^2$
I can subtitute the radius into the formula and then simplify.	$= \pi \cdot$ 21^2 $=$ 441 $\cdot \pi$
I can use a calculator to find the approximate area.	$\approx$ 1385.44236

11. The area of the wrestling region is about 1385 ft^2.

take note

Theorem 10-12 Area of a Sector of a Circle

The area of a sector of a circle is the product of the ratio $\frac{\text{measure of the arc}}{360}$ and the area of the circle.

Area of sector $AOB = \dfrac{m\widehat{AB}}{360} \cdot \pi r^2$

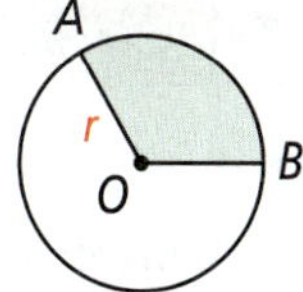

Complete.

	measure of the arc	$\frac{\textbf{measure of the arc}}{\textbf{360}}$	**area of the sector**
12.	60	$\frac{60}{360} = \frac{1}{6}$	$\frac{1}{6} \cdot \pi \cdot r^2$
13.	120	$\frac{120}{360} = \frac{1}{3}$	$\frac{1}{3} \cdot \pi \cdot r^2$

Problem 2 Finding the Area of a Sector of a Circle

Got It? **A circle has a radius of 4 in. What is the area of a sector bounded by a 45° minor arc? Leave your answer in terms of π.**

14. At the right is one student's solution. What error did the student make?

The student did not square the radius.

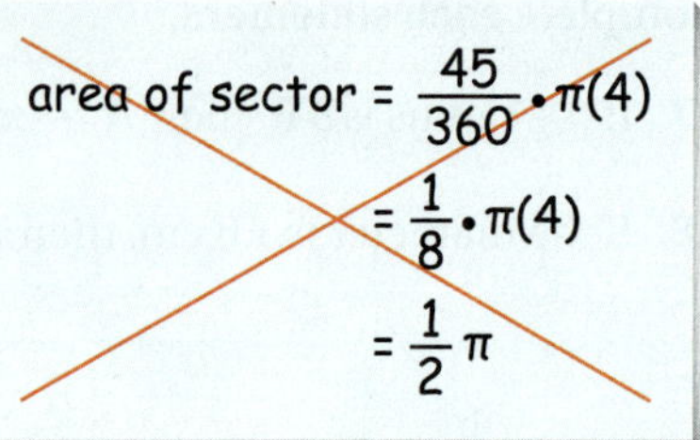

15. Find the area of the sector correctly.

$$\text{area of sector} = \frac{45}{360} \cdot \pi(4)^2 = \frac{1}{8} \cdot \pi(16) = 2\pi$$

16. The area of the sector is 2π in.².

take note — Key Concept Area of a Segment

The area of a segment is the difference of the area of the sector and the area of the triangle formed by the radii and the segment joining the endpoints.

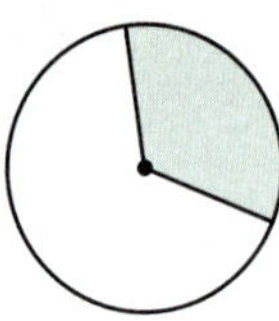 − 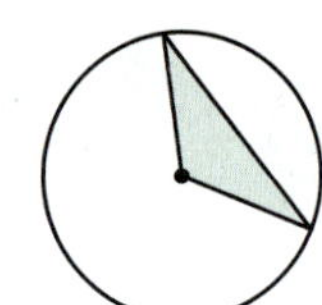 = 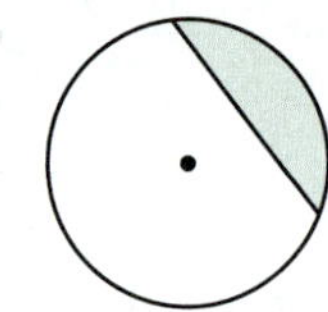

Area of sector − Area of triangle = Area of segment

Problem 3 Finding the Area of a Segment of a Circle

Got It? **What is the area of the shaded segment shown at the right? Round your answer to the nearest tenth.**

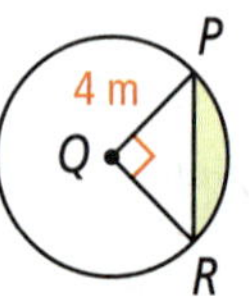

17. Use the justifications below to find the area of sector *PQR*.

area of sector $PQR = \frac{m\overparen{PR}}{360} \cdot \pi r^2$	Use the formula for the area of a sector.
$= \frac{90}{360} \cdot \pi(4)^2$	Substitute.
$= 4 \cdot \pi$	Simplify.

18. $\triangle PQR$ is a right triangle, so the base is 4 m and the height is 4 m.

19. Find the area of $\triangle PQR$.

$A = \frac{1}{2}bh$

$= \frac{1}{2}(4)(4)$

$= 8$

20. Complete to find the area of the shaded segment. Use a calculator.

area of shaded segment = area of sector PQR − area of $\triangle PQR$

$= 4 \cdot \pi - 8$

≈ 4.566370614

21. To the nearest tenth, the area of the shaded segment is 4.6 m^2.

Lesson Check • Do you UNDERSTAND?

Reasoning **Suppose a sector in $\odot P$ has the same area as a sector in $\odot O$. Can you conclude that $\odot P$ and $\odot O$ have the same area? Explain.**

Use the figures at the right for Exercises 22–24.

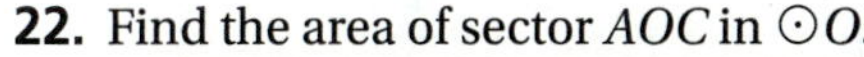

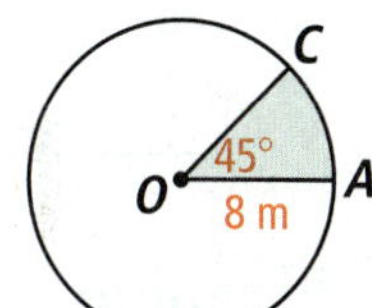

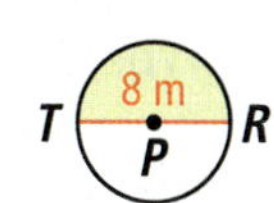

22. Find the area of sector AOC in $\odot O$.

area of sector $= \frac{45}{360} \cdot \pi(8)^2$

$= \frac{1}{8} \cdot \pi(64)$

$= 8\pi$

23. Find the area of sector RPT in $\odot P$.

area of sector $= \frac{180}{360} \cdot \pi(4)^2$

$= \frac{1}{2} \cdot \pi(16)$

$= 8\pi$

24. Do the sectors have the same area? Can you conclude that the circles have the same area? Explain. Explanations may vary. Sample:

Yes; no; the circles do not have the same area because their radii are different lengths.

Math Success

Check off the vocabulary words that you understand.

☐ sector of a circle ☐ segment of a circle ☐ area of a circle

Rate how well you can *find areas of circles, sectors, and segments.*

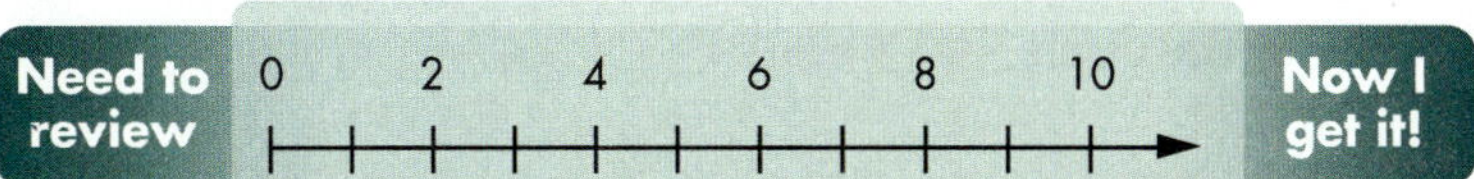

Name ______________________ Class ____________ Date ____________

10-7 Think About a Plan

Areas of Circles and Sectors

Industrial Design Refer to the diagram of the regular hexagonal nut. What is the area of the hexagonal face to the nearest millimeter?

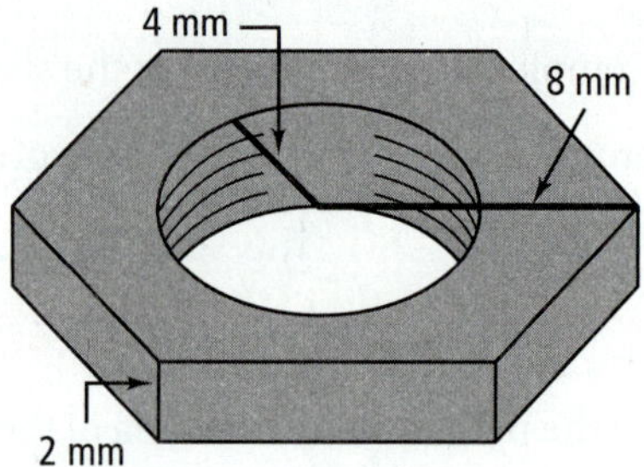

Understanding the Problem

1. On the diagram at the right, what is the area that you need to find?

   the top surface of the nut

2. How does this area differ from that of a regular hexagon?

   There is a circular area cut out of the center.

3. What two areas must you find to solve this problem?

   the area of the hexagon and the area of the interior circle

Planning the Solution

4. What is the formula for the area of a circle? $A = \pi r^2$

5. What is the formula for the area of a regular polygon? $A = \frac{1}{2}ap$

6. What information do you have about the hexagon? What information do you need?

   that the radius is 8 mm; the length of the apothem and the perimeter

7. What special triangle relationship can you use to find the information you need?

   the relationship between the sides of a 30°-60°-90° right triangle

Getting an Answer

8. Use this relationship to find the length of the shorter leg, the perimeter, and the apothem. 4 mm; 48 mm; $4\sqrt{3}$ mm ≈ 6.93 mm

9. Use the formula to calculate the area of the hexagon. 166.3 mm^2

10. Use the formula to calculate the area of the circle. 50.3 mm^2

11. What is the area of the hexagonal face? 116 mm^2

Name ______________________ Class ____________ Date ____________

10-7 Practice
Form K

Areas of Circles and Sectors

Find the area of each circle. Leave your answer in terms of π.

1.

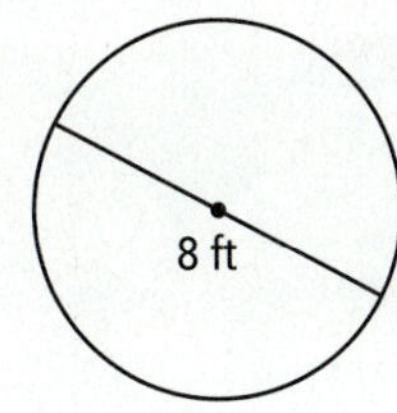

To start, find the radius. Then use the correct area formula.

$r = 8 \div 2 = \boxed{4}$; $A = \pi r^2 = \pi \cdot \boxed{4}^2$

16π ft^2

2.

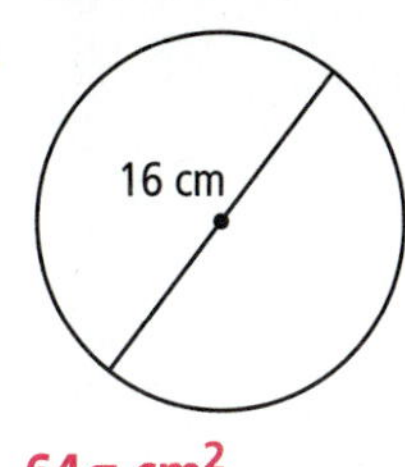

64π cm^2

3.

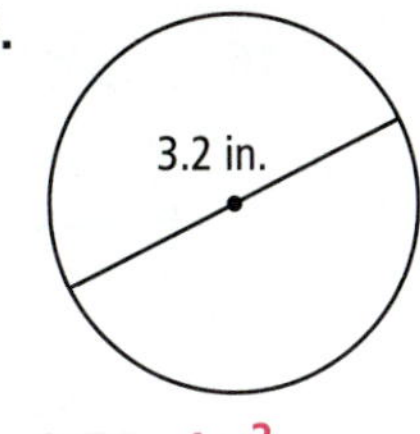

2.56π in.^{2}

4.

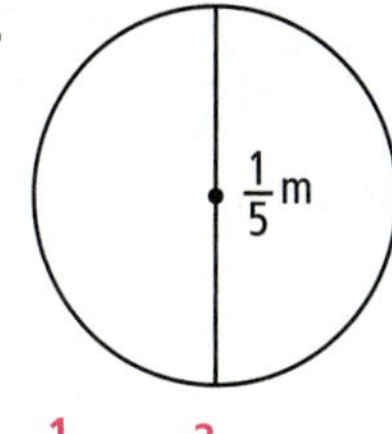

$\frac{1}{100}\pi$ m^2

5. Jerry has a lawn sprinkler that sprays water out into a circle. The diameter of the circle is 10 ft. What area can Jerry water with the sprinkler? Round to the nearest tenth. 78.5 ft^2

6. A dog is on a leash that is attached to a pole in the ground. If the leash is 8 ft long, in how much area can the dog move around? Round to the nearest tenth. 201.1 ft^2

Find the area of each shaded sector of a circle. Leave your answer in terms of π.

7.

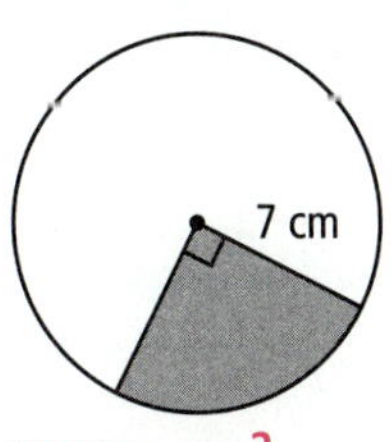

To start, find the ratio of the measure of the arc to 360.

$\frac{90}{360} = \frac{\boxed{1}}{\boxed{4}}$

12.25π cm^2

8.

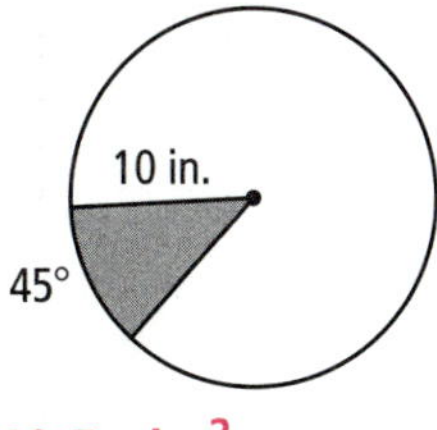

12.5π in.^{2}

9.

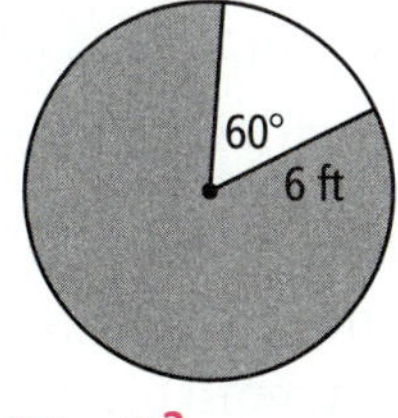

30π ft^2

10.

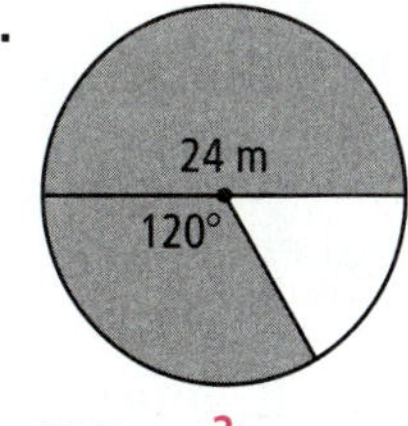

120π m^2

Find the area of sector *QRS* in $\odot R$ using the given information. Leave your answer in terms of π.

11. $r = 4$ in., $m\widehat{QS} = 135$ 6π in.^{2}

12. $r = 10$ cm, $m\widehat{QS} = 90$ 25π cm^2

Name ______________________ Class __________ Date __________

10-7 Practice (continued) *Form K*

Areas of Circles and Sectors

Find the area of each shaded segment. Round your answer to the nearest tenth.

13. 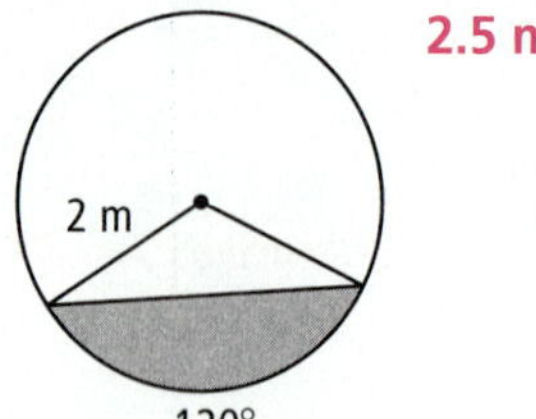

2.5 m^2

14. 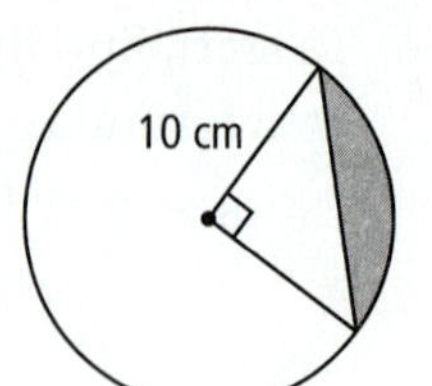

28.5 cm^2

15. 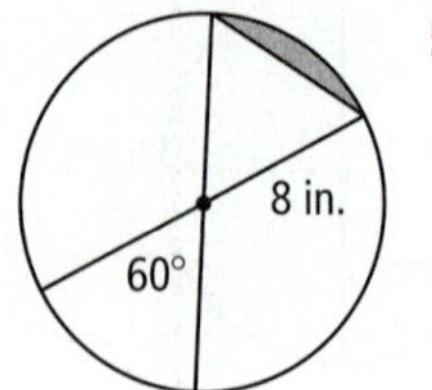

5.8 in.^{2}

16. 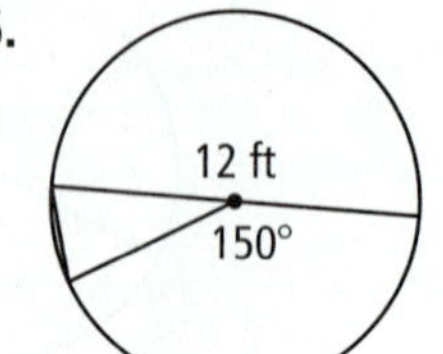

0.4 ft^2

Find the area of the shaded region. Leave your answer in terms of π and in simplest radical form.

17. 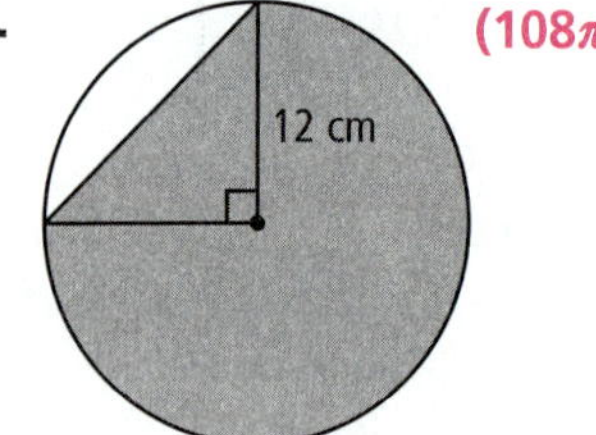

$(108\pi + 72)$ cm^2

18. 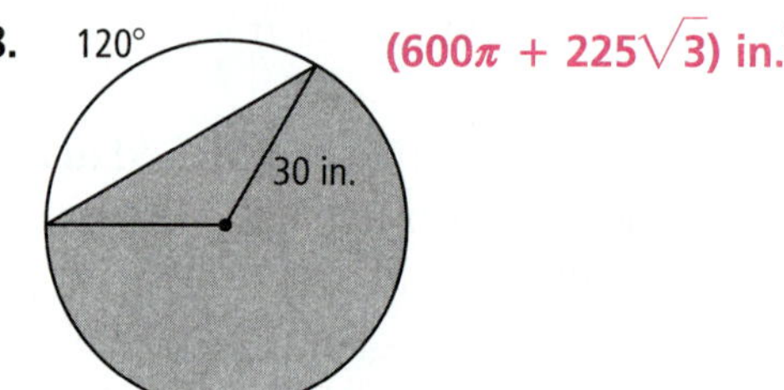

$(600\pi + 225\sqrt{3})$ in.^{2}

19. 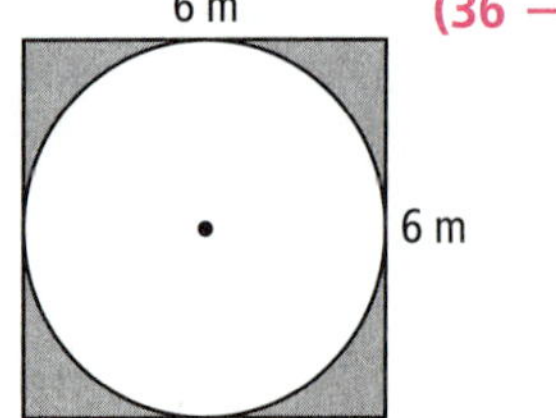

$(36 - 9\pi)$ m^2

20. 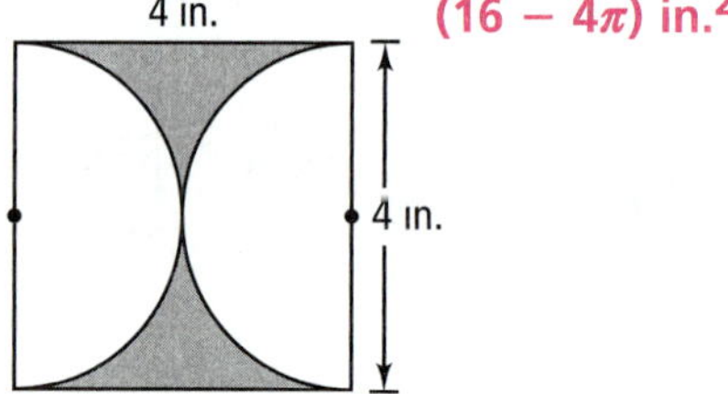

$(16 - 4\pi)$ in.^{2}

21. The school is planting a circular garden. If the diameter of the garden is 6 ft, what is the garden's area to the nearest tenth of a square foot? **28.3 ft^2**

22. An apartment complex is replanting grass seed in a play area. The area is a circle that is 30 ft in diameter. They need 1 lb of grass seed for every 300 square ft. Find the area to the nearest tenth of a square foot. Then calculate how many 1-lb bags of grass seed they need. **706.9 ft^2; 3 bags**

23. A circular fountain is surrounded by flowers. The fountain's diameter is 8 ft. The flowers extend 1.5 ft out from the fountain on all sides. What area do the flowers cover to the nearest tenth of a square foot? **44.8 ft^2**

Name ______________________ Class ____________ Date ____________

10-7 Standardized Test Prep

Areas of Circles and Sectors

Multiple Choice

For Exercises 1–4, choose the correct letter.

1. What is the area of a circle with a diameter of 8? C

Ⓐ 4π Ⓑ 8π Ⓒ 16π Ⓓ 64π

2. Which sector below has the greatest area? F

Ⓕ 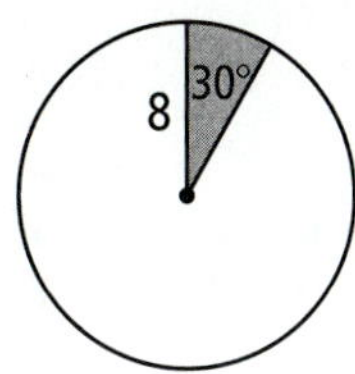

Ⓖ 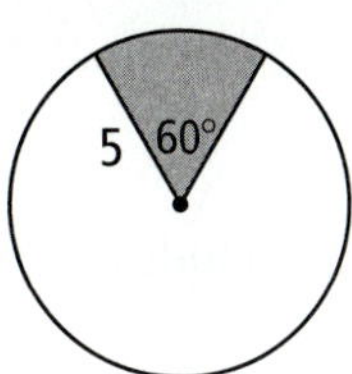

Ⓗ 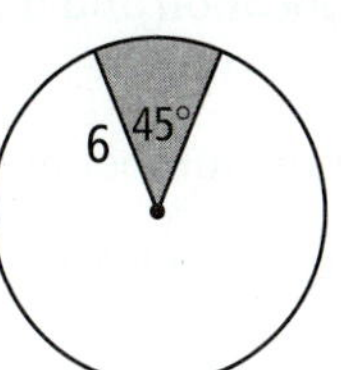

Ⓘ 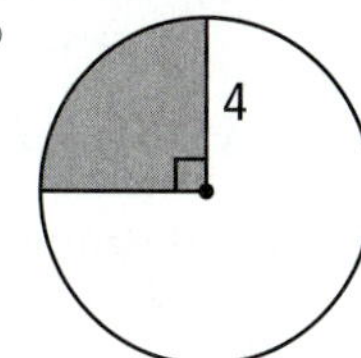

3. If $\odot B$ has a radius of 4 and $m\overarc{AC} = 36$, what is the area of sector ABC? D

Ⓐ $\frac{5}{8}\pi$ 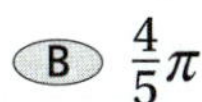 Ⓑ $\frac{4}{5}\pi$ 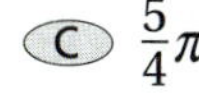 Ⓒ $\frac{5}{4}\pi$ Ⓓ $\frac{8}{5}\pi$

4. Which of the following is equal to the area of the sector ABC in the figure at the right? H

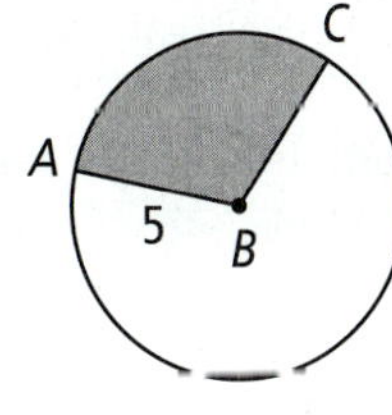

Ⓕ $\frac{m\overarc{AC}}{360} \cdot 10\pi$ Ⓗ $\frac{m\overarc{AC}}{360} \cdot 25\pi$

Ⓖ $\frac{360}{m\overarc{AC}} \cdot 5\pi$ Ⓘ $\frac{360}{m\overarc{AC}} \cdot 25\pi$

Short Response

5. What is the area of the shaded segment in the figure at the right? Use at least three steps. Show your work. Leave your answer in terms of π and in simplest radical form.

Answers may vary. Sample:

Step 1) area of sector $RST = \frac{m\overarc{RT}}{360} \cdot 3\pi = \frac{60}{360} \cdot 3\pi = \frac{1}{6} \cdot 3\pi = \frac{\pi}{2}$

Step 2) area of $\triangle RST = \frac{1}{2} \cdot bh = \frac{1}{2} \cdot \sqrt{3} \cdot \frac{3}{2} = \frac{3\sqrt{3}}{4}$

Step 3) area of segment = area of sector RST − area of $\triangle RST = \frac{\pi}{2} - \frac{3\sqrt{3}}{4}$

[2] Student response is complete and shows all steps clearly.
[1] Student shows one or two steps that are clearly worked out.
[0] Student has no steps correct.

10-8 Geometric Probability

Vocabulary

Review

Write T for *true* or F for *false*.

T 1. A *point* indicates a location and has no size.

F 2. A line contains a finite number of *points.*

3. Use the diagram at the right. Circle the segment that includes *point S*.

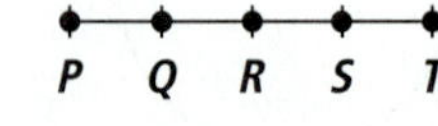

$\overline{PR}$  $\overline{PT}$ $\overline{QR}$

Vocabulary Builder

probability (noun) **prah buh BIL uh tee**

Related Term: geometric probability

theoretical **probability**

$$P(\text{event}) = \frac{\text{number of favorable outcomes}}{\text{number of possible outcomes}}$$

Definition: The **probability** of an event is the likelihood that the event will occur.

Main Idea: In geometric **probability,** numbers of favorable and possible outcomes are geometric measures such as lengths of segments or areas of regions.

Use Your Vocabulary

4. Underline the correct words to complete the sentence.

The *probability* of an event is the ratio of the number of favorable / possible outcomes to the number of favorable / possible outcomes.

5. There are 7 red marbles and 3 green marbles in a bag. One marble is chosen at random. Write the *probability* that a green marble is chosen.

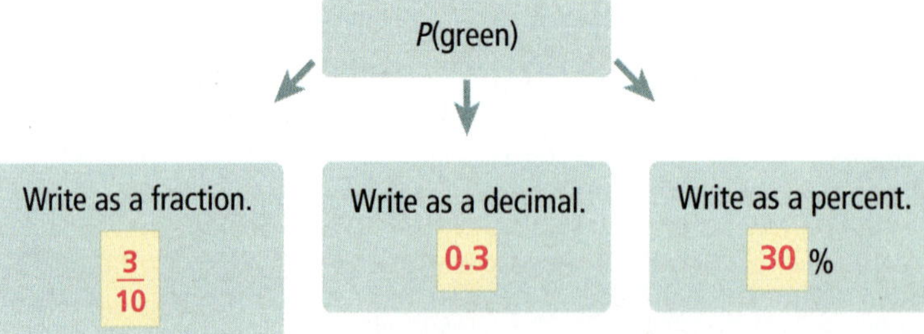

Key Concept Probability and Length or Area

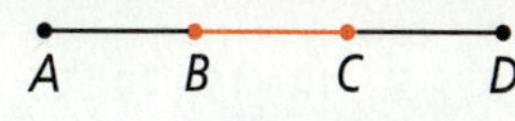

Probability and Length

Point S on $\overline{AD}$ is chosen at random. The probability that S is on $\overline{BC}$ is the ratio of the length of $\overline{BC}$ to the length of $\overline{AD}$.

$$P(S \text{ on } \overline{BC}) = \frac{BC}{AD}$$

Complete.

6. $P(S \text{ on } \overline{AC}) = \frac{AC}{AD}$

7. $P(S \text{ on } \overline{AB}) = \frac{AB}{AD}$

Probability and Area

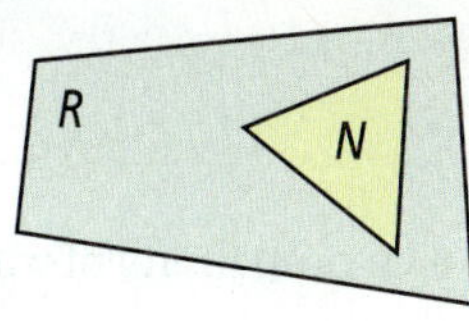

Point S in region R is chosen at random. The probability that S is in region N is the ratio of the area of region N to the area of region R.

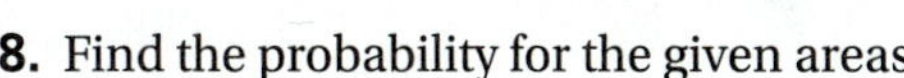

$$P(S \text{ in region } N) = \frac{\text{area of region } N}{\text{area of region } R}$$

8. Find the probability for the given areas.

area of region $R = 11 \text{ cm}^2$ area of region $N = 3 \text{ cm}^2$

$$P(S \text{ in } N) = \frac{3}{11}$$

Problem 1 Using Segments to Find Probability

Got It? **Point H on $\overline{ST}$ is selected at random. What is the probability that H lies on $\overline{SR}$?**

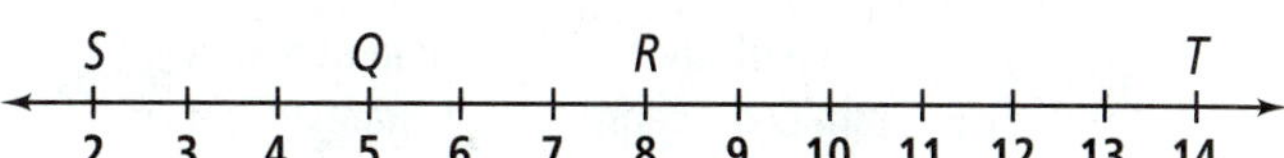

9. Find the length of each segment.

length of $\overline{SR} = |2 - 8| = 6$ length of $\overline{ST} = |2 - 14| = 12$

10. Find the probability.

$$P(H \text{ on } \overline{SR}) = \frac{\text{length of } \overline{SR}}{\text{length of } \overline{ST}} = \frac{6}{12} = \frac{1}{2}$$

11. The probability that H is on $\overline{SR}$ is $\frac{1}{2}$, or 50 %.

Problem 2 Using Segments to Find Probability

Got It? **Transportation** **A commuter train runs every 25 min. If a commuter arrives at the station at a random time, what is the probability that the commuter will have to wait no more than 5 min for the train?**

12. Circle the time t (in minutes) before the train arrives that the commuter will need to arrive in order to wait *no more than* 5 minutes.

$0 \leq t \leq 5$ (circled) $5 < t \leq 10$ $10 < t \leq 15$

$15 < t \leq 20$ $20 < t \leq 25$

13. Circle the diagram that models the situation.

A C B
0 5 10 15 20 25

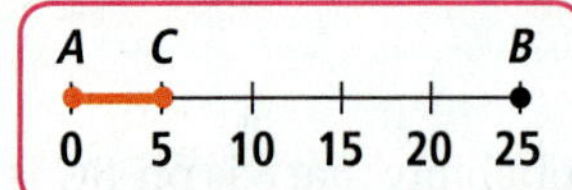

A C B
0 5 10 15 20 25

14. Complete.

length of favorable segment = **5** length of entire segment = **25**

15. Find the probability.

$$P(\text{waiting no more than 5 min}) = \frac{\text{length of favorable segment}}{\text{length of entire segment}}$$

$$= \frac{5}{25}, \text{ or } \frac{1}{5}$$

16. The probability of waiting no more than 5 min for the train is $\frac{1}{5}$, or **20** %.

Problem 3 Using Area to Find Probability

Got It? A triangle is inscribed in a square. Point T in the square is selected at random. What is the probability that T lies in the shaded region?

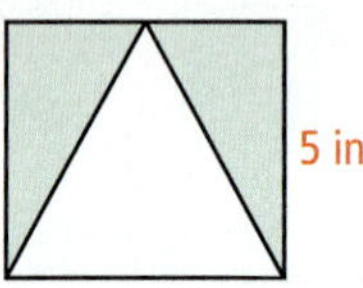

17. Complete the model below to write an equation.

Define Let s = the area of the shaded region.

Relate area of the shaded region is area of the square minus area of the triangle

Write $s = 5^2 - \frac{1}{2} \cdot 5 \cdot 5$

18. Now solve the equation to find the area of the shaded region.

$s = 5^2 - \frac{1}{2} \cdot 5 \cdot 5$
$= 25 - \frac{1}{2} \cdot 25$
$= 25 - 12.5$
$= 12.5$

19. Find the probability.

$$P(\text{point } T \text{ is in shaded region}) = \frac{\text{area of shaded region}}{\text{area of square}}$$

$$= \frac{12.5}{25}, \text{ or } \frac{1}{2}$$

20. The probability that T lies in the shaded region is $\frac{1}{2}$, or **50** %.

Problem 4 Using Area to Find Probability

Got It? Archery An archery target has 5 colored scoring zones formed by concentric circles. The target's diameter is 122 cm. The radius of the yellow zone is 12.2 cm. The width of each of the other zones is also 12.2 cm. If an arrow hits the target at a random point, what is the probability that it hits the yellow zone?

21. The radius of the target is $\frac{122}{2}$, or 61 cm.

22. Find the probability. Write the probability as a decimal.

$$P(\text{arrow hits yellow zone}) = \frac{\text{area of yellow zone}}{\text{area of entire target}}$$

$$= \frac{\pi(12.2)^2}{\pi(61)^2} = \frac{148.84}{3721} = 0.04$$

23. Explain why the calculation with π is not an estimate. Answers may vary. Sample:

I divide π out before finding the quotient.

24. The probability that the arrow hits the yellow zone is 0.04, or 4 %.

Lesson Check • Do you UNDERSTAND?

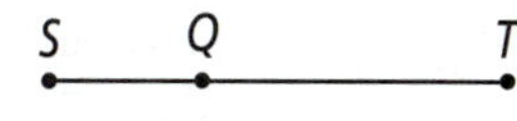

Reasoning In the figure at the right, $\frac{SQ}{QT} = \frac{1}{2}$. What is the probability that a point on $\overline{ST}$ chosen at random will lie on $\overline{QT}$? Explain.

25. If $SQ = x$, then $QT = 2x$ and $ST = 3x$.

26. What is $P(\text{point on } \overline{QT})$? Explain.

$\frac{2}{3}$; $\frac{\text{length of } QT}{\text{length of } ST} = \frac{2x}{3x} = \frac{2}{3}$

Math Success

Check off the vocabulary words that you understand.

☐ length ☐ area ☐ geometric probability

Rate how well you can *use geometric probability.*

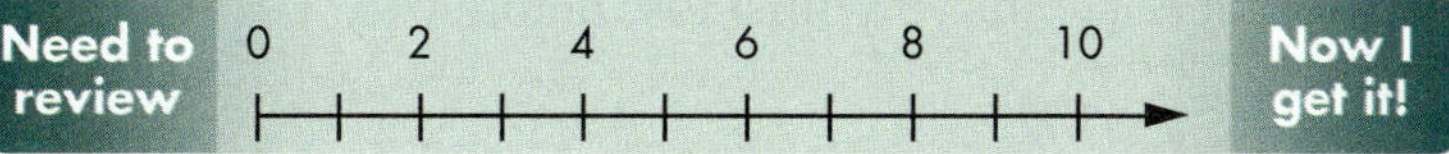

Name ______________________ Class ____________ Date ____________

10-8 Think About a Plan

Geometric Probability

Games To win a prize at a carnival game, you must toss a quarter so that it lands entirely within a 1-in. circle as shown at the right. Assume that the center of a tossed quarter is equally likely to land at any point within the 8-in. square.

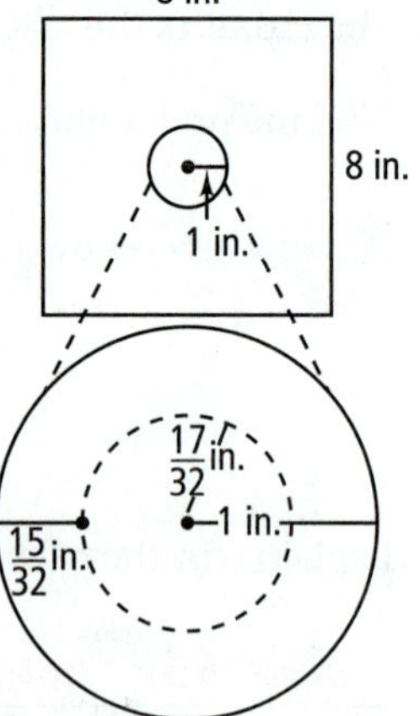

a. What is the probability that the quarter lands entirely in the circle in one toss?

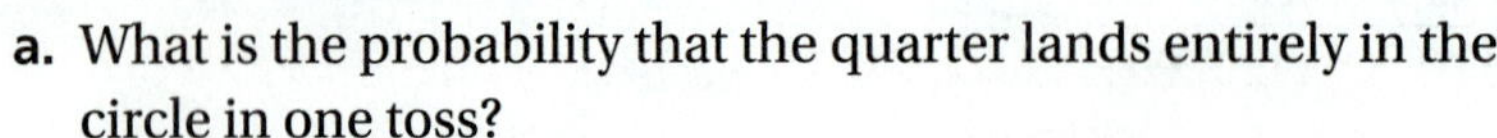

b. Reasoning On average, how many coins must you toss to win a prize? Explain.

1. In this problem, what represents the favorable outcome? Be specific.

The quarter lands within the circle.

2. In this problem, what represents all the possible outcomes?

The quarter lands anywhere within the square.

3. If a section of the quarter is in the circle, does this count as a favorable outcome?

No; the entire quarter must be in the 1-in. circle.

4. How can you determine a smaller circle within which the center of the quarter must land for the quarter to be entirely within the 1-in. circle? What is the radius of this circle? The radius of a quarter is $\frac{15}{32}$ in.

Subtract the radius of the quarter from the radius of the 1-in. circle to find the radius of the circle within which the center of the quarter must fall; the radius is $\frac{17}{32}$ in., or $\frac{15}{32}$ in. less than the 1-in. circle.

5. Use words to write a probability ratio. Then rewrite the ratio using the appropriate formulas. Substitute the appropriate measures and find the probability.

$P(\text{event}) = \frac{\text{area of smaller circle}}{\text{area of square}} = \frac{\pi r^2}{s^2} = \frac{\pi \cdot 0.53125^2}{8^2} \approx \frac{0.89}{64} \approx 0.014$

6. Based on this, what is the average number of coins you must toss before you can expect to win a prize? Explain.

72; $72 > \frac{1}{0.014} > 71$, so you cannot expect to win a prize with the toss of 71 or fewer coins.

Name ______________________ Class ____________ Date ____________

10-8 Practice

Form K

Geometric Probability

A point on $\overline{AM}$ is chosen at random. Find the probability that the point lies on the given segment.

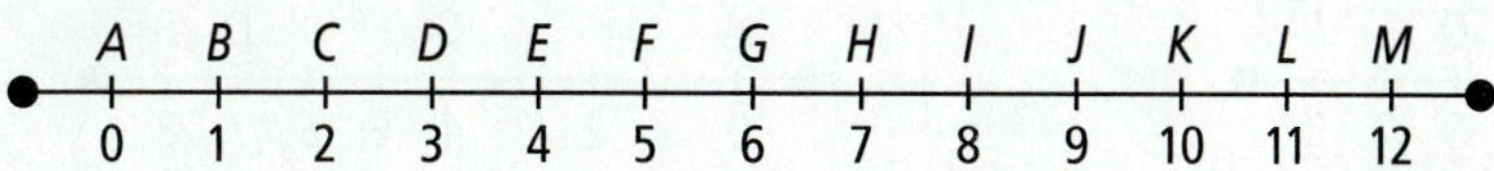

1. $\overline{DJ}$ $\frac{1}{2}$
2. $\overline{JL}$ $\frac{1}{6}$
3. $\overline{BE}$ $\frac{1}{4}$
4. $\overline{CK}$ $\frac{2}{3}$
5. $\overline{AJ}$ $\frac{3}{4}$
6. $\overline{BL}$ $\frac{5}{6}$
7. A fitness club set up an express exercise circuit. To warm up, a person works out on weight machines for 90 s. Next the person jogs in place for 60 s, and then takes 30 s to do aerobics. After this, the cycle repeats. If you enter the express exercise circuit at a random time, what is the probability that a friend of yours is jogging in place? What is the probability that your friend will be on the weight machines? $\frac{1}{3}$; $\frac{1}{2}$

A point in the figure is chosen at random. Find the probability that the point lies in the shaded region.

8. 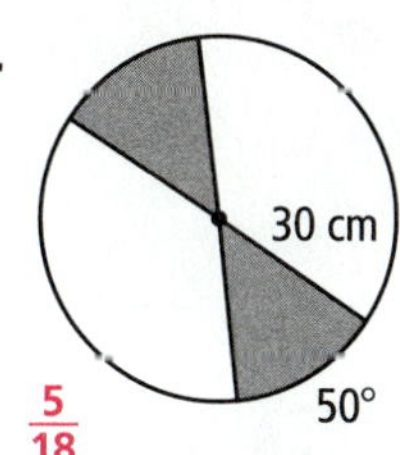

$\frac{5}{18}$

To start, find the area of the two shaded sectors.
Then find the total area.

Area of two sectors $= 2 \cdot \frac{50}{360} \cdot \pi \cdot \boxed{30}^2$

Total area $= \pi \cdot \boxed{30}^2$

9. 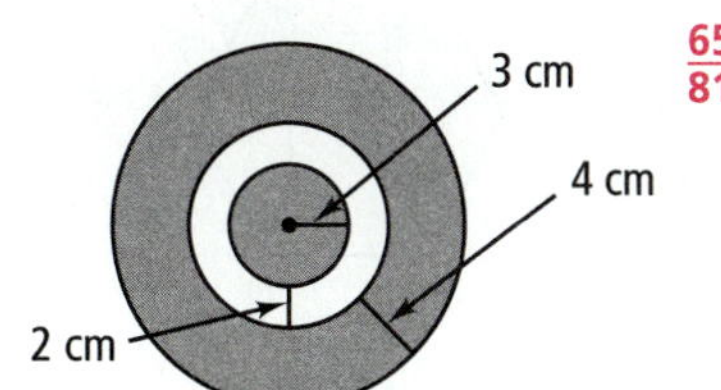

$\frac{65}{81}$

10. 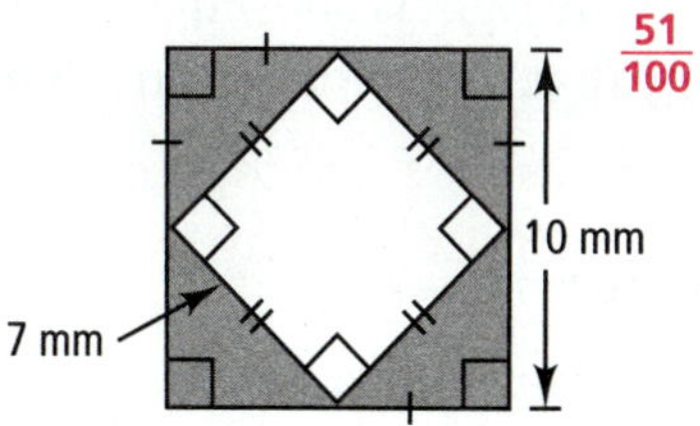

$\frac{51}{100}$

11. A Sunday night sports show is on from 10:00 P.M. to 10:30 P.M. You want to find out if your favorite team won this weekend, but forgot that the show was on. You turn it on at 10:14 P.M. The score will be announced at one random time during the show. What is the probability that you haven't missed the report about your favorite team? $\frac{8}{15}$

Name ______________________ Class ____________ Date ____________

10-8 Practice (continued) Form K

Geometric Probability

A point between *A* and *B* on each number line is chosen at random. What is the probability that the point is between *C* and *D*?

12. 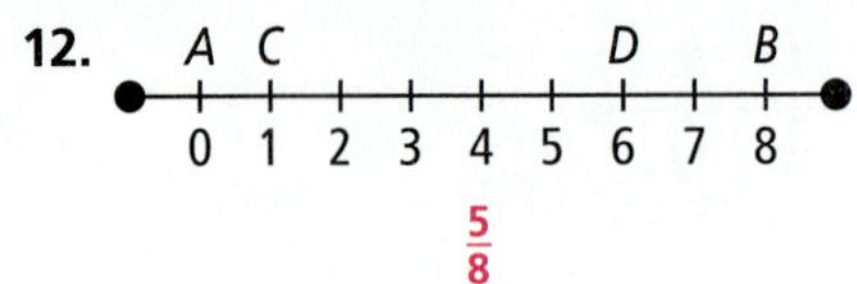

$\frac{5}{8}$

13. 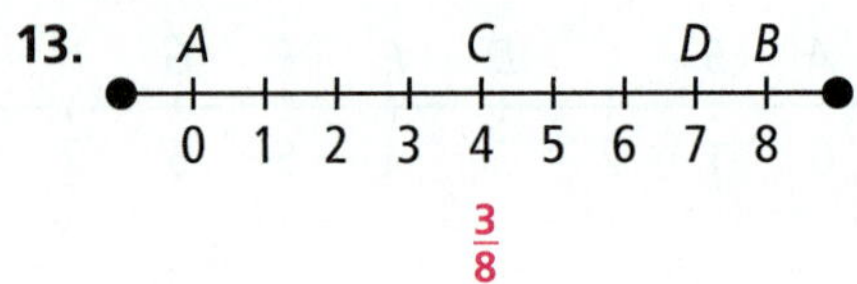

$\frac{3}{8}$

14. 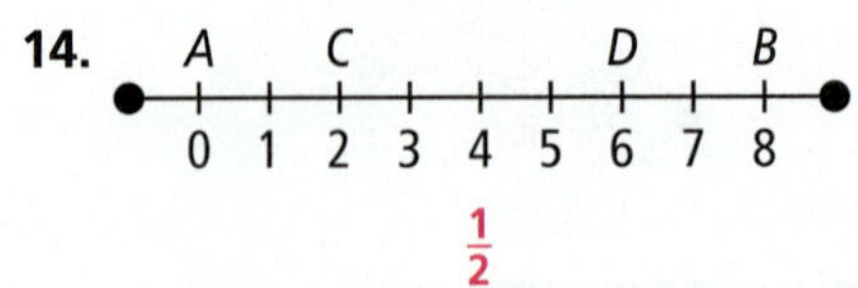

$\frac{1}{2}$

15. 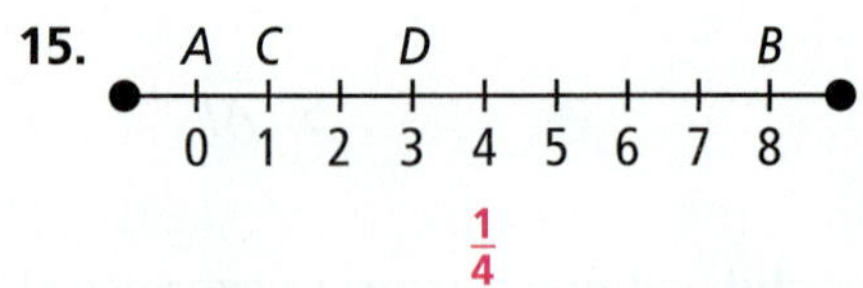

$\frac{1}{4}$

16. In the fundraiser game at the right, players toss darts at a board to try to get them into one of the holes. The diameter of the center hole is 8 in. The diameter of each of the four corner holes is 5 in. The board is a 20-in.-by-30-in. rectangle. Find the probability that a tossed dart will go through the indicated hole.

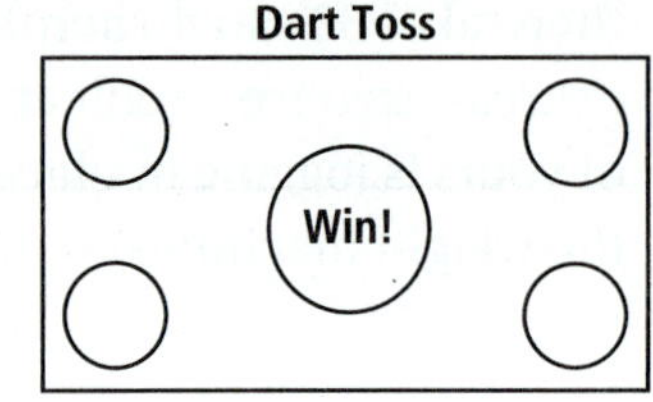

a. center hole $\frac{2}{75}\pi$

b. top right or left corner $\frac{1}{48}\pi$

c. any corner $\frac{1}{24}\pi$

d. lower left corner $\frac{1}{96}\pi$

17. Reasoning Suppose a point on the perimeter of the regular hexagon at the right is chosen at random. What is the probability that the point lies on $\overline{AB}$ or $\overline{BC}$? Explain.

$\frac{1}{3}$; the point has an equal chance of being on six congruent segments, so the probability of being on 2 segments is $\frac{2}{6}$, or $\frac{1}{3}$.

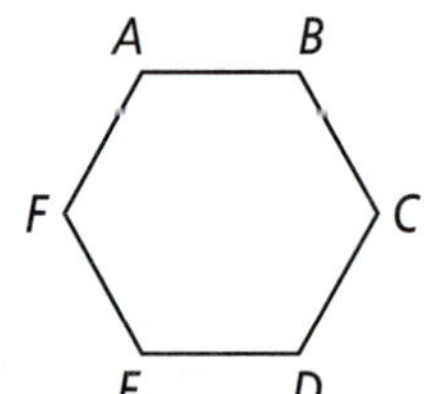

18. At the space museum, a movie starts every 15 min. There are 5 min between shows. If you enter the theater at a random time, what is the probability that you will have to wait more than 2 min. for the next movie to start? $\frac{13}{15}$

Name ______________________ Class ____________ Date ____________

10-8 Standardized Test Prep

Geometric Probability

Multiple Choice

For Exercises 1–4, choose the correct letter.

1. Point X on $\overline{QT}$ is chosen at random. What is the probability that X is on $\overline{ST}$? B

A $\frac{QT}{ST}$ B $\frac{ST}{QT}$ C $\frac{QS}{ST}$ D $\frac{ST}{QS}$

2. Point P on $\overline{AD}$ is chosen at random. For which of the figures below is the probability that P is on $\overline{BC}$ 25%? Note: Diagrams not drawn to scale. I

F 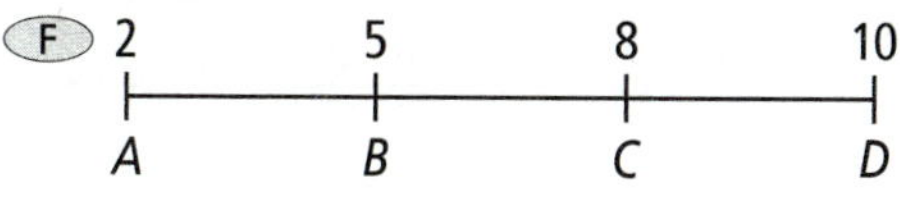

H 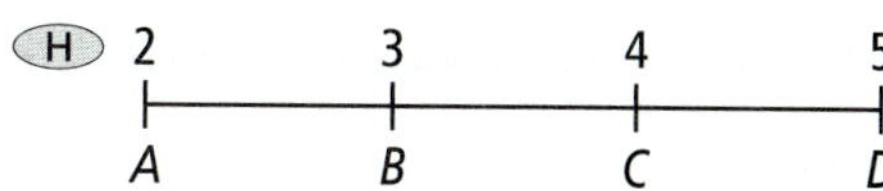

G 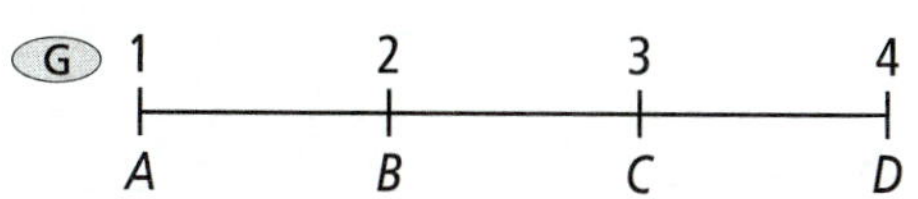

I 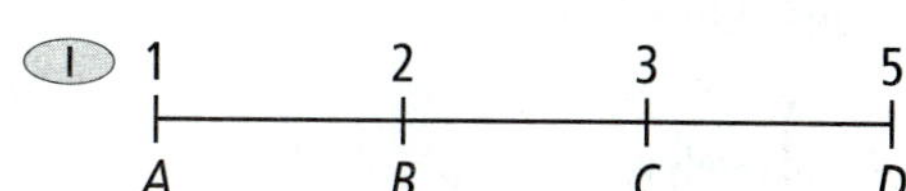

3. Point P is chosen at random in a circle. If a square is inscribed in the circle, what is the probability that P lies outside the square? B

A $1-\frac{1}{2\pi}$ B $1-\frac{2}{\pi}$ C $1-\frac{\pi}{2}$ D $1-\frac{1}{4\pi}$

4. You have a 7-cm straw and a 10-cm straw. You want to cut the 10-cm straw into two pieces so that the three pieces make a triangle. If you cut the straw at a random point, what is the probability that you can make a triangle? I

F 30% G 40% H 60% I 70%

Short Response

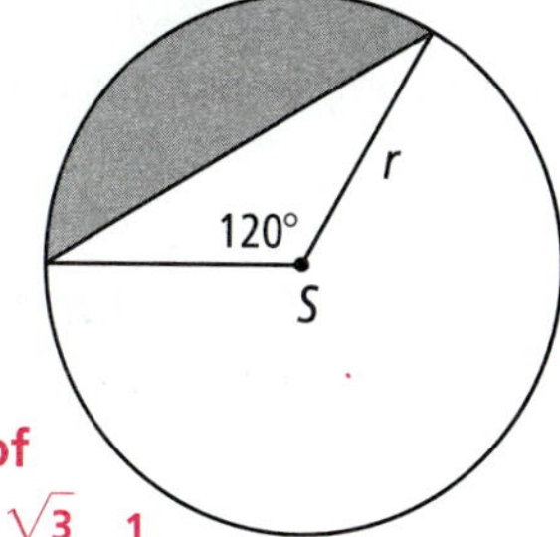

5. Point P is chosen at random in $\odot S$. What is the probability that P lies in the shaded segment shown in the diagram at the right? Show your work.

Answers may vary. Sample: Area of sector $= \frac{120}{360} \cdot \pi r^2 = \frac{1}{3}\pi r^2$; area of triangle $= \frac{1}{2} \cdot bh = \frac{1}{2} \cdot 2r \sin(60) \cdot r\cos(60) = r^2 \sin 60 \cdot \cos 60 = r^2 \frac{\sqrt{3}}{2} \cdot \frac{1}{2} = \frac{r^2\sqrt{3}}{4}$; area of segment = area of sector − area of triangle $= \frac{1}{3}\pi r^2 - \frac{r^2\sqrt{3}}{4}$;

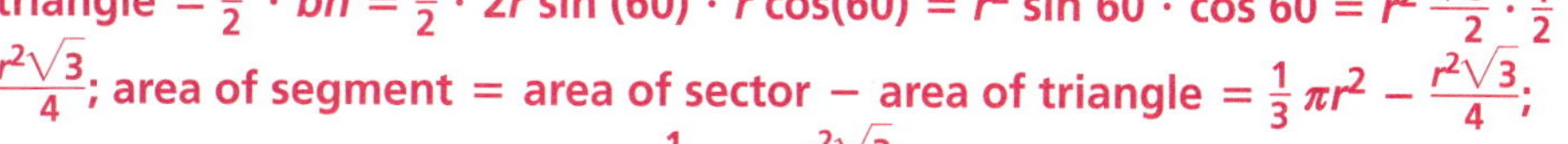

$$\text{probability} = \frac{\text{Area of segment}}{\text{Area of circle}} = \frac{\frac{1}{3}\pi r^2 - \frac{r^2\sqrt{3}}{4}}{\pi r^2} = \frac{1}{3} - \frac{\sqrt{3}}{4\pi} \approx 0.1955 \approx 19.55\%$$

[2] All answers correct [1] some answers correct [0] no answers correct

Space Figures and Cross Sections

Vocabulary

Review

Complete each statement with the correct word from the list.

edge edges vertex vertices

1. A(n) _?_ is a segment that is formed by the intersections of two faces. edge
2. A(n) _?_ is a point where two or more *edges* intersect. vertex
3. A cube has eight _?_. vertices
4. A cube has twelve _?_. edges

Vocabulary Builder

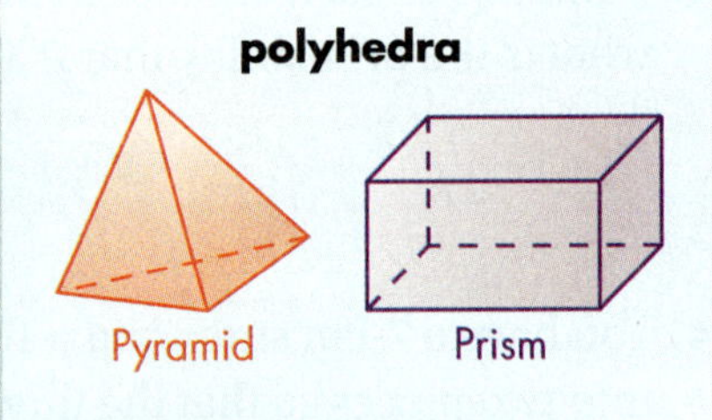

polyhedron (noun) pahl ih HEE drun (plural: polyhedra)

Related Words: face, edge, vertex

Definition: A *polyhedron* is a space figure, or three-dimensional figure, whose surfaces are polygons.

Origin: The word *polyhedron* combines the Greek prefix *poli-*, meaning "many," and *hedron*, meaning "base."

Examples: prism, pyramid

Non-Examples: circle, cylinder, sphere

Use Your Vocabulary

5. Cross out the figure below that is NOT a *polyhedron*.

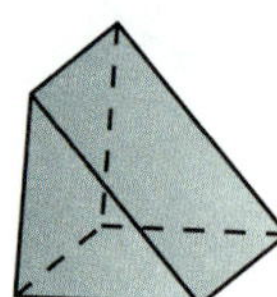
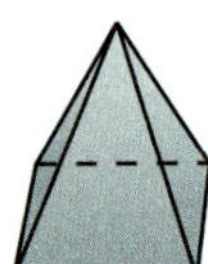
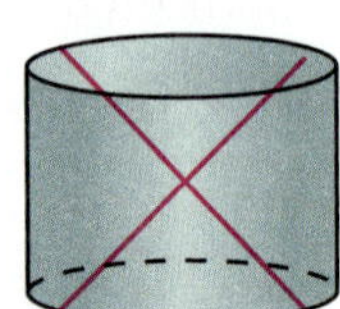
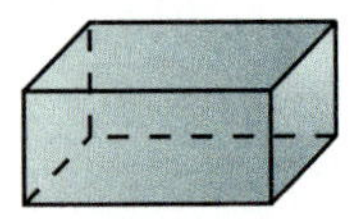

Problem 1 Identifying Vertices, Edges, and Faces

Got It? **How many vertices, edges, and faces are in the polyhedron at the right? List them.**

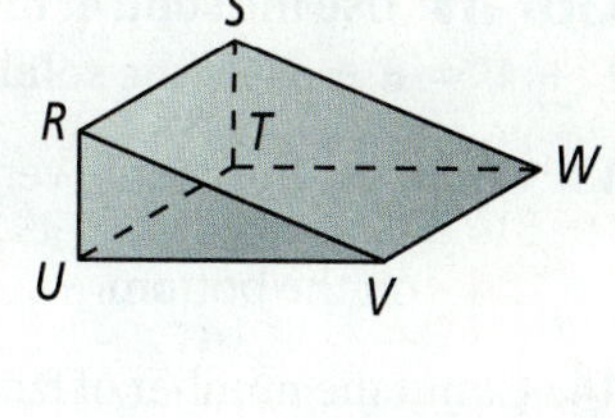

6. Identify each description as a *vertex*, an *edge*, or a *face*.

a point where three or more edges intersect	polygon	a segment where two or more faces intersect
vertex	face	edge

7. List the two vertices at the top of the polyhedron and the four vertices along the bottom of the polyhedron.

R, S, T, U, V, W

8. List the one edge at the top of the polyhedron, the four edges along the bottom, and the four edges that connect the top and bottom. Remember to list the dashed hidden edges.

$\overline{RS}, \overline{VW}, \overline{RU}, \overline{RV}, \overline{ST}, \overline{SW}, \overline{TU}, \overline{TW}, \overline{UV}$

9. List the faces. Remember to list the hidden faces.

quadrilateral *RSTU*, quadrilateral *RSWV* , quadrilateral *TUVW*, △*STW*, △*RUV*

10. The polyhedron has 6 vertices, 9 edges, and 5 faces.

take note

Key Concept Euler's Formula

The sum of the number of faces (F) and vertices (V) of a polyhedron is two more than the number of its edges (E).

$F + V = E + 2$

Problem 2 Using Euler's Formula

Got It? **Use Euler's Formula to find the number of faces for a polyhedron with 30 edges and 20 vertices.**

11. Use the justifications at the right to find the number of faces.

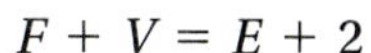

$F + V = E + 2$	Use Euler's Formula.
$F + 20 = 30 + 2$	Substitute the given information.
$F + 20 = 32$	Simplify.
$F = 32 - 20$	Subtraction Property of Equality
$F = 12$	Simplify.

12. A polygon with 30 edges and 20 vertices has 12 faces.

Problem 3 Verifying Euler's Formula in Two Dimensions

Got It? **Use the solid at the right. How can you verify Euler's Formula $F + V = E + 2$ for the solid?**

13. Count the number of vertices.

4 on the bottom + 4 on the top = 8 vertices

14. Count the number of faces.

2 bases + 4 lateral faces = 6 faces

15. Count the number of edges.

9 solid edges + 3 dashed hidden edges = 12 edges

16. Underline the correct word to complete the sentence.

You can verify Euler's Formula for a solid by showing that the equation is true / false for the values of F, V, and E.

17. Now verify Euler's Formula for the values you found.

$F + V = E + 2$	Write Euler's Formula.
$6 + 8 = 12 + 2$	Substitute.
$14 = 14$	Simplify.

Lesson Check • Do you UNDERSTAND?

Error Analysis **Your math class is drawing polyhedrons. Which figure does not belong in the diagram below? Explain.**

 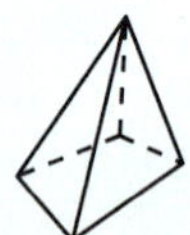  

18. Circle the figure(s) below that have edges that are line segments. Underline the figure(s) that are NOT polygons.

circle hexagon rectangle trapezoid triangle

19. Which figure does not belong in the diagram? Explain why it doesn't belong.

Cylinder. Explanations may vary. Sample: All surfaces of polyhedrons must be polygons. The cylinder does not belong because it has a surface that is not a polygon.

11-1 PART 2 Space Figures and Cross Sections

Vocabulary

Review

T 1. A *plane* extends without end.

F 2. A *plane* contains a finite number of lines.

T 3. A *plane* has no thickness.

T 4. A *plane* can be named using at least three noncollinear points.

F 5. Two different *planes* can intersect at more than one line.

T 6. Through any three noncollinear points there is exactly one *plane*.

Vocabulary Builder

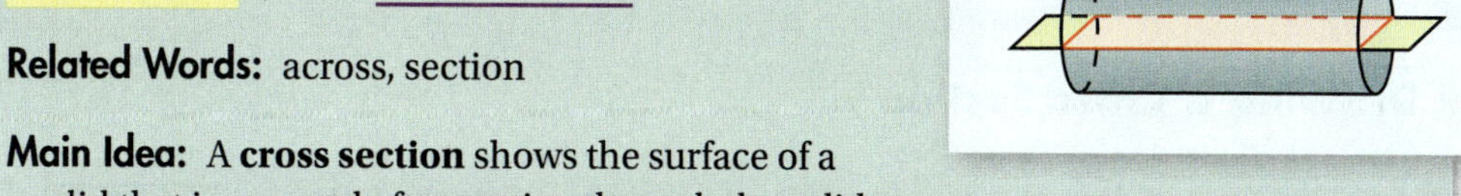

cross section (noun) **kraws** SEK **shun**

Related Words: across, section

Main Idea: A **cross section** shows the surface of a solid that is exposed after cutting through the solid.

Math Usage: A **cross section** is the intersection of a solid and a plane.

Use Your Vocabulary

Underline the correct word to complete each sentence.

7. A *cross section* is formed by a plane / solid and a solid.

8. A *cross section* looks like a very thin slice of a plane / solid .

9. A *cross section* may look like a circle / cube .

10. A *cross section* looks like a three-dimensional / two-dimensional figure.

Problem 4 Describing a Cross Section

Got It? **For the solid at the right, what is the cross section formed by a horizontal plane?**

Underline the correct word to complete each sentence.

11. A horizontal plane is parallel to the bottom / side of the solid.

12. A view from the side / top of the solid helps you see the shape of the cross section.

13. The cross section is a circle / trapezoid.

Got It? **Use the solid shown for Exercises 11–13 above. What is the cross section formed by a vertical plane that divides the solid in half?**

Underline the correct word(s) to complete each sentence.

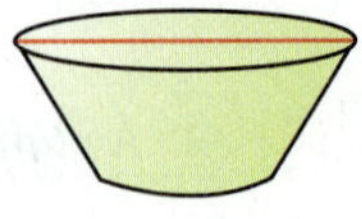

14. The red line in the figure at the right is the intersection of the top of the solid with a vertical plane that divides it in half. The vertical plane intersects the bottom of the solid in a line segment that is parallel / perpendicular to the red line segment.

15. The vertical plane intersects the bottom of the solid in a line segment that is / is not congruent to the red line segment.

16. The vertical plane intersects the side surface of the solid in one / two / four line segments.

17. The cross section formed is a triangle / quadrilateral.

18. Sketch the cross section in the space below.

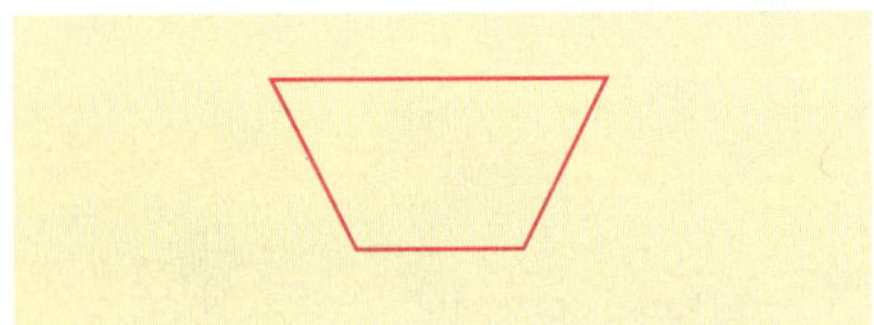

19. The cross section is a __?__.

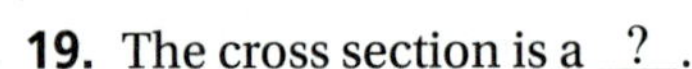

trapezoid

Problem 5 Drawing a Cross Section

Got It? **Draw the cross section formed by a horizontal plane intersecting the left and right faces of the cube. What shape is the cross section?**

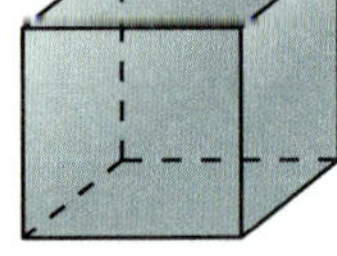

20. A *horizontal* plane is parallel to which faces of the cube? Circle your answer.

front and back　　　left and right　　　top and bottom

21. Circle the diagram that shows the intersection of the horizontal plane and the left and right faces of the cube.

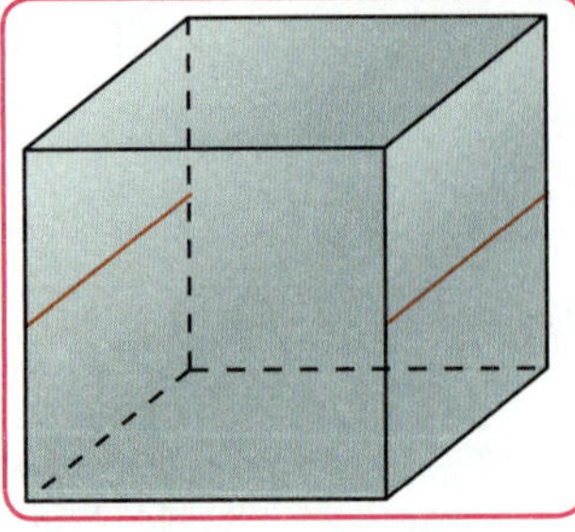

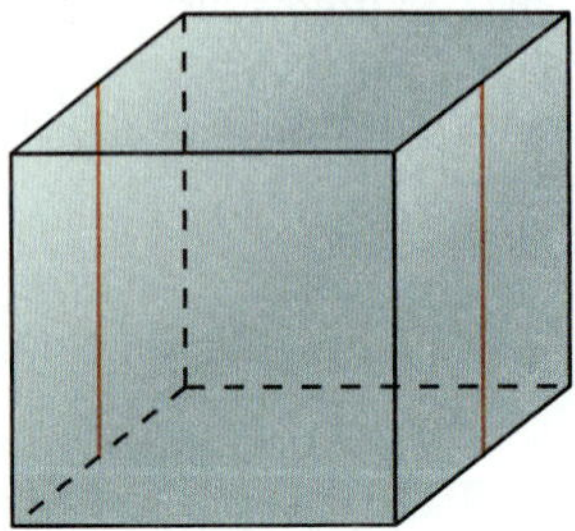

22. Use the cube below to draw and shade the cross section.

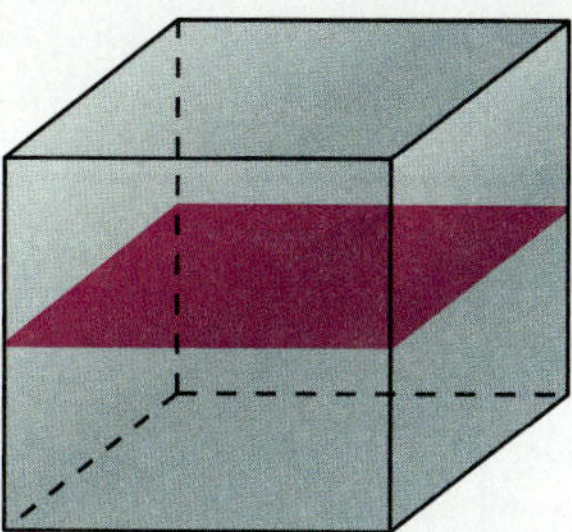

23. The cross section is a __?__.

square

Lesson Check • Do you know HOW?

What is the cross section formed by the cube and the plane containing the diagonals of a pair of opposite faces?

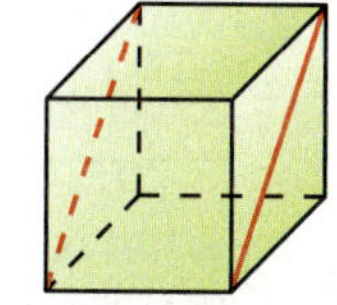

Underline the correct word(s) to complete each sentence.

24. Each diagonal and the sides of the face containing it form acute / obtuse / right triangles.

25. The length of each diagonal is less than / equal to / greater than the length of an edge.

26. The cross section is a rectangle / square / triangle .

Math Success

Check off the vocabulary words that you understand.

- ☐ polyhedron
- ☐ face
- ☐ edge
- ☐ vertex
- ☐ cross section

Rate how well you can *recognize polyhedra and their parts.*

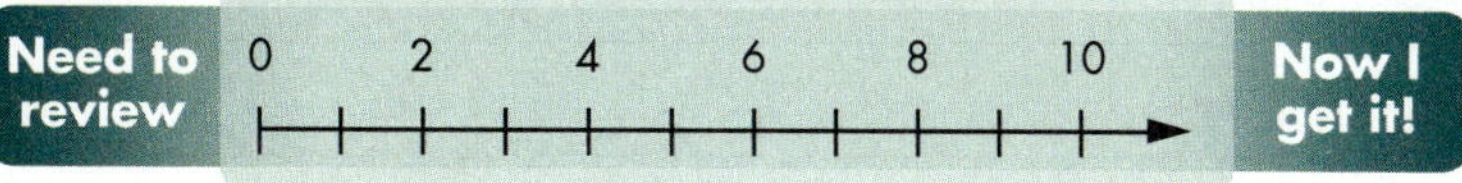

Name ______________________ Class ____________ Date ____________

11-1 Think About a Plan

Space Figures and Cross Sections

Visualization **Draw and describe a cross section formed by a plane intersecting the cube as follows.**

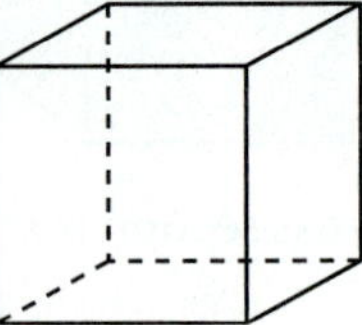

The plane is tilted and intersects the front and back faces of the cube perpendicular to the left and right faces.

Understanding the Problem

1. What is a cube? Draw a typical view of a cube and describe a cube.
   a rectangular prism with six square faces, all congruent

2. What is a plane? Draw a typical view of a plane and describe a plane.
   a two-dimensional surface unbounded in all directions

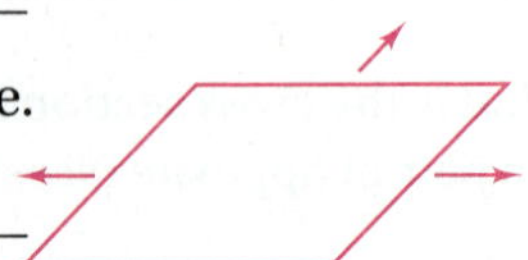

3. What is a cross section? Draw a plane passing through your cube that is parallel to the top and bottom faces of your cube. Explain why the cross section is a square. A cross section is an intersection of a solid and a plane. It is a very thin slice of the solid. Because the plane is parallel to two opposing faces, the cross section is congruent to the faces. So, the cross section is a square congruent to the faces.

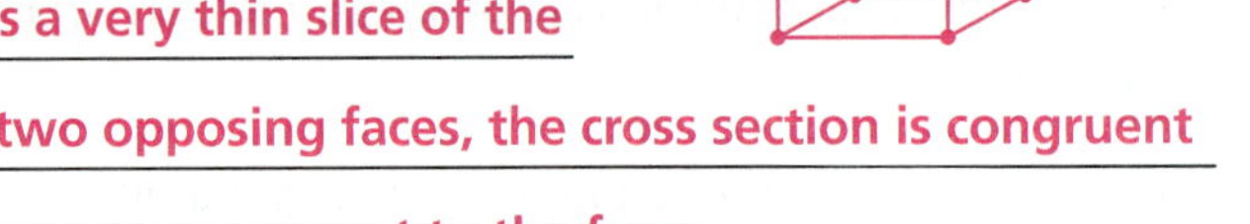

Planning the Solution

4. How can you use your understanding of cubes, planes, and cross sections to draw a plane that is tilted and intersects the front and back faces of the cube perpendicular to the left and right faces?
   Look at the drawing of a parallel plane to understand how a tilted plane is different.

5. You showed that if a plane is not tilted, the cross section is a square. How can you use this knowledge to predict what the cross section will look like if the plane is tilted? Contrast the cross section you get when the plane is parallel to the cross section you will get when the plane is tilted.

Getting an Answer

6. Prepare to draw a plane that is tilted and intersects the front and back faces of the cube perpendicular to the left and right faces by studying your drawing of a plane parallel to the top and bottom faces. Imagine the thin slice created when this tilted plane passes through the cube. Describe this cross section.
   The cross section is a rectangle. Two sides are the same length as the edges of the cube, and two sides are longer than the edges.

Name ______________________ Class ____________ Date ____________

11-1 Practice

Form K

Space Figures and Cross Sections

For each polyhedron, how many vertices, edges, and faces are there? List them.

1. 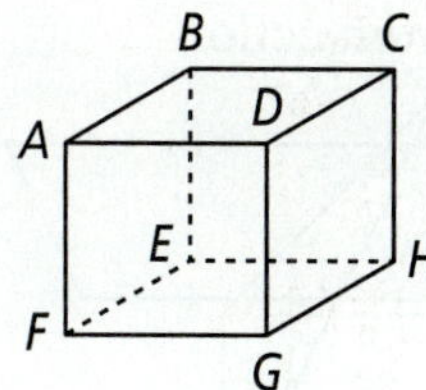

Vertices: *A, B, C, D, E, F, G, H; 8*

Edges: $\overline{AB}, \overline{AF}, \overline{AD}, \overline{BE}, \overline{BC}, \overline{CD}, \overline{CH}, \overline{HE}, \overline{HG}, \overline{GF}, \overline{EF}, \overline{DG}$ 12

Faces: *ABCD, ABEF, ADGF, DCHG, BCHE, EFGH; 6*

2. 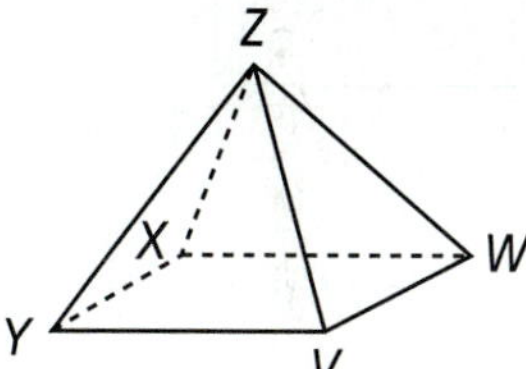

Vertices: *V, W, X, Y, Z; 5*

Edges: $\overline{XY}, \overline{XW}, \overline{XZ}, \overline{YV}, \overline{YZ}, \overline{VW}, \overline{VZ}, \overline{WZ}$ 8

Faces: *VWZ, XYZ, WXYV, XWZ, YVZ; 5*

For each polyhedron, use Euler's Formula to find the missing number.

3. Faces: [5] Edges: 8 Vertices: 5

To start, use Euler's formula, then identify the variables and any given values. $F + V = E + 2$

4. Faces: 6 Edges: [12] Vertices: 8

5. Faces: 4 Edges: 6 Vertices: [4]

Verify Euler's Formula for each polyhedron. Then draw a net for the figure and verify Euler's Formula for the two-dimensional figure.

6. 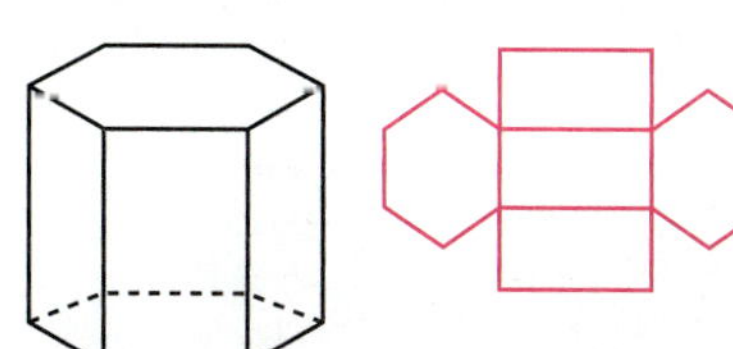

8 faces, 18 edges, 12 vertices; 8 + 12 = 18 + 2
8 faces, 29 edges, 22 vertices; 8 + 22 = 29 + 1

7. 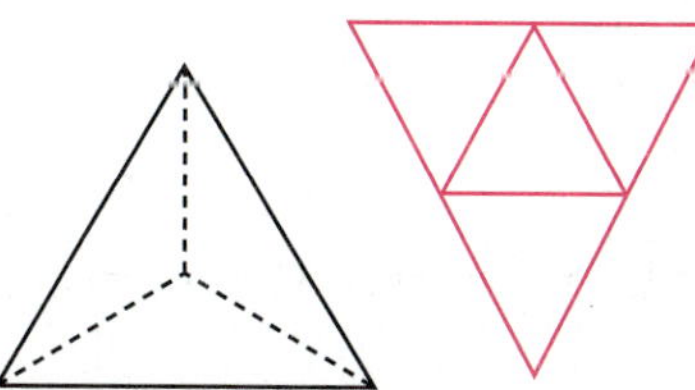

4 faces, 6 edges, 4 vertices; 4 + 4 = 6 + 2
4 faces, 9 edges, 6 vertices; 4 + 6 = 9 + 1

Use Euler's Formula to find the number of vertices in each polyhedron.

8. 6 faces that are all squares 8

9. 1 face that is a hexagon, 6 triangular faces 7

10. 2 faces that are pentagons, 5 rectangular faces 10

11. **Reasoning** Can a polyhedron have 20 faces, 30 edges, and 13 vertices? Explain. No; by Euler's Formula, there should be 31 edges, 19 faces, or 12 vertices.

12. **Reasoning** Is a cylinder a polyhedron? Explain.
No; all of the faces of a polyhedron are polygons. A cylinder has faces that are circles, and circles are not polygons.

11-1 Practice (continued)

Form K

Space Figures and Cross Sections

Describe each cross section.

13.

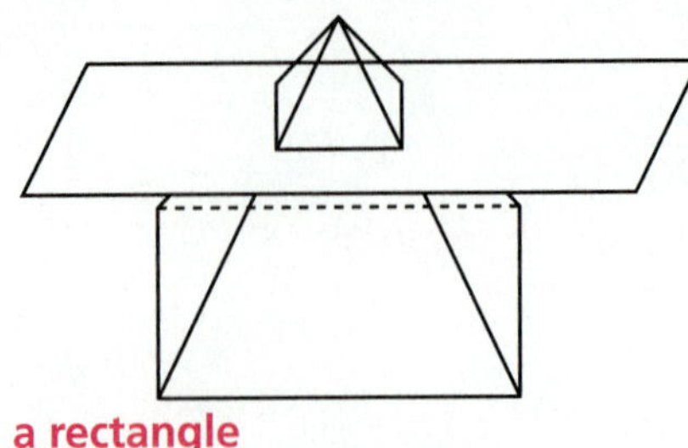

a rectangle

To start, visualize the plane's intersection with the solid.

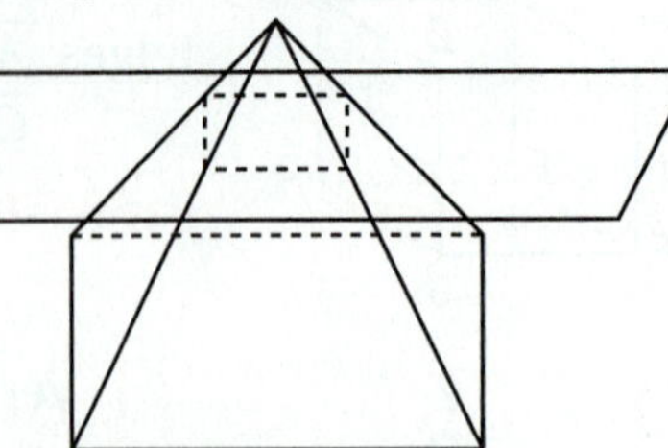

14.

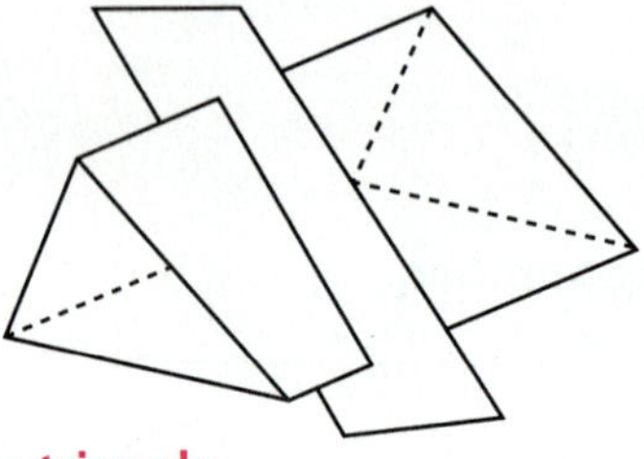

a triangle

15.

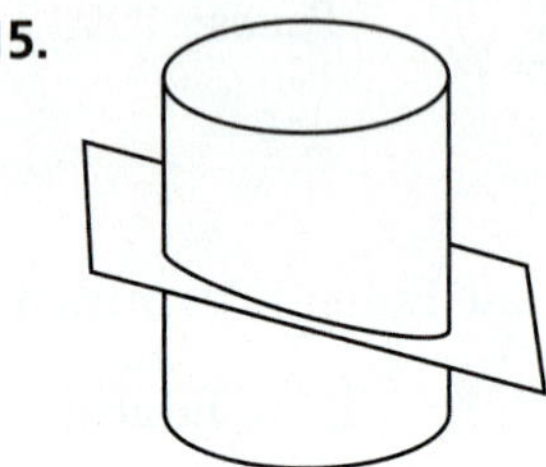

an oval (ellipse)

Reasoning Can you find a cross section of a square pyramid that forms the figure? Draw the cross section if the cross section exists. If not, explain.

16. isosceles triangle

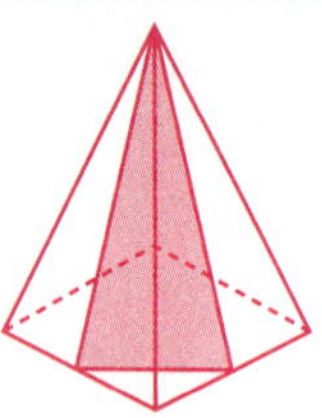

17. trapezoid

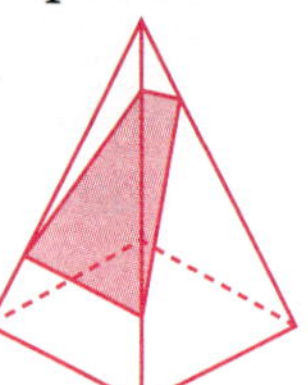

18. scalene triangle

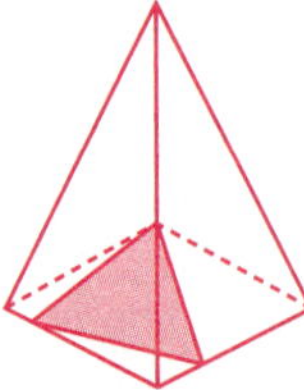

19. square

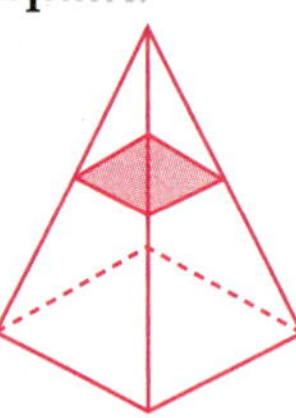

20. What is the cross section formed by a plane containing a vertical line of symmetry for the figure at the right? rectangle

21. What is the cross section formed by a plane that is parallel to the base of the figure at the right? hexagon

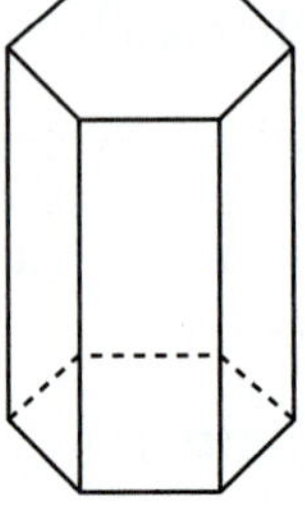

Name ______________________ Class __________ Date __________

11-1 Standardized Test Prep

Space Figures and Cross Sections

Multiple Choice

For Exercises 1–5, choose the correct letter.

1. A polyhedron has 6 vertices and 9 edges. How many faces does it have? B

(A) 3 (B) 5 (C) 7 (D) 9

2. A polyhedron has 25 faces and 36 edges. How many vertices does it have? H

(F) 11 (G) 12 (H) 13 (I) 14

3. Which of the following shows a net for a solid that has 8 faces, 12 vertices, and 18 edges? D

(A)

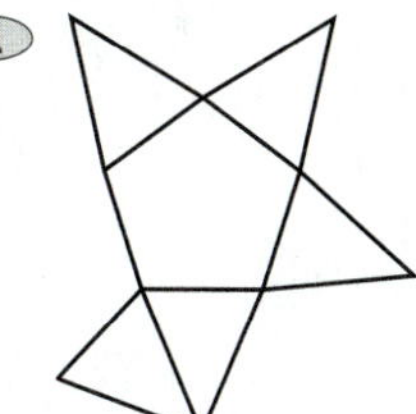

(C)

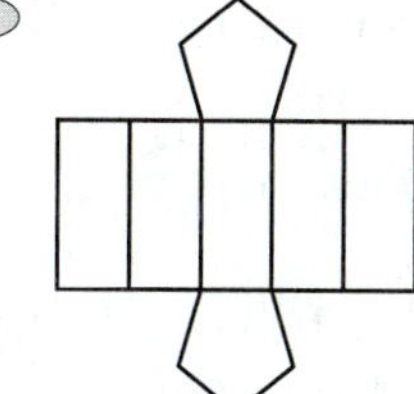

(B)

(D)

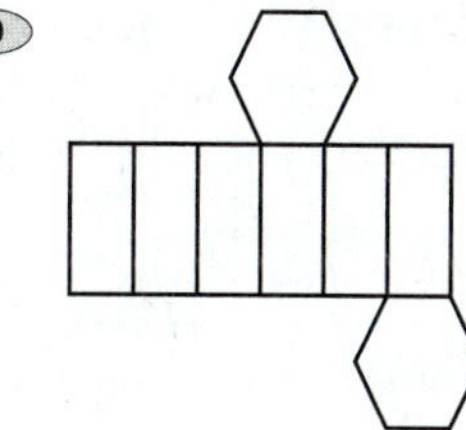

4. What is the cross section formed by a plane that contains a vertical line of symmetry for a tetrahedron? F

(F) triangle (G) square (H) rectangle (I) pentagon

5. What is the cross section formed by a plane that intersects three faces of a cube? A

(A) triangle (B) square (C) rectangle (D) pentagon

Short Response

6. How many edges and vertices are there for an octahedron, a polyhedron with eight congruent triangular faces?

[2] 12 edges AND 6 vertices
[1] 12 edges OR 6 vertices
[0] no correct response given

11-2 PART 1 Surface Areas of Prisms and Cylinders

Vocabulary

Review

Write T for *true* or F for *false*.

T **1.** A *lateral face* is shaped like a polygon.

T **2.** *Lateral faces* are surfaces of a polyhedron.

F **3.** A *lateral face* may be a circle.

F **4.** A base is a *lateral face*.

Vocabulary Builder

oblique (adjective) **oh BLEEK**

Other Word Forms: obliquely (adverb)

Main Idea: **Oblique** means indirect and not straight to the point.

Definition: An **oblique** object is slanting, not straight.

Math Usage: An **oblique** polyhedron has no vertical edge so an **oblique** prism is not a right prism.

Use Your Vocabulary

5. Circle the *oblique* prism.

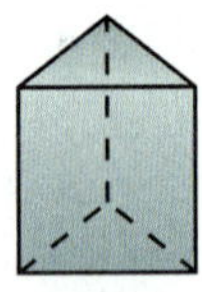

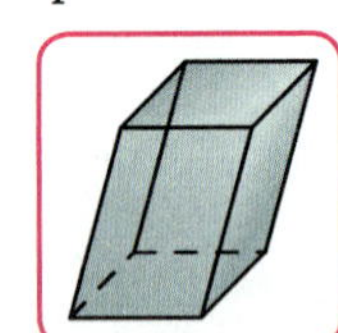

6. Circle the *oblique* cylinder.

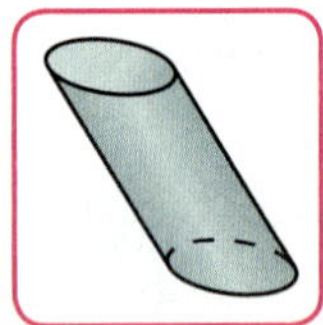

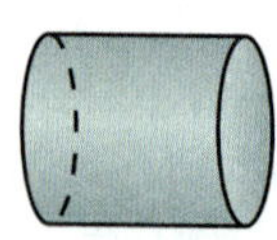

7. Complete with *oblique* or *obliquely*.

A right prism is not an __?__ prism. oblique

Your classmate answered the question __?__ . obliquely

Problem 1 Using a Net to Find Surface Area of a Prism

Got It? **What is the surface area of the triangular prism? Use a net.**

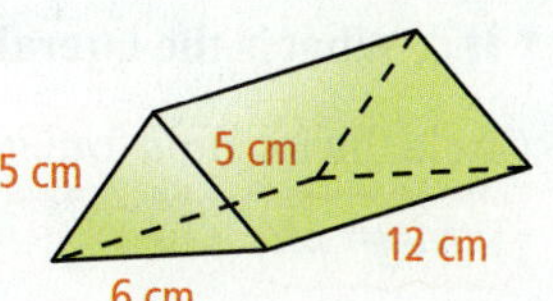

8. Label the missing dimensions in the net below.

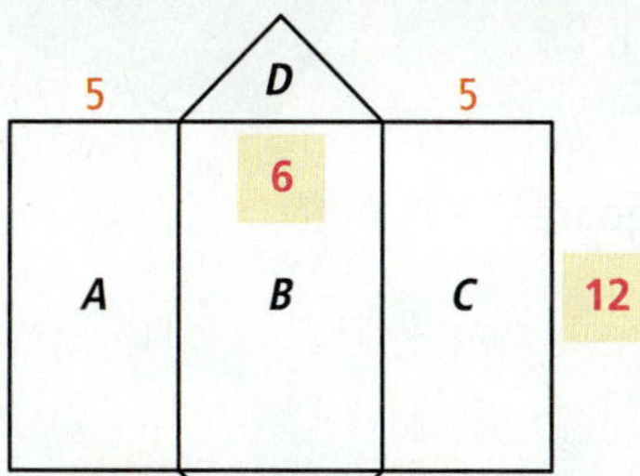

9. The altitude a of each triangle forms a right triangle with legs of lengths a cm and 3 cm.

10. Use the Pythagorean Theorem to find a.

$$3^2 + a^2 = 5^2$$

$$a^2 = 25 - 9$$

$$a^2 = 16$$

$$a = 4$$

11. Find the surface area of the prism.

S.A. = L.A. + area of base

= areas of two lateral rectangles + areas of two lateral triangles + area of base

= (Area A + Area C) + (Area D + Area E) + Area B

$= 5 \cdot 12 + 5 \cdot 12 + \frac{1}{2}(6 \cdot 4) + \frac{1}{2}(6 \cdot 4) + 6 \cdot 12$

$= 60 + 60 + 12 + 12 + 72$

$= 216$

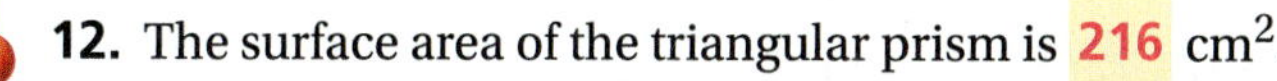

12. The surface area of the triangular prism is 216 cm^2.

take note

Theorem 11-1 Lateral and Surface Areas of a Prism

The lateral area of a right prism is the product of the perimeter of the base and the height of the prism.

L.A. = ph

The surface area of a right prism is the sum of the lateral area and the areas of the two bases.

S.A. = L.A. + $2B$

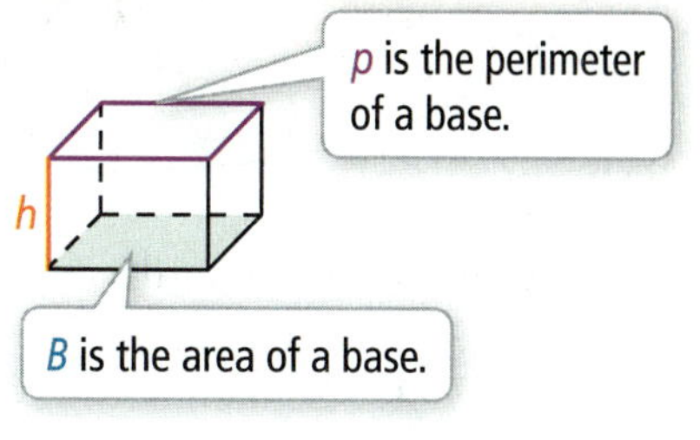

13. Write the formula for S.A. using p and h.

S.A. = ph + $2B$

Problem 2 Using Formulas to Find Surface Area of a Prism

Got It? **What is the lateral area of the prism at the right?**

12 m

6 m

14. Circle the formula for lateral area of a prism.

(L.A. $= ph$)   S.A. $=$ L.A. $+ 2B$ S.A. $= ph + 2B$

15. Circle the polygon that is the base of the prism.

(hexagon)   octagon   rectangle   square

16. Complete the flow chart below.

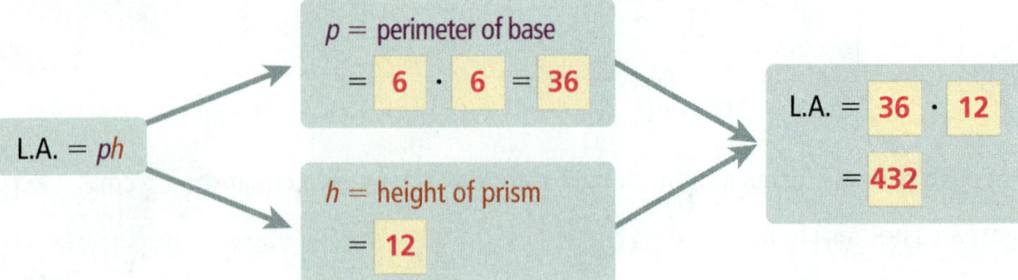

17. The lateral area of the prism is 432 m^2.

Lesson Check • Do you UNDERSTAND?

Vocabulary **Name the lateral faces and the bases of the prism at the right.**

18. The prism has 6 faces.

19. Is each base a face of the prism? (Yes) / No

20. Are the bases of the prism parallel and congruent? (Yes) / No

21. Write the name of each face of the prism in the correct region of the Venn diagram.

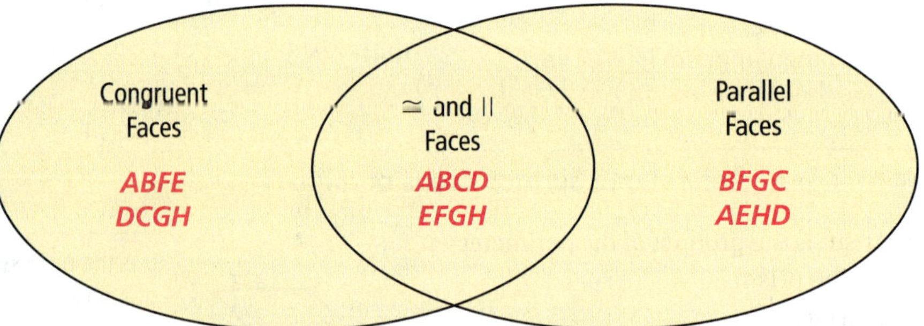

22. Circle the most accurate description of the bases of the prism.

congruent   parallel   (both congruent and parallel)

23. The bases of the prism are ABCD and EFGH.

24. Name the lateral faces of the prism. ABFE, DCGH, BFGC, AEHD

11-2 PART 2 Surface Areas of Prisms and Cylinders

Vocabulary

Review

Complete each statement with *always, sometimes,* or *never*.

1. The bases of a *cylinder* are _?_ circles. always

2. A *cylinder* _?_ has bases that are polygons. never

3. A *cylinder* is _?_ oblique. sometimes

4. Draw an example of a *cylinder*.

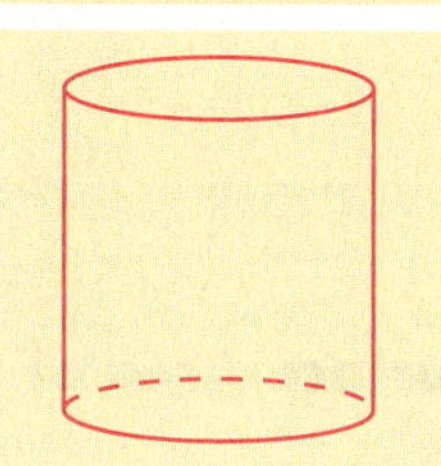

Vocabulary Builder

lateral area (adjective and noun) LAT ur ul EHR ee uh

Main Idea: **Lateral** means "side" and **area** is the measure, in square units, of a surface.

Math Usage: **Lateral area (L.A.)** is the sum of the areas of the lateral faces of a three-dimensional figure.

Example: The **lateral** faces of the prism above are rectangles, so the **lateral area** of the prism is the sum of the areas of three rectangles.

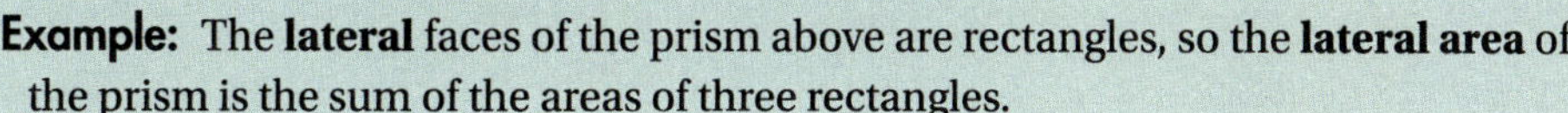

Use Your Vocabulary

Identify the number of faces to include in finding the *lateral area* of each figure.

5. 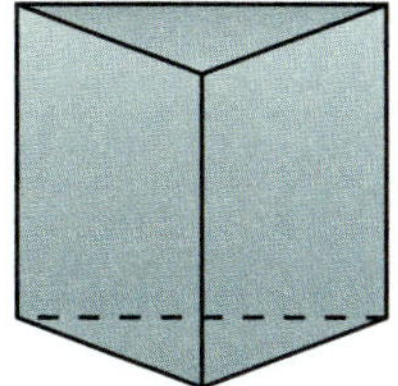 3

6. 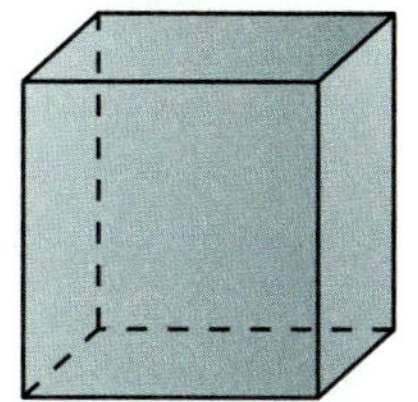 4

7. 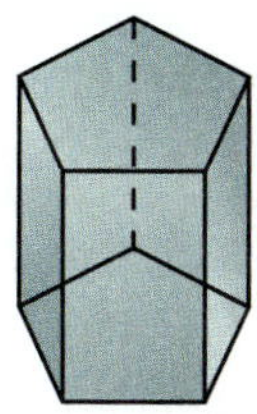 5

take note

Theorem 11-2 Lateral and Surface Areas of a Cylinder

8. Use the diagram at the right to complete the table below.

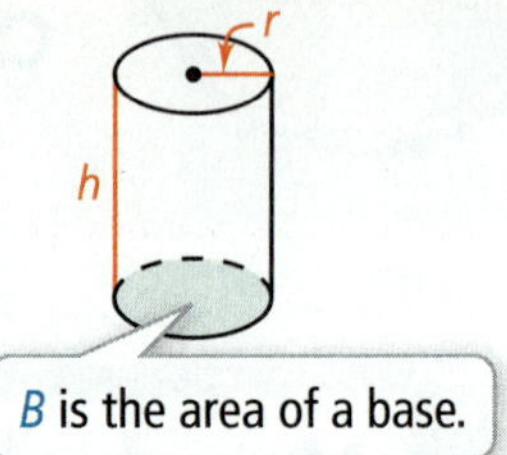

Lateral Area of a Right Cylinder	Surface Area of a Right Cylinder
Product of the circumference of the base and the height of the cylinder L.A. = $2\pi r \cdot h$, or L.A. = $\pi d h$	Sum of the lateral area and the areas of the two bases S.A. = L.A. + $2B$ = $2\pi rh$ + $2\pi r^2$ = πdh + $2\pi r^2$

Complete each statement with *circle* or *circumference*.

9. The lateral area of a cylinder is the product of the _?_ of the base and the height of the cylinder. circumference

10. The base of a cylinder is a _?_. circle

11. A cylinder has 2 bases.

Problem 3 Finding Surface Area of a Cylinder

Got It? **A cylinder has a height of 9 cm and a radius of 10 cm. What is the surface area of the cylinder in terms of π?**

12. Do you need to know the lateral area in order to find the surface area of a cylinder? Yes / No (Yes circled)

13. Use the information in the problem to complete the reasoning model below.

Think	Write
I can use the formula for the surface area of a cylinder.	S.A. = L.A. + $2B$
Then I can substitute the formulas for lateral area and area of a circle.	= $2\pi rh$ + $2 \cdot$ πr^2
Next I substitute 10 for the radius and 9 for the height.	$= 2\pi \cdot 10 \cdot 9 + 2\pi \cdot 10^2$
Now I simplify.	$= 180 \cdot \pi + 200 \cdot \pi$ $= 380 \cdot \pi$

14. The surface area of the cylinder is 380 π cm^2.

Problem 4 Finding Lateral Area of a Cylinder

Got It? **A stencil roller has a height of 1.5 in. and a diameter of 2.5 in. What area does the roller cover in one turn? Round your answer to the nearest tenth.**

15. The distance that is covered in one turn is the <u>circumference</u> / diameter of the circular base of the <u>cylinder</u> / prism .

16. Use your answer to Exercise 15 to find the area the roller covers in one turn.

$$\text{L.A.} = \pi dh$$
$$= \pi(2.5)(1.5)$$
$$\approx 11.78097245$$

17. The stencil roller covers about 11.8 in.^{2} in one turn.

Lesson Check • Do you UNDERSTAND?

Error Analysis **Your friend drew a net of a cylinder. What is your friend's error? Explain.**

Write T for *true* or F for *false*.

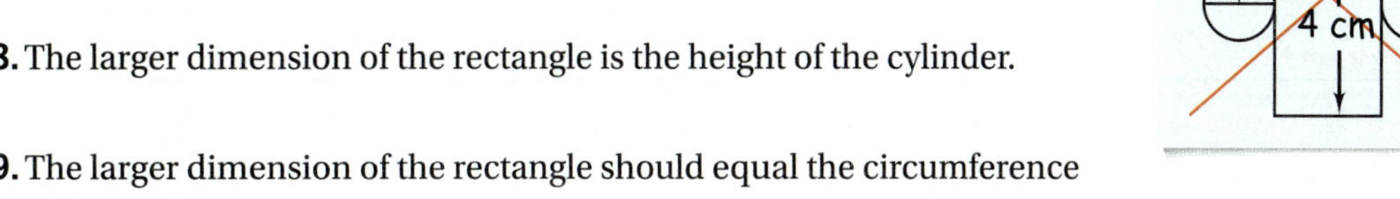

F **18.** The larger dimension of the rectangle is the height of the cylinder.

T **19.** The larger dimension of the rectangle should equal the circumference of the circle.

20. What is your friend's error? Explain. Answers may vary. Sample:

The larger dimension of the rectangle cannot be 4 cm if the diameter of the circle is 2 cm, because the circumference of the circle is $\pi \cdot d = 2\pi$, or about 6 cm.

Math Success

Check off the vocabulary words that you understand.

☐ right prism ☐ oblique prism ☐ right cylinder ☐ oblique cylinder

Rate how well you can *find the surface area of a prism and a cylinder*.

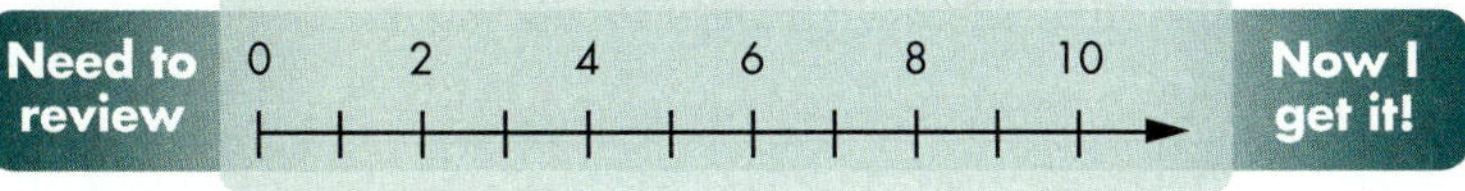

Name ______________________ Class __________ Date __________

11-2 Think About a Plan

Surface Areas of Prisms and Cylinders

Reasoning Suppose you double the radius of a right cylinder.

a. How does that affect the lateral area?

b. How does that affect the surface area?

c. Use the formula for surface area of a right cylinder to explain why the surface area in part (b) was not doubled.

Understanding the Problem

1. What is the formula for the lateral area of a right cylinder? **L.A. $= 2\pi rh$**

2. What is the formula for the surface area of a right cylinder? **S.A. $= 2\pi rh + 2\pi r^2$**

Planning the Solution

3. How does doubling the radius affect the formulas for the lateral and surface areas? In the formula for the surface area, where do you need to be most careful?

Replace r with $2r$ everywhere it appears in each formula; in the formula for surface area, be careful to apply the exponent of 2 to $2r$, not just r.

4. How do you compare the new formulas you get after doubling the radius in the original formulas?

Factor each formula or divide the new formula by the old formula.

Getting an Answer

5. Write the formula for the new lateral area after the radius has been doubled. Compare this to the original formula for the lateral area. What effect does doubling the radius have?

Original formula: L.A. $= 2\pi rh$; the formula after doubling the radius is New L.A. $= 2\pi(2r)h = 4\pi rh$; because $\frac{\text{New L.A.}}{\text{L.A.}} = \frac{4\pi rh}{2\pi rh} = 2$, doubling the radius doubles the lateral area.

6. Write the formula for the new surface area after the radius has been doubled. Compare this to the original formula for the surface area. What effect does doubling the radius have?

Original formula: S.A. $= 2\pi rh + 2\pi r^2$; the formula after doubling the radius is New S.A. $= 2\pi(2r)h + 2\pi(2r)^2 = 4\pi rh + 8\pi r^2$; the area of the base has been quadrupled. So, the surface area has more than doubled.

Name ______________________ Class ____________ Date ____________

11-2 Practice

Form K

Surface Areas of Prisms and Cylinders

Use a net to find the surface area of each prism.

1. $160\ m^2$

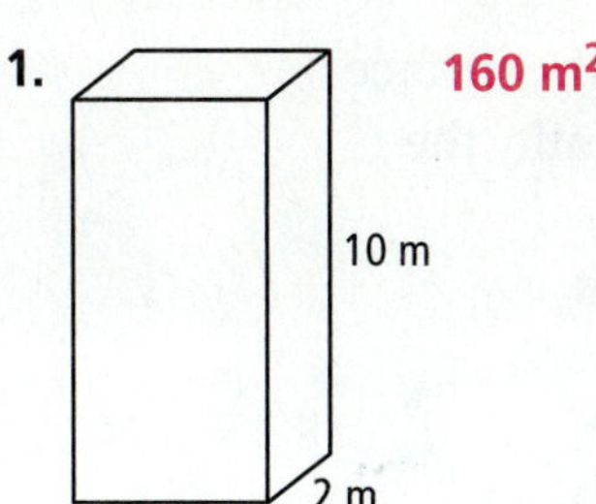

2. $84\ ft^2$

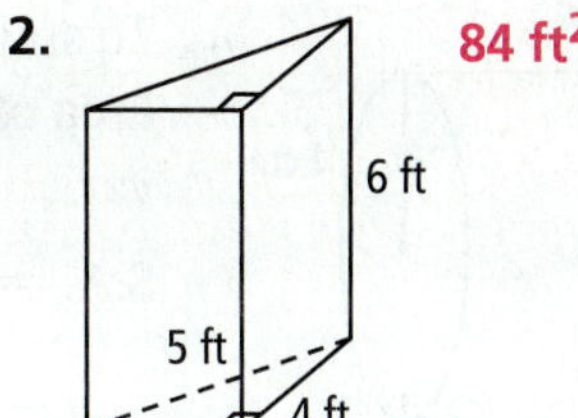

3. a. Classify the prism at the right. right hexagonal prism

b. Find the lateral area of the prism. $216\ cm^2$

c. The bases are regular hexagons. The area of each is about $41.6\ cm^2$. Find the sum of their areas. $83.2\ cm^2$

d. Find the surface area of the prism. $299.2\ cm^2$

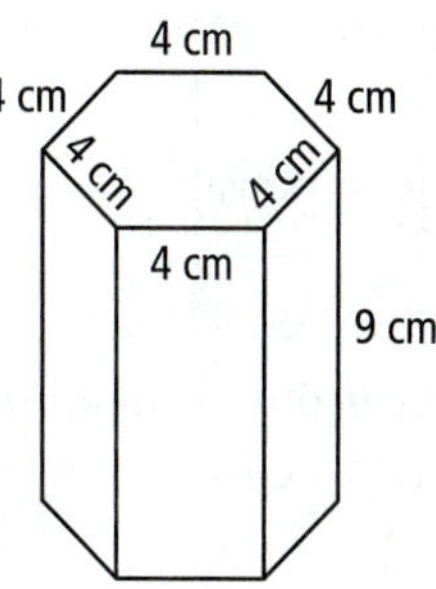

Use formulas to find the surface area of each prism. Round your answer to the nearest whole number.

4.

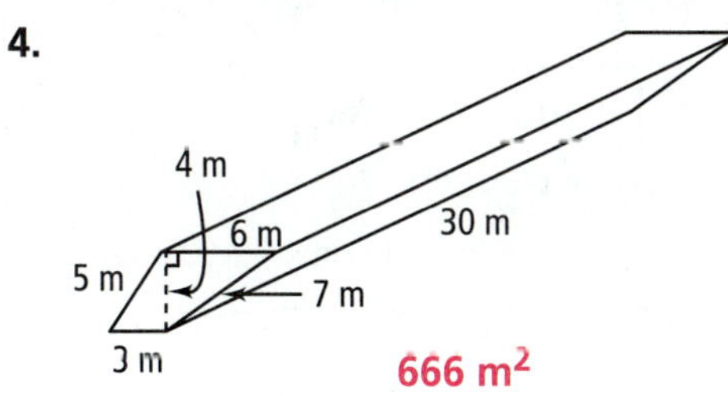

$666\ m^2$

To start, use the formula for the lateral area of a prism, then find the perimeter of the base trapezoid.

L.A. $= ph$

$p = \boxed{3} + \boxed{5} + \boxed{6} + \boxed{7}$

$= \boxed{21}$ m

5. $150\ m^2$

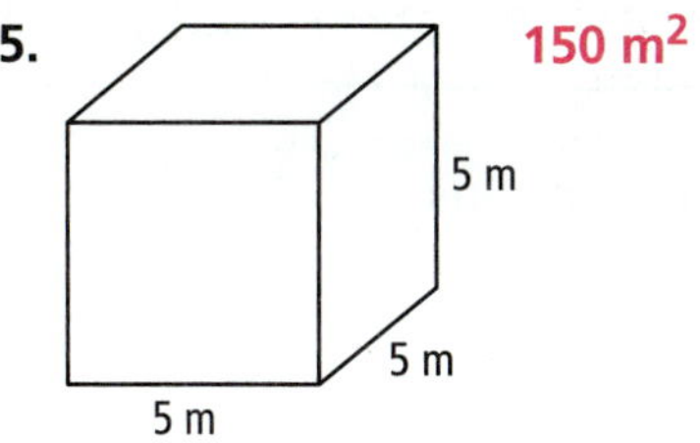

6. $48\ ft^2$

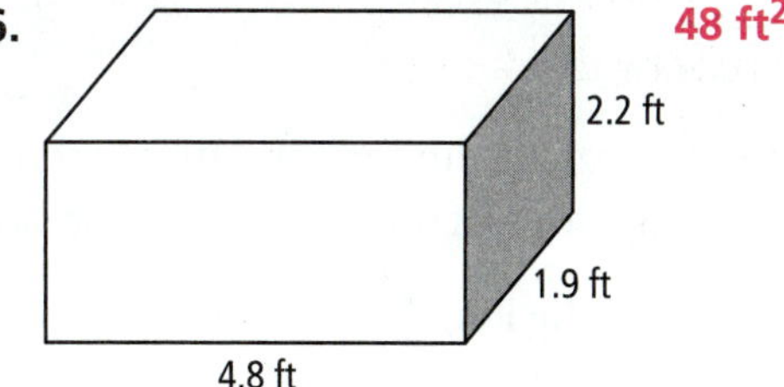

7. A box measures 10 in. wide, 12 in. high, and 14 in. deep. If all surfaces are made of cardboard, how much cardboard is used to make the box? $856\ in.^2$

8. An artist creates a right prism whose bases are regular pentagons. He wants to paint the lateral surfaces of the prism. One can of paint can cover $30\ ft^2$. How many cans of paint must he buy if the height of the prism is 15 ft and the length of each side of the pentagon is 5 ft? 13 cans

11-2 Practice (continued) Form K

Surface Areas of Prisms and Cylinders

Find the surface area of each cylinder in terms of π.

9. 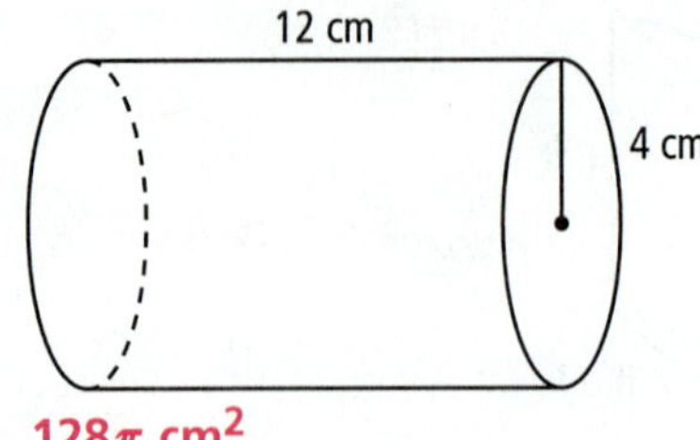

To start, use the formula for the surface area of the cylinder, then identify the variables and any given values.

$\text{S.A.} = 2\pi rh + 2\pi r^2$

$r =$ [4] cm, $h =$ [12] cm

$128\pi\ \text{cm}^2$

10. 

$522\pi\ \text{mm}^2$

11. 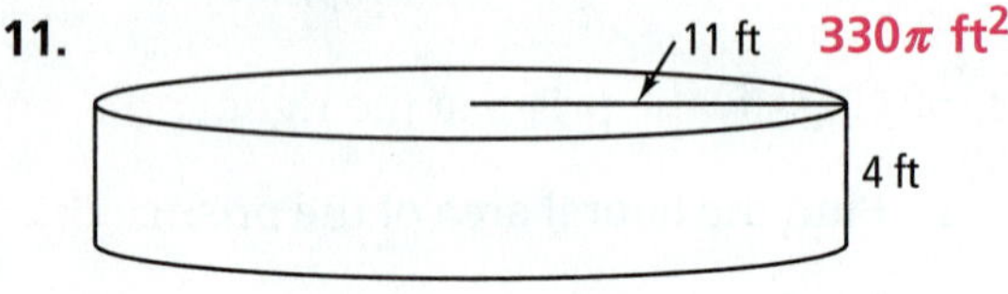

$330\pi\ \text{ft}^2$

Find the lateral area of each cylinder to the nearest whole number.

12. 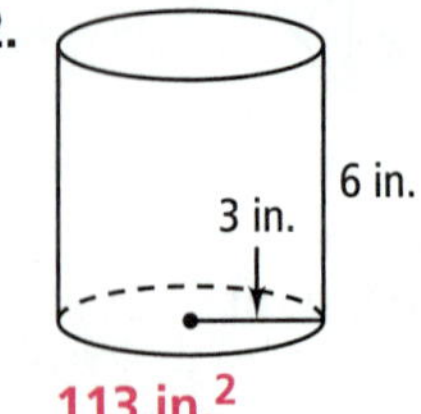

To start, use the formula for the lateral area of the cylinder, then identify the variables and any given values.

$\text{L.A.} = \pi dh$

$h = 6$ in., $d = 2 \cdot$ [3] in. $=$ [6] in.

113 in.^{2}

13. 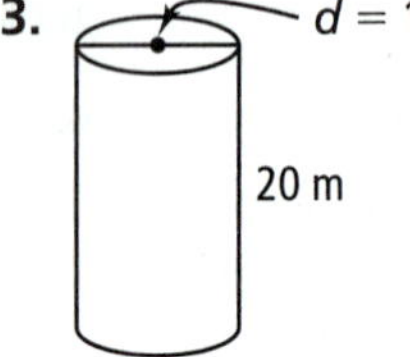

754 m^2

14. 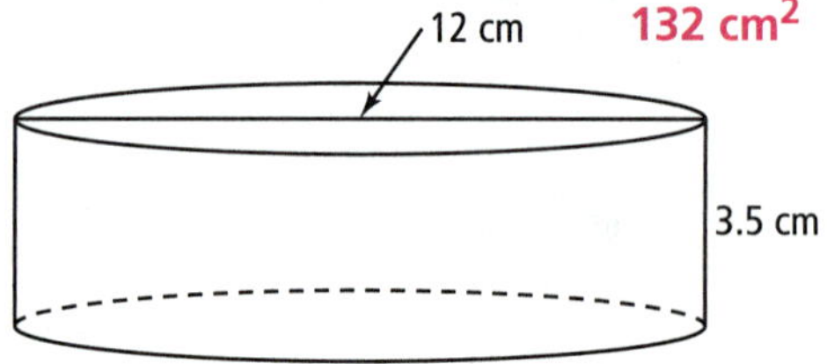

132 cm^2

15. Reasoning A cylinder has a height that is 2 times as large as its radius. The lateral area of the cylinder is 16π square units.

a. What is the length of the radius of the cylinder? 2 units

b. What is the height of the cylinder? 4 units

c. What is the surface area of the cylinder? Round your answer to the nearest square unit. 75 square units

16. Reasoning A triangular prism and a rectangular prism both have bases that are regular polygons with sides 2 units long. Which has a greater surface area? Explain.

The surface area of a rectangular prism is greater. It has a greater perimeter, and its bases have greater areas.

Name ______________________ Class ____________ Date ____________

11-2 Standardized Test Prep

Surface Areas of Prisms and Cylinders

Multiple Choice

For Exercises 1–8, choose the correct letter.

1. What is the lateral surface area of a cube with side length 9 cm? B

   A 72 cm^2 B 324 cm^2 C 405 cm^2 D 486 cm^2

2. What is the surface area of a prism whose bases each have area 16 m^2 and whose lateral surface area is 64 m^2? G

   F 80 m^2 G 96 m^2 H 144 m^2 I 160 m^2

3. A cylindrical container with radius 12 cm and height 7 cm is covered in paper. What is the area of the paper? Round to the nearest whole number. D

   A 528 cm^2 B 835 cm^2 C 1055 cm^2 D 1432 cm^2

For Exercises 4 and 5, use the prism at the right.

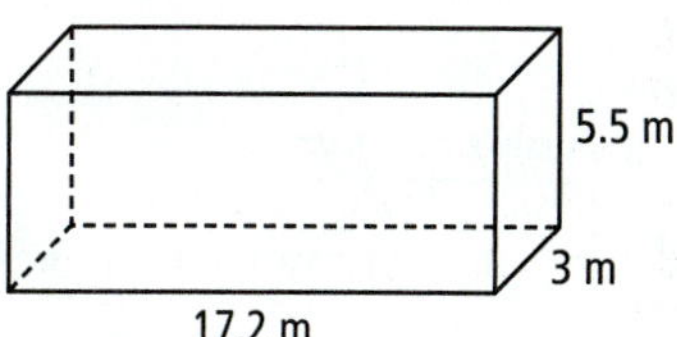

4. What is the surface area of the prism? H

   F 283.8 m^2 H 325.4 m^2
   G 292.4 m^2 I 407 m^2

5. What is the lateral surface area of the prism? B

   A 283.8 m^2 B 292.4 m^2 C 325.4 m^2 D 407 m^2

For Exercises 6 and 7, use the cylinder at the right.

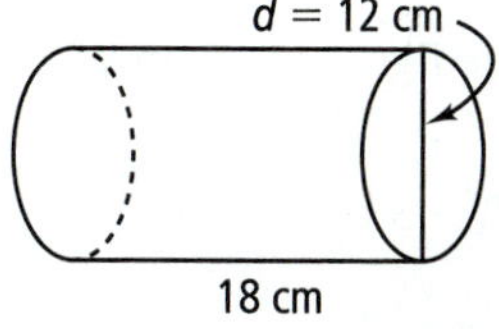

6. What is the lateral surface area of the cylinder? H

   F 12π cm^2 H 216π cm^2
   G 18π cm^2 I 288π cm^2

7. What is the surface area of the cylinder? D

   A 12π cm^2 B 18π cm^2 C 216π cm^2 D 288π cm^2

8. The height of a cylinder is three times the diameter of the base. The surface area of the cylinder is 126π ft^2. What is the radius of the base? F

   F 3 ft G 6 ft H 9 ft I 18 ft

Short Response

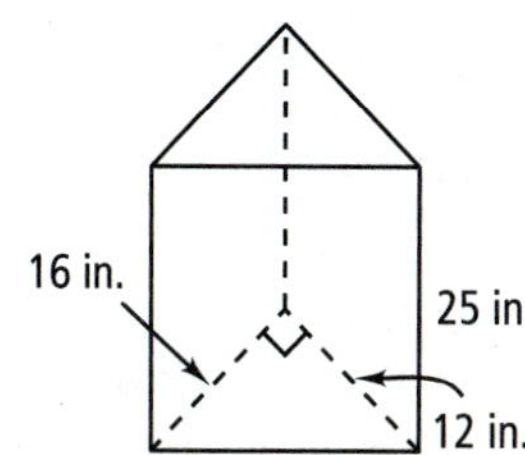

9. What are the lateral area and the surface area of the prism?

   [2] L.A. = 1200 $in.^2$; S.A. = 1392 $in.^2$ [1] one of two answers correct [0] no correct response given

11-3 PART 1 Surface Areas of Pyramids and Cones

Vocabulary

Review

Label each diagram *prism* or *pyramid*.

1. 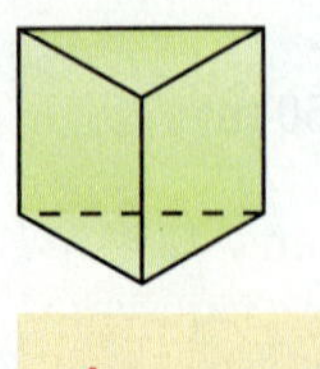 prism

2. 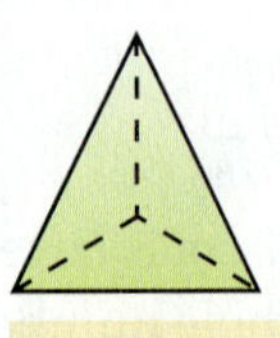 pyramid

3. 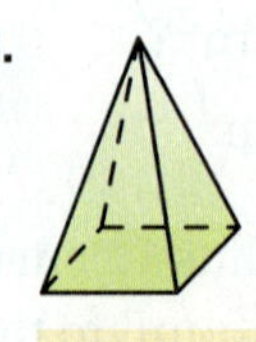 pyramid

4. 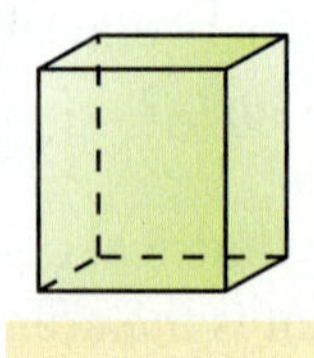 prism

Vocabulary Builder

slant height (noun) slant hyt

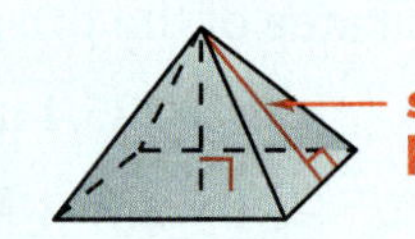

Related Words: regular pyramid, lateral face

Definition: The **slant height** ℓ of a regular pyramid is the length of the altitude of a lateral face of the pyramid.

Use Your Vocabulary

5. Circle the figure that shows a three-dimensional figure with *slant height* 5 m.

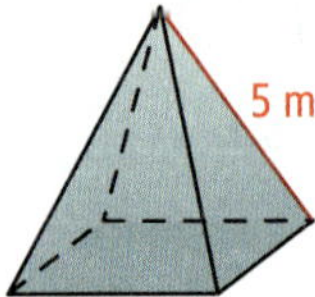

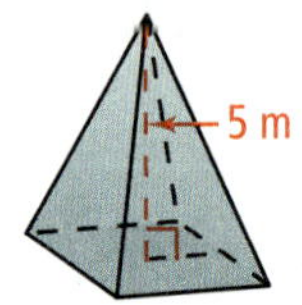

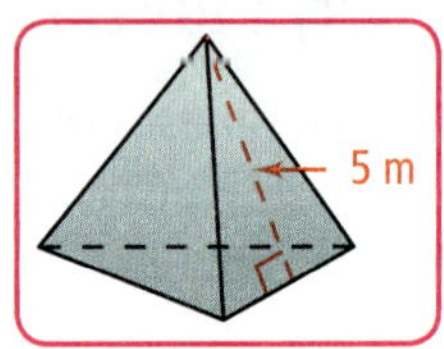

6. Is the *slant height* of a pyramid the same as its *height*? Yes / No

7. The *slant height* of the pyramid below is 5 in.

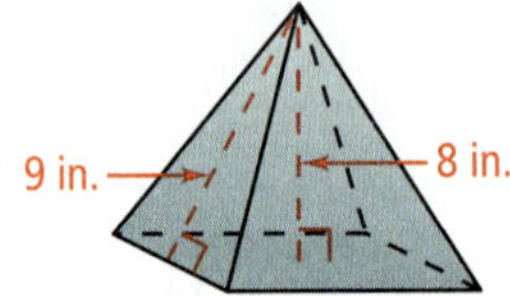

take note

Theorem 11-3 Lateral and Surface Areas of a Pyramid

The lateral area (L.A.) of a regular pyramid is half the product of the perimeter p of the base and the slant height ℓ of the pyramid.

The surface area (S.A.) of a regular pyramid is the sum of the lateral area and the area B of the base.

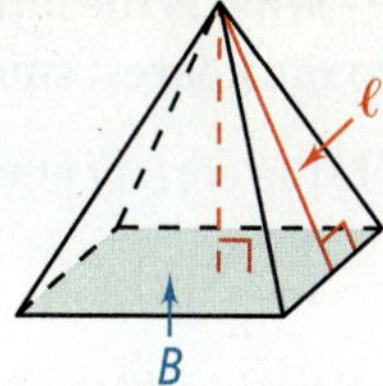

8. In a square pyramid with side lengths s, p = 4s .

9. If the base of a regular pyramid has a perimeter of $6q$ and its side length is 6, the pyramid has q sides.

Draw a line from each description in Column A to the corresponding formula in Column B.

	Column A	Column B
10.	lateral area (L.A.) of a pyramid	$\frac{1}{2}p\ell + B$
11.	surface area (S.A.) of a pyramid	$\frac{1}{2}p\ell$

Problem 1 Finding the Surface Area of a Pyramid

Got It? A square pyramid has base edges of 5 m and a slant height of 3 m. What is the surface area of the pyramid?

12. Complete the problem-solving model below.

Know	Need	Plan
The base is a square with side length 5 m. Slant height ℓ is 3 m.	Lateral area Surface area	Find the perimeter p of the base. Find the area B of the base. Use p and ℓ to find L.A. Use L.A. and B to find S.A.

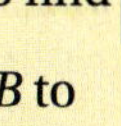

13. Find p.

$p = 4(s)$

$= 4(5)$

$= 20$

14. Find B.

$B = s^2$

$= 5^2$

$= 25$

15. L.A. $= \frac{1}{2}p\ell$

$= \frac{1}{2}(20)(3)$

$= 30$

16. S.A. = L.A. + B

$= 30 + 25$

$= 55$

17. The surface area of the pyramid is 55 m^2.

Problem 2 Finding the Lateral Area of a Pyramid

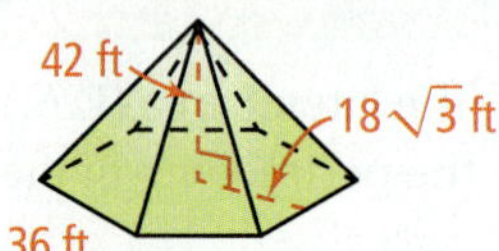

Got It? **What is the lateral area of the hexagonal pyramid at the right? Round to the nearest square foot.**

18. Circle the correct equation for the perimeter of the hexagonal base.

$42 \cdot 36 = 1512$ $\quad$ $6 \cdot 18 = 108$ $\quad$ $\frac{1}{2}(36)(18\sqrt{3}) \approx 561$ $\quad$ (circled) $6 \cdot 36 = 216$

19. The slant height ℓ of the pyramid is the hypotenuse of a right triangle. Label the legs of the right triangle at the right.

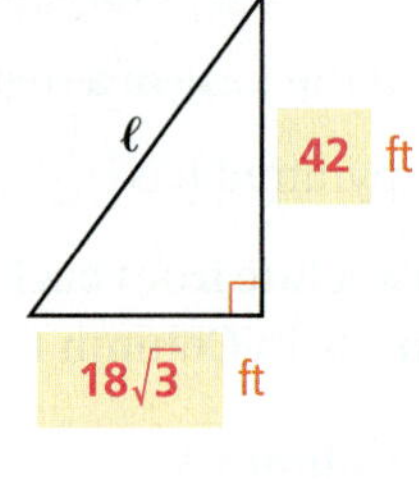

20. Use the Pythagorean Theorem to find the slant height ℓ of the pyramid.

$$\ell = \sqrt{(18\sqrt{3})^2 + 42^2}$$
$$= \sqrt{972 + 1764}$$
$$= \sqrt{2736}$$

21. Use the formula L.A. $= \frac{1}{2}p\ell$ to find the lateral area of the pyramid.

$$\text{L.A.} = \frac{1}{2}(216)(\sqrt{2736}) \approx 5649.133031$$

22. The lateral area of the hexagonal pyramid is about 5649 ft^2.

Lesson Check • Do you UNDERSTAND?

Compare and Contrast **How are the formulas for the surface area of a prism and the surface area of a pyramid alike? How are they different?**

23. Circle the formula for the surface area of a prism. Underline the formula for the surface area of a pyramid.

S.A. $= \frac{1}{2}p\ell$ $\quad$ S.A. $= ph$ $\quad$ (underlined) S.A. $= \frac{1}{2}p\ell + B$ $\quad$ (circled) S.A. $= ph + 2B$

24. Use the descriptions in the list at the right. Write the letter for each description under the correct polyhedron.

Prism	Pyramid
A B E F G	A C D G H

A. Base is a polygon.
B. Faces are rectangles.
C. Faces are triangles.
D. S.A. = L.A. + B
E. S.A. = L.A. + 2B
F. Uses height
G. Uses perimeter
H. Uses slant height

25. How are the formulas alike? How are they different?

Answers may vary. Sample: Alike: Bases are polygons; both use perimeter. Different: L.A. for pyramids uses triangular faces and slant height and S.A. has only one base. L.A. for prisms uses rectangular faces and height and S.A. has two bases.

11-3 PART 2 Surface Areas of Pyramids and Cones

Vocabulary

Review

1. Circle the *cone*(s).

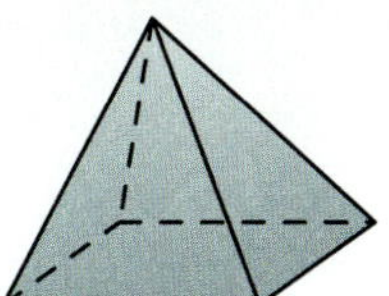

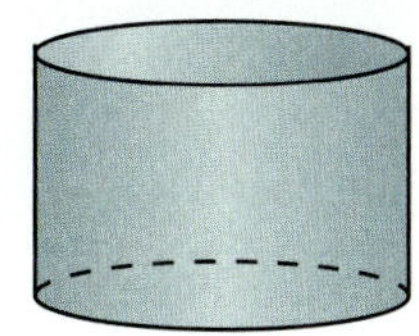

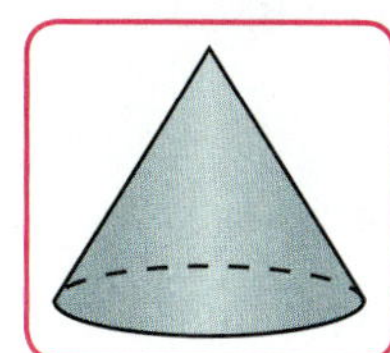

Vocabulary Builder

altitude (noun) AL tuh tood

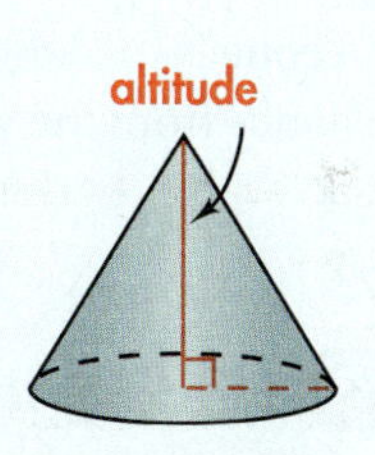

Related Word: height

Origin: **Altitude** comes from the Latin word *altus,* which means "high."

Math Usage: The **altitude** of a cone is a perpendicular segment from the vertex to the plane containing the base of the cone. In a right cone, the endpoints of the **altitude** are the vertex and the center of the base.

Use Your Vocabulary

2. Circle the cone that has an *altitude* of 5 cm.

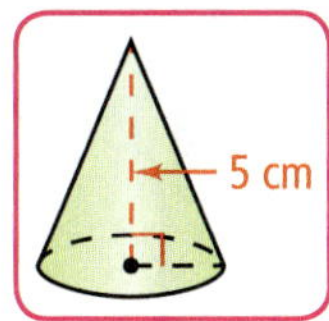

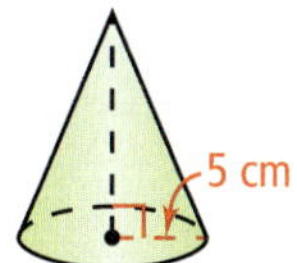

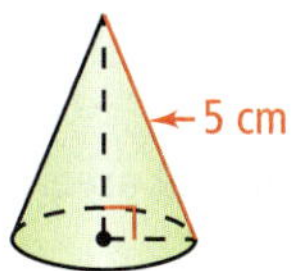

Complete each statement with *always, sometimes,* or *never.*

3. The *altitude* of a cone is ? equal to the slant height of the cone. never

4. The *altitude* of a cone is ? perpendicular to the base of the cone. always

5. The *altitude* of a cone ? has one endpoint at the center of the base. sometimes

take note

Theorem 11-4 Lateral and Surface Areas of a Cone

The lateral area of a right cone is half the product of the circumference of the base and the slant height of the cone.

L.A. $= \frac{1}{2} \cdot 2\pi r \cdot \ell$, or L.A. $= \pi r \ell$

The surface area of a cone is the sum of the lateral area and the area of the base.

S.A. = L.A. + B

Slant height
Vertex
Altitude
Base

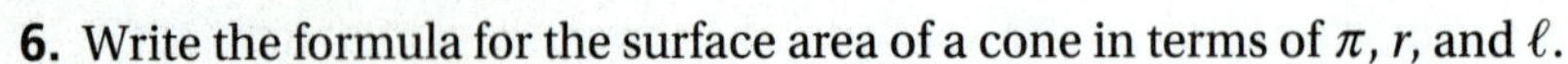

6. Write the formula for the surface area of a cone in terms of π, r, and ℓ.

S.A. = $\pi r \ell$ + πr^2

7. Draw a line from each description in Column A to the corresponding information needed in Column B.

Column A	Column B
surface area of a cone	perimeter of the base
surface area of a pyramid	circumference of the base

The *height h* of a cone is the length of the altitude of the cone. The *slant height* ℓ of a cone is the distance from the vertex of a cone to a point on the circumference of the base.

Problem 3 Finding the Surface Area of a Cone

Got It? The radius of the base of a cone is 16 m. Its slant height is 28 m. What is the surface area in terms of π?

8. Label the cone below.

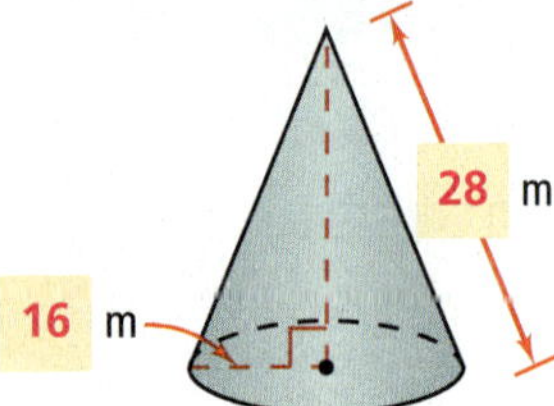

9. Circle the formula for the lateral area of a cone.

L.A. $= 2\pi r \ell$ L.A. $= \frac{1}{2}\pi r \ell$ L.A. $= \pi r \ell$

10. Use the justifications at the right to find the surface area.

S.A. = L.A. + B	Use the formula for surface area.
$= \pi r \ell + \pi r^2$	Substitute the formulas for L.A. and B.
$= \pi(16)(28) + \pi(16)^2$	Substitute for r and for ℓ.
$= \pi(448) + \pi(256)$	Simplify.
$= \pi(704)$	Add.

11. The surface area of the cone in terms of π is 704π m^2.

Problem 4 Finding the Lateral Area of a Cone

Got It? **What is the lateral area of a traffic cone with radius 10 in. and height 28 in.? Round to the nearest whole number.**

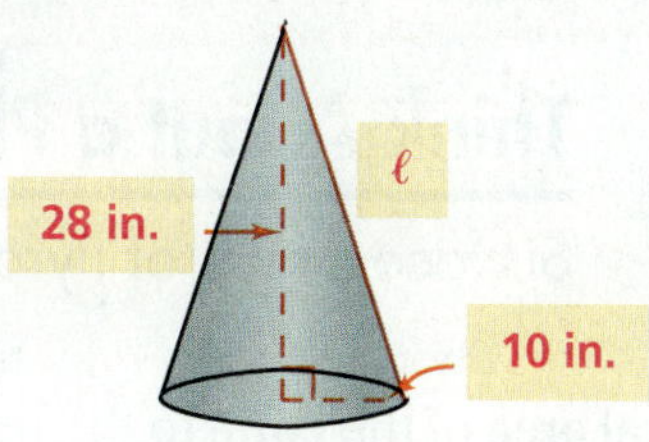

12. Let ℓ be the slant height of the cone. Label the missing dimensions on the cone at the right.

13. Use the Pythagorean Theorem to find ℓ.

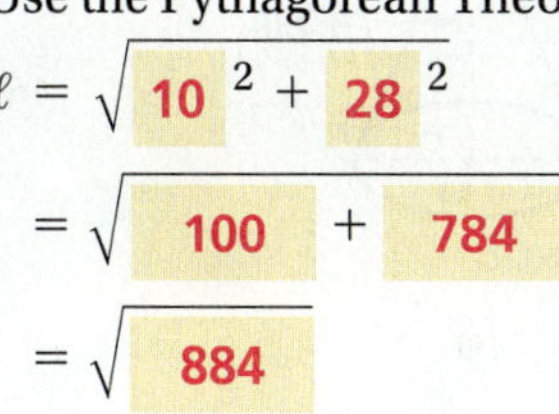

$\ell = \sqrt{10^2 + 28^2}$

$= \sqrt{100 + 784}$

$= \sqrt{884}$

14. Use the formula for lateral area of a cone.

L.A. $= \pi(r)(\ell)$

$= \pi(10)(\sqrt{884})$

≈ 934.0626473

15. To the nearest square inch, the lateral area of the traffic cone is 934 in.^{2}.

Lesson Check • Do you UNDERSTAND?

Error Analysis **A cone has height 7 and radius 3. Your classmate calculates its lateral area. What is your classmate's error? Explain.**

L.A. $= \pi r \ell$
$= \pi(3)(7)$
$= 21\pi$

16. Cross out the information that you are NOT given.

height	~~radius~~	slant height

17. Did your classmate use the correct formula? **Yes** / No

18. Explain your classmate's error.

Explanations may vary. Sample: My classmate used the height instead of the slant height in calculating the cone's lateral area.

Math Success

Check off the vocabulary words that you understand.

☐ pyramid ☐ slant height ☐ lateral area ☐ surface area ☐ cone

Rate how well you can *find the surface area of pyramids and cones.*

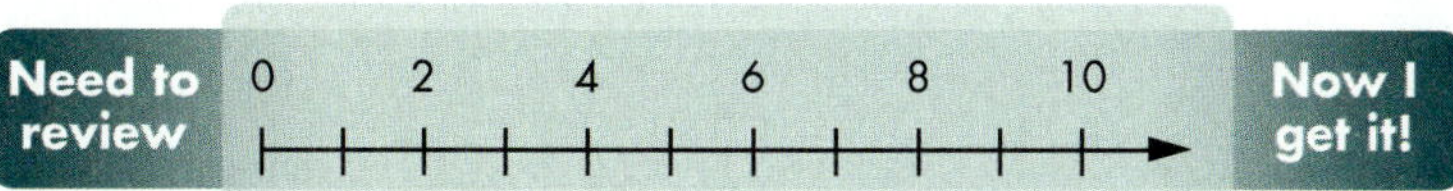

Name ______________________ Class ____________ Date ____________

11-3 Think About a Plan

Surface Areas of Pyramids and Cones

Find the lateral area of the cone to the nearest whole number.

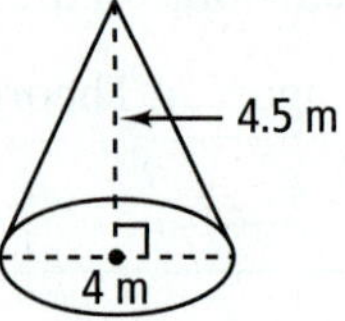

Understanding the Problem

1. What is the formula for the lateral area of a cone? L.A. = $\pi r\ell$

2. How are the two variables in this formula defined?
The radius, r, is the distance from the center of the circle to a point on the circle. The slant height, ℓ, is the distance from the vertex of the cone to a point on the circle.

3. What two pieces of information are given in the figure of the cone?
the diameter and the height

Planning the Solution

4. How can you use the given information to find the radius?
Divide the length of the diameter by 2.

5. How can you use the given information and the radius to find the slant height?
Substitute the height and the radius into the Pythagorean Theorem, $\ell = \sqrt{r^2 + h^2}$.

Getting an Answer

6. What is the radius? $r = \frac{1}{2} \cdot 4 \text{ m} = 2 \text{ m}$

7. What is the slant height of the cone? $\ell = \sqrt{2^2 + (4.5)^2} = \sqrt{24.25}$ m

8. What is the lateral area of the cone? L.A. = $\pi \cdot 2 \cdot \sqrt{24.25} = 2\sqrt{24.25}\pi \approx 31 \text{ m}^2$

Name ______________________ Class ____________ Date ____________

11-3 Practice — Form K

Surface Areas of Pyramids and Cones

Find the surface area of each pyramid to the nearest whole number.

1. 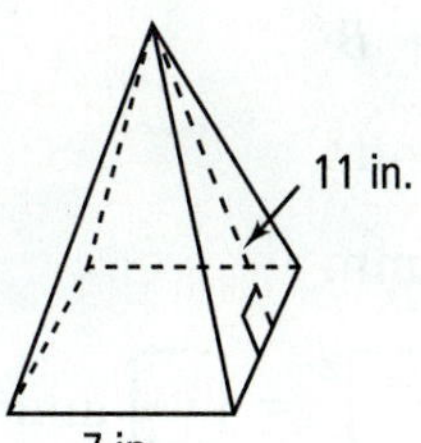

To start, use the formula for surface area of the pyramid, then identify the variables and any given values.

$S.A. = \frac{1}{2}p\ell + B$

$p = 4 \cdot \boxed{7} = \boxed{28}$ in.

$\ell = \boxed{11}$ in.

$B = \boxed{7} \cdot \boxed{7} = \boxed{49}$ in.^{2}

203 in.^{2}

2. 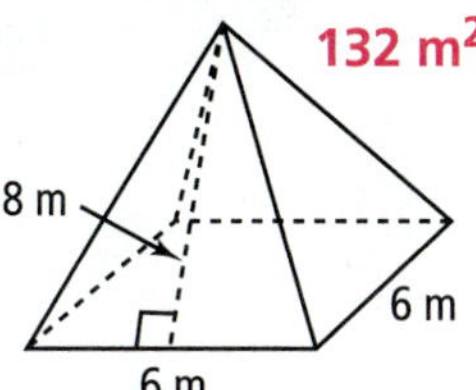

132 m^2

3. 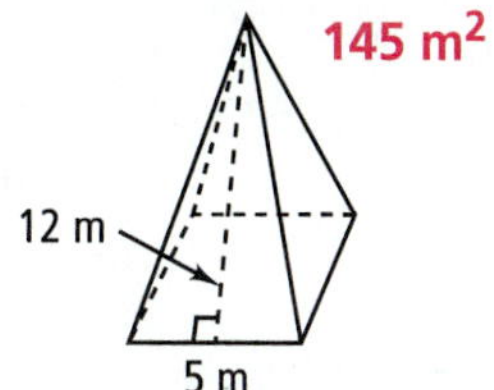

145 m^2

Find the lateral area of each pyramid to the nearest whole number.

4. 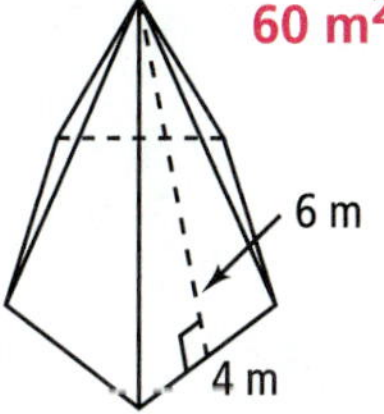

60 m^2

5. 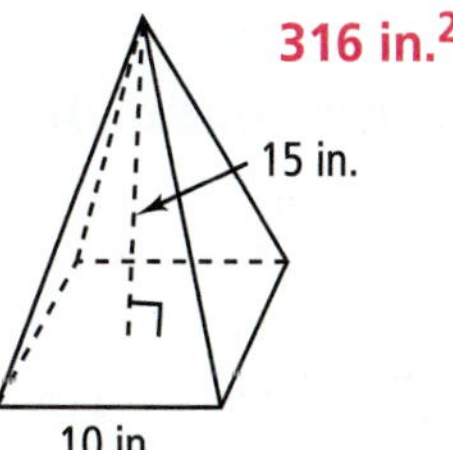

316 in.^{2}

6. The figure at the right has one base and eight lateral faces. Find its surface area to the nearest whole number. 320 m^2

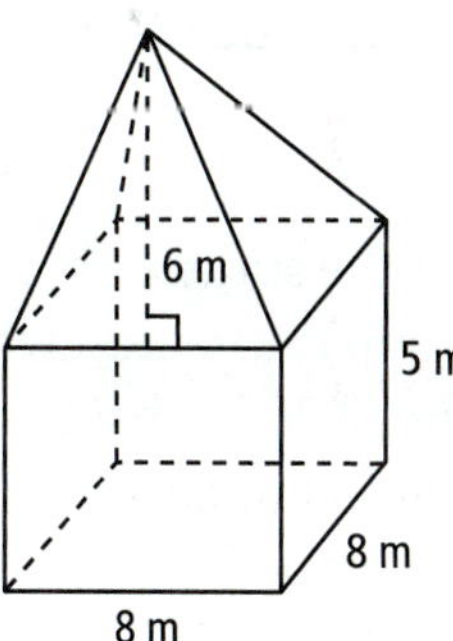

7. The roof of a clock tower is a square pyramid. Each side of the base is 16 ft long. The slant height is 22 ft. What is the lateral area of the roof? 704 ft^2

8. **Reasoning** Write a formula to show the relationship between surface area and the length of a side of the base (s) and slant height in a square pyramid. $S.A. = 2s\ell + s^2$

The length of a side (s) of the base, slant height (ℓ), height (h), lateral area (L.A.), and surface area (S.A.) are measurements of a square pyramid. Given two of the measurements, find the other three to the nearest tenth.

9. $s = 16$ cm, $\ell = 10$ cm $h = 6$ cm; L.A. $= 320$ cm^2; S.A. $= 576$ cm^2

10. L.A. $= 624$ m^2, S.A. $= 1200$ m^2 $s = 24$ m; $\ell = 13$ m; $h = 5$ m

11. $h = 7$ cm, $\ell = 25$ cm $s = 48$ cm; L.A. $= 2400$ cm^2; S.A. $= 4704$ cm^2

Name ______________________ Class ____________ Date ____________

11-3 Practice (continued)

Form K

Surface Areas of Pyramids and Cones

Find the surface area of each cone in terms of π.

12. 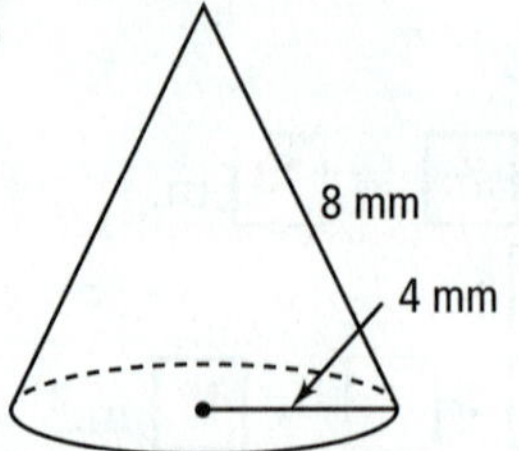

To start, use the formula for surface area of the pyramid, then identify the variables and any given values.

$S.A. = \pi r\ell + B$

$r =$ [4] mm

$\ell =$ [8] mm

$B = \pi \cdot [4]^2 =$ [16π] mm^2

48π mm^2

13. 95π cm^2

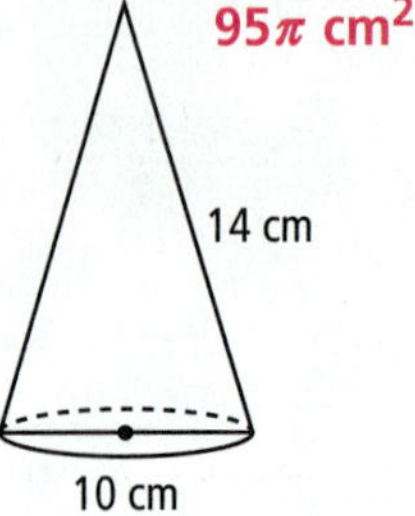

14. 39π ft^2

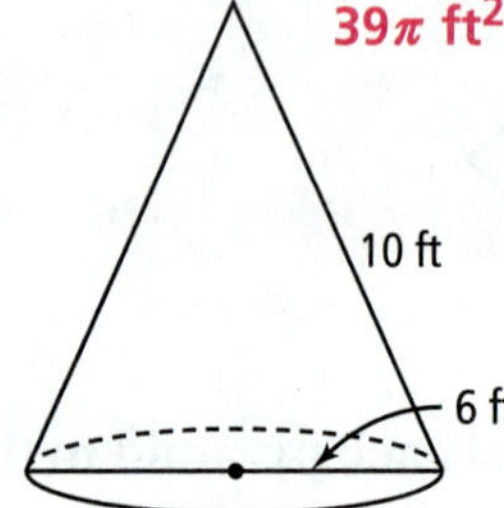

Find the lateral area of each cone to the nearest whole number.

15. 3299 in.^2

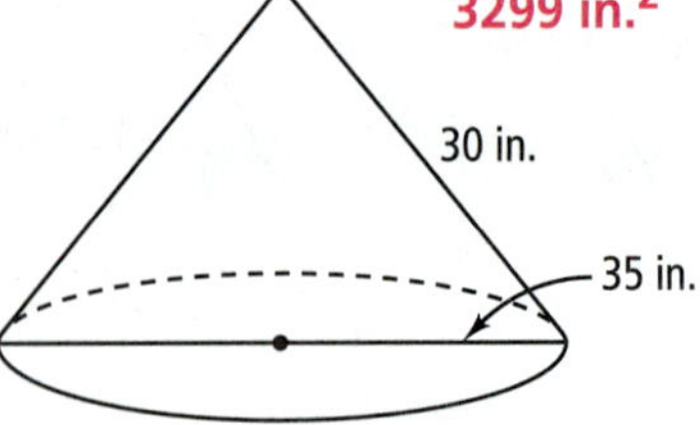

16. 204 m^2

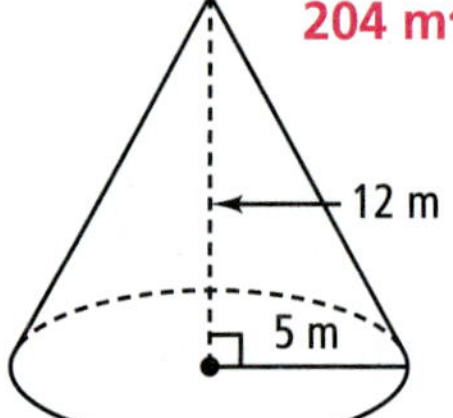

17. Find the surface area of the figure at the right to the nearest whole number. (*Hint:* Add the base, the lateral area of the cylinder, and the lateral area of the cone.) 547 mm^2

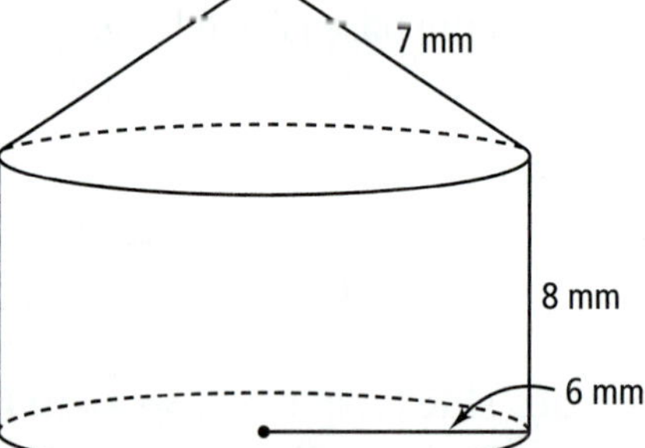

18. The lateral area of a cone is 60π m^2. The slant height is 15 m. What is the radius? 4 m

19. The surface area of a cone is 55π cm^2. The radius is 5 cm. What is the slant height? 6 cm

Name ______________________ Class __________ Date __________

11-3 Standardized Test Prep

Surface Areas of Pyramids and Cones

Multiple Choice

For Exercises 1–5, choose the correct letter.

1. What is the lateral surface area of a square pyramid with side length 11.2 cm and slant height 20 cm? B

   (A) 224 cm^2 (B) 448 cm^2 (C) 896 cm^2 (D) 2508.8 cm^2

2. What is the lateral surface area of a cone with radius 19 cm and slant height 11 cm? I

   (F) 19π cm^2 (G) 30π cm^2 (H) 200π cm^2 (I) 209π cm^2

3. What is the lateral area of the square pyramid, to the nearest whole number? D

   (A) 165 m^2 (C) 330 m^2

   (B) 176 m^2 (D) 351 m^2

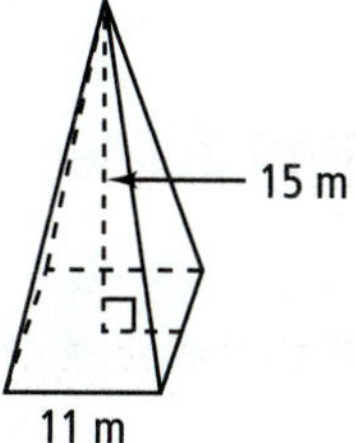

4. What is the surface area of the cone, to the nearest whole number? G

   (F) 221 cm^2 (H) 304 cm^2

   (G) 240 cm^2 (I) 620 cm^2

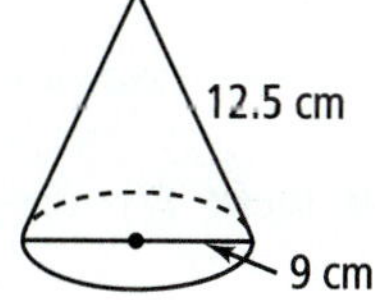

5. What is the surface area of a cone with diameter 28 cm and height 22 cm in terms of π? C

   (A) 196π cm^2 (B) 365π cm^2 (C) 561.1π cm^2 (D) 2202.8π cm^2

Extended Response

6. What are the perimeter of the base, slant height, lateral area, and surface area for the square pyramid, to the nearest tenth of a meter or square meter?

   [4] $p = 24$ m; $\ell = 12.4$ m; L.A. = 148.4 m^2; S.A. = 184.4 m^2
   [3] any three of the four values correctly given
   [2] any two of the four values correctly given
   [1] any one correct value given
   [0] no correct responses given

11-4 Volumes of Prisms and Cylinders

Vocabulary

Review

Label each diagram *cylinder* or *prism*.

1. 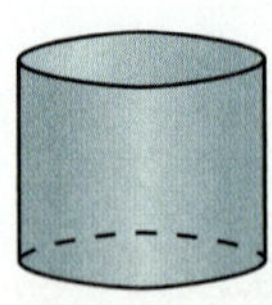 cylinder

2. 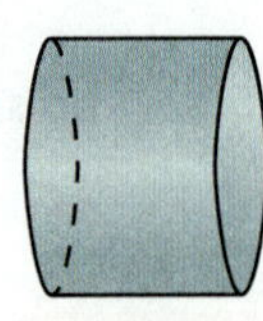 cylinder

3. 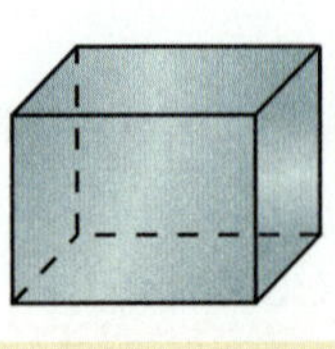 prism

4. 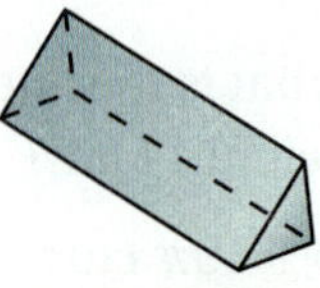 prism

Vocabulary Builder

composite (adjective, noun) **kum PAHZ it**

Related Words: compound, combination, component

Definition: **Composite** means put together with distinct parts.

Main Idea: A **composite** is a whole made up of different parts.

Use Your Vocabulary

Complete each statement with the correct phrase from the list below. Use each phrase only once.

composite function *composite* map *composite* number *composite* sketch

5. A _?_ combines different descriptions of features. composite sketch

6. A _?_ has factors other than one and the number. composite number

7. A _?_ shows the locations of shopping malls, houses, and roads in one illustration. composite map

8. A _?_ shows how to apply at least one function to another function. composite function

take note

Theorem 11-5 Cavalieri's Principle

If two space figures have the same height and the same cross-sectional area at every level, then they have the same volume.

9. The three prisms below have the same height and the same volume. The first is a square prism. Label the missing dimensions.

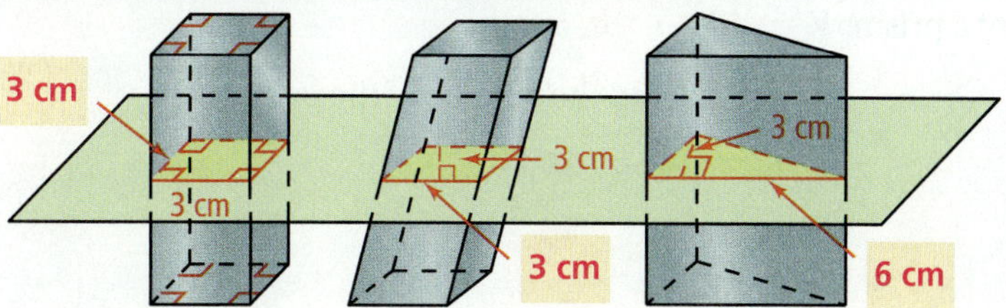

10. Circle the solid(s) that may have the same cross-sectional area at every level.

cone   (cylinder)   (prism)   pyramid

Theorem 11-6 Volume of a Prism

The volume of a prism is the product of the area of the base and the height of the prism.

$V = Bh$

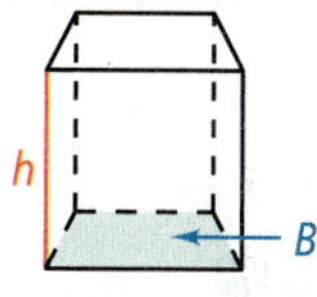

11. A prism with a base area of 15 m^2 and a height 4 m has a volume of 60 m^3.

12. A prism with a volume of 81 ft^3 and a height of 3 ft has a base area of 27 ft^2.

Problem 1 Finding the Volume of a Rectangular Prism

Got It? What is the volume of the rectangular prism at the right?

4 ft
3 ft
5 ft

13. Circle the measurements of a base of the prism.

3 ft × 4 ft   (3 ft × 5 ft)   4 ft × 5 ft

14. Underline the correct word to complete the sentence.

The base is a rectangle / square.

15. Find B.

$B = \ell \cdot w$

$= 5 \cdot 3$

$= 15$

16. Find V.

$V = B \cdot h$

$= 15 \cdot 4$

$= 60$

17. Underline the correct word to complete the sentence.

The units for this volume are cubic / square feet.

18. The volume of the prism is 60 ft^3.

Problem 2 Finding the Volume of a Triangular Prism

Got It? **What is the volume of the triangular prism at the right?**

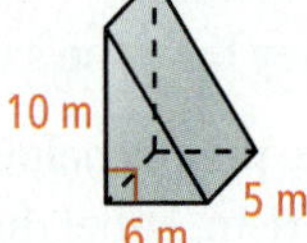

19. The base is a right triangle with legs of length 10 m and 6 m.

20. The height of the prism is 5 m.

21. Complete the formula for volume of a prism. $V = B \cdot h$

22. Find the area of the base.

$A = \frac{1}{2} \cdot 6 \cdot 10$

$= \frac{1}{2} \cdot 60$

$= 30$

23. Find the volume of the prism.

$V = 30 \cdot 5$

$= 150$

24. The volume of the triangular prism is 150 m^3.

take note — Theorem 11-7 Volume of a Cylinder

The volume of a cylinder is the product of the area of the base and the height of the cylinder.

$V = Bh$, or $V = \pi r^2 h$

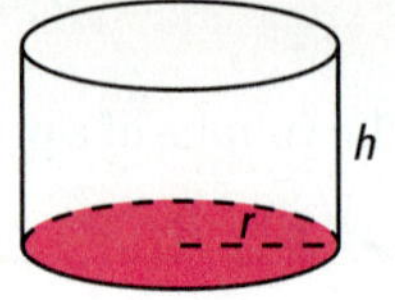

25. Shade a base of the cylinder at the right. Answers may vary. Sample:

26. Describe the shape of the base.

The base is a circle.

Problem 3 Finding the Volume of a Cylinder

Got It? **What is the volume of the cylinder at the right in terms of π?**

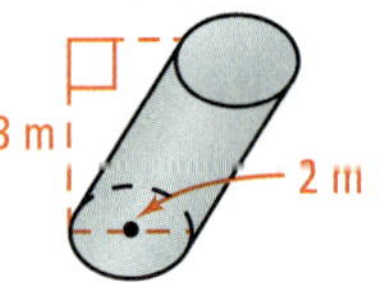

27. Compete the reasoning model below.

Think	Write
First I need to find the radius.	$r = \frac{2}{2} = 1$
I can use the formula $V = \pi r^2 h$ and substitute for r and h.	$V = \pi \cdot 1^2 \cdot 3$
Now I simplify.	$V = \pi \cdot 3$

28. The volume of the cylinder is 3π m^3.

Problem 4 Finding Volume of a Composite Figure

Got It? **What is the approximate volume of the lunch box shown at the right? Round to the nearest cubic inch.**

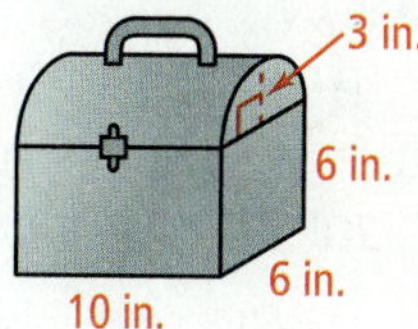

29. The top and bottom of the lunch box are sketched below. Label the dimensions.

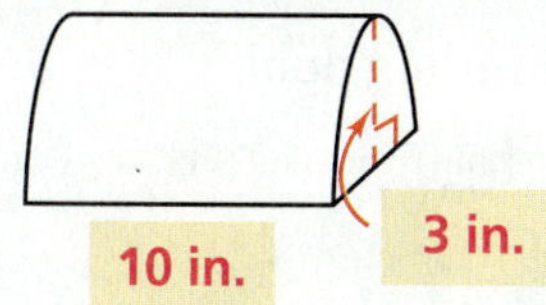

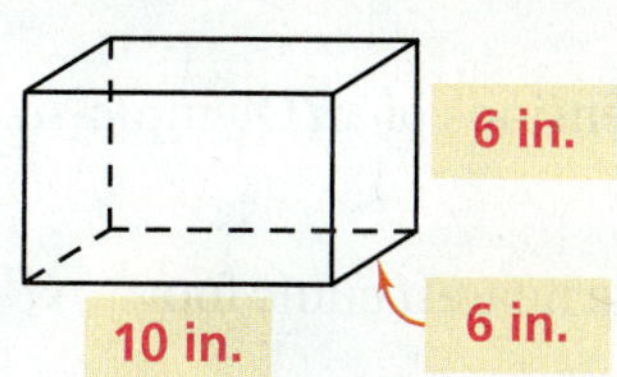

30. Find the volume of the top.

$V = \frac{1}{2}\pi r^2 h$

$= \frac{1}{2}\pi(\ 3\ ^2)(\ 10\ )$

$= 45\pi$

31. Find the volume of the bottom.

$V = Bh$

$= (\ 6 \cdot 6\ )(\ 10\ )$

$= 360$

32. Find the sum of the volumes.

$V = 45\pi + 360$

≈ 501.3716694

33. The approximate volume of the lunch box is 501 in.^{3}.

Lesson Check • Do you UNDERSTAND?

Reasoning **How is the volume of a rectangular prism with base 2 m by 3 m and height 4 m related to the volume of a rectangular prism with base 3 m by 4 m and height 2 m? Explain.**

34. Cross out the formula that does NOT give the volume of a rectangular prism.

$V = Bh$ 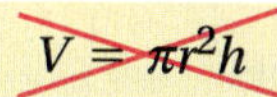 $V = \ell wh$

35. The Commutative / Identity Property of Multiplication states that the product of factors is the same when listed in a different order.

36. Now answer the question. Explanations may vary. Sample:

The volumes are equal by the Commutative Property of Multiplication.

Math Success

Check off the vocabulary words that you understand.

☐ volume ☐ composite space figure

Rate how well you can *find the volume of prisms and cylinders.*

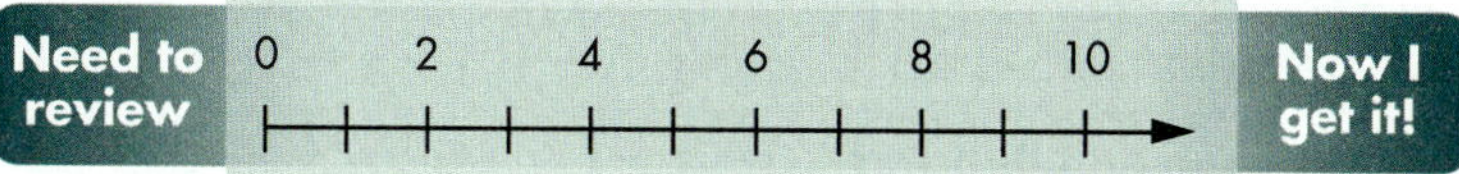

Name ______________________ Class ____________ Date ____________

11-4 Think About a Plan

Volumes of Prisms and Cylinders

Swimming Pool The approximate dimensions of an Olympic-size swimming pool are 164 ft by 82 ft by 6.6 ft.

a. Find the volume of the pool to the nearest cubic foot.

b. If 1 $ft^3 \approx 7.48$ gallons, about how many gallons does the pool hold?

Understanding the Problem

1. What are the dimensions of the pool?

   164 ft by 82 ft by 6.6 ft

2. How long is the pool? How wide is the pool? How deep is the pool?

   164 ft long; 82 feet wide; 6.6 ft deep

3. What are the dimensions of the base of the pool?

   164 ft-by-82 ft

4. How do you convert cubic feet to gallons?

   Multiply the number of cubic feet by 7.48.

Planning the Solution

5. How would you use the dimensions of the pool to find its volume?

   First find the area of the base of the pool by substituting the values of the dimensions into the formula $B = \ell \cdot w$, then find the volume by substituting the values for B and h into the formula $V = B \cdot h$.

6. How would you use the volume of the pool to find the number of gallons the pool holds?

   Multiply the volume of the pool by 7.48.

Getting an Answer

7. What is the area of the base of the pool? $B = \ell \cdot w = 164 \cdot 82 = 13{,}448 \text{ ft}^2$

8. What is the volume of the pool? $V = B \cdot h = 13{,}448 \cdot 6.6 = 88{,}756.8 \text{ ft}^3$

9. About how many gallons of water does the pool hold?

   The pool holds about $88{,}756.8 \times 7.48 \approx 663{,}901$ gallons.

Name ______________________ Class ____________ Date ____________

11-4 Practice

Form K

Volumes of Prisms and Cylinders

Find the volume of each rectangular prism.

1. 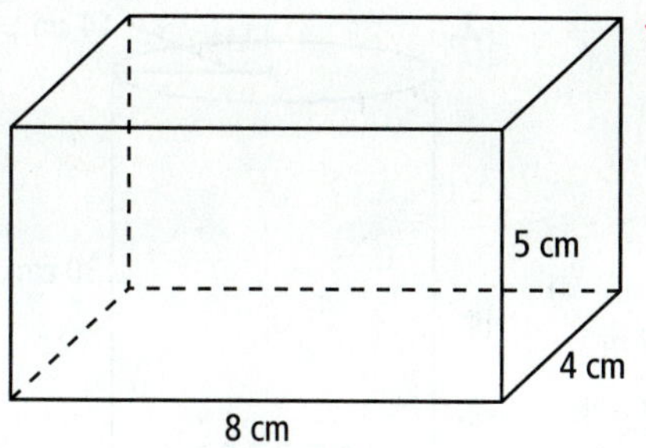

160 cm^3

2. 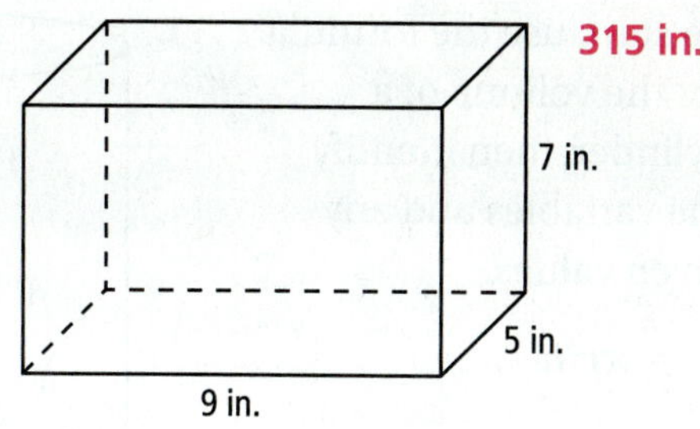

315 $in.^3$

3. 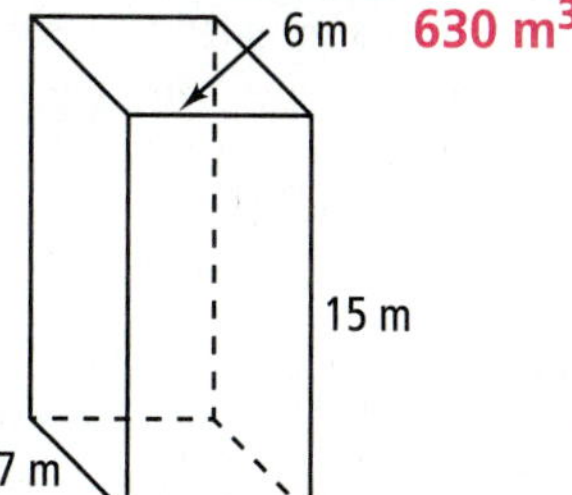

630 m^3

4. 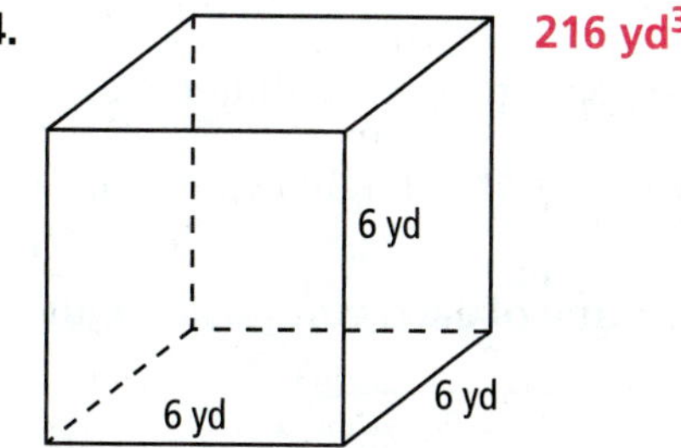

216 yd^3

5. The base is a square, 9.6 cm on a side. The height is 6.2 cm. 571.392 cm^3

6. The base is a rectangle with length 4.7 cm and width 7.5 cm. The height is 6.1 cm. 215.025 cm^3

Find the volume of each triangular prism to the nearest tenth.

To start, use the formula for the volume of a triangular prism and the formula for the base area of a triangle.

$V = BH, B = \frac{1}{2}bh$

7. 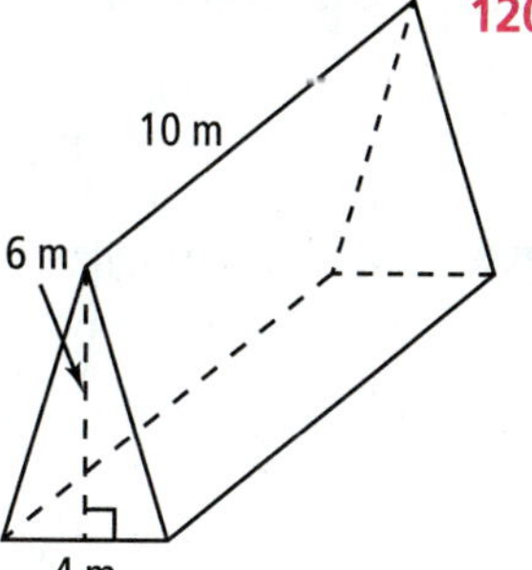

120 m^3

8. 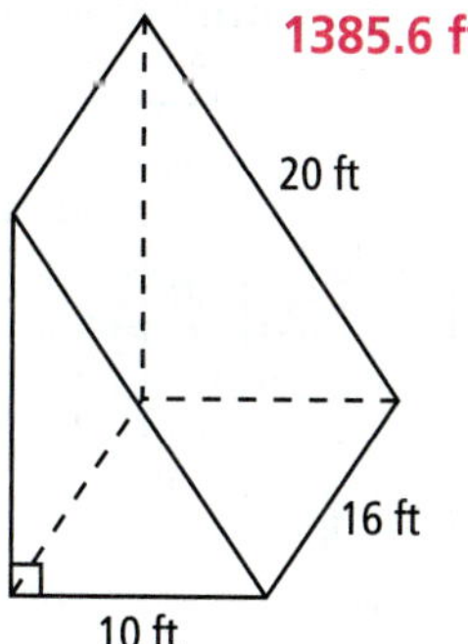

1385.6 ft^3

9. The base is a right triangle with a leg of 8 in. and hypotenuse of 10 in. The height of the prism is 15 in. (*Hint:* Use the Pythagorean Theorem to find the length of the other leg.) 360 $in.^3$

10. The base is a 30°-60°-90° triangle with a hypotenuse of 14 m. The height of the prism is 11 m. Find the volume to the nearest tenth. 466.8 m^3

Name ______________________ Class ____________ Date ____________

11-4 Practice (continued)

Form K

Volumes of Prisms and Cylinders

Find the volume of each cylinder in terms of π and to the nearest tenth.

To start, use the formula for the volume of a cylinder, then identify the variables and any given values.

$V = \pi r^2 h$

11.

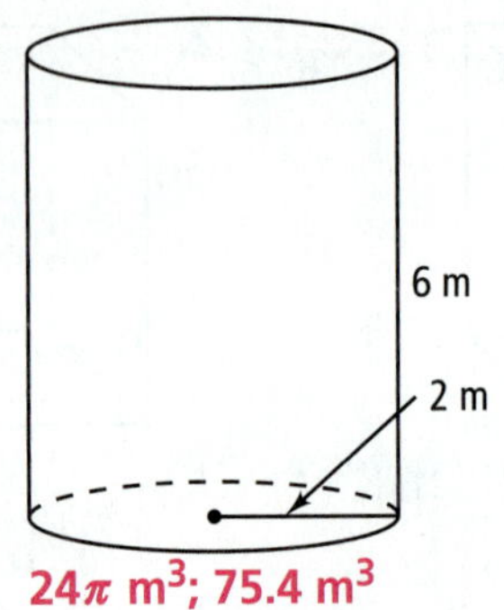

24π m³; 75.4 m³

12.

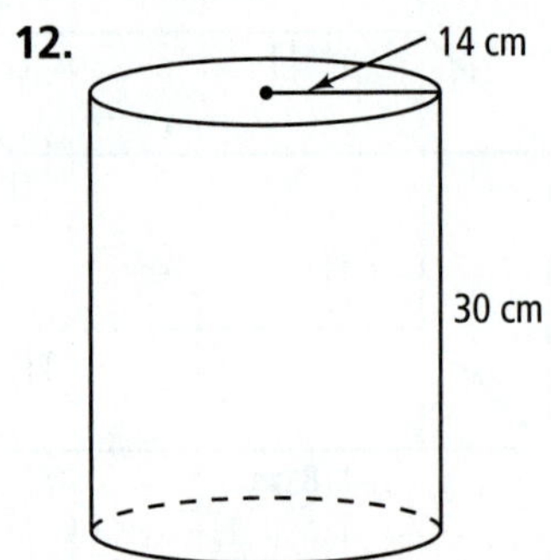

5880π cm³; 18,472.6 cm³

13. The radius of the right cylinder is 6.3 cm. The height is 14.5 cm. 575.5π cm³; 1808.0 cm³

14. The diameter of the right cylinder is 16 ft. The height is 7 ft. 448π ft³; 1407.4 ft³

Find the volume of each composite figure to the nearest whole number.

15.

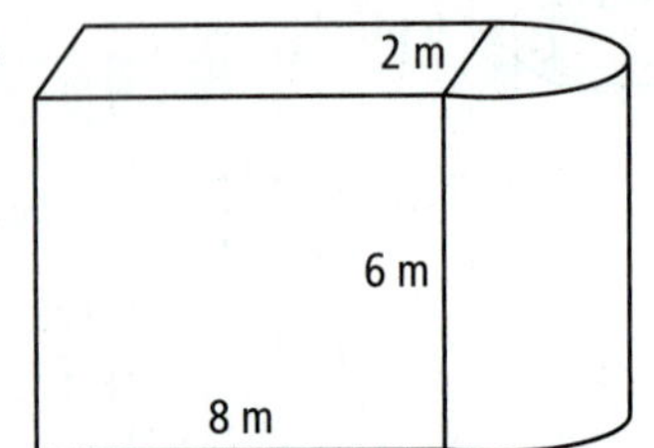

105 m³

16.

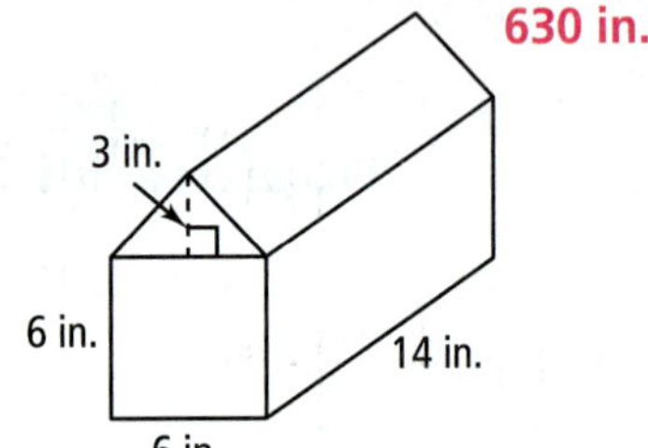

630 in.³

Find the volume of each figure to the nearest tenth.

17.

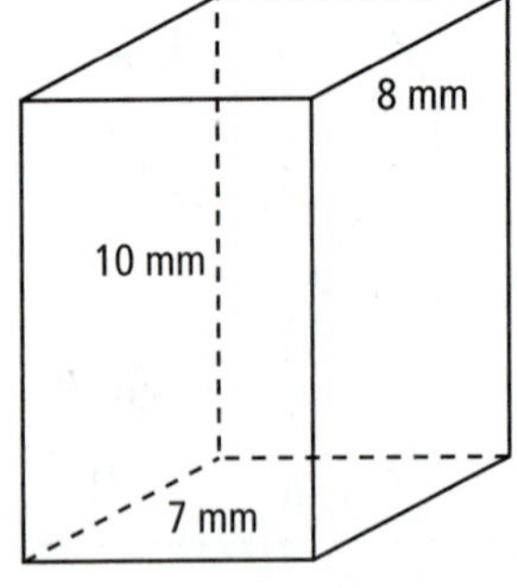

560 mm³

18.

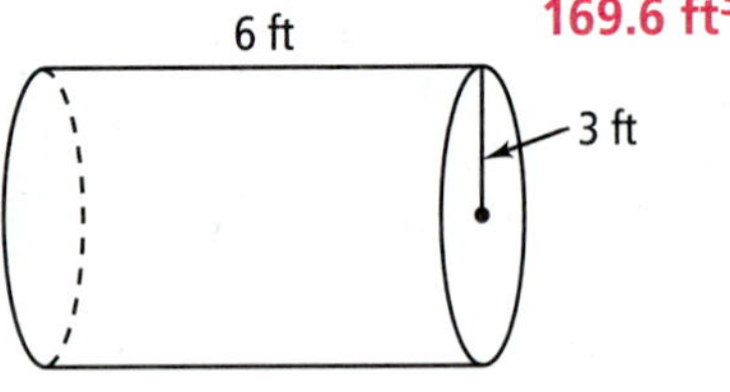

169.6 ft³

19. A cylindrical weather satellite has a diameter of 10 ft and a height of 6 ft. What is the volume available for carrying instruments and computer equipment, to the nearest tenth of a cubic foot? 471.2 ft³

20. Can A has a diameter of 6 cm and a height of 6.5 cm. Can B has a diameter of 16 cm and a height of 11.5 cm. What is the difference in volume of the two can types, to the nearest cubic centimeter? 2128 cm³

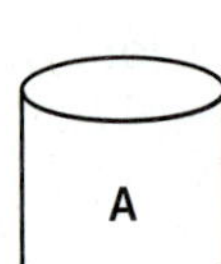

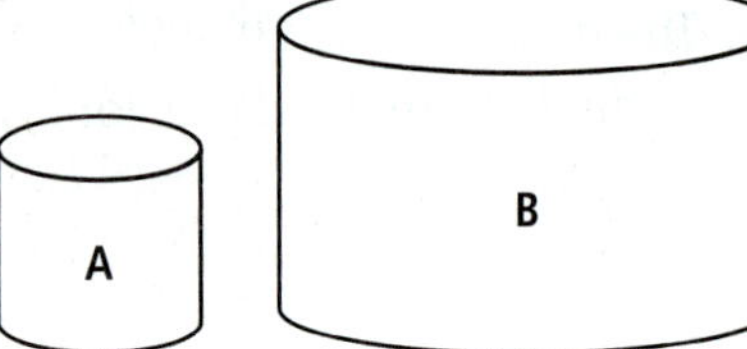

Name ______________________ Class ____________ Date ____________

11-4 Standardized Test Prep

Volumes of Prisms and Cylinders

Gridded Response

Solve each exercise and enter your answer on the grid provided.

1. What is the volume in cubic inches of the prism?

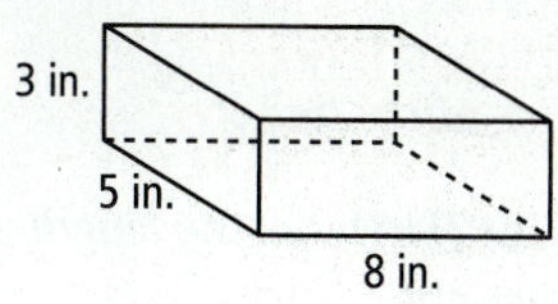

2. What is the volume in cubic feet of the prism, rounded to the nearest cubic foot?

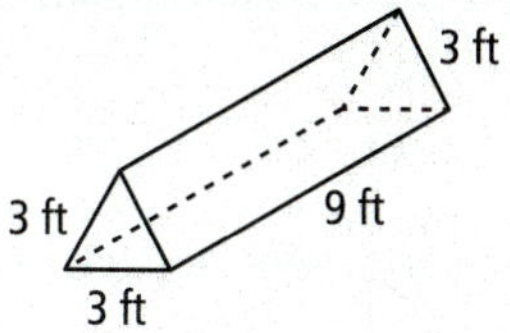

3. What is the volume in cubic inches of the cylinder, rounded to the nearest cubic inch?

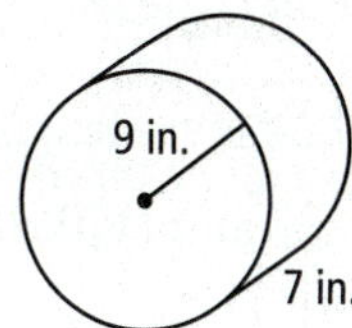

4. What is x, if the volume of the cylinder is 768π cm^3?

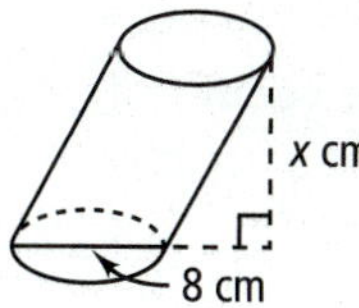

5. What is the volume in cubic inches of the solid figure, rounded to the nearest cubic inch?

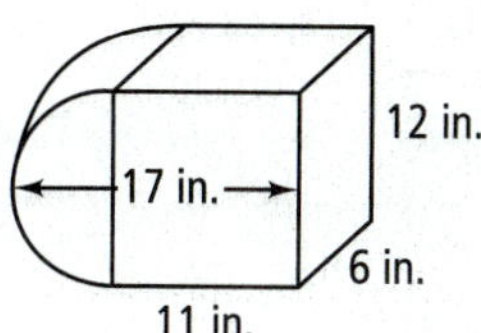

Answers

1. 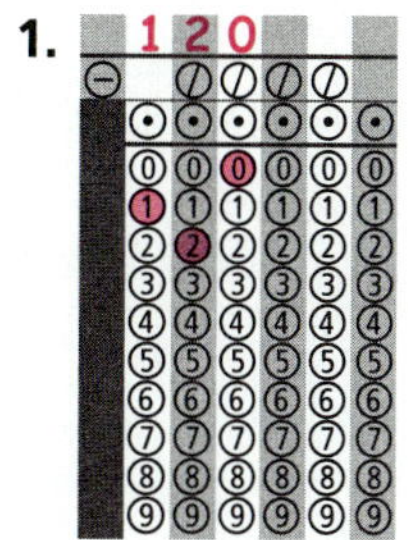

2. 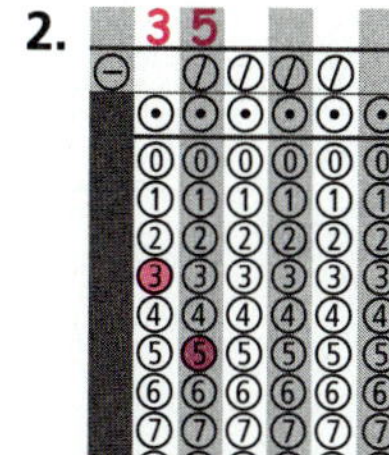

3. 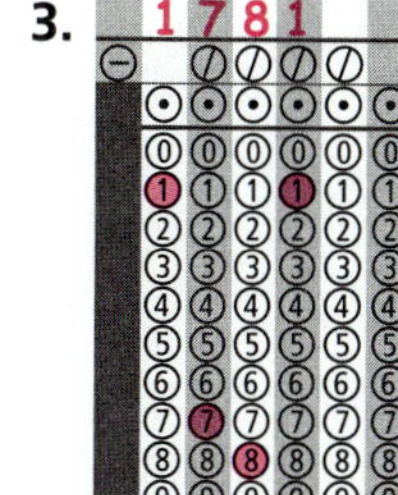

4. 

5. 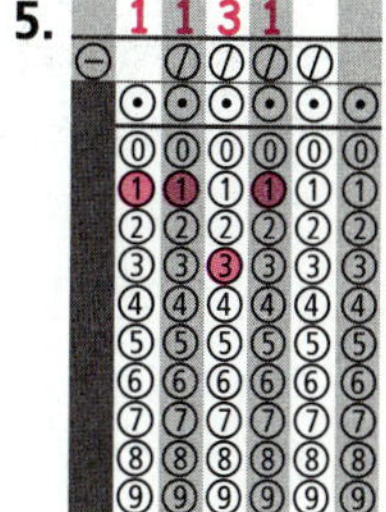

11-5 Volumes of Pyramids and Cones

Vocabulary

Review

1. Write *L*, *W*, or *H* to label the *length, width,* and *height* of the rectangular prism at the right.

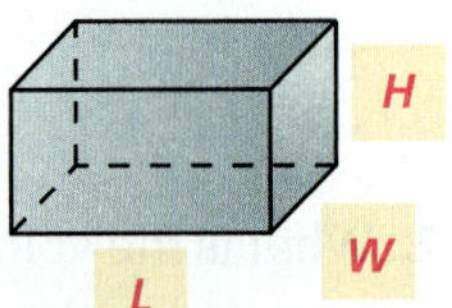

2. Explain how the *length, width,* and *height* of a cube are related.

   The length, width and height of a cube are equal.

Circle the correct statement in each exercise.

3. The *width* of a cylinder is the radius of a base of the cylinder.

   The *height* of a cylinder is the *length* of an altitude of the cylinder.

4. The *height* of a pyramid is the length of a segment perpendicular to the base.

   The slant *height* of a pyramid is the length of a segment perpendicular to the base.

Vocabulary Builder

volume (noun) VAHL yoom

Related Word: capacity

Main Idea: **Volume** measures quantity of space or amount, such as loudness of sound or a collection of books.

Definition: **Volume** is the amount of space that a three-dimensional figure occupies, measured in cubic units.

Example: The **volume** of a bottle of juice is 2 liters.

Use Your Vocabulary

Write T for *true* or F for *false*.

T 5. A synonym for *volume* is capacity.

F 6. *Volume* is measured in square units.

F 7. You can find the *volume* of a circle.

take note

Theorem 11-8 Volume of a Pyramid

The volume of a pyramid is one third the product of the area of the base and the height of the pyramid.

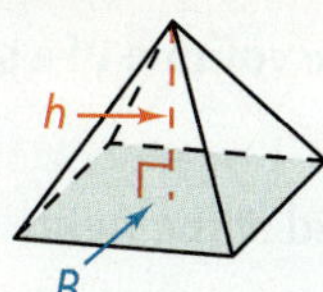

8. Complete the formula for the volume of a pyramid.

$V = \frac{1}{3} \cdot Bh$

take note

Theorem 11-9 Volume of a Cone

The volume of a cone is one third the product of the area of the base and the height of the cone.

$V = \frac{1}{3}Bh$

9. Circle an equivalent formula for the volume of a cone.

$V = \frac{1}{3}\pi r^2 h$ (circled) $\qquad V = \frac{1}{3} \cdot 2\pi r \cdot h$

Write the formula for the volume of each figure below.

10.

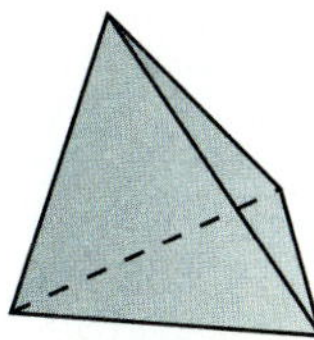

$V = \frac{1}{3} \cdot B \cdot h$

11.

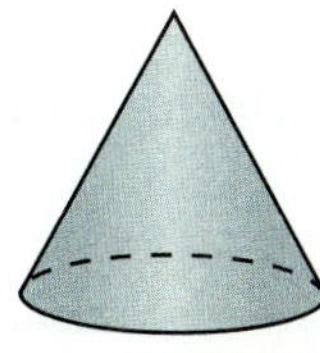

$V = \frac{1}{3}Bh$

Problem 1 Finding Volume of a Pyramid

Got It? **A sports arena shaped like a pyramid has a base area of about 300,000 ft^2 and a height of 321 ft. What is the approximate volume of the arena?**

12. Complete the problem-solving model below.

Know	Need	Plan
$B \approx$ 300,000 $h =$ 321	Volume of the pyramid	Substitute the given values into the formula $V = \frac{1}{3}Bh$.

13. Solve for V.

$$V = \frac{1}{3}Bh$$
$$\approx \frac{1}{3}(300{,}000)(321)$$
$$\approx 32{,}100{,}000$$

14. The approximate volume of the arena is 32,100,000 ft^3.

Problem 2 Finding the Volume of a Pyramid

Got It? **What is the volume of a square pyramid with base edges 24 m and slant height 13 m?**

15. Label the pyramid at the right.

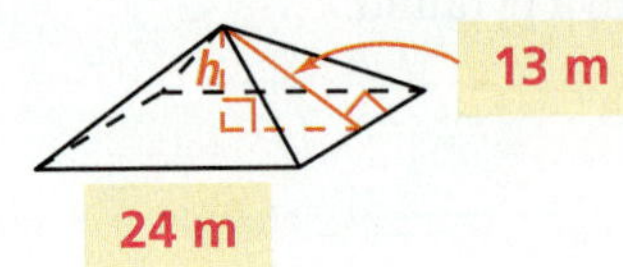

16. Find the height of the pyramid.

$13^2 = h^2 + 12^2$

$169 = h^2 + 144$

$h^2 = 25$

$h = 5$

17. Find the area of the base.

$B = 24 \cdot 24$

$= 576$

18. Find the volume of the pyramid.

$V = \frac{1}{3} \cdot Bh$

$= \frac{1}{3} \cdot 576 \cdot 5$

$= 960$

19. The volume of the pyramid is 960 m^3.

Problem 3 Finding the Volume of a Cone

Got It? **A small child's teepee is 6 ft high with a base diameter of 7 ft. What is the volume of the child's teepee to the nearest cubic foot?**

20. Label the cone at the right with the dimensions of the teepee.

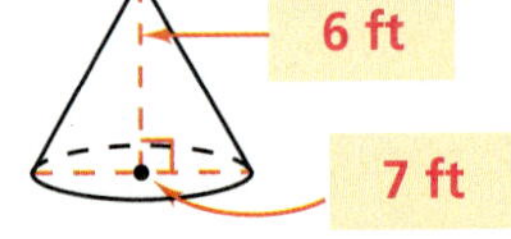

21. The radius of the teepee is 3.5 ft.

22. Use the justifications to find the volume of the teepee.

$V = \frac{1}{3}\pi r^2 h$	Use the formula with π for the volume of a cone.
$V = \frac{1}{3}\pi(3.5)^2(6)$	Substitute for r and h.
$= \frac{1}{3}\pi(12.25)(6)$	Square the radius.
$= 24.5\pi$	Simplify in terms of π.
≈ 76.96902001	Use a calculator.

23. The volume of the child's teepee to the nearest cubic foot is 77 ft^3.

Problem 4 Finding the Volume of an Oblique Cone

Got It? **What is the volume of the oblique cone at the right in terms of π and rounded to the nearest cubic meter?**

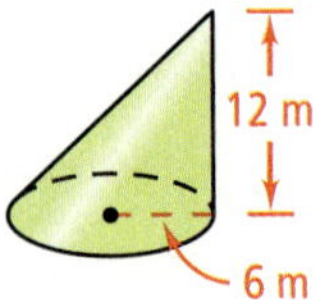

24. The radius of the base is 6 m and the height is 12 m.

25. Cross out the formula that is NOT a formula for the volume of a cone.

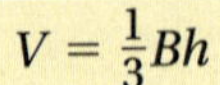 $V = \frac{1}{3}Bh$  ~~$V = Bh$~~ $V = \frac{1}{3}\pi r^2 h$

26. Find the volume of the cone.

$V = \frac{1}{3}\pi r^2 h$

$= \frac{1}{3}\pi(6)^2(12)$

$= 144\pi$

≈ 452.3893421

27. The volume of the cone in terms of π is 144π m^3.

Rounded to the nearest cubic meter, the volume of the cone is 452 m^3.

Lesson Check • Do you UNDERSTAND?

Error Analysis **A square pyramid has base edges 13 ft and height 10 ft. A cone has diameter 13 ft and height 10 ft. Your friend claims the figures have the same volume because the volume formulas for a pyramid and a cone are the same: $V = \frac{1}{3}Bh$. What is her error?**

28. Is $V = \frac{1}{3}Bh$ the volume formula for both a pyramid and a cone? Yes / No

Underline the correct word to complete each sentence.

29. The base of a square pyramid is a circle / polygon.

30. The base of a cone is a circle / polygon.

31. Circle the base used in the formula for the volume of a cone. Underline the base used in the formula for the volume of a square pyramid.

$B = \pi r^2$ $\qquad$ $B = \frac{1}{2}bh$ $\qquad$ $B = s^2$

32. Now explain your friend's error. Explanations may vary. Sample:

She forgot that the area formulas for the bases of pyramids and cones are different.

Math Success

Check off the vocabulary words that you understand.

☐ pyramid ☐ cone ☐ oblique ☐ volume

Rate how well you can *find the volumes of pyramids and cones.*

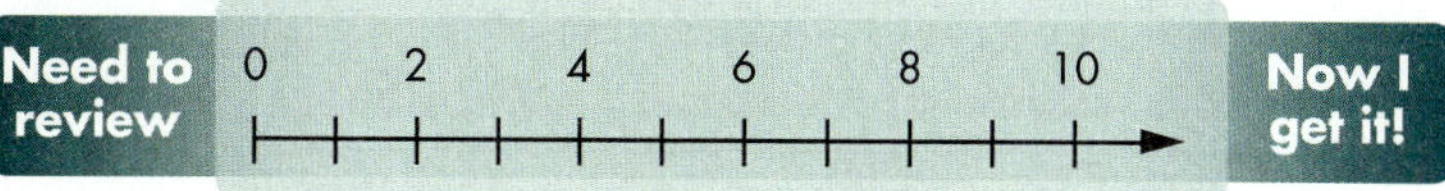

Name ______________________ Class ____________ Date ____________

11-5 Think About a Plan

Volumes of Pyramids and Cones

Writing The two cylinders pictured at the right are congruent. How does the volume of the larger cone compare to the total volume of the two smaller cones? Explain.

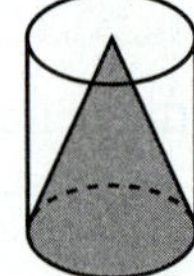
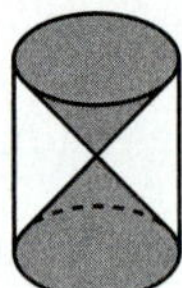

Understanding the Problem

1. You are told that the two cylinders are congruent. What does that tell you about the cones?

   It tells you that the larger cone is twice as tall as the smaller cones.

2. You are asked to compare the volumes of the cones. Can you find the exact volumes of the cones? In what other way can you compare their volumes?

   No; you can compare their volumes using the formulas for the volumes of the cones.

Planning the Solution

3. What are the variables in the formula for the volume of a cone? What do they represent?

   The variables are the radius of the base, r, and the height of the cone, h.

4. Let r represent the radius of the larger cone. What is the radius of the smaller cones in terms of r? Let h represent the height of the larger cone. What is the height of the smaller cones in terms of h? Explain.

   Because the radii are equal, the radius of the smaller cones is also r; because the height of the smaller cones is one-half the height of the larger cone, the height of the smaller cones is $\frac{1}{2}h$.

Getting an Answer

5. What is the formula for the volume of the larger cone? What is the formula for the volume of the smaller cones?

   larger cone: $V = \frac{1}{3}\pi r^2 h$; smaller cones: $V = \frac{1}{3}\pi r^2 (\frac{1}{2}h)$

6. How does the volume of the larger cone compare to the total volume of the smaller cones?

   Because $\frac{1}{3}\pi r^2(\frac{1}{2}h) + \frac{1}{3}\pi r^2(\frac{1}{2}h) = \frac{1}{3}\pi r^2 h$, the volume of the larger cone is equal to the total volume of the two smaller cones.

Name ______________________ Class __________ Date __________

11-5 Practice

Form K

Volumes of Pyramids and Cones

Find the volume of each square pyramid. Round to the nearest tenth if necessary.

To start, use the formula for the volume of a pyramid. Then find the area of the base of the pyramid.

$V = \frac{1}{3}Bh$

1\.

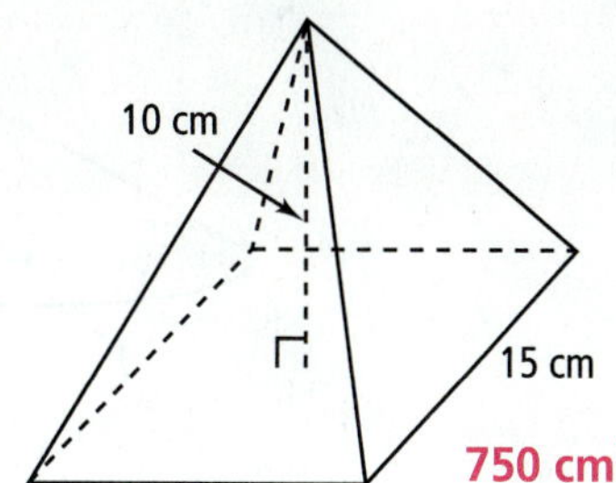

750 cm^3

2\.

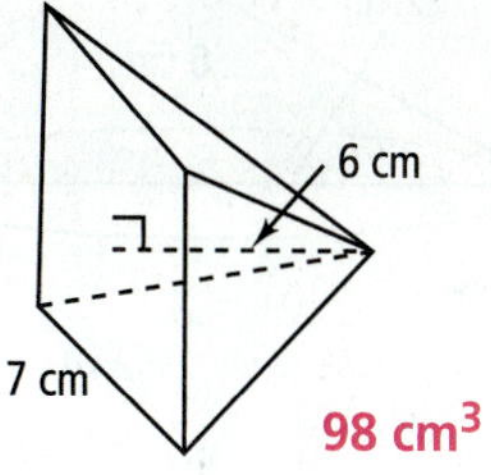

98 cm^3

Find the volume of each square pyramid, given its slant height. Round to the nearest whole number.

To start, find the height of the pyramid using the Pythagorean Theorem. Then use the formula for the volume of a pyramid.

3\.

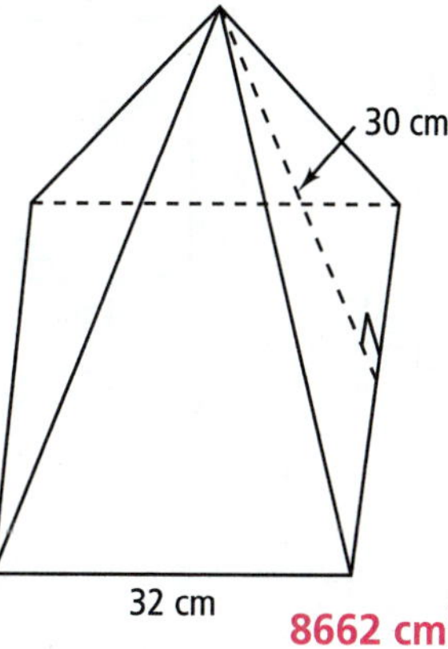

8662 cm^3

4\.

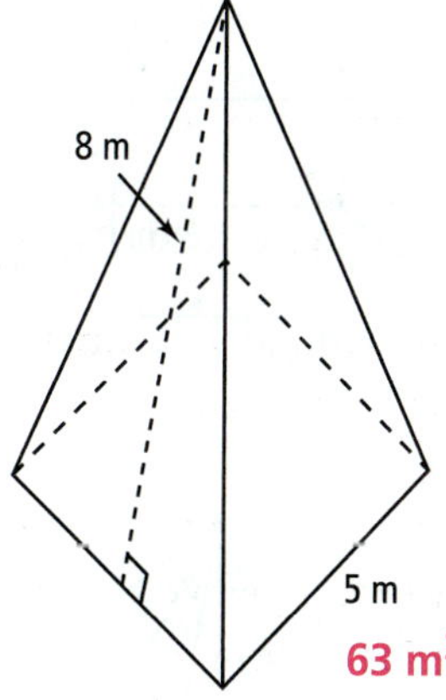

63 m^3

5. The base of a pyramid is a square, 24 cm on a side. The height is 13 cm. Find the volume. 2496 cm^3

6. The base of a pyramid is a square, 14 cm on a side. The height of the pyramid is 25 cm. Find the volume to the nearest whole number. 1633 cm^3

Find the volume of each cone in terms of π and also rounded as indicated.

7. nearest cubic foot

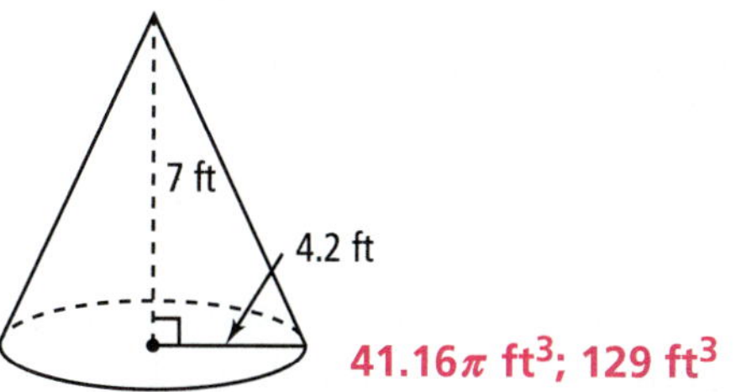

41.16π ft^3; 129 ft^3

8. nearest cubic inch

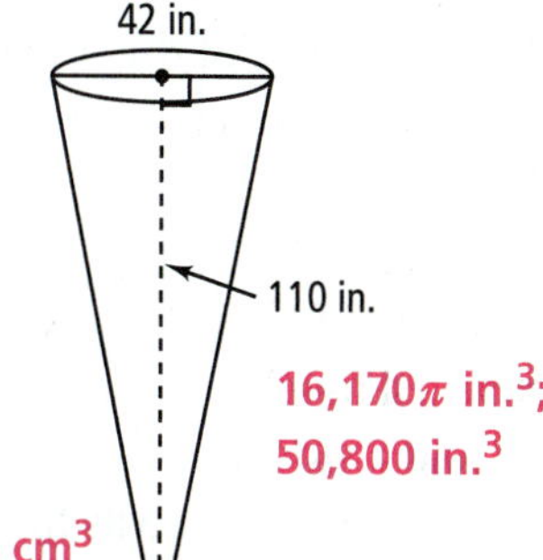

16,170π in.^{3}; 50,800 in.^{3}

9. The base has a radius of 8 cm and a height of 5 cm. Round to the nearest cubic centimeter. $106\frac{2}{3}\pi$ cm^3; 335 cm^3

10. The base has a diameter of 20 m and a height of 12.6 m. Round to the nearest cubic meter. 420π m^3; 1319 m^3

11-5 Practice (continued) Form K

Volumes of Pyramids and Cones

Find the volume of each figure to the nearest whole number.

11. 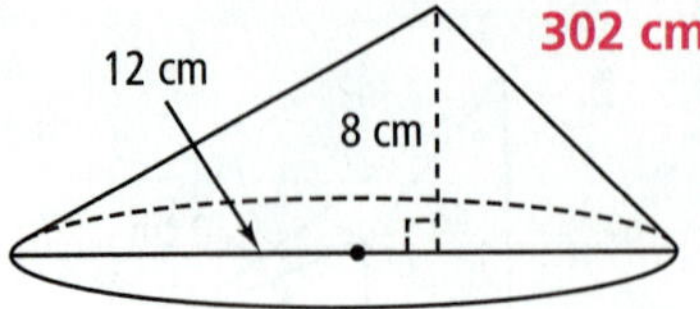

302 cm³

12. 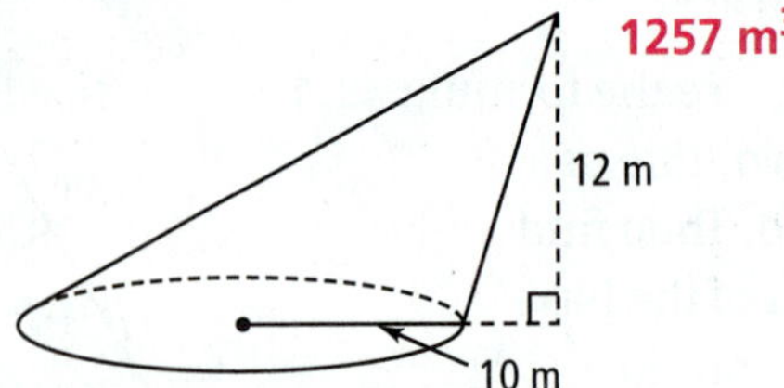

1257 m³

13. 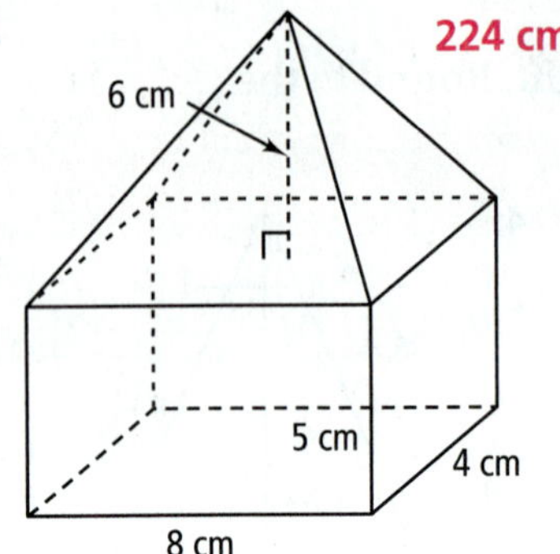

224 cm³

14. 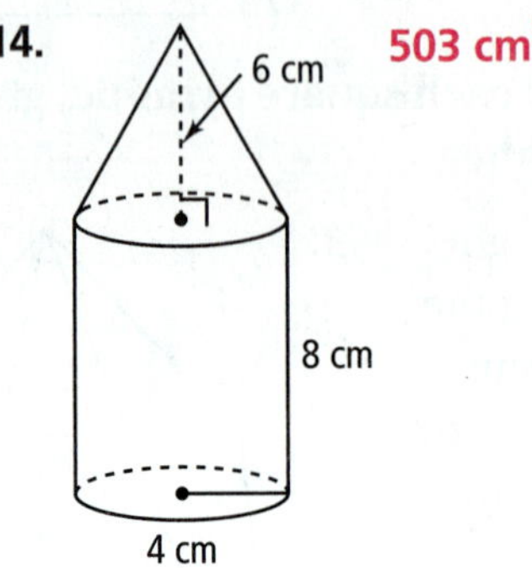

503 cm³

15. 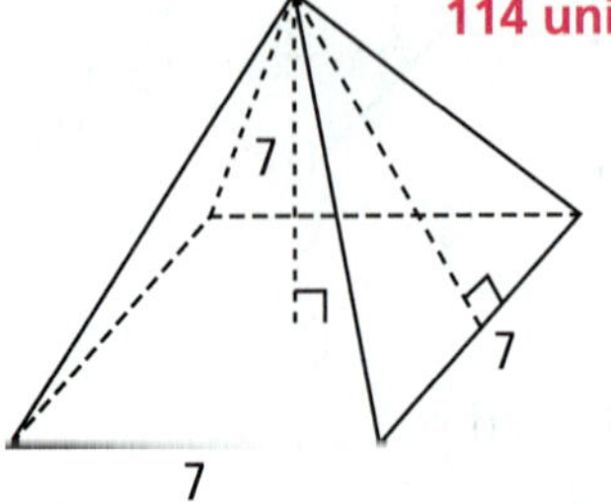

114 unit³

16. 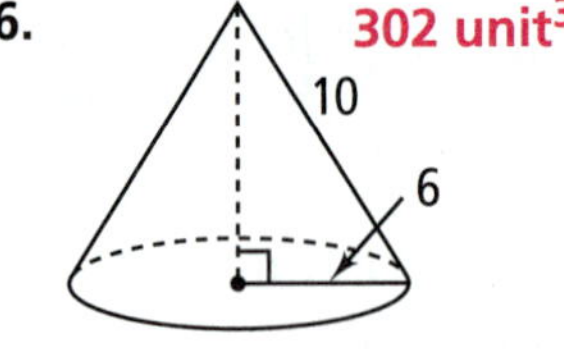

302 unit³

17. One right circular cone is set inside a larger right circular cone. Find the volume of the space between the cones if the diameter of the inside cone is 9 in., the diameter of the outside cone is 15 in., and the height of both is 8 in. Round to the nearest tenth. 301.6 in.^{3}

18. The Pyramid of Khufu is a square pyramid which had a side length of about 230 m and a height of about 147 m when it was completed. The Pyramid of Khafre had a side length of about 215 m and a height of about 144 m when it was completed. What was the approximate difference in the volume of the two pyramids upon completion? 373,300 m^3

Name ______________________ Class ____________ Date ____________

11-5 Standardized Test Prep

Volumes of Pyramids and Cones

Multiple Choice

For Exercises 1–5, choose the correct letter.

1. What is the volume of the pyramid? B

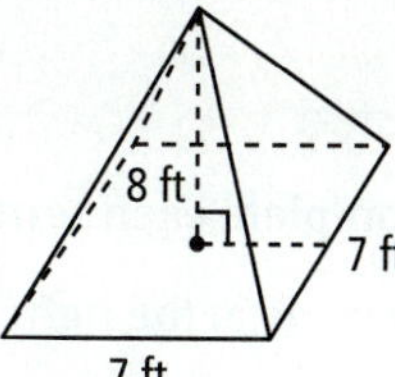

A 56 ft^3 C 196 ft^3

B $130\frac{2}{3}\text{ ft}^3$ D 392 ft^3

2. What is the volume of the cone, rounded to the nearest cubic inch? G

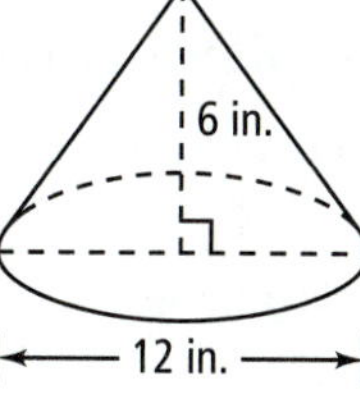

F 72 in.^3 H 905 in.^3

G 226 in.^3 I 2714 in.^3

3. What is the volume of the figure? B

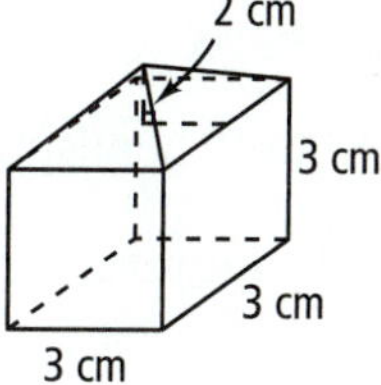

A 15 cm^3 C 45 cm^3

B 33 cm^3 D 54 cm^3

4. What is the value of x, if the volume of the cone is $12\pi\text{ m}^3$? F

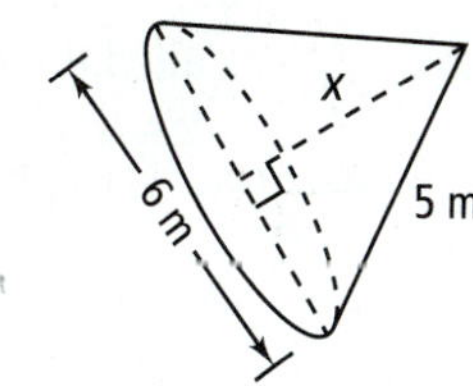

F 4 m H 6 m

G 5 m I 10 m

5. What is the diameter of a cone with height 8 m and volume $150\pi\text{ m}^3$? D

A 7.5 m B $5\sqrt{3}$ m C $7.5\sqrt{3}$ m D 15 m

Short Response

6. Error Analysis A student calculates the volume of the given cone as approximately 2094 cm^3. Explain the error in the student's reasoning and find the actual volume of the cone rounded to the nearest whole number.

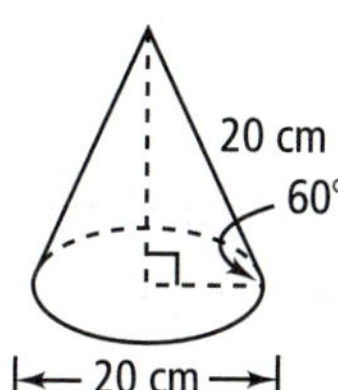

[2] The student uses slant height of the cone instead of the height to find the volume. The actual volume is approximately 1814 cm^3. [1] incorrect explanation or incorrect volume [0] no correct responses given

11-6 Surface Areas and Volumes of Spheres

Vocabulary

Review

Underline the correct word to complete each sentence.

1. The *diameter* / *radius* of the circle at the right is 5 cm.
2. The circumference of a circle is the product of its *diameter* / *radius* and π.
3. The *diameter* / *radius* of a circle is a segment containing the center with endpoints on the circle.

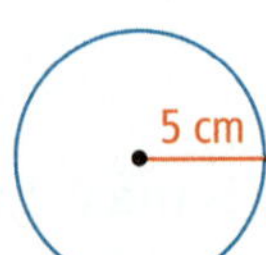

Vocabulary Builder

sphere (noun) sfeer

Related Words: spherical (adjective), hemisphere (noun)

Main Idea: A **sphere** is formed by the revolution of a circle about its diameter.

Definition: A **sphere** is the set of all points in space equidistant from a given point called the *center*.

Example: A basketball is a **sphere**.

Non-Example: A football is not a **sphere**.

sphere

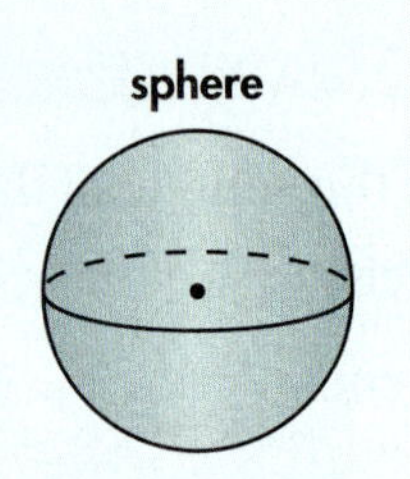

Use Your Vocabulary

4. Complete each statement with *sphere* or *spherical*.

ADJECTIVE Each _?_ candy looks like a rock. spherical

NOUN A baseball is in the shape of a _?_. sphere

Write T for *true* or F for *false*.

T 5. Celestial bodies such as the sun or Earth are often represented as *spheres*.

F 6. A *sphere* is a two-dimensional figure.

Name ______________________ Class ____________ Date ____________

11-6 Practice

Form K

Surface Areas and Volumes of Spheres

Find the surface area of the sphere with the given diameter or radius. Leave your answer in terms of π.

1. $r = 6$ ft 144π ft^2
2. $d = 10$ cm 100π cm^2
3. $r = 8$ in. 256π in.^{2}
4. $d = 4$ yd 16π yd^2

Find the surface area of each sphere. Leave each answer in terms of π.

5. 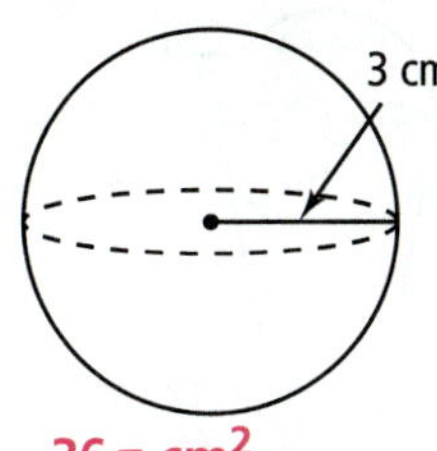

To start, use the formula for the surface area of a sphere. Then determine the radius and substitute it into the formula.

S.A. $= 4\pi r^2 = 4\pi \cdot \boxed{3}^2$

36π cm^2

6. 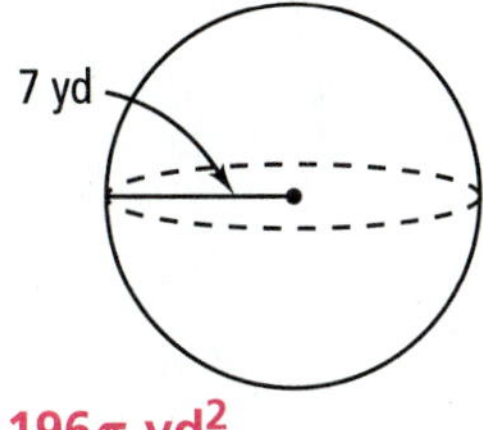

196π yd^2

7. 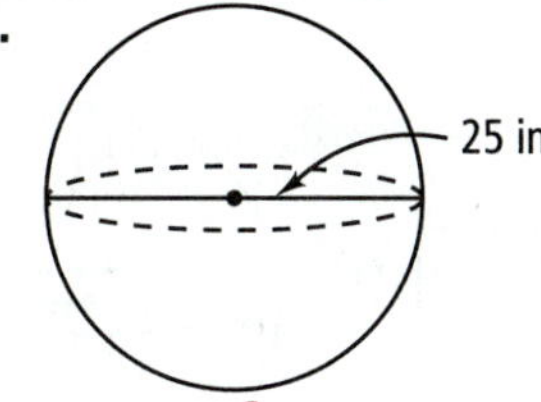

625π in.^{2}

8. 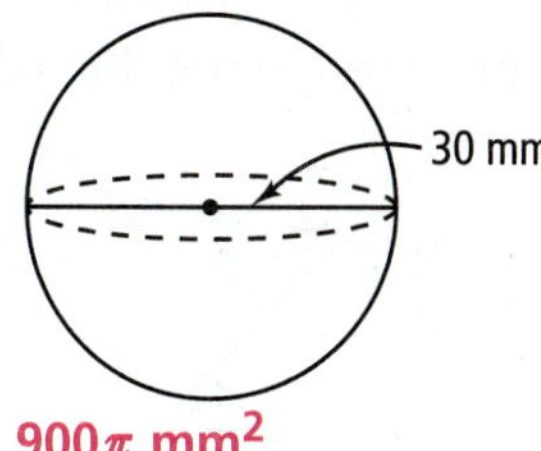

900π mm^2

Use the given circumference to find the surface area of each spherical object. Round your answer to the nearest tenth.

9. a baseball with $C = 9.25$ in. 27.2 in.^{2}
10. a softball with $C = 28.25$ cm 254.0 cm^2
11. a basketball with $C = 2.98$ ft 2.8 ft^2
12. a bowling ball with $C = 26.7$ in. 226.9 in.^{2}

Find the volume of each sphere. Give each answer in terms of π and rounded to the nearest cubic unit.

13. 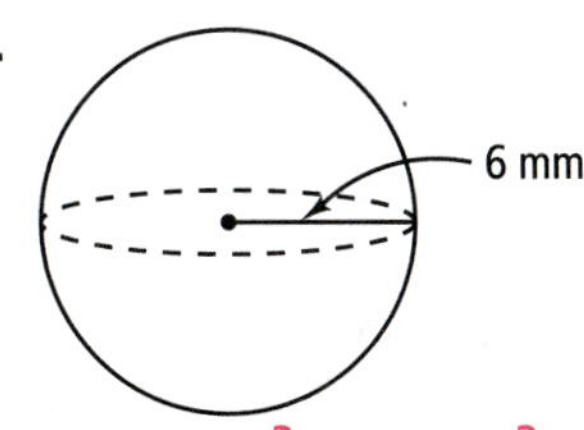

To start, use the formula for the surface area of a sphere. Then determine the radius, and substitute it into the formula.

$V = \frac{4}{3}\pi r^3 = \frac{4}{3}\pi \cdot \boxed{6}^3$

288π mm^3; 905 mm^3

14. 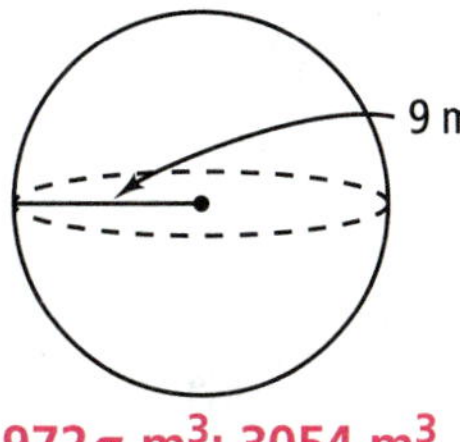

972π m^3; 3054 m^3

15. 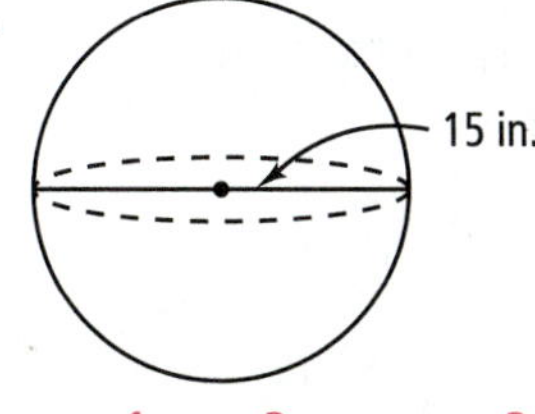

$562\frac{1}{2}\pi$ in.^{3}; 1767 in.^{3}

16. 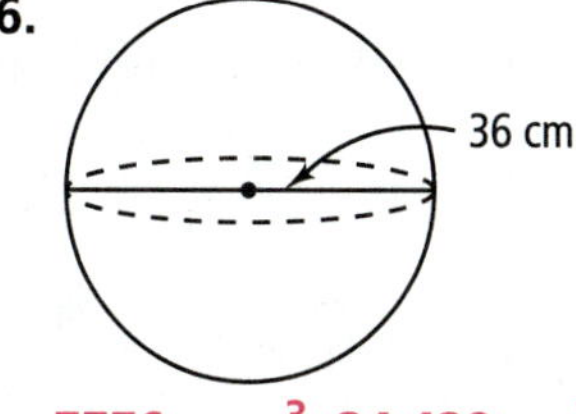

7776π cm^3; 24,429 cm^3

11-6 Practice (continued)

Form K

Surface Areas and Volumes of Spheres

A sphere has the volume given. Find its surface area to the nearest whole number.

17. $V = 14{,}130\text{ ft}^3$ 2826 ft^2

18. $V = 4443\text{ m}^3$ 1307 m^2

19. $V = 100\text{ in.}^3$ 104 in.^2

20. $V = 31{,}400\text{ mi}^3$ 4813 mi^2

21. A spherical scoop of ice cream with a diameter of 5 cm rests on top of a sugar cone that is 12 cm deep and has a diameter of 5 cm. If all of the ice cream melts into the cone, what percent of the cone will be filled? Round to the nearest percent. 83%

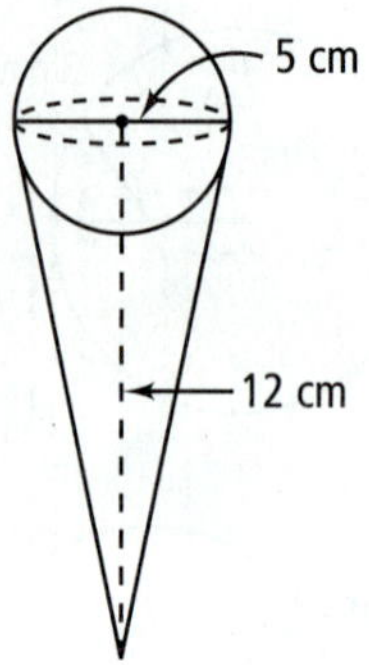

22. Writing A cylinder, a cone, and a sphere have the dimensions indicated in the diagram below.

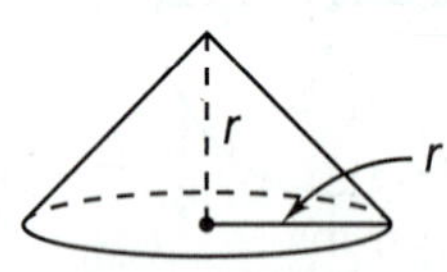

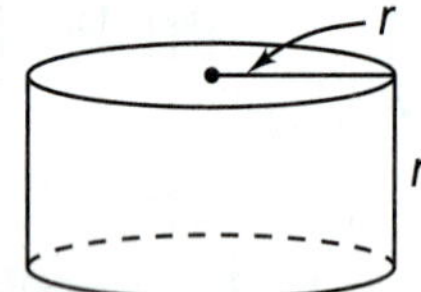

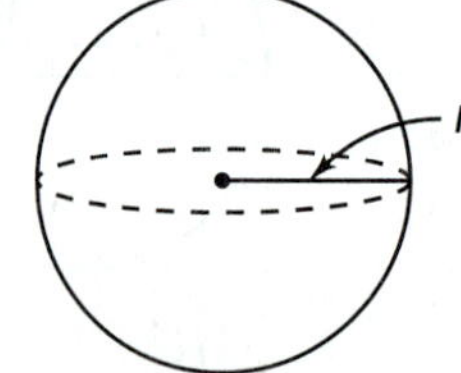

a. What are the formulas for the volume of the cone and the volume of the cylinder in terms of r? Give each answer in terms of π.
cone: $V = \frac{1}{3}\pi r^3$; cylinder: $V = \pi r^3$

b. If $r = 9$ in., what are the volumes of the cone, cylinder, and sphere? 243π, 729π, 972π

c. How are the volumes related? The volume of a sphere is equal to the sum of the volumes of the cone and the cylinder.

d. How can you show that this relationship is true for all values of r?
by using the formulas for the volumes to show that $\frac{1}{3}\pi r^3 + \pi r^3 = \frac{4}{3}\pi r^3$

23. A bowling ball must have a diameter of 8.5 in. If the bowling ball weighs 16 lb, find the density (lb/in.^{3}) of the bowling ball. Density is the quotient of weight divided by volume. Round your answer to the nearest hundredth. 0.05 lb/in.^3

24. Open-Ended Draw two spheres such that the volume of one sphere is eight times the volume of the other sphere. Answers may vary. The larger sphere's radius will be twice the radius of the smaller sphere.

Name ______________________ Class ____________ Date ____________

11-6 Standardized Test Prep

Surface Areas and Volumes of Spheres

Multiple Choice

For Exercises 1–5, choose the correct letter.

1. What is the approximate volume of the sphere? A

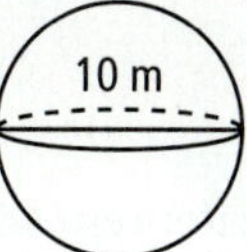

A $524\ m^3$ C $1256\ m^3$

B $1000\ m^3$ D $1570\ m^3$

2. What is the approximate surface area of the sphere? G

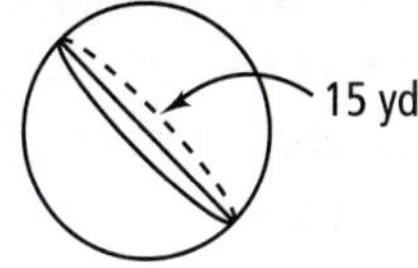

F $225\ yd^2$ H $1767\ yd^2$

G $707\ yd^2$ I $5301\ yd^2$

3. What is the approximate volume of the sphere if the surface area is $482.8\ mm^2$? A

A $998\ mm^3$ B $1126\ mm^3$ C $2042\ mm^3$ D $2993\ mm^3$

4. What is the approximate surface area of the sphere? G

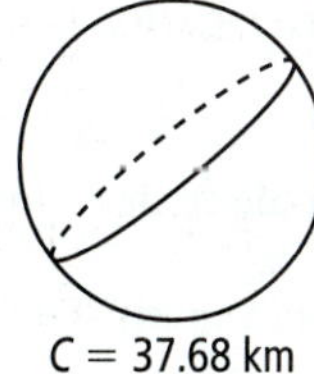

F $342.3\ km^2$ H $903.4\ km^2$

G $451.9\ km^2$ I $2713\ km^2$

5. What is the approximate radius of a sphere whose volume is $1349\ cm^3$? B

A 5.7 cm B 6.9 cm C 11 cm D 14.7 cm

Short Response

6. Suppose a wealthy entrepreneur commissions the design of a spherical spaceship to house a small group for a week in orbit around the Earth. The designer allocates $1000\ ft^3$ for each person, plus an additional $4073.5\ ft^3$ for various necessary machines. As in a recreational vehicle, the personal space is largely occupied by items such as beds, shower and toilet facilities, and a kitchenette. The diameter of the ship is 26.8 ft. What is the volume of the spaceship, and for approximately how many people is the ship designed?

[2] $V = 10{,}078.7\ ft^3$; 6 people
[1] incorrect volume or incorrect number of people
[0] no response or incorrect response

11-7 Areas and Volumes of Similar Solids

Vocabulary

Review

Complete each statement with the appropriate word from the list. Use each word only once.

similar   similarities   similarity   similarly

1. There are several _?_ house styles in the neighborhood. similar
2. The sequel may end _?_ to the original movie. similarly
3. There is not one _?_ between his first and second drawings. similarity
4. You could find several _?_ between the two video games. similarities

Vocabulary Builder

scale factor (noun) **skayl** FAK **tur**

Main Idea: The **scale factor** for similar polygons is the ratio of the lengths of their corresponding sides.

Definition: The **scale factor** for two similar solids is the ratio of their corresponding linear dimensions.

Example: The **scale factor** of a map may be 1 inch : 5 miles.

Use Your Vocabulary

Write T for *true* or F for *false*.

F 5. You can find the *scale factor* for any two figures.

T 6. You can find the *scale factor* for similar figures.

T 7. You can write a *scale factor* as a ratio $(a : b)$ or as a fraction $\left(\frac{a}{b}\right)$.

F 8. A *scale factor* is always written as the ratio $a : b$.

Problem 1 Identifying Similar Solids

Got It? **Are the two cylinders similar? If so, what is the scale factor of the first figure to the second figure?**

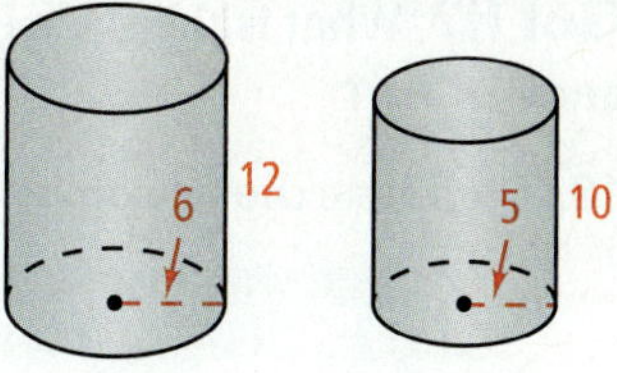

Underline the correct word to complete each sentence.

9. You can check whether prisms are similar by comparing the ratios of two / three dimensions.

10. You can check whether cylinders are similar by comparing the ratios of two / three dimensions.

11. Always compare the ratios of corresponding / similar dimensions.

12. The ratio of the height of the larger cylinder to the height of the smaller cylinder is $\frac{12}{10}$. Simplified, this ratio is $\frac{6}{5}$.

13. The ratio of the radius of the larger cylinder to the radius of the smaller cylinder is $\frac{6}{5}$.

14. Underline the correct words to complete the sentence. The ratios you found in Exercises 12 and 13 are/are not equal, so the cylinders are/are not similar.

15. The scale factor is $\frac{6}{5}$.

take note

Theorem 11-12 Areas and Volumes of Similar Solids

If the scale factor of two similar solids is $a : b$, then

- the ratio of their corresponding areas is $a^2 : b^2$
- the ratio of their volumes is $a^3 : b^3$

16. Complete the model below.

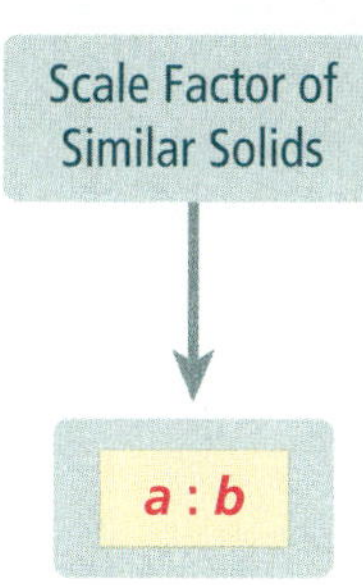

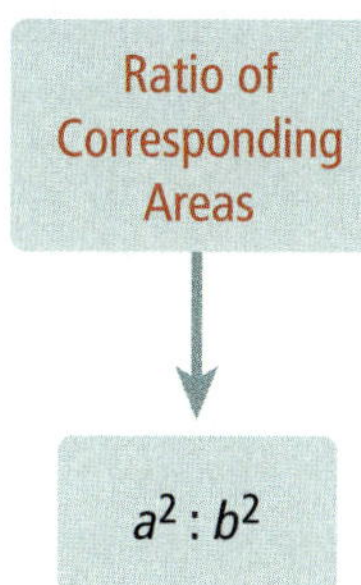

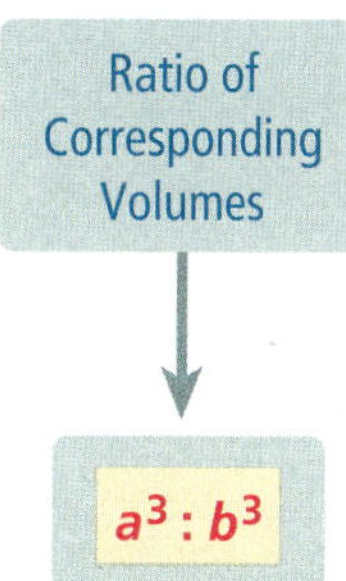

$a : b$ $a^2 : b^2$ $a^3 : b^3$

17. If the scale factor of two similar solids is 1 : 2, then the ratio of their corresponding areas is $1^2 : 2^2$, or $1 : 4$.

18. If the scale factor of two similar solids is 1 : 2, then the ratio of their corresponding volumes is $1^3 : 2^3$, or $1 : 8$.

Problem 2 Finding the Scale Factor

Got It? **What is the scale factor of two similar prisms with surface areas 144 m^2 and 324 m^2?**

19. Complete the reasoning model below.

Think	Write
I can write the ratio of the lesser surface area to the greater surface area.	$\frac{a^2}{b^2} = \frac{144}{324}$
I can take the square roots of the surface areas and write the scale factor as $a : b$.	$\sqrt{\frac{a^2}{b^2}} = \frac{a}{b} = \frac{12}{18}$

20. The scale factor is 12 : 18, which can be simplified to 2 : 3.

Problem 3 Using a Scale Factor

Got It? **The volumes of two similar solids are 128 m^3 and 250 m^3. The surface area of the larger solid is 250 m^2. What is the surface area of the smaller solid?**

21. Let $\frac{a}{b}$ represent the scale factor of the similar solids. Circle the simplified ratio of the volume of the smaller solid to the volume of the larger solid.

$\frac{a^3}{b^3} = \frac{64}{125}$ (circled) $\qquad \frac{a}{b} = \frac{64}{125} \qquad \frac{a^3}{b^3} = \frac{125}{64}$

22. Find the scale factor $a : b$.

$$\frac{a}{b} = \frac{\sqrt[3]{64}}{\sqrt[3]{125}} = \frac{4}{5}$$

23. Use the scale factor to find the ratio of surface areas.

$$\frac{a^2}{b^2} = \frac{4^2}{5^2} = \frac{16}{25}$$

24. Circle the proportion that compares the surface area of the smaller solid to the surface area of the larger solid.

$\frac{a^2}{b^2} = \frac{x}{250}$ (circled) $\qquad \frac{a}{b} = \frac{x}{250} \qquad \frac{a^2}{b^2} = \frac{250}{x}$

25. Now solve for x.

$$\frac{16}{25} = \frac{x}{250}$$
$$(250)(16) = 25x$$
$$4000 = 25x$$
$$\frac{4000}{25} = \frac{25x}{25}$$
$$x = 160$$

26. The surface area of the smaller solid is 160 m^2.

Problem 4 Using a Scale Factor to Find Capacity

Got It? **A marble paperweight shaped like a pyramid weighs 0.15 lb. How much does a similarly shaped marble paperweight weigh if each dimension is three times as large?**

27. The scale factor of small paperweight to large paperweight is 1 : 3.

28. Let x = the weight of the larger paperweight. Use the justifications at the right to find the value of x.

$$\frac{1^3}{3^3} = \frac{0.15}{x}$$ The weights are proportional to their volumes.

$$\frac{1}{27} = \frac{0.15}{x}$$ Simplify.

$$x = 4.05$$ Use the Cross Products Property.

29. The paperweight that is three times as large weighs 4.05 lb.

Lesson Check • Do you UNDERSTAND?

Error Analysis **Two cubes have surface areas 49 cm² and 64 cm². Your classmate tried to find the scale factor of the larger cube to the smaller cube. Explain and correct your classmate's error.**

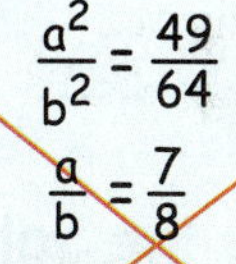

$\frac{a^2}{b^2} = \frac{49}{64}$

$\frac{a}{b} = \frac{7}{8}$

The scale factor of the larger cube to the smaller cube is 7 : 8.

Underline the correct word(s) to complete each sentence.

30. The larger cube has the greater / lesser surface area.

31. The scale factor of larger cube to smaller cube is greater / less than the scale factor of smaller cube to larger cube.

32. Your classmate found the scale factor of the smaller / larger cube to the smaller / larger cube.

33. Find the correct scale factor.

Begin with the proportion $\frac{a^2}{b^2} = \frac{64}{49}$. Then, $\frac{a}{b} = \frac{8}{7}$.

Math Success

Check off the vocabulary words that you understand.

☐ similar solids ☐ scale factor

Rate how well you can *find and use scale factors of similar solids.*

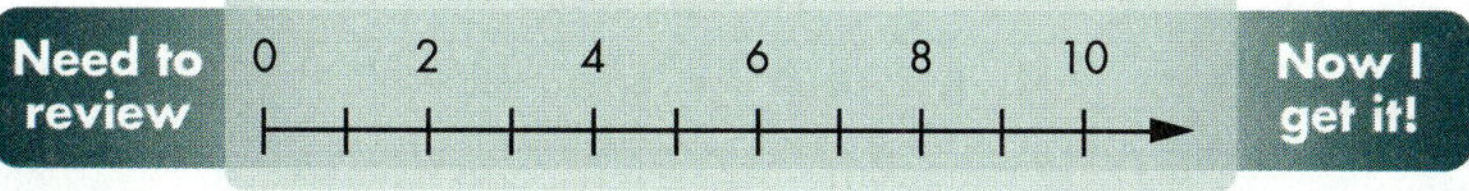

Name ______________________ Class ____________ Date ____________

11-7 Think About a Plan

Areas and Volumes of Similar Solids

Reasoning A carpenter is making a blanket chest based on an antique chest. Both chests have the shape of a rectangular prism. The length, width, and height of the new chest will all be 4 in. greater than the respective dimensions of the antique. Will the chests be similar? Explain.

Understanding the Problem

1. How much longer will the blanket chest be than the antique chest? How much wider will it be? How much taller will it be? Draw a diagram of the blanket chest showing the increase in each dimension.

   The new chest will be 4 in. longer, wider, and taller than the antique chest.

2. If two solids are similar, what must be true about their corresponding dimensions?

   Each pair of corresponding dimensions must satisfy the same ratio.

Planning the Solution

3. Practice explaining your reasoning. Imagine a chest has dimensions 3 ft-by-3 ft-by-3 ft. Add 4 in. to each dimension. Is the new chest similar to the old chest? Explain.

   Yes; the ratios between each pair of corresponding dimensions are equal.

4. Practice explaining your reasoning. Suppose a chest has dimensions 4 ft-by-3 ft-by-3 ft. Add 4 in. to each dimension. Is the new chest similar to the old chest? Explain.

   No; the new chest is not similar because the ratios between each pair of corresponding dimensions are not equal.

Getting an Answer

5. How can you generalize the dimensions of the old chest?

   Sample: The dimensions can be represented by the variables ℓ, w, and h.

6. Using the dimensions of the chest, determine whether the new chest and the old chest will be similar.

   Unless $\ell = w = h$, then the ratios between each pair of corresponding dimensions will not be equal, and they will not be similar.

Name ______________________ Class ____________ Date ____________

11-7 Practice
Form K

Areas and Volumes of Similar Solids

Are the two figures similar? If so, give the scale factor of the first figure to the second figure.

1.

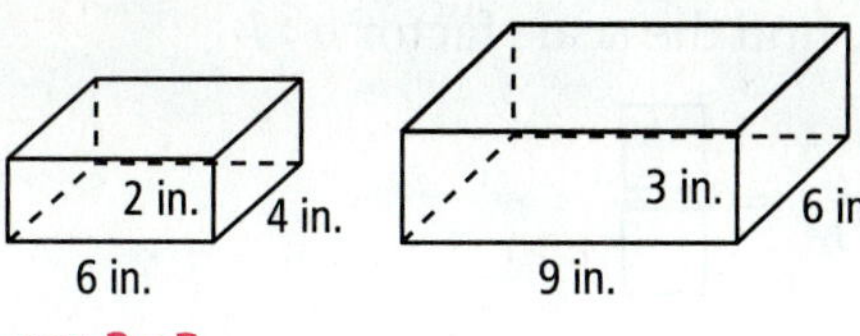

yes; 2 : 3

2.

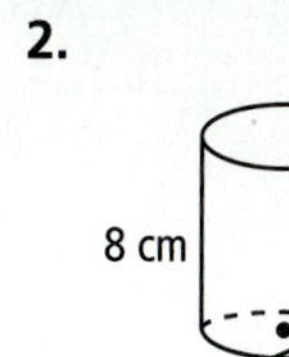

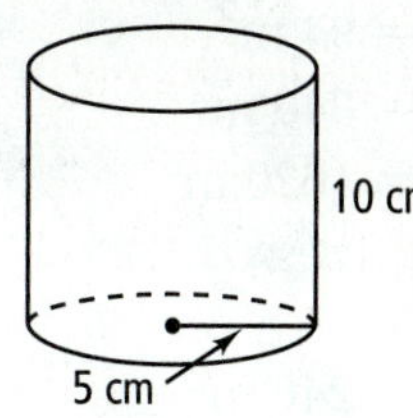

yes; 4 : 5

3.

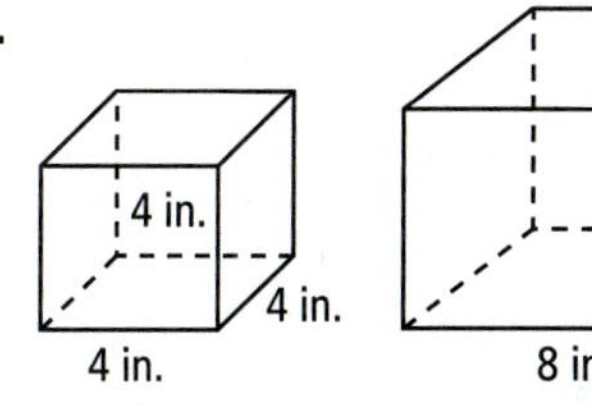

no

4.

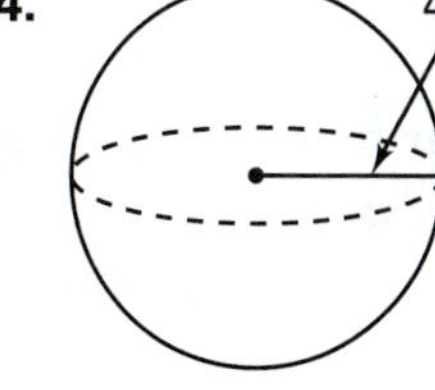

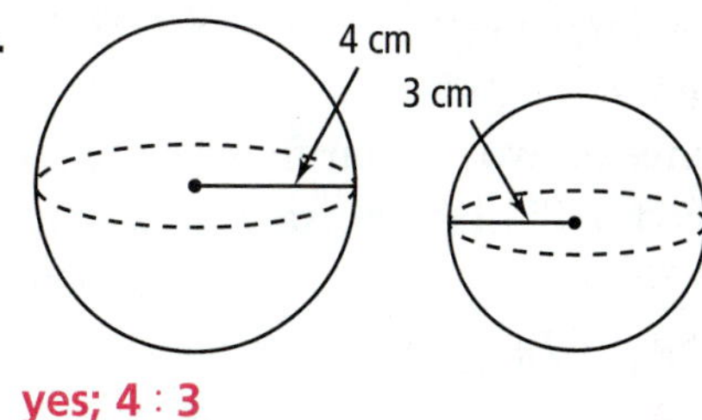

yes; 4 : 3

5. two cubes, one with 6-in. edges, the other with 8-in. edges yes; 3 : 4

6. a cylinder and a cone, each with 9-m radii and 5-m heights no

Each pair of figures is similar. Use the given information to find the scale factor of the smaller figure to the larger figure.

7.

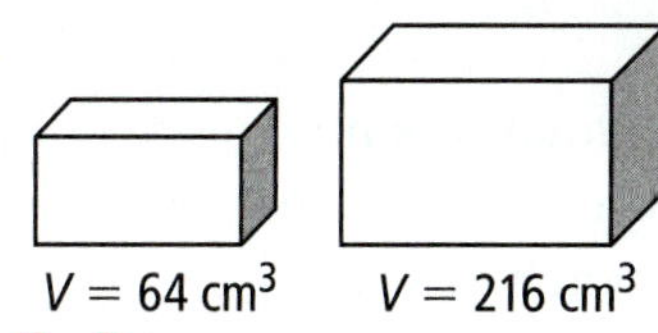

$V = 64\text{ cm}^3$ $V = 216\text{ cm}^3$

2 : 3

To start, write a proportion using the ratio of the volumes of the solids.

$$\frac{a^3}{b^3} = \frac{64}{216}$$

8.

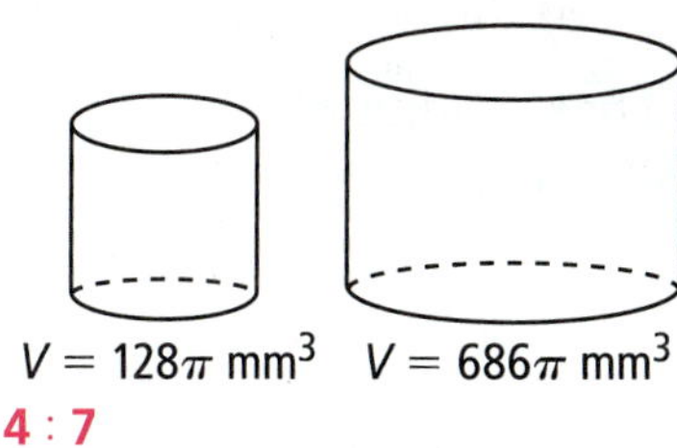

$V = 128\pi\text{ mm}^3$ $V = 686\pi\text{ mm}^3$

4 : 7

9.

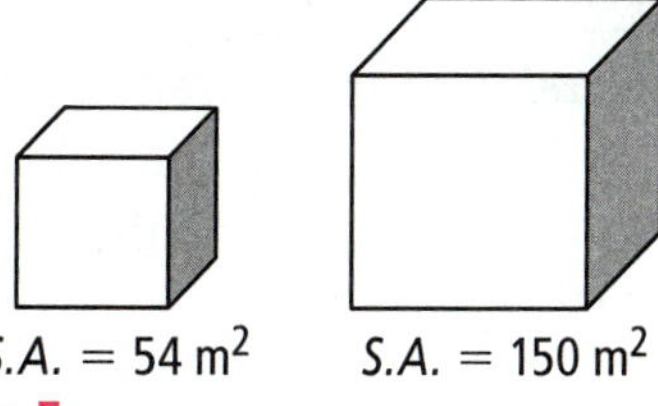

$S.A. = 54\text{ m}^2$ $S.A. = 150\text{ m}^2$

3 : 5

10. Two similar cones have heights 4 m and 12 m.

a. What is their scale factor? 1 : 3

b. What is the ratio of their surface areas? 1 : 9

c. What is the ratio of their volumes? 1 : 27

11. A shipping box holds 450 golf balls. A larger shipping box has dimensions triple the size of the other box. How many golf balls does the larger box hold? 12,150 balls

11-7 Practice (continued) Form K

Areas and Volumes of Similar Solids

The surface areas of two similar figures are given. The volume of the larger figure is given. Find the volume of the smaller figure.

12. S.A. = 94 m^2
S.A. = 846 m^2
V = 1620 m^3
60 m^3

To start, find the scale factor $a : b$.

$\frac{a^2}{b^2} = \frac{\square}{\square}$ 94 / 846

13. S.A. = 240 m^2
S.A. = 1500 m^2
V = 1562.5 m^3
100 m^3

14. S.A. = 96 $in.^2$
S.A. = 216 $in.^2$
V = 216 $in.^3$
64 $in.^3$

The volumes of two similar figures are given. The surface area of the larger figure is given. Find the surface area of the smaller figure.

15. V = 384 m^3
V = 10,368 m^3
S.A. = 3168 m^2 352 m^2

16. V = 216 $in.^3$
V = 1728 $in.^3$
S.A. = 864 $in.^2$ 216 $in.^2$

17. A cylindrical thermos has a radius of 3 in. and is 12 in. high. It holds 20 fl oz. To the nearest ounce, how many ounces will a similar thermos with a radius of 4 in. hold? 47 fl oz

18. You have a set of three similar gift boxes. Each box is a rectangular prism. The large box has 15-cm base edges. The medium box has 10-cm base edges. The small box has 5-cm base edges. How does the volume of each box compare to every other box? The ratio of the volume of the large box to that of the medium box is 27 : 8; the ratio of the volume of the large box to that of the small box is 27 : 1; the ratio of the volume of the medium box to that of the small box is 8 : 1.

19. A baseball and a softball are similar in shape. The baseball has a radius of 1.25 in. and a volume of 8.18 $in.^3$. If the volume of a softball is 65.44 $in.^3$, what is the radius of the softball? 2.5 in.

20. Error Analysis A classmate says that a rectangular prism that is 9 cm long, 12 cm wide, and 15 cm high is similar to a rectangular prism that is 12 cm long, 16 cm wide, and 21 cm high. Explain your classmate's error. The ratios of the dimensions are not the same. The ratio of the lengths is 3 : 4, the ratio of the widths is 3 : 4, but the ratio of the heights is 5 : 7.

21. The volumes of two similar prisms are 512 ft^3 and 8000 ft^3.

a. Find the ratio of their heights. 2 : 5

b. Find the ratio of the area of their bases. 4 : 25

Name ______________________ Class ____________ Date ____________

11-7 Standardized Test Prep

Areas and Volumes of Similar Solids

Multiple Choice

For Exercises 1–5, choose the correct letter.

1. Which of the figures shown below are similar? D

A 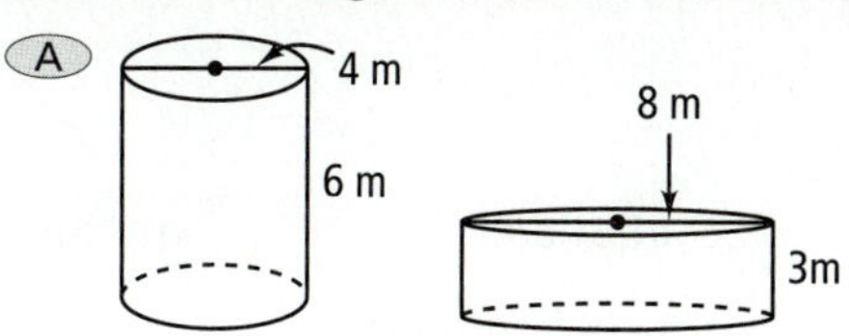

C 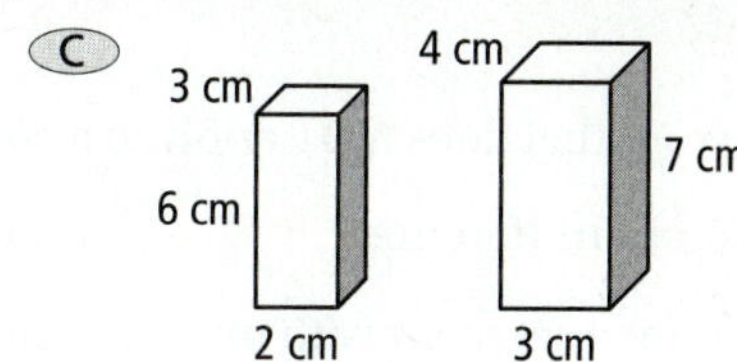

B 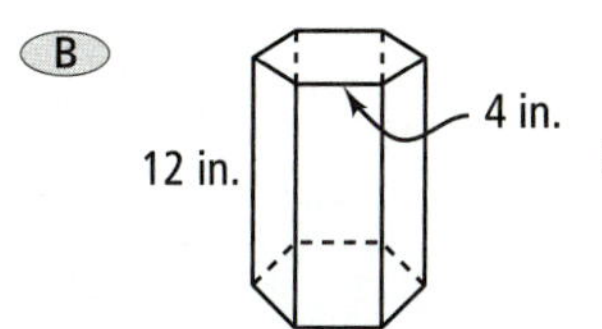

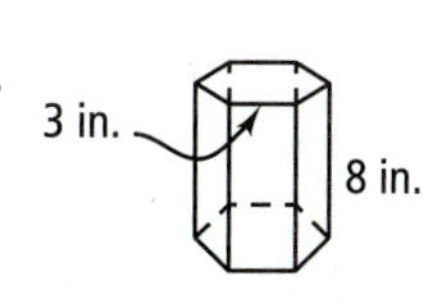

D 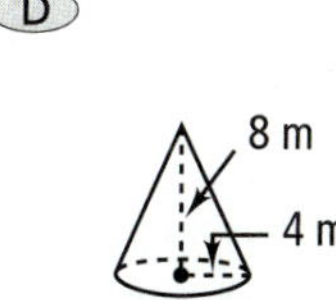

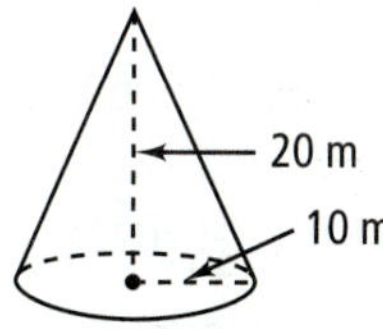

2. The measure of the side of a cube is 6 ft. The measure of the side of a second cube is 18 ft. What is the scale factor of the cubes? G

F 1 : 2 G 1 : 3 H 1 : 9 I 1 : 27

3. What is the ratio of the surface areas of the similar square pyramids at the right? C

A 4 : 5 C 16 : 25

B 8 : 10 D 64 : 125

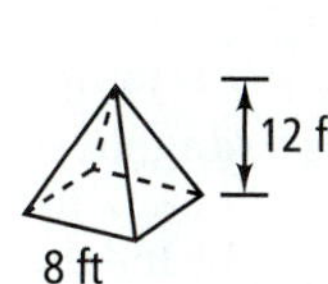

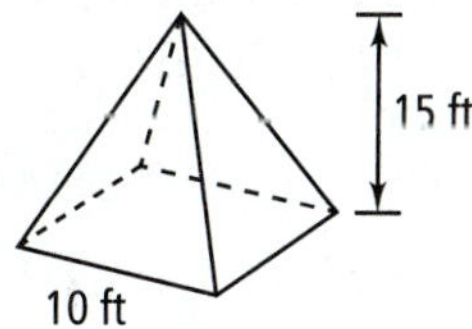

4. What is the ratio of the volumes of the similar square pyramids above? I

F 4 : 5 G 8 : 10 H 16 : 25 I 64 : 125

5. The surface areas of two similar triangular prisms are 132 m^2 and 297 m^2. The volume of the smaller prism is 264 m^3. What is the volume of the larger prism? B

A 594 m^3 B 891 m^3 C 1336.5 m^3 D 3007.125 m^3

Short Response

6. A medium-sized box can hold 55 T-shirts. If the dimensions of a jumbo box are three times that of the medium box, how many T-shirts can the jumbo box hold? Explain. [2] 1485 T-shirts; if the dimensions of the jumbo box are three times those of the medium box, the scale factor is 1 : 3. The ratio of the volumes is $1^3 : 3^3$, or 1 : 27. Set up a proportion to solve: $\frac{1}{27} = \frac{55}{x}$; $x = 27 \cdot 55 = 1485$. [1] error in calculation, or work not shown [0] incorrect or no response

12-1 PART 1 Tangent Lines

Vocabulary

Review

1. Cross out the word that does NOT apply to a *circle*.

arc	circumference	diameter	~~equilateral~~	radius

2. Circle the word for a segment with one endpoint at the center of a *circle* and the other endpoint on the *circle*.

arc	circumference	diameter	perimeter	(radius)

Vocabulary Builder

tangent (noun, adjective) TAN junt

Other Word Form: tangency (noun)

Definition: A **tangent** to a circle is a line, ray, or segment in the plane of the circle that intersects the circle in exactly one point.

tangent

A

B

Examples: In the diagram, $\overleftrightarrow{AB}$ is **tangent** to the circle at *B*. *B* is the *point of tangency*. $\overrightarrow{BA}$ is a **tangent** ray. $\overline{BA}$ is a **tangent** segment.

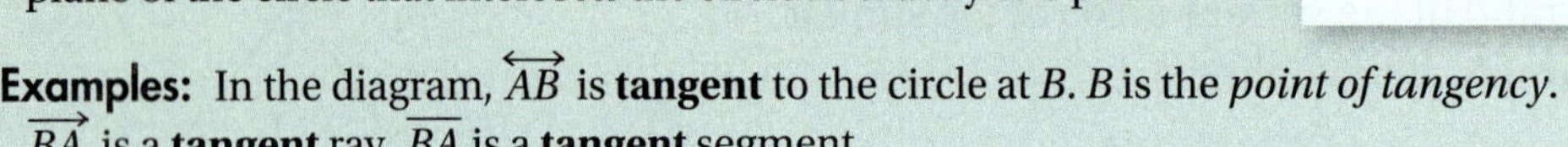

Other Usage: In a right triangle, the **tangent** is the ratio of the side opposite an acute angle to the side adjacent to the angle.

Use Your Vocabulary

3. Complete each statement with *always, sometimes,* or *never.*

A diameter is __?__ a *tangent.* never

A *tangent* and a circle __?__ have exactly one point in common. always

A radius can __?__ be drawn to the point of tangency. always

A *tangent* __?__ passes through the center of a circle. never

A *tangent* is __?__ a ray. sometimes

take note

Theorem 12-1

Theorem 12-1 If a line is tangent to a circle, then the line is perpendicular to the radius at the point of tangency.

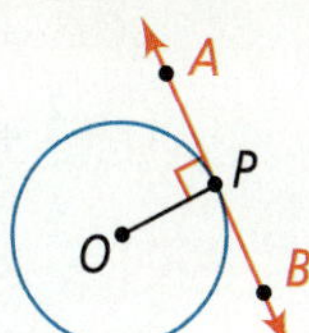

Use the diagram at the right.

4. If $\overleftrightarrow{AB}$ is tangent to $\odot O$ at P, then $\overleftrightarrow{AB}$ ⊥ $\overline{OP}$.

Problem 1 Finding Angle Measures

Got It? $\overline{ED}$ **is tangent to** $\odot O$**. What is the value of** x**?**

D
E
$x°$
O
38°

5. Circle the word that best describes $\overline{OD}$.

diameter — **radius** (circled) — tangent

6. What relationship does Theorem 12-1 support? Circle your answer.

$\overline{OD} \perp \overline{ED}$ (circled) — $\overline{OD} \parallel \overline{ED}$ — $\overline{OD} \cong \overline{ED}$

7. Circle the most accurate description of the triangle.

acute — isosceles — obtuse — **right** (circled)

8. Circle the theorem that you will use to solve for x.

Theorem 12-1 — **Triangle Angle-Sum Theorem** (circled)

9. Complete the model below.

Relate	sum of angle measures in a triangle	is	38	plus	measure of ∠D	plus	measure of ∠E
Write	180	=	38	+	90	+	x

10. Solve for x.

$180 = 38 + 90 + x$

$52 = x$

11. The value of x is 52 .

Problem 2 Finding Distance

Got It? What is the distance to the horizon a person can see on a clear day from an airplane 2 mi above Earth? Earth's radius is about 4000 mi.

12. The diagram at the right shows the airplane at point A and the horizon at point H. Use the information in the problem to label the distances.

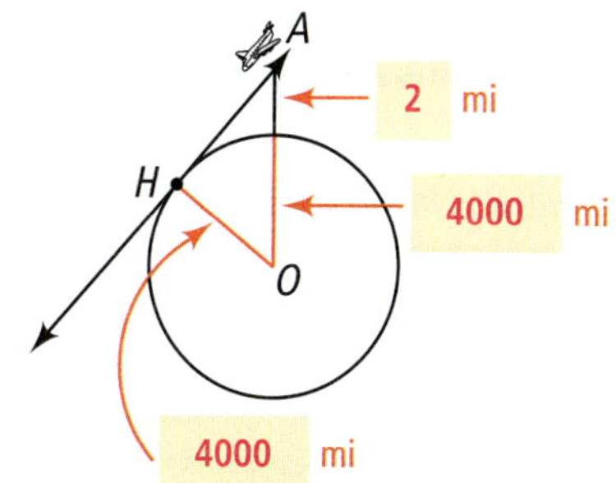

13. Use the justifications at the right to find the distance.

$\overline{OH} \perp \overline{AH}$	Theorem 12-1
$OH^2 + AH^2 = OA^2$	Pythagorean Theorem
$4000^2 + AH^2 = 4002^2$	Substitute.
$16{,}000{,}000 + AH^2 = 16{,}016{,}004$	Use a calculator.
$AH^2 = 16{,}004$	Subtract from each side.
$AH = \sqrt{16{,}004}$	Take the positive square root.
$AH \approx 126.5069168$	Use a calculator.

14. A person can see about 127 miles to the horizon from an airplane 2 mi above Earth.

Problem 3 Finding a Radius

Got It? What is the radius of $\odot O$?

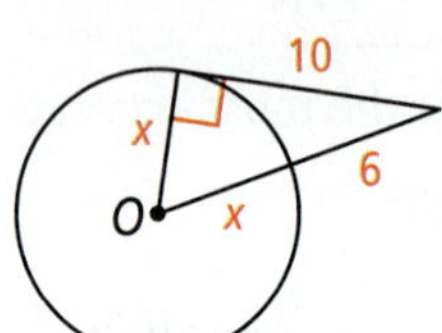

15. Write an algebraic or numerical expression for each side of the triangle.

x 10 $x + 6$

16. Use the Pythagorean Theorem to complete the equation.

$x^2 + 10^2 = (x + 6)^2$

17. Solve the equation for x.

$$x^2 + 10^2 = (x + 6)^2$$
$$x^2 + 100 = x^2 + 12x + 36$$
$$100 = 12x + 36$$
$$64 = 12x$$
$$5\tfrac{1}{3} = x$$

18. The radius is $5\frac{1}{3}$.

Lesson Check • Do you UNDERSTAND?

Error Analysis **A classmate is convinced that the length of the radius of $\odot C$ is 3. Explain how to show that your classmate has made a mistake.**

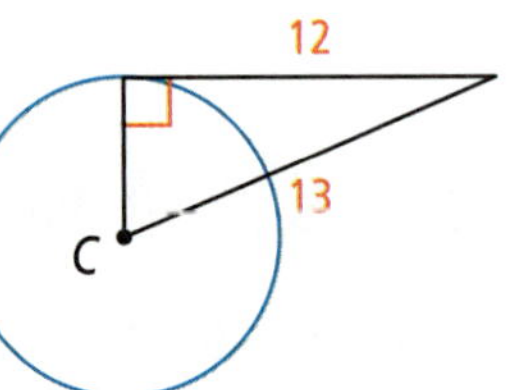

19. Is the radius *the hypotenuse* or *a leg* of the triangle? a leg

20. Circle the inequality that would show the mistake.

$3^2 + 12^2 \neq 13^2$ (circled) $3^2 + 13^2 \neq 12^2$ $12^2 + 13^2 \neq 3^2$

Tangent Lines

Vocabulary

Review

Use the triangle at the right for Exercises 1 and 2.

1. Circle the *congruent* segments in $\triangle RST$.

$\overline{RT}$

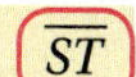

2. Circle the *congruent* angles in $\triangle RST$.

$\angle S$

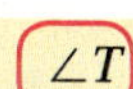

S R T

Write T for *true* or F for *false*.

T 3. Segments that are *congruent* have the same length.

T 4. Angles that are *congruent* have the same measure.

F 5. Polygons that are *congruent* have the same shape, but a different size.

Vocabulary Builder

horizon (noun) **huh** RY **zun**

Other Word Form: horizontal (adjective)

Definition: The **horizon** is the line at which Earth and the sky appear to meet.

Word Origin: **Horizon** comes from the Greek word *horos,* which means "boundary."

Use Your Vocabulary

Underline the correct word to complete each sentence.

6. You watched the sun set over the *horizon* / *horizontal*.

7. *Horizontal* lines are parallel / perpendicular to the *horizon*.

8. Circle the *horizontal* line(s).

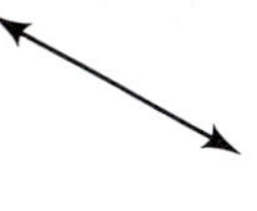

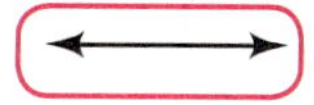

take note

Theorems 12-2 and 12-3

Theorem 12-2 If a line in the plane of a circle is perpendicular to a radius at its endpoint on the circle, then the line is tangent to the circle.

Theorem 12-3 If two tangent segments to a circle share a common endpoint outside the circle, then the two segments are congruent.

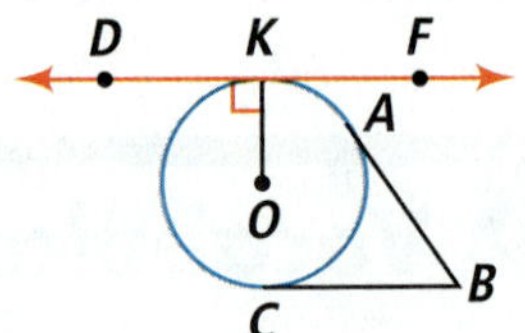

Use the diagram at the right. Complete each statement.

9. If $\overleftrightarrow{DF} \perp \overline{OK}$ at K, then $\overleftrightarrow{DF}$ is tangent to $\odot O$.

10. If $\overline{BA}$ and $\overline{BC}$ are tangent to $\odot O$, then $\overline{BA} \cong \overline{BC}$.

Problem 4 Identifying a Tangent

Got It? **Is $\overline{ML}$ tangent to $\odot N$ at L? Explain.**

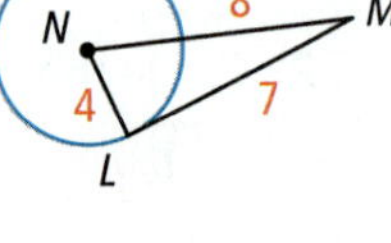

11. Use the Pythagorean Theorem to determine whether $\triangle LMN$ is a right triangle.

$4^2 + 7^2 \stackrel{?}{=} 8^2$

$16 + 49 \stackrel{?}{=} 64$

$65 \neq 64$

12. Is $\triangle LMN$ a right triangle?

Yes / No (circled: No)

13. Is $\overline{ML} \perp \overline{NL}$?

Yes / No (circled: No)

14. Underline the correct words to complete the sentence.

$\overline{ML}$ is / <u>is not</u> tangent to $\odot N$ at L because $\overline{ML}$ is / <u>is not</u> perpendicular to $\overline{NL}$.

Problem 5 Circles Inscribed in Polygons

Got It? **$\odot O$ is inscribed in $\triangle PQR$, which has a perimeter of 88 cm. What is the length of $\overline{QY}$?**

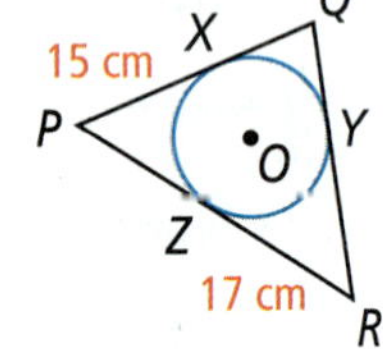

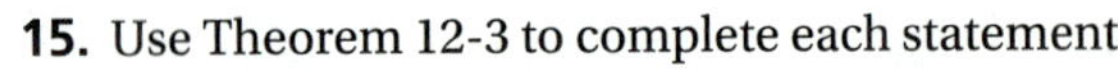

15. Use Theorem 12-3 to complete each statement.

$PX = PZ =$ 15 cm $\qquad RZ =$ RY $=$ 17 cm $\qquad QX =$ QY

16. The length of $\overline{QY}$ is found below. Justify each step.

$p = PQ + QR + RP$	definition of perimeter
$p = PX + QX + QY + RY + RZ + PZ$	Segment Addition Postulate
$88 = 15 + QY + QY + 17 + 17 + 15$	Substitute.
$88 = 64 + 2QY$	Simplify.
$24 = 2QY$	Subtract 64 from each side.
$12 = QY$	Divide each side by 2.

Lesson Check • Do you know HOW?

$\odot B$ is inscribed in $\triangle XYZ$. What is the perimeter of $\triangle XYZ$?

17. $YD = YE =$ 3 in.

18. $ZC = ZE =$ 13 in.

19. $XD =$ XC $=$ 2 in.

20. Find the perimeter of $\triangle XYZ$.

$P = 3 + 13 + 13 + 2 + 2 + 3$

$= 36$

21. The perimeter of $\triangle XYZ$ is 36 in.

Lesson Check • Do you UNDERSTAND?

Error Analysis **A classmate insists that $\overline{DF}$ is a tangent to $\odot E$. Explain how to show that your classmate is wrong.**

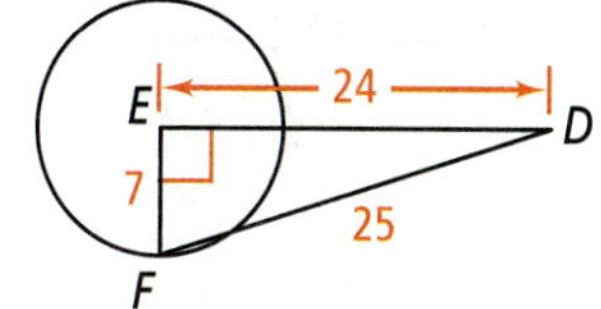

Underline the correct word or number to complete the sentence.

22. A tangent to a circle is parallel / perpendicular to a radius.

23. If $\overline{DF}$ is tangent to $\odot E$ at point F, then $m\angle EFD$ must be 30 / 90 / 180 .

24. A triangle can have at most 1 right angle(s).

25. Explain why your classmate is wrong.

Answers may vary. Sample: A triangle cannot have two right angles, so the segment is not a tangent.

Math Success

Check off the vocabulary words that you understand.

- ☐ circle
- ☐ tangent to a circle
- ☐ point of tangency

Rate how well you can *use tangents to find missing lengths.*

Need to review | 0 | 2 | 4 | 6 | 8 | 10 | Now I get it!

Name ______________________ Class ____________ Date ____________

12-1 Think About a Plan

Tangent Lines

a. A belt fits snugly around the two circular pulleys. $\overline{CE}$ is an auxiliary line from E to $\overline{BD}$. $\overline{CE} \parallel \overline{AB}$. What type of quadrilateral is $ABCE$? Explain.

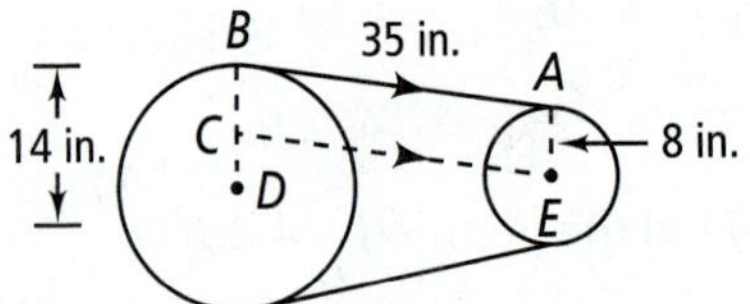

b. What is the length of $\overline{CE}$?

c. What is the distance between the centers of the pulleys to the nearest tenth?

1. What is the definition of a tangent line? a line that touches a circle at only one point

2. What is the relationship between a line tangent to a circle and the radius at the point of tangency (Theorem 12-1)? They are perpendicular.

3. Where is the point of tangency for $\overline{AB}$ on $\odot D$? On $\odot E$? B; A

4. What is the measure of $\angle CBA$? What is the measure of $\angle BAE$? Explain.

90°; 90°; they are formed by perpendicular line segments.

5. How can you use parallel lines to find the measure of $\angle CEA$?

Because $\overline{CE} \parallel \overline{AB}$, $\angle BAE$ and $\angle CEA$ are supplementary angles, so $m\angle CEA = 90°$.

6. How can you use parallel lines or the Polygon Angle-Sum Theorem to find the measure of $\angle BCE$?

Because $\overline{CE} \parallel \overline{AB}$, $\angle CBA$ and $\angle BCE$ are supplementary angles, so $m\angle BCE = 90°$. Or, $\angle BCE$ is the fourth angle in a quadrilateral in which the other angles sum to 270°, so its measure is 90°.

7. What type of quadrilateral has four right angles? a rectangle

8. What is the length of $\overline{BA}$? 35 in.

9. What is the length of $\overline{CE}$? 35 in.

10. What are the center points of the pulleys? D; E

11. How can you use the Segment Addition Postulate to find $\overline{CD}$?

$BD - BC = CD$, $BD = 14$ in., and $BC = 8$ in.

12. What is the measure of $\overline{CD}$? 6 in.

13. How can you use the Pythagorean Theorem to find the length of $\overline{DE}$?

$a^2 + b^2 = c^2$; if $CD = a$, $CE = b$, and $DE = c$, then $DE = \sqrt{(6^2) + (35^2)} = \sqrt{1261} \approx 35.5$ in.

Name ______________________ Class ____________ Date ____________

12-1 Practice

Form K

Tangent Lines

Lines that appear to be tangent are tangent. *O* is the center of each circle. What is the value of *x*?

1. 145

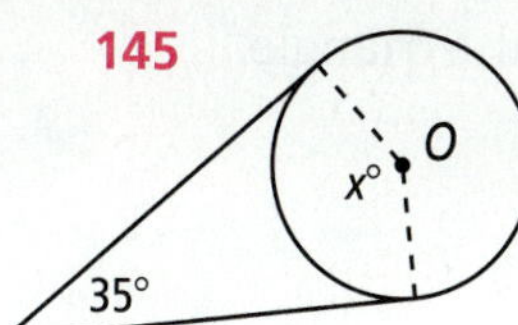

To start, identify the type of geometric figure formed by the tangent lines and radii.

The figure formed is a __?__. quadrilateral

2. 54

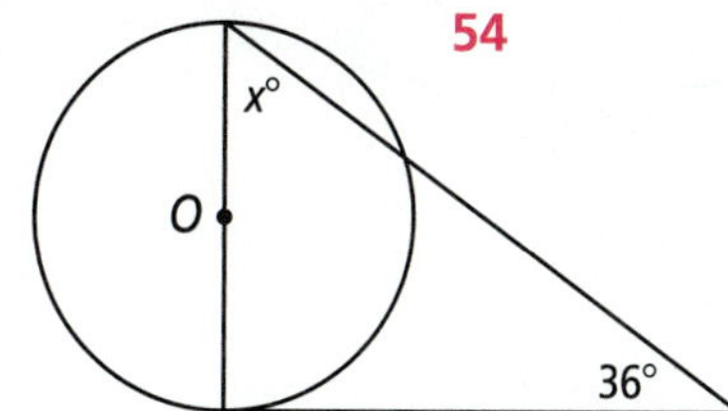

3. 16

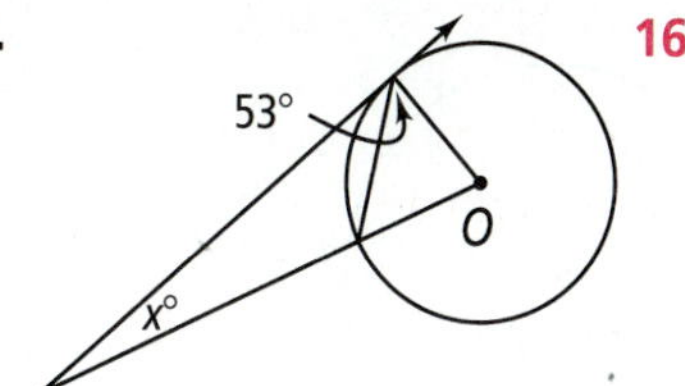

The circle at the right represents Earth. The radius of Earth is about 6400 km. Find the distance *d* to the horizon that a person can see on a clear day from each of the following heights *h* above Earth. Round your answer to the nearest tenth of a kilometer.

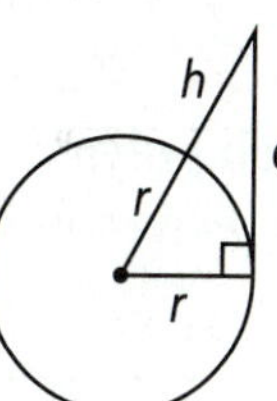

4. 7 km
299.4 km

5. 400 km
2297.8 km

6. 2000 m
160.0 km

Algebra **In each circle, what is the value of *x* to the nearest tenth?**

7. 6.8

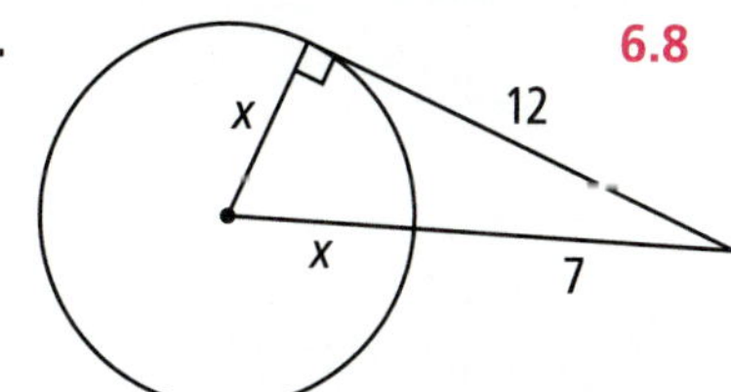

To start, use the Pythagorean Theorem.

$x^2 + 12^2 = (\underline{\ ?\ })^2$ $x + 7$

8. 3.9 in.

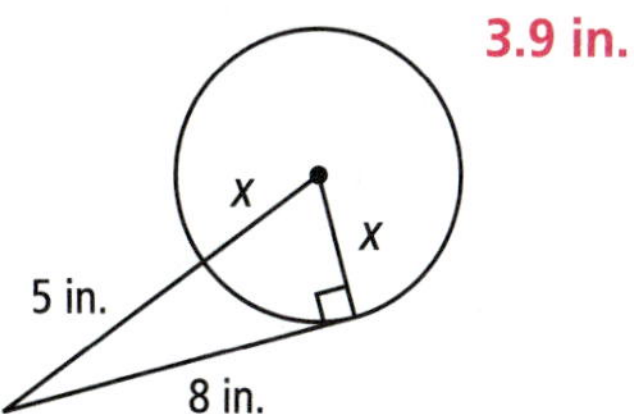

9. 9.7 m

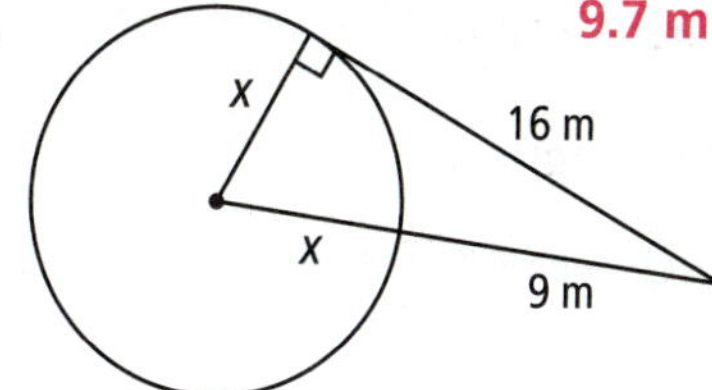

10. $\overline{QO}$ and $\overline{UR}$ are diameters of $\odot P$.
$\overline{RS}$ and $\overline{TS}$ are tangents of $\odot P$.
Find $m\angle UPT$ and $m\angle UQP$. 32; 53

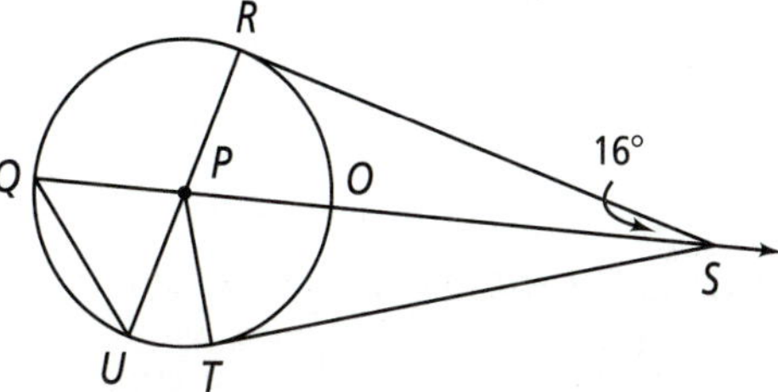

Name ______________________ Class ____________ Date ____________

12-1 Practice (continued) Form K

Tangent Lines

Determine whether a tangent is shown in each diagram. Explain.

11. 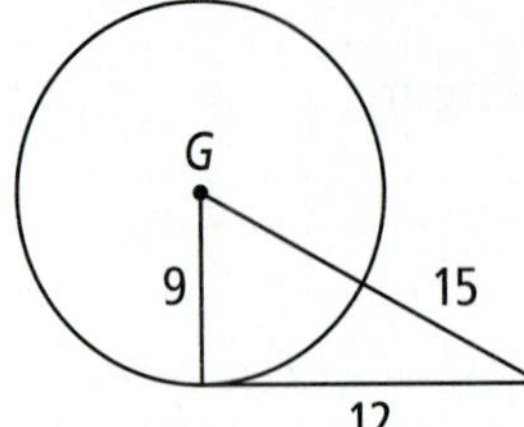

To start, use the Converse of the Pythagorean Theorem to relate the side lengths of the triangle.

$9^2 + 12^2 \stackrel{?}{=} \underline{\ ?\ }^2$ 15

yes; 81 + 144 = 225

12. 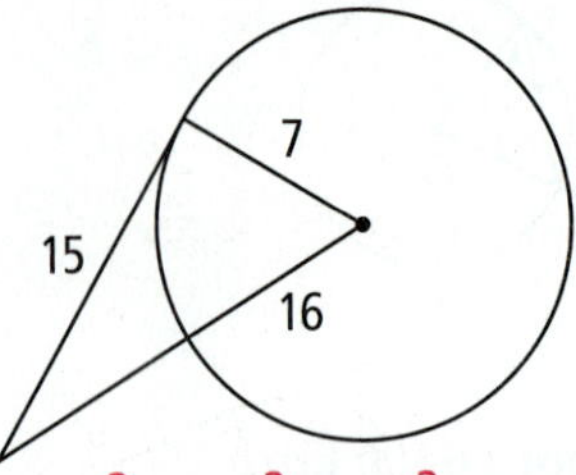

no; $7^2 + 15^2 \neq 16^2$

13. 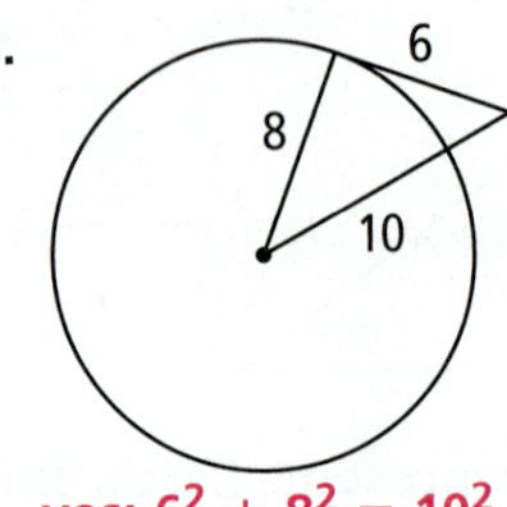

yes; $6^2 + 8^2 = 10^2$

Each polygon circumscribes a circle. What is the perimeter of each polygon?

14. 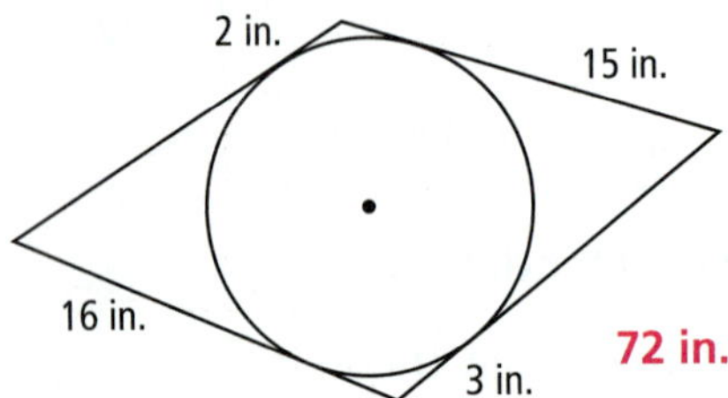

72 in.

To start, find the length of each unknown segment.

$P = 2 + \boxed{2} + 15 + \boxed{15}$

$+ 3 + \boxed{3} + 16 + \boxed{16}$

15. 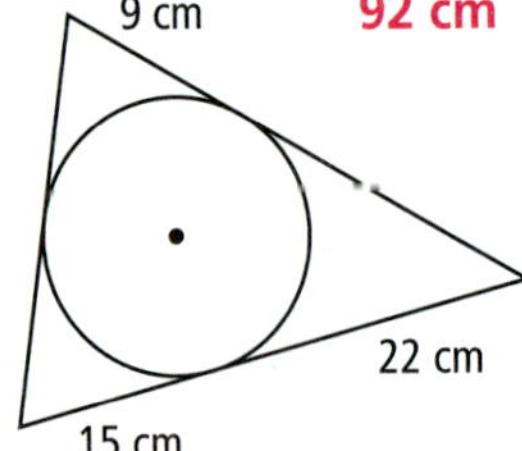

92 cm

16. 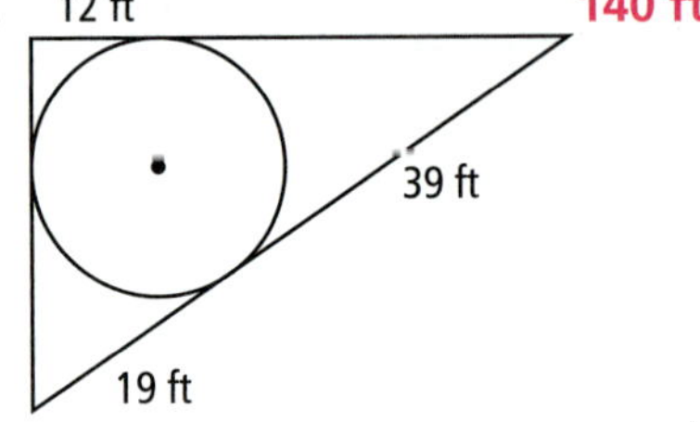

140 ft

17. $\odot B$ is inscribed in a triangle, which has a perimeter of 76 in. What is the value of x? 8 in.

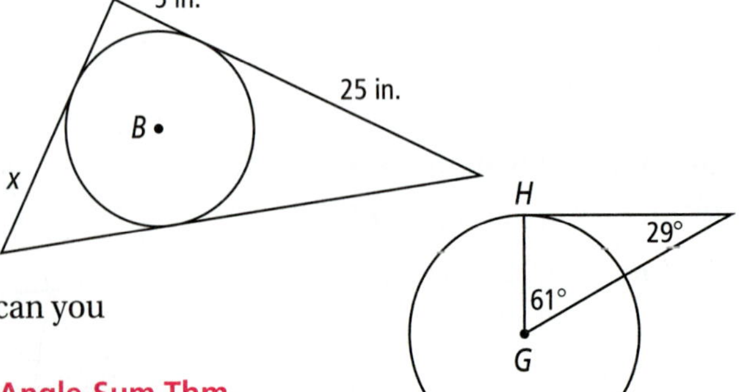

18. Reasoning GHI is a triangle. How can you prove that $\overline{HI}$ is tangent to $\odot G$?

$m\angle G + m\angle I = 90$. By the Triangle Angle-Sum Thm., $m\angle H = 90$, so $\overline{HI}$ is tangent to $\odot G$ by Thm. 12-2.

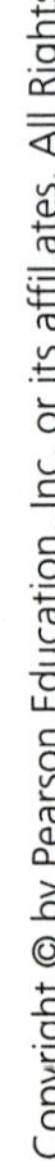

Name ______________________ Class ____________ Date ____________

12-1 Standardized Test Prep

Tangent Lines

Multiple Choice

For Exercises 1–5, choose the correct letter.

1. $\overline{AB}$ and $\overline{BC}$ are tangents to $\odot P$. What is the value of x? **B**

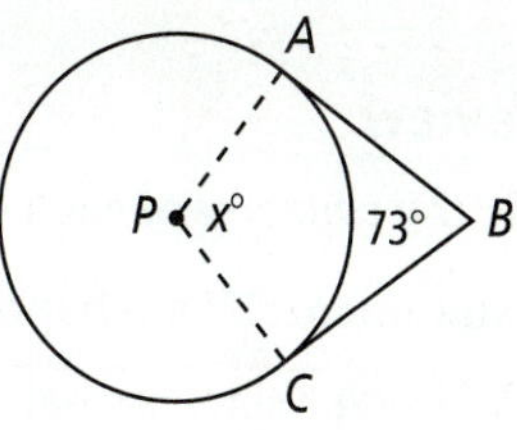

Ⓐ 73 Ⓒ 117

Ⓑ 107 Ⓓ 146

2. Earth's radius is about 4000 mi. To the nearest mile, what is the distance a person can see on a clear day from an airplane 5 mi above Earth? **G**

Ⓕ 63 mi Ⓖ 200 mi Ⓗ 4000 mi Ⓘ 5660 mi

3. $\overline{YZ}$ is a tangent to $\odot X$, and X is the center of the circle. What is the length of the radius of the circle? **B**

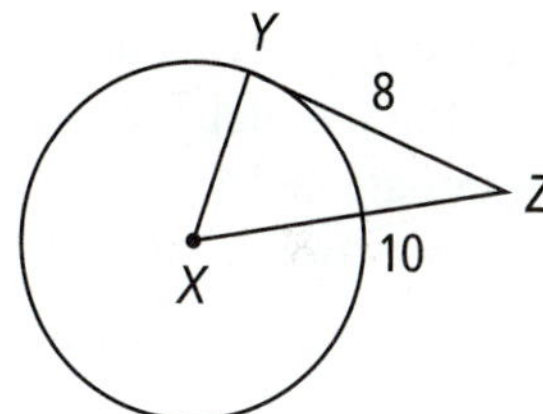

Ⓐ 4 Ⓒ 12

Ⓑ 6 Ⓓ 12.8

4. The radius of $\odot G$ is 4 cm. Which is a tangent of $\odot G$? **I**

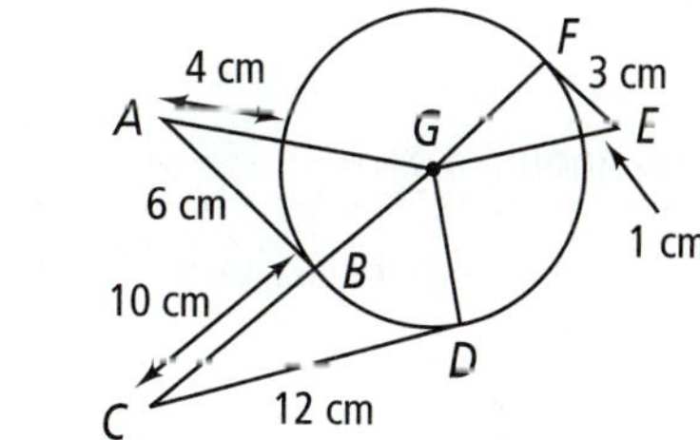

Ⓕ $\overline{AB}$ Ⓗ $\overline{BF}$

Ⓖ $\overline{CD}$ Ⓘ $\overline{FE}$

5. $\odot A$ is inscribed in a quadrilateral. What is the perimeter of the quadrilateral? **B**

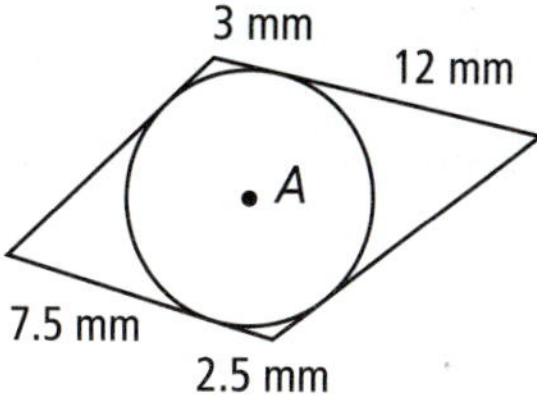

Ⓐ 25 mm Ⓒ 60 mm

Ⓑ 50 mm Ⓓ 150 mm

Short Response

6. **Given:** $\overline{GI}$ is a tangent to $\odot J$.

Prove: $\triangle FGH \cong \triangle FIH$ **[2] Statements: 1) $\overline{GI}$ is a tangent to $\odot J$; 2) $\overline{FH} \perp \overline{GI}$; 3) $\angle FHG$ and $\angle FHI$ are right ∠s; 4) $\angle FHG \cong \angle FHI$; 5) $\overline{FH} \cong \overline{FH}$; 6) $m\angle GFH = 42$, $m\angle FIH = 48$; 7) $m\angle HFI = 42$; 8) $\angle HFI \cong \angle HFG$; 9) $\triangle FGH \cong \triangle FIH$; Reasons: 1) Given; 2) Thm. 12-1; 3) Def. of ⊥; 4) Def. of ≅; 5) Refl. Prop.; 6) Given; 7) Triangle Angle-Sum Thm.; 8) Def. of ≅; 9) ASA Post. [1] proof missing steps [0] incorrect or missing proof**

42° F, J, 48°, G, H, I

12-2 PART 1 Chords and Arcs

Vocabulary

Review

Circle the *converse* of each statement.

1. **Statement:** If I am happy, then I sing.

If I sing, then I am happy. | If I am not happy, then I do not sing. | If I do not sing, then I am not happy.

2. **Statement:** If parallel lines are cut by a transversal, then alternate interior angles are congruent.

If lines cut by a transversal are not parallel, then alternate interior angles are not congruent.	If lines cut by a transversal form alternate interior angles that are not congruent, then the lines are not parallel.	If lines cut by a transversal form alternate interior angles that are congruent, then the lines are parallel.

Vocabulary Builder

chord (noun) kawrd

Definition: A **chord** is a segment whose endpoints are on a circle.

Related Word: arc

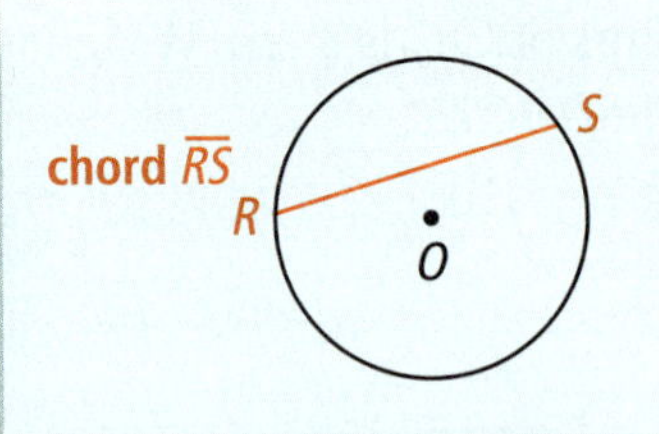

Use Your Vocabulary

3. Complete each statement with *always*, *sometimes*, or *never*.

A *chord* is _?_ a diameter. sometimes

A diameter is _?_ a *chord*. always

A radius is _?_ a *chord*. never

A *chord* _?_ has a related arc. always

An arc is _?_ a semicircle. sometimes

take note

Theorems 12-4, 12-5, 12-6 and Their Converses

Theorem 12-4 Within a circle or in congruent circles, congruent central angles have congruent arcs.

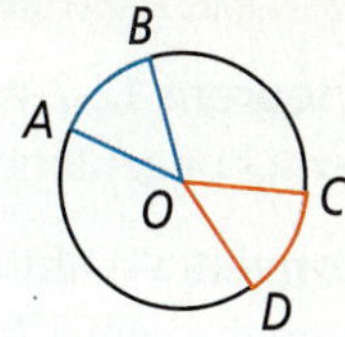

4. If $\angle AOB \cong$ **$\angle COD$**, then $\overset{\frown}{AB} \cong \overset{\frown}{CD}$.

Converse Within a circle or in congruent circles, congruent arcs have congruent central angles.

5. If $\overset{\frown}{AB} \cong \overset{\frown}{CD}$, then $\angle AOB \cong$ **$\angle COD$**.

Theorem 12-5 Within a circle or in congruent circles, congruent central angles have congruent chords.

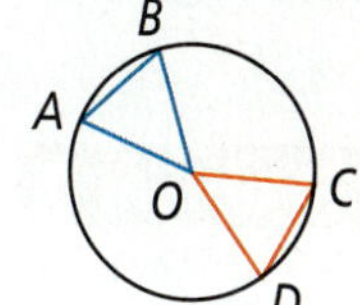

6. If $\angle AOB \cong \angle COD$, then $\overline{AB} \cong$ **$\overline{CD}$**.

Converse Within a circle or in congruent circles, congruent chords have congruent central angles.

7. If $\overline{AB} \cong \overline{CD}$, then **$\angle AOB$** $\cong \angle COD$.

Theorem 12-6 Within a circle or in congruent circles, congruent chords have congruent arcs.

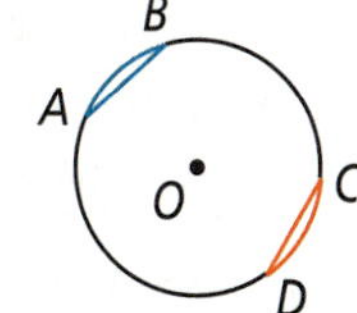

8. If $\overline{AB} \cong$ **$\overline{CD}$**, then $\overset{\frown}{AB} \cong \overset{\frown}{CD}$.

Converse Within a circle or in congruent circles, congruent arcs have congruent chords.

9. If $\overset{\frown}{AB} \cong$ **$\overset{\frown}{CD}$**, then $\overline{AB} \cong \overline{CD}$.

Problem 1 Using Congruent Chords

Got It? **Use the diagram at the right. Suppose you are given $\odot O \cong \odot P$ and $\angle OBC \cong \angle PDF$. How can you show $\angle O \cong \angle P$? From this, what else can you conclude?**

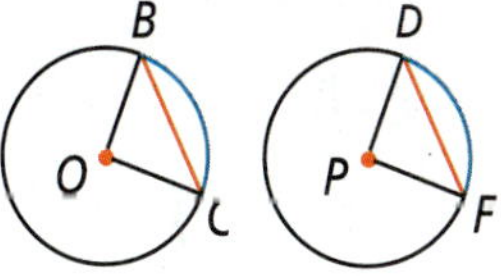

10. Complete the flow chart below to explain your conclusions.

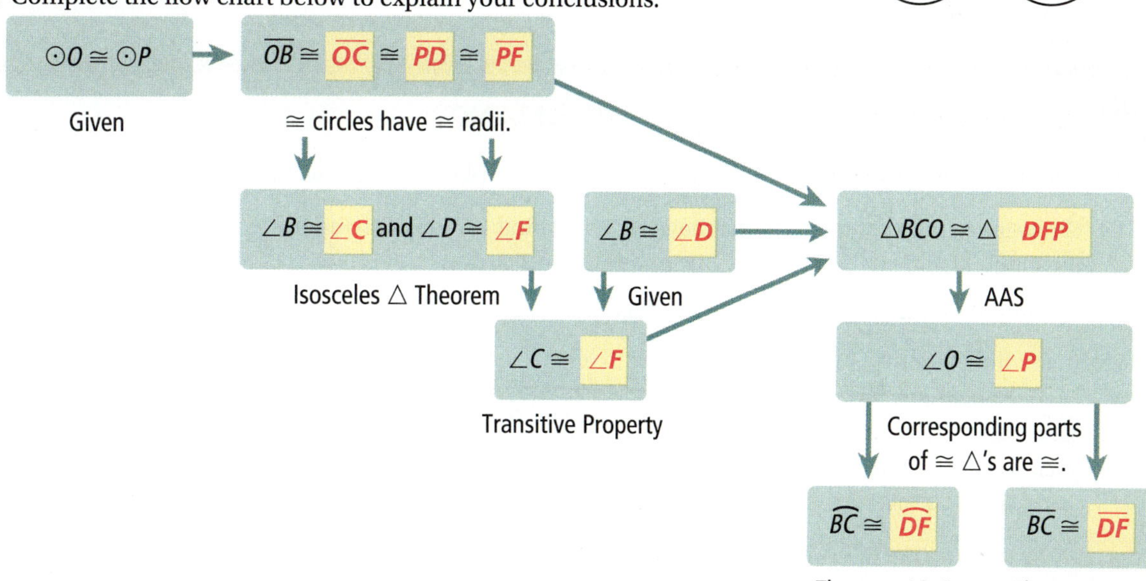

Take note: Theorem 12-7 and Its Converse

Theorem 12-7 Within a circle or in congruent circles, chords equidistant from the center or centers are congruent.

Converse Within a circle or in congruent circles, congruent chords are equidistant from the center (or centers).

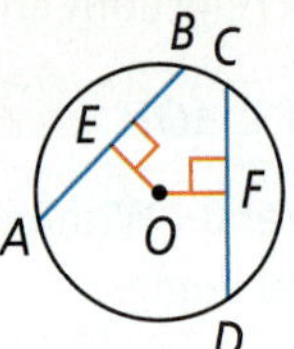

11. If $OE = OF$, then $\overline{AB} \cong$ CD. **12.** If $\overline{AB} \cong$ CD, then $OE =$ OF.

Problem 2 Finding the Length of a Chord

Got It? What is the value of x? Justify your answer.

13. What is the measure of each chord? Explain.

36. Explanations may vary. Sample: The length of one chord is 36 and the other chord has two segments with lengths 18, so, by the Segment Addition Postulate, it also has a length of 36.

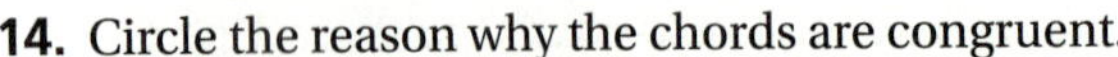

14. Circle the reason why the chords are congruent.

(Chords that have equal measures are congruent.) Chords that are equidistant from the center of a circle are congruent.

15. Circle the theorem that you will use to find the value of x.

Theorem 12-5 Theorem 12-7 (Converse of Theorem 12-7)

16. Circle the distances from the center of a circle to the chords.

(16) 18 36 (x)

17. The value of x is 16.

Lesson Check • Do you UNDERSTAND?

Vocabulary Is a radius a chord? Is a diameter a chord? Explain your answers.

18. Circle the name(s) of figure(s) that have two endpoints on a circle. Underline the name(s) of figure(s) that have one endpoint on a circle.

(chord) (diameter) <u>radius</u> ray segment

19. Is a radius a chord? Is a diameter a chord? Explain. Answers may vary. Sample:

A radius has only one endpoint on a circle, so it is not a chord.

A diameter has two endpoints on a circle, so it is a chord.

12-2 PART 2 Chords and Arcs

Vocabulary

Review

1. Describe what it means for two lines to be perpendicular.

Answers may vary. Sample: The lines intersect to form right, or 90°, angles.

2. Cross out the pairs(s) of lines that are NOT perpendicular.

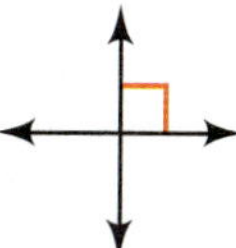
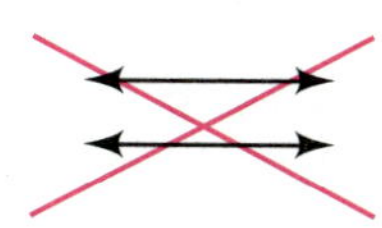
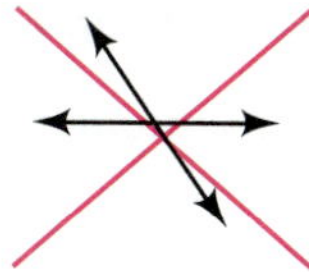

Vocabulary Builder

diameter (noun) dy AM ut ur

Related Word: radius

Definition: A **diameter** is a segment that passes through the center of a circle and has its endpoints on the circle.

Main Idea: In any circle, the length of a **diameter** is twice the length of a *radius.*

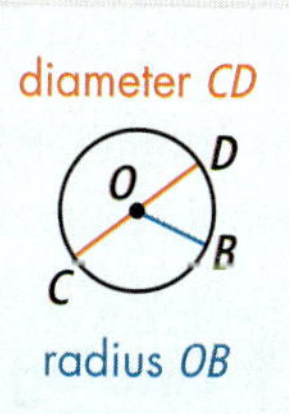

Use Your Vocabulary

Complete.

3. If the *diameter* of a circle is 6 in., then the *radius* is 3 in.

4. If the *radius* of a circle is 5.4 cm, then the *diameter* is 10.8 cm.

5. Circle the radii of $\odot P$. Underline the *diameters.*

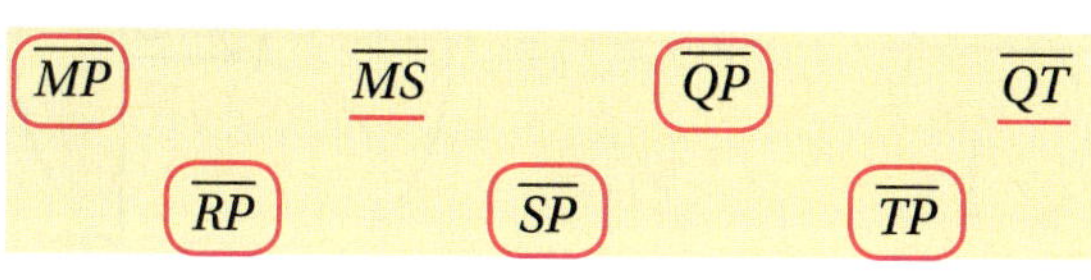

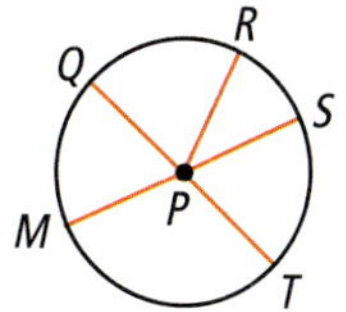

take note

Theorems 12-8, 12-9, and 12-10

Theorem 12-8 In a circle, if a diameter is perpendicular to a chord, then it bisects the chord and its arc.

6. If $\overline{AB}$ is a diameter and $\overline{AB} \perp \overline{CD}$, then $\overline{CE} \cong$ ED and $\overset{\frown}{CA} \cong$ AD.

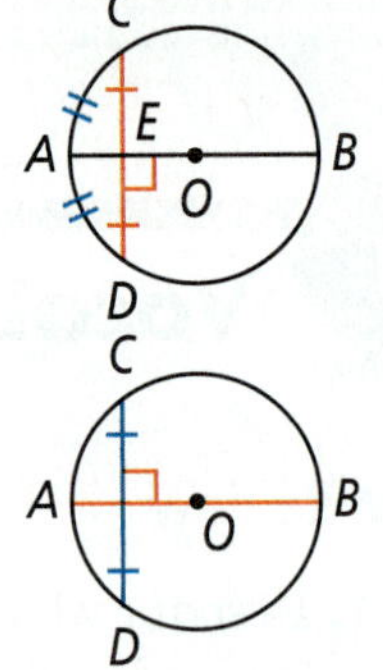

Theorem 12-9 In a circle, if a diameter bisects a chord (that is not a diameter), then it is perpendicular to the chord.

7. If $\overline{AB}$ is a diameter and $\overline{CE} \cong \overline{ED}$, then $\overline{AB} \perp$ CD.

Theorem 12-10 In a circle, the perpendicular bisector of a chord contains the center of the circle.

8. If $\overline{AB}$ is the perpendicular bisector of chord $\overline{CD}$, then AB contains the center of $\odot O$.

Problem 3 Using Diameters and Chords

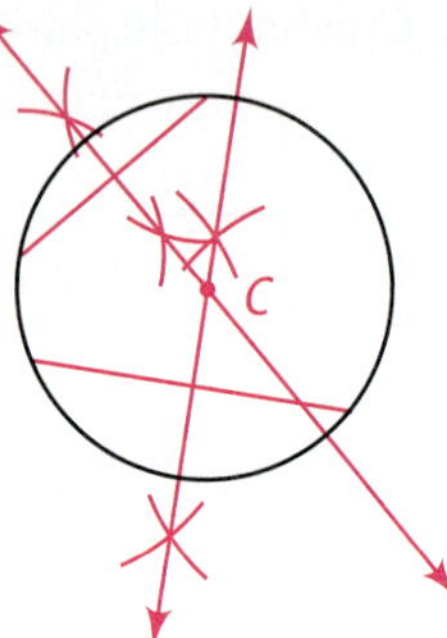

Got It? **The diagram shows the tracing of a quarter. What is its radius?**

Underline the correct word to complete each sentence. Then do each step.

9. First draw two chords / tangents.

10. Next construct one / two perpendicular bisector(s).

11. Label the intersection C. It is the circle's center / chord.

12. Measure the diameter / radius. **13.** The radius is about 12 mm.

Problem 4 Finding Measures in a Circle

Got It? **Reasoning** **In finding y, how does the auxiliary $\overline{BA}$ make the problem simpler to solve?**

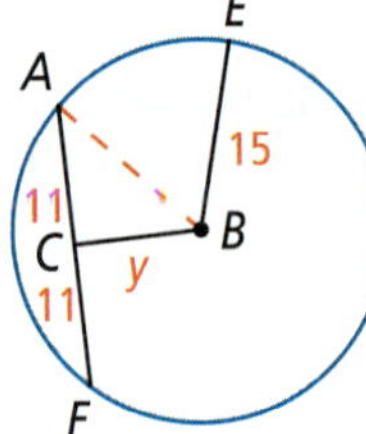

14. $\overline{BA}$ is the hypotenuse of a right _?_. triangle

15. You can use the _?_ Theorem to solve for y. Pythagorean

Lesson Check • Do you know HOW?

What is the missing length to the nearest tenth?

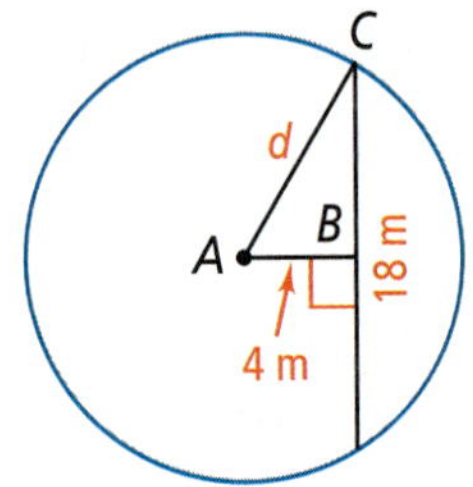

16. $\triangle ABC$ is a right triangle, so $AB^2 + BC^2 =$ d^2.

17. $\overline{AB}$ is a perpendicular bisector of the chord, so $BC = \frac{1}{2} \cdot$ 18 = 9.

18. Use the Pythagorean Theorem to find the value of d.

$$4^2 + 9^2 = d^2$$
$$16 + 81 = d^2$$
$$97 = d^2$$
$$\sqrt{97} = d$$
$$9.848857802 \approx d$$

19. To the nearest tenth, the missing length is 9.8 m.

Lesson Check • Do you UNDERSTAND?

Reasoning **A chemist gathered the pieces of a broken flask. He wanted to find the radius of the flask to determine the amount of liquid that was spilled when the flask broke. Explain how the chemist could determine the radius of the flask.**

20. Is the perpendicular bisector of a chord a diameter of the circle? (Yes) / No

21. Do the diameters of a circle intersect at the center? (Yes) / No

22. Is a radius the distance from the center of the circle to a point on the circle? (Yes) / No

23. The chemist traced a piece of the rim of the flask and then did the construction at the right to determine the radius. Describe each step.

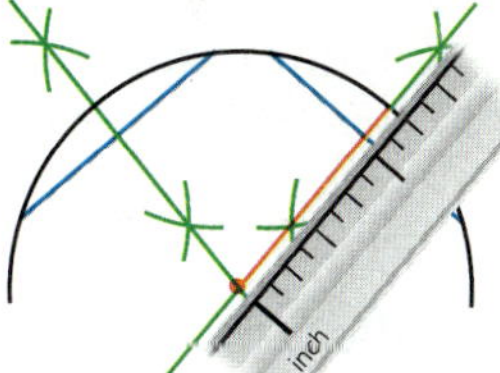

Step 1: Use a straightedge to draw two chords.

Step 2: Construct the perpendicular bisector of each chord.

Step 3: The perpendicular bisectors of the chords intersect at the center of the circle. Use a ruler to measure the radius.

Math Success

Check off the vocabulary words that you understand.

☐ circle ☐ chord ☐ radius ☐ diameter

Rate how well you can *use chords to find measures.*

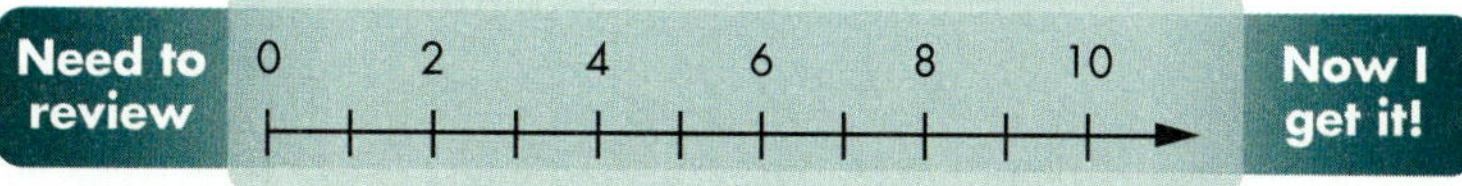

Name ______________________ Class ____________ Date ____________

12-2 Think About a Plan

Chords and Arcs

$\odot A$ and $\odot B$ are congruent. $\overline{CD}$ is a chord of both circles.
If $AB = 8$ in. and $CD = 6$ in., how long is a radius?

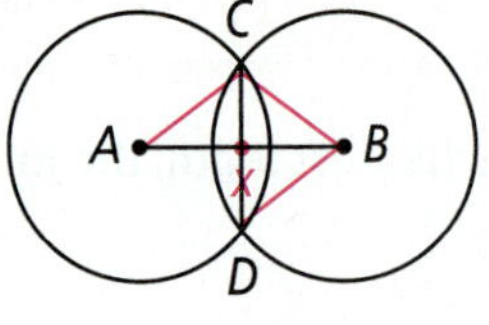

1. Draw the radius of each circle that includes point C. What is the name of each of the two line segments drawn?
   $\overline{AC}$, $\overline{BC}$

2. Label the intersection of $\overline{CD}$ and $\overline{AB}$ point X.

3. You know that $\overline{CD} \cong \overline{CD}$. How can you use the converse of Theorem 12-7 to show that $AX = XB$?
   Because congruent chords are equidistant from the centers of congruent circles, X is the same distance from A as it is from B. So, $AX = XB$.

4. How long is $\overline{XB}$? 4 in.

5. Draw in radius $\overline{BD}$. What is true about BC and BD? Explain.
   $BC = BD$; all radii of a circle have the same length.

6. Because $AD = AC = BD = BC$, $ACBD$ is a rhombus and its diagonals $\overline{AB}$ and $\overline{CD}$ are perpendicular.

7. What can you say about the diagram using Theorem 12-8? $\overline{AB}$ bisects $\overline{CD}$.

8. How long is $\overline{CX}$? 3 in.

9. How can you use the Pythagorean Theorem to find BC?
   $a^2 + b^2 = c^2$; if $CX = a$, $XB = b$, and $CB = c$, then $CB = \sqrt{3^2 + 4^2} = \sqrt{25} = 5$ in.

10. How long is the radius of each circle? 5 in.

Name ______________________ Class ____________ Date ____________

12-2 Practice

Chords and Arcs

Form K

In Exercises 1 and 2, the circles are congruent. What can you conclude?

1.

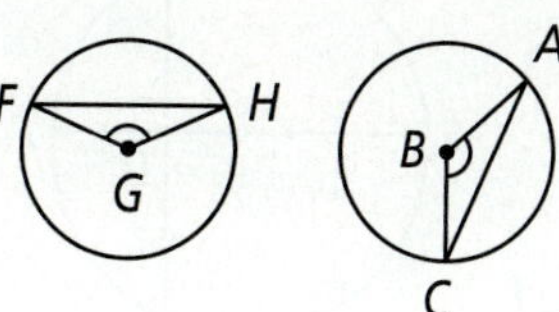

To start, look at the chords. If they are equidistant from the center of the circle, what can be concluded?

The chords must be _?_. congruent

$\overline{FH} \cong \overline{AC}$; $\overline{GF} \cong \overline{GH} \cong \overline{BA} \cong \overline{BC}$; $\overset{\frown}{FH} \cong \overset{\frown}{AC}$; $\angle FGH \cong \angle ABC$

2.

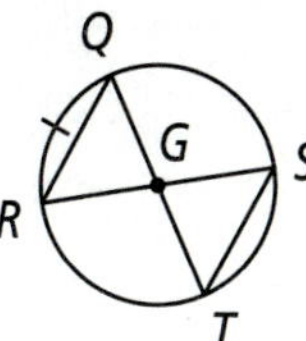

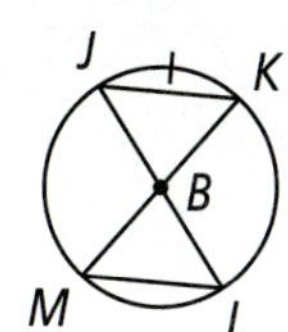

$\overline{QR} \cong \overline{TS} \cong$ _?_ $\cong$ _?_

$\overline{KJ}$; $\overline{LM}$

$\angle QGR \cong$ _?_ $\cong$ _?_ $\cong$ _?_

$\angle SGT$; $\angle JBK$; $\angle MBL$

$\overset{\frown}{QR} \cong$ _?_ $\cong$ _?_ $\cong$ _?_

$\overset{\frown}{KJ}$; $\overset{\frown}{ST}$; $\overset{\frown}{LM}$

$\angle QGS \cong$ _?_ $\cong$ _?_ $\cong$ _?_

$\angle RGT$; $\angle JBM$; $\angle KBL$

$\overset{\frown}{QS} \cong$ _?_ $\cong$ _?_ $\cong$ _?_

$\overset{\frown}{TR}$; $\overset{\frown}{KL}$; $\overset{\frown}{MJ}$

Find the value of *x*.

3. 30

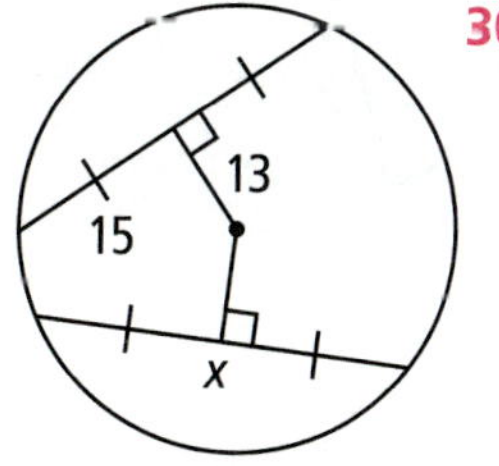

4. 8

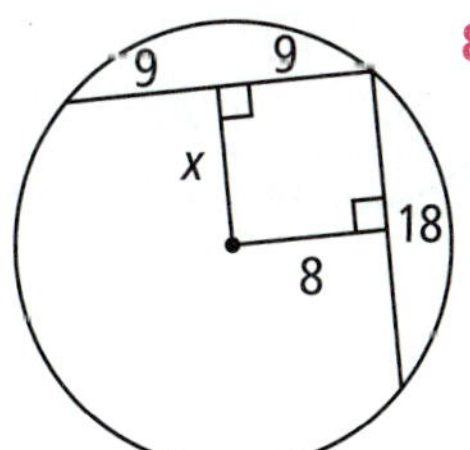

5. 12.5

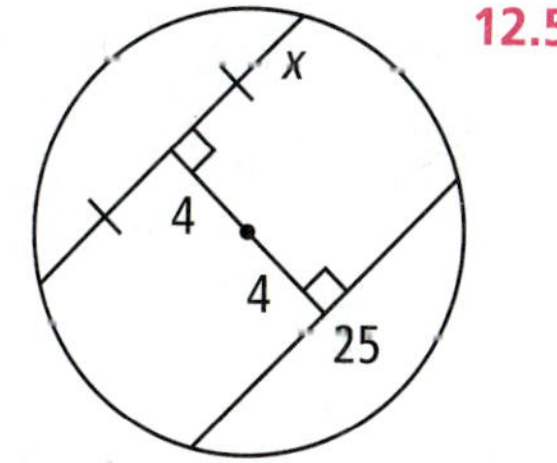

6. Reasoning $\angle QRS$ and $\angle TRV$ are vertical angles inscribed in $\odot R$. What must be true of $\overset{\frown}{QS}$ and $\overset{\frown}{TV}$? Explain.
They must be ≅ because vertical ∠s are ≅, and the arcs of ≅ central ∠s in the same circle are ≅.

Draw a Diagram **Tell whether the statement is *always, sometimes,* or *never* true.**

7. $\overset{\frown}{XY}$ and $\overset{\frown}{RS}$ are in congruent circles. Central $\angle XZY$ and central $\angle RTS$ are congruent. sometimes

8. $\odot I \cong \odot K$. The length of chord $\overline{GH}$ in $\odot I$ is 3 in. and the length of chord $\overline{LM}$ in $\odot K$ is 3 in. $\angle GIH \cong \angle LKM$. always

9. $\angle STU$ and $\angle RMO$ are central angles in congruent circles. $m\angle STU = 50$ and $m\angle RMO = 55$. $\overset{\frown}{SU} \cong \overset{\frown}{RO}$. never

Name ____________________ Class ____________ Date ____________

12-2 Practice (continued)

Form K

Chords and Arcs

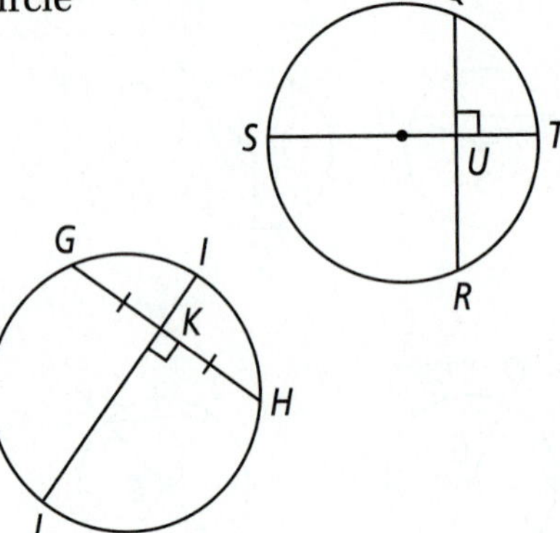

10. In the diagram at the right, $\overline{ST}$ is a diameter of the circle and $\overline{ST} \perp \overline{QR}$. What conclusions can you make?
$\overline{QT} \cong \overline{TR}$, $\overline{SQ} \cong \overline{SR}$, and $\overline{QU} \cong \overline{UR}$.

11. In the diagram at the right, $\overline{IJ}$ is a perpendicular bisector of chord $\overline{GH}$. What can you conclude?
Answers may vary. Sample: $\overline{IJ}$ contains the center of the circle.

Find the value of x to the nearest tenth.

12. 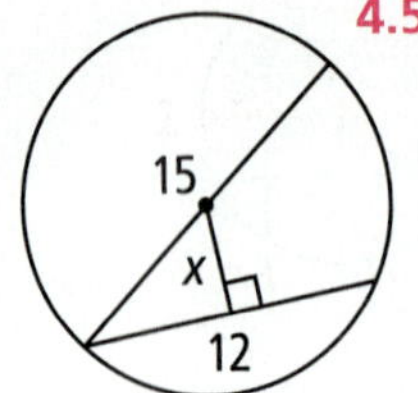

4.5

To start, since the radius is perpendicular to the chord, the chord is bisected.

The longer leg of the triangle is $12 \div 2 =$ 6.

13. 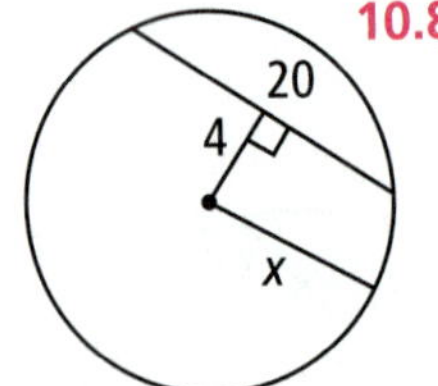

10.8

14. 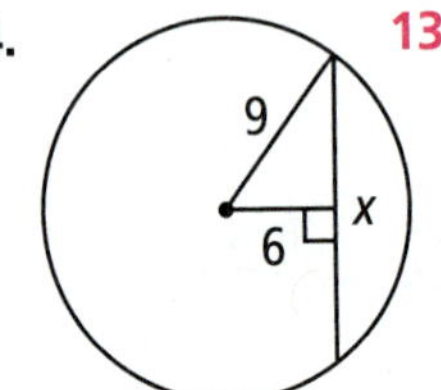

13.4

15. 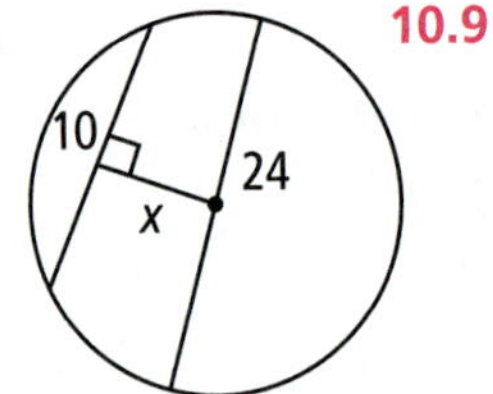

10.9

$\odot D$ and $\odot E$ are congruent. $\overline{GH}$ is a chord of both circles. Round all answers to the nearest tenth.

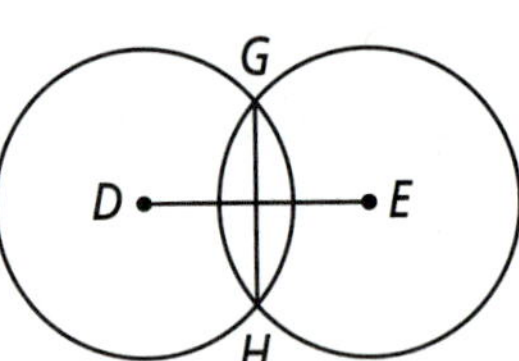

16. If $DE = 10$ in. and $GH = 4$ in., how long is a radius? 5.4 in.

17. If $DE = 22$ cm and radius $= 14$ cm, how long is $\overline{GH}$? 17.3 cm

18. If the radius $= 18$ ft and $GH = 32$ ft, how long is $\overline{DE}$? 16.5 ft

19. In the figure at the right, Sphere Z with radius 9 in. is intersected by a plane 4 in. from center Z. To the nearest tenth, find the radius of the cross section $\odot X$. 8.1 in.

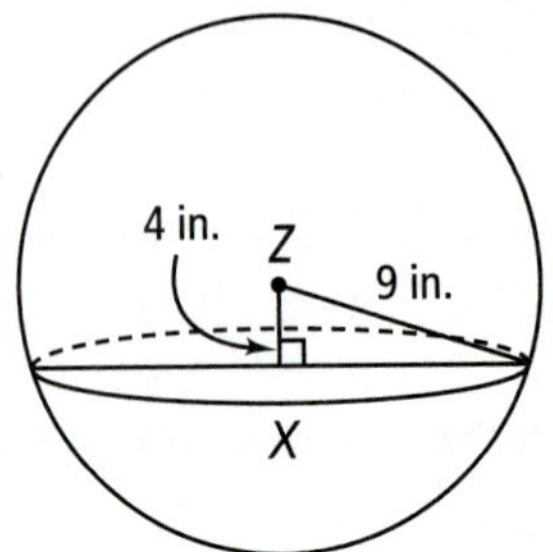

Name ______________________ Class ____________ Date ____________

12-2 Standardized Test Prep

Chords and Arcs

Multiple Choice

For Exercises 1–5, choose the correct letter.

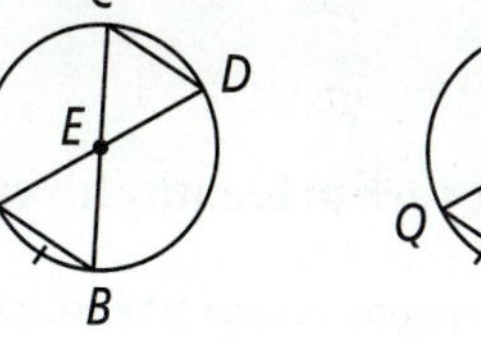

1. The circles at the right are congruent. Which conclusion can you draw? C

Ⓐ $\overline{CD} \cong \overline{ST}$ Ⓒ $\angle AEB \cong \angle QUR$

Ⓑ $\angle CED \cong \angle SUT$ Ⓓ $\overset{\frown}{BD} \cong \overset{\frown}{RT}$

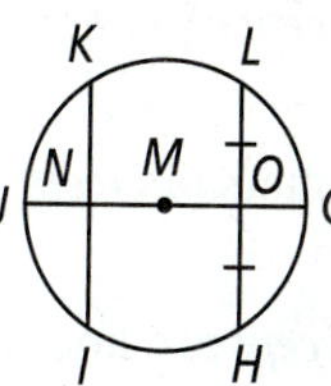

2. $\overline{JG}$ is the diameter of $\odot M$. Which conclusion *cannot* be drawn from the diagram? F

Ⓕ $\overline{KN} \cong \overline{NI}$ Ⓗ $\overline{JG} \perp \overline{HL}$

Ⓖ $\overset{\frown}{LG} \cong \overset{\frown}{GH}$ Ⓘ $\overset{\frown}{GH} \cong \overset{\frown}{GL}$

For Exercises 3 and 4, what is the value of *x* to the nearest tenth?

3. B

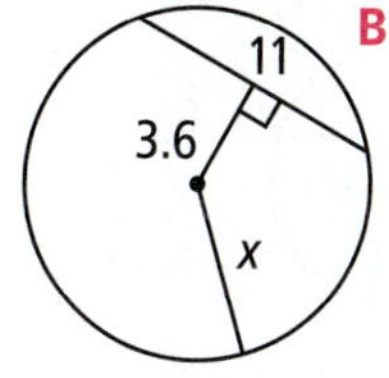

Ⓐ 4.2 Ⓒ 10.4

Ⓑ 6.6 Ⓓ 11.6

4. H

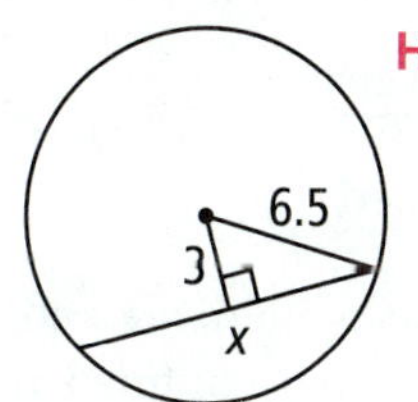

Ⓕ 3.6 Ⓗ 11.5

Ⓖ 5.8 Ⓘ 14.3

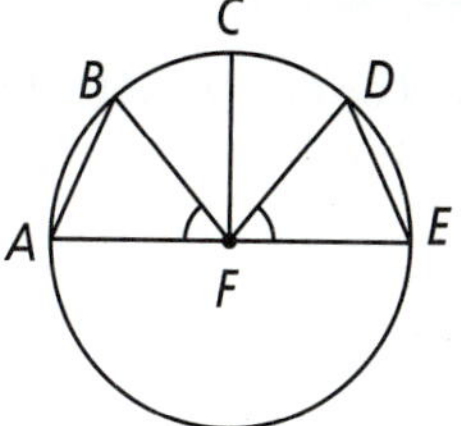

5. If $\angle AFB \cong \angle DFE$, what must be true? A

Ⓐ $\overset{\frown}{AB} \cong \overset{\frown}{DE}$ Ⓒ $\overline{CF} \perp \overline{AE}$

Ⓑ $\overset{\frown}{BC} \cong \overset{\frown}{DE}$ Ⓓ $\angle BFC \cong \angle DFC$

Short Response

6. Given: $\odot A \cong \odot C$, $\overset{\frown}{DB} \cong \overset{\frown}{EB}$

Prove: $\triangle ADB \cong \triangle CEB$

[2] Statements: 1) $\odot A \cong \odot C$, $\overset{\frown}{DB} \cong \overset{\frown}{EB}$; 2) $\overline{AB}$, $\overline{CB}$, $\overline{DA}$, and $\overline{CE}$ are all radii; 3) $\overline{AB} \cong \overline{CB} \cong \overline{CE} \cong \overline{AD}$; 4) $\overline{DB} \cong \overline{EB}$; 5) $\triangle ADB \cong \triangle CEB$; Reasons: 1) Given; 2) Def. of radius; 3) Radii of $\cong$ circles are $\cong$; 4) Converse of Thm. 12–6; 5) SSS [1] proof missing steps [0] incorrect or missing proof

12-3 PART 1 Inscribed Angles

Vocabulary

Review

Write *noun* or *verb* to identify how *intercept* is used.

1. Defense tries to *intercept* a touchdown pass. verb

2. The *y-intercept* of a line is the *y*-value at $x = 0$. noun

3. Cryptographers *intercept* and decipher code messages. verb

4. The *x-intercept* of a line is the *x*-value at $y = 0$. noun

Vocabulary Builder

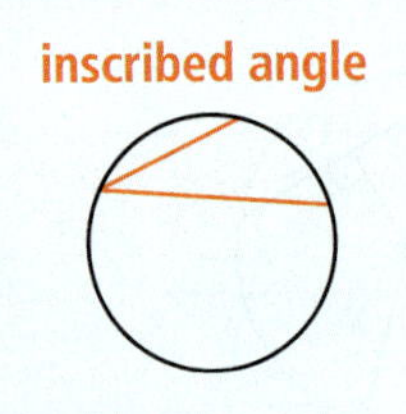

inscribed (adjective) in SKRYBD

Related Word: circumscribed

Definition: *Inscribed* means written, marked, or engraved on. *Circumscribed* means encircled, confined, or limited.

Math Usage: An **inscribed** angle is formed by two chords with a vertex on the circle.

Use Your Vocabulary

Write *circumscribed* or *inscribed* to describe each angle.

5. 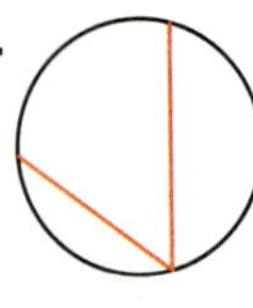
inscribed

6. 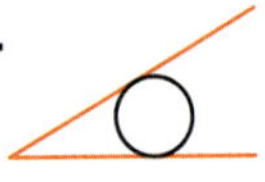
circumscribed

7. 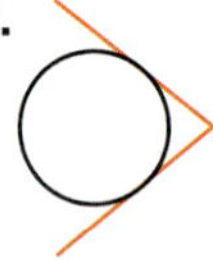
circumscribed

8. 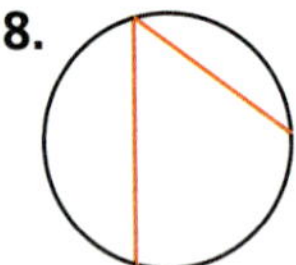
inscribed

Underline the correct word to complete each sentence.

9. $\angle ABC$ with points A, B, and C on a circle is a(n) circumscribed / inscribed angle.

10. An intercepted arc is between the sides of a(n) circumscribed / inscribed angle.

take note

Theorem 12-11 Inscribed Angle Theorem

The measure of an inscribed angle is half the measure of its intercepted arc.

$m\angle B = \frac{1}{2} m\overset{\frown}{AC}$

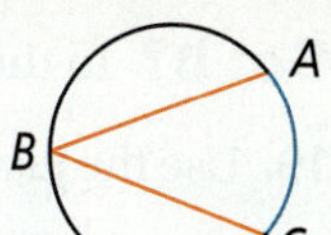

11. Suppose $m\overset{\frown}{AC} = 90$.

$m\angle B = \boxed{\frac{1}{2}} \cdot m\overset{\frown}{AC} = \boxed{45}$

12. Suppose $m\angle B = 60$.

$m\overset{\frown}{AC} = \boxed{2} \cdot m\angle B = \boxed{120}$

Problem 1 Using the Inscribed Angle Theorem

Got It? In $\odot O$, what is $m\angle A$?

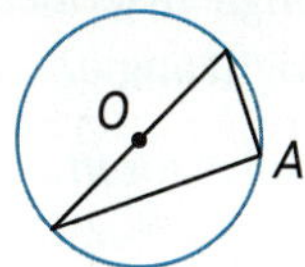

13. Complete the reasoning model below.

Think	Write
I know the sides of $\angle A$ are chords and the vertex is on $\odot O$.	$\angle A$ is an inscribed angle.
I can use the Inscribed Angle Theorem.	$m\angle A = \frac{1}{2}$(measure of the blue arc) $= \frac{1}{2} \cdot \boxed{180}$ $= \boxed{90}$

take note

Corollaries to Theorem 12-11 Inscribed Angle Theorem

Corollary 1

Two inscribed angles that intercept the same arc are congruent.

Corollary 2

An angle inscribed in a semicircle is a right angle.

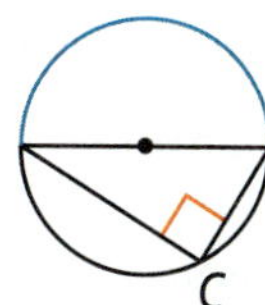

Corollary 3

The opposite angles of a quadrilateral inscribed in a circle are supplementary.

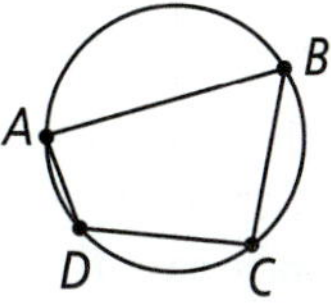

Use the diagram at the right. Write T for *true* or F for *false*.

T **14.** $\angle P$ and $\angle Q$ intercept the same arc.

F **15.** $\angle SRP$ and $\angle Q$ intercept the same arc.

T **16.** $\overset{\frown}{TSR}$ is a semicircle.

F **17.** $\angle PTS$ and $\angle SRQ$ are opposite angles.

T **18.** $\angle PTS$ and $\angle SRP$ are supplementary angles.

Problem 2 Using Corollaries to Find Angle Measures

Got It? **In the diagram at the right, what is the measure of each numbered angle?**

19. Use the justifications at the right to complete each statement.

$m\angle 4 = \frac{1}{2}($ **60** $+$ **80** $)$	Inscribed Angle Theorem
$m\angle 4 = \frac{1}{2}($ **140** $)$	Add within parentheses.
$m\angle 4 =$ **70**	Simplify.

20. Circle the corollary you can use to find $m\angle 2$.

An angle inscribed in a semicircle is a right angle.	(circled) The opposite angles of a quadrilateral inscribed in a circle are supplementary.

21. Now solve for $m\angle 2$.

$$m\angle 4 + m\angle 2 = 180$$
$$70 + m\angle 2 = 180$$
$$70 + m\angle 2 - 70 = 180 - 70$$
$$m\angle 2 = 110$$

22. Underline the correct word to complete the sentence.

The dashed line is a diameter / radius . (diameter underlined)

23. Circle the corollary you can use to find $m\angle 1$ and $m\angle 3$.

(circled) An angle inscribed in a semicircle is a right angle.	The opposite angles of a quadrilateral inscribed in a circle are supplementary.

Use your answer to Exercise 23 to find the angle measures.

24. $m\angle 1 =$ **90** **25.** $m\angle 3 =$ **90**

26. So, $m\angle 1 =$ **90** , $m\angle 2 =$ **110** , $m\angle 3 =$ **90** , and $m\angle 4 =$ **70** .

Lesson Check • Do you UNDERSTAND?

Error Analysis **A classmate says that $m\angle A = 90$. What is your classmate's error?**

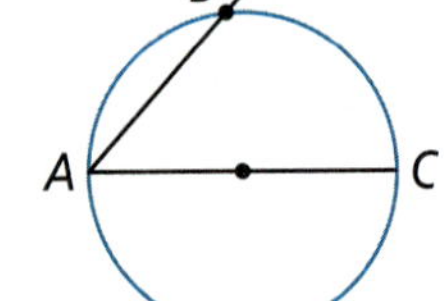

27. Is diameter $\overline{AC}$ a side of $\angle A$? (Yes) / No

28. Is $\angle A$ inscribed in a semicircle? Yes / (No)

29. What is your classmate's error? Explain.

Answers may vary. Sample: The error is in thinking that an angle with a diameter as a side intercepts a semicircle. $m\angle A \neq \frac{1}{2} \cdot 180$.

Inscribed Angles

Vocabulary

Review

Underline the correct word or letter to complete each sentence.

1. A *tangent* to a circle is a line, ray, or segment in the plane of the circle that intersects the circle in exactly one / two point(s).

2. If a line in the plane of a circle is parallel / perpendicular to a radius at its endpoint on the circle, then the line is tangent to the circle.

Use the diagram for Exercises 3-5.

3. $\overleftrightarrow{AC}$ is *tangent* to $\odot O$ at point A / B / C.

4. $\overline{BC}$ is a *tangent* ray / segment.

5. $\overrightarrow{BA}$ is a *tangent* ray / segment.

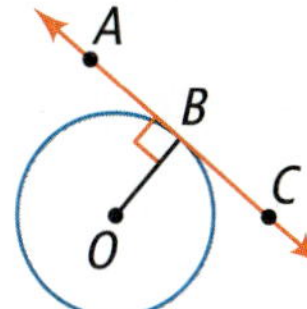

Vocabulary Builder

coincide (verb) **koh in SYD**

Related Word: coincidence (noun), coincidental (adjective)

Definition: **Coincide** means to occupy the same place in space or time.

Use Your Vocabulary

Complete each statement with the appropriate word from the list. Use each word only once.

coincide(s) coincidence coincidental

6. It was a _?_ that two friends bought the same color sweater at the same store. coincidence

7. This year, your birthday _?_ with the first day of school. coincides

8. Any similarity between my project and my friend's project is purely _?_. coincidental

take note

Theorem 12-12

The measure of an angle formed by a tangent and a chord is half the measure of the intercepted arc.

$m\angle C = \frac{1}{2}\, m\widehat{BDC}$

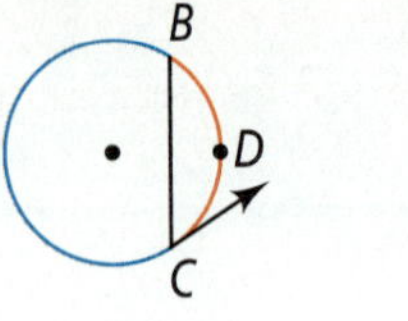

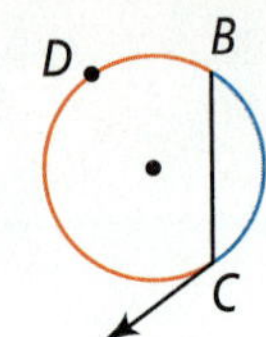

9. Suppose $m\angle C = 50$.

$m\,\widehat{BDC} = 2 \cdot m\angle C = 100$

10. Suppose $m\widehat{BDC} = 80$.

$m\angle C = \frac{1}{2} \cdot m\widehat{BDC} = 40$

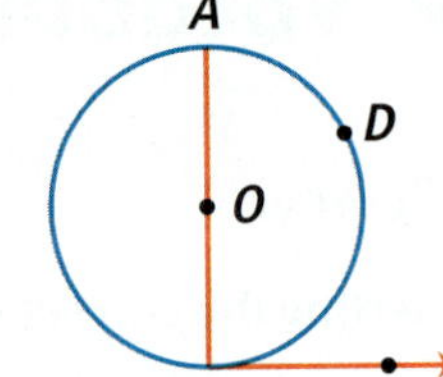

In the diagram at the right, $\overrightarrow{BC}$ is tangent to ⊙*O* at *B*. Use the diagram for Exercises 11–13.

11. $m\widehat{ADB} = 180$

12. $m\angle ABC = 90$

13. How does Theorem 12-12 relate to Theorem 12-1: If a line is tangent to a circle, then the line is perpendicular to the radius at the point of tangency?

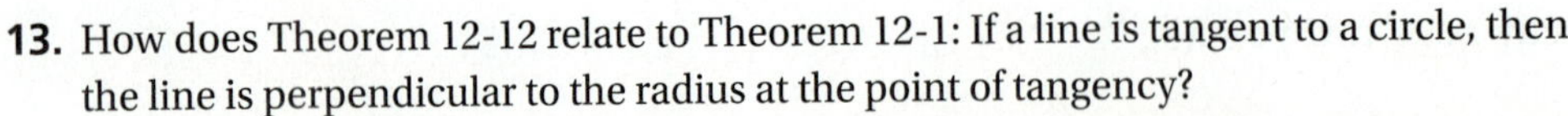

Answers may vary. Sample: If the chord in Theorem 12-12 is a diameter, Theorem 12-1 applies because the ray $\overrightarrow{BC}$ is a part of a line and the radius $\overline{OB}$ is a part of the diameter $\overline{AB}$.

Problem 3 Using Arc Measure

Got It? **In the diagram at the right, $\overline{KJ}$ is tangent to ⊙*O*. What are the values of *x* and *y*?**

14. Circle the arc intercepted by $\angle JQL$. Underline the arc intercepted by $\angle KJL$.

 $\widehat{JL}$  $\widehat{JQ}$ $\widehat{QL}$ $\widehat{QLJ}$

15. By the Inscribed Angle Theorem, $m\widehat{JL} = 2 \cdot 35 = 70$.

16. By Theorem 12-12, $x = \frac{1}{2} \cdot m\widehat{JL} = 35$.

17. The value of *x* is 35.

18. Underline the correct words to complete the sentence.

$\overline{QL}$ is a <u>diameter</u> / radius, so $\angle QJL$ is a(n) acute / <u>right</u> / obtuse angle.

19. Use the justifications at the right to complete each statement.

$m\angle QJL + m\angle JLQ + m\angle LQJ = 180$	Triangle Angle-Sum Theorem
$90 + y + 35 = 180$	Substitute.
$y + 125 = 180$	Simplify.
$y = 55$	Subtraction Property of Equality

20. The value of *x* is 35 and the value of *y* is 55.

Lesson Check • Do you know HOW?

In the diagram, $\overleftrightarrow{MN}$ is a tangent to $\odot O$ at T. If $m\widehat{TRS} = 246$, what is $m\angle STN$?

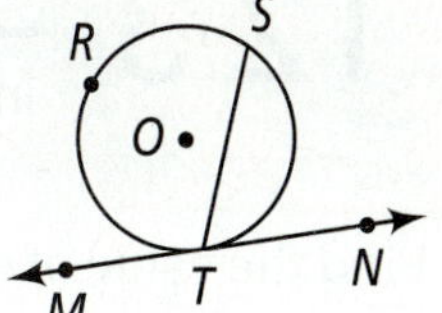

21. Use Theorem 12-12 to complete.

$m\angle MTS = \frac{1}{2} \cdot m\widehat{TRS} = 123$

22. Use the justifications to find $m\angle STN$.

$m\angle MTS + m\angle STN = 180$	Use the Linear Pair Postulate.
$123 + m\angle STN = 180$	Substitute.
$m\angle STN = 57$	Subtraction Property of Equality

Lesson Check • Do you UNDERSTAND?

Reasoning In the diagram, $\overleftrightarrow{JK}$ is a tangent to $\odot L$ at B. If $m\angle EBJ = 44$, explain how to find $m\widehat{BDE}$.

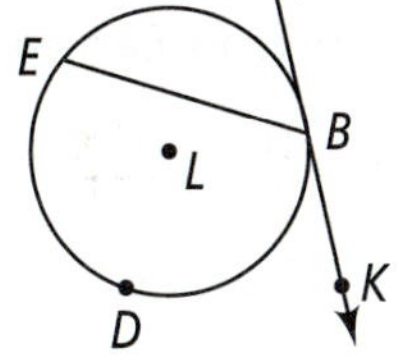

Write T for *true* or F for *false*.

T **23.** $m\angle EBJ + m\angle EBK = 180$

F **24.** $m\angle EBK = m\widehat{BDE}$

25. Explain how to find $m\widehat{BDE}$.

Explanations may vary. Sample: Subtract $m\angle EBJ$ from 180 to find $m\angle EBK$. Since $m\angle EBK = \frac{1}{2}m\widehat{BDE}$, multiply $m\angle EBK$ by 2 to find $m\widehat{BDE}$.

Math Success

Check off the vocabulary words that you understand.

☐ inscribed angle ☐ intercepted arc

Rate how well you can *find the measure of inscribed angles.*

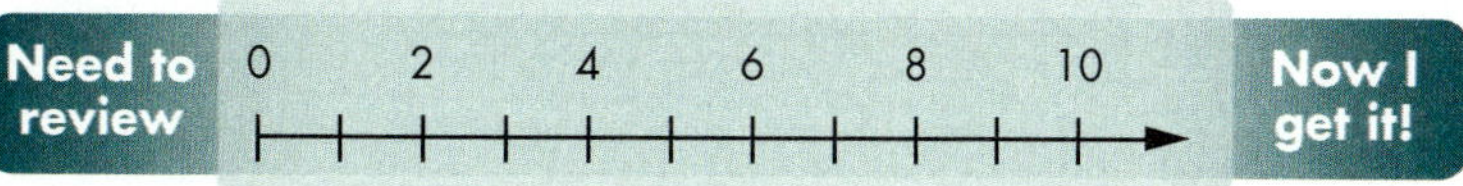

Name ______________________ Class ____________ Date ____________

12-3 Think About a Plan

Inscribed Angles

Find the value of each variable. The dot represents the center of the circle.

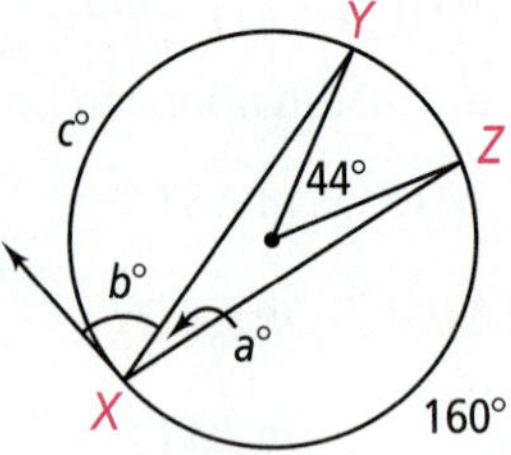

1. Draw in points X, Y, and Z on the circle so that the measure of $\angle YXZ$ is a, $\widehat{XY}$ is c, and $\widehat{XZ}$ is 160.

2. How is the measure of an inscribed angle related to the measure of its intercepted arc?

By Theorem 12-11, the measure of an inscribed angle is half the measure of its intercepted arc.

3. What is the measure of $\widehat{YZ}$, by the definition of an arc? **44**

4. How can you use Theorem 12-11 to find a?

Because a (the measure of $\angle YXZ$) is half the measure of its intercepted arc ($\widehat{YZ}$), it is equal to half of 44.

5. What is a? **22**

6. What is the sum of the measures of $\widehat{XY}$, $\widehat{YZ}$, and $\widehat{XZ}$? **360**

7. How can you use the sum of the measures of all these non-overlapping arcs of a circle to find c?

Because c is the measure of $\widehat{XY}$, and $m\widehat{XY} + m\widehat{YZ} + m\widehat{XZ} = 360$, $m\widehat{XY} = 360 - (m\widehat{YZ} + m\widehat{XZ})$. Then substitute the values for $m\widehat{YZ}$ and $m\widehat{XZ}$.

8. What is c? **156**

9. What is the arc that is intercepted by the angle measuring b? What is the measure of this arc? **$\widehat{XY}$; 156**

10. How can you use Theorem 12-12 to find b?

The measure of an angle that is formed by a tangent and a chord is half the measure of the intercepted arc. So, b is half of 156.

11. What is b? **78**

Name ______________________ Class ____________ Date ____________

12-3 Practice

Form K

Inscribed Angles

Find the value of each variable. For each circle, the dot represents the center.

1. 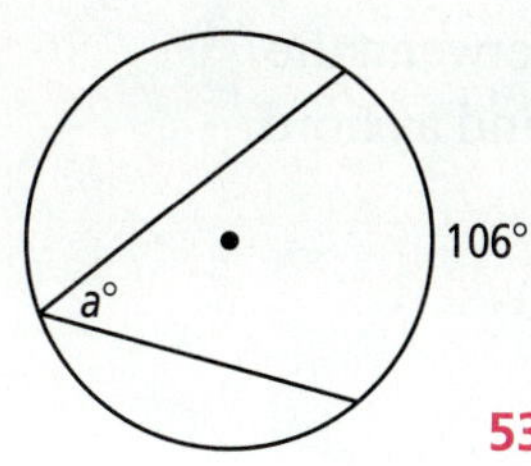

To start, describe the relationship between the inscribed angle and the intercepted arc.

The measure of the inscribed angle is __?__ the measure of the intercepted arc. half

53

2. 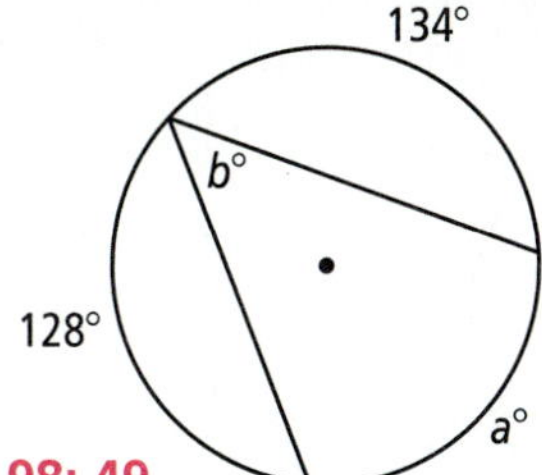

98; 49

3. 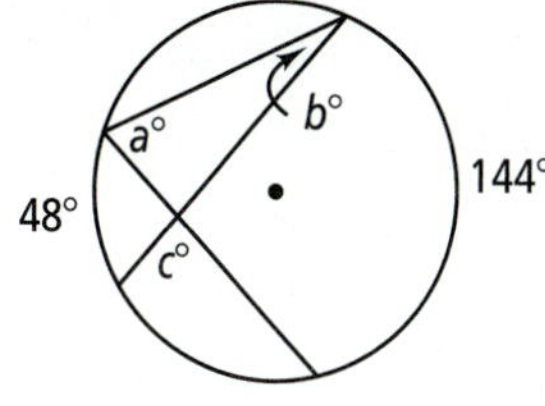

72; 24; 84

4. 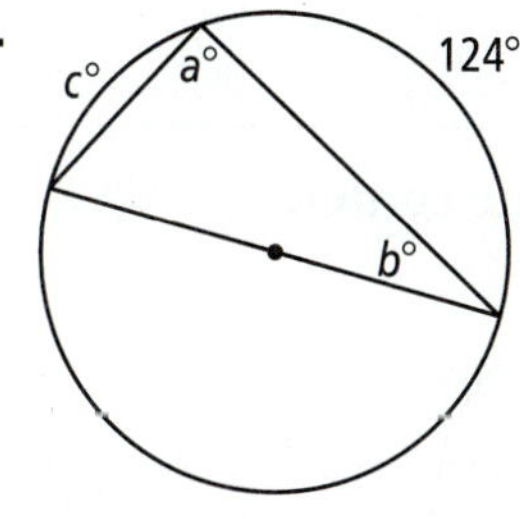

90; 28; 56

5. 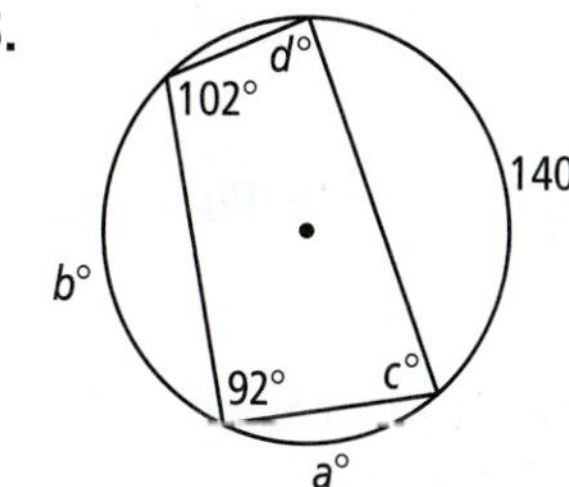

64; 112; 78; 88

Find each indicated measure for ⊙M.

6. a. $m\widehat{EF}$ 110

b. $m\angle E$ 77

c. $m\angle F$ 48

d. $m\widehat{DF}$ 154

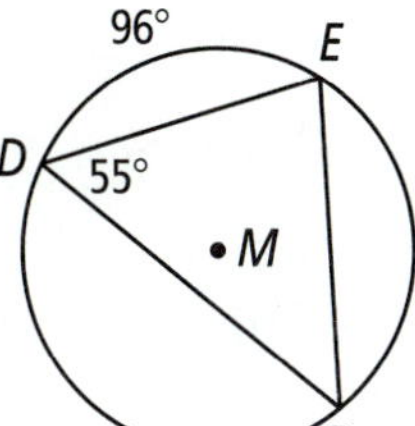

7. a. $m\angle S$ 33

b. $m\widehat{TS}$ 78

c. $m\widehat{QU}$ 66

d. $m\angle TMS$ 78

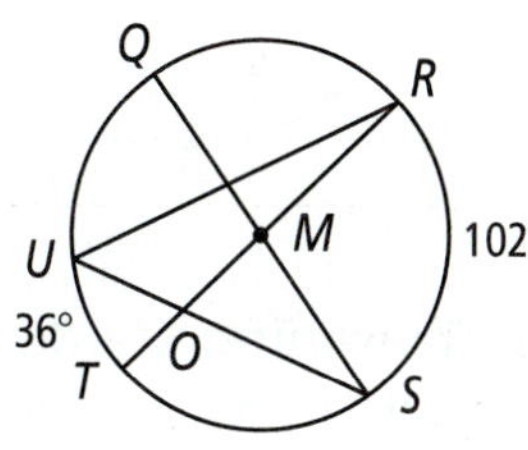

8. Reasoning A quadrilateral that is not a rectangle is inscribed in a circle. What is the least number of arc measures needed to determine the measures of each angle in the quadrilateral? Use drawings to explain.
Two; you can find the other measures using Corollary 3 of Theorem 12-11.

9. Open-Ended Draw a circle. Inscribe two angles in the circle so that the angles are congruent. Explain which corollary to Theorem 12-11 you can use to prove the angles are congruent without measuring them.
Check students' work. If Corollary 1 is cited, angles should intercept the same arc. If Corollary 2 is cited, angles should intercept a semicircle.

Name ______________________ Class ____________ Date ____________

12-3 Practice (continued)

Form K

Inscribed Angles

Find the value of each variable. Lines that appear to be tangent are tangent.

10.

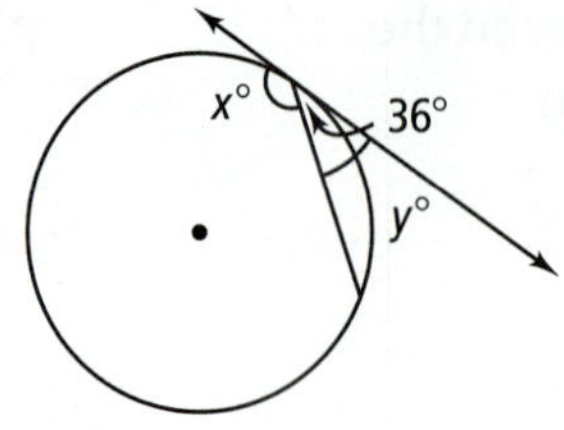

To start, determine the relationship between the inscribed angle formed by a tangent and a chord and the intercepted arc.

The measure of the intercepted arc is y.

$36 = \frac{1}{2} \cdot \boxed{y}$

144; 72

11.

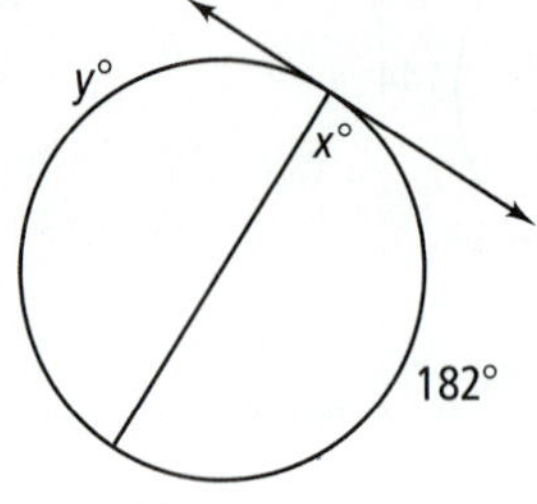

91; 178

12.

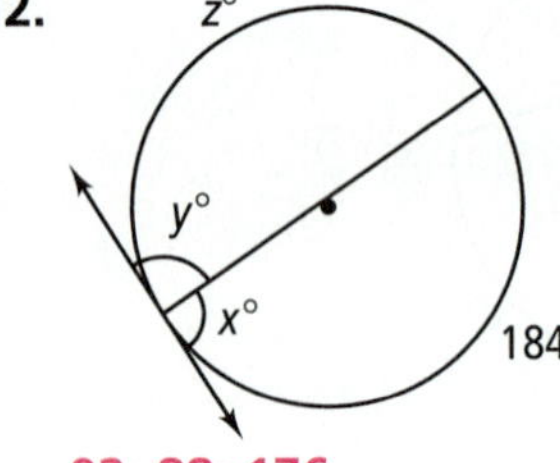

92; 88; 176

Find the value of each variable. For each circle, the dot represents the center.

13.

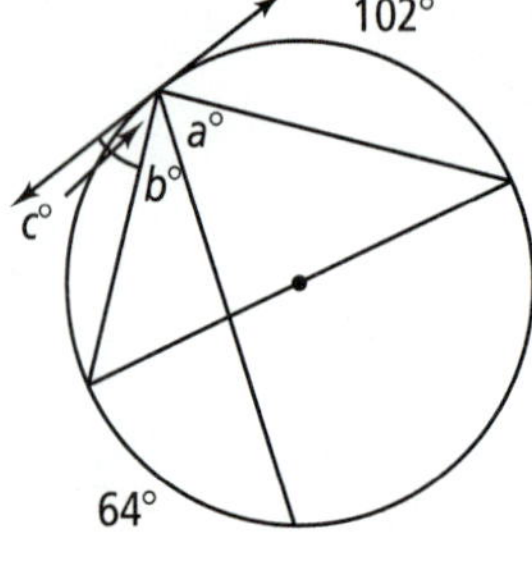

58; 32; 39

14.

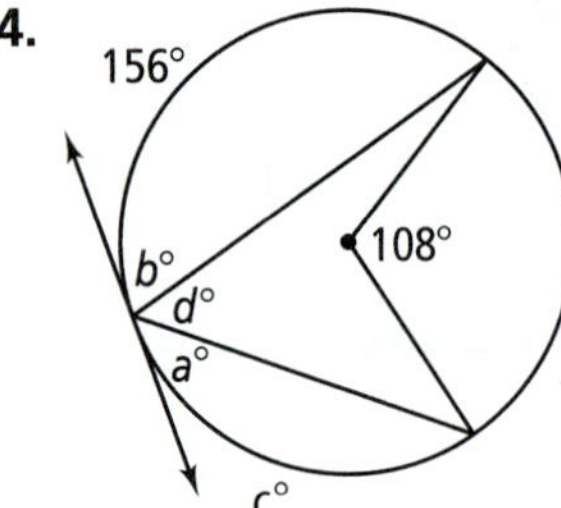

48; 78; 96; 54

15. Reasoning $\angle ABC$ is formed by diameter $\overline{AB}$ and a tangent to $\odot D$ containing point C. What is the measure of $\angle ABC$? Explain. 90; the intercepted arc is a semicircle, so the inscribed angle must be a right angle.

16. Draw a Diagram $\overline{GH}$ is a chord of $\odot Y$. $\overline{GH}$ forms angles with tangents at points G and H. What is the relationship between the angles formed? Use a drawing in your explanation. The inscribed angles on the same side of the tangents are congruent because they intercept the same arc.

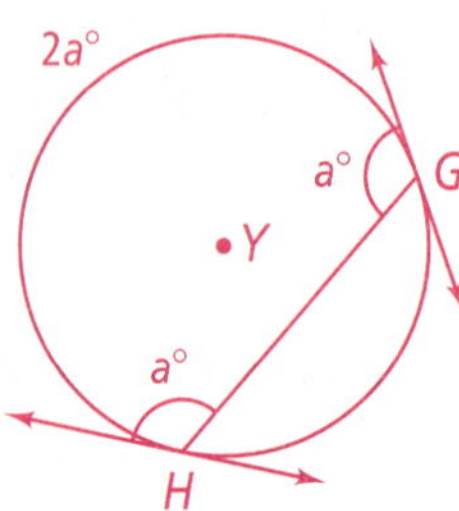

17. Writing Explain why the angle formed by a tangent and a chord has the same measure as an inscribed angle that intercepts the same arc.

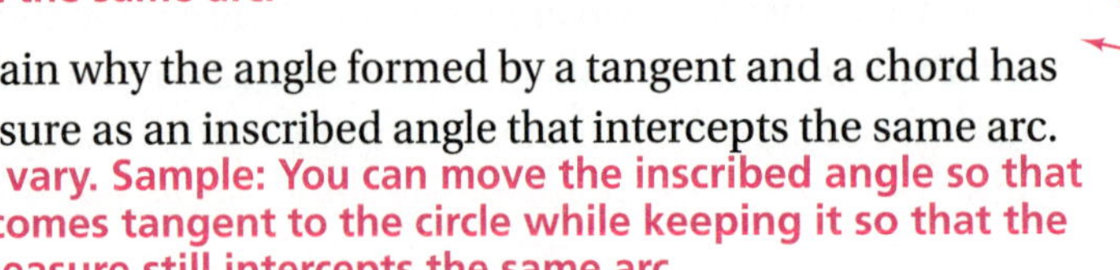

Answers may vary. Sample: You can move the inscribed angle so that one chord becomes tangent to the circle while keeping it so that the same angle measure still intercepts the same arc.

Name ______________________ Class ____________ Date ____________

12-3 Standardized Test Prep

Inscribed Angles

Multiple Choice

For Exercises 1–6, choose the correct letter.

1. What is the value of x? B

Ⓐ 19 Ⓒ 38

Ⓑ 31 Ⓓ 62

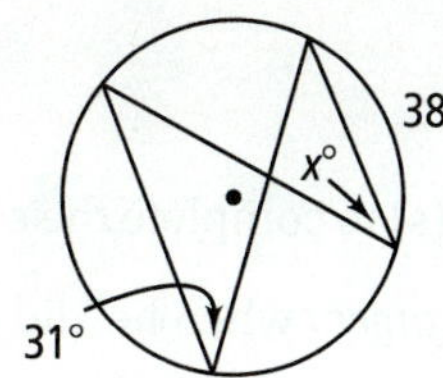

For Exercises 2–3, use the diagram at the right.

2. What is the value of a? H

Ⓕ 34 Ⓗ 68

Ⓖ 56 Ⓘ 146

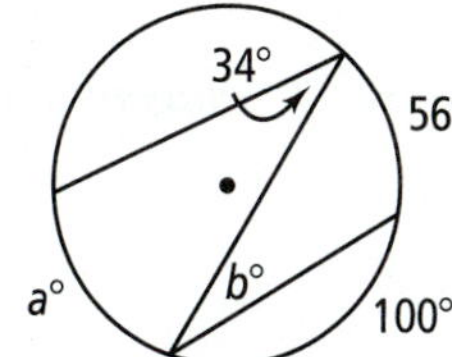

3. What is the value of b? A

Ⓐ 28 Ⓒ 56

Ⓑ 34 Ⓓ 112

4. What is the value of s? F

Ⓕ 35 Ⓗ 70

Ⓖ 55 Ⓘ 90

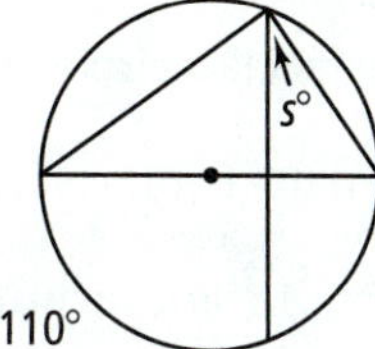

5. What is the value of y if the segment outside the circle is tangent to the circle? B

Ⓐ 85 Ⓒ 190

Ⓑ 95 Ⓓ cannot determine

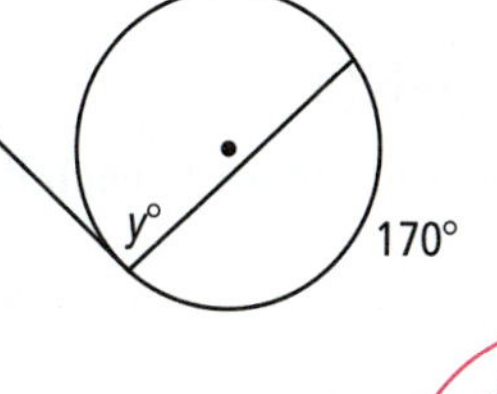

6. What is the value of z? H

Ⓕ 77 Ⓗ 126

Ⓖ 95 Ⓘ 154

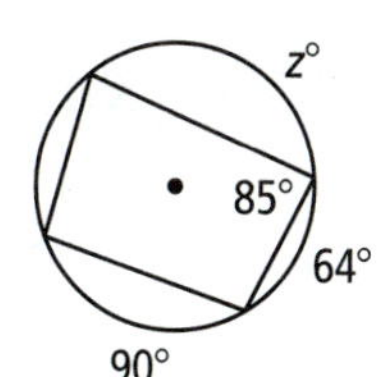

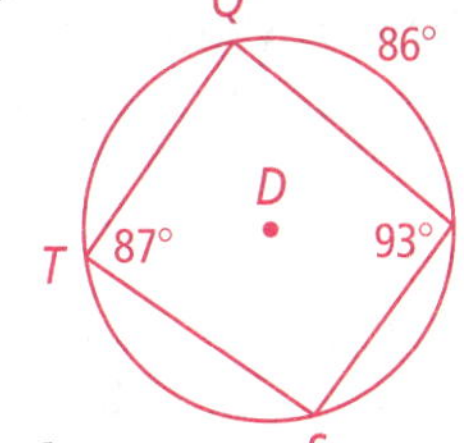

Extended Response

7. A student inscribes quadrilateral $QRST$ in $\odot D$ so that $m\overset{\frown}{QR} = 86$ and $m\angle R = 93$. What is the measure of $\overset{\frown}{RS}$? Draw a diagram and explain the steps you took to find the answer.

[4] 88; Explanations may vary. Sample: $m\angle R = 93$, $\angle T$ and $\angle R$ are suppl. according to Corollary 3 of Inscribed ∠ Thm, so $m\angle T = 180 - 93 = 87$. According to Inscribed ∠ Thm., $m\overset{\frown}{QRS} = 2m\angle T$, and $m\overset{\frown}{RS} = m\overset{\frown}{QRS} - m\overset{\frown}{QR}$, so $m\overset{\frown}{RS} = 2m\angle T - m\overset{\frown}{QR} = 2(87) - 86 = 88$. [3] appropriate methods, but incorrect answer [2] diagram incorrectly drawn [1] correct answer without work [0] incorrect answer and incomplete work

12-4 Angle Measures and Segment Lengths

Vocabulary

Review

1. Underline the correct word(s) to complete the sentence.

   The student went off on a *tangent* when he did / <u>did not</u> stick to the subject.

2. A *tangent* to a circle intersects the circle at exactly __?__ point(s). one

3. From a point outside a circle, there are __?__ *tangent(s)* to the circle. two

Vocabulary Builder

secant (noun) SEEK unt

Related Word: tangent (noun)

Definition: A **secant** is a line that intersects a circle at two points.

Source: The word **secant** comes from the Latin verb *secare*, which means "to cut."

Examples: In the diagram at the right, $\overleftrightarrow{AB}$ is a **secant**, $\overrightarrow{AB}$ and $\overrightarrow{BA}$ are **secant** rays, and $\overline{AB}$ is a **secant** segment.

Use Your Vocabulary

Write *secant* or *tangent* to identify each line.

4. 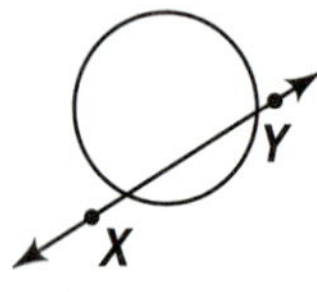

secant

5. 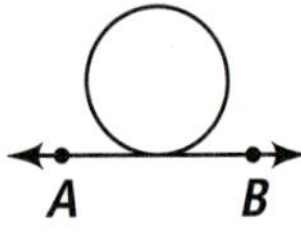

tangent

6. 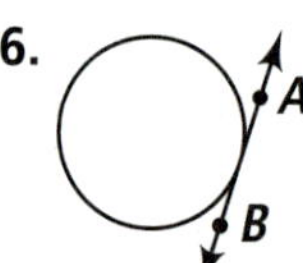

tangent

7. 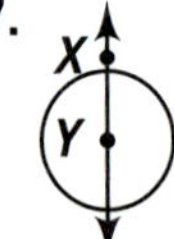

secant

8. Is a chord a *secant*? Explain.

   No. Explanations may vary. Sample: A secant contains points outside a circle, while a chord does not.

take note — Theorems 12-13, 12-14, and 12-15

Theorem 12-13 The measure of an angle formed by two lines that intersect inside a circle is half the sum of the measures of the intercepted arcs.

$m\angle 1 = \frac{1}{2}(x + y)$

9. In the diagram at the right, does $m\angle 2 = \frac{1}{2}(x + y)$? Explain.

Yes. Explanations may vary. Sample: $\angle 1$ and $\angle 2$ are vertical angles, so $m\angle 1 = m\angle 2$ and $m\angle 2 = \frac{1}{2}(x + y)$ by the Trans. Prop. of Equality.

Theorem 12-14 The measure of an angle formed by two lines that intersect outside a circle is half the difference of the measures of the intercepted arcs.

$m\angle 1 = \frac{1}{2}(x - y)$

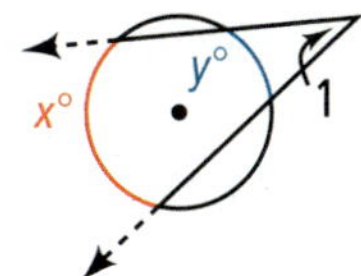

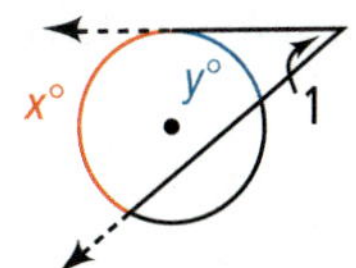

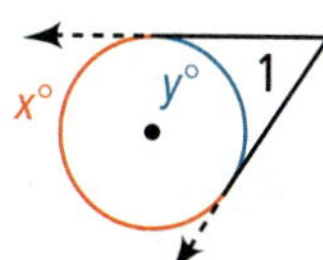

10. In the first diagam, the sides of the angle are a secant and a _?_. **secant**

11. In the second diagram, the sides of the angle are a secant and a _?_. **tangent**

12. In the third diagram, the sides of the angle are a tangent and a _?_. **tangent**

13. Is $m\angle 1 = \frac{1}{2}(y - x)$ equivalent to $m\angle 1 = \frac{1}{2}(x - y)$? Yes / (No)

Theorem 12-15 For a given point and circle, the product of the lengths of the two segments from the point to the circle is constant along any line through the point and the circle.

I.

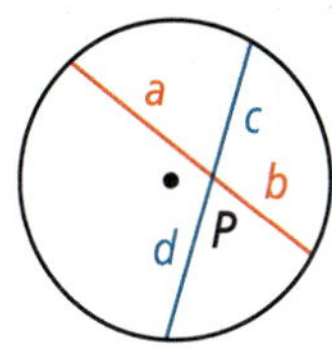

II.

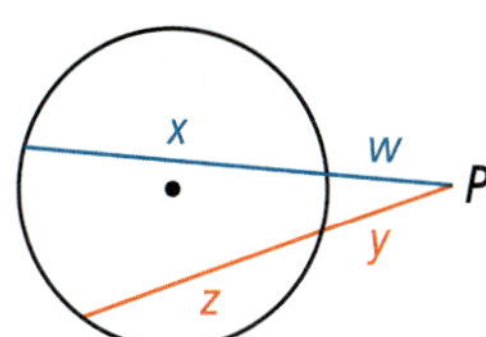

III.

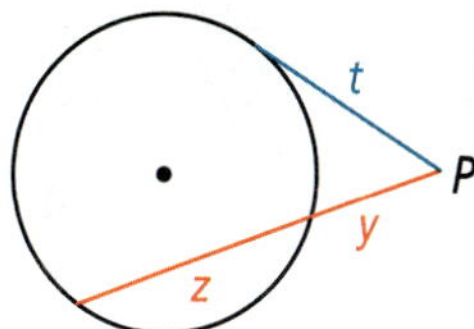

Complete each case of Theorem 12-15.

14. Case I $a \cdot b = c \cdot$ **d**

15. Case II $(w + x)w = ($ **y** $+ z)$ **y**

16. Case III $(y + z)$ **y** $= t^2$

Problem 1 Finding Angle Measures

Got It? What is the value of w?

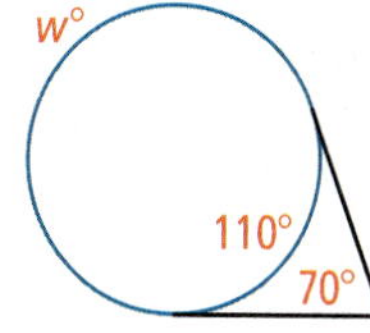

17. Use Theorem 12-14 to complete the equation.

70 $= \frac{1}{2}(w -$ **110**$)$

18. Now solve the equation.

$70 = \frac{1}{2}(w - 110)$

$140 = w - 110$

$250 = w$

19. The value of w is 250.

Problem 2 Finding an Arc Measure

Got It? **A departing space probe sends back a picture of Earth as it crosses Earth's equator. The angle formed by the two tangents to the equator is 20°. What is the measure of the arc of the equator that is visible to the space probe?**

20. Use 20, F, G, and the words *Earth* and *probe* to complete the diagram below.

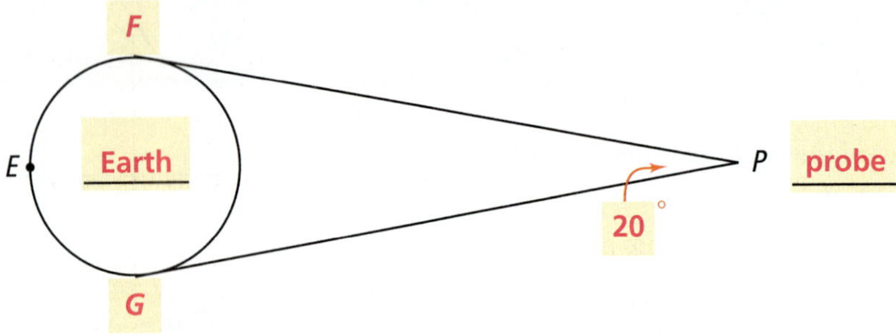

21. Complete the flow chart below.

Let $m\widehat{FG} = x$. Then $m\widehat{FEG} = 360 - x$.

The sum of the arc measures is 360°.

$m\angle FPG = \frac{1}{2}(m\widehat{FEG} - m\widehat{FG})$

Theorem 12-14

$20 = \frac{1}{2}(360 - x - x)$

Substitute.

$20 = \frac{1}{2}(360 - 2x)$

Simplify.

$20 = 180 - x$

Use the Distributive Property.

$-160 = -1x$

Subtract 180 from each side.

$160 = x$

Divide each side by –1.

22. A 160° arc of the equator is visible to the space probe.

Problem 3 Finding Segment Lengths

Got It? **What is the value of the variable to the nearest tenth?**

Underline the correct word to complete each sentence.

23. The segments intersect inside / <u>outside</u> the circle.

24. Write a justification for each statement.

$(14 + 20)14 = (16 + x)16$	Use Theorem 12–15 (II).
$476 = 256 + 16x$	Simplify.
$220 = 16x$	Subtract 256 from each side.
$13.75 = x$	Divide each side by 16.

25. To the nearest tenth, the value of x is 13.8 .

Lesson Check • Do you UNDERSTAND?

In the diagram at the right, is it possible to find the measures of the unmarked arcs? Explain.

26. You can use intercepted arcs to find the value of y. **Yes** / No

27. You can use supplementary angles to find the measures of the angles adjacent to $y°$. **Yes** / No

28. You can find the sum of the unmarked arcs. **Yes** / No

29. Is it possible to find the measure of each unmarked arc? Explain. Explanations may vary. Sample:

No. The sum of the unmarked angles is not enough information to find the measure of each unmarked arc.

Math Success

Check off the vocabulary words that you understand.

☐ chord ☐ circle ☐ secant ☐ tangent

Rate how well you can *find the lengths of segments associated with circles.*

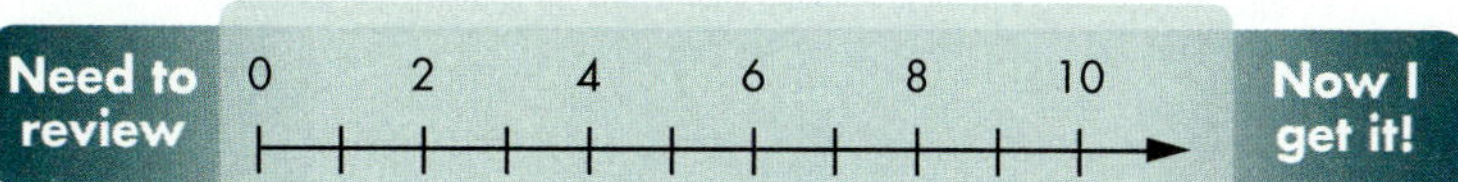

Name ______________________ Class ____________ Date ____________

12-4 Think About a Plan

Angle Measures and Segment Lengths

A circle is inscribed in a quadrilateral whose four angles have measures 85, 76, 94, and 105. Find the measures of the four arcs between consecutive points of tangency.

1. Draw a diagram of a circle inscribed in a quadrilateral. The diagram does not have to be exact; it is just a visual aid.

2. Label as $a°$ the intercepted arc closest to the angle measuring 85. Label as $b°$ the intercepted arc closest to the angle measuring 76. Label as $c°$ the intercepted arc closest to the angle measuring 94. Finally, label as $d°$ the intercepted arc closest to the angle measuring 105.

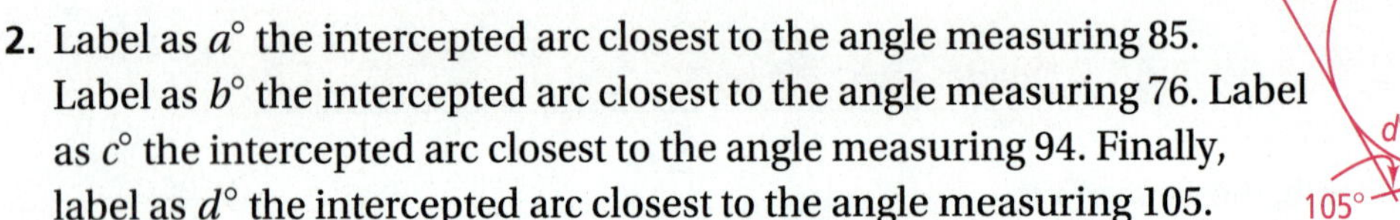

3. What is the sum of the measures of the four arcs $(a + b + c + d)$? **360**

4. Write an equation that relates a to the measures of the other arcs. **$a = 360 - (b + c + d)$**

5. Repeat Step 4 to write three more equations that relate the measure of each arc to the measures of the other arcs.
   $b = 360 - (a + c + d)$; $c = 360 - (a + b + d)$; $d = 360 - (a + b + c)$

6. How is the measure of each angle in the quadrilateral related to the measures of the intercepted arcs? (*Hint:* Use Theorem 12-14.)
   The measure is half the difference of the measures of the intercepted arcs.

7. Write expressions for the measures of the two arcs intercepted by the 85° angle. **a; $b + c + d$**

8. Using Theorem 12-14, write an equation that relates 85 to the measures of the intercepted arcs. **$85 = \frac{1}{2}(b + c + d - a)$**

9. Multiply each side of this equation by 2. **$170 = (b + c + d - a)$**

10. Look at your equation from Step 4. What is the value of $b + c + d$?
    $b + c + d = 360 - a$

11. How can you use the equations from Steps 9 and 10 to find a?
    Substitute $360 - a$ for $b + c + d$ into $170 = (b + c + d - a)$ to get $170 = 360 - 2a$.
    Isolate a and solve.

12. What is the value of a? **95**

13. Repeat this process to find b, c, and d. What are their values? **104; 86; 75**

Name ______________________ Class __________ Date __________

12-4 Practice

Form K

Angle Measures and Segment Lengths

Algebra **Find the value of each variable.**

1. 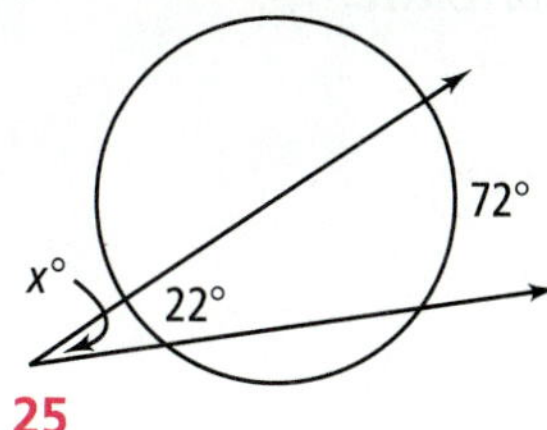

25

To start, identify the type of rays intersecting in the diagram.

Two __?__ rays intersect outside the circle. secant

Then write an equation using Theorem 12-14.

$x = \frac{1}{2} \cdot (\boxed{72} - \boxed{22})$

2. 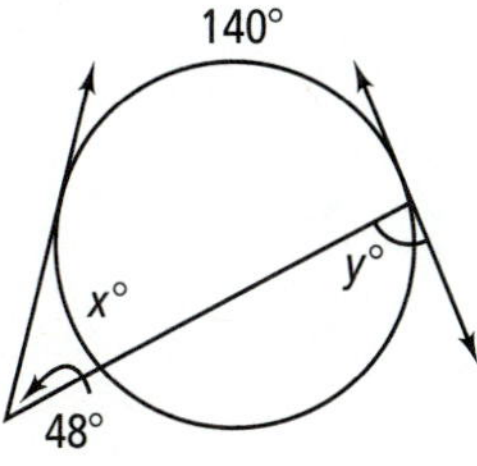

44; 88

3. 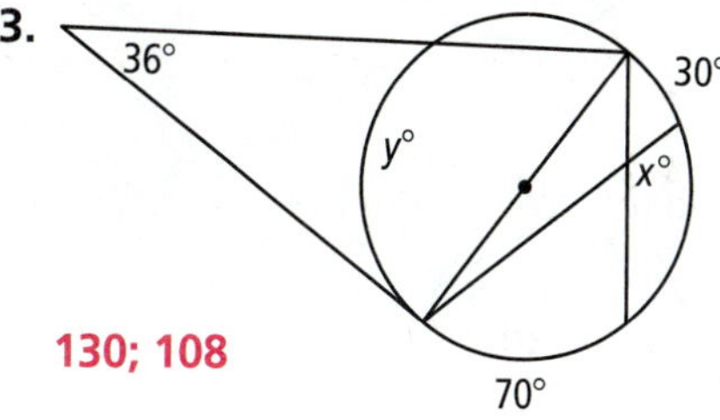

130; 108

Algebra **Find the value of each variable using the given chord, secant, and tangent lengths. If your answer is not a whole number, round it to the nearest tenth.**

4. 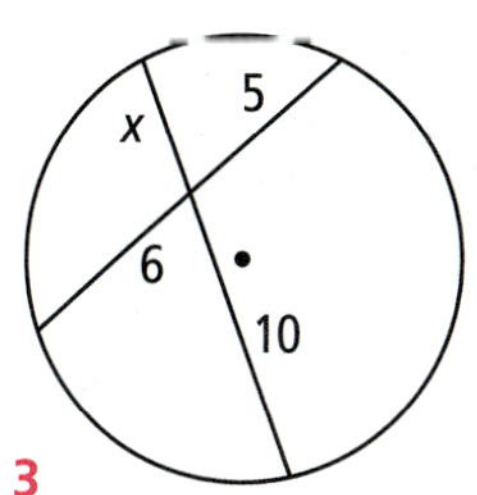

3

To start, identify the type of segments intersecting in the diagram.

Two __?__ intersect inside the circle. chords

Then write an equation using Theorem 12-12, Case I.

$\boxed{6} \cdot \boxed{5} = x \cdot \boxed{10}$

5. 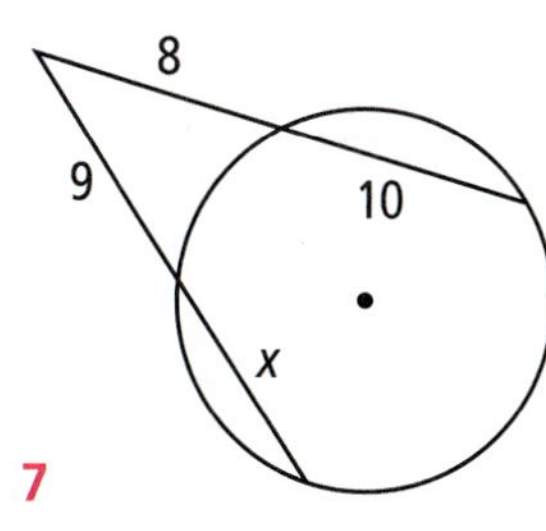

7

6. 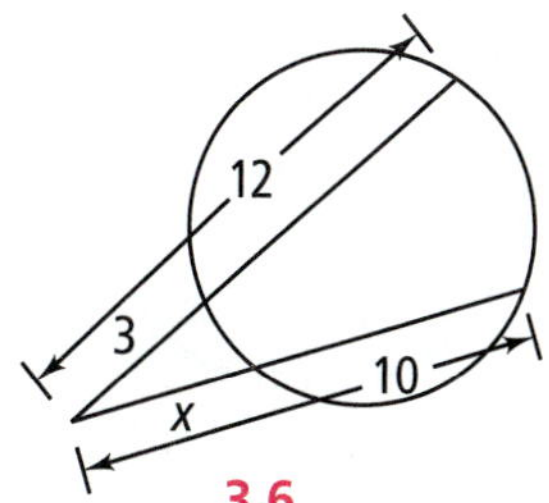

3.6

7. 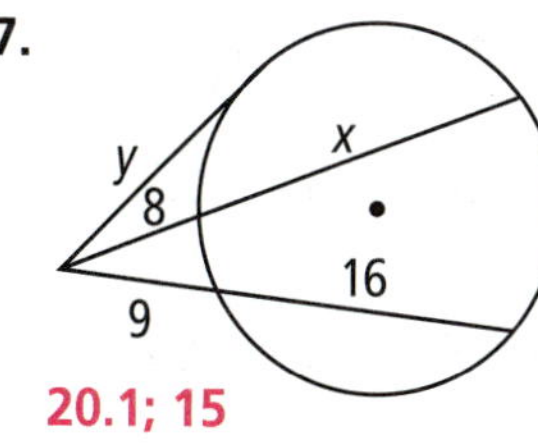

20.1; 15

8. **Algebra** $\overline{FH}$ and $\overline{GI}$ are chords in $\odot T$. Write an expression for $m\angle FJI$ in terms of x and y.

$\frac{1}{2}(x + y)$

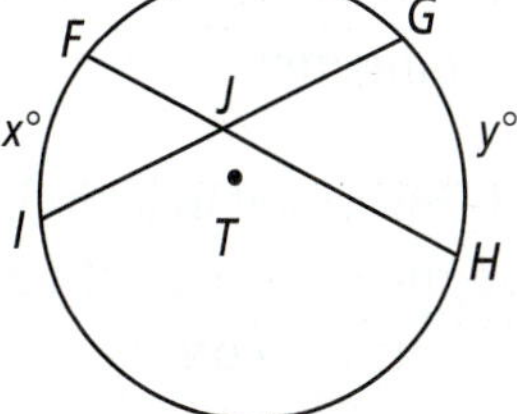

12-4 Practice (continued)

Form K

Angle Measures and Segment Lengths

Algebra Find the value of each variable using the given chord, secant, and tangent lengths. If your answer is not a whole number, round it to the nearest tenth.

9. 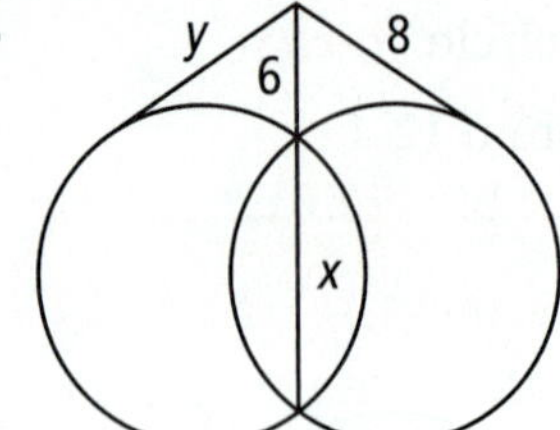

To start, write an equation using Theorem 12-15, Case III.

$\boxed{8} \cdot \boxed{8} = (x + 6) \cdot \boxed{6}$

4.7; 8

10. 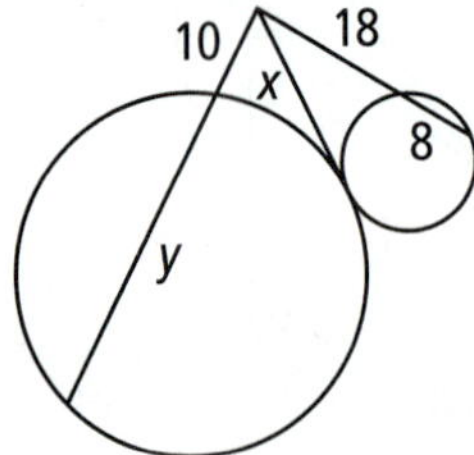

21.6; 36.8

11. 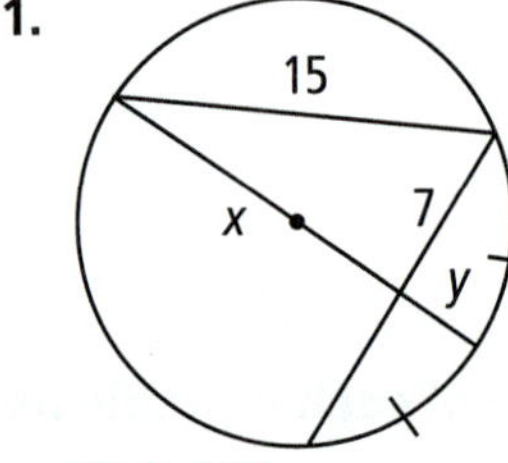

13.3; 3.7

12. You look through binoculars at the circular dome of the Capitol building in Washington, D.C. Your binoculars are at the vertex of the angle formed by tangents to the dome. You estimate that this vertex angle is 70°. What is the measure of the arc of the circular base of the dome that is visible? 110

Find the diameter of $\odot O$. A line that appears to be tangent is tangent. If your answer is not a whole number, round it to the nearest tenth.

13. 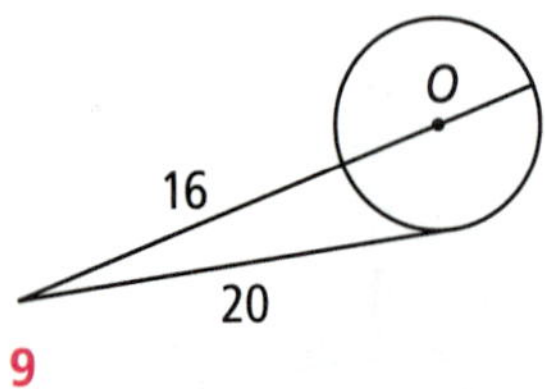

9

14. 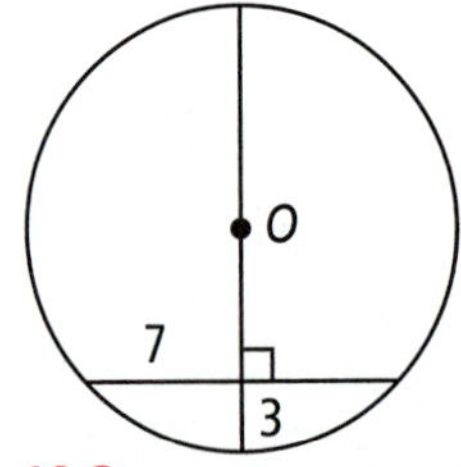

19.3

15. 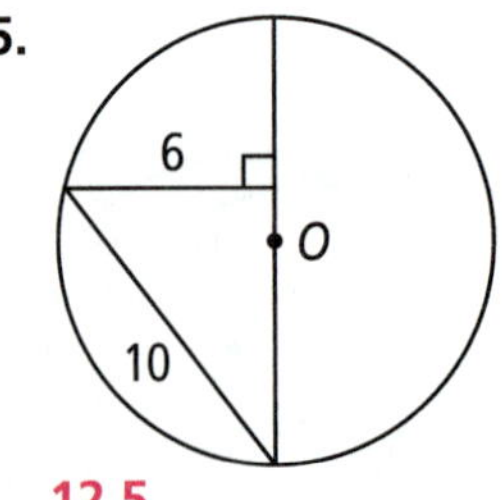

12.5

16. A circle is inscribed in a quadrilateral whose four angles have measures 74, 96, 81, 109. Find the measures of the four arcs between consecutive points of tangency. 106; 84; 99; 71

17. $\triangle CED$ is inscribed in a circle with $m\angle C = 40$, $m\angle E = 55$, and $m\angle D = 85$. What are the measures of $\overset{\frown}{CE}$, $\overset{\frown}{ED}$, and $\overset{\frown}{DC}$? Explain how you can check that your answers are correct. $m\overset{\frown}{CE} = 170$; $m\overset{\frown}{ED} = 80$; $m\overset{\frown}{DC} = 110$; to check, find the sum of the arc measures. The sum should be 360.

Name ______________________ Class ____________ Date ____________

12-4 Standardized Test Prep

Angle Measures and Segment Lengths

Multiple Choice

For Exercises 1–6, choose the correct letter.

1. Which of the following statements is false? C

   (A) Every chord is part of a secant.
   (B) Every diameter is part of a secant.
   (C) Every chord is a diameter.
   (D) Every diameter is a chord.

2. In the figure at the right, what is $m\angle C$? G

   (F) 15
   (G) 35
   (H) 50
   (I) 65

3. In the figure at the right, what is the value of x? D

   (A) 45
   (B) 60
   (C) 75
   (D) 90

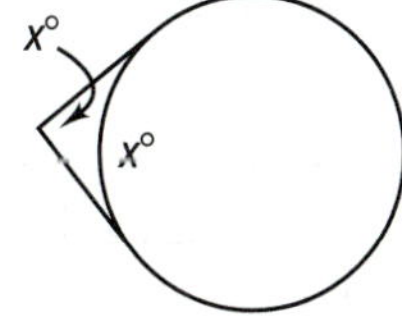

4. In the figure at the right, what is the value of z? G

   (F) 2.9
   (G) 5.6
   (H) 6
   (I) 8.75

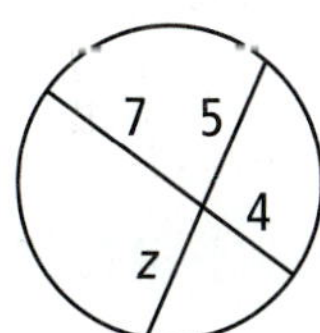

5. An equilateral triangle with sides of length 6 is inscribed in a circle. What is the diameter of the circle? C

   (A) 5.2
   (B) 6
   (C) 6.9
   (D) 7.5

6. In the figure at the right, what is $m\widehat{ABC}$ in terms of x? F

   (F) $180 + x$
   (G) $180 - x$
   (H) $2(180 + x)$
   (I) $360 - x$

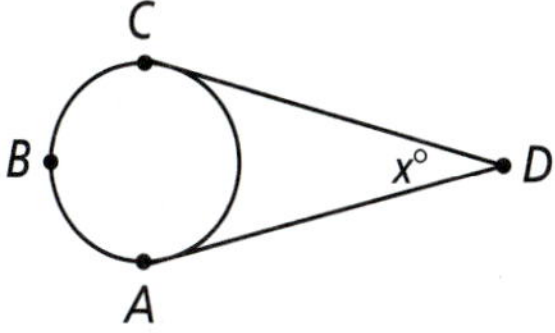

Short Response

7. Use $\odot O$ to prove that $\triangle AED \sim \triangle BEC$.

   By Thm. 12.15, $AE \cdot CE = DE \cdot BE$, and by division, $\frac{AE}{EB} = \frac{DE}{CE}$. $\angle AED \cong \angle CEB$. because they are vert. ∠s. The two △s are ~ by SAS similarity. [2] Student sets up proof correctly using SAS similarity. [1] one error in proof [0] proof incorrect or no proof given

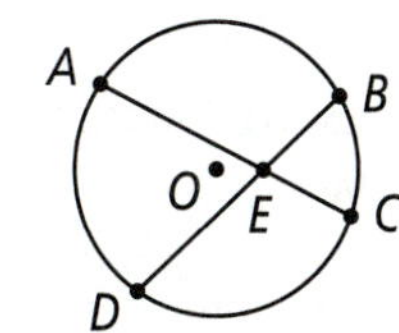

12-5 Circles in the Coordinate Plane

Vocabulary

Review

Write T for *true* or F for *false*.

T **1.** The *coordinate plane* extends without end and has no thickness.

F **2.** Only lines can be graphed in the *coordinate plane.*

T **3.** Any polygon can be plotted in the *coordinate plane.*

F **4.** (0, 5) and (5, 0) are the same point in the *coordinate plane.*

F **5.** The *coordinate plane* is three-dimensional.

T **6.** You can find the slope of a line in the *coordinate plane.*

Vocabulary Builder

standard form (noun) STAN durd fawrm

Main Idea: The **standard form** of an equation gives information that can help you graph the equation in the coordinate plane.

Examples: The **standard form** of an equation of a circle is $(x - h)^2 + (y - k)^2 = r^2$. The **standard form** of a linear equation is $Ax + By = C$. The **standard form** of a quadratic equation is $y = ax^2 + bx + c$.

Use Your Vocabulary

Draw a line from each equation in Column A to its *standard form* in Column B.

Column A	Column B
7. $y = 2x + 3$	$x + y = 0$
8. $y = \frac{3}{4}x - 2$	$2x - y = -3$
9. $y = -x$	$3x - 4y = 8$
10. $0 = 2y - 4x + 3$	$4x - 2y = 3$

(Answer lines drawn: 7 → $2x - y = -3$; 8 → $3x - 4y = 8$; 9 → $x + y = 0$; 10 → $4x - 2y = 3$.)

take note

Theorem 12-16 Equation of a Circle

An equation of a circle with center (h, k) and radius r is $(x - h)^2 + (y - k)^2 = r^2$.

Complete each sentence with *center, circle,* or *radius.*

11. Each point on a __?__ is the same distance from the center. circle

12. The equation of a circle with center $(-1, 0)$ and __?__ 6 is $(x + 1)^2 + (y - 0)^2 = 6^2$. radius

13. Each point on a circle is r units from the __?__. center

14. The Distance Formula is $d = \sqrt{(x_2 - x_1)^2 + (y_2 - y_1)^2}$.

15. How is d in the Distance Formula related to the radius r in the standard equation of a circle?

Answers may vary. Sample: The radius r is the distance d between center (h, k) and (x, y) on a circle and is also the hypotenuse of a right triangle with vertices (h, k), (x, y), and $(x - h, y - k)$.

16. How are the Distance Formula and the standard form of the equation of a circle alike?

Answers may vary. Sample: The standard form of the equation is the Distance Formula using (x, y) on a circle and the center (h, k). This distance is the radius r of the circle.

Problem 1 Writing the Equation of a Circle

Got It? **What is the standard equation of the circle with center (3, 5) and radius 6?**

17. The x-coordinate of the center is 3.

18. The y-coordinate of the center is 5.

19. Is the standard equation of a circle $(x - h)^2 + (y - k)^2 = d$? Yes / **No** (circled)

20. Identify the values of h, k, and r.

$h = 3$ $\quad k = 5$ $\quad r = 6$

21. Write the standard equation of the circle with center (3, 5) and radius 6.

$(x - 3)^2 + (y - 5)^2 = 6^2$

22. Simplify the equation in Exercise 21.

$(x - 3)^2 + (y - 5)^2 = 36$

Problem 2 Using the Center and a Point on a Circle

Got It? **What is the standard equation of the circle with center (4, 3) that passes through the point (−1, 1)?**

23. Complete the reasoning model below.

Know	Need	Plan
(h, k) is (4 , 3). (−1, 1) is a point on the circle.	The radius r The standard equation of the circle	Use the Distance Formula to find r. Then substitute for (h, k) and for r.

24. Use the Distance Formula to find r.

$d = \sqrt{(x_2 - x_1)^2 + (y_2 - y_1)^2}$ Write the Distance Formula.

$r = \sqrt{(4 - (-1))^2 + (3 - 1)^2}$ Substitute.

$r = \sqrt{(5)^2 + (2)^2}$ Simplify within parentheses.

$r = \sqrt{(25) + (4)}$ Square each number.

$r = \sqrt{29}$ Add.

25. Now write the standard form of the circle with center (4, 3) that passes through the point (−1, 1).

$(x - h)^2 + (y - k)^2 = r^2$ Use the standard form of an equation of a circle.

$(x - 4)^2 + (y - 3)^2 = \sqrt{29}^2$ Substitute.

$(x - 4)^2 + (y - 3)^2 = 29$ Simplify.

Problem 3 Graphing a Circle Given Its Equation

Got It? **Suppose the equation $(x - 7)^2 + (y + 2)^2 = 64$ represents the position and transmission range of a cell tower. What does the center of the circle represent? What does the radius represent?**

Place a ✓ in the box if the response is correct. Place an ✗ if it is incorrect.

✓ **26.** The transmission range is the same distance all around the cell tower.

✓ **27.** The center of the circle represents the position of the cell tower.

✗ **28.** The center of the circle represents the transmission range.

✗ **29.** The radius of the circle represents the position of the cell tower.

✓ **30.** The radius of the circle represents the transmission range.

Got It? **What is the center and radius of the circle with equation $(x-2)^2+(y-3)^2=100$? Graph the circle.**

31. The center of the circle is (2, 3).

32. $r^2 = 100$

33. The radius of the circle is 10.

34. Graph the circle on the coordinate plane at the right.

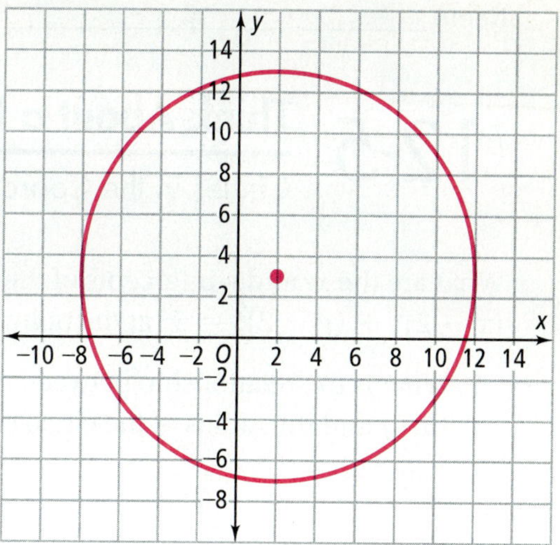

Lesson Check • Do you UNDERSTAND?

Suppose you know the center of a circle and a point on the circle. How do you determine the equation of the circle?

35. Do you know the value of h? **Yes** / No

36. Do you know the value of k? **Yes** / No

37. Do you know the value of r? Yes / **No**

38. How can you find the missing value?

Answers may vary. Sample: Use the Distance Formula to find the radius r of the circle.

39. Once you know h, k, and r, how do you determine an equation of the circle?

Answers may vary. Sample: Substitute the values in the standard equation of a circle.

Math Success

Check off the vocabulary words that you understand.

☐ circle ☐ Distance Formula ☐ standard form

Rate how well you can *use the standard form of a circle.*

Need to review 0 2 4 6 8 10 Now I get it!

Name ______________________ Class ____________ Date ____________

12-5 Think About a Plan

Circles in the Coordinate Plane

What are the *x*- and *y*-intercepts of the line tangent to the circle $(x - 2)^2 + (y - 2)^2 = 5^2$ at the point (5, 6)?

1. What is the relationship between the line tangent to the circle at the point (5, 6) and the radius of the circle containing the point (5, 6)?

   They are perpendicular.

2. What is the product of the slopes of two perpendicular lines or line segments? **−1**

3. What is the center of the circle? **(2, 2)**

4. How can you use the slope formula to find the slope of the radius of the circle containing the point (5, 6)? What is this slope?

   Use the slope formula with the points (5, 6) and (2, 2); $m = \frac{y_2 - y_1}{x_2 - x_1} = \frac{6 - 2}{5 - 2} = \frac{4}{3}$.

5. What is the slope of the line tangent to the circle at point (5, 6)? $-\frac{3}{4}$

6. What is the slope-intercept equation for a line? $y = mx + b$

7. How can you use the slope-intercept equation to find the *y*-intercept for the line tangent to the circle at point (5, 6)?

   Use the known slope, and the *x*-value and *y*-value for the point (5, 6) to solve for *b*; $6 = -\frac{3}{4}(5) + b$; $b = 9\frac{3}{4}$ or 9.75.

8. How can you use this equation to find the *x*-intercept for the line tangent to the circle at point (5, 6)?

   Find the *x* value of the *x*-intercept by setting $y = 0$ and substituting for *m* and *b*; $0 = -\frac{3}{4}x + 9\frac{3}{4}$; $x = 13$.

9. What are the *x*- and *y*-intercepts for the line tangent to the circle at point (5, 6)? **(13, 0) and $(0, 9\frac{3}{4})$**

Name ______________________ Class ____________ Date ____________

12-5 Practice

Form K

Circles in the Coordinate Plane

Write the standard equation of each circle.

1. center $(7, -3)$; $r = 9$ $(x - 7)^2 + (y + 3)^2 = 81$

To start, write the equation of a circle.

$(\boxed{x} - h)^2 + (\boxed{y} - k)^2 = \boxed{r}^2$

Identify the values of h, k, and r.

$h = \boxed{7}$ $k = \boxed{-3}$ $r = \boxed{9}$

2. center $(0, 4)$; $r = 3$
$x^2 + (y - 4)^2 = 9$

3. center $(-2, -8)$; $r = 4$
$(x + 2)^2 + (y + 8)^2 = 16$

4. center $(2, 6)$; $r = 12$
$(x - 2)^2 + (y - 6)^2 = 144$

5. center $(10, 0)$; $r = 7$
$(x - 10)^2 + y^2 = 49$

6. center $(-5, -4)$; $r = \sqrt{3}$
$(x + 5)^2 + (y + 4)^2 = 3$

7. center $(-3, 2)$; $r = \sqrt{10}$
$(x + 3)^2 + (y - 2)^2 = 10$

Write the standard equation for each circle in the diagram at the right.

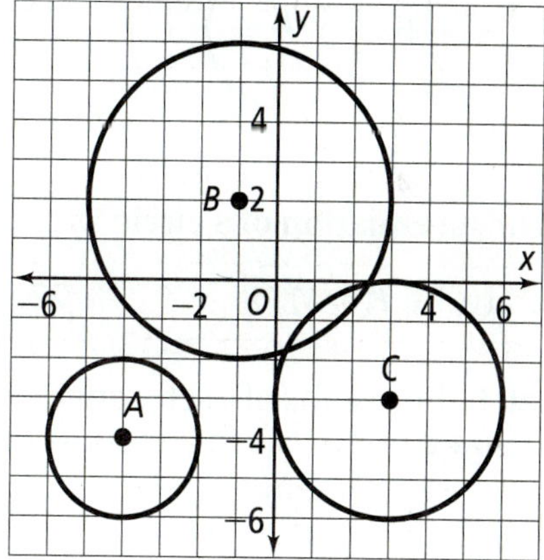

8. $\odot A$ $(x + 4)^2 + (y + 4)^2 = 4$

9. $\odot B$ $(x + 1)^2 + (y - 2)^2 = 16$

10. $\odot C$ $(x - 3)^2 + (y + 3)^2 = 9$

Write the standard equation of each circle with the given center that passes through the given point.

11. center $(6, 4)$; point $(9, 12)$
$(x - 6)^2 + (y - 4)^2 = 73$

12. center $(-2, 0)$; point $(5, 8)$
$(x + 2)^2 + y^2 = 113$

13. center $(-4, -1)$; point $(-6, 5)$
$(x + 4)^2 + (y + 1)^2 = 40$

14. center $(0, 6)$; point $(5, -2)$
$x^2 + (y - 6)^2 = 89$

15. center $(3, 0)$; point $(-5, -2)$
$(x - 3)^2 + y^2 = 68$

16. center $(0, 0)$; point $(\sqrt{5}, \sqrt{8})$
$x^2 + y^2 = 13$

Name ______________________ Class ____________ Date ____________

12-5 Practice (continued)

Form K

Circles in the Coordinate Plane

Find the center and radius of each circle. Then graph the circle.

17. $(x - 2)^2 + (y - 3)^2 = 9$

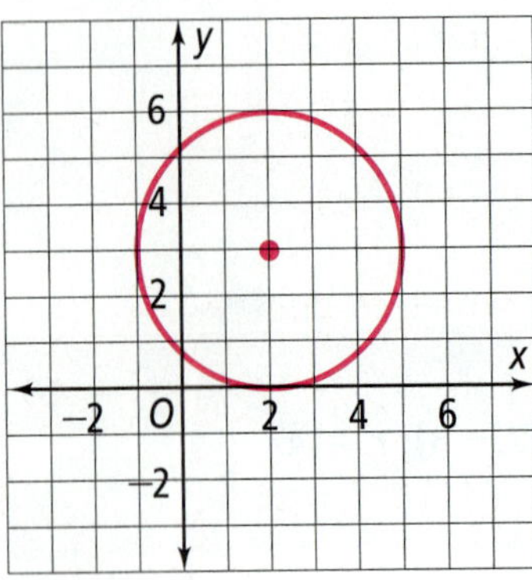

center (2, 3); $r = 3$

18. $(x - 1)^2 + (y + 5)^2 = 4$

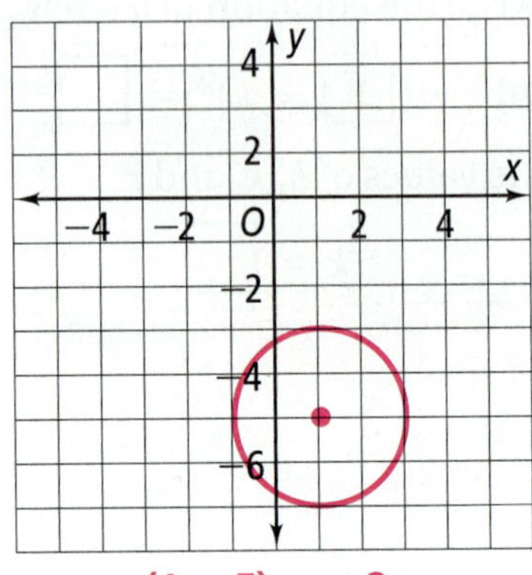

center (1, −5); $r = 2$

Write the standard equation of each circle.

19.

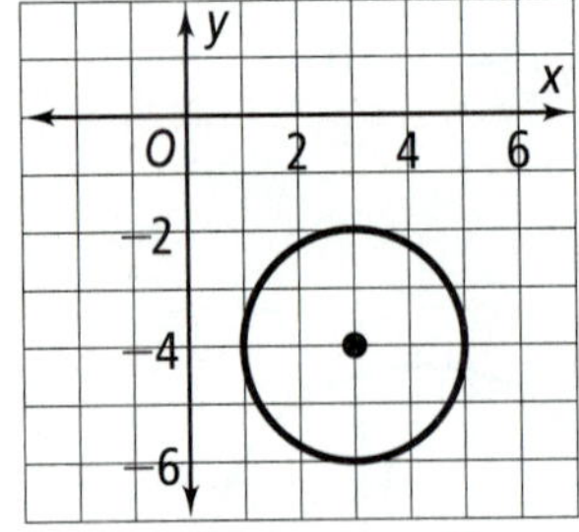

$(x - 3)^2 + (y + 4)^2 = 4$

20.

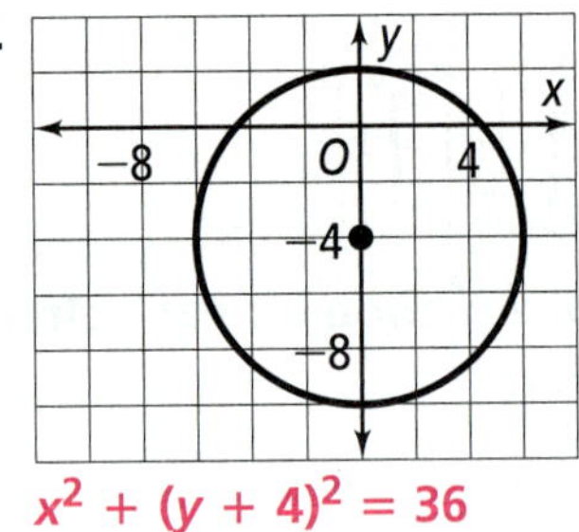

$x^2 + (y + 4)^2 = 36$

Write an equation of a circle with diameter $\overline{ST}$.

21. $S(0, 0)$, $T(6, 4)$ $(x - 3)^2 + (y - 2)^2 = 13$

22. $S(0, 2)$, $T(6, 10)$ $(x - 3)^2 + (y - 6)^2 = 25$

23. $S(5, 11)$, $T(9, 3)$ $(x - 7)^2 + (y - 7)^2 = 20$

Sketch the graphs of each equation. Find all points of intersection of each pair of graphs.

24. $(x + 2)^2 + y^2 = 9$

$y = -x + 1$ (1, 0), (−2, 3)

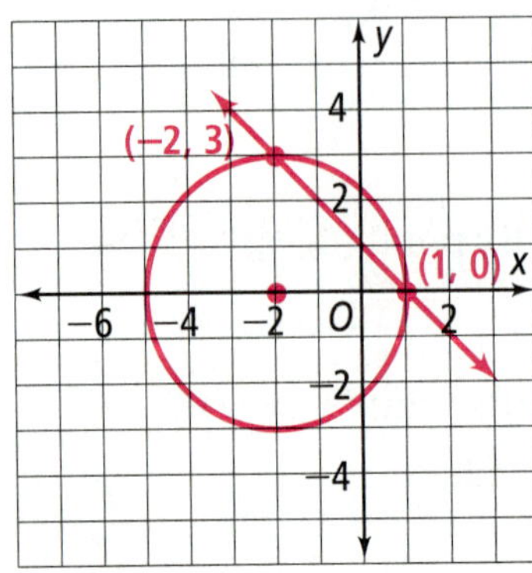

25. $(x - 1)^2 + (y - 1)^2 = 13$

$y = x + 1$ (3, 4), (−2, −1)

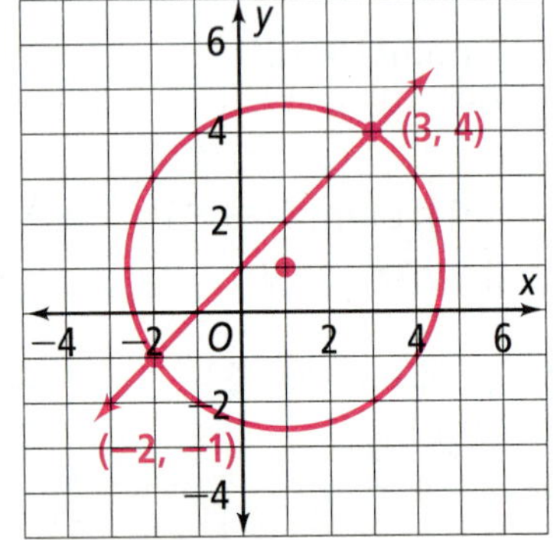

Name ______________________ Class ____________ Date ____________

12-5 Standardized Test Prep

Circles in the Coordinate Plane

Multiple Choice

For Exercises 1–4, choose the correct letter.

1. Which is the equation of a circle with center $(-2, 3)$ and radius $r = 5$? B

   A $(x + 2)^2 + (y - 3)^2 = 10$ C $(x - 2)^2 + (y + 3)^2 = 10$

   B $(x + 2)^2 + (y - 3)^2 = 25$ D $(x - 2)^2 + (y + 3)^2 = 25$

2. A circle with center $(-1, 2)$ passes through point $(2, -2)$. Which is true? G

   F The radius is $\sqrt{5}$. H The equation is $(x + 1)^2 + (y - 2)^2 = 10$.

   G The diameter is 10. I The circumference is 25π.

3. Which of the following is the graph of $(x - 2)^2 + (y + 1)^2 = 9$? D

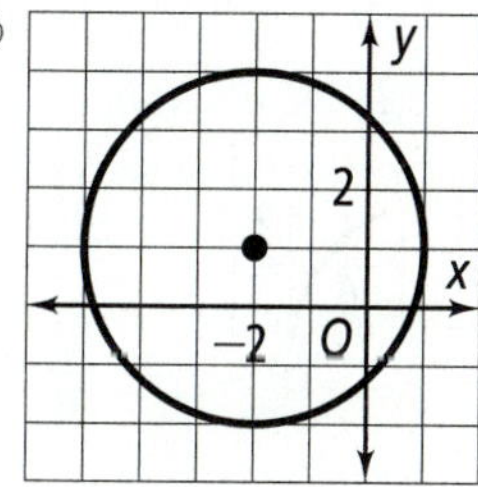

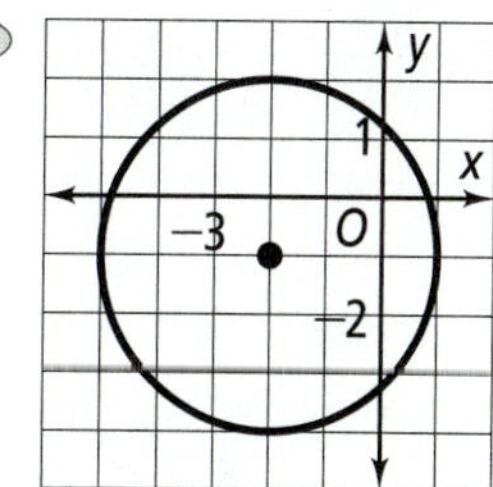

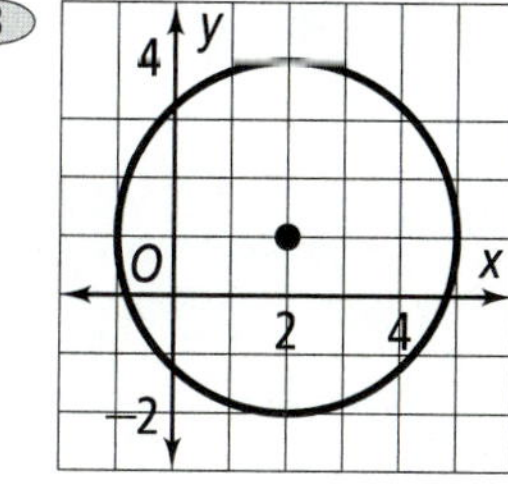

D
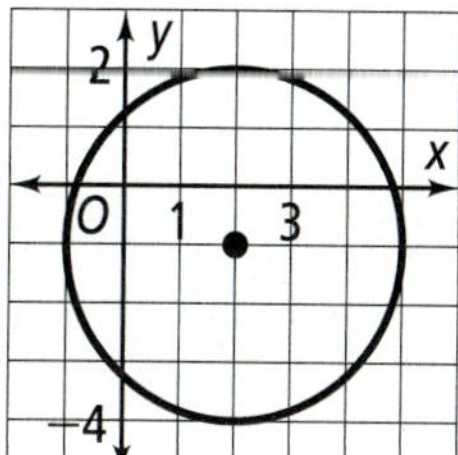

4. Which is the equation of a circle with diameter $\overline{AB}$ with $A(5, 4)$ and $B(-1, -4)$? H

   F $(x - 5)^2 + (y - 4)^2 = 10$ H $(x - 2)^2 + y^2 = 25$

   G $(x + 5)^2 + (y + 4)^2 = 100$ I $(x + 2)^2 + y^2 = 5$

Short Response

5. Write the standard equation of a circle with a circumference of 14π and center $(4, -1)$. (*Hint:* Use the formula for circumference.)

   $(x - 4)^2 + (y + 1)^2 = 49$ [2] correct equation in standard form [1] Student makes one error or equation not in standard form. [0] Equation is incorrect or no equation is given.